# Essential Law Revision from Oxford University Press

## The perfect pairing for exam success

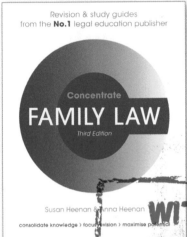

### Heenan & Heenan
### *Family Law Concentrate*

For students who are serious about exam success, it's time to Concentrate!

- **Written by experts**
- **Developed with students**
- **Designed for success**

Each guide in the *Concentrate* series shows you what to expect in a law exam, what examiners are looking for and how to achieve extra marks.

'This jam-packed book is a fantastic source, giving a clear, concise and understandable presentation of the law which is essential for revision'
*Stephanie Lawson, Law Student, Northumbria University*

'Every law student serious about their grades should use a *Concentrate*. I would not revise without it'
*Heather Walkden, Law Student, University of Salford*

### Gaffney-Rhys
### *Concentrate Q&A Family Law*

Unrivalled exam and coursework support for when you're aiming high.

- **Typical exam questions**
- **Model answers**
- **Advice on structure and exam technique**

Law examiners share the secrets of how to *really* answer typical law questions, giving you the confidence to tackle any essay or problem question.

'The content is exceptional; the best Q&A books that I've read'
*Wendy Chinenye Akaigwe, Law Student, London Metropolitan University*

'Since I started using the OUP Q&A guides my grades have dramatically improved'
*Glen Sylvester, Law Student, Bournemouth University*

For the full list of revision titles and additional resources visit: www.oup.com/lawrevision/

**\* Techniques for exam** **Written by experts**

# Hayes and Williams' Family Law

*Fifth Edition*

## STEPHEN GILMORE

*LL.B (Hons) Leics, LL.M (Family Law and Policy) UEA, M.St Oxon
of Lincoln's Inn, Barrister, Professor of Family Law, King's College London*

## LISA GLENNON

*LL.B, Ph.D*

OXFORD
UNIVERSITY PRESS

# OXFORD
UNIVERSITY PRESS

Great Clarendon Street, Oxford, OX2 6DP,
United Kingdom

Oxford University Press is a department of the University of Oxford.
It furthers the University's objective of excellence in research, scholarship,
and education by publishing worldwide. Oxford is a registered trade mark of
Oxford University Press in the UK and in certain other countries

Second edition 1999
Third edition 2012
Fourth edition 2014

Impression: 1

Public sector information reproduced under Open Government Licence v3.0
(http://www.nationalarchives.gov.uk/doc/open-government-licence/open-government-licence.htm)

Published in the United States of America by Oxford University Press
198 Madison Avenue, New York, NY 10016, United States of America

British Library Cataloguing in Publication Data
Data available

Library of Congress Control Number: 2016932532

ISBN 978–0–19–875308–7

Printed in Great Britain by
Bell & Bain Ltd., Glasgow

# Acknowledgements

We are very grateful to the team at OUP for all their encouragement and support with this new edition. In particular we would like to record our thanks to John Carroll and Tom Young for commissioning a new edition; to Amar Pannu, who saw us through the production process; to our copy-editor, Nicholas Bromley; and to our proofreader, Sarah Parker.

Friends and colleagues in family law have helped in various ways (in some cases perhaps unknown to them). As the new editions of this book now appear at short intervals, we continue to record our thanks to those who have assisted with recent previous editions. With regard to this edition, Stephen would in particular like to thank Professor Emeritus Chris Barton, for kind emails during the production process, highlighting very recent developments. Above all, Stephen would like to thank his wife, Penny, and children, Libby and Tom, for all their love and support.

Lisa would like to take this opportunity to thank all those who have helped and supported her academic pursuits including Anne Barlow, Mavis Maclean, John Eekelaar, Martha Fineman, Claire Archbold, David Capper and Norma Dawson. Of course Lisa would like to pay particular thanks to her husband, Brian, and children, Daniel and Evie (who was born during the writing of this new edition!), for their constant supply of love, laughter, and encouragement.

Lisa was responsible for the adult family law section of the book, and Stephen wrote the child law section, although we prefer to think of it all as a joint effort (and for which we are each grateful to the other).

Stephen Gilmore
Lisa Glennon
March 2016

# New to this Edition

The fifth edition of this book appears only two years after the last edition, which was published in July 2014. While this edition has not needed to contend with as many statutory amendments as the last (which addressed the changes effected by the Marriage (Same Sex Couples) Act 2013 and the Children and Families Act 2014), the case law in family law continues apace. Accommodating developments over even such a short time has required the addition of some 40,000 words to the text.

Some of the additional text represents our attempt to address reviewers' suggestions. For example, the introductory chapter now contains a more detailed overview of the meaning of private and family life within Article 8 of the European Convention for the Protection of Human Rights and Fundamental Freedoms, the workings of Article 8, and of Article 14. The introductory chapter also contains accounts of recent case law illustrating the difficulties which curtailment of legal aid by the Legal Aid, Sentencing and Punishment of Offenders Act 2012 has caused for litigants in family law cases. We appreciate that an account of family law cannot detach itself entirely from the context in which family lawyers are working, and there is a difficult line between what is 'practice' and what is 'substantive law'. However, as we have explained in previous editions, we can touch only briefly on practice issues, since our principal objective is to provide a clear account of substantive family law for undergraduate studies.

With students in mind, this edition, like earlier ones, highlights within the text various challenging issues or debates as 'talking points'. In this edition we have added to each 'talking point' a question for readers to consider in order to focus 'discussion'.

Part 1 of the book, on adult family law, outlines the most up-to-date statistics on the incidence of marriage, civil partnerships and divorce/dissolution of a civil partnership, as well as discussing recent initiatives which challenge the refusal to allow opposite-sex couples to enter into a civil partnership. This includes the Civil Partnerships Act 2004 (Amendment) Bill 2015–16, which had its first reading in the House of Commons on 21 October 2015, and had its second reading debate on 11 March 2016. Chapter 1 also discusses the recently published review of the differences in survivor benefits in occupational pension schemes between opposite-sex and same-sex couples in legal relationships. This review, which was published in June 2014, observed that removing the differences in survivor benefits would have an estimated capitalised cost of around £2.9 billion for schemes in the public sector, and £0.4 billion for those in the private sector. While many schemes have already equalised survivor benefits for all periods of service, regardless of the sexual orientation of the members to whom they apply, there is no compulsion to do so as confirmed by the recent Court of Appeal decision in *Walker v Innospec Ltd and Others* [2015] EWCA Civ 1000. Chapter 1 also discusses *R (Hodkin & Anor) v Registrar General of Births, Deaths and Marriages* [2013] UKSC 77 where the question before the Supreme Court was whether a church of the Church of Scientology is recordable as a 'place of meeting for religious worship' under section 2 of the Places of Worship Registration Act 1855, thus allowing a valid ceremony of marriage to be performed there. There is also discussion of the Law Commission's recent Scoping Paper 'Getting Married' which concluded that the law that governs how and where couples in England and Wales can marry is in need of reform as it is out of date, inconsistent, and overly restrictive. Chapter 1 also discusses the recent case law which elaborates on the guidance given by Bodey J in *Hudson v Leigh* [2009] EWHC 1306 (Fam) on the existence of a non-marriage. This includes *Asaad v Kurter* [2013] EWHC 3852 (Fam) where the court had to decide upon the nature of a ceremony which took place in a Syriac Orthodox Church in Syria.

Other reform initiatives discussed in Chapter 2 include the No-Fault Divorce Bill 2015–16, which seeks to add an additional fact on which a divorce can be granted to allow a couple who mutually agree to divorce to do so without having to establish the lengthy separation periods under the current law, or to fabricate one party's fault (such as adultery or unreasonable behaviour) in order to speed up the process. While there has been little case law development in the area of domestic violence, Chapter 3 outlines the recent report of the HM Inspectorate of Constabulary (HMIC), which found that, despite considerable improvement over the last decade, the overall police response to victims of domestic abuse was not good enough. In too many police forces, weaknesses were found in the service provided to victims, some of which were serious and put victims at unnecessary risk. In addition, the chapter highlights the new criminal offence of controlling and coercive behaviour under the Serious Crime Act 2015, which aims to tackle domestic abuse by criminalising patterns of repeated or continuous coercive or controlling behaviour where perpetrated against an intimate partner or family member, causing victims to feel fear, alarm, or distress. Finally, Chapter 3 draws attention to *JM v CZ* [2014] EWHC 1125 (Fam) where Mostyn J found that the usual practice of making an ex parte non-molestation order for 12 months with a provision for the respondent to request a return date hearing or apply on 48 hours' notice to vary or discharge the order did not comply with the statutory requirement for a full hearing 'as soon as just and convenient'.

The new edition also provides comprehensive discussion of three landmark decisions of the Supreme Court in the area of financial provision on divorce. In an unprecedented decision, the Supreme Court in *Wyatt v Vince* [2015] UKSC 14 allowed the wife to make a financial provision application almost 20 years after the divorce, and in *Sharland v Sharland* [2015] UKSC 60 and *Gohil v Gohil* [2015] UKSC 61 the Supreme Court had to consider the impact of fraudulent non-disclosure on a financial settlement agreed between the parties on divorce. In these latter cases, two former wives wanted their agreed financial settlements set aside on the ground that their respective husbands had fraudulently failed to make full and frank disclosure regarding their assets during the negotiations. The fact that the Supreme Court ruled in their favour attracted a considerable amount of media attention and commentary, and sent the clear message that fraudulent non-disclosure will not be tolerated. Chapter 5 discusses these cases in some length and seeks to place them in their legal context and beyond the sensationalist media headlines which followed in their wake.

In Part 2 of the book, on child law, there have also been many significant case law developments. There has been a flurry of cases clarifying the requirements in section 54 of the Human Fertilisation and Embryology Act 2008 for the making of a parental order, transferring legal parenthood from a surrogate mother to a commissioning couple: eg, *Re X (A Child) (Parental Order: Time Limit)* [2014] EWHC 3135 (Fam), [2015] Fam 186; *Re Z (A Child: Human Fertilisation and Embryology Act: Parental Order)* [2015] EWFC 73; *Re A and B (No 2) (Parental Order)* [2015] EWHC 2080 (Fam). These cases emerge from the courts' struggles with the tension between the statutory requirements and the overarching requirement that in deciding whether to make such an order the welfare of the child concerned is the court's paramount consideration.

In the law relating to child arrangements orders in section 8 of the Children Act 1989, the Court of Appeal in *Re C (Internal Relocation)* [2015] EWCA Civ 1305 provided important new dicta on relocation within the UK (internal relocation), clarifying that the use of the word 'exceptional' in earlier cases was not to import a criterion of exceptionality, and emphasising that the overarching principle is the paramountcy of the child's welfare. Thus the general approach to internal relocation is (perhaps always was!) the same as for international relocation. Recent Court of Appeal authority on the latter, *Re F (A Child) (International Relocation Cases* [2015] EWCA Civ 882, has also seen a move towards situating earlier guidance in *Payne v Payne* [2001] EWCA CIV 166, [2001] 1 FLR 1052 firmly within an holistic analysis of the welfare of the child.

In the related area of international child abduction, there have been important Supreme Court decisions on custody rights (*Re K (Abduction: Inchoate Rights)* [2014] UKSC 29, [2014] 2 FLR 629), and on the child's habitual residence (*AR v RN (Habitual Residence)* [2015] UKSC 35, [2015] 2 FLR 503; *Re B (A child)* [2016] UKSC 4); and the Court of Appeal has provided important authority on the child's objection to return (*Re M (Republic of Ireland) (Child's Objections) (Joinder of Children as Parties to Appeal)* [2015] EWCA Civ 26, [2015] 2 FLR 1074).

The Court of Appeal has also addressed the issue of long-term supervised contact between a child and parent, clarifying that there is no principle that such contact should not be ordered (*Re S (Child Arrangements Order: Effect of Long-Term Supervised Contact on Welfare)* [2015] EWCA Civ 689).

Within the public law relating to children, the Court of Appeal has issued guidance on the use of local authority accommodation under section 20 of the Children Act 1989 (*Re N (Children) (Adoption: Jurisdiction)* [2015] EWCA Civ 1112), following a number of cases in which judicial concerns have been expressed about inappropriate practices. In the law relating to care orders, the courts have been required to address the issue of 'significant harm' in new contexts of children's radicalisation (eg, *London Borough of Tower Hamlets v B* [2015] EWHC 2491 (Fam)), and female genital mutilation (*Re B and G (Care Proceedings: FGM) (No 2)* [2015] EWFC 3). The latter case contains interesting *obiter* comments comparing male circumcision with female genital mutilation, and concluding (perhaps controversially for some) that male circumcision (for non-medical reasons) constitutes significant harm, yet can be justified by reference to society's acceptance of its practice. The Court of Appeal has also been busy clarifying its holistic approach to the consideration of options for the child's placement in public law cases (eg, *Re R (Adoption)* [2014] EWCA Civ 1625; *CM v Blackburn with Darwen Borough Council* [2014] EWCA Civ 1479; and *Re T (Application to Revoke Placement Orders: Change in Circumstances)* [2014] EWCA Civ 1369).

In *Re P (Step-parent Adoption)* [2014] EWCA Civ 1174 the Court of Appeal provided important guidance on the approach to step-parent adoption, applying the European Court of Human Rights case of *Söderbäck v Sweden* [1999] 1 FLR 250.

As the foregoing brief account shows, keeping abreast of developments presents an ongoing challenge, but we have endeavoured to state the law as at 1 January 2016. We have managed, however, to incorporate some developments since that date during the production process.

We have sought in this edition to maintain the clear, logical, and straightforward account of the law for which earlier editions of this book were known, and locate this within relevant academic commentary and policy debate, in order to encourage students to engage critically with the law and debates about it. However, we also firmly believe that students must be able to situate their criticisms within a good, detailed understanding of the law. In the spirit of earlier editions, we have therefore sought, where possible, to provide quite full (student-friendly) accounts of case law. Our reasons are explained more fully in the Introduction. We have tried to ensure that students are able to identify the wood, whilst also maintaining awareness of the trees.

# Outline Contents

*Table of Cases*                                                                xxii

*Table of Statutes*                                                             xlvi

*Table of Statutory Instruments*                                                 lx

*Table of European and International Instruments*                               lxii

*Introduction: The Changing Family and Developing Family Law*                   lxiii


## Part 1  Adult Family Law

1  The Formation of Adult Relationships                                           3

2  The Dissolution of Adult Relationships                                        65

3  Protection from Domestic Violence and Occupation of the Family Home           97

4  Money and Property Distribution on Marriage Breakdown                        167

5  Property Disputes of Unmarried Cohabitants on Relationship Breakdown         253


## Part 2  Child Family Law

6  Financial Support for Children                                               319

7  A Child's Parents: Parentage, Parenthood, and Parental Responsibility        345

8  Children's Rights                                                            424

9  Private Law Disputes and Issues in Children Cases                            455

10  Children Needing Services, Care, and Protection                            593

11  Adoption and Special Guardianship                                          700


*Index*                                                                         751

# Detailed Contents

*Table of Cases*                                                                                    xxii

*Table of Statutes*                                                                                  xlvi

*Table of Statutory Instruments*                                                                      lx

*Table of European and International Instruments*                                                   lxii

**Introduction: The Changing Family and Developing Family Law**                                    **lxiii**

   Family law: an inherently interesting and dynamic subject                          lxiii

   A volatile time for family law; recent developments                                lxiii

      The family justice review recommendations                         lxvi

      The Government response to the family justice review              lxvii

      The new single family court for England and Wales                 lxvii

      The Children and Families Act 2014                                lxvii

   Setting the scene for the rest of the book                                         lxviii

   What is family law?                                                                lxviii

   Families today: the statistical picture and trends                                 lxix

   The legally recognised 'family': shifting over time                                lxix

   The impact of the Human Rights Act 1998 and international conventions               lxxii

   Some features of family law                                                        lxxvii

      Discretion                                                        lxxvii

      Interaction with other disciplines                                lxxviii

   The arrangement of the text                                                        lxxviii

## Part 1  Adult Family Law

**1  The Formation of Adult Relationships**                                                          **3**

   1  Marriage                                                                          3

      1.1  Marriage Today                                                   3

      1.2  The Right to Marry                                                 5

      1.3  The Creation of a Valid Marriage                                   5

      1.4  Capacity to Marry                                                  5

      1.5  The Law of Nullity                                                  6

   2  Void Marriages                                                                     7

      2.1  Marriage within the Prohibited Degrees of Relationship              8

      2.2  Marriage under the Age of 16                                        9

      2.3  Failure to Comply with the Required Formalities for Marriage         9

      2.4  A Party Must not Already be Married                                 16

3   Voidable Marriages                                                          16
    3.1   Non-Consummation                                                      17
    3.2   Lack of Consent to the Marriage                                       18
    3.3   Mental Disorder Rendering a Person Unfitted for Marriage              20
    3.4   Venereal Disease                                                      20
    3.5   Pregnancy by Another Man                                              20
    3.6   Gender Recognition as a Ground for Nullity                            21
    3.7   Bars to Relief                                                        21
    3.8   Should the Concept of the Voidable Marriage be Abolished?             22
4   Sham Marriages/Civil Partnerships                                          24
5   Forced Marriages                                                           25
    5.1   Annulment                                                             26
    5.2   Inherent Jurisdiction or Wardship                                     26
    5.3   Forced Marriage Protection Orders                                     27
6   Recognition of an Overseas Marriage                                        29
7   The Removal of Section 11(c) of the MCA 1973                               30
    7.1   Transsexual Persons and Marriage                                      30
    7.2   The Gender Recognition Act 2004                                       33
    7.3   Intersexuals and Marriage                                            35
8   The Development of Gay and Lesbian Rights                                  35
    8.1   The Road to Civil Partnership                                         36
    8.2   The Legal Formation of a Civil Partnership                            39
    8.3   Recognition of Overseas Civil Partnerships, Annulments, and Separations   40
    8.4   The Legal Consequences of Civil Partnerships                          41
9   The Road to Same-Sex Marriage                                             41
    9.1   The Marriage (Same Sex Couples) Act 2013                              44
    9.2   Other Aspects of the 2013 Act                                         47
10  The Legal Consequences of Marriage                                         50
11  Non-Formal Adult Relationships                                            51
    11.1   Cohabitation                                                         51
    11.2   Home-Sharers                                                         61

2  The Dissolution of Adult Relationships                                      65
1   The Law of Divorce                                                         65
    1.1   A Brief History of Divorce                                           65
    1.2   Developments in Divorce Procedure                                     67
    1.3   Trends in Divorce                                                    67
2   Obtaining a Divorce                                                       68
    2.1   Jurisdiction to Hear a Divorce                                        68
    2.2   Staying Divorce Proceedings in England and Wales                      70
    2.3   Divorce under the Matrimonial Causes Act 1973                         70
    2.4   The Legal Effects of Divorce                                          81
    2.5   Recognition of an Overseas Divorce                                    81

3    Criticisms of Divorce under the Matrimonial Causes Act 1973 and
     an Attempt at Reform                                                      83
     3.1    Introduction                                                       83
     3.2    Divorce under the Family Law Act 1996                              86
4    The Future of Divorce Law                                                 89
     4.1    Recent Proposals to Reform the Law of Divorce                      91
5    Other Decrees under the Matrimonial Causes Act 1973                       93
     5.1    Decree of Judicial Separation                                      93
     5.2    Decree of Presumption of Death and Dissolution of the Marriage     94
6    Dissolution of a Civil Partnership                                        94
7    The Termination of Cohabitation Relationships                            95

**3 Protection from Domestic Violence and Occupation of the Family Home**     97
1    What is Domestic Violence?                                               97
2    How Prevalent is Domestic Violence?                                     100
3    Explanations for Domestic Violence                                      103
     3.1    Psychological Explanations                                       103
     3.2    Social Structural Explanations                                   104
     3.3    Feminist Explanations—The Patriarchal Social Order               104
     3.4    A Multifaceted Phenomenon                                        105
4    The Response of the Law to Domestic Violence                           105
     4.1    The Role of the Criminal Law                                     106
     4.2    Criminal Injuries Compensation                                   112
     4.3    Civil Law Remedies                                               113
5    Occupation Orders                                                       127
     5.1    Some Preliminary Points about Occupation Orders                  127
     5.2    Who can Apply for an Occupation Order?                           128
     5.3    Entitled Applicants                                              129
     5.4    Non-Entitled Applicants                                          137
     5.5    Orders where Neither Party is Entitled to Occupy the Dwelling-House  142
     5.6    The Approach of the Courts to Occupation Orders                  143
     5.7    Enforcement of an Occupation Order                               147
     5.8    Undertakings                                                     149
     5.9    Ex Parte Orders                                                  150
     5.10   Provision for Third Parties to Act on Behalf of Victims of Domestic Violence  152
6    Persons Not Protected under the Family Law Act 1996                     153
7    Protection from Harassment Act 1997                                     154
     7.1    Harassment                                                       154
     7.2    Putting People in Fear of Violence                               155
     7.3    Restraining Orders                                               156
8    Domestic Violence and Local Authority Housing                          156
     8.1    'Homeless'                                                       157

| | | |
|---|---|---|
| 8.2 | 'Priority Need' | 158 |
| 8.3 | Intentionally Homeless | 159 |
| **9** | **Domestic Violence: Human Rights Implications** | **160** |
| 9.1 | The Human Rights Act 1998 | 161 |
| 9.2 | International Human Rights Law | 161 |
| **10** | **Domestic Violence and Child Contact** | **163** |

**4  Money and Property Distribution on Marriage Breakdown**  **167**

| | | |
|---|---|---|
| **1** | **Background to the Current Law** | **167** |
| **2** | **The Legislative Framework** | **169** |
| 2.1 | The Courts' Powers | 171 |
| **3** | **Undertakings** | **174** |
| **4** | **The Clean Break** | **175** |
| 4.1 | Section 25A(1) | 175 |
| 4.2 | Section 25A(2) | 176 |
| 4.3 | Section 25A(3) | 180 |
| **5** | **Exercise of the Court's Discretion** | **181** |
| 5.1 | Refusal to Exercise Discretion on Policy Grounds | 181 |
| 5.2 | The Court's General Direction in Section 25(1) | 181 |
| 5.3 | The Statutory Factors: Section 25(2) | 182 |
| 5.4 | The Courts' General Guidance | 196 |
| 5.5 | The Bases of Financial Provision Orders Following *Miller; McFarlane* | 202 |
| 5.6 | Rules or Guidelines? | 210 |
| 5.7 | The Law Commission Report: 'Matrimonial Property, Needs and Agreements' | 210 |
| **6** | ***Wyatt v Vince*: Is there a Time Limit for making an Application for Financial Provision?** | **212** |
| **7** | **Pensions** | **215** |
| 7.1 | Duty to Consider the Parties' Pension Entitlements | 215 |
| 7.2 | Pensions—The Options | 216 |
| **8** | **The Matrimonial Home—What Order is the Most Appropriate?** | **217** |
| 8.1 | The Powers of the Court | 218 |
| **9** | **Financial and Property Agreements** | **222** |
| 9.1 | Separation Agreements | 222 |
| 9.2 | Embodying the Agreement in a Consent Order | 224 |
| 9.3 | Pre-Nuptial Agreements | 229 |
| 9.4 | Debate Surrounding Pre-nuptial Agreements | 234 |
| **10** | **Appeals and Rehearings** | **237** |
| 10.1 | The Barder Test | 237 |
| 10.2 | Variation | 242 |
| **11** | **Financial Provision Orders During the Marriage** | **249** |

**5 Property Disputes of Unmarried Cohabitants on Relationship Breakdown**    **253**

1 Ownership of the Family Home: Property Law Principles    254

   1.1 Establishing Legal Ownership    254

   1.2 Establishing Beneficial Ownership    254

   1.3 The Resulting Trust    256

   1.4 The Constructive Trust    257

   1.5 Distinguishing Two Situations    258

2 Joint Names Cases    258

   2.1 *Stack v Dowden*: The Facts    259

   2.2 Sole Name Cases    272

   2.3 Quantification of the Beneficial Interest    287

   2.4 Proprietary Estoppel    290

   2.5 Orders under the Trusts of Land and Appointment of Trustees Act 1996    295

   2.6 Transfer of Tenancies between Cohabitants    298

   2.7 Schedule 1 to the Children Act 1989    300

   2.8 The Need for Reform    301

## Part 2   Child Family Law

**6 Financial Support for Children**    **319**

1 The Child Support Act 1991: Background and Recent Reforms    319

   1.1 Birth of the Child Support Act    319

   1.2 Problems    320

   1.3 Responding to Criticism    321

   1.4 Loss of Confidence and a Review of the System    321

2 The Child Support Act 1991: The Law    323

   2.1 Parents and Children to whom the Act Applies    323

   2.2 Each Parent's Duty to Maintain a Qualifying Child    323

   2.3 Applications for a Maintenance Calculation and Collection/Enforcement    324

   2.4 The Maintenance Calculation    324

   2.5 Enforcement    327

3 The Courts' Residual Role with Respect to Child Maintenance    328

   3.1 Section 8(3A): Existing Maintenance Orders    328

   3.2 Section 8(5): Existing Maintenance Agreements    328

   3.3 Section 8(6): A Topping up Order    328

   3.4 Section 8(7): Educational Expenses    329

   3.5 Section 8(8): Expenses attributable to a child's disability    329

   3.6 Section 8(10): Orders against a Person with Care    329

4 The Courts' Powers    330

   4.1 Matrimonial Causes Act 1973    330

| | 4.2 | Available Orders | 332 |
| | 4.3 | Exercise of the Court's Discretion | 332 |
| | 4.4 | Maintenance of a Child by a Party who is not the Child's Parent | 332 |
| | 4.5 | Duration of Orders | 333 |
| | 4.6 | Provision for Children as Dependants | 333 |
| | 4.7 | Children Act 1989, Section 15 and Schedule 1 | 335 |

**7  A Child's Parents: Parentage, Parenthood, and Parental Responsibility** **345**

| 1 | A Child's Parents | | 345 |
| | 1.1 | Different Senses of 'Parent': Biological, Social, and Legal | 345 |
| | 1.2 | Law's Distinctions: Parentage, Parenthood, and Parental Responsibility | 346 |
| 2 | Parentage | | 347 |
| | 2.1 | The Presumption of Paternity in Favour of the Mother's Husband | 347 |
| | 2.2 | Where Parentage is in Issue: Declarations of Parentage | 347 |
| | 2.3 | Directions for Scientific Testing under Section 20 of the Family Law Reform Act 1969 | 349 |
| | 2.4 | Legal Recognition of Persons' Interests in Knowing Genetic Origins | 351 |
| | 2.5 | Disclosure of Parentage to Children | 361 |
| 3 | Legal Parenthood | | 362 |
| | 3.1 | Motherhood | 362 |
| | 3.2 | Fatherhood | 363 |
| | 3.3 | The Human Fertilisation and Embryology Act 1990 | 364 |
| | 3.4 | Section 28: The Legal but not Biological Father | 366 |
| | 3.5 | The Human Fertilisation and Embryology Act 2008 | 369 |
| | 3.6 | Lesbian Couples, Assisted Conception, and Parenthood | 371 |
| | 3.7 | Biology: The Default Position | 372 |
| | 3.8 | Persons not Regarded in Law as a Parent | 373 |
| | 3.9 | Transsexual Persons and Parenthood | 374 |
| | 3.10 | Surrogacy and Parental Orders | 376 |
| 4 | Making Sense of the Law on Parenthood | | 385 |
| | 4.1 | Rationales for Attributing Parenthood | 385 |
| 5 | Criticism of the Law | | 387 |
| 6 | Allocation of Parental Responsibility | | 388 |
| | 6.1 | Acquisition of Parental Responsibility by an Unmarried Father | 390 |
| | 6.2 | Should Unmarried Fathers be Afforded Equal Treatment? | 405 |
| | 6.3 | Acquisition of Parental Responsibility by a Female Parent | 411 |
| | 6.4 | Acquisition of Parental Responsibility by a Step-Parent | 411 |
| | 6.5 | Further Methods of Acquiring Parental Responsibility | 412 |
| 7 | Duration of Parental Responsibility | | 414 |
| 8 | Removal of Parental Responsibility | | 415 |
| 9 | The Position of Persons without Parental Responsibility | | 416 |

10 The Nature and Scope of Parental Responsibility 418

10.1 The Complexity of Parental Responsibilities 418

10.2 Statutory Guidance on the Nature and Exercise of Parental Responsibility in Section 2 of the Children Act 1989 419

10.3 The Content and Scope of Parental Responsibility 420

11 The Link with Chapters that Follow 422

8 Children's Rights 424

1 Fundamental Debates Surrounding Children's Rights 424

1.1 Conceptions of a Right: Will Theory v Interest Theory 424

1.2 Should Children have Rights? 425

1.3 Children and Childhoods 427

1.4 Different Childhoods 428

2 Categorising Children's Rights: The Interests Children Might Plausibly Claim 429

2.1 Eekelaar's Future-Oriented Consent and Freeman's Liberal Paternalism 430

3 Legal Protection of Children's Interests 430

3.1 Recognition of Children's Autonomy Interest? 431

3.2 Interpreting *Gillick* 434

3.3 *Axon*: A Human Rights Challenge to *Gillick* 437

4 Children's Rights in Cases of Refusal of Medical Treatment 438

4.1 *Re R (A Minor) (Wardship: Consent to Treatment)* 439

4.2 *Re W (A Minor) (Medical Treatment: Court's Jurisdiction)* 442

4.3 Authorising the Use of Reasonable Force 444

4.4 Criticism of *Re R* and *Re W*: The Distinction between Consent and Refusal 445

4.5 The So-Called 'Retreat from *Gillick*' 446

4.6 Will a Child ever be Considered Sufficiently Competent to Refuse Life-Saving Treatment? 447

5 Children and the European Convention on Human Rights 451

6 Conclusion 453

9 Private Law Disputes and Issues in Children Cases 455

1 The Courts' Focus on Child Welfare: Background 455

1.1 Decision-Making Principles in Section 1 of the Children Act 1989 456

1.2 Section 1(2): 'Delay Likely to Prejudice the Child's Welfare' 458

1.3 Section 1(2A): The Presumption of Parental Involvement 459

1.4 Section 1(3): The Welfare Checklist 460

1.5 Section 1(5): No Order Unless Better for the Child 461

2 The Meaning of 'Welfare' and 'Paramountcy' 463

3 Is Section 1(1) of the Children Act 1989 Compatible with the Requirements of the Human Rights Act 1998? 471

4 Criticism of the Welfare Principle 472

4.1 'Welfare' as a Decision-Making Criterion 472

4.2 Criticisms of the Paramountcy of the Child's Welfare 474

5    Section 8 Orders                                                                     474
   5.1   Giving Directions and Imposing Conditions on Section 8 Orders               475
   5.2   The Family Assistance Order                                                 476
   5.3   The Courts' Powers to Make a Section 8 Order                                477
   5.4   Who May Apply for a Section 8 Order?                                        478
   5.5   Leave to Apply for a Section 8 Order                                        481
   5.6   Restrictions on Applications for, and the Use of, Section 8 Orders         491
   5.7   Child Arrangements Orders Dealing with a Child's Residence                 492
   5.8   Shared Residence                                                           499
   5.9   Attaching Conditions to an Order Dealing with Residence                    508
   5.10  The Legal Consequences of a Child Arrangements Order with Respect to
         the Child's Living Arrangements                                           510
   5.11  Child Arrangements Concerning Contact                                      512
   5.12  Facilitation and Enforcement of Child Arrangements                         531
   5.13  Prohibited Steps Order                                                     544
   5.14  Specific Issue Order                                                       545
   5.15  Restricting Applications for Section 8 Orders under Section 91(14)         566
   5.16  Local Authority Applications for Section 8 Orders                          571

6    International Child Abduction                                                    572
   6.1   A Criminal Offence: The Child Abduction Act 1984                           573
   6.2   Preventing Abduction                                                       573
   6.3   Recovery of Abducted Children                                              573
   6.4   The Hague Convention on the Civil Aspects of International
         Child Abduction                                                           574
   6.5   Non-Convention Countries                                                   587

7    The Inherent Jurisdiction of the High Court                                     588
   7.1   The Inherent Jurisdiction and Local Authorities                            589

10   Children Needing Services, Care, and Protection                                 593
   1    Background                                                                   594
       1.1   The Inadequacies of the Previous Law                                   594
       1.2   Ongoing Practice Concerns: The Climbié Report and the Children Act 2004   596
       1.3   The Children Act 2004                                                   597
   2    Part III of the Children Act 1989                                            598
       2.1   Who are 'Children in Need'?                                             599
       2.2   Provision of Services: Schedule 2 to the Children Act 1989             600
       2.3   Provision of Accommodation for Children                                601
       2.4   Ways in which the Child can be Accommodated                           604
       2.5   The Status of a 'Looked After' Child                                   604
       2.6   Representations and Complaints Relating to Part III                    607

| | | |
|---|---|---|
| 2.7 | The Voluntary Nature of 'Accommodation' | 609 |
| 2.8 | Some Qualifications to the Voluntary Nature of 'Accommodation' | 613 |
| **3** | **Significant Harm: The Threshold for Compulsory Intervention** | **617** |
| 3.1 | Health or Development: Comparison with Similar Child | 619 |
| **4** | **Investigation** | **623** |
| 4.1 | Investigating whether a Child is Suffering, or is Likely to Suffer, Significant Harm | 623 |
| 4.2 | Child Assessment Orders | 625 |
| 4.3 | The Power of a Court to Direct a Section 37 Investigation in Family Proceedings | 627 |
| 4.4 | Local Authority Responses to Significant Harm | 627 |
| **5** | **Emergency Protection Orders** | **628** |
| 5.1 | What is an Emergency Protection Order? | 628 |
| 5.2 | The Grounds for Making an Emergency Protection Order | 630 |
| 5.3 | Including an Exclusion Requirement in an Emergency Protection Order | 634 |
| 5.4 | Executing the Emergency Protection Order: The Assistance of the Police and Health Care Professionals | 635 |
| 5.5 | Applying to Discharge an Emergency Protection Order | 635 |
| 5.6 | Challenging the Making of, or Refusal to Make, an Emergency Protection Order | 636 |
| **6** | **Police Protection: Children Act 1989, Section 46** | **637** |
| **7** | **Interim Care and Supervision Orders** | **639** |
| 7.1 | Duration of Interim Orders and Renewal | 640 |
| 7.2 | Interim Care and Supervision Orders: The Threshold | 641 |
| 7.3 | Deciding whether or not to Grant the Order and whether Immediate Removal is Necessary | 641 |
| 7.4 | Interim Care Orders and Assessment | 644 |
| 7.5 | The Child's Right to Refuse to be Assessed | 650 |
| 7.6 | Interim Care Orders and Excluding the Alleged Abuser from the Home | 650 |
| 7.7 | The Role of the Children's Guardian | 651 |
| **8** | **The Final Hearing in Care Proceedings** | **653** |
| 8.1 | The Threshold Test | 653 |
| 8.2 | 'Is Suffering Significant Harm' | 654 |
| 8.3 | 'Or is Likely to Suffer Significant Harm' | 657 |
| 8.4 | Proving Actual or Likely Significant Harm | 658 |
| 8.5 | The Burden and Standard of Proof in Care Proceedings | 664 |
| 8.6 | Harm Attributable to Care not being what it Would be Reasonable to Expect a Parent to Give | 666 |
| 8.7 | The Harm is Attributable to the Child's being Beyond Parental Control | 677 |
| 8.8 | The Welfare Question in Care Proceedings | 678 |

8.9    Delay Likely to be Prejudicial: Sections 1(2) and 32                  680

8.10   Issues Surrounding Application of the Checklist in Care Proceedings   681

9    The Local Authority's Care Plan and Respective Roles of
the Local Authority and Court                                             683

9.1    Reviewing Implementation of the Care Plan                         685

10   The Legal Effect of a Care Order                                          685

11   Supervision Orders                                                        687

12   Deciding Between a Care Order or Supervision Order                        689

13   Discharge of Care Orders                                                  692

14   Contact with a Child in Care                                             693

14.1   Regulating Contact with a Child in Care in Cases of Disagreement   695

14.2   Authorising the Local Authority to Deny Contact                    695

**11  Adoption and Special Guardianship**                                     **700**

1    Adoption                                                                  700

2    The Adoption Service                                                      704

3    Decision Making in Relation to Adoption                                   704

3.1    The Welfare Principle                                              704

3.2    Delay Likely to Prejudice Child's Welfare                         705

3.3    The Welfare Checklist                                             705

3.4    The Child's Religion, Origin, and Background                      706

3.5    The Range of Powers Available                                     706

3.6    The No Order Principle                                            706

3.7    Section 1 of the Adoption and Children Act 2002 and Article 8 of
the ECHR                                                          707

4    Adoption Agencies' Role in Assessing Suitable Adoptions                   707

4.1    Can Information about Adoption be Withheld from the Child's Father
and Other Relatives?                                              708

5    Rules Relating to Parental Consent in Adoption Cases                      712

6    Placement for Adoption                                                    712

6.1    Meaning of 'Placing a Child for Adoption'                         713

6.2    Placement by Agency with Parental Consent (S 19)                  713

6.3    Placement Orders                                                  715

6.4    Consequences of a Placement Order                                 720

6.5    Placement and Contact                                             721

6.6    Effect of Placement or Authorisation to Place                     721

6.7    Duration, and Revocation, of a Placement Order                    723

7    Applications to Adopt                                                     726

7.1    Who may Adopt?                                                    726

7.2    Who may be Adopted?                                               731

7.3    Preliminaries to Adoption                                         731

7.4    Conditions for Making an Adoption Order                           733

7.5  Court's Leave Required to Oppose Making of Adoption Order                733

7.6  Effect of an Adoption Order                                              735

7.7  Setting Aside an Adoption Order                                          736

7.8  Openness in Adoption and On-Going Contact                               739

8    **Special Guardianship**                                                **744**

*Index*                                                                       751

# Table of Cases

A (A Child) (Contact: Sexual Abuse), Re [2002] EWCA Civ 1595 . . . 531

A (A Child) (Parental Order: Surrogacy Arrangement, Re [2015] EWHC 1756 . . . 381

A (A Child), Re [2015] EWFC 11 . . . 654

A (A Child), Re, Darlington Borough Council v M [2015] EWFC 11 . . . 610

A (A Minor) (Care Proceedings), Re [1993] 1 FCR 824 . . . 619

A (A Minor) (Custody), Re [1991] 2 FLR 394 . . . 493, 494

A (A Minor) (Paternity: Refusal of Blood Test), Re [1994] 2 FLR 463, CA . . . 359, 360

A (A Minor), Re [1996] 1 FCR 5, FD . . . 399

A (A Minor) (Residence Order: Leave to Apply), Re [1993] 1 FLR 425 . . . 485, 486

A (Abduction: Contempt), Re [2008] EWCA Civ 1138, [2009] 1 WLR 1482, [2009] 1 FLR 1 . . . 540

A (Adoption: Removal), Re [2009] EWCA Civ 41, [2010] Fam 9 . . . 732

A (Application for Leave), Re [1998] 1 FLR 1 . . . 570, 571

A (Care: Discharge Application by Child), Re [1995] 1 FLR 599 . . . 692

A (Care Proceedings: Learning Disabled Parent), Re [2013] EWHC 3502 (Fam) . . . 669

A (Change of Name), Re [2003] EWCA Civ 56, [2003] 2 FLR 1 . . . 562

A (Children) (Conjoined Twins: Surgical Separation), Re [2001] Fam 147 . . . 458

A (Children) (Interim Care Order), Re [2001] 3 FCR 402 . . . 643

A (Children) (Shared Residence), Re [2002] EWCA Civ 1343, [2003] 3 FCR 656 . . . 504

A (Contact: Section 91(14)), Re [2009] EWCA Civ 1548, [2010] 2 FLR 151 . . . 567

A (Father: Knowledge of Child's Birth), Re [2011] EWCA Civ 273, [2011] 2 FLR 123 . . . 709–11

A (Intractable Contact Dispute: Human Rights Violations), Re [2013] EWCA Civ 1104, [2014] 1 FLR 1185 . . . 515, 527, 539

A (Joint Residence: Parental Responsibility), Re [2008] EWCA Civ 867, [2008] 2 FLR 1593, CA . . . 499, 501, 503

A (Leave to Remove: Cultural and Religious Considerations), Re [2006] EWHC 421 (Fam), [2006] 2 FLR 572 . . . 558

A (Residence Order), Re [2007] EWCA Civ 899 . . . 541

A (Residential Assessment), Re [2009] EWHC 865 (Fam), [2009] 2 FLR 443 . . . 649

A (Sexual Abuse: Disclosure), Re [2012] UKSC 60, [2013] 1 FLR 948 . . . 520

A (Specific Issue Order: Parental Dispute), Re [2001] 1 FLR 121 . . . 547

A (Supervised Contact Order: Assessment of Impact of Domestic Violence), Re [2015] EWCA Civ 486 . . . 525

A (Supervision Order: Extension), Re [1995] 1 FLR 335, CA . . . 640, 687

A (Suspended Residence Order), Re [2009] EWHC 1576 (Fam), [2010] 1 FLR 1679 . . . 540

A (Termination of Parental Responsibility), Re [2013] EWHC 2963 (Fam) . . . 416

A and B (Children) (No 3), Re [2015] EWHC 818 (Fam) . . . 541

A and B (Contact) (No 1), Re [2013] EWHC 2305 . . . 541

A and B (Contact) (No 2), Re [2013] EWHC 4150 (Fam) . . . 541

A and B (Contact) (No 4), Re [2015] EWHC 2839 (Fam) . . . 541

A and B (No 2) (Parental Order), Re [2015] EWHC 2080 . . . 378–81

A and B (One Parent Killed by the Other), Re [2011] 1 FLR 783 . . . 654

A and B (Parental Order: Domicile), Re [2013] EWHC 426 (Fam) . . . 381, 411

A and D (Local Authority: Religious Upbringing), Re [2010] EWHC 2503 (Fam), [2011] 1 FLR 615 . . . 686

A and Others (Minors) (Residence Orders: Leave to Apply), Re [1992] Fam 182, [1992] 3 All ER 872 . . . 486, 487

A and S v Lancashire County Council [2013] 2 FLR 803 . . . 715

A Local Authority and NB [2013] EWHC 4100 (Fam) . . . 662

A Local Authority v GC and Others [2008] EWHC 2555 (Fam), [2009] 1 FLR 299 . . . 713, 714

A v A (A Minor: Financial Provision) [1994] 1 FLR 657 . . . 300, 339, 340

A v A (Family: Unborn Child) [1974] Fam 6 . . . 330, 331

A v A (Financial Provision) [1995] 1 FLR 345 . . . 195

A v A (Financial Provision) [1998] 2 FLR 180 . . . 176, 193

A v A (Maintenance Pending Suit: Provision for Legal Fees) [2001] 1 FLR 377 . . . 171, 336

A v A (Minors) (Shared Residence Order) [1994] 1 FLR 669, CA . . . 503, 505

A v A (Shared Residence) [2004] EWC 142 (Fam), [2004] 1 FLR 1195 . . . 500, 505

A v A and Another (Children: Habitual Residence) (Reunite International Child Abduction Centre and others intervening) [2013] UKSC 60, [2013] 3 WLR 761 . . . 575, 576, 578

A v B and Another (Contact: Alternative Families) [2012] EWCA Civ 285, [2012] 1 FCR 510 . . . 402

A v C [1985] FLR 445 . . . 517

A v East Sussex County Council and Chief Constable of Sussex Police [2010] EWCA Civ 743, [2010] 2 FLR 1596 . . . 638

A v J (Nullity Proceedings) [1989] 1 FLR 110 . . . 18

A v L [2010] EWHC 460 (Fam), [2010] 2 FLR 1418 . . . 83

A v L (Contact) [1998] 1 FLR 361 . . . 517

A v Liverpool City Council [1981] 2 All ER 385 . . . 491, 590

A v Liverpool City Council [1982] AC 363 . . . 442, 645

A v N (Committal: Refusal of Contact) [1997] 1 FLR 533 . . . 538

A v P (Surrogacy: Parental Order: Death of Application) [2011] EWHC 1738 (Fam), [2011] Fam Law 1080 . . . 377

A v SM and HB (Forced Marriage Protection Orders) [2012] EWHC 435 (Fam) . . . 27

A, Re; Coventry County Council v CC and A [2007] EWCA Civ 1383, [2008] 1 FLR 959 . . . 732

AAA v ASH, Registrar General for England and Wales and the Secretary for Justice [2009] EWHC 636 (Fam), [2010] 1 FLR 1 . . . 391

AB v BB and Children (Through their Children's Guardian) [2013] EWHC 227 (Fam) . . . 565

AB v CD [2016] EWHC 10 (Fam) . . . 228

AB v CD and the Z Fertility Clinic [2013] EWHC 1418 (Fam), [2013] 2 FLR 1357, [2013] 2 FLR 1357 . . . 371, 372

AB v CD (Surrogacy - Time Limit and Consent) [2015] EWFC 12 . . . 378, 381, 382

Abbott v Abbott [2007] UKPC 53 . . . 257, 272, 276, 280–2, 284, 287–90

A-C; Re A (Fact- Finding: Possible Perpetrators), Re [2013] EWCA Civ 1321 . . . 675

A City Council v M, F and C (By Her Children's Guardian) [2013] 1 FLR 517 . . . 617

A Council v M and Others (No 1) (Fact-finding; Adoptive Child; Artificial Insemination) [2012] EWHC 4241 (Fam) . . . 618

A Council v M and Others (No 2) (Welfare; Adoptive Children; Artificial Insemination) [2013] 2 FLR 126 . . . 618

Adekunle v Ritchie [2007] BPIR 1177 . . . 271

Adoption Application (Payments for Adoption), Re [1987] Fam 81 . . . 383

Agar-Ellis, Re (1883) 24 ChD 317 . . . 432

Agbaje v Akinnoye-Agbaje [2010] UKSC 13 . . . 82

AJ (Adoption Order or Special Guardianship Order), Re [2007] EWCA Civ 55, [2007] 1 FLR 507 . . . 746, 747

Alfonso-Brown v Milwood [2006] EWHC 642 (Fam), [2006] 2 FLR 265 . . . 13

Al Habtoor v Fotheringham [2001] 1 FLR 951 . . . 576

A Local Authority v DL [2012] EWCA 253 . . . 153

A-M v A-M (Divorce: Jurisdiction: Validity of Marriage) [2001] 2 FLR 6 . . . 13, 16

Ampthill Peerage Case [1977] AC 547 . . . 362

AMS v Child Support Officer [1998] 1 FLR 955 . . . 330

AMV v RM (Children: Judge's Visit to Private Home) [2012] EWHC 3629 (Fam), [2013] 2 FLR 150 . . . 492

Ansah v Ansah [1977] 2 All ER 638 . . . 149

AR (A Child: Relocation), Re [2010] EWHC 1346 (Fam), [2010] 2 FLR 1577 . . . 504, 552, 553, 557

AR v AR (Treatment of Inherited Wealth) [2011] EWHC 2717 (Fam) . . . 207, 210

AR v RN (Habitual Residence) [2015] UKSC 35, [2015] 2 FLR 503 . . . 579

Archer v Archer [1999] 1 FLR 327 . . . 79

AS (Unlawful Removal of a Child), Re [2015] EWFC B150 . . . 610

Asaad v Kurter [2013] EWHC 3852 (Fam) . . . 15

ASB and KBS v MQS (Secretary of State for the Home Department Intervening) [2009] EWHC 2491 (Fam) . . . 731

Ash v Ash [1972] 1 All ER 582 . . . 75

Ashley v Blackman [1988] FCR 699 . . . 175

Aspden v Elvy [2012] EWHC 1387 (Ch) . . . 273

Assicurazioni Generali SpA v Arab Insurance Group [2003] 1 WLR 577 . . . 653

Associated Provincial Picture Houses Ltd v Wednesbury Corp [1948] 1 KB 223, CA . . . 603

Atkinson v Atkinson (No 2) [1996] 1 FLR 51 . . . 185, 186, 249

Atkinson v Atkinson [1988] Fam 93 . . . 185, 186, 249

Attar v Attar [1985] FLR 649 . . . 189

Attorney-General ex rel Tilley v Wandsworth London Borough Council [1981] 1 WLR 854 . . . 603

B (A Child) (Care Order), Re (2013) UKSC 33 . . . 659

B (A Child) (Care Proceedings: Threshold Criteria), Re [2013] UKSC 33, [2013] 1 WLR 1911; 1911, sub nom Re B (Care Proceedings: Appeal) [2013] 2 FLR 1075 . . . 515, 653

B (A Child: Contact), Re [2001] EWCA Civ 1968 . . . 512

B (A Child: Evidence: Passport Order), Re [2014] EWCA Civ 843, [2015] 1 FLR 871 . . . 573

B (A Child) (Immunisation), Re [2003] EWCA Civ 1148, [2003] 2 FLR 1095 . . . 547

B (A Child), Re [2012] EWCA 1475 . . . 653

B (A Child), Re [2013] UKSC 33 . . . 659, 672, 673, 678, 680–2, 718

B (A Child), Re [2016] UKSC 4 . . . 576, 577

B (A Child) (Residence), Re [2009] UKSC 5 . . . 469

B (A Minor), Re, 17 October 1995, CA . . . 394

B (A Minor) (Abduction), Re [1994] 2 FLR 249 . . . 581

B (A Minor) (Access), Re 1984] FLR 648, CA . . . 528

B (A Minor) (Care Order: Criteria), Re [1993] 1 FLR 815 . . . 641

B (A Minor) (Care Order: Review), Re [1993] 1 FLR 421 . . . 683

B (A Minor) (Contact: Stepfather's Opposition), Re [1997] 2 FLR 579 . . . 516

B (A Minor) (Natural Parent), Re [2001] UKHL 70, [2002] 1 FLR 196 . . . 730

B (A Minor) (Wardship: Medical Treatment), Re
(1982) 3 FLR 717, FD . . . 589
B (A Minor) (Wardship: Sterilisation), Re [1987] 2
FLR 314 . . . 466, 589
B (A Minor) (Wardship: Sterilisation), Re [1988] 1 AC
199 . . . 463, 546
B (Abduction: Acquiescence), Re [1999] 2 FLR
818 . . . 584
B (Adoption by One Natural Parent to Exclusion of
Other), Re [2001] 1 FLR 589 . . . 730
B (Adoption Order: Nationality), Re [1999] 2 AC
136 . . . 732
B (Adoption: Natural Parent), Re [2001] UKHL 70,
[2002] 1 FLR 196 . . . 471
B (Adoption: Jurisdiction to Set Aside), Re [1995] Fam
239 . . . 737, 738
B (Care or Supervision Order), Re [1996] 2 FLR
693 . . . 689, 692
B (Care Proceedings: Interim Care Order), Re [2009]
EWCA Civ 1254, [2010] 1 FLR 1211 . . . 642
B (Care Proceedings: Proportionality Evaluation), Re
[2014] EWCA Civ 565 . . . 680
B (Care Proceedings: Standard of Proof), Re [2008]
UKHL 35, [2009] 1 AC 11 . . . 524, 593, 672, 698
B (Care: Interference with Family Life), Re [2003] 2
FLR 813 . . . 632
B (Case Management), Re [2012] EWCA Civ 1742,
[2013] 1 FLR 963 . . . 541
B (Change of Surname), Re [1996] 1 FLR 791,
CA . . . 563–65
B (Children) (Care: Interference with Family Life), Re
[2003] EWCA Civ 786, [2004] 1 FCR 463 . . . 717
B (Children) (Care Proceedings: Standard of Proof)
(Cafcass Intervening), Re [2008] UKHL 35, [2009]
AC 11 . . . 660, 665
B (Children) (Removal from Jurisdiction), Re; Re S (A
Child) (Removal from Jurisdiction) [2003] EWCA
Civ 1149, [2003] 2 FLR 1043 . . . 549, 550
B (Children) (Sexual Abuse: Standard of Proof), Re
[2008] UKHL 35 . . . 678
B (Contact: Child Support), Re [2006] EWCA Civ
1574, [2007] 1 FLR 1949 . . . 326
B (Contact: Stepfather's Opposition), Re [1997] [1997]
2 FLR 579, CA . . . 361, 531
B (Fact-Finding Hearing: Evidence), Re [2008] EWCA
Civ 1547, [2009] 2 FLR 14 . . . 667
B (Interim Care Order: Directions), Re [2002] 1 FLR
545 . . . 648
B (Interim Care Orders: Renewal), Re [2001] 2 FLR
1217, FD . . . 640
B (Leave to Remove), Re [2008] EWCA Civ 1034,
[2008] 2 FLR 2059 . . . 557
B (Leave to Remove: Impact of Refusal), Re [2004]
EWCA Civ 956, [2005] 2 FLR 239 . . . 549, 550
B (Minors: Access), Re [1992] 1 FLR 140, CA . . . 526
B (Minors) (Care: Contact: Local Authority's Plans),
Re [1993] 1 FLR 543 . . . 695–7
B (Minors) (Care Proceedings: Practice) [1999] 1
WLR 238 . . . 672
B (Non-Accidental Injury), Re [2002] EWCA Civ 752,
[2002] 2 FLR 1133 . . . 663

B (Parentage), Re [1996] 2 FLR 15 . . . 368
B (Paternal Grandmother: Joinder as Party), Re
[2012] 2 FLR 1358 . . . 484
B (Placement Order), Re [2008] EWCA Civ 835,
[2008] 2 FLR 1404 . . . 715
B (Prohibited Steps Order), Re [2007] EWCA Civ
1055, [2008] 1 FLR 613, CA . . . 509, 545
P (Prohibited Steps Order: Removal from
Jurisdiction), Re [2013] EWCA Civ 1869 . . . 545
B (Psychiatric Therapy for Parents), Re [1999] 1 FLR
701 . . . 647, 648
B (Refusal to Grant Interim Order), Re [2012] EWCA
Civ 1275, [2013] 2 FLR 153 . . . 644
B (Residence Order: Status Quo), Re[1998] 1 FLR
368 . . . 493
B (Role of Biological Father), Re [2007] EWHC
1952 (Fam) [2008] 1 FLR 1015, [2008] 1 FLR
1015 . . . 401, 402
B (Section 91(14) Order: Duration), Re [2003] EWCA
Civ 1966, [2004] 1 FLR 871 . . . 512, 569
B (Sexual Abuse: Standard of Proof), Re [2008]
UKHL 35 . . . 134
B (Wardship: Abortion), Re [1991] 2
FLR 426 . . . 589
B and L v UK (App No 36536/02) [2006] 1 FLR . . . 35,
8, 9
B, Re; RB v FB and MA (Forced Marriage: Wardship:
Jurisdiction) [2008] 2 FLR 1624 . . . 26, 576
B v B [2007] EWHC 2492 (Fam), [2008] 1 FLR
813 . . . 13, 240
B v B [2008] EWCA Civ 483 . . . 205
B v B (A Minor) (Residence Order) [1992] 2 FLR
327 . . . 452
B v B (Abduction: Child with Learning Difficulties)
[2011] EWHC 2300 . . . 586
B v B (Adult Student: Liability to Support) [1998] 1
FLR 373 . . . 333
B v B (Ancillary Relief) [2008] 1 FCR 613 . . . 206
B v B (Consent Order: Variation) [1995] 1 FLR
9 . . . 219, 223, 224, 243
B v B (Financial Provision) [1990] 1 FLR 20 . . . 177
B v B (Financial Provision: Leave to Apply) [1994] 1
FLR 219 . . . 237
B v B (Financial Provision: Welfare of Child and
Conduct) [2002] 1 FLR 555 . . . 182
B v B (Mesher Order) [2002] EWHC 3106
(Fam) . . . 177
B v B (Minors) (Custody, Care and Control) . . . 495
B v B (Occupation Order) [1999] 1 FLR
715 . . . 133, 135
B v B (Residence: Condition Limiting Geographic
Area) [2004] 2 FLR 979 . . . 509
B v B (Residence Order: Restricting Applications)
[1997] 1 FLR 139 . . . 495, 566, 568, 569
B v C (Surrogacy: Adoption) [2015] EWFC 17
(Fam) . . . 377, 728
B v Chief Constable of the Avon and Somerset
Constabulary [2001] 1 WLR 340 . . . 665
B v El-B (Abduction: Sharia Law: Welfare of Child)
[2003] 1 FLR 811 . . . 588
B v I [2010] 1 FLR 1721 . . . 27

B v P (Adoption by Unmarried Father) [2000] 2 FLR 717 . . . 730

B v S [2009] EWCA Civ 548 . . . 539

B v United Kingdom [2000] 1 FLR 1 . . . 405

B, Re; RB v FB [2008] EWHC 1436 (Fam), [2008] 2 FLR 1624 . . . 26

BB and FB v Germany (App Nos 18734/09 and 9424/11) [2013] 2 FLR 847 . . . 659

B and G (Care Proceedings: FGM) (No 2), Re [2015] EWFC 3 . . . 622

B- G (Parental Orders: Domicile), Re [2014] EWHC 444 (Fam) . . . 380

BN v MA [2013] EWHC 4250 (Fam) . . . 171

Baker v Baker [1995] 2 FLR 829 . . . 187

Balraj v Balraj (1981) 11 FL 110 . . . 80

Banbury Peerage Case [1803–13] All ER Rep 171, 1 Sim and St 153, 57 ER 62 . . . 347

Banks v Banks [1999] 1 FLR 726 . . . 122

Barca v Mears [2004] EWHC 2170 (Ch) . . . 298

Barder v Caluori [1987] 2 All ER 440 . . . 225, 237–42

Barlow Clowes International Ltd (In Liquidation) & Others v Henwood [2008] EWCA Civ 577 . . . 380

Barnardo v McHugh [1891] AC 388 . . . 389

Barnes v Phillips [2015] EWCA Civ 1056 . . . 270

Barrett v Barrett [1988] 2 FLR 516 . . . 176

Basham (Deceased), Re [1987] 1 All ER 405 . . . 291, 292, 295

Baxter v Baxter [1947] 2 All ER 886) . . . 17, 47

BC (A Minor) (Access), Re [1985] FLR 639, CA . . . 528

Beach v Beach [1995] 2 FLR 160 . . . 224

Bellinger v Bellinger [2003] UKHL 21 . . . 3, 32, 33, 38

Belton v Belton [1987] 2 FLR 343 . . . 548

Benham v UK (1996) 22 EHRR 293 . . . 540

Benson v Benson [1996] 1 FLR 692 . . . 239

Berkshire County Council v C and Others [1993] Fam 203, [1993] 1 FLR 569, [1993] 2 WLR 475, FD . . . 645, 646

Berry v Berry [1986] 1 FLR 618 . . . 187

Bhaiji v Chauhan (Queen's Proctor Intervening) [2003] 2 FLR 485 . . . 72

Birch v Birch [1992] 1 FLR 564 . . . 74, 75

Birmingham City Council v AB and Others [2014] EWHC 3090 (Fam) . . . 654

Birmingham City Council v AG and A [2009] EWHC 3720 (Fam) . . . 625

Birmingham City Council v Ali and Others; Moran v Manchester City Council [2009] UKHL 36, HL . . . 158

Birmingham City Council v D; Birmingham City Council v M [1994] 2 FLR 502 . . . 675

Birmingham City Council v H (A Minor) [1994] 2 AC 212 . . . 457, 696

Birmingham City Council v R [2006] EWCA Civ 1748, [2007] 1 FLR 563 . . . 745, 746

Birmingham City Council v S, R and A [2006] EWHC 3065 (Fam), [2007] 1 FLR 1223 . . . 710

Blackstock v Blackstock [1991] 2 FLR 308 . . . 132

Boylan v Boylan [1988] 1 FLR 282 . . . 177

Bremner (A Bankrupt), Re [1999] 1 LR 912 . . . 298

Brierley v Brierley and Williams [1918] P 257 . . . 348

Briody v St Helen's and Knowsley Area Health Authority [2001] EWCA Civ 1010, [2001] 2 FLR 1094 . . . 376

Bristol City Council v A and A and Others [2012] EWHC 2548 (Fam), [2013] 2 FLR 1153 . . . 661

Brixey v Lynas, 1994 SLT 847 . . . 494

Bronda v Italy (App No 22430/93) (2001) 33 EHRR 4 . . . 514

Brooks v Brooks [1995] 2 FLR 13 . . . 215

Brown v Brown (1981) 3 FLR 161 . . . 187

Bryant v Bryant (1976) 120 Sol Jo 165 . . . 194

B-S (Children), Re [2013] EWCA Civ 1146 . . . 678, 718, 719, 733

Buckland v Buckland [1968] P 296 . . . 19

Buffery v Buffery [1988] 2 FLR 365 . . . 71, 75

Burden and Burden v UK (App No 13378/05), [2008] 2 FLR 787 . . . 61, 62

Burgess v Burgess [1996] 2 FLR 981, [2000] 3 FCR 555 . . . 175

Burns v Azadani [1999] 1 FLR 266 . . . 131

Burns v Burns [1984] Ch 317 . . . 57, 278, 279, 303

Burris v Azadani [1995] 4 All ER 802 . . . 153

Burrow v Burrow [1999] 1 FLR 508 . . . 216, 217

C (A Child) (Adoption: Duty of Local Authority), Re [2007] EWCA Civ 1206, [2008] Fam 54 . . . 710, 711

C (A Child) (Direct Contact: Suspension), Re [2011] EWCA Civ 521 . . . 515, 518

C (A Child) (HIV Testing), Re [2000] Fam 48 . . . 547

C (A Child), Re [2006] EWCA Civ 235 . . . 504, 505

C (A Child), Re [2013] EWCA Civ 431 . . . 733

C (A Minor) (Adopted Child: Contact), Re [1993] 2 FLR 431 . . . 484

C (A Minor) (Adoption Order: Conditions), Re [1989] 1 AC 1 . . . 742

C (A Minor) (Leave to Seek Section 8 Orders), Re [1994] 1 FLR 26 . . . 488

C (A Minor) (Wardship: Surrogacy), Re [1985] FLR 846 . . . 589

C (Adoption: Disclosure to Father), Re [2005] EWHC 3385 (Fam), [2006] 2 FLR 589 . . . 710, 712

C (Adoption Proceedings: Change of Circumstances), Re [2013] EWCA Civ 431, [2013] 2 FLR 1393 . . . 707

C (Appeal from Care and Placement Orders), Re [2013] EWCA Civ 1257 . . . 718

C (Care: Contact), Re [2009] EWCA Civ 959, [2010] 1 FLR 895 . . . 641

C (Care: Discharge of Care Order), Re [2009] EWCA Civ 955, [2010] 1 FLR 774 . . . 692, 693

C (Care or Supervision Order), Re [1999] 2 FLR 621 . . . 691, 692

C (Care Proceedings: Parents with Disabilities), Re [2014] EWCA Civ 128 . . . 669

C (Change of Surname), Re [1998] 2 FLR 656 . . . 561, 564, 565

C (Child Abduction) (Unmarried Father: Rights of Custody), Re [2003] 1 FLR 252 . . . 580

C (Contact: No Order for Contact), Re [2000] 2 FLR 723 (Fam) . . . 526

C (Detention: Medical Treatment), Re [1997] 2 FLR 180 . . . 444

C (Direct Contact: Suspension), Re [2011] EWCA Civ
521 [2011] 2 FLR 912 . . . 518

C (Domestic Violence: Fact-Finding Hearing), Re
[2009] EWCA Civ 994, [2010] 1 FLR 1728 . . . 524

C (Family Assistance Order), Re [1996] 1 FLR 424,
FD . . . 476, 477

C (Family Proceedings: Case Management), Re [2012]
EWCA Civ 1489, [2013] 1 FLR 1089 . . . 493

C (Financial Provision), Re [2007] 2 FLR 13 . . . 340, 342

C (Foreign Adoption: Natural Mother's
Consent: Service), Re [2006] 1 FLR 318 . . . 728

C (HIV Test), Re [1999] 2 FLR 1004 . . . 547

C (Indirect Contact), Re [2012] EWCA Civ 128, [2013]
2 FLR 27, [2013] 2 FLR 272 . . . 744

C (Interim Care Order: Residential Assessment), Re
[1997] 1 FLR 1 . . . 646, 647, 649

C (Internal Relocation), Re [2015] EWCA Civ
1305 . . . 508

C (Litigant in Person: Section 91(14) Order), Re [2009]
EWCA Civ 674, [2009] 2 FLR 1461 . . . 567

C (Minors) (Parental Rights), Re [1992] 1 FLR 1,
CA . . . 396, 405

C (Permission to Remove from Jurisdiction),
Re [2003] EWHC 596 (Fam), [2003] 1 FLR
1066 . . . 550

C (Refusal of Medical Treatment), Re [1994] 1
FLR 31 . . . 440

C (Residence: Child's Application for Leave), Re
[1995] 1 FLR 927, FD . . . 488, 489

C (Residence Order), Re [2007] EWCA Civ 866,
[2008] 1 FLR 211 . . . 541

C (Welfare of Child: Immunisation), Re [2003]
EWHC 1376 (Fam), [2003] 2 FLR 1054 . . . 547

C and B (Children) (Care Order: Future Harm), Re
[2000] 2 FCR 614 . . . 717

C and M (Children), Re [1999] EWCA Civ
2039 . . . 552

C and V (Contact and Parental Responsibility), Re
[1998] 1 FLR 392, CA . . . 392, 394, 396, 397, 529

C v B (Abduction: Grave Risk) [2005] EWHC 2988
(Fam) . . . 585

C v C (A Minor) (Custody: Appeal) [1991] 1 FLR
223 . . . 495, 496

C v C (Financial Provision: Personal Damages) [1995]
2 FLR 171 . . . 183

C v C (Financial Relief: Short Marriage) [1997] 2 FLR
26 . . . 177, 335

C v C (Minors: Custody) [1988] 2 FLR 291, CA . . . 495

C v F (Disabled Child: Maintenance Orders) [1998] 2
FLR 1, CA . . . 329, 340

C v Solihull MBC [1993] 1 FLR 290 . . . 459

C v W (A Minor) (Contact: Leave to Apply) [1998] 1
FCR 618 . . . 485

Cackett v Cackett [1950] 1 All ER 677 . . . 17

Cambra v Jones [2014] EWHC 2264 (Fam) . . . 532

Camden LBC v Alexandrou (No 2) (1998) 30 HLR
534 . . . 254

Camm v Camm (1983) 4 FLR 577 . . . 222

Capehorn v Harris [2015] EWCA Civ 955 . . . 276, 281

Carroll, Re [1931] 1 KB 317 . . . 465

Carron v Carron [1984] FLR 805, CA . . . 331, 333

Carson v Carson [1983] 1 All ER 478 . . . 219, 220

Carter-Fea v Carter-Fea [1987] Fam Law 131 . . . 75

Cartwright v Cartwright (1983) 4 FLR 463 . . . 233

CB (A Child), Re [2015] EWCA Civ 888 . . . 610

CB (A Minor) (Parental Responsibility Order), Re
[1993] 1 FLR 920, FD . . . 393

CB and JB (Care Proceedings: Guidelines), Re [1998]
2 FLR 211 . . . 670, 671

CC (Adoption Application: Separated Applicants), Re
[2013] EWHC 4815 (Fam) . . . 728

CF v KM (Financial Provision for Child: Costs of
Legal Proceedings) [2010] EWHC 1754 (Fam),
[2011] 1 FLR 208 . . . 336

C-G (Contact Order: Staying Contact with Father)
[2013] EWCA Civ 301, [2013] 2 FLR 1307 . . . 512

CH (Contact: Parentage), Re [1996] 1
FLR 569 . . . 369

Chadwick v Chadwick [1985] FLR 606, CA . . . 191

Chalmers v Johns [1999] 1 FLR 392 . . . 133, 143, 146

Chamberlain v Chamberlain [1973] 1 WLR
1557 . . . 334, 335

Chamberlain v De La Mare (1982) 4 FLR
434 . . . 548, 550

Charman v Charman [2007] EWCA Civ 503, [2007] 1
FLR 1246 . . . 53, 69, 205–7, 210, 235

Chase v Chase (1983) 13 Fam Law 21 . . . 250

Chaudhuri v Chaudhuri [1992] 2
FLR 73 . . . 219, 240

Chechi v Bashier [1999] 2 FLR 489 . . . 117, 122

Cheshire County Council v M [1993] 1 FLR
463 . . . 483, 695

Chief Adjudication Officer v Bath [2000] 1
FLR 8. . . . 16

Churchard v Churchard [1984] FLR 635 . . . 538

Citro (A Bankrupt), Re [1991] 1 FLR 71 . . . 298

City of Westminster v IC (By His Litigation Friend
the Official Solicitor) and KC and NNC [2008]
EWHC 198, [2008] 2 FLR 267 . . . 30

C-J (Section 91(14) Order), Re [2006] EWHC 1491
(Fam), [2006] 2 FLR 1213 . . . 567, 569

CL v East Riding Yorkshire Council, MB and
BL (A Child) [2006] EWCA Civ 49, [2006] 2
FLR 24 . . . 667

Clark v Clark [1999] 2 FLR 498, CA . . . 195

Claughton v Charalambous [1999] 1 FLR 740 . . . 298

Cleary v Cleary [1974] 1 All ER 498 . . . 73

Clutton v Clutton [1991] 1 All ER 340 . . . 220

CM v Blackburn with Darwen Borough Council
[2014] EWCA Civ 1479 . . . 718, 719

Co v Co [2004] 1 FLR 1095 . . . 190

Coleman v Coleman [1972] 3 All ER 886 . . . 172

Conran v Conran [1997] 2 FLR 615 . . . 197

Coombes v Smith [1986] 1 WLR 808 . . . 293

Corbett v Corbett (Otherwise Ashley) [1971] P 83,
[1970] 2 WLR 1306 . . . 18, 22, 30–3, 35, 374

Cordle v Cordle [2002] 1 FCR 97 . . . 182, 188

Cornick v Cornick (No 3) [2001] 2 FLR 1240 . . . 245

Cornick v Cornick [1994] 2 FLR 530 . . . 238, 239

Cossey v UK [1991] 2 FLR 492 . . . 31

Coventry City Council v C, B, CA and CH1 [2012] EWHC 2190 (Fam), [2013] 2 FLR 987 . . . 609, 610, 616

Coventry City Council v O (Adoption) [2011] EWCA Civ 729, [2011] 2 FLR 936 . . . 713

Covezzi and Morselli v Italy (2003) 38 EHRR 28 . . . 632

Cowan v Cowan [2001] 2 FLR 192 . . . 208, 209

Crabb v Arun District Council [1976] Ch 179 . . . 295

Crago v Julian [1992] 1 WLR 372 . . . 254

Crake v Supplementary Benefits Commission [1982] 1 All ER 498 . . . 117

Crossley v Crossley [2007] EWCA Civ 1491 . . . 235, 287

Croydon London Borough Council v A (No 3) [1992] Fam 169, CA . . . 544, 690

Crozier v Crozier [1994] 1 FLR 126 . . . 320

Curley v Parkes [2004] EWCA Civ 1515 . . . 257

Curran v Collins [2015] EWCA Civ 404 . . . 274

Currey v Currey [2006] EWCA Civ 1338 . . . 171

CW v SG (Parental Responsibility: Consequential Orders) [2013] EWHC 854 (Fam), [2013] 2 FLR 655 . . . 416

D (A Child) (Care Order: Evidence), Re [2010] EWCA Civ 1000, [2011] 1 FLR 447 . . . 668

D (A Child) (IVF Treatment), Re [2001] 1 FLR 972, CA . . . 392

D (A Child) (Residence: Natural Parent), Re [2000] 1 FCR 97, FD . . . 470

D (A Child), Re [2010] EWCA Civ 470 . . . 570

D (A Child), Re [2014] EWHC 3388 (Fam) . . . 715

D (A Child), Re [2014] EWCA Civ 315 . . . 416

D (A Minor) (Care or Supervision Order), Re [1993] 2 FLR 423 . . . 690

D (A Minor) (Child: Removal from Jurisdiction), Re [1992] 1 All ER 892 . . . 573

D (A Minor) (Contact: Mother's Hostility), Re [1993] 2 FLR 1 . . . 528, 529

D (A Minor), Re [1995] 3 FCR 783, FD . . . 398

D (Abduction: Child's Objections), Re [2011] EWCA Civ 1294 . . . 586

D (Abduction: Rights of Custody), Re [2006] UKHL 51, [2007] 1 FLR 961 . . . 580, 581, 587

D (Adoption: Leave to Oppose), Re [2015] EWCA Civ 703 . . . 733

D (Adoption: Parent's Consent), Re [1977] 1 All ER 145 . . . 716

D (Article 13b: Non-Return), Re [2006] EWCA Civ 146, [2006] 2 FLR 305 . . . 585

D (Care Order: Evidence), Re [2010] EWCA Civ 1000, [2011] 1 FLR 447 . . . 662, 668

D (Children), Re [2009] EWCA Civ 1551 . . . 540

D (Contact and Parental Responsibility: Lesbian Mothers and Known Father), Re [2006] 1 FCR 556, FD . . . 399, 401, 402

D (Contact: Reasons for Refusal), Re [1997] 2 FLR 48, CA . . . 529

D (Habitual Residence: Consent and Acquiescence, Re [2015] EWHC 1562 . . . 580

D (Interim Care Order), Re [2011] EWCA Civ 1743, [2013] 1 FLR 173 . . . 641

D (Intractable Contact Dispute: Publicity), Re [2004] EWHC 727 (Fam), [2004] 1 FLR 1226 . . . 520, 532, 539

D (Jurisdiction: Programme of Assessment or Therapy), Re [1999] 2 FLR 632 . . . 648

D (Leave to Remove: Appeal), Re [2010] EWCA Civ 50, [2010] 2 FLR 1605 . . . 553, 554

D (Minors), Re, 20 March 1995, CA . . . 400

D (Minors) (Residence: Imposition of Conditions), Re [1996] 2 FLR 281, CA . . . 510

D (Paternity), Re [2006] EWHC 3545 (Fam), [2007] 2 FLR 26 . . . 349, 358, 361

D (Prohibited Steps Order), Re [1996] 2 FLR 273 . . . 510, 544

D (Unborn Baby), Re [2009] EWHC 446 (Fam), [2009] 2 FLR 313 . . . 638

D and H (Care: Termination of Contact), Re [1997] 1 FLR 841 . . . 698

D and L (Surrogacy), Re [2012] EWHC 2631 (Fam), [2013] 2 FLR 275 . . . 381

D v D (1982) 12 Fam Law 150 . . . 18

D v D (Child of the Family) (1981) 2 FLR 93, CA . . . 331

D v D (County Court Jurisdiction: Injunctions) [1993] 2 FLR 802 . . . 623

D v D (Nature of Recognition of Overseas Divorce) [2005] EWHC 3342 (Fam), [2006] 2 FLR 825 . . . 81

D v D (Nullity: Statutory Bar) [1979] Fam 70 . . . 21

D v D (Shared Residence Order) [2001] 1 FLR 495, CA . . . 503, 504

D v Hereford and Worcester County Council [1991] Fam 14, [1991] 1 FLR 205 . . . 394

D v N (Contact Order: Conditions) [1997] 2 FLR 797 . . . 476, 589

Dart v Dart [1996] 2 FLR 286 . . . 168, 181, 197, 202

Datec Electronics Holdings Ltd v United Parcels Service Ltd [2007] 1 WLR 1325 . . . 653

Daubney v Daubney [1976] 2 All ER 453 . . . 183

Davis v Johnson [1978] 1 All ER 1132 . . . 114, 139

Dawson v Wearmouth [1999] 2 AC 308 . . . 560, 562, 563, 565

DE v AG (1985) 1 Rob Eccl 279 . . . 17

De L v H [2009] EWHC 3074 (Fam), [2010] 1 FLR 1229 . . . 587

De Lasala v de Lasala [1979] 2 All ER 1146 . . . 224

De Lasala v de Lasala [1980] AC 546, PC . . . 224

De Manneville v De Manneville (1804) 10 Ves 54 . . . 455

Dean v Stout (Trustee in Bankruptcy) [2005] EWHC 3315 (Ch) . . . 298

Delaney v Delaney [1990] 2 FLR 457 . . . 319

Dellow's Will Trusts, Re [1964] 1 WLR 451 . . . 664

Den Heyer v Newby [2006] 1 FLR 1114 . . . 238

Dennis (Deceased), Re [1981] 2 All ER 140 . . . 335

Dennis v Dennis [1955] P 153 . . . 46, 72, 73

Devjee v Patel [2006] EWCA Civ 1211 . . . 125, 149

Devon County Council v EB and Others [2013] EWHC 968 (Fam) . . . 661

Devon County Council v S [1994] 1 FLR 355 . . . 589

DH (A Minor) (Child Abuse), Re [1994] 1 FLR 679 . . . 462, 683

Dharamshi v Dharamshi [2001] 1 FCR 492 . . . 206

Dickson v Rennie [2014] EWHC 4306 (Fam) [2015] 2 FLR 978 . . . 329

Din v Wandsworth London Borough Council [1983] 1 AC 657 . . . 160

Dixon v Marchant [2008] 1 FLR 655 . . . 238, 240, 242

Dodsworth v Dodsworth (1973) 228 EG 1115 . . . 295

Dolan v Corby [2011] EWCA Civ 664 . . . 146

Donohue v Ingram [2006] EWHC 282 . . . 298

Dorney-Kingdom v Dorney-Kingdom [2000] 2 FLR 855 . . . 220

Down Lisburn Health and Social Services Trust v H [2006] UKHL 36, [2007] 1 FLR 121 . . . 742

D-R (Adult: Contact), Re [1999] 1 FLR 1161, CA . . . 516

Drake v Whipp [1996] 1 FLR 826 . . . 287

DT v LBT (Abduction: Domestic Abuse) [2010] EWHC 3177, [2011] 1 FLR 1215 . . . 578, 585

Duhur-Johnson v Duhur-Johnson (Attorney-General Intervening) [2005] 2 FLR 1042 . . . 82

Dukali v Lamrani [2012] EWHC 1748 . . . 14, 16

Duxbury v Duxbury [1987] 1 FLR 7 . . . 172, 197

E (A Minor: Access), Re [1987] 1 FLR 368 . . . 529

E (A Minor) (Care Order: Contact), Re [1994] 1 FLR 146 . . . 696, 697

E (A Minor) (Wardship: Medical Treatment), Re [1993] 1 FLR 386 . . . 447–50

E (Abduction: Non-Convention Country), Re [1999] 2 FLR 642 . . . 588

E (An Alleged Patient), Re; Sheffield City Council v E and S [2004] EWHC 2808 (Fam), [2005] 1 FLR 965 . . . 5, 6

E (Children) (Abduction: Custody Appeal), Re [2011] UKSC 27, [2011] 2 FLR 758 . . . 572, 582, 585

E (Family Assistance Order), Re [1999] 2 FLR 512, FD . . . 476, 477

E (Parental Responsibility: Blood Tests), Re [1995] 1 FLR 392 . . . 349, 399

E (Relocation: Removal From the Jurisdiction), Re [2012] EWCA Civ 1893, [2013] 2 FLR 290 . . . 555

E (Residence: Imposition of Conditions), Re [1997] 2 FLR 638, CA . . . 421, 492, 509

E v E (Ouster Order) [1995] 1 FLR 224 . . . 131

EB v France (App No 43546/02) [2008] 1 FLR 850, ECtHR . . . 708

ECC (The Local Authority) v SM [2010] EWHC 1694 (Fam), [2011] 1 FLR 234 . . . 731

Edgar v Edgar [1980] 1 WLR 1410 . . . 222, 223, 230, 239

E-L (A Child) (Contact), Re [2003] EWCA Civ 1947 . . . 520

El Fadl v El Fadl [2000] 1 FLR 175 . . . 83

El Gamal v Al Maktoum [2011] EWHC 3763 . . . 13, 14

Elliott v Elliott [2001] 1 FCR 477 . . . 219, 220

Elsholz v Germany (App No 25735/94) (2002) 34 EHRR 58 . . . 471, 514, 515

E-R (A Child), Re [2015] EWCA Civ 405 . . . 465

Eroglu v Eroglu [1994] 2 FLR 287 . . . 82

Essex County Council v B [1993] 1 FLR 866 . . . 651

Essex County Council v F [1993] 1 FLR 847 . . . 636

Estate of Park, Re [1954] P 112 . . . 5

ET, BT and CT v Islington Borough Council [2013] EWCA Civ 323 . . . 623

ET (Parental Responsibility: Blood Tests), Re [1995] 1 FLR 392 . . . 394

ET (Serious Injuries: Standard of Proof) (Note), Re [2003] 2 FLR 1205 . . . 665

Evans v Evans [1989] 1 FLR 351 . . . 194, 195

Evans v UK [2007] 2 FCR 5, ECtHR . . . 365

Eve, Re 31 DLR (4th) 1 . . . 467

Evelyn, Re [1998] Fam 55, CA . . . 468

Evers Trust, Re; Papps v Evers [1980] 3 All ER 399 . . . 298

Eves v Eves [1975] 1 WLR 1338 . . . 274–6, 286, 302

F (A Child) (Contact Order), Re [2001] 1 FCR 422, CA . . . 524

F (A Child) (International Relocation Cases), Re [2015] EWCA Civ 882 . . . 555, 556

F (A Minor) (Blood Tests: Parental Rights), Re [1993] Fam 314, CA . . . 354, 355, 356

F (A Ward) (Leave to Remove Ward Out of the Jurisdiction), Re [1988] 2 FLR 116 . . . 548

F (Abduction: Removal Outside Jurisdiction), Re [2008] EWCA Civ 842 . . . 583

F (Abduction: Unmarried Father: Sole Carer), Re [2003] 1 FLR 839 . . . 581

F (Care Proceedings: Interim Care Order), Re [2010] EWCA Civ 826, [2010] 2 FLR 1455 . . . 643

F (Child Abduction: Risk if Returned), Re [1995] 2 FLR 31 . . . 585

F (Child: International Relocation), Re [2012] EWCA Civ 1364, [2013] 1 FLR 645 . . . 551, 552, 555

F (Child: Surname), Re [1993] 2 FLR 837 . . . 563

F (Children) (DNA Evidence), Re [2007] EWHC 3235 (Fam), [2008] 1 FLR 348 . . . 349

F (Children), Re [2003] EWCA Civ 592 . . . 499

F (Children) (Restriction on Applications), Re [2005] EWCA Civ 499, [2005] 2 FLR 950 . . . 568

F (Children) (Shared Residence Order), Re [2003] EWCA Civ 592, [2003] 2 FLR 397 . . . 500

F (Contact: Child in Care), Re [1995] 1 FLR 510, FD . . . 458, 694

F (Contact: Enforcement), Re [1998] 1 FLR 691 . . . 538

F (In Utero) (Wardship), Re [1988] Fam 122, [1988] 2 FLR 307 . . . 638

F (Infants) (Adoption Order: Validity), Re [1977] Fam 165 . . . 737

F (Interim Care Order), Re [2011] EWCA Civ 258, [2011] 2 FLR 856 . . . 671

F (Mental Patient: Sterilisation), Re [1990] 2 AC 1, [1989] 2 FLR 376 . . . 638

F (Minor: Abduction: Jurisdiction), Re [1991] Fam 25 . . . 588

F (Minors) (Denial of Contact), Re [1993] 2 FLR 677, CA . . . 526

F (Mother) v F (Father) [2013] EWHC 2638 (Fam) . . . 547

F (Placement Order), Re [2008] EWCA Civ 439, [2008] 2 FLR 550 . . . 703, 723

F (Shared Residence Order), Re [2003] EWCA Civ 592, [2003] 2 FLR 347 . . . 500

F (Specific Issue: Child Interview), Re [1995] 1 FLR 819 . . . 546, 547

F and H (Children: Relocation), Re [2007] EWCA Civ 692, [2008] 2 FLR 1667 . . . 556

F and R (Section 8 Order: Grandparent's Application), Re [1995] 1 FLR 524, FD . . . 481

F v Cambridgeshire County Council [1995] 1 FLR 516 . . . 492

F v G (Child: Financial Provision) [2004] EWHC 1848 (Fam), [2005] 1 FLR 261 . . . 343

F v Leeds City Council [1994] 2 FLR 60 . . . 458, 619

F v S (Adoption: Ward) [1973] Fam 203, [1973] 1 All ER 722 . . . 482

F v Wirral Metropolitan Borough Council [1991] 2 All ER 648 . . . 617

FH (Dispensing with Fact-Finding Hearing), Re [2008] EWCA Civ 1249, [2009] 1 FLR 349, CA . . . 524

F(R) (An Infant), Re [1970] 1 QB 385; Re RA (Minors) (1974) 4 Fam Law 182 . . . 737

FZ v SZ (Ancillary Relief: Conduct: Valuations) [2010] EWHC 1630 (Fam) . . . 207

Farley v Secretary of State for Work and Pensions and Another [2006] UKHL 31, [2006] 2 FLR 1243 . . . 327

Ferguson & Others v United Kingdom . . . 48

Ferrari v Romania (Application No 1714/10) [2015] 2 FLR 303, ECtHR . . . 574

Fisher v Fisher [1988] EWCA Civ 4 . . . 179, 188

Fitzpatrick v Sterling Housing Association Ltd [2001] AC 27, [2000] 1 FLR 271 . . . 36, 37, 43

Flavell v Flavell [1997] 1 FLR 353 . . . 243, 244

Fleming v Fleming [2003] EWCA Civ 1841 . . . 201

Fleming v Fleming [2004] 1 FLR 667 . . . 185, 186

Foley v Foley [1981] 2 All ER 857 . . . 189, 190

Fowler v Barron [2008] EWCA Civ 377 . . . 265, 266, 267

Foyle v Turner [2007] BPIR 43 . . . 298

Frary v Frary [1993] 2 FLR 696 . . . 185

Fraser v Children's Court Pretoria North and Others (CCT31/96) [1997] ZACC 1, 1996 (8) BCLR 1085, 1997 (2) SA 218 . . . 408

Frazer Harris v Scholfield Roberts & Hill (A Firm) [1998] 2 FLR 679 . . . 226

Frost v Clarke [2008] EWHC 742 (Ch) . . . 281

FS (Child Abuse: Evidence), Re [1996] 2 FLR 158 . . . 683


G (A Child), Re [2013] EWCA Civ 965 . . . 678, 718

G (A Minor) (Care Order: Threshold Conditions), Re [1995] Fam 16 . . . 670

G (A Minor) (Interim Care Order: Residential Assessment), Re [2006] 1 AC 576 . . . 646, 648

G (A Minor) (Parental Responsibility Order), Re [1994] 1 FLR 504, CA . . . 393, 394

G (Abduction: Children's Objections), Re [2010] EWCA Civ 1232, [2011] 1 FLR 1645 . . . 587

G (Abduction: Psychological Harm), Re [1995] 1 FLR 64 . . . 585

G (Adoption: Unmarried Couple), Re [2008] UKHL 38, [2009] 1 AC 173 . . . 376

G (Care: Challenge To Local Authority's Decision), Re [2003] EWHC 551 (Fam), [2003] 2 FLR 42 . . . 668, 687

G (Child Case: Parental Involvement), Re [1996] 1 FLR 857, CA . . . 483, 485, 570

G (Children Act 1989, Schedule 1), Re [1996] 2 FLR 171 . . . 337

G (Children) (Care Order: Evidence), Re [2001] EWCA Civ 968, [2001] 2 FCR 757 . . . 656

G (Children), Re [2005] EWCA Civ 1283, [2006] 1 FLR 771 . . . 462

G (Children) (Residence: Same-Sex Partner), Re [2006] UKHL 43, [2006] 4 All ER 241 . . . 362, 460, 467, 469–71

G (Children: Contact), Re [2002] EWCA Civ 761, [2002] 3 FCR 377 . . . 742

G (Contempt: Committal), Re [2003] EWCA Civ 489, [2003] 1 WLR 2051, [2003] 2 FLR 58 . . . 540

G (Education: Religious Upbringing), Re [2012] EWCA Civ 123, [2013] 1 FLR 677 . . . 463, 464, 497, 498

G (Financial Provision: Liberty to Restore Application for Lump Sum), Re [2004] 1 FLR 997 . . . 191

G (Interim Care Order: Residential Assessment), Re [2006] 1 AC 576 . . . 641

G (Intractable Contact Dispute), Re [2013] EWHC B16 (Fam) . . . 527

G (Leave to Remove), Re [2007] EWCA Civ 1497, [2008] 1 FLR 1587 . . . 547

G (Minors) (Interim Care Order), Re [1993] 2 FLR 839, CA . . . 640, 641

G (Parentage: Blood Sample), Re [1997] 1 FLR 360, CA . . . 360

G (Parental Responsibility Order), Re [2006] 2 FLR 1092, CA . . . 399

G (Parental Responsibility: Education), Re [1994] 2 FLR 964 . . . 419

G (Removal from Jurisdiction), Re [2005] EWCA Civ 170, [2005] 2 FLR 166 . . . 556

G (Residence: Restriction on Further Applications), Re [2008] EWCA Civ 1468, [2009] 1 FLR 894, CA . . . 474, 569

G (Residence: Same-Sex Partner), Re [2006] UKHL 43, [2006] 2 FLR 629, HL . . . 345, 505

G (Shared Residence), Re [2012] EWCA Civ 1434, [2013] 1 FLR 1323 . . . 467

G (Shared Residence Order: Biological Mother of Donor Egg), Re [2014] EWCA Civ 336, [2014] 2 FLR 897 . . . 403, 501

G (Special Guardianship Order), Re [2010] EWCA Civ 300, [2010] 2 FLR 696 . . . 746

G (Surrogacy: Foreign Domicile), Re [2007] EWHC 2814 (Fam), [2008] 1 FLR 1047 . . . 366, 381

G and A (Care Order: Freeing Order: Parents with a Learning Disability), Re [2006] NI Fam 8 . . . 668

G and M (Parental Orders), Re [2014] EWHC 1561 (Fam) . . . 376, 380

G and R (Child Sexual Abuse: Standard of Proof), Re [1995] 2 FLR 867 . . . 660

G v B [2013] EWHC 3414 (Fam) . . . 206

G v ED and DD (Parental Order: Time Limit) [2015] EWHC 911 (Fam) . . . 378

G v F (Non-Molestation Order: Jurisdiction) [2000] Fam 186 . . . 117

G v F (Shared Residence: Parental Responsibility) [1998] 2 FLR 799 . . . 485, 496

G v G [2012] EWHC 167 (Fam) . . . 169, 171, 177, 182

G v G (Occupation Order: Conduct) [2000] 2 FLR 36 . . . 144, 146

G v G (Ouster: Ex Parte Application) [1990] 1 FLR 3 95 . . . 151

G v G (Parental Order: Revocation) [2012] EWHC 1979 (Fam), [2013] 1 FLR 286 . . . 384

G v G (Periodical Payments: Jurisdiction) [1997] 1 All ER 272 . . . 243

G v Kirklees Metropolitan Borough Council [1993] 1 FLR 805 . . . 481

G v Netherlands (App No 16944/90) (1993) 16 EHRR CD 38 . . . 712

Gandolfo v Gandolfo [1980] 1 All ER 833 . . . 174

Garcia v Garcia [1992] 1 FLR 256 . . . 80

Gardner v Gardner (1877) 2 App Cas 723 . . . 347

Gaskin v UK (App No 10454/83) (1989) 12 EHRR 36 . . . 353

Gay v Sheeran [1999] 3 All ER 795 . . . 299

Geary v Rankine [2012] EWCA Civ 555 . . . 271, 273, 281

George v George [1986] 2 FLR 347 . . . 114

Gereis v Yagoub [1997] 1 FLR 854 . . . 13

Ghaidan v Godin-Mendoza [2004] UKHL 30, [2004] 2 FLR 600 . . . 37, 43

Ghandi v Patel [2002] 1 FLR 603 . . . 13

Gillet v Holt [2001] Ch 210 . . . 291, 292

Gillick v West Norfolk and Wisbech AHA [1986] AC 112 . . . 320, 357, 358, 406, 420, 431–42, 445–50, 453, 564, 565

Gissing v Gissing [1970] 2 All ER 780 . . . 256, 279

Glaser v United Kingdom (Case No 32346/96) (2000) 33 EHRR 1 . . . 535, 556

Glass v UK (App No 61827/00) [2004] 1 FLR 1019 . . . 422

Gloucestershire County Council v M and C [2015] EWFC B147 . . . 610

Gloucestershire County Council v P [1999] 2 FLR 61 . . . 477

Gloucestershire County Council v S [2015] EWFC B149 . . . 610

Gogay v Hertfordshire County Council [2001] 1 FLR 280, CA . . . 623

Gohil v Gohil [2015] UKSC 61 . . . 188, 226–28

Golubovich v Golubovich [2010] EWCA Civ 810 . . . 69

Goodman v Gallant [1986] 1 FLR 513 . . . 255, 259

Goodrich v Goodrich [1971] 2 All ER 1340 . . . 73

Goodwin v UK (2002) 35 EHRR 18, [2002] 2 FLR 487 . . . 31–3

Görgülü v Germany . . . 712

GR (Care Order), Re [2010] EWCA Civ 871, [2011] 1 FLR 669 . . . 641, 642

GR v CMEC (CSM) [2011] UKUT 101 (AAC), [2011] 2 FLR 962 . . . 324

Granatino v Radmacher (formerly Granatino) [2010] UKSC 42, [2011] 1 AC 534 . . . 223, 229–32, 234, 236, 251

Grant v Edwards [1986] 2 All ER 426 . . . 275, 286

Greasley v Cooke [1980] 3 All ER 710 . . . 292

Greenham v Greenham [1989] 1 FLR 105 . . . 189

GS v Georgia (Application No 2361/13) [2015] 2 FLR 647, ECtHR . . . 574

Grey v Grey [2010] 1 FCR 394 . . . 186

Griffiths v Dawson & Co [1993] 2 FLR 315 . . . 80

Griffiths v Griffiths [1984] Fam 70 . . . 334

Grocholewska-Mullins v Mullins [2014] EWCA Civ 148 . . . 179, 202, 211

Grubb v Grubb [2009] EWCA Civ 976 . . . 145, 146

GS v L [2011] EWHC 1759 . . . 233

Guerroudj v Rymarczyk [2015] EWCA Civ 743 . . . 299

Gulobovich v Gulobovich [2011] EWCA Civ 479 . . . 187

GW v RW (Financial Provision: Departure from Equality) [2003] 2 FLR 108 . . . 190, 192, 200, 204, 328

H (A Child) (Interim Order), Re [2002] EWCA Civ 1932, [2003] 1 FCR 350 . . . 642

H (A Child: Parental Responsibility), Re [2002] EWCA Civ 542 . . . 392, 529

H (A Child), Re [2002] EWCA Civ 2005 . . . 499

H (A Child: Residence), Re [2002] 3 FCR 277 . . . 471

H (A Minor) (Abduction: Rights of Custody), Re [2000] 2 AC 291, [2000] 1 FLR 374 . . . 580

H (A Minor) (Blood Tests: Parental Rights), Re [1997] Fam 89, CA . . . 355, 357, 361

H (A Minor) (Care Proceedings: Child's Wishes), Re [1993] 1 FLR 440 . . . 652

H (A Minor) (Contact), Re [1994] 2 FLR 776, CA . . . 516, 529

H (A Minor: Custody), Re [1990] 1 FLR 51 . . . 470

H (A Minor) (Custody: Interim Care and Control), Re [1991] 2 FLR 109, CA . . . 467, 468

H (A Minor) (Parental Responsibility), Re [1993] 1 FLR 484, CA . . . 531

H (A Minor) (Section 37 Direction), Re [1993] 2 FLR 541 . . . 627, 658

H (A Minor) (Shared Residence), Re [1994] 1 FLR 717 . . . 503

H (Application to Remove from the Jurisdiction), Re [1998] 1 FLR 848 . . . 549

H (Child Orders: Restricting Applications), Re [1991] FCR 896 . . . 566, 568

H (Children), Re [2003] EWCA Civ 369, [2003] All ER (D) 290 . . . 484

H (Children), Re [2009] EWCA Civ 902 . . . 486, 499, 500

H (Children: Residence Order: Condition), Re [2001] EWCA Civ 1338, [2001] 2 FLR 1277 . . . 509

H (Contact Order) (No 2), Re [2002] 1 FLR 22, FD . . . 471, 516, 530

H (Contact: Domestic Violence), Re [2005] EWCA Civ 1404, [2006] 1 FLR 943 . . . 523, 524

H (Leave to Apply for Residence Order), Re [2008] 2 FLR 848 . . . 483, 485, 523

H (Leave to Remove), Re [2010] EWCA Civ 915, [2010] 2 FLR 1875 . . . 552–54

H (Minors) (Abduction: Acquiescence), Re [1997] 1 FLR 872 . . . 584

H (Minors) (Access), Re [1992] 1 FLR 148, CA . . . 517

H (Minors) (Local Authority: Parental Rights), Re (No 3) [1991] Fam 151; sub nom. H (Illegitimate Children: Father: Parental Rights), Re (No 2) [1991] 1 FLR 214 . . . 394, 396

H (Minors), Re, CA (3 December 1999) . . . 527

H (Minors) (Sexual Abuse: Standard of Proof), Re [1996] AC 563 . . . 665, 682, 698

H (Parental Responsibility), Re [1998] 1 FLR 855, CA . . . 393, 395, 404, 410, 419

H (Parental Responsibility Maintenance), Re [1996] 1 FLR 867, CA . . . 395, 396, 404

H (Prohibited Steps Order), Re [1995] 1 FLR 638 . . . 544

H (Residence Order: Child's Application for Leave), Re [2000] 1 FLR 780 . . . 488, 489

H (Shared Residence: Parental Responsibility), Re [1995] 2 FLR 883 . . . 492, 501, 510

H (Supervision Order), Re [1994] 2 FLR 979 . . . 688

H (Termination of Contact), Re [2005] 2 FLR 408 . . . 696

H (Threshold Criteria: Standard of Proof), Re [1996] 1 All ER 1 . . . 134

HA (A Child), Re [2013] EWHC 3634 (Fam) . . . 719

H and A (Minors), Re, 19 January 1993, CA . . . 393

H and A, Re [2002] EWCA Civ 383, [2002] 2 FCR 469 . . . 347, 356

H and G (Adoption: Consultation of Unmarried Fathers), Re [2001] 1 FLR 745 . . . 710

H and Others (Minors) Sexual Abuse: Standard of Proof), Re [1996] AC 563 . . . 658, 664, 666

H v C [2009] 2 FLR 1540[2009] 2 FLR 1540 . . . 329

H v H [1989] 1 FLR 212, CA . . . 520

H v H [2014] EWHC 760 . . . 204

H v H (Child Abuse: Access) [1989] 1 FLR 212, CA . . . 520

H v H (Family Provision: Remarriage) [1975] Fam 19 . . . 241

H v H (Financial Provision) [2009] 2 FLR 795 . . . 207

H v H (Financial Provision: Conduct) [1994] 2 FLR 801 . . . 195

H v H (Financial Provision: Remarriage) [1975] 1 All ER 367 . . . 218

H v H (Financial Provision: Short Marriage) (1981) 2 FLR 392 . . . 189

H v H (Financial Relief: Attempted Murder as Conduct) [2005] EWHC 2911 (Fam), 2006 1 FLR 990 . . . 194

H v H (Financial Relief: Conduct) [1998] 1 FLR 971 . . . 194

H v H (Talaq Divorce) [2007] EWHC 2945, [2008] 2 FLR 857 . . . 83

H v H (The Queen's Proctor Intervening) (Validity of Japanese Divorce) [2006] EWHC 2989 (Fam), [2007] 1 FLR 1318 . . . 82

H v O (Contempt of Court: Sentencing) [2004] EWCA Civ 1691 . . . 125, 149

H v S (Disputed Surrogacy Agreement) [2015] EWFC 36 . . . 385

H v Trafford Borough Council [1997] 3 FCR 113 . . . 667

H, Barhanu and B v Wandsworth Hackney and Islington LBC [2007] EWHC 1082 (Admin), [2007] 2 FLR 822 . . . 607

Haase v Germany [2005] 3 FCR 666 . . . 632

Hadjimilitis (Tsavliris) v Tsavliris (Divorce: Irretrievable Breakdown) [2003] 1 FLR 81 . . . 73

Haines v Hill [2007] EWCA Civ 1284 . . . 225

Hale v Tanner [2000] 2 FLR 879 . . . 125, 149

Hale v Tanner [2000] 3 FCR 62 . . . 124

Hämäläinen v Finland (Application No 37359/09) . . . 34

Hamilton v Hamilton [2013] EWCA Civ 13 . . . 172

Hammerton v Hammerton [2007] EWCA Civ 248, [2007] 2 FLR 1133 . . . 539, 540

Hammond v Mitchell [1991] 1 WLR 1127 . . . 57, 274, 275

Hampshire County Council v S [1993] 1 FLR 559 . . . 642

Hanlon v Hanlon [1978] 2 All ER 889 . . . 218, 220

Hardy v Hardy (1981) 2 FLR 321 . . . 184

Harnett v Harnett [1973] Fam 156 . . . 334

Haroutunian v Jennings (1980) 1 FLR 62 . . . 339, 340

Harris v Harris [2001] 1 FCR 68 . . . 243

Harris v Harris; Attorney-General v Harris [2001] 2 FLR 895, FD . . . 567

Harris v Manahan [1997] 1 FLR 205 . . . 223, 225, 226

Harwood v Harwood [1991] 2 FLR 274 . . . 173, 259

H- B (Contact), Re [2015] EWCA Civ 389 . . . 346, 492, 531

H-C (Care Proceedings: Appeal from Care Order), Re [2014] EWCA Civ 536 . . . 680

Heard v Heard [1995] 1 FLR 970 . . . 237, 239

Hedges v Hedges [1991] 1 FLR 196 . . . 189

Hepburn v Hepburn [1989] 1 FLR 373 . . . 176

Hertfordshire County Council v H [2013] EWHC 4049 (Fam) . . . 663

Hewer v Bryant [1970] 1 QB 357 . . . 432

Hewitson v Hewitson [1995] 1 FLR 241 . . . 191

HFEA 2008 (Cases A, B, C, D, E, F, G and H Declaration of Parentage), In the Matter of [2015] EWHC 2602 (Fam) . . . 372

HG (Specific Issue Order: Sterilisation), Re [1993] 1 FLR 587, FD . . . 545, 546

Hill v Hill [1998] 1 FLR 198 . . . 191

Hillard v Hillard (1982) 12 Fam Law 176 . . . 194

Hipgrave and Hipgrave v Jones [2004] EWHC 2901 (QB) . . . 155

Hirani v Hirani (1983) 4 FLR 232 . . . 19

H-L (A Child) (Care Proceedings: Expert Evidence),
   In Re [2013] EWCA Civ 655, [2014] 1 WLR 1160,
   [2013] 2 FLR 1434 . . . 646
H-L (Expert Evidence: Test for Permission), Re [2013]
   EWCA Civ 655, [2013] 2 FLR 1434 . . . 662
Hobhouse v Hobhouse [1999] 1 FLR 961 . . . 175
Hodak v Newman (1993) 16 Fam LR 1 . . . 470
Hoffmann v Austria (App No 12875/87) [1993]
   ECHR 25, (1994) 17 EHRR 293, [1994] 1 FCR 193,
   ECtHR . . . 497
Hollens v Hollens (1971) 115 SJ 327 . . . 78
Holman v Howes [2007] EWCA Civ 877 . . . 287–9,
   292, 295
Holmes-Moorhouse v Richmond-Upon-Thames LBC
   [2009] UKHL 7, [2009] 1 FLR 904 . . . 502, 507
Hopes v Hopes [1949] P 227 . . . 77
Hoppe v Germany (App No 28422/95) [2003] 1 FLR
   384 . . . 515
Hornal v Neuberger Products Ltd [1957] 1 QB
   247 . . . 664
Horner v Horner [1982] 2 All ER 495 . . . 114
Horton v Horton [1947] 2 All ER 871 . . . 18
Howard v Bodington (1877) 2 PD 203 . . . 378
H-T (Contact: Sexual Abuse), Re [2012] EWCA Civ
   1215, [2013] EWCA Civ 1215 . . . 696
Hudson v Leigh [2009] EWHC 1306 (Fam) . . . 13, 29
Humberside County Council v B [1993] 1 FLR
   257 . . . 134, 618
Hunter v Canary Wharf Ltd [1997] 2 All ER
   426 . . . 154
Hunter v Murrow (Abduction: Rights of Custody)
   [2005] EWCA Civ 976, [2005] 2 FLR 1119 . . . 582
Huntingford v Hobbs [1993] 1 FLR 736 . . . 258,
   259, 287
Hyde v Hyde [1866] LR 1 P & D 130 . . . 3, 16, 18, 42
Hyett v Stanley [2003] EWCA Civ 942 . . . 289
Hyman v Hyman [1929] AC 601 . . . 222, 229

I (Abduction: Acquiescence), Re [1999] 1 FLR
   778 . . . 584
I (Adoption: Appeal: Special Guardianship), Re
   [2012] EWCA Civ 1217 . . . 747
IJ (A Child) (Overseas Surrogacy: Parental Order), Re
   [2011] EWHC 921 (Fam), [2011] 2 FLR 646 . . . 381
I v UK [2002] 2 FLR 518 . . . 31, 32
Ignaccolo-Zenide v Romania (App No 31679/96)
   (2001) 31 EHRR 7 . . . 515
Inwards v Baker [1965] 2 QB 29 . . . 295
Islington London Borough Council v EV [2010]
   EWHC 2340 (Fam), [2011] 1 FLR . . . 642
Ismailova v Russia [2008] 1 FLR 533 . . . 497

J (A Child) (Custody Rights: Jurisdiction, Re) [2006] 1
   AC 80 . . . 575, 578, 588
J (A Child), Re [2015] EWCA Civ 222 . . . 654
J (A Child) (Restriction on Applications), Re [2007]
   EWCA Civ 906, [2008] 1 FLR 369 . . . 568–70
J (A Minor) (Abduction: Custody Rights), Re [1990] 2
   AC 562 . . . 577, 580
J (A Minor) (Contact), Re [1994] 1 FLR 729,
   CA . . . 517, 528, 529

J (A Minor), Re, The Times, 14 May 1992 . . . 442
J (Abduction: Children's Objections), Re [2011]
   EWCA Civ 1448, [2012] 1 FLR 457 . . . 587
J (Care: Care Plan), Re [1994] 1 FLR 253 . . . 683
J (Care Proceedings: Injuries), Re [2009] 2 FLR
   99, FD . . . 667
J (Care Proceedings: Possible Perpetrators), Re [2013]
   UKSC 9, [2013] 1 FLR 1373 . . . 671, 674, 675
J (Child Returned Abroad: Convention Rights), Re
   [2005] UKHL 40, [2005] 2 FLR 802 . . . 552
J (Children) (Care Proceedings: Threshold Criteria),
   Re [2012] EWCA Civ 380, [2012] 2 FLR 842 . . . 672,
   673, 674
J (Costs of Fact-Finding Hearing), Re [2009] EWCA
   Civ 1350, [2010] 1 FLR 1893 . . . 524
J (Leave to Issue Application for Residence Order), Re
   [2003] 1 FLR 114, CA . . . 481–84
J (Leave to Remove: Urgent Case), Re [2006] EWCA
   Civ 1897, [2007] 1 FLR 2033 . . . 550
J (Minors), Re, 2 October 1997, CA . . . 526
J (Minors) (Care: Care Plan), Re [1994] 1 FLR
   253 . . . 684
J (Parental Responsibility), Re [1999] 1 FLR
   784, FD . . . 395
J, Re [2013] UKSC 9, [2013] 1 FLR 1373, [2013] 2 WLR
   649 . . . 659, 673, 698
J (Refusal of Contact), Re [2012] EWCA Civ 720,
   [2013] 2 FLR 1042 . . . 530
J (Residential Assessment: Rights of Audience), Re
   [2009] EWCA Civ 1210, [2010] 1 FLR 1290 . . . 649
J (Specific Issue Order: Leave to Apply), Re [1995] 1
   FLR 669 . . . 546
J (Specific Issue Orders: Child's Religious
   Upbringing and Circumcision), Re [2000] 1 FLR
   571 . . . 419, 547
J v C [1969] 1 All ER 788 at 821, [1970] AC
   668 . . . 465–7, 470, 471, 716
J v C [2006] EWHC 2837 (Fam), [2007] 1 FCR
   365 . . . 361
J v C and Another [2006] EWCA Civ 551, [2007] Fam
   1 . . . 366, 375
J v C (Child: Financial Provision) [1999] 1 FLR
   152 . . . 339, 340
J v G (Parental Orders) [2013] EWHC 1432
   (Fam) . . . 377, 381
J v J and C's Tutor, 1948 SC 636 . . . 737
J v J (A Minor: Property Transfer) [1993] 2
   FLR 56 . . . 337
J v J (Financial Orders: Wife's Long-term Needs
   [2011] EWHC 1010 (Fam) . . . 188
J v S (Leave to Remove) [2010] EWHC 2098
   (Fam) . . . 553, 557
JA (Child Abduction: Non-Convention Country), Re
   [1998] 1 FLR 231 . . . 588
J and Another v C and Others [1970] AC 668 . . . 464
Jackson v Bell [2001] EWCA Civ 387 . . . 298
Jackson v Jackson [1993] 2 FLR 848 . . . 80
Jäggi v Switzerland App No 58757/00,
   ECtHR . . . 353
James v Thomas [2007] EWCA Civ 1212 . . . 275, 281,
   283–6, 291, 292, 294, 302–4

JB v KS and E (Contact: Parental Responsibility)
[2015] EWHC 180 (Fam) [2015] 2 FLR 1180 . . . 402
Jennings v Rice [2002] EWCA Civ 159 . . . 291, 295
JKN v JCN [2010] EWHC 843(Fam) . . . 70
J-M (Contact Proceedings: Balance of Harm), Re
[2014] EWCA Civ 434 . . . 536
JM v CZ [2014] EWHC 1125 (Fam) . . . 151
Jodla v Jodla [1960] 1 WLR 236 . . . 18
Johansen v Norway (App No 17383/90) (1997) 23
EHRR 33 . . . 471, 472, 514, 515, 717
Johnson v Calvert, 5 Cal 4th 84, 851 P2d 776
(1993) . . . 385
Johnson v UK (1999) 27 EHRR 296 . . . 711
Johnson v Walton [1990] 1 FLR 350 . . . 121
Johnston v Republic of Ireland (1986) 9 EHRR
203 . . . 406
Jones v Challenger [1960] 1 All ER 785 . . . 298
Jones v Jones [1975] 2 All ER 12 . . . 194, 195
Jones v Jones [1976] Fam 8, CA . . . 193
Jones v Jones [2000] 2 FCR 201 . . . 244
Jones v Jones [2011] EWCA Civ 41, [2012] Fam
1 . . . 205–7, 210
Jones v Kernott [2011] UKSC 53 . . . 257, 259, 264,
268–70, 281, 287
JPC v SLW and SMW (Abduction) [2007] EWHC
1349 (Fam), [2007] 2 FLR 900 . . . 587
JP v LP and Others (Surrogacy
Arrangements: Wardship) [2014] EWHC 595
(Fam) . . . 376–78

K (Abduction: Case Management), Re [2010] EWCA
Civ 1546, [2011] 1 FLR 1268 . . . 582, 585
K (Abduction: Inchoate Rights), Re [2014] UKSC 29,
[2014] 2 FLR 629 . . . 581
K (Adoption and Wardship), Re [1997] 2 FLR
221 . . . 737
K, Re; A Local Authority v N and Others [2005]
EWHC 2956 (Fam), [2007] 1 FLR 399 . . . 25, 621
K (A Minor) (Custody), Re [1990] 2 FLR
64, CA . . . 467
K (A Minor) (Wardship: Adoption), Re [1991] 1
FLR 57 . . . 470
K (Care Order), Re [2007] EWCA Civ 697, [2007] 2
FLR 1066 . . . 649
K (Care Proceedings: Care Plan), Re [2007] EWHC
393 (Fam) . . . 683, 684
K (Care: Threshold Criteria), Re [2005] EWCA Civ
1226, [2006] 2 FLR 868 . . . 664
K (Contact), Re [2008] 2 FLR 581 . . . 697
K (Contact: Committal Order), Re [2002] EWCA Civ
1559, [2003] 1 FLR 277 . . . 540
K (Contact: Mother's Anxiety), Re [1999] 2 FLR
703 . . . 164, 529
K (Minors: Foreign Surrogacy), Re [2010] EWHC
1180 . . . 381
K (Post-Adoption Placement Breakdown), Re [2013] 1
FLR 1 . . . 677
K (Shared Residence Order), Re [2008] 2 FLR 380,
CA . . . 500, 502, 505
K (Special Guardianship Order), Re [2011] EWCA Civ
635 . . . 747

K (Specific Issue Order), Re [1999] 2 FLR 280 . . . 547
K and Another v FY and Another [2014] EWHC 3111
(Fam) . . . 720
K and H, Re [2006] EWCA Civ 1898, [2007] 1 FLR
2043 . . . 642
K and S (Children) (Contact: Domestic Violence), Re
[2005] EWCA Civ 1660, [2006] 1 FCR 316 . . . 524
K and T v Finland (2000) 31 EHRR 484, [2000] 2 FLR
79, [2001] 2 FLR 707 . . . 632, 661
K v H (Child Maintenance) [1993] 2 FLR 61 . . . 461
K v K [2010] EWCA Civ 125 . . . 194
K v K (A Minor) (Removal from Jurisdiction) [1992] 2
FLR 98 . . . 557
K v K (Children: Permanent Removal from
Jurisdiction), Re [2011] EWCA Civ 793, [2012] Fam
134 . . . 555
K v K (Conduct) [1990] 2 FLR 225 . . . 183
K v K (Financial Provision: Conduct) [1990] 2 FLR
225 . . . 195
K v K (Minors: Property Transfer) [1992] 2 All ER
727 . . . 338
K v K (Periodical Payment: Cohabitation) [2005]
EWHC 2886 (Fam) . . . 186
K v K (Relocation: Shared Care Arrangement) [2011]
EWCA Civ 793, [2011] 2 FLR . . . 551, 552, 554
K v L [2011] EWCA Civ 550 . . . 206–8, 210
K v L (Child Abduction: Declaration) [2012] EWHC
1234 (Fam), [2013] 1 FLR 998 . . . 580
K, W and H (Minors) (Medical Treatment) [1993] 1
FLR 854 . . . 444
Karner v Austria (App No 40016/98) (2004) 38
EHRR 24 . . . 37
Karoonian v CMEC; Gibbons v CMEC [2012]
EWCA Civ 1379[2013] 1 FLR 1121, [2013] 1 FLR
1121 . . . 327
Katz v Katz [1972] 1 WLR 955 . . . 74, 76
Kaur v Singh [1972] 1 WLR 10 . . . 18
Kautzor v Germany (App No 23338/ 09) [2012] 2 FLR
396 . . . 352
KD (A Minor) (Access: Principles), Re [1988] 2 FLR
139 . . . 420
KD (A Minor) (Ward: Termination of Access), Re
[1988] 1 AC 806 . . . 465, 467, 471, 517, 621
Kehoe v UK [2008] ECHR 528, [2008] 2 FLR
1014 . . . 327
Kelly v BBC [2001] 1 All ER 323 . . . 456
Kendrick v Kendrick [1990] 2 FLR 107 . . . 148
Kensington Housing Trust v Oliver (1997) 30 HLR
608 . . . 174
Kent County Council v A Mother and Others [2011]
EWHC 402 Fam) . . . 669
Kent County Council v C [1993] 1 FLR
308 . . . 683, 698
Kent County Council v PA-K and IA (A Child) [2013]
EWHC 578 (Fam) . . . 721
Kevin: Validity of Marriage of Transexual, Re [2001]
Fam CA 1074 . . . 32
Khoransandjian v Bush [1993] 3 All ER 669 . . . 153
Kiam v Crown Prosecution Service [2014] EWHC
1606 (Admin) . . . 637
Kiely v Kiely [1988] 1 FLR 248, CA . . . 334

Kim v Morris [2012] EWHC 1103 (Fam) . . . 72, 74
Kingdon v Kingdon [2010] EWCA Civ 1251 . . . 227
Klentzeris v Klentzeris [2007] EWCA Civ 533, [2007] 2 FLR 996 . . . 585
Kokosinski v Kokosinski [1980] 1 All ER 1106 . . . 190
Kosmopoulou v Greece (App No 60457/00) [2004] 1 FLR 800 . . . 514
Kremen v Agrest (No11) (Financial Remedy: Non-Disclosure: Post-Nuptial Agreement) . . . 234
KS v ND (Schedule 1: Appeal: Costs) [2013] EWHC 464 (Fam), [2013] 2 FLR 698 . . . 336
Kutzner v Germany (2002) 35 EHRR 653 . . . 661, 668
Kyte v Kyte [1988] Fam 145 . . . 194

L (Abduction: European Convention: Access), Re [1999] 2 FLR 1089 . . . 574
L (A Child) (Custody: Habitual Residence) (Reunite International Child Abduction Centre intervening), Re [2013] UKSC 75, [2013] 3 WLR 1597 . . . 578
L (A Child) (Parental Order: Foreign Surrogacy), Re [2010] EWHC 3146, [2011] Fam 106 . . . 383
L (A Child), Re [2009] EWCA Civ 1239, [2010] 2 FLR 188 . . . 359
L (A Minor), 18 March 1997 . . . 677
L (Adoption: Contacting Natural Father), Re [2007] EWHC 1771 (Fam), [2008] 1 FLR 1079 . . . 709, 710
L (Care: Assessment: Fair Trial), Re [2002] EWHC 1379 (Fam), [2002] 2 FLR 730 . . . 687
L (Care Proceedings: Human Rights Claims), Re [2003] EWHC 665 (Fam), [2003] 2 FLR 160 . . . 684
L (Care Proceedings: Removal of Child), Re [2008] 1 FLR 575 . . . 642
L (Care: Threshold Criteria), Re [2007] 1 FLR 2050 . . . 618, 620, 621, 656, 678
L (Children) (Care Proceedings: Significant Harm), Re [2006] EWCA Civ 1282, [2007] 1 FLR 1068 . . . 656, 663, 668
L (Children), Re [2012] EWCA Civ 721 . . . 147
L (Contact: Genuine Fear), Re [2002] 1 FLR 621, FD . . . 405, 530
L (Contact: Transsexual Applicant), Re [1995] 2 FLR 438 (Fam) . . . 526
L (Interim Care Order: Extended Family), Re [2013] EWCA Civ 179, [2013] 2 FLR 302 . . . 642, 645
L (Interim Care Order: Power of Court), Re [1996] 2 FLR 742 . . . 645
L (Medical Treatment: Gillick Competence), Re [1998] 2 FLR 810 . . . 449, 450
L (Minors) (Care Proceedings: Contact), Re [1998] 3 FCR 339 . . . 693
L (Minors), Re, CA (10 June 1998) . . . 526
L (Relocation: Shared Residence), Re [2012] EWHC 3069 (Fam), [2013] 1 FLR 777 . . . 555
L (Sexual Abuse: Standard of Proof), Re [1996] 1 FLR 116 . . . 684, 697
L (Shared Residence Order), Re [2009] EWCA Civ 20, [2009] 1 FLR 1157 . . . 509
L (Special Guardianship: Surname), Re [2007] EWCA Civ 196, [2007] 2 FLR 50 . . . 560, 746

L and H (Residential Assessment), Re [2007] EWCA Civ 213, [2007] 1 FLR 1370 . . . 648
L v Human Fertilisation and Embryology Authority and Secretary of State [2008] EWHC 2149 (Fam) . . . 365
L v L [2002] 1 FLR 642 . . . 209
L v L [2006] EWHC 956 (Fam) . . . 226
L v L [2008] 1 FLR 26 . . . 174, 242
L v L [2011] EWHC 2207 (Fam), [2011] EWHC 3399 (Fam) . . . 176
L v L (Child Abuse: Access) [1989] 2 FLR 16, CA . . . 520
L v L (Financial Remedies: Deferred Clean Break) [2011] EWHC 2207 (Fam) . . . 180
L v London Borough of Bromley [1998] 1 FLR 709 . . . 694, 695, 697
L v M [2014] EWHC 220 (Fam) . . . 223
L v P (Paternity Test: Child's Objection) [2011] EWHC 3399 (Fam) . . . 358, 446
L, V, M, H (Children) (Contact: Domestic Violence), Re [2001] Family Law 260 . . . 164, 517, 518, 519, 522, 523, 524, 531
LA (Care: Chronic Neglect), Re [2009] EWCA Civ 822, [2010] 1 FLR 80 . . . 641, 642, 643
Ladd v Marshall [1954] 1 WLR 1489 . . . 228
Lambert v Lambert [2003] 1 FLR 139 . . . 193, 208, 209
Lambeth London Borough v S, C, V and J (By His Guardian) [2006] EWHC 326 (Fam), [2007] 1 FLR 152 . . . 353, 356
Lancashire County Council v B [2002] 2 AC 147 . . . 666–8, 670, 671, 674, 682, 698
Lancashire County Council v D and E [2008] EWHC 832 (Fam) . . . 662
Lancashire County Council v R [2008] EWHC 2959 (Fam), [2010] 1 FLR 387 . . . 663
Lang v Lang [1955] AC 402 . . . 77
Langley v Liverpool City Council [2005] EWCA Civ 1173, [2006] 1 FLR 342 . . . 637, 638
Laskar v Laskar [2008] EWCA Civ 347 . . . 271
Lau v Director of Public Prosecutions [2000] 1 FLR 799 . . . 155
Lauder v Lauder [2007] 2 FLR 802 . . . 247, 248
Lawrence v Gallagher [2012] EWCA Civ 394 . . . 167, 206
L-B (Reversal of Judgment), Re [2013] UKSC 8 . . . 672
LBH (A Local Authority) v KJ and IH [2007] EWHC 2798 . . . 668, 669
LC (Children), Re [2014] UKSC 1 . . . 578
LC (Habitual Residence: Grave Risk of Harm), Re [2014] EWFC 8 (Fam), [2015] 1 FLR 1019 . . . 579
Le Foe v Le Foe [2001] 2 FLR 970 . . . 279, 280
Le Marchant v Le Marchant [1977] 3 All ER 610 . . . 174
Leadbeater v Leadbeater [1985] FLR 789 . . . 176, 177, 182, 193
Lee v Lee (1984) FLR 243 . . . 136
Leeds City Council v C [1993] 1 FLR 269 . . . 683
Leeds City Council v YX and ZX (Assessment of Sexual Abuse) [2008] EWHC 802 (Fam) . . . 662

Leeds Teaching Hospital NHS Trust v A and Others [2003] 1 FCR 599, [2003] EWHC 259 (QB) . . . 367, 372

Leicester City Council v S & Others [2014] EWHC 1575 (Fam) . . . 610

Leicestershire County Council v G [1994] 2 FLR 329 . . . 689

Lewis v Lewis [1978] 1 All ER 729 . . . 148

LG (Adoption: Leave to Oppose), Re [2015] EWFC 52 . . . 735

Lissimore v Downing [2003] 2 FLR 308 . . . 292

Livesey v Jenkins [1985] 1 All ER 106 . . . 174, 224–6

Livingstone-Stallard v Livingstone-Stallard [1974] Fam 47 . . . 75

Lloyds Bank v Rosset [1990] 1 All ER 1111 . . . 253–5, 273, 275–80, 282, 283

Local Authority, A v DL [2012] EWCA 253 . . . 153

Lomas v Parle [2004] 1 FLR 812 . . . 124, 125, 149, 156

London Borough of Hillingdon v AO [2014] EWHC 75 (Fam) . . . 676

London Borough of Southwark v B [1993] 2 FLR 559, CA . . . 663

London Borough of Southwark v D; sub nom R (On the Application of D) v A Local Authority [2007] EWCA Civ 182, [2007] 1 FLR 2181, [2007] Family Law 701 . . . 607

London Borough of Tower Hamlets v B [2015] EWHC 2491 (Fam) . . . 618

London Borough of Tower Hamlets v D, E and F . . . 679

London Borough of Wandsworth v W [2014] EWHC 3682 (Fam) . . . 679

Lonslow v Hennig [1986] 2 FLR 378 . . . 548

Lord Lilford v Glyn [1979] 1 All ER 441 . . . 195, 334, 335

LRP (A Child) (Care Proceedings: Placement Order), Re [2013] EWHC 3974 (Fam) . . . 719

Luckwell v Limata [2014] EWHC 502 (Fam) . . . 233, 236

LW (Children) (Enforcement and Committal: Contact), Re; CPL v CH-W and others [2010] EWCA Civ 1253, [2011] 1 FCR 78 . . . 512, 514, 539–43

M (A Child: Long-Term Fostering), Re [2014] EWCA Civ 1406 . . . 679, 718

M (A Child) (Prohibited Steps Order: Appeal), Re [2002] All ER (D) 401 (Nov) . . . 487, 544

M (A Minor) (Care Order: Threshold Conditions), Re [1994] 2 AC 424 . . . 676

M (A Minor) (Care Order: Threshold Conditions), Re [1994] 3 All ER 298 . . . 641, 654–6

M (A Minor) (Contact: Conditions), Re [1994] 1 FLR 272 . . . 513, 514

M (A Minor) (No 2) (Appeal), Re [1994] 1 FLR 59 . . . 689

M (A Minor) (Secure Accommodation Order), Re [1995] Fam 108 . . . 457

M (Abduction: Child's Objections), Re [2007] EWCA Civ 260, [2007] 2 FLR 72 . . . 586

M (Abduction: Habitual Residence), Re [1996] 1 FLR 887, CA . . . 575, 576, 578

M (Abduction: Psychological Harm), Re [1997] 2 FLR 690 . . . 585

M (Abduction: Zimbabwe), Re [2007] UKHL 55, [2008] 1 FLR 251 . . . 583

M (Adoption: Leave to Oppose), Re [2010] 1 FLR 238 . . . 734

M (Care: Challenging Decisions by Local Authority), Re [2001] 2 FLR 1300, FD . . . 687

M (Care: Contact: Grandmother's Application for Leave), Re [1995] 2 FLR 86, CA . . . 482, 483, 486, 695

M (Care: Leave to Interview Child), Re [1995] 1 FLR 825 . . . 590

M (Care Order: Parental Responsibility), Re [1996] 2 FLR 84 . . . 676

M (Care Proceedings: Judicial Review), Re [2003] EWHC 850 (Admin), [2003] 2 FLR 171 . . . 632

M (Child Abduction) (European Convention) [1994] 1 FLR 551 . . . 574

M (Child Support: Parentage), Re [1997] 2 FLR 90 . . . 323

M (Child's Upbringing), Re [1996] 2 FCR 473 . . . 470

M (Children) (Residence Order), Re [2004] EWCA Civ 1413 . . . 505

M (Contact: Family Assistance: McKenzie Friend), Re [1999] 1 FLR 75, CA . . . 398, 530

M (Contact: Long-Term Best Interests), Re [2006] 1 FLR 627, CA . . . 537

M (Contact) (Parental Responsibility), Re [2001] 2 FLR 342 . . . 394, 400

M (Contact), Re [2012] EWHC 1948 (Fam), [2013] 1 FLR 1403 . . . 540

M (Contact Refusal: Appeal), Re [2013] EWCA Civ 1147 . . . 515, 525

M (Contact: Violent Parent), Re [1999] 2 FLR 321 . . . 523

M (Contact: Welfare Test), Re [1995] 1 FLR 274, CA . . . 516

M (Education: Section 91(14) Order), Re [2007] EWCA Civ 1550, [2008] 2 FLR 404 . . . 567

M (Fact-Finding Hearing: Burden of Proof), Re [2008] EWCA Civ 1261, [2009] 1 FLR 1177 . . . 662, 672

M (Guardian's Appeal from Care Proceedings), Re [2014] EWCA Civ 226 . . . 680

M (Interim Care Order: Removal), Re [2005] EWCA Civ 1594, [2006] 1 FLR 1043 . . . 643, 644

M (Intractable Contact Dispute: Interim Care Order), Re [2003] EWHC 1024 (Fam), [2003] 2 FLR 636 . . . 527, 539, 541

M (Judge's Discretion), Re [2001] EWCA Civ 1428, [2002] 1 FLR 730 . . . 475

M (Medical Treatment: Consent), Re [1999] 2 FLR 1097 . . . 449

M (Minors) (Adoption), Re [1991] 1 FLR 458 . . . 738

M (Minors) (Care Proceedings: Child's Wishes), Re [1994] 1 FLR 749 . . . 652

M (Minors), Re, 11 October 1995, unreported, CA . . . 415, 416

M (Minors), Re, CA (26 January 2000) . . . 512, 527

M (Parental Responsibility Order), Re [2013] EWCA Civ 969 . . . 398

M (Republic of Ireland) (Child's Objections) (Joinder of Children as Parties to Appeal), Re [2015] EWCA Civ 26, [2015] 2 FLR 1074 . . . 586

M (Residential Assessment Directions), Re [1998] 2 FLR 371 . . . 646, 647

M and R (Child Abuse: Evidence), Re [1996] 2 FLR 195 . . . 658, 664, 682

M v A (Contact: Domestic Violence) [2002] 2 FLR 921 . . . 524

M v A (Wardship: Removal from Jurisdiction) [1993] 2 FLR 715 . . . 557

M v B (Ancillary Proceedings: Lump Sum) [1998] 1 FLR 53 . . . 188, 218, 233

M v B, A and S (By the Official Solicitor) [2005] EWHC 1681 (Fam), [2006] 1 FLR 117 . . . 6

M v Birmingham City Council [1994] 2 FLR 141 . . . 677

M v F and H (Legal Paternity) [2013] EWHC 1901 (Fam) . . . 369, 391

M v H (Education: Welfare) [2008] EWHC 324 (Fam), [2008] 1 FLR 1400 . . . 498

M v M (Child: Access) [1973] 2 All ER 81, DC . . . 517

M v M (Child of the Family) (1981) 2 FLR 39, CA . . . 331

M v M (Financial Misconduct; Subpoena against Third Party) [2006] 2 FCR 555 . . . 185

M v M (Financial Provision) [1987] 2 FLR 1 . . . 176

M v M (Financial Relief: Substantial Earning Capacity) [2004] EWHC 688 (Fam), [2004] 2 FLR 236 . . . 190

M v M (Minors) (Jurisdiction) [1993] Fam Law 396 . . . 557

M v M (Minors) (Removal from Jurisdiction) [1992] 2 FLR 303 . . . 552

M v M (Parental Responsibility) [1999] 2 FLR 737 . . . 394, 396

M v M (Property Adjustment: Impaired Life Expectancy) [1993] 2 FLR 723 . . . 191

M v M (Removal from Jurisdiction) [1993] 1 FCR 5 . . . 552

M v P (Contempt: Committal); Butler v Butler [1993] Fam 167, [1993] 1 FLR 773 . . . 540

M v Secretary of State for Work and Pensions [2006] UKHL 11, [2006] 2 AC 91 . . . 42

M v W (Ancillary Relief) [2010] EWHC 1155 (Fam) . . . 184

M v Warwickshire County Council [2007] EWCA Civ 1084, [2008] 1 FLR 1093 . . . 725, 726, 732, 746

M v Westminster City Council [1985] FLR 325 . . . 690

M, T, P, K and B (Care: Change of Name), Re [2000] 2 FLR 645 . . . 565

MA (Care Threshold), Re [2009] EWCA Civ 853, [2010] 1 FLR 431 . . . 621, 653

MA v JA [2012] EWHC 2219 (Fam) . . . 14

Mabon v Mabon [2005] EWCA Civ 634, [2005] Fam 366 . . . 438, 452

Macey v Macey (1981) 3 FLR 7 . . . 187

MacLeod v MacLeod [2008] UKPC 64, [2010] 1 AC 298 . . . 229, 230, 236

Majrowski v Guy's and St Thomas' NHS Trust [2005] EWCA Civ 251 . . . 154, 155

Makarskaya v Korchagin [2013] EWHC 4393 (Fam) . . . 171

Mansfield v Mansfield [2011] EWCA Civ 1056 . . . 183, 220

Marckx v Belgium (1979) 2 EHRR 330 . . . 711

Marckx v Belgium (1979–80) 2 EHRR 14 . . . 406

Mark v Mark [2005] UKHL 42, [2005] 2 FLR 1193, HL . . . 69, 380

Martin v Martin [1977] 3 All ER 625 . . . 174, 185, 220

Martin v Martin [1976] Fam 335 . . . 194

Masefield v Alexander [1995] 1 FLR 100 . . . 224

Maskell v Maskell [2003] 1 FLR 1138 . . . 240

Matter of C (A Child) [2002] EWHC 157 (Fam) . . . 382, 384

Matthews v Matthews [2013] EWCA Civ 1874 . . . 175, 176

McCabe v McCabe [1994] 1 FLR 410 . . . 29, 44

McCartney v McCartney Mills [2008] EWHC 401 (Fam) . . . 206

McEwan v McEwan [1972] 2 All ER 708 . . . 184

McFarlane v McFarlane; Parlour v Parlour [2004] EWCA Civ 872 . . . 199, 205

McGrath, Re [1893] 1 Ch 143 . . . 455, 463

McHardy and Sons (A Firm) v Warren [1994] 2 FLR 338 . . . 288

McLean v Nugent (1980) 1 FLR 26 . . . 148

McMichael v UK (1995) 20 EHRR 205 . . . 405

Medway Council v A and Others (Learning Disability: Foster Placement) [2015] EWFC B66 . . . 610

Medway Council v M and T (By Her Children's Guardian) [2015] EWFC B164 . . . 610

Medway Council v M, F and G (By her Children's Guardian) [2014] EWHC 308 (Fam) . . . 611

Mehta v Mehta [1945] 2 All ER 690 . . . 20

Mercredi v Chaffe Case, C-497/10 PPU, [2012] Fam 22 . . . 575

Mesher v Mesher and Hall [1980] 1 All ER 126n . . . 185, 219, 220

Metropolitan Borough Council v DB [1997] 1 FLR 767 . . . 440, 444

MF v SF [2015] EWHC 1273 (Fam) . . . 196

M-H (A Child) (Placement Order: Correct Test to Dispense with Consent), Re [2014] EWCA Civ 1396 . . . 718, 719

Michael v Michael [1986] 2 FLR 389 . . . 183

Midland Bank plc v Cooke [1995] 2 FLR 915 . . . 276, 287–9

Mikulić v Croatia (App No 53176/99) [2002] 1 FCR 720 . . . 351–53

Miller v Miller; McFarlane v McFarlane [2006] UKHL 24, [2006] 1 FLR 1186 . . . 53, 82, 169, 175, 177, 178, 182, 188, 189, 192, 193, 199–210, 247, 248, 251

Minton v Minton [1979] 1 All ER 79 . . . 175

Mirza v Mirza [2009] EWHC 3 (Ch) . . . 281

Mizzi v Malta (App No 2611/02) [2006] 1 FLR 1048, ECtHR . . . 352

M-J (Adoption Order or Special Guardianship Order), Re [2007] EWCA Civ 56, [2007] 1 FLR 691 . . . 746, 747

M-K (A Child) (Relocation Outside the Jurisdiction), Re [2006] EWCA Civ 1013, [2007] 1 FLR 432 . . . 557

ML v RW [2011] EWHC 2455 (Fam) . . . 402

Morgan v Hill [2006] EWCA Civ 1602, [2007] 1 FLR 1480 . . . 339, 343

Morgan v Morgan [1977] 2 All ER 515 . . . 185

Morris v Morris [2008] EWCA Civ 257 . . . 283, 284, 291, 292, 294

Mortgage Corporation v Shaire [2001] Ch 743 . . . 289

Mortimer v Mortimer-Griffin [1986] 2 FLR 315 . . . 218

M'P-P (Adoption Proceedings: Value to be Placed on Status Quo), Re [2015] EWCA Civ 584 . . . 706

MT v MT (Financial Provision: Lump Sum) [1992] 1 FLR 362 . . . 183

Munro v Munro [2007] EWHC 3315 (Fam), [2008] 1 FLR 1613 . . . 69

Murphy v Gooch [2007] EWCA Civ 603 . . . 296

Murphy v Murphy [2014] EWHC 2263 (Fam) . . . 176

M-W (Care Proceedings: Expert Evidence), Re [2010] EWCA Civ 12, [2010] 2 FLR 46 . . . 662

MW (Leave to Apply for Adoption), Re [2014] EWHC 385 (Fam) . . . 731

Myerson v Myerson [2009] EWCA Civ 282 . . . 242

N (Abduction: Appeal), Re [2013] 1 FLR 457 . . . 576

N (Abduction: Habitual Residence), Re [2000] 2 FLR 899 . . . 578

N (Adoption: Jurisdiction), Re [2015] EWCA Civ . . . 653

N (Children) (Adoption: Jurisdiction), Re [2015] EWCA Civ 1112 . . . 610, 612, 726

N (Children), Re [2015] EWFC 37 . . . 620

N (Minors) (Care Orders: Termination of Parental Contact), Re [1994] 2 FCR 1101 . . . 697

N (Section 91(14) Order), Re [1996] 1 FLR 356 . . . 566, 571

N v B and Others (Adoption by Grandmother) [2013] EWHC 820 (Fam) . . . 747

N v D [2008] 1 FLR 1629 . . . 300, 343

N v F [2011] EWHC 586 (Fam), [2012] 1 FCR 139 . . . 184, 207, 210

N v N (1928) 44 LR 324 . . . 168

NA v MA [2007] 1 FLR 1760 . . . 224

Nash v Nash [1973] 2 All ER 704 . . . 548

Neulinger and Shuruk v Switzerland (App No 41615/07) [2011] 1 FLR 122, ECHR . . . 582, 583

Newbold and Others v Coal Authority [2013] EWCA Civ 584, [2014] 1 WLR 1288 . . . 378

Newcastle City Council v WM and Others [2015] EWFC 42 . . . 610

Newham London Borough v AG [1993] 1 FLR 281 . . . 653, 658

NG v S G [2011] EWHC 3270 (Fam) . . . 187

North v North [2007] 2 FCR 601 . . . 188

North v North [2007] EWCA Civ 760 . . . 180, 214, 245, 247

North Yorkshire County Council v SA [2003] 2 FLR 849 . . . 672

Northamptonshire County Council v AS and Others [2015] EWHC 199 (Fam) . . . 610

Northamptonshire County Council v S [1993] Fam 136, [1992] 3 WLR 1010 . . . 676

Nottinghamshire County Council v P [1993] 2 FLR 134 . . . 544, 571, 627

Nottinghamshire County Council v P [1993] 3 All ER 815 . . . 487, 685

NS v MI [2006] EWHC 1646 (Fam), [2007] 1 FLR 444 . . . 19, 25, 26

NS-H v Kingston Upon Hull City Council and MC [2008] EWCA Civ 493, [2008] 2 FLR 918, CA . . . 726

Nutley v Nutley [1970] 1 WLR 217 . . . 77

Nuutinen v Finland (App No 32842/96) (2002) 34 EHRR 15 . . . 515

Nwogbe v Nwogbe [2000] 2 FLR 744 . . . 132

Nylund v Finland (App No 27110/ 95) (unreported) 29 June 1999 . . . 712

O (A Child) (Supervision Order: Future Harm), Re [2001] EWCA Civ 16, [2001] 1 FCR 289 . . . 717

O (A Minor) (Care Order: Education: Procedure), Re [1992] 2 FLR 7 . . . 619

O (A Minor) (Medical Treatment), Re [1993] 2 FLR 149 . . . 571, 572

O (Abduction: Settlement), Re [2011] EWCA Civ 128 . . . 583

O (Care or Supervision Order), Re [1996] 2 FLR 755 . . . 462, 632, 690, 691

O (Care Order: Discharge of Care Order), Re [1999] 2 FLR 119 . . . 692

O (Contact: Imposition of Conditions), Re [1995] 2 FLR 124, CA . . . 476, 513, 514, 516, 517, 528, 529, 540

O (Contact: Withdrawal of Application), Re [2003] EWHC 3031 (Fam), [2004] 1 FLR 1258 . . . 527, 528, 536

O (Minors) (Care or Supervision Order), Re [1997] 2 FCR 17 . . . 717

O (Minors) (Medical Examination), Re [1993] 1 FLR 860 . . . 646

O (Supervision Order), Re [2001] EWCA Civ 16, [2001] 1 FLR 923 . . . 632

O and Another (Minors) (Care: Preliminary Hearing); Re B (A Minor) [2003] UKHL 18, [2004] 1 AC 523 . . . 672, 681, 682, 698

O v L (Blood Tests) [1995] 2 FLR 930, CA . . . 355

O'D v O'D [1976] Fam 83 . . . 197, 204

O'Donoghue and Others v UK (App No 34848/07) [2011] 2 FCR 197 . . . 5

O'Hara, Re [1900] 2 IR 232 . . . 465

O'Neill v O'Neill [1975] 1 WLR 1118 . . . 75

Odièvre v France (App No 42326/98) [2002] 1 FCR 621, ECtHR (Grand Chamber) . . . 352

Olsson v Sweden (No 2) (App No 13441/87) (1994) 17 EHRR 134 . . . 515

O-M, GM (and KM) v The Local Authority,
    LO and EM [2009] EWCA Civ 1405, [2010] 2
    FLR 58 . . . 661
Omielan v Omielan [1996] 2 FLR 306 . . . 174, 219
Oxfordshire County Council v L (Care or
    Supervision Order) [1998] 1 FLR 70 . . . 462, 632,
    683, 690
Oxfordshire County Council v X, Y and J [2010]
    EWCA Civ 581, [2011] 1 FLR 272 . . . 743
Oxley v Hiscock [2004] EWCA Civ 546, [2004] 2 FLR
    669 . . . 95, 262, 274, 287, 288

P (A Child), Re [2013] EWCA Civ 963 . . . 678, 718
P (A Child) (Adoption: Leave Provisions), Re [2007]
    EWCA Civ 616, [2007] 2 FLR 1069 . . . 734
P (A Child: Use of S.20 CA 1989), Re[2014] EWFC
    775 . . . 610
P (A Minor) (Care: Evidence), Re [1994] 2 FLR
    751 . . . 660
P (A Minor) (Child Abduction: Non-Convention
    Country), Re [1997] 1 FLR 780 . . . 588
P (A Minor) (Leave to Apply: Foster Parents), Re
    [1994] 2 FCR 1093 . . . 490
P (A Minor) (Parental Responsibility Order), Re
    [1994] 1 FLR 578 . . . 396, 407
P (A Minor) (Residence Order: Child's Welfare), Re
    [2000] Fam 15 . . . 566–70
P (Adoption: Unmarried Couple) [2008] UKHL
    38, Re . . . 700
P (Child: Financial Provision), Re [2003] EWCA Civ
    837, [2003] 2 FLR 865 . . . 300, 334, 340–43
P (Children), Re [2008] EWCA Civ 1431, [2009] 1 FLR
    1056 . . . 518
P (Contact: Discretion), Re [1998] 2 FLR 696
    (Fam) . . . 529, 530
P (Contact: Supervision), Re [1996] 2 FLR 314 . . . 516
P (Emergency Protection Order), Re [1996] 1 FLR
    482 . . . 636
P (Identity of Mother), Re [2011] EWCA Civ 795,
    [2012] 1 FLR 351 . . . 358
P (Medical Treatment: Best Interests), Re [2003]
    EWHC 2327, [2004] 2 FLR 1117 . . . 450
P (Minors) (Contact with Children in Care), Re 1993]
    2 FLR 156 . . . 694
P (Parental Responsibility), Re [1997] 2 FLR 722,
    CA . . . 393, 394, 565
P (Parental Responsibility), Re [1998] 2 FLR
    96 . . . 393, 394, 398, 400, 401
P (Placement Orders: Parental Consent), Re [2008]
    EWCA Civ 535, [2008] 2 FLR 625 . . . 715, 716, 743
P, Re [2008] UKHL 38 . . . 701, 703, 708
P (Representation), Re [1996] 1 FLR 486 . . . 652
P (Residence: Appeal), Re [2007] EWCA Civ 1053,
    [2008] 1 FLR 198 . . . 385
P (Section 91(14) Guidelines) (Residence
    and Religious Heritage), Re [1999] 2 FLR
    573, CA . . . 498
P (Sexual Abuse: Standard of Proof), Re [1996] 2 FLR
    333, CA . . . 660, 682
P (Shared Residence Order), Re [2005] EWCA Civ
    1639, [2006] 2 FLR 347 . . . 502

P (Step-parent Adoption), Re [2014] EWCA Civ
    1174 . . . 729
P (Terminating Parental Responsibility), Re [1995] 1
    FLR 1048, FD . . . 415, 416
P v B [2003] EWHC 327 (Fam) . . . 520, 527
P v P [2006] EWHC 3409 (Fam) . . . 202, 527
P v P (Contempt of Court: Mental Capacity) [1999] 2
    FLR 897 . . . 121
P v P (Financial Provision) [1989] 2 FLR 241 . . . 174
P v P (Financial Provision: Lump Sum) [1978] 3 All
    ER 70 . . . 174
P v P (Inherited Property) [2004] EWHC 1364 (Fam),
    [2005] 1 FLR 576 . . . 206
P v R (Forced Marriage: Annulment: Procedure)
    [2003] 1 FLR 661 . . . 19, 26
P, C and S v UK (App No 56547/00) (2002) 35 EHRR
    31, [2002] 2 FLR 631, ECtHR . . . 632, 639
Padfield and Others v Minister of Agriculture,
    Fisheries and Food and Others [1968] AC
    997 . . . 637
Page v Page (1981) 2 FLR 198 . . . 197, 204
Pardy v Pardy [1939] P 288 . . . 77
Parry v UK (App No 42971/05) . . . 34
Pascoe v Turner [1979] 2 All ER 945 . . . 293–5
Pasha v Pasha [2001] EWCA Civ 466 . . . 187
Paton v British Pregnancy Advisory Service Trustees
    [1979] QB 276 . . . 50
Paulik v Slovakia (App No 10699/05) [2007] 1 FLR
    1090, ECtHR . . . 351, 352
Payne v Payne [2001] EWCA Civ 166, [2001] Fam
    473 . . . 471, 472, 508, 548–58
Pazpena de Vire v Pazpena de Vire [2001] 1
    FLR 460 . . . 16
P-B (Contact: Committal), Re [2009] 2 FLR
    66, CA . . . 695
P-B, Re [2006] EWCA Civ 1016 . . . 715
PC (Change of Surname), Re [1997] 2 FLR
    730 . . . 419, 564
Peacock v Peacock [1984] 1 All ER 1069 . . . 171
Pearce v Pearce [1980] 1 FLR 261 . . . 182
Pearce v Pearce [2003] 2 FLR 1144 . . . 244, 248
Pettitt v Pettitt [1969] 2 All ER 385 . . . 255, 256, 278
PG v TW (No 1) (Child: Financial Provision: Legal
    Funding) [2012] EWHC 1892 (Fam) . . . 336
Phillips v Peace [1996] 2 FLR 230 . . . 330
Pierce v Society of Sisters (1925) 268 US 510,
    535 . . . 593
Piglowska v Piglowski [1999] 3 All ER 632, [1999] 2
    FLR 763, HL . . . 170, 181, 218
Pini v Romania (2005) 40 EHRR 132, [2005] 2 FLR
    596 . . . 712
P-J (Abduction: Habitual Residence: Consent), Re
    [2009] EWCA Civ 588, [2009] 2 FLR 1051 . . . 575,
    578, 584
PK v Mr and Mrs K [2015] EWHC 2316 (Fam) . . . 738
Poel v Poel [1970] 1 WLR 1469 . . . 548, 552, 553
Popat v Popat [1991] 2 FLR 163 . . . 221
Pounds v Pounds [1994] 1 FLR 775 . . . 222, 225
Power v Power [1996] 3 FCR 338 . . . 237
Practice Direction Children Act 1989 (Applications
    By Children) [1993] 1 FLR 668 . . . 488

Practice Direction (Child: Removal from Jurisdiction) [1986] 1 All ER 983, [1986] 2 FLR 89 . . . 573

Practice Direction (Family Proceedings: Committal) [2001] 1 WLR 1253, sub nom President's Direction: (Committal Applications and Proceedings in which a Committal Order may be Made) [2001] 1 FLR 949 . . . 540

Practice Direction: Residence and Contact Orders: Domestic Violence and Harm [2009] All ER (D) 122 (Jan) . . . 164, 524

Practice Direction: Revised Private Law Programme [2010] 2 FLR 717 . . . 532

Prescott v Fellowes [1958] P 260 . . . 173

Prest v Petrodel [2013] UKSC 34 . . . 184

Preston v Preston [1982] 1 All ER 41 . . . 189, 197, 202, 204

Pulford v Pulford [1923] P 18 . . . 77

PW (Adoption), Re [2013] 1 FLR 96 . . . 738

Q (A Child), Re [2015] EWCA Civ 991 . . . 538

Q (A Minor) (Parental Order), Re [1996] 1 FLR 369 . . . 382

Q (Adoption), Re [2011] EWCA Civ 1610 . . . 716

Q (Parental Order), Re [1996] 1 FLR 369 . . . 368

Q (Parental Order: Domicile), Re [2014] EWHC 1307 (Fam), [2015] 1 FLR 704 . . . 379, 380, 381

Q v Q [2008] EWHC 1874 . . . 290

Quoraishi v Quoraishi [1985] FLR 780 . . . 77

R (A Child) (Adoption: Contact), Re [2005] EWCA Civ 1128, [2007] 1 FCR 149 . . . 742

R (A Child) (IVF: Paternity), Re [2005] UKHL 33, [2005] 2 AC 621 . . . 369, 370

R (A Child), Re [2009] EWCA Civ 1316 . . . 540

R (A Minor) (Blood Transfusion), Re [1993] 2 FLR 757 . . . 547, 571, 572

R (A Minor) (Child Abuse: Access), Re [1988] 1 FLR 206, CA . . . 520

R (A Minor), Re, CA (12 March 1998) . . . 527

R (A Minor) (Wardship: Consent to Treatment), Re [1992] Fam 11 . . . 438–42, 444–8, 453

R (A) v Croydon London Borough Council; R (M) v Lambeth London Borough Council [2008] EWCA Civ 1445, [2009] 1 FLR 1324 . . . 602

R (Adoption), Re [2014] EWCA Civ 1625, [2015] 1 FLR 715 . . . 679, 718, 719

R (Adoption: Contact), Re [2005] EWCA Civ 1128, [2006] 1 FLR 373 . . . 483, 484, 486

R (Appeal from Placement Order: Change of Circumstances), Re [2013] EWCA Civ 1240 . . . 724

R (Axon) v Secretary of State for Health [2006] EWHC 37 (Admin) . . . 437, 438, 452

R (Baiai and Others) v Secretary of State for the Home Department [2008] UKHL 53, [2008] 2 FLR 1462 . . . 5, 24

R (Care Order: Threshold Criteria), Re [2009] EWCA Civ 942, [2010] 1 FLR 673 . . . 658

R (Care Proceedings: Adjournment), Re [1998] 2 FLR 390 . . . 684

R (Care Proceedings: Welfare Analysis of Changed Circumstances), Re [2014] EWCA Civ 597 . . . 680

R (Family Proceedings: No Case to Answer), Re [2009] EWCA Civ 1619, [2009] 2 FLR 83 . . . 524

R (G) v Barnet London Borough Council; R (W) v Lambeth London Borough Council; R (A) v Lambeth London Borough Council [2003] UKHL 57, [2004] 2 AC 208, [2003] 3 WLR 1194, [2004] 1 FLR 454 . . . 600, 603

R (G) v Nottingham City Council [2008] EWHC 152 (Admin), [2008] 1 FLR 1660, QBD . . . 416, 417, 610, 615–17

R (G) v Southwark London Borough Council [2009] UKHL 26, [2009] 2 FLR 380 . . . 602, 603, 607

R (H) v Kingston Upon Hull City Council [2013] EWHC 388 (Admin) . . . 687

R (Hodkin & Anor) v Registrar General of Births, Deaths and Marriages [2013] UKSC 77 . . . 4, 11

R (IVF: Paternity of Child), Re [2003] Fam 129, CA . . . 368

R (L) v Nottinghamshire County Council [2007] EWHC 2364 (Admin), [2007] All ER (D) 158 (Sept) . . . 607

R (M) v Hammersmith and Fulham London Borough Council [2008] UKHL 14, [2008] 1 FLR 1384 . . . 603, 605–7

R (McCann) v Crown Court at Manchester [2003] 1 AC 787 . . . 665

R (No Order for Contact: Appeal), Re [2014] EWCA Civ 1664 . . . 536

R (On the Application of A) v Croydon London Borough Council; R (On the Application of M) v Lambeth London Borough Council [2009] UKSC 8, [2009] 3 FCR 607 . . . 602

R (On the Application of Kehoe) v Secretary of State for Work and Pensions [2005] UKHL 48 . . . 327

R (On the Application of Williamson) v Secretary of State for Education and Employment [2005] UKHL 15, [2005] AC 246 . . . 453

R (Parental Responsibility), Re [2011] EWHC 1535 (Fam), [2011] 2 FLR 1132 . . . 411, 412

R (Plumb) v Secretary of State for Work and Pensions [2002] EWHC 1125 (Admin) . . . 326

R (Quila and Another) v Secretary of State for the Home Department [2011] UKSC 45 . . . 9

R (Residence: Contact: Restricting Applications), Re [1998] 1 FLR 749 . . . 567–69

R (Residence: Religion), Re [1993] 2 FLR 163 . . . 497

R (Residence: Shared Care: Children's Views), Re [2005] EWCA Civ 542, [2006] 1 FLR 491 . . . 503

R (Rights of Women) v The Secretary of State for Justice [2016] EWCA Civ 91 . . . 103

R (S) v Sutton London Borough Council [2007] EWCA Civ 790, (2007) 10 CCLR 625 . . . 607

R (Surname: Using Both Parents'), Re [2001] EWCA Civ 1344, [2001] 2 FLR 1358, CA . . . 562, 563

R (S) v Swindon Borough Council and Another [2001] EWHC (Admin) 334, [2001] 3 FCR 702 . . . 623

R (Steinfeld and Keidan) v Secretary of State for Education [2016] EWHC 128 (Admin) . . . 49

R (Surname: Using Both Parents'), Re [2001] EWCA
    Civ 1344, [2001] 2 FLR 1358, CA . . . 562, 563
R (W) v Brent London Borough Council [2010]
    EWHC 175 (Admin), [2010] 1 FLR 1914 . . . 713
R and G (Minors) (Interim Care or Supervision
    Orders), Re [1994] 1 FLR 793 . . . 688, 691
R v Avon County Council, ex p M [1994] 2 FLR
    1006 . . . 609
R v Broxbourne Borough Council, ex p Willmoth
    (1989) 22 HLR 118 . . . 158
R v C [2007] EWCA Crim 3463 . . . 108
R v Cannings [2004] EWCA Crim 1, [2004] 1 All ER
    725 . . . 662
R v D [1984] AC 778 . . . 422
R v E and F (Female Parents: Known Father) [2010]
    EWHC 417 (Fam), [2010] 2 FLR 383 . . . 401
R v Ealing London Borough Council, ex p Sidhu
    (1982) 80 LGR 534 . . . 158
R v Gyngall [1893] 2 QB 232 . . . 455
R v Hills [2001] 1 FLR 580 . . . 155
R v Howes (1860) 3 E & E 332 . . . 433
R v Human Fertilisation and Embryology Authority,
    ex p Blood [1997] 2 All ER 687, CA . . . 365, 367
R v Mushtaq [2005] UKHL 25, [2005] 1 WLR
    1513 . . . 540
R v Northavon District Council, ex p Smith [1994] 2
    AC 402, [1994] 2 FLR 671 . . . 598, 603
R v Oldham MBC, ex p Garlick; R v Bexley LBC, ex
    p Bentham; R v Tower Hamlets LBC, ex p Begum
    [1993] AC 509 . . . 159
R v Pontlottyn Juvenile Court, ex p R [1990] FCR
    900 . . . 651
R v R (Divorce: Hemain Injunction) [2003] EWHC
    2113 (Fam), [2005] 1 FLR 386 . . . 83
R v R (Financial Provision: Reasonable Needs) [1994]
    2 FLR 1044 . . . 177
R v R (Financial Remedies: Needs and Practicalities)
    [2011] EWHC 3093 (Fam) . . . 207, 210
R v R (Otherwise F) [1952] 1 All ER 1194 . . . 17
R v R (Rape: Marital Exemption) [1992] 1 AC
    599 . . . 106
R v Rahman (1985) 81 Cr App R 349 . . . 422
R v Registrar General, ex p Segerdal [1970] 2
    QB 697 . . . 11
R v Registrar General, ex p Smith [1991] 1 FLR
    255, CA . . . 739
R v Royal Borough of Kingston upon Thames, ex p T
    [1994] 1 FLR 798 . . . 600
R v S [1988] 2 FLR 339 . . . 148
R v Secretary of State for Social Security, ex p W
    [1999] 2 FLR 604, FD . . . 392
R v Soneji and Another [2005] UKHL 49, [2006] 1 AC
    340 . . . 378
R v Tameside Metropolitan Borough Council, ex p J
    [2000] 1 FCR 173 . . . 611
R v UK (Case 6/1986/104/152), The Times, 9 July
    1987 . . . 465, 466
R v Westminster City Council, ex p Bishop [1993] 2
    FLR 780 . . . 160
R v Widdows [2011] EWCA Crim 1500 . . . 156
RA (Minors), Re (1974) 4 Fam Law 182 . . . 737

Radovanovic v Austria (App No 42703/98) (2005) 41
    EHRR 6, ECtHR . . . 570
Rahnema v Rahbari [2008] 2 P & CR DG5 . . . 296
Rampal v Rampal (No 2) [2001] EWCA Civ 989,
    [2002] Fam 85 . . . 181
Rees v UK (1986) 9 EHRR 56, [1987] 2 FLR 111 . . . 31
Reid v Reid [2003] EWHC 2878 (Fam) . . . 239
Rice v Miller (1993) 16 Fam LR 970 . . . 468
Richards v Richards [1972] WLR 1073 . . . 71, 76
Richards v Richards [1984] AC 174, [1983] 2 All ER
    807, HL . . . 132, 456, 457
Richardson v Richardson [1993] 4 All ER
    673 . . . 180, 243
Richardson v Richardson (No 2) [1994] 2 FLR
    1051 . . . 219
Riley v Riley [1986] 2 FLR 429 . . . 503
Ritchie v Ritchie [1996] 1 FLR 898 . . . 238
Robinson v Robinson [1982] 2 All ER 699n . . . 225
Robson v Robson [2010] EWCA Civ 1171 . . . 188, 202,
    207, 208, 210
Rochefaucauld v Boustead [1897] 1 Ch 196 . . . 255
Roddy (A Child) (Identification: Restrictions on
    Publication), Re [2003] EWHC 2927 (Fam), [2004]
    2 FLR 949 . . . 452
Rose v Secretary of State for Health and Human
    Fertilisation and Embryology Authority [2002]
    EWHC 1593 (Admin), QB . . . 352
Rossi v Rossi [2006] 2 FLR 1482 (Fam) . . . 206, 207
Rozanski v Poland (App No 55339/00) [2006] 2 FCR
    178 . . . 352, 711
RP and Others v UK (App No 38245/08) [2013] 1 FLR
    744, [2013] 1 FLR 744 . . . 668
RS v Poland (Application No 73777/ 09) [2015] 2 FLR
    848, ECtHR . . . 574
Rubin v Rubin [2014] EWHC 611 (Fam) . . . 171
Rukat v Rukat [1975] Fam 63 . . . 80
RY v Southend Borough Council [2015] EWHC 2509
    (Fam) . . . 722


S (A Child) (Abduction: Rights of Custody), Re [2012]
    UKSC 10, [2012] 2 FLR 442 . . . 583, 585
S (A Child), In the Matter of [2010] EWCA Civ
    705 . . . 512
S (A Child), Re [2013] EWCA Civ 1835 . . . 719
S (A Child) (Residence Order: Condition), Re [2001]
    EWCA Civ 847, [2001] 3 FCR 154 . . . 470
S (A Child) (Residence Order: Condition) (No
    2), Re [2002] EWCA Civ 1795, [2002] 1 FCR
    138 . . . 509, 510
S (A Child) v Nottingham City Council and Others
    [2013] EWCA Civ 771 . . . 663
S (A Minor) (Access Application), Re [1991] 1 FLR
    161 . . . 695
S (A Minor) (Adopted Child: Contact), Re [1999] Fam
    283 . . . 488
S (A Minor) (Adoption: Blood Transfusion), Re [1995]
    2 FCR 177, CA . . . 736
S (A Minor) (Care: Contact Order), Re [1994] 2 FLR
    222 . . . 693, 695
S (A Minor) (Change of Surname), Re [1999] 1 FCR
    304 . . . 686

S (A Minor) (Consent to Medical Treatment), Re [1994] 2 FLR 1065 . . . 448

S (A Minor) (Custody), Re [1991] 2 FLR 388, CA . . . 494

S (A Minor) (Custody: Habitual Residence), Re [1997] 4 All ER 251 . . . 575

S (A Minor), Re, 5 October 1994, CA . . . 400

S (A Minor) (Stay of Proceedings), Re [1993] 2 FLR 912, CA . . . 395, 396

S (Abduction: Custody Rights), Re [2002] EWCA Civ 908 . . . 575, 585

S (Abduction: Hearing the Child), Re [2014] EWCA Civ 1557, [2015] 2 FLR 588 . . . 587

S (Adoption Order or Special Guardianship Order), Re [2007] EWCA Civ 54, [2007] 1 FLR 819 . . . 744–47

S (Adult Patient: Sterilisation), Re [2001] Fam 15 . . . 463

S (Care Order: Appeal), Re [2013] EWCA Civ 1835 . . . 679

S (Care Order: Immigration), Re [2014] EWHC 529 (Fam) . . . 679

S (Care or Supervision Order), Re [1996] 1 FLR 753 . . . 691

S (Care: Parental Contact), Re [2004] EWCA Civ 1397, [2005] 1 FLR 469 . . . 697

S (Care: Parenting Skills: Personality Tests), Re [2004] EWCA Civ 1029, [2005] 2 FLR 658 . . . 663

S (Care Proceedings: Evaluation of Grandmother), Re [2015] EWCA Civ 325 . . . 680

S (Change of Names: Cultural Factors), Re [2001] Fam 1, CA . . . 566

S (Change of Surname), Re [1999] 1 FLR 672 . . . 560

S (Child Arrangements Order: Effect of Long- Term Supervised Contact on Welfare), Re [2015] EWCA Civ 689 . . . 521

S (Children), Re [2014] EWCA Civ 135 . . . 718

S (Contact: Application by Sibling), Re [1998] 2 FLR 897 . . . 458, 489

S (Contact: Children's Views), Re [2002] EWHC 540 (Fam), [2002] 1 FLR 1156 . . . 527

S (Contact Dispute: Committal), Re [2004] EWCA Civ 1790, [2005] 1 FLR 812 . . . 539

S (Contact: Promoting Relationship with Absent Parent), Re [2004] EWCA Civ 18, [2004] 1 FLR 1279 . . . 471, 518, 536, 537

S (Discharge of Care Order), Re [1995] 2 FLR 639 . . . 692

S (Habitual Residence and Child's Objections), Re [2015] EWCA Civ 2, [2015] 2 FLR 1338 . . . 586

S (Infants), Re [1967] 1 All ER 202 . . . 588

S (J) (A Minor) (Care or Supervision Order), Re [1993] 2 FLR 919, FD . . . 689–91

S (Minors: Access), Re [1990] 2 FLR 166 . . . 539

S (Minors) (Care Order: Implementation of Care Plan), Re; Re W (Minors) (Care Order: Adequacy of Care Plan) [2002] 2 AC 291 . . . 683, 685

S (Minors) (Child Abduction: Wrongful Retention), Re [1994] Fam 70 . . . 576

S (Parental Order), Re [2009] EWHC 2977, [2010] 1 FLR 1156 . . . 377, 383

S (Parental Responsibility), Re [1995] 2 FLR 648, CA . . . 394, 396–98

S (Parental Responsibility: Jurisdiction), Re [1998] 2 FLR 921 . . . 392

S (Parenting Assessment), Re [2014] 2 FLR 575 . . . 679

S (Permission to Seek Relief), Re [2006] EWCA Civ 1190, [2007] 1 FLR 482 . . . 567, 569–71

S (Placement Order: Revocation), Re [2008] EW CA Civ 1333, [2009] 1 FLR 503 . . . 713, 723

S (Practice: Muslim Women Giving Evidence), Re [2007] 2 FLR 461 . . . 26

S (Relocation: Interests of Siblings), Re [2011] EWCA Civ 454, [2011] 2 FLR 678, [2011] 2 FLR 678 . . . 552

S (Relocation: Parental Responsibility), Re [2013] EWHC 1295 (Fam), [2013] 2 FLR 1453, [2013] 2 FLR 1453 . . . 391, 412

S (Transfer of Residence), Re [2010] EWHC 192 (Fam), [2010] 1 FLR 1785 . . . 541

S (Unmarried Parents: Financial Provisions), Re [2006] EWCA Civ 479, [2006] 2 FLR 950 . . . 342

S and D (Children: Powers of Court), Re [1995] 2 FLR 456 . . . 684

S, K v The London Borough of Brent [2013] EWCA Civ 926 . . . 718

S and P (Discharge of Care Order), re [1995] 2 FLR 782 . . . 692

S v AG (Financial Orders: Lottery Prize) [2011] EWHC 2637 (Fam) . . . 207

S v F (Occupation Order) [2000] 1 FLR 255 . . . 145

S v H (Abduction: Access Rights) [1997] 1 FLR 971 . . . 580

S v Oxfordshire County Council [1993] 1 FLR 452 . . . 683

S v P (Contact Application: Family Assistance Order) [1997] 2 FLR 277, FD . . . 477

S v R [1993] 1 FCR 331, FD . . . 399, 340

S v S [1962] 1 WLR 445 . . . 517

S v S [1977] 1 All ER 56 . . . 189, 199

S v S [1987] 1 FLR 71 . . . 186

S v S (Ancillary Relief: Consent Order) [2002] EWHC 223 (Fam) . . . 226, 238

S v S (Child Abuse: Access) [1988] 1 FLR 213, CA . . . 520

S v S (Divorce: Staying Proceedings) [1997] 2 FLR 100 . . . 70

S v S (Interim Contact) [2009] EWHC 1575 (Fam), [2009] 2 FLR 1586 . . . 524

S v S (Otherwise W) (No 2) [1962] 3 All ER 55 . . . 17

S v S (Rescission of Decree Nisi: Pension Sharing Provision) [2002] 1 FLR 457 . . . 72

S v S; W v Official Solicitor [1972] AC 24 . . . 349, 350, 351, 357, 358, 457

S v T (Permission to Relocate to Russia) [2012] EWHC 4023 (Fam), [2013] 2 FLR 457 . . . 555

S and Others (By their Children's Guardian) v Nottingham City Council and Others [2013] EWCA Civ 771 . . . 672

SA (Vulnerable Adult with Capacity: Marriage), Re [2005] EWHC 2942 (Fam), [2006] 1 FLR 867 . . . 26

SA v PA [2014] EWHC 392 (Fam) . . . 203

Sahin v Germany (App No 30943/96) [2003] 2 FLR
    671 . . . 515
Salgueiro da Silva Mouta v Portugal (App No
    33290/96) [1999] ECHR, [2001] 1 FCR 653,
    ECtHR . . . 495, 496
Sanchez Cardenas v Norway (App No 12148/03)
    [2007] ECHR 763 . . . 520
Santos v Santos [1972] Fam 247 . . . 79
Saunders v UK (1996) 23 EHRR 313 . . . 540
Sawden v Sawden [2004] 1 FCR 776 . . . 219, 220
S-B (Children) (Care Proceedings: Standard
    of Proof), Re [2009] UKSC 178, [2010] 1 AC
    678 . . . 671–73
SB v RB [2008] EWHC 938 (Fam), [2008] 2 FLR
    1588 . . . 26
SC (A Minor) (Leave to Seek Residence Order), Re
    [1994] 1 FLR 96 . . . 487, 488
S-C (Contempt), Re [2010] EWCA Civ 21, [2010] 1
    FLR 1478 . . . 540
Scallon v Scallon [1990] 1 FLR 194 . . . 176
Schalk and Kopf v Austria (App No 30141/04), 24
    June 2001 . . . 36, 41, 42
Schuller v Schuller [1990] 2 FLR 193 . . . 218
Scozzari and Giunta v Italy (2000) 35 EHRR
    243 . . . 661
Secretary of State for Work and Pensions v Jones
    [2003] EWHC 2163 (Fam), [2004] 1 FLR
    282 . . . 356
SH (Care Order: Orphan), Re [1995] 1 FLR
    746 . . . 675
SH v NB [2009] EWHC 3274 (Fam) . . . 21
Sharland v Sharland [2015] UKSC 60 . . . 188,
    226, 227
Shaw v Shaw [2002] 2 FLR 1204 . . . 238
Sheffield and Horsham v UK [1998] 2 FLR 92 . . . 31
Shipp v Shipp [1988] 1 FLR 345 . . . 132
Shofman v Russia (App No 74826/01) [2006] 1 FLR
    680, ECtHR . . . 351
Singh v Bhakar [2007] 1 FLR 880 . . . 154, 155
Singh v Kaur (1981) 11 Fam Law 152 . . . 19
Singh v Singh [1971] 2 WLR 963 . . . 18, 19
Smith v Bottomley [2013] EWCA Civ 953 . . . 285
Smith v McInerney [1994] 2 FLR 1077 . . . 222
Söderbäck v Sweden [1999] 1 FLR 250 . . . 729
Sorrell v Sorrell [2005] EWHC 1717 (Fam) . . . 209
Soulsbury v Soulsbury [2007] EWCA
    969 . . . 224, 225
South Glamorgan County Council v W and B [1993] 1
    FLR 574 . . . 437, 445, 650
Southwark London Borough Council v B [1999] 1
    FCR 550, FD . . . 656
SP v EB and KP [2014] EWHC 3964 (Fam) . . . 586
Spencer v Camacho (1984) 4 FLR 662 . . . 114
Springette v Defoe [1992] 2 FLR 388 . . . 258, 287
Squire v Squire [1905] P 4 . . . 249
SS v NS (Spousal Maintenance) [2014] EWHC
    4183 . . . 179, 188, 202, 211
Stack v Dowden [2007] UKHL 17, [2007] 1 FLR
    1858 . . . 54, 95, 255–69, 271, 272, 276, 280–85,
    287–90, 296, 302
Standley v Stewkesbury [1998] 2 FLR 610 . . . 222

Stringer v Stringer [2006] EWCA Civ 1617, [2007] 1
    FLR 1532 . . . 567
Sulaiman v Juffali [2002] 1 FLR 479 . . . 83
Surrey County Council v S [2014] EWCA Civ
    601 . . . 692
Suter v Suter and Jones [1987] Fam 111 . . . 175,
    176, 182
Sutton v Gray and Others No 1 [2012] EWHC 2604
    (Fam), [2013] 1 FLR 833 . . . 667
Sutton v Mischon De Reya and Gawor and Co [2003]
    EWHC 3166 (Ch), 2004] 1 FLR 837 . . . 56, 234
SW (A Minor) (Care Proceedings), Re [1993] 2 FLR
    609 . . . 697
S-W (Care Proceedings: Case Management Hearing)
    [2015] EWCA Civ 27 . . . 679
Szechter v Szechter [1970] 3 All ER 905 . . . 19

T (A Child: Contact), Re [2002] EWCA Civ 1736,
    [2003] 1 FLR 531 . . . 527
T (A Child) (Early Permanence Placement), Re [2015]
    EWCA CIv 983 . . . 714
T (A Minor) (Care or Supervision Order), Re [1994] 1
    FLR 103 . . . 683, 690, 691
T (A Minor) (Care Order: Conditions), Re [1994] 2
    FLR 423 . . . 645, 649, 684
T (A Minor) (Contact after Adoption) [1995] 2 FCR
    537 . . . 742
T (A Minor) (Guardian ad Litem: Case Record), Re
    [1994] 1 FLR 632 . . . 652
T (A Minor) (Parental Responsibility: Contact), Re
    [1993] 2 FLR 450, CA . . . 403
T (Abduction: Child's Objections to Return), Re
    [2000] 2 FLR 192 . . . 586
T (Accommodation by Local Authority), Re [1995] 1
    FLR 15 . . . 613
T (Adopted Children: Contact), Re [1995] 2 FLR
    792 . . . 484
T (Adoption: Contact), Re [1995] 2 FLR 251 . . . 461
T (Adoption Order), Re [2012] EWCA Civ 191, [2013]
    1 FLR 360 . . . 737
T (An Adult) (Consent to Medical Treatment), Re
    [1993] Fam 95 . . . 449
T (Application to Revoke Placement Orders: Change
    in Circumstances), Re [2014] EWCA Civ
    1369 . . . 724
T (Change of Surname), Re [1998] 2 FLR 620 . . . 563
T (Interim Care Order: Removal of Children Where
    No Immediate Emergency), Re [2015] EWCA Civ
    453 . . . 643
T (Minors) (Custody: Religious Upbringing), Re
    (1981) 2 FLR 239 . . . 497, 498
T (Paternity: Ordering Blood Tests), Re [2001] 2 FLR
    1190, FD . . . 356, 357, 452
T (Placement Order), Re [2008] EWCA Civ 248,
    [2008] 1 FLR 1721 . . . 720
T (Termination of Contact: Discharge of Order), Re
    [1997] 1 FLR 517 . . . 644
T and E (Proceedings: Conflicting Interests), Re
    [1995] 1 FLR 581, FD . . . 458
T and M (Adoption), Re [2010] EWHC 964 (Fam),
    [2011] 1 FLR 1487 . . . 727

T v B (Parental Responsibility: Financial Provision) [2010] EWHC 1444 (Fam), [2010] 2 FLR 1966 . . . 337

T v S (Financial Provision for Children) [1994] 2 FLR 883 . . . 300, 340

T v T (Consent Order: Procedure to Set Aside) [1996] 2 FLR 640 . . . 225

T v T (Financial Provision) [1988] 1 FLR 480 . . . 180, 243

T v T (Financial Relief: Pensions) [1998] 1 FLR 1072 . . . 215–17

T v T (Shared Residence) [2010] EWCA Civ 1366 . . . 502, 504

T v W (Contact: Reasons For Refusing Leave) [1996] 2 FLR 473, FD . . . 481

Tavli v Turkey [2007] 1 FLR 1136, ECtHR . . . 351, 352

Tavoulareas v Tavoulareas [1998] 2 FLR 418 . . . 334, 335

TB, In the Matter of, A Community and Hospitals Trust, Transcript GILF3498, 25 September 2001 . . . 393, 400

TC and JC (Children: Relocation), Re [2013] EWHC 292 (Fam), [2013] 2 FLR 484 . . . 555

Teeling v Teeling [1984] FLR 808, CA . . . 331

TG (Care Proceedings: Case Management: Expert Evidence), Re [2013] EWCA Civ 5, [2013] 1 FLR 1250 . . . 646, 662

Thomas v News Group Newspapers [2002] EMLR 78 . . . 154

Thomas v Thomas [1995] 2 FLR 668 . . . 183

Thompson v Hurst [2012] EWCA Civ 1752 . . . 281

Thompson v Thompson [1985] 2 All ER 243 . . . 238, 239

Thorner v Major [2009] UKHL 18 . . . 290, 291

Thurlow v Thurlow [1975] 2 All ER 979 . . . 76

Thwaite v Thwaite [1982] Fam 1 . . . 224

Tibbs v Dick [1998] 2 FLR 1118 . . . 226

TL v ML [2006] 1 FCR 465 . . . 183

Tommey v Tommey [1983] Fam 15 . . . 225

Tuck v Nicholls [1989] 1 FLR 283 . . . 131

TW v TM (Minors) (Child Maintenance: Jurisdiction and Departure from Formula) [2015] EWHC 3054 (Fam) . . . 328

Turner v Avis [2009] 1 FLR 74 . . . 298

Tyler v Tyler [1989] 2 FLR 158 . . . 557

U (A Child) (Department for Education and Skills intervening) [2005] Fam 134 . . . 665

U (Serious Injury: Standard of Proof), Re; Re B [2004] EWCA Civ 567, [2004] 2 FLR 263 . . . 662, 663, 665

U v W (Attorney General Intervening) [1998] Fam 29 . . . 367

U-B (Abduction: Objections to Return), Re [2015] EWCA Civ 60 . . . 586

V (A Minor) (Adoption: Dispensing with Agreement), Re [1987] 2 FLR 89 . . . 742

V (Care or Supervision Order), Re [1996] 1 FLR 776, CA . . . 691

V (Children), Re [2013] EWCA Civ 913 . . . 718

V (Long- Term Fostering or Adoption), Re [2013] EWCA Civ 913, [2014] 1 FLR 1009 . . . 680

V v V [2011] EWHC 3230 . . . 232, 234

V v V (Children) (Contact: Implacable Hostility) [2004] EWHC 1215 (Fam), [2004] 2 FLR 851 . . . 527, 532

Vaughan v Vaughan [1973] 1 WLR 1159 . . . 114

VB v JP [2008] 1 FLR 742 . . . 202, 248

Venema v Netherlands [2003] 1 FLR 552 . . . 632

W (A Child) (Illegitimate Child: Change of Surname), Re; Re A (A Child); Re B (Children) [2001] Fam 1, CA . . . 563, 565

W (A Child) (Parental Contact: Prohibition), Re [2000] Fam 130 . . . 698

W (A Child) (Removal from Jurisdiction), Re [2005] EWCA Civ 1614, [2006] 1 FCR 346 . . . 558

W (A Minor) (Contact), Re [1994] 2 FLR 441 . . . 400, 499, 529

W (A Minor) (Interim Care Order), Re [1994] 2 FLR 892 . . . 642, 690

W (A Minor) (Medical Treatment: Court's Jurisdiction), Re [1993] Fam 64 . . . 438, 439, 441, 442, 444–48, 452, 453, 589

W (A Minor) (Residence Order), Re [1992] 2 FLR 332, CA . . . 467, 493

W (A Minor) (Residence Order), Re [1993] 2 FCR 589, CA . . . 467

W (Abduction: Acquiescence: Children's Objections), Re [2010] EWHC 332, [2010] 2 FLR 1150 . . . 584

W (Abduction: Child's Objections), Re [2010] EWCA Civ 520, [2010] 2 FLR 1165 . . . 586

W (Abduction: Domestic Violence), Re [2004] EWHC 1247 (Fam) [2004] 2 FLR 499 . . . 585

W (Adoption Order: Set Aside and Leave to Oppose), Re [2010] EWCA Civ 1535, [2011] 1 FLR 2153 . . . 733, 734, 735

W (An Infant), Re [1971] 2 All ER 49, [1971] AC 682 . . . 716

W (Application for Leave: Whether Necessary), Re [1996] 3 FCR 337 . . . 488

W (Assessment of Child), Re [1998] 2 FLR 130 . . . 645, 646

W (Care Proceedings: Functions of Court and Local Authority, Re [2013] EWCA Civ 1227 . . . 679

W (Care: Threshold Criteria), Re [2007] EWCA Civ 102, [2007] 2 FLR 98 . . . 667

W (Children), Re [2014] EWCA Civ 1065 . . . 610

W (Children) (Residence Order), Re [2003] EWCA Civ 116 . . . 500

W (Contact Application: Procedure), Re [2000] 1 FLR 263 . . . 487

W (Contact Dispute) (No 2), Re [2014] EWCA Civ 401 . . . 536

W (Direct Contact), Re [2012] EWCA Civ 999, [2013] 1 FLR 494 . . . 531, 532

W (Inherent Jurisdiction: Permission Application: Revocation of Adoption Order), Re [2013] 2 FLR 1609 . . . 738

W (Parental Responsibility Order: Inter-Relationship with Direct Contact), Re [2013] EWCA Civ 335, [2013] 2 FLR 1337 . . . 392

W (Relocation: Removal Outside Jurisdiction), Re [2011] EWCA Civ 345, [2011] 2 FLR 409 . . . 551, 554

W (Residence Order), Re [1999] 1 FLR 869, CA . . . 421

W (RJ) v W (SJ) [1971] 3 All ER 303 . . . 480

W (RJ) v W(SJ) [1972] Fam 152 . . . 331

W (Shared Residence Order), Re [2009] EWCA Civ 370, [2009] 2 FLR 436, CA . . . 500, 504, 505

W (Welfare Reports), Re [1995] 2 FLR 142, CA . . . 459

W (Withdrawal of Allegations of Abuse), Re [2012] EWCA Civ 1307 . . . 459

W v Ealing London Borough Council [1993] 2 FLR 788, CA . . . 396, 400, 483

W v J (Child: Variation of Financial Provision) [2003] EWHC 2657 (Fam), [2004] 2 FLR 300 . . . 336

W v W (Ancillary Relief: Non-Disclosure) [2003] 3 FCR 385 . . . 187

W v W (Child of the Family) [1984] FLR 796, CA . . . 331

W v W (Disclosure by Third Party) (1981) 2 FLR 291 . . . 185

W v W (Financial Provision: Lump Sum) [1976] Fam 107 . . . 193

W v W (Physical Inter-Sex) [2001] Fam 111, FD . . . 18, 35

W and B, Re; Re W (Care Plan) [2001] EWCA Civ 757, [2001] 2 FLR 582 . . . 684

Wachtel v Wachtel [1973] Fam 72 . . . 193

Wagstaff v Wagstaff [1992] 1 All ER 275 . . . 183

Walker v Hall [1984] FLR 126 . . . 258, 287

Walker v Innospec Ltd and Others [2015] EWCA Civ 1000 . . . 47

Walsh v Rother District Council [1978] ICR 1216 . . . 666

Waterman v Waterman [1989] 1 FLR 380 . . . 176, 180, 182

Wayling v Jones [1995] 2 FLR 1029 . . . 292

WB (Residence Orders), Re [1995] 2 FLR 1023 . . . 545

Webster v Norfolk County Council and the Children (By their Children's Guardian) [2009] EWCA Civ 59, [2009] 1 FLR 1378 . . . 737

Weisz v Weisz (1975) Times, 16 December . . . 194

Wellesley v Duke of Beaufort (1827) 2 Russ Rep 1 . . . 455

Wells v Wells [1992] 2 FLR 66 . . . 219, 240, 241

West v West [1977] 2 All ER 705 . . . 193, 194, 195

Westbury v Sampson [2001] EWCA Civ 4807 . . . 172

Whiston v Whiston [1995] 2 FLR 268 . . . 181

White v White [1948] 2 All ER 151 . . . 17

White v White [2001] 1 AC 596, [2000] 2 FLR 981 . . . 53, 69, 82, 172, 189, 192, 197–200, 204, 205, 208–10, 219, 251

Whiting v Whiting [1988] 2 All ER 275 . . . 176

Widdowson v Widdowson (1982) 4 FLR 121 . . . 148

Wilcox v Tait [2006] EWCA Civ 1867 . . . 296

Wilkinson v Kitzinger [2006] EWHC 2022 (Fam), [2007] 1 FLR 295 . . . 31, 41–43

Wilkinson v Kitzinger [2006] EWHC 835 (Fam), [2006] 2 FLR 397 . . . 95

Wilkinson v Wilkinson (1980) 10 Fam Law 48 . . . 187

Williams and Another v London Borough of Hackney [2015] EWHC 2629 (QB) . . . 610

Williams v Lindley [2005] EWCA Civ 103 . . . 237, 240, 241

Williams v Williams [1974] 3 All ER 377 . . . 184

Wilson v Webster [1998] 1 FLR 1097 . . . 149

Wiseman v Simpson [1988] All ER 245 . . . 132

WM (Adoption: Non-Patrial), Re [1997] 1 FLR 132, FD . . . 727, 728

Wookey v Wookey [1991] 3 All ER 365 . . . 122

Wooton v Wooton (1984) FLR 871 . . . 121

Wright v Wright [1970] 1 WLR 1219 . . . 223

Wright v Wright [1981] 2 FLR 276 . . . 498

Wright v Wright [2015] EWCA Civ 201 . . . 179, 202, 211

WT (Foreign Surrogacy), Re [2014] EWHC 1303 . . . 377, 383

Wyatt v Vince [2015] UKSC 14 . . . 212–15

Wynne v Wynne and Jeffers [1980] 3 All ER 659 . . . 185

X (A Child) (Injunctions Restraining Publication), Re [2001] 1 FCR 541 . . . 456

X (A Child) (Parental Order: Time Limit), Re [2014] EWHC 3135 (Fam), [2015] Fam 186, [2015] 1 FLR 349 . . . 377, 379, 383

X (A Minor) (Adoption Details: Disclosure), Re [1994] 2 FLR 45 . . . 588

X (Adopted Child: Access to Court File), Re [2014] EWFC 33 . . . 740

X (Care: Notice of Proceedings), Re [1996] 1 FLR 186 . . . 710

X (Children) and Y (Children) (No 1), Re [2015] EWHC 2265 (Fam) . . . 618

X (Children) and Y (Children) (No 2), Re [2015] EWHC 2358 (Fam) . . . 618

X (Children) (Parental Order: Foreign Surrogacy), Re [2008] EWHC 3030 (Fam), [2009] Fam 71 . . . 377, 379, 381, 382

X (Emergency Protection Orders), Re [2006] EWHC 510 (Fam), [2006] 2 FLR 701 . . . 629, 633

X (Minors) (Care Proceedings: Parental Responsibility), Re [2000] Fam 156 . . . 392

X, Re; Barnet London Borough Council v Y and X [2006] 2 FLR 998 . . . 684

X v Latvia (App No 27853/09) [2012] 1 FLR 860 . . . 583

X and Another v Z (Children) and Another, Re [2015] EWCA Civ 34 . . . 354

X and Y, Re [2001] 2 FCR 398 . . . 461

X and Y (Children: Foreign Surrogacy), Re [2011] EWHC 3147 (Fam) . . . 383

X and Y v A Local Authority (Adoption: Procedure) [2009] EWHC 47 (Fam) . . . 484

X City Council v MB, NB and Mab (By His Litigation Friend The Official Solicitor) [2006] EWHC 168 (Fam), [2006] 2 FLR 968 . . . 6

X Council v B (Emergency Protection Order) [2004] EWHC 2015 (Fam), [2005] 1 FLR 341 . . . 631–33, 636

X County Council v B (Abduction: Rights of Custody in the Court) [2009] EWHC 2635 (Fam) . . . 580

X v X (Y and Z Intervening) [2002] 1 FLR 508 . . . 223

X v Y (St Bartholomew's Hospital Centre for Reproductive Medicine (CRM intervening) [2015] EWFC 13 . . . 372

X, Y and Z v UK [1997] 2 FLR 892 . . . 375

Xydhias v Xydhias [1999] 1 FLR 683 . . . 225

Y (Care Proceedings: Proportionality Evaluation) [2014] EWCA Civ 1553 . . . 679

Y (Children), Re [2014] EWCA Civ 1553 . . . 718, 719

Y (Children) (Occupation Order), Re [2000] 2 FCR 470 . . . 143

Y (Leave to Remove From Jurisdiction), Re [2004] 2 FLR 330 . . . 551

Y and Z (Care Proceedings: Genetic Testing), Re [2013] EWHC 953 (Fam), [2013] 2 FLR 249 . . . 737

Yates v Yates [2012] EWCA Civ 532 . . . 180

YC v United Kingdom (App No 4547/10) [2012] 2 FLR 332[2012] 2 FLR 332 . . . 707, 717

Yemshaw v Hounslow London Borough Council [2011] UKSC 3 . . . 157

Yeoman's Row Management Ltd v Cobbe [2008] UKHL 55, HL . . . 291

Young v Lauretani [2007] EWHC 1244 (Ch) . . . 296

Young v Young [1962] P 27 . . . 173

Young v Young [2013] EWHC 34 (Fam) . . . 187

Yousef v The Netherlands (Application No 33711/96), 36 EHRR 20 . . . 471, 472

Z (A Child: Human Fertilisation and Embryology Act: Parental Order), Re [2015] EWFC 73 . . . 376

Z (A Child: Independent Social Work Asssessment, Re [2014] EWHC 729 (Fam) . . . 679

Z (A Child) (Specific Issue Order: Religious Education), Re [2002] EWCA Civ 501 . . . 547

Z (A Minor) (Freedom of Publication), Re [1997] Fam 1 . . . 456

Z (Children), Re [2008] EWCA Civ 1556 . . . 405

Z (Children: Sperm Donors: Leave to Apply for Children Act Orders), Re [2013] EWHC 134 (Fam), [2013] 1 FLR 1334 . . . 485

Z (In the Matter of) (Children) [2008] EWCA Civ 1556 . . . 393

Z, Re (Unsupervised Contact: Allegations of Domestic Violence) [2009] EWCA Civ 430 . . . 164

Z (Unsupervised Contact: Allegations of Domestic Violence), Re [2009] EWCA Civ 430, [2009] 2 FLR 877 . . . 164, 524

Z and B v C (Parental Order: Domicile) [2011] EWHC 3181 (Fam), [2012] 2 FLR 797 . . . 380, 381

Z and Others v UK [2000] 2 FLR 603 . . . 628

Z County Council v R [2001] 1 FLR 365 . . . 709, 710

Z v B v C (Parental Order: Domicile) [2011] EWHC 3181 (Fam) . . . 380

Z v Z (No 2) [2011] EWHC 2878 (Fam) . . . 232

ZA and PA v NA (Abduction: Habitual Residence) [2012] EWCA Civ 1369, [2013] 1 FLR 1041 . . . 575

Zaffino v Zaffino (Abduction: Children's Views) [2005] EWCA Civ 1012, [2006] 1 FLR 410 . . . 586

# Table of Statutes

## United Kingdom

Adoption Act 1976 . . . 116, 117, 588, 727, 728, 732
   s 15(3) . . . 730
Adoption and Children Act 1926 . . . 700
Adoption and Children Act 2002 . . . 36, 43, 116,
   390, 413, 478, 588, 652, 700–6, 708, 712, 726, 728,
   739, 744
   s 1 . . . 377, 704, 706, 707, 710, 711, 716, 717, 725, 734
   s 1(1) . . . 704
   s 1(2) . . . 704, 705, 716
   s 1(4) . . . 705, 716, 717
   s 1(4)(f) . . . 716
   s 1(5) . . . 706
   s 1(6) . . . 706
   s 1(7) . . . 704, 725
   s 1(8) . . . 706
   s 2 . . . 705
   s 2(1) . . . 704
   s 2(2) . . . 704
   s 3(2) . . . 704
   s 4 . . . 704
   s 7 . . . 705
   s 8 . . . 704
   s 9 . . . 704
   s 10 . . . 704
   s 12 . . . 704, 708
   s 18 . . . 712
   s 18(1)(b) . . . 713
   s 18(2) . . . 712
   s 18(4) . . . 726
   s 18(5) . . . 713
   s 19 . . . 712–14, 721, 722
   s 19(1) . . . 713
   s 20 . . . 713, 714, 733
   s 20(1) . . . 713
   s 20(4) . . . 713
   s 21 . . . 712, 714, 715
   s 21(1) . . . 715
   s 21(3)(a) . . . 716
   s 22(1) . . . 715
   s 22(1)(d) . . . 715
   s 24 . . . 723, 724
   s 24(2) . . . 723, 725, 732
   s 24(2)(a) . . . 724
   s 24(2)(b) . . . 723, 724
   s 24(3) . . . 724, 725, 746
   s 24(4) . . . 723, 746
   s 24(5) . . . 723, 724
   s 25 . . . 721
   s 26 . . . 721, 743
   s 26(1) . . . 721
   s 26(2) . . . 721

   s 26(4) . . . 721
   s 26(5) . . . 721, 743
   s 26(6) . . . 721
   s 27 . . . 721, 743
   s 27(4) . . . 721
   s 27(5) . . . 721
   s 28(1) . . . 722
   s 28(2) . . . 721
   s 28(3) . . . 721
   s 28(4) . . . 721
   s 29(1) . . . 720
   s 29(2) . . . 720
   s 29(3) . . . 720
   s 29(4) . . . 720
   s 29(5) . . . 720
   s 30(1) . . . 722
   s 30(2) . . . 722
   s 30(3) . . . 722
   ss 31–33 . . . 722
   s 31(2) . . . 722
   s 31(3) . . . 722
   s 32 . . . 722
   s 33 . . . 722
   s 35 . . . 722
   s 35(2) . . . 722
   s 42 . . . 731
   s 42(2) . . . 731
   s 42(3) . . . 731
   s 42(4) . . . 731
   s 42(5) . . . 731
   s 42(6) . . . 731
   s 42(7) . . . 732
   s 43 . . . 732
   s 44(1) . . . 732
   s 44(2) . . . 732
   s 44(3) . . . 732
   s 44(4) . . . 732
   s 44(5) . . . 732
   s 44(6) . . . 732
   s 44(8) . . . 713
   s 45 . . . 708
   s 46 . . . 413, 700
   s 46(1) . . . 735
   s 46(2) . . . 735, 742
   s 46(2)(d) . . . 736
   s 46(3)(a) . . . 735
   s 46(4) . . . 735
   s 46(5) . . . 731
   s 46(6) . . . 743
   s 47 . . . 413, 418, 700, 733, 735
   s 47(2) . . . 733
   s 47(2)(d) . . . 735
   s 47(3) . . . 733

s 47(4) . . . 714, 733
s 47(5) . . . 733, 735
s 47(7) . . . 733, 734
s 47(8) . . . 731
s 47(8A) . . . 731
s 47(9) . . . 731
s 49 . . . 726
s 49(2) . . . 726
s 49(3) . . . 726
s 49(4) . . . 731
s 50 . . . 727, 735
s 50(1) . . . 727
s 50(7) . . . 728
s 51 . . . 728, 735
s 51(1) . . . 728
s 51(2) . . . 728, 729, 736
s 51(3) . . . 728
s 51(3A) . . . 728
s 51(4) . . . 729
s 51A . . . 743
s 52 . . . 712, 714
s 52(1) . . . 716
s 52(1)(a) . . . 720
s 52(1)(b) . . . 716, 717
s 52(2) . . . 712
s 52(3) . . . 712
s 52(4) . . . 713
s 52(5) . . . 712
s 52(6) . . . 418, 712
s 52(7) . . . 714
s 52(8) . . . 714
s 52(9) . . . 712
s 52(10) . . . 712
s 56 . . . 739
s 57 . . . 739
s 58 . . . 739
s 59 . . . 739
s 60 . . . 739, 740
s 61 . . . 739, 740
s 62 . . . 739, 740
s 63 . . . 739, 740
s 64 . . . 739
s 65 . . . 739
s 67 . . . 736
s 67(1) . . . 736
s 67(2) . . . 736
s 67(3) . . . 736
s 67(3)(a) . . . 729
s 67(3)(b) . . . 736
s 67(4) . . . 736
s 67(5) . . . 736
s 67(6) . . . 736
s 68 . . . 736
s 74(1)(a) . . . 736
s 74(1)(b) . . . 736
s 74(2) . . . 736
s 79(4) . . . 740
s 80 . . . 739
s 83 . . . 380
s 84 . . . 412, 686

s 84(2) . . . 381
s 103 . . . 652
s 111 . . . 390
s 115 . . . 744
s 120 . . . 521
s 144(4) . . . 727
s 144(4)(b) . . . 727
s 144(5) . . . 727
s 144(6) . . . 727
s 145(5) . . . 727
Anti-Social Behaviour, Crime and Policing Act
    2014 . . . 28
Attachment of Earnings Act 1971 . . . 132

Births and Deaths Registration Act 1953
    s 2A . . . 391
    s 2B . . . 391
    s 2B(3) . . . 391
    s 2B(4) . . . 391
    s 2C . . . 391
    s 2D . . . 391
    s 2E . . . 391
    s 10(1)(a)–(c) . . . 391
    s 10A(1) . . . 391
    s 14A . . . 403
Borders, Citizenship and Immigration Act 2009
    s 55 . . . 597
British Nationality Act 1981 . . . 736

Care Standards Act 2000
    Pt 2 . . . 604, 704
Child Abduction Act 1984 . . . 511, 547, 573, 581
    s 1 . . . 511, 545, 573
    s 1(2) . . . 573
    s 1(3) . . . 547
    s 1(4) . . . 545
    s 1(5) . . . 573, 581
    s 13(2) . . . 530
Child Abduction and Custody Act
    1985 . . . 573, 574
    s 18 . . . 574
Child Care Act 1980 . . . 595
    s 3 . . . 595
Child Care Act 2006
    s 40 . . . 597
Child Maintenance and Other Payments Act
    2008 . . . 321, 322, 324, 343
Child Support Act 1991 . . . 54, 250, 319–24, 327, 329,
    330, 333, 335, 343, 367, 418
    s 1 . . . 388, 418
    s 1(1) . . . 323, 324
    s 1(2) . . . 324
    s 1(3) . . . 324
    s 3 . . . 323
    s 3(1) . . . 323
    s 3(2) . . . 323
    s 3(3) . . . 323
    s 3(3)(b) . . . 324
    s 3(5) . . . 323
    s 3(6) . . . 324

s 4 . . . 324
s 4(1) . . . 324
s 4(2) . . . 324
s 4(2A) . . . 324
s 4(10) . . . 328
s 4(10)(a) . . . 324
s 4(10)(aa) . . . 324
s 5 . . . 324
s 6 . . . 324
s 7(10) . . . 328
s 8 . . . 250, 328, 329, 397
s 8(1) . . . 328, 330
s 8(3) . . . 328, 330
s 8(3A) . . . 328
s 8(4) . . . 328
s 8(5) . . . 328
s 8(6) . . . 328, 329
s 8(6)(a) . . . 328
s 8(6)(b) . . . 328, 329
s 8(7) . . . 329
s 8(8) . . . 329
s 8(9) . . . 329
s 8(10) . . . 329
s 8(11) . . . 328, 330
s 9(2A) . . . 322
s 9A . . . 322
s 26(2) . . . 323
s 27 . . . 323
s 27A . . . 323
s 28A(1) . . . 326
s 28E . . . 326
s 28F . . . 321, 326
s 28F(1) . . . 326
s 28F(2) . . . 326
s 31 . . . 327
s 32M . . . 327
s 35 . . . 327
s 36 . . . 327
s 39A . . . 327
s 39B . . . 327
s 44 . . . 323
s 44(2A) . . . 323
s 54 . . . 323
s 55(1) . . . 323
s 55(1)(b) . . . 418
s 55(2) . . . 323
s 55(7) . . . 418
s 55(8) . . . 418
Sch 1 . . . 319, 324, 325, 328
Sch 1 para 2(3) . . . 325
Sch 1 para 4 . . . 324
Sch 1 para 5A . . . 325
Sch 1 para 6 . . . 326
Sch 1 para 7(6) . . . 326
Sch 1 para 7(7) . . . 326
Sch 1 para 8(2) . . . 326
Sch 1 para 10(3) . . . 325
Sch 1 para 10A(1)(b) . . . 328
Sch 1 para 10C . . . 325
Sch 4B . . . 326, 327
Sch 4B Pt1 . . . 321, 326

Child Support Act 1995 . . . 321
Child Support, Pensions and Social Security Act
    2000 . . . 250, 322
    Pt 1 . . . 321
Children Act 1948 . . . 594, 595
Children Act 1975 . . . 701, 744
Children Act 1989 . . . 26, 73, 116, 117, 120, 134, 164,
    320, 329, 330, 335, 337, 343, 384, 388, 393, 408, 418,
    419, 437, 439, 457, 468, 476–8, 487, 489, 490, 521,
    523, 538, 567, 572, 577, 588, 594–6, 598, 602, 603,
    607, 616, 617, 624, 629, 638, 678, 693, 702, 706, 720,
    721, 744
    Pt 1 . . . 94, 478
    Pt 2 . . . 94, 476, 478
    Pt 3 . . . 457, 546, 595, 598, 600, 601, 607, 609, 611,
        676, 686, 690
    Pt 4 . . . 421, 430, 458, 460, 478, 571, 595, 669, 678,
        680, 681
    Pt 5 . . . 421, 430, 571, 595, 596, 651
    s 1 . . . 338, 452, 455, 456, 459, 470, 471, 641, 678,
        704, 705
    s 1(1) . . . 393, 415, 418, 443, 456, 457, 460, 461, 469,
        471, 472, 474, 482, 492, 502, 503, 516, 551, 561,
        568, 590
    s 1(2)–(5) . . . 456
    s 1(2) . . . 458, 652, 680, 696
    s 1(2A) . . . 393, 416, 459, 515, 518
    s 1(2B) . . . 459
    s 1(3) . . . 164, 393, 443, 460, 471, 492, 516, 523, 551,
        652, 678, 681, 716, 743
    s 1(3)(a)–(g) . . . 460
    s 1(3)(a) . . . 516
    s 1(3)(b) . . . 516
    s 1(3)(d) . . . 498
    s 1(3)(e) . . . 516, 681, 682, 692
    s 1(3)(g) . . . 681, 682
    s 1(4) . . . 393, 460, 678
    s 1(5) . . . 393, 457, 461, 462, 561, 613, 678
    s 1(6)(a) . . . 459
    s 1(6)(b) . . . 416, 459
    s 1(7) . . . 460
    s 2 . . . 419
    s 2(1) . . . 388, 389
    s 2(1A)(a), (b) . . . 41
    s 2(1A) . . . 43
    s 2(1B) . . . 43
    s 2(2) . . . 388, 389
    s 2(3) . . . 388
    s 2(5) . . . 419, 613
    s 2(6) . . . 419
    s 2(7) . . . 419
    s 2(8) . . . 419
    s 2(9) . . . 419
    s 2(11) . . . 419
    s 3 . . . 346, 358, 416, 418, 546
    s 3(1) . . . 388
    s 3(2) . . . 388
    s 3(3) . . . 388
    s 3(4) . . . 418
    s 3(5) . . . 417, 616
    s 4 . . . 354, 389, 390, 392, 393, 403

s 4(1)(a) . . . 390, 391
s 4(1)(b) . . . 390, 392, 411
s 4(1)(c) . . . 390, 392
s 4(1A) . . . 391
s 4(2A) . . . 414, 416
s 4(3) . . . 415
s 4(4) . . . 415
s 4ZA . . . 41, 411, 501
s 4ZA(5) . . . 414
s 4ZA(6) . . . 415
s 4ZA(7) . . . 415
s 4A . . . 41, 411, 412, 479, 501, 686, 694, 701
s 4A(1)(a) . . . 411
s 4A(1)(b) . . . 411, 412
s 4A(3) . . . 414, 415
s 4A(4) . . . 415
s 5 . . . 676
s 5(1) . . . 413
s 5(2) . . . 413
s 5(5) . . . 413
s 5(6) . . . 413
s 5(7) . . . 511
s 5(7)(a) . . . 414
s 5(7)(b) . . . 414
s 5(9) . . . 413, 414
s 5(10) . . . 413
s 5(13) . . . 413
s 6(1) . . . 414
s 6(2) . . . 414
s 6(3) . . . 414
s 6(3A) . . . 414
s 6(3B) . . . 414
s 7 . . . 73
s 8 . . . 41, 56, 120, 354, 375, 384, 412, 418, 453,
   460, 474–82, 487, 488, 490, 492, 510, 512, 514,
   515, 546, 566, 568, 571, 572, 654, 657, 695, 720,
   721, 745
s 8(1) . . . 512, 720
s 8(3) . . . 478
s 8(4) . . . 478
s 9 . . . 448, 491, 571
s 9(1) . . . 480, 482, 491, 571, 572, 590
s 9(2) . . . 491
s 9(3) . . . 489, 490, 745
s 9(3)(a) . . . 490
s 9(3)(c ) . . . 490
s 9(5) . . . 475, 545, 685
s 9(5)(a) . . . 544
s 9(6) . . . 492
s 9(6B) . . . 491
s 9(7) . . . 614
s 10 . . . 354, 477
s 10(1)(a) . . . 477
s 10(1)(b) . . . 447
s 10(2) . . . 478
s 10(3) . . . 491
s 10(4) . . . 375, 418, 479, 570
s 10(5) . . . 479, 480, 570
s 10(5)(b) . . . 480
s 10(5)(c) . . . 511
s 10(5)(c)(i)–(iii) . . . 481

s 10(5A) . . . 480, 490, 491
s 10(5B) . . . 480
s 10(5C) . . . 480
s 10(7) . . . 546
s 10(8) . . . 482, 488, 489
s 10(9) . . . 481–5, 488, 489, 491, 570, 695
s 10(9)(b) . . . 484
s 10(9)(c) . . . 485
s 10(9)(d)(ii) . . . 487
s 10(10) . . . 480
s 11(4) . . . 499
s 11(7) . . . 475, 476, 510, 514
s 11(7)(b) . . . 534, 535, 542, 543
ss 11A–11P . . . 533
s 11A . . . 533, 721
s 11A(1) . . . 533
s 11A(1A) . . . 533
s 11A(2A) . . . 533
s 11A(2B) . . . 533
s 11A(3) . . . 533
s 11A(4) . . . 533, 534
s 11A(5) . . . 534
s 11A(6) . . . 534
s 11A(7) . . . 533
s 11A(9) . . . 534
s 11B(1) . . . 533
s 11B(2) . . . 534
s 11B(4) . . . 533, 535
s 11B(5) . . . 533
s 11B(7) . . . 534
s 11C . . . 534
s 11C(2) . . . 534
s 11C(3) . . . 534
s 11C(4) . . . 534
s 11D(1) . . . 534
s 11D(3) . . . 534
s 11E(2)–(4) . . . 534
s 11E(5) . . . 534
s 11E(6) . . . 535
s 11F(1) . . . 534
s 11G . . . 535
s 11G(3) . . . 535
s 11H . . . 535
s 11H(3) . . . 535
s 11H(5) . . . 535
s 11H(6) . . . 535
s 11H(8) . . . 535
s 11H(10) . . . 535
s 11I . . . 535, 542, 543
s 11J . . . 535, 542
s 11J(2) . . . 542
s 11J(3) . . . 542
s 11J(4) . . . 542
s 11J(5) . . . 542
s 11J(6) . . . 542
s 11J(7) . . . 542
ss 11J(8) . . . 542
s 11J(9) . . . 543
s 11J(10) . . . 542
s 11K . . . 542
s 11K(1) . . . 542

s 11K(2) . . . 542
s 11K(4) . . . 542
s 11L . . . 542
s 11L(1) . . . 543
s 11L(2) . . . 543
s 11L(3) . . . 543
s 11L(4) . . . 543
s 11L(7) . . . 543
s 11M . . . 543
s 11N . . . 543
s 11O(2)–(4) . . . 543
s 11O(7)–(11) . . . 543
s 11O(14) . . . 543
s 11P . . . 543
s 12(1) . . . 412
s 12(1A) . . . 412
s 12(2) . . . 412, 501, 510, 654
s 12(2A) . . . 412, 479, 480
s 12(3) . . . 412
s 12(4) . . . 412
s 13 . . . 419, 511, 545, 548, 555
s 13(1)(b) . . . 547, 548, 549
s 13(2) . . . 548, 573
s 13(3) . . . 548
ss 14A–14F . . . 413, 744
s 14A . . . 391, 745
s 14A(1) . . . 744
s 14A(2) . . . 744
s 14A(4) . . . 745
s 14A(5) . . . 745
s 14A(6) . . . 745
s 14A(7) . . . 745
s 14A(11) . . . 745
s 14B(2) . . . 745, 746
s 14C(1), (2) . . . 745
s 14C(3), (4) . . . 746
s 14D . . . 746
s 14D(4), (5) . . . 746
s 15 . . . 54, 55, 335
s 16 . . . 476, 477
s 16(1) . . . 476
s 16(2) . . . 476
s 16(3) . . . 476
s 16(5) . . . 476
s 16(7) . . . 476
s 17 . . . 546, 598–604, 607, 611, 623, 627
s 17(1) . . . 600, 612, 686
s 17(3) . . . 599
s 17(6) . . . 599
s 17(10) . . . 599
s 17(11) . . . 599
s 17(14A) . . . 599
s 17A . . . 599
s 18 . . . 601
s 20 . . . 417, 600–7, 609–11, 616, 640, 675
s 20(1) . . . 602–4, 607
s 20(1)(a)–(c) . . . 603
s 20(3) . . . 613
s 20(5) . . . 613
s 20(6) . . . 602
s 20(7) . . . 511, 609, 612–14

s 20(8) . . . 417, 511, 609–15, 617
s 20(9) . . . 511, 613
s 20(10) . . . 613
s 20(11) . . . 613, 614
ss 22–22G . . . 686
s 22 . . . 604, 675, 690
s 22(1) . . . 604
s 22(1)(a), (b) . . . 604
s 22(2) . . . 604
s 22(3) . . . 486, 686
s 22(3A) . . . 604
s 22(4) . . . 605
s 22(5) . . . 605
s 22A . . . 604
s 22B . . . 604
s 22B(3) . . . 604
s 22C . . . 604
s 22C(4) . . . 604
s 22C(7) . . . 604
s 22C(8) . . . 604
s 22C(9) . . . 604
s 22C(9B)(c) . . . 714
s 22G . . . 601
s 23 . . . 487, 675
s 23A . . . 605–7
s 23B . . . 604, 605
s 23B(8), (9) . . . 605
s 23C . . . 604, 607
s 23C(1) . . . 607
s 23C(2) . . . 606
s 23C(5A) . . . 606
s 23C(6) . . . 606
s 23C(7) . . . 606
s 23CA(1) . . . 606
s 23CA(5) . . . 606
s 24B . . . 604
s 24B(1) . . . 606
s 24B(2) . . . 606, 607
s 24D . . . 607
s 25 . . . 457, 602, 614
s 25(1) . . . 457
s 25(1)(b) . . . 457
s 26 . . . 608, 685
s 26(3) . . . 607, 608
s 26(3B) . . . 608
s 26(3C) . . . 608
s 26(8) . . . 608
s 26A . . . 608
s 26A(1) . . . 608
s 26A(2) . . . 608
s 27 . . . 598
s 27(1) . . . 598
s 27(2) . . . 598
s 31 . . . 26, 134, 458, 478, 521, 621, 622, 625,
    641, 659
s 31(2) . . . 589, 639, 641, 653, 654, 657–9, 664, 667,
    668, 698, 715
s 31(2)(a) . . . 656, 658, 672
s 31(2)(b) . . . 658, 666, 667, 670, 672
s 31(2)(b)(ii) . . . 677
s 31(8) . . . 687

s 31(9) . . . 164, 486, 617
s 31(10) . . . 486, 619
s 31(11) . . . 645
s 31A . . . 679, 683, 685
s 32 . . . 680, 681
s 33 . . . 413, 685, 686
s 33(3)(a) . . . 687
s 33(3)(b) . . . 392, 657
s 33(5) . . . 686
s 33(6)(a) . . . 686
s 33(6)(b) . . . 686
s 33(6)(b)(i), (ii) . . . 686
s 33(7) . . . 560, 686
s 34 . . . 482, 491, 510, 630, 651, 683, 693, 695, 696,
    698, 721, 746
s 34(1) . . . 694, 696, 698
s 34(1)(a)–(d) . . . 695
s 34(2) . . . 458, 693, 695, 698
s 34(3) . . . 457, 458, 482, 483, 693, 695
s 34(3)(a), (b) . . . 695
s 34(4) . . . 457, 458, 696, 697
s 34(5) . . . 693
s 34(6) . . . 696
s 34(6A) . . . 696
s 34(8) . . . 695
s 34(9) . . . 697
s 34(10) . . . 693
s 34(11) . . . 685, 693
s 35 . . . 688
s 35(1) . . . 657
s 35(1)(a) . . . 688
s 35(1)(b) . . . 688
s 35(1)(c) . . . 688
s 36 . . . 651
s 37 . . . 541, 542, 627
s 37(1) . . . 542, 640, 658
s 38 . . . 616, 640
s 38(1)(b) . . . 541, 640
s 38(2) . . . 641, 681
s 38(3) . . . 640, 698
s 38(6) . . . 437, 644–50, 737
s 38(7) . . . 645–7, 650
s 38(7A) . . . 645
s 38(7B) . . . 645
s 38(8) . . . 645
s 38A . . . 640, 650
s 38A(2) . . . 650
s 38A(5) . . . 651
s 38A(8) . . . 651
s 38B . . . 650, 651
s 39 . . . 683
s 39(1) . . . 511, 692
s 41 . . . 651
s 41(1) . . . 542, 651
s 41(2) . . . 651
s 41(2)(a), (b) . . . 651
s 41(3) . . . 652
s 41(6) . . . 651
s 41(6)(b) . . . 542
s 42 . . . 652
s 43 . . . 625, 658

s 43(1) . . . 626
s 43(2) . . . 625
s 43(3) . . . 627
s 43(4) . . . 626
s 43(5) . . . 626
s 43(6) . . . 625, 626
s 43(7) . . . 626
s 43(8) . . . 437, 626
s 43(9), (10) . . . 626
s 43(13) . . . 625
s 44 . . . 572, 616, 628, 637, 658
s 44(1) . . . 630
s 44(1)(a) . . . 630, 631, 634
s 44(1)(b) . . . 630, 631, 634
s 44(1)(c) . . . 630, 634
s 44(3) . . . 631
s 44(4) . . . 628
s 44(4)(c) . . . 628
s 44(5) . . . 413, 633
s 44(5)(a) . . . 629, 635
s 44(6)(b) . . . 629, 629
s 44(7) . . . 437, 629
s 44(8) . . . 629
s 44(9) . . . 629
s 44(10) . . . 629, 635
s 44(10)(a) . . . 633
s 44(11) . . . 629
s 44(11)(a) . . . 633
s 44(12) . . . 629
s 44(13) . . . 629, 630
s 44(15) . . . 628
s 44A . . . 650
s 44A(1) . . . 634
s 44A(2) . . . 634
s 44A(3) . . . 634
s 44A(5) . . . 635
s 44A(8) . . . 635
s 44A(10) . . . 635
s 44B . . . 634, 635, 650
s 44B(3)(a) . . . 635
s 45(1) . . . 629, 637
s 45(5) . . . 629, 635, 637
s 45(6) . . . 629
s 45(7) . . . 630
s 45(8) . . . 635
s 45(10) . . . 636
s 45(11) . . . 635
s 45(12) . . . 635
s 46 . . . 602, 637, 638, 658
s 46(1) . . . 637
s 46(6) . . . 637
s 46(7) . . . 624, 637
s 47 . . . 26, 623–5, 628, 631, 720
s 47(1) . . . 623
s 47(1)(b) . . . 623, 630, 631
s 47(2) . . . 623
s 47(3) . . . 624
s 47(4) . . . 624, 625, 631
s 47(6) . . . 624, 625
s 47(7) . . . 625
s 47(8) . . . 625

s 47(9) . . . 624
s 47(10) . . . 624
s 47(11) . . . 624
s 48(3) . . . 635
s 48(4) . . . 635
s 48(9) . . . 635
s 87 . . . 597
s 91(1) . . . 511, 683
s 91(5A) . . . 746
s 91(10) . . . 492
s 91(12) . . . 684
s 91(13) . . . 745
s 91(14) . . . 566–70, 747
s 93(13) . . . 569
s 100 . . . 439, 448, 588, 589, 616
s 100(2) . . . 589, 636
s 100(2)(b) . . . 685
s 100(2)(d) . . . 589
s 100(3) . . . 572
s 100(4) . . . 589, 636
s 100(5) . . . 589, 650
s 102 . . . 690
s 105 . . . 338, 456
s 105(1) . . . 337, 418, 457, 479, 480, 486, 602
s 188 . . . 607
Sch 1 . . . 54, 55, 142, 232, 253, 300, 318, 328–30,
    335–8, 340, 341, 343, 370, 461
Sch 1 para 1 . . . 343
Sch 1 para 1(1) . . . 335
Sch 1 para 1(1)(b) . . . 336
Sch 1 para 1(2) . . . 335, 336
Sch 1 para 1(2)(a) . . . 335, 336
Sch 1 para 1(2)(b) . . . 335, 336
Sch 1 para 1(2)(c) . . . 336
Sch 1 para 1(2)(d) . . . 138, 140, 336
Sch 1 para 1(2)(e) . . . 336
Sch 1 para 1(3) . . . 336
Sch 1 para 1(4) . . . 335
Sch 1 para 1(5) . . . 336
Sch 1 para 1(6) . . . 335
Sch 1 para 1(7) . . . 335
Sch 1 para 2 . . . 335, 336, 339
Sch 1 para 2(2) . . . 336
Sch 1 para 2(3) . . . 336
Sch 1 para 2(4) . . . 336
Sch 1 para 3(1) . . . 337
Sch 1 para 3(2) . . . 337
Sch 1 para 4 . . . 338
Sch 1 para 4(1) . . . 338, 343
Sch 1 para 4(2) . . . 338
Sch 1 para 4(3) . . . 338
Sch 1 para 5(2) . . . 336
Sch 1 para 10(3) . . . 343
Sch 1 para 16 . . . 337
Sch 2 . . . 599, 600, 601
Sch 2 para 1 . . . 599
Sch 2 para 4(1) . . . 601
Sch 2 para 5 . . . 601, 640
Sch 2 para 6 . . . 601
Sch 2 para 7 . . . 601
Sch 2 para 8 . . . 601

Sch 2 para 8A . . . 601
Sch 2 para 9 . . . 601
Sch 2 para 10 . . . 601
Sch 2 paras 15(1)–(4) . . . 693
Sch2 para 15(1) . . . 696
Sch 2 para 15(1)(c) . . . 695
Sch 2 para 16 . . . 693
Sch 2, para 19 . . . 642
Sch 2 para 19A . . . 605
Sch 2 para 19B . . . 605
Sch 2 para 19B(2) . . . 605, 607
Sch 2 para 19B(4), (5) . . . 605
Sch 3 . . . 688
Sch 3 para 1 . . . 688
Sch 3 para 2(1) . . . 688
Sch 3 para 2(3) . . . 688
Sch 3 para 3 . . . 688
Sch 3 para 4(4), (5) . . . 688
Sch 3, para 6(1) . . . 687
Sch 3 para 6(3), (4) . . . 687
Sch 3 para 8(1) . . . 688
Sch 3 para 8(2) . . . 688
Sch 3 para 9(1) . . . 687
Children Act 2004 . . . 421, 596, 597
    Pt 2 . . . 597
    s 9A . . . 597
    s 10 . . . 597
    s 10(3) . . . 597
    s 10(4) . . . 597
    s 10(5) . . . 597
    s 11 . . . 597
    s 11(1) . . . 597
    ss 13–16 . . . 597
    s 13 . . . 597
    s 13(2) . . . 597
    s 13(4) . . . 597
    s 14 . . . 597
    s 18 . . . 597
    s 35 . . . 651
    s 58 . . . 421
Children and Adoption Act 2006 . . . 476, 533
    Part I . . . 533
    s 6(1) . . . 476, 533
    s 6(3) . . . 533
    s 6(4) . . . 476
Children and Families Act 2014 . . . 459, 475, 478,
    499, 681
    Pt I . . . 705
    s 3 . . . 706
    s 9 . . . 743
    s 11 . . . 393, 459
    s 13 . . . 662, 681
    s 14 . . . 640, 681
    s 14(4)–(8) . . . 681
    s 15 . . . 685
    s 17 . . . 478
Children and Young Persons Act 1933
    s 1(7) . . . 421
Children and Young Persons Act 1969 . . . 595
    s 1 . . . 595
    s 28 . . . 595, 654

Children and Young Persons Act 2008
   s 22(2) . . . 606
Children (Scotland) Act 1995
   s 1 . . . 420
   s 2 . . . 420
Civil Partnership Act 2004 . . . 33, 36–40, 42, 43, 48,
   62, 94, 95, 116, 250, 309, 319, 330, 478
   s 1(1) . . . 39
   s 2(1) . . . 40
   s 2(5) . . . 40
   s 3 . . . 39
   s 3(1) . . . 39
   s 8 . . . 39
   s 12 . . . 39
   s 14 . . . 39
   ss 18, 19 . . . 40
   ss 37–64 . . . 94
   s 41 . . . 95
   s 42 . . . 95
   s 44(5) . . . 95
   s 47 . . . 95
   s 48 . . . 95
   ss 49–54 . . . 40
   ss 65–72 . . . 41
   s 72 . . . 95
   s 72(4) . . . 40, 95
   s 73 . . . 40, 116
   s 74 . . . 40
   s 74(5) . . . 40
   s 75(2) . . . 411
   ss 212–218 . . . 42
   s 215 . . . 42
   s 218 . . . 40
   ss 233–238 . . . 40, 95
   Sch 5 . . . 95, 167, 253, 296, 300, 328, 330, 478
   Sch 5 Pt 9 . . . 250
   Sch 6 . . . 328, 478
   Sch 7 . . . 40, 95, 328
   Sch 8 para 13 . . . 37
   Sch 9 . . . 221
Contempt of Court Act 1981
   s 14 . . . 123
   s 14(1) . . . 148
Crime and Disorder Act 1998
   s 11 . . . 478
   s 12 . . . 478
Crime and Security Act 2010 . . . 109
   s 24 . . . 109
Criminal Injuries Compensation Act 1995 . . . 112
Criminal Justice Act 2003 . . . 36
Criminal Justice and Court Services Act
   2000 . . . 597
   s 12 . . . 651

Debtors Act 1869 . . . 132
Divorce Reform Act 1969 . . . 66, 67, 88, 167, 319
Divorce (Religious Marriages) Act 2002 . . . 80
Domestic Proceedings and Magistrates' Courts Act
   1978 . . . 50, 113, 249, 478
   s 1 . . . 250
   s 2 . . . 250

s 3 . . . 250
s 20 . . . 250
Domestic Violence and Matrimonial Proceedings Act
   1976 . . . 113, 147
Domestic Violence, Crime and Victims Act
   2004 . . . 114, 116, 118, 120, 122–4, 126, 132,
   140, 156
   s 1 . . . 123
   s 2(1) . . . 140
   s 2(2) . . . 140
   s 3 . . . 118
   s 4 . . . 116
   s 10 . . . 155
   s 12 . . . 156
   s 58(1) . . . 116
   Sch 10 para 36 . . . 115
Domicile and Matrimonial Proceedings Act
   1973 . . . 69, 70
   s 5 . . . 68
   s 5(2) . . . 68, 69
   s 5(6) . . . 70
   Sch 1 para 9(1) . . . 70

Education Act 1996
   s 548 . . . 453
Equality Act 2010 . . . 46
   s 12 . . . 708
   s 29 . . . 708
   s 199 . . . 257
   s 202 . . . 38–40
   Sch 9 para 18(1) . . . 47

Family Law Act 1975
   s 51 . . . 22
Family Law Act 1986 . . . 82, 83
   Pt II . . . 72
   s 25 . . . 574
   s 55 . . . 32, 42
   s 55A . . . 349, 358, 370
   s 55A(1) . . . 348
   s 55A(2) . . . 348
   s 55A(3) . . . 348
   s 55A(4) . . . 348
   s 55A(5) . . . 348
   s 56 . . . 349
Family Law Act 1996 . . . 53, 67, 83, 86, 88–91, 96, 97,
   116, 118, 134, 137, 139, 143, 148–50, 153, 156, 165,
   244, 253, 297, 478, 544
   Pts 1–3 . . . 85, 86
   Pt 1 . . . 85, 88
   Pt 2 . . . 81, 83, 88
   Pt 4 . . . 27, 36, 40, 41, 50, 51, 53, 55, 56, 61, 81, 85,
      87, 96, 113, 114, 116, 118, 121, 218, 457, 568, 571
   Pt 4A . . . 27, 56, 85, 86
   s 30 . . . 41, 50, 55, 81, 96, 129, 253
   s 30(1)(a)(i), (ii) . . . 129
   s 30(2) . . . 130
   s 30(8) . . . 131
   s 31 . . . 130
   s 32 . . . 130
   s 33 . . . 128–30, 132, 138, 142, 144, 299

s 33(1)(b) . . . 130
s 33(2) . . . 129
s 33(2A) . . . 129
s 33(3) . . . 130, 133, 134
s 33(3)(c) . . . 130
s 33(3)(e) . . . 131
s 33(3)(g) . . . 131
s 33(4) . . . 130, 133
s 33(5) . . . 131, 134, 137
s 33(6) . . . 133–5, 142, 144–6, 297
s 33(6)(a)–(c) . . . 222
s 33(6)(c) . . . 136
s 33(6)(d) . . . 136
s 33(7) . . . 133, 134, 142, 146, 147, 297
s 33(8) . . . 134
s 33(10) . . . 132, 137
s 35 . . . 128, 132, 137, 145
s 35(5) . . . 138
s 35(6) . . . 138
s 35(7) . . . 138
s 35(8) . . . 138
s 35(9) . . . 139
s 35(10) . . . 132, 139
s 36 . . . 128, 132, 137, 139, 299
s 36(3) . . . 139, 140
s 36(4) . . . 139, 140
s 36(5) . . . 141
s 36(6) . . . 139
s 36(a)–(e) . . . 140, 141
s 36(8) . . . 141
s 36(10) . . . 132, 142
s 37 . . . 128, 129, 142
s 37(5) . . . 142
s 38 . . . 128, 129, 142
s 38(6) . . . 142
s 39(2) . . . 128
s 39(3) . . . 128
s 40 . . . 132
s 40(l) . . . 132
s 40(3) . . . 132
s 41 . . . 140
s 42 . . . 114, 117
s 42(2)(b) . . . 115
s 42(4A) . . . 115
s 42(5) . . . 120
s 42(6) . . . 114
s 42(7) . . . 115
s 42(8) . . . 115
s 42A . . . 114, 123–6, 150, 152
s 42A(2) . . . 123, 152
s 42A(3) . . . 124
s 42A(4) . . . 124
s 42A(4A) . . . 127
s 42A(5) . . . 120, 123, 124
s 43 . . . 120
s 45 . . . 150, 161
s 45(3) . . . 151, 161
s 46 . . . 150
s 46(2) . . . 150
s 46(3) . . . 150

s 46(3A) . . . 150
s 46(4) . . . 149, 150
s 47 . . . 148
s 47(2) . . . 118, 122, 148
s 47(3) . . . 152
s 47(4) . . . 152
s 47(6) . . . 148
s 47(7) . . . 148
s 47(8) . . . 124, 148
s 47(12) . . . 148
s 52 . . . 634
s 53 . . . 221, 298
s 60 . . . 115, 116, 152
s 62 . . . 157
s 62(1) . . . 116
s 62(1)(a) . . . 139
s 62(2) . . . 116
s 62(2)(b) . . . 116
s 62(2)(c) . . . 116
s 62(3) . . . 116
s 62(3)(ea) . . . 117
s 63 . . . 117, 118
s 63(1) . . . 134
s 63A(1) . . . 27
s 63A (2) . . . 28
s 63A(3) . . . 28
s 63A(4) . . . 27
s 63A(6) . . . 27
s 63B(1) . . . 27
s 63B(2) . . . 27
s 63C(1) . . . 27
s 63CA . . . 28
s 63D . . . 28
s 63E . . . 28
s 63F . . . 27
s 63G . . . 27
s 63H . . . 28
s 63Q(1) . . . 27
Sch 6 para 1 . . . 650
Sch 6 para 3 . . . 634
Sch 7 . . . 221, 222, 298, 300, 338
Sch 7 para 1 . . . 221
Sch 7 para 2 . . . 298
Sch 7 para 3 . . . 299
Sch 7 para 4 . . . 299
Sch 7 para 5 . . . 299
Sch 7 para 5(c) . . . 299
Sch 7 para 10(1) . . . 299
Sch 7 para 10(2) . . . 299
Sch 7 para 10(4) . . . 299
Sch 7 para 10(5) . . . 299
Sch 7 para 11(1) . . . 299
Sch 7 para 11(2) . . . 300
Sch 7 para 12 . . . 221
Sch 7 para 14(1) . . . 299
Sch 8 para 16 . . . 244
Family Law Reform Act 1969
    Pt III . . . 348, 350, 357, 358
    s 1 . . . 427
    s 8 . . . 432, 441, 442, 448

s 8(3) . . . 442
s 20 . . . 349, 351, 354, 357, 359
s 20(1) . . . 350, 357, 359
s 20(1A) . . . 349
s 20(2A) . . . 349
s 21 . . . 359
s 21(1) . . . 357
s 21(2) . . . 357
s 21(3) . . . 357, 358
s 21(4) . . . 357
s 22 . . . 349
s 23 . . . 360
s 23(1) . . . 359
s 23(2) . . . 359
s 25 . . . 357
s 26 . . . 347, 350
Family Law Reform Act 1987 . . . 347, 363
s 1 . . . 388
s 1(3)(b) . . . 388
s 1(3)(c), (d) . . . 389
s 4 . . . 389, 393
s 27 . . . 363, 366, 375
s 27(2) . . . 375
Family Law (Scotland) Act 2006 . . . 311
s 10 . . . 91
Forced Marriage (Civil Protection) Act
2007 . . . 26, 27, 28

Gender Recognition Act 2004 . . . 17, 18, 21, 33, 34,
34, 375, 408
s 1(1) . . . 33
s 2(1) . . . 33
s 3 . . . 33
s 4 . . . 33
s 5 . . . 33
s 9(1) . . . 33
s 9(2) . . . 374, 375
s 12 . . . 374
Guardianship of Infants Act 1925
s 1 . . . 455, 464
Guardianship of Minors Act 1971
s 1 . . . 455
s 11B(2)(d) . . . 338

Homelessness Act 2002 . . . 157, 160
Housing Act 1980 . . . 338
Housing Act 1985
s 60(1) . . . 598
s 79 . . . 221, 299
Housing Act 1988
Pt 1 . . . 221, 299
Housing Act 1992
s 191 . . . 160
Housing Act 1996 . . . 98, 157, 158, 502
s 175(1) . . . 157
s 175(2)(a) . . . 157
s 175(3) . . . 157
s 177(1) . . . 98, 157
s 178 . . . 157
s 182 . . . 607

s 188(1) . . . 135, 606
s 189(1) . . . 158, 502
s 189(1)(c) . . . 159
s 190(2) . . . 160
s 191(3) . . . 160
s 193(2) . . . 158, 160
s 195(2) . . . 158
s 196 . . . 160
Human Fertilisation and Embryology Act
1990 . . . 363–9, 372, 375, 376
s 2(1) . . . 367
s 13 . . . 335
s 13(5) . . . 364
s 13(6) . . . 365
s 25 . . . 364
ss 27–29 . . . 363, 364
s 27 . . . 362
s 28 . . . 366, 369, 372, 729
s 28(2) . . . 363, 366–8, 372, 375
s 28(3) . . . 364, 366–70, 372
s 28(4) . . . 369
s 28(5) . . . 366, 369
s 28(5A)–(5I) . . . 374, 729
s 28(6) . . . 385
s 28(6)(a) . . . 373
s 28(6)(b) . . . 374
s 28(7) . . . 366
s 29(1) . . . 369
s 29(3B) . . . 374
s 30 . . . 376, 383
s 30(7) . . . 381
s 31ZA . . . 373
s 31ZA(2)(a) . . . 373
s 31ZC . . . 373
s 31ZE . . . 373
s 31ZF . . . 373
s 49(4) . . . 363
Sch 3 . . . 365
Sch 3 para 1 . . . 365
Sch 3 para 3 . . . 365
Sch 3 para 5 . . . 365, 373
Sch 3 para 5(1) . . . 365
Sch 3 para 5(3) . . . 365
Sch 3 para 8 . . . 365
Sch 3ZA Pt I . . . 365
Human Fertilisation and Embryology Act
2008 . . . 337, 362–64, 370, 375–7, 387, 501,
576, 729
Pt II . . . 364
ss 33–48 . . . 364
s 33 . . . 362, 728
s 33(2) . . . 362
s 33(3) . . . 362
ss 35–37 . . . 729
ss 35–38 . . . 369
s 35 . . . 369–71, 374, 375, 382, 728
s 36 . . . 370, 371, 374
s 37 . . . 370–2
s 38(2)–(4) . . . 370
s 39 . . . 374, 729

s 40 ... 729
s 41 ... 385, 391
s 41(1) ... 373
s 41(2) ... 374
ss 42–44 ... 371
s 42 ... 41, 43, 338, 370, 389, 485
s 43 ... 41, 43, 338, 371, 375, 389, 411, 412
s 44 ... 371, 375
s 44(1)(b) ... 371
s 45 ... 485
s 46 ... 374, 729
s 48 ... 485
s 49 ... 375
s 54 ... 364, 376, 377, 380, 383, 384, 387
s 54(1) ... 376
s 54(2) ... 376
s 54(3)–(8) ... 377
s 54(3) ... 378, 379
s 54(4) ... 379
s 54(4)(a) ... 379
s 54(4)(b) ... 380
s 54(5) ... 381
s 54(6) ... 381, 382
s 54(8) ... 381, 382, 383
s 54(10) ... 377
s 54(11) ... 377
s 55 ... 376
s 57(1) ... 364
s 57(2) ... 364
Human Rights Act 1998 ... 32, 37, 161, 356, 437, 451,
    469–72, 483, 548, 609, 680
s 2(1) ... 32
s 3 ... 376, 724
s 3(1) ... 32
s 4 ... 32
s 4(2) ... 42
s 6 ... 161, 451
s 6(1) ... 515
s 7 ... 32, 638, 685

Immigration Act 1971 ... 69, 736
Immigration Act 2014 ... 24
Immigration and Asylum Act 1999 ... 24
s 24 ... 24
Inheritance (Provision for Family and
    Dependants) Act 1975 ... 41, 51, 53, 55, 81, 94,
96, 217, 335, 339
Insolvency Act 1986
s 335A(3) ... 298

Land Registration Act 1925 ... 277
s 70(1)(g) ... 277
Land Registration Act 2002 ... 277
Law of Property Act 1925
s 30 ... 297
s 52(1) ... 254, 293
s 53(1) ... 255
s 53(1)(b) ... 255, 256
s 53(2) ... 256
Law Reform (Husband and Wife) Act 1962
s 1 ... 50

Law Reform (Married Women and Tortfeasors ) Act
    1935 ... 50
Legal Aid, Sentencing and Punishment of Offenders
    Act 2012 ... 103, 171
Sch 1 para 12 ... 103
Legitimacy Act 1976
s 1(1) ... 388
s 1(4) ... 388
s 10 ... 388
Local Authority Social Services Act 1970
s 7 ... 598
Local Government Act 1986
s 2A ... 36
Local Government Act 2003
s 28 ... 36, 38
s 122 ... 36

Marriage Act 1949 ... 4, 7, 8, 10, 11, 16, 511
s 1 ... 9
s 3 ... 9, 511
s 49 ... 16
Sch 1 Pt I ... 8, 9
Sch 1 Pts II–III ... 8
Marriage Act 1983 ... 10
Marriage Act 1994 ... 7, 10
Marriage (Prohibited Degrees of Relationship)
    Act 1986 ... 8
Marriage (Same Sex Couples) Act 2013 ... 3, 4, 7, 11,
    21, 30, 34, 35, 44–8
s 1(1) ... 45
s 1(3) ... 46
s 2 ... 45
s 4 ... 45
s 5 ... 45
s 9 ... 35
s 11 ... 4, 46
s 12 ... 34
s 14 ... 11
s 15 ... 48
Sch 1 ... 45
Sch 3 ... 4, 46
Sch 4 ... 4, 46
Sch 5 ... 34
Sch 7 paras ... 26–27 45
Married Women's Property Act 1882 ... 50, 81
Matrimonial and Family Proceedings Act
    1984 ... 168, 478
Pt III ... 82, 478
s 31F(6) ... 227
Matrimonial Causes Act 1923 ... 65
Matrimonial Causes Act 1937 ... 65
Matrimonial Causes Act 1857 ... 65
Matrimonial Causes Act 1973 ... 61, 67, 80, 83–6, 93,
    191, 222, 236, 319, 330, 335, 337, 339, 478
Pt 1 ... 6, 70, 71, 93
Pt 2 ... 6, 7, 13, 17, 50, 60, 69, 70, 81, 82, 94, 168,
    253, 296, 300, 328, 330
s 1(1) ... 70
s 1(2) ... 70, 73
s 1(2)(a) ... 73, 77
s 1(2)(b) ... 22, 73–7

s 1(2)(c) . . . 76
s 1(2)(d) . . . 78
s 1(2)(e) . . . 78
s 1(4) . . . 71
s 2 . . . 66
s 2(1) . . . 66, 74
s 2(2) . . . 74
s 2(5) . . . 77, 79
s 2(6) . . . 78
s 2(7) . . . 78
s 3 . . . 7
s 3(1) . . . 71
s 3(2) . . . 71
s 3(2)(b) . . . 94
s 4(1) . . . 94
s 5 . . . 78, 79, 94
s 6(1) . . . 66, 72
s 6(2) . . . 66, 72
s 8 . . . 72
s 9(2) . . . 72
s 10 . . . 79, 80, 94
s 10(1) . . . 78, 80
s 10(2) . . . 80
s 10(3) . . . 80
s 10(4) . . . 80
s 10A . . . 80
s 11 . . . 5, 7, 94
s 11(a)(i) . . . 8
s 11(a)(ii) . . . 9
s 11(a)(iii) . . . 13
s 11(b) . . . 16
s 11(c) . . . 7, 30, 32, 33, 42, 45, 375
s 12 . . . 17, 21, 26
s 12(a) . . . 17, 46
s 12(b) . . . 17, 46
s 12(c) . . . 18, 26
s 12(d) . . . 20, 22
s 12(e) . . . 20, 22
s 12(f) . . . 20, 22
s 12(g) . . . 17, 21
s 12(h) . . . 17, 21
s 13 . . . 21
s 13(1) . . . 21, 22
s 13(2) . . . 20, 21, 27
s 13(2A) . . . 21
s 13(3) . . . 21
s 13(4) . . . 21
s 16 . . . 6
s 17 . . . 93
s 17(2) . . . 93
s 18(1) . . . 94
s 18(2) . . . 94
s 19 . . . 94
ss 21–25D . . . 224
s 21A(1) . . . 217
s 22 . . . 171
s 22A(3) . . . 249
s 22ZA . . . 171, 213
s 22ZA(3), (4) . . . 171
s 22ZB . . . 171
ss 23–24A . . . 169

s 23 . . . 169, 171, 332
s 23(1)(b) . . . 172
s 23(1)(c) . . . 172, 243
ss 23(1)(d)–(f) . . . 332
s 23(2) . . . 332
s 23(3)(c) . . . 172
s 23(4) . . . 332
s 23(6) . . . 172
s 23A . . . 138
s 23B(1) . . . 221
s 24 . . . 138, 173, 184, 332
s 24(1)(a) . . . 173, 218
s 24(1)(b) . . . 173
s 24A . . . 169, 173, 218, 330, 332
s 24A(2)(b) . . . 174
s 24A(4) . . . 173
s 24A(5) . . . 174
s 24A(6) . . . 174
s 24B . . . 243
s 24B(5) . . . 217
s 25 . . . 174, 181, 185, 190, 198, 217, 224, 225,
   233, 250
s 25(1) . . . 169, 181, 182, 190, 213, 331, 335, 338, 457
s 25(2) . . . 169, 170, 181, 182, 195, 332
s 25(2)(a) . . . 182–85, 189, 195, 216, 335
s 25(2)(b) . . . 188, 195
s 25(2)(c) . . . 188, 338
s 25(2)(d) . . . 195
s 25(2)(e) . . . 183, 195, 338
s 25(2)(f) . . . 190, 192, 195
s 25(2)(g) . . . 192, 195
s 25(2)(h) . . . 196
s 25(3) . . . 332
s 25(3)(e) . . . 338
s 25(4) . . . 332, 333
s 25A . . . 170, 175, 177, 184, 195
s 25A(1) . . . 175
s 25A(2) . . . 176, 180
s 25A(3) . . . 180
ss 25B–25D . . . 169, 216, 217
s 25B . . . 217
s 25B(1)(a) . . . 216
s 25B(1)(b) . . . 216
s 25B(4) . . . 216
s 25B(5) . . . 216
s 25B(7) . . . 217
s 25B(7B) . . . 217
s 25C(2) . . . 216
s 27 . . . 50, 249, 250
s 28 . . . 216
s 28(1)(a) . . . 171, 185
s 28(1)(b) . . . 172
s 28(1A) . . . 180, 243, 244, 246, 249
s 29(1) . . . 333
s 29(2)(a) . . . 333
s 29(2)(b) . . . 333
s 29(3) . . . 333
s 31 . . . 176, 180, 216, 242–6
s 31(1) . . . 172
s 31(2) . . . 242
s 31(7) . . . 180, 244

s 31(7)(a) ... 244
s 31(7)(b) ... 244
s s 31(7A)–(7G) ... 244
s 31(7B) ... 180
s 31(7B)(c) ... 244
s 33 ... 185
s 33A ... 224, 227
s 33A(3) ... 224
ss 34–36 ... 222
s 34(1) ... 222
s 35 ... 222, 230
s 41 ... 54, 478
s 41(1) ... 73
s 41(2) ... 73
s 46(1) ... 82
s 46(2) ... 82
s 51(3) ... 82
s 52 ... 82, 181, 331
Matrimonial Homes Act 1983 ... 113, 457
s 1(3) ... 132
Matrimonial Proceedings and Property Act
1970 ... 67, 81, 167, 168, 191
s 5(1) ... 168
s 37 ... 285
Mental Capacity Act 2005 ... 153, 357, 391, 716
Mental Health Act 1983 ... 17, 20, 444, 445
s 2 ... 439
s 3 ... 439

Offences Against the Person Act 1861 ... 97, 421
s 57 ... 16

Pensions Act 1995 ... 216
Pensions Act 2014 ... 217
Places of Worship Registration Act 1855 ... 11
s 2 ... 11
Police and Criminal Evidence Act 1984
s 17(1)(e) ... 635
s 22 ... 354
s 24(1) ... 123
s 24(6) ... 156
s 64(1A) ... 354
Poor Relief Act 1601 ... 594
Presumption of Death Act 2013 ... 94
s 1 ... 94
s 3 ... 94
Sch 2 para 1 ... 94
Protection from Harassment Act 1997 ... 25, 119,
124, 125, 149, 154, 156
s 1(1) ... 154
s 1(2) ... 154
s 2 ... 154, 156
s 3 ... 154, 155
s 3(1) ... 155
s 3(2) ... 154, 155
s 3(6) ... 155
s 3(7) ... 155
s 3(8) ... 155
s 4 ... 155, 156
s 5 ... 155, 156

s 5(4) ... 156
s 5A ... 156
s 7(2) ... 154
Public Bodies Act 2011 ... 322

Rent Act 1977 ... 36, 43, 221, 299
Sch 1 para 2(2) ... 37
Sch 1 para 3(1) ... 37
Rent (Agriculture) Act 1976 ... 221, 299

Serious Crime Act 2015 ... 111
s 76 ... 111
Sex Disqualification (Removal) Act 1919 ... 465
Sexual Offences Act 1956
s 5 ... 432
s 6 ... 432
s 28(1) ... 432
Sexual Offences Act 1967 ... 35
Sexual Offences Act 2003
s 1 ... 106
s 64 ... 736
s 65 ... 736
Sexual Offences (Amendment) Act 2000 ... 35
Social Security Contributions and Benefits Act 1992
Pt IX ... 325
Surrogacy Arrangements Act 1985 ... 376
s 1 ... 376
s 1A ... 376
s 2 ... 376
s 3 ... 376

Terrorism Act 2000 ... 618
Trusts of Land and Appointment of Trustees Act
1996 ... 295–8
s 13 ... 296, 297
s 13(2) ... 297
s 14 ... 296–8
s 14(1) ... 297
s 15 ... 296, 297
s 15(1)(d) ... 298
s 15(2) ... 297

Welfare Reform Act 2009
Sch 6 ... 391, 411
Welfare Reform Act 2012 ... 321, 322
ss 136–142 ... 321
s 136 ... 322
s 137 ... 324
s 138 ... 322
Welfare Reform and Pensions Act 1999 ... 216, 217
s 27(1) ... 217
s 29 ... 217
Wills Act 1837
s 18A ... 94

## Austria

Federal Act on the Religious Education of Children
Art 2(2) ... 497

## Australia

Family Law Act 1975 . . . 60
Family Law Amendment (De Facto Financial
  Matters and Other Measures)
  Act 2008 . . . 60

## New Zealand

Bill of Rights Act 441
  s 11 . . . 441
Domestic Violence Act 1995 . . . 522
Property (Relationships) Act 1976 . . . 60

# Table of Statutory Instruments

Adoption Agencies Regulations 2005
(SI 2005/389) . . . 707, 715
reg 3 . . . 707
reg 4 . . . 707
reg 6 . . . 707
reg 12 . . . 707
reg 13 . . . 707
reg 14 . . . 707
reg 15 . . . 707
reg 16 . . . 707, 709
reg 17 . . . 707
reg 17(3) . . . 707
reg 18 . . . 708
reg 22 . . . 708
reg 23 . . . 708
reg 24 . . . 708
reg 25 . . . 708
reg 26 . . . 708
reg 31 . . . 708
reg 32 . . . 708
reg 33 . . . 708
reg 35 . . . 708, 712, 713
Sch 1 . . . 707, 708
Sch 1 para 3 . . . 709
Adoption Agencies (Wales) Regulations 2005
(SI 2005/1313) . . . 715
Adoption Support Services Regulations 2005
(SI 2005/691) . . . 704

Blood Tests (Evidence of Paternity) Regulations 1971
(SI 1971/1861) . . . 349

Care Planning, Placement and Case Review
(England) Regulations 2010 (SI 2010/959) . . . 605,
614, 683, 687, 690, 695
reg 8(4) . . . 695
reg 28 . . . 690
reg 30 . . . 690
reg 40 . . . 605
reg 48 . . . 605
Child Maintenance and Other Payments Act
2008 (Commencement No 10 and Transitional
Provisions) Order 2012 (SI 2012/ 3042) . . . 322
Child Support (Applications: Prescribed Date)
Regulations 2003 (SI 2003/194)
reg 10(1)(a) . . . 324
Child Support (Maintenance Calculation Procedure)
Regulations 2000 (SI 2001/157) . . . 323
Sch1 para 5(1) . . . 418
Child Support (Miscellaneous Amendments)
Regulations 1993 (SI 1993/913) . . . 323
Child Support (Miscellaneous Amendments)
(No 2) Regulations 2009 (SI 2009/2909) . . . 323

Children Act 1989 Representations Procedure
(England) Regulations 2006 (SI 2006/1738) . . . 608
reg 9(1) . . . 608
reg 14 . . . 608
reg 14(1) . . . 608
reg 15(2) . . . 608
reg 17 . . . 608
reg 18 . . . 608
reg 19(3) . . . 608
reg 20 . . . 608
Children (Leaving Care) (England) Regulations 2001
(SI 2001/2874)
reg 4(5) . . . 693
Children (Secure Accommodation) Regulations 1991
(SI 1991/1505)
reg 10(1) . . . 614
Civil Legal Aid (Procedure) Regulations 2012
(SI 2012/3098) . . . 103
Community Care, Services for Carers and Children's
Services (Direct Payments) (England) Regulations
2009 (SI 2009/1887) . . . 599
Community Care, Services for Carers and Children's
Services (Direct Payments) (Wales) Regulations
2004 (SI 2004/1748) . . . 599
Contact with Children Regulations 1991 (SI 1991/891)
reg 3 . . . 698

Determinations (Adoption and Fostering)
Regulations 2009 (SI 2009/ 395) . . . 708
Disclosure of Adoption Information (Post-
Commencement Adoptions) Regulations 2005
(SI 2005/888) . . . 739
reg 4 . . . 739
reg 5 . . . 739
reg 6 . . . 739
reg 16 . . . 740
reg 21 . . . 739
Divorce etc (Pensions) (Scotland) Regulations 2000
(SI 2012/212) . . . 215

Employment Equality (Sexual Orientation)
Regulations 2003 (SI 2003/1661) . . . 35

Family Procedure Rules 2010 (SI 2010/2955) . . . 70, 71
r 4.4 . . . 213
Pt 6 . . . 73
r 6.2 . . . 652
r 6.3 . . . 652
r 7.6 . . . 72
r 7.12(12) . . . 78
r 7.12(13) . . . 78
r 7.33 . . . 72
Pt 12 . . . 524

r 12.6 . . . 651
PD 12J . . . 525
Pt 16 . . . 652
r 16.3 . . . 651
r 16.17 . . . 651
r 16.20(1) . . . 652
r 16.20(2) . . . 652
r 16.20(5) . . . 652
Pt 16A PD . . . 652
Pt 16A PD Pt 3 . . . 652
Pt 16A PD para 6.1(a), (b) . . . 652
Pt 16A PD para 6.6 . . . 652
Pt 16A PD para 6.8(a) . . . 652
Pt 16A PD para 6.10 . . . 652
Fostering Services (England) Regulations 2011
(SI 2011/581) . . . 683
Fostering Services (Wales) Regulations 2003
(SI 2003/237)
reg 38(2) . . . 649

Homeless (Priority Need for Accommodation)
(England) Order 2002 (SI 2002/2051) . . . 158, 606
art 3 . . . 606
Homeless (Priority Need for Accommodation)
(Wales) Order 2002 . . . 158
Human Fertilisation and Embryology Authority
(Disclosure of Donor Information) Regulations
2004 (SI 2004/1511) . . . 352, 373
reg 2(2) . . . 373
reg 2(3) . . . 373
Human Fertilisation and Embryology (Parental
Orders) Regulations 2010 (SI 2010/985) . . . 377
reg 2 . . . 377, 383
Sch 1 . . . 377, 383

Local Safeguarding Children Boards Regulations
2006 (SI 2006/90) . . . 597

Local Safeguarding Children Boards (Amendment)
Regulations 2010 (SI 2010/622) . . . 597

Marriage Act 1949 (Remedial Order) 2007
(SI 2007/438) . . . 9
Marriage and Civil Partnerships (Approved
Premises) (Amendment) Regulations 2011
(SI 2011/2661) . . . 38, 40
Marriage of Same Sex Couples (Conversion of
Civil Partnership) Regulations 2014
(SI 2014/3181) . . . 47

Occupational Pension Schemes (Disclosure of
Information) Regulations 1996
(SI 1996/ 1655) . . . 215
Occupational Pension Schemes (Disclosure of
Information) Amendment Regulations 2002
(SI 2002/1383) . . . 215

Parental Responsibility Agreement Regulations 1991
(SI 1991/1478) . . . 392
Parental Responsibility Agreement (Amendment)
Regulations 2005 (SI 2005/2808) . . . 392
Parental Responsibility Agreement (Amendment)
Regulations 2009 (SI 2009/2026) . . . 392
Pensions on Divorce etc (Provision of Information)
Regulations 2000 (SI 2000/1048) . . . 215
Personal and Occupational Pension Schemes
(Indexation and Disclosure of Information)
(Miscellaneous Amendments) Regulations 2005
(SI 2005/704) . . . 215
Public Bodies (Child Maintenance and Enforcement
Commission: Abolition and Transfer of Functions)
Order 2012 (SI 2012/2007) . . . 322

Suitability of Adopters Regulations 2005
(SI 2005/1712) . . . 708

# Table of European and International Instruments

## Conventions and Treaties

Convention on the Elimination of All Forms
of Discrimination Against Women 1979
(CEDAW) . . . 161–3
European Convention on Human Rights 1950 . . . 5,
161, 451, 452, 556
Art 2 . . . 161, 365, 451
Art 3 . . . 161, 451, 628, 715
Art 5 . . . 152, 451
Art 6 . . . 151, 152, 161, 327, 451, 483, 536, 538, 539,
548, 556, 566, 641, 649, 668, 715
Art 6(1) . . . 351
Art 6(3)(c) . . . 540
Art 8 . . . 31, 32, 34, 36, 42, 152, 161, 185, 298, 351–3,
356, 365, 375, 376, 406, 416, 438, 451–3, 465, 466,
470–2, 483, 496, 497, 514–16, 519, 536, 538, 548,
553, 556, 558, 574, 582, 583, 593, 612, 616, 641,
659, 672, 678, 686, 703, 707, 711, 712, 715, 717,
730, 743, 744
Art 8(1) . . . 438, 472, 669
Art 8(2) . . . 161, 438, 472, 515, 526, 669
Art 9 . . . 453, 686
Art 10 . . . 452
Art 12 . . . 5, 8, 9, 24, 31, 32, 34, 42, 43, 365
Art 13 . . . 31
Art 14 . . . 5, 34, 37, 42, 43, 62, 365, 376, 406, 416,
496, 497, 703
Protocol 1—
Art 1 . . . 62
European Convention on Recognition and
Enforcement of Decisions concerning Custody of
Children and Restoration of Custody of Children
1980 . . . 574
European Convention on the Adoption of Children
1967 . . . 714
Hague Convention on the Civil Aspects of
International Child Abduction . . . 572–4, 578,
579–84, 586, 588
Art 1(1) . . . 574
Art 3 . . . 580, 581
Art 4 . . . 574
Art 5 . . . 580
Art 5a . . . 580

Art 7 . . . 582
Art 8 . . . 582
Arts 9, 10 . . . 574
Art 12 . . . 583, 587
Art 12(2) . . . 583
Art 13 . . . 583, 585–7
Art 13a . . . 584
Art 13b . . . 584, 585
Art 15 . . . 581
Art 16 . . . 574
Art 18 . . . 578, 583
Art 20 . . . 587
International Covenant on Civil and Political Rights
1968 . . . 593
Art 23 . . . 593
Treaty of Rome 1950 . . . 36
Art 59 . . . 367
United Nations Convention on the Rights of the
Child (UNCRC) . . . 351, 353, 514, 587
Art 3 . . . 474
Art 7 . . . 351, 353–5, 514
Art 8 . . . 514
Art 9(3) . . . 514
Art 12 . . . 587
Art 12(1) . . . 438
Art 16(1) . . . 438
Art 18(1) . . . 514

## Directives and Regulations

Council Directive 2000/78/EC establishing a general
framework for equal treatment in employment and
occupation . . . 35
Council Regulation (EC) No 2201/ 2003 concerning
jurisdiction and the recognition and enforcement
of judgments in matrimonial matters and in
matters of parental responsibility ('Brussels II
Revised') . . . 68, 70, 81, 574, 582, 585
Art 8 . . . 653
Art 11 . . . 574, 582
Art 11.2 . . . 587
Art 11.3 . . . 582
Art 11.4 . . . 585

# Introduction: the changing family and developing family law

## Family law: an inherently interesting and dynamic subject

The subject matter of family law is inherently interesting to many because the issues it addresses are often personal matters to which we can relate in our own lives, whether directly, or indirectly through the experiences of those we know. The courts tend to get involved with families when things go wrong, when relationships break down, and there are disputes, and when emotions are running high. The focus of much of family law is thus on the pathology of family life.[1] Not surprisingly, therefore, the family law reports are strewn with mini-dramas, with striking facts, revealing the messiness and complexity of family life.[2] The issues raised are often controversial. By way of examples, take just the following issues which appear within this book. For how long, if at all, should one spouse be ordered to supplement a former spouse's income after divorce, or provide the other with a home? What financial provision should be made on divorce to a wife who has incited others to kill her husband? How should the law respond to the issue of domestic violence? Can a child have two female parents? Can a female-to-male transsexual person be the father of a child? Could that person be the mother of one child and the father of another? To what extent should a child be permitted to make his or her own decisions? Can a child be taken into state care in circumstances where it is unclear whether a parent or a childminder has caused injury to a child? Can a child be adopted without a parent's knowledge? In addition to specific questions like these, family law raises many interesting broader issues and debates,[3] such as how the law can meet the needs of diverse cultures and religions within an increasingly plural society; the extent to which the law should regulate the affairs of unmarried cohabitants; the extent to which families should be permitted to order their family matters privately without law's interference; the extent to which family members' conduct should be material to decision making.[4] In short, the subject matter of family law is rarely dull. It is, we believe, one of the most fascinating legal subjects of study. Of course, as teachers of the subject, we might be expected to hold that view. We hope, however, that once you have read this book you will fully understand what we mean. One of the reasons is that there is little time to stand still with family law, which develops at a pace, attracting a large body of case law and much policy debate.

## A volatile time for family law; recent developments

This is a volatile time for family law, with family justice encountering a period of major uncertainty and change. Indeed, in recent years the family justice system was the subject of an extensive review,

---

[1] This is of course only a partial view of family law, see R. Probert (ed), *Family Life and the Law Under one Roof* (Aldershot: Ashgate, 2007), exploring law and the intact family.

[2] For in-depth accounts of the fascinating stories behind some of the landmark cases in family law, see S. Gilmore, J. Herring, and R. Probert, (eds), *Landmark Cases in Family Law* (Oxford: Hart Publishing, 2011).

[3] See J. Herring, R. Probert, and S. Gilmore, *Great Debates in Family Law* (Basingstoke: Palgrave MacMillan, 2015).

[4] See A. Bainham, 'Men and Women Behaving Badly: Is Fault Dead in English Family Law?' (2001) 22(1) Oxford Journal of Legal Studies 219–38.

and the Government responded with proposals for change.[5] A new single family court was established and major changes to family and child law[6] were made by the Children and Families Act 2014.

In addition, and controversially, the Legal Aid, Sentencing and Punishment of Offenders Act 2012 (LASPO 2012) drastically curtailed legal aid for legal advice and representation in private family law matters,[7] with significant implications for access to family justice.[8] The main exceptions are cases involving domestic violence or unlawful removal of a child from the UK. In relation to domestic violence cases, paragraph 12 of Schedule 1 to LASPO 2012 makes provision for civil legal services to be provided to an adult (A) 'in relation to a matter arising out of a family relationship between A and another individual (B) where (a) there has been, or is a risk of, domestic violence between A and B, and (b) A was, or is at risk of being, the victim of that domestic violence'. However, the evidential requirements for qualification for legal aid are arguably narrowly drawn in the accompanying Civil Legal Aid (Procedure) Regulations 2012. Indeed there has already been a challenge in judicial review. In *R (Rights of Women) v The Secretary of State for Justice*,[9] a charity, *Rights of Women*, challenged Regulation 33 of the Civil Legal Aid (Procedure) Regulations 2012.[10] In broad outline, this regulation provides that legal aid will not be available in cases of domestic violence unless documentary verification is provided 'within the 24 month period before the application for legal aid is made save for instances of an unspent conviction, un-concluded criminal proceedings and existing police bail for a domestic violence criminal offence'.[11] *Rights of Women* claimed that Regulation 33 is ultra vires the statute and alternatively, that in imposing the 24-month time period, it frustrates the purpose of the Act[12] (which is that persons suffering from domestic violence should be eligible for legal aid provided they qualify in respect of their financial resources and the merits of their case). The Court of Appeal held that the regulation was not made ultra vires. However, the Court held that it did frustrate the purpose of the legislation in imposing the 24-month limitation with respect to evidence.[13] The Court could see 'no obvious correlation between the passage of such a comparatively short period of time as 24 months and the harm to the victim of domestic violence disappearing or even significantly diminishing.'[14] The court therefore declared in principle that Regulation 33 is invalid in so far as it frustrates the purpose of the legislation.[15] Clearly this is a significant victory for victims of domestic violence, a wider category of whom will now be eligible for legal aid.

There is evidence that the restrictions in legal funding are causing significant hardship in other areas too. In *Re D (Non-Availability of Legal Aid)*[16] Sir James Munby P was concerned that, whereas in proceedings to take a child into the care of a local authority parents automatically are entitled to legal

---

[5] *Family Justice Review Final Report* (Ministry of Justice, November 2011), and see Ministry of Justice and Department for Education, *The Government Response to the Family Justice Review: A System with Children and Families at its Heart* (Cm 8273, February 2012).

[6] For a comprehensive and detailed consideration of child law, see A. Bainham and S. Gilmore, *Children: The Modern Law* (Bristol: Family Law, 2013).

[7] See Sch 1 to the 2012 Act. A case for exceptional funding can be made under s 9. For the human rights implications, see J. Miles, 'Legal Aid, Article 6 and "Exceptional Funding" under the Legal Aid Etc Bill 2011' [2011] Fam Law 1003 and 'Legal Aid and "Exceptional" Funding: A Postscript' [2011] Fam Law 1268. See also M. Maclean and J. Eekelaar, 'Legal Representation in Family Matters and the Reform of Legal Aid: A Research Note on Current Practice' [2012] Child and Family Law Quarterly 223.

[8] Research shows that litigants in person 'have considerable needs for support across several dimensions': see L. Trinder, R. Hunter, E. Hitchings, J. Miles, R. Moorhead, L. Smith, M. Sefton, V. Hinchly, K. Bader and J. Pearce, *Litigants in person in private family law*, (Ministry of Justice Analytical Series, November 2014). See https://www.gov.uk/government/uploads/system/uploads/attachment_data/file/380479/litigants-inperson-in-private-family-law-cases.pdf.

[9] [2016] EWCA Civ 91 (Longmore, Kitchin, Macur LJJ).

[10] Which came into force on 1 April 2013, as amended by the Civil Legal Aid (Procedure) (Amendment) Regulations 2014 which came into force on 22 April 2014.

[11] *R (Rights of Women) v The Secretary of State for Justice* [2016] EWCA Civ 91, [29].

[12] Ibid, [47]. This was in breach of the principles to be found in *Padfield v Minister of Agriculture* [1968] A.C. 997.

[13] The court also held that there was also a frustration of the purpose of the legislation insofar as the Regulation makes no provision for victims of financial abuse.

[14] *R (Rights of Women) v The Secretary of State for Justice* [2016] EWCA Civ 91, [45].

[15] Ibid, [51].     [16] [2014] EWFC 39.

funding, no such funding was available to fund an application under section 39 of the Children Act 1989 to discharge an existing care order. In that case a two-year-old child was placed with his parents under a care order and the local authority subsequently removed the child. The parents did not qualify for means-tested legal aid because the father's income was just above the threshold. The parents, however, had learning disabilities and were incapable of conducting the proceedings without legal assistance.[17] Munby P concluded that in these circumstances a failure to provide funding would breach the parents' procedural rights under Articles 6 and 8 of the European Convention on Human Rights (ECHR). Accordingly, his lordship indicated that a further hearing might need to take place at which it would be decided whether or not the costs were to be funded by one, some, or all of: the local authority, as the public authority bringing the proceedings; the legal aid fund, on the basis that the child's interests and human rights protections required it; or Her Majesty's Courts and Tribunals Service (HMCTS).[18] Fortunately, subsequently the father's means were reassessed and he was granted legal aid up to the hearing, and Munby P gave directions that the cost of an intermediary to permit the parents to communicate effectively be funded by HMCTS and an expert report be funded by the Legal Aid Agency.[19]

Similarly, in *Re K and H (Children: Unrepresented Father: Cross-Examination of Child)*[20] HHJ Bellamy, sitting as a deputy High Court Judge, felt compelled to order HMCTS to meet the costs of a father's representation where he did not otherwise qualify for funding. In proceedings concerning the father's two children aged five and four, a fact-finding hearing was required in order to address allegations by a 17-year-old 'step-daughter' that the father had sexually abused her. Without the court's funding, the young woman would have been compelled to endure cross-examination by the father in person.

On the Lord Chancellor's appeal, however, the Court of Appeal held that the judge's approach amounted to impermissible judicial legislation.[21] LASPO provides a comprehensive code and the court has to respect the boundaries drawn by Parliament for public funding of legal representation set out in such a detailed scheme.[22] The Master of the Rolls (with whom the other members of the court agreed) indicated that 'in a simple straightforward case, questioning by the judge is likely to be the preferred option and it should present no difficulties'.[23] He concluded this was such a case and the judge should probably have decided to conduct the questioning himself. The court was clear that there were 'options available to the judge which would have ensured a fair hearing and vindicated the Article 6 and 8 rights of the father and K and H'.[24] It was appreciated, however, that the position may be different in other cases, for example involving complex medical or expert evidence, where lack of legal representation might result in the proceedings not being conducted in compliance with Articles 6 or 8 of the ECHR.[25] Lord Dyson MR commented that:

> In order to avoid the risk of a breach of the Convention, consideration should be given to the enactment of a statutory provision for (i) the appointment of a legal representative to conduct the cross-examination and (ii) the payment out of central funds of such sums as appear to be reasonably necessary to cover the cost of the legal representative …[26]

In *NJDB v United Kingdom*[27] the applicant claimed that the denial to him of legal aid to pursue his case to the Supreme Court of the United Kingdom breached Article 6(1) of the ECHR. He

---

[17] There may be similar issues for parents with mental health problems. For a discussion of the prevalence of mental health problems amongst adults with family law problems, suggesting a higher than anticipated proportion of disputants seeking exceptional funding, see J. Miles, N. J. Balmer, and M. Smith, 'When Exceptional is the Rule: Mental Health, Family Problems and the Reform of Legal Aid in England and Wales' (2012) 24(3) Child and Family Law Quarterly 320.

[18] See also *Q v Q; Re B; Re C (Private Law: Public Funding)* [2014] EWFC 31 (order of last resort would be that costs, such as the cost of an expert report, would be borne by HMCTS if no other funding was possible).

[19] See *Re D (Non-Availability of Legal Aid (No 2)* [2015] EWFC 2.      [20] [2015] EWFC 1.

[21] *Re K and H (Children)* [2015] EWCA Civ 543 (The Master of the Rolls, McFarlane and Black LJJ). For comment, see J. Eekelaar, 'Litigants in person – the struggle for justice' (2015) 37(4) Journal of Social Welfare and Family Law 463–6.

[22] *Re K and H (Children)* [2015] EWCA Civ 543, at [31].      [23] Ibid, [61].      [24] Ibid, [61].

[25] Ibid, [62].      [26] Ibid.      [27] Application No 76769/12, [2016] 1 FLR 186.

had been granted funding at first instance and before the Inner House of the Court of Session, but the Scottish Legal Aid Board declined to fund a further appeal to the Supreme Court. In the end the applicant was represented pro bono before the Supreme Court by experienced lawyers who were familiar with his case and the Supreme Court waived its fees. The ECtHR found in these circumstances no violation of Article 6(1). The court noted the role of the Scottish Legal Aid Board as 'an independent body charged with acting in the general interest in order to ensure that the limited amount of public money made available to the legal aid scheme is spent fairly and sensibly',[28] and commented that 'the court cannot lose sight either of this general interest or of the fact that in the particular case the impugned denial of scarce legal aid funding came after the applicant's claims had been thoroughly examined by the domestic courts at two levels of jurisdiction in proceedings in which the applicant had received legal aid and been represented by highly qualified lawyers.'[29]

Many of the changes made to the family justice system in recent years represent responses to the major review by the Family Justice Review (FJR),[30] conducted by a panel of civil servants and independent members from across the family justice service, and chaired by David Norgrove. The FJR panel began work in March 2010.[31] A year later, having taken evidence from over 700 individuals and organisations, an interim report was published for consultation.[32] With the benefit of 668 responses to the consultation, and of the Justice Select Committee's report on the operation of the family courts,[33] a final report was presented in November 2011.[34] The Government's response to the final report was published in February 2012.[35]

### The family justice review recommendations

The FJR found the family law legal framework robust, but had deep concern that it does not operate as a cost-effective, coherent, managed system.[36] The FJR had four main strands of recommendations. The first was the establishment of a new Family Justice Service, with responsibility for court social work services, provision of mediation and out-of-court resolution services, and for monitoring the use of expert witnesses. A second strand of recommendations was directed to judicial leadership and culture. It suggested that judges with leadership responsibilities should have clearer management responsibilities; judicial continuity should be the aim in all family law cases; judges and magistrates should be encouraged to specialise in family matters; and the judiciary should review and plan how to deliver consistently effective case management in the courts. Thirdly, the FJR recommended that, without prejudice to the special position of the Family Division of

---

[28] Ibid, at para [77].     [29] Ibid.

[30] For a good overview of recent policy developments, see A. Bainham and S. Gilmore, *Children: The Modern Law* (Jordan Publishing, 2013), at pp 42–6.

[31] The terms of reference were not entirely neutral: mediation was to be preferred over court intervention and the court's role should be 'focused on protecting the vulnerable . . . and should avoid intervening except where there is clear benefit to children or vulnerable adults in doing so'. As John Eekelaar observes, this is 'a startlingly limited view of the role of a court, and hence of the law which courts apply': J. Eekelaar, ' "Not of the Highest Importance": Family Justice Under Threat' (2011) 33(4) Journal of Social Welfare and Family Law 311.

[32] https://www.gov.uk/government/publications/family-justice-review-interim-report.

[33] *Operation of the Family Courts* Sixth Report of Session 2010–12, Vol 1 (2011) House of Commons Justice Committee (July 2011).

[34] https://www.gov.uk/government/publications/family-justice-review-final-report.

[35] Ministry of Justice and Department for Education, *The Government Response to the Family Justice Review: A System with Children and Families at its Heart* (Cm 8273, February 2012).

[36] For comparative perspectives, see M. Maclean, R. Hunter, F. Wasoff, L. Ferguson, B. Bastard, and E. Ryrstedt, 'Family Justice in Hard Times: Can We Learn from Other Jurisdictions?' (2011) 33(4) Journal of Social Welfare and Family Law 319.

the High Court,[37] there should be a single family court, with family friendly facilities, in which all levels of the family judiciary (including magistrates) should sit. Fourthly, the FJR suggested a workforce strategy to improve interdisciplinary understanding, including interdisciplinary inductions and training.

Specifically, in relation to private law disputes when parents separate (see Chapter 9), the FJR concluded that there should be no change to the substantive approach to deciding post-separation parenting issues, but recommended a new 'child arrangements order' (setting out arrangements for the upbringing of the child in cases of dispute), which would represent a move away from what it saw as the current loaded terminology of 'residence' and 'contact' with a non-resident parent that had become a source of contention. The FJR also recommended that parents should have ready access to a wide range of information and support.

In relation to the public law by which a child may be taken into state care (see Chapter 10), the FJR made several recommendations to tackle delay in the system, including that proceedings should be concluded, where possible, within 26 weeks.

## The Government response to the family justice review

The Government's response to the FJR largely agreed with the FJR's recommendations, including that the court process would be simplified by the establishment of a single family court.[38] Controversially, the Government, in contrast to the FJR's conclusion, opined that 'there should be a legislative statement of the importance of children having an ongoing relationship with both their parents after family separation, where that is safe, and in the child's best interests'.[39]

## The new single family court for England and Wales

The FJR's recommendation for a single family court for England and Wales was enacted by section 17 of the Crime and Courts Act 2013. This inserts a new Part 4A into the County Courts Act 1984, which introduces a new section 31A, as follows:

> (1) There is to be a court in England and Wales, called the family court, for the purpose of exercising the jurisdiction and powers conferred on it—
>     (a) by or under this or any other Act, or
>     (b) by or under any Act, or Measure, of the National Assembly for Wales.
> (2) The family court is to be a court of record and have a seal.[40]

## The Children and Families Act 2014

Most of the legislative changes suggested in the Government's response to the FJR were brought before Parliament in the Children and Families Bill 2013/14.[41] The Bill also contained proposals relating to adoption in the Government's Action Plan published in March 2012, which aims to speed up the process of adoption and matching children with prospective adoptive parents. The Children and Families Act 2014 (which the Bill became) received Royal Assent on 13 March 2014, and relevant provisions of the Act are explained at appropriate points in the text.

---

[37] With its inherent jurisdiction, and jurisdiction over international family law matters.

[38] Ministry of Justice and Department for Education, *The Government Response to the Family Justice Review: A System with Children and Families at its Heart* (Cm 8273, February 2012), para 75.

[39] Ibid, at paras 61 and 62; and see Department for Education and Ministry of Justice consultation paper, *Co-operative Parenting Following Family Separation: Proposed Legislation on the Involvement of Both Parents in a Child's Life* (launch date 13 June 2012).

[40] Schedules 10 and 11 to the 2013 Act make further provisions.

[41] See www.education.gov.uk/inthenews/inthenews/a00208753/childrens-bill-family-support.

## Setting the scene for the rest of the book

In this introductory chapter we briefly set the scene for the chapters that follow by exploring some general features of family law and its study, and providing some background information, including a statistical picture of families in England and Wales. So far, we have assumed that the term 'family law' is understood, but our first task must be to seek to explain what is meant by this subject—family law—that you are beginning to study.

## What is family law?

What is family law? This is a question which is difficult, if not impossible, to answer directly. What one can do is give some reasons why it is difficult to answer. First, understandings of 'family' may be contingent on the particular society concerned, influenced by cultural, economic, ideological, or other circumstances and, as illustrated in some of the case law discussed later, such understandings can shift over time. Furthermore, as illustrations given by Lords Nicholls and Slynn in *Fitzpatrick v Sterling Housing Association*[42] show, the word 'family' itself has different connotations depending on how it is used: 'we are thinking of having a family'; 'accommodation suitable for families' (adults and children); 'family tree'; 'we're having a family gathering' (wider family/friends); the Christian family (religious community). As these examples show, the meaning may depend on the context, and the purpose for which a definition of family is required. For example, we might give different answers if we are asked to define family in terms of those who should be responsible to each other for economic support, or inheritance, compared with those who should be regarded as family for the purpose of protection from domestic violence.[43] A further difficulty is that a great variety of areas of law impact on the family, so deciding what 'family law' is, as distinct from other areas of law, is essentially a matter of line-drawing. There is a traditional core of study in family law which examines the formation and dissolution of legally recognised relationships, their legal consequences, and protection of individuals in the family. Some areas of law which have important impacts on family life (like taxation or social security law) are not usually included within standard accounts of family law, perhaps because these are also regarded as detailed areas of law in their own right. Alison Diduck has observed, however, that while family law displays this incoherence, there is a glimmer of a thread of normative consistency in family law's role as shaper of responsibility for responsibility.[44] In other words, family law decides who has responsibility for caring for others (the state or individuals), and who within the family is so responsible. The fact that family law is merely a collection of different areas of law collected around the family has led others to suggest that family law might be replaced, for example by a 'personal law'[45] or by a law of domestic relations.[46]

The core areas of study tend to reflect the major functions of family law: defining legally recognised relationships; protection; adjustment; and support.[47] This is one way of ordering, reflecting on, and assessing family law. If anything, the trend has been towards increased focus on the

---

[42] [1999] 3 WLR 1113, HL.

[43] Compare those who have a claim under s 1 of the Inheritance (Provision for Family and Dependants) Act 1975, with the definition of associated persons for the purpose of protection from domestic violence in the Family Law Act 1996, s 63(2).

[44] A. Diduck, 'Family Law and Family Responsibility' in J. Bridgeman, H. Keating, and C. Lind (eds), *Responsibility, Law and the Family* (Aldershot: Ashgate, 2008).

[45] J. Eekelaar, *Family Law and Personal Life* (Oxford: Oxford University Press, 2006).

[46] R. Probert, 'Family Law—A Modern Concept?' [2004] Family Law 901.

[47] See eg J. Eekelaar, *Family Law and Social Policy* (London: Weidenfeld & Nicholson, 1984).

functions carried out within relationships.[48] Another way of interrogating family law is to look at its impact. In this respect, the work of feminist writers has been particularly influential, drawing attention to the gender dimension of many family laws.[49] A recent striking example of this perspective at work in the courts is Baroness Hale's judgment in *Granatino v Radmacher (formerly Granatino)*[50] in which she pointedly remarked that the legal recognition of ante-nuptial agreements has a gender dimension 'which some may think ill-suited to decision by a court consisting of eight men and one woman'.[51]

## Families today: the statistical picture and trends

There were 26.3 million households in the UK in 2011, at the time of the last census. The trend is towards smaller household sizes.[52] Twenty-nine per cent of households in 2011 consisted of only one person and only about 20 per cent consisted of four or more people. In 2011, 7.7 million people in UK households lived alone.

In 2011 there were 17.9 million families in the UK, of which 12 million consisted of a married couple with or without children. So married couple families are still the most common family type in the UK. The most common family type is a married or civil partner couple family without dependent children (7.6 million in 2011), then such families with dependent children (4.5 million in 2011).

However, the long-term picture for UK marriages has been one of decline since 1972, although the marriage rate has remained relatively stable in the last few years. Statistics show that people are marrying at an older age than in the past; the provisional mean age for men marrying in 2011 was 36.3 years, and for women was 33.8 years. The percentage of marriages ending in divorce increased for those marrying between the 1970s and the early 1990s, 22 per cent of marriages in 1970 ending in divorce by the fifteenth wedding anniversary compared with 33 per cent of marriages in 1995. However, since 2003 there has been a consistent downward trend in divorces in England and Wales.

Cohabitation outside marriage, however, is on the increase. The number of opposite-sex cohabiting couple families increased from 2.1 million in 2001 to 2.9 million in 2011. Thirty-eight per cent of cohabiting couples had dependent children.

Lone parenthood is also on the increase. There were 2 million lone parents with dependent children in the UK in 2011 (92 per cent of them women), a figure which has grown significantly from 1.7 million in 2001.

The birth rate is in decline. In 2009 there were 706,200 live births registered in England and Wales, compared with 783,200 in 1971 and 708,700 in 2008. The age distribution for childbirth has changed considerably and women are having children older than they used to.[53]

## The legally recognised 'family': shifting over time

Many of the cases providing some indication of law's view of what constitutes a family, have arisen in the context of the question whether a person could succeed to a tenancy by reason of being

---

[48] For discussion, see L. Glennon, 'Obligations Between Adult Partners: Moving From Form to Function' (2008) 22 International Journal of Law, Policy and the Family 22.

[49] See A. Diduck and K. O'Donovan (eds), *Feminist Perspectives on Family Law* (Abingdon: Routledge-Cavendish, 2006); J. Bridgeman and D. Monk, *Feminist Perspectives on Child Law* (London: Cavendish, 2000); K. O'Donovan, *Family Law Matters* (London: Pluto Press, 1993); R. Hunter, C. McGlynn, and E. Rackley (eds), *Feminist Judgments From Theory to Practice* (Oxford: Hart, 2010); A. Diduck and F. Kaganas, *Family Law, Gender and the State: Text, Cases and Materials* (Oxford: Hart, 2012).

[50] [2010] UKSC 42, [2011] 1 AC 534.     [51] Ibid, para 137.

[52] The information in this section is taken from ONS national statistics, and from Social Trends, No 41, 2011 edn.

[53] Social Trends, No 41, 2011 edn.

a member of the deceased's family,[54] where unusually the word 'family' appears in the relevant statutes. The courts initially adopted the test of the ordinary man's view in determining whether someone was a member of another's family. The cases illustrate how notions of the legally recognised 'family' have shifted over time. It was soon established that family was not confined to *de jure* relationships, but also included some *de facto* equivalents. So, by 1949, in *Brock v Wollams*,[55] a child who had been adopted as a matter of fact but not law was regarded as a member of her adoptive family. Around the same time, however, application of the same test resulted in the view that to say that unmarried cohabitants of 20 years were members of each other's family would be 'an abuse of the English language'.[56] Where, however, an unmarried couple had children, their family life together was recognised.[57] Yet, by the mid-1970s, in *Dyson Holdings v Fox*[58] the popular view of family had shifted to include unmarried cohabitants without children, although the Court of Appeal cautioned that relationships 'of a casual or intermittent character and those bearing indications of impermanence would not come within the popular concept of a family unit'.[59] In *Joram Developments Ltd v Sharratt*,[60] however, the House of Lords, approving a dictum of the Court of Appeal in *Ross v Collins*,[61] made clear that

> two strangers cannot … ever establish artificially … a familial nexus by acting as brothers or as sisters, even if they call each other such and consider their relationship to be tantamount to that. Nor … can an adult man and woman who establish a platonic relationship establish a familial nexus by acting as a devoted brother and sister or father and daughter would act, even if they address each other as such and even if they refer to each other as such and regard their association as tantamount to such.

Thus a 24-year-old man and 75-year-old woman who had a platonic aunt/nephew-type relationship were not members of each other's family.[62]

The 'ordinary person test' was rejected, however, and the *Joram Developments* case distinguished, by a majority of the House of Lords[63] in *Fitzpatrick v Sterling Housing Association*.[64] Mr Thompson was the tenant of a flat. The appellant, Mr Fitzpatrick, lived with Mr Thompson from 1976 until Mr Thompson's death in 1994. They had been 'partners in a longstanding, close, loving and faithful, monogamous, homosexual relationship'. Mr Fitzpatrick had nursed Mr Thompson 24 hours a day for the final eight years of his life, after Mr Thompson had suffered an accident resulting in a blood clot on his brain. Mr Fitzpatrick claimed protection of the Rent Act 1977 either as a statutory tenant because he and Mr Thompson had been living as husband and wife, or as an assured tenant by reason of being a member of Thompson's family.[65] The House held unanimously that the words 'husband and wife' are gender specific, so could not apply, but by a majority found that Mr Fitzpatrick was a member of Mr Thompson's family. Lord Slynn emphasised that 'family' is not a term of art, and needs to be understood in context. The relevant questions were: what were the characteristics of a family as understood by the legislation and could two same-sex partners satisfy those characteristics? His Lordship saw the hallmarks of the relationship as 'essentially that there should be a degree of mutual

---

[54] In statutes going back to the 1920s, amended several times over the years.

[55] *Brock v Wollams* [1949] 2 KB 388.          [56] *Gammans v Ekins* [1950] 2 All ER 140 at 142.

[57] *Hawes v Evenden* [1953] 2 All ER 737.          [58] [1976] QB 503.

[59] Ibid, per James LJ.          [60] [1979] 1 WLR 928, HL.

[61] [1964] 1 WLR 425 at 432 (woman who began living in an elderly man's property when she was in her 30s, and who subsequently acted as his housekeeper and nurse, not a member of the man's family).

[62] See also *Sefton Holdings v Cairns* [1988] 2 FLR 109, CA (no family relationship in case of *de facto* adoption of an adult 'child', distinguishing member of family and member of household).

[63] Lords Slynn, Nicholls, and Clyde; Lords Hutton and Hobhouse dissenting on the basis that the *Joram Developments* case was binding on the House and any change was a matter for Parliament.

[64] [1999] 3 WLR 1113, HL. For a detailed comment, see L. Glennon, '*Fitzpatrick v Sterling Housing Association: A Perfectly Pitched Stall*' in S. Gilmore, J. Herring, and R. Probert (eds), *Landmark Cases in Family Law* (Oxford: Hart, 2011).

[65] Rent Act 1977, Sch 1, paras 2 and 3.

inter-dependence, of the sharing of lives, of caring and love, of commitment and support.' Lord Nicholls, although disapproving the 'ordinary person test', approved the *Dyson Holdings* case and concluded that 'there can be no rational or other basis on which the like conclusion can be withheld from a similarly stable and permanent sexual relationship between two men or between two women'. Lord Clyde explained that each case 'will require to depend eventually upon its own facts'. He saw the bond as 'one of love and affection, not of a casual or transitory nature, but in a relationship which is permanent or at least intended to be so' and commented that it would be difficult to establish 'without an active sexual relationship between them or at least the potentiality of such a relationship' and unless the couple were living together in the same house. Fitzpatrick was a seminal case in family law because it recognised, for the first time, that same-sex couples could form a family unit. As such it represented a powerful endorsement of gay and lesbian relationships at a time when such relationships were not fully legitimised either in law or social consciousness.

In *Ghaidan v Godin-Mendoza*[66] the question was whether the ruling in *Fitzpatrick* on the applicability of the term 'living together as husband and wife' to homosexual relationships could survive in the light of implementation of the Human Rights Act (HRA) 1998. Unanimously, the House ruled that the exclusion of homosexual relationships would not pursue a legitimate aim and constituted a breach of Articles 14 and 8 of the European Convention on Human Rights (ECHR).[67] A majority of the House[68] was prepared to reinterpret those words pursuant to section 3 of the HRA 1998 to mean 'living together *as if they were* husband and wife'. As can be seen, therefore, the law adopts a mixture of form and function to determine the existence of family relationships. Formally legally recognised relationships, such as marriage or civil partnership, are included. Such relationships will usually be loving, caring ones, but need not necessarily be so to qualify. The *de facto* equivalents of such relationships are included, in certain contexts, provided there is the necessary stability, caring, and mutual interdependence. Usually it will be necessary for the parties to be living under the same roof, and for there to be at least the potential for a sexual relationship. There can be no overarching meaning of 'family'; the meaning attributed depends upon the context, and each case depends upon its facts. Indeed, one of the broadest definitions of the term 'family' can be seen in domestic violence legislation where it has been deemed important to cast the net wide to ensure that all those who need protection from violence within families, receive it.

However, it must be said that the state preference is to give legal recognition to relationships based upon 'form' and not 'function'. Relying upon functional approaches, whilst allowing greater individualised justice, is said to lack clarity and predictability with family members perhaps not realising that they have mutual rights and responsibilities until declared by a court. Indeed, the functional approach which was taken by the House of Lords in *Fitzpatrick* and in *Ghaidan* was quickly followed by the legislature cementing the rights of same-sex couples firmly within a form-based approach by the enactment of the Civil Partnership Act 2004. Following the trend in other European countries, this Act established a registered partnership system for same-sex couples giving those who register their partnership effectively the same legal incidents as those attaching to marriage. This commitment to the 'form' approach was developed further when same-sex marriage was legalised in 2013. Although civil partners have practically the same legal rights as spouses, both public and political support grew in favour of same-sex marriage. In February 2011, an application was filed in the European Court of Human Rights challenging the prohibition on same-sex civil marriages[69] and it became clear that the government was resolute in its intention

---

[66] [2004] UKHL 30.

[67] As Baroness Hale observed, 'the legitimate aim cannot be the protection of the traditional family. The traditional family is not protected by granting it a benefit that is denied to people who cannot, or will not, become a traditional family . . . it is difficult to see how heterosexuals will be encouraged to form and maintain . . . marriage-like relationships by the knowledge that the equivalent benefit is being denied to homosexuals.' Ibid, para [143].

[68] Lords Nicholls, Steyn, Rodger, and Baroness Hale; Lord Millett dissenting.

[69] *Ferguson & Others v United Kingdom*, a copy of the submission can be found at http://equallove.org.uk/wp-content/uploads/2011/02/equalloveapplicationtoechr.pdf.

to legalise same-sex marriage within this Parliament. On 17 July 2013 the Marriage (Same Sex Couples) Act 2013 received its Royal Assent with the first same-sex marriages taking place on 29 March 2014. Under the provisions of the Act same-sex couples can marry either in a civil ceremony or, provided that the governing body of the religious organisation concerned has opted in to that process, on religious premises with the marriage being solemnised through a religious ceremony.[70]

Thus there are now three formalised relationship structures which are open to couples: opposite-sex marriage; same-sex marriage; and same-sex civil partnership. The state preference is for couples to opt in to one of these structures as it is seen to be the easiest method of regulating relationships and defining the parties' mutual rights and responsibilities. Legal consequences simply attach to these relationships by virtue of the parties opting in. While it may be the most straightforward way to give legal recognition to relationships, it does produce harsh consequences for those relationships that fall outside this regulatory net.[71] Unmarried and unregistered cohabitants are given some recognition in family law but not to the same extent as married couples and civil partners. In particular, in respect of property and financial matters, there are no special family law provisions for unmarried cohabitants who must turn instead to the general principles of the law of property and contract. As we shall see in Chapter 5, this makes them particularly vulnerable on relationship breakdown: cohabiting partners have no duty to provide each other with financial provision and any dispute about the family home must be determined by property law principles where the outcome may operate harshly. This is quite different from marriage and civil partnerships where the court can make financial orders according to the needs of the parties and by applying principles of fairness and non-discrimination. Thus the fact of being married or in a civil partnership carries determinative weight in family law, and the legitimacy of this approach (which prioritises relationship form over relationship functions) has generated much debate from family law scholars and policy-makers.[72]

## The impact of the Human Rights Act 1998 and international conventions

As *Ghaidan v Godin-Mendoza* illustrates, English law must now take account of the ECHR as implemented by the HRA 1998. Domestic courts must take account of the case law of the European Court of Human Rights (ECtHR),[73] statutory provisions must be interpreted so far as possible in a way which is consistent with Convention rights,[74] and a public authority (including a court or tribunal) must not act in a way which is inconsistent with the Convention rights.[75] Several Articles of the Convention, particularly Articles 3 (protection from inhuman and degrading treatment), 6 (right to a fair trial), 8 (private and family life), 12 (right to marry and found a family), and 14 (non-discrimination in application of Convention rights), will often be encountered in family law and their implications are discussed at various points in this book. Article 8 of the ECHR is particularly pertinent since it protects the right to respect for private and family life, and it is convenient at the outset of this book to provide a short general account of its nature and scope.

---

[70] With the exception of the Church of England and the Church of Wales.

[71] See R. Leckey (ed.), *After Legal Equality: Family, Sex and Kinship* (Abingdon: Routledge, 2014).

[72] See, for example, L. Glennon, 'Obligations Between Adult Partners: Moving From Form to Function' (2008) 22 International Journal of Law, Policy and the Family 22, and R. Leckey, *Contextual Subjects, Family, State and Relational Theory* (Toronto: University of Toronto Press, 2008). See also the Law Commission of Canada, *Beyond Conjugality: Recognising and supporting close personal adult relationships* (LC, 2001) for interesting policy proposals in Canada which sought to challenge the centrality of the 'conjugal family' in law and thus respond more accurately to the functional attributes of particular relationships rather than their form.

[73] HRA 1998, s 2.      [74] Ibid, s 3.      [75] Ibid, s 6.

Article 8 provides:

> 1. Everyone has the right to respect for his private and family life, his home and his correspondence.
> 2. There shall be no interference by a public authority with the exercise of this right except such as is in accordance with the law and is necessary in a democratic society in the interests of national security, public safety or the economic well-being of the country, for the prevention of disorder or crime, for the protection of health or morals, or for the protection of the rights and freedoms of others.

To be able to rely upon Article 8 the applicant must first demonstrate that a complaint falls within its scope, in other words that aspects of private and family life etc are engaged.

The scope of 'private life' is broad, covering such matters as personal identity and development, psychological and physical integrity, and personal engagement with others. For example, there are many cases in which the right to respect for private life has been invoked by parents or children seeking to establish their biological connection with the other,[76] or by transgender persons seeking recognition of their transgender identity.[77] Article 8 was invoked in relation to physical and psychological integrity in, for example, *Hajduova v Slovakia*,[78] where a violation was found in the state's failure to provide necessary psychiatric treatment for a husband, which had led to the husband's ongoing abusive behaviour to the wife, including threats to kill her.[79] In *Dickson v United Kingdom*[80] Article 8 was pleaded to seek to protect a 'right of procreation'. There a violation of Article 8 was found in the state's not permitting a prisoner's attempt to father a child by artificial insemination.

In order to rely upon the notion of 'family life' within Article 8 it is necessary to demonstrate existing family relationships as opposed to merely a desire to found family relationships.[81] De jure relationships such as those arising from marriage are automatically recognised.[82] However, 'family life' may also encompass de facto 'family' ties, for example where the parties are living together outside of marriage, including in same-sex relationships whether or not such couples have children.[83] Where the circumstances warrant it, 'family life' may also extend to the potential relationship which may develop between a child and a parent. In such cases, the necessary close personal ties in practice[84] can be demonstrated through the nature of the parents' relationship and a demonstrable interest in and commitment by the parent to the child both before and after the birth.[85] In *Lebbink v The Netherlands*[86] the father had been in a relationship with the mother for two years prior to the birth of their daughter, although the couple had never cohabited. He visited the mother and daughter regularly and babysat on occasions, but did not formally recognise the baby because of the mother's refusal of permission. The parents' relationship broke down when the child was 16 months old and the father applied to the court for contact with his daughter. The domestic court held the application inadmissible, finding that no family life existed between father and daughter. The ECtHR, however, held that while 'a mere biological kinship, without any further legal or factual elements indicating

---

[76] See eg, *Mikulić v Croatia* (App no 53176/99) [2002] 1 FCR 720 and *Odièvre v France* (App no 42326/98) [2002] 1 FCR 621, ECtHR (Grand Chamber). These and other cases are discussed in Chapter 7.

[77] Eg, *Goodwin v United Kingdom* (Application No 28957/95), ECHR, discussed in Chapter 1.

[78] Application No 2660/03, [2011] 1 FLR 1247.

[79] See also *A v Croatia* (Application No 55164/08) [2011] 1 FLR 407.

[80] Application No 44362/04, 2008 1 FLR 135.          [81] *Fretté v France* (Application No 36515/97), ECHR.

[82] See eg, *Marckx v Belgium* (A/331, ECHR) (1979–80).

[83] *Schalk and Kopf v Austria* (Application no. 30141/04) and *Vallianatos and Others v Greece* (Applications nos. 29381/09 and 32684/09).

[84] *K and T v Finland* (2000) 31 EHRR 484, [2000] 2 FLR 79.

[85] See *Ahrens v Germany* (Application No 45071/09) [2012] 2 FLR 483, at [58]. See *Nylund v Finland; Nekvedavicius v Germany* (Application No 46165/99); *Lebbink v The Netherlands* (Application No 45582/99) [2004] 2 FLR 463, [36]; and *Anayo v Germany* (Application No 20578/07) [2011] 1 FLR 1883.

[86] Application No 45582/99, [2004] 2 FLR 463.

the existence of a close personal relationship' is insufficient to attract the protection of Article 8, the necessary close relationship evidencing 'family life' was demonstrated on the facts of the case.[87] Accordingly the domestic court had been wrong not to consider the merits of the father's claim for contact. The court has also indicated that, exceptionally, intended family life may fall within the ambit of Article 8, notably where the fact that family life has not yet fully been established is not attributable to the applicant.[88] For example in *Pini and Bertani; Manera and Atripaldi v Romania*[89] two Italian couples had obtained lawful adoption orders in respect of Romanian children, whom they had selected from photographs in accordance with the procedure put in place by the Romanian authorities. Although the Italian parents had written letters to the children in Romanian, there was no established actual family life between the adoptive parents and children because the orphanage in which the children were staying had refused to hand over the children. The adoptive parents claimed a breach of Article 8. While on the facts the ECtHR did not find a violation, it deemed the relationship arising here from a lawful and genuine adoption sufficient to attract such respect as may be due for family life under Article 8 of the ECHR.[90]

In *Anayo v Germany*[91] the biological father of twins had a two-year relationship with the children's mother which ended when she was pregnant. The twins had been brought up since birth by the mother and her husband, who was the legal father. Despite the biological father's requests to see the children, both before and after their birth, the mother and her husband refused him any contact with the children. The German courts held that the father had no right of contact, there never having been a family relationship between the father and children, and therefore the court did not see the need to consider the merits with reference to the children's interests. However, the ECtHR noted the father's expressed wish to have contact, his speedy pursuit of legal proceedings, and that the children 'emanated from a relationship which lasted some 2 years and was, therefore, not merely haphazard'. The court concluded that 'this conduct was sufficient to demonstrate the applicant's interest in his children'[92] and the court therefore did 'not exclude that the applicant's intended relationship with his biological children attracts the protection of 'family life' under Art 8'.[93] In any event, the court held that the determination of the issues raised concerned an important part of the applicant's identity and thus his 'private life' within the meaning of Article 8(1). The domestic courts' decision to refuse him contact with his children thus interfered with his right to respect, at least, for his private life. The ECtHR ultimately found a violation of Article 8, holding that the domestic court had failed to balance the competing interests and to give sufficient reasons to justify interference with the biological father's interests protected under Article 8, in particular by not giving any consideration to whether contact was in the best interests of the twins.[94]

In *Ahrens v Germany*[95] the biological father's relationship with the mother ended about a year before the child was conceived. The mother had been cohabiting with a new partner when for a brief period she had what were described as relations of a 'purely sexual nature' with the father. The child was brought up by the mother and her new partner, who acknowledged paternity. The German court held that the biological father did not have a right to challenge the social and family relationship of the legal father. The ECtHR noted that there was no intention to found a family with the biological father and that he had not shown signs of commitment prior to the child's birth. On these facts, the ECtHR found that the father's relationship with the child was not within the scope of 'family life'. However, the decision to reject his request to establish paternity interfered with his right to respect for private life. The ECtHR noted that the father's proceedings here would seek to challenge, and remove, the paternity of the mother's partner and must be considered to have a 'fundamentally different and more far-reaching objective than the mere establishment of biological paternity for the purpose of having contact',[96] as was at stake in the *Anayo* case. The court found no settled consensus among states on challenging paternity

---

[87] Ibid, [37] to [40].
[88] Applications Nos 78028/01 and 78030/01, (2004) 40 EHRR 312, [2005] 2 FLR 596, [143] and [146].
[89] Applications Nos 78028/01 and 78030/01, (2004) 40 EHRR 312, [2005] 2 FLR 596.     [90] Ibid, [148].
[91] Application No 20578/07, [2011] 1 FLR 1883.     [92] Ibid, [61].     [93] Ibid, [62].
[94] Ibid, [71] to [73].     [95] Application No 45071/09, [2012] 2 FLR 483.     [96] Ibid, [67].

as between social and biological parents which would narrow the state's margin of appreciation. The ECtHR held that its ruling in *Anayo* did 'not necessarily imply a duty under the European Convention to allow the biological father to challenge the legal father's status'[97] and the decision whether the biological father should be permitted to challenge paternity fell within the state's margin of appreciation.[98]

As these cases illustrate, Article 8 is often invoked to protect existing family ties between parent and child. Such cases arise often because there can be interference with the rights of one parent by the other in private law disputes, and an interference more directly by the state in public law cases in which the state may intervene to protect a child. The ECtHR has been clear that 'the mutual enjoyment by parent and child of each other's company constitutes a fundamental element of family life, even if the relationship between the parents has broken down, and domestic measures hindering such enjoyment amount to an interference with the right protected by Art 8 of the Convention.'[99]

As Article 8(2) makes clear, any interference must be 'in accordance with the law', pursue legitimate aims within the meaning of Article 8(2), and be 'necessary in a democratic society', in other words a proportionate response. States are accorded a certain margin of appreciation in the choice of means to secure compliance with the ECHR. The width of the margin depends on the circumstances. In determining whether a measure is necessary, the court 'will consider whether, in the light of the case as a whole, the reasons adduced to justify this measure were relevant and sufficient for the purposes of Art 8, para 2'.[100] The review requires a fair balance to be struck between the interests of the child and parent.[101] However, particular importance must be attached to the best interests of a child which, depending on their nature and seriousness, may override those of the parent. In particular, the parent cannot be entitled under Article 8 of the Convention to have such measures taken as would harm the child's health and development.[102]

Where the existence of family life has been established, the state must, in principle, act in a manner calculated to enable the tie to be maintained. In *Nazarenko v Russia*[103] a child was born during the parents' marriage and the husband was registered as the child's father. The spouses had shared the care of the child until the marriage broke down. There were proceedings concerning the child's residence, during which a DNA test revealed that the husband was not the father. The Russian court terminated the man's paternity, removed his name from the child's birth certificate, and dismissed his application for residence, the overall effect of which was to terminate the relationship, including contact. The European Court of Human Rights found a violation of Article 8, holding that the relationship could not be terminated unless there were relevant reasons relating to the welfare of the child, and no such reasons had been advanced.[104] The ECtHR commented:

> The court is not convinced that the best interests of children in the sphere of contact rights can be truly determined by a general legal assumption. Having regard to the great variety of family situations possibly concerned, the court considers that a fair balancing of the rights of all persons involved necessitates an examination of the particular circumstances of the case ... Accordingly, Art 8 of the European Convention can be interpreted as imposing on the Member States an obligation to examine on a case-by-case basis whether it is in the child's best interests to maintain contact with the person, whether biologically related or not, who has taken care of him or her for a sufficiently long period of time.[105]

In cases in which a measure will result in the severance of family ties, strict scrutiny is employed. In *YC v United Kingdom*[106] the ECtHR reiterated that in cases which entail the permanent severance

---

[97] Ibid, [74].     [98] Ibid, [75].

[99] *Johansen v Norway* (App no 17383/90) (1997) 23 EHRR 33 at para 52; *Bronda v Italy* (App no 22430/93) (2001) 33 EHRR 4 at para 51; *Elsholz v Germany* (App no 25735/94) (2002) 34 EHRR 58 at [43]; *Kosmopoulou v Greece* (App no 60457/00) [2004] 1 FLR 800, [47].

[100] *Elsholz*, [48].     [101] *Olsson v Sweden* (No 2) (App no 13441/87) (1994) 17 EHRR 134, [90]; *Elsholz*, [50].

[102] *Johansen v Norway* (App no 17383/90) (1997) 23 EHRR 33 at para 78; *Elsholz*, [50].

[103] Application No 39438/13, [2015] 2 FLR 728.     [104] Ibid, at para [67].

[105] Ibid, at para [66].     [106] Application No 4547/10, [2012] 2 FLR 332.

of family ties, such as the placement of a child for adoption, 'family ties may only be severed in very exceptional circumstances and that everything must be done to preserve personal relations and, where appropriate, to "rebuild" the family.'[107] It is 'not enough to show that a child could be placed in a more beneficial environment for his upbringing'.[108]

Article 8 places positive obligations on the state to ensure that family members are reunited when ties are severed, although it is not an absolute obligation.[109] However, the state will be in breach of Article 8 where, without good reason, it fails to enforce court orders relating to with whom the child is to live or have contact.[110]

The ECHR provides not only substantive protections but also procedural protections. The ECtHR will consider whether the decision-making process was fair. There may be a breach of the Convention where a case is not dealt with diligently,[111] or where there is a failure to involve persons sufficiently in the decision-making process,[112] or where the decision making process is not sufficiently rigorous. For example, in *MD and Others v Malta*[113] breaches of Articles 6 and 8 were found where Maltese law provided for the automatic removal of children from parents who had been found guilty of criminal offences relating to child cruelty, with no procedure to challenge the automatic making of care orders.

Article 14 of the ECHR provides that:

> The enjoyment of the rights and freedoms set forth in this Convention shall be secured without discrimination on any ground such as sex, race colour, language, religion, political or other opinion, national or social origin, association with a national minority, property, birth or other status.

This non-discrimination provision provides further protection from discrimination in the enjoyment of the Convention rights. It is not freestanding, but rather must be used in conjunction with other rights. For an issue to arise under Article 14 there must be a difference in the treatment of persons in relevantly similar situations, such difference being based on one of the grounds expressly or implicitly covered by Article 14. In *Burden v The United Kingdom*,[114] for example, the Grand Chamber of the ECtHR held that two sisters could not be compared for the purposes of Article 14 to a married couple or civil partners and accordingly there was no discrimination in their enjoyment of property under Article 1 of Protocol 1. The sisters, who lived together inter-dependently, claimed that they should be able to claim exemption from inheritance tax as would be the case if they were in a civil partnership.

A difference in treatment covered by the Convention is discriminatory if it lacks reasonable and objective justification. It will be discriminatory, therefore, if it does not pursue a legitimate aim or if there is no reasonable relationship of proportionality between the means employed and the aim pursued. States have a margin of appreciation in assessing whether and to what extent differences in otherwise similar situations justify a different treatment. The width of the margin depends on the circumstances but it has been said that in cases of discrimination on grounds of

---

[107] Ibid, at [134]. The court explained: 'In identifying the child's best interests in a particular case, two considerations must be borne in mind: first, it is in the child's best interests that his ties with his family be maintained except in cases where the family has proved particularly unfit; and secondly, it is in the child's best interests to ensure his development in a safe and secure environment': ibid, at [134].

[108] Ibid.

[109] See eg, *Glaser v United Kingdom* (Application No 32346/96) [2001] 1 FLR 153; *Kaleta v Poland* (Application No 11375/02).

[110] See eg, *VP v Russia* (Application No 61362/12), [2015] 2 FLR 240 (Russian authorities' failure to enforce a Moldovan residence order in favour of the father, despite the fact that the mother was living openly with the child in Russia); and for a similar case, see *Pakhomova v Russia* (Application No 22935/11) [2014] 2 FLR 44.

[111] See eg, *Kopf and Liberda v Austria (Application No 1598/06)* [2012] 1 FLR 1199 (procedural breach of Article 8).

[112] See eg, *Jucius and Juciuviene v Lithuania* (Application No 14414/03); and *Venema v The Netherlands* (Application No 35731/97) [2003] 1 FLR 552.

[113] Application No 64791/10, [2013] 1 FLR 586.  [114] Application No 13378/05, [2008] 2 FLR 787.

sexual orientation, the margin is narrow, and particularly convincing and weighty reasons are required.[115]

There are many examples of complaints where Article 14 is taken together with Article 8. For example, some cases have claimed discrimination in relation to acquisition of citizenship on the basis of marital status.[116] Several cases have drawn attention to discrimination on the ground of sexual orientation, in, for example, matters of child adoption,[117] contact,[118] and child support. In *JM v United Kingdom*,[119] for example, the ECtHR found a violation of Article 14, in conjunction with Article 1 of Protocol 1, in English child support legislation's failure to take account of the housing costs of a mother's cohabitation with a woman, where the law did so in relation to cohabitation with a man. Several cases have involved alleged discrimination as between parents on the basis of one parent's religion, particularly in disputes about a child's residence.[120]

There is an increasing internationalisation of family law, and no comprehensive account of family law can legitimately ignore the impact of international conventions,[121] even where not directly part of English law (such as the United Nations Convention on the Rights of the Child). Mention is made of such provisions at various points in the text where relevant to matters under discussion. However, it is important for us to make clear at the outset that our focus in this book is upon domestic family law in the sense of family law issues within this jurisdiction (as opposed to international aspects of family law involving disputes as between jurisdictions). We have eschewed an encyclopaedic treatment in favour of a clear, detailed examination of domestic case law and statutes and critical commentary thereon. Our focus is on the needs of undergraduate law students commencing their family law studies, by way of providing a foundation for further study. We believe that overload at this stage can easily undermine that foundation.

## Some features of family law

### Discretion

There is another reason why our focus is heavily on the domestic law, and particularly the case law. Family law is different from many other law subjects in that much of family law decision making is discretionary in nature. Appellate courts cannot interfere with a judge's discretion unless he or she has taken into account an irrelevant matter, has omitted a relevant matter, or the judge's balancing of factors in a case is plainly wrong.[122] Frequently, therefore, knowledge of family law involves understanding how judges exercise their wide discretion, which is often guided by statutory frameworks.[123] Unlike in subjects like tort or contract, where students are concerned to learn the *ratio decidendi* or particular legal principle represented by each case, in family law the cases are often not setting precedents in the same sense. Appellate judgments will often merely set guidelines for

---

[115] See eg, *EB v France* (Application No 43546/02) [2008] 1 FLR 850, at [91] (sexual orientation of adopter).

[116] See eg, *Genovese v Malta (Application No 53124/09)* [2012] 1 FLR 10 (discrimination in relation to citizenship by descent based on whether parents were married or not). See also *Sporer v Austria* (Application No 35637/03) [2011] 2 FLR 294.

[117] Eg, *EB v France* (Application No 43546/02) [2008] 1 FLR 850.

[118] Eg, *Salgueiro Da Silva Mouta v Portugal* (Application no. 33290/96), ECHR.

[119] Application No 37060/06, [2011] 1 FLR 491.

[120] See eg, *Gineitiene v Lithuania* Application No 20739/05 [2010] 2 FLR 1837 (complaint not upheld); *Palau-Martinez v France* Application No 64927/01 [2004] 2 FLR 810; *Hoffman v Austria* (App no 12875/87) [1993] ECHR 25, (1994) 17 EHRR 293, [1994] 1 FCR 193, ECtHR; *Ismailova v Russia* [2008] 1 FLR 533.

[121] For example, as part of Chapter 9 on private law disputes concerning children, we explore the law on relocation from the jurisdiction and, with reference to the Hague Convention on Civil Aspects of International Child Abduction, measures to ensure the child's return when unlawfully abducted.

[122] *G v G (Minors) (Custody Appeal)* [1985] FLR 894, as explained in *Re B (A Child)* [2013] UKSC 33.

[123] See eg the Children Act 1989, s 1 or the Matrimonial Causes Act 1973, s 25.

judges in the exercise of their discretion.[124] In order to understand family law it is necessary therefore to get a feel for how judges are likely to exercise their discretion. This comes with experience and with reading a large number of judgments. That is why we have tried, wherever possible, to deal with the cases in some detail and give as many examples as space permitted.

That is not to say that all of family law relies merely on discretion. Some areas are more rule-based, for example the calculation of child support maintenance.[125] The choice between the use of rules and discretion in family law has provoked debate as to the respective advantages and disadvantages of those approaches, and whether there is any coherence to such choices or whether the responses of family law are nothing more than chaotic.[126] Where the court's exercise of discretion is dictated by welfare considerations, as for example in matters with respect to children's upbringing,[127] there is also a tension between utility and rights.[128]

## Interaction with other disciplines

Another feature of family law is the role that other disciplines play, particularly in children cases. In child protection cases, paediatricians, child psychiatrists, and other specialists may provide valuable expert evidence. Social workers will also be closely professionally involved. Even in private law cases there may be a need for the child's welfare to be safeguarded in the proceedings and for the court to receive professional advice. The Children and Family Court Advisory and Support Service (Cafcass)[129] has statutory duties[130] in family law cases involving children: to safeguard and promote child welfare; to give advice to the court; to represent children where necessary; and to provide information and support to families. Officers of the service have various roles: preparing court reports; representing children in public law child protection and adoption cases, and ensuring parents understand what is happening in adoption cases; and, where appropriate,[131] providing separate representation for children in private law cases. The focus in such cases on the welfare of children, and the interaction which law has here with other disciplines, raises issues concerning the use of knowledge from other disciplines in court decision making. To what extent are the courts, and should they be, influenced by social science research evidence on child well-being?[132] At various points in this book we examine the connections between research evidence and the law.

## The arrangement of the text

The text is arranged as follows. In the first chapter, we begin by examining the law surrounding the formation of the formal relationships of marriage and civil partnership, including the law on nullity. This chapter also explores, by way of contrast, non-formal cohabiting relationships. Chapters 2 and 3 then move on to examine how the law regulates the breakdown of relationships, Chapter 2 exploring the law of divorce and dissolution of civil partnership, before Chapter 3 explores more specifically the problems and legal responses to relationships in which there is domestic violence. Chapters 4 and 5 then consider the financial consequences of relationships (which usually come to

---

[124] For further discussion, see S. Gilmore, 'The *Payne* Saga: Precedent and Family Law Cases' [2011] Family Law 970, esp at 973 et seq.

[125] Child Support Act 1991, Sch 1.

[126] J. Dewar, 'The Normal Chaos of Family Law' (1998) 61 Modern Law Review 467.

[127] Children Act 1989, s 1(1).

[128] See S. Parker, 'Rights and Utility in Anglo-Australian Family Law' (1992) 55 Modern Law Review 311.

[129] Set up pursuant to the Criminal Justice and Court Services Act 2002, s 11.

[130] Criminal Justice and Court Services Act 2000, s 12.         [131] Usually only in difficult cases.

[132] Indeed, to what extent is law capable of managing knowledge from other disciplines? See for a discussion of autopoietic theory in this context, M. King and C. Piper, *How the Law Thinks About Children*, 2nd edn (Aldershot: Ashgate, 1995).

the fore on breakdown). Chapter 4 examines the courts' powers to make financial provision and adjust property as between spouses or civil partners ancillary to divorce or dissolution. Chapter 5 explores how the family finances are dealt with in the absence of such a discretionary regime, which particularly affects cohabitants in non-formal relationships. In the case of a former cohabitant who has no entitlement to the former family home, one way of obtaining support may be in his or her role as carer of any child of the relationship. Thus, Chapter 6 follows with a discussion of financial support for children. Having examined parental duties relating to child support, Chapter 7 then examines in more detail the law on parenthood and parental responsibility. Chapters 8, 9, and 10 then examine different areas of law which may result in an interference with parental responsibility. Chapter 8 explores the issue of children's rights, with a particular focus on the child's right to make his or her own decisions as a possible limitation on parental responsibility. Chapter 9 examines how the courts deal with private law issues or disputes relating to children's upbringing, such as post-separation residence or contact disputes, or other specific issues. Chapter 10 examines the relationship between children, parents, and the state, looking at how the law responds to children needing services, care, and protection. The book ends by examining in Chapter 11 the legal mechanisms by which children can be provided with long-term alternative secure family placements: the law on adoption and special guardianship.

It may be helpful to view the arrangement of the text in this book as two halves. The first half (Chapters 1 to 5 inclusive) deals principally with the legal regulation of adult family relationships, and the second (Chapters 6 to 11) focuses on the law relating to children, with the linking point in this arrangement of the book being the chapter on child support. Each half of the book has its own logical arrangement, however, and in this way the book is particularly suitable not only for modules that cover both aspects of family law (or a little of each), but also allows it to be used conveniently in cases where separate family law and child law modules are taught.

# PART 1

# Adult Family Law

1 The formation of adult relationships ........................................................................................................... 3

2 The dissolution of adult relationships .................................................................................................. 65

3 Protection from domestic violence and occupation of the family home ................................ 97

4 Money and property distribution on marriage breakdown ......................................................... 167

5 Property disputes of unmarried cohabitants on relationship breakdown ............................ 253

# 1

# The formation of adult relationships

## INTRODUCTION

At one time family law recognised only one sort of status relationship between adult partners, namely marriage between persons of the opposite sex. Today, however, same-sex relationships are similarly recognised in that such couples can register a civil partnership, and since the enactment of the Marriage (Same Sex Couples) Act 2013, can enter into a same-sex marriage. Over time, the law has also given increasing recognition to couples who cohabit outside marriage or civil partnership, although as we shall see cohabitants have fewer rights and remedies in family law than married couples or civil partners.[1] This chapter looks at the creation of these adult relationships and their legal consequences.

Marriage and civil partnership are regarded as 'formal' in nature, since certain legal formalities must be complied with for their creation (and indeed dissolution). A failure to do so may mean that the legal relationship of marriage or civil partnership will not have been created and the parties will not have the legal rights, obligations, and privileges which attach thereto. By contrast, other relationships, such as cohabitation outside marriage and civil partnership, or home-sharer relationships, are 'informal' in nature. Whether such informal relationships exist depends on the factual nature of the relationship. Proposals for reform of the law to give cohabitants rights on relationship breakdown have struggled with the difficulty of defining cohabitation.[2] Marriage and civil partnership, on the other hand, are proved simply by evidencing the status, for example by production of a marriage certificate.

This chapter deals first with formal relationships of marriage and civil partnership, and then with cohabitation and finally with other home-sharer relationships.

## 1 Marriage

### 1.1 **Marriage today**

Although Lord Nicholls stated in *Bellinger v Bellinger (Lord Chancellor Intervening)*[3] that marriage is 'an institution, or a relationship, deeply embedded in the religious and social culture of this country', marriage is no longer as popular as it was, and increasing numbers of couples opt to cohabit rather than marry.[4] Also, the nature of marriage has changed over the years. In 1886, Lord Penzance in the case of *Hyde v Hyde*[5] said: 'I conceive that marriage, as understood in Christendom, may . . . be defined as the voluntary union for life of one man and one woman, to the exclusion of all others.' Today, this definition[6] is no longer accurate. First, the Christian conception of marriage

---

[1] For discussion of the differences and of legal developments and policy, see A. Barlow, S. Duncan, G. James, and A. Park, *Cohabitation, Marriage and the Law: Social Change and Legal Reform in the 21st Century* (Oxford: Hart, 2005).

[2] See Chapter 2.    [3] [2003] UKHL 21.    [4] See Chapter 2.    [5] [1866] LR 1 P & D 130.

[6] Or a defence of a particular view of marriage, see R. Probert, '*Hyde v Hyde*: Defining or Defending Marriage?' [2007] Child and Family Law Quarterly 322.

no longer predominates. Many marriages today are civil marriages,[7] and it is possible to marry in a Muslim mosque or a Hindu temple, not just in a Christian church.[8] Marriage is also not necessarily regarded as being for life, as many marriages end in divorce. Also, some polygamous marriages are recognised in this country where the parties have come from an overseas jurisdiction where such marriages are lawful. Furthermore, since the enactment of the Marriage (Same Sex Couples) Act 2013, same-sex couples can enter into a legally valid marriage which has the same effect as opposite-sex marriage, extending both existing and future legislation applicable to opposite-sex spouses to same-sex spouses.[9] The only part of Lord Penzance's definition, therefore, which remains material today is that marriage involves a voluntary union, a fact which has been reinforced in recent years by reforms giving greater protection to victims of forced marriage.[10]

---

### The Law in Context

According to Government statistics,[11] the long-term picture for UK marriages has been one of decline, from a peak of 480,285 marriages in 1972, with figures for 2010 showing the first increase since 2004. This general decline has been attributed to two main social factors. First, the growing number of men and women delaying marriage, or not marrying at all. Secondly, the increasing number of couples choosing to cohabit rather than entering into a marriage, either as a precursor to marriage or as an alternative.[12] While the rate of marriage has remained relatively stable in the last few years, recent statistics reveal an upward trend. The provisional number of marriages registered in England and Wales rose by 1.7 per cent in 2011, and 5.3 per cent in 2012 to 262,240 (from 249,133 in 2011).[13] The largest percentage increase in the number of marriages between 2011 and 2012 was for men and women aged 65 to 69, rising by 25 per cent and 21 per cent respectively. In 2012, the provisional male marriage rate was 23.2 men marrying per 1,000 unmarried men aged 16 and over (from 22.1 in 2011 and 27.4 in 2002), and the provisional female marriage rate was 21.0 women marrying per 1,000 unmarried women aged 16 and over (from 19.9 in 2011 and 23.9 in 2002).

The average age of marriage has increased over the years: in 2012, the number of marriages was greatest among men and women aged 25 to 29; the provisional mean age for men marrying in 2012 was 36.5 years, and for women was 34.0 years. Due to the high incidence of marriage breakdown, many marriages are second marriages. In 2012, provisional figures show that 33 per cent of all marriages in England and Wales were remarriages for one or both of the parties. Since 1992, there have been more civil ceremonies in England and Wales than religious ceremonies. In 2012, civil ceremonies accounted for 70 per cent of all marriages, an increase from 64 per cent in 2001. Increasing numbers of marriages now take place in approved premises, such as hotels, stately homes, and historic buildings. In 2012, 60 per cent of all marriages took place in such premises.

---

[7] Recent statistics reveal that civil ceremonies accounted for 70 per cent of all marriages that took place in 2012, an increase from 66 per cent in 2002, Office for National Statistics, Marriages in England and Wales (Provisional) 2012 (2014).

[8] In *R (Hodkin & Anor) v Registrar General of Births, Deaths and Marriages* [2013] UKSC 77, the Supreme Court decided that the Church of Scientology was a 'place of meeting for religious worship' which meant that a valid ceremony of marriage could be performed there under the Marriage Act 1949.

[9] Section 11 and Schs 3–4 of the Marriage (Same Sex Couples) Act 2013. There are some differences between same- and opposite-sex marriages which will be explained later in this chapter.

[10] See Section 5 of this chapter.    [11] Published by the Office for National Statistics (www.statistics.gov.uk).

[12] Office for National Statistics, Marriages in England and Wales (Provisional) 2012 (2014) citing B. Wilson and S. Smallwood, (2007) Understanding recent trends in marriage, *Population Trends* 128.

[13] Office for National Statistics, Marriages in England and Wales (Provisional) 2012 (2014). Marriage statistics for 2012 are provisional and will be finalised in 2015 when the majority of marriage returns have been received from register offices and the clergy.

## 1.2 **The right to marry**

### Key legislation

The right to marry is a human right under Article 12 of the European Convention for the Protection of Human Rights (ECHR),[14] which provides that: 'Men and women of marriageable age have the right to marry and to found a family according to the national laws governing the exercise of this right.'

This is a 'strong' right, as illustrated by the House of Lords decision in *R (Baiai and Others) v Secretary of State for the Home Department*.[15] In that case a legal challenge was made to the immigration rules which required persons subject to immigration control to obtain the written permission of the Home Secretary to marry in the UK, unless they intended to enter into an Anglican marriage. These provisions were held to breach Article 12 and Article 14 (discrimination in respect of a Convention right) of the ECHR. The House of Lords held that, although the right to marry under Article 12 can be regulated by national laws both as to procedure and substance, such laws must not deprive persons of full legal capacity of the right to marry, or substantially interfere with their exercise of that right.[16]

## 1.3 **The creation of a valid marriage**

Marriage is an arrangement in which the state has an interest and thus it is not a contract which can be created and terminated at the will of the parties. For this reason there are legal rules governing its formation and dissolution.[17] In order to create a valid marriage in England and Wales, both parties must have the capacity to marry, and the marriage must not fall foul of various grounds in section 11 of the Matrimonial Causes Act (MCA) 1973 upon which a marriage may be regarded as void.

## 1.4 **Capacity to marry**

As marriage involves a *voluntary* union between a man and a woman, each party must consent to the marriage and thus have the capacity to consent. In *Re E (An Alleged Patient); Sheffield City Council v E and S*[18] a local authority sought to prevent E, a young woman of 21 who was functioning at the level of a 13-year-old, from marrying a 37-year-old man who had a substantial history of sexually violent crimes. The local authority were concerned that the relationship was an abusive one. As a preliminary issue, the question arose as to the test for capacity to marry. Munby J, drawing on earlier authority,[19] explained that the test for capacity is whether a person is able to understand the nature of the marriage contract, and whether he or she is mentally capable of understanding the duties and responsibilities that normally attach to marriage.[20] His Lordship went on, however, to indicate that this requires merely an understanding of the essence of the agreement, which is 'to live together, and to love one another as husband and wife, to the exclusion of all others. It creates a relationship of mutual and reciprocal obligations, typically involving the sharing of a common home and a common

---

[14] On the right to marry, see R. Probert, 'The Right to Marry and the Impact of the Human Rights Act 1998' [2003] International Family Law 29.

[15] [2008] UKHL 53, [2008] 2 FLR 1462.

[16] See also *O'Donoghue and Others v UK* (App no 34848/07) [2011] 2 FCR 197.      [17] See Chapter 2.

[18] [2004] EWHC 2808 (Fam), [2005] 1 FLR 965.      [19] *Re Estate of Park* [1954] P 112.

[20] *Re E (An Alleged Patient); Sheffield City Council v E and S* [2004] EWHC 2808 (Fam), [2005] 1 FLR 965. See R. Gaffney-Rhys, '*Sheffield City Council v E & Another*—Capacity to Marry and the Rights and Responsibility of Married Couples' [2006] 18 Child and Family Law Quarterly 139.

domestic life and the right to enjoy each other's society, comfort and assistance.' Munby J was concerned not to set the test of capacity to marry too high, 'lest it operate as an unfair, unnecessary and indeed discriminatory bar against the mentally disabled'[21] or become 'too easy to challenge the validity of what appear on the surface to be regular and seemingly valid marriages'.[22]

The High Court's inherent jurisdiction[23] can be invoked to protect vulnerable adults who lack the capacity to marry but who may be at risk of being forced into a marriage. For instance, in *M v B, A and S (By the Official Solicitor)*,[24] the local authority was concerned that the parents of a young woman aged 23 with a severe learning difficulty were organising a marriage for her in Pakistan. The High Court, exercising its inherent jurisdiction, granted declarations, on the local authority's application, that she lacked the capacity to marry and that it was not in her best interests to leave the jurisdiction of the UK.[25]

## 1.5  The law of nullity

### Key legislation

The law of nullity of marriage is laid down in Part I of the MCA 1973.[26] This is where a marriage is ended by being declared not valid. This can either be because the marriage was void (not allowed by law) or because the marriage was voidable (the marriage was legal but there are circumstances that mean it can be treated as if it never took place).

A void marriage is one which is not valid because of a fundamental defect. The marriage is void *ab initio*; there never was a valid marriage right from the beginning. Parties to a void marriage are therefore free to marry, and there is no need to apply for a decree to annul the 'marriage'.[27] However, the advantage of obtaining a decree of nullity is that it removes any uncertainty as to the status of the parties, and the grant of a decree gives the court jurisdiction under Part II of the MCA 1973 to grant finance and property orders equivalent to those which can be made on divorce.[28] Third parties, not just the parties to the marriage, can apply for a decree of nullity on the ground that the marriage is void and they can do so during the lifetime of the spouses or after their deaths.[29] In some circumstances, a marriage may be regarded as a 'non-marriage', one which departs so far from the formalities required to contract a valid marriage in England and Wales that it cannot even be regarded as a void marriage.[30]

A voidable marriage, on the other hand, is a valid and subsisting marriage unless and until it is annulled by the court on application of one of the parties during the lifetime of both parties.[31]

---

[21]  *Re E (An Alleged Patient); Sheffield City Council v E and S* [2004] EWHC 2808 (Fam), [2005] 1 FLR 965, para [144].

[22]  Ibid, para [145].

[23]  The High Court's inherent jurisdiction is a parental sort of jurisdiction, of which wardship is also a part, see Chapter 9.

[24]  [2005] EWHC 1681 (Fam), [2006] 1 FLR 117.

[25]  See also *X City Council v MB, NB and Mab (By His Litigation Friend The Official Solicitor)* [2006] EWHC 168 (Fam), [2006] 2 FLR 968 where an autistic man (aged 25) who lacked capacity to marry was given protection by Munby J under the inherent jurisdiction of the High Court on the application of the local authority, in order to prevent him being taken abroad by his parents to be married in Pakistan.

[26]  Which also governs the law of divorce (and judicial separation), see Chapter 4.

[27]  The parties to a void first 'marriage' will not commit the crime of bigamy if they enter into a second one without annulling the first.

[28]  See Chapter 4.

[29]  Eg a third party who wishes to prove there is no valid marriage in order to establish that the children of the relationship have no automatic right to succeed to any property on the death of a party to the 'marriage' who has died intestate.

[30]  See Section 2.3.1 of this chapter.         [31]  MCA 1973, s 16.

---

**The Law in Context**

Nullity petitions are rarely sought and are much less commonly sought than divorce. According to Government statistics, only 290 nullity decrees were filed in the courts in England and Wales in 2009 compared with 132,144 petitions for divorce.[32]

---

A decree of nullity is granted in two stages: decree nisi followed by a decree absolute. On or after the grant of a decree of nullity, the court has jurisdiction to make finance and property orders under Part II of the MCA 1973 equivalent to those which can be made on divorce. Nullity differs from divorce, however, in that the grounds for nullity are different, and there is no prohibition on bringing nullity proceedings in the first year of marriage as there is for divorce.[33] Also, the procedure for nullity is very different from that of divorce. Thus, whereas undefended divorces are dealt with by what is essentially an administrative procedure with little judicial involvement and there usually being no need to attend court, nullity proceedings, whether or not defended, are heard in open court with the parties giving oral evidence. This can be distressing and embarrassing for the parties, particularly in forced marriage cases where the petitioner may already be considerably distressed by the experience of being forced into marriage. There has been discussion about whether the law should be changed to remove the need for nullity proceedings to be heard in open court, and a significant majority of persons who responded to a Government consultation were in favour of the court having the power to make nullity orders without hearing oral evidence, but having a discretion to require a hearing where appropriate.[34]

## 2 Void marriages

**Key legislation**

The grounds on which a marriage may be void are laid down in section 11 of the MCA 1973, which provides that:

A marriage celebrated after 31 July 1971 shall be void on the following grounds only, that is to say—

(a) That it is not a valid marriage under the provisions of the Marriage Acts 1949–1986 (that is to say where—
   (i) the parties are within the prohibited degrees of relationship;
   (ii) either party is under the age of sixteen; or
   (iii) the parties have intermarried in disregard of certain requirements as to the formation of the marriage);
(b) that at the time of the marriage either party was already lawfully married . . .[35]
(d) in the case of a polygamous marriage entered into outside England and Wales, that either party was at the time of the marriage domiciled in England and Wales.

For the purposes of paragraph (d) of this subsection a marriage may be polygamous although at its inception neither party has any spouse additional to the other.

---

[32] *Judicial and Court Statistics 2009* (Ministry of Justice, 2010), Ch 2, Table 2.5.    [33] See MCA 1973, s 3.
[34] See the consultation document, *Family Procedure Rules: A New Procedural Code for Family Proceedings*, CP 19/06.
[35] Section 11(c), which stated that the parties must be respectively male and female, has been deleted by the Marriage (Same Sex Couples) Act 2013. As a result, marriage is now available to same-sex couples. This will be discussed later in the chapter, see Section 7.

The grounds which render a marriage void are considered in more detail in the following sections.

## 2.1 Marriage within the prohibited degrees of relationship

A marriage is void under section 11(a)(i) of the MCA 1973 if the parties are within the prohibited degrees of relationship. The law of England and Wales prohibits marriage between certain relationships of consanguinity (blood relations) and affinity (family relationship created by marriage). The rules governing relationships of consanguinity are more restrictive than those for relationships of affinity.

Under the rules which apply to relationships of consanguinity,[36] a person may not marry his or her parent, grandparent, child, grandchild, sibling, aunt or uncle, niece or nephew. These prohibitions on marriages between persons related closely by blood are founded on biological, moral, and social reasons. The biological reasons are based on genetic factors, as inherited disorders are more liable to arise within the same genetic pool. The moral and social policy reasons which prohibit such marriages relate to what is acceptable to public opinion. People have a strong sense of taboo about sexual relationships taking place between persons who are closely related. Marriage between cousins is permitted, however, despite evidence to show that children of cousin-parents are more likely to suffer from genetic diseases which may cause disability or death. Cousin marriage is particularly common in the Pakistani and Bangladeshi immigrant community, and Baroness Deech has expressed the view that, although human rights and religious and cultural practices are respected by not prohibiting such marriages, those cousins who do marry should be made aware of the possible genetic consequences for their children.[37]

There are also prohibitions on marriages taking place between persons who are related by reason of marriage.[38] These prohibitions are based on social policy considerations designed to discourage sexual relations within the family which cut across taboos of what is generally regarded as acceptable behaviour. However, these prohibitions were made less restrictive by the Marriage (Prohibited Degrees of Relationship) Act 1986, which amended the relevant provisions of the Marriage Act 1949 and permitted certain persons related by marriage to enter into a valid marriage. Thus, it became possible for a step-parent to marry his or her stepchild (the son or daughter of his or her former spouse), provided both parties were over the age of 21 and the step-parent had not treated the stepchild as a child of the family before the stepchild reached the age of 18. It also became possible to marry a former in-law provided both parties to the marriage were over 21 and the parties' former spouses were dead. Thus, for example, a man could marry his mother-in-law, provided his former wife and his former father-in-law were both dead. However, the restrictions on former in-law marriages were removed on 1 March 2007, as they were held by the European Court of Human Rights (ECtHR) in *B and L v UK*[39] to be in breach of the right to marry under Article 12 of the ECHR.

---

### Key case

In *B and L*, a father-in-law (B) and his daughter-in-law (L) wished to marry after each of their marriages had ended in divorce, but the superintendent registrar at the register office refused to give them permission to marry as they were prohibited from doing so on the ground that both their former spouses were alive. B and L took their case to the ECtHR claiming that this bar on 'in-law' marriages was a breach of their fundamental right to marry under Article 12.

---

[36] See the Marriage Act 1949, Sch 1, Pt I.          [37] R. Deech, 'Cousin Marriage' [2010] Family Law 619.
[38] See Marriage Act 1949, Sch 1, Pts II and III.          [39] (App no 36536/02) [2006] 1 FLR 35.

> The Court allowed their claim, holding that the relevant sections of the Marriage Act 1949 were incompatible with Article 12 of the ECHR as the prohibition was neither rational nor logical and served no useful purpose of public policy.[40]

After the decision in *B and L v UK*, the UK Government was forced to change the law and remove the restrictions that both former spouses should be dead.[41] Although the UK Government was not obliged to remove the age restriction, as the ECtHR had not considered this matter (as B and L were both over 21), it nonetheless decided to remove the incompatibility with Article 12 'across the board' by removing the age restriction.[42]

## 2.2 Marriage under the age of 16

Under section 11(a)(ii) of the MCA 1973, a marriage is void if either party to the marriage is under the age of 16.[43] One of the reasons for making 16 the minimum age for marriage is that it is a criminal offence for a man to have sexual intercourse with a girl aged under 16, and the notion that a man could nonetheless be entitled to have sexual intercourse with a girl under 16 under the cloak of marriage was regarded as offensive to law reformers. The view was taken that it was 'essential that the minimum age of marriage and the age of consent for sexual intercourse should be the same'.[44]

If a party is aged 16 but under 18, the age of majority, the consent of certain persons is required as a preliminary formality. These persons include each parent with parental responsibility (or guardian), a special guardian, anyone with whom the young person lives or is to live under a child arrangements order, and a local authority if the child is in care.[45] The absence of parental consent does not render a marriage void although it does mean that the celebrant can refuse to marry the couple; if the child is a ward of court, the court's consent is required. Consent can be dispensed with, however, if a person whose consent is needed is absent, inaccessible, or suffers from a disability.

## 2.3 Failure to comply with the required formalities for marriage

As marriage changes the status of the parties and gives them various rights and responsibilities it is important to make sure that a marriage has been contracted. For this reason, various formalities must be complied with. The aim of these formalities is to ensure that the parties have the capacity

---

[40] For a discussion of *B and L v UK* and whether the decision has other implications for the law on the prohibited degrees of relationship, see L. Schäfer, 'Marrying an In-Law: The Future of Prohibited Degrees of Affinity and Consanguinity in English Law' [2008] Child and Family Law Quarterly 219.

[41] It did so by passing the Marriage Act 1949 (Remedial Order) 2007, which amended s 1 of and Sch 1 to the Marriage Act 1949, and applied to marriages solemnised on or after 1 March 2007.

[42] The Government was of the view that there would be very few cases involving a party under 21 (because the younger person must have been 16 or over to enter into the first marriage, and could not divorce for at least one year afterwards; and because very few couples marry at so young an age).

[43] Immigration rules contain certain restrictions on the settlement of foreign spouses or civil partners in the UK. Paragraph 277 of the Immigration Rules states that the spousal visas required to enter the UK will only be granted where both parties are over the age of 21. The purpose of this restriction was to deter forced marriages, where at least one party enters the marriage without his or her free and full consent through force or duress, including coercion by threats or other psychological means. However, while the Supreme Court in *R (Quila and another) v Secretary of State for the Home Department* [2011] UKSC 45 held that this was a legitimate aim, its efficacy was, according to the majority, highly debatable [58]. The Supreme Court held that the Secretary of State had failed to produce robust evidence that the restriction had any substantial deterrent effect on the number of forced marriages. It was concluded that the restriction would keep a substantial number of bona fide young couples apart or force them to live outside the UK [54], far exceeding the number of forced marriages that would be deterred. Thus the Supreme Court held that the restriction was an infringement of the parties' rights under Article 8 of the ECHR.

[44] *Report of the Committee on the Age of Majority*, Latey Committee (Cmd 3342, 1967), para 177.

[45] See Marriage Act 1949, s 3.

to marry and consent to doing so, that there are no impediments to the marriage, and that there is proof by registration that a marriage has taken place. These rules are complex and breach of certain formality requirements can attract criminal sanctions.[46]

The exact nature of the formalities differs depending on whether the marriage is a civil or religious marriage, and whether it takes place in a religious building, a register office, or approved premises. With respect to religious marriages, there are also different rules depending on whether or not the marriage is an Anglican marriage, in other words one celebrated in the Church of England. The different formalities are explained in the following sections.

**Preliminary formalities:**  the parties must satisfy certain preliminary formalities before the marriage can take place. The rules are the same for all marriages, except those which are to be celebrated in the Church of England.

In the case of a non-Anglican marriage, the parties must first obtain a superintendent registrar's certificate giving them approval to marry. Various requirements must be satisfied before the certificate can be granted, and these are laid down in the Marriage Act 1949. Thus, the parties must give notice of the marriage in prescribed form to the superintendent registrar in the district(s) in which each of them has resided for at least the previous seven days, and to the register office where the ceremony is to take place (if this is different). The parties must declare that: there are no lawful impediments to the marriage; the residence requirements have been satisfied; and the required consents have been given. Notice of the marriage is then entered in the marriage notice book and publicly displayed in the register officer for 15 days after which the superintendent registrar issues a certificate (provided there has been no objection to the marriage). The marriage must take place within three months of notice in the marriage notice book. The Registrar-General has the power in exceptional circumstances to reduce the 15-day period; and under the Marriage Act 1983 special provisions permit a person who is housebound due to illness or disability, or who is detained in prison or due to mental ill-health, to marry in the place where he or she is residing or is detained.

A Church of England marriage can only be solemnised after the publication of banns,[47] or after the completion of one of the formalities listed earlier. In the case of other religious marriages, a superintendent registrar's certificate must be obtained, but there are additional preliminary formalities for some religions. Thus, under the provisions of the Marriage Act 1949, Quakers must make special declarations when giving notice; and both parties to a Jewish marriage must profess to belong to the Jewish faith.

**The marriage ceremony:**  in England and Wales the ceremony of marriage can take place in a register office, a religious building (such as a church or mosque), or in approved premises.[48]

A marriage ceremony in England and Wales must comply with certain legal formalities which differ depending on whether the marriage is civil or religious. In the case of a civil marriage, once the parties have satisfied the preliminary formalities (see earlier) and obtained the approval of the superintendent registrar (or the Registrar-General) to marry, the marriage can take place in a register office or in 'approved premises', or, in special cases, at the location where a person is housebound or detained. 'Approved premises' are premises which have been approved by the local authority for the purpose of conducting a civil marriage,[49] and include premises such as hotels, stately homes, castles, and other approved places. The civil ceremony, which is public and secular, may be followed by a

---

[46] Eg giving a false declaration constitutes the criminal offence of perjury.

[47] An announcement of the intended marriage made by the vicar or rector on three successive Sundays in the parish church of each of the parties.

[48] According to statistics published by the Office for National Statistics, civil ceremonies are more popular than religious ceremonies, and many marriages now take place in approved premises.

[49] Under the provisions of the Marriage Act 1994 and in government regulations.

religious ceremony, but it is the civil ceremony which creates the marriage. At the civil ceremony, the parties must declare that there are no lawful impediments to the marriage and they must exchange vows. At least two witnesses must attend.

In the case of a religious marriage, once the preliminary formalities have been complied with, the marriage is celebrated according to the rites of the particular religion and in the presence of at least two witnesses. Quaker and Jewish marriages are celebrated according to their own religious rites, but they need not take place in a registered building or in public or before an authorised person. There are special rules for the registration of Quaker and Jewish marriages. In the case of other religious marriages, the superintendent registrar's certificate will state where the ceremony is to be held, which will usually be a registered building in the district where at least one of the parties resides. Under the Marriage Act 1949, a 'registered building' is one which is registered by the Registrar-General as a place of meeting for religious worship, and includes not only Christian churches but also Sikh and Hindu temples and Muslim mosques.[50] In *R (Hodkin & Anor) v Registrar General of Births, Deaths and Marriages*[51], the question before the Supreme Court was whether a church of the Church of Scientology is recordable as a 'place of meeting for religious worship' under section 2 of the Places of Worship Registration Act 1855, thus allowing a valid ceremony of marriage to be performed there.[52] The Court of Appeal had previously rejected such a claim on the basis that Scientology did not involve 'religious worship' as it did not involve 'reverence or veneration of God or of a Supreme Being', but rather instruction in a philosophy.[53] In reaching a different conclusion, the Supreme Court decided that Scientology is a religion.[54] The court observed that religion should not be confined to faiths involving a supreme deity, since to do so would exclude Buddhism, Jainism, and others, and involve the Court in difficult theological territory.[55] Instead, and for the purposes of the legislation, religion could be described as 'a spiritual or non-secular belief system, held by a group of adherents, which claims to explain mankind's place in the universe and relationship with the infinite, and to teach its adherents how they are to live their lives in conformity with the spiritual understanding associated with the belief system'.[56] On this approach to religion, Scientology was clearly a religion. It followed that as the Church of Scientology held religious services, its church is a 'place of meeting for religious worship, which meant that it could be registered for the solemnisation of marriages under the Marriage Act 1949.

**Marriages by non-religious belief organisations:** Currently, The Marriage Act 1949 makes provision for both religious and civil marriage ceremonies. However, during the passage of the Marriage (Same Sex Couples) Act 2013, the question arose as to whether the law should allow humanists, and possibly other non-religious belief organisations, to solemnise marriages. As a result, section 14 of the 2013 Act required a review to be carried out on this issue. The Ministry of Justice published its consultation on the topic in 2014.[57] Currently, it is estimated that the British Humanist Association carries out between six and eight hundred humanist weddings each year in England and Wales but these do not have legal force. The Consultation asked whether there was a substantial

---

[50] A non-Anglican religious marriage must be attended by a registrar or an 'authorised person' (such as a religious cleric) and must take place in the presence of at least two witnesses and be open to the public. The ceremony can take any form, provided that during the ceremony the required declarations are made.

[51] [2013] UKSC 77.

[52] This statute provides that every 'place of meeting for religious worship' may be certified to the Registrar General which then entitles the building to be registered for the solemnisation of marriages under the Marriage Act 1949.

[53] *R v Registrar General, ex parte Segerdal* [1970] 2 QB 697.       [54] [2013] UKSC 77, at [50].

[55] Ibid, at [51]–[52].       [56] Ibid, at [57].

[57] Ministry of Justice, Marriages by non-religious belief organisations, (2014) https://consult.justice.gov.uk/digital-communications/marriages-by-non-religious-belief-organisations/supporting_documents/beliefmarriagesconsultation.pdf.

case for changing the law to permit non-religious belief ceremonies which would, in effect, allow a third type of legal ceremony (alongside religious and civil ceremonies) for getting married in England and Wales. A related question was where, if permitted, such marriages would take place. The Government response to the Consultation revealed that the majority of respondents were in favour of changing the law to allow non-religious belief ceremonies, and for those ceremonies to take place in unrestricted locations.[58] However, no change to the law was proposed as the consultation was said to raise a number of complex issues which had wider implications for the law on marriage ceremonies.

Instead the Government asked the Law Commission to consider the law governing how and where people can marry in England and Wales. The aim was to consider 'whether the current law, which has evolved over a long period of time, provides a fair and coherent legal framework for enabling people to marry. Does the law allow people to marry in a way which meets their needs and wishes while recognising the interests of society and the state in protecting the status of marriage?'[59] The Commission published its initial scoping paper, 'Getting Married', in December 2015, concluding that the law that governs how and where couples in England and Wales can marry is in need of reform as it is out of date, inconsistent, and overly restrictive.[60] According to the Law Commission, marriage law in England and Wales was designed to meet the needs of the early nineteenth century and, as such, it fails to cater for the many faiths and non-religious beliefs that make up the twenty-first century. Not only is it out of date, but it is also too complex as there are different rules for different groups at every stage of getting married. Thus, according to the Law Commission, the current system governing where and how marriages can take place is needlessly over-regulated. Civil marriages must take place in a register office or on approved premises and, with certain exceptions, religious ceremonies must take place within a registered place of religious worship. By contrast, many couples would like the opportunity to marry in a more meaningful alternative location, or to have a ceremony according to particular beliefs (such as humanism) that are not currently recognised for the purposes of solemnising a legal marriage. The Commission point to evidence which shows that couples may seek out organisations or individuals who are willing to conduct non-binding ceremonies in accordance with their wishes, which is usually either preceded or followed by a binding ceremony. The complexity of the law also leads to uncertainty, which can make it difficult to know whether a valid marriage has taken place or not. The Commission conclude that full-scale reform of this area of the law is necessary, 'a reformed law should, while taking account of the history of marriage, strike the right balance between freedom for couples to get married in a way and in a location that they want and that is meaningful to them, while protecting against the abuses involved in sham and forced marriages'.[61] At this stage, however, the Commission did not making specific reform proposals, instead its scoping study outlines the questions that would need to be examined, and the guiding principles to be followed in order to achieve a modern law of marriage.

### 2.3.1 'Non-marriages'

A failure to comply with the formalities required for contracting a valid marriage will usually mean that the marriage is void, but in some circumstances the court may hold that there was no marriage at all; in other words there was a 'non-marriage'.[62] The distinction between a void

---

[58] Ministry of Justice, Marriages by non-religious belief organisations: Summary of Written Responses to the Consultation and Government Response (2014).

[59] See http://www.lawcom.gov.uk/project/marriage-law/. The Law Commission will not, as part of this review, consider who can be married (thus there will be no consideration of changing the age of consent or the restrictions on marrying within prohibited degrees); neither will it consider whether or not religious groups should be obliged to solemnise same-sex marriages, or the rights and responsibilities flowing from marriage.

[60] Law Commission, 'Getting Married: A Scoping Paper', 17 December 2015.

[61] Law Commission, 'Getting Married: A Scoping Paper', Executive Summary, 17 December 2015, para 1.64.

[62] See R. Probert, 'When Are We Married? Void, Non-Existent and Presumed Marriages' [2000] 22 Legal Studies 398.

marriage and a 'non-marriage' is important because, if there is a 'non-marriage', then a party will not be entitled to a decree of nullity and will therefore be unable to apply for finance and property orders under Part II of the MCA 1973. A 'non-marriage' is one where the formation of the 'marriage' is so flawed that it cannot even be considered a void marriage; it is meaningless in the eyes of the law.

Whether there is a non-marriage depends on the facts of the case, including, for instance, whether the participants, in particular the celebrant, reasonably believed and intended the ceremony to be one which created a lawful marriage. In *Ghandi v Patel*,[63] for instance, a Hindu marriage ceremony conducted by a Brahmin priest in a London restaurant was held to be a 'non-marriage'.[64] The court came to the same conclusion in *Alfonso-Brown v Milwood*[65] as the parties had lacked the necessary intent at the time of the ceremony. Neither party had believed that the ceremony, which took place in Ghana, was anything other than an engagement ceremony. By contrast in *Gereis v Yagoub*[66] a couple went through a marriage ceremony at a Coptic Orthodox Church which was not licensed for marriage. The ceremony was conducted by a priest who was not licensed to conduct marriages, and who told the couple that they would also require a civil ceremony to effect a valid marriage. The court held that the ceremony bore all the hallmarks of an ordinary Christian marriage[67] and that the marriage had been treated as a subsisting marriage by all those who had attended. The court rejected the submission that there was no marriage at all, and granted a decree of nullity under section 11(a)(iii) of the MCA 1973, on the basis that the parties had knowingly and wilfully disregarded the formalities.[68]

These authorities were reviewed in *Hudson v Leigh*[69] by Bodey J who took the opportunity to outline the factors which should be considered when deciding whether a marriage was a void marriage or a non-marriage. In this case, Miss Hudson was religious and wanted a religious marriage, but Mr Leigh was an atheist. The couple therefore agreed to have a religious ceremony for Miss Hudson's benefit to be followed by a civil ceremony of marriage. The religious ceremony took place but Mr Leigh subsequently refused to go through with the civil ceremony and the question arose as to the status of the religious ceremony. That ceremony was conducted by a minister who was aware of the couple's intentions with respect to the two ceremonies. It was agreed that he would omit the usual words required by law to effect a lawful marriage. So the minister did not ask if the parties knew of any lawful impediments to the marriage, made no reference to them as 'lawful husband or wife', and did not declare that they were 'lawfully married'. Bodey J found on the facts that the ceremony was a non-marriage. Neither the parties at the time of the ceremony, nor the celebrant, intended or believed it to be legally binding. While Bodey J emphasised that the test for non-marriage is a flexible one, with questionable ceremonies being addressed on a case-by-case basis, he provided a non-exhaustive list of factors for consideration. First, whether the ceremony or event set out or purported to be a lawful marriage;[70] secondly, whether it bore all or enough of the hallmarks of marriage; thirdly, whether the three key participants (most especially the officiating official) believed, intended, and understood the ceremony as giving rise to the status of lawful marriage; and finally the reasonable perceptions, understandings, and beliefs of those in attendance.[71]

---

[63] [2002] 1 FLR 603. See also *A-M (Divorce: Jurisdiction: Validity of Marriage)* [2001] 2 FLR 6.

[64] The law's classifications are arguably unsatisfactory. A father/daughter marriage is void, yet the ceremony in *Ghandi v Patel* is merely a non-marriage. See R. Probert, 'When Are We Married? Void, Non-Existent and Presumed Marriages' [2000] 22 Legal Studies 398.

[65] [2006] EWHC 642 (Fam), [2006] 2 FLR 265.     [66] [1997] 1 FLR 854.

[67] See R. Probert, 'When Are We Married? Void, Non-Existent and Presumed Marriages' [2000] 22 Legal Studies 398 for criticism of this arguably unjustifiable emphasis on the Christian nature of the ceremony.

[68] See also *B v B* [2007] EWHC 2492 (Fam), [2008] 1 FLR 813.     [69] [2009] EWHC 1306 (Fam).

[70] Bodey J subsequently clarified in *El Gamal v Al Maktoum* [2011] EWHC 3763 that he was referring here to a lawful marriage under English law, at [81].

[71] For a discussion of this case, see R. Gaffney-Rhys, '*Hudson v Leigh*—The Concept of Non-Marriage' (2010) Child and Family Law Quarterly 351.

Bodey J had the opportunity to consider the issue again in *El Gamal v Al Maktoum*[72] where a private Muslim ceremony was conducted by an Imam in a flat. It was argued by the wife that the most important factor was whether the parties intended to create a valid marriage, and that if they did then this could convert a ceremony which was, in effect, a non-marriage into a void marriage. Bodey J gave this short shrift, dismissing the submission that the parties' belief or intent that a ceremony would be valid could convert something which would otherwise have been a non-marriage into a marriage, albeit a void one.[73] Clarifying the role of the parties' intention in deciding such matters, Bodey J said 'I have no doubt that intention is relevant to the status achieved or not achieved by a questionable ceremony, as being one of the many considerations which need to be taken into account. It is particularly relevant in the presumably unusual circumstances where the parties did not intend to create a valid marriage, or where they realised that for some reason they would not be able to do so. But the converse does not apply. It is not the law, in my judgment, where no or minimal steps are taken to comply with the Marriage Acts and so the marriage does not set out or purport to be a marriage under those Acts, that it nevertheless suffices if the participants hopefully intended, or believed, that the ceremony would create one.'[74]

It can be said with some certainty, therefore, that the intention of the parties, while a relevant consideration, cannot convert a ceremony which had little or no purported compliance with the legal formalities under the Marriage Acts into either a valid or a void marriage. In *Dukali v Lamrani*,[75] for example, the parties married in a civil ceremony at the Moroccan Consulate. While the ceremony fully complied with Moroccan law, it did not comply with the formalities required under English law even though both parties and the staff of the Moroccan Consulate believed that it did. Relying on *El Gamal v Maktoum*,[76] the court held that just because the parties believed in the validity of the marriage under English law did not mean that it was valid. Due to the wholesale failure to comply with the formalities, the ceremony could not be regarded as giving rise to a valid marriage.[77] Further, it was not a void marriage because it did not even purport to be a marriage under the Marriage Acts. The judge concluded therefore that this was a 'non-marriage'.

Whether the ceremony or event in question is held either to be a non-marriage, a valid marriage, or a void marriage depends not only on the extent to which the purported marriage bore any of the hallmarks of a valid marriage under English law, but also on the extent to which the parties were aware that the ceremony did not comply with the legal formalities. In *MA v JA*[78] the parties underwent a marriage ceremony, conducted by an authorised celebrant in a registered mosque. The parties believed that the ceremony would create a valid marriage under English law. While the celebrant was aware that the ceremony did not comply with the legal requirements, he did not inform the couple of this. Moylan J held that, while all the formalities were not complied with, the marriage was in its character 'of the kind' contemplated by the Marriage Acts. In other words, it bore the hallmarks of a valid marriage. It was conducted in an authorised building in the presence of an authorised person, and there was no lawful impediment to the marriage. The marriage was, therefore, valid as the parties did not 'knowingly and wilfully breach' the requirements of the Marriage Acts.[79]

In short, therefore, it seems that a non-marriage will be found where the ceremony or event bears no resemblance to the requirements of a valid marriage under English law, regardless of the

---

[72] [2011] EWHC 3763.     [73] [2011] EWHC 3763, [86].     [74] Ibid.     [75] [2012] EWHC 1748.

[76] [2011] EWHC 3763.

[77] The parties did not give notice, the Consulate was not registered as approved premises, and the celebrant was not an authorised person, ibid, [36].

[78] [2012] EWHC 2219 (Fam).

[79] For an in-depth discussion of these cases see R. Probert, 'The Evolving Concept of Non-marriage' (2013) Child and Family Law Quarterly 314.

intention of the parties. A valid marriage will be found where the ceremony meets some of the requirements of the Marriage Acts and the parties intended to create a valid marriage. A void marriage will be found where there was some compliance with the formalities (to distinguish it from a non-marriage) but the parties knowingly and wilfully disregarded the full extent of the formal requirements.

If the ceremony took place abroad, but the question of nullity has to be decided under English law, it is arguable that the court has more lee-way to rule that the ceremony created a void marriage as opposed to a non-marriage. This may be so if the formal validity of the marriage is to be determined with reference the law in another jurisdiction where there may be fewer legal requirements to effect a valid marriage, or where the foreign law has no separate concepts of a marriage being void or voidable or a non-marriage. In *Asaad v Kurter*,[80] for example, the court had to decide upon the nature of a ceremony which took place in a Syriac Orthodox Church in Syria. Following the ceremony, the couple moved to the UK and separated two years later. Although the wife, who was petitioning for a decree of nullity, argued that the celebrant, the parties, and the guests all understood and intended the ceremony to be a legal marriage and was able to produce a 'marriage certificate', the marriage had not been registered with the Syrian authorities, nor had permission for the marriage been obtained. The husband sought dismissal of the petition on the basis that there had never been a marriage as the ceremony was merely a 'blessing'. The wife sought a decree of nullity on the basis that, although the failure to comply with the formalities of Syrian law rendered the marriage not valid, it was still sufficient to entitle her to a decree of nullity. Moylan J agreed, holding that the ceremony created a void marriage under English law and that the petitioner was entitled to a decree of nullity. In reaching his decision, Moylan J ruled that the ceremony had been intended by both parties and all the relevant participants to be a marriage ceremony. The question then became the effect upon the ceremony, under Syrian law, of the failure to either register the ceremony or seek permission for it. Moylan J ruled that as no legal marriage was effected, there was no marriage under Syrian law. That, however, was not the end of the matter as he then had to consider whether the petitioner was entitled to any remedies under English law, specifically, whether she was entitled to a decree of nullity. In other words, did the ceremony create a non-marriage or a void marriage under English law? While under Syrian law no legal marriage had been effected, Syrian law had no separate concepts of a marriage being void or voidable or a non-marriage. This was particularly relevant because in the absence of these classifications under Syrian law, the principles of English law could determine the remedy.[81] Moylan J thus ruled that the ceremony was not 'so deficient' that it could be described in English law as a 'non-marriage'. It was a ceremony that had all the 'hallmarks' of a marriage capable of conferring the legal status of husband and wife had the parties complied with the necessary formalities. He concluded, therefore, that it was a marriage which was not valid as a result of a failure to comply with the required formalities and was thus, under English law, a void marriage. Accordingly, the petitioner was entitled to a decree of nullity. This has led one commentator to conclude that 'if an invalid marriage was conducted in a country where the venue and officiator need not have a specific marriage licence (or where the requirements for creating a valid marriage are very few), it would be easier for the English court to categorise, as it did here, that marriage as a void marriage rather than 'non-marriage' as there are less key formalities (from the English perspective) to fall foul of'.[82]

### 2.3.2 The presumptions of marriage

In some cases it may be necessary to rely on the common law presumptions of marriage in order to make a finding that there is a valid marriage.[83] There are two presumptions of marriage.

---

[80] [2013] EWHC 3852 (Fam).   [81] Ibid, at [87].

[82] L. Mottahedan, 'Asaad v Kurter: The latest round in 'non-marriage' cases – is the tide turning?' Family Law Week, http://www.familylawweek.co.uk/site.aspx?i=ed127612.

[83] See A. Borkowsi, 'The Presumption of Marriage' [2002] Child and Family Law Quarterly 251.

There is a presumption of marriage arising from cohabitation after a ceremony of marriage. In such cases, everything necessary for the validity of the marriage is presumed in the absence of decisive evidence to the contrary.[84] A second presumption arises merely from long cohabitation, where a couple have cohabited for such a length of time and in such circumstances as to acquire the reputation of being married, even though there is no positive evidence of a ceremony. This presumption can be rebutted only by strong and weighty evidence. In *Chief Adjudication Officer v Bath*[85] the respondent, Kirpal Bath had gone through a marriage ceremony with Mr Bath at a Sikh Temple in 1956 when she was 16. The couple believed the marriage ceremony to be legally valid and were ignorant of the requirements of the Marriage Acts. They had two children and lived together for 37 years until Mr Bath's death. Mr Bath had paid National Insurance contributions as a married man. On his death, however, Mrs Bath was refused a state widow's pension on the ground that there was not a valid marriage ceremony, since there was no evidence that the Sikh temple was registered at the material time. However, there was also no positive evidence that it was not registered. In those circumstances, the Court of Appeal held that the presumption of marriage from long cohabitation was not rebutted and Mrs Bath was entitled to her pension.[86] Evans and Schiemann LJJ also held that since Mr and Mrs Bath had not knowingly and wilfully married in disregard of the formalities contrary to section 49 of the Marriage Act 1949, there was no provision in the Marriage Act which rendered the marriage void.[87]

### 2.4  **A party must not already be married**

Under section 11(b) of the MCA 1973, a marriage is void if at the time of the marriage either party was already lawfully married. As Lord Penzance said in 1866 in *Hyde v Hyde*,[88] marriage is 'the voluntary union for life of one man and one woman to the exclusion of all others'. A person who enters into a subsequent marriage, without the previous marriage being terminated by annulment, divorce, or death, may commit the criminal offence of bigamy.[89] If a spouse has disappeared and is thought to be dead, the other spouse should therefore consider applying for a decree of presumption of death and dissolution of marriage which, if granted, prevents the second marriage being void or possibly bigamous even if the first spouse reappears.

## 3  Voidable marriages

A voidable marriage is a valid and subsisting marriage unless and until a decree of nullity is granted. Unlike a void marriage, a voidable marriage can only be annulled during the lifetime of both parties and only the parties to the marriage can petition for a decree. However, like a void marriage, on a

---

[84]  See *Asaad v Kurter* [2013] EWHC 3852 (Fam).     [85]  [2000] 1 FLR 8.

[86]  The parties, in this case, had lived together as man and wife for 37 years. By contrast, in *Dukali v Lamrani* [2012] EWHC 1748, the parties had only lived together for seven years. The court held that this was insufficient to give rise to the presumption of marriage based on the parties' long cohabitation. While Holman J did not specify what would constitute sufficient length, he said that 'a longer period then seven or eight years must be required', [33].

[87]  See also *Pazpena de Vire v Pazpena de Vire* [2001] 1 FLR 460 (marriage by proxy in Uruguay with neither party present at the ceremony was held to be valid by applying the presumption of long cohabitation, as the parties had lived in England for 35 years as husband and wife); and *A-M v A-M (Divorce: Jurisdiction: Validity of Marriage)* [2001] 2 FLR 6.

[88]  (1866) LR 1 P & D 130.

[89]  Offences Against the Person Act 1861, s 57. See C. Barton, 'Bigamy and Marriage—Horse and Carriage?' [2004] Family Law 517.

decree being granted the court has jurisdiction under Part II of the MCA 1973 to make finance and property orders equivalent to those which can be made on divorce.[90]

The grounds upon which a marriage may be declared voidable are laid down in section 12 of the MCA 1973, which provides that:

---

### Key legislation

A marriage celebrated after 31st July 1971 shall be voidable on the following grounds only, that is to say—

(a) that the marriage has not been consummated owing to the incapacity of either party to consummate it;

(b) that the marriage has not been consummated owing to the wilful refusal of the respondent to consummate it;

(c) that either party to the marriage did not validly consent to it, whether in consequence of duress, mistake, unsoundness of mind or otherwise;

(d) that at the time of the marriage either party, though capable of giving a valid consent, was suffering (whether continuously or intermittently) from mental disorder within the meaning of the Mental Health Act 1983 of such a kind or to such an extent as to be unfitted for marriage;

(e) that at the time of the marriage the respondent was suffering from venereal disease in a communicable form;

(f) that at the time of the marriage the respondent was pregnant by some person other than the petitioner;

(g) that an interim gender recognition certificate under the Gender Recognition Act 2004 has, after the time of the marriage, been issued to either party to the marriage;

(h) that the respondent is a person whose gender at the time of the marriage had become the acquired gender under the Gender Recognition Act 2004.[91]

---

Each of these grounds is now considered in turn.

## 3.1 Non-consummation

A marriage is voidable under section 12(a) of the MCA 1973 if there is non-consummation owing to the incapacity of either party to the marriage; or, under section 12(b), if non-consummation is due to wilful refusal on the part of the respondent. Sexual intercourse for the purposes of consummation must be 'ordinary and complete, and not partial and imperfect'.[92] Incapacity to consummate, unlike wilful refusal to consummate, can be brought by either party to the marriage and can therefore be based on either the petitioner's or respondent's incapacity. The incapacity must be permanent and incurable. It is unclear whether a transsexual person can

---

[90] See Chapter 4.    [91] Sections 12(g) and 12(h) were inserted by the Gender Recognition Act 2004.

[92] *DE v AG* (1985) 1 Rob Eccl 279, *per* Dr Lushington. This should be contrasted with the law of rape, and adultery, where sexual intercourse occurs where the penis makes the slightest penetration of the vagina. Case law has established that a marriage is consummated where there is *coitus interruptus* (where the husband withdraws before ejaculation (*White v White* [1948] 2 All ER 151 and *Cackett v Cackett* [1950] 1 All ER 677)); or where the husband is not capable of ejaculation (*R v R (Otherwise F)* [1952] 1 All ER 1194). The use of contraceptives does not prevent consummation occurring (*Baxter v Baxter* [1947] 2 All ER 886); and it is the fact of intercourse which is the sole issue, not whether it is qualitatively satisfactory (*S v S (Otherwise W) (No 2)* [1962] 3 All ER 55).

consummate a marriage. In *Corbett v Corbett*[93] Ormrod J stated *obiter* that a male-to-female transsexual person with an artificially constructed vagina was incapable of consummating. However, the courts may not take the same view now that the Gender Recognition Act 2004 permits transsexual marriage. In *W v W (Physical Inter-Sex)*[94] Charles J distinguished *Corbett* in holding that an intersexual person who had had surgery was not necessarily incapable of consummating.

It has been held that incapacity to consummate can include not just physical incapacity, but also 'an invincible repugnance to the respondent due to a psychiatric or sexual aversion'.[95] With wilful refusal to consummate, 'a settled and definite decision not to consummate without just excuse' must be established.[96]

Incapacity to consummate and wilful refusal to consummate are closely linked even though the two grounds are conceptually quite different. A petitioner who wishes to plead that the marriage has not been consummated may be unsure which of the two grounds is the relevant one, and may decide to plead them in the alternative. The question of whether a marriage had not been consummated due to incapacity or wilful refusal sometimes arose in the earlier case law on forced marriage.[97] In some religions, it is the practice to have a civil ceremony of marriage followed by a religious ceremony. Only after the religious ceremony are the parties deemed to be married in the eyes of their religion whereupon consummation can take place. In some of these cases there was held to be wilful refusal to consummate if a party refused to go through with the religious ceremony,[98] refused to make arrangements for the religious ceremony when it was his duty to do so,[99] or postponed the religious ceremony indefinitely.[100] Such behaviour has been held to be wilful refusal because the defaulting party knew that, by failing to satisfy the religious requirements, he or she was in effect refusing to have sexual intercourse.[101] However, a woman who has been forced into marriage and who refuses to consummate the marriage cannot petition on the basis of her own wilful refusal to consummate, but must instead prove incapacity to consummate, which can include not just a physical incapacity but 'an invincible repugnance to the respondent due to a psychiatric or sexual aversion'.[102]

## 3.2  Lack of consent to the marriage

Consent is regarded as an essential component of marriage. As Lord Penzance said in *Hyde v Hyde*[103] marriage involves a '*voluntary* union' between a man and a woman. Under section 12(c) of the MCA 1973 a marriage is voidable if 'either party to the marriage did not validly consent to it, whether in consequence of duress, mistake, unsoundness of mind or otherwise'. Most of the reported case law has concerned duress, mistake, and lack of capacity to marry.

---

[93]  [1971] P 83.        [94]  [2001] Fam 111, FD, *per* Charles J.

[95]  See *Singh v Singh* [1971] 2 WLR 963 (see further at n 83), where the Court of Appeal held that the evidence was not sufficient to prove an invincible repugnance.

[96]  *Horton v Horton* [1947] 2 All ER 871, *per* Lord Jowitt LC.        [97]  See further at p 25 (Section 5).

[98]  *Jodla v Jodla* [1960] 1 WLR 236.        [99]  *Kaur v Singh* [1972] 1 WLR 105.

[100]  *A v J (Nullity Proceedings)* [1989] 1 FLR 110.

[101]  In *Kaur v Singh* [1992] 1 WLR 105 the husband's refusal to arrange the Sikh wedding ceremony after the civil ceremony was held to constitute wilful refusal to consummate the marriage and his wife was successful in obtaining a nullity decree.

[102]  In *Singh v Singh* [1971] 2 WLR 963 the wife petitioned on the ground of her husband's incapacity to consummate due to her invincible repugnance to him (she had never met him until the civil ceremony and went back to live with her parents and refused to take part in a Sikh religious ceremony). Her petition was dismissed, as her refusal to go through with the religious ceremony was held to be a very long way away from having an invincible repugnance to sexual intercourse. See *D v D* (1982) 12 Fam Law 150.

[103]  (1886) LR 1 P & D 130 at 133.

### 3.2.1 Duress

With regard to duress, the question is what degree of duress suffices to vitiate consent. At one time, the test for establishing duress was much more stringent. In *Szechter v Szechter*[104] Simon P said that the test was whether the will of one of the parties had been 'overborne by a genuine and reasonably held fear caused by threat of immediate danger (for which the party is not himself responsible), to life, limb or liberty'.[105] This test was approved and adopted by the Court of Appeal in *Singh v Singh*[106] in refusing the claim of a 17-year-old Sikh woman that she had been forced by her parents into an arranged marriage to a man whom she had never met and who was neither handsome nor intelligent as she had been told. The *Szechter* test made it particularly difficult for victims of forced marriages to obtain a decree on this ground.[107] However, in *Hirani v Hirani*[108] a different and less stringent test for establishing duress was adopted.

---

**Key case**

In *Hirani v Hirani* the petitioner, a woman aged 19, formed an association with an Indian Muslim. Her parents, who were Hindus, were horrified at this relationship and quickly arranged for her to marry a Hindu man, Mr Hirani, whom she had never met. Reluctantly, and crying throughout, she went through a ceremony of marriage with Mr Hirani. After the marriage, the wife petitioned for nullity on the ground of lack of consent owing to duress. She claimed that she was wholly dependent on her parents and that they had threatened to throw her out of the house if she did not go through with the marriage. The Court of Appeal held that a threat to life, limb, or liberty, as required in *Szechter*, was no longer required. Instead, the crucial question was whether the threats, pressure, or other acts were sufficient 'to destroy the reality of consent and overbear the will of the individual'.[109] This test is a subjective test, considering whether the particular petitioner's will has been overborne, not whether a reasonable person would find there to be lack of consent due to duress. As the Court of Appeal found that the petitioner's will had been clearly overborne by parental pressure, it held that she had not consented to the marriage and was therefore entitled to have the marriage annulled.

---

In *NS v MI*[110] Munby J drew attention to the different approaches in the cases and preferred the *Hirani* approach, declaring that the *Szechter* approach no longer represents the law, if it ever did. The preferred approach in practice is certainly the subjective approach in *Hirani*.[111] However, the conflict as a matter of doctrine at Court of Appeal level[112] has not been resolved, since the Court of Appeal decision in *Singh v Singh* (which adopted the objective test) was not cited in *Hirani*. In *NS v MI* the petitioner had been taken to Pakistan by her parents when she was 16, supposedly for a two-month holiday. She was stranded in a remote region of Pakistan for over a year, because her mother held her passport, and eventually it emerged that arrangements had been made for her to marry a cousin there. She went through the ceremony under great family pressure to go ahead with the marriage. Upon her return to England, she sought a decree of nullity

---

[104] [1970] 3 All ER 905. See also *Buckland v Buckland* [1968] P 296.     [105] [1970] 3 All ER 905, 915.

[106] [1971] 2 All ER 828.

[107] In *Singh v Kaur* (1981) 11 Fam Law 152 a young man petitioned for a decree on the basis that the pressure put upon him by his parents was so great that his consent had no validity. The Court of Appeal dismissed his case holding that it did not wish to see the *Szechter* test watered down.

[108] (1983) 4 FLR 232.     [109] Ibid, *per* Ormrod LJ at 234.     [110] [2007] 1 FLR 444.

[111] See eg *P v R (Forced Marriage: Annulment: Procedure)* [2003] 1 FLR 661, *per* Coleridge J.

[112] See A. Bradney, 'Duress, Family Law and Coherent Legal System' [1994] Modern Law Review 963.

on the ground of lack of consent. Applying a subjective approach, Munby J granting the decree, commenting:

> where the influence is that of a parent or other close and dominating relative, and where the arguments and persuasion are based upon personal affection or duty, religious beliefs, powerful social or cultural conventions, or asserted social, familial or domestic obligations, the influence may . . . be subtle, insidious, pervasive and powerful. In such cases, moreover, very little pressure may suffice to bring about the desired result.[113]

The 'overborne will' test for duress has made it easier for victims of forced marriage to succeed in obtaining a decree of nullity based on lack of consent. Forced marriages are condemned by the courts and by the Government, and various provisions in addition to nullity exist to protect victims.[114]

### 3.2.2 Mistake

Consent to marriage may be vitiated where there is mistake, and this may entitle either party to the marriage to a decree of nullity. Mistake can relate either to the identity of the other person or to the nature of the ceremony. However, with respect to identity, a mistake as to a party's attributes or characteristics does not constitute a mistake and will not invalidate a marriage. Mistake as to the nature of the ceremony could include, for example, a situation where a party mistakenly believes that he or she is taking part in an engagement ceremony, not a marriage ceremony.[115]

## 3.3 Mental disorder rendering a person unfitted for marriage

Under section 12(d) of the MCA 1973 a marriage is voidable on the ground that 'either party, though capable of giving a valid consent, was suffering (whether continuously or intermittently) from mental disorder within the meaning of the Mental Health Act 1983 of such a kind or to such an extent as to be unfitted for marriage'. This ground differs from unsoundness of mind for the purposes of consent discussed earlier, in that a party is capable of giving a valid consent, but the state of his or her mental health is such that it would be appropriate to annul the marriage. A petitioner may rely on his or her own mental disorder for the purpose of petitioning for a decree of nullity on this ground.

## 3.4 Venereal disease

Under section 12(e) a marriage is voidable where the respondent was suffering from venereal disease in a communicable form at the time of the marriage. The basis of this ground clearly ties in with the non-consummation grounds, as it is looked upon as an impediment to sexual intercourse.

## 3.5 Pregnancy by another man

Section 12(f) provides a husband with a ground for nullity if he can prove that at the time of the marriage his wife was pregnant by some person other than himself. Thus, if, at the time of the marriage, the wife conceals from her husband the fact that she is pregnant by another man, he can subsequently seek an annulment. The petition must be presented within three years of the marriage,[116]

---

[113] [2007] 1 FLR 444 at [34].    [114] See Section 5.
[115] See eg *Mehta v Mehta* [1945] 2 All ER 690 where the wife mistakenly thought that the marriage ceremony was one of conversion to the Hindu religion, and who was granted a decree of nullity on this basis.
[116] MCA 1973, s 13(2).

so that if a wife keeps the child's true paternity secret for more than three years, the marriage cannot be annulled on this ground.

## 3.6 Gender recognition as a ground for nullity

Two new grounds for establishing a voidable marriage were introduced into section 12 of the MCA 1973 by the Gender Recognition Act 2004, which was passed to give transsexual persons new rights, including the right to enter into a valid marriage in their acquired gender on the issue of a full gender recognition certificate granted by a Gender Recognition Panel.[117] If a person who applies to a Gender Recognition Panel meets the statutory criteria and is unmarried, the Panel will issue a full gender recognition certificate, which will entitle this person to a new birth certificate reflecting their acquired gender, thus allowing marriage in this new gender. However, if a married applicant applies to the Gender Recognition Panel for recognition of his or her 'acquired' gender, the Panel, on the satisfaction of the criteria, will only issue an interim gender recognition certificate (due to the existing marriage). This becomes a ground for annulment of the existing marriage as under section 12(g) of the MCA 1973 a marriage is voidable if an interim gender recognition certificate has, after the time of the marriage, been issued to either party to the marriage.[118] Under section 12(h) a marriage is voidable if the respondent is a person whose gender at the time of the marriage had become the acquired gender under the Gender Recognition Act 2004. In other words, a marriage is voidable if at the time of the marriage one party to the marriage did not know that the other was previously of another gender and had obtained a gender recognition certificate.

## 3.7 Bars to relief

There are certain statutory prohibitions (bars) to relief in respect of voidable marriages. Thus, under section 13 of the MCA 1973, there are time limits for certain nullity petitions, and for all petitions there is a general bar based on the approbation of the petitioner.

A nullity petition must be instituted within three years of the date of the marriage unless the petitioner is relying on incapacity or wilful refusal to consummate the marriage.[119] Where the ground relied on is venereal disease or pregnancy by another man, the petitioner must be ignorant of those facts at the date of the marriage.[120] Where a decree is sought on the basis of the issue of an interim gender recognition certificate,[121] the proceedings must be instituted within six months of the interim gender recognition certificate being issued.[122]

A general bar based on approbation by the petitioner applies to all nullity petitions brought on the basis that a marriage is voidable.[123] Thus, the court must not grant a decree if the respondent proves that the petitioner knew that it was open to him or her to have the marriage annulled but led the respondent reasonably to believe that he would not seek to do so; *and* that it would be unjust to the respondent to grant the decree. It will be very difficult to satisfy this test, as the facts of *D v D (Nullity: Statutory Bar)*[124] illustrate. The wife had a physical impediment, preventing consummation. It could have been cured by a comparatively common operation but the wife refused and the marriage was never consummated. Although the husband knew he could have the marriage annulled,

---

[117] See Section 7.1.

[118] Where a person obtains a decree absolute of nullity on this ground, the court must issue that person with a full gender recognition certificate. This has been amended by the Marriage (Same Sex Couples) Act 2013 to allow transsexual people to change their gender without having to legally end their existing marriage, see Section 7.2 which explains the situation more fully.

[119] See s 13(2). This is subject to the proviso that the period may be extended where the petitioner has suffered from a mental disorder during the three years, and it is just to do so (s 13(4)). For a case involving the non-availability of a nullity petition after three years (on the ground of lack of consent), see *SH v NB* [2009] EWHC 3274 (Fam).

[120] Section 13(3).    [121] Under s 12(g).    [122] Section 13(2A).    [123] Section 13(1).

[124] [1979] Fam 70.

the couple fostered, then adopted, two children at the request of the Church of England Children's Society. The husband subsequently sought a decree of nullity. Dunn J found that the first limb of section 13(1) was fulfilled but it could not be shown that there would be any injustice to the wife. She would have access to the same orders for financial provision as on divorce.

### 3.8 **Should the concept of the voidable marriage be abolished?**

There are arguments in favour of abolishing the concept of the voidable marriage, something which has been done in Australia.[125] One argument is that there are so few nullity petitions today that it would cause no great hardship if the voidable grounds were abolished. In 2009, only 290 nullity petitions were filed in the courts in England and Wales, with 199 decrees absolute of nullity being granted, whereas 116,576 decrees absolute of divorce were granted in that year.[126] The reasons why there are so few nullity petitions is partly because the facts upon which a nullity petition can be based do not often arise, and partly because of the ease with which it is now possible to obtain a divorce. Also, divorce no longer carries the stigma that it once did.[127]

Another argument is that some of the grounds seem rather archaic and with little or no relevance today. Thus, for instance, should non-consummation be abolished as a ground for nullity on the basis that it is an archaic relic of medieval ecclesiastical law? In the view of the Church, marriage is important for begetting children, and hence there is a need to consummate the marriage. However, some couples may choose to marry for companionship and may not consider consummation to be particularly important, whether or not they are capable of it. Probert[128] has argued that it might be better if non-consummation were abolished in order to 'define marriage in a way that is relevant for the twenty-first century'[129] since it is arguably too intrusive and embarrassing for the law to examine parties' sexual lives in this way. Furthermore, doing away with the grounds based on non-consummation would remove the possibility that transsexual marriages are always voidable for lack of capacity. If non-consummation were abolished as a ground for nullity, a person who wished to terminate the marriage could still do so by petitioning for a divorce on the ground of unreasonable behaviour[130] due to the respondent's failure to consummate the marriage. The only disadvantage of this would be that a petitioner would have to wait for one year after the marriage to do so as there is a statutory prohibition on divorce in the first year of marriage. A decree of judicial separation, on the other hand, is available at any time after the marriage.

Some of the other grounds for rendering a marriage voidable are also open to criticism, and might justifiably be abolished. Thus mental disorder as a ground for nullity under section 12(d) seems somewhat outmoded and offensive, as it stems from the days when mental illness was misunderstood and those suffering from such illness were regarded with fear and suspicion. It is also difficult to understand why mental illness should be singled out as a ground for nullity when an adult who is prone to violence or paedophilia, for example, may also be equally unfit for marriage. The venereal disease ground in section 12(e) is also out of touch with developments in medical science and is also somewhat limited. It is difficult to know what to make of this ground today as, when it was first introduced in 1937, antibiotics were not available. Medical practitioners today no longer talk about 'venereal diseases' but about 'sexually transmitted diseases'.

The pregnancy by another man ground for nullity under section 12(f) is also questionable. The Law Commission's original explanation for this ground was that a husband who marries in these

---

[125] By the Family Law Act 1975, s 51.

[126] *Judicial and Court Statistics 2009* (Ministry of Justice, 2010), Ch 2, Table 2.5.

[127] The Law Commission's claim in its 1970 *Report on Nullity of Marriage* (Law Com No 33), about the stigma associated with divorce, but not with nullity, is no longer true today.

[128] R. Probert, 'How Would *Corbett v Corbett* Be Decided Today?' [2004] Family Law 382.

[129] It should also be noted that consummation has no relevance to the annulment of a civil partnership.

[130] Under the MCA 1973, s 1(2)(b), see Chapter 2.

circumstances has given conditional consent only to the marriage. The ground therefore appears to rest on one of two bases. Either the husband has married a woman knowing her to be pregnant and believing that he is the father of the child, in which case he might then argue that, but for the pregnancy, he would not have married her. Alternatively, he might argue that he was marrying a woman who was chaste, but the lack of chastity has self-evidently been demonstrated. Whichever of these two bases applies, it is suggested that such thinking has no place in the law today. In 1937, when the ground was first introduced, men might well be forced to marry if they were believed to be responsible for the pregnancy of a woman. This would not normally be the case nowadays; but if it was, the ground of duress might apply. The chastity basis is not relevant or sensible in today's society. There are other forms of behaviour by a spouse which could just as easily be said to strike at the fundamental root of a marriage, in the sense that a spouse is giving conditional consent to the marriage. For example, the woman who marries a man not knowing that he is a convicted rapist, or paedophile, could claim her consent to the marriage should be characterised as conditional. However, her escape route is to use the law of divorce. It is suggested that, similarly, divorce is a more appropriate response in the case of pregnancy by another man.

Nevertheless, the fact that the woman is pregnant by another man undoubtedly strikes at the heart of the marriage. A man is unquestionably entitled to say that he certainly would not have married his wife had he known she was carrying another man's child. But is a woman not equally entitled to state that she would not have married her husband if, at the time of the marriage, she had known that another woman was pregnant by him? It is suggested that the law should treat spouses in an equal manner in this regard.

If voidable marriages were abolished, the parties to a marriage would instead have to seek a divorce. The question which therefore arises is whether divorce can provide an adequate alternative to nullity in the case of voidable marriages. In its 1970 *Report on Nullity of Marriage*[131] the Law Commission referred to the stigma associated with divorce. Today, however, there is little stigma attached to divorce, and it could be argued that greater stigma may attach to the grounds for nullity. Thus, there may be a stigma attached to a finding that a person has wilfully refused to consummate the marriage or a woman has deceived a man into marrying by concealing the true paternity of the baby. For these reasons, the Law Commission's arguments about stigma are no longer so valid. As regards the Law Commission's comments in its Report about the Christian Church's distinction between nullity and divorce, it can be argued that this distinction is no longer so valid now that society is more secular and multicultural. It could be argued that it is inappropriate for the Christian Church to have such a large influence on the law relating to marriage when only a minority of the population attend organised Christian worship and when many people today are either of a religious persuasion which is not Christian, or have no religion at all.

The Law Commission's argument in its *Report on Nullity of Marriage* in favour of retaining the concept of voidable marriage—because there was no advantage to be achieved in abolishing it—is perhaps the strongest argument for retaining the concept. Thus, if the concept of voidable marriage is useful for a few parties to a marriage, then why do away with it? Although the number of nullity decrees compared with decrees of divorce is small, they do show that nullity is still useful for some people. One of the main advantages of nullity is that a petition can be brought straightaway after a marriage whereas with divorce there is an absolute bar on bringing a petition in the first year of marriage. Also, there may be a small number of persons who choose to have their marriage annulled for religious reasons, perhaps because they may wish to marry in the future and be able to marry in a church or other religious building. Some religions will not allow a divorced person to marry in church, but other religions are now less strict about this. Thus, while the Church of England teaches that marriage is for life, it recognises that marriages do break down and since 2002 has permitted divorced persons to marry

---

[131] Law Com No 33.

in church provided the local parish priest agrees to this. Other churches are more lenient about remarriage after divorce, but the Catholic Church's view on this matter is much stronger and it does not tolerate divorce. Another important reason in favour of retaining the concept of a voidable marriage is that it allows victims of forced marriages to have their marriage annulled, for instance on the ground that there was no consent as a result of duress. However, if consent is regarded as a fundamental flaw existing at the inception of a marriage, which the formalities for marriage show it to be, then lack of consent should be a ground for rendering a marriage *void*, not voidable. This would give victims of forced marriages the option of nullity, instead of having to rely on divorce. It would also send out a strong message that consent is a requirement going to the root of a marriage in England and Wales and that lack of consent will not be tolerated.

## 4  Sham marriages/civil partnerships

A 'sham' marriage or 'sham' civil partnership, or what is sometimes called a 'marriage or civil partnership of convenience', is a marriage or civil partnership which is entered into for an ulterior motive, such as to gain British citizenship and/or to enter the UK. The Home Office has described sham marriages and sham civil partnerships as posing 'a significant threat to UK immigration control',[132] and thus the immigration authorities are keen to ensure that these sorts of marriages do not take place as they allow the parties to circumvent the immigration rules. For this reason, the immigration rules attempt to prevent such marriages taking place. However, although this is a legitimate role for immigration law, it was held by the House of Lords in *R (Baiai and Others) v Secretary of State for the Home Department*[133] that the powers of the immigration authorities must not interfere with the right to marry in Article 12 of the ECHR. Thus, the immigration authorities must exercise their powers in a proportionate and non-discriminatory way.

The Home Affairs Select Committee has recently said that it is not convinced that the Home Office has a true understanding of the scale of the problem relating to sham marriages.[134] It observed that the organisation of sham marriages is an industry, which is increasing at an alarming rate, noting that such a marriage does not just provide UK residence rights to one person but to a range of family members. As such, the Committee made recommendations to strengthen the controls on such marriages taking place. Currently, if a registrar has reasonable grounds for suspecting that a marriage of which notice has been given[135] will be a sham marriage, they have a duty under the Immigration and Asylum Act 1999[136] to report their suspicions to the Home Office without delay. The Committee recommends that the law be changed so that if the Home Office enforcement team do not act upon the section 24 report, and the registrar is confident the wedding is a sham, then the registrar should have the power to not proceed with the wedding. Further recommendations include the provision of additional training to registrars on how to identify potential shams, and the publication by the Home Office of the number of people removed from the UK in order to deter people from involvement in these activities.

---

[132] The Home Office, Sham Marriages and Civil Partnerships, November 2013.

[133] [2008] UKHL 53, [2008] 2 FLR 1462.

[134] Home Affairs Committee—Third Report: The work of the Immigrations Directorates (October – December 2013), http://www.publications.parliament.uk/pa/cm201415/cmselect/cmhaff/237/23702.htm.

[135] Under the provisions of the Immigration Act 2014, this notice period has been extended from 15 days to 28 days.

[136] Section 24.

# 5 Forced marriages

A forced marriage is a marriage which is entered into without the true consent of one or both of the parties and where some degree of duress is involved, which may include, for example, physical, psychological, financial, sexual, and emotional pressure, and even violence. A forced marriage is different from an 'arranged marriage', which is one where the families of both parties take a leading role in choosing a marriage partner but where consent to the arrangement remains with the parties themselves. The courts are not opposed to arranged marriages but are strongly opposed to forced marriages. In *NS v MI*[137] Munby J said that while forced marriages were utterly unacceptable, arranged marriages were to be respected and supported. Forced marriages are common in some religious and ethnic groups and are sometimes used for immigration purposes, such as to enable a foreign relative to gain entry into the UK. Forced marriage victims can suffer traumatic and distressing experiences, which may include physical and emotional threats, violence, blackmail, abduction, and imprisonment in the home.

In recent years there has been increasing recognition of the problem of forced marriages and the need to prevent them happening and to protect victims. A special unit, the Forced Marriage Unit (FMU) based in the Foreign & Commonwealth Office,[138] was established in 2005 as a joint initiative with the Home Office. It is responsible for developing Government policy on forced marriages and for providing support, information, and advice for actual and potential victims and for practitioners working in the field. Most cases of forced marriage in the UK involve South Asian families, particularly families of Pakistani and Bangladeshi origin, which is partly due to the fact that there is a large South Asian population in the UK.[139] Some cases occur within the UK and have no overseas element, but others involve a party coming from overseas or a British citizen being sent abroad. Most cases involve young women, but some cases involve the coercion of men. Many cases go unreported.

Forced marriages are not tolerated in England and Wales, being regarded by the Government and the courts as a gross abuse of human rights and as a form of domestic violence. In *NS v MI*[140] where a nullity decree was granted to the petitioner who had entered into a forced marriage, Munby J said that 'the court must not hesitate to use every weapon in its protective arsenal if faced with what is, or appears to be, a case of forced marriage.' In *Re K; A Local Authority v N and Others*[141] Munby J described forced marriage as an 'appalling practice' and 'a gross abuse of human rights'. He said it was 'a form of domestic violence that dehumanises people by denying them their right to choose how to live their lives'. In addition to remedies for victims under the general law,[142] the Government has taken steps to give greater protection to victims. Family law provides actual and potential victims of forced marriage with the following remedies: annulment of the marriage; protection under the High Court's inherent and wardship jurisdictions; and forced marriage

---

[137] [2006] EWHC 1646 (Fam), [2007] 1 FLR 444.

[138] See the Foreign & Commonwealth Office website: https://www.gov.uk/guidance/forced-marriage#forced-marriage-unit https. The Unit, together with relevant government departments and agencies, has published practice guidelines for police officers, health professionals, social workers, and education professionals on how to deal with forced marriage cases.

[139] Figures published by the Forced Marriage Unit (FMU) in 2016 (see its website, www.gov.uk/forced-marriage) show that the unit gave advice and support to 1,220 cases in 2015, 80 per cent of which involved females and 20 per cent males. The majority of reportings to the FMU involved families of Pakistani (44 per cent) and Bangladeshi (7 per cent) origin, with smaller percentages of those of Indian, Middle Eastern, European, and African origin. Where the age was known, 14 per cent involved victims below 16 years, 13 per cent involved victims aged 16–17, 20 per cent involved victims aged 18–21, 15 per cent involved victims aged 22–25, 9 per cent involved victims aged 26–30, and 8 per cent involved victims over the age of 31.

[140] [2006] EWHC 1646 (Fam), [2007] 1 FLR 444.   [141] [2005] EWHC 2956 (Fam), [2007] 1 FLR 399.

[142] With regard to the criminal law, there are various criminal offences which can be committed by those perpetrating a forced marriage (such as assault, abduction, kidnapping, and false imprisonment). In addition to the criminal law there are remedies which can be sought under the civil law. Forcing a person to marry can constitute a tort of trespass to the person, false imprisonment, or harassment under the Protection from Harassment Act 1997, and may give the victim a right to obtain damages by way of compensation and/or protection by way of injunctive relief.

protection orders under the Forced Marriage (Civil Protection) Act 2007. A multi-agency approach is taken in forced marriage cases involving a wide range of agencies, such as social workers, the police, and health authorities. If a victim is under 18, the Children Act 1989 will be relevant, as forcing someone to marry may constitute significant harm for the purposes of that Act.[143]

## 5.1 Annulment

A person who enters into a forced marriage can have the marriage annulled on the ground that the marriage is voidable under section 12 of the MCA 1973. In most cases, victims will petition on the ground of lack of consent to the marriage as a result of duress caused by parental and/or family pressure.[144] Thus, for example, in *P v R (Forced Marriage: Annulment)*[145] a 20-year-old woman who had been forced to enter into a marriage in Pakistan successfully petitioned for a decree of nullity on the ground of lack of consent as a consequence of duress. Her brother had threatened her with violence and she believed that if she failed to go ahead with the marriage she would be unable to return to England. She was told by her parents that she would bring shame and disgrace on the family if she did not go ahead with the marriage. During the ceremony in Pakistan, she was forced to nod in agreement to the marriage by her mother pushing her head forward three times, and she signed the marriage certificate out of fear. When she returned to the UK, she successfully petitioned for a decree of nullity. Coleridge J found that she had not validly consented to the marriage as her consent had been vitiated by physical and emotional force.

Although a petitioner for a decree of nullity will have to give oral evidence in open court, the court will do whatever it can to protect the petitioner (eg where the petitioner is reluctant to give evidence because of the presence of family members).[146]

## 5.2 Inherent jurisdiction or wardship

The inherent jurisdiction of the High Court can be invoked to protect a person who is being forced into marriage, or the High Court's wardship jurisdiction if the victim is under 18. Because of the flexible and parental nature of these jurisdictions, they can be invoked, in exceptional circumstances, even though the victim is not present or living in the UK but is living overseas, for instance in Pakistan[147] or Bangladesh.[148] These 'parental' jurisdictions of the High Court can also be invoked where there is merely a risk that someone will be forced into a marriage, and where a person needs protection even though they may have capacity.[149] Forced marriage protection orders

---

[143] Where there is significant harm, or a risk of significant harm, a local authority has a duty to make enquiries (under s 47) to decide whether to take action to safeguard or promote the welfare of a child; and where there is an actual or potential risk of significant harm, a local authority can bring care proceedings (under s 31) to protect a child or young person who is being forced into marriage. See Chapter 10.

[144] See MCA 1973, s 12(c). In some of the older reported cases, non-consummation was sometimes used as a ground.

[145] [2003] 1 FLR 661. See also *Re S (Practice: Muslim Women Giving Evidence)* [2007] 2 FLR 461 where a young Muslim woman was granted a decree of nullity because she had entered into a forced marriage after a two-year campaign of family pressure.

[146] *Per* Munby J in *NS v MI* [2006] EWHC 1646 (Fam), [2007] 1 FLR 444.

[147] See *Re B; RB v FB* [2008] EWHC 1436 (Fam), [2008] 2 FLR 1624, where a girl (aged 15) who was a British national living in Pakistan was made a ward of court as it considered her to be a British national who was in desperate need of help, even though her only connection with the UK was that her late father was British.

[148] See *SB v RB* [2008] EWHC 938 (Fam), [2008] 2 FLR 1588 where a girl (aged 11) was made a ward of court because she had been forced to marry a 20-year-old man in Bangladesh. She was subsequently returned to the UK with the assistance of the FMU in London, and the marriage was subsequently annulled.

[149] See *Re SA (Vulnerable Adult With Capacity: Marriage)* [2005] EWHC 2942 (Fam), [2006] 1 FLR 867 where the inherent jurisdiction of the High Court was successfully invoked by the local authority as it feared that the girl (aged 17, who was profoundly deaf, unable to speak, and had an intellect of a 13- or 14-year-old) might be taken by her family to Pakistan for the purposes of an arranged marriage.

(see Section 5.3) now provide protection for such persons but, where there is an overseas element, the High Court's inherent and wardship jurisdictions may be more appropriate because of their more flexible jurisdictional rules. This may include, for instance, the High Court under its inherent jurisdiction making a declaration that a forced marriage entered into overseas is not capable of being recognised as a valid marriage in England and Wales. The inherent jurisdiction may also prove useful in a case where a victim of a forced marriage is unable to petition for a decree of nullity on the ground of lack of consent because of being statute barred under section 13(2) of the MCA 1973.[150]

## 5.3 **Forced marriage protection orders**

Under Part 4A of the Family Law Act 1996, the Family Division of the High Court and county courts have jurisdiction to make a forced marriage protection order, which is an order providing legal protection for an actual or potential victim of a forced marriage or an attempted forced marriage.[151] These provisions were introduced by the Forced Marriage (Civil Protection) Act 2007.[152] The remedies are modelled on those available under Part 4 of the Family Law Act 1996 to protect victims of domestic violence.[153] A multi-agency approach is adopted for dealing with forced marriages, and Government guidance sets out the responsibilities of the various agencies involved in protecting victims.[154] Part 2 of the guidance is issued as statutory guidance under section 63Q(1) of Part 4A of the Family Law Act 1996, and must be taken into account by those exercising a public function.[155]

'Forced marriage' is defined in the Act as a marriage where a person has not given full and free consent;[156] and 'force' is defined to include not just physical coercion but coercion by threats or other psychological means.[157] The court has wide powers to include in the order such prohibitions, restrictions, or requirements, or other such terms as are considered appropriate, and the terms of the order can relate to conduct outside and/or within England and Wales.[158] Thus, for example, an order could be made to prohibit a potential victim being taken outside the UK for the purpose of marrying overseas (which could include handing over a passport), or to prevent a family member from molesting or contacting a victim who has escaped from her family and taken refuge elsewhere. An order can be made for a specified period or until varied or discharged.[159]

An application for an order can be made by: a victim, a person on the victim's behalf with permission of the court, or a relevant third party. Local authorities have been specified as relevant third parties. As with certain other family proceedings, the court has the power to make an order of its own motion (in other words, where no application has been made for an order but it is appropriate to make one).[160]

---

[150] See *B v I* [2010] 1 FLR 1721 where an English woman of Bangladeshi origin who had been forced into a marriage in Bangladesh but who was unable to petition for nullity, as the 'marriage' had taken place in 2005, was granted a declaration under the court's inherent jurisdiction that the ceremony in Bangladesh had not given rise to a marriage capable of recognition in England and Wales.

[151] Section 63A(1). Between November 2008 (when the 2007 Act came into force) and June 2011, 339 orders were recorded, see Home Office, Forced Marriage Consultation (December 2011), p 6, www.gov.uk/government/uploads/system/uploads/attachment_data/file/157827/forced-marriage-consultation.pdf.

[152] See G. Vallance-Webb, 'Forced Marriage: A Yielding of the Lips Not the Mind' [2008] Family Law 565.

[153] See Chapter 3.

[154] *The Right to Choose: Multi-Agency Statutory Guidance for Dealing with Forced Marriage* (available at www.fco.gov.uk).

[155] Eg persons performing a child protection function, teachers, police, local authorities, police authorities, youth offending teams, Cafcass, Local Safeguarding Children Board, and NHS Trusts.

[156] Section 63A(4).

[157] Section 63A(6). There does not have to be violence or a threat of violence, see *A v SM and HB (Forced Marriage Protection Orders)* [2012] EWHC 435 (Fam).

[158] Section 63B(1) and (2).     [159] Sections 63F and 63G.     [160] Section 63C(1).

When deciding whether to exercise its powers to make an order and, if so, in what manner, the court must consider all the circumstances of the case including the need to secure the health, safety, and well-being of the victim; and, when ascertaining 'well-being', it must have regard in particular to the victim's wishes and feelings (so far as they are readily ascertainable) as the court considers appropriate in light of the victim's age and understanding.[161]

Orders can be made without the respondent having been given notice of the proceedings, provided it is just and convenient to do so.[162] In appropriate cases the court can, instead of making an order, accept an undertaking from the respondent, but not if the respondent has used or threatened violence.[163] The court can attach a power of arrest to an order (but not to an order without notice) if the respondent has used or threatened violence against the victim or otherwise in connection with the matters being dealt with in the order.[164] If a power of arrest is attached, a police officer can arrest the respondent without warrant if there is reasonable cause for suspecting that person to be in breach of a forced marriage protection order. Breach of a forced marriage protection order is now a criminal offence.[165]

### 5.3.1 The new criminal office of forced marriage

Following a public consultation on the issue of forced marriage in 2011,[166] the Government announced its intention to criminalise both forced marriage and breach of a forced marriage protection order. These offences came into force on 16 June 2014 under the Anti-social Behaviour, Crime and Policing Act 2014.[167] This is not the first time that the issue of criminalising forced marriage has been raised. However after an earlier consultation in 2005,[168] the Government decided not to introduce any new criminal offence as there was little support from the Crown Prosecution Service and the Probation Service for such a move. Although the Government recognised that an offence of forcing someone to marry would have advantages (such as creating a change of culture, having a deterrent effect, and empowering young people), it considered that these advantages were outweighed by the disadvantages. In other words, it was of the view that the introduction of a criminal offence of forcing someone to marry might drive forced marriages underground and isolate victims, and also cause racial problems at a time of heightened racial tension. The Government instead introduced civil remedies under the Forced Marriage (Civil Protection) Act 2007.

However, concerns continued to be raised that not enough was being done to tackle forced marriage. In 2011, the Home Affairs Select Committee published a report on the issue which called on the Government to consider, once again, criminalising forced marriage.[169] Aligned with this was the growing trend of criminalising forced marriage across Europe and countries such as Denmark, Germany, Austria, and Belgium had already taken this step. The Government responded decisively by indicating its intention to criminalise breach of a Forced Marriage Protection Order and to consult on making the act of forcing someone to marry a specific criminal offence. In response to the public consultation in 2011, 54 per cent of respondents were in favour of criminalising forced marriage and only 37 per cent were opposed.[170] Further, 80 per cent of respondents felt that the current civil remedies and criminal sanctions are not being used as effectively as they could in tackling forced marriage, indicating the very strong feeling that more needed to be done.[171] Not

---

[161]  Section 63A(2) and (3).      [162]  Section 63D.      [163]  Section 63E.      [164]  Section 63H.

[165]  Section 120, Anti-social Behaviour, Crime and Policing Act 2014, which inserts section 63CA into the Family Law Act 1996.

[166]  Home Office, Forced Marriage Consultation (December 2011) www.gov.uk/government/uploads/system/uploads/attachment_data/file/157827/forced-marriage-consultation.pdf

[167]  www.gov.uk/government/news/forced-marriage-to-become-criminal-offence.

[168]  See the consultation paper, *Forced Marriage: A Wrong Not a Right*, published by the Home Office and the Foreign & Commonwealth Office in September 2005.

[169]  Home Affairs Select Committee, Report Forced Marriage, 17 May 2011 (Eighth Report, Session 2010–11, HC 880).

[170]  Home Office, Forced Marriage – A Consultation: Summary of Responses (June 2012) www.gov.uk/government/uploads/system/uploads/attachment_data/file/157829/forced-marriage-response.pdf.

[171]  Ibid, p 8.

only, therefore, has breach of a forced marriage protection order become a criminal offence, but a specific criminal offence of forcing someone to marry has been created.[172]

---

### Talking point

The Prime Minister, David Cameron, said: 'Forced marriage is abhorrent and is little more than slavery. To force anyone into marriage against their will is simply wrong and that is why we have taken decisive action to make it illegal.'[173]

**Q.** Does criminalising forced marriages send an important message that such behavior will not be tolerated?

**Q.** Will this have an impact on the incidence of such marriages taking place, or will victims be deterred from reporting these offences due to the fear of criminalising family members?

---

## 6  Recognition of an overseas marriage

A marriage contracted in a country outside the jurisdiction of the UK is recognised as valid in the UK provided each party had the capacity to marry according to his or her place of domicile and the formalities required by the law of the place where the marriage was celebrated were complied with.[174] Thus, even though the formalities might be invalid under the law of England and Wales, the court can still recognise the marriage as valid, provided it complied with the rules laid down in the place in which it was celebrated. For this reason an overseas marriage celebrated by local custom can be recognised in the UK.[175] These rules, however, are subject to the overriding rule that an overseas marriage will not be recognised in the UK if it is manifestly unjust or contrary to public policy. Special legal provisions apply to certain overseas marriages, for instance where persons are serving abroad in HM Forces. If the marriage is recognised in England and Wales, then recognition of the marriage will affect the legitimacy of children and the availability of divorce or other marital claims, as well as nationality, immigration rights, inheritance rights, and tax and welfare benefits.

---

### Key case

Whether the courts in England and Wales will recognise an overseas marriage as a valid marriage in the UK depends on the facts of each case. In *Hudson v Leigh*,[176] for example, Bodey J made a declaration that a 'marriage' conducted in South Africa was not a valid marriage in England and Wales as the formal requirements for a valid marriage had not been satisfied. Furthermore, both the parties and the minister who had conducted the religious ceremony did not at the time of the ceremony intend or believe it to be legally binding. Bodey J held that, while the ceremony had the trappings of a marriage, it had fundamentally failed to effect a valid one. Lack of capacity to marry may invalidate an overseas marriage. Thus, for

---

[172] See C. Proudman, The Criminalisation of Forced Marriage (2012) 42 Fam Law 460.      [173] Ibid.

[174] See *Dicey, Morris and Collins on the Conflict of Laws*, 14th edn (London: Sweet & Maxwell, 2010).

[175] As it was, eg, in *McCabe v McCabe* [1994] 1 FLR 410, where a marriage in Ghana between a Ghanaian woman and an Irish man, involving a bottle of gin and a sum of money, was upheld as valid by the English court, even though the parties were not present at the ceremony. The Court of Appeal held that on the evidence of local law, the essential components of a marriage ceremony (ie, the consent of both parties and of their families) was present and so it was a valid marriage ceremony and would be recognised in the UK.

[176] [2009] EWHC 1306 (Fam), [2009] 2 FLR 1129.

> instance, in *City of Westminster v IC (By His Litigation Friend the Official Solicitor) and KC and NNC*,[177] a Muslim arranged marriage which had taken place over the telephone between an autistic man (aged 26, but with a mental age of 3) in England and a woman in Bangladesh, was held to be invalid even though it was agreed by all the parties that the marriage had validly taken place in Bangladesh under Shariah law. The Court of Appeal refused to recognise the marriage as valid as the man, due to his disability, lacked capacity under the law of England and Wales and was therefore unable to give valid consent.[178]

## 7  The removal of section 11(c) of the MCA 1973

Until recently, section 11(c) of the MCA 1973 stated that the parties to a marriage must be respectively male and female otherwise the marriage is void.[179] This had two main consequences. First, it meant that same-sex marriage was not permitted in law. Secondly, it gave rise to the thorny issue of whether a transsexual person could validly marry in his or her acquired gender, and how to deal with intersexual persons. The issue of same-sex marriage will be discussed later in the chapter. The next sections will consider the development of the law relating to transsexual and intersexual persons.

### 7.1  Transsexual persons and marriage

Transsexualism is a medically recognised gender identity disorder, gender dysphoria, whereby a person who appears to be biologically of a particular sex believes or feels that he or she is psychologically a member of the opposite sex. Some persons with gender dysphoria opt to have a gender reassignment, which involves hormone treatment and in some cases surgery.[180] The starting point for discussion of the law relating to transsexual persons and marriage is the case of *Corbett v Corbett (Otherwise Ashley)*.[181] April Ashley, a male-to-female transsexual person, had gone through a ceremony of marriage with Arthur Corbett, who at the time was fully aware of Ashley's background. Subsequently, however, Corbett sought a decree of nullity on the basis that Ashley was male. Ormrod J heard medical evidence which accepted at least four criteria for determining a person's sex, namely: (i) chromosomal factors; (ii) gonadal factors (ie, presence or absence of testes or ovaries); (iii) genital factors (including internal sex organs); and (iv) psychological factors. The witnesses were clear, however, that 'the biological sexual constitution of an individual is fixed at birth (at the latest)'. Having regard to this evidence and the essentially heterosexual nature of marriage, Ormrod J concluded that the law 'should adopt in the first place, the first three of the doctors' criteria, i.e. the chromosomal, gonadal and genital tests, and if all three are congruent, determine the sex for the purpose of marriage accordingly, and ignore any operative intervention'.[182] Accordingly, even though Ashley had undergone gender reassignment surgery and hormone treatment and lived as a woman, 'she' was male, and 'her' marriage to the petitioner was void.

---

[177] [2008] EWHC 198, [2008] 2 FLR 267.

[178] See R. Probert, 'Hanging on the Telephone: *City of Westminster v IC*' (2008) Child and Family Law Quarterly 395.

[179] This has been deleted by the Marriage (Same Sex Couples) Act 2013 and thus marriage can now take place between two people of the same sex. See Section 8.

[180] Gender reassignment is available on the National Health Service.

[181] [1971] P 83, [1970] 2 WLR 1306. For a detailed discussion of this case and its impact, see S. Gilmore, '*Corbett v Corbett*: Once a Man, Always a Man?' in S. Gilmore, J. Herring, and R. Probert, *Landmark Cases in Family Law* (Oxford: Hart, 2011).

[182] [1971] P 83 at 106.

The biological test propounded in *Corbett* made it impossible for transsexual persons to have their acquired gender legally recognised and to enter into a valid marriage in that gender. In a series of cases, transsexual persons took their cases to the ECtHR arguing that UK laws breached their human rights.[183] It was argued that the UK Government was in breach of Article 8 (the right to respect for family life) and Article 12 (the right to marry) of the ECHR taken in conjunction with Article 14 (the right not to be discriminated against in respect of a Convention right). At first the claims failed, the ECtHR affording the UK a wide margin of appreciation on these issues. However, the Court had stressed the need for the law to be kept under review by contracting states and by the European Court itself, having regard to scientific and societal developments. In *Sheffield and Horsham v UK*[184] the Court stressed the importance of the increasing social acceptance of transsexualism and the growing recognition of the problems which post-operative transsexuals encountered.

---

### Key case

Eventually, taking account of these factors, in *Goodwin v UK*[185] (heard with *I v UK*[186]), the ECtHR changed its approach. In *Goodwin*, the applicant, a male-to-female transsexual, claimed that the UK had violated her rights under Articles 8 and 12 of the ECHR because UK law was failing to recognise the legal status of transsexual persons in respect of a wide range of matters, such as employment, social security, the state pension, car insurance, and marriage. The UK's defence was that it enjoyed a margin of appreciation in respect of legislating on such matters. However, the European Court refused to accept this argument and unanimously held that both Articles 8 and 12 had been breached.

---

With regard to Article 8, the ECtHR held that the unsatisfactory situation whereby post-operative transsexuals lived in an intermediate zone where they were not quite one gender or another was no longer sustainable. The UK could no longer claim it enjoyed a margin of appreciation in such matters. As there were no significant factors of public interest which weighed against the interest of the applicant in obtaining legal recognition of her reassignment, the Court held that the fair balance inherent in the European Convention tilted in her favour. It held that a 'serious interference with private life can arise where domestic law conflicts with an important aspect of personal identity, and that the stress and alienation'[187] suffered by a post-operative transsexual could not be considered as a minor inconvenience arising from a formality. The Court also recognised that developments in medical science necessitated a change of approach, and that it was not apparent that chromosomal tests alone should necessarily be decisive for the purposes of attributing gender identity.

With regard to Article 12, the ECtHR held that the term 'man and woman' in relation to the right to marry could no longer be assumed to refer to a test of gender based on purely biological criteria, as had been laid down in *Corbett v Corbett*.[188] It held that such a test was no longer appropriate to the current understanding of transsexualism and could no longer be decisive in denying legal recognition to the change of gender of a post-operative transsexual. Another factor which influenced the

---

[183]  *Rees v UK* (1986) 9 EHRR 56, [1987] 2 FLR 111; *Cossey v UK* [1991] 2 FLR 492; *Sheffield and Horsham v UK* [1998] 2 FLR 928.

[184]  [1998] 2 FLR 928.

[185]  (2002) 35 EHRR 18, [2002] 2 FLR 487. *Goodwin* was used in argument in *Wilkinson v Kitzinger* [2006] EWHC 2022 (Fam), [2007] 1 FLR 295, see p 31 (Section 8).

[186]  [2002] 2 FLR 518.    [187]  (2002) 35 EHRR 18, [2002] 2 FLR 487 at [77].

[188]  That a person's biological sex is fixed at birth and could only be established by chromosomal, gonadal, and genital criteria, see earlier.

Court to find in favour of the applicants was that the condition of gender identity disorder was rec-ognised by the medical profession and treatment, including surgery, was available on the National Health Service. It held that, as the applicant had no possibility of marrying a man even though she lived as a woman and was in a relationship with a man and would only wish to marry a man, the very essence of her right to marry had been infringed and there was no justification for barring her from enjoying that right in the circumstances.[189] The reasoning in *Goodwin* was adopted by the ECtHR in *I v UK*,[190] heard with *Goodwin*, where the applicant, a male-to-female transsexual, had not been admitted to a nursing course because she had failed to show her birth certificate which stated she was male. The ECtHR found in her favour.

---

### Key case

Around the same time as the *Goodwin* decision, a case involving a transsexual person and the right to marry was progressing through the domestic courts, reaching the House of Lords in 2003. In *Bellinger v Bellinger (Lord Chancellor Intervening)*,[191] the House of Lords had to consider the legal position of transsexuals in light of its obligations under the Human Rights Act (HRA) 1998. The *Bellinger* case was different from the transsexual cases cited earlier in that it involved an application by a transsexual person, Mrs Bellinger, for a declaration under section 55 of the Family Law Act 1986 that her 1981 marriage was a valid and subsisting marriage, even though she was a male-to-female transsexual and had married a man. The High Court and the Court of Appeal by a majority (Thorpe LJ dissenting) refused to grant the declaration as, applying the biological test of gender laid down in *Corbett*, they had not entered into a valid marriage, as section 11(c) of the MCA 1973 required the parties to be respectively male and female.

Mrs Bellinger appealed to the House of Lords arguing that the Court of Appeal's decision was incompatible with the ECHR and was therefore unlawful under section 7 of the HRA 1998. As section 2(1) of the HRA 1998 requires courts in the UK to take account of the judgments of the ECtHR when determining any question arising in connection with a Convention right, the House of Lords had to take into account the decision in *Goodwin v UK* (and *I v UK*), which had been decided after the decision of the Court of Appeal in *Bellinger* but before the case was heard by the House of Lords. As the courts are required by section 3(1) of the HRA 1998 to read and give effect to primary legislation in a way which is compatible with the ECHR, the House of Lords was obliged to consider whether section 11(c) of the MCA 1973, which requires the parties to a marriage to be male and female, was incompatible with the European Convention. However, despite the provisions of the HRA 1998 and the decisions of the European Court in *Goodwin* and *I v UK*, the House of Lords dismissed Mrs Bellinger's appeal on the ground that such an important change in the law was better left to Parliament not the courts, particularly as the UK Government had already said it would introduce legislation to change the law. The House of Lords, however, made a declaration of incompatibility under section 4 of the HRA 1998 that section 11(c) of the MCA 1973 was incompatible with Articles 8 and 12 of the ECHR.

---

[189] In *Goodwin*, the European Court was referred to the case of *Re Kevin: Validity of Marriage of Transsexual* [2001] Fam CA 1074 where Chisholm J in the Family Court of Australia had strongly criticised the reasoning in *Corbett* and had upheld the validity of a marriage between a woman and a female-to-male transsexual on the basis that sex was to be determined at the date of marriage having regard not just to biological factors but to all other relevant factors, such as life experiences and self-perception.

[190] [2002] 2 FLR 518.

[191] [2003] UKHL 21, [2003] 1 FLR 1043. See S. Gilmore, '*Bellinger v Bellinger*—Not Quite Between the Ears and Between the Legs—Transsexualism and Marriage in the Lords' (2003) 15(3) Child and Family Law Quarterly 295; C. Bessant, 'Transsexuals and Marriage after *Goodwin v United Kingdom*' [2003] Family Law 111; A. Bradney, 'Developing Human Rights? The Lords and Transsexual Marriages' [2003] Family Law 585.

## 7.2 **The Gender Recognition Act 2004**

After the decisions of the ECtHR in *Goodwin v UK* and *I v UK*,[192] and *Bellinger v Bellinger (Lord Chancellor Intervening)*,[193] the UK was forced to comply with its Convention obligations and change the law to give transsexuals new rights. The UK Government announced that it would introduce new laws which would include not only changes in respect of birth certificates, inheritance provision, and pension rights, but also give transsexuals the right to enter into a valid marriage or civil partnership in their acquired sex. These changes were enacted in the Gender Recognition Act 2004, which came into force on 4 April 2005, and which gives legal recognition to transsexuals who have shown that they have taken decisive steps towards living fully and permanently in their acquired gender.

Under the Gender Recognition Act, a transsexual person aged 18 who has lived in the other gender or who has changed gender under the law or a country or territory outside the UK can apply for a gender recognition certificate from the Gender Recognition Panel,[194] which it must grant if it is satisfied that the applicant has or has had gender dysphoria; has lived in the acquired gender for two years ending on the date on which the application is made; intends to continue to live in the acquired gender until death; and complies with certain evidential requirements laid down in section 3 of the Act.[195] There is no requirement that the applicant must have had gender reassignment surgery or have been sterilised. The effect of a full gender recognition certificate[196] is that the applicant's gender 'becomes for all purposes the acquired gender'.[197] Thus, the practical effect of a gender recognition certificate is to provide a transsexual person with legal recognition in the acquired gender, so that he or she is entitled to various rights, which include a new birth certificate reflecting the acquired gender and the right to enter into a valid marriage or civil partnership in the acquired gender.[198] In the absence of a gender recognition certificate, however, the common law in *Corbett* still applies; indeed it was apparently endorsed by the House of Lords in *Bellinger*.

### 7.2.1 **Application for a GRC by a spouse or civil partner**

One consequence of section 11(c) of the MCA 1973, which prohibited a marriage between two persons of the same sex, was that if the applicant was married, the panel would only issue an interim gender recognition certificate.[199] However, the applicant could seek a full gender recognition certificate if the existing marriage was brought to an end by divorce or dissolution within six months of the issue of the interim certificate.[200] This was to ensure that there could be no marriage between persons of the same sex. The same legal requirements apply to a civil partner who applies for a gender recognition certificate. A full certificate will only be issued once the existing civil partnership had been brought to an end. This is to ensure that the requirements of the Civil Partnership Act 2004 are met, that is, that an opposite-sex couple cannot form a civil partnership. In short, if someone who was in a marriage or civil partnership wished to apply for a Gender Recognition Certificate to legally change their gender, the existing marriage or civil partnership would have to be terminated because the law did not allow same-sex couples to be married,[201] or opposite-sex couples to be in a civil partnership.

---

[192] See earlier in this section.     [193] [2003] UKHL 21, [2003] 1 FLR 1043.

[194] Section 1(1). The Panel is comprised of lawyers and medical practitioners.     [195] Section 2(1).

[196] If the applicant is a spouse or civil partner, only an interim gender recognition certificate can be issued (s 4), but, if the marriage or civil partnership is terminated by divorce or dissolution within six months of the issue of the interim certificate, the applicant can seek a full gender recognition certificate (s 5).

[197] Section 9(1).

[198] With regard to parenthood, however, the grant of a gender recognition certificate does not affect the applicant's parental status as a father or mother, so that it is not thereby possible to remove parental rights and responsibilities: see s 12, and S. Gilmore, 'The Gender Recognition Act 2004' [2004] Family Law 741.

[199] Section 4.     [200] Section 5.

[201] This was prior to the introduction of same-sex marriage by the Marriage (Same Sex) Couples Act 2013.

This was challenged before the European Court of Human Rights in *Parry* v *UK*.[202] In this case a husband and wife were married. The husband subsequently changed gender and wanted to apply for a full gender recognition certificate but also wished to remain married. It was argued that the requirement to end the existing marriage before the certificate could be issued was in breach of the parties' rights under the ECHR. The ECtHR rejected this complaint on the basis that English law did not permit same-sex marriage, thus explaining the legal requirement to annul the existing marriage before a full gender recognition certificate could be issued. Once these steps were followed and the parties were both legally of the same sex, it was open to them to formalise their relationship by entering into a civil partnership. This meant that their rights under the ECHR had not been violated. The European Court of Human Rights confirmed this approach in *Hämäläinen v. Finland*.[203] The case concerned that complaint of a male-to-female transsexual that she could only obtain full legal recognition of her new gender by having her existing marriage turned into a civil partnership. It was argued that this violated her rights under Article 8 (right to respect for private and family life), Article 12 (right to marry) and Article 14 (prohibition of discrimination). The European Court of Human Rights held by a majority that no violation had occurred. The Court found that it was not disproportionate to require the conversion of a marriage into a civil partnership as a precondition to the legal recognition of an acquired gender as that gave the applicant a genuine option which provided her with the legal protection that was almost identical to that of marriage.

---

### Talking point

Alecs Recher, co-chair of the organisation Transgender Europe said that this judgment:

> is a missed chance to bring the practise of the Court in line with the calls from many human rights specialists not to put trans persons in a dilemma to choose between legal gender recognition and other human rights like the right to marry. Today, those European States still forcing trans persons to give up their most basic rights have been told that their approach is acceptable—that is not acceptable.[204]

**Q.** Do you agree? Or, do you agree with the majority view of the court that forcing a couple to convert their marriage to a registered partnership which provides 'almost identical' legal protection to marriage was not disproportionate?

---

In any event, this position has now been altered in England and Wales by the legalisation of same-sex marriage under the Marriage (Same Sex Couples) Act 2013. Section 12 of the 2013 Act brings into effect Schedule 5 which amends the Gender Recognition Act 2004 to allow individuals to change their legal gender without first having to end their existing marriage, which, according to the LGBT Partnership, caused great distress to the transsexual community: 'for many trans people, same-sex civil marriage will mean an end to the distressing and inconvenient practice of having to dissolve one's existing marriage to obtain a GRC'.[205] Permitting same-sex marriage now

---

[202]  App no 42971/05.        [203]  (Application no. 37359/09).

[204]  Transgender Europe, Press Statement: European Human Rights Court confirms forced divorce of trans people is legal, 16 July 2014, http://www.tgeu.org/sites/default/files/2014-07-16_TGEU_PR_Hamalainen_v_Finland.pdf.

[205]  Equal Marriage: The Government's response (December 2012), para 8.7. For a discussion of the impact of the legalisation of same-sex marriage on the Gender Recognition Act 2004 see S. Gilmore, 'The Legal Status of Transsexual and Transgender Persons in England and Wales' in J. M. Scherpe (ed), *The Legal Status of Transsexual and Transgender Persons* (Intersentia, 2014).

enables those in a marriage, when one of the couple legally changes their gender, to remain married, should the parties wish to do so. However, as an opposite-sex couple still cannot form a civil partnership, it remains the case that an existing civil partnership must be brought to an end if one of the parties wishes to apply for a GRC. An alternative option made possible by the 2013 Act is for such a couple to convert their civil partnership into a marriage[206] which would then allow one of the couple to apply to change their gender.[207]

### 7.3 **Intersexuals and marriage**

The law treats transsexual and intersexual persons differently. An intersexual person is one whose biological sex is ambiguous at birth and in *W v W (Physical Inter-Sex)*[208] Charles J distinguished *Corbett* on that basis. In *W v W* the respondent to an application for a decree of nullity had been diagnosed with a physical intersex condition. At birth her chromosomal sex was male, but the external genital appearance was ambiguous. She had no internal sex organs or genitalia of a woman and no vaginal opening, although she subsequently had gender reassignment surgery. Her body now looked more female than male, and she chose to live as a woman. Charles J concluded that the decision whether the respondent was male or female was to be ascertained at the time of the marriage, having regard to her development and all of the indicia of sex listed in *Corbett* (ie, the biological factors, psychological factors, hormonal factors, and secondary sexual characteristics, such as distribution of hair, breast development, physique, etc)[209] Applying those criteria, the respondent was female and the decree was refused.

## 8 **The development of gay and lesbian rights**

The development of same-sex rights in England and Wales mirrors the 'standard sequence' of events usually associated with gay and lesbian emancipation in most countries.[210] This sequence tends to move from the protection of the *individual rights* of gays and lesbians to recognising the *partnership status* of same-sex relationships. Broadly speaking, the protection of individual rights in the gay and lesbian reform agenda begins with the decriminalisation of homosexual acts[211] and the equalisation of the age of consent for sexual activity between adults.[212] It is usually followed by legislation which protects the rights of gay and lesbian individuals in different contexts. For example, legislation was passed in 2003 which outlawed discrimination in the workplace on the grounds of sexual orientation,[213] greater protection from homophobic hate crimes was

---

[206] Section 9 of the Marriage (Same Sex Couples) Act 2013.

[207] Equal Marriage: The Government's response (December 2012), para 8.5.

[208] [2001] Fam 111, FD, *per* Charles J. See A. Barlow, '*W v W (Nullity: Gender) and B v B (Validity of Marriage: Transsexual)*—A New Approach to Transsexualism and a Missed Opportunity?' [2001] Child and Family Law Quarterly 225 and also P.-L. Chau and J. Herring, 'Defining, Assigning and Designing Sex' (2002) 16 International Journal of Law, Policy and the Family 327 and J. Herring and P.-L. Chau, 'Assigning Sex and Intersexuals' [2001] Family Law 762.

[209] [2001] Fam 111, FD, 146.

[210] K. Waaldijk, 'Standard Sequence in the Legal Recognition of Homosexuality—Europe's Past, Present and Future' (1994) 4 Australasian Gay and Lesbian Law Journal 50; K. Waaldijk, 'Civil Developments: Patterns of Reform in the Legal Position of Same-Sex Partners in Europe' (2000) 17 Canadian Journal of Family Law 62. See also L. Glennon, 'Displacing the Conjugal Family in Legal Policy—A Progressive Move?' (2005) 17 Child and Family Law Quarterly 141.

[211] Homosexual activity was decriminalised in England and Wales by the Sexual Offences Act 1967.

[212] The Sexual Offences (Amendment) Act 2000 equalised the age of consent for homosexual and heterosexual activity.

[213] The Employment Equality (Sexual Orientation) Regulations 2003, which implemented Council Directive 2000/78/EC, made it unlawful to discriminate on grounds of sexual orientation in employment and vocational training.

developed in 2003,[214] and it was in the same year that the infamous section 28 was abolished.[215] These measures, which aim to protect the rights of gay and lesbian individuals, tend to be followed in most countries by legal moves to recognise the *partnership status* of same-sex relationships either through civil partnership legislation or the introduction of same-sex marriage. This evolutionary process can be seen in England and Wales with the introduction of civil partnerships for same-sex couples in 2004, followed by the legalisation of same-sex marriage almost a decade later in 2013. The following sections will discuss each in turn.

## 8.1  **The road to civil partnership**

Persons in a same-sex relationship have been able to enter into a registered civil partnership since the enactment of the Civil Partnership Act 2004.[216] However, even before the introduction of civil partnership, the law had begun to give same-sex couples various rights. Same-sex partners could seek protection against domestic violence under Part IV of the Family Law Act 1996,[217] and gay and lesbian couples have been able to adopt children jointly since 2002.[218] One of the most significant milestones in the development of gay and lesbian rights was *Fitzpatrick v Sterling Housing Association Ltd*[219] where the House of Lords held that a same-sex partner was capable of being a member of the other partner's family for the purpose of the Rent Act 1977 thus enabling the applicant to succeed to a tenancy held in the name of their deceased partner.[220] This was a seminal case in family law policy because it recognised, for the first time, that same-sex couples could form a family unit. As such, it represented a powerful endorsement of the sexual partnership of gay and lesbian relationships at a time when such relationships were not fully legitimised either in law or social consciousness. Indeed, section 28 was still on the statute books, which meant that the House of Lords legitimised same-sex partnerships at a time when 'official discourse' still referred to them as 'pretended family relationship[s]'. It is also noteworthy that the decision pre-empted the jurisprudence of the European Court of Human Rights, which has more recently accepted that same-sex couples can be classed as a 'family' for the purposes of Article 8 of the ECHR.[221] Thus, as well as contrasting starkly with the demeaning representation of same-sex relationships under section 28, *Fitzpatrick* also contrasted with human rights jurisprudence which, at the time, required respect for the 'sexual identity of lesbians and gays but not their relationships'.[222]

---

[214] The Criminal Justice Act 2003 imposed a statutory requirement on judges to treat as an aggravating factor when sentencing, assaults involving or motivated by hostility based on sexual orientation (or presumed sexual orientation).

[215] Section 122 of the Local Government Act 2003 repealed section 2A of the Local Government Act 1986 (known as section 28) which prohibited local authorities from intentionally promoting homosexuality or publishing material with the intention of doing so or from promoting teaching in schools of the acceptability of homosexuality as a 'pretended' family relationship.

[216] The Act came into force in December 2005. See R. Deech, 'Civil Partnership' [2010] Family Law 468. On the history of the legal treatment of homosexuality, see S. Cretney, *Same Sex Relationships: From 'Odious Crime' to 'Gay Marriage'* (Oxford: Oxford University Press, 2006). See also the government consultation paper, *Civil Partnership: A Framework for the Legal Recognition of Same-Sex Couples* (Women and Equality Unit of the Department of Trade and Industry, June 2003), which set out the proposals for reform.

[217] See Chapter 3.     [218] Under the Adoption and Children Act 2002, see Chapter 11.

[219] [2001] 1 AC 27, [2001] 1 FLR 271.

[220] The decision was reached by a narrow three-to-two majority with Lords Hutton and Hobhouse of Woodborough dissenting. For a discussion of *Fitzpatrick* see L. Glennon, '*Fitzpatrick v Sterling Housing Association*: A Perfectly Pitched Stall' in S. Gilmore, J. Herring, and R. Probert (eds), *Landmark Cases in Family Law* (Oxford: Hart, 2011).

[221] *Schalk and Kopf v Austria* (App no 30141/04) 24 June 2010.

[222] B. Hale, 'Same-Sex Relationships and the House of Lords' Incorporated Council of Law Reporting Lecture 2007, 14.

> ## The Law in Context
>
> The timing of *Fitzpatrick* coincided with the liberalisation of attitudes towards homosexuality. Indeed, surveys have shown that attitudes towards homosexuality have gradually liberalised since 1998.[223] In 1983, 62 per cent of respondents to a survey though that sexual relations between two people of the same sex were 'always' or 'mostly wrong'.[224] This rose to 75 per cent in 1987 but steadily declined to 36 per cent in 2007.[225] In 1999, the year of the *Fitzpatrick* decision, 49 per cent of respondents still felt that homosexual sex was wrong but by 2003 this had dropped to 40 per cent.[226]

The next major legal development in the gay and lesbian rights agenda was the decision of the House of Lords in *Ghaidan v Godin-Mendoza*.[227] In *Fitzpatrick* it was held that a same-sex partner could succeed to his deceased's partners tenancy by being classed as a member of his family,[228] but that he could not be classed as 'living with the original tenant as his or her husband or wife'.[229] In *Ghaidan*, this difference in treatment was considered in light of the Human Rights Act 1998 where the House of Lords held that it infringed Article 14 of the ECHR. In reaching this decision the court accepted that both opposite- and same-sex relationships can be marriage-like in nature, with the result that any difference in treatment between the two was based upon sexual orientation which had no objective or reasonable justification.[230] Baroness Hale said '[h]omosexual couples can have exactly the same sort of inter-dependent couple relationships as heterosexuals can . . . Some people, whether heterosexual or homosexual, may be satisfied with casual or transient relationships. But most human beings eventually want more than that. They want love . . . And many couples also come to want the stability and permanence which go with sharing a home and a life together, with or without the children who for many people go to make a family. In this, people of homosexual orientation are no different from people of heterosexual orientation.'[231] This was significant. Although the decision in *Ghaidan* related to a specific statutory provision, it called into question the legitimacy of other provisions which conferred rights on unmarried opposite-sex but not same-sex couples.[232] It thus brought same-sex rights within the mainstream political agenda and a short time later the Civil Partnership Act 2004 was passed.

The Consultation Paper preceding the Civil Partnership Act 2004 Act highlighted the plight of same-sex couples: '[s]ame-sex couples face many problems in their day-to-day lives because there is no legal recognition of their relationship. In many areas, each partner in the couple is treated as a separate individual; they are denied rights and responsibilities that could help them to organise their lives together. Opposite-sex couples have the choice to marry and have the relationship recognised by law. Same-sex couples have no such choice.'[233] The Civil Partnership Act 2004 thus established a same-sex registered partnership system and gave registrants marital-like rights and duties. This followed the trend in other European countries to enact registered

---

[223] A. Ross and A. Stacker, 'Understanding the Dynamics of Attitude Change' in A. Park et al (eds), *British Social Attitudes 2009–2010: the 26th Report* (Sage Publications, 2010), pp 115–33.

[224] Ibid.    [225] Ibid.    [226] Ibid.    [227] [2004] UKHL 30, [2004] 2 AC 557, [2004] 2 FLR 600.

[228] Under para 3(1) of Sch 1 to the Rent Act 1977.

[229] Under para 2(2) of Sch 1 to the Rent Act 1977, which states that 'a person who was living with the original tenant as his or her wife or husband shall be treated as a spouse of the original tenant'. This has now been amended by the Civil Partnership Act 2004 (Sch 8, para 13) to include 'a person who was living with the original tenant as if they were civil partners'.

[230] Applying *Karner v Austria* (App no 40016/98) (2004) 38 EHRR 24.    [231] [2004] UKHL 30, p 142.

[232] R. Bailey-Harris and J. Wilson, '*Mendoza v Ghaidan* and the Rights of de facto Spouses' (2003) 33 Family Law 575–9.

[233] DTI, Women and Equality Unit, 'Civil Partnership: A framework for the legal recognition of same-sex couples', 2003, p 10.

partnership schemes for same-sex couples.[234] As such, it was a significant milestone in the gay and lesbian reform agenda in England and Wales. In the parliamentary debates during the passage of the Civil Partnership Bill, the Deputy Minister for Women and Equality noted the evolutionary nature of legal developments in this area: '[w]e have equalised the age of consent, outlawed discrimination in the workplace on the grounds of sexual orientation, secured protection from homophobic hate crimes and supported the abolition of section 28 . . . The Civil Partnership Act, in [representing an] historic step on what has been a long journey to respect and dignity for lesbians and gay men in Britain . . . [creates] a new legal relationship for same-sex couples.'[235]

The Government's intention in introducing civil partnership in 2004 was to create an institution which would be parallel, but not identical, to marriage. It was keen to emphasise that civil partnership would not undermine the institution of marriage or offend religious beliefs. Marriage, at this time, was still regarded as a union which was only possible between a man and a woman. As Lord Nicholls said in *Bellinger v Bellinger (Lord Chancellor Intervening)*, marriage is 'deeply embedded [in the religious and social culture of this country] as a relationship between two persons of the opposite sex'.[236]

---

### Talking point

Baroness Scotland, introducing the second reading of the Civil Partnership Bill in the House of Lords, said:

> The Bill offers a secular solution to the disadvantages which same-sex couples face in the way they are treated by our laws . . . This Bill does not undermine or weaken the importance of marriage and we do not propose to open civil partnership to opposite-sex couples. Civil partnership is aimed at same-sex couples who cannot marry. However, it is important for us to be clear that we continue to support marriage and recognise that it is the surest foundation for opposite sex couples raising children.[237]

**Q.** Do you agree that limiting civil partnership registration to same-sex couples (and thus not offering opposite-sex couples an alternative structure to marriage) was the Government's attempt to safeguard the privileged position of marriage?

---

Although the Government has been keen to stress that civil partnership is not 'gay marriage', civil partnership is in fact almost identical to marriage as it creates a status from which virtually the same rights and responsibilities flow. One of the reasons for refusing to equate civil partnership with marriage is that marriage is considered by many to be a religious sacrament, and the law of marriage has ecclesiastical origins. This approach is questionable given that, first, we live in a multi-ethnic and multi-religious society and, secondly, civil partnerships can be celebrated in religious premises.[238] Civil partnership does, however, have the following differences from marriage. Adultery is not a ground for the dissolution of a civil partnership as it is in the case of divorce; and non-consummation and venereal disease are not available as grounds for the voidability of a civil partnership.[239] In essence, there is therefore very little difference between the status relationship of civil partnership and that of marriage.

---

[234] Registered partnership legislation was first introduced in Denmark in 1989.
[235] Hansard, HC Deb, vol 425, col 174 (12 October 2004).    [236] [2003] UKHL 21.
[237] Hansard, HL 22 April 2004, col 388.
[238] See s 202 of the Equality Act 2010. The Marriage and Civil Partnerships (Approved Premises) (Amendment) Regulations 2011.
[239] See Sections 3.1 and 3.4.

---

### The Law in Context

The Government Equalities Office originally predicted that there would be between 11,000 and 22,000 civil partners in Great Britain by 2010, but there were over 79,000 people in civil partnerships at the start of 2010. The number of civil partnerships peaked in the first quarter of 2006 at 4,869. This is likely to be explained by the number of same-sex couples in long-standing relationships who took the opportunity to formalise their relationship as soon as the legislation was implemented in December 2005. During 2008 to 2013 civil partnerships had fallen to an average of around 1,400 to 1,600 per quarter. Similar trends can be seen in other jurisdictions such as Norway and Sweden where there was a high number of civil partnerships immediately after legislation was introduced, followed by a few years of stable numbers at a lower level.[240] Following the introduction of same-sex marriage in March 2014, the number of civil partnerships formed in England and Wales fell by 70 per cent from 5,646 in 2013 to 1,683 in 2014.[241]

Initially the numbers of males forming civil partnerships were much higher than females, but now there is little difference. In line with trends in other European countries, the numbers of male and female civil partnerships converged in 2009/10. In 2014, 57 per cent of civil partnerships formed were between male couples. This is a change from 2013 when only 47 per cent were between males. The Office for National Statistics reports that the statistics on marriages of same-sex couples show that more female couples are marrying than male couples, which may account for the difference.

The mean age at formation of civil partnership in 2014 increased by nearly 3 years for men to 43.6 years and over 4 years for women to 42.3 years. These increases represent the largest annual increase in the average age at formation since civil partnerships were introduced in 2005.

In 2014, 76 per cent of civil partnerships formed in England and Wales were to couples where both partners were single. However, 11 per cent of men and 17 per cent of women forming a civil partnership had been in a previous marriage or civil partnership. These were similar to the proportions for 2013.

---

## 8.2 The legal formation of a civil partnership

A civil partnership is defined in the Civil Partnership Act 2004 as 'a relationship between two people of the same sex . . . which is formed when they register as civil partners of each other'.[242] To be able to register a civil partnership, the parties must be of the same sex, and each party must not be under 16, not be within the prohibited degrees of relationship, and not be already civil partners or lawfully married.[243] The ban on opposite-sex couples forming a civil partnership is another example of the Government's attempt to safeguard the privileged position of marriage. By limiting registration to same-sex couples, it ensured that an alternative legal structure was not offered to opposite-sex partners.

Local registration services are responsible for registration, which involves a process similar to that for a civil marriage. Like a civil marriage, various preliminary formalities must be satisfied, such as residence and notice requirements. Each party must declare that there is no impediment to the formation of the partnership and that the residence requirements are satisfied.[244] Notice of the proposed registration will be published and, after a 15-day waiting period and in the absence of any objections, the registration authority will issue a 'civil partnership schedule' authorising registration to take place.[245] The 15-day waiting period can be reduced in special cases;[246] and special provision exists for housebound persons, hospital patients, and prisoners.[247] Once these preliminary formalities have been satisfied, registration can take place. The Civil Partnership Act 2004 prohibited civil partnership registrations taking place on religious premises. However, section 202

---

[240] Office for National Statistics, Civil Partnerships in England and Wales, 2014.
[241] Office for National Statistics, Civil Partnerships in England and Wales, 2014.   [242] Section 1(1).
[243] Section 3(1).    [244] Section 3.    [245] Section 8.    [246] Section 14.    [247] Section 12.

of the Equality Act 2010 and the Marriages and Civil Partnerships (Approved Premises) (Amendment) Regulations 2011 enable civil partnerships to be registered on approved religious premises where permitted by religious organisations, although there must be no religious service at the registration.[248] Registration is completed when each party has signed the civil registration document at the invitation of, and in the presence of, the civil partnership registrar; and in the presence of each other and two witnesses.[249]

### 8.2.1 Civil partnership agreements

Civil partners can enter into a civil partnership agreement. This is the equivalent of an engagement to marry and the rules which apply are the same as those which apply to engagements. Thus, a civil partnership agreement does not have contractual effect, and the same rules about rights in property apply on the termination of a civil partnership agreement as apply on the termination of an engagement.[250] A party to a civil partnership agreement can also seek protection against domestic violence under Part IV of the Family Act 1996.[251]

### 8.2.2 Termination of a civil partnership

Under the Civil Partnership Act 2004 a civil partner can apply to have the partnership annulled (on the ground that it is void or voidable) or have it dissolved. These legal processes and the laws which apply are virtually the same as those for married couples who are applying to have their marriage annulled or terminated by divorce. Civil partners can also apply for a separation order, which is equivalent to a decree of judicial separation in the case of married persons; and an order equivalent to the decree of presumption of death.

### 8.2.3 Annulment of a civil partnership

Under the Civil Partnership Act 2004 the court has the power to make nullity orders in respect of void and voidable civil partnerships. These provisions are virtually the same as those for nullity of marriage.[252] Unlike nullity of a marriage,[253] however, there are no non-consummation and venereal disease grounds to render a civil partnership voidable.

### 8.2.4 Dissolution of a civil partnership

Dissolution of a civil partnership is the same as the termination of a marriage by divorce, except that there is no adultery ground.

## 8.3 Recognition of overseas civil partnerships, annulments, and separations

The Civil Partnership Act 2004 makes provision[254] for the recognition of overseas civil partnerships in the UK, and also the recognition of overseas civil partnership dissolutions, annulments, and separations. These are equivalent to the provisions governing the recognition of overseas marriages, divorces, annulments, and separations. This is subject, however, to the provision that an overseas civil partnership will not be recognised if it 'would be manifestly contrary to public policy to recognise the capacity, under the relevant law, of one or both of them to enter into the relationship.'[255] The court has jurisdiction to make finance and property orders after an overseas dissolution, annulment, or legal separation of a civil partnership.[256]

---

[248] Sections 18–19.    [249] Sections 2(1) and 2(5).

[250] See ss 73 and 74. Thus, where a party makes a gift to the other party on the condition (express or implied) that it is to be returned if the civil partnership agreement is terminated, that party is not prevented from recovering the property merely because he or she was responsible for terminating the agreement (s 74(5)).

[251] See Chapter 3.    [252] See Section 1.5.    [253] Sections 49–54.    [254] See ss 233–238.

[255] Section 218.    [256] See s 72(4) and Sch 7.

## 8.4 **The legal consequences of civil partnerships**

Civil partners have virtually the same rights, responsibilities, and privileges as married couples both during the partnership and on and after its breakdown. Thus, the effect of registration is to give the partners various rights, responsibilities, and obligations broadly analogous to those of married couples.

During the partnership, civil partners, like spouses, have a mutual duty to maintain each other, and a civil partner can apply against the other partner for financial provision in the family proceedings court.[257] Civil partners have the same pension rights as married couples; and they are treated in the same way as married couples for tax and state benefit purposes.

On the grant of a dissolution order or a decree of annulment, the family courts have jurisdiction to make finance and property orders in favour of civil partners equivalent to those which it can make on divorce.

On the death of a civil partner, the surviving partner is in the same position as a surviving spouse. Thus, if a civil partner dies intestate, then the surviving partner is treated in the same way as a surviving spouse in respect of inheriting the deceased's estate. The survivor is also entitled to inherit a tenancy belonging to the deceased partner in the same way as a surviving spouse, and the surviving partner can also bring a claim for financial provision on the death of a partner under the Inheritance (Provision for Family and Dependants) Act 1975 in the same way as a married person.

In respect of children and parenting, a civil partner who is not the biological parent can obtain parental responsibility for his or her civil partner's child by entering into a parental responsibility agreement with his or her partner or by obtaining a parental responsibility order from the court.[258] Provisions have recently been introduced which give lesbian partners (whether or not they are civil partners) 'automatic' parental responsibility for a child of the partnership conceived as a result of assisted reproduction or surrogacy;[259] and which allow a lesbian partner (whether or not a civil partner) of a child's mother to acquire parental responsibility where the partners have a child by means of assisted reproduction or surrogacy.[260] Civil partners can apply for child arrangements orders and other orders under section 8 of the Children Act 1989.[261] They have a duty to provide maintenance for any child of the family; and they can apply for financial provision for a child in the same way as married couples. Like a married couple, they can apply to adopt a child jointly and, in some circumstances, solely.

Civil partners who are actual or potential victims of domestic violence can apply for non-molestation orders and occupation orders under Part IV of the Family Act 1996 in the same way as married couples, and a non-owning civil partner has 'home rights' (a statutory right of occupation in the home) under section 30 of the 1996 Act.[262]

# 9 **The road to same-sex marriage**

While the legal obligations between civil partners are based on marriage, same-sex marriage remained unlawful. In *Wilkinson v Kitzinger*, it was held that this was not in violation of the principles of the ECHR.[263] It was also held that a same-sex marriage validly entered into in an overseas

---

[257] Sections 65–72.    [258] See Children Act 1989, s 4A and Chapter 7.

[259] See the Children Act 1989, s 2(1A)(a) and (b) and the Human Fertilisation and Embryology Act 2008, ss 42 and 43. 'Automatic' means that parental responsibility arises 'automatically' in the sense that there is no need to apply for it. On parental responsibility generally, see further Chapter 7.

[260] See Children Act 1989, s 4ZA.    [261] See Chapter 9.    [262] See Chapter 3.

[263] [2006] EWHC 2022 (Fam), [2007] 1 FLR 295. See also *Schalk and Kopf v Austria* (App no 30141/04), 24 June 2010. For commentary on *Wilkinson v Kitzinger*, see N. Bamforth, '"The Benefits of Marriage in All But Name"? Same-Sex Couples and the Civil Partnership Act 2004' [2007] Child and Family Law Quarterly 133 and R. Auchmuty, 'What's so Special about Marriage? The Impact of *Wilkinson v Kitzinger*' [2008] Child and Family Law Quarterly 475.

jurisdiction is not recognised as a valid marriage in the courts in this country, although it can be recognised as a valid civil partnership.[264]

---

**Key case**

In *Wilkinson v Kitzinger* the parties, Ms Kitzinger and Ms Wilkinson, two feminist scholars who lived and worked in England, applied to the English court to have their Canadian marriage, which had been validly entered into in British Columbia, recognised in the UK. They applied for a declaration as to marital status under section 55 of the Family Law Act 1986. They argued that the provisions of the Civil Partnership Act 2004,[265] which treated an overseas marriage as a civil partnership, and section 11(c) of the MCA 1973, which required, at the time, that the parties to a valid marriage in England and Wales be respectively male and female,[266] violated their human rights under the ECHR. They argued that the provisions breached their rights to respect for private and family life (Article 8), to marry (Article 12), and not to suffer discrimination in respect of those Convention rights (Article 14). In the alternative they contended that the common law definition of marriage in English law as a union between a man and a woman[267] should be developed so as to recognise same-sex marriages. They also sought a declaration under section 4(2) of the HRA 1998 that the statutory provisions were incompatible with Articles 8, 12, and 14 of the ECHR.

---

Potter P dismissed the petition on the basis that there had been no violation of their human rights. He said that this was a controversial topic, which lacked consensus throughout Europe, with the result that the ECtHR had declared itself slow to trespass into this area. Potter P rejected the Article 8 argument on the basis that Strasbourg jurisprudence did not regard relationships between same-sex partners as 'family life'.[268] (It should be noted that this view no longer holds following the ECtHR's ruling in *Schalk and Kopf v Austria*.[269]) Insofar as the claim was based on a 'private life', Potter P referred to *M v Secretary of State for Work and Pensions*[270] in which the majority of the House of Lords had guarded against an expansive interpretation of Article 8. For the same reasons, Potter P found no breach of Article 8 taken together with Article 14.

Potter P also held that there was no breach of Article 12, the right to marry, because Strasbourg jurisprudence referred to marriage in the traditional sense, in other words as a marriage between a man and a woman. The petitioner in *Wilkinson v Kitzinger* relied on *Goodwin v UK*[271] (a case on transsexuals) to argue that it was possible to apply the 'living instrument' doctrine (which requires the Convention to be interpreted in light of present-day conditions) and to interpret and extend the right to marry in Article 12 to recognise the unqualified right of a man or a woman to marry a person of the same, as well as the opposite, sex. Potter P rejected this argument, holding that there were 'clear limitations' to the 'living instrument' doctrine and that it could not be said that this was an area where there was European-wide consensus on the matter. Potter P therefore declined to find a violation of Article 12. He held that the 'living instrument' doctrine could not be applied to Article 12 to bring issues within the scope of the Convention which were plainly outside its contemplation.

By contrast, Potter P held that Article 12 was engaged for the purpose of Article 14. He concluded, however, that the difference in treatment of same-sex couples pursued a legitimate aim and represented a proportionate response to achieving that aim. Potter P referred to the Civil

---

[264] Provided the parties had the capacity to marry in the overseas jurisdiction and complied with the required overseas formalities, see the Civil Partnership Act 2004, s 215.

[265] Sections 212–18.          [266] See Section 7.

[267] The common law definition of marriage, as stated by Lord Penzance in *Hyde v Hyde* (1866) LR 1 P & D 130 at 133, 35 LJP & M 57, is: 'The voluntary union for life of one man and one woman, to the exclusion of all others'.

[268] See paras 70–5.          [269] (App no 30141/04), 24 June 2010.          [270] [2006] UKHL 11, [2006] 2 AC 91.

[271] (2002) 35 EHRR 18, [2002] 2 FLR 487. See further at Section 7.1.

Partnership Act 2004, which he said Parliament had enacted as a policy choice to create a legal status for same-sex partners while at the same time demonstrating support for marriage. Prefacing his comments with the observation that same-sex relationships are not inferior, he nevertheless adopted a traditional view of marriage to justify his conclusion. He held that marriage is a heterosexual institution, the primary (although not exclusive) aim of which is procreation in a family environment where children are nurtured by both maternal and paternal influences.[272] To allow same-sex couples to marry would, he concluded, 'fail to recognise physical reality'.[273]

Potter P's reasoning in *Wilkinson v Kitzinger* has been criticised as being unconvincing, in particular for its adoption of a 'traditional' view of marriage, which, it has been argued, is out of step with other areas of the law and societal trends.[274] The traditional view that marriage can only be a relationship between opposite-sex partners, because one of the main functions of marriage is to have children, is open to challenge now that same-sex couples can adopt children[275] and a lesbian woman who has a child by artificial reproduction or surrogacy, whether or not she is a civil partner, now has parental responsibility for a child of the partnership.[276] If marriage is the best environment for raising children, why deny it to same-sex couples who have children? Bamforth has criticised Potter P for choosing to ignore a line of authority in English law which found that childless same-sex couples were 'family' in other contexts, for instance in the context of the Rent Acts.[277] He also argues that Potter P's view that the parties were adequately compensated by having their union recognised as a civil partnership is unconvincing. Potter P's insistence that marriage is the relationship that 'best encourages stability in a well regulated society' means that 'anything else must be second-best, or worse', yet the thrust of Wilkinson and Kitzinger's argument was that they were not being treated equally to those who marry because civil partnership was considered to be different from marriage.

At this time other countries[278] permitted same-sex marriages, and Auchmuty[279] predicted that English law would have to accept same-sex marriage. She said that *Wilkinson v Kitzinger* 'bears all the hallmarks of law in transition' and that same-sex marriage 'will doubtless come to the UK, one way or another'. She concluded that a declaration of incompatibility was 'a likely route' as, while Potter P ruled that Article 12 was engaged by Article 14, he nevertheless offered 'a fairly feeble justification for discrimination which should be easy to demolish'.

There are arguments for and against allowing same-sex marriages in England and Wales, and difficult policy issues are involved. Some argue that marriage is for heterosexuals, and same-sex couples should not be 'landed' with the religious 'baggage' and gender dimensions that marriage carries. It can be argued that some same-sex couples have lifestyles different from heterosexual couples and should not be required to conform to norms that are designed for heterosexuals.[280] Indeed, some gay and lesbian activists argue that same-sex marriage is far from a liberating concept. Ettlebrick, for example, argues that same-sex marriage will do little more than reinforce the status of marriage as the primary trigger for the conferment of rights and responsibilities within the law, thus furthering the gap between the privileged position of those couples who formalise

---

[272] [2006] EWHC 2022 (Fam), [118] and [120].     [273] Ibid, [120].

[274] By Bamforth and Auchmuty (n 266).     [275] Under the Adoption and Children Act 2002, see Chapter 11.

[276] See the Children Act 1989, ss 2(1A) and 2(1B) and the Human Fertilisation and Embryology Act 2008, ss 42 and 43.

[277] He referred to *Fitzpatrick v Sterling Housing Association Ltd* [2001] AC 27, [2000] 1 FLR 271 where, as we have seen, the House of Lords had held that a same-sex couple should be considered 'family' for the purposes of tenancy succession, and to *Ghaidan v Godin-Mendoza* [2004] UKHL 30, [2004] 2 FLR 600 where Lord Nicholls had stated that the existence of children should not be used as a means of differentiating between heterosexual and homosexual couples.

[278] Such as in Holland, Spain, South Africa, Mexico City, and in some provinces of Canada (Ontario, Quebec, and British Columbia).

[279] Auchmuty (n 266).

[280] K. McK. Norrie, 'Marriage is for Heterosexuals—May the Rest of Us be Saved From It' [2000] Child and Family Law Quarterly 363.

their relationship and those who do not (such as unmarried cohabitants).[281] Critics also argue that extending marriage to same-sex couples forces such couples to structure their relationships within a marriage-like framework.[282] Stoddard, in response, cites a number of reasons to support same-sex marriage. First, on a practical level, the status of marriage carries economic and practical benefits which are withheld from those who cannot marry. Secondly, from a political perspective, it is the issue which 'most fully tests the dedication of people who are not gay to full equality for gay people'.[283] In other words, given the privileged position of marriage in social and legal thinking, denying access to gays and lesbians suggests that same-sex relationships are somehow 'less significant, less valuable' than opposite-sex relationships. This is a very compelling argument and given the historic prejudice suffered by gays and lesbians, it is suggested that legalising same-sex marriage is a very powerful state endorsement of gay and lesbian relationships. Thus, although civil partnership is effectively same-sex marriage in all but name, very strong arguments can be made in favour of same-sex marriage.[284] In the era of emerging equality and human rights dialogue, both public and political support grew in favour of same-sex marriage.

---

### The Law in Context

In a YouGov poll carried out for the *Sunday Times* in 2013, 54 per cent of respondents supported changing the law to allow same-sex couples to marry,[285] and it became clear that the Government was resolute in its intention to legalise same-sex marriage by 2015. David Cameron said: 'I think marriage is a great institution – I think it helps people to commit, it helps people to say that they're going to care and love for [sic] another person. It helps people to put aside their selfish interests and think of the union that they're forming. It's something I feel passionately about and I think if it's good enough for straight people like me, it's good enough for everybody and that's why we should have gay marriage and we will.'[286]

---

## 9.1 The Marriage (Same Sex Couples) Act 2013

In March 2012 the Government Equalities Office published a consultation on 'Equal Civil Marriage', which considered how to enable same-sex couples to marry.[287] The consultation closed on 14 June 2012 and received over 228,000 responses, together with 19 petitions, which is the largest response ever submitted to a Government consultation. As expected the proposals attracted much public and political controversy, with strong opposition being mounted by some religious groups. In the initial consultation the Government intended to remove the ban on civil marriage for same-sex couples but

---

[281] P. Ettlebrick, 'Since When Is Marriage a Path to Liberation' in *Lesbian and Gay Marriage: Private Commitments, Public Ceremonies*, ed S. Sherman (Philadelphia: Temple University Press, 1992) 21.

[282] See N. Barker, 'For Better or Worse? The Civil Partnerships Bill [HL] 2004' (2004) 36 Journal of Social Welfare and Family Law 313.

[283] T. Stoddard, 'Why Gay People Should Seek the Right to Marry' in Lesbian and Gay Marriage: Private Commitments, Public Ceremonies, ed. S. Sherman (Philadelphia: Temple University Press, 1992) 14.

[284] The case for recognising a same-sex marriage validly entered into in an overseas jurisdiction as a valid marriage in England and Wales seems even stronger, particularly as increasing numbers of countries are beginning to accept and permit such marriages. It seems rather strange that Wilkinson and Kitzinger could not have their valid Canadian marriage recognised in this country whereas in *McCabe v McCabe* [1994] 1 FLR 410 a marriage in Ghana between a Ghanaian woman and an Irish man involving a bottle of gin and a sum of money, was recognised as valid by the English court even though the parties were not present at the ceremony.

[285] https://yougov.co.uk/news/2013/05/20/voters-back-same-sex-marriage/.

[286] C. Hope, 'We will legalise gay marriage by 2015, says David Cameron', *The Telegraph*, 24 July 2012.

[287] Government Equalities Office (2012), Equal civil marriage: a consultation paper, www.gov.uk/government/uploads/system/uploads/attachment_data/file/133258/consultation-document_1_.pdf.

it did not intend to allow religious organisations to conduct religious same-sex marriage ceremonies. This received a mixed response, with some respondents raising concerns that the continued ban on same-sex religious marriage could be legally challenged.[288] On 11 December 2012, the Government issued its response to the consultation confirming that it would proceed with its intention to legalise same-sex marriage making clear that while it would permit religious organisations to carry out same-sex marriages if they wished to do so, it would provide protections for religious organisations who did not wish to marry same-sex couples.[289] On 17 July 2013, the Marriage (Same Sex Couples) Act 2013 received its Royal Assent with the first same-sex marriages taking place on 29 March 2014.[290] Under the provisions of the Act, same-sex couples can marry either in a civil ceremony or, provided that the governing body of the religious organisation concerned has opted in to that process, on religious premises with the marriage being solemnised through a religious ceremony.[291]

---

**The Law in Context**

The first same-sex marriages took place on 29 March 2014. A total of 7,366 marriages were formed between same sex couples between 29 March 2014 and 30 June 2015. Of these, 55 per cent (4,059 marriages) were between female couples and 45 per cent (3,307 marriages) were between male couples.[292] Statistics reveal that the number of civil partnerships formed has been affected by the legalisation of same-sex marriage. From February 2014, the number of civil partnerships formed each month began to fall notably when compared with the same month in 2013. In December 2014, only 58 civil partnerships were formed compared with 314 in December 2013, a fall of 82 per cent.[293]

---

### 9.1.1 Religious protections

The Marriage (Same Sex Couples) Act 2013 seeks to balance equality between same- and opposite-sex couples with protection of religious freedom. Thus, religious organisations that wish to conduct marriages for same-sex couples can 'opt in' without their being any obligation to do so. It is unlawful for an individual church or place of worship belonging to that faith to marry same-sex couples without the agreement of its governing body. In addition, no religious organisation, or individual, can be compelled to conduct marriage ceremonies for same-sex couples. The Act sets out a 'quadruple lock' of measures to put this 'utterly beyond doubt'. The legislation:

1. states clearly that no religious organisation, or individual, can be compelled to marry same-sex couples or permit this to take place on their premises;[294]

2. provides an 'opt-in' system for religious organisations who wish to conduct marriages for same-sex couples;[295]

---

[288] See, for example, Church of England's response to the consultation: Church of England, A Response to the Government Equalities Office Consultation—'Equal Civil Marriage'—from the Church of England, 11 June 2012.

[289] HMG (2012), Equal Marriage: the Government's response, www.gov.uk/government/uploads/system/uploads/attachment_data/file/133262/consultation-response_1_.pdf.

[290] Large numbers of Conservative MPs were opposed to the legislation and the Government had to rely on the votes of Labour and Liberal Democrat MPs to defeat a series of amendments tabled by Conservative opponents during the passage of the Bill through Parliament. The Act permits same-sex marriage by simply deleting s 11(c) from the MCA 1973. See s 1(1) of and Sch 7, paras 26–7 to the 2013 Act.

[291] With the exception of the Church of England and the Church of Wales.

[292] ONS, 'How have marriages of same sex couples affected the number of civil partnership formations, and how many couples have converted their civil partnership into a marriage?', 20 October 2015, http://www.ons.gov.uk/ons/rel/vsob1/marriages-in-england-and-wales--provisional-/for-same-sex-couples--2014/sty-for-same-sex-couples-2014.html.

[293] Ibid.     [294] Section 2.     [295] Sections 4–5 and Sch 1.

3. amends the Equality Act 2010 to ensure that no discrimination claims can be brought against religious organisations or individual ministers for refusing to marry a same-sex couple or allowing their premises to be used for this purpose;

4. ensures that the legislation will not affect the Canon law of the Churches of England or the Church of Wales.[296]

### 9.1.2 Does same-sex marriage have the same legal effect as opposite-sex marriage?

The 2013 Act gives same-sex marriages the same legal effect as opposite-sex marriages.[297] However, somewhat disappointingly, it fails to fully equalise same- and opposite-sex marriages in relation to the grounds upon which a marriage can be brought to an end through divorce or annulment.

#### 9.1.2.1 Grounds for ending a marriage through divorce or annulment

There are currently some differences in the grounds for ending a marriage and a civil partnership. While married couples can cite adultery as evidence that the marriage has broken down irretrievably for the purposes of divorce law,[298] and non-consummation in order to petition for annulment,[299] these grounds (which are based on definitions of sexual intercourse) are not available to civil partners. Under the 2013 Act, these grounds for ending a marriage similarly do not apply in the case of same-sex marriages. The Government had originally intended that in removing the ban on same-sex marriage, all aspects of current marriage and divorce law would apply to same-sex couples. In other words, that the reasons for ending a marriage would be the same for all couples, both same- and opposite-sex, and it was expected that case law would develop in this area in order to create 'new' definitions of non-consummation and adultery for same-sex couples:[300]

> Specifically, non-consummation and adultery are currently concepts that are defined in case law and apply only to marriage law, not civil partnership law. However, with the removal of the ban on same-sex couples having a civil marriage, these concepts will apply equally to same-sex and opposite-sex couples and case law may need to develop, over time, a definition as to what constitutes same-sex consummation and same-sex adultery.[301]

This position, which provided the opportunity to reflect upon the sexuality of same-sex relationships, changed after the consultation. Influenced by some responses received to the consultation, such as from the Catholic Bishops' Conference of England and Wales and the Family Bar Association, which raised concerns about having such uncertainty in the law, the Government decided to mirror the law on civil partnerships. As such, same-sex couples are not able to cite non-consummation as a basis for annulling their marriage. This position was taken in order to address the concerns of some that having uncertainty in the law on this issue would end up removing the concept of consummation from marriage law in its entirety.[302] One could argue, however, this is an out-of-date concept and that an

---

[296] This is to avoid conflict with the Canon law of the Church of England in relation to marriage which specifies that marriage is between one man and one woman. Section 1(3) of the 2013 Act provides that the nature of marriage in the Anglican Canon law is unaltered and that this is not contrary to the general law which enables same-sex couples to marry.

[297] Section 11 and Schs 3–4. Sch 4, Part 2, para 2 makes it clear, however, that the legislation does not extend the common law presumption that a child born to a woman during her marriage is also the child of her husband. Thus, where a child is born to a woman during her marriage to another woman, it will not be presumed that the latter is a parent of the child.

[298] Adultery requires at least partial penetration of the female by the male, see *Dennis v Dennis* [1955] 2 All ER 51.

[299] Under s 12(a) and (b) of the MCA 1973, opposite-sex couples can apply to annul their marriage where the marriage has not been consummated due to either the incapacity of either party to consummate it or to the wilful refusal of the respondent to consummate it.

[300] Equal Marriage: The Government's response (December 2012), para 9.8.

[301] Government Equalities Office (2012), Equal civil marriage: a consultation paper, para 2.16.

[302] Equal Marriage: The Government's response (December 2012), para 9.9.

opportunity was missed to reflect, through case law, upon its utility in modern matrimonial law. Its origins can be traced to historic theories of marriage as having the purpose of procreation. However, marriage can no longer be considered to be just about the possibility of procreation[303] and one could argue that consummation is an antiquated concept based upon historic notions of conjugal rights within marriage. In relation to adultery, same-sex couples can cite adultery to end a marriage provided that the behaviour complained of meets the common law definition of adultery. In other words, if a same-sex spouse had sexual intercourse with someone of the opposite sex, the other spouse could cite adultery as grounds for divorce. However, if the adulterous affair was with a member of the same sex, this could only be cited as unreasonable behaviour, as is currently the case with civil partnerships.[304] One could argue that the law's refusal to engage with the definitions of homosexual sex, evidenced by its failure to include such behaviour within the definition of adultery, is unfortunate and could be taken to suggest that heterosexual sex retains a more privileged position within legal ideology.

### 9.1.2.2 Pensions

Under the 2013 Act, same-sex married couples are given fewer pension inheritance rights than opposite-sex spouses. For the purposes of occupational pension rights, the Act treats same-sex spouses the same as civil partners. This means that a surviving same-sex spouse is not entitled to the full value of the deceased spouse's pension as the law only requires employers to pay same-sex survivor pensions based on contributions made since 2005.[305] The Government amended the Marriage (Same Sex Couples) Bill 2013 to require a review of the differences in survivor benefits in occupational pension schemes between opposite-sex and same-sex couples in legal relationships. This review which was published in June 2014 observed that removing the differences in survivor benefits would have an estimated capitalised cost of around £2.9 billion for schemes in the public sector, and £0.4 billion for those in the private sector.[306] On 18 March 2015, Work and Pensions Minister Lord Freud, said that a response to the review would be issued in due course.[307] On 4 August 2015, Pensions Minister, Baroness Altmann, said that the Government needed to take account of the cost and other effects of reducing or eliminating discrimination before deciding whether the law should be changed.[308] It seems that many schemes have already equalised survivor benefits for all periods of service, regardless of the sexual orientation of the members to whom they apply. However, schemes that have not taken this step will not currently be compelled to do so. This was confirmed by the recent Court of Appeal decision in *Walker v Innospec Ltd and Others*[309] where the court ruled that same-sex survivors' pensions may be restricted to post-2005 service. This meant that Mr Walker's surviving husband would, in the event of the former's death, be entitled to a pension of only £500 a year, whereas a surviving widow's annual pension would be around £41,000.

## 9.2  Other aspects of the 2013 Act

### 9.2.1  Civil partnerships

The Act does not prohibit same-sex couples from entering into a civil partnership and from 10 December 2014, same-sex couples in a civil partnership have been able to convert that relationship to marriage if they choose to do so.[310] While same-sex couples now have the choice of marrying or entering into a civil partnership, opposite-sex couples who wish to formalise their relationship

---

[303] *Baxter v Baxter* [1948] AC 274.

[304] Equal Marriage: The Government's response (December 2012), para 9.11.

[305] Under Sch 9, para 18(1) to the Equality Act 2010.

[306] HM Government, Review of Survivor Benefits in Occupational Pension Schemes, June 2014, p22.

[307] PQ HL5724, 13 March 2015.

[308] PQHL 1778, Occupational Pensions: LGBT People, 4 August 2015. See also D. Thurley, Pensions: civil partnerships and same sex marriages, HC Briefing Paper Number SN03035, 27 October 2015.

[309] [2015] EWCA Civ 1000.

[310] Under the Marriage of Same Sex Couples (Conversion of Civil Partnership) Regulations 2014. Provisional data on civil partnership conversions show that between 10 December 2014 and 30 June 2015 there have been 7,732 couples

only have the option of marriage. An opposite-sex civil partnership is still not legally possible despite the fact that 61 per cent of respondents to the Government's consultation on equal marriage supported the right of opposite-sex couples to enter a civil partnership.[311] Only 24 per cent of respondents disagreed. Other countries, such as the Netherlands and South Africa, allow both opposite- and same-sex couples to enter into civil partnerships. However, the Government made it clear during the passage of the 2013 Act that it had no plans to allow opposite-sex couples to enter into a civil partnership as it was 'unclear of the need for civil partnerships for opposite-sex couples and had seen no evidence that opposite-sex couples suffered any detriment as a result of not being able to have a civil partnership'.[312]

Amendments to the Marriage (Same Sex Couples) Bill which would have extended civil partnerships to opposite-sex couples were rejected by the House of Commons. Instead, a review of civil partnerships was promised.[313] On 26 June 2014, the Government Equalities Office and Department for Culture, Media and Sport published a report on the conclusions of this review. The Government concluded that in light of the lack of consensus on the way forward for civil partnerships, no changes were being recommended. In particular it was pointed out that over three-quarters of respondents were opposed to opening up civil partnerships to opposite-sex couples.[314]

It remains the case, therefore, that same-sex couples now have greater choice in terms of relationship status than opposite-sex couples as they can either enter into a civil partnership, a same-sex marriage, or convert an existing civil partnership to marriage. This is a strange and anomalous position but one that is not entirely surprising. Making civil partnerships available to opposite-sex couples is perceived as a threat to the institution of marriage by diverting opposite-sex couples away from the preferred family relationship (marriage) in favour of an alternative legal structure. Legal challenges to this position have not, thus far, made any headway. An application made to the ECtHR to challenge the prohibition on opposite-sex civil partnerships in the UK[315] was declared inadmissible.[316] However, closer to home, an opposite-sex couple have now been granted permission to proceed with a legal challenge against the government's refusal to allow them to register their relationship as a civil partnership.[317] The couple, who were strong advocates for same-sex

---

choosing to convert their civil partnership to same-sex marriage. Roughly equal numbers of male and female couples converted their civil partnerships to a marriage (3,856 male couples and 3,876 female couples). The number of conversions taking place has decreased each month from a peak of 2,401 in December 2014, with the exception of May 2015 when there was a small rise: ONS, 'How have marriages of same sex couples affected the number of civil partnership formations, and how many couples have converted their civil partnership into a marriage?', 20 October 2015, http://www.ons.gov.uk/ons/rel/vsob1/marriages-in-england-and-wales--provisional-/for-same-sex-couples--2014/sty-for-same-sex-couples-2014.html Couples who do so will have their marriage certificate backdated to the date of registration of the civil partnership, and thus will not merely receive a conversion certificate as originally suggested, see Pink News, Couples converting from civil partnerships will get backdated marriage certificates, 3 October 2013, http://www.pinknews.co.uk/2014/10/03/couples-converting-from-civil-partnerships-will-get-backdated-marriage-certificates/.

[311] HMG (2012), Equal Marriage: The Government's response, Annex B, p 42. www.gov.uk/government/uploads/system/uploads/attachment_data/file/133262/consultation-response_1_.pdf.

[312] Equal Marriage: The Government's response (December 2012), para 7.2.

[313] Grice & Morris, 'Gay Marriage Bill: David Cameron offers civil partnership review and seeks to smooth relations with angry activists as Bill clears major hurdle', *The Independent*, 21 May 2013. Section 15 of the 2013 Act requires the Secretary of State to arrange for a review to be carried out on the operation and future of the Civil Partnership Act in England and Wales.

[314] Department for Culture, media & Sport, Civil Partnership Review (England and Wales)—Report on Conclusions (2014).

[315] *Ferguson & Others v United Kingdom*, a copy of the submission can be found at http://equallove.org.uk/wp-content/uploads/2011/02/equalloveapplicationtoechr.pdf. See also See N. Barker, 'Civil Partnership: An Alternative to Marriage? An Analysis of the Application in Ferguson & Others v UK' (2012) Family Law. The application also sought to challenge the ban on same-sex civil marriages prior to the enactment of the 2013 Act.

[316] See F. Cranmer, 'Opposite-sex civil partnerships and judicial review [updated], Law & Religion UK, 6 December 2014.

[317] The High Court also issued a Protective Costs Order in order to limit the couple's liability for the Government's legal costs should they be unsuccessful. The High Court later rejected the couple's claim for judicial review. Mrs Justice

marriage, do not want to enter into traditional marriage which they believe is patriarchal and contrary to feminist principles.

---

**Talking Point**

The couple explained their reasons for seeking a civil partnership as follows: 'For us, as for thousands of other opposite-sex couples, entering into a civil partnership would be a serious, lifelong commitment that will give us the legal rights and responsibilities that we need to protect ourselves and our families while formalising our relationship within a modern social institution'.[318] An online petition supporting their stance has attracted almost 3,000 signatures. It is hard to disagree with the point that full relationship equality will not be achieved until all couples have the same options regarding relationship formation, regardless of sexual orientation.

**Q.** Do you agree with the view that both institutions (marriage and civil partnerships) can co-exist without one being a threat to the other? More precisely, does it matter? Is it a legitimate purpose of the law to attempt to mould social behavior in order to protect the institution of marriage?

---

This legal challenge coincides with the Private Member's Bivll, sponsored by Tim Loughton, the former Conservative Children's Minister, which also seeks to remove the prohibition on opposite-sex civil partnerships. The Civil Partnership Act 2004 (Amendment) Bill 2015–16 had its first reading in the House of Commons on 21 October 2015, and is due to have its second reading debate on 11 March 2016.[319] During the Bill's first reading, two core arguments were put forward for change. First, it was argued that it is necessary to remove the 'glaring inequality' resulting from the introduction of same-sex marriage whereby 'same-sex couples are still entitled to continue in a civil partnership, to take up a civil partnership or to enjoy the recent extension of marriage, while opposite-sex couples have only the option of conventional marriage, albeit by a larger range of religious institutions'.[320] This argument is strong and hard to refute. Secondly, given the growing number of cohabiting opposite-sex couples, the availability of civil partnership registration it is argued would encourage family stability by giving those couples who avoid formal marriage for a variety of reasons, the opportunity to have the same legal rights, responsibilities and protections by entering into a civil partnership.[321]

---

**Talking Point**

The case was put as follows:

> We know that marriage works, but we also know that civil partnerships are beginning to show evidence of greater stability for same-sex couples, including those who have children . . . If just one in 10 cohabiting opposite-sex couples entered into a civil partnership, that would amount to some 300,000 couples and their children. It would offer the prospect of yet greater security, greater stability, less likelihood of family breakdown, better social outcomes and better financial outcomes. That, surely, is progress.[322]

---

Andrews ruled that the law on civil partnerships had not become imcompatible with the ECHR 'just because same-sex couples now have two routes to achieving legal recognition of their relationship by the state and opposite-sex couples continue to only have one', *R (Steinfeld and Keidan) v Secretary of State for Education* [2016] EWHC 128 (Admin), at [84]. The couple have, however, been given permission to appeal to the Court of Appeal.

[318] Pink News, High Court judges permits straight civil partnerships legal challenge to proceed, 24 February 2015, http://www.pinknews.co.uk/2015/02/24/high-court-judge-permits-straight-civil-partnerships-legal-challenge-to-proceed/

[319] Hansard, HC Debates, Column 960 (21 October 2015).      [320] Ibid.

[321] Hansard, HC Debates, Column 961 (21 October 2015).      [322] Ibid.

There is no doubt that the law has to change in this area in order to achieve full relationship equality. However, as will be explained later in this chapter, the law in England and Wales has thus far failed to adequately address the needs of unmarried cohabitants. Do you think that making provision for opposite-sex civil registration will help to resolve this by encouraging couples who have avoided conventional marriage, to enter into a civil partnership?

## 10  The legal consequences of marriage

Married persons, as a result of their marital status, have various legal rights and responsibilities, which are prescribed by the state. There is no statutory list of these rights and responsibilities but they are found in a wide range of statutory provisions and cover a wide range of matters, such as taxation, inheritance, immigration, social security, financial obligations, and tenancies. On marriage breakdown, married persons also have various rights and responsibilities, for instance to provide financial provision for the other spouse in certain circumstances. However, despite their rights and responsibilities, which are outlined in the following text, husbands and wives have separate legal personalities. This means that they can own property in their sole name (or jointly) and can bring proceedings in tort and contract separately against each other or against third parties.[323] They can also enter into contracts with each other, make unilateral decisions about their own medical treatment,[324] and make their own decisions on how their property is to be administered on their death.

Married persons have the following rights and responsibilities.

**Financial obligations:** the parties to a marriage have financial obligations to each other during their marriage and, depending on the circumstances, on the termination of the marriage by divorce or annulment. They can seek orders from the court in respect of financial provision during marriage[325] and on divorce. Married couples, like all parents, have a duty to provide maintenance for any child of the family during the marriage and on and after marital breakdown. They can enter into agreements about maintenance provision for themselves and also their children, but they cannot exclude the jurisdiction of the court in respect of the terms of such agreements; and any provision in an agreement restricting the right of either spouse or any other relevant person to apply for child support maintenance for a relevant child is void.

**Property rights:** each spouse can own property solely or jointly with the other spouse. During the marriage the rules governing property ownership are the same as those which apply to other persons, with the exception of some special statutory provisions which apply only to spouses,[326] of particular importance being the statutory right to occupy the family home ('home rights').[327] Thus, who owns what during marriage depends on which spouse bought the property or to whom the property was given, subject in all cases to a contrary intention. On divorce, however, the position is different, as the divorce court has wide powers to adjust the property rights of spouses, irrespective of who owns what but according to the circumstances of the case.[328] In respect of property

---

[323] Law Reform (Married Women and Tortfeasors) Act 1935; Law Reform (Husband and Wife) Act 1962, s 1.

[324] This includes the right of a wife to make a unilateral decision to abort a child born of the marriage (see *Paton v British Pregnancy Advisory Service Trustees* [1979] QB 276 where the husband's application for an injunction to prohibit the defendant carrying out an abortion on his wife failed).

[325] In the family proceedings court (under the Domestic Proceedings and Magistrates' Courts Act 1978) and in the county court or High Court (under the MCA 1973, s 27).

[326] Such as the Married Women's Property Act 1882.      [327] Under the Family Law Act 1996, Part IV, s 30.

[328] Under the MCA 1973, Pt II, see Chapter 4.

on death, each spouse is free to make a will leaving his or her property to whomsoever he or she wishes. On intestacy the surviving spouse will succeed to the estate of the deceased spouse, subject to certain restrictions and financial limits. A surviving spouse can apply to the court for reasonable financial provision from the other spouse's estate under the Inheritance (Provision for Family and Dependants) Act 1975, and is treated more favourably than other applicants.[329]

**Children:** parents who are married have 'automatic' parental responsibility in law for their children[330] unlike unmarried parents, where only the unmarried mother has automatic parental responsibility. In respect of any stepchild of either party, parental responsibility is not 'automatic' but can be acquired. Married parents, like all parents, have a duty to provide maintenance for any child of the family. They can adopt a child jointly, and in some circumstances solely, and they also have a right to give or refuse consent to the adoption of their child.

**Other miscellaneous rights:** spouses (and former spouses) can seek remedies under Part IV of the Family Law Act 1996 to protect themselves against domestic violence. Special rules apply to spouses in respect of giving evidence in criminal proceedings. The marriage of a non-British person to a British citizen may provide a way of acquiring British citizenship and/or the right to enter the UK. Married couples enjoy certain tax and pension privileges. For instance, transfers between parties to a marriage are exempt from inheritance tax, and a transfer between spouses does not give rise to a chargeable gain for the purpose of capital gains tax. A married person can also benefit from a deceased spouse's pension rights.

## 11  Non-formal adult relationships

The only two formal adult relationships in family law are marriage and civil partnership. These are relationships which can only be created by complying with various statutory formalities. These requirements have been considered earlier. Family law also recognises the non-formal relationship of cohabitation, but not to the same extent as marriage and civil partnership. There is also another type of non-formal adult relationship, that between home-sharers, but although these relationships have been considered by law reformers, such as by the Law Commission, and provision was made for them in the Cohabitation Bill 2008, no recognition has been given to such relationships in family law.

### 11.1  Cohabitation

Cohabitation[331] is an increasingly popular relationship choice whether between heterosexual or homosexual partners, and social attitudes to cohabitation have changed over the years. Although

---

[329]  The applicant spouse (or former spouse) can do so without having to prove dependency on the deceased or that he or she was being maintained by the deceased.

[330]  On parental rights and responsibilities and children, see Chapter 7.

[331]  On cohabitation, see A. Barlow, S. Duncan, G. James, and A. Park, *Cohabitation, Marriage and the Law: Social Change and Legal Reform in 21st Century Britain* (Oxford: Hart, 2005); C. Burgoyne and S. Sonnenberg, 'Financial Practices in Cohabiting Heterosexual Couples: A Perspective from Economic Psychology' in J. Miles and R. Probert (eds), *Sharing Lives, Dividing Assets, An Inter-Disciplinary Study* (Oxford: Hart, 2009), pp 89–108; K. Kiernan, 'Unmarried Cohabitation and Parenthood in Britain and Europe' (2004) 26(1) Journal of Law and Policy 33–55; C. Grant Bowman, *Unmarried Couples, Law, and Public Policy* (Oxford: Oxford University Press, 2010); C. Vogler, M. Brockmann, and R. Wiggins, 'Intimate Relationships and Changing Patterns of Money Management at the Beginning of the 21st Century' (2008) 37 British Journal of Sociology 455; G. Douglas, J. Pearce, and H. Woodward, *A Failure of Trust: Resolving Property Disputes on Cohabitation Breakdown* (2007) A. Barlow, C. Burgoyne, and J. Smithson, *The Living Together Campaign: An Investigation of its Impact on Legally Aware Cohabitants* (Ministry of Justice, 2007), available at http://www.lawcom.gov.uk/wp-content/

cohabitation is on the increase, while marriage is on the decline, it is difficult to measure accurately how many people are actually living in cohabiting relationships and also how many relationships break down. This is because there is no proof by public record, as there is with marriage and civil partnership, as to the existence of a cohabitation relationship. Also, there is no proof of the termination of a cohabiting relationship as there is with divorce and dissolution of a civil partnership. The problem of estimating the number of cohabiting relationships and how many break down is particularly difficult because of the difficulty of defining what the terms 'cohabitants' and 'cohabitation' mean.[332]

---

**The Law in Context**

In 2012, there were 5.9 million people cohabiting in the UK, double the 1996 figure. Over the same period, the percentage of people aged 16 or over who were cohabiting steadily increased, from 6.5 per cent in 1996 to 11.7 per cent in 2012.[333] The 2015 Families and Households Survey reveals that there were 3.1 million opposite-sex cohabiting couple families and 90,000 same-sex cohabiting couple families in the UK in 2015. Together, cohabiting couple families account for 17 per cent of all families in the UK, making this relationship the fastest growing family type in the UK.[334]

---

### 11.1.1 Defining cohabitants and cohabitation

One of the difficulties for the law, and for any law reform, is defining what the terms 'cohabitant' and 'cohabitation' mean. Defining these terms is important for determining whether the parties possess, or should possess, various legal rights and responsibilities. But defining them is difficult because cohabitation relationships can take many forms. In fact, the parties to a relationship may themselves have divergent views about whether or not they are cohabiting, and whether or not they should be subject to mutually enforceable legal obligations.

Persons cohabit for different reasons. Some couples may cohabit in preference to marriage. Some may cohabit as a precursor to marriage. In some cohabiting relationships, the parties may not be in agreement—one of the parties may be committed to the relationship whereas the other party might not be, or not to the same degree. A study by Barlow and Smithson[335] found that cohabitants are of the following four psychological types: 'idealogues' (those who cohabit as they have an ideological objection to marriage); 'romantics' (those for whom cohabitation is a step towards marriage); 'pragmatists' (those who make decisions about whether to marry or cohabit on legal or financial grounds); and 'uneven couples' (those where one party to the relationship wishes to marry and the other does not, thereby leaving the person who wishes to marry in a vulnerable position). Barlow and Smithson concluded that these different styles of cohabiting relationship underlined the need for any legal reforms to provide a range of legal options for cohabitants.

---

uploads/2015/03/living-together-research-report.pdf; A. Barlow, 'Legal Rationality and Family Property: What has Love Got to Do With It?' in J. Miles and R. Probert (eds), *Sharing Lives, Dividing Assets: An Interdisciplinary Study* (Oxford: Hart, 2009); A. Dnes, 'Rational Decision-Making and Intimate Cohabitation' in J. Miles and R. Probert (eds), *Sharing Lives, Dividing Assets: An Interdisciplinary Study* (Oxford: Hart, 2009); A. Barlow, C. Burgoyne, E. Clery, and J. Smithson, *Cohabitation and the Law: Myths, Money and the Media, British Social Attitudes 24th Report* (London: Sage, 2008); S. Duncan, A. Barlow, and G. James, 'Why Don't They Marry? Cohabitation, Commitment and DIY Marriage' [2005] Child and Family Law Quarterly 383.

[332]  See further Section 11.1.1.

[333]  ONS, Short Report: Cohabitation in the UK, 2012, http://www.ons.gov.uk/ons/dcp171776_284888.pdf.

[334]  ONS, Families and Households, 2015.

[335]  A. Barlow and J. Smithson, 'Legal Assumptions, Cohabitants' Talk and the Rocky Road to Reform' [2010] Child and Family Law Quarterly 328.

How the terms 'cohabitation' and 'cohabitants' are defined raises certain policy issues. Some argue that a wide definition giving a wide category of cohabitants new legal rights and remedies similar, or identical, to those of married couples and civil partners would undermine the institution of marriage. Such presumptive-based recognition (ie, where rights and duties arise by virtue of the cohabiting relationship itself and not through the parties opting in to marriage or civil partnership) would, it is argued, also undermine the autonomy of cohabiting couples, some of whom may have made a conscious decision not to marry in order to avoid the rights and obligations which the state imposes on married couples or civil partners. On the other hand, one could argue that such presumptive-based legal recognition is necessary in order to protect economically vulnerable parties in cohabiting relationships.

Current statutory provisions giving cohabitants rights do not adopt a consistent definition of the term 'cohabitants'. Although they define 'cohabitants' as persons living in a quasi-marital or civil partnership relationship, there is not necessarily a minimal duration and residence requirement. Thus, to apply for financial provision from a deceased cohabiting partner's estate under the Inheritance (Provision for Family and Dependants) Act 1975, a cohabitant must have lived in the same household as the deceased for at least two years as if he or she were the spouse or civil partner of the deceased; but for the purposes of obtaining protection against domestic violence under Part IV of the Family Law Act 1996 the term 'cohabitant' is defined less restrictively as there is no minimum duration requirement. The reason for this is to ensure that persons who are living together come under the umbrella of the 1996 Act and are able to gain protection against violence.

Determining the length of a cohabitation relationship for the purpose of reforming the law and giving cohabitants new rights is difficult, and there have been divergent views on this. Lord Lester's Cohabitation Bill 2008 initially recommended two years, but this was increased to five when the Bill was debated in the House of Lords. Deech, however, has suggested that ten years is a better 'gateway', if there is to be one at all, on the basis that 'only 5 per cent of cohabiting unions in this country last for more than 10 years'.[336] There is also the question of whether short periods of separation should be ignored when calculating the duration of a cohabiting relationship and whether the nature of the parties' commitment should be taken into account, although that would be virtually impossible to assess. Difficulties about whether someone is or is not a cohabitant could result in protracted and expensive litigation being brought, which would result in the assets of cohabitants being significantly reduced and be counterproductive in any attempt to give them new rights.

### 11.1.2 The vulnerability of cohabitants and their children

Cohabitants are given some recognition in family law but not to the same extent as married couples and civil partners. Thus, for instance, they can seek orders from the court to protect themselves against domestic violence[337] and make a claim for financial provision from the estate of their deceased partner.[338] In respect of property and financial matters, however, there are no special family law provisions and cohabitants must turn instead to the general principles of the law of property and contract. This makes them particularly vulnerable on relationship breakdown as cohabiting partners have no duty to provide each other with financial provision (maintenance); and any dispute about the family home must be determined by property law principles and in the ordinary courts where the outcome may be uncertain and the cost of litigation prohibitive. This is quite different from marriage and civil partnerships where the family court has a wide discretion to make property and finance orders according to the needs and resources of the parties and by applying principles of fairness and non-discrimination.[339] In a property dispute involving cohabitants, on the other hand, the court will exercise its jurisdiction by looking at the express or inferred

---

[336] R. Deech, 'Cohabitation' [2010] Family Law 39.
[337] Under the Family Law Act 1996, Part IV, see Chapter 3.
[338] Under the Inheritance (Provision for Family and Dependants) Act 1975.
[339] See, in particular, *White v White* [2001] 1 AC 596, [2000] 2 FLR 981; *Miller v Miller; McFarlane v McFarlane* [2006] UKHL 24, [2006] 1 FLR 1186; and *Charman v Charman* [2007] EWCA Civ 503, [2007] 1 FLR 1246. See Chapter 4.

intentions of the parties,[340] and not base its decision on what is fair in the circumstances. The only remedy cohabitants have in family law is that, if they have a child, they can apply for a property order for the benefit of the child under Schedule 1 to the Children Act 1989.[341]

There is also the problem that there is a widespread but erroneous belief that there exists something in English law called a 'common law marriage' which gives cohabiting couples after a period of time the same rights and remedies as married couples.[342] Cohabiting couples need to be informed and made aware that this is a myth. Probert[343] argues that the origin of the 'common-law marriage myth' can be traced back to no earlier than the 1970s, basing her hypothesis on the fact that the media used this term during the 1970s when Parliament and the courts began to confer rights on such couples. A two-year study by Barlow, Burgoyne, Clery, and Smithson (2008)[344] found that cohabitation is a popular choice of relationship in Britain but that, despite the Living Together Campaign,[345] few cohabitants had taken steps to safeguard their legal position. Thus, only 15 per cent of those who owned their accommodation had a written agreement about their share of the ownership; and only 19 per cent had sought advice about their legal position.

Children of cohabiting couples are also likely to be in a more vulnerable position than children whose parents are married, not only because cohabiting relationships are more prone to breakdown,[346] but because the court has no power to oversee the residence and contact arrangements for children of cohabiting parents on family breakdown, whereas it has if parents are divorcing.[347] Children may also be vulnerable if one of their cohabiting parents loses a right to remain in the family home on relationship breakdown, and also because there is no maintenance obligation between unmarried partners.

### 11.1.3 The rights and obligations of cohabitants

Cohabitants have some legal rights and obligations but these are much more limited than those of married couples and civil partners.

**Financial obligations:** unlike married couples and civil partners, cohabitants have no duty during their relationship or on its breakdown to provide each other with financial support, and therefore have no right to apply for court orders in respect of financial provision during their relationship or on its breakdown. They do, however, have a right to seek financial provision in certain circumstances from the estate of their deceased partner on his or her intestacy.[348] In respect of their children, cohabiting parents, whether or not they have parental responsibility, have a duty to provide financial provision for their children and, if a parent fails to do so, an application can be made to the Child Maintenance and Enforcement Commission[349] and, in certain circumstances, to the court, where they can apply not just for maintenance but also lump sum orders for the benefit of a child.[350]

---

[340] See, in particular, Baroness Hale in *Stack v Dowden* [2007] UKHL 17, [2007] 1 FLR 1858 at [61]. See further at Chapter 5.

[341] See Chapter 5.

[342] In fact some 53 per cent of the 2006 British Social Attitudes survey's nationally representative sample believed there was something called a 'common law marriage' (see A. Barlow, C. Burgoyne, E. Clery, and J. Smithson, 'Cohabitation and the Law: Myths, Money and the Media' in A. Park, J. Curtice, K. Thompson, M. Phillips, and E. Clery (eds), *British Social Attitudes—The 24th Report* (London: Sage, 2008), pp 29–51).

[343] See R. Probert, 'Common-Law Marriage: Myths and Misunderstandings' [2008] Child and Family Law Quarterly 1.

[344] See n 331.

[345] Its website provides cohabitants with information about their legal rights and remedies.

[346] See K. Kiernan, Childbearing outside marriage in Western Europe, (1999) Population Trends 98.

[347] A petitioner to a divorce must present a Statement of Arrangements for the Children to the divorce court and the district judge has an obligation under the MCA 1973, s 41, to consider those arrangements. See further Chapter 9.

[348] Under the Inheritance (Provision for Dependants) Act 1975.

[349] Under the Child Support Act 1991, as amended, see Chapter 6.

[350] Under the Children Act 1989, s 15 and Sch 1.

**Property rights:** cohabitants, unlike married couples and civil partners, have no special property rights in family law either during the relationship or on relationship breakdown. To establish an interest in property, such as the family home, cohabitants must rely on equitable doctrines, such as trusts and proprietary estoppel.[351] This is quite different from divorce or dissolution of a civil partnership.[352] This may mean that, on relationship breakdown, cohabitants may find themselves without any entitlement to the former family home and with no right to any pension provision from their former cohabiting partner. Also, cohabitants, unlike married couples and civil partners, have no statutory rights of occupation of the family home ('home rights'), which means that they will only have a right to occupy the home if they have a right of ownership in the property, a licence to live there, a right under a tenancy, or they have been granted an occupation order permitting them to reside in the home where there is domestic violence.[353] However, if cohabitants have children they are in a slightly better position as they can seek property orders for the benefit of a child under section 15 of and Schedule 1 to the Children Act 1989, which give the court power to transfer, for instance, the family home to the non-owning cohabitant during a child's dependency which may enable the child and the residential parent to continue living in the home after the age of majority.[354]

**Property rights on the death of a cohabiting partner:** on the death of a cohabiting partner who dies intestate, the surviving cohabitant is in a vulnerable position compared to a married person or civil partner, as the survivor has no right to inherit from the deceased partner's estate. Instead, any property goes to the deceased's children or parents. There has, however, been discussion about whether the rules of intestacy should be reformed to give cohabitants a right to succeed to their deceased partner's estate.[355] In 2007 the Law Commission in its report on cohabitation law reform was not in favour of this, as it considered it would be difficult to reflect appropriately the diverse range of cohabiting relationships.[356] It proposed instead making better provision for cohabitants by amending the Inheritance (Provision for Family and Dependants) Act 1975. However, in 2008 the Law Commission announced that it would carry out a general review of the law of intestacy and the 1975 Act, and in 2009 it published a consultation paper in which it reviewed the law and discussed options for reform including a proposal that unmarried couples who had lived together for at least two years should be automatically entitled to half their deceased partner's estate on intestacy, which would put them in the same position as surviving spouses and civil partners.[357]

Because of the danger that a surviving cohabitant may be left with nothing on his or her partner's death, it is particularly important for cohabiting partners to make a will even though the surviving cohabitant can apply to the court for financial provision from the deceased partner's estate under the Inheritance (Provision for Family and Dependants) Act 1975. Under this Act, however, cohabitants are not treated as favourably as spouses and civil partners. It is also possible to bring a claim against a deceased partner's estate by applying to the court to establish a beneficial interest in the deceased cohabitant's property under a trust or proprietary estoppel. A surviving partner can succeed to a tenancy belonging to a deceased cohabitant.

---

[351] See Chapter 5.    [352] See Chapter 4.

[353] Married couples and civil partners have 'home rights' under the Family Law Act 1996, Pt IV, s 30 in certain circumstances, see Chapter 3.

[354] See Chapter 5.

[355] See C. Williams, G. Potter, and G. Douglas, 'Cohabitation and Intestacy: Public Opinion and Law Reform' [2008] Child and Family Law Quarterly 499 which considers the position of cohabitants whose partners die, and also the approach of the courts to claims under the Inheritance (Provision for Family and Dependants) Act 1975.

[356] Law Commission, *Cohabitation: The Financial Consequences of Relationship Breakdown* (Law Com No 307, 2007), Part 6.

[357] *Intestacy and Family Provision Claims on Death* (Law Com CP No 191, 2009).

**Cohabitants and their children:** cohabiting parents have virtually the same rights and responsibilities with regard to their children as married couples, but with the important exception that the unmarried father has no 'automatic' parental responsibility in law for his children, although he can acquire it in various ways.[358] Cohabitants have the same maintenance obligations to their children as married couples, and all other parents, irrespective of whether the father has parental responsibility, and cohabiting parents (including fathers without parental responsibility) can apply for child arrangements orders and other orders under section 8 of the Children Act 1989.[359] Eligibility to apply for section 8 orders is based on parenthood, not on whether a parent has parental responsibility. Only the unmarried mother, not the father, has a duty to register the child's birth, but both parties can choose to do so jointly whereupon the father acquires parental responsibility. Under the law of adoption[360] a cohabiting couple can make a joint application to adopt a child, but an unmarried father without parental responsibility has no statutory right to consent to the adoption of his child.

**Other rights:** cohabitants and former cohabitants, opposite-sex and same-sex, can apply for non-molestation orders and occupation orders under Part IV of the Family Law Act 1996 to protect themselves and their children against domestic violence. Cohabitants have a right to enter into a contract to regulate their affairs, for example to make arrangements about the allocation of property and other matters should their relationship break down, but in practice few do so.[361]

### 11.1.4 Reforming the law

For many years there has been discussion about reforming the law to give cohabitants rights in respect of property and finance on relationship breakdown, and on the death of their partner. Proposals for reform have come not only from the Law Commission[362] but from the Law Society[363] and from Resolution, the body of family lawyers.[364] At the end of 2008, Lord Lester of Herne Hill[365] introduced the Cohabitation Bill into the House of Lords,[366] a Bill which was supported by Resolution. The Bill had its second reading in the House of Lords in March 2009, but met with resistance from some members of the House and went no further. However, a new Private Member's Bill, The Cohabitation

---

[358] Eg by registering his child's birth with the mother, by entering into parental responsibility agreement with the mother, or obtaining a parental responsibility order from the court (see Children Act 1989, s 4), or by subsequently marrying the child's mother (see further Chapter 7).

[359] Such as for residence and contact, see Chapter 9.    [360] See Chapter 11.

[361] See *Sutton v Mishcon de Reya and Gawor & Co* [2003] EWHC 3166 (Ch), [2004] 1 FLR 837 where a cohabitation agreement was held not to be valid in the circumstances of the case, as it was an agreement about sexual relations not one about the parties' property, and see commentary by R. Probert, 'Sutton v Mishcon de Reya and Gawor & Co: Cohabitation Contracts and Swedish Sex Slaves' [2004] Child and Family Law Quarterly 453.

[362] In 2002 it published *Sharing Homes: A Discussion Paper* (Law Com No 278), in which it discussed reforming the law not just for cohabitants but home-sharers generally. It did so by discussing a 'contribution-based' model for reform, but it found it to be unworkable in practice. In 2006 the Law Commission published a Consultation Paper, *Cohabitation: The Financial Consequences of Relationship Breakdown* (Law Com CP No 179) making proposals for reform of the law relating to the property and financial consequences of cohabitation breakdown. This was followed in 2007 by the publication of its Report, *Cohabitation: The Financial Consequences of Relationship Breakdown* (Law Com No 307).

[363] See *Cohabitation: The Case for Clear Law; Proposals for Reform.*

[364] In 2000 the Solicitors' Family Law Association (now called Resolution) published *Fairness for Families*, in which it recommended reforms similar to those recommended by the Law Society.

[365] A human rights lawyer, and the person who was responsible for driving the reforms giving victims of forced marriages greater protection under the Family Law Act 1996, Pt 4A.

[366] The Bill was drawn up after a consultation paper, *Reforming the Law for People Who Live Together*, had been published in 2008 setting out two main options for reform: one similar to that proposed by the Law Commission in 2007 being based on economic disadvantage; and the other a more discretionary scheme similar to that on divorce under the MCA 1973. It was the latter option which was chosen and incorporated into the Bill. For details of the Bill, see R. Probert, 'The Cohabitation Bill' [2009] Family Law 150.

Rights Bill 2014–15, was introduced into the House of Lords in 2014 by Liberal Democrat MP Lord Marks. The Bill received its second reading in the House of Lords on 12 December 2014 and, at the time of writing, was at the Committee stage, during which time its provisions will be subjected to greater scrutiny by the House. The Bill proposes to implement the recommendations of the Law Commission in 2007 by making provision for an 'opt-out' system that would automatically bring cohabiting couples (who had lived together as a couple for two or more years, or had a child together) within its regulatory remit unless they opted out. The Bill, amongst other things, seeks to provide a legal remedy in the situation where one party is left financially disadvantaged following the breakdown of an unmarried relationship. However, as discussions around the extension of civil partnerships to opposite-sex couples have shown, the Government remains fearful of being seen to undermine marriage. In the absence of Government support, this Bill is likely to be destined to the same fate as prior initiatives in this area.

There are several arguments for and against reforming the law to give cohabitants new rights on relationship breakdown and on the death of a partner. One of the main arguments given in favour of reform is that under the current law cohabitants and their children are vulnerable and suffer unfairness and injustice particularly on relationship breakdown.[367] Lord Marks summarised the case for reform in the following terms: '[when an unmarried couple separate], there are no legal rights at all for the woman who has given up her career to look after her partner's children—or their joint children—once they are older and independent. There are no rights for the woman who gives up working to keep house for her family and then does so for many years before the relationship breaks down. There is no redress for the man who has worked for years and used up his savings to help establish his partner's business and is then left with nothing when they break up. Then again, if one partner dies without leaving a will, the other will inherit nothing as of right from the estate— not even the home they lived in together'[368]. In a similar vein, Lord Lester of Herne Hill, when presenting the Cohabitation Bill to Parliament at the end of 2008, said it is 'a scandal in modern Britain that existing law does almost nothing to prevent such people from losing their home or sliding into poverty if their relationship breaks down or their partner dies'.

Other arguments are posited as reasons for reforming the law. One is that the law should keep up to date with changing social conditions and provide new rights for cohabitants, as cohabitation is increasingly popular and is predicted to increase even further in the future. Another argument is that the law of property, which cohabitants must use to determine property disputes, is unsatisfactory and their property rights should be determined by a family law, not a property law, regime. The drawbacks of the law of property were referred to by the Law Commission in its 2006 Consultation Paper[369] where it stated that in cohabitation cases the rules 'have proved to be relatively rigid and extremely difficult to apply, and their application can lead to what many would regard as unfairness between the parties.' The Law Commission said that any claim based on these rules was time-consuming and expensive and resulted in protracted hearings. It also said that the inherent uncertainty of the underlying principles made effective bargaining difficult to achieve as parties found it difficult to predict the outcome of contested litigation.

There are, however, arguments against reforming the law, such as that cohabitants can, if they wish, enter into a marriage or, if in a same-sex relationship, a civil partnership and thereby acquire the rights which attach to that status. One of the major arguments against reform is that it would

---

[367] The 'classic' case of unfairness which is often cited is that of *Burns v Burns* [1984] Ch 317 where the female cohabitant (she had taken her partner's name) failed on relationship breakdown to gain an interest under a trust in the home owned by her male partner, even though they had cohabited for nearly 20 years and she had looked after the house and brought up the children. Cf *Hammond v Mitchell* [1991] 1 WLR 1127 where the female cohabitant obtained an interest in the home under a trust on facts similar to those in *Burns*, except that a conversation she had had with her partner (even though brief and many years earlier) was held to be sufficient evidence of an inferred intention that she was to have a half-share.

[368] HL Debates, Column 2069, 12 December 2014.

[369] *Cohabitation: The Financial Consequences of Relationship Breakdown* (Law Com No 179, 2006).

undermine the autonomy of cohabitants, some of whom may have consciously chosen to cohabit in order to avoid the state imposing on them legal obligations which they do not wish to have. Deech,[370] for instance, is of the view that the autonomy and privacy of those who live together should be respected and that, rather than reforming the law, any disputes should be 'dealt with by the ordinary law of the land, of agreements, wills, property and so on'. She argues that any reform of the law degrades the emancipation of women and that any legal reform 'should build on cohabitants' autonomy rather than take it away'. Indeed, during the second reading debate of Lord Mark's Cohabitation Rights Bill in 2014, Baroness Deech told the House that the Bill 'is an attack on the liberty of two people who have refrained from marrying. Either they have good reasons not to—for example, preserving property from a previous relationship—or they are trying out the relationship before cementing it. It may well be that one of them would like to marry and the other holds back, but we do not have forced marriage in this country . . . it is illiberal to impose on couples an intrusive contractual obligation, not freely entered into, and it will encourage inherently more unstable relationships. We should encourage contracts between those who share property'.[371] Thus, this approach favours the use of cohabitation contracts and advocates that cohabitants be encouraged to make wills leaving their property to each other if that is what they wish.[372] In other words, Deech is in favour of maintaining the autonomy and contractual freedom of cohabitants, but ensuring that they know what their rights and remedies are.

Herring, on the other hand, is of the view that individual conceptions of autonomy 'are inconsistent with the realities of family life; are dissonant with how people understand their intimate lives; and work against the interests of women.'[373] Instead, he argues that a vision of autonomy is needed which recognises the interdependency and vulnerability of both children and adults within family relationships.[374] In a similar vein, speaking in favour of the Cohabitation Rights Bill 2014, Baroness Butler-Sloss said that she 'profoundly disagreed' with the view of Baroness Deech and others who opposed the Bill on the basis of respecting the autonomy of unmarried cohabitants. She correctly points out that the decision to avoid marriage may not reflect the mutual will of the parties, and may leave one party in a financially vulnerable position on relationship breakdown:

> marriage requires the consent of both parties, of an age and ability to make that consent. The freedom that is talked about is very often a freedom for one cohabitant but a sentence for the other, who is left on an inadequate income to cope with the children . . . It is important to remember that there is a major detriment to children from the parting of any couple. In my view, the detriment is as much from the parting of a couple who are not married as a couple who are, and, as I have already said, there is the added detriment that the mother may not have very much money and may not be able to get much from the father.[375]

This a strong argument, and it is worth remembering that the parties' autonomy can still be respected as any legal reform giving cohabitants new rights could include provisions allowing cohabitants to contract out of any new regime should they wish to do so.[376]

---

[370]　R. Deech, 'Cohabitation' [2010] Family Law 39.

[371]　HL Debates, Column 2073-2075, 12 December 2014.

[372]　Deech is also not in favour of the proposals providing for automatic inheritance on intestacy for cohabitants (see Law Commission Consultation Paper, *Intestacy and Family Provision* (Law Com CP No 191, 2009), Part 4).

[373]　J. Herring, 'Relational Autonomy in Family Law' in J. Wallbank, J. Herring, and S. Choudhry (eds), *Rights, Gender and Family Law* (Abingdon: Routledge, 2009), p 275.

[374]　See also L. Glennon, 'The Limitations of Equality Discourses on the Contours of Intimate Obligations' in J. Wallbank, J. Herring, and S. Choudhry (eds), *Rights, Gender and Family Law* (Abingdon: Routledge, 2009), pp 169–98.

[375]　HL Debates, Column 2079, 12 December 2014.

[376]　Provision was made for this in both the Law Commission's proposals for reform in 2007, the Cohabitation Bill in 2008, and the Cohabitation Rights Bill 2014–15 which is currently before the House of Lords.

Away from the autonomy argument, others point to statistics which suggest that unmarried relationships are more unstable and prone to breakdown, thus leading to negative outcomes for children of the relationship. Statistics show that unmarried couples account for more than half of all family breakdowns, even though they make up only one fifth of all couples with children.[377] This leads Harry Benson of the Marriage Foundation to conclude that 'we have an epidemic of family breakdown in this country because so few people realise how badly the odds of success are stacked against unmarried cohabitees'.[378] On this view, it is argued that in the interests of family stability and the economic well-being of children, the law should not encourage cohabitation and should instead take positive steps to promote the institution of marriage. This can be seen in recent Government policy. For example, Iain Duncan-Smith MP, the Secretary of State for Work and Pensions, said in a speech to the Marriage Foundation Conference in January 2014 that any government that was serious about tackling poverty and promoting a strong, cohesive society must seek to strengthen families, and the institution of marriage. He outlined the various steps that the Coalition Government have taken in this respect. This includes the introduction of a transferable tax allowance for married couples and civil partners from April 2015, which will reduce the annual tax bill of around 4 million such couples who pay the basic rate of tax by up to £200 a year. He justified such steps on the basis that 'there is something special about the commitment that marriage involves, which needs to be acknowledged publicly . . . the willingness to openly and actively plan for the future—in turn, promoting responsibility and stability in other aspects of the relationship and family life'.[379]

---

### The Law in Context

One cannot dispute that there is evidence to suggest that cohabiting relationships are more likely to break down[380] thus leading to negative outcomes for children.[381] However, is there a causal connection between a couple not getting married and eventual relationship breakdown? Or, are there other social and behavioural factors within these relationship which make them more prone to breakdown, irrespective of the fact that the parties did not marry. A recent study found that parents who are married differ from those who are cohabiting in very substantial ways, particularly relating to their ethnicity, education, and socio-economic status, and their history of relationship stability. In other words, 'couples that choose to marry in the first place will have different characteristics from those that choose to cohabit'.[382] The researchers suggest that it is these traits that are more likely to lead to the differences in outcomes between the children of married and unmarried parents, rather than the parents' formal marriage status itself.[383] If this is the case, then two points can be made. First, encouraging the parties to marry, rather than cohabit, may have no impact on the outcome of the relationship. Secondly, if there are particular features of cohabiting relationships which make them more prone to breakdown, then surely the law should provide greater legal protection on relationship breakdown and thus an adequate safety net to

---

[377] Marriage Foundation, Cohabiting couples will account for half of all family breakdown in 2013, 29 November 2013: http://www.marriagefoundation.org.uk/Web/News/News.aspx?news=152

[378] Ibid.

[379] Iain Duncan-Smith MP, Secretary of State for Work and Pensions, Speech to the Marriage Foundation Conference, 8 January 2014, https://www.gov.uk/government/speeches/marriage-foundation-conference

[380] See A. Goodman and E. Greaves, Institute for Fiscal Studies, Cohabitation, marriage and child outcomes, IFS Commentary C114 citing J. Ermisch, and C. Pronzato, 'Intra-household allocation of resources: inferences from non-resident fathers' child support payments' (2008) 118 Economic Journal 347–62 which uses evidence from the British Household Panel Survey that only around 35 per cent of children born into a cohabiting relationship will live with both parents until their 16th birthday, compared with 70 per cent of children born within a marriage.

[381] A recent study showed that the children of married parents do better than the children of cohabiting parents in a number of areas, particularly on measures of social and emotional development at the ages of three and five, A. Goodman and E. Greaves, Institute for Fiscal Studies, Cohabitation, marriage and child outcomes, IFS Commentary C114.

[382] Ibid.        [383] Ibid.

improve the economic outcomes for each of the parties and their children. As a consequence of this, it is suggested that it is misplaced optimism to think that using legal policy to simply divert couples away from unmarried cohabitation will have any impact on the prevalence of unmarried cohabitation, and resulting outcomes for the parties and any children.

As can be seen, reforming the law to give greater rights to unmarried cohabitants is a contentious issue, which attracts strong polarised opinions. Even if there were agreement on the need for reform, difficult policy issues would have to be decided upon. For example, how should the law define the terms 'cohabitants' or 'cohabitation' for the purpose of giving those who live together new rights and obligations. Should there be a minimum duration requirement and, if so, how long should the relationship have lasted; and should the fact the couple have children automatically bring them within the definition of cohabitants? As previously noted, the Cohabitation Rights Bill 2014–15 defines cohabitants as those couples who have lived together as a couple for two or more years, or have a child together.[384]

Another difficult policy issue is whether cohabitants who are eligible should have the same rights and remedies as married couples and civil partners on relationship breakdown. In other words, what should be the scope of any new rights? Should, for instance, cohabitants be entitled to maintenance, property orders, and a share of their partner's pension on relationship breakdown in the same way as spouses and civil partners? The Law Commission in its 2007 Report and the Cohabitation Bill 2008 took different approaches in respect of what entitlements cohabitants should have.

The Law Commission was against cohabitants having the same rights as divorcing couples as it would 'impose an equivalence with marriage which many people would find inappropriate' and which would be 'politically unattainable'.[385] The Law Commission therefore recommended a statutory discretionary regime for adjusting the property of cohabitants, although limited to addressing the need to adjust for any disadvantage or retained benefit arising from the relationship. There would be no power to order periodical payments as cohabitants do not necessarily give each other a commitment of future support.[386]

The Cohabitation Bill 2008, on the other hand, would have given cohabitants rights which were similar, although not identical, to those of married couples on divorce. Reforms in Australia and New Zealand have also given cohabitants virtually the same rights as married couples on relationship breakdown. Thus, in Australia[387] cohabiting couples (those who are able to prove according to various statutory criteria that they living in a '*de facto*' relationship) have rights equivalent to those of married couples on relationship breakdown, and which are similar to those which married couples have on divorce in England and Wales.[388] In New Zealand, 'relationship property' (home, chattels, post-relationship acquisitions) are shared equally after three years' cohabitation, subject to the parties contracting out.[389]

---

[384] The Cohabitation Bill 2008 originally defined cohabitants as persons who live together as a couple (opposite-sex or same-sex) for a continuous period of at least two years; or live together as a couple and are the parents of a minor child or have a joint residence order in respect of a child. However, the two-year requirement was later amended to five after debate in the House of Lords.

[385] See the Law Commission Report, paras 4.5–4.10.

[386] S. Bridge, 'Financial Relief for Cohabitants: How the Law Commission's Scheme would Work' [2007] Family Law 998 and S. Bridge, 'Financial Relief for Cohabitants: Eligibility, Opt-Out and Provision on Death' [2007] Family Law 1076. For criticism, see G. Douglas, J. Pearce, and H. Woodward, 'The Law Commission's Cohabitation Proposals: Applying them in Practice' [2008] Family Law 1076.

[387] Under the Family Law Amendment (De Facto Financial Matters and Other Measures) Act 2008, which amends the Family Law Act 1975, and which came into force in March 2008. See H. Baker, 'Family Law Down Under: Can the Old World Learn from the New?' [2009] International Family Law 165 (for an edited version of this article, see [2009] Family Law 1201).

[388] Under the MCA 1973, Pt II, see Chapter 4.          [389] See the Property (Relationships) Act 1976.

The provisions of the more recent Civil Partnerships Bill 2014–15 seek to implement the recommendations of the Law Commission. Under the Bill, where the parties have a child together or where they have lived together for two years, the court would have the power to make a 'Financial Settlement Order' providing certain conditions are met. Although in the interests of achieving a clean break between the parties, there is no provision for the payment of periodical payments (commonly known as maintenance) as is available to married couples under the Matrimonial Causes Act 1973. Thus, although the Bill would give cohabiting couples rights similar to those available for married couples, they are not as extensive. Some feel that, while a welcome attempt to give cohabiting couples greater legal protection, these provisions do not go far enough. The organisation Resolution, the body that represents family solicitors, points out that the provisions of Lord Marks' Bill does not include 'payments for child care costs to enable a primary carer parent to work. This is a major obstacle for separating cohabiting families and can be a factor in driving some into poverty and state dependence.'[390] As an alternative Resolution proposes a new cohabitation law which includes provision for time-limited maintenance.

Despite differing views about whether the law should be reformed to give cohabitants new rights, and the advantages and disadvantages of reforming the law, it is not disputed that cohabitants should have access to easily understandable information about their rights and remedies and about their lack of them compared with married couples, including the fact that there is no such thing as a 'common law marriage'. The Government's 'Living Together Campaign', launched in 2004, aimed to provide information and guidance for cohabitants,[391] and a survey conducted for the Ministry of Justice by Barlow, Burgoyne, and Smithson[392] found that those who used the Living Together Campaign's website were of the view that they had become better informed about their rights and obligations as cohabitants as a result of visiting it.

## 11.2 **Home-sharers**

Some people live together in informal relationships but are not cohabitants. Thus, some people live together as companions, or as friends, or because they have a family relationship.[393] Such 'home-sharers' may live together for different reasons. Some may live together because this is the only way they can afford to buy a house. Some may do so for companionate reasons, and others may live together to care for another person or a family member. Persons living in informal home-sharing relationships do not have those family law rights which are available to married couples and civil partners except in respect of protection from domestic violence when they can apply for remedies under Part IV of the Family Law Act 1996 in certain circumstances.[394] 'Home-sharers' can be vulnerable in the same was as cohabitants can be in respect of ownership of the home when the home-sharing arrangement comes to an end and also when the other home-sharer dies. They can also suffer tax disadvantages as the case of *Burden and Burden v UK*,[395] which follows, has shown. The Law Commission has considered whether the law should be changed to give home-sharers certain property rights, and in 2002 published a discussion paper[396] in which it discussed a

---

[390]  Resolution, Cohabitation Rights Bill goes to Committee Stage, 12 December 2014, http://www.resolution.org.uk/news-list.asp?page_id=228&n_id=259.

[391]  Its website (www.advicenow.org.uk/living-together) provides advice and guidance for cohabitants which explains what rights cohabitants have and how they differ from those of married couples.

[392]  See para 5, p 7, in A. Barlow, C. Burgoyne, and J. Smithson, *The Living Together Campaign: An Investigation of its Impact on Legally Aware Cohabitants* (Ministry of Justice, 2007).

[393]  See L. Glennon, 'Displacing the "Conjugal" Family in Legal Policy—A Progressive Move?' (2005) Child and Family Law Quarterly 17.

[394]  As associated persons, which includes persons who 'live or have lived in the same household, otherwise than merely by reason of one of them being the other's employee, tenant, lodger or boarder' and persons who are relatives (s 62(3)).

[395]  (App no 13378/05), [2008] 2 FLR 787.     [396]  *Sharing Homes: A Discussion Paper* (Law Com No 278).

'contribution-based' model of reform, but in which it came to the conclusion that this was unwork-able in practice and the discussion was taken no further.

---

### Key case

In the *Burden* case, two unmarried sisters (aged 90 and 82) considered that they were discriminated against in respect of inheritance tax under UK law as they did not have the same inheritance rights as same-sex couples even though they had lived together for the whole of their adult lives in the same home which they owned in their joint names. On the death of one of them, the survivor would be forced to sell the house to pay the 40 per cent inheritance tax owed on its value. After their claim failed before the English courts they took their case to the ECtHR, arguing that UK inheritance tax laws discriminated against them under Article 14 of the ECHR taken in conjunction with Article 1 of Protocol 1 to the Convention which provides that '[e]very natural or legal person is entitled to the peaceful enjoyment of his possessions'. They also argued that the Civil Partnership Act 2004 breached their human rights under the ECHR as it was discriminatory in that it gave rights to same-sex, but not opposite-sex, couples. Their claim failed. The Grand Chamber of the ECtHR held by 15 votes to 2 that there had been no violation of the Convention, as the UK had not exceeded the wide margin of appreciation afforded to it; and the difference of treatment for the purposes of the grant of inheritance tax exceptions was reasonably and objectively justified for the purpose of Article 14. It was of the view that any workable tax system was bound to create marginal situations and individual cases of apparent hardship or injustice; and it was up to national authorities to decide how to strike the right balance between raising revenue and pursuing social policy objectives.

---

The outcome of the decision in *Burden* was that the UK was justified in not treating siblings in the same way as married couples and civil partners for the purpose of inheritance tax, even though they had lived together for all their adult lives.[397] The UK was entitled to differentiate between marriage and other relationships in respect of tax. However, some commentators have been critical of the decision. Deech, for instance, considered it 'inequitable' that the Burden sisters, who had lived 'at least as companionably and interdependently as any two same sex partners' were denied any sort of benefits.[398] She referred to other carer situations, such as the child who looks after a parent and does not inherit, or if he or she inherits has to pay inheritance tax. Deech proposes that a 'sensible reform' would be 'to grant deferral of IHT to any two family members who are co-dependent and are within the prohibited degrees so that the option of civil partnership or marriage is not open to them.' Lord Lester's Cohabitation Bill[399] put before Parliament at the end of 2008 made provision for sibling home-sharers but the Bill went nowhere and there are currently no proposals for reform.

## Discussion Questions

1. Is the 'legal' family becoming more fragmented in the face of greater cohabitation between adults?
2. Compile the arguments for and against same-sex marriage.

---

[397]  See R. Auchmuty, 'Beyond Couples' (2009) 17 Feminist Legal Studies 205.

[398]  See R. Deech. 'Sisters Sisters—And Other Family Members' [2010] Family Law 375.

[399]  Lord Lester of Herne Hill introduced a Private Member's Bill in the House of Lords on 11 December 2008. See Chapter 5.

3. Do you agree with the view that legalising same-sex marriage reinforces the use of 'marriage' to confer rights and responsibilities within family law and that other ways of recognising relationships need to be found?

4. Should civil partnerships be made available to opposite-sex couples?

5. Is nullity a relevant remedy in the twenty-first century?

# Further Reading

AUCHMUTY, R., 'Beyond Couples' (2009) 17 Feminist Legal Studies 205

BAMFORTH, N., ' "The Benefits of Marriage in All But Name"? Same-Sex Couples and the Civil Partnership Act 2004' [2007] Child and Family Law Quarterly 133

BARKER, N., *Not the Marrying Kind: A Feminist Critique of Same-Sex Marriage* (London: Macmillan, 2012)

BARLOW, A., BURGOYNE, C., CLERY, E., and SMITHSON, J., *Cohabitation and the Law: Myths, Money and the Media*, British Social Attitudes 24th Report (London: Sage, 2008)

BARLOW, A., DUNCAN, S., JAMES, G., and PARK, A., *Cohabitation, Marriage and the Law: Social Change and Legal Reform in 21st Century Britain* (Oxford: Hart, 2005)

BESSANT, C., 'Transsexuals and Marriage after *Goodwin v United Kingdom*' [2003] Family Law 111

BRADNEY, A., 'Developing Human Rights? The Lords and Transsexual Marriages' [2003] Family Law 585

CRETNEY, S., *Same-Sex Relationships* (Oxford: Oxford University Press, 2006)

DIDUCK, A. and O'DONOVAN, K. (eds), *Feminist Perspectives on Family Law* (London: Routledge, 2007)

DUNCAN, S., BARLOW, A., and JAMES, G., 'Why Don't They Marry? Cohabitation, Commitment and DIY Marriage' [2005] Child and Family Law Quarterly 383

EEKELAAR, J., *Family Life and Personal Life* (Oxford: Oxford University Press, 2006)

EEKELAAR, J., and MACLEAN, M., 'Marriage and the Moral Bases of Personal Relationships' (2004) Journal of Law and Society 244

GILMORE, S., '*Bellinger v Bellinger*—Not Quite Between the Ears and Between the Legs—Transsexualism and Marriage in the Lords' (2003) 15(3) Child and Family Law Quarterly 295

GILMORE, S., 'The Gender Recognition Act 2004' [2004] Family Law 741

GILMORE, S. 'The Legal Status of Transsexual and Transgender Persons in England and Wales' in Scherpe, J.M., (ed), *The Legal Status of Transsexual and Transgender Persons* (Intersentia, 2014).

GLENNON, L., 'Displacing the Conjugal Family in Legal Policy—A Progressive Move?' (2005) 17(2) Child and Family Law Quarterly 141

GLENNON, L., 'Strategizing for the Future through the Civil Partnership Act' (2006) 33(2) Journal of Law and Society 244

GLENNON, L., 'The Limitations of Equality Discourses on the Contours of Intimate Obligations' in J. Wallbank, J. Herring, and S. Choudhry (eds), *Rights, Gender and Family Law* (Abingdon: Routledge, 2009), 169

GRANT BOWMAN, C., *Unmarried Couples, Law, and Public Policy* (Oxford: Oxford University Press, 2010)

PROBERT, R., 'When Are We Married? Void, Non-Existent and Presumed Marriages' (2002) Legal Studies 398

PROBERT, R., *The Changing Legal Regulation of Cohabitation* (Cambridge: Cambridge University Press, 2012)

PROBERT, R., 'The Evolving Concept of Non-marriage' (2013) 3 Child and Family Law Quarterly 314

PROUDMAN, C., 'The Criminalisation of Forced Marriage' (2012) 42 Family Law 460

Visit the Online Resource Centre at **www.oxfordtextbooks.co.uk/orc/gilmore_glennon5e/** for a range of further features including a detailed bibliography and self-test questions.

online
resource
centre

# 2

# The dissolution of adult relationships

## INTRODUCTION

This chapter deals with the termination of adult relationships, in particular divorce. It also considers the dissolution of civil partnerships, and the termination of cohabitation. The property and financial consequences of termination and arrangements for children on relationship breakdown are dealt with in other chapters in the book.

## 1 The law of divorce

### 1.1 A brief history of divorce

Divorce has only been generally available as a means of ending a marriage since the middle of the nineteenth century. Prior to that, the Ecclesiastical Courts could grant a decree *a mensa et thoro*, a decree which, like the current decree of judicial separation, relieved the parties of the duty to live together but did not terminate the marriage. For a very few couples, it was possible to end a marriage and thereby obtain the right to remarry, but this could only be achieved by means of a private Act of Parliament.[1] It was not until the Matrimonial Causes Act 1857 that a law of divorce applicable to the public at large was introduced.[2] This Act, and subsequent divorce legislation until 1969, was strictly fault-based.[3] Divorce law was built around the notion that one spouse was guilty of a matrimonial offence.[4] Parties were referred to as 'guilty' and 'innocent', and divorce was a remedy for a legal wrong. This conceptual base led to the inclusion in legislation, and the development by case law, of a legal infrastructure of rules and principles which often bore little relationship to the physical, mental, and emotional circumstances of marriage breakdown. The matrimonial offences were difficult to prove whether or not the petition was defended. Divorce was barred where the respondent had connived at the commission of the offence relied on. An attempt at reconciliation was regarded as condonation (evidence that a party approved of the divorce), which could also provide a defence to divorce. Thus, evidence that the parties were in agreement that divorce was the solution to their matrimonial difficulties resulted in the decree being denied on the ground of collusion, polarising the position of the parties. It led to spurious cases where the husband provided

---

[1] For discussion of the first ever divorce, see R. Probert, 'The *Roos* Case' in S. Gilmore, J. Herring, and R. Probert (eds), *Landmark Cases in Family Law* (Oxford: Hart, 2011).

[2] For an account of the history of the law of divorce, see L. Stone, *Road to Divorce* (Oxford: Oxford University Press, 1991).

[3] Matrimonial Causes Act 1923; Matrimonial Causes Act 1937.

[4] Between 1937 and 1969 the grounds for divorce were adultery, cruelty, desertion for a continuous period of three years or more, and incurable insanity on the part of the respondent. This last ground was the only concession to the notion that a marriage could be terminated despite there being no 'fault' by either party.

false evidence of adultery (often allegedly committed in a hotel), and to snooping and gross invasions of privacy in order to obtain evidence of adultery where this was denied. It prevented divorces where marriages had clearly broken down and it prevented spouses from making realistic attempts at reconciliation. In short, the law was out of touch with natural human responses to matrimonial difficulties and positively encouraged acrimony. It allowed the notion that one spouse was guilty and the other innocent to influence arrangements about the children, and it penalised sensible agreements arrived at by consent. Moreover, it made no provision for those persons who had left their spouses and formed a new family unit. It was impossible for such persons to marry for a second time where their first spouse refused to divorce them. By the middle of the twentieth century change was clearly long overdue.

In 1956 a Royal Commission, the Morton Commission,[5] published a report which advocated reform of the law and recommended the introduction of the concept of no-fault divorce. In 1966, a group appointed by the Archbishop of Canterbury published a report, *Putting Asunder*, which advocated that divorce should be based on a single concept, namely the irretrievable breakdown of the marriage. *Putting Asunder* recommended that in every case there should be a judicial enquiry to ensure that breakdown had really occurred and that no abuse of the system had taken place. *Putting Asunder* was followed shortly afterwards by a discussion paper issued by the Law Commission,[6] which similarly advocated proof of marital breakdown as the basis for dissolving a marriage, but recommended that this should be inferred from one or more of five specified facts. The law was amended in 1969 by the Divorce Reform Act 1969, which represented a compromise between the positions taken by the Archbishop of Canterbury's group and the Law Commission.

The underlying purpose of the reformed divorce law was:

(i) to buttress, rather than to undermine, the stability of marriage; and

(ii) when, regrettably, a marriage has irretrievably broken down, to enable the empty shell to be destroyed with the maximum fairness, and the minimum bitterness, distress and humiliation.[7]

Provisions were therefore introduced which were designed to assist parties to remain together and resolve their differences. Parties were no longer to be barred from petitioning if they continued to live together after a party committed adultery or after other behaviour which under the old law would have prevented them from obtaining a decree of divorce.[8] Some encouragement was given to parties to consider reconciliation rather than proceeding to a divorce. A solicitor acting for the petitioner would be obliged to file a certificate stating whether or not he or she had discussed reconciliation with the client or had given the client names and addresses of people qualified to help.[9] A court could adjourn the proceedings at any time if it appeared that there was a reasonable prospect of successful reconciliation.[10]

Parliament properly took the view that it would be wrong to liberalise divorce law without at the same time ensuring that dependent spouses were protected from suffering some of the more serious economic consequences of divorce.[11] Therefore, legislation was introduced, the Matrimonial

---

[5] *Royal Commission on Marriage and Divorce* (Cmd 9678, 1956).

[6] *Reform of the Grounds of Divorce: the Field of Choice* (Cmd 3123, 1966).     [7] Ibid, para 15.

[8] MCA 1973, s 2, although, in relation to adultery, s 2(1) creates a bar where the parties live together for longer than six months after the discovery of the adultery.

[9] MCA 1973, s 6(1).

[10] Section 6(2). It was subsequently established that these provisions had limited value, see the Booth Report (*Report of the Matrimonial Causes Procedure Committee*, Matrimonial Causes Procedure Committee, chaired by Hon Mrs Justice Booth (HMSO, 1985), paras 4.42–4.43; Law Com No 170, para 3.9; and G. Davis and M. Murch, *Grounds for Divorce* (Oxford: Clarendon Press, 1988), Ch 4.

[11] There was particular concern about the so-called 'Casanova's charter' provision, which enabled an 'innocent' spouse to be divorced against his or her will after the parties had lived apart for at least five years.

Proceedings and Property Act 1970, which gave the courts wide powers to make financial provision and property adjustment orders on the grant of a decree.[12] Implementation of the new law by the Divorce Reform Act 1969 was delayed and the two Acts came into force together. The 1969 Act and the 1970 Act were subsequently consolidated in the Matrimonial Causes Act (MCA) 1973, which remains the law today.

## 1.2 **Developments in divorce procedure**

Changes to the procedure for obtaining a divorce have been made over the years. At one time, all divorces, undefended and defended, were heard in London and only by senior judges. This was because divorce was considered a serious matter. Divorces were heard in open court with the petitioner giving oral evidence to prove the ground and fact alleged. This was not only distressing for the parties, but also costly and time-consuming. With the huge increase in divorces, particularly after the more liberal grounds for divorce were introduced by the Divorce Reform Act 1969, the courts became overloaded with divorces, even though undefended divorces were taking only a short time to be heard. Owing to these difficulties, a new procedure called the 'special procedure' was introduced in the 1970s with the aim of simplifying the divorce process, making it quicker and less costly. It was initially introduced, in 1973, for childless couples divorcing with consent, but in 1975 was extended to all childless couples, except those petitioning on the basis of unreasonable behaviour. In 1977 it was extended to all undefended divorces. All undefended divorces today are therefore dealt with by what is an essentially administrative procedure, a 'paper exercise' whereby the district judge in the divorce court examines the papers to establish whether the marriage has irretrievably broken down and whether the fact alleged in the divorce petition (eg adultery, behaviour etc) is proved and whether there is any reason for refusing to grant the divorce. A list of those petitioners who have satisfied the district judge that a decree nisi of divorce should be granted is drawn up and read out in open court, after which the district judge pronounces decrees nisi of divorce en bloc. If a divorce is undefended there is usually no need for the parties to attend court. Defended divorces, on the other hand, which are virtually non-existent because of the futility of doing so, are still heard in open court with the parties giving oral evidence.

From time to time, there has been discussion about reforming the divorce procedure. For instance in the 1980s, the Matrimonial Causes Act Committee, chaired by Hon Mrs Justice Booth (the 'Booth Committee')[13] was requested by the Government to look at the divorce procedure and to make recommendations for reform. The recommendations were not implemented, but the attempt at divorce reform in the Family Law Act 1996 included some of the Booth Committee's recommendations, such as changes of terminology to make divorce law more understandable.

## 1.3 **Trends in divorce**

---

### The Law in Context

Statistics show a sharp decline in the numbers of divorces. In 2013, the number of divorces in England and Wales was 114,720, a drop of 2.9 per cent since 2012.[14] There was a sharp decline in the number of divorces between 2003 and 2009, and a 4.9 per cent increase in divorces in 2010. The number of divorces remained stable until 2012 before falling again in 2013.[15] The likelihood of a marriage ending in divorce has increased over the years. 20 per cent of marriages in 1968 had ended in divorce by the 15th wedding

---

[12] See Chapter 4.

[13] See *Report of the Matrimonial Causes Procedure Committee*, Matrimonial Causes Procedure Committee, chaired by Hon Mrs Justice Booth (HMSO, 1985).

[14] Office for National Statistics, Divorces in England and Wales 2013 (London: 2015).      [15] Ibid.

anniversary, whereas 32 per cent of marriages in 1998 had ended after the same period of time. In 2011, it was estimated that 42 per cent of all marriages end in divorce.[16]

In 2013, there were 9.8 men divorcing per thousand married males and 9.8 women divorcing per thousand married females.[17] The average age of those who divorce has risen over the years and in 2012 the number of divorces was highest amongst men and women aged 40 to 44. Since 1985, the mean ages for divorce have risen for both men and women, figures which partly reflect the rise in the age at which people marry. In 2013, the mean age of men divorcing was 45.1 years, and the mean age of women divorcing was 42.6 years.[18]

The median duration of marriage for divorces granted in 2013 was 11.7 years. This is an increase from 1985 where the median duration of marriage for divorces granted in that year was 8.9 years. Since 1985 the median duration of marriage increased steadily up to 2005 but has remained relatively stable since.[19]

Many divorces involve persons who have had a previous divorce. In 2013, 19 per cent of men and women divorcing had their previous marriage end in divorce, a proportion which has almost doubled since 1980 when the comparable figures were 10 per cent.

48 per cent of couples divorcing in 2013 had at least one child aged under 16. There were 94,864 children aged under 16 who were in families where the parents divorced in 2013, a decrease of 38 per cent from 2003 when there were 153,088 children.[20] These changes may reflect the increasing proportion of children born to cohabiting rather than married couples.[21]

More divorces are brought by and granted to wives (66 per cent of divorces in 2013); and for all divorces the behaviour of the respondent is the most common fact relied on for divorce.[22]

The number of civil partnership dissolutions in England and Wales increased by 20 per cent to 974 dissolutions in 2013.[23] It is predicted that the number of dissolutions is likely to fall due to the introduction of same-sex marriage from March 2014.

## 2 Obtaining a divorce

### 2.1 Jurisdiction to hear a divorce

#### Key legislation

The rules governing the jurisdiction of the courts in England and Wales to hear a divorce (and annulment and judicial separation) are laid down in section 5 of the Domicile and Matrimonial Proceedings Act 1973, as amended by Council Regulation (EC) No 2201/2003 Concerning Jurisdiction and the Recognition and Enforcement of Judgments in Matrimonial Matters and in Matters of Parental Responsibility ('Brussels II Revised'). Section 5(2) of the Domicile and Matrimonial Proceedings Act 1973 sets out, with reference to Brussels II, the circumstances when the courts have jurisdiction to entertain proceedings for divorce.

These jurisdictional rules are complex, but in very general terms the courts in England and Wales have jurisdiction in divorce proceedings if either spouse is domiciled in England or Wales when the proceedings are begun, or is habitually resident in England or Wales throughout the period of one year ending with the date on which proceedings are

---

[16] Ibid.    [17] Ibid.    [18] Ibid.    [19] Ibid.
[20] Ibid.    [21] Ibid.    [22] Ibid.    [23] Ibid.

begun.[24] The issue of jurisdiction can be complex and may involve difficult questions, for instance about domicile.[25]

Establishing whether England and Wales has jurisdiction to hear a divorce is particularly important for parties in 'big money' cases, because if a decree of divorce is granted by the divorce court in England and Wales then the courts in England and Wales also have jurisdiction to make property and finance orders on divorce under Part II of the MCA 1973.[26] Because the divorce courts in England and Wales have wide discretionary powers to make property and financial orders depending on the circumstances of the case and exercise an approach based on fairness and equality,[27] some parties to a marriage, particularly those where there are substantial property assets to distribute, are keen to divorce in England and Wales. In 'big money' international cases, the parties may compete with each other to have their case heard in the country whose court will give them the more favourable award. Thus, even though it is time-consuming and expensive, parties to 'international' marriages will sometimes engage in what is called 'forum shopping' and there will be a race between the parties so that one of them (usually the wife) can win the race and have the divorce dealt with in London or in another part of England and Wales. Such disputes are not about which jurisdiction is the better one for obtaining the actual divorce, but about which jurisdiction will provide a better finance and property award on divorce. The former President of the Family Division, Sir Mark Potter, in a postscript to his decision in *Charman v Charman*[28] drew attention to this: 'Thus, in very big money cases, the effect of the decision in *White* was to raise the aspirations of the claimant hugely. In big money cases the *White* factor has more than doubled the levels of award and it has been said by many that London has become the divorce capital of the world for aspiring wives'.

---

### Key case

Attempts by the husband and wife to hear their cases in different jurisdictions were the subject of the litigation, for example, in *Golubovich v Golubovich*,[29] which provides an example of how parties are willing to engage in complex and costly jurisdictional disputes in order to gain a financial advantage on divorce. In this case, the husband (who came from a hugely wealthy Russian family) and his Russian wife had lived in London following their marriage. On marriage breakdown, he invoked the jurisdiction of the Russian courts and she the jurisdiction of the English courts. It was therefore a question of which court had priority to hear their divorce. The husband won the race to the divorce decree but, it appeared, by allegedly forging documents. The English court subsequently made a '*Hemain* injunction'[30] precluding him from

---

[24] In *Mark v Mark* [2005] UKHL 42, [2005] 2 FLR 1193 the House of Lords held that, for the purpose of jurisdiction to entertain a divorce petition under s 5(2) of the Domicile and Matrimonial Proceedings Act 1973, residence in England and Wales need not be lawful residence. Thus a person can be habitually resident or domiciled in England and Wales even if his or her presence in the UK is a criminal offence under the Immigration Act 1971.

[25] See eg *Munro v Munro* [2007] EWHC 3315 (Fam), [2008] 1 FLR 1613 where Bennett J had to decide whether the wife should be allowed to petition for divorce in England and Wales even though she and her husband had moved to Spain shortly after marrying in England. On the facts, Bennett J held that the English court had jurisdiction.

[26] See Chapter 4.

[27] See *White v White* [2001] 1 AC 596 where the House of Lords held that fairness and non-discrimination were the principles to be applied by the courts in ancillary relief proceedings on divorce and that the court should apply a 'yardstick of equality' and not just make an award limited to the reasonable needs of the applicant. After *White*, in big money cases, wives in particular were successful in gaining a much bigger share of the matrimonial assets on divorce than had hitherto been the case, as the court was no longer restricted to making an order that merely satisfied their reasonable needs. See Chapter 4 on finance and property on divorce.

[28] [2007] EWCA Civ 503 at [116]. See Chapter 4 on finance and property on divorce.

[29] [2010] EWCA Civ 810.

[30] This is an 'anti-suit' injunction requiring a person not to take steps to bring proceedings in another jurisdiction.

taking any further steps in the Russian courts to have his divorce decided there. However, despite being aware of the injunction, the Russian court, on his application, granted him a divorce. The wife thereupon sought an order in the English court asking for the Russian divorce decree to be refused recognition in England and Wales. She was successful at first instance but the Court of Appeal allowed the husband's appeal, holding that the Russian court had found itself with jurisdiction to dissolve the marriage and, absent any treaty with the jurisdiction of England and Wales, the Russian court had found itself unfettered by the existence of the *Hemain* injunction.

## 2.2 Staying divorce proceedings in England and Wales

In connection with jurisdiction, the divorce courts in England and Wales have jurisdiction to stay proceedings for divorce if they consider the matter would be better dealt with in another jurisdiction. Thus, if divorce proceedings are pending in a country outside England and Wales, then, under the Domicile and Matrimonial Proceedings Act 1973,[31] the divorce courts in England and Wales have a discretionary jurisdiction to stay the English divorce proceedings which they will usually do if they consider the foreign court to be the more appropriate forum for hearing the divorce.[32] With regard to EU divorces, even though Brussels II governs the jurisdiction of divorces in England and Wales, a party to a marriage can nevertheless apply for a stay of the English proceedings under the Domicile and Matrimonial Proceedings Act 1973.[33]

## 2.3 Divorce under the Matrimonial Causes Act 1973

The current law governing the substantive law of divorce is set out in Part I of the MCA 1973, and the rules governing divorce procedure are laid down in the Family Procedure Rules 2010. Part II of the 1973 Act deals with property and financial matters on divorce, which are discussed in detail in Chapter 4. Other statutory provisions apply to disputes about children on divorce, whether it be about residence, contact, or child maintenance.[34]

### 2.3.1 The ground for divorce

### Key legislation

Under section 1(1) of the MCA 1973, irretrievable breakdown of marriage is the sole ground for divorce, but irretrievable breakdown is only established on proof of at least one of the five facts listed in section 1(2) of the Act.[35] Section 1(2) provides as follows:

The court hearing a petition for divorce shall not hold the marriage to have broken down irretrievably unless the petitioner satisfies the court of one or more of the following facts, that is to say—

(a) that the respondent has committed adultery and the petitioner finds it intolerable to live with the respondent;

(b) that the respondent has behaved in such a way that the petitioner cannot reasonably be expected to live with the respondent;

---

[31] See Domicile and Matrimonial Proceedings Act 1973, s 5(6) and Sch 1, para 9(1).
[32] See eg *S v S (Divorce: Staying Proceedings)* [1997] 2 FLR 100 (and see *JKN v JCN* [2010] EWHC 843 (Fam)).
[33] See *JKN v JCN* [2010] EWHC 843 (Fam).       [34] See Chapters 9 and 6.
[35] In discussions leading up to the current law of divorce, it was recognised by the Law Commission and accepted by Parliament that it would be impossible for courts to adjudicate on the individual circumstances of every marriage to establish whether the marriage had irretrievably broken down. Hence the introduction of the five facts.

(c) that the respondent has deserted the petitioner for a continuous period of at least two years immediately preceding the presentation of the petition;

(d) that the parties to the marriage have lived apart for a continuous period of at least two years immediately preceding the presentation of the petition . . . and the respondent consents to a decree being granted;

(e) that the parties to the marriage have lived apart for a continuous period of at least five years immediately preceding the presentation of the petition.

---

### Summary

These five facts are commonly referred to as the 'grounds' for divorce, when, technically speaking, there is only one ground for divorce, irretrievable breakdown of the marriage. However, both irretrievable breakdown *and* at least one of the five facts must be proved,[36] requirements which have provoked criticism, and have caused some rather strange decisions in the earlier case law.[37]

---

In Section 2.3.3 we examine in some detail how the five facts have been judicially interpreted. Before doing so, however, it is convenient to outline some procedural matters relating to obtaining a divorce.

### 2.3.2 Divorce procedure

The divorce petition is the key document in the divorce proceedings, as it informs the respondent and the court of the basis on which the petitioner is seeking the divorce and of any orders that he or she will be seeking as part of the divorce. It must contain specified information,[38] and also a statement that the marriage has broken down and brief particulars of the fact(s) relied on. The petition must conclude with a prayer for dissolution of the marriage, any claim for costs, and a prayer setting out any claims for property and finance orders and any child support maintenance claimed. To begin proceedings, the petition, and other required documents, must be presented to a divorce county court (or the Principal Registry in London).[39]

#### 2.3.2.1 The one-year bar on petitions

A petition for divorce cannot be presented within the first year of marriage.[40] This is an absolute bar. In other words, there is no discretion to waive or reduce the time limit, however extreme a petitioner's case. But, despite the one-year bar, a petition can be based on matters which occurred during the first year of marriage,[41] such as any evidence of adultery or unreasonable behaviour.

#### 2.3.2.2 Encouraging reconciliation

One of the policy objectives of the law of divorce is to encourage the saving of saveable marriages and in order to promote this objective, certain provisions in Part I of the MCA 1973 encourage

---

[36] Section 1(4).

[37] See eg *Richards v Richards* [1972] WLR 1073 and *Buffery v Buffery* [1988] 2 FLR 365, where in both cases the Court of Appeal found that the marriage had irretrievably broken down but that the fact alleged ('unreasonable behaviour') had not been satisfied.

[38] See the Family Procedure Rules (FPR) 2010 and the supporting notes to the divorce petition.

[39] The marriage certificate, the Statement of Arrangements for the Children, certified copies of any court orders, and any certificate in respect of public funding.

[40] MCA 1973, s 3(1).

[41] Ibid, s 3(2). In the law prior to the current law there was as a bar on divorce in the first three years of marriage, unless a party could prove exceptional hardship on the part of the petitioner or depravity on the part of the respondent. There is no bar in respect of nullity proceedings; a petition for nullity can be sought at any time after a marriage.

reconciliation. Thus, the court can adjourn divorce proceedings at any stage if there is a reasonable possibility of a reconciliation being effected between the parties;[42] and certain periods of resumed cohabitation are ignored when establishing whether a fact is proved in order to satisfy the court that the marriage has irretrievably broken down.[43] If a solicitor is acting in the proceedings, then a reconciliation certificate must be filed with the court stating whether or not the solicitor has discussed with the client the possibility of a reconciliation and has given the client details of persons qualified to help effect a reconciliation.[44] The solicitor is not obliged to discuss reconciliation with the client.[45]

Divorce involves a two-stage procedure: a decree nisi followed by a decree absolute.[46] The marriage is not terminated until the grant of decree absolute, which is automatically granted on the application of the petitioner who can apply for it six weeks or later after the grant of decree nisi. If the petitioner fails to apply, the respondent can do so after three months have passed from the earliest day on which the petitioner could apply,[47] but the decree cannot be granted without a hearing by a judge or district judge.[48] If no application has been made after 12 months, the court may require the applicant to provide evidence accounting for the delay. The court then has discretion whether to make the decree absolute or to rescind it altogether. These rules are strict; a decree absolute obtained in breach of the rules is void.[49] When a divorce is sought on either of the separation grounds, a decree absolute can be refused if the respondent has not been satisfactorily financially provided for by the petitioner.[50]

The period between decree nisi and decree absolute can be used to sort out outstanding issues relating to financial and property matters and children, but there is no requirement that these should be resolved before the divorce is finalised. The purpose of the gap between decree nisi and decree absolute is to enable a respondent to appeal and for the Queen's Proctor and other persons to show just cause why the decree should not be made absolute.[51] Intervention by the Queen's Proctor is rare, but was more common under the 'old' law when a decree could be refused if the parties had colluded in obtaining the divorce, for instance by fabricating adultery.[52] If a decree nisi is issued but there is a delay in the application for the decree absolute, the court may rescind the decree nisi. In *Kim v Morris*[53] the wife issued a petition for divorce in 2006. However, the parties reconciled and cohabited for four years after the decree nisi was issued. When the relationship subsequently broke down the wife sought to conclude the divorce proceedings and applied for the decree nisi to be made absolute. Parker J refused the wife's application and rescinded the decree nisi. The wife had to start proceedings again and petition for a new decree.

As one of the policy objectives of divorce law is to protect the interests of children, if there are children under 16, or over 16 but receiving higher education or training, then the divorce cannot be made absolute until the judge[54] is satisfied with the arrangements for the children as set down in the Statement of Arrangements for the Children, a form containing specified information and which must be submitted to the court with the divorce petition.[55] The purpose of the 'Statement' is

---

[42] Section 6(2).        [43] See Section 2.3.3.2.3.        [44] See FPR 2010, r 7.6.        [45] MCA 1973, s 6(1).

[46] A decree nisi may be rescinded by the court if both spouses agree to this and are of sound mind (see eg *S v S (Rescission of Decree Nisi: Pension Sharing Provision)* [2002] 1 FLR 457, where the parties wished to do so in order that they could be subject to the new legislation on pensions which had just come into force).

[47] MCA 1973, s 9(2)).        [48] See FPR 2010, r 7.33.        [49] See *Dennis v Dennis* [2000] 2 FLR 231.

[50] See Section 2.3.4.        [51] MCA 1973, s 8.

[52] See *Bhaiji v Chauhan (Queen's Proctor Intervening)* [2003] 2 FLR 485 where the Queen's Proctor intervened and opposed the grant of decrees absolute in cases where bogus allegations of unreasonable behaviour had been made to obtain divorces in respect of five marriages which had been entered into solely for the purpose of circumventing the immigration rules.

[53] [2012] EWHC 1103 (Fam).

[54] The word 'judge' is used here, but in practice it is usually a district judge who hears divorces.

[55] The Statement of Arrangements for the Children (Form D8A) must include details relating to the child's home, education and training, care, child maintenance, contact, and health. The form is available on the HM Courts Service website.

to enable the court to fulfil its duty under section 41(1) of the MCA 1973 which requires the judge to consider whether, in light of the actual or proposed arrangements made for the children, the court should exercise any of its powers under the Children Act 1989 with respect to them. If the court is satisfied with the arrangements, the judge will certify to that effect. If not, he or she can direct that further evidence be filed, or order a welfare report under section 7 of the Children Act 1989, or order the parent(s) to attend court. If the child's welfare requires it, and the court is not able to exercise any of its powers under the Children Act 1989 without further consideration of the case, the judge can exceptionally direct that the decree of divorce should not be made absolute.[56] In practice this rarely happens.

In the case of undefended divorces (virtually all divorces because of the futility of defending a divorce), there is usually no need for the parties or their legal representatives to attend court. The judge may request further information or evidence, if needed. The judge, sitting in private in the divorce court, scrutinises the divorce application and, if satisfied that the ground is made out, files a certificate to that effect, and a date, time, and place are fixed for the judge to pronounce decree nisi. Both parties receive a certificate and notice of the date and place for the pronouncement, which takes place in open court, but which neither the parties nor their legal representatives need attend. The process of pronouncement of decree nisi is a mere formality. The decrees are listed together in batches and collectively read out by the clerk of the court (or by the judge), with the judge pronouncing decrees nisi orally or by nodding.

Defended divorces begin in the same way as an undefended divorce, but the respondent will indicate in the Acknowledgement of Service his or her intention to defend the divorce. Once various notice requirements have been satisfied,[57] there is an exchange of pleadings and the hearing takes place in open court with the parties giving oral evidence and with there being cross-examination of the parties.[58]

### 2.3.3 The five facts in section 1(2)

#### 2.3.3.1 Adultery by the respondent and intolerability

A petition based on adultery must establish that the respondent has committed adultery *and* that the petitioner finds it intolerable to live with the respondent.[59] A petitioner cannot rely on his or her own adultery. The requirement of intolerability was added to buttress the stability of marriage, one of the policy aims of the law, so that adultery on its own would not be sufficient to terminate a marriage. Adultery involves a voluntary act of sexual intercourse between a married person and another person not being married to him or her and who is of the opposite sex, and who may or may not be married.[60] Thus, homosexual intercourse will not constitute adultery but may be regarded as unreasonable behaviour under section 1(2)(b).

Adultery may be proved in a number of ways. The Acknowledgment of Service form used in relation to petitions based on adultery asks the question: 'Do you admit the adultery alleged in the petition?' If the respondent answers 'Yes', and signs the form, that is sufficient proof. Where the respondent does not admit the adultery, and fails to file an answer, the petitioner will have to prove the adultery in other ways, such as by providing evidence that the respondent is living with another person.

In addition to adultery, the petitioner must also prove that he or she finds it intolerable to live with the respondent. The intolerability need not follow from the adultery,[61] but it may well be the adultery which makes living with the respondent intolerable. The test to be applied when establishing intolerability is subjective,[62] in other words it depends on the petitioner's view of the matter.

---

[56] Section 41(2).  [57] See FPR 2010, Pt 6.
[58] For a rare case involving a defended divorce, see *Hadjimilitis (Tsavliris) v Tsavliris (Divorce: Irretrievable Breakdown)* [2003] 1 FLR 81.
[59] Section 1(2)(a).  [60] *Dennis v Dennis* [1955] P 153.  [61] See *Cleary v Cleary* [1974] 1 All ER 498.
[62] *Goodrich v Goodrich* [1971] 2 All ER 1340.

To encourage reconciliation, one of the policy objectives of divorce, if the parties continue living together for a period of up to six months after the discovery of the adultery this period must be disregarded in determining whether the petitioner finds it intolerable to live with the respondent.[63] However, if the parties live together for a period in excess of six months after the discovery of adultery then this operates as a complete bar to the presentation of a petition based on adultery.[64]

### 2.3.3.2 Behaviour by the respondent

The petitioner must prove, in addition to establishing irretrievable breakdown of the marriage, that 'the respondent has behaved in such a way that the petitioner cannot reasonably be expected to live with the respondent'.[65] The Court of Appeal had held that behaviour can take the form of an act or an omission.[66]

---

**Summary**

This fact is often referred to colloquially as 'unreasonable behaviour', but this is not strictly correct. Rather, it is a question of whether the respondent's behaviour is such that it is unreasonable for this *petitioner* to continue living with the respondent, not whether the respondent's behaviour is unreasonable per se. Thus, the court can take the parties' personalities into account to decide whether any right-thinking person would consider whether this particular petitioner could reasonably be expected to continue to live with the respondent.[67]

---

The respondent's behaviour is the most commonly alleged ground for divorce.[68] This is regrettable, since the policy of terminating a marriage with the minimum bitterness, distress, and humiliation is undermined when either party sets out to prove the behaviour fact. Petitions often contain a catalogue of incidents in support of the allegation so that they add up cumulatively to sufficient behaviour to satisfy the court. Also, because of its pejorative connotations, a petition based on behaviour may be hotly contested in respect of ancillary matters. Allegations of behaviour may make settlement more difficult which is often contrary to the best interests of the parties and any children. As long ago as 1985, the Booth Committee, which was asked by the Government to look at divorce procedure with a view to reform, found that allegations of unreasonable behaviour made it worse for the parties and their children. Those findings still hold good today, perhaps even more so, as since 1985 there has been an even greater emphasis on the parties to divorce settling matters in a civilised and non-hostile way and with solicitors having an obligation to deal with family matters in a conciliatory way.[69] In its Report, the Booth Committee stated:[70]

> We are satisfied that the bitterness and unhappiness of divorcing couples is frequently exacerbated and prolonged by the fault element in divorce and that this is particularly so where the fact relied upon is behaviour, whether or not the suit is defended. Great hostility and resentment may be generated by the recital in the petition of allegations of behaviour, often exaggerated and

---

[63] Section 2(2).     [64] Section 2(1). See *Kim v Morris* [2012] EWHC 1103 (Fam).     [65] Section 1(2)(b).

[66] *Katz v Katz* [1972] 1 WLR 955.     [67] *Birch v Birch* [1992] 1 FLR 564.

[68] For example, in over half of the cases where the divorce was granted to the wife in 2013, the husband's behaviour was the fact proven. Office for National Statistics, *Divorces in England and Wales 2013* (London: 2015).

[69] Members of Resolution (an association of family lawyers) adhere to a Code of Practice which requires them to 'see the advantages of a constructive and non-confrontational approach as a way of resolving differences' (r 2). The principles of the Code have been adopted by the Law Society as rules of good practice for family law solicitors generally (see the *Family Law Protocol*, 2nd edn (2006), Appendix 2).

[70] *Report of the Matrimonial Causes Procedure Committee*, para 2.8, under the chairmanship of Hon Mrs Justice Booth (HMSO, 1985).

sometimes stretching back over many years, to the extent that no discussion can take place between the parties or any agreement be reached on any matter relating to their marriage or their children.

'Unreasonable behaviour' can cover a wide range of behaviour and be of varying degrees of severity. In some cases, a single serious incident of behaviour may be sufficient to establish the petitioner's case. However, it is important to appreciate that the focus is not on the gravity of the behaviour per se but on its impact on the petitioner. An accumulation of trivial incidents may suffice.[71] There must, however, be some behaviour from which the court can conclude that the petitioner cannot reasonably be expected to live with the respondent, and more than a mere drifting apart of the parties. In *Buffery v Buffery*,[72] for instance, a decree was denied where the wife alleged that her husband was insensitive and never took her out, and that they had nothing to talk about and nothing in common after their children had grown up and left home.

In some circumstances, conduct which is not actually directed at the marriage itself, but which has a serious effect on the petitioner, will be sufficient. Thus, a conviction for a serious criminal offence would undoubtedly give the petitioner the facts on which to base a petition, but minor acts of violence might require more than one incident to satisfy the court. Behaviour such as drunkenness, alcoholism, and drug addiction are frequently relied on by petitioners. Causing financial difficulties can constitute unreasonable behaviour,[73] and so may even a failure to finish 'DIY' jobs over a long period.[74]

### 2.3.3.2.1 *The test under section 1(2)(b)*

The question to be asked under section 1(2)(b) is: 'Can this particular petitioner be expected to live with this particular respondent?'[75]

---

**Key case**

When considering the subsection in *Ash v Ash*[76] Bagnall J stated:

> Can this petitioner, with his or her character and personality, with his or her faults and other attributes, good and bad, and having regard to his or her behaviour during the marriage reasonably be expected to live with the respondent?

In *O'Neill v O'Neill* the Court of Appeal endorsed Dunn J's formulation of the test in *Livingstone-Stallard v Livingstone-Stallard*:[77]

---

[71] As they did in *Livingstone-Stallard* [1974] Fam 47 where Dunn J held that the wife 'was subjected to a constant atmosphere of criticism, disapproval and boorish behaviour on the part of her husband'.

[72] [1988] 2 FLR 365.

[73] See *Carter-Fea v Carter-Fea* [1987] Family Law 131 where the wife complained that her husband was incapable of managing his own affairs, and she was faced with mounting debt due to his failure to take any action in response to his financial difficulties. She was held to be entitled to a decree of divorce.

[74] As it did in *O'Neill v O'Neill* [1975] 1 WLR 1118 where the husband's DIY behaviour caused the wife so much stress that her health suffered. The final straw was when his renovation work on their bungalow involved mixing cement on the living room floor and leaving the lavatory door off for eight months. He had also written to the wife's solicitors casting doubt on the paternity of the children which the Court of Appeal thought of itself was sufficient to establish the ground alleged.

[75] *Birch v Birch* [1992] 1 FLR 564.     [76] [1972] 1 All ER 582.

[77] [1974] Fam 47. The test in *Livingstone-Stallard* was approved by the Court of Appeal in *O'Neill v O'Neill* (n 71); and endorsed by the Court of Appeal in *Buffery v Buffery* [1988] 2 FLR 365. See also *Birch v Birch* [1992] 1 FLR 564.

> would any right-thinking person come to the conclusion that the husband has behaved in such a way that this wife cannot reasonably be expected to live with him, taking into account the whole of the circumstances and the characters and personalities of the parties?
>
> These judicial statements show how the test for behaviour combines both an objective and a subjective approach.

It is objective in that the court must decide whether the petitioner can *reasonably* be expected to live with the respondent, but the essence of section 1(2)(b) is subjective in its focus on the parties concerned.

### 2.3.3.2.2 Behaviour arising through illness

Cases involving illness, particularly mental illness, have posed problems for the courts as they have had to grapple with the difficulty of deciding whether to grant a decree where a respondent is not morally responsible for his or her behaviour. Whilst it is generally accepted that marriage entails taking on certain obligations, including the burden of illness, the court will recognise the strain that illness can impose on the other spouse. The courts have made it clear that granting a decree of divorce does not necessarily involve blameworthiness.

> ### Key case
>
> In *Thurlow v Thurlow*[78] Rees J held that, in cases involving illness, the court must take into account:
>
> all the circumstances including the disabilities and temperaments of both parties, the causes of the behaviour and whether the causes were or were not known to the petitioner, the presence or absence of intention, the impact of it on the petitioner and the family unit, its duration, and the prospects of cure or improvement in the future.

Each case depends on its facts, and a divorce may be granted even though the respondent is not responsible for his or her own behaviour, particularly if the behaviour is serious or harmful. In *Katz v Katz*[79] despite making allowances for the husband's manic depression, the impact on his wife was held to be sufficiently serious to justify granting her a decree. She was so distressed by the situation that she had attempted suicide. But in *Richards v Richards*[80] where the husband was very moody, sat staring into space, and had assaulted the wife on two occasions (one incident was very trivial), the court held that this was not sufficient for granting a decree.

### 2.3.3.2.3 Living together after the behaviour

Where a petitioner continues to live with the respondent for a period of up to six months after the date of the last incident of behaviour relied on in the petition, this period must be disregarded by the court when determining whether the petitioner can reasonably be expected to live with the respondent.[81] The aim of this provision is to facilitate a reconciliation between the parties. Where the period of living together exceeds six months, the court must take it into account, but this does not provide an automatic bar to the granting of a decree. It depends on the facts of the case.

### 2.3.3.3 Desertion for two years by the respondent

To establish desertion under section 1(2)(c), the respondent must have deserted the petitioner for a continuous period of at least two years immediately preceding the presentation of the petition.

---

[78] [1975] 2 All ER 979 at 988.    [79] [1972] 1 WLR 955.    [80] [1972] 3 All ER 695.    [81] Section 2(3).

Desertion occurs where one spouse abandons the other spouse and leaves the household[82] with the intention of not returning. In practice, desertion is rarely used as a fact because the petitioner will normally use the two years' separation fact if the respondent consents to the divorce. Therefore a petitioner will only need to use this fact where the deserting spouse refuses to consent to a divorce and has not behaved in such a way as to enable the petitioner to petition under either section 1(2) (a) or (b).

Desertion requires the following to be proved:

— factual separation;
— an intention to desert on the part of the respondent;
— no consent by the petitioner to the desertion; and
— no just cause to desert.

The first element, the parties' physical separation, is most obviously established by one spouse leaving the family home. However, the parties can still be regarded as separated even if they are still living under the one roof if one spouse has deliberately retreated from the common household. In *Pulford v Pulford*,[83] desertion was described as 'not the withdrawal from a place, but from a state of things'. Thus desertion can be established where there is a total cessation of cohabitation between the parties, even though they remain living under the same roof. In *Hopes v Hopes*,[84] Denning LJ said that a husband who 'shuts himself up in one or two rooms of his house, and ceases to have anything to do with his wife, is living separately and apart from her as effectively as if they were separated by the outer door of a flat'.[85] To satisfy this test, however, the parties must be living separate lives under one roof and no longer operating as one household but two.

The second element requires the deserting spouse to intend to leave the marriage permanently and not to be absent for any other reason such as work commitments, holiday, or imprisonment. Where the parties are forcibly absent from one another, for example because the respondent is in prison, or on a posting abroad, or where the parties agree to separate, that will not normally amount to desertion, unless evidence can be brought to show that the respondent intended to have nothing more to do with the petitioner.[86] The third element requires it to be shown that the innocent spouse does not consent to the desertion.[87] Finally, there must be no justification for the deserting party's absence from the marriage.[88] In circumstances where the behaviour of the non-deserting spouse (ie, the spouse left behind) can be called into question, 'constructive' desertion may be possible. This occurs when a spouse is physically forced out of the household or feels compelled to leave because of the respondent's actions.[89] In these circumstances it is not the party who leaves the household who is in desertion, but his or her spouse whose actions have resulted in the former's absence. To establish constructive desertion, the petitioner must show that the respondent's behaviour was sufficiently serious to drive him or her out. In *Lang v Lang*, Lord Porter said that the course of conduct leading to one spouse leaving must be 'grave and convincing'.[90]

Desertion can come to an end in various ways, for example by a spouse moving back into the home or by the parties agreeing to separate. In order to encourage reconciliation, a period of up to six months' cohabitation does not terminate the desertion, but the period of failed reconciliation must be added on to the two years required to establish desertion.[91]

---

[82] See *Hopes v Hopes* [1949] P 227.     [83] [1923] P 18.     [84] [1949] P 227.     [85] Ibid, 235.
[86] See *Nutley v Nutley* [1970] 1 WLR 217.     [87] *Pardy v Pardy* [1939] P 288.
[88] See eg *Quoraishi v Quoraishi* [1985] FLR 780 where the husband took a second wife which justified his first wife's desertion of the marriage when she left him.
[89] *Lang v Lang* [1955] AC 402.     [90] Ibid, 418.     [91] See s 2(5).

### 2.3.3.4 Two years' separation with the respondent's consent and five years' separation

A divorce can be granted on the basis of two years' separation with the respondent's consent to the divorce (s 1(2)(d)) or on the basis of five years' separation (s 1(2)(e)). These are the only no-fault facts but, due to the delay involved in proving these grounds, they are much less relied on by petitioners than the fault facts of adultery and unreasonable behaviour.

A petitioner who relies on two years' separation must show that the parties have been 'living apart' for two years and must also obtain the respondent's consent to the divorce before a decree will be granted. Prior to 1969, when the current law was enacted, divorce by consent was completely forbidden.[92] When the ground of two years' separation with consent to the divorce was introduced, it was the hope of law reformers that this simple, non-judgemental state of affairs, with no allegations of any kind against the respondent being required, would become the main fact relied on for divorce purposes, but this has not been the case. The fact that few petitioners rely on these two no-fault separation grounds has provided one of the arguments for reforming the law.

The positive consent of the respondent is required under section 1(2)(d) and mere passive non-objection is not sufficient. Consent must be freely given with an understanding of what it entails,[93] and it can be withdrawn at any time before decree nisi is pronounced whereupon the proceedings must be stayed.[94] At any time before decree absolute is granted, the respondent can apply to have the decree nisi rescinded if he or she has been misled by the petitioner in respect of any matter which the respondent took into account in deciding whether to give consent.[95] The usual way in which notice of consent is given is by the respondent signifying to that effect in the Acknowledgement of Service form.

With the five years' separation ground under section 1(2)(e), all that is required is proof that the parties have 'lived apart' for a period of five years. This was highly controversial when first introduced because it permitted divorce against the respondent's will even though the respondent had done nothing 'wrong', a consideration of particular significance for those who were opposed to divorce on religious grounds. Such a respondent was, and still is, helpless to prevent such a divorce, unless he or she is able to raise a defence under section 5 that he or she will suffer grave financial or other hardship; a defence which is highly unlikely to succeed.[96]

### 2.3.3.4.1 Living apart

The parties will not be held to be living apart for the purpose of the two or five years' separation grounds merely by reason of physical separation (eg, where a spouse is abroad on military service or in prison). Living apart also requires a mental element, the belief by one of the parties that the marriage is at an end, although it is not necessary for this belief to be communicated to the other.

For the purpose of establishing physical separation, section 2(6) provides that a husband and wife 'shall be treated as living apart unless they are living with each other in the same household'. This is a question of fact in each case, but 'living with each other in the same household' is not the same as living with each other in the same *house*. For this reason, it is possible for the parties to be separated even if they are living under the same roof. It depends on whether or not they have a communal life together. Thus, where there has been no communal life under the same roof, the parties may succeed in obtaining a decree of divorce on the basis of separation. In *Hollens v Hollens*,[97] for example, the husband and wife continued living in their two-bedroomed council house, but had not spoken or eaten together since a violent quarrel more than two years previously. Neither party had done anything for the other since the quarrel. This degree of separation was sufficient to satisfy the court that all common life between them had ceased and that they were living apart. By contrast, in *Mouncer v Mouncer*,[98] it was held that the parties were not living

---

[92] See Section 1.1.    [93] See s 2(7) and the FPR 2010, r 7.12(12) and (13).
[94] FPR 2010, r 7.12(12) and (13).    [95] Section 10(1).    [96] See Section 2.3.4.
[97] (1971) 115 SJ 327.    [98] [1972] 1 All ER 289.

apart as, although they were on very bad terms and slept in separate bedrooms, they continued to eat meals together and in the company of their children. In other words, they enjoyed some communal life together. It is unfortunate that the more civilised the parties, and the more willing they are to behave well, cooperate with each other, and share the care of their children, the less chance there is of them obtaining a divorce under one of the separation grounds. This is because the court will consider that they have a communal life together and are not therefore living separately. This is likely to affect, in particular, those couples who, due to financial constraints, cannot afford to separate and live in separate dwellings. The Law Commission has described it as being 'unjust and discriminatory of the law to provide for a civilised "no fault" ground for divorce which, in practice, is denied to a large section of the population'.[99] Thus, some petitioners are forced to rely on the fault grounds of adultery and unreasonable behaviour because of the difficulty of separating even though allegations of fault may create hostility and bitterness and may make sorting out the consequences of divorce much more difficult.

As previously indicated, physical separation will not be enough by itself to establish that the parties are living apart. This must be accompanied by a belief by one of the parties that the marriage is over although this need not be communicated to the other.[100]

The period where the parties are deemed to be living apart must be continuous. However, to facilitate attempts at reconciliation, the spouses are permitted to resume living together for one or more periods totalling up to six months without the continuity of the period being broken.[101] Although such a period will not stop the time running, neither will it count towards the living apart time frame.

### 2.3.4 Special protection for respondents in separation divorces

Sections 5 and 10 of the MCA 1973 provide protection for respondents in petitions brought on the separation grounds. These provisions were introduced with the aim of protecting 'innocent' and vulnerable spouses, in other words those who were respondents to a 'no-fault' divorce and who had therefore committed no matrimonial offence.

> ### Key legislation
>
> Where the only fact relied on for divorce is five years' separation, the petitioner can be refused a decree under section 5 of the MCA 1973 if the respondent establishes that dissolution of the marriage will cause him or her to suffer grave financial or other hardship *and* that it would be wrong in all the circumstances to dissolve the marriage.

This provision, however, is rarely used in practice and, if used, rarely succeeds, but it may be useful for putting pressure on a petitioner to offer the respondent a reasonable financial settlement.[102] In respect of the 'other hardship' part of the 'defence' in section 5, this might include, for example,

---

[99] See Law Com No 192, para 2.12.

[100] See *Santos v Santos* [1972] Fam 247. It is worth noting that Parliament did not intend there to be any mental element to 'living apart' for the purposes of the two- and five-year separation facts. This requirement was introduced by the Court of Appeal in *Santos v Santos* [1972] Fam 247 where it held that to establish living apart not only must there be a physical separation, but there must also be a mental element of wishing to live apart as respects at least one of the spouses.

[101] See s 2(5).

[102] At one time it was sometimes used to put pressure on a petitioner to make pension provision for the respondent (see eg *Archer v Archer* [1999] 1 FLR 327), but now that the court has the power to make pension orders on divorce (see Chapter 4), this is no longer necessary.

religious or social hardship that a respondent might suffer due to ostracism in the community as a result of religious or social objections to the divorce.[103]

---

### Key legislation

The court has jurisdiction under section 10 to protect a respondent in a divorce case where a decree nisi has been obtained on the basis of two or five years' separation. Thus, under section 10(1) the court has jurisdiction to rescind the decree nisi where a respondent can prove that the petitioner misled the respondent (intentionally or unintentionally) about any matter which the respondent took into account in deciding to give consent to the decree being granted in a two-year separation case. Under section 10(2), a respondent may apply to the court for his or her financial position after divorce to be considered, in which case the court hearing the application shall by virtue of section 10(3) consider all the circumstances including a list of circumstances in section 10(3); and can refuse to grant a decree absolute unless it is satisfied that 'the petitioner should not be required to make any financial provision for the respondent, or that the financial provision made by the petitioner for the respondent is reasonable and fair or the best that can be made in the circumstances.' However, the court has an overriding discretion (under s 10(4)) to make a decree absolute, notwithstanding the requirements of section 10(3), if there are circumstances making it desirable that the decree should be made absolute without delay and the court has obtained a satisfactory undertaking from the petitioner that he or she will make such financial provision for the respondent as the court may approve.

---

These provisions therefore afford a respondent valuable protection where a petitioner is, for example, being unreasonable or obdurate over financial arrangements or is in arrears with payments due under an existing order.[104] The effect of section 10 is to delay decree absolute while financial matters are looked into. These provisions were at one time occasionally used to protect respondents who were at risk of losing their entitlement to pension rights on divorce,[105] but now that the divorce court has wider powers to make orders with respect to pensions, this is no longer necessary.

### 2.3.5 Religious decrees of divorce and the Matrimonial Causes Act 1973

The MCA 1973 was amended[106] to provide protection to those requiring a religious as well as a civil decree of divorce as there were a number of cases of women being refused a religious divorce by their spouse. Section 10A will apply where a decree of divorce has been granted but not made absolute and the parties to the marriage:

(a)  were married in accordance with—

(i)  the usages of the Jews, or

(ii)  any other prescribed religious usages; and

(b)  must cooperate if the marriage is to be dissolved.

Either party can apply to the court for an order that the divorce decree is not to be made absolute until a declaration by both parties that they have taken such steps as are required to dissolve the marriage in accordance with those usages is produced to the court. Such an order will be made if the court believes it is just and reasonable to do so considering all the circumstances of the case.

---

[103]  See eg *Rukat v Rukat* [1975] Fam 63 and *Balraj v Balraj* (1981) 11 FL 110.

[104]  In *Garcia v Garcia* [1992] 1 FLR 256, for instance, the wife successfully invoked s 10(3) to delay the grant of decree nisi because her Spanish husband owed her a substantial sum in unpaid child maintenance.

[105]  See eg *Griffiths v Dawson & Co* [1993] 2 FLR 315 and *Jackson v Jackson* [1993] 2 FLR 848.

[106]  Divorce (Religious Marriages) Act 2002.

This will prevent the dissolution of the marriage until the court is satisfied that all steps have been taken to secure a religious divorce. This clearly would be a bargaining point for the party wishing to obtain a religious decree of divorce. Currently there are no other prescribed religious usages. In future, other religious marriages, for example under Islamic law, may come within the ambit of this section.

## 2.4 **The legal effects of divorce**

The status of being married gives rise to various rights, and responsibilities.[107] Termination of the marriage by decree absolute of divorce therefore has important legal consequences.

On the grant of decree absolute, the marriage is dissolved and each party is free to remarry. The decree has other legal consequences. Thus, any finance and property orders made under Part II of the MCA 1973 in favour of a party to a marriage take effect and orders for the settlement or variation of a settlement can take effect in respect of any child of the family. All other orders for children take effect as soon as they are made. Divorce also has an effect on a will made by either party so that, subject to any contrary intention in a will, any legacies and gifts to a former spouse lapse. However, a former spouse can make a claim for reasonable financial provision from the deceased's estate under the Inheritance (Provision for Family and Dependants) Act 1975.[108] Termination of the marriage also affects social security, pension, and taxation rights. Both parties also lose their rights under legislation governing their 'matrimonial' rights, in particular the statutory right of occupation of the family home,[109] although they still have a right to apply for protection against domestic violence under Part IV of the Family Law Act 1996 in their status as former spouse.[110] With regard to children, divorce does not terminate the parties' parental responsibility, and the obligation to provide financial support for their children continues after divorce.[111]

## 2.5 **Recognition of an overseas divorce**

In certain circumstances divorces obtained in an overseas jurisdiction are recognised in the UK. Part II of the Family Law Act 1986 makes provision for the recognition of overseas divorces (and annulments and separations), but special rules apply to the recognition of divorces obtained in other member states of the European Union.[112]

Disputes about the recognition of an overseas divorce usually arise in the context of 'big money' international marriage cases. This is because if an overseas divorce is recognised as valid in England and Wales, then a party to the marriage will not be able to apply for a divorce in the English courts and will therefore have no access to the financial order jurisdiction of the divorce court in England and Wales under Part II of the MCA 1973, which requires a divorce decree to be granted in the divorce court in England and Wales. If the divorce has already been granted overseas then a party to the marriage may attempt to argue before the courts in England and Wales that the overseas divorce should not be recognised. If successful, then the divorce may be able to be heard in the English courts with the 'reward' possibly being a more lucrative finance and property award than the one that would have been awarded in the court of the overseas jurisdiction.

---

[107] See Chapter 1.

[108] A provision can be included in the divorce settlement precluding such an application.

[109] Under the Family Law Act 1996, Pt IV, s 30. They also lose rights under, for instance, the Matrimonial Proceedings and Property Act 1970 and the Married Women's Property Act 1882.

[110] See Chapter 3.     [111] See Chapter 6.

[112] See Council Regulation (EC) No 2201/2003 Concerning Jurisdiction and the Recognition and Enforcement of Judgments in Matrimonial Matters and in Matters of Parental Responsibility (Brussels II Revised); and see eg *D v D (Nature of Recognition of Overseas Divorce)* [2005] EWHC 3342 (Fam), [2006] 2 FLR 825 where a Greek divorce was recognised in England and Wales under Brussels II.

It is usually wives who argue that an overseas divorce should not be recognised in England and Wales, because the English courts adopt a generous approach in financial proceedings and apply principles of fairness and non-discrimination.[113] If, on the other hand, the overseas divorce is recognised by the courts in this country as being valid in England and Wales, then a party will have to apply instead for financial orders under Part III of the Matrimonial and Family Proceedings Act 1984, which gives the English court jurisdiction to grant financial relief after a marriage has been dissolved (or annulled) in a foreign country, but where the award may not be as great as that which might be obtained in the divorce court under Part II of the MCA 1973.[114]

### Key legislation

The law governing the recognition in England and Wales of overseas divorces is found in the Family Law Act 1986 (which applies to all overseas divorces other than those obtained in the EU).

The Act makes a distinction between divorces obtained in proceedings (judicial or other proceedings) and those which are not. For divorces obtained in proceedings, recognition is much broader and such a divorce will be recognised as a valid divorce in this country if it is effective under the law of the country where it was obtained and, at the commencement of the proceedings, either party was habitually resident or domiciled in that country or was a national of that country.[115] An overseas divorce not obtained in proceedings is recognised in this country if it is effective in the country where it was obtained, and on the date it was obtained one or both parties were domiciled in that country, or one party was domiciled there and the other party was domiciled in a country which recognised the divorce, and in any case neither party was habitually resident in the UK for one year immediately preceding the divorce.[116]

Notwithstanding these rules, the court in England and Wales has an overriding discretion to refuse recognition of an overseas divorce where, in the case of a divorce obtained by proceedings, reasonable steps were not taken to give notice of the proceedings to a party to the marriage or to give a party to the marriage an opportunity to take part in those proceedings;[117] and, in all cases, where recognition would be manifestly contrary to public policy.[118] It is often difficult to succeed in arguing that a divorce should not be recognised on grounds of public policy.[119] Cases are decided on their own facts, but the courts are keen to ensure that the principles of international law are upheld, in particular the principle of comity which requires the courts to respect the jurisdiction of courts in countries overseas.

In some cases the courts have had to consider whether a talaq should be recognised in England and Wales. A talaq is an Islamic divorce whereby the husband can divorce his wife by uttering the words 'I divorce you' three times without being in the presence of another person and without his wife giving consent. A talaq made *within* the jurisdiction of England and Wales is not valid, as

---

[113] See *White v White* [2001] 1 AC 596, [2000] 2 FLR 981 and *Miller v Miller; McFarlane v McFarlane* [2006] UKHL 24, [2006] 1 FLR 1186. See Chapter 4.

[114] See *Agbaje v Akinnoye-Agbaje* [2010] UKSC 13.     [115] Section 46(1).     [116] Section 46(2).

[117] Section 51(3). See eg *Duhur-Johnson v Duhur-Johnson (Attorney-General Intervening)* [2005] 2 FLR 1042 where a Nigerian divorce was refused recognition as the husband had not taken reasonable steps to give his wife notice of the divorce proceedings.

[118] Section 52.

[119] See Thorpe LJ in *Eroglu v Eroglu* [1994] 2 FLR 287 where the wife's argument that her Turkish divorce should not be recognised on the ground that it had been obtained by fraud was dismissed. See also *H v H (The Queen's Proctor Intervening) (Validity of Japanese Divorce)* [2006] EWHC 2989 (Fam), [2007] 1 FLR 1318 where a Japanese divorce by agreement (a Kyogi rikon) was recognised as a valid divorce, as there was no reason to refuse recognition on public policy grounds.

only divorces obtained in court proceedings are recognised in this country.[120] On the other hand, a talaq validly made *outside* the UK may, at the discretion of the court, be recognised as a valid divorce in the UK, and is likely to be recognised unless the court considers there are public policy reasons for refusing to do so.

---

### Key case

In *H v H (Talaq Divorce)*[121] where a talaq divorce validly announced in Pakistan was upheld by the High Court, Sumner J said it was important that marriages and divorces recognised in one country should be recognised in another unless there were good reasons for not doing so, particularly where many people moved freely between the two countries. However, in *A v L*,[122] where the husband applied to the High Court for his wife's petition for divorce to be adjourned on the ground that the Egyptian court had made an order confirming that he had already divorced his wife by talaq over the telephone, the High Court refused to accept his argument. Although a talaq is not normally regarded as a divorce by means of proceedings, in this case it was regarded as being granted in proceedings because the Egyptian court had been involved. As the wife had not been given notice of the proceedings or been able to attend them, recognition was refused.[123]

---

Where the court in England and Wales considers that a party to a marriage has acted unconscientiously, oppressively, or vexatiously by stealing a forensic advantage by disputing that England is the appropriate forum to hear the divorce proceedings and thereby holds up the English proceedings while at the same time pursuing his or her own proceedings abroad, then the court in England and Wales can grant a '*Hemain*' injunction to prevent this happening.[124]

## 3  Criticisms of divorce under the Matrimonial Causes Act 1973 and an attempt at reform

### 3.1  Introduction

The current law of divorce has been criticised by judges, academics, and politicians for many reasons. In 2000 a radical reform of divorce was due to come into force under Part II of the Family Law Act 1996 but it was shelved at the eleventh hour much to the relief of those who had argued against it. This part of the chapter considers the criticisms of the current law of divorce and gives an overview of the radical reform of divorce which was due to come into force under the Family Law Act 1996 but which was never implemented.

---

[120]  See eg *Sulaiman v Juffali* [2002] 1 FLR 479 where a talaq pronounced in England, and subsequently registered in Saudi Arabia, was held not to be a valid divorce under the provisions of the Family Law Act 1986 as the court held that it had been obtained in England, not Saudi Arabia.

[121]  [2007] EWHC 2945, [2008] 2 FLR 857. See also *El Fadl v El Fadl* [2000] 1 FLR 175 where a talaq divorce registered with the Shariah court in Lebanon was recognised by the High Court in England and Wales, as registration constituted proceedings for the purpose of the Family Law Act 1986.

[122]  [2010] EWHC 460 (Fam), [2010] 2 FLR 1418.          [123]  See earlier in this section.

[124]  See eg *S v S (Hemain) Injunction* [2009] EWHC 3224 (Fam), [2010] 2 FLR 502 where the wife's application for a *Hemain* injunction (an 'anti-suit' injunction) against her husband to order him not to take any further steps to register a talaq divorce in the Sunnite Shariah Court of Beirut was dismissed as she had started the English proceedings with the deliberate aim of frustrating the Lebanese process in which she had previously participated. It was held that to order a *Hemain* injunction against the husband would also offend the principles of comity and the principles and policy underpinning the *Hemain* injunction procedure. See also *R v R (Divorce: Hemain Injunction)* [2003] EWHC 2113 (Fam), [2005] 1 FLR 386.

In the years following the implementation of the current law there was growing disquiet in some quarters that the aims of the new law were not being achieved in practice. This disquiet, coupled with a significant increase in the divorce rate, provided fertile ground for a fresh examination of the legal framework. Thus, in 1982 a committee chaired by Hon Mrs Justice Booth was established to examine the procedure associated with matrimonial causes. The committee was displeased with what it discovered, particularly with regard to divorces based on the behaviour fact, and in its Report published in 1985[125] recommended that changes be made which would lead to a reduction in acrimony between the parties. The Law Commission, taking the lead from the Booth Report, carried out an examination of the law governing the grounds for divorce, against the background of the divorce law's professed objectives, and found it to be wanting. The Law Commission's findings were published in a discussion paper in 1988.[126] These findings were that the law had failed to satisfy its original objectives. Indeed the criticisms were devastating. The law was found to be confusing and misleading; to be discriminatory and unjust; to exacerbate hostility; to distort the parties' bargaining positions; to do nothing to save the marriage; and to make matters worse for the children. In its discussion paper the Law Commission invited views on different suggestions for how the law might be altered. In light of the responses, the Law Commission made proposals for the reform of divorce in its report, *Family Law: The Ground for Divorce*.[127]

---

**Summary**

The aims of the law of divorce as expressed in both Law Commission papers were encapsulated in the following four propositions: (i) to support those marriages capable of being saved; (ii) to enable those not so capable of being saved to be dissolved with the minimum of avoidable distress, bitterness, and hostility; (iii) so far as possible, to encourage the amicable solution of practical issues relating to the couple's home, finances, and children, and the proper discharge of their responsibilities to one another and their children; and (iv) to minimise the harm the children of the family might suffer, both at the time of the divorce and in the future, and to promote, so far as possible, the continued sharing of parental responsibility for them.

---

The Law Commission's 1988 discussion paper contained three possible models for reform: a mixed system with both fault and no-fault grounds for divorce, as under the current law in the MCA 1973, but with some modifications; divorce after a fixed minimum period of separation; and divorce after a fixed minimum period of reflection and consideration, in other words a divorce involving a process over time. The last model was chosen as the Law Commission's preferred option and it recommended that in its final report.

The Lord Chancellor's Department[128] took up many of the Law Commission's suggestions and in 1993 published a Consultation Paper, *Looking to the Future: Mediation and the Ground for Divorce*.[129] In the introduction, the Government's objectives in relation to the law and procedure surrounding the dissolution of marriage were expressed rather differently from those put forward by the Law Commission. These objectives were: (i) to support the institution of marriage; (ii) to include practicable steps to prevent the irretrievable breakdown of marriage; (iii) to ensure that the parties understand the practical consequences of divorce before taking any irreversible decision;

---

[125] *Report of the Matrimonial Causes Procedure Committee* (1985).
[126] *Facing the Future: A Discussion Paper on the Ground for Divorce* (Law Com No 170, 1988).
[127] Law Com No 192.
[128] In 2003 the Lord Chancellor's Department was renamed the Department for Constitutional Affairs, but the responsibilities of the latter were in May 2007 transferred to the newly formed Ministry of Justice.
[129] HMSO, 1993.

(iv) where divorce is unavoidable, to minimise the bitterness and hostility between the parties and to reduce the trauma for the children; and (v) to keep to the minimum the cost to the taxpayer.

In the Government's Consultation Paper, the objections to the divorce law in the MCA 1973 and the reasons for wishing for change, were spelled out in some detail.[130] The Government claimed that the law in the 1973 Act, particularly the manner in which it was applied in practice, allowed divorce to be obtained too quickly and too easily without the parties being required to consider the consequences. It claimed that the system did nothing to save a marriage; it could make things worse for the children; it was unjust and exacerbated bitterness and hostility; it was confusing, misleading, and open to abuse; it was discriminatory; and it distorted the parties' bargaining positions. The Consultation Paper listed nine possible options for reform but with the preferred option being the Law Commission's recommended model, namely that the sole ground for divorce should be irretrievable breakdown of the marriage to be established by the passage of time, during which time the parties would be expected to consider and reflect on the divorce and its consequences.

A considerable number of comments were received in response to the Consultation Paper, and. in the spring of 1995, the Government published a White Paper, *Looking to the Future: Mediation and the Ground for Divorce*[131] setting out fresh proposals for change.

## Summary

The White Paper stated, *inter alia*, that the proposals would:

- require couples to attend a compulsory information session before starting the divorce process;
- remove the incentive to make allegations of fault in order to divorce quickly;
- require a 12-month period of reflection by the parties on whether the marriage could be saved;
- require couples to think through and face up to the consequences of divorce before it happened;
- ensure that arrangements for children and other matters were settled before a divorce was granted;
- allow divorces to be barred where the dissolution of the marriage would cause grave financial or other grave hardship; and
- introduce comprehensive family mediation as part of the divorce process.

The Government's proposals had a strong marriage-saving rhetoric. The aim of the reforms was not to make divorce easier: key aspects of the Government's proposals concentrated as much on 'marriage saving' as 'marriage ending'. Thus, it was proposed that:[132] saveable marriages would be identified; referrals for marriage guidance, and opportunities to explore reconciliation, would be facilitated; adequate time would be given to test whether the marriage had genuinely broken down; acrimony, hostility, and conflict would be removed or minimised, thereby reducing the worst effects of divorce on children; parents would be encouraged to focus on their joint responsibility to support and care for their children; couples would be encouraged to meet these responsibilities before the marriage was dissolved; and couples would be assisted in this process through family mediation.

The resultant Family Law Bill had a difficult progress through Parliament. A large number of amendments were made in response to pressure from both Houses. However, the Lord Chancellor was determined that the Bill would become law and it received the Royal Assent in July 1996. However, the reforms, which were contained in Parts I–III of the Family Law Act 1996,[133] were

---

[130]  *Looking to the Future* (1993), Ch 5.      [131]  Cm 2799.      [132]  See the Preface to the White Paper.
[133]  Part IV contains provisions providing protection against domestic violence. Part 4A contains provisions giving protection to victims of forced marriage.

never introduced and were eventually repealed.[134] For this reason, only an outline of the reforms is given next.[135]

## 3.2 Divorce under the Family Law Act 1996

### 3.2.1 An outline of the reform

The new divorce law laid down in Parts I–III of the Family Law Act 1996[136] would have radically reformed the law of divorce, in both substance and procedure. It would have swept away the provisions in the MCA 1973. The 1996 Act introduced 'divorce over a process of time', in fact a significant period of time, in which divorcing parties were required to face up to the emotional and practical consequences of divorcing. Under the 1996 Act, divorce law, like the current law, required proof that the marriage had irretrievably broken down, but instead of requiring factual evidence to prove breakdown (such as adultery, behaviour, or separation), the parties were required to follow and complete a complex sequence of procedural steps before being able to obtain a divorce. If the process was complied with, this provided evidence of irretrievable breakdown. The main stages in the process involved: attendance at an information meeting; making a statement of marital breakdown; passing a period of time for reflection and consideration; and finally the granting of a divorce order. Orders were also available to protect vulnerable parties to divorce, similar to those which exist under the current law.

One of the main differences between the current law and the proposed new law was that the parties were required to sort out arrangements ancillary to the divorce (such as arrangements about their children and in respect of property and financial matters) *before* being able to obtain a divorce. Under the current law, on the other hand, a divorce can be obtained relatively quickly (in a matter of weeks) but sorting out the consequences may take several years. The Government took the view in discussions leading to the enactment of the Family Law Act 1996 that, by making the parties settle their arrangements for the future, it would emphasise the responsibilities of marriage and parenthood.[137] The new law also included a much greater use of mediation in divorce and related disputes. There were also changes in the terminology used for divorce law and joint applications for divorce were possible.

**Attendance at an information meeting:** the spouse (or both spouses) contemplating divorce would first have to attend an information meeting where information about matters relating to divorce would be given, including not only information about the divorce and separation process but on other matters, such as: marriage counselling and marriage support services; the importance of the welfare needs of any children; the nature of the financial issues which might arise; mediation; and legal aid. The actual details about the content and length of these information meetings, however, proved to be complex and unclear, and because of these concerns the Government decided to conduct pilot studies before the new law came into force. The results of the pilot studies found that there were various problems relating to the information meetings, and it was these results which eventually led to the reforms being 'ditched' and the relevant Parts of the Family Law Act 1996 being repealed.

---

[134] Except for some general principles by which the law should be guided, set out in s 1, which remain in force.

[135] For a detailed account of the divorce provisions of the 1996 Act, see S. M. Cretney and R. Bird, *Divorce: The New Law* (Bristol: Family Law, 1996).

[136] Part I laid down a set of general principles governing the divorce legislation. Part II contained provisions relating to divorce and separation. Part III laid down provisions relating to legal aid for mediation.

[137] The Law Commission, by contrast, had recommended that making arrangements should not be a precondition of divorce, as this might rush the parties into making unsuitable arrangements and play into the hands of one of the parties.

**Statement of marital breakdown:** three months or more after attendance at an information meeting, one spouse (or both) would be required to make a 'statement of marital breakdown' declaring that the party (or parties) were aware of the purposes of the period of reflection and consideration and wished to make arrangements for the future. A statement of breakdown could not be made in the first year of marriage.

**A period for reflection and consideration:** once the statement of marital breakdown had been made, a period for reflection and consideration would begin to run. The purpose of this period was to give the parties time to reflect on whether their marriage could be saved, to have an opportunity to effect a reconciliation, and to consider what arrangements should be made for the future. The minimum period for reflection and consideration in all cases was nine months, but this was automatically extended for a further six months (making 15 months in total) where there was a child of the family aged under 16, unless a non-molestation or occupation order[138] had been made to protect a party and/or a child against domestic violence by the other party, or where delay in making a divorce order would be significantly detrimental to the welfare of any child of the family. The period could also be extended by six months if the party who had not applied for the divorce order applied to the court for further reflection.

During the period for reflection and consideration the parties were required to make financial arrangements for the future and arrangements about their children, because, unless they did so to the court's satisfaction by the end of the required period, a divorce order would not be made. However, in certain circumstances, this requirement to make arrangements could be waived (eg where the other party was obstructive or where there was ill health, disability, or domestic violence or where delay would be significantly detrimental to the welfare of a child of the family).

**The divorce order:** after complying with the above requirements, one or both parties (irrespective of who set the divorce in motion) could then apply for a divorce order which the court could make if the marriage had irretrievably broken down; the requirements listed earlier had been satisfied; and the application had not been withdrawn. Irretrievable breakdown was proved if the parties had complied with the process for obtaining a divorce. The effect of a divorce order was to dissolve the marriage, although it could not be made if an order preventing divorce was in force.

**Orders preventing divorce:** the court could make an order preventing divorce if dissolution of the marriage would result in substantial financial or other hardship to the other party or to a child of the family; and it would be wrong in the circumstances for the marriage to be dissolved.

### 3.2.2 The decision not to implement the reform

The proposed radical reforms of divorce law were due to come into force on 1 January 1999, but implementation was suspended until 2000—after the Government had received the results of pilot projects to see how the information meetings would work in practice. However, the results of these pilot projects turned out to be disappointing,[139] as it was found that the information meetings failed to achieve their aims, which were to save marriages and promote mediation. The results showed that only a minority of couples were diverted to marriage counselling, that few people attended a meeting with a view to saving their marriage, and that the meetings were not very successful in diverting couples into mediation.

---

[138]   Under the Family Law Act 1996, Pt IV, see Chapter 3.

[139]   Only 7 per cent of those attending information meetings were diverted into mediation and very few couples attended the meetings together. The information meetings had therefore failed to achieve the Government's stated objectives of saving saveable marriages and encouraging mediation.

Although the aim of the pilot projects was simply to test the format for information delivery, the Government evaluated the results of the pilots by reference to the likelihood of the parties electing to use mediation rather than seeking legal advice. Thus, the Law Commission's original scheme changed its emphasis as it developed in the hands of successive Governments. The use of mediation had not been central to the scheme as was originally proposed by the Law Commission, but it became central to the Government's scheme, particularly when the Conservative Government took over the reform. As marriage-saving and cost-saving had become the new rhetoric, the Government came to the conclusion that the proposed reform would fail to fulfil the policy objectives laid down in Part I of the 1996 Act, namely to save saveable marriages and, where they had broken down, to bring them to an end with the minimum of distress to the parties and any children. For this reason, the reforms were never introduced and Parts I and II of the 1996 Act were eventually repealed.

### 3.2.3  Reaction to the proposed reform

The proposed reform of divorce law by the Family Law Act 1996 generated fierce debate; and the decision not to implement the new law was greeted with considerable relief by those who had considered the reforms to be inherently flawed and unworkable in practice. Some of the main criticisms were that the new divorce law was unnecessarily complicated and that it would place impossible demands on divorcing couples to sort out arrangements about their property and children, often at a time of emotional turmoil, before they would be able to get a divorce. The Solicitors' Family Law Association (now called Resolution) considered the reforms to be cumbersome and confusing, and said that they would create delay and uncertainty which were contrary to the best interests of divorcing couples and their children.

Some commentators considered the length of the period of reflection and consideration to be much too long. Freeman,[140] for example, was critical of the length of the process because, among other things, it would create more conflict, more tension, more domestic violence, and unnecessary abortions. Cretney[141] considered the Government to be 'curiously naive' about what was likely to happen during the period of reflection. He said that some couples would not spend time considering whether their marriage could be saved or making arrangements for the future, but would instead spend the time conceiving children, or exploiting their emotional or financial advantage, or brooding on their grievances. Eekelaar[142] was critical of the need for information meetings and considered them to be a form of 'social engineering'. His main objection was that the reforms had strong implications for the rule of law, in that the Government was using 'the institutions of law itself to obstruct individuals from access to the rights conferred on them by law'.[143] He said that this could be 'deeply corrupting of the law itself', and that it should not be forgotten that both marriage and divorce were legal rights. In other words, Eekelaar found the requirement that those wishing to divorce should be compulsorily required to attend an information meeting was obstructive of justice.

Thus, despite more than ten years of debate and an attempt to devise and introduce 'divorce over a period of time' (a rather appropriate name for a divorce law which took so long to gestate),[144] divorce law in England and Wales remains the same as it was in 1971 when the Divorce Reform Act 1969 introduced the current grounds for divorce.

---

[140]  M. Freeman, 'Divorce Gospel Style' [1997] Family Law 413 at 414.
[141]  S. Cretney, 'The Divorce White Paper—Some Reflections' [1995] Family Law 302 at 304.
[142]  J. Eekelaar, 'Family Law—Keeping Us "On Message"' [1999] Child and Family Law Quarterly 387.
[143]  Ibid.
[144]  It was 1988 when the Law Commission first 'set the ball rolling' with it discussion paper, and it was 1999 when the divorce reforms under the Family Law Act 1996 were due to come into force.

# 4 The future of divorce law

The law of divorce has been criticised by many commentators,[145] and some have argued for it to be reformed. Concerns about divorce law cover a range of issues and there is also the added difficulty of deciding what form any new law should take. As the attempt at divorce reform by the Family Law Act 1996 showed in the previous section, any reform of the law is difficult and raises difficult policy issues.

However, the criticisms which led to the reforms under the 1996 Act still remain true today; and, after the Government's decision not to implement the reforms, some judges, practitioners, academics, and politicians have continued to voice concerns about the current law. For instance, the Rt Hon Elizabeth Butler-Sloss, a former President of the Family Division, described obtaining a divorce on the ground of unreasonable behaviour as a 'hypocritical charade', and she said there was a need to introduce a truly no-fault divorce.[146] In 2001, the Lord Chancellor's Advisory Board on Family Law in its final report[147] said that it regretted the missed opportunity to reform divorce, and it urged that serious consideration be given to replacing the current adversarial system and partly fault-based divorce regime. The Advisory Board stated that serious defects identified by the Law Commission in discussions leading up to reform in the Family Law Act 1996 still remained, in particular that allegations of fault (unreasonable behaviour and adultery) caused unnecessary conflict between the parties, and that their distress and anger impacted on their children.

Resolution, a group of family lawyers which adopts a non-confrontational approach to family disputes, is also in favour of reform and has spent many years campaigning for the introduction of no-fault divorce on the basis that the current system does not sit well with the non-confrontational settlement culture which is encouraged and promoted in the rest of the family justice system. Resolution has asked for divorce reform to be put back on the political agenda in order to end the 'blame game'.[148] Cretney[149] has described the law of divorce as being in 'a state of confusion', because the theory of divorce (that the state has a vital interest in the matter and divorce is only available on proof of irretrievable breakdown) does not match up with the practical reality (which is that divorce should be readily and quickly available, whether or not the parties agree, because 'there is no point in denying that the marriage has broken down if one party firmly asserts it has').

One of the main criticisms of divorce relates to the fault element, which is particularly pertinent as most divorces are brought on the fault grounds of adultery and unreasonable behaviour, partly because these grounds, unlike the separation grounds, enable the marriage to be terminated quickly. Allegations of fault increase bitterness and hostility which may make agreement between the parties about the consequences of divorce more difficult. Allegations of fault also run counter to the settlement culture which is adopted in respect of ancillary matters on divorce. Also, fault has little relevance to arrangements for children and to finance and property matters, unless behaviour is of an extreme kind, a fact which some parties find difficult to understand. There is also the worry

---

[145] On divorce reform, see eg R. Deech, 'Divorce—A Disaster?' [2009] Family Law 1048; E. Hasson, 'Setting a Standard or Reflecting Reality? The "Role" of Divorce Law, and the Case of the Family Law Act 1996' [2003] International Journal of Law, Policy and the Family 338; R. Kay, 'Whose Divorce is it Anyway? The Human Rights Aspect' [2004] Family Law 892; E. Hasson, 'Wedded to "Fault": The Legal Regulation of Divorce and Relationship Breakdown' (2006) Legal Studies 267; S. Cretney, 'Marriage, Divorce and the Courts' [2002] Family Law 900; M. Freeman (ed), *Divorce: Where Next?* (Aldershot: Dartmouth, 1996).

[146] At her inaugural speech on being appointed President of the Family Division.

[147] See its final report, *Making Contact Work*, in which it made a number of serious criticisms of the family justice system, particularly, but not exclusively, relating to contact proceedings.

[148] See [2007] Family Law 1053; and N. Shepherd, 'Ending the Blame Game: Getting No Fault Divorce Back on the Agenda' [2009] Family Law 122.

[149] S. Cretney, *Family Law in the Twentieth Century* (Oxford: Oxford University Press, 2003), p 391.

that allegations of fault are fabricated by the parties in order to expedite the divorce process and avoid the long delays associated with the separation facts.

Another concern relates to the speed with which a divorce can be granted. A divorce can be obtained in a matter of weeks, but sorting out disputes relating to finance and property and children involves separate court proceedings which can sometimes drag on for years. One of the few advantages of the reforms under the Family Law Act 1996 was that obtaining a divorce and sorting out the consequences were integrated, and the requirement of a 'period of reflection and consideration' meant that couples were not 'steamrollered' into divorce and regretted it later.

Reforming divorce raises difficult questions, and there is no point in reforming the law unless any reform is a significant improvement on the current system. However, reforming the law and getting the balance right is difficult. Thus, some argue that if divorce is made too easy it may send out a message that marriage can be treated lightly but, on the other hand, if it is made too difficult then people may decide not to marry and opt instead for cohabitation. In terms of the substantive law, one of the most important policy decisions is whether there should be fault, no fault, or a mixed system of fault and no fault. Allegations of fault may make marriage breakdown and divorce more difficult for the parties and make things worse for the children. However, one possible advantage of fault is that it sends out a message that marriage involves a moral code, although this raises the question of whether it is the function of family law to provide a moral code of behaviour and also whether the law can actually influence human conduct. Also, ascribing and apportioning fault to parties to a marriage is difficult and complex. In many cases, both parties may be to blame, but only one of them can petition for divorce.

It seems to be generally agreed that fault divorce is not the preferred option, but then it becomes a question of what the alternative is. Should, for instance, divorce be available on the unilateral demand of one of the parties or by mutual consent of the parties? Divorce on unilateral demand is the most liberal form of divorce, but it may give too much freedom to the individual and possibly send out a message that divorce is something which is easy to obtain. However, on the basis that a divorce is relatively easy to obtain today, it could be argued that we already have what is in effect divorce on unilateral demand. Divorce by mutual consent[150] seems to be a 'civilised' way of permitting a divorce, and would tie in with the settlement culture which pervades the rest of the family justice system. But, there are also problems with mutual consent. Thus, for instance, procedural safeguards would have to be put in place to ensure that consent has been truly and freely given and also to ensure that both parties have the capacity to consent. Divorce by mutual consent might also threaten the balance of power between the parties and act as a bargaining chip whereby one party may agree to succumb to an unfavourable divorce settlement in relation to, say, the family home and the children, in order to 'escape' from the marriage. Grounds other than mutual consent would also be needed to provide a basis for divorce for those persons not able to consent.

Another policy issue is whether divorce law should promote the institution of marriage. However, whether the law can actually do this is questionable, for marriages may break down despite divorce law, not because of it. Some commentators, on the other hand, have argued that the more liberal the divorce law, the more likely it is that the number of divorcing couples will rise. Deech,[151] for example, is against any wholesale reform of the grounds for divorce as those whose marriage has broken down 'can easily obtain divorces under the existing law, so there is no need to "liberalise" it'; and she is of the view that any reform is 'dangerous' as '[e]ach successive attempt in the twentieth century to bring the statute law into line with "reality" has resulted in an increase in the divorce rate'.[152]

---

[150] The Law Commission, when it was considering reform of divorce in the early 1990s, found substantial support for divorce on the basis of mutual consent, with a survey showing that 90 per cent of those persons who responded to a survey thought that divorce should be available on this basis (see Law Com No 183, 1990).

[151] R. Deech, 'Divorce—A Disaster?' [2009] Family Law 1048.     [152] Ibid.

Other difficulties relate to the process of divorce. One difficulty is deciding whether there should be a 'cooling off' period before the parties are permitted to divorce and, if so, how long this period should be. Resolution[153] has recommended *inter alia* that there should be a 'waiting period' of six months before one party (or both) is able to file a declaration that the marriage has broken down. Deech[154] recommends that a waiting period should be introduced to delay divorces based on adultery or unreasonable behaviour being processed so quickly, which she says would be achieved by adding to those grounds 'a provision that no decree shall be granted until at least 12 months have elapsed from the service of the petition'.

There are other questions to be addressed, such as whether joint applications for divorce should be permitted[155] and whether there should be a purely administrative form of divorce without judicial and court involvement. Cretney[156] has questioned the need for judicial involvement in the divorce process:

> Should we not accept that the routine processing of marriage breakdown is no longer a judicial function and that it should accordingly be removed altogether from the courts and the judicial system, leaving them with more time to deal with the problems that do require their expertise and procedures? If we believe that respect for the law and the legal system is important, and that the 1996 reforms would have made the law even more complex and difficult to understand, should we not begin to ask whether there is not a simpler and better alternative?

Other issues relate to the role to be played by mediation, and whether it should be compulsory, and the role played by marriage counselling and information provision for those persons contemplating divorce. Another issue is whether marriage and divorce education should be made part of the national curriculum.

One change which could easily be implemented in England and Wales would be for the Government to follow the lead of the Scottish Parliament[157] which has made a simple adjustment to the law of divorce (which is virtually the same as divorce law in England and Wales) so that the period of two years' separation and consent to the divorce has been reduced to one, and the five-year separation ground reduced to three. Scotland has also abolished desertion as a ground for divorce. The aim of these simple reforms is to encourage the use of the separation grounds and thereby lessen the acrimony and conflict which can be associated with fault-based divorces, and to allow parents and children to move on.

## 4.1 Recent proposals to reform the law of divorce

Recently reforms have been proposed to change the divorce process, and the grounds for divorce. Dealing with proposed administrative changes to the divorce process first, the Family Justice Review proposed to enable couples to divorce and reach agreement about their financial arrangements without using a court.[158] Instead, under the proposed process, where a person seeks a divorce they will go to an online information hub where they will access a divorce portal. The person initiating the divorce would complete the application online and would be prompted to consider arrangements for children, as well as financial and religious issues about the divorce. The online form would then be submitted to a centralised court processing centre, along with the appropriate

---

[153] See N. Shepherd, 'Ending the Blame Game: Getting No Fault Divorce Back on the Agenda' [2009] Family Law 122.
[154] R. Deech, 'Divorce—A Disaster?' [2009] Family Law 1048.
[155] Resolution is in favour of joint applications, and joint applications were available under the reforms proposed in the Family Law Act 1996.
[156] S. Cretney, 'Marriage, Divorce and the Courts' [2002] Family Law 900.
[157] By the Family Law (Scotland) Act 2006, s 10.   [158] D. Norgrave, *Family Justice Review* (London, 2012).

fee. A court officer would check that the application was correct and would then serve notice on the other party. Where the divorce is uncontested, the court officer would issue the parties with a decree nisi, and after six weeks the applicant would be able to apply for a decree absolute. If the other party did contest the divorce, the application would be transferred to the local court for judicial consideration. The judge would examine the case and determine whether the decree nisi should be issued.[159] These proposals, which have not yet been implemented, are eminently sensible and give recognition to the fact that the current procedure for divorce where the ground for divorce is uncontested is largely administrative anyway. In a recent speech about family law reform, President of the Family Division, Sir James Munby, posed the question 'may the time not come when we should at least consider whether the process of divorce still needs to be subject to judicial supervision?'[160]

Turning to more substantive reform of the actual grounds for divorce, Sir James Munby said in the same speech: 'has the time not come to legislate to remove all concepts of fault as a basis for divorce and to leave irretrievable breakdown as the sole ground?' This is a much more politically sensitive issue than administrative reform of the divorce process and it is unlikely that the current Government has the appetite for it. Certainly no-fault divorce was beyond the remit of the Family Justice Review. However, a Private Member's Bill aimed at reforming divorce law was introduced into the House of Commons on 13 October 2015. The No-Fault Divorce Bill 2015–16 seeks to allow the dissolution of a marriage or civil partnership when each party has separately made a declaration that the marriage or civil partnership has irretrievably broken down without a requirement by either party to satisfy the court of any other facts. The Bill was due to have its second reading in January 2016 although this was postponed until the next parliamentary session which commenced on 18 May 2016. The aim of the Bill is not to remove the current 'facts' on which a divorce can be granted, or to abolish the option of fault-based divorce. Instead the Bill proposes to add an additional fact to allow a couple who mutually agree to divorce to do so without having to establish the lengthy separation periods under the current law, or to fabricate one party's fault (such as adultery or unreasonable behaviour) in order to speed up the process. The Bill also proposes a one-year cooling off period before a decree of divorce is granted to allow the parties to reflect on whether a divorce was what they really wanted.

---

### Talking Point

A recent survey carried out by YouGov on behalf of Resolution showed that 27 per cent of couples who cited unreasonable behaviour in their divorce petition admitted that this claim was untrue, but simply the easiest way of getting a divorce.[161] Speaking during the introduction of the Bill to Parliament, Richard Bacon MP, said: 'Plainly there is a public interest in the justice system not encouraging people to make things up. There is also a contradiction in the current law. Although the whole thrust of current policy is supposedly about taking disputes away from the courts and towards reconciliation, mediation and alternative dispute resolution, people seeking a divorce who wish to avoid apportioning blame often find themselves required by the law to follow a path they do not wish to take. In effect, they are required to throw mud at each other.'[162]

**Q.** Do you think that the introduction of the No-Fault Divorce Bill would reduce the reliance on the fault-based facts for proving irretrievable breakdown of a marriage? Would it reduce the number of people who make false claims of 'fault' in order to expedite the divorce process?

---

[159] Ibid, Appendix H.
[160] President of the Family Division, The Family Justice Reforms, 29 April 2014, https://www.judiciary.gov.uk/wp-content/uploads/2014/05/family-justice-reforms-29042014.pdf.
[161] HC Debates, 13 October 2015, Col 190.        [162] Ibid.

Concerns were raised during the first reading of the Bill that changing the introduction of no-fault divorce would make divorce easier and thus increase the number of divorces. However, as Resolution point out, there is no evidence to suggest that no-fault divorce would have any long-term impact on the divorce rate and certainly evidence from other jurisdictions that have intro-duced non fault-based divorce is that any increase after the new legislation is only temporary, reflecting those who have waited for the new legislation to come in.[163]

---

**Talking Point**

Resolution point out: '. . . the vast majority of people know little about the divorce process and their decision to divorce is therefore unaffected by process . . . People divorce for many different reasons, not because of the nature of the divorce process itself. It is not the divorce process which saves saveable marriages, it is the information and support available.'[164]

**Q.** Do you agree?

---

Resolution feel that while the Bill is a welcome move towards a non-fault based system, it does not go far enough.[165] By contrast, Resolution proposes to remove fault completely from the divorce process by recommending a system where divorce could be granted where one or both of the par-ties to a marriage give notice that their marriage has broken down irretrievably and one or both of them are still of that view after six months.

# 5 Other decrees under the Matrimonial Causes Act 1973

There are two decrees other than divorce (and nullity) which can be made by the court under Part I of the MCA 1973. These are a decree of judicial separation and a decree of presumption of death and dissolution of marriage.

## 5.1 Decree of judicial separation

Some spouses may have objections to divorce (eg because of their religious beliefs), but if their mar-riage has come to an end they may wish to separate from the other spouse. A decree of judicial sepa-ration, which the court has jurisdiction to make under section 17 of the MCA 1973, provides such spouses with the judicial assistance they need. It may also be useful for persons who cannot divorce because one year of marriage has not elapsed, as the one-year bar which applies to divorce does not apply. In practice, compared with divorce, the number of petitions for a decree of judicial separation each year is small and the trend over the years has been downwards.[166]

A decree can be obtained in reliance on the same facts as those for divorce (adultery, unrea-sonable behaviour etc), but there is no need to prove that the marriage has irretrievably broken down.[167] If one of the facts is made out, the court must grant the decree, which comes into effect immediately. There is no two-stage process as there is in divorce. It is also not possible to raise the

---

[163] Ibid.  [164] Ibid.

[165] Resolution, No Fault Divorce Bill, House of Commons – Second Reading, http://www.resolution.org.uk/site_content_files/files/resolution_briefing_no_fault_divorce_bill_hc_2r_december_2015.pdf

[166] In 2009, 360 petitions were filed, a drop of 14 per cent on the previous year, and continuing the steady downward trend (see *Judicial and Court Statistics 2009* (Ministry of Justice, 2010), Ch 2, Table 2.5).

[167] See s 17(2).

defence of grave financial or other hardship in section 5; and section 10[168] does not apply because the parties' status as a married couple does not alter. A petitioner who successfully petitions for a decree of judicial separation is entitled to petition for divorce in reliance on the same facts.[169]

A decree of judicial separation does not terminate the marriage but merely relieves the parties of the duty to live with each other,[170] although they are not obliged to separate. Once a decree has been obtained, neither party is in desertion for refusing to live with the other party and so desertion cannot be relied upon as a fact for divorce. A spouse may decide to seek a decree of judicial separation in order to take advantage of the court's ancillary powers to make financial provision and property orders[171] and, where appropriate, orders in relation to the upbringing of the children.[172] For succession purposes, the parties are treated as if they have pre-deceased one another. Consequently, they are not entitled to succeed to one another's property on intestacy.[173] However, where one party is a beneficiary under the other party's will the position is different from divorce. On divorce any gift made to a spouse in a will automatically lapses,[174] but this rule does not extend to where the parties are judicially separated.

### 5.2  Decree of presumption of death and dissolution of the marriage

A difficult situation arises where a spouse disappears and the other spouse does not know whether the spouse who has disappeared is alive or dead. If the spouse marries again and the other spouse is not dead, the second 'marriage' is void as section 11 of the MCA 1973 provides that the parties must not be already married.[175] Also, to enter into another marriage when a spouse is not dead and where the first marriage has not been annulled or terminated by divorce, may result in a party being convicted of the criminal offence of bigamy.[176] In a case of this kind, a spouse can be assisted by obtaining a declaration of presumption of death under the Presumption of Death Act 2013.

The 2013 Act introduced a new court-based procedure enabling those left behind to obtain a declaration from the High Court that the missing person is presumed to have died. Section 1 provides that the ground for making a declaration is that the missing person is thought to have died or has not been known to be alive for at least seven years. Under section 3, a declaration is conclusive proof of the missing person's presumed death and brings an end to the missing person's marriage.[177] The 2013 Act repeals section 19 of the MCA 1973[178] under which the court could made a decree of presumption of death if the petitioner was able to prove that there were reasonable grounds for supposing that the other party to the marriage was dead. For this purpose, the other party was presumed dead if, after a period of seven years or more, he or she had been continually absent from the petitioner and the petitioner had no reason to believe that the other party had been alive during that period.

## 6  Dissolution of a civil partnership

A civil partnership can be terminated by a dissolution order made under the Civil Partnership Act 2004 in virtually same way as a divorce. The court also has the power to make separation orders and presumption of death orders.[179]

---

[168]  Which makes provision for the rescission or withholding of a decree of divorce when the petitioner has misled the respondent to a petition based on the two- or five-year fact.

[169]  MCA 1973, s 4(1).

[170]  Section 18(1).    [171]  Under the MCA 1973, Pt II, see Chapter 4.

[172]  Under the Children Act 1989, Pts I and II.

[173]  MCA 1973, s 18(2). However, they can make an application for reasonable financial provision under the Inheritance (Provision for Family and Dependants) Act 1975.

[174]  Wills Act 1837, s 18A.    [175]  See Chapter 1.    [176]  Ibid.    [177]  Section 3(2)(b).

[178]  Schedule 2, paragragh 1 of the 2013 Act.    [179]  Under the Civil Partnership Act 2004, ss 37–64.

Dissolution is a court-based process like that of divorce and, with the exception of adultery, the ground and the fact(s) which must be proved to obtain a dissolution order are the same as those for divorce. Thus, the applicant must prove that the partnership has irretrievably broken down on the basis of:[180] 'unreasonable behaviour'; two years' separation with consent to the dissolution; five years' separation; and desertion for at least two years. Like divorce, an application for a dissolution order cannot be made until one year has passed from the date on which the civil partnership was created[181] and attempts at reconciliation are permitted when calculating the periods of separation and desertion.[182] Provision is also made for the refusal of a dissolution order in five-year separation cases and for the protection of respondents in separation cases, just as there is in separation cases on divorce.[183] Dissolution, like divorce, involves a two-stage procedure: a conditional order followed by a final order.[184] The civil partnership is not terminated until the final order is made.

Like divorce, the court has the power on or after making a dissolution order to make finance and property orders equivalent to those which the court can make on divorce.[185] Thus, the court has a discretionary jurisdiction to make periodical payments and lump sum orders, orders for the sale and transfer of property, and pension orders. The court also has the power to make finance and property orders after the overseas dissolution (annulment and legal separation) of a civil partnership.[186]

Under the Civil Partnership Act 2004,[187] the family courts in England and Wales have the power to recognise overseas civil partnerships and overseas civil partnership dissolutions (and annulments and separations), and these powers are the same as those governing the recognition of overseas marriages and divorces. However, overseas same-sex marriages are not recognised in the UK, as the case of *Wilkinson v Kitzinger*[188] shows, although they may be converted to a civil partnership within this jurisdiction.

## 7 The termination of cohabitation relationships

There are no special legal provisions governing the termination of cohabitation relationships as there are for marriage and civil partnership. Thus, there is nothing equivalent to divorce or the dissolution of a civil partnership. This makes cohabitants particularly vulnerable on relationship breakdown because there is no discretionary jurisdiction, as there is on divorce and civil partnership dissolution, to distribute the parties' financial and property assets according to the present and future needs and resources of the parties. Instead any dispute about property, for instance ownership of the family home, must be dealt with in the civil courts, not the family courts, using the general principles of property and contract law, in particular the law of equity.[189] Ownership of property will depend largely on the intentions of the parties, and proving the existence of intention can involve costly and protracted litigation. Cohabitants are also at a disadvantage, compared with

---

[180] Section 44(5).      [181] Section 41.

[182] Eg a period of up to six months' cohabitation can be disregarded when calculating periods of separation or desertion (see s 42).

[183] Sections 47 and 48.

[184] It should be noted that the terminology for dissolution of a civil partnership is different from that of divorce in order to make the terms less archaic and the law more understandable, eg applicant (not petitioner) and order (not decree).

[185] Under the Civil Partnership Act 2004, s 72 and Sch 5. For more details on these orders and the principles governing the making of them, see Chapter 4 which deals with the courts' power to make finance and property orders in ancillary proceedings on divorce.

[186] See s 72(4) and Sch 7.      [187] See ss 233–238.

[188] [2006] EWHC 835 (Fam), [2006] 2 FLR 397, and see Chapter 1.

[189] See eg *Oxley v Hiscock* [2004] EWCA Civ 546, [2004] 2 FLR 669; *Stack v Dowden* [2007] UKHL 17, [2007] AC 432, [2007] 1 FLR 1858; and see further Chapter 5.

spouses and civil partners, in that they have no statutory right of occupation of the family home,[190] although they can apply under Part IV of the Family Law Act 1996 for non-molestation orders and occupation orders if they are actual or potential victims of domestic violence.

Cohabitants are also vulnerable on the death of their partner, for on their partner's intestacy they have no right to succeed to their deceased partner's property, as is the case for married persons and civil partners, although they can apply for financial provision from their deceased partner's estate under the Inheritance (Provision for Family and Dependants) Act 1975. However, applications by cohabitants under that Act are not treated as favourably as applications by married couples and civil partners.

Although there has been a great deal of debate about reforming the law to give cohabitants new family law rights on relationship breakdown and also on a partner's intestacy, there has been no political will to reform the law in this area, despite the fact that there is some considerable support for change.[191]

## Discussion Questions

1. Given the relative ease with which a divorce can be obtained under the special procedure, is there 'divorce on demand'?

2. Does the current law on divorce allow the empty shell of a marriage which has irretrievably broken down to be brought to an end with the maximum fairness, and the minimum bitterness, distress, and humiliation?

3. The Family Law Act 1996 attempted to reform the law on divorce. Discuss the failure to implement the Act and the reasons for this.

4. Would the provisions contained in the 1996 Act in relation to the divorce procedure have been an improvement on the current law?

## Further Reading

CRETNEY, S., 'Marriage, Divorce and the Courts' [2002] Family Law 900

DEECH, R., 'Divorce—A Disaster?' [2009] Family Law 1048

FREEMAN, M. (ed), *Divorce: Where Next?* (Aldershot: Dartmouth, 1996)

HASSON, E., 'Setting a Standard or Reflecting Reality? The "Role" of Divorce Law, and the Case of the Family Law Act 1996' [2003] International Journal of Law, Policy and the Family 338

HASSON, E., 'Wedded to "Fault": The Legal Regulation of Divorce and Relationship Breakdown' (2006) 26 Legal Studies 267

KAY, R., 'Whose Divorce is it Anyway? The Human Rights Aspect' [2004] Family Law 892

REECE, H., *Divorcing Responsibly* (Oxford: Hart, 2003)

 Visit the Online Resource Centre at **www.oxfordtextbooks.co.uk/orc/gilmore_glennon5e/**
**online resource centre** for a range of further features including a detailed bibliography and self-test questions.

---

[190] See the Family Law Act 1996, Pt IV, s 30, and see further Chapter 3.
[191] For details of these reforms, see Chapters 1 and 5.

# 3

# Protection from domestic violence and occupation of the family home

## INTRODUCTION

The purpose of this chapter is to consider the civil law remedies which are designed to protect a victim from domestic violence. While domestic violence resulting in a physical assault can be prosecuted as a crime such as common assault or under the Offences Against the Person Act 1861, there may be particular reasons why the victim may not want to have the perpetrator prosecuted and classed as a criminal. The civil law provides a range of remedies which are specifically designed to tackle the problem of family violence and abuse. The two primary protective orders under Part IV of the Family Law Act (FLA) 1996 are the non-molestation order and the occupation order. They can be applied for and obtained in conjunction with each other, or separately. In addition, it is important to be aware that the occupation order can also be used to regulate occupation of the family home in non-violent situations when a dispute arises between family members about who is entitled to occupy it, and on what basis.

## 1 What is domestic violence?

In 2013, the Government extended its definition of domestic violence. Up to this point the government definition of domestic violence was: 'Any incident of threatening behaviour, violence or abuse (psychological, physical, sexual, financial or emotional) between adults who are or have been intimate partners or family members, regardless of gender or sexuality'.[1] Following a commitment set out in the Government's *Violence Against Women and Girls Action Plan*,[2] and a Home Office consultation,[3] the Government announced changes to this official definition of domestic abuse. While this is not a statutory or legal definition and thus does not signal any change in the law, its importance lies in the fact that it is used by Government departments to inform policy development and by other agencies such as the police to inform the identification of domestic violence cases.[4] The new definition states that domestic violence is:

Any incident or pattern of incidents of controlling, coercive, threatening behaviour, violence or abuse between those aged 16 or over who are or have been intimate partners

---

[1] *Domestic Violence: National Plan* (London: Home Office, 2005).

[2] www.gov.uk/government/uploads/system/uploads/attachment_data/file/118153/vawg-action-plan.pdf.

[3] Home Office, *Cross-Government Definition of Domestic Violence* (2011).

[4] Home Office, *Cross-Government Definition of Domestic Violence – A Consultation, Summary of Responses* (2012), p 3.

or family members regardless of gender or sexuality. The abuse can encompass but is not limited to:

psychological

physical

sexual

financial

emotional

Controlling behaviour is: a range of acts designed to make a person subordinate and/or dependent by isolating them from sources of support, exploiting their resources and capacities for personal gain, depriving them of the means needed for independence, resistance and escape and regulating their everyday behaviour.

Coercive behaviour is: an act or a pattern of acts of assault, threats, humiliation and intimidation or other abuse that is used to harm, punish, or frighten their victim. This definition includes so called 'honour' based violence, female genital mutilation (FGM) and forced marriage, and is clear that victims are not confined to one gender or ethnic group.

This means that young people, aged 16–17 (including boys) are now recognised as victims of domestic abuse, and that such abuse includes patterns of controlling or coercive behaviour. 85 per cent of respondents to the Government consultation supported the inclusion of 16 and 17-year-olds in the official definition of domestic violence on the basis that early intervention in abusive relationships is essential, and that young people need to be made aware of what constitutes abuse. Some respondents commented that many young people, entering their first adult-type relationship, may be unaware of what constitutes acceptable and unacceptable behaviour. As such, teenage relationships may actually constitute a high-risk group in terms of the incidence of abusive relationships.[5]

## The Law in Context

This is backed up by research carried out by the NSPCC which showed that 33 per cent of girls and 16 per cent of boys aged 13–17 had experienced some form of sexual abuse.[6] It also found that 25 per cent of girls and 18 per cent of boys aged 13–17 had suffered some form of physical abuse, and that 75 per cent of girls and 50 per cent of boys reported some form of emotional abuse.[7]

The Supreme Court has recently held that 'domestic violence' for the purposes of the Housing Act 1996[8] is not limited to violence involving physical contact but also includes threatening or intimidating behaviour and any other form of abuse which, directly or indirectly, may give rise to the risk of harm.[9] Thus, it is clear that domestic violence is not simply understood as physical violence but that it encompasses a broad spectrum of abusive and controlling behaviour from actual violence, and the threat of such, to psychological, sexual, financial, and emotional abuse. As will be seen in this chapter, the legal

---

[5] Home Office, *Cross-Government Definition of Domestic Violence A Consultation, Summary of Responses* (2012), p 12.

[6] C. Barter, M. McCarry, D. Berridge, and K. Evans, *Partner Exploitation and Violence in Teenage Intimate Relationships* (2009) London, NSPCC.

[7] Ibid. The 2009/10 British Crime Survey found that women aged 16–24 and men aged 16–34 were more likely to suffer relationship abuse that any other age range, see K. Smith (ed), K. Coleman, S. Eder, and P. Hall (2011), *Homicides, Firearm Offences and Intimate Violence 2009/10* (Supplementary volume 2 to Crime in England and Wales 2009/10 2nd Edition). Home Office Statistical Bulletin 01/11.

[8] Section 177(1). See at Section 8.1.    [9] *Yemshaw v Hounslow London Borough Council* [2011] UKSC 3.

understanding of domestic violence which entitles a victim to seek a protective civil order is similarly broad.[10]

The words which are used to describe or define the abuse which takes place within the family are important. This terminology has changed over the years. In the nineteenth century, the common term used was 'wife beating'. However, as the phenomenon came to be understood as involving a wide-ranging type of controlling abuse which can occur between different family members and not just between a husband and a wife, other terms such as 'family violence' and 'domestic violence' came to be used.[11] The selection of appropriate terminology is important because it can affect a victim's perception of her own situation and the abuse which she suffering. For example, if the term 'battered wives' is used, then individuals who either are not married to the perpetrator or who are suffering non-physical mental or emotional abuse may not identify with this term and thus may not feel that they are suffering from domestic violence for which help is available.[12] Some argue that the use of the modifier 'domestic' to describe violence between family members should be avoided because it locates this form of abuse within the private sphere of the family, and marks a distinction between violence which occurs between strangers and violence between family members, leading to the perception that the latter is not as serious.[13] It has been suggested that the term 'domestic violence' be replaced by terminology which underpins the serious nature of the abuse. Marcus, for example, argues that domestic violence should be seen as a form of 'terrorism' because of the parallels between terrorism, in its conventional usage, and gender-based violence.[14] Terrorists use three tactics to achieve their goals: unannounced and calculated attacks of violence; psychological as well as physical warfare; and the creation of an atmosphere of intimidation. Marcus argues that perpetrators of violence against women in intimate relationships use similar tactics to maintain domination, control, and superiority within the relationship.

The use of a more general term such as 'family violence' is also problematic because it obscures the fact that the most prevalent and severe form of domestic violence is that perpetrated by men against women in a marriage or a marriage-like relationship.[15] While there is no doubt that domestic violence can, and does, take place between a variety of family members and that the perpetrators are not always men, some definitions of domestic violence are deliberately gendered. For example, the UN Declaration on the Elimination of Violence against Women says that domestic violence is:

Any act of gender-based violence that results in, or is likely to result in, physical, sexual or psychological harm or suffering to women, including threats of such acts, coercion or arbitrary deprivations of liberty, whether occurring in public or private life.

While this chapter will use the term 'domestic violence' as this is the term which is most commonly used to describe violence within the home, cognisance is taken of the fact that the most recurrent and severe form of domestic violence takes place by men against women.[16]

---

[10] See Section 4.3.1 for a description of the non-molestation order which is available to protect the victim from all forms of abuse including non-physical harassment.

[11] R. Dobash and R. Dobash, 'Violence Against Women in the Family' in S. A. Katz, J. Eekelaar, and M. Maclean, *Cross-Currents: Family Law Policy in the US and England* (Oxford: Oxford University Press, 2000), p 495.

[12] A. Mullender, *Rethinking Domestic Violence* (Abingdon: Routledge, 1996), p 26.

[13] I. Marcus, 'Reframing "Domestic Violence": Terrorism in the Home' in M. Fineman and R. Mykitiuk (eds), *The Public Nature of Private Violence: The Discovery of Domestic Abuse* (Abingdon: Routledge, 1994), pp 11–36.

[14] Ibid.

[15] R. Dobash and R. Dobash, 'Violence Against Women in the Family' in S. A. Katz, J. Eekelaar, and M. Maclean, *Cross-Currents: Family Law Policy in the US and England* (Oxford: Oxford University Press, 2000), p 496.

[16] See the following section.

## 2 How prevalent is domestic violence?

Domestic violence occurs in all types of families and is not confined to any particular social class, racial or religious group, or age group. Commentators agree that it is very difficult to be precise about the prevalence of domestic violence, largely due to victim under-reporting, and the absence of a single criminal offence covering domestic violence. Another difficulty in collecting precise statistical evidence is that some data only portrays violence between intimate partners and not that which occurs between other family members.[17] In addition, the fact that domestic violence not only refers to physical violence but also to other forms of abuse, such as emotional abuse and financial deprivation, makes it hard to quantify as the incidence of these non-physical forms of abuse are difficult to measure.

---

**The Law in Context**

Statistical evidence does give us some idea of the prevalence of domestic violence, although certainly not its full extent. In the UK, one in four young people, aged 10 to 24, reported that they had experienced domestic violence and abuse during their childhood.[18] Evidence shows that in 2013/14, 8.5 per cent of women and 4.5 per cent of men were estimated to have experienced domestic abuse, equivalent to around 1.4 million female and 700,000 male victims.[19] Overall, 28.3 per cent of women and 14.7 per cent of men had experienced any domestic abuse since the age of 16, equivalent to an estimated 4.6 million female victims and 2.4 million male victims. For women the most commonly experienced types of intimate violence since age 16, covered by the survey, were non-sexual partner abuse (22.0 per cent), stalking (21.5 per cent) and sexual assault (19.9 per cent). For men, the most commonly experienced types of abuse were stalking (9.8 per cent) and non-sexual partner abuse (9.6 per cent). Studies also show that 1 in 5 teenagers have been physically abused by their boyfriends or girlfriends.[20] It is estimated that 130,000 children live in households with high-risk domestic abuse.[21] Children exposed to domestic violence are more likely to have behavioural and emotional problems.[22]

---

Domestic violence accounted for 15 per cent of all violent incidents in 2011/12.[23] In the same year, the police recorded nearly 800,000 domestic violence incidents.[24] Domestic violence is the largest cause of morbidity worldwide in women aged 19–44, greater than deaths caused by war, cancer, or motor accidents, costing public services in the UK £25.3 billion in one year alone.[25] In 2012-13, seventy seven women were killed by their partners or ex-partners.[26]

Recent research by the national domestic abuse charity, SafeLives, shows that around a quarter of victims suffering domestic abuse are experiencing medium- or high-risk abuse and that more than 100,000 victims are at imminent risk of being murdered or seriously injured.[27] The study also showed that victims suffer on average for nearly three years before seeking help, and that a quarter of the children living with high-risk domestic abuse are under three years of age. The research also

---

[17] Home Affairs Select Committee (2008).

[18] L. Radford, S. Corral, C. Bradley et al, *Child Abuse and Neglect in the UK Today* (London: NSPCC, 2011).

[19] ONS, *Crime Statistics, Focus on Violent Crime and Sexual Offences, 2013/14*, February 2015, Chapter 4.

[20] Barter et al, *Partner Exploitation and Violence in Teenage Intimate Relationships* (NSPCC and Bristol University, 2009).

[21] CAADA, *A Place of Greater Safety: Insights into Domestic Abuse* (2012).

[22] C. Humphreys, 'Relevant Evidence for Practice' Chapter 1 in C. Humphreys and N. Stanley (eds) *Domestic Violence and Child Protections: Directions for Good Practice*, (Jessica Kingsley Publishers, 2006).

[23] P. Strickland, *Domestic Violence*, London: House of Commons Library (2012).

[24] ONS, *Focus on Violent Crime and Sexual Offences*, 2011/12.

[25] Home Affairs Select Committee (2008). See also *Domestic Violence: A National Report* (London: Home Office, 2005).

[26] HMIC, *Everyone's Business: Improving the Police Response to Domestic Abuse* (London, 2014).

[27] SafeLives, *Getting it Right First Time*, http://www.safelives.org.uk/sites/default/files/resources/Getting%20it%20 right%20first%20time%20-%20complete%20report.pdf

found that there are far too many missed opportunities to get help for victims of domestic abuse. 85 per cent of victims sought help five times on average from professionals, such as the police, GP or A&E department, in the year before they got effective help to stop the abuse.

While there is evidence to show that men are at times the victims of domestic violence at the hands of their female partners, it remains the case that there is *asymmetry* in domestic violence with men more likely to be the perpetrator and women more likely to be the victim.[28] Others take a different view and argue that intimate partner violence is just as likely to involve a female perpetrator and a male victim. In light of this, some argue that the focus should be on 'family violence' as opposed to constructing the problem primarily as one of 'violence against women'.[29] However, studies continue to show that men are more likely than women to perpetrate violence against an intimate partner, and that women's violence to men does not equate in terms of frequency, severity, or in terms of its impact on the victim's sense of safety and well-being.[30] Dobash and Dobash reject evidence which suggests that domestic violence is gender-neutral arguing that it is based on narrow research methodologies which rely on the measurement of individual 'acts' of abuse such as a slap or a punch. The problem with this type of approach is that it measures these individual acts out of context and does not consider either the history of violence and abuse which may have preceded the act in question, or the outcome of the specific act. For example, they point to the fact that this approach will equate 'the physical impact/consequences of a "slap" delivered by a slight, 5 ft 4 inch woman with the "slap" of a heavily built man of 6 ft 2 inches'.[31] In addition, this approach simply looks at the fact of an act of violence taking place but does not consider the motives or intentions of the perpetrator such as whether it took place in the context of self-defence.

Statistics from the British Crime Survey also reveal that while less serious violence tends to be gender-neutral, the majority of serious and recurring violence is carried out by men against women.[32] A study in 2004 revealed that while 45 per cent of women and 26 per cent of men had experienced at least one incident of domestic violence in their lifetime, women were much more likely to be the victims of repeat incidents, and more severe attacks. Recent research based on studies of 96 cases reported by the Northumbrian police over a six-year period, found that the majority of perpetrators of domestic violence in cases which were reported to the police were men, and that the majority of repeat incidents were recorded for male rather than for female perpetrators.[33] Men were also more likely to use physical violence, threats, and harassment. The authors noted that:

> Men's violence tended to create a context of fear and related to that, control. This was not similarly the case where women were perpetrators.

Incidents where women were the perpetrators usually involved verbal abuse, some physical violence, and only a small proportion of threats or harassment. Women were, however, more likely

---

[28] R. Dobash and R. Dobash, 'Violence Against Women in the Family' in S. A. Katz, J. Eekelaar, and M. Maclean, *Cross-Currents: Family Law Policy in the US and England* (Oxford: Oxford University Press, 2000).

[29] R. Dobash and R. Dobash, 'Women's Violence to Men in Intimate Relationships: Working on a Puzzle' (2004) British Journal of Criminology, 324.

[30] Ibid. See also M., Hester, 'Gender and Sexuality' in Itzin et al., *Tackling the Health Effects of Abuse and Violence* (London: Routledge, 2010).

[31] R. Dobash and R. Dobash, 'Women's Violence to Men in Intimate Relationships: Working on a Puzzle' (2004) British Journal of Criminology, 329.

[32] S. Walby and J. Allen, *Domestic Violence, Sexual Assault and Stalking: Findings from the British Crime Survey*, Home Office Research Study 276 (London: Home Office, 2004). See also Home Affairs Select Committee (2008).

[33] M. Hester, *Who Does What to Whom? Gender and Domestic Violence Perpetrators* (Bristol: University of Bristol in association with the Northern Rock Foundation, 2009). However, the study found that women were arrested to a 'disproportionate degree' given that they were much less likely to be perpetrators of violence than men. During the six-year period of the study, men were arrested once in every ten incidents, and women were arrested every three incidents. See also M. Hester and N. Westmarland, *Tackling Domestic Violence: Effective Interventions and Approaches*, Home Office Research Study 290 (London: Home Office, 2005).

to use a weapon although this was, at times, in an attempt to stop further violence from their partners. The study also found that in over half of the cases, children were recorded as having been present when the violence or other abuse took place.

Crime and other statistics only provide a rough estimate of the nature and extent of domestic violence, but it is very clear that those living in households where abuse and violence occur are damaged by this behaviour, both physically and emotionally. It is estimated that at least 750,000 children a year witness domestic violence.[34] There is also evidence to show that witnessing domestic violence has a detrimental impact on a child's health and well-being.[35] Children who have lived in a household where domestic violence occurs are more likely to have behavioural problems and other such difficulties. Mullender observes that:

> children are likely to be affected by the fear, disruption and distress in their lives. Children show distress in their own ways, depending on their age and developmental stage. They may have physical, emotional, learning, behavioural or developmental problems, and their educational performance and achievement may also be affected. These symptoms can easily be misdiagnosed or wrongly assessed as illness, permanent learning difficulties or naughtiness.[36]

Given the very damaging consequences of domestic violence, one question which is often asked is: Why did the victim not leave the relationship? Victims of such violence and abuse very often do not report the violence or seek help, either through fear of the repercussions or because they may be too embarrassed to tell anyone what is happening to them. One of the most notable characteristics of domestic violence is that it rarely occurs as an isolated incident. It is much more likely to occur as an ongoing process of abuse and intimidation with the attacks escalating in both frequency and severity. Parmar and Sampson note that:

> [a] particular feature of domestic violence is that it occurs as part of a continuum of violence; sometimes there may be serious physical violence, and at other times there are verbal taunts about the incompetence of the woman and her 'ugliness' . . . The forms of abuse can include controlling behaviour, such as limiting a woman's contact with her family and friends, scrutiny of and restriction of her actions, threats to hurt, rape and murder.[37]

Repeat victimisation, particularly against female victims, is very common. Hester describes domestic violence whether physical, psychological, emotional, verbal, or financial as an 'ongoing pattern of fear and coercive control'.[38] She continues:

> Such 'archetypal' domestic violence . . . will usually involve one partner being violent, involve frequent abuse, and is likely to escalate and to result in serious injury.[39]

At the start of the abuse, the victim is unlikely to report it as she may believe the abuser's promises that it will not happen again and is likely to be committed to the relationship.[40] However, as the

---

[34] *Secure Futures for Women: Making a Difference* (London: Department of Health, 2002).

[35] *Domestic Violence: A National Report* (London: Home Office, 2005), para 39.

[36] A. Mullender, *Tackling Domestic Violence: Providing Support for Children Who Have Witnessed Domestic Violence* (London: Home Office, 2005).

[37] A. Parmar and A. Sampson, 'Evaluating Domestic Violence Initiatives' (2007) British Journal of Criminology 671 at 674. The authors cite R. Dobash et al, *Research Evaluation Programmes for Violent Men* (Edinburgh: The Scottish Office Central Research Unit, 1996); S. Edwards, 'Police Attitudes and Dispositions in Domestic Disputes: The London Study' (1986) Police Journal, July; J. Hanmer and S. Saunders, *Well-Founded Fear* (London: Hutchinson, 1984); L. Kelly, *Surviving Sexual Violence* (Cambridge: Polity Press, 1987); B. Stanko, *Intimate Intrusions: Women's Experience of Male Violence* (London: Routledge, 1985).

[38] M. Hester, *Who Does What to Whom? Gender and Domestic Violence Perpetrators* (Bristol: University of Bristol in association with the Northern Rock Foundation, 2009), p 4.

[39] Ibid.     [40] A. Mullender, *Rethinking Domestic Violence* (Abingdon: Routledge, 1996).

abuse continues and escalates in severity, a victim may become less confident in her ability to leave the situation and regain her independence, and more fearful of the abuser and of the repercussions of leaving. The victim may also blame herself, and many victims do not regard the abuse which they suffer as a crime, or as something with which the law can help. There may also be very practical reasons why a person remains in an abusive relationship, especially if the victim has few independent economic resources and is financially dependent on the abuser.[41] Also, leaving the relationship does not mean that the abuse will come to an end. Studies show that women are at the greatest risk of being killed by their former partner after they leave a violent relationship,[42] and that women find the first six months after they leave their partner to be the most dangerous.[43] It should also be pointed out that querying why the victim did not leave removes the focus of attention from the perpetrator. This places responsibility on the victim for not leaving and, in doing so, implicates her in the allocation of blame for what has taken place.[44]

# 3  Explanations for domestic violence

There are several schools of thought around the reasons why domestic violence takes place.[45]

## 3.1  Psychological explanations

Some argue that domestic violence is perpetrated by deviant individuals who, for a variety of reasons connected with their background, character, and psychology, are predisposed to violence.[46] Risk factors such as alcohol or drug abuse may also explain the violence, as might the fact that the perpetrator has also suffered abuse and is repeating the cycle of violence. According to the British Crime Survey, 32 per cent of incidents of domestic violence occurred when the perpetrator was under the influence of alcohol.[47] A study in 2003 of 336 convicted domestic violence offenders

---

[41] The victim may face obstacles in securing legal aid funding to support an application for a legal remedy. The Legal Aid, Sentencing and Punishment of Offenders Act 2012 (LASPO 2012) dramatically curtailed legal aid for legal advice and representation in private family law matters. However, one main exception is cases involving domestic violence. Paragraph 12 of Schedule 1 to LASPO 2012 makes provision for civil legal services to be provided to an adult (A) 'in relation to a matter arising out of a family relationship between A and another individual (B) where – (a) there has been, or is a risk of, domestic violence between A and B, and (b) A was, or is at risk of being, the victim of that domestic violence. However, the accompanying Civil Legal Aid (Procedure) Regulations 2012 provide that legal aid will not be available in cases of domestic violence unless documentary verification is provided 'within the 24-month period before the application for legal aid is made save for instances of an unspent conviction, un-concluded criminal proceedings and existing police bail for a domestic violence criminal offence'. This has been the subject of a recent judicial review. In *R (Rights of Women) v The Secretary of State for Justice* [2016] EWCA Civ 91 it was claimed, in the first instance, that this regulation was ultra vires the statute and, alternatively, that the imposition of the 24-month time period frustrates the purpose of the Act (which is that persons suffering from domestic violence should be eligible for legal aid provided they qualify in respect of their financial resources and the merits of their case). The Court of Appeal held that the regulation was not made ultra vires. However, the Court held that the 24-month limitation did frustrate the purpose of the legislation with respect to evidence and in failing to make provision for victims of financial abuse. The Court could see 'no obvious correlation between the passage of such a comparatively short period of time as 24 months and the harm to the victim of domestic violence disappearing or even significantly diminishing' (*R (Rights of Women) v The Secretary of State for Justice* [2016] EWCA Civ 91, [45]).

[42] S. Lees, 'Marital Rape and Marital Murder' in J. Hanmer and C. Itzin (eds), *Home Truths about Domestic Violence: Feminist Influences on Policy and Practice: A Reader* (Abingdon: Routledge, 2002).

[43] C. Humphreys and R. K. Thiara, 'Neither Justice nor Protection: Women's Experiences of Post-Separation Violence' (2003) 25 Journal of Social Welfare and Family Law 195.

[44] See E. M. Schneider, *Battered Women and Feminist Lawmaking* (New Haven, CT: Yale University Press, 2000).

[45] For an interesting discussion see J. Miles, 'Domestic Violence' in J. Herring (ed), *Family Law: Issues, Debates, Policy* (Cullompton: Willan Publishing, 2001), pp 78–124.

[46] Ibid, p 80.

[47] C. Mirrlees-Black, *Domestic Violence: Findings from a New British Crime Survey Self-Completion Questionnaire*, Home Office Research Study 191 (Home Office, 1999). See *Alcohol and Intimate Partner Violence* (London: Home Office, 2004).

identified two main types of perpetrator of domestic violence.[48] First, there were 'borderline/emotionally dependent offenders' who tended to display high levels of anger and jealousy, formed intense relationships with high levels of interpersonal dependency, and tended to suffer from depression and/or anxiety and have low self-esteem. Secondly, the study identified 'antisocial/narcissistic' offenders who had hostile attitudes towards women, had difficulty empathising with others, and who also had the highest rate of alcohol dependence and previous convictions.

### 3.2 Social structural explanations

From another perspective, broader social and environmental factors, such as unemployment, poverty, and bad housing, are said to contribute to the occurrence of domestic violence. From this sociological perspective, the more social stress that individuals and families face, the greater the likelihood of conflict occurring within the family.[49] According to Straus and Gelles, the family as a social institution has unique features which make it prone to violence.[50] These characteristics include the sheer amount of time spent with family members engaging in a wide-ranging number of activities; the intensity of this involvement; the age and sex differences of family members and the ascribed roles of individuals within the family; the perception of the family as a private institution; and the stresses and strains associated with family life and the dependency of ageing family members. However, this approach can also be criticised because it downplays the gendered nature of violence within families, and suggests that violence only occurs in families facing poverty and other social stresses, which we know not to be the case. It also fails to answer the question of why such social and environmental stresses should lead to violence against women.[51]

### 3.3 Feminist explanations–the patriarchal social order

Another school of thought frames the problem of domestic violence within the patriarchal social order where male violence against women is viewed as a mechanism of control and domination within marriage and marriage-like relationships.[52] On this view, domestic violence is the product of the unequal power relationship between men and women in society and is used to perpetuate a female subordination which is central to the patriarchal social order.[53] Many argue that male violence against women is characterised by the desire to control the victim's behaviour.[54] The historical legitimisation of domestic violence and the reluctance of the law to take it seriously give credence to the abuser's belief that he is entitled to use force, either physical or otherwise, in order to exercise power and control within the relationship. Thus while the law has changed and domestic violence is no longer lawful, attitudes about female subordination in society and within intimate relationships persist.

---

[48] *Domestic Violence Offenders: Characteristics and Offending Related Needs* (London: Home Office, 2003).

[49] See R. Gelles, 'Through a Sociological Lens: Social Structures and Family Violence' in R. Gelles and D. Loseke (eds), *Current Controversies on Family Violence* (Thousand Oaks, CA: Sage, 1993), pp 31–47.

[50] R. Gelles and M. Straus, 'Determinants of Violence in the Family: Toward a Theoretical Integration' in R. Burr et al (eds), *Contemporary Theories About the Family*, vol. 1 (New York: Free Press, 1979), pp 549–81.

[51] A. Mullender, *Rethinking Domestic Violence* (Abingdon: Routledge, 1996).

[52] See D. Martin, *Battered Wives* (New York: Pocket Books, 1976); R. Dobash and R. Dobash, *Violence Against Wives: A Case Against the Patriarchy* (New York: Free Press, 1979); J. Radford and E. Stanko, 'Violence Against Women and Children: The Contradictions of Crime Control under Patriarchy' in M. Hester, L. Kelly, and J. Radford (eds), *Women, Violence and Male Power* (Buckingham: Open University Press, 1996) pp 65–80.

[53] Ibid.

[54] P. Romito, *A Deafening Silence: Hidden Violence against Women and Children* (Bristol: Policy Press, 2008); R. B. Felson and S. F. Messner, 'The Control Motive in Intimate Partner Violence' (2000) 63 Social Psychology Quarterly 86.

## 3.4 **A multifaceted phenomenon**

While focusing on pathological explanations is a limited viewpoint because it means that the response to domestic violence will be based upon the need to address the individual deviance of the abuser, one must be careful that the personal responsibility of the perpetrator is not diminished by an approach which blames broader social factors. Thus, the preferred approach may be to view domestic violence as caused by a combination of factors. According to Dobash and Dobash:

> Men's violence towards their partners has been part of a world culture for most of written history and should be understood both as an individual and as a sociocultural phenomenon.[55]

In addition, looking at the social structural explanations for domestic violence recognises that the family, as an institution, can be a dangerous environment. Moreover, the prevalence of male violence against women cannot be ignored and thus domestic violence must also be understood within the context of the patriarchal social order. Viewing domestic violence as a product of the patriarchal social structure 'that is built on male superiority and female inferiority, sex-stereotyped roles and expectations, and economic, social and political predominance of men and dependency of women'[56] means that social and political structures which perpetuate female inequality must be challenged. Not only does this involve strategies to maximise women's economic independence, but also a break from notions which legitimise male domination of women in intimate relationships. Madden Dempsey forcefully argues that domestic violence reflects the intersection between three key elements—violence, domesticity, and structural inequality.[57] She uses a conceptual framework which defines violence in the home by its location within the private sphere of the family, and by the relationship between the parties which is usually characterised by intimacy, familial ties, or a shared household. In addition, the two key concepts which underpin the structural inequalities within relationships which form part of her analytical framework are power and control. Power is defined as the 'ability or entitlement to exercise control over another person'. For Madden Dempsey, domestic violence can manifest itself on a continuum from a 'strong' to a 'weak' representation of the phenomenon. The location of different acts of violence and abuse on this continuum depends on the extent of the intersection between the three key elements of violence, domesticity, and structural inequalities. Domestic violence in its 'strong' sense refers to illegitimate violence which occurs in a domestic context and which sustains or perpetuates the structural inequalities between the parties. The classic example of this is 'wife beating'. On the other end of the spectrum is domestic violence in its 'weak' sense, which refers to illegitimate violence in a domestic context which does not sustain or perpetuate structural inequalities. An example of this is the actions of a victim of domestic violence in its 'strong' sense who engages in violent actions against his or her abuser. This work is interesting as it shows how the power differentials within relationships impact on the interpretation of violence between the parties, and confirms the notion that dominance, power, and control are at the heart of domestic violence.

# 4 **The response of the law to domestic violence**

It is only in recent years that domestic violence has been regarded as a social problem requiring state intervention to protect victims. The fact that it occurred within the private realm of the family

---

[55] R. Dobash and R. Dobash, *Violence Against Wives: A Case Against the Patriarchy* (New York: Free Press, 1979).

[56] R. Copelon, 'Intimate Terror: Understanding Domestic Violence as Terror' in R. Cook (ed), *Human Rights of Women* (Philadelphia, PA: University of Pennsylvania Press, 1994).

[57] M. Madden-Dempsey, 'What Counts as Domestic Violence: A Conceptual Analysis' [2006] 12 William and Mary Journal of Women and the Law 301.

meant that in social consciousness and by law it was regarded as a private matter. Historically, a husband was responsible for his wife's behaviour and, as such, he had the right to apply moderate chastisement to her.[58] This did not begin to change until the mid-nineteenth century when legal provisions were introduced to protect women from violence. However, these provisions were largely ineffective and it was not until the late 1960s that the pernicious nature of domestic violence became an issue for policy-makers. The first women's refuge was opened in Chiswick in 1971 by Erin Pizzey who subsequently published a dramatic account of the true nature of domestic violence and the failure of the law to provide safeguards for its victims.[59] In the 1970s, domestic violence came to be recognised as a serious social problem. The growing women's movement in the 1970s led to the creation of the Select Committee on Violence in Marriage in 1974, which resulted in a legislative framework of civil remedies to meet the needs of victims of domestic violence. Before looking at these civil remedies in detail, we must first look at how the criminal justice system responds to domestic violence.

## 4.1 The role of the criminal law

While there is no specific offence of 'domestic violence', domestic assaults are criminal offences and the perpetrator can be prosecuted under the criminal justice system for offences such as assault, harassment, and rape. Until relatively recently, a husband could not be charged with the rape of his wife because, on marriage, she was deemed to give irrevocable consent to sexual intercourse throughout the marriage. However, following the decision of the House of Lords in *R v R (Rape: Marital Exemption)*[60] this common law rule was abolished and a man can now be charged with raping his wife.[61] In terms of other forms of assault, there is nothing to prevent a perpetrator of domestic abuse from being dealt with by the criminal justice system, and guidelines issued by the Sentencing Guidelines Council state that domestic violence offences are just as serious as offences committed in a non-domestic context.[62] In addition, the Guidelines make it clear that because the offence took place between family members, there are likely to be aggravating factors to make it more serious when it comes to sentencing. The court will consider, in particular, whether the perpetrator abused his position of trust and power within the relationship or exploited the victim's vulnerability and whether there has been a proven history of violence or threats of violence by the offender in a domestic setting. Offences involving serious violence will result in a prison sentence in the majority of cases.[63]

However, domestic violence has not always been regarded as a serious problem by the criminal justice system. The official attitudes of the police and criminal justice agencies towards domestic violence have changed dramatically in the latter half of the twentieth century. Throughout the 1970s and 1980s, the police were reluctant to intervene in situations of domestic violence, which tended to be regarded as a private family matter, or a mere 'domestic'. The fact the victims quite often withdrew complaints led to a perception that they were 'fickle', and that this type of violence was less serious than violence between strangers.[64] By 1990, however, criminal justice agencies were taking domestic violence much more seriously and emphasis was placed on pro-arrest policies and prosecution. A Home Office Circular was issued to all police forces in England and Wales in 1990 directing a more proactive response to incidents of domestic violence.[65] However, subsequent research found that putting these policies into practice had not been that successful.[66]

---

[58] W. Blackstone, *Commentaries on the Laws of England* (1765).

[59] E. Pizzey, *Scream Quietly or the Neighbours Will Hear* (Harmondsworth: Penguin Books, 1974).

[60] [1992] 1 AC 599.      [61] See Sexual Offences Act 2003, s 1.

[62] Sentencing Guidelines Council, 'Overarching Principles: Domestic Violence' (2006).      [63] Ibid.

[64] See S. Edwards, *Policing 'Domestic' Violence: Women, the Law and the State* (London: Sage Publications, 1989).

[65] Home Office Circular 60/1990.

[66] S. Grace, *Policing Domestic Violence in the 1990s*, Home Office Research Study 139 (London: Home Office, 1995).

A revised circular was introduced in 2000 which emphasised, once again, the need for proactive policing of domestic violence, with a focus on pro-arrest policies.

Official government policy is also focused on improving the criminal justice response to domestic violence in order to achieve justice for victims and to bring perpetrators to account.[67] This change in emphasis has had some success. Reports show an increase in the number of domestic violence offenders being convicted, and pleading guilty. In 2012–13, the overall pattern of domestic violence prosecutions indicated that since 2005, a higher proportion of domestic violence cases were charged, prosecuted, and convicted, with fewer cases discontinued and more defendants pleading guilty.[68] Figures from the Crown Prosecution Service (CPS) reveal a 65 per cent increase in the volume of domestic violence prosecutions from 2005–06 to 2010–11,[69] and, between 2005–06 and 2012–13, conviction rates have risen from 59.7 per cent to 74.3 per cent.[70] Notably, this is the highest recorded conviction rate.[71] Central to the more proactive government policy on domestic violence is the introduction of a network of Specialist Domestic Violence Courts (SDVCs), which have developed a specialist way of dealing with domestic violence cases.[72] These specialist courts offer a combined approach to tackling domestic violence by bringing together the police, the Crown prosecutors, magistrates, courts, and specialist support services for victims. This integrated system aims to enhance the effectiveness of court and support services for victims, to improve victim participation and satisfaction, and to increase public confidence in the criminal justice system.[73]

However, despite these improvements, there are still problems with the criminal justice response to domestic violence. Domestic violence remains an under-reported crime.[74] The proportion of domestic violence cases remains only 8.9 per cent of all court prosecutions.[75] The two main problems are under-reporting of the abuse and victim retraction. 'One of the main problems in domestic violence cases relates to victim retraction due to the close and often intimate relationship between the defendant and victim. 6,741 domestic violence cases failed in 2012–13 because the victim either failed to attend court or retracted their evidence . . .'[76]

### 4.1.1 Failure to report the abuse

In the 2004 British Crime Survey, the police were only aware of 1 in 4 of the worst cases of domestic violence.[77] When asked why victims did not report the domestic violence to the police:

- 41 per cent of women and 68 per cent of men thought that it was too trivial;

- 38 per cent of women and 39 per cent of men thought that it was a private family matter;

- 7 per cent of women and 5 per cent of men said that they did not want to suffer any more humiliation; and

- 13 per cent of women (and no discernible percentage of men) feared more violence or that the situation would deteriorate if the police were involved.

---

[67] *Safety and Justice: the Government's Proposals on Domestic Violence* (Cm 5847, 2003); HM Government, National Domestic Violence Delivery Plan: Annual Progress Report 2008–09. See also HM Government, *A Call to End Violence against Women and Girls: Action Plan 2013.*

[68] CPS, *Violence against Women and Girls: Crime Report 2012–2013* (London: CPS, 2013).

[69] CPS, *Violence against Women and Girls: Crime Report 2010–2011* (London: CPS, 2011).

[70] CPS, *Violence against Women and Girls: Crime Report 2012–2013* (London: CPS, 2013).          [71] Ibid.

[72] *Domestic Violence: A National Report* (London: Home Office, 2005), para 51.

[73] Ibid, para 53. See D. Cook et al, *Evaluation of Specialist Domestic Violence Courts/Fast Track Systems* (London: CPS/Department of Constitutional Affairs, 2004); A. Robinson and D. Cook, 'Understanding Victim Retraction in Cases of Domestic Violence: Specialist Courts, Government Policy, and Victim-Centred Justice' (2006) 9 Contemporary Justice Review 189.

[74] See Home Affairs Select Committee, Domestic Violence, Forced Marriage and 'Honour'-Based Violence, Sixth Report of Session 2007-08 (2008).

[75] Ibid.          [76] Ibid, p 23.

[77] S. Walby and J. Allen, *Domestic Violence, Sexual Assault and Stalking: Findings from the British Crime Survey,* Home Office Research Study 276 (London: Home Office, 2004).

There are a range of reasons why a victim may be reluctant to report the abuse.[78] Some may have low expectations of the police and criminal justice system, others may feel fear and shame, or regard the abuse to be their own fault. A person may also be deterred by the fact that, once an attack is reported to the police, the matter is no longer under her control. It will be up to the police to decide whether and how they wish to investigate the complaint, and it will be the decision of the CPS whether or not to go ahead and press charges. This loss of control acts as a disincentive to women to report incidents of violence as they may fear the consequences of their actions if the police and the CPS fail to respond in an appropriate fashion. Other factors which may deter a victim from becoming involved in the criminal process include the fear of further, and perhaps more vicious, assaults in retaliation for reporting the abuse; anxiety about the financial hardship which the family may suffer if the perpetrator were to lose his job; and a more general reluctance to be instrumental in the perpetrator obtaining a criminal record, and perhaps being sent to prison.

### 4.1.2 High levels of 'attrition'

In relation to incidents that are reported to the police, very few make it through the criminal justice system. A Home Office report on domestic violence noted that while there are estimated to be some 500,000 domestic violence-related calls to the police, only around 7,000 incidents result in prosecution.[79] The occurrence where cases fall out of the criminal justice system is known as 'attrition'. There are a variety of reasons why cases do not progress through the system from arrest to conviction. Not only might the police fail to obtain the necessary evidence, but victims may withdraw from the system.[80] Some victims may have concerns about giving evidence in court against a partner or a former partner. For example, a victim could be concerned that even if her partner is convicted, a non-custodial sentence may be imposed which could place her in immediate danger for giving evidence.[81] A study in 2003 examined the attrition rate in domestic violence cases entering the criminal justice system in Northumbria.[82] Of the 869 domestic violence incidents recorded by the police during the sample period, only 3.6 per cent resulted in conviction for criminal offences and there were only four custodial sentences. The researchers found that the victims were considered by the police as key to attrition. If the victim was unable or unwilling to provide a statement, there was little chance of a successful prosecution. However, it is possible for a prosecution to proceed even without the victim's testimony and the policy of the CPS is to consider other evidence which may be available either to support the victim's evidence or as an alternative to the victim's evidence.[83] If the victim does not wish to give evidence, the CPS will decide whether to proceed with the case on public interest grounds, taking into account a number of factors such as whether the defendant used a weapon, the seriousness of the attack, the nature of the victim's injuries, and the effect of the violence on any children living in the household. Given this, the police are encouraged to gather all evidence, such as photographic evidence and witness statements, which may make prosecution possible even if the victim does not wish to provide evidence. This is called 'enhanced evidence gathering'. However, in the Northumbrian study it was found that enhanced evidence was only rarely collected, and the extent to which the police

---

[78] See A. Mullender, *Rethinking Domestic Violence* (Abingdon: Routledge, 1996), p 33.

[79] *Domestic Violence: A National Report* (London: Home Office, 2005).

[80] See M. Hester, 'Making It Through the Criminal Justice System: Attrition and Domestic Violence' (2005) 5(1) Social Policy and Society 79.

[81] See B. James, 'In Practice: Prosecuting Domestic Violence' [2008] Family Law 456. See also *R v C* [2007] EWCA Crim 3463.

[82] M. Hester et al, *Domestic Violence: Making it Through the Criminal Justice System* (University of Sunderland, Northern Rock Foundation and the International Centre for the Study of Violence and Abuse, 2003); M. Hester, 'Making it Through the Criminal Justice System: Attrition and Domestic Violence' (2005) 5(1) Social Policy and Society 79.

[83] M. Burton, *Legal Responses to Domestic Violence* (Abingdon: Routledge-Cavendish, 2008), p 98.

gathered other evidence (such as CCTV footage and interviews with neighbours) depended on what was requested by the CPS.[84]

Despite the changes in the criminal justice system concerning pro-arrest policies and the need to take domestic violence seriously, improvements are still required to translate this rhetoric into practice. However, some argue that regardless of the criminal sanction imposed on a violent partner, women can benefit from simply engaging with the criminal justice system.[85] Lewis says that:

> the process of 'going public' can make women feel that their attempts to challenge their partner's violence are acknowledged and validated. It can offer women immediate and longer-term support, represent a challenge to their partner's tactic of isolation, and/or facilitate a shift in the balance of power in the relationship as men reduce their violence and abuse under the threat of further intervention.[86]

However, from another perspective, some point out that there are negative aspects of pro-arrest and prosecution policies. For example, some argue that such policies may result in the arrest of women who have used violence in retaliation and defence, which may contribute to the emergence of statistics which show than women are also the perpetrators of domestic violence.[87] Others point out that engaging with the criminal justice system means that the victim loses control of how the case is managed which could 'further disempower and endanger the victim' if prosecution is not what she wants.[88] Evidence has shown that court outcomes of domestic violence cases did not stop chronic offenders from continuing their course of violence and harassment.[89]

### 4.1.3 Domestic violence protection orders

While there have been improvements in the response of the criminal justice system to domestic violence cases, problems remain. In particular, the high levels of attrition mean that many cases fail to progress through the criminal justice system. This can put victims at even more risk especially in situations where a suspected offender who is not charged or is released on bail returns to the family home in the aftermath of a domestic violence incident. Research has shown that victims are particularly vulnerable at this time.[90] It has been noted that '[t]here is no readily available, consistent, affordable and timely access to civil court orders in the immediate aftermath of a domestic violence incident and therefore a gap exists between how the criminal justice system and civil law processes interact to provide immediate safety and a seamless service to victims at on-going risk of violence'.[91] Provisions of the Crime and Security Act 2010, which introduce the 'domestic violence protection notice' and 'domestic violence protection order' have now been enacted in an effort to address this gap.

Under section 24 of the Act, the police may issue, without court proceedings, a 'domestic violence protection notice' to a person over 18 if there are reasonable grounds for believing that the person

---

[84] M. Hester, 'Making it Through the Criminal Justice System: Attrition and Domestic Violence' (2005) 5(1) Social Policy and Society 79 at 86.

[85] R. Lewis, 'Making Justice Work: Effective Legal Interventions for Domestic Violence' (2004) British Journal of Criminology 204.

[86] Ibid.

[87] M. Chesney-Lind, 'Patriarchy, Crime and Justice: Feminist Criminology in an Era of Backlash' (2006) 1 Feminist Criminology 6. See also S. Walklate, 'What is to be Done About Violence Against Women? Gender, Violence, Cosmopolitanism and the Law' (2008) British Journal of Criminology 39.

[88] M. Burton, 'Civil Law Remedies for Domestic Violence: Why are Applications for Non-Molestation Orders Declining?' (2009) 31(2) Journal of Social Welfare and Family Law 109.

[89] M. Hester, 'Making it Through the Criminal Justice System: Attrition and Domestic Violence' (2005) 5(1) Social Policy and Society 79.

[90] Home Office. 'Interim Guidance Document for Police Regional Pilot Schemes' (2011) www.gov.uk/government/uploads/system/uploads/attachment_data/file/97864/DV-protection-orders.pdf.

[91] Ibid, at para 1.5.

'has been violent towards, or has threatened violence towards, an associated person'. The victim's consent is not needed for this notice to be issued. The notice prohibits the suspected perpetrator from molesting the victim and may even require him to leave the home. The police then have to apply to the magistrates' court for a 'domestic violence protection order' within 48 hours to limit the length of time for which the suspected perpetrator can be excluded from his home in the absence of a court order. The 'domestic violence protection order' is a court order lasting between 14 and 28 days, which prohibits the perpetrator from molesting the victim and it may also oust the perpetrator from the home. The court can make the order if it is satisfied on the balance of probabilities that the respondent was violent towards or had threatened violence towards an 'associated person' and that the order is necessary to protect that person from violence or a threat of violence from the perpetrator.

In 2011, pilot schemes were set up in three locations to review the operation of these orders before their full implementation. While it could be argued that allowing the police to remove a suspected perpetrator from the family home in the absence of a court order is an invasion of that person's family and property rights, it should be remembered that this is only for a short period of up to 48 hours and that it is designed to give the victim some time to decide what actions to take. It has been noted that the Home Office evaluation of the pilot schemes suggests that these new orders 'were generally seen positively by practitioners and victim-survivors and were associated with a reduction in re-victimisation, particularly when used in "chronic" cases'.[92] On 25 November 2013 Theresa May, the Home Secretary, announced in a written ministerial statement that both domestic violence protection orders would be rolled out across England and Wales from March 2014.[93]

### 4.1.4  Domestic Violence Disclosure Scheme (DVDS)

In 2013, the Home Secretary also announced that a scheme allowing police to disclose to individuals details of their partners' abusive pasts would be rolled out across England and Wales from March 2014. Under the domestic violence disclosure scheme (also known as Clare's Law), an individual can ask the police to check whether a new or existing partner has a violent past ('right to ask'). If police checks show that a person may be at risk of domestic violence from their partner, the police will consider disclosing the information ('right to know').

These recent initiatives show that the government does take domestic violence seriously and will introduce measures to try to tackle it. However, in reality, the success of the criminal justice response to domestic abuse depends on the attitude and actions of individual police officers and police forces, and recent research has shown that the police response to domestic abuse is still not good enough.

### 4.1.5  HMIC report (2014): 'police response to domestic abuse is not good enough'

In February 2014, HM Inspectorate of Constabulary (HMIC) published the findings from its review of the police's response to domestic violence across England and Wales. It concluded that the current police response to domestic abuse is failing victims, and made a number of recommendations.[94] The report found that, despite considerable improvement made over the last decade, the overall police response to victims of domestic abuse was not good enough. In too many police forces weaknesses were found in the service provided to victims, some of which were serious and put victims at unnecessary risk. It found that while domestic abuse was a priority on paper, this had not translated into operational reality in the majority of forces, and that domestic abuse was too often the poor relation of other policing activity, such as acquisitive crime and serious organised crime. The report said that these failings were the result of, among other things:

- a lack of visible leadership and clear direction set by senior officers;
- alarming and unacceptable weaknesses in some core policing activity, in particular the collection of evidence by officers at the scene of domestic abuse incidents;

---

[92] P. Strickland, *Domestic Violence* (London: House of Commons Library, 2012).     [93] Ibid.
[94] HMIC, *Everyone's Business: Improving The Police Response to Domestic Abuse*, March 2014.

- poor management and supervision that fails to reinforce the right behaviours, attitudes and actions of officers;
- officers lacking the skills and knowledge necessary to engage confidently and competently with victims of domestic abuse; and
- extremely limited systematic feedback from victims about their experience of the police response.

The report made a series of recommendations to improve the service provided to victims of domestic violence by the police. It called for a renewed national effort to tackle domestic abuse, the creation of a national oversight group to report quarterly on the progress made in implementing the report's recommendations, and for each police force to establish an action plan setting out how it would improve its approach to domestic violence.

Recent research suggests that police forces have begun to address the criticisms outlined in the HMIC Report. Between June and August 2015, HMIC visited every police force in England and Wales to assess the progress they had made in responding to and protecting victims of domestic violence. The findings from this inspection show that progress has been made and that the police service now sees tackling domestic abuse as an important priority.[95] HMIC noted that there has been a 31 per cent increase in domestic-abuse related recorded crime which is deemed to be due, in part, to police forces getting better at identifying and recording domestic abuse. More work is still be to done, however, and HMIC made a series of further recommendations to ensure that the momentum for change which has been demonstrated so far continues apace.[96]

### 4.1.6  A new criminal offence of 'controlling or coercive behaviour'

As outlined at the beginning of this chapter, coercive and controlling behavior has been included within the non-statutory Government definition of domestic abuse. However, up to now there has been no specific offence of domestic abuse which provides that coercive and controlling behaviour in an intimate relationship is criminal. Instead, these behaviours are covered by the legislation on stalking and harassment, which do not explicitly apply to intimate relationships. In order to strengthen the law in this area, the Home Office has announced that, under the Serious Crime Act 2015, a new criminal offence of controlling and coercive behaviour will come into force on 29 December 2015.[97] This new measure aims to tackle domestic abuse by criminalising patterns of repeated or continuous coercive or controlling behaviour where perpetrated against an intimate partner or family member, causing victims to feel fear, alarm, or distress.[98]

---

[95]  HMIC, *Increasingly Everyone's Business: A Progress Report on the Police response to Domestic Abuse*, December 2015, https://www.justiceinspectorates.gov.uk/hmic/wp-content/uploads/increasingly-everyones-business-domestic-abuse-progress-report.pdf

[96]  Ibid.

[97]  Section 76 of the Serious Crime Act 2015. The offence carries a maximum sentence of 5 years' imprisonment, a fine, or both.

[98]  The offence is constituted by behaviour on the part of the perpetrator which takes place 'repeatedly or continuously', and the victim and the alleged perpetrator must be 'personally connected' at the time the behaviour takes place. The behaviour must have had a serious effect on the victim, meaning that it has caused the victim to fear violence will be used against them on 'at least two occasions', or it has had a 'substantial adverse effect on the victims' day to day activities'. The alleged perpetrator must have known that their behaviour would have had a serious effect on the victim, or the behaviour must have been such that he or she 'ought to have known' it would have that effect. The Home Office has published statutory guidance concerning the offence, see Home Office, Controlling or Coercive Behaviour in an Intimate or Family Relationship, Statutory Guidance Framework, December 2015, https://www.gov.uk/government/uploads/system/uploads/attachment_data/file/482528/Controlling_or_coercive_behaviour_-_statutory_guidance.pdf.

---

**Talking Point**

The Consultation Paper which preceded this development outlined the arguments for and against making a specific domestic abuse offence:

On the one hand, 'victims of domestic abuse often fear the consequences of reporting their abuse for their families and even their perpetrators. Accessing the criminal justice system can be intimidating, particularly where a victim is likely to remain emotionally involved with their perpetrator. In making new laws we must carefully consider the concerns victims may have about accessing the criminal justice system. Creating a new offence may also be seen as duplicating existing legislation relating to stalking and harassment, and distracting frontline agencies from the fundamental operational changes that are urgently needed to use the existing framework effectively'.[99]

The Report continues, 'conversely, the HMIC report on domestic abuse makes clear that the police fail to see domestic abuse, particularly in its non-violent form, as a serious crime. Acts that are clearly criminal are not referred for prosecution and [the] arrest rate varies widely. Creating a specific offence of domestic abuse may send a clear, consistent message to frontline agencies that non-violent control in an intimate relationship is criminal. Explicitly capturing this in legislation may also help victims identify the behaviour they are suffering as wrong and encourage them to report it, and cause perpetrators to rethink their controlling behaviour'.[100]

**Q.** Do you think that the provision of a new criminal offence of coercive control within intimate relationships will strengthen the law on domestic abuse?

Some argue that such initiatives are introduced in order for the Government to appear to be pro-active in tackling domestic violence, but that what really needs to happen is for the police and others within the criminal justice system to receive proper training in current laws and how best to implement them, 'and for those tasked with protection and prosecution to be held accountable when they fail to do their jobs to an acceptable standard'.[101]

**Q.** Do you agree?

---

### 4.2 Criminal injuries compensation

A victim of domestic violence may be able to claim compensation from the state for the injuries sustained (both physical and mental) as a result of domestic violence. An application can be made to the Criminal Injuries Compensation Scheme which is established under the Criminal Injuries Compensation Act 1995. Compensation may be paid to an individual who has sustained personal injury as a direct result of an act of violence (including arson, fire-raising, or an act of poisoning).[102] A claim should be made as soon as possible, and not usually more than two years after the incident giving rise to the injury.[103] It is not necessary for the assailant to have been convicted of a criminal offence in connection with the injury.[104] However, a claims officer may withhold or reduce an award if the applicant failed to take, without delay, all reasonable steps to inform the police of the circumstances giving rise to the injury;[105] or if the applicant failed to cooperate with the police in attempting to bring the assailant to justice or other disqualifying criteria.[106] In addition, an award will only be made where there is no likelihood that an assailant would benefit from the award.[107] If, at the time the injury was sustained, the victim and the assailant were living in the same household as members of the same family, an application for compensation will be rejected unless:

---

[99] Home Office, Strengthening the Law on Domestic Abuse—A Consultation, August 2014.   [100] Ibid.
[101] J. Bindel, Criminalising coercive control will not help victims of domestic abuse, The Guardian, 27 August 2014,
[102] Criminal Injuries Compensation Scheme (2008), para 8.   [103] Ibid, para 18.   [104] Ibid, para 10.
[105] Ibid, para 13(1)(a).   [106] Ibid, para 13(1)(b).   [107] Ibid, para 16(a).

(a) the assailant has been prosecuted in connection with the offence, or a claims officer considers that there are practical, technical, or other good reasons why a prosecution has not been brought; and

(b) in the case of violence between adults in the family, a claims officer is satisfied that the applicant and the assailant stopped living in the same household before the application was made and are unlikely to share the same household again.[108]

For the purposes of the scheme, a man and woman living together as husband and wife (whether or not they are married) or same-sex partners living together (whether or not they are civil partners) will be treated as members of the same family.[109] Where the applicant is entitled to compensation for a series of assaults, she will qualify for an award as the victim of a pattern of abuse, rather than for a separate award for each incident.[110]

## 4.3 Civil law remedies

The criminal law and civil law have very different objectives. The criminal law is concerned with identifying and punishing criminals, whereas the civil law is designed to respond to the needs of the victim. This is an important distinction, particularly in this area where the victim has an emotional attachment to the abuser which may affect how she wishes the matter to be dealt with. It is often the case that a victim of domestic violence does not wish to bring the relationship to an end permanently, but wants the violence to stop and to receive protection from further assaults. The civil law is designed to take account of the victims' differing needs, and civil law orders are prospective in nature. In other words, they are designed to protect the victim from future violence, as opposed to punishing the abuser for past behaviour.[111]

---

### Key legislation

The civil law remedies for domestic violence are found in Part IV of the FLA 1996. Before the enactment of this legislation, the relevant civil law orders were contained in two pieces of legislation: the Domestic Violence and Matrimonial Proceedings Act 1976 and the Domestic Proceedings and Magistrates' Court Act 1978. Another piece of legislation, the Matrimonial Homes Act 1983, gave the courts the power to regulate occupation of the family home, and to enforce and restrict the respective rights of spouses to occupy the family home.

---

The Law Commission reviewed the law in 1992 and concluded that the civil remedies were complex, confusing, and lacked integration.[112] Different remedies were available to different applicants in different courts. The legislation also failed to give protection to a number of family members (such as siblings and former cohabitants) who fell outside of the categories of person who were eligible to apply for relief under the various pieces of legislation. The Law Commission made recommendations to deal with two 'distinct but inseparable problems'. First, it sought to provide protection for one member of the family against molestation or violence by another. Secondly, it sought to design provisions to regulate occupation of the family home when a relationship had broken down whether temporarily or permanently. The Law Commission recommended that a new legislative code be enacted to provide a single and consistent set of remedies which are available in all courts to deal with these two situations. The result was the Family Homes and Domestic

---

[108] Ibid, para 17.　　[109] Ibid, para 17(2).　　[110] Ibid, p 33.

[111] See B. James, 'In Practice: Prosecuting Domestic Violence' [2008] Family Law 456.

[112] Law Com No 207 (1992).

Violence Bill 1995. However, this draft legislation was withdrawn due to political pressure after a high-profile campaign led by Conservative backbench Members of Parliament and the tabloid press complained that its provisions gave unmarried cohabitants the same property rights as married parties.[113] The draft legislation was amended and the final version was enacted as Part IV of the FLA 1996.

The two main orders under Part IV of the FLA 1996 are the non-molestation order and the occupation order. Not only was the law streamlined under the 1996 Act to ensure that these orders are available in all courts, but enforcement mechanisms were strengthened to provide that powers of arrest should be attached to orders if the victim or a child had been subjected to violence or threats of violence unless the court was satisfied that this was not necessary. In addition, the legislation introduced a new category of 'associated persons' who are entitled to apply for an order under the legislation although, as we shall see, there are differences between the list of persons who can apply for the two orders.

The law has been amended again in recent years. The enactment of the Domestic Violence, Crime and Victims Act 2004 sought to enhance the criminal justice response to domestic violence. One of the primary changes brought about by this Act was in making a breach of a non-molestation order made under Part IV of the FLA 1996 a criminal offence.[114]

### 4.3.1 Non-molestation orders

Section 42 of the FLA 1996 allows the court to make a non-molestation order which is an order which prohibits the respondent from molesting an 'associated person' or a 'relevant child'. The non-molestation order is aimed at providing a speedy remedy for a victim of domestic violence, and the Domestic Violence, Crime and Victims Act 2004 makes breach of this civil order a criminal offence.[115] 'Molestation' is not defined in the FLA 1996 as it was feared that this would be over-restrictive and lead to borderline results.[116] Thus, molestation is an 'umbrella term which covers a wide range of behaviour'.[117] It covers the most obvious type of case where the victim is subject to a physical assault or battery which could also give rise to criminal proceedings. However, it is much wider than this as the courts have accepted that while:

> violence is a form of molestation . . . molestation may take place without the threat or use of violence and still be serious and inimical to mental and physical health.[118]

Molestation can take a variety of forms such as writing abusive letters and shouting obscenities[119] or following the applicant around and making a 'perfect nuisance' of oneself.[120] In *Horner v Horner*[121] the molestation by the husband took the form of handing the wife upsetting notes, and intercepting her on her way to work. Ormrod LJ said that molestation did not 'imply necessarily either violence or threats of violence. It applies to any conduct which can properly be regarded as such a degree of harassment as to call for the intervention of the court.' In *Spencer v Camacho*[122] after a series of other activities for which the woman had obtained non-molestation orders, riffling through her handbag was held to be sufficient conduct to amount to molestation.

Where a non-molestation order is made, the actual wording of the order can be tailored to meet the needs of the particular case and can prohibit the respondent from carrying out very specific acts of molestation such as sending emails or letters.[123] However, a more generally phrased prohibition

---

[113] This incorrect assessment of the legislation led to a campaign against its enactment, which was instigated by the *Daily Mail*, 23 October 1995.
[114] See the following sections.       [115] Section 42A.
[116] Following the recommendation of the Law Commission (Law Com No 207), para 3.1.       [117] Ibid.
[118] *Davis v Johnson* [1978] 1 All ER 1132, *per* Viscount Dilhorne at 1144.
[119] *George v George* [1986] 2 FLR 347.       [120] *Vaughan v Vaughan* [1973] 1 WLR 1159.
[121] [1982] 2 All ER 495.       [122] (1984) 4 FLR 662.       [123] Section 42(6).

can be used and a usual form of wording is that the respondent is restrained from 'assaulting, molesting, annoying or otherwise interfering with the applicant or any relevant child living with the applicant'. Some have argued that the term 'non-molestation order' should have been replaced with clearer words which accurately portray the harm at which the order is aimed.[124] At the time the legislation was enacted, the police had concerns about the term 'non-molestation' because they had information to suggest that either the people seeking protection, or those to whom they turned for assistance, did not fully understand what the term means. They took the view that some kind of definition, designed to be inclusive not exclusive, could usefully have been provided containing such words as 'pester', 'threaten', or 'harass'.[125] There is a risk that the phrase may be narrowly interpreted by victims and those working within the legal system because of a lack of a clear indication of how wide the term's meaning is meant to be. Unfortunately, recent evidence confirms this. It seems that some solicitors are informing their clients that the non-molestation order only covers physical violence which leads to physical injury, and not non-physical forms of abuse such as emotional abuse.[126] In taking this narrow interpretation, some clients who are suffering from non-physical abuse are being incorrectly advised that they cannot apply for a non-molestation order. One of the problems which may cause such misapprehensions is the lack of specialisation of family law solicitors and the 'large number of untrained lawyers and judges operating in domestic violence cases'.[127]

### 4.3.2 Some preliminary points about non-molestation orders

A non-molestation order can be made in the magistrates' family proceedings court, county court, and the High Court. The order can be made by the court on application by an eligible person. However, even if no such application has been made, the court has the power to make an order of its own motion in any family proceedings to which the respondent is a party where it considers that the non-molestation order should be made for the benefit of any other party to the proceedings or any relevant child.[128] In addition, the court can make the order when it is considering whether to make an occupation order.[129] The Law Commission had recommended that, on occasion, certain third parties (such as the police) should be able to bring proceedings on behalf of a victim of domestic violence.[130] While section 60 of the FLA allows prescribed persons to bring such proceedings on behalf of another, this provision has not yet been enacted.[131] The non-molestation order can be made for a specified period or until further order.[132]

The order can prohibit the respondent from molesting an 'associated person' or any 'relevant child'. The Law Commission considered that the court should have the discretion to make orders in relation to as wide a range of children as possible.[133] Thus, a 'relevant child' is given a very broad definition and does not just relate to the biological child of the applicant or the respondent but to any child whose interests the court considers relevant. Children who are living, or expected to

---

[124] Eg see the written evidence of M. L. Parry to the Special Committee on the Family Homes and Domestic Violence Bill (1994–95) HL Paper 55, p 66. He suggested that terms like 'no harm', 'non-abuse', or 'protection' orders would be more appropriate.

[125] Ibid, oral evidence, p 41.

[126] M. Burton, 'Civil Law Remedies for Domestic Violence: Why are Applications for Non-Molestation Orders Declining?' (2009) 31(2) Journal of Social Welfare and Family Law 109 at 115.

[127] Home Affairs Committee, 'Domestic Violence, Forced Marriage and "Honour"-Based Violence', Sixth Report of Session 2007–08, vol I, HC 263-I.

[128] Section 42(2)(b). Such an order which is made under the court's own motion powers ceases to have effect if the family proceedings in which it is made are withdrawn or dismissed (s 42(8)).

[129] Section 42(4A), inserted by the Domestic Violence, Crime and Victims Act 2004, Sch 10, para 36.

[130] Law Com No 207 (1992), paras 5.18–5.23.

[131] For an assessment of the views of service providers on third party applications, see M. Burton, 'Third Party Applications for Protection Orders in England and Wales: Service Provider's Views on Implementing Section 60 of the Family Law Act 1996' (2003) 25(2) Journal of Social Welfare and Family Law 137–50.

[132] Section 42(7).     [133] Law Com No 207 (1992), para 3.27.

live, with either the applicant or the respondent will be considered by the court,[134] as will children whose welfare is already before the court (under the Adoption Act 1976, the Adoption and Children Act 2002, or the Children Act 1989).[135] In addition, Parliament was so concerned to ensure that all relevant children fell within the scope of the protection afforded by non-molestation injunctions that it included a catch-all provision which gives the court the discretion to make orders to protect 'any other child whose interests the court considers relevant'.[136] The gate-keeping role in relation to this provision is vested in the court which will decide whether the interests of any other child are relevant to the application.

### 4.3.3  Who can apply for a non-molestation order?

A non-molestation order can be made in respect of any relevant child (s 62(2)), or any person associated with the respondent. Under section 62(3), persons will be 'associated' with one another if:

(a)  they are spouses and civil partners, former spouses, and former civil partners;

(b)  they are cohabitants or former cohabitants: the definition of cohabitants was amended by the Civil Partnership Act 2004 and the Domestic Violence, Crime and Victims Act 2004 to include same-sex cohabitants. Under section 62(1) cohabitants are now defined as 'two persons who are neither married to each other nor civil partners of each other but are living together as husband and wife or as if they were civil partners';

(c)  they live or have lived in the same household, otherwise than merely by reason of one of them being the other's employee, tenant, lodger, or boarder;

(d)  they are relatives: the term relatives is defined in section 63 as:

   (i)  the father, mother, stepfather, stepmother, son, daughter, stepson, stepdaughter, grandmother, grandfather, grandson, or granddaughter of that person or of that person's spouse or former spouse, or

   (ii)  the brother, sister, uncle, aunt, niece, nephew, or first cousin[137] (whether of the full blood or of the half blood or by affinity) of that person or of that person's spouse or former spouse, and includes, in relation to a person who is cohabiting or has cohabited with another person, and any person who would fall within paragraph (i) or (ii) if the parties were married to each other;

(e)  they are engaged or formerly engaged couples: to come within this definition the parties must produce evidence that there was actually an agreement to marry or enter into a civil partnership. First, the parties can produce written evidence of the agreement to marry or enter into a civil partnership.[138] Secondly, the agreement can be proven by the gift of an engagement ring by one party to the other in contemplation of their marriage. In the case of an agreement to enter into a civil partnership, this can be proven by a gift by one party to the other as a token of the agreement.[139] Thirdly, a ceremony entered into by the parties in the presence of one or more other persons assembled for the purpose of witnessing the ceremony can evidence such an agreement. The application must be made within three years of the agreement to marry or enter into a civil partnership being terminated;[140]

(f)  they have or have had an intimate personal relationship with each other which is or was of significant duration: this category was inserted by the Domestic Violence, Crime and Victims Act 2004[141] and it plugs a gap in the law whereby dating couples who had neither lived together nor been engaged were not classed as 'associated persons'. No statutory guidance is

---

[134]  Section 62(2).      [135]  Section 62(2)(b).      [136]  Section 62(2)(c).

[137]  First cousins were included within the definition of relative by the Domestic Violence, Crime and Victims Act 2004, s 58(1).

[138]  For the definition of a civil partnership agreement, see the Civil Partnership Act 2004, s 73.

[139]  Civil Partnership Act 2004, Sch 9.      [140]  Sections 42(4) and 42(4ZA).      [141]  Section 4.

given on what constitutes an 'intimate personal relationship' or what length of time will suffice to constitute 'significant duration'. Case law will determine the scope of these terms. However, the explanatory notes accompanying the legislation make it clear that this category covers 'a long-standing relationship which may, or may not, be a sexual relationship, but which is an intimate and personal one. It does not include long-term platonic friends or "one-night stands" ';[142]

(g) in relation to any child, persons who are either a parent of the child or have parental responsibility for the child: if a child has been adopted, two persons are also associated with each other if one is a natural parent of the child or a parent of such a natural parent; and the other is the child or any person who has become a parent of the child by virtue of an adoption order or has applied for an adoption order; or with whom the child has at any time been placed for adoption;

(h) parties to the same family proceedings other than proceedings under Part IV of the FLA 1996. Family proceedings are defined under section 63 of the FLA 1996 and include proceedings under the Matrimonial Causes Act 1973, the Adoption Act 1976, and the Children Act 1989.

### 4.3.4 The approach of the courts to defining 'associated persons'

In *G v F (Non-Molestation Order: Jurisdiction)*[143] the court emphasised that a purposive construction should be taken when deciding whether an applicant was associated with the respondent for the purposes of the legislation. In this case the applicant did not live with the respondent but they stayed with each other two or three nights of the week and for a time had a joint back account. Wall J held that the parties were cohabitants within the meaning of the FLA 1996. The characteristics of their relationship met three of the six 'signposts' which had been set out in *Crake v Supplementary Benefits Commission*[144] to assist in determining what amounts to cohabitation. The signposts were (i) whether they are members of the same household; (ii) whether the relationship is stable; (iii) whether there is financial support; (iv) whether there is a sexual relationship; (v) whether they have children; and (vi) whether there is public acknowledgement of the relationship. In the present case, the parties were in a sexual relationship, they lived in the same household part of the time, and operated a joint bank account. As such, the court held that there was sufficient evidence to demonstrate that they had been cohabitants and therefore 'associated persons' for the purpose of section 42. The general approach of the court in this case is important because it illustrates that in borderline cases where there is some uncertainty about whether an applicant falls into one of the categories of 'associated person', a purposive interpretation will be taken. Wall J said that:

> where domestic violence is concerned [judges] should give the statute a purposive construction and not decline jurisdiction, unless the facts of the case before them are plainly incapable of being brought within the statute.

The legislation is designed to provide 'swift and accessible protective remedies' to victims of domestic violence which mandates against a narrow interpretation of associated persons. In light of recent amendments, this approach may be important when the courts are called upon to decide whether a potential applicant was in an 'intimate relationship' with the respondent which is, or was, of 'significant duration'.[145]

Case law also illustrates that an applicant who is associated with the respondent can apply for a non-molestation order even where the disharmony is not borne from the family relationship between the parties but from a civil dispute. In *Chechi v Bashier*[146] a bitter family dispute over land in

---

[142] www.opsi.gov.uk/acts/acts2004/en/ukpgaen_20040028_en.pdf.     [143] [2000] Fam 186.
[144] [1982] 1 All ER 498.     [145] FLA 1996, s 62(3)(ea).     [146] [1999] 2 FLR 489.

Pakistan led to the applicant's claim for a non-molestation order against his brother and nephews, all of whom were resident in the UK. Even though this was a dispute over land, the court held that it had been intensified by the family relationship between the parties. As such, it was genuinely within the ambit of the FLA 1996 and the applicant was eligible to apply for a non-molestation order against his brother and nephews because he was 'associated' with them under the wide definition of relative in the legislation.[147] However, even though he was entitled to apply for this order, the court rejected his application. Under section 47(2), the court is mandated to attach a power of arrest to a non-molestation order if the respondent has used or threatened violence against the applicant or relevant child unless it is satisfied in all the circumstances that the applicant or child will be adequately protected without such a power of arrest. In the circumstances, the court felt compelled to attach a power of arrest to the order in line with this provision but it feared that in doing so the applicant would have unacceptable power over the respondents. The application for a non-molestation order was rejected on that basis. Some are critical of this decision. Burton, for example, points out that section 47(2) which was designed to strengthen the enforcement of non-molestation orders operated to deny the applicant an order in the first place.[148] She says that in the alternative:

> the court could have granted the order but exercised the discretion afforded by the legislation to not attach a power [of arrest] in circumstances where the applicant is adequately protected without it. If they did not think that the applicant would have been adequately protected without a power of arrest then the case for a non-molestation order was compelling and the courts were arguably wrong to refuse one.

As we shall see later in this chapter, amendments made by the Domestic Violence, Crime and Victims Act 2004 ensure that breach of a non-molestation order is now a criminal offence, which means that the police have, in all cases, the power of arrest.[149]

### 4.3.5 The arguments for and against the wide definition of 'associated persons'

One of the most significant changes brought about by Part IV of the FLA 1996 was the creation of the new category of 'associated persons' where the aim was to ensure that a much wider range of person was eligible to apply for the civil remedies under the legislation.[150] As we have seen, this statutory list has been extended even further by the Domestic Violence, Crime and Victims Act 2004 to include 'those who have or have had an intimate personal relationship with each other which is or was of significant duration',[151] and to include same-sex couples within the definition of cohabitant.[152] The reason for such a wide category of eligible applicants was the recognition that domestic violence can occur in many types of family relationship, and not just between spouses or cohabitants, and that those who fell outside the legislation were not receiving the protection which they may need.[153] The Law Commission originally mooted the idea of removing all eligibility requirements to ensure that any person who required protection from abuse was able to obtain it. In effect, this would have created a new tort of harassment or molestation where the protective orders could be used to resolve disputes between neighbours or harassment in the workplace where 'there is no domestic or family relationship to justify special remedies or procedures'.[154] However, this approach was rejected on the grounds that the special nature of family relationships, the strength of the emotions involved in these relationships, and the stresses and strains of family life meant that

---

[147]  FLA 1996, s 63.

[148]  M. Burton, *Legal Responses to Domestic Violence* (Abingdon: Routledge-Cavendish, 2008), p 27.

[149]  See Section 4.3.9.

[150]  See A. Bainham, 'Changing Families and Changing Concepts—Reforming the Language of Family Law' (1998) 10 Child and Family Law Quarterly 1.

[151]  Domestic Violence, Crime and Victims Act 2004, s 3.        [152]  Ibid, s 3.

[153]  Law Com No 207 (1992), para 2.28.        [154]  Ibid, para 3.19.

violence and molestation within the family has to be considered as a special case. Thus, the Law Commission adopted a 'middle path' and widened the range of applicants to include anyone who is associated with the respondent by virtue of a family relationship or something closely akin to such a relationship.[155] No longer are the protective remedies only available to spouses and cohabitants, but also to those within family relationships of sufficient proximity to require the flexibility of a specialist family law regime.

However, this approach can be criticised and some have argued that the protective orders should be available to whoever needs them, regardless of the relationship between the parties. As the Law Commission recognised, restricting the law's remedies to pre-determined categories of persons associated through a family relationship can give rise to strange results. It gave the example of four friends sharing a flat. If they are all joint tenants then any one of them would be able to apply for a non-molestation order as they all live in the same household. However, if one party took the tenancy and then sub-let to his friends, the order would not be available in relation to him because the category of co-residents in a household excludes those who share a household on a commercial basis (such as tenant, lodger, or boarder).[156] It seems unfortunate to legislate knowing in advance the difficult problems that are liable to arise, particularly if those difficulties can be avoided. Limiting the scope of the Act's provisions to associated persons may prevent the court from dealing in an even-handed manner with potential litigants where one is being molested but, in failing to come within the definition of associated person, is unable to avail herself of the court's injunctive powers. Where the behaviour is such that the law should provide a remedy, and given that the legislation focuses on the effect of the conduct in question on the victim rather than on its intrinsic nature, one could question the efficacy of limiting the remedies to certain classes of applicant.[157] Some argue that a simple, accessible remedy available to all who are subject to molestation, not just those in a familial relationship, should have been provided. Of course, it is worth pointing out that another option for such persons is to seek a remedy under the Protection from Harassment Act 1997 where there are no limitations on who can apply for an order.[158]

Others take the opposite view and argue that the definition of 'associated person' is too widely drawn in the legislation. Reece, for example, argues that the category of 'associated person' upon whom enhanced civil protection for domestic violence is conferred, is misguided. Not only is there little evidence to suggest that the breadth of 'family members' identified as associated persons are vulnerable to domestic violence, but their inclusion within the legislation gives rise to the perception that domestic violence occurs in every type of family relationship. This, Reece argues, obscures the 'true character of the phenomenon' and the fact that domestic violence is typically perpetuated by men against women in partnering relationships. Pointing to statistics which show that domestic violence is usually carried out by men against their present or former female partners, Reece argues that the range of associated persons do not share the features of wives and female heterosexual cohabitants which make them particularly vulnerable to domestic violence. These features include:

- the victim's isolation;
- the victim's unequal power relations with her spouse or partner;
- the presence of barriers to leaving the relationship (such as one's identity being fixed on the relationship to the extent that it becomes impossible to consider leaving);
- the victim's financial dependence on her spouse or partner.

---

[155] Ibid, para 3.19.        [156] Ibid, para 3.22.

[157] Eg if a university student becomes the object of the obsessive attentions of an unbalanced lecturer (or vice versa) why should not he or she be able to obtain a non-molestation order? See M. Hayes and C. Williams, 'Domestic Violence and Occupation of the Family Home: Proposals for Reform' [1992] Family Law 497 at 498; M. Hayes, 'Non-Molestation Protection—Only Associated Persons Need Apply' [1996] Family Law 134.

[158] See Section 7.

While some associated persons may face similar issues, for example an elderly person who is being abused in the family home, Reece concludes that for the most part those included within the statutory list do not have these characteristics. In short, she argues that the wide category of associated persons 'endangers the specificity of the category of domestic violence'.

### 4.3.6  The child as applicant for a non-molestation order

Under section 43, children under the age of 16 can apply for a non-molestation order provided that the child obtains the leave of the court. The court will grant leave only if it is satisfied that the child has sufficient understanding to make the proposed application. No statutory guidance is provided to the court on what criteria should apply to such a leave application. However, it is likely that parallels will be drawn with applications for leave to apply for section 8 orders made by children under the Children Act 1989, where the same restriction applies. Persuading a parent or other adult associated with the respondent to apply for a non-molestation order, particularly where the application is coupled with an application for an occupation order, might sometimes avoid the necessity of instituting care proceedings on behalf of a child who is suffering, or likely to suffer, significant harm as a result of domestic violence. It also avoids the child becoming embroiled in taking legal proceedings against his or her own parent.

### 4.3.7  Criteria for granting non-molestation orders

Under the pre-1996 domestic violence legislation, protection orders could only be granted by the court where the respondent had used, or threatened to use, violence against the applicant or a child of the family.[159] However, the 1996 legislation heralded a change in emphasis. The Law Commission took the view that the criteria for granting a non-molestation order should focus on the *effect* of the respondent's behaviour on the applicant and any relevant child.[160]

---

**Key legislation**

Thus under section 42(5) of the 1996 Act:

In deciding whether to exercise its powers under this section and, if so, in what manner, the court shall have regard to all the circumstances including the need to secure the health, safety and well-being—

(a) of the applicant or in a case [where the court proposes to make an order of its own motion], the person for whose benefit the order would be made; and

(b) of any relevant child.

---

For the purposes of this provision, 'health' includes both physical and mental health. This victim-focused provision mandates the court to consider the *effect* of the respondent's behaviour on the applicant or any relevant child rather than on the nature of the conduct itself. It is clear that the purpose of the legislation is to provide protection from harm rather than to assign punishment or blame. The court has a wide discretion when deciding whether to grant a non-molestation order. No specific evidence of violence or threats of violence is required before the court will make an order. The standard of proof required to obtain a non-molestation order is the civil standard (the balance of probabilities) even though breach of this order is a criminal offence.[161]

---

[159]  Under the Domestic Proceedings and Magistrates' Court Act 1978.

[160]  Law Com No 207 (1992), para 3.6.

[161]  The Government said that 'in criminalising the breach of the non-molestation order it is not the Government's intention to affect the law in respect of the making of such orders, in particular the standard of proof required for the courts to grant orders', House of Commons Standing Committee E, Hansard, 22 June 2004, col 27. See S. Gore, 'In Practice: The Domestic Violence, Crime and Victims Act 2004 and Family Law Act 1996 Injunctions' [2007] Family Law 739.

A very wide definition of molestation, and a victim-focused approach to the criteria to be applied to the exercise of judicial discretion, is to be welcomed. Any conduct which has the effect of harassing or pestering the applicant or any relevant child will come under the scope of a non-molestation order if sufficiently serious. However, as previously indicated, while a non-molestation order can be made to protect the victim from non-physical abuse, research has called into question the extent to which orders are made to protect against this sort of behaviour.[162] While, technically, a non-molestation order is available to protect against non-physical forms of abuse, there may be practical reasons why a victim of such abuse may find it hard to obtain a legal remedy. In particular, the victim might face obstacles in securing legal aid funding to support their case.[163] Research has shown through interviews with representatives from the Legal Services Commission that victims of non-physical violence would not be considered as a priority for public funding and that those suffering from mental abuse would have to produce medical documentation to verify the effect that this had on their health.[164]

### 4.3.8 Can an order be made to protect the applicant against unintentional conduct?

One question which has arisen is whether it is a requirement that the conduct complained of be intentional on the part of the respondent. In *Johnson v Walton*,[165] a case which was decided under the pre-1996 legislation, the court took the view that molestation involving harassment includes an intent to cause distress or harm. However, earlier case law confirmed that where the respondent is physically violent towards the applicant an order can be granted regardless of intention. In *Wooton v Wooton*[166] the respondent only became violent during epileptic episodes. The Court of Appeal held that the court had jurisdiction to grant an injunction because it was the actual violence and the consequences suffered by the applicant which were the important factors to be considered by the court.

However, what is the position under Part IV of the FLA 1996: Must the respondent have the 'intent' to molest for a victim to obtain a non-molestation order? The answer to this question appears to be that an order can be made regardless of the respondent's actual intent. This, it is suggested, is the correct approach. Given that the criteria for making non-molestation orders are deliberately focused on the *effect* of the conduct on the victim as opposed to the actual nature of the respondent's actions, it would be contradictory for the courts to impose a requirement that the conduct was carried out with the deliberate intention of harassing the applicant. Although the respondent's behaviour in a large number of instances of domestic violence may well satisfy a threshold of intent, making this a pre-requisite to obtaining an order would give the respondent the scope to put forward a defence on the ground that due to a medical condition or drug/alcohol consumption he was unable to control his actions. Given the statistical evidence which shows the clear link between alcohol/drug abuse and domestic violence,[167] such a requirement would limit the scope of the non-molestation order. An abuser who, perhaps due to mental illness, is behaving in such a way that the court would normally intervene, may be causing as much distress as an abuser who is deliberately acting out of spite. As Sedley LJ observed in *P v P (Contempt of Court: Mental Capacity)*:[168] 'The court has an invidious choice to make in a situation like this between the compulsive behaviour of a most unfortunate individual and the safety and well-being of his family.' It is also arguable that this same principle should

---

[162] See Section 4.3.1.

[163] M. Burton, 'Civil Law Remedies for Domestic Violence: Why are Applications for Non-Molestation Orders Declining?' (2009) 31(2) Journal of Social Welfare and Family Law 109.

[164] M. Burton, *Legal Responses to Domestic Violence* (Abingdon: Routledge-Cavendish, 2008), p 40.

[165] [1990] 1 FLR 350.     [166] (1984) FLR 871.

[167] See eg C. Mirrlees-Black, *Domestic Violence: Findings from a New British Crime Survey Self-Completion Questionnaire*, Home Office Research Study 191 (London: Home Office, 1999); K. E. Leonard and B. M. Quigley, 'Drinking and Marital Aggression in Newlyweds: An Event-Based Analysis of Drinking and the Occurrence of Husband Marital Aggression' (1999) 60(4) Journal of Studies on Alcohol 537–45.

[168] [1999] 2 FLR 897.

apply where the abuser was behaving whilst under the influence of drugs or alcohol. Thus it seems that a non-molestation order can be made against someone whose actions are not deliberately wilful, but are unintentional.

However, this gives rise to a related issue. If the respondent is suffering from a mental illness or some other disability which impairs their understanding of the nature of the order and the fact that it prohibits certain conduct, the court may refuse to grant the order on the ground that it could not be effectively enforced. In such circumstances, the order would have no deterrent effect because the respondent would not be capable of complying with it, and any breach could not be subject to effective enforcement proceedings.[169]

---

### Key case

In *Banks v Banks*,[170] which was a decision of the Oxford County Court, the court refused to grant a non-molestation order against a 79-year-old woman who suffered from manic depression and dementia. The woman had been looked after by her husband and other carers for many years in the matrimonial home. When her condition deteriorated, she was admitted to hospital but after responding to treatment, the hospital wished to discharge her and send her home as it was felt to be best for her to be in familiar surroundings rather than in residential care. Her husband, who was aged 75 and both physically and emotionally frail, petitioned for divorce on the ground that he could no longer cope with her illness. She had been both physically and verbally abusive towards him although at no point had he suffered any physical injury. According to the wife's consultant psychiatrist, it was unlikely that she posed a threat to his health and the intention was that she was to be looked after by a team of daily carers. The husband's application for a non-molestation order was refused by the court. Judge Geddes held that her behaviour was a symptom of her condition and thus outside her control. He concluded that an order would serve no practical purpose, even if she were capable of understanding it.[171]

---

In short, therefore, when dealing with a respondent whose actions are caused by a medical condition, or some other ailment which impairs his judgement, the fact that the abuse may be unintentional will not prevent the court from making the order. However, if the respondent's condition affects his ability to understand the nature of the order, the court may refuse to grant the order on the ground that it would serve no useful purpose. But an order will be made if the respondent understands that an order prohibits him or her from doing certain things and that if this is ignored punishment will follow.

### 4.3.9 Enforcement of the non-molestation order

The non-molestation order is designed to protect the applicant against violence and other forms of molestation. However, this order may be worthless unless it is backed up by strong enforcement powers which courts are prepared to use, and the police to operate in practice. One of the major changes introduced by the Domestic Violence, Crime and Victims Act 2004 concerns the enforcement of a non-molestation order. Under the old law, breach of this order was dealt with as a civil contempt of court and the exact method of enforcement depended on whether the court had attached a power of arrest to the order. While this was a matter for the court's discretion, section 47(2) of the 1996 Act compelled the court to attach a power of arrest to a non-molestation order if it appeared that the respondent had used or threatened violence against the applicant or relevant child unless it was satisfied in all the circumstances that the applicant or child would be adequately protected without such a power of arrest.[172] A power of arrest allowed the police to arrest the

---

[169] *Wookey v Wookey* [1991] 3 All ER 365.   [170] [1999] 1 FLR 726.
[171] See *Wookey v Wookey* [1991] 3 All ER 365.   [172] See *Chechi v Bashir* [1999] 2 FLR 489.

respondent without warrant if there was reasonable cause to suspect that the respondent was in breach of the order to which the power of arrest was attached. If no power of arrest was attached to the order, the victim had to apply to the civil court for an arrest warrant and then enforce the order through the contempt of court procedure.

In line with the general trend to take domestic violence more seriously and to use the criminal justice system to punish domestic violence offenders, the Government sought to strengthen the legal protection afforded to victims of domestic violence.[173] A new provision was introduced by the Domestic Violence, Crime and Victims Act 2004 which criminalised the breach of a non-molestation order.

### Key legislation

Under the new section 42A in the 1996 Act:[174]

> a person who without reasonable excuse does anything that he is prohibited from doing by a non-molestation order is guilty of an offence.

This means that breach of a non-molestation order is now an arrestable offence.[175] Enforcement of this order no longer depends on whether a power of arrest has been attached, nor does the victim have to apply to the civil court to get an arrest warrant.[176]

### 4.3.10  Why was the law changed?

There were various reasons put forward to justify the criminalisation of non-molestation orders.[177] First, enforcing a non-molestation order through the criminal courts takes the matter out of the hands of the victim. It is the police and the CPS who will decide whether to proceed with the prosecution and it was thought that this would be helpful to victims who may not want to have the responsibility of instigating proceedings against a husband or partner. The aim was to encourage greater use of the criminal justice system and the application of criminal sanctions for domestic violence. Secondly, it was hoped that this would address the uncertainty which police officers faced around whether they could arrest someone for an alleged breach of a non-molestation order. Previously this depended on whether a power of arrest was attached to the order and it was not always clear to police officers who were called to an incident of domestic violence whether or not this power was in existence. The matter is now much more straightforward. Under section 42A, the police in all cases have the power to arrest a person who is in breach of a non-molestation order. Thirdly, as an action under section 42A will be taken by the police, the cost of enforcing the non-molestation order will not fall to the victim. The victim may be a witness but she will not be enforcing the action personally. In addition, the available sanctions are much more extensive in the criminal courts. While the maximum custodial sentence for breach of a non-molestation order under section 42A is five years,[178] the maximum period of imprisonment for breach of an injunction in civil contempt cases is two years.[179]

---

[173] *Safety and Justice: The Government's Proposals on Domestic Violence* (Cm 5847, 2003).

[174] Inserted by the Domestic Violence, Crime and Victims Act 2004, s 1.

[175] Under the Police and Criminal Evidence Act 1984, s 24(1).

[176] Note: for orders made without notice, an individual will only be guilty of a criminal offence if he is aware of the existence of the order (s 42A(2)).

[177] See C. Bessant, 'Enforcing Non-Molestation Orders in the Civil and Criminal Courts' [2005] Family Law 640.

[178] Section 42A(5).     [179] Contempt of Court Act 1981, s 14.

### 4.3.11 **Can a victim still enforce the order in the civil courts?**

The court no longer has the power to attach a power of arrest to a non-molestation order. However, a victim who wishes to enforce the order in the civil courts can apply for a warrant to arrest the respondent[180] or make an application for committal proceedings.[181] This may be particularly relevant where the police have decided not to arrest the alleged abuser, or where the CPS does not proceed with the prosecution. In such circumstances, the victim retains the option of enforcing the non-molestation order through civil proceedings for contempt of court.

However, the legislation makes it clear that the non-molestation order cannot be enforced as *both* a civil and criminal matter. Section 42A(4) and (5) states that a person cannot be convicted of breach of a non-molestation order under section 42A where the conduct has already been dealt with under contempt of court proceedings. The converse is also true. If a respondent has been convicted for breach of a non-molestation order under section 42A, the victim cannot subsequently bring proceedings for contempt of court in the civil courts.[182] In other words, the order can be enforced in one of two ways, under section 42A or as a contempt of court, but not both.

This does give rise to some concerns surrounding the extent to which a victim of domestic violence can control the manner in which any breach of a non-molestation order is dealt with. It has already been pointed out that a victim of domestic violence may want to salvage the relationship with the abuser, or may fear the practical consequences of the abuser being labelled a criminal and the impact which this may have on the family (eg if the abuser loses his job). It is these sorts of factors which may have led the victim to apply for a civil order in the first place, as opposed to seeking the protection of the criminal law. However, breach of a non-molestation order is now a criminal offence. Thus, what is to happen if the police decide to pursue the matter through the criminal courts but the victim opposes this and prefers, in the alternative, to enforce the order through the civil courts? While, in theory, the legislation preserves the right of the victim to enforce the order through the civil courts, in practice this option will be denied to the victim if the police and CPS adopt a rigorous policy of prosecuting breaches as a criminal offence under section 42A. Some have criticised this change to the law on the grounds that it undermines the autonomy of the victim and fails to appreciate the very particular nature of domestic violence. Indeed, some point out that the enforcement of non-molestation orders could have been strengthened by simply extending the penalties available in civil proceedings for contempt.[183] However, this may be little more than a hypothetical problem as evidence on the implementation of section 42A suggests that the police are using cautions to deal with perpetrators who have breached a non-molestation order under section 42A,[184] and that the CPS is not charging perpetrators with a criminal offence.[185]

While a breach of a non-molestation order cannot be dealt with through both civil and criminal enforcement proceedings, there is nothing to prevent a perpetrator whose actions in breaching the order also constitute a substantive criminal offence from being prosecuted under the criminal law for this offence,[186] and also being prosecuted for breach of the non-molestation order under section 42A (or facing contempt of court proceedings).

---

[180] Under s 47(8).

[181] J. Platt, 'The Domestic Violence, Crime and Victims Act 2004 Part 1: Is it Working?' [2008] Family Law 642.

[182] Section 42A(3). See *Hale v Tanner* [2000] 3 FCR 62; *Lomas v Parle* [2004] 1 FLR 812.

[183] M. Burton, 'Criminalising Breaches of Civil Orders for Protection from Domestic Violence' [2003] Crim LR 301.

[184] J. Platt, 'The Domestic Violence, Crime and Victims Act 2004 Part 1: Is it Working?' [2008] Family Law 642.

[185] Home Affairs Committee, 'Domestic Violence, Forced Marriage and "Honour"-Based Violence', Sixth Report of Session 2007–08, volume I, HC 263-I.

[186] Including under the Protection from Harassment Act 1997.

### 4.3.12 Sentencing for breach of a non-molestation order in the civil courts

A range of orders may be made in civil contempt cases and every case must be considered on its own facts.[187] In particular, the court will consider the nature of the breach, the presence of children, and whether the order was breached more than once.[188] The sentence imposed by the civil courts has a dual function. It will indicate the court's disapproval of the respondent's breach of the order, and will also attempt to secure the perpetrator's future compliance with the order.[189] A custodial sentence can be imposed, the maximum of which is two years. While there are no precise tariffs set for the appropriate sentence to be handed down when enforcing breach of a non-molestation order as a contempt of court,[190] case law shows that the courts take such breaches very seriously. In *Lomas v Parle*,[191] for example, the court indicated that the sentence imposed for breach of a non-molestation order as a civil contempt matter should not be 'manifestly discrepant' with the sentences imposed for criminal offences for breach of the orders under the Protection from Harassment Act 1997.[192] Where the respondent has used violence in breach of a non-molestation order, the court is likely to order imprisonment.

### 4.3.13 Sentencing for breach of a non-molestation order in the criminal courts

Under section 42A breach of a non-molestation order is an arrestable offence which can be enforced in the criminal courts. The sentences which can be imposed by the criminal courts are more extensive than those available to the civil courts and include fines, imprisonment, or community sentences and rehabilitation orders. Guidance issued by the Sentencing Guidelines Council on the approach to be taken to breach of a non-molestation order under section 42A makes it clear that the aim of the order is to protect the victim from harm. Thus, the sentence imposed for breach of this order should be primarily concerned with 'ensuring that the order is complied with and that it achieves the protection that it was intended to achieve'.[193]

One question which arises on sentencing is the relevance of the nature and context of the conduct which led to the non-molestation order being made in the first place. The Sentencing Guidelines state that the nature of the original conduct is relevant to the extent that it allows an assessment to be made regarding the severity of the breach. For example, if the non-molestation order was made in relation to very serious behaviour, then even relatively minor conduct which constitutes a breach (emails, telephone calls) could cause significant anxiety for a victim. Notwithstanding this, it must be remembered that the sentence following a breach is for the actual breach and is not designed to punish the offender for the original conduct which led to the order being made.

The nature of the conduct which caused the breach will also be considered and where the order is breached by the use of physical violence, the Guidelines make it clear that the starting point should normally be a custodial sentence. Non-violent behaviour that causes a high degree of harm or harassment can also result in a custodial sentence.

---

[187] *Devjee v Patel* [2006] EWCA Civ 1211. For guidance see *Hale v Tanner* [2000] 2 FLR 879; *Lomas v Parle* [2004] 1 FLR 812; *H v O (Contempt of Court: Sentencing)* [2004] EWCA Civ 1691.

[188] *Lomas v Parle* [2004] 1 FLR 812.     [189] *Hale v Tanner* [2000] 2 FLR 879.     [190] Ibid.

[191] [2004] 1 FLR 812.

[192] See also *H v O (Contempt of Court: Sentencing)* [2004] EWCA Civ 1691. Although this approach has been criticised on the basis that there are discrepancies between the range of remedies which are available in the civil and criminal courts respectively, and that the two systems have different objections and functions. While civil orders are designed to mark the court's disapproval at the respondent's breach of the civil order and ensure future compliance, the criminal courts are primarily concerned with punishing the offender. See M. Burton, 'Case Commentary—*Lomas v Parle*—Coherent and Effective Remedies for Victims of Domestic Violence: Time for an Integrated Domestic Violence Court' [2004] Child and Family Law Quarterly 317.

[193] Breach of a Protective Order, Sentencing Guidelines Council (2006), para 3.3.

### 4.3.14  Recent research on the use of non-molestation orders

Burton observes that an increase in the number of non-molestation orders sought may have been expected after the implementation of the Domestic Violence, Crime and Victims Act 2004 given that a greater number of people could apply for this order, and the fact that it had strengthened enforcement mechanisms.[194] However, this has not been the case. Recent studies have revealed that since the criminalisation of the non-molestation order, there has been a reduction in the number of applications for this order.[195] His Honour Justice Platt notes that across six courts during a six-month period after the changes introduced by the Act, the drop in applications for a non-molestation order varied from 15–30 per cent, with an average drop of around 25 per cent. Judge Platt suggests that there may be several possible explanations for this trend. First, the more severe sanctions for domestic violence may have led to a reduction in the incidence of such abuse, which means that fewer people actually need to apply for protective orders. However, this optimistic view is unlikely. As Platt points out, the new provisions only affect the sanctions for breach and not the criteria for initially making the order. Secondly, it may be that more victims are choosing to initiate criminal proceedings to tackle domestic violence. The fact that there has been an increase in the number of criminal prosecutions adds weight to this argument. However, the most likely explanation for the drop in applications is that the criminalisation of a breach of a non-molestation order has discouraged some victims from applying for the order. Platt regards this as entirely possible saying that:

> there are serious shortcomings in the way the 2004 Act has been implemented and there remains, as the Government acknowledged, serious disagreement as to whether the civil or criminal route is more effective in achieving the common goal which is to get the domestic abuse to stop.[196]

Even though these enhanced measures have been designed to increase the level of protection afforded to victims, the factors which deter victims from seeking the prosecution of the perpetrator may now act as a similar deterrence when deciding whether to initiate civil proceedings. However, it has also been pointed out that there may be other reasons which help to explain the reduction in the number of applications. For example, the perception that seeking an order is an expensive business,[197] the reduction in the availability of legal aid, and the fact that some victims may simply be receiving poor legal advice may all be relevant factors.[198] In addition, it is worth pointing out that even before the enactment of the 2004 Act there had been a steady decrease in the number of applications for non-molestation orders, which may mean that the current reductions may be a 'consolidation of the previous downward trend'.[199] Indeed, both applications and orders made for

---

[194]  M. Burton, 'Civil Law Remedies for Domestic Violence: Why are Applications for Non-Molestation Orders Declining?' (2009) 31(2) Journal of Social Welfare and Family Law 109 at 112.

[195]  J. Platt, 'The Domestic Violence, Crime and Victims Act 2004 Part 1: Is it Working?' [2008] Family Law 642. Platt also notes, however, that during the same period there was a significant increase in the number of applications for occupations orders under s 33(3)(g), which 'are non-molestation orders in all but name and to which a power of arrest can be attached'. M. Burton, 'Civil Law Remedies for Domestic Violence: Why are Applications for Non-Molestation Orders Declining?' (2009) 31(2) Journal of Social Welfare and Family Law 109.

[196]  Platt notes that police training in the aftermath of the new changes was inadequate as police were still using the civil courts when arresting someone for breach of a non-molestation order. Also it is unclear whether a person is charged under the new s 42A, charged with a criminal offence (if their conduct also constitutes an existing criminal offence), or both. There is also evidence that the police are using cautions to deal with those arrested under s 42A. See J. Platt, 'The Domestic Violence, Crime and Victims Act 2004 Part 1: Is it Working?' [2008] Family Law 642.

[197]  C. Humphreys and R. K. Thiara, *Routes to Safety: Protection Issues Facing Abused Women and Children and the Role of Outreach Services* (Bristol: Women's Aid Federation England, 2002); M. Burton, 'Civil Law Remedies for Domestic Violence: Why are Applications for Non-Molestation Orders Declining?' (2009) 31(2) Journal of Social Welfare and Family Law 109.

[198]  Ibid.

[199]  M. Hester, N. Westmarland, J. Pearce, and E. Williamson, *Early Evaluation of the Domestic Violence, Crime and Victims Act 2004*, Ministry of Justice Research Series 14/08 (2008), p 27 cited in Burton, 'Civil Law Remedies' at 112.

domestic violence have been declining since 2002. Recent statistics reveal the continuation of this trend. Applications made in the county courts for domestic violence remedies fell from 23,000 in 2010 to 20,700 in 2011, a 14 per cent decrease. Within this overall decrease, applications for non-molestation orders decreased by 13 per cent (from 17,843 to 15,573).[200]

# 5 Occupation orders

The breakdown of a personal relationship often occurs after a long period of time and it may be punctuated by incidents of violence and molestation. Victims of domestic assaults do not necessarily want their relationship with their spouse or partner to end, rather they may want it to continue but for the violence and threatening behaviour to stop. A spouse or partner who is being assaulted, harassed, threatened, or otherwise abused and molested may reach the stage where it is no longer tolerable to live under the same roof as the perpetrator. Indeed, many victims of domestic violence are forced to flee the family home because of the risks to which they, and their children, may be exposed. The question of whether an order can be obtained to force the abuser to leave the home and, where the victim has already been driven from the home, whether an order can be obtained which will entitle this person to return to the property, arises as a matter of real urgency. This is particularly true where the parties have few assets and a relatively low income. In such cases, the parties often cannot agree about who should stay in the home and who should leave, because the person who leaves may have nowhere suitable to go. The occupation order is, therefore, an important protective order. As noted by the Law Commission: 'in cases of domestic violence as where the parties live together, an occupation order ousting the respondent from the home will often be the only way of supporting a non-molestation order and giving the applicant effective protection.'[201] It is worth noting that when the court is considering whether to make an occupation order, it is also under a duty to consider whether to make a non-molestation order.[202]

The issue may be more complicated where children are living in the home. In this situation, a spouse or partner may insist on remaining in the home because they feel that to leave would impact on their relationship with their children, and would prejudice any chance they have of obtaining a child arrangements order in respect of the children's residence.[203] In addition, where allegations of violence have been made against one of the parties, the alleged perpetrator may refuse to leave the home on the basis that this would amount to an admission of guilt. While non-molestation orders can be granted which focus solely on the person of the victim, these may have little value if the perpetrator of an assault (or other form of molestation) is living in the same household as the victim. By giving the court the power to make occupation orders, the law therefore makes provision for the temporary removal of one of the parties from the home. The occupation order can also be used to give one party the right to enter the home and remain in occupation.

## 5.1 Some preliminary points about occupation orders

While an occupation order will usually be sought by a victim of domestic violence, it is not limited to these situations. The occupation order can be used to regulate occupation of the family home where a non-violent dispute arises between the parties as to who is entitled to occupy the property. However, due to the temporary nature of the order, it is unlikely that parties will seek an occupation order to resolve the long-term consequences of a relationship breakdown. Case law shows that the courts do not regard an occupation order as being designed to fulfil this function but instead view it as a serious interference with one's occupation rights in the family home.

---

[200] Ministry of Justice, *Judicial and Court Statistics 2011* (London: Ministry of Justice, 2012).
[201] Law Com No 207 (1992), para 4.6.     [202] Section 42(4A).
[203] On residence orders and the status quo principle, see Chapter 9.

Not all those who are entitled to apply for a non-molestation order can apply for an occupation order. Occupation orders interfere with the parties' property rights and the law takes such interference very seriously. Thus, the legislation restricts eligibility to apply for occupation orders to a narrow range of persons. There are two categories of applicant: entitled and non-entitled applicants. Entitled applicants have some existing legal rights in the property, while non-entitled applicants do not.[204]

An occupation order can only be made in relation to a dwelling-house which is, was, or was intended by both of them at any time to be the home of the parties.[205] Under section 39(2), an occupation order may be made on a free-standing application brought under section 33 or sections 35–38 of the FLA 1996. An occupation order can also be made in other family proceedings,[206] but the court does not have the power to make an occupation order by its own motion.[207]

There are two types of occupation orders. First, a 'declaratory occupation order', which declares, confers, or extends occupation rights in the home. This order must be obtained as a preliminary order by non-entitled applicants who have no pre-existing right to occupy the home. Secondly, a 'regulatory occupation order' which controls the exercise of the parties' existing rights of occupation. For example, this order can require one party to leave the home, or require one party to allow the other to enter and/or remain in the home.

### 5.2  Who can apply for an occupation order?

Entitled applicants are those who have an existing right of occupation in the home arising from a legal or beneficial interest in the property, or spouses/civil partners who have a statutory right of occupation in the home (known as 'home rights'). Entitled applicants can seek an occupation order against anyone with whom they are 'associated'. Non-entitled applicants are persons who do *not* have any existing legal or beneficial interest in the property, nor do they have 'home rights'. The legislation provides that non-entitled applicants can only seek an occupation order against a former spouse/civil partner, cohabitant, or former cohabitant. However, for non-entitled applicants the order is simply a short-term protective measure to give the applicant time to find suitable alternative accommodation or to 'await the outcome of an application for a property law remedy'.[208]

Thus, there are five categories of person who are eligible to apply for an occupation order. They are:

(i) those entitled to occupy the property (s 33);

(ii) a former spouse/civil partner with no existing rights of occupation in the property where the other former spouse/civil partner is so entitled (s 35);

(iii) a cohabitant or former cohabitant with no existing rights of occupation in the property where the other partner/former partner is so entitled (s 36);

(iv) a spouse or civil partner who has no existing right to occupy the property where the other spouse/civil partner also has no entitlement to remain in occupation (s 37);

(v) a cohabitant or former cohabitant who has no existing right to occupy the property where the other cohabitant or former cohabitant also has no entitlement to remain in occupation (s 38).

It is very important to establish which category a person falls under as this will affect the manner of their application, and the nature of any order made. Where an application is made under the wrong section the court may make an order under the correct section.[209] The following sections will detail the situation for each category of applicant.

---

[204] See Section 5.2.

[205] Under the previous law, the court had no power to make an order in respect of property which the parties intended to be their home but where they never actually lived together. This was amended by the FLA 1996 and thus an occupation order can be made in relation to property which the parties intended to be their joint home.

[206] Section 39(2).     [207] Section 39(2).     [208] Law Com No 207 (1992), para 4.7.     [209] Section 39(3).

## 5.3 **Entitled applicants**

Entitled applicants have an existing estate or interest in the family home and already have an entitlement to occupy the property.

---

### Key legislation

The provision dealing with entitled applicants is section 33 which provides that:

(1) If—

    (a) a person (the person entitled)—

        (i) is entitled to occupy a dwelling-house by virtue of a beneficial estate or interest or contract or by virtue of any enactment giving him the right to remain in occupation, or

        (ii) has home rights in relation to a dwelling-house, and

    (b) the dwelling-house—

        (i) is or at any time has been the home of the person entitled and of another person with whom he is associated, or

        (ii) was at any time intended by the person entitled and any such other person to be their home,

    (c) the person entitled may apply to the court for an order containing any of the provisions specified in subsections (3), (4) and (5).

---

Thus, under section 33 there are two types of entitled applicant. First, those who are already entitled to occupy the home by virtue of a beneficial estate or other interest in the property provided that the respondent is an 'associated person'.[210] This covers someone who is the sole or joint legal owner of the property or has a beneficial interest in the property by virtue of a resulting or constructive trust, or proprietary estoppel.[211] Under this provision, an application for an occupation order can be made between a variety of associated persons, for example siblings, unmarried partners, and engaged couples. This has nothing to do with the nature of the applicant's personal status but instead depends on whether the applicant has an existing estate or interest in the property which he or she shared, or intended to share, as a home with the respondent. Secondly, a spouse or civil partner is almost always entitled to apply for an occupation order under section 33 because he or she has a personal right to occupy the family home, known as 'home rights'.[212] Under section 30 of the 1996 Act, 'home rights' automatically arise in the following situation. Where one spouse or civil partner ('A') is entitled to occupy the home,[213] but the other spouse or civil partner ('B') is not so entitled, B, by virtue to being married or in a civil partnership with A obtains 'home rights' in the home. 'Home rights' are basically a statutory right of occupation: that is, a right to remain living in the home.[214]

---

[210] The meaning of 'associated person' is found in s 62(3); it is discussed in Section 4.3.3 in relation to non-molestation orders. Persons who have agreed to marry or enter into a civil partnership (whether or not that agreement has been terminated) are associated, but where the agreement has been terminated no application for an occupation order may be made under s 33 by reference to that agreement after three years beginning with the day on which it is terminated (s 33(2) and (2A)).

[211] See Chapter 5.

[212] Where the spouses or civil partners are bare licensees or squatters they are both non-entitled and will not be able to apply for an occupation order against each other under s 33. Instead, an application may be made under either s 37 or s 38.

[213] This entitlement can arise by virtue of a beneficial estate or interest or contract, or any enactment giving that person the right to remain in occupation (s 30(1)(a)(i) and (ii)).

[214] Spouses and civil partners have 'home rights' simply by being married to, or in a civil partnership with, the person who is entitled to occupy the home under s 30. For the purposes of obtaining occupation orders it does not matter whether these rights have been registered. It is only where a third party is claiming rights in the family home that notification of matrimonial home rights becomes a crucial issue.

**Key legislation**

The precise nature of this personal right is described in section 30(2) of the 1996 Act:

  (a) if in occupation, a right not to be evicted or excluded from the dwelling-house or any part of it by the other spouse/civil partner except with the leave of the court given by an order under section 33;
  (b) if not in occupation, a right with the leave of the court to enter into and occupy the dwelling-house.

This is a crucial provision because it not only gives a non-owning spouse/civil partner the right to live in the family home, it also gives that person certain rights against third party purchasers. Any purchaser from the entitled owning spouse/civil partner will take the property subject to the other spouse/civil partner's 'home rights' (provided that these have been registered in accordance with the Act's provisions).[215]

### 5.3.1  What order(s) can be made?

In terms of the property to which the order applies, it must be a dwelling-house that either is, or at any time has been, or was intended to be, the home of the applicant and of the person with whom she is associated.[216] The court, under section 33(4), can make a preliminary order which simply declares that the applicant falls into one of the earlier mentioned categories of entitled applicant. That is, that the applicant already has an estate or interest in the dwelling-house or has 'home rights' in the property. This may be particularly useful in situations where it may not be clear whether an applicant who is not a spouse or civil partner has a sufficient property interest to be entitled to apply for an order under section 33. This can be clarified by an order under section 33(4) declaring that the applicant is so entitled.

In the case of any entitled applicant the court can make a variety of orders to *regulate* occupation of the family home.

**Key legislation**

Section 33(3) provides that the court may:

  (a) enforce the applicant's entitlement to remain in occupation as against the other person ('the respondent');
  (b) require the respondent to permit the applicant to enter and remain in the dwelling-house or part of the dwelling-house;
  (c) regulate the occupation of the dwelling-house by either or both parties;
  (d) if the respondent is entitled as mentioned in subsection (1)(a)(i), prohibit, suspend or restrict the exercise by him of his right to occupy the dwelling-house;
  (e) if the respondent has home rights in relation to the dwelling-house and the applicant is the other spouse, restrict or terminate those rights;
  (f) require the respondent to leave the dwelling-house or part of the dwelling-house; or
  (g) exclude the respondent from a defined area in which the dwelling-house is included.

Together these provisions give the court wide powers to control the occupation of the home. It is important to understand that an occupation order is not simply confined to removing the respondent from the home. That may, indeed, be one manifestation of the order but it is much more flexible than that. For example, under section 33(3)(c) the court can make an order which regulates the

---

[215] Sections 31 and 32.      [216] Section 33(1)(b).

occupation of the home by either or both parties. This gives the court considerable flexibility to impose certain arrangements about how the property is to be used by the parties. In some instances the court may order that while the respondent is to remain living in the home, he is only allowed to use certain rooms. Indeed, the court may be more inclined to make such an order to carve up the parties' living arrangements rather than remove the respondent from the home, particularly in view of the general approach of the courts which has been to view the actual removal of one party from the home as being draconian.[217] It may also make sense for the applicant to accept such an arrangement as the difficulties in obtaining an occupation order removing the respondent from the property mean that the parties are frequently left living together. Thus, to have an order restricting occupation may be better than no order at all. While this type of remedy may be considered to be inappropriate in situations of violence because the applicant may remain at risk, there are cases which show that even in these sorts of circumstances the court may refuse to remove the respondent from the property. In *E v E (Ouster Order)*,[218] despite accepting the evidence of the wife that the husband attempted to rape her, the Court of Appeal confirmed the trial judge's decision simply to exclude the husband from one of the two bedrooms in the house. In her evidence-in-chief the wife had said: 'separate rooms would help, yes. I don't necessarily want him to go. I want my safety and peace. I don't want any more aggravation.' The Court of Appeal considered that normally it should be expected that an order removing the respondent from the property would follow where the judge finds allegations of rape or attempted rape. However, the evidence of the wife, coupled with other factors,[219] indicated that it was not possible for them to say that the judge had been plainly wrong in the exercise of his discretion.

Section 33(3)(g) which permits the court to 'exclude the respondent from a defined area in which the dwelling-house is included' is also useful as it allows the court to throw a ring around the property and order the respondent not to come within its vicinity. For example, if the home was located in a block of flats, the respondent could not only be ordered to keep away from the home, but also the block in which the home is situated. In *Tuck v Nicholls*[220] the order stated that the respondent should not enter 'that area of King's Lynn in which lies the matrimonial home'.[221] This broad exclusionary order confers considerable protection on the applicant as she can take action to have the respondent brought before the court for breach of the order before he comes near enough to attack her. So, for example, if he is hanging around in the road outside the house, or threatening her when she goes out, and an injunction is in force prohibiting him from being in that area, she can have him brought back before the court for breach of the order.[222]

In the case of spouses and civil partners two additional orders are available, and each may have a radical effect on the applicant's position in relation to the property. Section 33(3)(e) allows the court to restrict or terminate the 'home rights' of a respondent spouse or civil partner. In other words, if the respondent simply has 'home rights' in relation to the property, the court can restrict or even terminate those rights. Such an order not only ends the respondent's right to live in the home, but also frees the applicant spouse/civil partner who is the sole owner of the property to dispose of the property as he or she wishes. By contrast, section 33(5) is a protective provision which enables a court to order that the 'home rights' of a spouse or civil partner are not brought to an end by the death of the other spouse/civil partner, or the termination (otherwise than by death) of the marriage or civil partnership.[223]

---

[217] See Section 5.6.     [218] [1995] 1 FLR 224.

[219] This included a living pattern whereby the parties were not in the house together very often, no children, and the wife's uncertain immigration status, which meant she might be reluctant to bring divorce proceedings. This latter consideration meant that the wife was in a particularly vulnerable position, but still the court was willing to accept at face value her evidence that separate bedrooms would give her adequate protection.

[220] [1989] 1 FLR 283.     [221] The order was discharged on appeal, but not for excess of powers in this regard.

[222] See also *Burns v Azadani* [1999] 1 FLR 266.

[223] Which is when they would normally terminate (s 30(8)).

Section 40 specifies additional orders which may be included where an occupation order is made under section 33.[224] Under this provision either party can be obliged to take responsibility for the repair and maintenance of the dwelling-house, or the discharge of rent, mortgage repayments, or other outgoings.[225] One of the main concerns of a person who is in a financially vulnerable position is to keep a roof over her head and not to fall behind with payments owed to third parties, as default may entitle them to take possession proceedings. Thus, section 40 aims to address this concern by giving the court the power to require either party to take responsibility for the rent or mortgage repayments in relation to the house. For example, if one party has been ousted from the home under an occupation order, that person can be ordered to pay the rent, mortgage, or other outgoings in relation to the property. When deciding whether to make an order under section 40, the court is directed to have regard to all the circumstances of the case including the financial needs and resources of the parties and their present and future financial obligations. Section 40 orders are likely to be less useful to unmarried partners and other persons entitled to apply for orders under sections 35 and 36, as any provision ceases to have effect when the occupation order to which it relates comes to an end.[226] While section 40 orders appear to be very useful, they have a serious defect. Orders made under section 40 lack effective enforcement mechanisms: there is no provision for enforcement under the FLA 1996 and they cannot be enforced under other enforcement legislation, namely, the Debtors Act 1869 and the Attachment of Earnings Act 1971. The Court of Appeal identified this gap in the law in *Nwogbe v Nwogbe*[227] and recommended that courts do not exercise their powers under section 40 until an effective enforcement procedure is provided by legislation. Despite the fact that this plea for reform was made in 2000, no action has yet been taken and section 40 remains a toothless provision.

### 5.3.2  Criteria for making an occupation order

Before the introduction of occupation orders under the FLA 1996, the court had the power to make an ouster order under the Domestic Violence and Matrimonial Proceedings Act 1976. The criteria for making such an order were contained in section 1(3) of the Matrimonial Homes Act 1983. This provision directed the court:

> to make such order as it thinks just and reasonable having regard to the conduct of the spouses in relation to each other and otherwise, to their respective needs and financial resources, to the needs of any children and to all the circumstances of the case.

These factors were not listed in any kind of hierarchy[228] and the courts made it very clear that an order ousting someone from their home was a very serious order, which required strong justification. Indeed, it was felt by the courts that such an order should only be made where the judge was satisfied that no lesser measure would suffice to protect the welfare of the applicant and any child.[229] This approach was criticised on a number of grounds. First, it was argued that it did not give sufficient priority to the applicant's need for personal protection but instead balanced this against other factors, such as the hardship to the respondent.[230] Secondly, it was felt that the requirement to consider the

---

[224] Section 40 also applies to orders made under ss 35 and 36.　　　[225] Section 40(1).

[226] Section 40(3). Orders for entitled applicants under s 33 may be made for a specified period, until the occurrence of a specified event or until further order (s 33(10)). In the first instance orders relating to former spouses under s 35 cannot last for longer than six months, although they may be extended on one or more occasion for a further six months (s 35(10)). However, orders between unmarried partners made under s 36 may be extended by six months on one occasion only (s 36(10)).

[227] [2000] 2 FLR 744.

[228] In *Richards v Richards* [1983] 2 All ER 807 the House of Lords rejected the submission that in cases where children were involved their needs were paramount and held that each of the factors listed in s 1(3) should be given equal weight.

[229] *Wiseman v Simpson* [1988] All ER 245; *Shipp v Shipp* [1988] 1 FLR 345; *Blackstock v Blackstock* [1991] 2 FLR 308.

[230] Law Com No 207 (1992), para 4.23.

conduct of the parties encouraged parties to make allegations of fault which conflicts with the general trend in family law to remove recrimination and fault-finding from decision making. Thirdly, it was also thought that the test gave insufficient weight to the welfare of children as each of the factors listed in the legislation were given equal weight. It was pointed out that this was inconsistent with the emerging ethos of family law to give priority to the interests of children.[231] While the statutory criteria for making an occupation order was amended in light of these shortcomings, it could be argued that very similar concerns can be levelled at the current criteria and its interpretation by the courts. The fear by some that the test which was recommended by the Law Commission would lead to 'occupation orders almost on demand' has certainly proved to be far from the case.[232]

The court can make a declaratory occupation order under section 33(4) or a regulatory occupation order under section 33(3). A declaratory order will simply confirm that the applicant either has 'home rights' or has an existing interest in the property. However, to enforce the entitled applicant's existing right of occupation or to restrict the respondent's use of the property a regulatory occupation order must be obtained. There are two tests for the court to consider when deciding whether to grant a regulatory occupation order. The first test,[233] if met in favour of the applicant, confers a mandatory duty on the court to make an order, while the second[234] gives the court the discretion whether to make the order or not. Initially there was some confusion over the relationship between these two sets of criteria with early authority suggesting that they fed into one another. In other words, the general checklist of factors outlined in section 33(6) was used by the court when considering the test under section 33(7).[235] However, it is now clear that these tests are applied separately.[236] In practical terms, when deciding whether to make a regulatory occupation order for an entitled applicant the court will approach the matter in the following way:

(i) it will first consider the 'balance of harm' test under section 33(7) and if this is satisfied in favour of the applicant or any child, then the court will be under a mandatory duty to make the order;

(ii) if the 'balance of harm' test does not apply or is not met in favour of the applicant, the court will consider whether to make an order at its discretion by considering the general checklist of factors under section 33(6).

### 5.3.3 The 'balance of harm' test

The first set of criteria that the court will consider when deciding whether to make an occupation order in favour of an entitled applicant is the 'balance of harm' test under section 33(7).

---

**Key legislation**

Under this provision:

If it appears to the court that the applicant or any relevant child is likely to suffer significant harm attributable to the conduct of the respondent if an order under this section containing one or more of the provisions mentioned in subsection (3) is not made, the court shall make the order unless it appears to it that—

(a) the respondent or any relevant child is likely to suffer significant harm if the order is made; and

(b) the harm likely to be suffered by the respondent or child in that event is as great as, or greater than, the harm attributable to conduct of the respondent which is likely to be suffered by the applicant or child if the order is not made.

---

[231] Ibid, para 4.23.   [232] Ibid, para 4.23.   [233] Under s 33(7).
[234] Under s 33(6).   [235] See eg *B v B (Occupation Order)* [1999] 1 FLR 715.
[236] *Chalmers v Johns* [1999] 1 FLR 392.

This test mandates the court to carry out a balancing exercise which weighs the harm likely to be suffered by the applicant and any relevant child if the order is not made against the harm likely to be suffered by the respondent and any relevant child if the order is made. This test states that the court *must* make an order where it appears that the applicant or any relevant child is likely to suffer significant harm attributable to the conduct of the respondent if the order is not made. The court must make an order in favour of the applicant in these circumstances although section 33(7) leaves open the type of protective action the court should take. The orders under section 33(3) range from simply enforcing the applicant's right to live in the house to excluding the respondent.[237] However, where the harm likely to be suffered by the respondent or child if the order were to be made is as great as, or greater than, the harm which is likely to be suffered by the applicant or child if the order is not made, then the court has a choice about what order, if any, to make. Where the likelihood of significant harm to both parties is deemed to be equal, then the court is not obliged to make an order but can do so at its discretion by applying the general checklist under section 33(6).

There are several points which are worth noting about this provision. First, if this test is established in favour of the applicant or any relevant child then the court is under a duty to make the order. However, this test only applies where 'likely significant harm attributable to the conduct of the respondent' is established. 'Harm' in relation to both adults and children is defined as the ill-treatment or the impairment of physical or mental health; but in relation to a child it also includes the impairment of a child's development.[238] The legislation also states that ill-treatment in relation to children includes sexual abuse, although why this is specified in relation to children and not adults is not entirely clear. While the term 'significant' is not defined in the FLA 1996, for the purposes of the Children Act 1989, 'significant' has been taken to mean 'considerable, noteworthy or important'.[239] It is clear from the case law that a similarly high threshold applies to the definition of 'significant harm' in the 1996 Act, which means that minor types of harm will not be considered. While the standard of proof required to establish the likelihood of significant harm has not been made clear in the FLA 1996, the term 'likely' in section 31 of the Children Act 1989 has been interpreted to mean 'a real possibility' which is to be established on the balance of probabilities.[240]

Contrary to the prevailing ethos of other family law provisions, the welfare of any children is not the paramount consideration under the 'balance of harm' test. The Law Commission considered this point head on and did not find it easy to strike an acceptable balance between what it termed a 'balance of hardship' test and a test which made the welfare of the children paramount.[241] In the end it recommended a middle-ground approach as it was felt that the paramountcy principle was not appropriate to occupation order cases.

Unfortunately, while the Law Commission was careful not to link the test to the respondent's conduct, Parliament thought otherwise and introduced conduct as an element to be considered.[242] Not only must significant harm to the applicant or child be shown before the balance of harm test comes into play, but the test only applies where it is established that the harm is *attributable* to the respondent's conduct. This means that the balancing exercise is immediately weighted in favour of the respondent. It is only where the respondent's conduct is causative of the likely harm that the court is under a duty to make an order. There is no similar requirement to show that the harm to the respondent is caused by the applicant's conduct: any type of harm which the respondent may suffer on making the order can be taken into account. This means that the test does not apply in a morally neutral fashion.

---

[237] It could be maintained that it is implicit that a finding of hardship to the applicant under s 33(7) must lead to an order which, at a minimum, regulates the respondent's occupation of the home, because this is what the court must do in a case of an applicant former spouse or civil partner with no existing right to occupy: s 33(5), (8).

[238] Section 63(1).    [239] *Humberside County Council v B* [1993] 1 FLR 257 at 263, *per* Booth J.

[240] *Re H (Threshold Criteria: Standard of Proof)* [1996] 1 All ER 1; *Re B (Sexual Abuse: Standard of Proof)* [2008] UKHL 35.

[241] Law Com No 207 (1992), paras 4.20–4.34.    [242] And under the general criteria in s 33(6).

The test's concentration on conduct and causation in addition to proof of significant harm gives ample scope for argument on behalf of the respondent that the order should not be made. It also means that the test will not apply where the significant harm is brought about by the applicant's decision to move out of the home without good cause. Further, if the harm is caused by the poor accommodation in which the applicant finds herself after moving out of the home, the court may not regard this harm as attributable to the conduct of the respondent even though it was this conduct that may have caused the applicant to leave the home in the first place.[243]

A useful example which shows how the courts weigh up the competing interests of the parties is *B v B (Occupation Order)*.[244] This case also illustrates how the courts can face some difficult decisions about the needs of different children. In this case the wife had been forced out of council property she shared with her husband due to his serious violence. She left the home with her baby and was temporarily housed by the local authority in bed and breakfast accommodation. The husband remained in the property with his 6-year-old son from a previous relationship. Allowing the husband's appeal against an occupation order made in favour of the wife, the Court of Appeal found that all that the baby needed was to be securely with her mother. Although the baby's present accommodation was unsuitable it was likely to be temporary as the local authority were bound to treat the wife as homeless and in priority need for suitable accommodation.[245] However, the local authority's duty to the husband, at its highest, was simply to provide advice and to secure temporary accommodation for him after which he would have to source accommodation for himself.[246] Applying the balance of harm test, the court found that if the husband were ordered out of the house this would cause his son to suffer significant harm. It would result in the boy changing school for the fifth time in 18 months, and this would be very damaging and disruptive to his mental and emotional well-being. The boy's security depended not only on being with his father, but on his other day-to-day support systems of which his home and school were plainly the most important. Thus, when the respective likelihoods of harm to the two children were weighed, the balance came down on the son suffering the greater harm if the occupation order were made. One should not take from this case that the court tolerated the husband's violence in the home: the Court of Appeal was emphatic that the husband's behaviour had been disgraceful, and it stressed that perpetrators of domestic violence cannot expect to remain in shared accommodation. However, the interests of all the parties had to be weighed against each other and a critical factor in this case was that the son was not the child of both parties, and that there was no question of him being cared for by anyone other than the father.

### 5.3.4 The general checklist

> **Key legislation**
>
> If the 'balance of harm' test is not met in favour of the applicant, the court can still make an order at its discretion taking into account all of the circumstances of the case including:[247]
>
> (a) the housing needs and housing sources of each of the parties and of any relevant child;
> (b) the financial resources of each of the parties;
> (c) the likely effect of any order, or of any decision by the court not to exercise its powers . . . on the health, safety or well-being of the parties and of any relevant child; and
> (d) the conduct of the parties in relation to each other and otherwise.

---

[243] M. Burton, *Legal Responses to Domestic Violence* (Abingdon: Routledge-Cavendish, 2008), pp 21–2.
[244] [1999] 1 FLR 715.    [245] Housing Act 1996, s 188(1). See Section 8.1 on homelessness.
[246] See Section 8.1 on homelessness.    [247] Section 33(6).

These factors are given equal weight and, once again, the welfare of the children is not the court's paramount consideration.

### 5.3.4.1 *Housing and financial needs and resources*

The court will consider the parties' respective housing and financial needs and their available resources. One issue will be what alternative accommodation each party has open to them. The court will, therefore, consider the ability of the respondent to rehouse himself. However, even where this is thought to be feasible, it is no guarantee that the court will make an occupation order, despite the fact that the court may accept that it is undesirable for the two parties to continue living together under the same roof.

Where the parties live in accommodation provided by the local authority, the court may be influenced by the authority's housing policies in determining whether or not to make an occupation order. Where the court is satisfied that suitable alternative accommodation will be provided for the respondent, the decision to remove him from the home becomes less draconian. However, if the order will effectively render him homeless, then this is an extremely serious matter.[248] In these sorts of situations much will depend on whether the local authority would rehouse the respondent if he were forced to leave the family home. If the local authority were under no obligation to rehouse the respondent, but the applicant would be treated by the local authority as in priority need for housing were *she* to leave the family home, then this may persuade the court that no order should be made.

### 5.3.4.2 *The likely effect of the court's decision on the health, safety, or well-being of the parties or a child*

Under section 33(6)(c), when exercising its discretion whether to make an order, the court must take into account the effect of its decision to grant, or refuse to grant, an order. Even though the welfare of any child is not the court's paramount consideration, there are some instances where their interests may persuade the court that an order should be made. In *Lee v Lee*,[249] for example, the wife had left the home and was unable to find accommodation for herself and her children to live together as a family. The court held that the needs of the children to be together, and to be with their mother, were sufficient to establish the necessity for an order. However, the prevailing judicial view is that occupation orders are draconian measures because they interfere with the respondent's property rights and, as such, they should only be made in exceptional circumstances. Indeed, in general, the courts have been more concerned about the impact of an occupation order on the respondent than on the impact of a refusal to make an order on the applicant and children. In other words, removing the respondent from his home tends to be viewed as more serious than the applicant fleeing the home to live in unsuitable accommodation.

### 5.3.4.3 *Conduct*

Under the old law, the courts tended to focus almost entirely on whether the respondent's conduct was sufficiently grave to justify exclusion from the home. The Law Commission considered that this placed too much emphasis on allegations of the parties' behaviour at the expense of giving priority to the applicant's personal protection and the interests of the children.[250] However, the conduct of the parties is specifically listed as one of the factors to consider under the general checklist.[251] This means that there remains a tension in the law between those cases where, after balancing all the factors, decisive weight is given to whether the respondent's conduct has been sufficiently serious to justify making an order removing him from the home, and those cases where the financial and housing needs of the applicant and her children appear to demand an order requiring the respondent to leave. Burton argues that the case law suggests that 'occupation orders will be difficult to obtain in the

---

[248]  See Section 8.1 on homelessness.   [249]  (1984) FLR 243.
[250]  Law Com No 207 (1992), para 4.23.   [251]  Section 33(6)(d).

absence of serious physical violence'.[252] One could say, therefore, that unless the court is satisfied that the respondent has been blameworthy in carrying out physical violence an order may not be made. Arguably this gives greater priority to the conduct element in the criteria than to the other considerations, such as the harm caused to the children in witnessing domestic violence and, if the applicant moves out of the home, the harm caused by living in unsuitable accommodation. It is suggested that the courts should re-focus on the role of the civil law which is to afford protection in cases of domestic violence, in contrast with the role of criminal law which is to apportion blame and to punish. While the Law Commission sought to prioritise the welfare of the applicant and children in the decision-making process, one can question whether the provisions under the FLA 1996 (as interpreted by the courts) 'do in fact tip the balance away from conduct and towards the welfare of applicant and child'.[253]

### 5.3.5 Duration of orders made in favour of entitled applicants

The Law Commission recommended that a distinction be made between entitled and non-entitled applicants in relation to the duration of the order.[254] They took the view that where an applicant is entitled to occupy the home, it is inappropriate to impose statutory time limits on the duration of the order. Thus, section 33(10) provides that '[a]n order under this section may, in so far as it has continuing effect, be made for a specified period, until the occurrence of a specified event or until further order'. This means that an occupation order can be made in favour of an entitled application for an unlimited duration, or until further order.

## 5.4 Non-entitled applicants

An occupation order can also be sought by a limited range of persons who are not entitled to occupy the home. There are two types of non-entitled applicant. First, those who are seeking an order against a respondent who is entitled to occupy the property. Secondly, there are those who are seeking an order against a respondent who is also non-entitled. As the Law Commission noted, in the latter case 'the court is only adjusting occupation rights as between the parties themselves, both of whom may well be subject to almost immediate ejection at the behest of a third party'.

In situations where the respondent is entitled to occupy the property, only a former spouse or civil partner (s 35) or a cohabitant or former cohabitant can apply for an order (s 36).[255]

### 5.4.1 One former spouse with no existing right to occupy (s 35)

When a marriage or a civil partnership is brought to an end by divorce or dissolution, the non-entitled party's 'home rights' come to an end unless they have been extended under section 33(5). The non-entitled spouse or civil partner can, therefore, be in a vulnerable position if the entitled person asserts his sole right to occupy the former family home while any pending financial provision and property adjustment arrangements within the divorce/dissolution proceedings are resolved.[256] The applicant may wish to take steps to obtain the right to remain in the property, and may wish to remove the respondent from the property in situations of domestic violence or to reduce the tension associated with the breakdown of the parties' relationship.

A non-entitled former spouse can make an application for an occupation order under section 35. However, this is a two-stage process as the court must first decide whether to make a declaratory order which will give this person rights of occupation in the property: that is, the right not to be evicted from the home or if she is not currently in occupation of the property, the right to enter the property and remain in occupation. If occupation rights are granted, the court will then decide whether to make a regulatory order.

---

[252] M. Burton, *Legal Responses to Domestic Violence* (Abingdon: Routledge-Cavendish, 2008), p 25.
[253] Ibid, p 21.     [254] Law Com No 207 (1992), paras 4.35–4.37.
[255] The legislation makes provision for the situation where neither party is entitled to occupy the home: see Section 5.5.
[256] See Chapter 4.

### Key legislation

In deciding whether to make a declaratory order, the court will have regard to all the circumstances of the case including the range of factors listed under section 35(6). These are:

(a) the housing needs and housing resources of each of the parties and of any relevant child;

(b) the financial resources of each of the parties;

(c) the likely effect of any order, or of any decision by the court not to exercise its powers under sub-section (3) or (4), on the health, safety or well-being of the parties and of any relevant child;

(d) the conduct of the parties in relation to each other and otherwise;

(e) the length of time that has elapsed since the parties ceased to live together;

(f) the length of time that has elapsed since the marriage was dissolved or annulled; and

(g) the existence of any pending proceedings between the parties—

(i) for an order under section 23A or 24 of the [1973 c. 18.] Matrimonial Causes Act 1973 (property adjustment orders in connection with divorce proceedings etc.);

(ii) for an order under paragraph 1(2)(d) or (e) of Schedule 1 to the [1989 c. 41.] Children Act 1989 (orders for financial relief against parents); or

(iii) relating to the legal or beneficial ownership of the dwelling-house.

Thus the court will take into account the general checklist of factors, paragraphs (a) to (e), before considering certain issues pertinent to the situation of a former spouse: that is, the length of time since the parties ceased to live together; the length of time since the marriage/civil partnership was brought to an end; and the existence of any pending proceedings between the parties. The latter point may be particularly important to the court.

If the court makes a declaratory occupation order giving the non-entitled former spouse the right to live in the home, it will then consider whether to make a regulatory order regulating this right of occupation. The regulatory order in favour of a former spouse/civil partner can do all of the things which can be done for the entitled applicant under section 33. For example, it can remove the respondent from the home or exclude the respondent from a defined area around the home.[257]

### Key legislation

Under section 35(7), the court will decide whether to make a regulatory order by taking into account all the circumstances of the case including:

(a) the housing needs and housing resources of each of the parties and of any relevant child;

(b) the financial resources of each of the parties;

(c) the likely effect of any order, or of any decision by the court not to exercise its powers under sub-section (3) or (4), on the health, safety or well-being of the parties and of any relevant child;

(d) the conduct of the parties in relation to each other and otherwise;

(e) the length of time that has elapsed since the parties ceased to live together.

The balance of harm test also applies under section 35(8) which means that the court is under a duty to make an order if the applicant or any relevant child is likely to suffer significant harm attributable to the conduct of the respondent if the order is not made, unless the respondent or relevant child would suffer harm as great or greater.

---

[257] See s 35(5).

The occupation order for a non-entitled former spouse/civil partner will only last for six months initially under section 35(10). However, the order may be extended on one or more occasion for a further period of six months although the Law Commission made it clear that an occupation order for a non-entitled applicant is designed to be a short-term measure to give the applicant time to find suitable alternative accommodation or to await the outcome of financial and property proceedings between the parties.[258] Under section 35(9), an order cannot be made after the death of either party and ceases to have effect on the death of either party.

### 5.4.2 Cohabitant or former cohabitant with no existing right to occupy (s 36)

A cohabitant or former cohabitant with no existing rights in the property can apply as a non-entitled applicant against an entitled respondent under section 36. Under section 62(1)(a) cohabitants are defined as 'two persons who are neither married to each other nor civil partners of each other but are living together as husband and wife or as if they were civil partners'.

The Select Committee on Violence in Marriage,[259] which produced its report in 1975, revealed that there were grounds for serious concern about the lack of protective safeguards for women abused by their violent husbands or partners. The home continues to be a dangerous place, and cohabitants and former cohabitants have an undoubted need for protection from eviction and to be able to evict their abusive partners. However, the thrust of the House of Lords' ruling in *Davis v Johnson*[260] was that the purpose of domestic violence relief is to provide a swift but temporary response to an urgent situation and to give the applicant a secure roof over her head while she looks for alternative accommodation. Consequently, the courts were normally unwilling to interfere with the undoubted right of the respondent to live in his own home except on the most temporary of bases. The FLA 1996 continues to reflect this view.

The application of a non-entitled cohabitant or former cohabitant is similar to the application of a non-entitled former spouse. That is, there is a two-step process. First the court will decide whether to grant the applicant occupation rights. Secondly, if these are granted, the court will then decide whether to regulate those rights by making a regulatory occupation order.

#### 5.4.2.1 Granting occupation rights

Under section 36(3) a non-entitled cohabitant who is in occupation may apply for an order:

(a) giving the applicant the right not to be evicted or excluded from the dwelling-house or any part of it by the respondent for the period specified in the order; and

(b) prohibiting the respondent from evicting or excluding the applicant during that period.

Subsection (4) covers the converse situation, and provides that where the cohabitant is not in occupation, an order must contain provisions:

(a) giving the applicant the right not to be evicted or excluded from the dwelling-house or any part of it by the respondent for the period specified in the order; and

(b) requiring the respondent to permit the exercise of that right.

---

### Key legislation

When the court is determining whether to make an order under either of these subsections and, if so, in what manner, section 36(6) directs it to have regard to all the circumstances including:

(a) the housing needs and housing resources of each of the parties and of any relevant child;
(b) the financial resources of each of the parties;

---

[258] Law Com No 207 (1992), para 4.19.    [259] HC 553 (1974–75).    [260] [1978] 1 All ER 1132.

(c) the likely effect of any order, or of any decision by the court not to exercise its powers under sub-section (3) or (4), on the health, safety or well-being of the parties and of any relevant child;

(d) the conduct of the parties in relation to each other and otherwise;

(e) the nature of the parties' relationship and in particular the level of commitment involved in it;

(f) the length of time during which they have lived together as husband and wife;

(g) whether there are or have been any children who are children of both parties or for whom both parties have or have had parental responsibility;

(h) the length of time that has elapsed since the parties ceased to live together; and

(i) the existence of any pending proceedings between the parties—

  (i) for an order under paragraph 1(2)(d) or (e) of Schedule 1 to the Children Act 1989 (orders for financial relief against parents); or

  (ii) relating to the legal or beneficial ownership of the dwelling-house.

Orders under section 36(3) and (4) give the applicant the right to live in the property but do not otherwise interfere with the owning cohabitant's rights. They are thus the least intrusive on the respondent's sole right of occupation. The criteria governing the exercise of the court's discretion in paragraphs (a) to (d) are identical to those which apply to entitled applicants and non-entitled former spouses/civil partners. The additional criteria in paragraphs (e) to (i) focus on the nature and duration of the personal relationship between the cohabitants, whether they have children, and whether proceedings designed to resolve the financial and property-owning issues stemming from their joint occupation and joint parenthood are pending. These criteria enable the court to take account of matters which reflect the parties' legitimate expectations according to the circumstances of the case.[261] In cases where the cohabitation has lasted for a short period of time, the claim of the non-entitled cohabitant is relatively weak. However, the court is also directed to take account of both the respondent's conduct and the applicant's needs and these considerations may strengthen the applicant's case for immediate relief.

Particular note should be taken of paragraph (e). This requires the court to consider the nature of the parties' relationship and the 'particular level of commitment involved in it'. Originally the court had to take into account the fact that the parties had not given each other the commitment involved in marriage.[262] This provision was included to pacify those opposed to legislation on the ground that it gave increased protection to unmarried cohabitants, thus undermining the institution of marriage. However, its inclusion can be criticised as being unhelpful to courts when deciding upon the civil remedies which may be necessary to protect a victim of domestic violence. It also involves a sweeping judgement of unmarried relationships as lacking the commitment of marriage when research illustrates that the level of commitment involved in relationships does not simply depend on marital status.[263] It is to be welcomed that this provision was repealed by the Domestic Violence, Crime and Victims Act 2004[264] although it added to section 36(6)(e) that when the court is considering the nature of the parties' relationship, it should consider the 'particular level of commitment involved in it'.[265] Quite how the court should assess this level of commitment is unclear, particularly when one considers that the court is, in another subsection, directed to consider the length of the parties' relationship and whether they had children. One could argue that this direction to consider the functional characteristics of the parties' relationship is quite sufficient for the court to draw a conclusion on the nature of the relationship without having to assess the 'level of commitment' under a separate provision.

---

[261] Law Com No 207 (1992), para 4.12.

[262] FLA 1996, s 41: repealed by the Domestic Violence, Crime and Victims Act 2004.

[263] See eg M. Maclean and J. Eekelaar, 'The Obligations and Expectations of Couples Within Families' (2004) 26(2) Journal of Social Welfare and Family Law 117.

[264] Section 2(1).    [265] Inserted by the Domestic Violence, Crime and Victims Act 2004, s 2(2).

### 5.4.2.2 Regulatory orders

> **Key legislation**
>
> Section 36(5) is a more draconian order because it allows the court to interfere directly with the entitled cohabitant's right to occupy the home. A regulatory order may:
>
> (a) regulate the occupation of the dwelling-house by either or both of the parties;
>
> (b) prohibit, suspend or restrict the exercise by the respondent of his right to occupy the dwelling-house;
>
> (c) require the respondent to leave the dwelling-house or part of the dwelling-house; or
>
> (d) exclude the respondent from a defined area in which the dwelling-house is included.

When deciding whether to grant a regulatory order, the court takes into account the general checklist of factors under section 36(6)(a)–(d)—that is: the housing needs and housing resources of each of the parties and of any relevant child; the financial resources of each of the parties; the effect of the court's decision whether to make an order on the health, safety, or well-being of the parties and of any relevant child; and the conduct of the parties in relation to each other and otherwise. This excludes the matters mentioned in paragraphs (e) to (h) of subsection (6).[266] This is important, because those paragraphs contain considerations which may be unhelpful to the applicant's case. It is plain that once paragraphs (e) to (h) have been overcome, and an order has been made allowing the applicant to enter and remain in the dwelling-house, they should not be revisited when consideration is given to making a harsher order containing a subsection (5) provision.

The court must also consider the balance of harm test, but this applies in a very different way to the other category of applicants. Under section 36(8) the court considers the following questions:

(a) whether the applicant or any relevant child is likely to suffer significant harm attributable to conduct of the respondent if the subsection (5) provision is not included in the order; and

(b) whether the harm likely to be suffered by the respondent or child if the provision is included is as great as or greater than the harm attributable to conduct of the respondent which is likely to be suffered by the applicant or child if the provision is not included.

There is a crucial distinction between the application of the balance of harm test for non-entitled cohabitants and the other applicants (ie, an entitled applicant and a non-entitled former spouse/civil partner). For other applicants, the court is under a duty to make an order where the harm to the applicant or child exceeds the likely harm to the respondent or child. However, in the case of non-entitled cohabitants or former cohabitants, the balance of harm provision in section 36(8) merely provides a set of questions for the court to take into account when exercising its discretion: they do not determine what, if any, order should be made. This means that even if the applicant or child is likely to suffer greater significant harm than the respondent, the court is not under a duty to make an order but instead retains its discretion in this matter. It is argued that this is an unacceptable distinction which elevates the status of the parties' relationship, or former relationship, over the applicant's need for protection. Surely the balance of harm test which seeks to safeguard the welfare of the applicant and children in situations where inaction will result in significant harm should apply in exactly the same way for all applicants, especially in light of the fact that all applicants are 'entitled' applicants by the time the court comes to make a decision on an application for a regulatory occupation order.

### 5.4.2.3 Duration and nature of an order for a non-entitled cohabitant or former cohabitant

Another significant difference between the position of a spouse and civil partner (who will always been an entitled applicant) and a non-entitled cohabitant is that an order made in favour of the

---

[266] See the previous section.

latter will be limited in duration. In the first instance they can last for up to six months, but may be extended on one occasion for a further maximum period of six months.[267] This means that an order for a non-entitled cohabitant can only last for a maximum of one year irrespective of the length of the parties' cohabitation, their relative need for accommodation, or the nature of the conduct which led to the order being made.

The court has no residual discretion so, for example, where the couple have lived together for many years and have brought up children who are now no longer dependent, the non-entitled partner must leave at the end of the specified period.[268] The six-month period, with the possibility of its extension, is intended to give the applicant time in which to sort out her financial affairs, to claim a beneficial entitlement to the property where evidence to support this is disputed, or otherwise to make new housing arrangements. It should be remembered that if a cohabitant already has either a legal or beneficial interest in the property, then she will be an entitled applicant under section 33 and will be treated in the same way as a spouse or civil partner. This illustrates the extent to which the legislation both prioritises and seeks to protect the proprietary interests of the parties. There is no distinction made between a spouse/civil partner and a cohabitant where the latter has an interest in the property because both have an equal right to occupy and, in this situation, the Law Commission did not think that it was appropriate to impose a time limit on the regulation of occupation between such entitled parties. However, where a cohabitant does not have an interest in the property, the occupation order is simply designed as a temporary measure and is thus subject to a statutory time limit. The maximum total period for which this order can be made is one year, and the Law Commission considered this sufficient time to enable the applicant to find alternative accommodation. Whatever the circumstances which initially led to the order being granted, the length of the parties' relationship and the applicant's need for protection, the fact that the applicant does not have an interest in the property and the respondent does, means that the interests of the latter take priority.

## 5.5  Orders where neither party is entitled to occupy the dwelling-house

In a case where neither party is entitled to occupy the home, the court is not interfering with property rights, it is merely adjusting occupation rights as between the parties. This situation may arise, for example, if the couple is living with relatives or friends. Section 37 governs the situation where the parties are spouses or former spouses, and section 38 where they are cohabitants or former cohabitants. Either party may obtain an order against the other containing the usual regulatory provisions, but this order will have no effect on a third party who may also be occupying the property or who may own it.

In the case of spouses and former spouses, the court's discretion is governed by exactly the same criteria which apply to entitled applicants under section 33(6) and (7). That is, the balance of harm test is applied and, if not met in favour of the applicant, the general checklist of factors is taken into account by the court in the exercise of its discretion. The order must initially be limited to six months, but may be extended on one or more occasion for a further specified period of not more than six months.[269]

In the case of cohabitants and former cohabitants, the Act continues to distinguish these applicants from their married counterparts[270] even though, in this instance, there are no property rights involved. The balance of harm test does not result in a mandatory duty to make an order and must merely be considered as a series of questions affecting the exercise of the court's discretion. In addition, the six-month maximum duration of any order applies, and may be extended on one occasion only for a period of not more than six months.[271]

---

[267]  Section 36(10).
[268]  Where the children continue to be dependent, she may be able to obtain an order maintaining a roof over the children's (and therefore her own) heads until their dependency ends: see the Children Act 1989, Sch 1, and Chapter 5.
[269]  Section 37(5).     [270]  And civil partners.     [271]  Section 38(6).

## 5.6 **The approach of the courts to occupation orders**

The courts regard occupation orders as an extremely serious invasion of the rights of the respondent, and thus considerations relating to the well-being of the applicant and any children will not, on their own, persuade the court to grant an occupation order; more will be required. Despite the intention of the Law Commission that the criteria for making occupation orders should remove the focus on the parties' conduct and concentrate, more specifically, on the needs of the parties, the courts have confirmed earlier authorities which took the view that such orders were draconian. In *Chalmers v Johns*[272] the Court of Appeal held that the string of authorities which emphasise the harsh nature of the occupation order had not been overtaken by the new provisions in the 1996 Act, and that an order which overrides proprietary interests was only justified in exceptional circumstances. In addition, the courts have been adamant that where divorce is imminent an occupation order should not be made as a short-term measure to give the parties breathing space from the tension surrounding the marital breakdown.

In *Chalmers v Johns*[273] the parties, who were not married, lived together for 25 years and occupied the family home as joint tenants. They had two children, an adult son and a daughter aged 7. The relationship between the parties had always been volatile and the year before they separated, the police had been called to the house on four occasions to investigate complaints of assault, by both the mother and the father, which resulted in minor injuries. The mother subsequently left the home with her daughter and moved into temporary council accommodation which was a mile and a half from the daughter's school. By contrast, the family home was approximately a ten-minute walk from the school. The judge made an interim occupation order in the mother's favour but the father successfully appealed against this decision. The Court of Appeal first considered the balance of harm test and held that neither the mother nor the child would be likely to suffer significant harm attributable to the conduct of the father if the order were not made. There was no risk of the child suffering violence and the inconvenience involved in her longer journey to school could not amount to harm. Thorpe LJ did not regard the facts of this case as coming anywhere near the level of harm required which would place the court under a duty to make the order on the balance of harm test.[274] The court then had to decide whether to make the order at its discretion under section 33(6). In light of the pending family law proceedings between the parties to decide upon the residence of the daughter, the court held that it was not appropriate to make an occupation order as an interim measure given, in particular, its severe consequences. Thus the fact that the final issues regarding the couple's separation and residence of the daughter had yet to be decided was of great relevance when the court was exercising its discretion.

In *Re Y (Children) (Occupation Order)*,[275] the parties had been married for 20 years and had four children. Two of the children, a boy aged 13 and a girl aged 16 who was pregnant, remained with them in the family home. The wife began divorce proceedings which had become protracted and, in the meantime, the husband applied for an occupation order against the wife. The husband had diabetes, had lost his sight in one eye, and was registered disabled. The family was described as dysfunctional with the mother and the daughter allied against the son and the father. In particular, the father and daughter had an appalling relationship. The parties lived in separate camps in the house, with the mother and daughter on one side and the father and son on the other. The Court of Appeal allowed the mother's appeal against the granting of an occupation order saying that this order was a draconian remedy which should only be used as a last resort. In making the order, the judge at first instance was persuaded by the fact that the local authority would more easily accommodate the mother and her pregnant 16-year-old daughter than the father and son thus concluding that the father and son would suffer greater harm. The Court of Appeal disagreed holding that the balance of harm test was not established. First, the court was not persuaded that the father would suffer significant harm if the order were not made. Secondly, even if this could be established, the balance of

---

[272] [1999] 1 FLR 392.　　[273] Ibid.　　[274] Ibid, 396.　　[275] [2000] 2 FCR 470.

harm test would fail because the harm to the husband was associated with his disability and thus was not attributable to the wife's conduct—there was no evidence that she had been violent towards the husband. The court also felt that the judge had failed to consider the harm which would be caused to the daughter if she were to be rehoused with the mother, and considered that the father would be in a stronger position to be rehoused by the local authority given his disability. However, the court did not wish to allow this to become the determinative factor when applying the balance of harm test.

It then considered the matter under section 33(6). First, when considering the housing needs and resources of the parties, the court felt that the matrimonial home could be divided to meet the needs of both parties. The family factions had already established their separate camps within the house and given that the issues would be resolved on a permanent basis when the parties divorced, the court held that there was no reason why the current arrangements could not continue until that time. In terms of financial resources, while the wife was working there was nothing to suggest that this income would provide enough for her to rent accommodation privately. The likely effect of the order on the health, safety, and well-being of the parties and of any relevant child may have tipped the balance in favour of the husband in light of his health. However, the court concluded that any potential effect on his health was not due to the wife's misconduct but rather was more to do with his poor relationship with his daughter. In relation to the conduct of each of the parties, the court felt that they were as bad as each other. In light of emphasis placed on the fact that an occupation order is a harsh remedy which should only be used as a 'last resort',[276] the court held that the judge had been wrong to make the order to bring to an end the atmosphere in the house during the pro-tracted divorce proceedings. That was not the purpose of an occupation order. As Sedley LJ noted:

> The purpose of an occupation order . . . is not to break matrimonial deadlock by evicting one of the parties . . . nor is it to use publicly-funded emergency housing as a solution for domestic strife.[277]

That the occupation should not be used as a 'weapon in domestic warfare'[278] is further illustrated in *G v G (Occupation Order: Conduct).*[279] In this case the wife had issued divorce proceedings against the husband. They had two children, aged 15 and 12, and the parties continued to live in the family home during the divorce proceedings. This caused considerable tension and the wife sought an oc-cupation order to remove the husband from the property. The judge at first instance refused to make the order on the ground that the husband's conduct was unintentional. However, the Court of Appeal held that this approach was incorrect. The court clarified that when considering under the balance of harm test whether any harm likely to be suffered by the applicant or child was attributable to the conduct of the respondent, the important factor was the effect of the conduct rather than the intention of the respondent. Lack of intent may be a relevant consideration, but even if the respond-ent's conduct had been unintentional, this did not mean that any resulting harm could not be attrib-uted to the respondent. Thorpe LJ said:

> the court's consideration must be upon the effect of the conduct rather than the intention of the doer. Whether misconduct is intentional or unintentional is not the question. An applicant under section 33 is entitled to protection from unjustifiable conduct that causes harm to her or the chil-dren of the family.[280]

However, on the facts there was no significant harm and so the balance of harm test did not apply. The court considered whether the occupation order should be made at its discretion under section 33(6). The answer was no. The husband had not been violent to the wife and this was not one of those exceptional cases which justified such a draconian order. Of significance was the fact that the wife had made applications for residence of the children and financial relief orders against the husband. As these substantive issues would be determined within a short time, an occupation

[276] Ibid, 477.        [277] Ibid, 478.        [278] Ibid, 480.        [279] [2000] 2 FLR 36.        [280] Ibid, 40.

order was not warranted in the meantime. It is clear that an occupation order will not be made to deal with the 'heightened tensions that any family has to live with whilst the process of divorce and separation is current'.[281] This is especially the case when a substantive hearing will take place within a short time to resolve the parties' affairs in the aftermath of the divorce or separation.

### 5.6.1  Are the courts becoming more willing to make an occupation order in the absence of physical violence?

In *S v F (Occupation Order)*[282] an occupation order was made in the absence of physical violence. In this case the parties had divorced and the children lived with their mother in the matrimonial home in London. When the mother remarried she wanted to sell the family home and move to the country. One son was opposed to the move and wished to remain living in London so that he could continue with his examinations. The father, who had been living in Kuala Lumpur, applied for an occupation order which would allow him to move back into the matrimonial home in London in order to provide a home for his son.[283] The court made the order allowing the father to return to the property for six months or until the ancillary relief proceedings between the parties were resolved, whichever was the sooner. Even though the court was prepared to make an occupation order in the absence of the respondent's violence, it should be remembered that, on the facts, the order operated in a positive as opposed to a negative way. In other words, it permitted the father to move into the former matrimonial home to provide a home for his son who wished to remain in London to continue his education, as opposed to removing the mother from the home. The mother was already living in another property in the country and so this is not an example of the occupation order at its most draconian. The restriction on the wife's proprietary rights was simply that her wish to sell the property was delayed for a short time and so, given these facts, one cannot take this case as evidence, on its own, of the court's willingness to make occupation orders removing the respondent from the property in the absence of serious physical violence.

Indeed, the courts have consistently taken the view that occupation orders are not designed to provide respite for the parties from the usual tensions associated with relationship breakdown. However, in *Grubb v Grubb*,[284] the Court of Appeal refused the husband's application for leave to appeal against an occupation order which removed him from the property which was his family's ancestral home. They parties were married for over 25 years and had five children, the youngest of whom was 13. The children were to remain living with the mother which meant that she required accommodation with at least five bedrooms. The matrimonial home was a large six-bedroom property in an estate which had been in the husband's family for over a century. The husband, who had substantial wealth, also had other properties on the estate. The wife sought an occupation order under section 33(6), the general checklist, and did not argue that the either she or the children were likely to suffer significant harm if the order were not made. While the wife accepted that the husband was never physically violent towards her, she alleged that he was verbally abusive and was domineering and controlling.

The judge at first instance accepted that the wife was under stress: she was diagnosed with a moderately severe depressive disorder and was on medication. It was agreed that the current living arrangements were intolerable and that a separation was required. Thus, the judge made an occupation order removing the husband from the family home. The Court of Appeal refused leave to appeal against this decision despite accepting existing authority that an occupation order is 'always serious, and no doubt can sometimes be particularly serious when it relates to a spouse's removal from what one might almost call his ancestral home'.[285] However, the court indicated that the

---

[281] Ibid, 41.    [282] [2000] 1 FLR 255.

[283] Note the father, as a former spouse, had to apply for an occupation order as a non-entitled applicant: a former spouse with no existing right to occupy the home under s 35. This was because the property was in the mother's name and as a former spouse he no longer had 'home rights' in the property and there was insufficient evidence to satisfy the court that he was entitled to occupy the property by virtue of having a beneficial interest in it.

[284] [2009] EWCA Civ976.    [285] Ibid, [26].

seriousness of the order was compounded when the evicted party did not have alternative accommodation readily available. In this case, the husband had another property at his disposal which was big enough for his needs but too small for the wife and children. In addition, he also had sufficient resources to fund comfortable accommodation elsewhere. The court noted, and was most likely persuaded by the fact that, the husband's removal from the home was simply a short-term interim measure, the duration of which was within his control as the wife was willing to move out when suitable accommodation had been found for the family. The husband was ordered to leave the property within 28 days and the order was to last until financial order proceedings between the parties were finalised.

A couple of points are worth noting. First, the fact that a case was not mounted under section 33(7) and that no 'significant harm' was alleged, but that the applicant was successful under section 33(6) confirms that significant harm is not a necessary threshold for making the order at the court's discretion.[286] Secondly, that the respondent was not guilty of any physical violence, and yet he was still removed from the home, could be taken to suggest a liberalisation of the criteria.[287] Thirdly, this case suggests that an occupation order can be used to resolve the tensions associated with relationship breakdown. It has been observed that:

> This decision may have the consequent effect of making it easier to persuade a judge to grant an occupation order under s 33(6), where conduct is not really the main issue, but a solution is needed to difficult living arrangements. Essentially, it would appear that if the applicant can demonstrate the existence of credible alternative accommodation for the other party, or rely upon that party's greater financial resources, then he or she need not cite very much by way of conduct to justify the order. Where the line is drawn, as to what may constitute credible alternative accommodation or adequate financial resources, remains to be seen.[288]

However, rather than 'putting the brakes' on the development of a more liberal approach to the making of an occupation order, two further Court of Appeal decisions illustrate that the courts will grant occupation orders in the absence of physical violence. In *Dolan v Corby*[289] the parties began living together in the property as joint tenants in 1980. In 2011, Ms Dolan was awarded an occupation order excluding Mr Corby from the property. The trial judge found that Ms Dolan, who had a history of drug abuse, was a 'very disturbed lady in need of immediate psychiatric help' and that she was a 'vulnerable woman who finds herself unable to live with the respondent'. Although the parties had similar housing needs, the judge made the order excluding Mr Corby from the property as he was better able to find alternative accommodation. Mr Corby appealed on the basis that such a draconian order should not have been made in the absence of any finding of violence. His appeal was dismissed by the Court of Appeal. Black LJ made it clear that nothing in *Chalmers v Johns* or *G v G* suggested that an occupation order could only be made where there is violence or a threat of violence. That would put an inappropriate gloss on the statute.[290] Black LJ continued that an occupation order 'requiring a respondent to vacate the family home and overriding his property rights is a grave or draconian order and one which would only be justified in exceptional circumstances, but exceptional circumstances can take many forms and are not confined to violent behaviour on the part of the respondent or the threat of violence and the important thing is for the judge to identify and weigh up all the relevant features of the case whatever their nature'.[291] On the facts, Ms Dolan's psychiatric state made the case exceptional. Black LJ also noted that 'exercising

---

[286] B. James, 'Occupation Orders after *Grubb*', available at www.familylawweek.co.uk.
[287] Although there were very particular facts which persuaded the court that an order should be made. Most notably, the husband owned another property which was readily available to him and which met his needs. In addition, the court noted the fact that the wife was willing to move out of the property but the husband had not made the necessary arrangements for her accommodation at another property on the estate which was large enough for the family.
[288] See B. James (n 286).     [289] [2011] EWCA Civ 664.     [290] Ibid, [27].     [291] Ibid.

discretion . . . is not a matter of considering the behaviour of the parties and awarding occupation of the property in question to the one who has behaved less inappropriately. All of the circumstances must be considered, of which conduct is only one.'[292] Given the finding that Mr Corby was less vulnerable than Ms Dolan and thus better equipped to find alternative accommodation, Black LJ concluded that the trial judge was entitled to exercise the discretion in the way that he had. Similarly in *Re L (Children)*[293] the Court of Appeal made it clear that reprehensible conduct is not a prerequisite for making an occupation order.[294] In this case the parties had been married for 20 years and had twins aged 8. When their relationship broke down, the trial judge found that the children were likely to suffer significant emotional harm by the arguments and hostility between the parents.[295] He made an occupation order requiring the husband to leave the family home for a period of three months. The husband appealed, alleging that this was too draconian a response to the domestic situation, drawing particular attention to the fact that no violence was alleged. The Court of Appeal dismissed the appeal. Black LJ made it clear that there is nothing in the legislation to limit the discretion to make occupation orders to cases where there has been physical violence. Further, there is no authority for the proposition that a spouse can only be excluded from the home if reprehensible conduct on his or her behalf is found. Black LJ made it clear that occupation orders are draconian and only to be made in exceptional circumstances,[296] but the fact that the children were found likely to suffer significant harm if the parents remained under the same roof made this case exceptional, and justified ordering the husband to vacate the family home. These cases illustrate that when considering whether to make an occupation order, the court will look at all the circumstances of the cases and not just the conduct and behaviour of the parties. While it remains the case that an occupation order will only be made in exceptional circumstances, this does not mean that it is limited to cases where there is violence or a threat of violence. Other 'non-violent' features of a case can make it exceptional enough to justify the making of an order.

## 5.7 **Enforcement of an occupation order**

Where the court has issued an occupation order requiring the respondent to permit the applicant to enter and remain in the home, excluding the respondent from the home, or forbidding him from a specified area in which the home is included, such orders will only be effective if steps can be readily taken to enforce them should the respondent choose to ignore them. Unlike the situation with the non-molestation order, breach of an occupation order is not a criminal offence. Instead breach of the order will be enforced as a contempt of court.

Historically there were problems with the enforcement of civil orders as the correct procedures had to be followed before the respondent was brought before the court for contempt. Normally the respondent must be served personally with notice of an application to commit him for breach and then must be arrested by officers of the court, all of which took time when the applicant required protection. The lack of speedy enforcement mechanisms was recognised by the Select Committee on Violence in Marriage, and it recommended that the police should become involved in the enforcement of the civil orders made to protect against domestic violence. This recommendation was accepted, and since 1976[297] courts have been able to attach a power of arrest to these civil orders. However, although the introduction of the power of arrest assisted victims of domestic violence, the Law Commission found that powers of arrest were being attached to a relatively small proportion of orders.[298]

---

[292] Ibid, [28].    [293] [2012] EWCA Civ 721.    [294] Ibid, [22].

[295] As this harm was not solely attributable to either parent, section 33(7) was not triggered and the case fell to the court's discretion under section 33(6).

[296] Ibid, [29].    [297] Domestic Violence and Matrimonial Proceedings Act 1976.

[298] In 1989, the latest year for which figures were available to the Law Commission, powers of arrest were attached to only 29 per cent of orders made under the 1976 Act: Law Com No 207 (1992), para 5.11.

Reluctance to make use of the power of arrest stemmed from the Court of Appeal's decision in *Lewis v Lewis*[299] where the court ruled that attaching a power of arrest to an injunction should not be a routine remedy and that the use of this power was quite plainly intended for the exceptional situation 'where men or women persistently disobey injunctions and make nuisances of themselves to the other party and to others concerned'.[300] This set the pattern for the approach in subsequent cases, and the courts consistently stated that the power of arrest should only be attached in exceptional circumstances.[301]

This gate-keeping attitude failed to recognise the very real dangers associated with domestic violence and suggested that speedy enforcement was only essential in the most extreme cases. Such an approach failed to recognise that a power of arrest is a 'simple, immediate and inexpensive means of enforcement which underlines the seriousness of the breach to the offending party'.[302] The FLA 1996 creates a presumption in favour of attaching a power of arrest in certain cases. Under section 47(2), the court shall attach a power of arrest to an occupation order if it appears that the respondent has used or threatened violence against the applicant or relevant child unless it is satisfied that the applicant will be adequately protected without this measure.[303] 'Violence' is undefined in relation to this provision. Under the previous legislation, 'actual bodily harm' to the applicant or child had to be established although this was held to encompass both physical and psychological violence.[304] However, the 1996 Act has extended the occasions when a power of arrest shall be attached by including threatened as well as actual violence. This is an important change because it recognises that the applicant or child should not have to be physically assaulted before a power of arrest can be attached to the order. Statistics show that the majority of occupation orders have a power of arrest attached.[305] Given that the power of arrest will only be attached where violence or threats of violence have been used, this illustrates the extent to which the occupation order is made to deal with this type of situation.

If a power of arrest is attached, a constable can arrest a person without warrant where there is reasonable cause to suspect that he or she is in breach of the order.[306] The respondent must be brought before the relevant judicial authority within 24 hours from the time of the arrest, and where the matter is not disposed of forthwith he may be remanded either in custody or on bail (to which conditions may be attached).[307] If the court has not attached a power of arrest to the order, then the applicant will have to apply to the court for a warrant for arrest if she considers that the respondent has breached the order.[308] The court will not issue a warrant unless the application is substantiated by a statement under oath and there are reasonable grounds to suspect that the respondent has been in breach.

If the respondent is arrested under section 47 for breaching an occupation order, he will be punished for contempt of court. The sanctions that can be imposed for contempt are a fine or imprisonment although the maximum sentence which can be imposed is two years.[309] The court does not have the power in contempt proceedings to impose other sanctions such as enforced enrolment

---

[299] [1978] 1 All ER 729. Similarly in *Widdowson v Widdowson* (1982) 4 FLR 121, it was held that magistrates should only attach a power of arrest where it was really necessary, and that they should specifically state their reasons for doing so.

[300] [1978] 1 All ER 729 at 731.     [301] See *R v S* [1988] 2 FLR 339; *McLean v Nugent* (1980) 1 FLR 26.

[302] Law Com No 207 (1992), para 5.13.

[303] Section 47(2). The legislation originally provided that the court should attach a power of arrest to a non-molestation order where there was violence or threats of violence. This is no longer the case because breach of a non-molestation order is now a criminal offence.

[304] *Kendrick v Kendrick* [1990] 2 FLR 107.

[305] In 2004, 90 per cent of occupation orders had a power of arrest attached; in 2005 and 2006 it was 91 per cent; in 2007 it was 81 per cent and in 2008 it was 66 per cent.

[306] Section 47(6).

[307] Section 47(7) and (12). No account is taken of Christmas Day, Good Friday, or any Sunday in reckoning this period of time.

[308] Section 47(8).     [309] Contempt of Court Act 1981, s 14(1).

on anger management or rehabilitation programmes. A range of orders may be made in civil contempt cases and every case must be considered on its own facts.[310] In particular, the court will consider the nature of the breach, the presence of children, and whether the order was breached more than once.[311] There have been some cases where the courts have appeared reluctant to impose a custodial sentence. In *Ansah v Ansah*,[312] for example, the court thought that committal orders are remedies of last resort, particularly in family cases because they could damage the applicant as much as the respondent. However, the position today is that the court will impose a sanction which reflects the gravity of the breach. While there are no precise tariffs set for the appropriate sentence to be handed down when enforcing breach of a civil order,[313] case law shows that the courts take such breaches very seriously. In *Lomas v Parle*,[314] for example, the court indicated that the sentence imposed for breach of a non-molestation order as a civil contempt matter should not be 'manifestly discrepant' with the sentences imposed for criminal offences for breach of the orders under the Protection from Harassment Act 1997.[315] Where the respondent has used violence when breaching an order, the court is likely to order imprisonment.[316]

It may be the case that breach of the civil order also gives rise to criminal proceedings. In these circumstances the civil and criminal proceedings may run concurrently, although it is likely that the civil proceedings will be dealt with more swiftly. One issue is whether the respondent is punished twice for the same offence. In *Lomas v Parle*,[317] the Court of Appeal laid down some guidelines for sentencing in concurrent proceedings. First the Court of Appeal said that it is 'essential that the second court should be fully informed of the factors and circumstances reflected in the first sentence' in order to ensure that the defendant is not punished twice.[318] The first court, which is most likely to be dealing with the civil proceedings, is not to try to second-guess the likely outcome of the subsequent proceedings or alter its sentence to take account of these proceedings, but must explain its reasoning fully for the benefit of the second court. The civil contempt proceedings must be dealt with swiftly and decisively in order to ensure that this information is available to the court dealing with the criminal proceedings.

## 5.8 **Undertakings**

An undertaking is a promise given by the respondent to the court which is enforceable like a court order. Prior to the FLA 1996, when an application was made for a non-molestation order it was frequently the case that pressure was put on the applicant to withdraw her application in return for the respondent giving an undertaking to the court not to molest her. Similarly, when faced with an application for an occupation order, the respondent often agreed to leave the home, thus obviating the need for the court to make an order. In theory, the protection afforded by such an undertaking to the court is just as effective as a court order, and breach of an undertaking can give rise to proceedings for contempt.[319] It was often to the respondent's advantage to give an undertaking because the court did not then make any findings of fact about his alleged behaviour.

---

[310] *Devjee v Patel* [2006] EWCA Civ 1211. For guidance see *Hale v Tanner* [2000] 2 FLR 879; *Lomas v Parle* [2004] 1 FLR 812; *H v O (Contempt of Court: Sentencing)* [2004] EWCA Civ 1691.

[311] *Lomas v Parle* [2004] 1 FLR 812.     [312] [1977] 2 All ER 638.

[313] See *Hale v Tanner* [2000] 2 FLR 879.     [314] [2004] 1 FLR 812.

[315] See also *H v O (Contempt of Court: Sentencing)* [2004] EWCA Civ 1691. Although this approach has been criticised on the basis that there are discrepancies between the range of remedies which are available in the civil and criminal courts respectively, and that the two systems have different objections and functions. While civil orders are designed to mark the court's disapproval at the respondent's breach of the civil order and ensure future compliance, the criminal courts are primarily concerned with punishing the offender. See M. Burton, 'Case Commentary—*Lomas v Parle*—Coherent and Effective Remedies for Victims of Domestic Violence: Time for an Integrated Domestic Violence Court' [2004] Child and Family Law Quarterly 317.

[316] *Wilson v Webster* [1998] 1 FLR 1097.     [317] [2004] 1 FLR 812.     [318] Ibid, [48].

[319] Section 46(4).

The FLA 1996 makes provision for the practice of accepting undertakings in non-molestation and occupation order cases to continue. Under section 46, in any case where the court has the power to make an occupation order or a non-molestation order, it may accept an undertaking from any party to the proceedings.[320] However, while the undertaking is enforced through contempt proceedings,[321] no power of arrest can be attached to the order.[322] As a result, the occasions when the court can accept an undertaking appear to be limited by provisions which prohibit the court's acceptance of an undertaking where a power of arrest would be attached to an occupation order,[323] or where it is necessary to make a non-molestation order which is enforceable as a criminal offence under section 42A.[324] This suggests that an undertaking will not be accepted by the court instead of making a non-molestation or occupation order in cases where the respondent has used or threatened violence against the applicant or relevant child. Thus there is still scope for a court to accept an undertaking from the respondent instead of making an order even though the legislation discourages this in cases of violence or threatened violence. There is evidence to suggest that undertakings are still used and that solicitors remain keen to deal with domestic violence cases by undertakings.[325]

## 5.9 **Ex parte orders**

Normally a respondent to an application for an order in civil proceedings must be given adequate notice of the proceedings in accordance with the rules of court. However, in an emergency, the normal notice procedures can be dispensed with and the court can make an order ex parte (without notice).

---

### Key legislation

Section 45 provides that in any case where the court considers it just and convenient to do so it may grant a non-molestation order or an occupation order in ex parte proceedings. In determining whether to do so the court must have regard to all the circumstances including:

(a) any risk of significant harm to the applicant or a relevant child, attributable to the conduct of the respondent if the order is not made immediately;

(b) whether it is likely that the applicant will be deterred or prevented from pursuing the application if an order is not made immediately; and

(c) whether there is reason to believe that the respondent is aware of the proceedings but is deliberately evading service and the applicant or a relevant child will be seriously prejudiced by the delay involved—

　　(i) where the court is a magistrates' court, in effecting service of proceedings; or

　　(ii) in any other case, in effecting substituted service.

These criteria stress that ex parte applications should only be granted where there are compelling reasons for doing so. As the Law Commission pointed out:

> The danger of a misconceived or malicious application being granted or the risk of some other injustice being done to the respondent is inevitably greater where the court has only heard the applicant's side of the story and the respondent has had no opportunity to reply.[326]

---

[320] Section 46 did not appear in the Law Commission's Draft Bill, or in the original Family Homes and Domestic Violence Bill 1995, but was introduced into the final legislation at the Committee stage of the legislative process.

[321] Section 46(4).　　[322] Section 46(2).　　[323] Section 46(3).　　[324] Section 46(3A).

[325] M. Burton, 'Civil Law Remedies for Domestic Violence: Why are Applications for Non-Molestation Orders Declining?' (2009) 31(2) Journal of Social Welfare and Family Law 109 at 115.

[326] Law Com No 207 (1992), para 5.6.

Other drawbacks in ex parte orders were pointed out such as the fact that 'the judge has no opportunity to try to resolve the parties' differences by agreed undertakings or otherwise to try to reduce the tension of the dispute'; and 'there is no opportunity to bring home the seriousness of the situation to the respondent and to underline the importance of complying with the order or undertaking'.[327] Accordingly, ex parte orders will be rare, although the courts are more likely to be willing to make an ex parte non-molestation order than an occupation order. The former restrains the respondent from carrying out an act(s) which he is prohibited from doing under the general law, while the latter involves a balancing exercise which is difficult to carry out without the respondent having the opportunity to present evidence. Evidence confirms that the courts are reluctant to grant ex parte occupation orders.[328]

The criteria for making an ex parte order concentrate on those situations where it is necessary or desirable. Paragraph (a) focuses on cases where the respondent's conduct creates a risk of significant harm to the applicant or relevant child unless the order is made immediately. It is more likely that this threshold of 'significant harm' will be met in cases where physical violence has taken place, or there is a threat of imminent violence. In addition, an ex parte order may be particularly appropriate where the applicant is frightened that the respondent will react violently to service of the proceedings. Paragraph (b) is a significant provision as it recognises the real risk that many applicants may be deterred from pursuing an application if an order is not made immediately. It also ties in with paragraph (c), which is aimed at the difficult situation where the respondent is deliberately evading service, sometimes as a device to wear down the applicant's resolve to press ahead with proceedings by causing delay.[329]

Where an ex parte order is granted it should be strictly limited in time and section 45(3) makes it clear that the respondent must be given an opportunity to make representations relating to the order as soon as just and convenient at a full hearing. Provided the court fulfils its obligations to secure a full hearing as soon as just and convenient, Article 6 of the European Convention on Human Rights (ECHR) which provides that everyone is entitled to a fair and public hearing of the determination of his civil rights, will not be breached. In *JM v CZ*[330] Mostyn J found that the usual practice of making an ex parte non-molestation order for 12 months with a provision for the respondent to request a return date hearing or apply on 48 hours' notice to vary or discharge the order did not comply with the statutory requirement under section 45(3) for a full hearing 'as soon as just and convenient'. He outlined the general principles that should apply on an *ex parte* application, in particular, that *ex parte* relief could only be justified where the matter was one of 'exceptional urgency'. In addition he noted that, at the very least, 'short informal notice should be given to the respondent', and that the court should make it clear why it is satisfied that the application was made *ex parte*. Subsequent to this decision, and in response to concerns raised by the Magistrates' Association and the National Bench Chairs' Forum about the duration of *ex parte* non-molestation orders, the President of the Family Division released Practice Guidance relating to the duration of such orders.[331] The President confirmed within the guidance that the practice of granting any *ex parte* injunctive order in the Family Court or by the Family Division for an unlimited time must stop. Instead, the guidance confirmed there must be a fixed end date, and that the duration of the order should not normally exceed 14 days.

---

[327] Ibid.

[328] J. Barron, *'Five Years On: A Review of Legal Protection from Domestic Violence'* (Bristol: Women's Aid, 2002); M. Burton, *Legal Responses to Domestic Violence* (Abingdon: Routledge-Cavendish, 2008), pp 38 and 41. See eg *G v G (Ouster: Ex Parte Application)* [1990] 1 FLR 395.

[329] The Law Commission was informed by a number of respondents that this evasion gives rise to considerable problems and expense, Law Com No 207 (1992), para 5.9.

[330] [2014] EWHC 1125 (Fam).

[331] President's Practice Guidance: Family Court—Duration of Ex Parte (Without Notice) Orders, https://www.judiciary.gov.uk/wp-content/uploads/2013/03/practice-guidance-family-court-duration-of-ex-parte-orders.pdf.

If a non-molestation order is made in ex parte proceedings, breach of that order will only constitute a criminal offence under section 42A if the respondent was aware of the existence of the order at the time the conduct was carried out.[332] It has been pointed out that the respondent simply has to be aware of the existence of the order, but not its terms[333] which means that a respondent could be guilty of a criminal offence (for breaching a non-molestation order) without knowing that he was prohibited from carrying out the precise conduct in question in the first place.[334] This has led to the observation that this may constitute an infringement of the respondent's rights under Articles 5,[335] 6,[336] and 8[337] of the ECHR.[338] It is also worth noting that the court's powers to attach a power of arrest to an occupation order are more circumscribed in ex parte proceedings than in a full hearing.[339] A power of arrest may be attached if it appears that the respondent has used or threatened violence against the applicant or a relevant child, and that there is a risk of significant harm to them attributable to the conduct of the respondent if a power of arrest is not attached to the order immediately.[340] In these circumstances, the court may order that the power of arrest is to last for a shorter period than other provisions in the order.[341]

### 5.10  Provision for third parties to act on behalf of victims of domestic violence

Section 60 of the FLA 1996, which has not been implemented, states that rules of court may provide for prescribed persons to apply for a non-molestation order or an occupation order on behalf of another. This provision stems from the Law Commission's recommendation that where the police have been involved in an incident of domestic violence or its aftermath, they should have the power to apply for civil remedies on behalf of the victim.[342] The Commission modelled its recommendation on similar provisions which apply in several Australian states where it has been found to serve a useful and valuable function.[343] The purpose behind involving the police is to remove the burden of taking action from the victim, to reduce the scope for further intimidation by the perpetrator, and to lead to fewer cases being withdrawn: 'The fact that the police are initiating the proceedings also has the beneficial effect of bringing home to the respondent the seriousness of the matter and giving civil proceedings the "weight" they can lack in the eyes of some of the less law abiding members of society.'[344]

The Commission found the question whether the victim's consent should be necessary before the police can bring civil proceedings a difficult one to resolve.[345] It concluded that the best solution was to require the police to consult the victim and take account of her views, but not to make her consent or approval the decisive factor in determining whether or not civil proceedings are issued. Research carried out by the Lord Chancellor's Department, which investigated the views of service providers on whether section 60 should be enacted, revealed clear support for this provision.[346] It was felt that third party applicants would remove the burden on the victim to seek protective remedies, which would be useful in cases where the victim was discouraged from taking such action for fear of reprisals. Despite the anticipated advantages of this provision, it has not yet been enacted. However, in a recent Court of Appeal decision it was confirmed that a local authority can use another legal method

---

[332] Section 42A(2).

[333] B. Soni, 'Domestic Violence and Family Law: A New Era', available at http://www.familylawweek.co.uk.

[334] Ibid.        [335] Right to respect for liberty and security of person.

[336] Right to a fair and public hearing.        [337] Right to respect for one's private and family life.

[338] B. Soni, 'Domestic Violence and Family Law: A New Era', available at www.familylawweek.co.uk.

[339] Section 47(3).        [340] Section 47(3).        [341] Section 47(4).

[342] Law Com No 207 (1992), paras 5.18–5.23.

[343] The Australian Law Reform Commission, Domestic Violence, Report No 30 (1986); D. Chappell and H. Strang, 'Domestic Violence—Findings and Recommendations of the National Committee on Violence' [1990] Australian Journal of Family Law 211.

[344] Law Com No 207 (1992), para 5.18.        [345] Ibid, para 5.22.

[346] M. Burton, 'Third Party Applications for Protections Orders in England and Wales: Service Provider's Views on Implementing Section 60 of the Family Law Act 1996' (2003) 25(2) Journal of Social Welfare and Family Law 137–50. Two-thirds of the respondents supported the implementation of s 60.

to seek injunctive relief to protect victims of domestic violence who do not wish to initiate proceedings themselves. In *A Local Authority v DL*,[347] the Court of Appeal held that the inherent jurisdiction of the court may be invoked by a local authority in order to obtain an injunction to protect vulnerable adults, that is, adults who have mental capacity under the Mental Capacity Act 2005 but who are nevertheless held to be vulnerable.[348]

# 6 Persons not protected under the Family Law Act 1996

As we have seen, the FLA 1996 sought to achieve a balance between widening the scope of the protective remedies to a wider class of family member whilst maintaining the requirement that a familial link exist between the parties. One could argue, however, that if the objective of the legislation is to provide protection to those suffering violence or molestation, it is counterproductive to restrict the availability of the protective remedies. Whilst recognising this, the Law Commission did not wish to create a new tort of harassment or molestation and thus took the view that it was inappropriate to remove all restrictions on applicants and open the legislation to all in need of protection, as has been done in some Australian states.[349] Consequently, the protective remedies in the FLA 1996 are limited to certain categories of applicant who are connected by family ties on the grounds that 'violence and molestation within family relationships need to be treated as a special case'.[350] This means that neighbours, work colleagues, tenants, doctors, teachers, and others who may be vulnerable to threats of violence, sexual harassment, and other forms of molestation are excluded from the Act's provisions. Unless the behaviour was criminal or tortious, such as where there had been violence, those falling outside the scope of the 1996 Act were not protected under the general criminal or civil law either. This left a gap in the law because as there was no distinct tort of harassment, a person who was harassed in a non-physical way by someone with whom they were not 'associated' (such as neighbours) may not be able to obtain the protection afforded by the general law.

Attempts were made to create a tort of harassment. In *Khoransandjian v Bush*[351] the Court of Appeal moved away from limiting an action in nuisance to those who had an interest in land, and opened up the possibility of future developments. In this case the plaintiff was a young woman whose relationship with the defendant had come to an end. Despite this, the defendant persecuted the plaintiff with telephone calls to her mother's house. The defendant conceded that the mother could complain about the persistent telephone calls made to the parental home if she had a freehold or leasehold interest in the property as such conduct would fall within the tort of private nuisance. However, he claimed that as the plaintiff was a mere licensee in her mother's property, with no proprietary interest, she did not fall within the scope of the law. This argument was rejected by the Court of Appeal. Dillon LJ commented:

> to my mind, it is ridiculous if in this present age the law is that the making of deliberately harassing and pestering telephone calls to a person is only actionable in the civil courts if the recipient of the calls happens to have the freehold or a leasehold proprietary interest in the premises in which he or she has received the calls.[352]

---

[347] [2012] EWCA 253.

[348] MacFarlane LJ said that '[t]he jurisdiction . . . is in part aimed at enhancing or liberating the autonomy of the vulnerable adult whose autonomy has been compromised by a reason other than mental incapacity', at [54]. This can be as a result of constraint, coercion, or undue influence, or some other circumstance which deprives them of the capacity to make the relevant decision or disables them from expressing a real and genuine consent, ibid.

[349] Eg in New South Wales it has been possible since 1989 for anyone to apply for an 'apprehended violence order' regardless of their connection with the applicant.

[350] Law Com No 207 (1992), para 3.16.

[351] [1993] 3 All ER 669. See also *Burris v Azadani* [1995] 4 All ER 802.    [352] [1993] 3 All ER 669 at 675.

He went on to approve the wording of the injunction granted by the judge which prohibited the defendant from 'using violence to, harassing, pestering or communicating with' the plaintiff. However, the potential of this development in the common law was short-lived because the decision was overruled by the House of Lords in *Hunter v Canary Wharf Ltd*.[353] Their Lordships held that a person who has no right in the land affected by the nuisance, such as a licensee or occupier, cannot bring an action in nuisance. Moreover, it was wrong to treat actions in respect of discomfort, interference with personal enjoyment, or personal injury by the plaintiff as actions in nuisance.

# 7 Protection from Harassment Act 1997

Fortunately many of the limitations of both the 1996 Act and the common law have been addressed by the Protection from Harassment Act 1997. The 1997 Act came into force after public concern about stalking.[354] Although it can cover situations where there is no relationship or connection between the parties, the Act can also be used in domestic disputes and, notably, breach of the orders under the legislation attracts both civil and criminal remedies. The Act creates two new criminal offences and a statutory tort of harassment.

## 7.1 Harassment

Section 1(1) creates an arrestable offence of harassment and gives victims of harassment both criminal[355] and civil remedies,[356] including the right to claim damages.[357] A victim does not have to pursue both civil and criminal sanctions. Civil enforcement may be particularly useful where there is insufficient evidence to satisfy the standard of proof required for a criminal prosecution (beyond reasonable doubt) but where there is sufficient evidence to meet the civil standard (on the balance of probabilities). The defendant can try to defend the allegations of harassment by showing that it was pursued for the purpose of preventing or detecting crime, it was pursued under an enactment or rule of law, or in the particular circumstances the conduct was reasonable.

Section 1 states that a person must not pursue a course of conduct which amounts to harassment of another, and which he knows or ought to know amounts to harassment of the other.[358] Such a person will be taken to know that his behaviour amounts to harassment 'if a reasonable person in possession of the same information would think the course of conduct amounted to harassment of the other'.[359] This provision focuses on the defendant's behaviour as well as its impact on the victim. The concept of harassment has no statutory definition but it appears to be very broad as it includes 'alarming the person or causing the person distress'.[360] This was considered by the Court of Appeal in *Majrowski v Guy's and St Thomas' NHS Trust*[361] where May LJ said that:

> [t]he conduct . . . has to be calculated, in an objective sense, to cause distress and has to be oppressive and unreasonable. It has to be conduct which the perpetrator knows or ought to know amounts to harassment, and conduct which a reasonable person would think amounted to harassment.[362]

In addition, a 'course of conduct' must involve conduct on at least two occasions and 'conduct' includes speech. It seems that harassment also encompasses the same types of behaviours as those which amount to molestation for the purposes of the 1996 Act, although unlike for the

---

[353] [1997] 2 All ER 426.   [354] *Stalking—The Solutions: A Consultation Paper* (London: Home Office, 1996).
[355] Section 2.   [356] Section 3.   [357] Section 3(2).
[358] Section 1(1).   [359] Section 1(2).
[360] Section 7(2). See *Thomas v News Group Newspapers* [2002] EMLR 78.   [361] [2005] EWCA Civ 251.
[362] See R. Noon, 'Compensation for Domestic Abuse after *Singh v Bhaker*', available at www.familylawweek.co.uk.

non-molestation order, a one-off act will not suffice. In addition, while the focus for the court when deciding whether to make a non-molestation order is on the effect of the behaviour on the victim, the court when deciding whether conduct amounts to harassment under the 1997 legislation, must consider the fact that this is a criminal offence which means that 'a series of very minor annoyances may not meet the criteria'.[363] To constitute a 'course of conduct' it seems that there must be some connection between the incidents complained of. In *R v Hills*,[364] the incidents of alleged harassment were six months apart and in this intervening period the parties had cohabited and had sexual relations. The Court of Appeal held that this prevented the assaults from constituting a course of conduct as they did not possess the 'necessary cogent linkage'.[365] It could be argued, therefore, that the 'fewer the number of incidents and the wider the time lapse between them, the less likely that they give rise to a "course of conduct"'.[366] A person who pursues a course of conduct which amounts to harassment is guilty of an offence, the penalty for which is imprisonment for up to six months, or a fine, or both. The court can also make a restraining order when someone is convicted of harassment, and breach of the order will be a further offence.[367]

A civil action for damages may also be brought by the victim of an actual or apprehended offence of harassment.[368] Various responses are open to the civil court. Damages may be awarded for (among other things) any anxiety or financial loss caused by, or resulting from, the harassment.[369] In *Singh v Bhakar*[370] the claimant was a Sikh woman who married a Hindu and subsequently moved in with her mother-in-law who disliked her and caused her 'four months of hell'. As a result of this abuse the claimant was diagnosed with a moderate depressive episode and sought damages from her mother-in-law under the 1997 legislation. Given the nature of the harassment and the fact that the claimant was the deliberate target of this conduct, the judge awarded her £35,000. This led some to point out that lawyers acting on behalf of victims of domestic violence should no longer be reticent about seeking damages from their client under the 1997 legislation either as a free-standing application or in conjunction with an injunction application.[371] Injunctions may also be granted to restrain the defendant from pursing the course of conduct, any breach of which may be enforced by the issue of an arrest warrant in proceedings brought by the victim. Breach of an injunction prohibiting harassment under section 3 amounts to an offence as well as contempt of court, but where the defendant is convicted he may not also be punished for contempt, and vice versa.[372] Even though the breach of this civil injunction is a criminal offence, the standard of proof required for making the injunction remains the civil standard (on the balance of probabilities).[373]

## 7.2 Putting people in fear of violence

Section 4 of the Act makes it an offence for a person to carry out a course of conduct on at least two occasions which causes another person to fear that violence will be used against him, if the perpetrator knows or ought to know that he will cause such a fear on each occasion. No warrant

---

[363] *Majrowski v Guy's and St Thomas' NHS Trust* [2005] EWCA Civ 251; R. Noon, 'Compensation for Domestic Abuse after *Singh v Bhaker*', available at www.familylawweek.co.uk.

[364] [2001] 1 FLR 580.

[365] R. Noon, 'Compensation for Domestic Abuse after *Singh v Bhaker*', available at www.familylawweek.co.uk. See also *Lau v Director of Public Prosecutions* [2000] 1 FLR 799 where the fact that the incidents were four months apart prevented the court from viewing them as a 'course of conduct'.

[366] R. N. Hill, 'Protection from Harassment' [2005] Family Law 364. Hill points out that in such circumstances, and where appropriate, a charge of assault may be the preferred course of action. Domestic Violence, Crime and Victims Act 2004, s 10 makes common assault an arrestable offence.

[367] Section 5.     [368] Section 3(1).     [369] Section 3(2).     [370] [2007] 1 FLR 880.

[371] J. Rosley, 'In Practice: Mother-in-law Harassment: *Singh v Bhakar*' [2006] Family Law 968.

[372] Section 3(6), (7), and (8). Breach of an injunction under s 3 is an arrestable offence which means that an arrest can be made without a warrant.

[373] *Hipgrave and Hipgrave v Jones* [2004] EWHC 2901 (QB).

is needed where there is a breach because the offence falls within the normal arrest powers given to the police.[374] It is a defence to show that the conduct was pursued for the purpose of preventing or detecting crime, was pursued under a statutory provision, or was reasonable for the protection of himself or someone else or for the protection of property. The courts seem unwilling to use section 4 in cases where, although there is a dispute between the parties, they want to continue the relationship. In *R v Widdows*[375] the Court of Appeal held that section 4 of the 1997 Act 'was not normally appropriate for use as a means of criminalizing conduct, not charged as violence, during incidents in a long and predominantly affectionate relationship in which both parties persisted and wanted to continue'.

### 7.3 **Restraining orders**

A court sentencing a person convicted of an offence under section 2 (harassment) or section 4 (putting people in fear of violence) may also make a restraining order, and breach of it will be further offence.[376] The restraining order can be used to prohibit the offender from engaging in conduct which amounts to harassment or will cause a fear of violence. It is an arrestable offence for the offender to breach this order without reasonable excuse.[377] The Domestic Violence, Crime and Victims Act 2004 inserted a new provision (s 5A) into the 1997 legislation giving the court the power to issue a restraining order in a wider range of circumstances.[378] If a defendant is acquitted in criminal proceedings of an offence, the court now has the power to make a restraining order where it considers it necessary to do so to protect a person from harassment from the defendant.[379] While the victim could, of course, apply for a non-molestation order and/or an injunction under the 1997 legislation, the court's power to make a restraining order 'would not only avoid delay and increased costs to the legal aid budget, but also provide a more seamless protection for the victim'.[380]

The 1997 Act clearly has widespread civil and criminal law implications, and where the victim wishes to pursue an action in damages it may be advantageous to apply under this Act even though she is entitled to apply for orders under the FLA 1996. Further, there is nothing to prevent a victim of domestic violence from making applications under both pieces of legislation.[381] In such a situation, the application should be issued in the same court and tried by a judge with jurisdiction in both sets of proceedings.[382] Despite the benefits of making an application under the 1997 legislation, which offers the potential of being awarded damages which are not available under the FLA 1996, research shows that the remedies under the 1997 Act are not pursued on many occasions.[383]

## 8 **Domestic violence and local authority housing**

Victims of domestic violence who have been forced to leave, or otherwise been driven, from the family home, may turn to their local housing authority for assistance. Statistics show that domestic

---

[374] Police and Criminal Evidence Act 1994, s 24(6).     [375] [2011] EWCA Crim 1500.

[376] Section 5.     [377] Section 5(4).     [378] Home Office Circular 017/2009.

[379] Protection from Harassment Act 1997, s 5A, inserted by the Domestic Violence, Crime and Victims Act 2004, s 12. This provision came into force on 30 September 2009.

[380] Home Office Circular 017/2009.

[381] *Lomas v Parle* [2004] 1 FLR 812 at [44]. For a comparison of the two pieces of legislation see R. N. Hill, 'Protection from Harassment' [2005] Family Law 364.

[382] *Lomas v Parle* [2004] 1 FLR 812.

[383] M. Burton, 'Civil Law Remedies for Domestic Violence: Why are Applications for Non-Molestation Orders Declining?' (2009) 31(2) Journal of Social Welfare and Family Law 109. In 2012–13, there were 4,217 offences identified as domestic violence charged under s 2 of the 1997 legislation, compared with 4,710 in 2011–12. In the same year there were 775 offences identified as domestic violence charged under s 4 of the 1997 legislation, compared with 1,056 in 2011–12. See CPS, *Violence against Women and Girls: Crime Report 2012–2013* (London: CPS, 2013).

violence is one of the primary causes of homelessness: in 2002, 40 per cent of homeless women indicated that domestic violence was a factor which led to their homelessness.[384] Under the Housing Act 1996, as amended by the Homelessness Act 2002, a local authority is obliged to provide accommodation for certain categories of person who are deemed to be 'unintentionally homeless'.[385]

## 8.1 **'Homeless'**

A person is homeless if they have no accommodation which is available for their occupation in the UK or elsewhere,[386] or if they have such accommodation but cannot secure entry to it.[387] If accommodation is available and accessible but it is not reasonable for the applicant to continue to occupy this property, they will also be deemed to be homeless.[388]

---

### Key legislation

Whether it is reasonable to continue to occupy accommodation is defined in section 177(1), which states:

It is not reasonable for a person to continue to occupy accommodation if it is probable that this will lead to domestic violence against him, or against—

(a) a person who normally resides with him as a member of his family, or
(b) any other person who might reasonably be expected to reside with him.

For this purpose 'domestic violence', in relation to a person, means violence from a person with whom he is associated, or threats of violence from such a person which are likely to be carried out.

---

This means that if a person is forced to flee the family home due to violence, or threats of violence, from an associated person, they will be deemed to be homeless and thus entitled to the help of the local authority. 'Associated person' is defined in section 178, the definition being almost identical to that contained in section 62 of the FLA 1996.[389] It is worth noting that the legislation does not actually require the perpetrator of the domestic violence to be living in the same property as the victim, merely that the parties are within an associated relationship. The Code of Guidance accompanying the legislation makes it clear that domestic violence does not just refer to incidents which take place within the home, but also covers violence outside the home.[390] The legislation follows the ethos of the FLA 1996 by giving 'domestic violence' a wide meaning. It includes:

threatening behaviour, violence or abuse (psychological, physical, sexual, financial or emotional) between persons who are, or have been, intimate partners, family members or members of the same household, regardless of gender or sexuality.[391]

The definition of domestic violence in section 177(1) of the Housing Act 1996 has now been considered by the Supreme Court in *Yemshaw v Hounslow London Borough Council*.[392] In this case the

---

[384] Shelter Scotland, *Repeat Homelessness and Domestic Abuse* (2002) cited in T. Rubens, 'Domestic Violence and Priority Need' (2008) Journal of Housing Law 28.

[385] Although research suggests that local authorities are failing to provide persons leaving a situation of domestic violence with the help which they need: Crisis, *Homeless Women: Still Being Failed Yet Striving to Survive* (London: Crisis, 2006).

[386] Housing Act 1996, s 175(1).   [387] Section 175(2)(a).   [388] Section 175(3).

[389] See Section 4.3.3. The only significant difference is that where the parties live or have lived in the same household, then employees, tenants, lodgers, and boarders are not excluded.

[390] Department for Communities and Local Government, *Homelessness Code of Guidance for Local Authorities* (2006), para 8.19.

[391] Ibid, para 8.21.   [392] [2011] UKSC 3.

court unanimously ruled that 'domestic violence' includes physical violence, threatening or intimidating behaviour, and any other form of abuse which, directly or indirectly, may give rise to the risk of harm. In this case the appellant left the matrimonial home in which she lived with her husband, taking her two young children with her. She sought assistance from the local housing authority, saying that her husband would shout at her in front of the children and that she was scared that if she confronted him he might hit her. The housing authority in this case felt that there was a low risk of domestic violence against her as her husband had never actually hit her or threatened to do so, and therefore that it was reasonable for her to continue to live in the matrimonial home. This meant that she had, in the housing authority's eyes, made herself intentionally homeless and, as such, it had no duty to provide her with alternative accommodation. The Supreme Court held unanimously that the Housing Act's definition of domestic violence should include not just physical violence, but also threatening or intimidating behaviour and other abuse that may give rise to the risk of harm. As such, the court held that the appellant had not made herself intentionally homeless and ruled that the case should be remitted to the local housing authority to make a fresh decision.

The Code of Guidance accompanying the legislation also makes it very clear that the safety of the applicant is the primary consideration, and thus the threat of violence is not based on whether there has been violence in the past.[393] Nor should any value judgement be made about the conduct of the applicant or the extent to which action could have been taken to mitigate the threat of violence.[394] While the applicant may be able to seek a non-molestation order to prevent future molestation, or an occupation order to remove the abuser from the home, there is no obligation on them to do this. The Code of Guidance recognises that victims may not have the confidence in these measures to prevent future abuse and thus their potential availability does not detract from the duty on the Local Authority to provide assistance to the victim as a homeless person.[395] In short, the Act makes provision both for a person who has been locked out of the home, and for a person who is too frightened either to stay in the home[396] or to return there, to seek accommodation from the local authority as a homeless person. A person who takes shelter in a refuge is still regarded as homeless.[397]

### 8.2 'Priority need'

The local authority will owe 'stronger' duties to homeless people who are deemed to have a priority need for accommodation. This includes the duty to secure accommodation for the homeless person[398] and to take reasonable steps to prevent the loss of accommodation.[399] Those in priority need of accommodation include:[400]

(i) a pregnant woman or a person with whom she resides or might reasonably be expected to reside;

(ii) a person with whom dependent children reside or might reasonably be expected to reside;

(iii) a person who is vulnerable as a result of old age, mental illness, or handicap or physical disability or other special reason, or with whom such a person resides or might reasonably be expected to reside;

---

[393] Department for Communities and Local Government, *Homelessness Code of Guidance for Local Authorities* (2006), paras 8.22 and 8.24.

[394] Ibid, para 8.22.          [395] Ibid, para 8.23.

[396] *R v Broxbourne Borough Council, ex p Willmoth* (1989) 22 HLR 118.

[397] *R v Ealing London Borough Council, ex p Sidhu* (1982) 80 LGR 534; *Birmingham City Council v Ali and Others; Moran v Manchester City Council* [2009] UKHL 36. The House of Lords accepted that while a 'refuge is a safe haven in which to find peace and support . . . it is not a place to live' [2009] UKHL 36 at [43].

[398] Section 193(2).          [399] Section 195(2).

[400] Section 189(1) as amended by the Homeless (Priority Need for Accommodation) (England) Order 2002 and the Homeless (Priority Need for Accommodation) (Wales) Order 2002.

(iv) a person who is vulnerable as a result of ceasing to occupy accommodation because of violence from another person or threats of violence from another person which are likely to be carried out;

(v) a person who is vulnerable for any other special reason, or with whom such a person resides or might reasonably be expected to reside.

Dependent children do not qualify as being in priority need in their own right, neither will they qualify as being vulnerable either because of their youth or because of some sort of disability.[401] However, applicants who have dependent children who live with them, or who might reasonably be expected to live with them, have a priority need. The Code of Guidance states that while the child need not be wholly and exclusively resident with the applicant, there must be actual residence (or a reasonable expectation of residence) with some degree of permanence or regularity as opposed to just a temporary arrangement.[402] The legislation does not define 'dependent child' but the Code of Guidance suggests that it should cover children under 16, and those aged 16–18 who are still in full-time education or training, or who are unable to support themselves and live at home.[403]

A person who has been forced out of accommodation because of violence, or threats of violence, from another will be classed as 'vulnerable' and in priority need for accommodation. The Code of Guidance specifies that when considering if a victim of actual or threatened domestic violence is 'vulnerable', the housing authority may wish to consider:

(i) the nature of the violence or threats of violence;

(ii) the impact of the violence/threats of violence on the applicant's current and future well-being;

(iii) whether the applicant has any existing support networks, particularly by way of family and friends.[404]

Thus, a person who leaves the family home due to violence may not be considered to be 'vulnerable' by the housing authority if they have a network of family and friends to support them. Of course, if they have dependent children residing with them, or expected to reside with them, they will already be in priority need of housing without having to show vulnerability. It may also be possible for a person to establish that they are in priority need under the category of vulnerability where they have a child living with them, but that child is now over the age of 18, if the child himself is vulnerable. Where the child is severely handicapped he may not be able to make an application for housing on his own behalf, as he may be considered to lack the capacity to do so.[405] However, section 189(1)(c) also encompasses the carer of a vulnerable person. Provided that the applicant's homelessness is not intentional, she will qualify for an offer of accommodation which will enable her to continue to look after her vulnerable child.

## 8.3 Intentionally homeless

If the applicant is found to be homeless and in priority need, a local authority must then assess whether or not they are intentionally homeless. Where their homelessness is unintentional,

---

[401] *R v Oldham MBC, ex p Garlick; R v Bexley LBC, ex p Bentham; R v Tower Hamlets LBC, ex p Begum* [1993] AC 509.

[402] Department for Communities and Local Government, *Homelessness Code of Guidance for Local Authorities* (2006), para 10.6.

[403] Ibid, para 10.7. The Guidance also stresses that dependency can be non-financial and thus a child who is over 16 and financially dependent may still lack the maturity to live independently from their parents (para 10.7).

[404] Ibid, para 10.29.

[405] *R v Oldham MBC, ex p Garlick; R v Bexley LBC, ex p Bentham; R v Tower Hamlets LBC, ex p Begum* [1993] AC 509.

the authority are under a duty to secure accommodation that becomes available for her occupation.[406] If, however, the local authority decides that they are intentionally homeless[407] their duty is limited to providing only temporary accommodation simply in order to enable her to have a reasonable opportunity of securing her own accommodation, and to furnishing her with advice and assistance.[408] The relevant date for determining whether or not homelessness is intentional is the date the person leaves the accommodation, and the cause of homelessness must be assessed as at that date.[409] Under section 191(3), a person becomes homeless intentionally if he deliberately does or fails to do anything as a result of which he ceases to occupy accommodation which is available for his occupation and which it would be reasonable for him to continue to occupy.[410]

Local authorities are anxious to preserve scarce resources for those who cannot make housing provision for themselves. For victims of domestic violence, there is evidence to suggest that some authorities will not assist a person if they have not taken steps to attempt to secure an exclusive right to occupy their present accommodation through seeking an occupation order.[411] However, the Code of Guidance suggests that a different view is taken. It states that:

> [i]n cases where there is a probability of violence against an applicant if they continue, or had continued, to occupy their accommodation, and the applicant was aware of measures that could have been taken to prevent or mitigate the risk of violence but decided not to take them, their decision cannot be taken as having caused the probability of violence, and thus, indirectly, having caused the homelessness. Authorities must not assume that measures which could have been taken to prevent actual or threatened violence would necessarily have been effective.[412]

The safety of the applicant is deemed to be the paramount consideration and the Guidance continues that 'in assessing whether it is likely that threats of violence are likely to be carried out, a housing authority should only take into account the probability of violence, and not actions which the applicant could take (such as injunctions against the perpetrators)'.[413] In light of this it would be counter-intuitive to then suggest that an applicant who does not attempt to remain in their current accommodation by seeking an occupation order is intentionally homeless and thus only entitled to temporary accommodation and the advice of the local authority.[414]

## 9  Domestic violence: human rights implications

As we have seen, domestic violence is a significant social problem which has not always been taken seriously by the police or the courts. One question which arises is whether domestic violence can be seen as a human rights issue. While theorising such violence under a human rights framework may help the victim, it should be remembered that it may also help the perpetrator of the violence, who could argue, for example, that legal sanctions (such as an occupation order) violate his or her property rights. Once a human rights framework is initiated, the rights of the victim must be balanced against the competing rights of the alleged perpetrator.[415]

---

[406] Section 193(2).    [407] Housing Act 1992, s 191, as amended by the Homelessnes Act 2002.
[408] Section 190(2).    [409] *Din v Wandsworth London Borough Council* [1983] 1 AC 657.
[410] See also ss 191(3) and 196.    [411] See *R v Westminster City Council, ex p Bishop* [1993] 2 FLR 780.
[412] Department for Communities and Local Government, *Homelessness Code of Guidance for Local Authorities* (2006), para 11.13.
[413] Ibid, para 10.29.    [414] See *R v Westminster City Council, ex p Bishop* [1993] 2 FLR 780.
[415] See J. Herring and S. Choudhry, 'Domestic Violence and the Human Rights Act 1998: A New Means of Legal Intervention' (2006) Public Law 752. See also S. Choudhry and J. Herring, *European Human Rights and Family Law* (Oxford: Hart, 2010), ch 9.

Domestic violence has several implications under international human rights law, as well as under the Human Rights Act 1998, which incorporates the principles of the ECHR into domestic law.

## 9.1 The Human Rights Act 1998

Several provisions of the ECHR are relevant to domestic violence. Article 2 requires everyone's right to life to be protected by the law and Article 3 protects individuals from torture or inhuman or degrading treatment or punishment. Section 6 of the Human Rights Act 1998 requires courts and other public authorities to act compatibly with parties' rights under the ECHR. This means that if the police or the courts fail to take reasonable steps to protect family members from violence or abuse which falls within the ambit of Article 2 or 3, they may be violating the victim's rights under the ECHR. This is the case even though it is another private individual, and not an agent of the state, who is carrying out the abuse. Indeed, the European Court of Human Rights made it very clear in *A v UK*[416] that the state is under a positive obligation to take measures to ensure that no one is subjected to inhuman or degrading treatment or punishment at the hands of another private individual.

Article 8 requires protection for an individual's right to respect for their private and family life and it could be argued that failing to protect a person from violence in the home, breaches their rights under Article 8. Balanced against this, however, are the alleged perpetrator's rights under the same Article which could be infringed by an occupation order which interferes with their property rights in the home and thus with their enjoyment of their private and family life. Indeed, unlike Articles 2 and 3 of the ECHR (which are absolute rights), a person's rights under Article 8 are qualified. Interference with one's right to a private and family life may be justified under Article 8(2) if it is in accordance with the law and is deemed to be necessary on the grounds of public safety; prevention of disorder or crime; protection of health or morals; or for the protection of the rights and freedoms of others. This means that the court must conduct a balancing exercise considering both the rights of the victim and the rights of the perpetrator under Article 8.

The human rights implications of an ex parte order have already been mentioned earlier in the chapter. Under Article 6 of the ECHR, a respondent has a right to a fair and public hearing of the determination of his civil rights. This has implications for ex parte orders that are made in emergency situations where the normal notice procedures are dispensed with.[417] However, section 45(3) of the Family Law Act 1996 makes it clear that where an ex parte order is granted, the respondent must be given an opportunity to make representations relating to the order as soon as just and convenient at a full hearing. Provided the court fulfils its obligations to secure a full hearing as soon as just and convenient, Article 6 of the ECHR is unlikely to be breached.

## 9.2 International human rights law

The Human Rights Act (and the ECHR) is not the only human rights law relevant to domestic violence. The subject is also dealt with in several UN treaties, notably the Convention on the Elimination of All Forms of Discrimination Against Women (CEDAW). The Convention, and several later declarations and statements, set out detailed guidelines as to what steps states should take to tackle domestic violence, among other problems. While such international human rights treaties do not give individuals direct rights in domestic courts, their provisions (if ratified) are binding on the UK Government. The UN monitors compliance with the provisions of the

---

[416] [1998] 2 FLR 959.    [417] Family Law Act 1996, s 45.

various treaties by requiring the production of periodic national reports to a committee, which then issues a report stating its concerns about the state of compliance in that country. This means that while the UN cannot force a state to change its policies or laws on a particular issue, the monitoring procedure can be used to try to persuade states to comply with their international obligations.[418]

International human rights law has not always been concerned with domestic violence. Thomas and Beasley suggest that there are various reasons why domestic violence has, in the past, been excluded from international human rights practice.[419] One of the main reasons is that international human rights law was historically designed to protect individuals from abuses carried out by the state as opposed to other private individuals. Domestic violence, by contrast, occurs in private and, as such, was regarded as being outside the scope of international human rights law. However, thinking began to change as it became accepted that abuse which takes place in the private sphere between private citizens is also a human rights violation for which the state is accountable.[420] As Thomas and Beasley note:

> the concept of state accountability has expanded to include not only actions directly committed by states, but also states' systemic failure to prosecute acts committed by . . . private actors.[421]

The extension of state accountability to cover abuse which takes place in the private sphere, coupled with the growth in information about the gender-specific nature of domestic violence and typical low rates of prosecution, have made it possible to consider domestic violence under international human rights law.[422] Indeed, many commentators argue that gender-based violence *must* be seen as a human rights issue as this shifts conceptions of such violence from being seen as an individual problem or simply part of 'family dynamics' to a more intense focus on the actions of the perpetrator and the 'traditional complicity of law and custom in giving license to violent "impulses" against women'.[423]

As already mentioned, one of the most important UN treaties to deal with domestic violence is CEDAW. CEDAW (also known as the Women's Convention) was adopted by the UN General Assembly in 1979 and is the only international human rights treaty to focus exclusively on the rights of women. The UK ratified CEDAW in 1986. However, the provisions of CEDAW do not deal directly with the issue of domestic violence. The Committee on the Elimination of Discrimination against Women (which monitors state compliance with CEDAW) recognised that the failure explicitly to address the issue of domestic violence within the Convention was a serious omission. Thus, in 1992 the Committee issued General Recommendation No 19 which makes it clear that violence against women is a form of discrimination which falls within the remit of CEDAW:

> The definition of discrimination includes gender-based violence, that is, violence that is directed against a woman because she is a woman or that affects women disproportionately. It includes acts that inflict physical, mental or sexual harm or suffering, threats of such acts, coercion and other

---

[418] R. McQuigg, 'The Responses of States to the Comments of the CEDAW Committee on Domestic Violence' (2007) 11(4) International Journal of Human Rights 461.

[419] D. Thomas and M. Beasley, 'Domestic Violence as a Human Rights Issue' (1993) 15 Human Rights Quarterly 36–62.

[420] See A. S. Fraser, 'Becoming Human: The Origin and Development of Women's Human Rights Law' (1999) 21 Human Rights Quarterly 853–906.

[421] D. Thomas and M. Beasley, 'Domestic Violence as a Human Rights Issue' (1993) 15 Human Rights Quarterly 36–62 at 41.

[422] Ibid.

[423] R. Copelon, 'Intimate Terror: Understanding Domestic Violence as Torture' in R. Cook (ed), *Human Rights of Women: National and International Perspectives* (Philadelphia, PA: University of Pennsylvania Press, 1994).

deprivations of liberty. Gender-based violence may breach specific provisions of the Convention, regardless of whether those provisions expressly mention violence.[424]

This means that the Committee, when monitoring state compliance with CEDAW, will seek information on how the problem of domestic violence is being addressed at state level. It also means that states must include in their reports to the Committee details on the prevalence of such violence and on the measures which have been taken to deal with it. This is significant for a number of reasons. First, it is symbolically important in conceptualising domestic violence as a gendered issue and a form of discrimination against women. Secondly, the monitoring procedures may encourage governments to take domestic violence seriously in order to avoid the criticism of the Committee. Thirdly, it gives activists and lobbyists working within the area the leverage to apply pressure on governments to develop strategies to tackle domestic violence in order to ensure compliance with CEDAW.[425] However, as enforcement is limited to these reporting procedures, much depends on the will of the state to comply with the provisions of the UN treaties. If a state does not comply then there is little that can be done as the UN has no real way of forcing states to alter their policies or change their laws.[426]

## 10  Domestic violence and child contact

The fact that a parent has perpetrated domestic violence does not constitute a bar to contact with his/her children.[427] Moreover, many agree that the extent to which children are harmed by domestic violence has not always received the attention which it deserves. Certainly, until recent years, allegations or findings of domestic violence had little impact at all on the issue of child contact in the aftermath of parental separation.[428] Courts tended to view violence against a parent and contact with children as separate issues and there was insufficient recognition of the effects of the violence on either the parent or the child. A presumption in favour of contact, the assumed benefits of continued contact between a child and the non-residential parent, and the suspicion that allegations of violence were being made or encouraged by a hostile parent who opposed contact out of spite or revenge operated to minimise the impact of domestic violence on child contact arrangements.[429]

However, in recent years increased attention has been paid to the issue of contact between parents who are perpetrators of domestic violence and their children following separation. The Department of Health recognised in 2003 that:

[a]t least 750,000 children a year witness domestic violence. Nearly three quarters of children on the 'at risk' register live in households where domestic violence occurs.[430]

---

[424] The Committee on the Elimination of Discrimination against Women, General Recommendation No 19, para 6: http://www.un.org/womenwatch/daw/cedaw/recommendations/recomm.htm.

[425] When Governments submit their reports to the Committee, NGOs and other lobbyists are also encouraged to submit their own 'shadow' reports outlining their own views on the compliance of the state with the provisions of CEDAW.

[426] R. McQuigg, 'The Responses of States to the Comments of the CEDAW Committee on Domestic Violence' (2007) 11(4) International Journal of Human Rights 461. It is worth noting that CEDAW has been augmented by an Optional Protocol, introduced in 1999, which provides for an individual complaints and inquiry procedure. Under the complaints procedure, the Committee can receive claims of state violations of CEDAW by individuals or groups. However, before hearing a complaint the Committee must be satisfied that all domestic remedies in relation to the issue have been exhausted. In addition, an inquiry procedure allows the Committee to initiate inquiries into situations of 'grave or systematic' violations of women's rights under CEDAW.

[427] The issue of child contact is considered more fully in Chapter 9.

[428] J. Barron, *Not Worth the Paper . . . ? The Effectiveness of Legal Protection for Women and Children Experiencing Domestic Violence* (Bristol: Women's Aid Federation England, 1990).

[429] R. Bailey-Harris, J. Barron, and J. Pearce, 'From Utility to Rights? The Presumption of Contact in Practice' (1999) 13 International Journal of Law, Policy and the Family 111–31.

[430] *Into the Mainstream—Strategic Development of Mental Health Care for Women* (London: Department of Health, 2003).

Studies have also highlighted the dangers of allowing perpetrators of domestic violence to have contact with their children. Indeed, domestic violence does not end when a relationship breaks down as victims can be exposed to even greater risk from an ex-partner. Research has established that post-separation contact between children and a violent parent, particularly during handovers, can be particularly dangerous.[431] In addition, there has been a growing awareness of the harmful effects of domestic violence on children. Not only have researchers established a clear connection between domestic violence and child abuse,[432] but it is clear that children who witness such violence (either through seeing or hearing it) also suffer significant harm. An influential report by child psychiatrists Drs Sturge and Glaser highlighted the dangers to children of witnessing domestic violence and the potential harm caused by allowing contact between a child and a violent parent.[433] They found that domestic violence was a 'very serious and significant failure in parenting' which meets any definition of child abuse.

Despite these recommendations, there is still no presumption against contact in situations of domestic violence, and allegations or findings of such violence will not constitute a bar to contact.[434] However, judicial attitudes have changed in recent years as the courts now recognise the harmful effects of domestic violence on children and their primary carers.[435] In one of the most important cases on the relevance of allegations of domestic violence on child contact disputes, the Court of Appeal laid down guidelines which direct a court to consider, amongst other things, whether the allegations are well founded and, if so, the impact of the violence on the child.[436] These guidelines reflect the need to take allegations of domestic violence more seriously and to recognise that children who are exposed to violence indirectly (through seeing or hearing incidents of abuse) as opposed to being directly involved in it also suffer harm.[437] The danger associated with indirect exposure to domestic violence is also recognised in legislation. The definition of 'harm' in the Children Act 1989 for the purposes of the welfare checklist[438] and for making a care or supervision order[439] has been amended to include the 'impairment suffered from seeing or hearing the ill-treatment of another'. This means that, when making decisions regarding a child's welfare, there is a statutory obligation to consider the harm a child will suffer through witnessing domestic violence. However, it has been argued that this does not go far enough to challenge the entrenched view that contact is almost always in the best interests of the child.[440]

Despite changes in both judicial attitudes and official thinking about the seriousness of domestic violence and its impact on children, many argue that little has changed in practice and that

---

[431] L. Richards, *Domestic Violence Murder Review Analysis of Findings* (London: Metropolitan Police Service, 2003).

[432] M. Hester, C. Pearson, and N. Harwin, *Making an Impact: Children and Domestic Violence—A Reader* (London: Jessica Kingsley, 2007).

[433] C. Sturge and D. Glaser, 'Contact and Domestic Violence—The Experts' Report' (2000) 30 Family Law 615.

[434] *Re L, V, M, H (Children) (Contact: Domestic Violence)* [2001] Family Law 260. See F. Kaganas, 'Re L (Contact: Domestic Violence) . . . Contact and Domestic Violence' (1999) 12 Child and Family Law Quarterly 311.

[435] *Re K (Contact: Mother's Anxiety)* [1999] 2 FLR 703; *Re M (Minors) (Contact: Violent Parent)* [1999] 2 FLR 231.

[436] *Re L, V, M, H (Children) (Contact: Domestic Violence)* [2001] Fam 260. See also Practice Direction: Residence and Contact Orders: Domestic Violence and Harm [2009] All ER(D) 122 (Jan). The Court of Appeal made it clear in *Re Z (Unsupervised Contact: Allegations of Domestic Violence)* [2009] EWCA Civ 430 that while the Practice Direction was not designed to tell judges what to decide in an application for contact or residence, its purpose was to inform them of how to go about deciding such issues where there were allegations of domestic violence. For a fuller discussion of the approach of the courts when determining child contact and residence disputes, see Chapter 9.

[437] Although evidence suggests that the implementation of these guidelines has been 'patchy', DCA, DfES, and DTI, 'Parental Separation: Children's Needs and Parents' Responsibilities' (Cm 6273, London: HMSO, 2004), para 48.

[438] Children Act 1989, s 1(3), see Chapter 10.    [439] Children Act 1989, s 31(9), see Chapter 10.

[440] H. Saunders, 'Twenty-Nine Child Homicides: Lessons Still to be Learnt on Domestic Violence and Child Protection' (Bristol: Women's Aid, 2004).

contact between a child and a violent partner is still too readily ordered. Indeed, less than 1 per cent of applications for child contact are rejected.[441] In a study for Women's Aid, Hilary Saunders compiled a list of 29 children in 13 families who were killed by their fathers during contact arrangements between 1994 and 2004.[442] It was established that domestic violence was involved in at least 11 out of the 13 families. In addition, in five of the cases contact had been ordered by the court, and in three of these cases the court granted orders for unsupervised contact or residence to very violent fathers against professional advice. It was also found that in five cases the father killed the children in order to take revenge on his ex-partner for leaving him. As such, there have been calls for the introduction of a rebuttable statutory presumption, as in New Zealand, that contact should not be granted to a perpetrator of domestic violence unless the court is satisfied that it will be safe for the child and the other parent[443] although the government remains resistant to such a change.

## Discussion Questions

1. Domestic violence has historical, patriarchal, and multifaceted explanations for its prevalence. Describe the theories which attempt to explain domestic violence.

2. Do the civil law remedies available in the Family Law Act 1996 adequately protect victims of domestic violence?

3. Occupation orders differentiate between applicants according to their legal right to occupy a property. Discuss whether this is satisfactory and what issues arise from this situation.

4. Critically evaluate the courts' approach to granting occupation orders.

## Further Reading

BURTON, M., 'Criminalising Breaches of Civil Orders for Protection from Domestic Violence' [2003] Crim LR 301

BURTON, M., *Legal Responses to Domestic Violence* (Abingdon: Routledge-Cavendish, 2008)

CHOUDRY, S. and HERRING, J., 'Righting Domestic Violence' (2006) 20 International Journal of Law, Policy and the Family 95

HERRING, J. and CHOUDHRY, S., 'Domestic Violence and the Human Rights Act 1998: A New Means of Legal Intervention' (2006) Public Law 752

HESTER, M., *Who Does What to Whom? Gender and Domestic Violence Perpetrators* (Bristol: University of Bristol in association with the Northern Rock Foundation, 2009)

HOME OFFICE, *Domestic Violence: A National Report* (London: Home Office, 2005)

HUMPHREYS, C. and THIARA, R. K., 'Neither Justice nor Protection: Women's Experiences of Post-Separation Violence' (2003) 25 Journal of Social Welfare and Family Law 195

MADDEN-DEMPSEY, M., 'What Counts as Domestic Violence: A Conceptual Analysis' [2006] 12 William and Mary Journal of Women and the Law 301

---

[441] DCA, DfES and DTI, 'Parental Separation: Children's Needs and Parents' Responsibilities, Cm 6273 (London: HMSO, 2004), para 25.

[442] H. Saunders, *Twenty-Nine Child Homicides: Lessons Still to be Learnt on Domestic Violence and Child Protection* (Bristol: Women's Aid, 2004).

[443] See eg Refuge, *Response to Domestic Violence, Crimes and Victims Bill* (July 2004); L. Radford, S. Sayers, and Aid for Mothers Involved in Contact Action (AMICA), *Unreasonable Fears? Child Contact in the Context of Domestic Violence: A Survey of Mothers' Perception of Harm* (Bristol: Women's Aid Federation England, 1999).

Mullender, A., *Rethinking Domestic Violence* (Abingdon: Routledge, 1996)

Reece, H., 'The End of Domestic Violence' (2006) 69(5) Modern Law Review 770

Walby, S. and Allen, J., *Domestic Violence, Sexual Assault and Stalking: Findings from the British Crime Survey*, Home Office Research Study 276 (London: Home Office, 2004)

**online resource centre**

Visit the Online Resource Centre at **www.oxfordtextbooks.co.uk/orc/gilmore_glennon5e/** for a range of further features including a detailed bibliography and self-test questions.

# 4

# Money and property distribution on marriage breakdown

## INTRODUCTION

When relationships break down, questions invariably arise about whether, and if so how, the parties' property will be divided. A further issue is whether one party should be required to provide ongoing financial support to the other. The answers depend on how legal and social policy views the now-ended relationship. For spouses and civil partners there are statutory regimes which allow the courts to respond flexibly to their specific circumstances by way of orders for financial provision and property adjustment. No similar scheme applies to cohabitants who are not in a marriage or civil partnership[1] and, as we shall see in the next chapter, disputes between such cohabitants on relationship breakdown are governed by strict property law principles. This chapter will examine the legal framework which determines how money and property are distributed between spouses or civil partners when the relationship ends. The focus will be on spouses since it is in that context that the guideline case law has emerged, and the relevant statutory provisions are similar for civil partners.[2] As in many areas of family law, the legal and social policy preference is for parties to reach agreement on these issues. However, in the absence of such agreement, the courts have very wide powers to resolve disputes, and of course agreements are reached in the shadow of knowledge of how the courts are likely to exercise discretion.

## 1 Background to the current law

Legislation was introduced in the early 1970s which gave the courts much greater powers to distribute the parties' assets following divorce, nullity, or judicial separation. The impetus for change was the introduction of no-fault divorce in the Divorce Reform Act 1969. The removal of 'fault' as the conceptual basis for divorce necessitated a new way of thinking about post-divorce economic obligations. It was feared that the new legislation would prove a 'Casanova's Charter', with innocent wives being divorced against their will and left in poverty. The Matrimonial Proceedings and Property Act 1970 thus introduced wide-ranging powers to adjust property as well as to make orders for financial provision following decrees of divorce, nullity, or judicial separation. The

---

[1] Although there have been proposals for a scheme: see Law Commission's proposals (Law Commission, *Cohabitation: The Financial Consequences of Relationship Breakdown* (Law Com No 307, 2007). See Chapter 5.

[2] Civil Partnership Act 2004, Sch 5. The Court of Appeal heard the first financial provision case involving the dissolution of a civil partnership in 2012. In *Lawrence v Gallagher* [2012] EWCA Civ 394, the Court of Appeal confirmed that the principles of financial provision following the dissolution of a civil partnership are to be applied in the same way as financial provision on divorce.

power to adjust property was one of the main innovations of the new legislation.[3] The provisions of the 1970 Act were consolidated with the substantive law of divorce in the Matrimonial Causes Act (MCA) 1973, and are now contained in Part II of that Act.[4] They have been amended on several occasions, most notably by the Matrimonial and Family Proceedings Act 1984.

When the legislation was first enacted in 1970, it stated that the court's powers should, as far as possible, be exercised in such a way as to place the parties in the financial position which they would have been in had the marriage not broken down and had each properly discharged his or her financial obligations and responsibilities towards the other.[5] This was known as the 'minimal loss principle'. However, it was criticised as being inconsistent with the modern notions of the dissoluble marriage and proved unworkable in practice.[6] There was a growing dissatisfaction with the law among a powerful lobby of former husbands who resented having to support their former wives for life (so-called 'alimony drones'),[7] and the Law Commission examined the law again in the early 1980s. The Law Commission reported that the consensus was for a change of emphasis rather than a radical restructuring of the law. Its recommendations, which were enacted by the Matrimonial and Family Proceedings Act 1984, were that: (i) emphasis should be on giving priority to the needs of children; (ii) greater weight should be attached to the wife's earning capacity and to the desirability of both parties becoming self-sufficient (the idea of seeking to effect a clean break); and (iii) that the principle of minimal loss should be repealed to allow more emphasis to be given to the individual facts of cases. The removal of the principle of minimal loss, however, signalled the advent of an even more unpredictable discretionary system as it was not replaced by an alternative overriding objective. Instead, the statute instructed the courts to give first consideration to the welfare of any minor children and to consider the appropriateness of a 'clean break', two objectives which can pull in different directions. In the absence of an overriding objective, it has been left to the judiciary to interpret the statutory criteria. This means that we must pay close attention to case law in this area, although as we shall see much uncertainty has arisen due to the lack of a clear principled basis upon which financial provision orders are made.[8]

### Summary

The Law Commission recently stated that '[m]arriage and civil partnership are an expression of commitment and of shared lives; they are also legal statuses which generate both privileges and responsibilities. The ending of marriage by divorce, or of civil partnership by dissolution, inevitably has financial consequences.'[9]

However, one of the core problems is that there is no clear idea of the rights and responsibilities which flow from marriage and civil partnership. The fact that the legislation provides no guiding objective and no indication of what former spouses' financial responsibilities to each other are, or should be, gives rise to the following thorny issues, as identified recently by the Law Commission:[10]

---

[3] Introducing the remedy of 'equitable distribution' of matrimonial property reflecting 'social change and compelling social need': see *Dart v Dart* [1996] 2 FLR 286 at 294.

[4] As Glendon observed, this 'sounded the death knell for the old marital property system of separation of assets, so far as divorce was concerned': see M. A. Glendon, *The Transformation of Family Law; State, Law, and Family in the United States and Western Europe* (Chicago, IL: University of Chicago Press, 1989), p 199.

[5] Matrimonial Proceedings and Property Act 1970, s 5(1). There was little discussion of this but it seems the approach taken was from the common law: see *N v N* (1928) 44 LR 324 at 328, quoted in Law Commission, *Family Law: The Financial Consequences of Divorce: The Basic Policy: A Discussion Paper* (Law Com No 103, 1980), para 9.

[6] See Law Com No 103 (1980), para 24.

[7] Cf C. Smart, *The Ties That Bind* (Abingdon: Routledge, 1984), who argues that the alimony drone was a myth.

[8] In 2010, the Family Procedure Rules 2010 introduced new terminology and the system is now described as 'proceedings for financial orders'. Previous terminology referred to ancillary relief orders.

[9] Law Commission Consultation Paper 208, *Matrimonial Property, Needs and Agreements* (2012), para 1.5.

[10] Ibid, at para 2.12.

— what is to be achieved by the financial order on divorce?
— why might a particular order be made?
— for how long, if at all, should one spouse be ordered to supplement a former spouse's income after divorce, or provide the other with a home?

It is these issues, amongst others, with which the courts have had to grapple and provide guidance. In *Miller; McFarlane*,[11] one of the seminal cases in this area, Lady Hale said that when making financial orders on divorce the 'ultimate objective is to give each party an equal start on the road to independent living'.[12] While economic self-sufficiency is an important goal, the courts have balanced this with the need to make provision for the economically weaker former spouse. Thus, as the Law Commission points out, while the current law tries to encourage independence, there is also the 'recognition that independence is impractical in circumstances where the financial commitment of the marriage has effects that reach a long way into the future'.[13] The courts have, therefore, had to deal with wider issues of social policy and the result has been a raft of case law from which it is not easy to discern what the law actually is. This, in turn, makes it difficult to predict what awards will be made in individual cases which hinders the parties' ability to 'bargain in the shadow of the law'. A related problem is that the reported case law in this area is generated largely by the disputes of wealthy couples and 'it is not straightforward to translate that case law into guidance for ordinary cases'.[14] Before looking at the approach of the courts in more detail, the next section will discuss the legislative framework.

## 2 The legislative framework

The court's powers are contained principally in sections 23 to 24A of the MCA 1973. Section 23 contains what are known as 'financial provision orders': powers to make orders for periodical payments, secured periodical payments, and lump sums. Section 24 contains powers to adjust property by way of transfer or settlement of property. Section 24A gives the court power to order the sale of property. In addition, there are powers to deal specifically with a party's pension in sections 25B–25D of the Act. The orders are discussed in detail in later sections of this chapter.

Section 25(1) and (2) gives guidance to the court on the matters to which it must have regard when deciding whether, and if so how, to exercise its powers.

---

### Key legislation

Section 25(1) provides the court with the general direction that:

It shall be the duty of the court in deciding whether to exercise its powers . . . and, if so, in what manner, to have regard to all the circumstances of the case, first consideration being given to the welfare while a minor of any child of the family who has not attained the age of eighteen.

---

[11] [2006] UKHL 24.

[12] Ibid, [144]. See also the comments by Mr Justice Charles in *G v G* [2012] EWHC 167 (Fam).

[13] Law Commission Consultation Paper No 208, *Matrimonial Property, Needs and Agreements* (2012), para 5.9.

[14] Ibid, para 3.33. See E. Hitchings, 'The Impact of Recent Ancillary Relief Jurisprudence in the "Everyday" Ancillary Relief Case' (2010) 22 Child and Family Law Quarterly 93; E. Hitchings, 'Chaos or Consistency? Ancillary Relief in the "Everyday" Case' in J. Miles and R. Probert (eds), *Sharing Lives, Dividing Assets: An Inter-Disciplinary Study* (Oxford: Hart Publishing, 2009).

Section 25(2) then highlights particular matters, providing that:

> As regards the exercise of the powers of the court . . . in relation to a party to the marriage, the court shall in particular have regard to the following matters—
>
> (a) the income, earning capacity, property and other financial resources which each of the parties to the marriage has or is likely to have in the foreseeable future, including in the case of earning capacity any increase in that capacity which it would in the opinion of the court be reasonable to expect a party to the marriage to take steps to acquire;
>
> (b) the financial needs, obligations and responsibilities which each of the parties to the marriage has or is likely to have in the foreseeable future;
>
> (c) the standard of living enjoyed by the family before the breakdown of the marriage;
>
> (d) the age of each party to the marriage and the duration of the marriage;
>
> (e) any physical or mental disability of either of the parties to the marriage;
>
> (f) the contributions which each of the parties has made or is likely in the foreseeable future to make to the welfare of the family, including any contribution by looking after the home or caring for the family;
>
> (g) the conduct of each of the parties, if that conduct is such that it would in the opinion of the court be inequitable to disregard it;
>
> (h) in the case of proceedings for divorce or nullity of marriage, the value to each of the parties of any benefit which by reason of the dissolution or annulment of the marriage, that party will lose the chance of acquiring.

In *Piglowska v Piglowski*[15] the House of Lords made clear that the considerations in section 25(2) (a)–(h) are not ranked in any hierarchy; consequently some factors will assume great importance in some cases, and lesser or no importance in others.

In addition, when a court is exercising its powers to make financial provision between the parties, it must consider whether a clean break or a deferred clean break order would be appropriate. The relevant legislative provisions are laid out below.

### Key legislation

Section 25A provides:

(1) Where on or after the grant of a decree of divorce or nullity of marriage the court decides to exercises its powers under [the legislation] in favour of a party to a marriage . . . it shall be the duty of the court to consider whether it would be appropriate so to exercise those powers that the financial obligations of each party towards the other will be terminated as soon after the grant of the decree of nullity as the court considers just and reasonable.

(2) Where the court decides in such a case to make a periodical payments or secured periodical payments order in favour of a party to the marriage, the court shall in particular consider whether it would be appropriate to require those payments to be made or secured only for such term as would in the opinion of the court be sufficient to enable the party in whose favour the order is made to adjust without undue hardship to the termination of his or her financial dependence on the other party.

(3) Where on or after the grant of a decree of divorce or nullity of marriage an application is made by a party to the marriage for a periodical payments or secured periodical payments order in his or her favour, then, if the court considers that no continuing obligation should be imposed on either party

---

[15] [1999] 3 All ER 632, [1999] 2 FLR 763, HL.

to make or secure periodical payments in favour of the other, the court may dismiss the application with a direction that the applicant shall not be entitled to make any further application in relation to that marriage for an order [for periodical payments or secured periodical payments].

## 2.1 **The courts' powers**

The court can make a variety of income-based orders and property adjustment orders which redistribute the parties' capital assets on divorce, which can be combined if necessary to achieve what it considers to be a fair settlement between the parties.

### 2.1.1 Maintenance pending suit

Under section 22 of the MCA 1973 the courts can, on a petition for divorce, nullity, or judicial separation, order either spouse to make such periodical payments to the other pending suit as it thinks reasonable. The court will take account of all the circumstances of the case although the applicant's immediate financial needs and the needs of the children will be particularly relevant.[16] Prior to April 2013, a maintenance pending suit order could include a component for legal costs in situations where the applicant had no other legal means to fund the litigation.[17] However, the court's power to make a costs allowance as part of a maintenance pending suit order has been abolished and replaced by a new statutory scheme which enables the court to make a legal services payment order (LSPO). Given the restrictions on the availability of legal aid for private cases, the new legal services payment order has become increasingly important. This power has been created by the insertion of section 22ZA into the MCA 1973 which allows the court to make an order requiring one party to the marriage to pay the other an amount to enable him or her to obtain legal services for the purposes of the proceedings.[18] The court cannot make an order unless it is satisfied that the applicant is not reasonably able to secure a loan to pay for the legal services, and the applicant is unlikely to be able to obtain the legal services by granting a charge over any assets recovered in the proceedings.[19] Section 22ZB MCA 1973 sets out the matters to which the court must have regard in deciding how to exercise its power under section 22ZA.[20]

### 2.1.2 Periodical payments order

Under section 23 of the MCA 1973, the court can make a periodical payments order in favour of a spouse and/or for the benefit of any child. These payments simply amount to ongoing payments of maintenance from the payer to the payee. They can be made for any amount, including a nominal sum which can be increased should the payer's circumstances change. Under section 28(1)(a) of the MCA 1973, the payments will end on the death of either party or the remarriage of the payee. The payments may be paid at any regular interval, including annually and may be for a fixed period or

---

[16] *Peacock v Peacock* [1984] 1 All ER 1069.

[17] See *A v A (Maintenance Pending Suit: Provision for Legal Fees)* [2001] 1 FLR 377; *G v G (Maintenance Pending Suit: Costs)* [2002] EWHC 306 (Fam); *Currey v Currey* [2006] EWCA Civ 1338.

[18] The Legal Aid, Sentencing and Punishment of Offenders Act 2012 inserted sections 22ZA and ZB into the MCA 1973 from 1 April 2013.

[19] Sections 22ZA(3) and (4) MCA 1973.

[20] These include the income, earning capacity, property and other financial resources which each of the applicants and the paying party has or is likely to have in the foreseeable future; the financial needs, obligations and responsibilities which each of the applicant and the paying party has or is likely to have in the foreseeable future; the subject matter of the proceedings; whether the paying party is legally represented in the proceedings; any steps taken by the applicant to avoid all or part of the proceedings; the applicant's conduct in the proceedings, and any amount owed by the applicant to the paying party in respect of costs in the proceedings. Recent case law on the operation of the new legal services payment orders include *BN v MA* [2013] EWHC 4250 (Fam); *Makarskaya v Korchagin* [2013] EWHC 4393 (Fam), and *Rubin v Rubin* [2014] EWHC 611 (Fam).

until further order. Any order for periodical payments, however small,[21] is capable of being varied upwards should either of the spouses' circumstances alter in the future. Thus, if at the time of divorce, the parties' resources are limited, the court could make an order for a nominal sum which can be increased should the parties' circumstances change.

### 2.1.3 Secured periodical payments order

A secured periodical payments order can be made under section 23(1)(b). Under a secured periodical payments order, payments are secured against specific property belonging to the payer. Sometimes the chosen property is income-producing, and sometimes it is property against which the charge can be enforced with the sum due should the payer default on the payments. The security reverts to the payer on the payee's death or remarriage;[22] or to his estate when these events occur after the payer's death.

The main advantage of a secured order over an unsecured order is that it can last for the payee's lifetime,[23] which means that when the payer dies the payee can still look to the security as a source of income. Despite the advantages of the secured periodical payments order, they are now rarely made. If there is sufficient capital to provide security for periodical payments, the preferred option is to use the capital to make a clean break transfer between the parties. This can be achieved by either a lump sum or property adjustment order.

### 2.1.4 Lump sum

A lump sum order is 'an order that either party to the marriage shall pay to the other such lump sum or sums as may be so specified'.[24] Although the legislation refers to sums in the plural, only one lump sum order can be made.[25] The plural allows for it to be paid in instalments[26] in which case the payments can be secured[27] and interest can be ordered on the amount deferred.[28] The lump sum order is designed to represent a final order and, as such, it will not usually be varied. However, as confirmed by the Court of Appeal in *Westbury v Sampson*,[29] the court has the power under section 31(1) to re-timetable and adjust the amounts of individual instalments under a lump sum order payable by instalments[30] and can also vary, suspend, or discharge the principal lump sum itself under such an order. However, the latter power should only be used sparingly.[31]

Where there are sufficient resources, a lump sum order may be used to capitalise an applicant's maintenance requirements in line with the clean break principle. The *Duxbury* formula can be used to calculate the quantum to be paid via a lump sum which will be sufficient to meet the applicant's income needs. Taken from the case of *Duxbury v Duxbury*,[32] this arithmetical formula will take into account factors such as the applicant's life expectancy, the rate of inflation, and interest rates, to generate a lump sum which when invested will provide a sufficient income for the remainder of the recipient's life. However, this formula is only a guide when assessing the quantum of a lump sum order, it is not determinative. The House of Lords in *White v White*[33] referred to the 'Duxbury paradox' which means that reliance on these actuarial calculations could result in unfair outcomes on the basis that 'the longer the marriage and hence the older the wife, the less the capital sum required for a Duxbury type fund'.[34] Thus, while the Duxbury calculation may be a useful tool to capitalise maintenance requirements, it is not determinative of the final award.

---

[21] Even 1p a year.    [22] MCA 1973, s 28(1)(b).
[23] By contrast, an unsecured order can last only for the spouses' joint lives.    [24] MCA 1973, s 23(1)(c).
[25] *Coleman v Coleman* [1972] 3 All ER 886.    [26] MCA 1983, s 23(3)(c).    [27] Section 23(3)(c).
[28] Section 23(6).    [29] [2001] EWCA Civ 4807.    [30] *Hamilton v Hamilton* [2013] EWCA Civ 13.
[31] *Westbury v Sampson* [2001] EWCA Civ 4807 at [18].    [32] [1987] 1 FLR 7.    [33] [2001] AC 596.
[34] Ibid, 609.

### 2.1.5 **Property adjustment orders**

Section 24 enables a court to adjust the spouses' interests in the ownership of property, such as the family home, a car, furnishings, and investments,[35] so that it can make provision for the current circumstances of all the family members. It cannot be emphasised too strongly that there is no power subsequently to vary a property adjustment order. A property adjustment order can take various forms.

#### 2.1.5.1 *Property transfer orders*

Section 24(1)(a) provides that the court may order that 'a party to the marriage shall transfer to the other party, to any child of the family or to such person as may be specified in the order' any property to which that party is entitled either in possession or reversion. Property transfer orders, like lump sum orders, may be used to bring about a clean break between the parties. This order may be made in respect of any property of the spouses, although it usually takes the form of an order that one party transfer a share in the matrimonial home to the other.

#### 2.1.5.2 *Settlement orders*

Section 24(1)(b) provides that the court can order a spouse to settle property for the benefit of the other party and of the children of the family, or either or any of them. A settlement arises where any property has been purchased in the spouses' joint names, or where they each have a beneficial interest in it.[36] A settlement creates successive interests in land, and can be invaluable where the spouses' resources are insufficient to make adequate provision for them both, and where one spouse needs the immediate use of property more urgently than the other. It may, for example, be appropriate to direct that the matrimonial home be jointly owned, that one spouse should have exclusive use of the property for a period of time, and that the other should become entitled to his or her share in the proceeds of sale of the property when the settlement period comes to an end. In this way a settlement enables a court to make provision for one of the party's needs without entirely taking away the other party's rights in the property concerned.

### 2.1.6 **Power of sale**

Section 24A provides that:

> [w]here the court makes . . . a secured periodical payments order, an order for the payment of a lump sum or a property adjustment order, then, on making that order or at any time thereafter, the court may make a further order for the sale of such property as may be specified in the order, being property in which or in the proceeds of sale of which either or both of the parties to the marriage has or have a beneficial interest, either in possession or reversion.

This provision is an essential adjunct to those other orders, and used imaginatively it can extend and complement the court's other powers. For example, it may only be possible to order a lump sum payment if property is sold to raise the necessary cash. Sometimes one spouse is obdurate about complying with an existing lump sum order. In these circumstances, provisions in section 24A may come to the assistance of the other spouse. Thus, the court can order sale but direct that the sale shall not take effect until a specified event occurs or until after a specified period of time has expired.[37] This power could be used to coerce the obdurate spouse into compliance. Clearly there are some situations in which sale of property may be unwise: for example if ordering the sale of the former matrimonial home will result in both spouses and their children being homeless or if

---

[35] Including property owned with a third party: see eg *Harwood v Harwood* [1991] 2 FLR 274 in which the husband was ordered to assign to the wife the whole of his share of the assets of a dissolved partnership.

[36] *Young v Young* [1962] P 27. However, an outright transfer is not a settlement, see *Prescott v Fellowes* [1958] P 260.

[37] Section 24A(4).

liquidating assets which are income-producing will destroy the owning spouse's means of earning his livelihood.[38]

Where a sale order is made, it can contain a provision requiring the proceeds to be invested in a fund designed to secure an order for periodical payments for one of the parties, but such an order will cease to have effect on the death or remarriage of that party.[39] The court can require specified property to be offered for sale to a specified person.[40]

In effect, this means that the court can give one spouse the first option to buy out the other spouse's share in the matrimonial home (or other specified property). This is a valuable provision where one spouse is hostile to the other acquiring a particular family asset, and where he or she plans to dispose of it to someone else. Where someone other than the spouses has a beneficial interest in the property in question, this does not prevent an order for sale being made. However, the court must give that person the opportunity to make representations in relation to the order which are then taken into account alongside the other matters it is required to consider under section 25.[41]

## 3  Undertakings

Undertakings given to the court enable spouses to promise the court to do certain things which the court cannot order them to do because they fall outside the scope of the statutory framework.[42] As put by Butler-Sloss LJ (as she then was) in *Kensington Housing Trust v Oliver*:[43]

> Undertakings are convenient since a party can promise to do or abstain from that which a court would be unable to order. In that way an undertaking may cover a situation not capable of being the subject of a court order.

For example, it is commonplace for a husband to undertake to make the mortgage repayments on the former matrimonial home, to use his best endeavours to secure the release of the wife from her own obligations to the mortgagee, and to indemnify her should she be pursued for payments owing. Or he might undertake to take out insurance on his life in order to compensate his wife for her loss of expectation of a widow's pension,[44] to pay the children's school fees,[45] or to be solely responsible for specified debts. The advantage of arrangements agreed in this manner is that they can be more flexible, and more imaginative, than the range of orders available to courts. For example, Munby J held in *L v L*[46] that while the court was prohibited from awarding a spouse periodical payments beyond their remarriage, neither the legislation nor public policy prevented a former spouse from voluntarily assuming to pay maintenance beyond the payee's remarriage. Such a promise could be embodied in a formal undertaking.[47] Importantly, such undertakings are enforceable just as effectively as direct orders,[48] but of course a court cannot require a party who is not willing to do so to give undertakings. Undertakings, particularly when combined with consent orders, allow for consideration of a wide range of proposals about how best to untangle spouses' financial affairs, and how best to make financial and property provision for their future.

---

[38]  *Martin v Martin* [1976] 3 All ER 625; *P v P (Financial Provision: Lump Sum)* [1978] 3 All ER 70; *P v P (Financial Provision)* [1989] 2 FLR 241.

[39]  Section 24A(5).     [40]  Section 24A(2)(b).     [41]  Section 24A(6).

[42]  For a general review on undertakings, see D. Burrows, 'Undertakings and Consent Orders' [1998] Family Law 158.

[43]  (1997) 30 HLR 608 at 611.     [44]  *Le Marchant v Le Marchant* [1977] 3 All ER 610.

[45]  *Gandolfo v Gandolfo* [1980] 1 All ER 833. See too *Omielan v Omielan* [1996] 2 FLR 306 where the husband gave up his share altogether in the house, and the wife's share was reduced from 50 per cent to 25 per cent, the children to gain the remaining 75 per cent. Such an arrangement was one which could not properly have been ordered by the court.

[46]  [2008] 1 FLR 26.     [47]  [2008] 1 FLR 26 at [101].     [48]  *Livesey v Jenkins* [1985] 1 All ER 106.

# 4  **The clean break**

The introduction of the clean break provisions in the legislation marked a shift in thinking away from the desirability of requiring a husband to provide continuing maintenance for his wife for the rest of her life, which had previously been a commonplace feature of court orders, towards an approach which, in appropriate cases, leads to each spouse becoming financially independent of the other. This shift had already started to permeate the reasoning of the courts before it received legislative approval. The motive was expressed by Lord Scarman in *Minton v Minton*[49] when he said:

> The law now encourages spouses to avoid bitterness after family breakdown and to settle their money and property problems. An object of the modern law is to encourage the parties to put the past behind them and to begin a new life which is not over-shadowed by the relationship which has broken down.[50]

The following features should be noted about the clean break provisions.

## 4.1  **Section 25A(1)**

Section 25A(1) imposes a duty on a court to consider, in all cases, whether the parties' obligations towards each other should be terminated as soon after the decree as the court considers just and reasonable.[51] This is a strong directive, but it is ameliorated by the language in which the court's discretion is couched. The court must ask itself whether it is *appropriate* so to exercise its powers; and whether the outcome will be *just and reasonable*. It can be seen that neither spouse is given preferential treatment. Rather the requirement is framed in terms which allow the court to consider the circumstances of both parties. Lady Hale described the approach under section 25A(1) as follows:

> It assumes that the court has decided that some award is appropriate . . . The court is then required to consider whether it could achieve an appropriate result by bringing their mutual obligations to an end. This is a clear steer in the direction of lump sum and property adjustment orders with no continuing periodical payments. But it does not tell us much about what an appropriate result would be.[52]

There is no presumption for a clean break but there may be some circumstances when a clean break may be appropriate and the courts strive for 'independent finances and self-sufficiency'.[53] The Court of Appeal made it clear in *Matthews v Matthews*[54] that, pursuant to section 25A, there is a 'statutory steer' towards a clean break order and that it should be made whenever possible. In some cases, a continuing set of orders may not offer any benefit to the spouse, for example where periodical payments in a small sum are accompanied by a similar reduction in welfare benefits.[55] In such cases the policy of the clean break is in tension with the policy that spouses should make financial provision for each other and not the state. Where, however, the latter policy would tie the spouses together in the long term with little advantage, the policy of the clean break may prevail. If the marriage is very short and childless,[56] or the parties are in established careers,[57] the court may be persuaded that the parties can reach a state of financial independence. If the parties are very wealthy, the courts may be able to find sufficient capital to produce a clean break.

---

[49] [1979] 1 All ER 79.       [50] Ibid, 87.       [51] See *Suter v Suter and Jones* [1987] 2 All ER 336.
[52] *Miller; McFarlane* [2006] UKHL 24 at [130].       [53] Ibid, [39].       [54] [2013] EWCA Civ 1874.
[55] *Ashley v Blackman* [1988] FCR 699.       [56] *Hobhouse v Hobhouse* [1999] 1 FLR 961.
[57] *Burgess v Burgess* [1996] 2 FLR 981, [2000] 3 FCR 555.

### 4.1.1 **Nominal orders**

The courts have held that it will be unusual for a clean break order to be made where there are young children of school age.[58] In these circumstances, the court can make a nominal sum periodical payments order (of say, 1p annually), to keep in place the possibility of variation upwards should the parties' circumstances change.[59] For example, in *Whiting v Whiting*[60] the Court of Appeal held that the trial judge had been entitled to take the view that periodical payments should be kept alive by a nominal sum order in case unforeseen contingencies, such as illness or redundancy, should prevent the wife from making adequate provision for her own needs, and made it necessary for her to look again to her ex-husband for support. However, much depends on the facts of each case and the Court of Appeal made it clear in *Matthews v Matthews*[61] that there is no presumption in favour of a continuing periodical payments order in favour of the parent with care of minor children.

## 4.2 **Section 25A(2)**

The court's duty under subsection (2) arises in a case when a clean break order is not appropriate and an order for periodical payments has been made. The court is then required to consider whether it would be appropriate to limit the term of these payments only to such term as would be sufficient to enable the recipient to adjust *without undue hardship* to the termination of his or her financial dependence on the other. In *Barrett v Barrett*[62] the Court of Appeal made clear that this provision does not say that there must be termination unless there are good reasons for there not to be. Rather the court must be satisfied on the evidence of the spouse's ability to adjust without undue hardship within any proposed term to be set.[63] As the Court of Appeal commented in *Flavell v Flavell*,[64] there is:

> often a tendency for these orders to be made more in hope than in serious expectation. Especially in judging the case of ladies in their middle years, the judicial-looking into a crystal ball very rarely finds enough of substance to justify a finding that adjustment can be made without undue hardship. All too often these orders are made without evidence to support them.

To what extent then are non-working claimants expected to obtain employment and become economically self-sufficient on divorce? The answer to this question depends on the circumstances of the case, in particular the reasons for lack of employment, their age, and the length of time for which they have been out of the labour market. A spouse who is not hampered by childcare responsibilities is not entitled simply to lapse into apathy with regard to obtaining employment; he or she is expected to make real efforts to obtain work. However, if the claimant is middle-aged and has been absent from the labour market for some time, the courts will not usually expect her to be able to secure full-time employment on divorce.[65] Thus the courts recognise the difficulties middle-aged spouses face in obtaining employment. As Heilbron J said of the wife in *M v M (Financial Provision)*:[66]

> The wife (and she will not mind my saying so) is no longer a young woman and she is beginning to enter the world of work from a base of 46 or 47 years of age. She is embarking on a difficult and

---

[58] See *Suter v Suter and Jones* [1987] 2 FLR 232; *Waterman v Waterman* [1989] 1 FLR 380.

[59] See s 31 for variation.

[60] [1988] 2 All ER 275; see also *Scallon v Scallon* [1990] 1 FLR 194; *Hepburn v Hepburn* [1989] 1 FLR 373.

[61] [2013] EWCA Civ 1874.     [62] [1988] 2 FLR 516.

[63] See *Murphy v Murphy* [2014] EWHC 2263 (Fam).

[64] [1997] 1 FLR 353. See *L v L* [2011] EWHC 2207 (Fam).

[65] *M v M (Financial Provision)* [1987] 2 FLR 1; *Leadbeater v Leadbeater* [1985] FLR 789; *Barrett v Barrett* [1988] 2 FLR 516; *A v A (Financial Provision)* [1998] 2 FLR 180.

[66] [1987] 2 FLR 1.

> unpredictable life in an increasingly difficult world of work—things do not get easier—and the older she gets, in all probability, the more difficult will it be for her, in my opinion, to work and make her way in that world of employment.

In *Boylan v Boylan*[67] it was held that it would be wrong to construe the words 'undue hardship' as referring solely to the bare needs of a former wife when assessing her ability to adjust to the termination of periodical payments. Rather, her reasonable requirements should be judged by the standard that she was the former wife of a man of substantial wealth.[68] As these cases show, one spouse's *past* contributions as primary caretaker may justifiably limit their economic self-sufficiency as their age and lack of recent training or qualifications may hinder their opportunities to re-enter the labour market.

The same may apply where the spouse currently has childcare responsibilities. In *Miller; McFarlane*[69] Lady Hale indicated that prioritising the children's welfare 'should also involve ensuring that their primary carer is properly provided for, because it is well known that the security and stability of children depends in large part upon the security and stability of their primary carers'.[70] Thus, although the clean break provisions in section 25A encourage the court to promote each party's self-sufficiency on divorce, the children's welfare will impact on the court's assessment of the financial needs of the residential parent. Indeed, it is unlikely that a court would expect a parent who is caring for young children to seek employment on divorce.[71] Much will depend on the facts of each individual case, but if the residential parent is caring for young children at the time of the divorce, then there may well be uncertainty about her capacity to achieve economic independence. As such, the court may not be able to predict when it would be appropriate to bring the maintenance obligation to an end and, in these circumstances, the court is likely to impose no time limit on the periodical payments order and to leave the payer to seek a variation of the order.[72] Even after a short marriage, the court may reach the same conclusion. In *C v C (Financial Relief: Short Marriage)*,[73] the wife's marriage to a very wealthy man had only lasted for a little over nine months, but the parties had a child who had health problems. The wife, too, had a 'fragile personality', and 'at the age of 40 [was] in that uncertain period in which it may be said she is not young and so her position in the labour market is obviously less favourable than when she was 30'.[74] The Court of Appeal, while acknowledging that the judge's award was at the very top end of the bracket, refused to interfere with the trial judge's decision to award her a lump sum of £195,000, and secured periodical payments of £19,500 per annum for herself, without limit of time.[75]

In *G v G*[76] the parties had been married for five years and had one child aged 4 at the time of the divorce. The parties' capital assets were divided equally but this was insufficient to meet the wife's

---

[67] [1988] 1 FLR 282.

[68] It was therefore held that the only way in which the wife's right to periodical payments could be terminated, in such a way as not to cause her undue hardship, would be by the payment to her of a lump sum sufficient to provide her with an income comparable to the amount she was receiving in periodical payments; see too *B v B (Financial Provision)* [1990] 1 FLR 20; *R v R (Financial Provision: Reasonable Needs)* [1994] 2 FLR 1044.

[69] [2006] UKHL 24.

[70] Ibid, [128]. Baroness Hale cited the work of Lewis in support of this argument. See J. Lewis, 'Debates and Issues Regarding Marriage and Cohabitation in the British and American Literature' (2001) 15(1) International Journal of Law, Policy and the Family 159.

[71] *Leadbetter v Leadbetter* [1985] 1 FLR 789.    [72] Ibid.    [73] [1997] 2 FLR 26.    [74] Ibid, 32.

[75] The husband was determined to pay his wife very little. He had met her when she was working as a 'high-class call-girl'. The husband deliberately concealed the extent of his assets and income. This led the judge to assume that he had capital assets of £1 million and an income of £100,000. Ward LJ commented more than once that he would not necessarily have made the same high level of provision as the trial judge. He emphasised the point which applies to all appeals, namely that it does not matter what the appeal court would have done, the question is whether the trial judge was plainly wrong. See also *B v B (Mesher Order)* [2002] EWHC 3106 (Fam).

[76] [2012] EWHC 167.

needs. The wife therefore claimed substantial periodical payments to be paid on a joint lives basis. While the wife had earning capacity—she worked as a barrister before the birth of the child—she argued that she should choose whether or not to return to work. The key question before the court, therefore, was the appropriate duration of the periodical payments order. Charles J rejected the wife's claim that she was entitled to remain at home indefinitely to care for the couple's child. He said that the objective of achieving a fair result as laid down by the House of Lords in *Miller; McFarlane*:

> i) is not met by an approach that seeks to achieve a dependence for life (or until re-marriage) for the payee spouse to fund a lifestyle equivalent to that enjoyed during the marriage (or parity if that level is not affordable for two households), but
>
> ii) is met by an approach that recognises that the aim is independence and self sufficiency based on all the financial resources that are available to the parties. From that it follows that:
>
> iii) generally, the marital partnership does not survive as a basis for the sharing of future resources (whether earned or unearned). But, and they are important buts:
>
>     a) the lifestyle enjoyed during the marriage sets a level or benchmark that is relevant to the assessment of the level of the independent lifestyles to be enjoyed by the parties,
>
>     b) the length of the marriage is relevant to determining the period for which that level of lifestyle is to be enjoyed by the payee (so long as this is affordable by the payor), and so also, if there is to be a return to a lesser standard of living for the payee, the period over which that transition should take place,
>
>     c) if the marriage is short, this supports the conclusion that the award should be directed to providing a transition over an appropriate period for the payee spouse to either a lower long term standard of living than that enjoyed during the marriage, or to one that is not contributed to by the other spouse,
>
>     d) the marriage, and the choices made by the parties during it, may have generated needs or disadvantages in attaining and funding self sufficient independence that (i) should be compensated, and (ii) make continuing dependence/provision fair,
>
>     e) the most common source of a continuing relationship generated need or disadvantage is the birth of children and their care,
>
>     f) a continuing relationship generated need is often reflected in a continuing contribution to the day to day care of the children of the relationship, that contribution being recognised by the continuing financial contribution of the paying spouse (which is a continuing contribution to the day to day care of the children),
>
>     g) the choices made by the parties as to the care of their children are an important factor in determining how that care should be provided and shared both by reference to day to day care and the funding of the independent households, and
>
>     h) the provisions of s. 25A must be taken into account.[77]

After considering the parties' common understandings about their working arrangements once their child was born, Charles J. awarded the wife periodical payments starting at £95,000 per annum. This was to be reduced after two, four, and six years respectively to take account of her increased earnings. After six years her periodical payments would reduce to £35,000 and this was to continue to be awarded as compensation for the relationship-generated disadvantage that she suffered as a result of her ongoing childcare obligations.

What is interesting in this case is the rejection of the wife's claim that she could simply choose not to return to work. On the facts of the case, she was young and had earning potential and

---

[77] Ibid, [136].

thus was expected to work, at least on a part-time basis. It was also relevant that the couple had a common understanding that the wife would not work while any of their children were of pre-school age, but after this point it was agreed that she would want to and would return to work on a part-time basis to allow her to continue to be the main day-to-day carer of the children.[78] This is not to suggest, however, that all caregiving wives will be expected to return to work. As noted by Charles J: 'Naturally, I recognise that in many cases where a wife has stayed at home to look after the children she will be awarded a joint lives periodical payments order, but this is not because she can simply choose whether or not to work. Rather, it is because she cannot fairly be expected to do so having regard to her earning capacity and her past and continuing care of the children.'[79]

However, there is no absolute principle that a caregiver can expect a joint lives periodical payments order, or can use the fact of caregiving to justify lifelong financial support from a former spouse. Indeed, the approach of the courts has shifted in this respect, and there is clear judicial encouragement for the use of clean break orders. Not only is there an increased use of term orders for spousal maintenance, but the courts now seem to favour terminating spousal maintenance at the earliest opportunity once the payee has had an opportunity to acclimatise herself to financial independence.[80] In *Wright v Wright*,[81] for example, the wife, who was 51, was expected to obtain employment as her childcare responsibilities reduced. Mr Wright was an equine surgeon, while Mrs Wright had worked prior to the marriage as a legal secretary but had left work to care for their two children, aged 16 and 10. They divorced in 2008 and Mr Wright was ordered to pay joint lives spousal maintenance of £33,200 per annum, and child maintenance of £10,400 per child per annum until they were 17. He was also ordered to pay school fees. In 2012 Mr Wright applied for a downwards variation of the order on two grounds. First, he argued that his financial circumstances had deteriorated. He reported that had planned to retire at 60 but as he had been unable to make sufficient pension contributions, that would be postponed until he was 65. Secondly, under the original order, Mrs Wright was expected to begin working again and make a contribution towards her expenditure within two years of the order being made, which she had not done. The judge was critical of the wife's failure to find employment and concluded that by the time of the husband's retirement he should no longer be paying spousal maintenance. The judge, therefore, concluded that spousal maintenance should be varied downwards over a 6 year period, after which the payments would cease. During this time, Mrs Wright was expected to gain experience and training to improve her earning capacity as her childcare responsibilities reduced. Mrs Wright sought permission to appeal which was refused.

The desire to end maintenance and achieve a clean break between the parties as soon as possible can also be seen in *SS v NS (Spousal Maintenance)*[82] where Mostyn J set out some key principles in respect of spousal maintenance.[83] On the issue of a clean break, Mostyn J said: 'In every case the court must consider a termination of spousal maintenance with a transition to independence as soon as it is just and reasonable. A term should be considered unless the payee would be unable to adjust without undue hardship to the ending of payments. A degree of (not undue) hardship in making the transition to independence is acceptable'.[84] He continued, 'if the choice between an extendable term and a joint lives order is finely balanced the statutory steer [towards a clean

---

[78] Ibid, [154].      [79] Ibid, [139].

[80] See, for example, *Grocholewska-Mullins v Mullins* [2014] EWCA Civ 148.      [81] [2015] EWCA Civ 201.

[82] [2014] EWHC 4183.

[83] For example, Mostyn J observed that the most common rationale to justify spousal maintenance was to meet the needs which the relationship has generated. He found it hard to see why a former spouse should have to meet one party's needs which were not causally connected to the marriage, unless these needs were looked at in a wider economic context (for example, to reduce reliance on the taxpayer). In these circumstances, he observed that an award should generally be aimed at alleviating significant hardship (Mostyn J referred to the decision of *Fisher v Fisher* [1988] EWCA Civ 4). He also noted that while the marital standard of living was relevant to the quantum of spousal maintenance, it was not decisive.

[84] [2014] EWHC 4183, at [46].

break] should militate in favour of the former'.[85] Thus, in order to achieve financial independence between the parties, we may see an increased use of term orders for spousal maintenance, although it remains the case that these can be extended in appropriate circumstances.

### 4.2.1 Extension of the term

An order will come to an end when its term expires. However, the initial decision to set a time limit on the periodical payments is not necessarily final, for there is a possibility of the order being varied in the future under section 31, and this could include the extension of the term during which payments are to be made, provided the application for extension is made during the currency of the term.[86] If a spouse applies for an extension of the periodical payments order, the court is again under a duty to consider bringing the payments to an end as soon as possible,[87] and it can order a lump sum, property adjustment order, or pension sharing order instead in order to achieve a clean break.[88]

### 4.2.2 A section 28(1A) direction

Clearly, the knowledge that such an application might be made could undermine the purpose of a clean break order which is intended to bring finality to the financial dependence of the payee, albeit postponed for the duration of the order.[89] Section 25A(2) should therefore be considered alongside section 28(1A). This provides:

> Where a periodical payments or secured periodical payments order in favour of a party to a marriage is made on or after the grant of a decree of divorce or nullity of marriage, the court may direct that that party shall not be entitled to apply under section 31 below for the extension of the term specified in the order.

Where such a direction is made, it prevents the party in receipt of periodical payments from applying in variation proceedings for an extension of the order.[90] In this way a postponed or deferred clean break can truly be achieved. In *Waterman v Waterman*[91] a judge set a term of five years in the case of a 38-year-old former secretary who had recently undertaken a computer course to obtain employment, and who had a 5-year-old child. The judge also attached a section 28(1A) direction. The Court of Appeal held that, while the five-year term was not of itself wrong, the section 28(1A) direction was inappropriate in such a case given a 'child of tender years' and uncertainty regarding the mother's future employment.

## 4.3 Section 25A(3)

Subsection (3) of section 25A contains the most draconian provision from the point of view of an applicant for a periodical payments order. It entitles a court to dismiss an application for periodical payments, and to direct that the applicant shall not be entitled to make any further application for an order for either secured or unsecured periodical payments. There are no words of guidance in subsection (3) on how a court should determine whether or not a continuing obligation should be imposed on one party to make, or secure, periodical payments in favour of the other, which seems to be a weakness in the drafting of this provision. The court will, of course, follow the statutory

---

[85]　Ibid.

[86]　*T v T (Financial Provision)* [1988] 1 FLR 480; *Richardson v Richardson* [1993] 4 All ER 673; *Yates v Yates* [2012] EWCA Civ 532; *North v North* [2007] EWCA Civ 760.

[87]　MCA 1973, s 31(7).　　[88]　Section 31(7B).

[89]　For discussion, see E. Cooke, 'Making the Clean Break Squeaky Clean' [1994] Family Law 268.

[90]　*L v L (Financial Remedies: Deferred Clean Break)* [2011] EWHC 2207 (Fam). See also N. Allen and V. Taylor, 'Till Death or Remarriage do our Finances Part: *L v L*' (2012) Family Law 665.

[91]　[1989] 1 FLR 380.

guidelines provided in section 25 in the exercise of its powers in general, but they are not specifically focused on periodical payments orders. It seems paradoxical that a court must consider the issue of the payee's adjustment without undue hardship to an order being terminated when limiting the duration of a periodical payments order, but not when refusing to make one altogether.

# 5 Exercise of the court's discretion

## 5.1 Refusal to exercise discretion on policy grounds

On rare occasions, the court may refuse to exercise its discretion for reasons of public policy. In *Whiston v Whiston*[92] the 'wife' was a bigamist and applied for financial orders ancillary to nullity proceedings. The Court of Appeal refused to exercise its discretion in her favour, holding that as a matter of public policy the 'wife' should not benefit from her crime. The court held that the fact that conduct is one of the factors in section 25(2) of the MCA 1973 should not prevent the application of this doctrine. There is, however, no universal rule precluding the exercise of the court's discretion in favour of a bigamist, for example where both spouses are knowing parties to a bigamous marriage.[93]

## 5.2 The court's general direction in section 25(1)

### 5.2.1 All the circumstances

Section 25(1) requires the court to have regard to all the circumstances of the case. The courts are given a very wide discretion to make financial orders which suit the needs of individual cases, albeit guided by the various factors in the statutory framework.[94] The legislation 'provides the jurisdiction for all applications for financial relief from the poverty-stricken to the multimillionaire'[95] and so the application of the statutory criteria will depend very much on the facts and circumstances of each individual case. Thus the value of precedent is limited. The Court of Appeal can only interfere with the judge's exercise of discretion if he or she has taken into account an irrelevant matter or failed to take into account a relevant matter, or the judge's weighing of factors is plainly wrong. As Lord Hoffmann observed in *Piglowska v Piglowski*[96] appellate courts must permit pluralism in these matters. Thus there is no easy and straightforward answer to the question: 'How will the parties' property and income be divided and distributed between the spouses when their marriage is terminated by divorce?' Moreover, in many cases there will be a range of possible solutions which could either be negotiated between the spouses or ordered by a court. So the law in this area can be unpredictable, with obvious impact on the length of time sometimes needed to reach a negotiated settlement, if at all.

### 5.2.2 First consideration to welfare of children of the family

Section 25(1) provides that 'first' consideration must be given to the welfare while a minor of any child of the family who has not attained the age of 18. A child of the family is defined in section 52 of the MCA 1973 as a child of both of the parties; and any other child, not being a child who is placed with those parties as foster parents by a local authority or voluntary organisation, who has been treated by both of those parties as a child of their family. Whether a child has been so treated is a matter of fact, determined according to how the parties have behaved towards the child.[97]

---

[92] [1995] 2 FLR 268.    [93] See *Rampal v Rampal (No 2)* [2001] EWCA Civ 989, [2002] Fam 85.
[94] See *Dart v Dart* [1996] 2 FLR 286 at 294 where Thorpe LJ commented: 'Parliament might have opted for a community of property system or some fraction approach. It opted instead for a wide judicial discretion that would produce a bespoke solution to fit the infinite variety of individual cases.'
[95] *Dart v Dart* [1996] 2 FLR 286 at 303, *per* Butler-Sloss LJ.    [96] [1999] 2 FLR 763, HL.
[97] See further discussion in Chapter 6 on child support.

In *Suter v Suter and Jones*[98] the Court of Appeal explained that the words 'first consideration' mean that the child's welfare is to be 'regarded as of first importance to be borne in mind throughout consideration of all the circumstances' but that it is not the overriding consideration.[99] The section requires 'the court to consider all the circumstances . . . always bearing in mind the important consideration of the welfare of the children, and then try to attain a financial result which is just as between husband and wife'.[100]

The focus on the welfare of the children required by section 25(1) means that 'in the ordinary case the court's first concern will be to provide a home for the primary carer and the children' and 'in many cases the satisfaction of that need may absorb all that is immediately available'.[101] Although financial support for children themselves is dealt with in law as a separate issue, the welfare of the children will be integrally bound with the appropriate level of financial provision for the spouse who is continuing to provide the primary care for the children.[102] This will usually mean that the spouse who is looking after the children will need an appropriate home, if possible by way of retention of the use of the former matrimonial home.[103] The presence of young children will also mean that it is unlikely that the court would expect a parent who is caring for the children to find full-time employment.[104]

### 5.3 **The statutory factors: section 25(2)**

After considering the welfare of the children, section 25(2) provides a list of factors to which the court must have regard when considering the appropriate financial provision order to make.

### 5.3.1 **Financial resources of each spouse**

#### Key legislation

Section 25(2)(a) provides that the court must have regard to:

> the income, earning capacity, property and other financial resources which each of the parties to the marriage has or is likely to have in the foreseeable future, including in the case of earning capacity any increase in that capacity which it would in the opinion of the court be reasonable to expect a party to the marriage to take steps to acquire.

Section 25(2)(a) concentrates attention on the spouses' resources. In *Pearce v Pearce*[105] Ormrod LJ commented that:

> [t]he word 'resources' in s. 25 is entirely unqualified, there are no words of limitation upon it, and so the court should approach the matter realistically, taking into account all the available resources and doing justice in all the circumstances of the case between the spouses in a realistic fashion, dealing with real figures and not with artificially produced figures.[106]

---

[98]  [1987] Fam 111.       [99]  Ibid, 123.       [100]  Ibid.

[101]  *Cordle v Cordle* [2002] 1 FCR 97 at [33], *per* Thorpe LJ; and see E. Jackson, F. Wasoff, M. Maclean, and R. Dobash, 'Financial Support on Divorce: The Right Mixture of Rules and Discretion?' (1993) 7 International Journal of Law and the Family 230.

[102]  See eg *Waterman v Waterman* [1989] 1 FLR 380.

[103]  See *B v B (Financial Provision: Welfare of Child and Conduct)* [2002] 1 FLR 555. See also the recognition in *Miller; McFarlane* [2006] UKHL 24 at [142], that the law has been extremely 'successful in retaining a home for the children'.

[104]  *Leadbetter v Leadbetter* [1985] 1 FLR 789. See also *G v G* [2012] EWHC 167.       [105]  [1980] 1 FLR 261.

[106]  Ibid, 267.

Thus, for example, the court has taken account of inherited wealth acquired after the parties separated, and which in no way formed part of the original matrimonial assets.[107] Expectations of inheritance give rise to difficulty because there is no knowing when the testator will die and whether his or her will may be altered. These expectations have therefore sometimes been deemed too uncertain to be included.[108] In some cases, however, the court may adjourn the proceedings pending receipt of the inheritance.[109] However, the courts have been prepared, in principle, to take account of all present and future resources and they have been prepared to widen the purse to the maximum extent. Thus, for example, personal injury damages can be taken into account.[110] The manner of the distribution of such damages is, of course, still a matter within the court's discretion, and likely to be influenced by section 25(2)(e), which looks to any mental or physical disability of either party. Moreover, where the injured party has very considerable needs there may be no readily available capital which is transferable to the other party.[111]

A difficulty occurs where a spouse enjoys access to wealth but is not entitled to it, or where he or she has substantial means but has an immediate liquidity problem. In *Thomas v Thomas*[112] the husband was a prosperous businessman and the court would normally have made a substantial financial order for the benefit of the wife and children. However, he had a large loan secured on the family home and he claimed that he was unable to offer any alternative security which would be acceptable to the bank. He also stated that his immediate income was modest. However, this was because it was derived from a family business of which he was joint managing director, and the company had a policy of ploughing back profits and paying relatively modest salaries to the directors, while at the same time making very generous provision for them by way of pension provision. The Court of Appeal adopted a robust approach. Waite LJ made it plain that 'the court is not obliged to limit its orders exclusively to resources of capital or income which are shown actually to exist. The availability of unidentified resources may, for example, be inferred from a spouse's expenditure or style of living, or from his inability or unwillingness to allow the complexity of his affairs to be penetrated with the precision necessary to ascertain his actual wealth or the degree of liquidity of his assets.' Moreover 'there will be occasions when it becomes permissible for a judge deliberately to frame his orders in a form which affords judicious encouragement to third parties to provide the maintaining spouse with the means to comply with the court's view of the justice of the case'.[113] However, this must be viewed alongside the general rule that, when assessing resources, the court cannot take account of the assets of a third party. As such, the willingness of the court to make an award which can only be met through the provision of funds from a third party is limited. In *TL v ML*[114] the claimant wife argued that the court should take into account the husband's parents' resources under section 25(2)(a) and that the court should 'judicially encourage' his parents to make funds available to meet her award. The court rejected this claim on the basis that the husband had no beneficial interest in these assets and, as such, it would be wrong in principle to make an award which ranged outside resources which were the husband's as of right.[115] In *TL v ML* the court commented:

> [I]f the court is satisfied on the balance of probabilities that an outsider will provide money to meet an award that a party cannot meet from his absolute property then the court can, if it is fair to do

---

[107] *Schuller v Schuller* [1990] 2 FLR 193.

[108] *Michael v Michael* [1986] 2 FLR 389; *K v K (Conduct)* [1990] 2 FLR 225.

[109] See eg *MT v MT (Financial Provision: Lump Sum)* [1992] 1 FLR 366 where the husband was entitled to a substantial inheritance from his elderly father under German law. Bracewell J adjourned the proceedings until the inheritance vested, although it seems that this power will only be exercised in unusual cases.

[110] *Mansfield v Mansfield* [2011] EWCA Civ 1056; *Daubney v Daubney* [1976] 2 All ER 453; *Wagstaff v Wagstaff* [1992] 1 All ER 275.

[111] *C v C (Financial Provision: Personal Damages)* [1995] 2 FLR 171.     [112] [1995] 2 FLR 668.

[113] Ibid, 670. The husband was appealing against a lump sum order of £150,000 plus £8,000 for a car and periodical payments of £1,500 per month on the ground that he had neither the capital nor income to pay because his resources were all absorbed by the family business. His appeal was dismissed.

[114] [2006] 1 FCR 465.

[115] The court noted that, by contrast, in *Thomas v Thomas* [1996] 2 FLR 668 'no part of the ancillary relief award ranged over assets or income that were not Mr Thomas' as of right', at [82].

so, make an award on that footing. But if it is clear that the outsider, being a person who has only historically supplied bounty, will not, reasonably or unreasonably, come to the aid of the payer then there is precious little the court can do about it.[116]

Another issue is the extent to which assets belonging to a limited company (which one party to the divorce may control) can be used to fund a settlement on divorce. It is important to note that a limited company has a separate legal personality from its members, and can hold property in its own name. Thus, one question which the Supreme Court recently had to address is whether property which is vested in companies which are owned and controlled by one spouse can be transferred to the other spouse in a financial provision order on divorce. In other words, are assets belonging to companies substantially owned by one party to the marriage available for distribution under section 24 of the MCA 1973? In *Prest v Petrodel*[117] the Supreme Court unanimously answered this question in the affirmative holding that, in the circumstances of the case, the properties were held by the husband's companies on a resulting trust for him since they was purchased from funds supplied by him rather than from the resources or profits of the company. As such, he was beneficially entitled to the properties and they could therefore be transferred to his wife on divorce. However, the Supreme Court made it clear that a company does have a separate legal personality, and that the court will not, as a matter of routine, 'pierce the corporate veil' to access property belonging to the company in order to fund a divorce settlement. Indeed, this will only be done in certain limited circumstances, in particular where a company structure has been set up deliberately by one party in an attempt to keep assets out of the reach of their former spouse on divorce.

### 5.3.1.1 Income and earning capacity

The court must have regard to any income and earning capacity of the parties, and the reference to an increase in earning capacity in section 25(2)(a) reinforces the clean break provisions in section 25A, and the thinking that, where appropriate, the aim should be to enable the spouses to become financially independent of one another. This is discussed further in Section 4 on the clean break.

If a spouse deliberately reduces his working hours, gives up a job, or is paid less than the normal rate for the work he is doing, the court can base its order on what he or she could earn.[118] A court may deem a person to be deliberately unemployed and make an order on the assumption that they could obtain work if they tried.[119] However, there is a risk that a court will make the assumption that a spouse could obtain work if he or she makes the effort, without there being any real evidence to substantiate this approach. The danger to the spouse who is wrongly labelled as 'work shy' by a court, and being ordered to make periodical payments on the basis of what the court believes him to be capable of earning, was graphically spelled out by Finer J in *Williams v Williams*,[120] when he reminded courts that the ultimate sanction for non-payment of periodical payments is imprisonment. He also stated that it is wrong for courts to make decisions on the footing of impressions about demeanour or generalised local knowledge, important as these factors may be, unchecked by all the hard information that may be available about a man's earning capacity and his chances of employment.[121] These were salutary words, which should be borne in mind particularly at times of high unemployment. There is a real risk that orders may be based on hunch and prejudice, especially if the political climate is one in which those persons who cannot obtain work are labelled as lacking the requisite initiative and drive to seek the employment which is allegedly available.

---

[116] [2006] 1 FCR 465 at [101]. See also *M v W (Ancillary Relief)* [2010] EWHC 1155 (Fam).
[117] [2013] UKSC 34.    [118] *Hardy v Hardy* (1981) 2 FLR 321.
[119] *McEwan v McEwan* [1972] 2 All ER 708.    [120] [1974] 3 All ER 377.
[121] See *N v F* [2011] EWHC 586 (Fam), [2012] 1 FCR 139 (evidence required, not anecdotal scraps).

### 5.3.1.2 Resources provided by a new spouse or partner

One of the most difficult issues of principle and policy which a court may have to grapple with is to what extent, if at all, it should take account of a new partner's resources when considering the spouses' resources. This difficulty is exacerbated when the new relationship is an unmarried relationship.[122] The simple answer to the question whether property belonging to a new spouse or partner can be treated as a resource under section 25(2)(a) is 'yes'. However, the extent to which a new spouse or partner's resources will influence the way the parties' own assets are distributed is a question for the discretion of the judge, 'not to be circumscribed by declarations of principle which run the risk of fettering the future exercise of what was meant to be a very flexible discretion indeed'.[123]

Where the resources available for distribution are being stretched then the actual, or anticipated, contribution by a new spouse or partner will assume greater significance and may need to be taken fully into consideration by the court when it decides what orders to make. It will normally not be possible for a court accurately to quantify the extent of a new spouse's, or partner's, assets, because he or she cannot usually be compelled to give precise evidence of means to the court.[124] However, as the court pointed out in *Frary v Frary*,[125] where the husband cannot persuade his partner to give such evidence, he takes the risk that the court will base its order on general assertions and assumptions about the extent of the new partner's means.[126]

For example, the fact that one spouse has accommodation provided by a new spouse may lead to the postponement of the realisation of his or her interest in the matrimonial home, and to the quantification of his or her share in the value of the home being reduced. In *Martin v Martin*[127] the husband was living with a woman, whom he intended to marry, in her council house. He gave evidence that the tenancy could be transferred into their joint names. The court took account of the husband's occupation of the council house and treated it as part of his resources affecting his needs. Consequently, it gave the wife a life interest in the former matrimonial home, followed by an equal division of the proceeds of sale.[128] Provision made for the husband by a second partner was taken into account in *Mesher v Mesher and Hall*.[129] Here the woman whom the husband intended to marry had provided a deposit for their new home. Her injection of these resources meant that the husband's housing needs were being met, whereas the wife needed to live in the former matrimonial home. The wife's greater needs led to the husband's entitlement to receive his share in the proceeds of sale of the former matrimonial home being postponed until the spouses' youngest child reached 17.

### 5.3.1.3 Periodical payments where a spouse is living with a new partner

Under section 28(1)(a) of the MCA 1973, an order for periodical payments automatically comes to an end when the recipient spouse remarries. This rule does not apply to a party's mere cohabitation with another. However, the court can take the recipient's new living arrangements into consideration which may result in the payments being varied or brought to an end under section 33.[130]

---

[122] Given that unmarried couples, in legal terms, do not owe each other mutual obligations of financial support, it would be inconsistent then to *assume* that the cohabiting couple will share their resources and provide for each other.

[123] *Atkinson v Atkinson (No 2)* [1996] 1 FLR 51 at 54.

[124] *Wynne v Wynne and Jeffers* [1980] 3 All ER 659; *Frary v Frary* [1993] 2 FLR 696; *Morgan v Morgan* [1977] 2 All ER 515. The court held in *M v M (Financial Misconduct; Subpoena Against Third Party)* [2006] 2 FCR 555, that Article 8 of the European Convention on Human Rights (right to respect for private and family life, home and correspondence) reinforces the 'principle that an order for disclosure is an intrusion into an individual's privacy that is oppressive and unwarranted unless it can be shown to be both necessary and proportionate to the issues in the case', at [115].

[125] [1993] 2 FLR 696.    [126] See also *W v W (Disclosure by Third Party)* (1981) 2 FLR 291.

[127] [1977] 3 All ER 762.

[128] This case was heavily influenced by the policy target under s 25 as originally drafted. However, the principle is clear, namely that housing provided by a new partner is a relevant consideration.

[129] [1980] 1 All ER 126n.    [130] *Atkinson v Atkinson* [1988] Fam 93; *Fleming v Fleming* [2004] 1 FLR 667.

In *Atkinson v Atkinson*[131] it was argued that a wife who cohabits permanently with another man should not be in a better position than a wife who remarries, especially if the motive for cohabitation rather than remarriage is financial. In *Atkinson* the wife was receiving £6,000 per annum in periodical payments which she would automatically lose if she remarried. The man with whom she was living had only a very modest income, and she was therefore heavily reliant on the money she was receiving from her ex-husband. The Court of Appeal held that the fact of cohabitation is a matter to be taken into account by the court, and is conduct which it would be inequitable to disregard under paragraph (g). Thus, according to the court, the financial consequences of cohabitation may be such that it would be inappropriate for maintenance to continue because the cohabitant can be expected to contribute to the running costs of the household. However, the court stated that, in general, there is no statutory requirement to give decisive weight to the fact of cohabitation and that it should *not* be equated with remarriage without legislative sanction.[132]

Another attempt to persuade the Court of Appeal that it was manifestly unjust for a cohabiting wife of a wealthy ex-husband to receive anything other than nominal periodical payments was made in *Atkinson v Atkinson (No 2)*.[133] The court rejected this submission, stating that it was 'too crude a view', and held that Thorpe J had been entitled to take into account 'the length of the marriage, the contribution made during the marriage by the wife to the care of the home, the upbringing of the children . . . and the opportunity she provided to the husband to pursue his very successful business activities'.[134] On the broader policy issue of the proper principles to be adopted in cases where a spouse is living in a new and permanent relationship, the Court of Appeal responded that Parliament had intended that this should be a matter for the discretion of the judge, and that the discretion should not be circumscribed by declarations of principle which ran the risk of fettering the exercise of what was meant to be a very flexible discretion indeed.[135] In *Fleming v Fleming*,[136] the Court of Appeal similarly rejected the argument that marriage should be equated with cohabitation for the purposes of bringing a periodical payments order to an end. However, in *K v K (Periodical Payment: Cohabitation)*[137] Coleridge J observed that the social acceptance of cohabitation had changed dramatically over the last 30 years, commenting:

> The concept of cohabitation is now as normal, commonplace and acceptable as marriage. At every level of society and amongst all adult age groups people cohabit without a second thought. It carries no social stigma whatever. Nor for that matter does the birth of children outside marriage.[138]

Given this 'social revolution',[139] he questioned why the consequences of cohabitation should not be the same as the consequences of a remarriage on an existing periodical payments order.[140] As Moor notes, 'for the first time in any reported judgment' the court considered that 'as a matter of principle, cohabitation was a relevant factor on an application to vary/terminate a spousal maintenance order'.[141] The court also considered that there was nothing in the legislation to prevent a court from making an order with would terminate on cohabitation after a certain period. However, more recently in *Grey v Grey*[142] the Court of Appeal approved the position in *Fleming*. Thorpe LJ observed that this approach is still 'sufficiently flexible to enable the court to do justice

---

131 [1987] 3 All ER 849.     132 On the facts of the case, the wife's payments were reduced to £4,500.
133 [1996] 1 FLR 51.     134 Ibid, 54.
135 See too *S v S* [1987] 1 FLR 71 where Waite J held that the weight given to a new partner's income will turn on such factors as the permanency of the relationship, the amount of support the wife is obtaining, and how much she needs.
136 [2004] 1 FLR 667.     137 [2005] EWHC 2886 (Fam).     138 Ibid, [2].     139 Ibid.
140 In this case, the husband and wife had been divorced for seven years. On divorce the wife had been awarded periodical payments of £16,000 per annum index linked (currently worth £18,955 per annum) and the husband now sought a downward variation of the payments to take account not only of his changed financial circumstances but of his former wife's settled cohabitation for three years. In taking account of the wife's cohabitation, the court reduced the periodical payments to £12,000 per annum, capitalising the payment at the sum of £100,000.
141 P. Moor, 'Key Developments in Ancillary Relief' [2008] Family Law 44 at 46.     142 [2010] 1 FCR 394.

and to reflect social and moral shifts within our society'.[143] Thus while it remains the case that cohabitation with another will not automatically bring a periodical payments order to an end, the recipient's new living arrangements will be taken into account along with a consideration of what the new partner should be contributing to the household when assessing the level of periodical payments.

A different question arises when the respondent to an application for periodical payments, usually the husband, has remarried or is living with another woman who has an income of her own. To what extent can the new partner's income be taken into account when assessing how much the husband ought to pay for the support of his first family? It has been held that a court cannot require a second wife directly to contribute to the periodical payments paid by a husband for the support of his former wife and children. Consequently, if the husband has no income at all of his own, and his second wife is the breadwinner in the family, no order for periodical payments can be made against the husband.[144] In *Macey v Macey*[145] it was held that a magistrates' court had erred in law when taking into account the second woman's income as part of the available funds from which an order for periodical payments could be paid. However, the position is a subtle one. The court held that where the husband derives benefits from his new partner's income, which means that a greater part of his own income is available to pay maintenance to his first wife and children, an order can be made on the basis that the husband may need less money to support his new family.[146] While the new partner's income cannot be brought directly into account, it can be taken into consideration as a cushion for the spouse's expenses. This has the practical consequence that a husband can be ordered to pay more by way of periodical payments to his first family when his new partner has her own income, than he would be required to do where she has not.

### 5.3.1.4 Full and frank disclosure of resources is required

Each party is under a duty to make full and frank disclosure of all material facts to the other party and to the court. What can a judge do where he or she forms the opinion that one party has deliberately failed or refused to make full and frank disclosure and has concealed his true financial position from the other party? Courts have been encouraged to adopt a robust response to deliberate non-disclosure, to draw adverse inferences against the recalcitrant party,[147] and to make findings about their actual financial circumstances applying a simple balance of probabilities test. Where this results in the non-disclosing party being assumed to have more assets than is the true position, they have only themselves to blame.[148] A costs penalty can also be imposed on the dishonest party. The courts are conscious that the integrity of the legal process would be severely undermined if a party were able deliberately to evade the duty to disclose.[149] Indeed, a recent case shows that, in extreme cases, an individual who fails to disclose the full extent of their assets can find themselves in contempt of court and at risk of imprisonment. In *Young v Young*[150] the husband alleged that he was penniless and bankrupt but his wife argued that he was a very wealthy man with assets of up to £400m. She alleged that he had hidden his entire resources to evade his financial obligations to her and their children. On the facts of the case, the husband had consistently failed to provide any details of his income and resources for five years. Mr Justice Moor found that this was a 'flagrant and deliberate contempt over a very long period' which justified imprisonment for a period of six months. While this is an extreme case and the other sanctions at the court's disposal mean that it will not usually be necessary to impose a term of imprisonment for failure to comply with an order

---

[143] Ibid, [43].    [144] *Brown v Brown* (1981) 3 FLR 161; *Berry v Berry* [1986] 1 FLR 618.    [145] (1981) 3 FLR 7.
[146] See also *Wilkinson v Wilkinson* (1980) 10 Fam Law 48.    [147] *Pasha v Pasha* [2001] EWCA Civ 466.
[148] *Baker v Baker* [1995] 2 FLR 829; *Gulobovich v Gulobovich* [2011] EWCA Civ 479; *NG v SG* [2011] EWHC 3270 (Fam).
[149] In *W v W (Ancillary Relief: Non-Disclosure)* [2003] 3 FCR 385 the court said that 'where it is found that a party has deliberately . . . misrepresented facts then he must expect judicial censure and penalties in costs', at [3].
[150] [2013] EWHC 34 (Fam).

for disclosure, it illustrates that repeatedly failing to make full and frank disclosure can result in such drastic measures.[151]

### 5.3.2 Financial needs, obligations, and responsibilities

Section 25(2(b) requires the court to take account of:

> the financial needs, obligations and responsibilities which each of the parties to the marriage has or is likely to have in the foreseeable future.

The court's first consideration will be the parties' housing needs.[152] Where there is sufficient to go beyond housing provision for children and a primary caretaker, 'the court's concern will be to provide the means for the absent parent to rehouse'.[153] As Thorpe LJ has commented:

> [I]n any case where there is, by stretch and a degree of risk-taking, the possibility of a division to enable both to rehouse themselves, that is an exceptionally important consideration and one which will almost invariably have a decisive impact on outcome.[154]

It is usually only the financial needs which have been generated by the marriage which become the responsibility of a former spouse on divorce.[155] Moreover, it is only financial obligations which have been reasonably assumed which will be taken into account, although the courts have accepted that the words 'obligations and responsibilities' embrace obligations not only to the ex-spouse and children, but also other family obligations, such as to elderly parents or other relatives. The inclusion of these words allows the claims of any new dependants to be brought into the weighing-up process. Thus, if by the time the court makes its order one of the parties has remarried and undertaken financial responsibility for a new spouse and her children, or if he is cohabiting and has taken on similar obligations, this will be taken into account. However, the court will not allow one party to live a lavish or extravagant lifestyle and claim this as a source of needs.[156]

### 5.3.3 The standard of living before the breakdown of the marriage

Paragraph (c) of section 25(2) requires the court to take account of:

> the standard of living enjoyed by the family before the breakdown of the marriage.

In the case of families of limited or average means, it is inevitable that the standard of living of each spouse will fall because resources which are adequate to keep one family at a standard of living which allows for small luxuries, when divided between two households will often barely keep each household in necessities. In the case of a wealthy spouse, there will be greater scope for the standard

---

[151] See the recent decision of the Supreme Court in *Sharland v Sharland* [2015] UKSC 60; *Gohil v Gohil* [2015] UKSC 61, discussed in section 9.2.

[152] *Cordle v Cordle* [2002] 1 FCR 97 at [33], *per* Thorpe LJ.

[153] Ibid, [33]. The court will attempt to house the children at a similar standard to that which was enjoyed during the marriage, *Robson v Robson* [2010] EWCA Civ 1171.

[154] *M v B (Ancillary Proceedings: Lump Sum)* [1998] 2 FLR 53 at 60.

[155] *Miller; McFarlane* [2006] UKHL 24 at [11], *per* Lord Nicholls. Baroness Hale said the three strands of fairness which underpin resource distribution on divorce are 'linked to the parties' relationship, either causally or temporally, and not to extrinsic, unrelated factors, such as a disability arising after the marriage has ended', at [137]. See also *J v J (Financial Orders: Wife's Long-term Needs)* [2011] EWHC 1010 (Fam). In *SS v NS* [2014] EWHC 4183 (Fam) Mostyn J found it hard to see why a former spouse should have to meet one party's needs which were not causally connected to the marriage, unless these needs were looked at in a wider economic context (for example, to reduce reliance on the taxpayer). In these circumstances, he observed that an award should generally be aimed at alleviating significant hardship (see *Fisher v Fisher* [1988] EWCA Civ 4).

[156] *North v North* [2007] 2 FCR 601.

of living enjoyed during the marriage to impact on the outcome. In *Preston v Preston*,[157] Ormrod LJ said 'the wife of a millionaire and 23 years married is entitled to expect a very high standard of living which would include a home in a house or flat at the top end of the market, and probably a second home in the country or abroad, together with a very high spending power'.[158] Thus, where resources permit such an assessment, the marital standard of living is important when determining the level of award to which the claimant is entitled. However, while the marital standard of living is a consideration, the House of Lords made it clear in *Miller; McFarlane*,[159] that there is no legitimate expectation that a particular standard of living will be maintained.

### 5.3.4 The age of each party and the duration of the marriage

Section 25(2)(d) directs the court's attention to:

> the age of each party to the marriage and the duration of the marriage.

A person's age is likely to impact on their financial prospects and, in particular, their 'earning capacity' to which the court has specific regard under section 25(2)(a). Thus, in light of these provisions, a court is likely to want to be given information about the following matters: the impact of an unemployed wife's age on whether she can be expected to obtain work; how old she will be when the children cease to be dependent; where the husband is unemployed, whether at his age he can expect to gain further employment; and where both parties are in middle age, what their financial positions will be on retirement. The age of the husband was an important consideration in *Greenham v Greenham*.[160] The trial judge had ordered that the former matrimonial home, in which the husband was living, should be sold when the husband attained the age of 70. The Court of Appeal held, however, that the judge had been wrong to include this provision. Even though the husband would probably be in a secure financial position at that age, and would be able to afford to pay the wife her share in the property, it was unreasonable to force him to move house at the age of 70.[161]

Following the jurisprudence of the House of Lords in *White v White*[162] and *Miller; McFarlane*,[163] the idea of marriage as a partnership of equals applies to all marriages.[164] Thus, financial awards in short marriage cases are no longer limited to the pre-*White* position of simply getting the wife back on her feet,[165] or to compensate her for any financial disadvantage arising as a result of the marriage.[166] If one party makes substantial assets during the marriage, whatever its length, then the other is entitled to some share in these assets. Thus in *Miller v Miller*,[167] the marriage lasted just three years but the wife was awarded a hefty £5 million on divorce. The court justified this on the grounds that this money was generated during the marriage.

#### 5.3.4.1 Can pre-marital cohabitation be taken into account?

It is becoming increasingly commonplace for couples to cohabit before they marry, and consequently various cases have had to consider whether pre-marital cohabitation can be taken into account, either as part of the circumstances of the case or, more interestingly, as part of the duration of the marriage.

In *Foley v Foley*[168] the Court of Appeal made clear that the statute refers to the 'duration of the marriage' and that periods of cohabitation and marriage are not the same. In that case, the parties

---

[157] [1982] 1 All ER 41.     [158] Ibid, 48.     [159] [2006] 1 FCR 213.     [160] [1989] 1 FLR 105.

[161] See also *S v S* [1977] 1 All ER 56, where the parties married over the age of 50 and the wife had pressing housing needs.

[162] [2001] 1 AC 596.     [163] [2006] UKHL 24.     [164] See Section 5.4.

[165] *Attar v Attar* [1985] FLR 649.

[166] As in the earlier case law such as *H v H (Financial Provision: Short Marriage)* (1981) 2 FLR 392, *Attar v Attar* [1985] FLR 649, and *Hedges v Hedges* [1991] 1 FLR 196. Of course, cases of limited financial resources will still have to focus primarily on meeting the parties' needs: *Miller; McFarlane* [2006] UKHL 24 at [55], *per* Lord Nicholls.

[167] [2006] 2 FCR 213.     [168] [1981] 2 All ER 857.

had lived together for seven years and had three children. They subsequently married but the marriage broke down and they divorced eight years later. The court treated the period when they were living together as 'one of the circumstances' to which the court was required to have regard, the weight to be attached to it being a matter for the court's discretion. The court held that it was entitled to give less weight to the period of cohabitation than to events occurring during the marriage, although the court also said that, where the parties cannot marry, the court could regard their cohabitation as a very weighty factor. This was the case in *Kokosinski v Kokosinski*,[169] where the husband had a wife in his native Poland from whom he was unable to obtain a divorce. The parties lived together for 25 years and had a son. They subsequently married but then only lived together for about four months. Wood J held that the 'welfare of the family' in section 25(2)(f) referred only to events which had occurred after the marriage took place. However, that did not mean that, on these exceptional facts, the 25 years' cohabitation was to be disregarded. Wood J pointed out that the court must also have regard to conduct,[170] and to all the circumstances of the case, and under both of these he could take account of behaviour which had occurred outside the span of marriage, at least in a case where the conduct had affected the finances of the other spouse.[171]

In *GW v RW*,[172] however, the court counted a period of 18 months pre-marital cohabitation as part of the duration of the marriage. Nicholas Mostyn QC said that:

> where a relationship moves seamlessly from cohabitation to marriage without any major alteration in the way the couple live, it is unreal and artificial to treat the periods differently.[173]

This approach has been criticised,[174] and in *Co v Co*[175] Coleridge J, whilst agreeing with the sentiment of Mostyn QC in *GW v RW*, preferred a different route.[176] Instead of treating the eight years' pre-marital cohabitation as part of the duration of the marriage, he viewed it as an important factor which could be considered as part of 'all the circumstances of the case', or if necessary under a 'specific section 25 pigeonhole', either as a species of contribution or conduct.[177] Similarly in *M v M (Financial Relief: Substantial Earning Capacity)*[178] Baron J regarded a 12-year marriage preceded by four years' cohabitation as a 16-year relationship, commenting:

> I take fully into account the precise wording of the Statute but I am clear that in modern society it is a couple's commitment to each other by co-habiting that is the relevant start date for consideration in most cases. Indeed, I consider that it is the norm for most couples to live together for a period before marriage . . . I am well aware of the decision in *Foley -v- Foley* [1981] 3 WLR 284 and the dicta of Eveleigh LJ at page 290. There are many other old cases dealing with the importance of the married years per se but I consider that society has moved on and it would be old-fashioned (indeed, senseless) to ignore the manner in which people now choose to order their lives. I prefer the modern view and draw a measure of comfort from *GW -v- RW* [2003] 2 FLR 108 . . .[179]

Thus the courts have more routinely regarded seamless preceding cohabitation as akin to the duration of the marriage.[180]

---

[169] [1980] 1 All ER 1106.     [170] Now under para (g), then under the final target in s 25(1).
[171] But it should be noted that the wife did not obtain the type of order she would have obtained had the marriage lasted for 25 years. She obtained a lump sum which was less than the amount she was seeking, and might have expected to obtain, and no periodical payments.
[172] [2003] 2 FLR 108.     [173] Ibid, [33].
[174] S. Gilmore, 'Duration of Marriage *and* Seamless Preceding Cohabitation?' [2004] Family Law 205.
[175] [2004] 1 FLR 1095.
[176] Ibid, [47], commenting that the exact method was perhaps little more than 'a distinction without a difference'. See *contra*, S. Gilmore, 'Duration of Marriage *and* Seamless Preceding Cohabitation?' [2004] Family Law 205.
[177] [2004] 1 FLR 1095 at [45].     [178] [2004] EWHC 688 (Fam), [2004] 2 FLR 236.     [179] Ibid, [55].
[180] See J. Edwards, 'Duration of Marriage: From "I Do", "I Promise" or "I May"?' [2004] Family Law 726.

Cases of post-divorce cohabitation between former spouses can also give rise to the question whether such cohabitation should be taken into account. If at the time of the divorce a clean break order was made between the spouses, then property and financial disputes which arise from any subsequent cohabitation between them are likely to be dealt with under the normal rules governing cohabitation.[181] However, where there has been no final settlement the applicant can ask for leave to apply for financial relief under the MCA 1973. In *Hill v Hill*[182] the parties had cohabited for 25 years after they divorced. Commenting on the relevance of this, Ward LJ said that since pre-marital cohabitation could be taken into account when the court was doing justice between the parties on ancillary relief, 'then I do not see how the court can deny that cohabitation after the divorce is not a similar circumstance to take into account'. Thus the court concluded that the wife should be granted leave to apply for a property adjustment order, where the husband and wife had divorced in 1969, prior to the availability of the remedy of property adjustment.[183] According to the court, this claim was based not on the parties' cohabitation but on the decree of divorce, the wife's claims from which were 'put in abeyance during the subsequent cohabitation'.

### 5.3.5 Any physical or mental disability of either of the parties to the marriage

Paragraph (e) requires the court to take account of:

> any physical or mental disability of either of the parties to the marriage.

The courts have yet to determine to what extent the needs of a disabled party should impose an obligation on the other spouse to provide financial support which exceeds the norm.[184] For example, should there be a life-long obligation to provide periodical payments for a disabled spouse where the marriage has been relatively short-lived, and where an immediate or deferred clean break order would normally be considered appropriate? This raises the broader question of when the private obligations of ex-spouses to one another should end, and when those of the welfare state should take over. This is an issue of principle which has not yet received a settled answer. In line with the clean break ideal, it seems that the courts will strive to achieve a full and final settlement at the time of the divorce in order to avoid burdening the respondent with a continuing obligation. However, sometimes this will not be possible. For example in *M v M (Property Adjustment: Impaired Life Expectancy)*,[185] the wife suffered a brain tumour which reduced her life expectancy. When the parties divorced, after a 13-year marriage, the court held that the wife's ill-health and its effect on her income-earning capacity meant that a clean break was not appropriate. She was always going to require periodical payments from her former husband. She was also awarded 75 per cent of the proceeds of sale of the matrimonial home, although this sum was charged back to the husband in the event of the wife's death. A spouse's illness may also impact upon the nature or quantum of an award. In *Re G (Financial Provision: Liberty to Restore Application for Lump Sum)*,[186] the wife, who suffered from multiple sclerosis, had run up debts to pay for her children's education and had had to move into rented accommodation. The husband

---

[181] See Chapter 5. See *obiter* comments of Butler-Sloss LJ in *Hewitson v Hewitson* [1995] 1 FLR 241 at 245 that there has to be finality and an end to litigation. In my view the umbrella of the dissolved marriage which covers the post-divorce period cannot remain open forever. Upon the making and implementing of a 'clean break' order between spouses with no children, that umbrella has to be closed. Thereafter the relationship which may develop between former spouses is to be dealt with under civil law. Balcombe J said that 'cohabitation subsequent to an English divorce is not the basis for the English court to grant matrimonial financial relief' (at 246).

[182] [1998] 1 FLR 198.

[183] Which was introduced on 1 January 1971 by the Matrimonial Proceedings and Property Act 1970, the Act having retrospective effect.

[184] In *Chadwick v Chadwick* [1985] FLR 606 the Court of Appeal declined to take account of the wife's disability when determining what order to make in respect of the matrimonial home.

[185] [1993] 2 FLR 723.          [186] [2004] 1 FLR 997.

inherited £2.1 million, and the court awarded the wife a lump sum of £460,000, noting that one of the wife's health needs was to avoid stress.

### 5.3.6 Contributions made to the welfare of the family

Under section 25(2)(f), the court has regard to:

> the contributions which each of the parties has made or is likely in the foreseeable future to make to the welfare of the family, including any contribution by looking after the home or caring for the family.

---

**Summary**

This factor has become very significant since the House of Lords' decision in *White v White*[187] articulated the non-discrimination principle which states that:

> whatever the division of labour chosen by the husband and wife, or forced upon them by circumstances . . . [i]f in their different spheres, each contributed equally to the family, then in principle it matters not which of them earned the money and built up the assets. There should be no bias in favour of the money earner and against the home-maker and child-carer.[188]

This principle equalised the value to the family of the parties' financial and non-financial contributions. Thus, a wife who stayed at home to look after the children became entitled to share in the 'pool of assets that is the fruit of the marital partnership'.[189] By equalising the value of financial and non-financial contributions, the House of Lords introduced much stronger presumptions of capital sharing on divorce which are implicitly based upon the parties' contributions to the joint marital enterprise. This was developed further by the House of Lords in *Miller; McFarlane*.[190] These cases will be discussed at length later in Section 5.4.

---

### 5.3.7 Conduct

Under section 25(2)(g), the court shall have regard to:

> the conduct of the parties, if that conduct is such that it would in the opinion of the court be inequitable to disregard it.

At one time, the provision of maintenance on divorce was linked to the attribution of blame for the marital breakdown and a wife who was guilty of a matrimonial offence lost her right to maintenance. However, the introduction of no-fault divorce in the 1970s reduced the significance of fault in both the availability of divorce and financial provision in its aftermath. However, the extent to which the conduct of the parties should be taken into account when making financial provision and property adjustment orders has been a controversial issue. When, in 1980, the Law Commission issued a discussion paper which included the question of what policy ought to be adopted on the impact of conduct,[191] it received a large amount of conflicting comment in response. Many individuals felt a considerable sense of injustice because the court had not been prepared to take account of the other spouse's behaviour on divorce.[192] Despite this, the Law Commission expressed the view that courts cannot reasonably be expected to apportion responsibility for marriage breakdown,

---

[187] [2001] AC 596.    [188] Ibid, at 605.    [189] GW v RW [2003] EWHC 611 (Fam), at para 85.
[190] [2006] UKHL 24.    [191] Law Com No 103 (1980).    [192] Law Com No 112 (1980), para 36.

save in exceptional circumstances. It relied in particular on the words of Ormrod J in *Wachtel v Wachtel*[193] when he said:

> The forensic process is reasonably well adapted to determining in broad terms the share of responsibility of each party for an accident on the road or at work because the issues are relatively confined in scope, but it is much too clumsy a tool for dissecting the complex inter-actions which go on all the time in a family. Shares in responsibility for breakdown cannot be properly assessed without a meticulous examination and understanding of the characters and personalities of the spouses concerned, and the more thorough the investigation the more the shares will, in most cases, approach equality.

The Law Commission also gave more pragmatic reasons for rejecting an inquiry into the parties' mutual recriminations in other than exceptional cases. These included that it would be expensive of court time and legal aid; that resurrecting past matters, sometimes stretching back over many years, for forensic investigation would not assist the parties to come to terms with their deep feelings about the breakdown of their marriage; and that such feelings are better dealt with during conciliation.[194] As Thorpe LJ explained in *Lambert v Lambert*,[195] considering the parties' conduct during the marriage requires a 'detailed retrospective at the end of a broken marriage just at a time when the parties should be looking forward not back'.[196] Not only does this involve a determination of fact, but it calls for 'a value judgement of the worth of each side's behaviour and translation of that worth into actual money'.[197] Thus, despite recognising the 'widespread feeling' that 'when making orders for financial ancillary relief the judge should know who was to blame for the breakdown of the marriage' and take it into account,[198] the courts will not 'seek to unravel mutual recriminations about happenings within the marriage'.[199] As such, conduct will only be relevant to the financial provision order in a minority of cases where the conduct is such that it would be inequitable to disregard it. Consequently, judges have refused to penalise a spouse who has committed adultery,[200] or otherwise behaved in a manner which has caused offence or distress to the other party, taking the view that the conduct is not of sufficient seriousness and that this would be to 'impose a fine for supposed misbehaviour in the course of an unhappy married life'.[201] If conduct is not of a serious enough nature to be considered 'inequitable to disregard', then it will not be taken into account.

### 5.3.7.1 What type of conduct is 'inequitable to disregard'?

As Lady Hale explained in *Miller; McFarlane*, conduct will only be material where 'one party is much more to blame than the other' through misconduct which is both 'obvious and gross'.[202] In *Leadbeater v Leadbeater*[203] Balcombe J found that the spouses had both behaved as badly as each other and left conduct out of account.

Relevant conduct is not confined to conduct during the marriage and can relate to behaviour after the marriage has broken down.[204] The conduct need not be morally blameworthy. In *West v*

---

[193] [1973] 1 All ER 113 at 119. For detailed discussion, see G. Douglas, 'Bringing an End to the Matrimonial Post Mortem: *Wachtel v Wachtel* and its Enduring Significance for Ancillary Relief' in S. Gilmore, J. Herring, and R. Probert, *Landmark Cases in Family Law* (Oxford: Hart, 2011).

[194] Law Com No 112 (1980), para 37.     [195] [2003] 1 FLR 139.     [196] Ibid, [20].     [197] Ibid, [20].

[198] *Miller; McFarlane* [2006] UKHL 24 at [60].     [199] Ibid, [61].

[200] *Miller; McFarlane* [2006] UKHL 24.

[201] *Wachtel v Wachtel* [1973] 1 All ER 829; *A v A (Financial Provision)* [1998] 2 FLR 180.

[202] *Miller; McFarlane* [2006] UKHL 24, at [146], *per* Baroness Hale borrowing the words of Ormrod J in *Wachtel v Wachtel* [1973] Fam 72 at 80. As Sir George Baker P put it: conduct 'of the kind that would cause the ordinary mortal to throw up his hands and say, "surely that woman is not going to be given any money" or "is not going to get a full award" ': *W v W (Financial Provision: Lump Sum)* [1976] Fam 107 at 114.

[203] [1985] FLR 789.     [204] *Jones v Jones* [1976] Fam 8, CA (discussed later in this section).

*West*,[205] for example, account was taken of a wife's refusal to cohabit after the marriage in the house purchased by the husband, preferring instead to remain living at her parents' home. In several of the cases, however, conduct which has been seen as material has been seriously morally wrong.

Some examples may help to illustrate the type of conduct which has been seen as 'inequitable to disregard'. In *Kyte v Kyte*[206] the wife, knowing that her husband had attempted suicide on previous occasions, complied with his request to help him to commit suicide by taking a bottle of whisky and some drugs to his office and did not try to dissuade him. She stood to gain from the husband's death and wanted him out of the way so that she could set up home with her new partner. The Court of Appeal reduced the wife's award of £14,000 by £5,000, holding that this was conduct which was inequitable to disregard. In *Evans v Evans*[207] the husband had conscientiously paid maintenance for his ex-wife for many years. She was then convicted of inciting others to kill him. Balcombe LJ commented that if 'the courts were in these circumstances not to discharge the order, the public might think that we had taken leave of our senses'.

Similarly, in *K v K*[208] a husband had sexually abused his wife's grandchildren. The 'legacy of misery' caused by his conduct justified the Court of Appeal's decision to award him nothing from his wife's assets which were substantial. Also, in *H v H (Financial Relief: Attempted Murder as Conduct)*[209] the husband attacked the wife with knives in front of the children inflicting serious wounds to her neck, face, and hands. He was convicted of attempted murder and sentenced to 12 years' imprisonment. The court held that the husband's conduct should be taken into account when assessing the financial outcome on divorce. In relation to the effect of the conduct on the final award, the court held that it 'should not be punitive or confiscatory for its own sake'.[210] According to Coleridge J:

> the proper way to have regard to conduct is as a potentially magnifying factor when considering the wife's position under the other subsections and criteria. It is the glass through which the other factors are considered. It places her needs, as I judge them, at a much higher priority to those of the husband because the situation the wife now finds herself in is, in a very real way, his fault. It is not just that she is in a precarious position, which she might be for a variety of medical reasons, but that he has created this position by his reprehensible conduct. So she must, in my judgment and in fairness, be given a greater priority in the share-out.[211]

Sometimes a spouse's behaviour (as well as being morally wrong) may have a direct financial impact, as in *Jones v Jones*,[212] where, after the marriage had ended, the husband maliciously attacked his wife with a knife, injuring her wrist so severely that he impaired her earning capacity as a nurse. The Court of Appeal found that it would be repugnant to justice not to take the husband's conduct into account when securing the position of the wife in the future. In *H v H (Financial Provision: Conduct)*,[213] where the husband violently assaulted his wife as a result of which he was sent to prison for wounding and attempted rape, the husband was no longer able to support his wife and children to the standard which had preceded the attack. Furthermore, the wife had been left in a psychologically vulnerable position. The husband's conduct was one of the factors which influenced Thorpe J to transfer the husband's half share in the matrimonial home to the wife. There was a causative link between the conduct of one of the spouses and the parties' current financial circumstances which it was inequitable for a court to disregard.[214]

---

[205] [1978] Fam 1.     [206] [1988] Fam 145.     [207] [1989] 1 FLR 351.     [208] [2010] EWCA Civ 125.

[209] [2005] EWHC 2911 (Fam), [2006] 1 FLR 990.     [210] Ibid, [44].

[211] Ibid. Douglas notes that the husband's conduct in this case was exceptionally grave and that the question for the future is 'how far less serious forms of criminal misconduct should "colour" the court's assessment' of the statutory factors: [2006] Family Law 265.

[212] [1975] 2 All ER 12.     [213] [1994] 2 FLR 801.

[214] See for other examples: *Martin v Martin* [1976] Fam 335; *Bryant v Bryant* (1976) 120 Sol Jo 165; *Weisz v Weisz* (1975) Times, 16 December; *Hillard v Hillard* (1982) 12 Fam Law 176.

The fact that a spouse has behaved very badly will not necessarily mean that he or she will lose all provision. A striking example is provided by *Clark v Clark*,[215] in which Thorpe LJ commented that it 'would be hard to conceive graver marital misconduct', and that the history was 'as baleful as any to be found in the family law reports'. As the judge found, the wife had married a wealthy man 36 years her senior for his money, and spent considerable sums on luxury items such as a boat, a Bentley car, and an expensive home. The marriage had never been consummated and at one stage the wife required the husband to live in a caravan in her garden. She had made him a virtual prisoner in their home and he was eventually rescued by his niece and nephew. The Court of Appeal reduced the judge's award of just over £500,000 to reflect the marital misconduct, but nevertheless the wife still received a lump sum of £125,000.

In *A v A (Financial Provision)*[216] the husband's violent conduct was partly attributable to his uncontrollable psychological state. Allowing the husband's appeal against an order which reduced his share in the parties' jointly owned property to 10 per cent, and increasing it to one-third, Thorpe J held that although an incident of serious violence could not be disregarded, particularly where it had long-standing effects on the psychological well-being of the injured spouse, conduct was only one of the factors to be considered, and it should not drive the court to conclude that a violent husband should be deprived of his entire capital.[217]

In *H v H (Financial Relief: Conduct)*[218] the husband in the last three years of an 18-year marriage had deceitfully used capital provided by his father-in-law (who was very wealthy) for his own purposes, including placing some of it in a Swiss bank account and financing an adulterous relationship. However, the court found that his breach of trust was out of character, and that the children had a good relationship with him. Singer J held that it was in the children's interests that their father should be securely and adequately housed even if this meant selling the former matrimonial home in which the children lived with their mother. Accordingly he ordered that £375,000 should be settled on the husband for the purchase of a house to be held on trust. However, because it was inequitable to disregard the husband's conduct, Singer J ordered that the property should revert to the children on the husband's death, and not pass to his estate.[219]

Section 25(2)(g) may be criticised as possibly inviting further animosity between the parties. An argument can certainly be made that it may be more beneficial for issues of conduct to be subsumed within the other paragraphs in section 25(2). For example, where one spouse refuses to cohabit as in *West v West*,[220] those allegations could have been considered under paragraph (d) or (f), which focuses on the duration of the marriage, and each spouse's contributions to the welfare of the family. Even extreme cases like *Jones v Jones*,[221] in which the husband attacked the wife with a knife, or *H v H (Financial Provision: Conduct)*,[222] where the husband's attack on his wife had led to his imprisonment, and to her being psychologically harmed, could probably have been adequately considered under paragraphs (a), (b), and (e) which focus respectively on each spouse's earning capacity, resources, needs, and any physical or mental disabilities. Where a spouse has squandered resources, this could be considered as a matter relating to the spouses' resources. While some situations would not easily fall within the other paragraphs in the section,[223] abolishing conduct as a separate category may be more in keeping with the desire to keep the parties from making allegations and counter-allegations of fault. The counter-argument to this is that there ought to be the opportunity for

---

[215] [1999] 2 FLR 498, CA.   [216] [1995] 1 FLR 345.

[217] See eg *K v K (Financial Provision: Conduct)* [1990] 2 FLR 225.   [218] [1998] 1 FLR 971.

[219] The husband also received a lump sum of £100,000, principally to cover his debts. The exceptional nature of the capital order for the benefit of the children was emphasised. Cf *Lord Lilford v Glyn* [1979] 1 All ER 441.

[220] [1977] 2 All ER 705.   [221] [1975] 2 All ER 12.   [222] [1994] 2 FLR 801.

[223] It is hard to see where *Evans v Evans* [1989] 1 FLR 351 would fall, but it might have been considered under the clean break provisions in s 25A.

the types of reprehensible conduct examined earlier to be positively condemned in proceedings ancillary to the divorce itself.

Litigation misconduct can also affect the quantum of the award. In the recent case of *MF* v *SF*,[224] Mostyn J made a considerable downward adjustment to the wife's final award on the basis of her unreasonable litigation conduct. The parties had been married for over 20 years and had two children. The total assets were just over £3million. The husband was an accountant for a private family company earning approximately £550,000 per annum. He was made redundant and was now employed by a different company at a rate of £145,000 per annum. The wife was a beauty therapist who gave up full-time work when the eldest child was born. When the parties separated the wife applied for financial provision. The case progressed through the courts, generating legal fees of around £980,000. The wife argued that she should receive a settlement of £3.8million, as the husband's shares were worth £6million. He argued, on the other hand, that the total matrimonial assets were worth only £3.1million. He agreed that she should receive half of this as the wealth had been created during the marriage. However, he also argued that the amount should be adjusted in his favour to reflect the fact that she had refused to accept his previous offer, and the disparity in legal costs.

The wife asserted, amongst other things, that the husband's redundancy was a sham designed to frustrate her claims for financial provision on divorce. This, according to the court, was merely 'groundless suspicion' which was not supported by any evidence. She also made other accusations of dishonesty against her husband and his business partner, none of which had any merit. While Mr Justice Moylan found the wife to be an honest witness, he considered that her 'deep distrust' of her husband prevented her from bringing 'any sensible objectivity' to the case. He held that she should have accepted her husband's original offer and, had she done so, she would have avoided her subsequent legal costs which he found to be 'grossly disproportionate'. Thus, a cost adjustment was made to ensure that the husband was not required to fund these in full. The parties' wealth had been created during the marriage so the starting point was equal division. However, in terms of division of the capital assets, the adjustment for cost totalled £400,000 which meant that the wife received £900,000 and the husband received £1.3million.[225]

### 5.3.8 Loss of pension

Section 25(2)(h) directs the court to have regard to:

> the value to each of the parties to the marriage of any benefit which, by reason of the dissolution or annulment of the marriage, that party will lose the chance of acquiring.

A spouse's expectation under a pension scheme is often considered under this provision and the court has specific powers to re-allocate prospective pension entitlements on divorce. This is discussed further in Section 7.

## 5.4 The courts' general guidance

As we have seen, there are a considerable amount of factors for the court to take into account when deciding upon a financial provision order. The complexity of the assessment is compounded by the fact that the legislation does not provide any overriding objective to be achieved, nor does it provide any indication of what the mutual responsibilities of former spouses are, or should be. In the absence of such direction, the House of Lords has provided some general guidance on how the statutory framework should be applied.

---

[224] [2015] EWHC 1273 (Fam).

[225] An equal pension sharing order was also made, and the husband was ordered to pay periodical payments of £30,000 per annum in respect of the wife, and £10,000 per annum per child.

## Key case

In *White v White*[226] the husband and wife had been married for over 30 years. Both came from farming families and during their marriage they ran a dairy farm business in partnership. One farm belonged to the couple jointly, having been purchased with the assistance of a mortgage and a loan from Mr White's father; and the other, which had been inherited from the husband's father, was in the husband's sole name. The couple's net assets were worth £4.6 million, £1.5 million of which belonged to the wife. When the marriage broke down, the trial judge awarded Mrs White £980,000, to meet what were seen as her 'reasonable requirements' by way of provision of a home and a lump sum to provide her with an income for life.[227] Thus, under the order the wife was to receive slightly over one-fifth of the parties' total assets. In adopting this approach, the judge was following Court of Appeal authority,[228] which had established that even in big money cases a spouse's award would be limited to 'reasonable requirements' assessed in light of the available wealth and the marital standard of living. On the wife's appeal to the Court of Appeal, the amount of the husband's payment was increased to £1.5 million, which meant that, after deducting the parties' costs, her share was increased to about two-fifths. The husband appealed to the House of Lords seeking the restoration of the trial judge's order, and the wife cross-appealed seeking an order giving her an equal share in all the assets. The key issue for the House of Lords was the principles that should determine applications for financial relief in so-called 'big money' cases where the assets exceed the parties' financial needs in terms of housing and income. The facts of the case starkly called into question the 'reasonable requirements' approach, since Mrs White received less than her share of jointly owned property, and she would have fared better under partnership law than she did in the ancillary relief jurisdiction.

The House of Lords could find no justification for departing from the outcome reached by the Court of Appeal. Lord Nicholls of Birkenhead delivered an opinion with which all their Lordships agreed.[229] He indicated that 'the objective must be to achieve a fair outcome'[230] and the courts' 'powers must always be exercised with this objective in view, giving first consideration to the welfare of the children'.[231] His Lordship recognised, however, that 'fairness, like beauty, lies in the eye of the beholder'.[232] He therefore stressed the desirability of identifying guiding principles as clearly as possible in order to 'promote consistency in court decisions and in order to assist parties and their advisers and mediators in resolving disputes by agreement as quickly and inexpensively as possible'.[233]

By way of guidance, the House of Lords introduced a non-discrimination principle, indicating that in 'seeking to achieve a fair outcome, there is no place for discrimination between husband and wife and their respective roles'.[234] As Lord Nicholls explained:

> whatever the division of labour chosen by [the parties] . . . if, in their different spheres, each contributed equally to the family, then in principle it did not matter which of them earned the money and built up the assets. There should be no bias in favour of the money-earner and against the home-maker and the child-carer.[235]

He then went on to advise that:

> a judge would always be well advised to check his tentative views against the yardstick of equality of division. As a general guide, equality should be departed from only if, and to the extent that, there is good reason for doing so. The need to consider and articulate reasons for departing

---

[226] [2001] 1 AC 596.      [227] A Duxbury fund: see *Duxbury v Duxbury (Note)* [1992] Fam 62.

[228] See *O'D v O'D* [1976] Fam 83; *Page v Page* (1981) 2 FLR 198 at 201; *Preston v Preston* [1982] Fam 17 at 25; *Dart v Dart* [1996] 2 FLR 286; and cf *Conran v Conran* [1997] 2 FLR 615. As Baroness Hale has described the practice, 'the wife was entitled to her "reasonable requirements" (preferably capitalised) and the husband got the rest': *Miller; McFarlane* [2006] UKHL 24 at [135].

[229] Lord Cooke of Thorndon added a short judgment by way of supplement and emphasis.

[230] [2001] 1 AC 596 at 604.      [231] Ibid, 605.      [232] Ibid, 599.      [233] Ibid, 600.      [234] Ibid, 605.

[235] Ibid.

from equality would help the parties and the court to focus on the need to ensure the absence of discrimination.[236]

Lord Nicholls was clear that this was 'not to introduce a presumption of equal division under another guise'[237] since 'a presumption of equal division would go beyond the permissible bounds of interpretation of section 25'.[238] Neither is there a starting point of equality since 'a starting point principle of general application would carry a risk that in practice it would be treated as a legal presumption'.[239]

The House of Lords rejected the 'reasonable requirements' ceiling as expressed in the earlier Court of Appeal authorities. Lord Nicholls commented that the statutory provisions 'lend no support to the idea that a claimant's financial needs, even interpreted generously and called reasonable requirements, are to be regarded as determinative' and that there was 'much to be said for returning to the language of the statute'.[240]

The final issue addressed related to inherited property or property brought into a marriage by one spouse. Lord Nicholls explained the view that such property comes from a source external to the marriage and that, in fairness, the owning spouse should be permitted to keep it. He pointed out that in English law, when present, this factor is one of the circumstances of the case and the judge should assess its importance, and other relevant matters including the 'nature and value of the property, and the time when and circumstances in which the property was acquired'.[241] However, 'in the ordinary course, this factor can be expected to carry little weight, if any, in a case where the claimant's financial needs cannot be met without recourse to this property'.[242] Applying this approach to the facts of the case, Lord Nicholls concluded that the 'initial cash contribution made by Mr White's father in the early days cannot carry much weight 33 years later'.[243]

## Summary

The decision in *White* got a mixed reception amongst commentators. One leading commentator, Stephen Cretney,[244] wondered whether it might have been a trifle rash for the House of Lords to overrule, in an untypical case like *White*, the well-settled practice of the courts. He was led to the view that legislation was now required. He commented that it does not follow that a spouse should be entitled to the division of assets which might have been made had Parliament in 1970 not specifically rejected the incorporation of community of property in marriage. He argued that it may be rather simplistic to equate home-making contributions with commercially motivated money-making activity. Other commentators were more welcoming of the decision, but pointed out, as Professor Cooke did, that *White* raised a whole host of further issues (eg whether and how it would apply to shorter marriages, to the not-so-diligent spouse, or in cases of scarce resources).[245] Professor Bailey-Harris welcomed the case as a step towards marriage as an equal partnership but questioned the extent to which it provides workable guidance.[246] Did it, she asked, elevate contributions in the same way as the reasonable requirements approach had elevated needs? She predicted (correctly as we shall see) that there would be scope in future for argument over whether there had been equality of contribution.

---

[236] Ibid.       [237] Ibid.       [238] Ibid, 606.

[239] Ibid. Lord Cooke doubted 'whether the labels "yardstick" or "check" will produce any result different from "guidelines" or "starting point"' ([2001] 1 AC 596 at 615).

[240] Ibid, 608.

[241] Ibid, 610.       [242] Ibid.       [243] Ibid, 611.       [244] [2001] Family Law 3.

[245] See E. Cooke, 'White v White—A New Yardstick for the Marriage Partnership' [2001] Child and Family Law Quarterly 81.

[246] R. Bailey-Harris, 'Dividing the Assets on Family Breakdown: The Content of Fairness' [2001] Current Legal Problems 533.

Bailey-Harris pointed out that the House's analysis of equality was simple formal equality, and that substantive equality may require more than equal division. She questioned the ability of the statute to provide justice or equality given the lack of any clear objective. While inappropriate, at the very least the reasonable requirements approach provided some certainty in predicting and assessing the likely outcome of cases.[247]

---

### Key case

An opportunity for the House of Lords to clarify the law further arose in two cases heard together, *Miller v Miller; McFarlane v McFarlane*.[248] In *Miller*, the spouses were married for two years and nine months and had no children. The marriage broke down because of the husband's relationship with another woman. The husband was a very wealthy accountant and unit trust fund manager. In 2000 he had earned a cash payment of £13 million and subsequently acquired shares worth £12–18 million. The wealth creation in relation to the shares took place during the period of the marriage. The wife, who had a good career before giving it up during the marriage to concentrate on renovation projects, had net assets in the region of £100,000. At first instance Singer J awarded the wife £5 million (£2.3 million for a home and a £2.7 million lump sum). He said that Mr Miller had given his wife a legitimate expectation that she would be living on a higher financial plain in the future, and took into account that it was the husband's marital misconduct which had brought the marriage to an end. The husband's appeal was dismissed by the Court of Appeal, which similarly held that the judge had been entitled to take into account that the husband was responsible for the breakdown of the marriage as a 'defence' to the shortness of the marriage. The husband further appealed to the House of Lords.

In *McFarlane v McFarlane* the parties were married for 16 years and had three children. Both were professionally qualified, the wife as a solicitor and the husband as an accountant. After the second child was born, the wife gave up her job. The husband proceeded in his career to a partnership in an accountant's firm, earning £753,000 net per annum. The parties' assets were valued at £3 million and they agreed an equal share, the wife retaining the matrimonial home worth £1.5 million. The only dispute was as to the level of the wife's periodical payments. The husband's income represented a significant surplus after the parties' needs had been satisfied and the key question was the basis upon which this should be distributed, if at all. In the first instance, the district judge ordered £250,000 per annum (which was approximately 33 per cent of husband's current net income). Bennett J reduced this to £180,000 per annum and, on appeal, the Court of Appeal restored the original order, albeit for a five-year extendable term to enable the wife to accumulate a capital reserve.[249]

---

#### MORE GENERAL GUIDANCE

Two main opinions were delivered, by Lord Nicholls and Lady Hale respectively.

Lord Nicholls made clear that the principles in *White* are applicable to all marriages. He acknowledged, however, that the removal of the needs-based approach had 'accentuated the need for some further

---

[247]  See *per* Ormrod LJ in *S v S* [1977] 1 All ER 56.

[248]  [2006] UKHL 24, [2006] 2 AC 618. For comment see E. Cooke, 'Miller/McFarlane: Law in Search of Discrimination' [2007] Child and Family Law Quarterly 98; District Judge Glen Brasse, 'It's Payback Time! Miller, McFarlane and the Compensation Culture' [2006] Family Law 647; L. Glennon, 'Obligations between Adult Partners: Moving from Form to Function?' (2008) 22(1) International Journal of Law, Policy and the Family 22.

[249]  For commentary on the Court of Appeal decision in *McFarlane*, see K. O'Donovan, 'Flirting with Academic Categorizations—*McFarlane v McFarlane and Parlour v Parlour*' [2005] Child and Family Law Quarterly 418.

judicial enunciation of general principle'.[250] He pointed out that an important aspect of fairness is that 'like cases are decided alike' and therefore the court must articulate, if only in the broadest fashion, what the applicable principles are.[251] Lord Nicholls then set out three underlying rationales for a seeking to achieve fairness:

(i) *The needs of the parties*, reflecting their interdependence. Most cases will end here.[252]

(ii) *Compensation* aimed at addressing any significant prospective economic disparity due to the manner in which the marriage was conducted.[253] Lord Nicholls acknowledged that there is potential overlap between needs and compensation and indicated that there is no invariable rule on how they are to be approached.

(iii) *Sharing*: the idea of marriage as a partnership of equals right from the outset, which means that when the marriage partnership ends, each spouse is 'entitled to an equal share in the assets of the partnership, unless there is a good reason to the contrary'.[254] Lord Nicholls made clear that this applies equally to a short marriage as a long one[255] and the House disapproved of the idea that a non-earning spouse would accrue a share in the marital assets over time.[256]

Lord Nicholls said that the court must have regard to all property but need not treat all property the same. Here Lord Nicholls distinguished, as he had done in *White*, between marital and non-marital property (eg gifts, inheritances, or other property brought into the marriage), but he was of the opinion that the courts should be slow to introduce a distinction between 'family assets' and 'business assets'. Lord Nicholls indicated that the position in relation to non-marital assets was summarised in *White*. He added:

24 In the case of a short marriage fairness may well require that the claimant should not be entitled to a share of the other's non-matrimonial property. The source of the asset may be a good reason for departing from equality. This reflects the instinctive feeling that parties will generally have less call upon each other on the breakdown of a short marriage.

25 With longer marriages the position is not so straightforward. Non-matrimonial property represents a contribution made to the marriage by one of the parties. Sometimes, as the years pass, the weight fairly to be attributed to this contribution will diminish, sometimes it will not. After many years of marriage the continuing weight to be attributed to modest savings introduced by one party at the outset of the marriage may well be different from the weight attributable to a valuable heirloom intended to be retained *in specie*.

He added another relevant matter, the way the parties organised their financial affairs, and that the court can distinguish property with the necessary degree of particularity or generality as the circumstances dictate.

Addressing some of the general issues raised by the *McFarlane* case, Lord Nicholls held that periodical payments are not confined to maintenance and can be made for the purpose of affording compensation. The desirability of the clean break should be a sufficient reason for depriving the claimant of compensation.

Lady Hale delivered an opinion which, in the main, reflected what Lord Nicholls had said. However, Lady Hale indicated that arguments about the provenance of some business assets could not be ignored. Unlike Lord Nicholls, she made a distinction between family assets and non-family business assets. Family assets are the home and its contents, other assets obviously acquired for the benefit of the family, for example holiday homes, furniture, caravans, family savings, including family businesses/joint ventures. By contrast, business or investment assets generated solely or mainly by the efforts of one party, that is, 'non-business partnership non-family assets' are not to be treated as family assets.[257] The distinction is

---

[250]  Ibid, [8].        [251]  Ibid, [6]. See also *per* Baroness Hale at [122].

[252]  Ibid, [11]; [138]–[139] *per* Lord Nicholls and Baroness Hale.

[253]  Ibid, [13]; [140] *per* Lord Nicholls and Baroness Hale.

[254]  Ibid, [16]–[17]; [141]–[143] *per* Lord Nicholls and Baroness Hale.        [255]  Ibid, [17].

[256]  Ibid, [19]. This approach had been suggested in *GW v RW (Financial Provision: Departure from Equality)* [2003] 2 FLR 108 at 121–2, and see J. Eekelaar, 'Asset Distribution on Divorce—The Durational Element' (2001) 117 LQR 552. Cf R. Bailey-Harris, 'Comment on *GW v RW (Financial Provision: Departure from Equality)*' [2003] Family Law 388.

[257]  [2006] UKHL 24, [2006] 2 AC 618 at [150].

founded on the basis that there is no obvious causal connection between the home-making contributions of the primary carer and the creation of these assets. The balance of opinion amongst the Lords appeared to favour the approach of Lady Hale.[258]

### The specific issues raised by the facts of *Miller* and *McFarlane*

Having set out the general principles, the House then addressed the specific issues raised in the cases. In *Miller* the marriage was less than three years in duration. Prior to this case the courts' approach in such cases tended to try to restore the parties to their position had the marriage not existed. The House made clear that, in light of the principles discussed earlier, that approach is no longer valid. The House also held that Singer J had been wrong to talk of the legitimate expectation of wealth that the husband had given the wife, since this would be tantamount to re-introducing the principle of minimal loss. In addition, the judge and the Court of Appeal had been wrong to take account of the husband's matrimonial conduct (in having an affair). The statute draws the line at conduct which it would in the opinion of the court be inequitable to disregard. As we shall see later in this chapter, by this is meant conduct which is material to the fairness of the proceedings, sometimes characterised as 'obvious and gross' conduct. It does not include 'run-of-the-mill' marital misconduct leading to a divorce. The House of Lords agreed with the judge's overall assessment. Having regard to the marital standard of living and the accretion of wealth during the marriage, the House considered the award of £5 million, amounting to less than one-sixth of the value of the husband's total worth,[259] was not inappropriate.

However, basing the decision on the career sacrifices made by Mrs McFarlane, the House of Lords restored the joint lives order in that case on the grounds that, over and above her financial needs, she was entitled to compensation for her economic disadvantage arising as a result of the division of labour within the marriage. This, according to Lord Nicholls, resulted in the double-loss of a 'diminution in her earning capacity and the loss of a share in husband's enhanced income'.[260] Thus, it seems that a compensatory award can mitigate both opportunity costs and expectation losses.[261] The House concluded that the five-year limitation on the periodical payments order should be removed. The Lords considered that the responsibility of applying for any variation to the term should rest with the husband, especially in light of the high threshold which is set for justifying an extension of the term.[262]

Reading the two leading decisions together, the ethos of the guiding principles in *White* (the non-discrimination principle and the yardstick of equal division) have now been incorporated within three bases of wealth distribution: needs, compensation, and equal sharing. Financial need, once the ceiling in big money cases, is now just one part of a more complex financial award. The net result is a more complex, layered approach to the redistribution of assets which has required, and continues to require, further clarification by the courts.

---

[258] Lord Hoffmann agreed with Lady Hale, as did Lord Mance who noted that in relation to 'non-business partnership, non-family assets' the yardstick of equal sharing 'may not apply with the same force especially in the case of short marriages' (p 168). Lord Hope agreed with both Lord Nicholls *and* Lady Hale.

[259] [2006] UKHL 24, at [73] *per* Lord Nicholls.

[260] Ibid, [13] *per* Lord Nicholls.

[261] At [13]. However, the interaction between the two is unclear. Can these elements operate independently of one another? Eg a wife who did not ostensibly sacrifice a lucrative career will still, on divorce, lose the opportunity to share in her husband's enhanced income. Will this only be compensable for a wife whose commitment at home, which allowed the husband to concentrate on his career unfettered by daily caring responsibilities, resulted in a tangible (non-speculative) loss in her own earning capacity? For a wife who did not make such a clear sacrifice, will the expectation loss associated with the divorce simply evidence her financial needs as she loses the opportunity to enjoy the resource of her husband's income?

[262] See *Fleming v Fleming* [2003] EWCA Civ 1841.

## 5.5  The bases of financial provision orders following *Miller; McFarlane*

### 5.5.1  Meeting the parties' needs

In cases where the parties have few assets, their financial circumstances will dictate the outcome as the assessment of the parties' needs will 'lean heavily in favour of the children and the parent with whom they live'.[263] Thus, in the majority of cases, the parties' needs will determine the redistribution of the assets on divorce.[264] However, in cases where the parties have assets which go beyond their financial needs, 'policy' questions become much more visible and 'it becomes necessary to consider the ultimate limits of the court's discretionary powers'.[265] In such situations, difficult questions have to be answered about the underlying rationale for the distribution of these assets.[266] Case law reveals that although the courts have a wide discretion when making awards to meet the applicant's financial needs, in practice the financial orders tend to lead the parties to independence.[267]

### 5.5.2  Compensation

In *McFarlane*, it was held that the wife's award had to reflect the fact that she had given up a very lucrative career which was as highly paid as her husband's. Thus, not only were the financial needs created by her absence from the labour market to be met, but she deserved to be compensated for the 'comparable position which she might have been in had she not compromised her own career for the sake of [the family]'.[268] As the capital assets were insufficient at the time of the divorce to meet this claim, this aspect of the financial award had to come from the husband's future income.

However, it should not be assumed that such a compensatory award will routinely be made. In an early first instance decision after *Miller; McFarlane*, Coleridge J cautioned against treating lost career opportunities as an independent consideration leading to a claim for damages.[269] Noting that it would be both undesirable and costly to embark upon a speculative 'what if' exercise in respect of career sacrifices, Coleridge J viewed such sacrifices as part of the parties' respective contributions to the marriage which gave rise to mutual obligations between the parties. Thus, in that case the wife's contribution in giving up a career did not give rise to an independent or additional layer of the award, but was reflected within an award which provided her with a secure future whilst allowing the husband to re-establish himself. In *VB v JP*,[270] Sir Mark Potter held that while the wife had clearly suffered lost earning potential as a result of the marriage and was entitled to compensation, this was difficult to quantify. Thus, he held that it was not necessary to quantify the element of compensation separately. Instead, it was considered as part of the assessment of the wife's needs generously assessed against the standard of living during the marriage and husband's increased income. The Law Commission has recently observed that the concept of compensation, that is the 'making up of loss arising from the marriage' has always been part of the court's assessment of the parties' needs, and that since *Miller; McFarlane* it has not featured much in case

---

[263] *Dart v Dart* [1996] 2 FLR 286 at 303, *per* Butler-Sloss LJ. See J. Eekelaar, 'Some Principles of Financial and Property Adjustment on Divorce' (1979) Law Quarterly Review 253; E. Jackson, F. Wasoff, M. Maclean, and R. Dobash, 'Financial Support on Divorce: The Right Mixture of Rules and Discretion?' (1993) 7 International Journal of Law and the Family 230.

[264] The level of the parties' needs in this context will be assessed in accordance with the marital standard of living. See, for example, *Robson v Robson* [2010] EWCA Civ 1171 where the wife's needs included the property and income which allowed her to continue her equestrian activities.

[265] *Preston v Preston* [1982] 1 All ER 41 at 47, *per* Ormrod LJ.

[266] See J. Eekelaar, 'Uncovering Social Obligations: Family Law and the Responsible Citizen' in M. Maclean (ed), *Making Law for Families* (Oxford: Hart, 2000), p 19 on the difficulty the courts found with identifying underlying rationales for provision.

[267] See, for example, *Wright v Wright* [2015] EWCA Civ 201; *Grocholewska-Mullins v Mullins* [2014] EWCA Civ 148; *SS v NS (Spousal Maintenance)* [2014] EWHC 4183.

[268] [2006] UKHL 24, at [154], *per* Baroness Hale.          [269] *P v P* [2006] EWHC 3409 (Fam).

[270] [2008] 2 FCR 682.

law.[271] It was noted that ' it is rare for the claimant, as the economically weaker party, to be able to demonstrate that he or she would in fact have been better off if not married, and so where needs are awarded at something referable to the marital standard of living a separate claim for compensation does not arise'.[272]

Thus, the extent to which compensation stands as a separate thread of distribution, or is merely considered to be part of the recipient's needs is a matter of some debate, and conflicting case law. In the recent case *SA* v *PA*[273] Mostyn J was very critical of the concept of compensation. In this case, the parties had been married for 18 years and had four teenage children. The husband was a solicitor earning £600K net. The wife claimed that she had given up a high powered career to look after the children while her husband's career flourished and that, as such, her periodical payments award should be significantly enhanced to compensate her for this. Mostyn J. reviewed the law relating to the compensation principle since the House of Lords' decision in *McFarlane* and took the view that the concept was 'extremely problematic and challenging both conceptually and legally'.[274] He gave a number of reasons for this. First, the term 'compensation' usually denotes a payment made by a wrongdoer to a victim to make amends for harm caused by the wrongdoer to the victim. But in these typical situations, the victim is not usually an active enthusiastic voluntary participant in the events that give rise to the claim. In financial provision cases, however, Mostyn J could not see how the free choice made by an individual to give up work could be characterised as a loss 'suffered' by her entitling her to an award in excess of her reasonable needs. Secondly, calculating a compensatory award in these cases was highly speculative. He said that this 'is extremely difficult and dangerous territory which is not based on any kind of hard evidence but usually on hunch, guesswork and speculation'. Thirdly, the exercise is highly arbitrary depending on whether the wife gave up a high-paid or low-paid job. Fourthly, experience has shown that it is extremely difficult to compute rationally, let alone predictably, how the wife's career would have progressed and the value of her loss of earnings/earning capacity caused by her marriage. Finally, he concluded that the ultimate award in *McFarlane* could be explained as no more than a conventional needs-based award without reference to the principle of compensation. Concluding that it was hard to identify any case where compensation had been separately reflected as a premium or additional element in the financial award, he said that there were now four guiding principles concerning a compensation claim:

- first, it will only be in a very rare and exceptional case where the principle will be capable of being successfully invoked;
- secondly, such a case will be one where the court can say without any speculation (that is, with almost near certainty) that the claimant gave up a very high earning career which had it not been foregone would have led to earnings at least equivalent to that presently enjoyed by the respondent;
- thirdly, such a high earning career will have been practised by the claimant over an appreciable period during the marriage. According to Mostyn J. proof of this track-record is key;
- finally, once these findings have been made, compensation will be reflected by fixing the periodical payments award towards the top end of the discretionary bracket applicable for a needs assessment on the facts of the case. He continued that 'compensation ought not to be reflected by a premium or additional element on top of the needs based award'.

Mostyn J found that the present case was one that could not be regarded as a compensation case as the wife had no appreciable track record by the time she gave up work and it was not known what her earnings were. He also concluded that except in highly exceptional cases, an award for periodical payments should be assessed by reference to the principle of need alone.

---

[271] Law Commission Consultation Paper 208, *Matrimonial Property, Needs and Agreements* (2012), para 2.18.
[272] Ibid.     [273] [2014] EWHC 392 (Fam).     [274] Ibid, at [24].

This can be contrasted with the approach of Coleridge J in *H v H*,[275] who said in relation to compensation: 'there remain a very small number of cases where it stares the court in the face and to ignore it and simply approach the case on the basis of the more simplistic 'needs' argument does not do full justice to a wife who has sacrificed the added security of generating her own generating earning capacity, as this wife undoubtedly did'.[276] The parties in this case had been married for 22 years. The wife was an accountant who left her career to look after the couple's children. Her husband was also an accountant who earned around £475,000 net per annum. He had remarried after the divorce and his new wife was suffering from terminal cancer. As such, he wanted to terminate a joint lives periodical payments order which had been made in favour of his former wife to allow him to retire in 2015 in order to care for their young children. His former wife argued that he should pay her a further lump sum to achieve a clean break and to compensate her for the career sacrifices she made during their marriage for the sake of the family. Coleridge J held that it was desirable for the parties to achieve a clean break, and that there was a 'tangible, obvious compensation element to the case which deserves recognition'.[277] To reflect this, the husband was ordered to make a lump sum payment to his former wife on his retirement.[278] It seems, therefore, that the compensation principle, albeit reigned in to apply to only a very small number of cases where one party has suffered tangible economic losses due to sacrificing a career to care for children, remains part of the law, and can be reflected in a separate strand of a financial award. However, we will have to wait and see the extent to which the courts, in future cases, will be willing to quantify the economic losses suffered by one party to a marriage within such a compensatory award.

### 5.5.3 The equal sharing principle

As previously outlined, the equal sharing principle means that when the marriage partnership ends each spouse is 'entitled to an equal share of the assets of the partnership, unless there is a good reason to the contrary'.[279] Prior to the decision of the House of Lords in *White*, the claimant's award on divorce was limited to satisfying his or her 'reasonable requirements' which were assessed in light of the available resources and the marital standard of living.[280] The House of Lords disparaged this approach in cases where there was a surplus of assets after the parties' needs had been satisfied (so called big-money cases). This altered the rationale of financial provision orders. While in the pre-*White* era of 'reasonable requirements', a homemaker wife sought resources from the assets of her wealthy spouse, on the principle of *White* and *Miller; McFarlane*, the function of financial provision orders is to 'determine the parties' unascertained shares in the pool of assets that is the fruit of the marital partnership'.[281] The courts, in their quest for gender equality, have thus initiated a shift from a welfare-based rationale for financial provision on divorce to an entitlement-based model,[282] and there is now a much stronger presumption of capital sharing on divorce, which is based on the notion of marriage as a collaborative partnership. However, this has given rise to a host of questions to which we will now turn.

---

[275] [2014] EWHC 760.     [276] Ibid, at [66].     [277] Ibid, at [49].

[278] The wife appealed and the Court of Appeal allowed her appeal, ordering a re-hearing before a different judge of the Family Division, *H v H* [2014] EWCA Civ 1523. On the compensation point, Ryder LJ in the Court of Appeal had no problem with the application of the compensation principle in the ways identified by Coleridge J although he questioned whether compensation was adequately reflected in the award given the overall asset distribution between the parties. He considered that the judge had not adequately identified the parties' assets which made it impossible to cross-check the fairness of the award, at [45]. Thus a re-hearing was necessary.

[279] [2006] UKHL 24 at [16].

[280] *O'D v O'D* [1976] Fam 83; *Page v Page* (1981) 2 FLR 198; *Preston v Preston* [1982] Fam 17.

[281] *GW v RW* [2003] EWHC 611 (Fam) at [85].

[282] See J. Eekelaar, 'Back to Basics and Forward into the Unknown' [2001] Family Law 30.

### 5.5.3.1 Is equal sharing an end-of-assessment yardstick or a starting point?

In *White*, the House of Lords viewed the principle of equal sharing as an end-of-assessment yardstick. Thus judges were to reach a provisional view on financial provision and then check this against the yardstick of equal division which should be departed from only if there are good reasons for doing so. However, in *Miller; McFarlane* the equal sharing principle was regarded by the House of Lords as a starting point (once the parties' assets had been established), which means that the court will assume that equal division should take place unless there is a good reason for departing from it. This approach was confirmed by the Court of Appeal in *Charman v Charman*.[283] Thus, the yardstick of equality propounded in earlier cases is now a principle of financial provision law[284] and any departure is not from the principle but takes place within the principle.[285]

---

**Summary**

To summarise, the starting point of every inquiry in an application for financial orders is the financial position of the parties. The inquiry is always in two stages, namely computation and distribution; the court must decide what assets are available to the parties and then decide how they should be distributed. The Court of Appeal confirmed in *Charman* that once the parties' assets have been established, the equal sharing principle is now a starting point for the distributive exercise rather than an end-of-assessment yardstick.

---

### 5.5.3.2 Does the sharing principle apply to the parties' income?

A further issue which arose was whether the *White* principles apply to the division of income, or put another way, should the parties' earning capacity be viewed as a capital asset of the marriage. In *McFarlane v McFarlane; Parlour v Parlour*[286] Thorpe LJ posed the following question:

> If the decision in [*White*] introduces the yardstick of equality for measuring a fair division of capital, why should the same yardstick not be applied as the measure for the division of income?[287]

While the Court of Appeal did not provide a clear answer, it seemed to draw a distinction between the distribution of capital and income on the basis that while the division of capital can be seen as the division of the 'accumulated fruits of past-shared endeavours' the same could not be said of future income.[288] The Court of Appeal in *Charman v Charman*[289] accepted that certain dicta of Lady Hale in *Miller; McFarlane*[290] could be relied upon to construct an argument that a spouse's earning capacity might be considered as a capital asset. However, the court concluded that this was an issue of 'complexity and potential confusion' which did not fall to be determined in the context of the case.

---

[283] [2007] EWCA Civ 503. For commentary, see J. Miles, '*Charman v Charman (No 4)*—Making Sense of Need, Compensation and Equal Sharing after *Miller/McFarlane*' [2008] Child and Family Law Quarterly 378.

[284] [2007] EWCA Civ 503, [65]. For criticism, see S. Davis, 'Equal Sharing: A Judicial Gloss Too Far?' [2008] Family Law 428 (arguing that the working wife suffers a detriment relative to the non-working wife, in that if she works she will not be compensated for loss of a career, ie, the non-working wife is rewarded for not working).

[285] Unhelpfully, however, in *B v B* [2008] EWCA Civ 543 the Court of Appeal appeared to suggest that the principle should be applied as a yardstick although emphasised that the decision depended on the unusual facts of the case and thus should not be regarded as establishing any new point of principle.

[286] [2004] EWCA Civ 872.     [287] Ibid, [4].

[288] J. Eekelaar, 'Shared Income After Divorce: A Step too Far' (2005) LQR 1. See *Jones v Jones* [2011] EWCA Civ 41.

[289] [2007] EWHC Civ 503.     [290] See *Miller; McFarlane* at [149].

In *Jones v Jones*[291] the Court of Appeal clarified that a spouse's earning capacity is not to be capitalised or otherwise brought into account for the purpose of the sharing principle.

### 5.5.3.3 *Non-matrimonial property*

One of the main questions which has arisen is when will it be appropriate to depart from equal sharing in order to achieve a fair outcome? The most obvious reason for departing from equal division is when this is required to satisfy the parties' needs. However, what are the other situations when this will occur? Can one party argue, for example, that they should keep assets which they brought into the marriage, or which they accumulated by their sole efforts during the marriage? The courts have made it clear that none of the parties' assets will be ring-fenced or quarantined to make them unavailable for distribution (especially where they are required to meet the parties' needs). However, their source will be a relevant factor for the court when making its assessment and may justify a departure from equal division, in the sense that 'there is likely to be better reason for departure from equality' in relation to non-matrimonial property.[292] Thus the court will need to consider more carefully than perhaps in the past, the nature of property and particularly whether it is matrimonial or non-matrimonial property.[293]

This may raise some difficult questions as to which side of the line resources lie. It is clear that the family home is generally considered to be marital property whatever its origin (for example, even if it was owned by one spouse prior to the marriage).[294] However, outside of this, if one party has substantial assets which were earned prior to the marriage[295] or the property held by the couple at the time of divorce has been largely generated by one person's inheritance,[296] for example by starting a business using inherited capital,[297] the courts may use this as a reason to depart from equality. In *B v B (Ancillary Relief)*,[298] the husband built a business based on the wife's inheritance and the court justified a departure from equality on this basis. The fact that the assets in question were inherited carried some weight in *G v B*,[299] but the main reason that equality was departed from was the fact that grandchildren were beneficiaries of the assets and thus it was considered to be wrong to benefit the wife at the expense of them. The parties married in 2004 and had one child, although the husband had three children from another marriage. The family's resources came from the husband's father who had been a successful businessman before his death in 1995. The husband, who was an only child, had never worked and the family's assets (which totalled around £6.5million) came from his father. These were primarily made up of equity in the matrimonial home and a foundation set up by the father in Liechtenstein. This fund was to benefit not only the husband, but the grandchildren (including the three children from the husband's previous marriage). The origin of the funds (that is, the fact that they were inherited from the husband's father) carried 'some but not great weight' in determining the wife's financial claim.[300] Instead, the wife's award was limited to satisfying her needs on the ground that the resources were intended to benefit all of the grandchildren as beneficiaries of the foundation. This led Blair J to conclude: 'it would not be fair or proper for the court to fix the wife's award at such a level so as to deplete the resources of the foundation to an extent which deprives the other beneficiaries of future support'.[301] This the wife received a portion of the income from the fund, but none of the capital.

The nature of the property may also be important. For example, in *P v P (Inherited Property)*[302] farming land had been in the husband's family for generations and had been brought into the

---

[291] [2011] EWCA Civ 41, [2012] Fam 1.     [292] *Charman v Charman* [2007] EWHC Civ 503.

[293] In *Rossi v Rossi* [2006] EWHC 1482 (Fam) Mostyn QC (sitting as deputy High Court judge) held that in all cases it is now a 'primary function' of the court to identify the matrimonial and non-matrimonial property.

[294] *Miller; McFarlane* [2006] UKHL 24 at [22]. See also *Lawrence v Gallagher* [2012] EWCA Civ 394.

[295] For example, *McCartney v McCartney Mills* [2008] EWHC 401 (Fam).

[296] *B v B (Ancillary Relief)* [2008] EWCA Civ 284; *K v L* [2010] EWHC 1234 (Fam).

[297] *Dharamshi v Dharamshi* [2001] 1 FCR 492.     [298] [2008] 1 FCR 613.

[299] [2013] EWHC 3414 (Fam).     [300] Ibid, at [82].     [301] Ibid, at [78].

[302] [2004] EWHC 1364 (Fam), [2005] 1 FLR 576.

marriage with the expectation that it would remain *in specie* for future generations. For these reasons, and since an order for sale of the farm would be little short of devastating to the husband, Munby J held that fairness required an order which merely addressed the wife's needs, which could be achieved without recourse to the farm assets. One issue over which there is considerable uncertainty is where a spouse receives a bonus shortly after the marriage breakdown. In *Rossi v Rossi*,[303] a limit of one year from the date of the break-up was suggested as a cut-off point and thereafter any bonus should not be regarded as matrimonial in nature. However, in *H v H (Financial Provision)* the idea of such a fixed cut-off point was disapproved.[304] The nature of the property and the use it is put to will need to be assessed in all the circumstances.

As the Law Commission have pointed out, 'the law is *not* that non-matrimonial property is exempt from sharing'.[305] As always, the parties' needs will take priority and so the court will order that non-matrimonial property is to be shared if it is required to meet need.[306] As Mr Justice Mostyn observed in *S v AG (Financial Orders: Lottery Prize)*[307] 'we await the first decision where the sharing principle has led to an award from non-matrimonial property in excess of needs'.[308] Outside of this there is some uncertainty about how non-matrimonial property is subtracted from the pool of assets which are available for distribution. In *Robson v Robson*[309] the Court of Appeal favoured the approach taken previously in *Charman v Charman*[310] in which the court applied the sharing principle to all of the parties' property whatever its origin, and then adjusted (as it saw fit) the proportions in which this property is shared to take account of the fact that some of the assets are non-matrimonial. By contrast, in *Jones v Jones*[311] the Court of Appeal took a more structured approach and simply excluded non-matrimonial property from the sharing exercise (subject, of course, to the parties' needs). Under this latter approach, which seems to be favoured by lower courts,[312] the equal sharing principle applies to matrimonial property and non-matrimonial property is only shared if it is required to satisfy needs.

A further question, however, is whether non-matrimonial property can become matrimonial property over time. Lady Hale said in *Miller; McFarlane* that in lengthy marriages 'the source of the assets may be taken into account but its importance will diminish over time'.[313] In other words, in a lengthy marriage the distinction between matrimonial and non-matrimonial property becomes less relevant, thus making it more likely that all of the parties' assets would be shared equally between the parties.

### Summary

The Law Commission explain the rationale behind this: '[t]he point is not that the status of the assets changes by virtue of time alone, but that as time goes on the lives of the two people become more intermingled, and it may cease to matter to them (at least while the relationship continues) who first owned (say) the shares or the piano'.[314]

---

[303] [2006] 2 FLR 1482 (Fam).    [304] [2009] 2 FLR 795.

[305] Law Commission Consultation Paper 208, Matrimonial Property, Needs and Agreements (2012), para 6.10.

[306] *Robson v Robson* [2010] EWCA Civ 1171; *AR v AR (Treatment of Inherited Wealth)* [2011] EWHC 2717 (Fam); *Jones v Jones* [2011] EWCA Civ 41.

[307] [2011] EWHC 2637 (Fam).

[308] Noted by the Law Commission in their Consultation Paper 208, Matrimonial Property, Needs and Agreements (2012), para 6.7. See also M Weldstead, 'The Sharing of Pre-matrimonial Property on Divorce: *K v L*' (2012) Family Law 185.

[309] [2010] EWCA Civ 1171.    [310] [2007] EWCA Civ 503.    [311] [2011] EWCA Civ 41.

[312] Law Commission Consultation Paper 208, Matrimonial Property, Needs and Agreements (2012), para 6.10. This approach has been followed by recent High Court decisions such as *FZ v SZ (Ancillary Relief: Conduct: Valuations)* [2010] EWHC 1630 (Fam); *N v F (Financial Orders: Pre-Acquired Wealth)* [2011] EWHC 586 (Fam) and *R v R (Financial Remedies: Needs and Practicalities)* [2011] EWHC 3093 (Fam).

[313] [2006] UKHL 24 at [152].

[314] Law Commission Consultation Paper 208, *Matrimonial Property, Needs and Agreements* (2012), para 6.62.

However, this is not to say that in lengthy marriage non-matrimonial property is shared between the parties, and in short marriages it is not. Indeed, there are no hard-and-fast rules on the length of time which it takes to convert a non-matrimonial asset into a matrimonial one, if at all.[315] It is instructive to look at the approach of Lord Justice Wilson in *K v L*[316] who rejected the argument that non-matrimonial property would *always* be shared in a lengthy marriage. He said:

> . . . I believe that the true position is that the importance of the source of the assets may diminish over time. Three situations come to mind:
>
> (a) Over time matrimonial property of such value has been acquired to diminish the significance of the initial contribution by one spouse of non-matrimonial property.
> (b) Over time the non-matrimonial property initially contributed has been mixed with matrimonial property in circumstances in which the contributor may be said to have accepted that it should be treated as matrimonial property or in which, at any rate, the task of identifying its current value is too difficult.
> (c) The contributor of non-matrimonial property has chosen to invest it in the purchase of a matrimonial home which, although vested in his or her sole name, has—as in most cases one would expect—come over time to be treated by the parties as a central item of matrimonial property.[317]

On the facts of the case, the wife's primary assets were shares in a family business. When the parties married the shares were worth only £300,000 but by the time of the parties' divorce (21 years later), they were valued at almost £59 million. The shares represented virtually the entire wealth of the parties. However despite their wealth, the parties' standard of living was 'extraordinarily modest'. Indeed, the former matrimonial home was worth only £225,000. On divorce, the husband was awarded just £5 million out of the total assets. It was accepted that neither party had earned any income during the marriage but both had contributed equally to family life during the marriage. Thus the husband appealed on the grounds that the departure from equal division was discriminatory. Wilson LJ rejected this argument holding that the wife had, at all times, kept the shares in her sole name and separate from the matrimonial assets. The length of the marriage did not alter the fact that as the shares were not mixed with the matrimonial assets, it was clear that the wife did not regard them as part of the matrimonial property. Thus the husband's award which although a small percentage of the assets was not discriminatory and, given the marital standard of living, recourse to the value of the shares was not required to meet his needs. When deciding whether to share non-matrimonial property, therefore, the court will look not only at the length of the marriage, but also the extent to which such property has been mingled with the parties' matrimonial assets.

### 5.5.3.4 *The 'special contribution' argument*

Much of the case law after *White* and *Miller; McFarlane* explored the circumstances when it will be fair to depart from equal division of the assets. A body of case law emerged in the immediate aftermath of *White* in which claims were made, usually by wealthy husbands, that their wealth creation was exceptional and, as such, they should be regarded as having made a 'special contribution' to the marriage which justified them being awarded more of the assets on divorce. In *Cowan v Cowan*,[318] for example, the Court of Appeal said that the husband should receive a greater share of the capital assets on divorce because his contribution to the welfare of the family in building up a very successful business was 'exceptional'. However, this approach was criticised by the Court of Appeal in *Lambert v Lambert*.[319] The parties' marriage had lasted 23 years and at the time of the divorce the wife was 49 and the husband was 57. There were two children of the marriage, aged 19 and 20 respectively. Both were at university and were very wealthy as a result of a trust created for them by their parents. Prior to the marriage, the husband had started a business which became very

---

[315] See *Robson v Robson* [2010] EWCA Civ 1171.     [316] [2011] EWCA Civ 550.
[317] Ibid, [18].     [318] [2001] 2 FLR 192.     [319] [2003] 1 FLR 139.

successful and which generated the family's substantial wealth. In 1999, shares in the husband's company were sold for £75 million. Of this, the husband received £19.7 million, the wife received £500,000, and the trust in favour of the children received £6 million. At the date of the ancillary relief hearing, the total assets amounted to £20.2 million. The wife sought 50 per cent of the assets on the basis that her contribution to the family had been equal to that of the husband. Throughout the marriage the wife had been the primary homemaker and parent although she also claimed that she had played an important role in the success of the husband's business. By contrast, the husband argued that the family's assets had been generated as a result of his labour, that his wife's involvement in the business had been more or less ornamental, and that this should be reflected in the settlement. The first instance judgment of Connell J gave the wife 37.5 per cent of the family's assets, which included the marital home; the departure from equal division being justified on the basis of the husband's special contributions.[320] Relying on the Court of Appeal decision in *Cowan v Cowan*, Connell J concluded that the husband's contribution, although not the product of genius, was a 'special achievement, via special business skills, acumen and effort'. Against this, the wife's contributions could not be described as 'really special' and despite Connell J's admission that there was nothing more that she could have done to justify equal division, this did not mean that an award of less than 50 per cent was unfair. This approach was strongly criticised by the Court of Appeal where Thorpe LJ emphasised that it was unacceptable to place greater value on the contribution of the breadwinner than that of the homemaker as justification for unequal division of assets.[321] He said:

> there must be an end to the sterile assertion that the breadwinner's contribution weighs heavier than the homemaker's.[322]

In addition, the court did not accept that its duty to assess the statutory criteria when making an order for financial provision required a detailed critical appraisal of the performance of each of the parties during the marriage. Indeed, the court foresaw that it was only a matter of time before this 'forensic analysis' approach led to arguments about a spouse's substandard contributions thus resulting in the re-emergence of conduct which, under the legislation, can only be considered if it is 'inequitable to disregard'. To avoid this, the court preferred to *assume* that the parties' contributions to this 23-year marriage had been equal.[323] This is not to suggest that finding that one party has made a special contribution will never be possible.[324] However, refusing to engage in a discussion as to the circumstances which would justify such a finding, Thorpe LJ preferred to leave the issue open-ended stating that it would only be successful in exceptional circumstances to be explored in future case law.

The House of Lords considered the 'special contributions' argument in *Miller; McFarlane* and, in doing so, approved *Lambert* and emphasised that the ethos of *White* must be followed. That is, domestic and financial contributions should be treated equally.[325] This meant that the while it still remains possible for one spouse to argue that they have made a 'special contribution', this will only be successful in exceptional cases. Lord Nicholls said that:

> [p]arties should not seek to promote a case of 'special contribution' unless the contribution is so marked that to disregard it would be inequitable. A good reason for departing from equality is not to be found in the minutiae of married life.[326]

---

[320]  *L v L* [2002] 1 FLR 642.      [321]  [2003] 1 FLR 139.      [322]  Ibid, [38].

[323]  Note, however, that equality of contributions does not mean equal division: 'a distinction must be drawn between an assessment of equality of contribution and an order for equality of division. A finding of equality of contribution may be followed by an order for unequal division because of the influence of one or more of the other statutory criteria as well as the over-arching search for fairness.' Ibid, [38].

[324]  Eg in *Sorrell v Sorrell* [2005] EWHC 1717 (Fam) the wife was awarded 40 per cent of the assets on the ground that her husband has made an exceptional contribution in building up a business worth £546 million.

[325]  [2006] UKHL 24 at [146].      [326]  Ibid, [67].

This approach was followed by the Court of Appeal in *Charman v Charman*.[327] The husband in this case, through his work in the insurance industry, had built up assets of approximately £130 million and he argued, amongst other things, that he had therefore made a 'special contribution' to the family. On this point, the Court of Appeal confirmed that a special contribution to the welfare of the family could be non-financial as well as financial although the court pointed out that, in practice, the claim of 'special contribution' has only been made by someone who has generated great wealth during the marriage. When assessing such claims the court said that:

> the court will no doubt have regard to the amount of the wealth; and in some cases, perhaps including the present, its amount will be so extraordinary as to make it easy for the party who generated it to claim an exceptional and individual quality which deserves special treatment. Often, however, he or she will need independently to establish such a quality, whether by genius in business or in some other field. Sometimes, by contrast, it will immediately be obvious that substantial wealth generated during the marriage is a windfall—the proceeds, for example, of an unanticipated sale of land for development or of an embattled takeover of a party's ailing company—which is not the product of a special contribution.[328]

While the Court of Appeal did not set a threshold of wealth which would evidence a special contribution, it did offer some guidance on how the finding of a special contribution on behalf of one party would affect the award. According to the court, in such circumstances, as a guideline the departure from equal division should be somewhere between 66.6/33.3 per cent and 55/45 per cent. In the case of *Charman* itself, the husband's contribution in generating the massive wealth was regarded as special and, as such, he was awarded 63.5 per cent of the assets.

## 5.6 **Rules or guidelines?**

As we have seen there has been a considerable amount of case law following *White* and *Miller; McFarlane* which attempts to clarify and apply the principles enunciated by the House of Lords. Two schools of thought have emerged in the Court of Appeal on the role of these judicially constructed principles when the court is deciding upon a financial provision order. One school sees the principles as offering structured guidelines within which the court exercises its discretion in order to promote consistency and predictability in terms of outcomes. We have already seen that such an approach was advocated in *Jones v Jones*[329] in relation to the distinction between matrimonial and non-matrimonial property. Other cases taking this approach include *N v F*,[330] and *K v L*.[331] The alternative approach regards the principles as mere guidelines, not rules, which inform the court when considering the section 25 factors and the circumstances of the case. Preferring a more fact-specific analysis, this approach emphasises the discretionary nature of the exercise and the need 'to find the right answer to suit the circumstances of the case'.[332] Cases which favour this approach include *Robson v Robson*,[333] *AR v AR*,[334] and *R v R*.[335] Thus, not only is there uncertainty surrounding the *content* of the judicial principles, but there is also disagreement about the *status* of these principles when the court is exercising its discretion.

## 5.7 **The Law Commission Report: 'Matrimonial Property, Needs and Agreements'**

The Law Commission carried out a project on marital property agreements and published a Consultation Paper on this topic in 2011. While this paper focused on the enforceability of

---

[327] [2007] EWCA Civ 503.     [328] Ibid, [80].     [329] [2011] EWCA Civ 11.
[330] [2011] EWHC 586.     [331] [2011] EWCA Civ 550.
[332] *Robson v Robson* [2010] EWCA Civ 1171 at [43].     [333] [2010] EWCA Civ 1171.
[334] [2011] EWHC 2717.     [335] [2011] EWHC 3093.

pre-nuptial agreements, it raised broader issues about financial provision orders. Thus, the Commission extended the remit of the project to include an examination of two areas of the law on financial provision:

1. the definition of 'needs' in the post-divorce context, and

2. the definition and treatment of non-matrimonial property.

A final report was published by the Commission in 2014.[336]

### 5.7.1 The law relating to 'needs'

While the meaning of 'financial needs' is not defined in the legislation, it is the determining factor in most divorces.[337] In small-asset cases, this will usually dictate the outcome as once the parties are re-housed and have their needs met, there may be nothing left to distribute. In big-money cases, the equal sharing principle is subject to the parties' needs, and the significance of property being non-matrimonial will carry less weight where needs cannot be met without recourse to that property. As the Law Commission point out '[t]he law is clear that former spouses have a responsibility for each other's needs after divorce or dissolution. But it does not state clearly how much, and for how long, a former spouse has to pay or contribute for this purpose.'[338] The Commission concluded in their Consultation Paper in 2011 that the lack of a principled basis governing this area of the law leads to problems. It makes it hard for legal advisers to give clear guidance to clients in the negotiation of settlements, particularly as there is evidence that different outcomes can be obtained in different courts and different regions. This is compounded by the fact that cuts to the legal aid budget mean that an increasing number of divorcing couples are negotiating settlements without legal representation. It is hard to bargain in the shadow of the law when one cannot discern what the law is. Thus, the Commission originally intended to 'to make recommendations for law reform which would introduce a clear principled basis for meeting needs after divorce and dissolution—a principle that would state what had to be paid and why'.[339]

However, in their Final Report published in 2014, the Commission concluded that the law relating to responsibilities of former spouses to meet each other's 'financial needs' is not in need of statutory reform. Although the courts have a wide discretion when making awards for needs, in practice the financial orders tend to lead the parties to independence.[340] This, according to the Commission, was the correct approach and, therefore, no fundamental change was required.

However, in order to ensure that the law was applied in a consistent fashion, the Commission recommended that the meaning of 'financial needs' be clarified in guidance to be published by the Family Justice Council.[341] The intention is not to change in any way the current law relating to financial needs, but rather to make the law, and the courts' practice more transparent. It is worth setting out the aims of the Commission in this regard:

> Our recommendation is that the Family Justice Council guidance should not only make clear the elements involved in assessing financial needs but also make explicit and endorse the courts' practice of making orders that lead to independence, to the extent that that is possible in the light of choices made within the marriage, the length of the marriage, the marital standard of living, the parties' expectation

---

[336] Law Commission, *Matrimonial Property, Needs and Agreements* (Law Com No 343, 2014), http://lawcommission. justice.gov.uk/docs/lc343_matrimonial_property.pdf.

[337] Ibid, para 1.22.

[338] Law Commission Consultation Paper 208 (Summary), *Matrimonial Property, Needs and Agreements: An Overview* (2012), para 4.

[339] Ibid, at para 44.

[340] See, for example, *Wright v Wright* [2015] EWCA Civ 201; *Grocholewska-Mullins v Mullins* [2014] EWCA Civ 148; *SS v NS (Spousal Maintenance)* [2014] EWHC 4183.

[341] The Ministry of Justice has agreed that the Family Justice Council should do this, 'Ministry of Justice, divorce myths to be dispelled', (2014, London: Ministry of Justice).

> of a home, and their continued shared responsibilities in the future, particularly for children. Couples making their own settlements, in the light of the courts' practice, can be informed by that guidance and will have an indication of the outcome that they should be aiming for.[342]

While this clarifies, to an extent, the objective of the law of financial provision on divorce, it is suggested that the Commission missed an opportunity to state more definitively the definition of financial needs in the post-divorce context.

### 5.7.2 The law relating to non-matrimonial property

As we have seen, the current law on financial provision distinguishes between matrimonial and non-matrimonial property. The courts' approach at present is generally not to make orders requiring former spouses to share non-matrimonial property (that is, property acquired by gift or inheritance, or acquired before marriage or civil partnership) unless that property is required to meet financial needs. A range of complexities exists when dealing with non-matrimonial property and the Commission previously highlighted this as an area in need of clarification.[343] For example, what rules should apply if inherited property is sold and the proceeds used to buy property that is used by the whole family?[344] However, the final Report makes no recommendations with regard to non-matrimonial property. This lack of guidance is justified by the Commission on the grounds that there was no consensus amongst consultees on how to treat non-matrimonial property and to deal with the myriad of issues which arise. The Commission took the view that as the question of how to deal with non-matrimonial property only arises in the minority of cases where the parties' assets exceed their financial needs, it is preferable to enable couples who have non-matrimonial property to make their own arrangements by making qualifying nuptial agreements.[345] However, the Commission concludes that, once more cases have reached the courts and the implications of non-matrimonial property have been further explored, there may be an opportunity for statutory provision.[346] This is a somewhat disappointing view. There is no doubt that the distinction between matrimonial and non-matrimonial property is a contentious issue, but rather than wait on the issues being teased out by the courts through expensive litigation, the Commission could have taken a stronger line in directing policy in this area. This issue may become even more relevant as parties in the future take the opportunity to protect non-matrimonial property from availability in the financial settlement on divorce through making a pre-nuptial agreement.

## 6 *Wyatt v Vince*: is there a time limit for making an application for financial provision?

The Supreme Court has recently had to consider whether there is any time limit on an application for financial relief. In *Wyatt* v *Vince*,[347] in a set of circumstances regarded by Lord Wilson as 'highly unusual'[348], the wife made an application for financial provision from her former spouse 27 years after they separated and 18 years after they divorced. The parties married in 1981 and had a son. Ms Wyatt also had a daughter from a previous relationship who was treated by Mr Vince as a child of the family. They separated in 1984. For a number of years after the parties' separation, Mr Vince lived as a new age traveller and was in no position to make any substantial payments of maintenance for either of the two children. During this time, Ms Wyatt lived in very difficult financial circumstances, struggling to 'maintain a home for them in circumstances of real privation bordering upon poverty'.[349] The couple

---

[342] Ibid, para 1.27.
[343] Law Commission, *Matrimonial Property, Needs and Agreements: A Supplementary Consultation Paper* (Consultation Paper No 208, 2012), http://lawcommission.justice.gov.uk/docs/cp208_matrimonial_property.pdf.
[344] Law Commission, *Matrimonial Property, Needs and Agreements* (Law Com No 343, 2014), para 1.39.
[345] Ibid.    [346] Ibid, para 1.40.    [347] [2015] UKSC 14.
[348] Ibid, at [2].    [349] Ibid, at [17].

divorced in 1992 although as the court file was mislaid it was unknown whether any order was made at the time regarding financial provision. The court, however, had no reason to believe that Ms Wyatt's claims were dismissed. From the late 1990s, Mr Vince's green energy business, Ecotricity, which he founded in 1995, became extremely successful and he became a muilti-millionaire. The court noted that he had achieved 'brilliant success' and was clearly a 'remarkable man'. In 2001, the couple's son went to live with him and to work for his company. By contrast, Ms Wyatt, who went on to have two more children, continues to live in very modest circumstances. She lives partly on her wages generated during periods of low-paid employment, although interrupted by periods of ill-health, and partly on state benefits. The court noted that the three adult children resident in her household make no more than modest contributions to its running expenses.[350]

In 2011, Ms Wyatt applied for financial provision from Mr Vince seeking a lump sum award of around £1.9million plus an order for her legal costs to be paid by him. Mr Vince argued that her application should be struck out pursuant to Rule 4.4 of the Family Procedure Rules 2010, which provides that the court may strike out an application if it appears to the court either that there are no reasonable grounds for bringing or defending the application, or it is an abuse of the court's process or is otherwise likely to obstruct the just disposal of the proceedings. In 2012, a deputy High Court judge dismissed Mr Vince's strike-out application and ordered him to make interim periodical payments to cover Ms Wyatt's legal costs. However, the Court of Appeal struck out Ms Wyatt's application for financial provision and ordered her to repay part of the money received under the costs allowance order. She appealed to the Supreme Court. The Supreme Court unanimously allowed the appeal which means that the wife's application for financial provision will now proceed in the High Court. The costs allowance order was also restored and the Court of Appeal's repayment order was set aside, with the result that Ms Wyatt's legal costs will be met by Mr Vince.[351]

In reaching this decision, the Supreme Court observed that in civil proceedings, the court has the power to give summary judgment when the claimant or defendant has no real prospect of success and there is no other compelling reason why the case should go to trial.[352] However, there is no corresponding power in family proceedings. This is a deliberate omission because when a former spouse makes an application for financial provision, the court has a duty under section 25(1) of the MCA 1973 to determine that application having regard to all the circumstances, and the statutory criteria listed for consideration. This assessment is not appropriate for summary determination. Thus, when construing Rule 4.4 of the Family Procedure Rules 2010, it did not matter whether or not the application had any real prospect of success. An application has 'no reasonable grounds' for the purposes of these rules only if it is not legally recognisable, for example, because there has already been a final determination of the proceedings, or the applicant has remarried.[353] Neither should an application be regarded as an 'abuse of process' on the ground that it has no real prospect of success.[354] As such, Ms Wyatt's application was regarded as legally recognisable and her appeal was successful.

Lord Wilson then decided to conduct a 'provisional evaluation of the issues' for the purposes of securing efficient future case management.[355] In doing so, we have been given an insight into the Court's thinking on the likelihood of success for Ms Wyatt on the substantive issues (which will be determined in the High Court). According to Lord Wilson, she faces 'formidable difficulties' in seeking to establish that a financial order should be made in her favour. He outlined five factors which would go against her.[356] First, the marital cohabitation lasted for little more than two years.

---

[350] Ibid, at [6].

[351] The test for making this order was whether Ms Wyatt could reasonably secure legal services by any other means. Given that it would be unreasonable to expect her solicitors to continue to act without payment until the determination of her substantive application, this test was satisfied, ibid, at [39–40]. The court now has a statutory jurisdiction to make a legal services payment order (under section 22ZA of the Matrimonial Causes Act 1973), which replaces the costs allowance order. In this case, however, the deputy judge made his order before this came into force. However, the Supreme Court noted that there is a 'close parallel' between the criteria for making a legal services payment order and the criteria for making a costs allowance order under the preceding jurisdiction, ibid, at [39].

[352] Ibid, at [24].    [353] Ibid, at [27].    [354] Ibid.    [355] Ibid, at [29].    [356] Ibid, at [30].

Second, the marriage broke down 31 years ago. Third, the standard of living enjoyed by the parties prior to the breakdown could not have been lower. Fourth, the husband did not begin to create his current wealth until 13 years after the breakdown. Finally, the wife has made no contribution, direct or indirect, to the husband's wealth creation. Lord Wilson was doubtful whether the wife would be able to secure financial provision from Mr Wyatt based on her 'financial needs'. He said that '[i]t is a dangerous fallacy . . . that the current law always requires rich men to meet the reasonable needs of their ex-wives'.[357] His Lordship continued, '[i]n order to sustain a case of need, at any rate if made after many years of separation, a wife must show not only that the need exists but that it has been generated by her relationship with her husband'.[358] This may prove fatal to the wife's claim on the basis of need. According to Lord Wilson, a more powerful argument may lie in the contributions she made to the welfare of the family, in particular, looking after the couple's children over many years in very difficult financial circumstances and without financial assistance from Mr Vince. It is these contributions which Lord Wilson considered may justify a financial order for a comparatively modest sum in comparison with the £1.9 million sought, perhaps enabling her to purchase a somewhat more comfortable, and mortgage-free, home for herself and her remaining dependants.[359] However, it remains to be seen whether her very lengthy delay in bringing a claim will have an impact on her final award.[360]

The decision to allow a wife to claim financial relief from her former spouse almost 20 years after the divorce is unprecedented. Unsurprisingly, it attracted a considerable amount of media attention, which, at times, sensationalised the decision[361] and missed the crucial point that it did not actually give Ms Wyatt any financial award, but simply gave her the right to make a financial provision application notwithstanding the time lapse from the date of the divorce. It confirmed that provided a final order has not already been made, or the applicant has not remarried, there is no time limit on making an application for financial provision from a former spouse. Thus it serves as a useful reminder to divorcing spouses to ensure that all financial matters are finalised at the time of the divorce and a court order obtained. If the parties reach an agreed settlement, which is the preferred option, this should be turned into a consent order in order to make it final.[362] If this is not done, it is now clear that it remains open to one party to make a claim for financial provision at a future date.

---

### Talking Point

Resolution, the organisation representing family lawyers, said of the decision:

> The Supreme Court has made it clear that the draconian power to strike out family proceedings simply does not exist, but stress that the court will consider the merits of such applications on a case by case basis . . . If Ms Wyatt had lost her appeal, Resolution was concerned that people without access to legal advice as a result of the legal aid cuts would have been at risk of having their applications struck out without proper consideration simply because of delay, along arbitrary lines.[363]

---

[357]  Ibid, at [33]. See also *North v North* [2007] EWCA Civ 760.     [358]  [2015] UKSC 14.

[359]  Ibid, at [36].

[360]  It is worth pointing out that as Mr Vince is responsible for Ms Wyatt's legal fees, it is very likely that the case will settle out of court and thus we may never know the extent of her financial award.

[361]  For example, the headline in the Daily Mail said: "Ex-wife of hippy turned wind farm tycoon who became a millionaire AFTER they split wins right to fight for £2million divorce payout', 11 March 2015, http://www.dailymail.co.uk/news/article-2989511/Ex-wife-hippy-turned-wind-farm-tycoon-millionaire-split-wins-right-fight-2million-divorce-payout.html.

[362]  See Section 9.2.

[363]  Resolution, Vince divorce case shows need for reform, 16 March 2015, http://www.resolution.org.uk/news-list.asp?page_id=228&n_id=277.

**Q.** Do you agree that the decision in *Vince v Wyatt* is to be applauded for ensuring that everyone has the opportunity for their application for financial provision to be fully heard?

However, Resolution also sounded a note of caution saying that the decision illustrates the need for reform of the law in this area to ensure greater certainty regarding the outcome of financial provision applications. Resolution Chair, Jo Edwards, said:

> 'But it's also important that people who have become wealthy over time are not exposed to potentially opportunistic claims many years after a marriage has broken down. We want to see reform of the law around financial provision on divorce. Part of that is a desire for greater clarity and a clearer intention to get couples to financial independence sooner.'[364]

**Q.** Do you think that the current discretionary-based system allows the court to take account of 'unusual circumstances', such as those in *Vince v Wyatt*, as they arise in individual cases? Or, do you think that injecting a greater degree of certainty into the system would reduce the amount and cost of litigation associated with the current broad discretion?

# 7 Pensions

For many people who are divorcing, the two most valuable assets they possess are the matrimonial home and any expectation they may have under a pension scheme.[365] Divorce has serious implications in relation to the parties' pension rights, particularly in cases where one spouse has substantial pension provision and the other has not. For example, a divorced wife will lose the opportunity to share in her husband's pension once it becomes payable and further, because a divorced wife is no longer her husband's widow for the purposes of his pension scheme, if he should predecease her, she will not obtain a widow's pension. Similarly, if the wife has a pension scheme which pays benefits to a widower, the husband will not be able to benefit from it if the parties divorce. The loss of pension entitlements therefore usually represents a real financial deprivation to a spouse, particularly one divorced in middle age who may not have a pension scheme of their own.

There are many types of benefit which can accrue under pension schemes. These include lump sum benefits, a regular income entitlement, a widow/widower's pension, death in service benefits, and life cover. The valuation of a person's interest in his pension scheme is by no means problem-free even though the process of gathering information is assisted by regulations.[366] For example, future interest, inflation, and taxation rates can only be predicted. This can therefore give rise to differing valuations, depending on the expectations and assumptions of the actuary doing the calculation.[367] This necessarily makes it difficult for any adviser to reach a conclusion as to the worth of a pension.

## 7.1 Duty to consider the parties' pension entitlements

The court, when making financial and property arrangements on divorce, is mandated to have regard to 'any benefits under a pension scheme which a party to the marriage has or is likely to have' when

---

[364] Ibid.    [365] See the comments of Lords Nicholls in *Brooks v Brooks* [1995] 2 FLR 13 at 15.

[366] See Occupational Pension Schemes (Disclosure of Information) Regulations 1996; Occupational Pension Schemes (Disclosure of Information) Amendment Regulations 2002; Personal and Occupational Pension Schemes (Indexation and Disclosure of Information) (Miscellaneous Amendments) Regulations 2005; Divorce etc. (Pensions) Regulations 2000; Pensions on Divorce etc. (Provision of Information) Regulations 2000.

[367] For a helpful analysis of how to assess the value of a pension, see *T v T (Financial Relief: Pensions)* [1998] 1 FLR 1072.

considering the spouses' resources under paragraph (a) of section 25(2);[368] and when considering paragraph (h) the court must have regard to 'any benefits under a pension scheme which, by reason of the dissolution or annulment of the marriage, a party to the marriage will lose the chance of acquiring'.[369] However, while the parties' respective pension entitlements and any loss of pension rights have to be considered, the court is not bound to make an order distributing the value of the pension between the parties.[370] Rather, redistributing the parties' pension rights on divorce is just one tool at the court's disposal to do justice between the parties in the exercise of its overall discretion. However, should the court wish to compensate one party for loss of pension rights or distribute the capital value of the pension fund between the parties as part of the financial settlement, there are a number of options available to it. The law relating to pensions after divorce was amended by the Pensions Act 1995, which inserted sections 25B–25D into the MCA 1973 and introduced the 'earmarking order', and by the Welfare Reform and Pensions Act 1999 which established pension splitting, which is the most effective means of redistributing the value of a pension on divorce.

## 7.2 Pensions–the options

### 7.2.1 Compensation to offset the loss of pension entitlements

The simplest means by which a court can take account of the potential loss of pension rights is to compensate the loser when adjusting the division of the parties' present financial and property assets. For example, where the husband can anticipate a lump sum payment and a regular income under his pension scheme, this might persuade a court to transfer the entire beneficial interest in the former matrimonial home to the wife, and/or to order that her periodical payments should last for the parties' joint lives, and/or to make a lump sum order. In appropriate cases, it could defer payment of the lump sum until the pension lump sum becomes payable. In many cases, however, it is not possible to make present provision for lost pension rights which adequately takes account of the pensioner's future entitlement and so this is only an option where resources permit such a compensatory award to be made.

### 7.2.2 Earmarking order

Sections 25B–25D give the court the power to earmark part of the pensioner's entitlement for the benefit of the other spouse and to order that the trustees or managers of the pension make payments to that person from the pension fund once it becomes payable. Thus under section 25B(4) the court 'may require the person responsible for the pension arrangement in question, if at any time any payment in respect of any benefits under the arrangement becomes due to the party with pension rights, to make a payment for the benefit of the other party'.[371] Thus, once the pensioner begins to draw benefits, a proportion of the pension can immediately become payable to his ex-spouse.[372] Similarly, the court may require the trustees or managers to pay the whole or part of a lump sum, when it becomes due, to the other party.[373] A disadvantage of earmarking arrangements is that it ties the parties together financially although their marriage has ended, and the receiving spouse is vulnerable should the pensioner spouse die prematurely as this brings any earmarking arrangements to an end. There may also be vulnerability where the pensioner delays taking his pension entitlement or stops paying into the scheme prematurely. Given these difficulties, greater powers were given to the court by the Welfare Reform and Pensions Act 1999 which provides for full pension splitting at the time of the divorce proceedings.

---

[368] Section 25B(1)(a).     [369] Section 25B(1)(b).     [370] See *Burrow v Burrow* [1999] 1 FLR 508.

[371] Under s 25B(5), an earmarking order must be expressed in percentage terms.

[372] Pension payments are periodical payments and therefore they do not survive the death or remarriage of the payee (s 28). Applications to vary the order can be made under s 31. See also *T v T (Financial Relief: Pensions)* [1998] 1 FLR 1072 at 1085.

[373] Section 25C(2). In common with ordinary lump sums, lump sum payments from a pension are treated as capital payments and are therefore unaffected by the remarriage of the recipient spouse.

### 7.2.3 **Pension splitting**

Pension splitting allows the court to split the pension between the parties at the time of the divorce. In other words, the pension is split into two sections (in equal or unequal proportions) to be allocated to each party who thereafter will be responsible for making their own pension arrangements from their provision. As it splits the pension at the time of the divorce it ties in with the principle that it is normally desirable to achieve a clean break between the parties at the time of the divorce. Pension splitting is available 'in relation to a person's shareable rights under any pension arrangement other than an excepted public service pension scheme'.[374] Under the order, a percentage of one party's rights under a pension scheme is transferred to the other party to enable her to establish her own pension provision either within or outside the current scheme.[375] The transferee is credited with the percentage value of the pension ordered by the court and the transferor's fund is reduced accordingly.[376] It should be noted that pension splitting, while a more effective remedy, does not replace the earmarking order, which can still be made. However, a pension splitting order cannot be made where an earmarking order is already in force in relation to the pension.[377] Also, an earmarking order cannot be made where a pension splitting order is already in force.[378]

In short, under section 25B the court *must* consider the current and/or likely pension entitlements of the parties on divorce and, in particular, any pension benefits which a spouse will lose on divorce. However, that is not to say that the court must make an order which either compensates the spouse for this loss or splits the value of the pension fund between the parties. In *T v T (Financial Relief: Pensions)*[379] it was argued on behalf of a wife that the earmarking provisions of section 25B–25D did not merely enable the court to compensate her for loss of pension benefits, they *required* the court to compensate her. Singer J rejected this argument.[380] He stated that giving consideration to pension provision was simply included as part of the conventional discretionary balancing exercise the court was required to perform.[381] Thus whether the court makes an order in relation to the pension is simply part of the court's discretionary powers under section 25 which will be exercised to achieve a fair result between the parties.

## 8 The matrimonial home—what order is the most appropriate?

Often the parties' only major asset is the matrimonial home and it may require some ingenuity to make adequate provision for each spouse from one main resource, particularly where they have dependent children. The dilemma faced by those assisting the parties to reach an agreement in

---

[374] Welfare Reform and Pensions Act 1999, s 27(1). Thus pension splitting can be applied to private and occupational pension schemes, as well as State Earnings Related Pension Scheme (SERPS) contributions, but not the basic state pension. This remains the case under the Pensions Act 2014 which introduces a new flat-rate, single tier pension.

[375] MCA 1973, s 21A(1).      [376] See the Welfare Reform and Pensions Act 1999, s 29.

[377] MCA 1973, s 24B(5).      [378] Section 25B(7B).      [379] [1998] 1 FLR 1072.

[380] In this case the wife had applied for an order directing the trustees of the husband's pension fund to pay her a proportion of his pension. Singer J declined to earmark part of the husband's pension in this fashion as he foresaw that such a direction could give rise to a number of potential 'pitfalls, disadvantages, complications and distractions'. These included the fact that it was impossible to predict the appropriate quantum of periodical payments so far ahead; the husband might delay the date when he took his pension rights; an application to vary the order could be made even before it came into effect; the court would be in a far better position to determine the amount of an order at the time when the husband took his pension rights; and there was no reason for supposing that the husband would not meet an appropriate periodical payments order from his pension receipts after retirement. For similar reasons, the court declined to require the husband to commute part of his pension benefits (s 25B(7)) so that a deferred lump sum could be paid to the wife. However, the pension trustees were ordered to pay a lump sum equal to ten times her annual maintenance payable from any death in service benefits, as these benefits might not fall into the husband's estate and would therefore not be available to the wife as a dependant in an application made under the Inheritance (Provision for Family and Dependants) Act 1975.

[381] See also *Burrow v Burrow* [1999] 1 FLR 508.

such circumstances, and by the court in determining what order to make, is how arrangements can be made which give proper recognition to the rights of both spouses in the property, protect a financially dependent spouse and any children of the family, create a clean break where appropriate, and allow for an adjustment of the position if the circumstances of the parties should significantly alter. Clearly, these very different objectives nearly always conflict. Moreover, there is a real risk that any property they own will be worth much less than it was originally by the time the parties have finished negotiating over what should happen to it, because of escalating legal costs.

As we have already seen, the court will endeavour to ensure that the children are adequately housed with the residential parent and that sufficient resources are left to house the non-residential parent.[382] However, in cases where resources are limited, this may not always be possible and thus it is not the case that both spouses 'invariably have a right to purchase accommodation'.[383]

## 8.1 The powers of the court

The options in relation to distribution of the family home are not limited to simply transferring the property into the sole name of one spouse or ordering immediate sale and distribution of the proceeds between the parties. Rather, the courts have a variety of options to achieve the immediate housing of the children and residential parent, whilst preserving the rights of the non-residential parent in the property. The following sections will discuss the main methods of disposition of the matrimonial home on divorce in situations where the property is owned by the parties (it may, of course, be subject to a mortgage). The court's power to order the transfer of tenancies under Part IV of the Family Law Act 1996 will also be highlighted.

### 8.1.1 The property to be sold and the proceeds of sale divided (s 24A)

The attractive feature of an agreement, or order, under which the matrimonial home is sold and the proceeds of sale divided between the parties is that each spouse is able to realise his or her investment in the property. The court can order that the proceeds of sale be divided in whatever proportions it sees fit in the exercise of its overall discretion to achieve fairness between the parties. This solution is particularly appropriate where there are no children and where each spouse can be adequately housed in alternative accommodation from his or her share of the proceeds. It is also appropriate where the spouses are young. They can go their separate ways, using their shares in the money realised as a down payment on fresh property should they so wish.

### 8.1.2 The property to be transferred into the sole name of one of the spouses (s 24(1)(a))

Transferring the matrimonial home into the sole name of one spouse, like sale, has the advantage that it helps to achieve a clean break. It also has the beneficial outcome that the owning spouse is not in the position of being fearful that he or she will have to sell the property at some date in the future in order that the other spouse can have his share.[384] Courts have been willing to order that the matrimonial home should belong solely to one of the parties where, in the circumstances of the case, the other party has alternative accommodation or sufficient resources to secure accommodation. Thus where one spouse enjoyed secure accommodation as part of his employment, as in *Hanlon v Hanlon*,[385] or had acquired an interest in property through marriage to another, as in *H v H (Financial Provision: Remarriage)*,[386] or had additional wealth as a result of inheritance, as in *Schuller v Schuller*,[387] the property was vested in the name of the other spouse alone.

---

[382] See *M v B (Ancillary Proceedings: Lump Sum)* [1998] 1 FLR 53.
[383] *Piglowska v Piglowski* [1999] 3 All ER 632 at 642–43.
[384] See *Hanlon v Hanlon* [1978] 2 All ER 889; *Mortimer v Mortimer-Griffin* [1986] 2 FLR 315.
[385] [1978] 2 All ER 889. The husband lived rent-free in a police flat.     [386] [1975] 1 All ER 367.
[387] [1990] 2 FLR 193.

When transferring the matrimonial home to one spouse on divorce, the court can order that the other spouse be compensated for his or her loss by a lump sum payment, raised perhaps through the property being mortgaged or remortgaged. An order requiring the spouse to whom the property is transferred to pay the other spouse a lump sum is similar in effect to one in which sale of the home is ordered, because in each case both acquire a share in the value of the property.[388] However, a transfer of property has the advantage that the original property is retained thus preserving familiarity of surroundings and continuity for any children of the family.

The disadvantage of an order which transfers the parties' only substantial asset into the name of only one spouse is that, unless it is made with compensating provisions, it may give unfair weight to one spouse's needs at the expense of the other spouse's rights. This position is exacerbated when the order has been based on the parties' respective needs, and if the needy spouse's circumstances change for the better after the order in her favour has been finalised, for example if she remarries,[389] comes into an inheritance, or obtains gainful employment. At this stage there is no way of reopening the matter and correcting the imbalance of the original distribution of the property.[390] In the interests of fairness, the court may find it preferable to shape the order to allow both spouses to retain an interest in the former matrimonial home. Thus, satisfying the immediate needs of one spouse at the time of divorce should not necessarily outweigh the legitimate expectation of the other spouse to have some share in the property. Indeed, the principles of equality and non-discrimination inherent in *White v White* strengthen the argument that the fairest solution is that each spouse should retain, or be awarded, a proprietary interest in the former matrimonial home.[391] There are particular legal devices which can be used to facilitate this.

### 8.1.3 Postponing the sale of the property until a specified event

Where the parties are joint owners of the property at the time of the divorce a court can order that their co-ownership should continue, but that the right of occupation should be given solely to the spouse who remains in occupation. Sale of the property would then be deferred until a specified event has occurred. There are two main ways of achieving this.

#### 8.1.3.1 A Mesher Order

This is an order that the property remain in co-ownership with the sale postponed until the youngest child reaches a specified age, or finishes their full-time education including further and higher education whichever is the later.[392] The original *Mesher* order involved a settlement of the property on the spouses on trust for sale in equal shares, sale postponed until the youngest child reached 17.[393] But the term a '*Mesher* order' has been used by lawyers and judges to describe any order under which one of the spouses is kept out of his or her share in the former matrimonial home until a specified event relating to the children occurs.[394] An even more generous approach was taken by the Court of Appeal in *Sawden v Sawden*[395] where the sale of the property was postponed until the adult children had left the family home and had settled in homes of their own.

It was suggested that *Mesher* orders would become more popular in the aftermath of *White v White* where the need to ensure fairness between the parties could be achieved by meeting the

---

[388] In many instances, however, the owner spouse will not have sufficient resources to make any, or any substantial, payment.

[389] *Wells v Wells* [1992] 2 FLR 66.

[390] *Chaudhuri v Chaudhuri* [1992] 2 FLR 73; *Omielan v Omielan* [1996] 2 FLR 306.

[391] See S. Gerlis, 'White—The Unlearned Lesson' [2002] 32 Family Law 628; L. Fisher, 'The Unexpected Impact of White—Taking "Equality" Too Far' [2002] Family Law 108 at 111–12. See also *Elliott v Elliott* [2001] 1 FCR 477.

[392] *Richardson v Richardson (No 2)* [1994] 2 FLR 1051; *B v B* [1995] 1 FLR 9.

[393] *Mesher v Mesher and Hall* [1980] 1 All ER 126n.

[394] See eg *Carson v Carson* [1983] 1 All ER 478, in which the property was ordered to be held on trust for sale for the spouses jointly until the youngest child attained 18, or completed full-time education.

[395] [2004] 1 FCR 776.

immediate housing needs of the wife and children by giving them occupancy of the property, but allowing the husband to retain an interest in its capital. Such thinking led to the making of a *Mesher* order in *Elliott v Elliott*.[396] A *Mesher* order was also made in *Mansfield v Mansfield*.[397] This case involved an appeal by the husband against a financial order where most of the family assets originated from personal injury damages received by him prior to the marriage. The Court of Appeal held that while the amount of the wife's award would not be altered, there should be a *Mesher* order giving the husband a charge-back for one-third of the award which was realisable on the children's maturity. The Court of Appeal made it clear that the while the origin of the assets did not exclude them from the court's dispositive powers, it was the exceptional factor which made the case 'particularly suitable for the application of a Mesher order'.[398]

However, in general terms, *Mesher* orders are not popular with the judiciary. They have dropped out of favour, not only because they contradict the ideal of producing finality between the parties at the time of divorce but also because they are said to store up problems for the future.[399] *Obiter dicta* in *Clutton v Clutton*[400] suggest that a *Mesher* order may be appropriate where the spouses' assets are amply sufficient to house both parties if the home is sold immediately, but where it is in the interests of the children that they remain in the same home for the time being.[401] In such a case, said Lloyd LJ, it may be sensible and just to postpone sale until the children have left home, since the wife's share in the proceeds of sale when that time arrives will be sufficient to enable her to rehouse herself. However, he continued, 'where there is doubt as to the wife's ability to rehouse herself, on the charge taking effect, then a *Mesher* order should not be made'.[402] This statement highlights the reservations which the courts have expressed about *Mesher* orders in recent years. When the children reach the specified age, the parent who has been looking after them in the former matrimonial home may not have enough remaining money after sale of the property, or redemption of the charge, to buy a new property.[403]

Another disadvantage of a *Mesher* order is that children do not stop needing a family home merely because they leave school, complete further education, or start work. Whilst it may be realistic to expect a child to be able to earn a living once he attains his majority, it is may not be realistic to expect him to earn sufficient income to rent or buy adequate accommodation. It is interesting that in *Sawden v Sawden*,[404] the Court of Appeal added to the list of trigger events which would realise the husband's charge on the property when the children (aged 28 and 21) had left home and settled independently in homes of their own.[405]

### 8.1.3.2 A Martin Order

One spouse, usually the wife, may have a particularly pressing need to be accommodated in the former matrimonial home. Sometimes this need is likely to continue for the rest of her life. Because one of the main concerns of the court is to make sure that, wherever possible, each spouse is securely housed, it has sometimes been thought appropriate to order that while the matrimonial home remains jointly owned, the wife should be allowed to live in the property for the rest of her life. This means that the husband will never himself obtain his share in the property if he predeceases her. However, usually such an order contains the contingencies that the property should be sold 'if the wife should remarry or cohabit with another man'. This is often described as a *Martin*[406] order.

In *Clutton v Clutton* both spouses were aged 48 and were divorcing after a 20-year marriage. Their only asset of substance was the matrimonial home, the equity in which was about £50,000. The husband was earning about £20,000 per annum but had substantial debts. The

---

[396] [2001] 1 FCR 477. See S. Gerlis, '*White*—The Unlearned Lesson' [2002] 32 Family Law 628; L. Fisher, 'The Unexpected Impact of *White*—Taking "Equality" Too Far' [2002] Family Law 108 at 111–12.

[397] [2011] EWCA Civ 1056.     [398] Ibid, [23].     [399] *Carson v Carson* [1983] 1 All ER 478.

[400] [1991] 1 All ER 340.     [401] See also *Dorney-Kingdom v Dorney-Kingdom* [2000] 2 FLR 855.

[402] [1991] 1 All ER 340 at 343.     [403] *Hanlon v Hanlon* [1978] 2 All ER 889.     [404] [2004] 1 FCR 76.

[405] See [2005] Family Law 116.     [406] After *Martin v Martin* [1977] 3 All ER 762.

wife had an income of £66 per week working part time as a typist. She was in a stable sexual relationship with a man, but she said that she did not intend either to marry him or to cohabit with him. The Court of Appeal considered whether remarriage, or cohabitation, should affect the wife's future position, and found that it should. The essence of the court's judgment was that it would be unfair to the husband if he lost his entire interest in the property through the wife obtaining an outright transfer order, if she was later joined in the house by a new husband, the latter having contributed nothing towards its acquisition. In relation to cohabitation, Lloyd LJ said that if the reason underlying the clean break principle is the avoidance of bitterness, 'then the bitterness felt by the husband when he sees the former matrimonial home occupied by the wife's cohabitee must surely be greater than the bitterness felt by the wife being subject, as she fears, to perpetual supervision'.[407] The court therefore ordered that the sale of the house should be postponed until the wife died, remarried, or cohabited with another man, and that the proceeds should then be divided on the basis of two-thirds to the wife and one-third to the husband.

### 8.1.4  A charge over the property

We have seen that where the parties are joint owners of the property at the time of the divorce a court can order that their co-ownership should continue, but that the right of occupation should be given solely to the spouse who remains in occupation. Alternatively, one sole or co-owner can be ordered to transfer his or her interest in the property to the other. In return, the (now) sole owner spouse can be required to execute a charge over the property in favour of the other spouse to secure to him the payment of a sum of money. This is particularly popular where the property is mortgaged. Many mortgagees, that is the banks and building societies, will release a husband from his personal covenants under the mortgage on the wife giving an undertaking to take full responsibility for these, provided that she is in the financial position to do so. If the husband should then wish to obtain a fresh mortgage to purchase a new home, he will be in a better position to do so because he has no liabilities. Indeed, he may even be able to claim that he is particularly credit-worthy because he has a charge on property which he will be able to enforce at some time in the future. Thus a charge order is usually advantageous for the husband.

The advantage of a charge order from the wife's point of view is that she now has full control over the property, and can deal with it without consulting the husband. This is in contrast to her position where there is co-ownership. She is also entitled to redeem the charge at any time, thereby ending the husband's claim over the property.[408]

### 8.1.5  Transfer of tenancies

A court has power under section 53 of the Family Law Act 1996 to make an order transferring a relevant tenancy from one spouse/civil partner to the other at any time where it has the power to make a property adjustment order.[409] Consequently, the order may not take effect before a divorce/dissolution or separation order is made, or a decree of nullity is made absolute, unless the circumstances are exceptional.[410] A relevant tenancy means a protected or statutory tenancy within the meaning of the Rent Act 1977, a statutory tenancy within the meaning of the Rent (Agriculture) Act 1976, a secure tenancy within the meaning of section 79 of the Housing Act 1985, or an assured tenancy or assured agricultural occupancy within the meaning of Part I of the Housing Act 1988.[411] The provisions in Schedule 7 to the Family Law Act 1996 only apply if one spouse/civil partner is entitled, either in his own right or jointly with the other spouse/civil

---

[407] Ibid, 345.     [408] *Popat v Popat* [1991] 2 FLR 163.

[409] See the Family Law Act 1996, Sch 7, as amended by the Civil Partnership Act 2004, Sch 9. Thus, a civil partner is treated in exactly the same way as a spouse and all references to spouse in this section should be taken to include civil partners.

[410] MCA 1973, s 23B(1); Family Law Act 1996, Sch 7, para 12.     [411] Family Law Act 1996, Sch 7, para 1.

partner, to occupy a dwelling-house by virtue of a relevant tenancy.[412] As with any other property adjustment order, an application for a tenancy transfer cannot be made if the applicant has remarried or entered into another civil partnership.[413] The court is given guidelines on the matters to which it must have regard when determining whether to make a tenancy transfer order.[414] These are not the same as those detailed in the MCA 1973. Rather, the court's attention is directed towards the circumstances in which the tenancy was granted, the criteria for making occupation orders specified in section 33(6)(a), (b), and (c),[415] and the suitability of the parties as tenants[416] but, interestingly, conduct is not a relevant consideration.

## 9 Financial and property agreements

### 9.1 Separation agreements

Instead of using the courts to resolve their post-divorce financial and property arrangements, it is possible for the parties to enter into a separation agreement to govern those matters. Indeed spouses are encouraged to settle their financial and property affairs without recourse to litigation, and most arrangements are arrived at through negotiation, mediation, and agreement, such bargaining taking place in the shadow of what a court would be likely to do.[417] Privately negotiated agreements are preferable for a variety of reasons. Not only can they reduce legal costs, but parties may have a greater sense of ownership of a negotiated agreement and may thus be more likely to abide by its terms.

Subject to the general principles of contract law, a separation agreement is enforceable.[418] However, in *Hyman v Hyman*,[419] the House of Lords held that no agreement can oust the jurisdiction of the court since the court's powers are designed not only to protect a spouse's interest but also the public interest.[420] Section 34(1) of the MCA 1973 clarifies that any provision within such an agreement which purports to do so is void.[421] Such a term will not, however, render the rest of the agreement void. Sections 34–36 of the MCA 1973 regulate agreements between spouses, and either party can apply to the court under section 35 to vary the terms of the agreement. A privately negotiated agreement cannot prevent an application to the court to vary the agreement or an application for a financial order. Even an express agreement by one spouse not to apply for financial and property provision after divorce does not preclude that spouse from seeking such relief in the courts. Thus the parties are in the paradoxical position that the court may refuse to give effect to an agreement but the parties themselves are not able to resile from the agreement except where normal contractual principles would allow this, such as fraud, misrepresentation, or undue influence.[422]

This is not to say, however, that the court will ignore the terms of the parties' agreement. On the contrary, the agreement reached may be highly relevant to the court's deliberations. *Edgar v Edgar*[423] is the leading case on the weight to be given to a separation agreement. The husband and wife executed a deed of separation under which the wife agreed not to apply for a lump sum or

---

[412] Ibid, para 2.    [413] Ibid, para 13.    [414] Ibid, para 5.    [415] See Chapter 3.

[416] The Family Law Act 1996 extends the court's property adjustment jurisdiction to cohabitants where they are tenants of property, and the details of the provisions in Sch 7 are more fully discussed in Chapter 3.

[417] G. Davis, S. M. Cretney, and J. Collins, *Simple Quarrels* (Oxford: Clarendon Press, 1994).

[418] Such arrangements are normally embodied in a deed, which resolves any difficulties over whether there was a final binding agreement, cf *Standley v Stewkesbury* [1998] 2 FLR 610, or whether the agreement was supported by consideration.

[419] [1929] AC 601.

[420] Ibid, 644. The state has an interest in ensuring that divorce settlements are just and reasonable, and that arrangements are not made which improperly impose the burden of providing housing and income for a spouse and children onto income support or other state funds.

[421] MCA 1973, s 34(1).

[422] The unsatisfactory nature of the law in this area is neatly analysed by Hoffmann LJ in *Pounds v Pounds* [1994] 1 FLR 775 at 791.

[423] [1980] 1 WLR 1410. See also *Camm v Camm* (1983) 4 FLR 577; *Smith v McInerney* [1994] 2 FLR 1077.

property transfer order on divorce. The husband was very wealthy and the wife's solicitors advised her that she could obtain a far better settlement in divorce proceedings. The wife, however, was eager to separate from the husband and therefore was insistent upon concluding matters between the parties. Nearly three years later the parties divorced and the wife sought a lump sum payment. The trial judge declined to give effect to the agreement and ordered the husband to pay the wife £670,000. The Court of Appeal allowed the husband's appeal. With regard to the weight to be given to a separation agreement, Ormrod LJ said:

> To decide what weight should be given, in order to reach a just result, to a prior agreement not to claim a lump sum, regard must be had to the conduct of both parties, leading up to the prior agreement, and to their subsequent conduct, in consequence of it. It is not necessary in this connection to think in formal legal terms, such as misrepresentation or estoppel; all the circumstances as they affect each of two human beings must be considered in the complex relationship of marriage. So, the circumstances surrounding the making of the agreement are relevant. Undue pressure by one side, exploitation of a dominant position to secure an unreasonable advantage, inadequate knowledge, possibly bad legal advice, an important change of circumstances, unforeseen or overlooked at the time of making the agreement, are all relevant to the question of justice between the parties.[424] Important too is the general proposition that formal agreements, properly and fairly arrived at with competent legal advice, should not be displaced unless there are good and substantial grounds for concluding that an injustice will be done by holding the parties to the terms of their agreement. There may well be other considerations which affect the justice of this case; the above list is not intended to be an exclusive catalogue.

His Lordship went on to comment that, where there is an agreement, prima facie evidence of material facts which show that justice requires that the spouse should be relieved from the effects of the agreement will be required.[425]

Oliver LJ concluded that:

> the court must . . . start from the position that a solemn and freely negotiated bargain by which a party defines her own requirements ought to be adhered to unless some clear and compelling reason, such as, for instance, a drastic change of circumstances, is shown to the contrary.[426]

Since there was no evidence of pressure by the husband to force the wife to accept the terms of the deed, and since the wife had received advice from her lawyers which she had refused to take, it had not been shown that justice required the court to relieve her of her agreement.

Thus where a separation agreement has been arrived at with the benefit of legal advice and with none of the vitiating factors outlined by the Court of Appeal,[427] a court will normally make a financial provision and property adjustment order in identical terms.[428] However, where a party to

---

[424] See *B v B (Consent Order: Variation)* [1995] 1 FLR 9, where a consent order was set aside because the wife was in a depressed and confused state when agreeing to it. She was also given bad legal advice, but cf *Harris v Manahan* [1997] 1 FLR 205. The difficulty with allowing a spouse to repudiate an agreement where she has received bad legal advice is that the other spouse has not been responsible for the wrongful advice being given, yet it is he who will be affected by the agreement being overturned.

[425] Agreeing with Sir Gordon Willmer in *Wright v Wright* [1970] 1 WLR 1219 at 1224.

[426] [1980] 1 WLR 1410 at 1424.

[427] Such as non-disclosure, change of circumstances, duress, or lack of legal advice.

[428] The fact that one party would have achieved a better outcome by going to court is not usually a ground for allowing them to resile from the terms of the agreement, *per* Munby J in *X v X (Y and Z Intervening)* [2002] 1 FLR 508 at [103]. *L v M* [2014] EWHC 220 (Fam) made it clear that the test in *Edgar* which is used to determine whether a separation agreement should be made into an order of the court, must now be considered in light of the decision of the Supreme Court in *Radmacher v Granatino* [2010] UKSC 42 (see Section 9.3). This means that one party's lack of legal advice may no longer be a vitiating factor. The test is whether the party freely entered into the agreement with a full appreciation of its implications.

an agreement is not wilfully or capriciously seeking to depart from a formal agreement freely ne-gotiated, and where the circumstances are totally different from the circumstances contemplated by the contracting parties, the court may not adhere rigidly to the agreement as this would be to depart from the criteria in section 25.[429] Further, if there is evidence of unfair or improper pres-sure applied to one party to sign the agreement, then it is unlikely to be upheld by the court. In *NA v MA*,[430] for example, the court found that improper pressure had been exerted on the wife by the husband to sign a post-nuptial agreement. After the husband had discovered that the wife had committed adultery, he gave her an ultimatum that she either sign the agreement (the terms of which had not been properly negotiated between the parties) or the marriage was over. The court held that the wife's free will was overborne and that the terms of the agreement were unfair. Accordingly, it was not factored into the exercise of the court's discretion under section 25.

## 9.2 Embodying the agreement in a consent order

In order to make the terms of any agreement 'watertight' and not subject to a further claim for court provision, it is necessary to embody the agreement in an order of the court, known as a 'consent order' (an order made with the consent of the parties). When this is done, the agreed terms derive their authority not from the contract but from the order of the court,[431] and can be enforced in the same way as a non-consensual order. A consent order cannot increase the range of possible disposals of the parties' assets.[432] The order may only contain terms which fall within the court's powers to make financial provision and property adjustment orders under the MCA 1973.[433] Where parties agree to the provisions of a consent order, and the court subsequently gives effect to their agreement by approving the provisions and embodying them in an order of the court, it is important to appreciate that the legal effect of those provisions is derived from the court order itself. It no longer depends on the agreement between the parties.[434] Consequently, consent orders do not have a contractual basis, they are court orders just like any other court orders.[435] Therefore they must be treated in the same way as non-consensual orders.[436]

On an application for a consent order, the court retains the power to examine the agreement and to consider the factors in section 25. Parties are wrong, however, to rely on judges being assiduous in examining the terms of a consent order. Section 33A provides:

> (1) . . . [O]n an application for a consent order for financial relief[437] the court may, unless it has reason to think that there are other circumstances into which it ought to inquire, make an order in the terms agreed on the basis only of the prescribed information[438] furnished with the application.

Thus, although a judge is no 'mere rubber stamp', he is under no obligation to make inquiries or re-quire evidence. The effect of section 33A is to confine the function of the court to a broad appraisal

---

[429] *Beach v Beach* [1995] 2 FLR 160.     [430] [2007] 1 FLR 1760.

[431] *De Lasala v de Lasala* [1980] AC 546, PC, and see also *Soulsbury v Soulsbury* [2007] EWCA 969 at [35].

[432] *Livesey v Jenkins* [1985] 1 All ER 106.

[433] MCA 1973, ss 21–25D.     [434] *De Lasala v de Lasala* [1979] 2 All ER 1146.

[435] *Thwaite v Thwaite* [1982] Fam 1. Although, as the court has not adjudicated on the evidence, a consent order cannot be challenged on the ground that the court has reached a wrong conclusion on the evidence before it.

[436] So, for example, in *Masefield v Alexander* [1995] 1 FLR 100 an application to extend the agreed period under which a lump sum payment should be made was granted by the court. As Butler-Sloss LJ explained, if the order had been imposed by a court and not made by consent there would have been no doubt that the time could be extended. See also *B v B (Consent Order: Variation)* [1995] 1 FLR 9 where a periodical payments order was extended contrary to the terms of the original agreement.

[437] This means any financial provision order, any property adjustment order, any order for sale of property, or any interim order for maintenance: s 33A(3).

[438] That is prescribed by rules of court. The information which must be given includes the duration of the marriage; the parties' ages and the ages of their dependent children; an estimate of the value of their property and their respective net incomes; their intended accommodation arrangements; and whether either party has remarried or intends to remarry.

of the parties' financial circumstances, and only to probe more deeply where that survey puts the court on inquiry.[439] Thus, '[t]he fact that [the judge] was not told facts which, had he known them, might have affected his decision to make a consent order, cannot of itself be a ground for impeaching the order'.[440] The judge's position was neatly summed up by Ward LJ in *Harris v Manahan*:[441] 'Whilst the court is no rubber stamp, nor is it some kind of forensic ferret.'[442]

Very often the parties will negotiate their position with a view to the court incorporating it in a consent order, and in *Xydhias v Xydhias*[443] Thorpe LJ opined that an agreement reached in such negotiations to compromise an ancillary relief application is not intended to give effect to an enforceable agreement and does not do so.[444] Of course, where there are no pending proceedings for ancillary relief before the court, a valid agreement will be binding.[445]

With the growing pressure on parties to reach a consensual settlement of their property and financial affairs, it is all the more important that the strictures of the House of Lords in *Livesey v Jenkins*[446] concerning full and frank disclosure are properly observed. Parties are under a duty in both contested proceedings and where a consent order is being negotiated to make proper disclosure of all the material facts. Material facts include those matters in section 25 to which the court must have regard when exercising its discretion, for unless the court has such information it is not in the position properly to exercise that discretion. In *Livesey v Jenkins*, the parties reached a final agreement about the form and the terms of a consent order under which the husband agreed to transfer his half share of the matrimonial home to the wife for the express purpose of providing her and their two children with a home. A week later the wife became engaged to be married, but she failed to disclose this fact either to her solicitor or the husband or his solicitor. Shortly afterwards the agreement was embodied in a consent order, the wife remarried, and within two months she advertised the matrimonial home for sale. Setting aside the consent order, the House of Lords held that the wife's engagement was a material circumstance which was directly relevant to the parties' agreement. She had therefore been under a duty to disclose her engagement and her failure to do so invalidated the consent order which would accordingly be set aside.[447] However, Lord Brandon concluded his speech with 'an emphatic word of warning':

> It is not every failure of frank and full disclosure which would justify a court setting aside an order of the kind concerned in this appeal. On the contrary, it will only be in cases when the absence of full and frank disclosure has led to the court making, either in contested proceedings or by consent, an order which is substantially different from the order which it would have made if such disclosure had taken place that a case for setting aside can possibly be made good.[448]

It is clear that a consent order will be set aside where there has been fraud[449] or mistake, as well as where there has been non-disclosure, as in *Livesey v Jenkins*. Outside these rather extreme

---

[439] *Pounds v Pounds* [1994] 1 FLR 775.

[440] *Tommey v Tommey* [1983] Fam 15 at 21. This statement was approved by the House of Lords in *Livesey v Jenkins* [1985] 1 All ER 106 (although the implication that there was no duty to make full and frank disclosure was disapproved).

[441] [1997] 1 FLR 205 at 213.

[442] As Ward LJ explained, 'officious inquiry may uncover an injustice but it is more likely to disturb a delicate negotiation and produce the very costly litigation and the recrimination which conciliation is designed to avoid.' Ibid.

[443] [1999] 1 FLR 683.      [444] Ibid, 691.

[445] See eg *Soulsbury v Soulsbury* [2007] EWCA 969 in which *Xydhias* was distinguished. There a contract was upheld where there was agreement that if the wife did not make a claim for periodical payments during the husband's lifetime she would receive £100,000 on his death. See also *Haines v Hill* [2007] EWCA Civ 1284 at [31]: while 'the jurisdiction of the court . . . cannot be ousted by the agreement of the spouses . . . [e]qually such an agreement is not devoid of any legal effect'.

[446] [1985] 1 All ER 106.      [447] See also *Robinson v Robinson* [1982] 2 All ER 699n.

[448] [1985] 1 All ER 106 at 119.

[449] See eg *T v T (Consent Order: Procedure to Set Aside)* [1996] 2 FLR 640, where the husband, by his deliberate concealment that he was engaged in active negotiations to acquire shares in a private company at the time when the consent order was being negotiated, was held to have acted fraudulently. Where there is fraudulent non-disclosure, the court is deprived of the opportunity properly to exercise its powers under s 25. Thus the situation is different from where there is a supervening event after the original order was made, as in *Barder v Caluori* [1987] 2 All ER 440.

circumstances, however, there is a deep reluctance to interfere with such orders. Consequently in *Harris v Manahan*,[450] despite having real sympathy for the wronged wife, the Court of Appeal reiterated that only in the most 'exceptional case of the cruellest injustice' would the public interest in the finality of litigation be overridden, and that the bad legal advice which the wife had clearly been given was no reason for setting the consent order aside.[451]

---

### Key Case

Recent Supreme Court jurisprudence has examined the extent to which a court is *bound* to set aside a consent order in cases of fraud. In *Sharland v Sharland*[452] and *Gohil v Gohil*[453], cases which were heard by the Supreme Court at the same time, two former wives wanted their agreed financial settlements set aside on the ground that their respective husbands had fraudulently failed to make full and frank disclosure regarding their assets during the negotiations. The fact that the Supreme Court ruled in their favour attracted a considerable amount of media attention and commentary, and sent the clear message that fraudulent non-disclosure will not be tolerated.

The core question before the Supreme Court in *Sharland v Sharland*[454] was whether, following *Livesey v Jenkins*,[455] it was appropriate for the court to refuse to set aside a consent order that was reached following one party's fraudulent non-disclosure on the ground that it would not have made a substantially different order in the financial proceedings. This was the decision of the judge at first instance, a decision which was upheld by the Court of Appeal. In this case, the parties married in 1993 and separated in 2010. They had three children, one of whom had severe autism and required ongoing care from Mrs Sharland. The issue during the financial proceedings between the parties was the value of the husband's shareholding in the software business, AppSense Holdings Ltd, which he developed. During the proceedings, the valuation of the company was conducted on the basis that there was no plans for an Initial Public Offering (IPO). The parties reached a financial settlement in 2012 under which Mrs Sharland was to receive 30 per cent of the net proceeds of sale of the shares in the company whenever that took place, along with other assets. Before this was turned into a consent order, however, Mrs Sharland became aware that the company was being actively prepared for an IPO which was expected to value the company at a much higher figure than the valuations relied upon during the negotiations leading to the settlement. As such, Mrs Sharland applied for the hearing to be resumed. The judge found that Mr Sharland had been dishonest and that, had he disclosed the IPO plans, the court would have adjourned the financial proceedings to establish whether it was going ahead. By the time of the hearing, however, the IPO had not taken place and it was not now in prospect. Thus, the judge declined to set aside the draft consent order on the ground that he would not have made a substantially different order in the financial proceedings.[456] This decision was upheld by the Court of Appeal (Briggs LJ dissenting).[457] Although the judges agreed that the husband had been guilty of fraudulent non-disclosure, the majority ruled that the original settlement could not be overturned because although the husband's evidence was 'seriously misleading', Mrs Sharland could not show that, in the absence of such fraud, the court would have made a significantly different order. The Supreme Court took a different view, however, and unanimously allowed Mrs Sharland's appeal which meant that her application for financial relief returned to the High Court for consideration.

Lady Hale, giving judgment for the Supreme Court, emphasised that it is in the interests of all members of a family that matrimonial disputes should be settled by agreement rather than adversarial battles in

---

[450] [1997] 1 FLR 205.

[451] See also *Tibbs v Dick* [1998] 2 FLR 1118, where the Court of Appeal held that bad or negligent legal advice per se could never be a ground for setting aside a consent order. This was applied in *S v S (Ancillary Relief: Consent Order)* [2002] EWHC 223 (Fam) and *L v L* [2006] EWHC 956 (Fam). However, a party may have a remedy in negligence, *Frazer Harris v Scholfield Roberts & Hill (A Firm)* [1998] 2 FLR 679.

[452] [2015] UKSC 60.     [453] [2015] UKSC 61.     [454] [2015] UKSC 60.

[455] [1985] AC 424.     [456] [2013] EWHC 991 (Fam).     [457] [2014] EWCA Civ 95.

court.[458] Her Ladyship emphasised the existing position that such agreement cannot oust the jurisdiction of the court, but that it will be turned into a consent order by the court unless it has reason to think that there are circumstances into which it ought to inquire.[459] This is what we already know. The court can make a consent order reflecting the terms of the parties' agreement, but it can also make further inquiries or suggest amendments to the parties.[460] Central to this whole process, however, is the duty on the parties to make full and frank disclosure of all relevant information (including their assets and income) to each other and to the court. This duty always arises and it goes to the heart of the parties' consent to the agreement. If there is a reason which vitiates a party's consent, there may also be good reason for the court to set aside the order. In other words, the court cannot make a consent order without the valid consent of the parties. The question before the Supreme Court was the extent to which a court is bound to set aside an order in such circumstances.[461] As Lady Hale observed, however, this depends on the nature of the vitiating factor. It was critical for the Supreme Court that this was a case concerning fraud. It was not simply a matter of one party negligently failing to disclose information. The husband positively set out to deceive Mrs Sharland and the court. According to the Supreme Court, Briggs LJ had been correct to apply, in the Court of Appeal, the principle that 'fraud unravels all' and should lead to the setting aside of a consent order procured by fraud. According to Lady Hale, the only exception to this general principle is 'where the court is satisfied that, at the time when it made the consent order, the fraud would not have influenced a reasonable person to agree to it, nor, had it known then what it knows now, would the court have made a significantly different order, whether or not the parties had agreed to it'.[462] The key point, however, is that the burden of proving this lies with the perpetrator of the fraud (in this case, Mr Sharland). Thus, it was wrong to place upon Mrs Sharland the burden of showing that the fraudulent non-disclosure about the husband's plans for the company would have made a difference to the order made by the court.

Applying this to the facts of the case, Lady Hale concluded that the husband's deception in deliberately withholding information about a possible IPO was 'highly material' to the terms of the settlement, it had coloured both valuers' approach to the valuation of the husband's shareholding. That in turn had coloured the wife's approach to the proportionality of the balance struck between her present share in the liquid assets and her future share in the value of the husband's shareholding. Thus, the judge would not have made the order he did, when he did, had the truth been known.[463] As such, the draft consent order should have been set aside and Mrs Sharland was entitled to re-open the case.[464] The final question concerned the correct procedure to the followed by parties seeking to challenge the final order of a court in family proceedings. Lady Hale made it clear that as the court retains jurisdiction over a marriage even after it has been dissolved,[465] and it remains open to the parties either to make a fresh application or to appeal against the consent order. However, Lady Hale emphasised that that the fact that there has been misrepresentation or non-disclosure justifying the setting aside of an order does not mean that the renewed financial remedy proceedings must necessarily start from scratch. Instead, the court may be able to isolate the issues to which the misrepresentation or non-disclosure relates and deal only with those.[466]

In *Gohil v Gohil*[467] the wife applied to set aside a consent order made in 2004 on the grounds of alleged serious material non-disclosure, fraud, and misrepresentation by the husband. In 2007 the husband was convicted of fraud and money laundering valued at an estimated £25million. He was sentenced to 10 years' imprisonment. One of the main questions before the Supreme Court was whether evidence from the husband's criminal proceedings, which exposed his fraudulent activity, could be relied upon by Mrs Gohil to overturn the settlement.[468] In 2012, Moylan J, sitting in the High Court, ruled that the settlement should

---

[458]  [2015] UKSC 60, at [17].

[459]  Under section 33A of the Matrimonial Causes Act 1973, [2015] UKSC 60, at [20].      [460]  Ibid.

[461]  Ibid, at [29].      [462]  [2015] UKSC 60, at [33].      [463]  Ibid, at [34].      [464]  Ibid, at [35].

[465]  Under section 31F(6) of the Matrimonial and Family Proceedings Act 1984, the family court has the power to vary, suspend, rescind or revive any order by it.

[466]  See *Kingdon v Kingdon* [2010] EWCA Civ 1251.      [467]  [2015] UKSC 61.

[468]  During his criminal trial, further evidence of the extent of his deliberate non-disclosure in the original divorce proceedings emerged.

be set aside on the ground of the husband's non-disclosure.[469] The Court of Appeal disagreed and held that Mrs Gohil's evidence to establish non-disclosure was inadmissible. The Supreme Court overruled the Court of Appeal describing its judgment as a 'rare aberration',[470] and reinstated the decision of the High Court. While the Court of Appeal appeared to consider that all of the evidence produced by Mrs Gohil was inadmissible, the Supreme Court held that this approach was erroneous.[471] While evidence from the criminal proceedings obtained from sources outside the UK was clearly inadmissible, Moylan J had not based his decision on this evidence alone. Other evidence was put forward by Mrs Gohil and relied upon by Moylan J to reach the conclusion that the husband was guilty of material non-disclosure during the divorce proceedings in 2004. Thus, even if Moylan J had referred only to the remaining admissible evidence,[472] he would, in the light of his findings on it, still have concluded that the husband was guilty of material non-disclosure.[473]

Importantly, the Supreme Court made it clear that the duty to make full and frank disclosure is absolute. The consent order in this case (which provided that the husband should make a lump sum payment in final settlement of the wife's capital claims (which was eventually paid), and periodical annual payments (which the husband stopped paying in 2008), also contained a recital that 'the [wife] believes that the [husband] has not provided full and frank disclosure of his financial circumstances (although this is disputed by the [husband]), but is compromising her claims in the terms set out in this consent order despite this in order to achieve finality'. Notwithstanding this, the Supreme Court ruled that the order should be set aside on the ground of the husband's material non-disclosure and the words used in the recital had no legal effect in a financial order in divorce proceedings. The husband owed a duty to the court to make full and frank disclosure of his resources and the court made it clear that one party cannot exonerate the other from complying with this duty.[474]

These cases attracted a lot of media attention and speculation that they will open the floodgates to wronged wives seeking to challenge existing financial settlements. However, it should be remembered that the husband in both cases had been guilty of fraudulent non-disclosure. Outside of such fraudulent behaviour, it remains the case that the court will be reluctant to interfere with properly negotiated divorce settlements. However, one hopes that these cases will serve as an important reminder to divorcing parties that they are under a duty to make full and frank disclosure not only to the other party, but to the court. The decision of the Supreme Court in *Gohil* also makes it clear that this is an absolute duty which cannot be avoided by the parties by agreement. It is now clear that a dishonest failure to make full and frank disclosure will not be tolerated. The only exception to this is where the court is satisfied that, at the time when it made the consent order, the fraud would not have resulted in the court making a significantly different order. In other words, not all incidents of non-disclosure will result in orders being set aside. Much depends on whether the non-disclosure is material to the decision of the court. Importantly, however, in cases involving fraud, the burden of establishing that a reasonable person would not have been influenced by the deceit, or that the court would not have made a different order, lies with the perpetrator of the fraud. By contrast, in cases of accidental or negligent non-disclosure, there is no presumption that it was material and thus the burden of proof is on the person seeking to set aside the order to show that proper disclosure would, on the balance of probabilities, have led to a different order.[475]

---

[469] [2012] EWHC 2897 (Fam).     [470] [2015] UKSC 61, at [31].

[471] The Supreme Court ruled that the criteria in *Ladd v Marshall* [1954] 1 WLR 1489 which govern when fresh evidence may be adduced on appeal, have no relevance to the determination of an application to set aside a financial order on grounds on fraudulent non-disclosure.

[472] [2015] UKSC 61, at [36–40].     [473] Ibid, at [42].

[474] Ibid, at [19-22]. The Supreme Court ruled that the criteria in *Ladd v Marshall* [1954] 1 WLR 1489 which govern when fresh evidence may be adduced on appeal, have no relevance to the determination of an application to set aside a financial order on grounds on fraudulent non-disclosure, [2015] UKSC 61, at [32].

[475] *Gohil v Gohil* [2015] UKSC 61, at [44]. The High Court has now handed down its decision in *AB v CD* [2016] EWHC 10 (Fam) where Mrs Justice Roberts made it clear that materiality is still an ingredient in any application to set aside a consent order where the non-disclosure does not amount to deliberate fraud. The High Court in this case upheld the husband's appeal to set aside a consent order on the basis that the wife had failed to provide full and frank disclosure. The court did not consider that there had been deliberate fraud or deception by the wife but upheld the husband's claim

## 9.3 **Pre-nuptial agreements**

Another form of private ordering is where the parties agree *before* the marriage how their property and assets should be split in the event of their marriage breaking down (a pre-nuptial agreement). Historically, such agreements, being in anticipation of, and thereby possibly encouraging, separation and divorce, were considered void as contrary to public policy.[476]

---

### Key case

Following the Supreme Court decision in *Granatino v Radmacher (formerly Granatino)*,[477] however, the status of pre-nuptial agreements is a little more complex to discern. In that case, the appellant Mr Granatino, a French national, and Ms Radmacher, a German national, signed a pre-nuptial agreement in Germany in August 1998. Mr Granatino did not take advantage of the wish of the German notary who had drafted the agreement, to postpone execution of the agreement until after Mr Granatino had taken advice, and neither did Mr Granatino take any advice after signing but prior to the marriage. The couple married in November 1998. The couple lived together in London and had two children, before separating after eight years of marriage. The pre-nuptial agreement was instigated by the wife who came from a very rich family and whose father had insisted upon it as the wife was to receive a portion of the family wealth in due course. It provided that the effects of the marriage were to be subject to German law.[478] The effect of the agreement was that 'neither party was to derive an interest in or benefit from the property of the other during the marriage or on its termination'.[479] The agreement made no mention of children. At the time of the agreement Mr Granatino earned about £120,000 per annum in the banking industry, and in subsequent years achieved higher earnings, until 2002 when he gave up his career to embark on a DPhil degree at Oxford University. Despite the terms of the agreement, the husband sought periodical payments and a lump sum against the wife ancillary to the divorce. Baron J concluded that, having regard to the circumstances surrounding the conclusion of the agreement, reduced weight should be given to it, and she awarded the husband approximately £5.5 million to provide a home and income. On the wife's appeal, the Court of Appeal[480] held that Baron J's approach to the circumstances of the agreement was wrong and she should have given the agreement decisive weight, in that there should be provision for Mr Granatino in his role as the children's father but not otherwise in his own right.

Mr Granatino appealed to the Supreme Court, where the issue was what weight should be given to the pre-nuptial agreement. However, the case provided the court with an opportunity to consider more widely the issue of nuptial agreements, particularly in light of the then recent decision of the Privy Council in *MacLeod v MacLeod*,[481] and nine Justices heard the case.

---

Before explaining the reasoning in *Granatino v Radmacher (formerly Granatino)*, it is convenient first briefly to outline what was said in the *MacLeod* case. In that case the Privy Council heard an appeal from the High Court of Justice of the Isle of Man, where the law on financial orders on divorce is similar to that in England and Wales. The husband and wife married after signing a pre-nuptial agreement. Substantial variations to that agreement were made by a deed executed during

---

that her failure to disclose the fact that an investment of £3.5million was going to be made to the company of which she was a director and shareholder deprived him of the opportunity of deciding whether to agree to the terms of the consent order on a fully informed basis.

[476] *Hyman v Hyman* [1929] AC 601.

[477] [2010] UKSC 42, [2011] 1 AC 534. For comment, see J. M. Scherpe, 'Fairness, Freedom and Foreign Elements—Marital Agreements in England and Wales After *Radmacher v Granatino*' [2011] Child and Family Law Quarterly 513.

[478] Although, as the Supreme Court found, the issues in the case were governed exclusively by English law: see [2010] UKSC 42, [2011] 1 AC 534 at [108].

[479] Ibid, [12].     [480] [2009] 2 FLR 1181.     [481] [2008] UKPC 64, [2010] 1 AC 298.

the marriage (a post-nuptial agreement). Lady Hale, who delivered the Board's advice, referred to the position of pre-nuptial agreements, commenting:

> The Board takes the view that it is not open to them to reverse the long standing rule that pre-nuptial agreements are contrary to public policy and thus not valid or binding in the contractual sense.[482]

However, the Board drew a distinction between pre-nuptial and post-nuptial agreements. It noted that there is no statutory power to vary a pre-nuptial agreement, and it would be unfair to render them enforceable if they could not be varied. By contrast, the Board interpreted the relevant statutory provision (the equivalent of the MCA 1973, s 35) to include power to vary a post-nuptial agreement. The Board also noted that the reasoning which led to the rule that agreements during marriage which anticipated breakdown of the relationship were void relied on an enforceable duty of husband and wife to live together, which had since been abolished. Consequently, since the reasoning had disappeared, it was time for the rule itself also to disappear.[483] It held that in the case of a post-nuptial agreement, the agreement is no longer the price which one party may extract for willingness to marry.[484]

In *Granatino v Radmacher (formerly Granatino)*[485] the Supreme Court delivered its view by way of a majority judgment of seven members of the court, together with a concurring separate judgment by Lord Mance. Lady Hale was the sole dissentient. The majority endorsed the view that the reasons given in *MacLeod* for declaring post-nuptial agreements void were obsolete, but could see no reason for maintaining a distinction in this regard between a post-nuptial and a pre-nuptial agreement.[486] The court did not accept that the protection of 'section 35 must be a precondition to holding that a nuptial agreement takes effect as a contract',[487] nor that there was any material distinction between the two types of agreement (eg one made the day before the wedding and one the day after). The court pointed out that, in any event, the issue did not arise for decision in *MacLeod*, any more than it arose in *Granatino*. Furthermore, it was a red herring: regardless of whether these types of nuptial agreement are enforceable, the court in ancillary relief proceedings should apply the same principles to pre-nuptial agreements as it applies to post-nuptial agreements.[488] The court indicated that the approach in *Edgar v Edgar* with regard to a separation agreement will not necessarily be appropriate for all post-nuptial agreements.[489]

As to disclosure of information, the Supreme Court held that the Court of Appeal had been 'correct in principle to ask whether there was any *material* lack of disclosure'.[490] What is important is that each party should have all the information material to the decision and intend the agreement to govern the end of the relationship.[491] As to factors detracting from the weight given to an agreement, the court commented:

> The first question will be whether any of the standard vitiating factors: duress, fraud or misrepresentation, is present. Even if the agreement does not have contractual force, those factors will negate any effect the agreement might otherwise have. But unconscionable conduct such as undue pressure (falling short of duress) will also be likely to eliminate the weight to be attached to the agreement, and other unworthy conduct, such as exploitation of a dominant position to secure an unfair advantage, would reduce or eliminate it.[492]
>
> The court may take into account a party's emotional state, and what pressures he or she was under to agree. But that again cannot be considered in isolation from what would have happened had he or she not been under those pressures. The circumstances of the parties at the time of the agreement will be relevant. Those will include such matters as their age and maturity, whether either or both had been married or been in long-term relationships before. For such couples, their experience

---

[482] Ibid, [31].      [483] Ibid, [38] and [39].      [484] Ibid, [36].      [485] [2010] UKSC 42, [2011] 1 AC 534.
[486] Ibid, [52]. See also [51].      [487] Ibid, [56].      [488] Ibid, [63].      [489] Ibid, [65].      [490] Ibid, [69].
[491] Ibid.      [492] Ibid, [71].

of previous relationships may explain the terms of the agreement, and may also show what they foresaw when they entered into the agreement. What may not be easily foreseeable for less mature couples may well be in contemplation of more mature couples. Another important factor may be whether the marriage would have gone ahead without an agreement, or without the terms which had been agreed. This may cut either way.

As to factors enhancing the weight to be given to the agreement, the court commented that the 'fact of the agreement is capable of altering what is fair. It is an important factor to be weighed in the balance.'[493] The court set out the following proposition:

The court should give effect to a nuptial agreement that is freely entered into by each party with a full appreciation of its implications unless in the circumstances prevailing it would not be fair to hold the parties to their agreement.

The court explained that the circumstances in which it will not be fair to hold the parties to their agreement will depend on the particular facts of the case.[494] However, the court gave the following guidance:[495]

(i) A nuptial agreement cannot be allowed to prejudice the reasonable requirements of any children of the family.

(ii) The court should accord respect to the parties' autonomy, and should not override the agreement simply on the basis that the court knows best.

(iii) There is nothing inherently unfair in an agreement which seeks to preserve non-matrimonial property for one party.

(iv) There is scope for what happens to the parties over time to make it unfair to hold them to an agreement. It is unlikely that the parties will have intended that one party should be left in a predicament of real need.

(v) It is in relation to the sharing of assets beyond those addressing need that the court will be most likely to make an order in the terms of the nuptial agreement.

The Supreme Court concluded that it was fair in this case for Mr Granatino to be held to the agreement and unfair to depart from it. It could detect no error of principle on the part of the Court of Appeal.[496]

Lady Hale delivered a dissenting judgment, in which she observed that the law was in a mess and ripe for systematic review and reform.[497] She observed that a court can all too easily lose sight of the fact that the object of a pre-nuptial agreement is to deny the economically weaker spouse provision to which he (and usually she) would otherwise be entitled, and that 'there is a gender dimension to the issue which some may think ill-suited to decision by a court consisting of eight men and one woman'.[498] She disagreed with the view that pre-nuptial agreements are legally enforceable, and that there are no relevant differences between post-nuptial and pre-nuptial agreements. She also saw the majority's formulation of the test to be applied for considering the effect of a pre-nuptial agreement (at para 75 of the judgment) as placing an impermissible gloss on the statute. Instead, she would ask: 'Did each party freely enter into an agreement, intending it to have legal effect and with a full appreciation of its implications? If so, in the circumstances as they now are, would it be fair to hold them to their agreement?'[499] In Lady Hale's view the Court of Appeal also erred in principle when it treated Mr Granatino in the same way as a parent who was not married to the other parent,[500] namely by making similar provision to that which he could have obtained in such

---

[493] Ibid, [75].    [494] Ibid, [76].    [495] Ibid, [77]–[83].    [496] Ibid, [123].
[497] Ibid, [133].    [498] Ibid, [137].    [499] Ibid, [169].    [500] Ibid, [193].

circumstances under Schedule 1 to the Children Act 1989.[501] As she commented: 'Marriage still counts for something in the law of this country and long may it continue to do so.'[502]

Lord Mance delivered a separate judgment, concurring in the conclusion of the majority. However, like Lady Hale, he expressed no view on the binding or other nature of a pre-nuptial agreement.[503] Lord Mance agreed with the majority view, expressed at paragraph 75 of the judgment, as to the onus or starting point for considering the effect of a pre-nuptial agreement, but did not 'think the difference in wording likely to be important in practice'.[504] He commented that 'the ultimate question remains on any view what is fair, and the starting point or onus is . . . unlikely to matter once all the facts are before the court'.[505]

The courts have now had the opportunity to consider and apply the principles of *Radmacher* and, in particular, to consider whether the parties freely entered into the agreement with a full appreciation of its implications, and when it will be considered unfair to hold the parties to the agreement. In *Z v Z (No 2)*,[506] which was the first contested case in the High Court to consider *Radmacher*, Moor J observed that the Supreme Court had 'changed the position fundamentally'[507] regarding pre-nuptial agreements. In this case the parties, a French couple, were married for 14 years and had three children. Before marrying, they entered into a standard pre-nuptial agreement in France (known as a *separation de biens*). The couple relocated to England during their marriage and when the marriage broke down, the weight to be given to the pre-nuptial agreement had to be decided according to the principles of English law. The parties' assets totalled £15 million and the wife argued that it would be unjust to hold the parties to the French agreement and that everything should be shared equally. There was no dispute that the agreement was entered into by the parties freely and with a full understanding of its implications. The husband argued, following the *Radmacher* decision, that the agreement, which excluded the equal sharing principle, should be upheld. He accepted, however, that the agreement did not exclude maintenance claims and that the wife's claim should be determined on the basis of a pre-*White* assessment of her needs (which, he argued, should result in an award to her of approximately 35 per cent of the assets). Moor J held that this would have been an appropriate case for equal division of the assets in the absence of the French agreement. However, he upheld the agreement insofar as it excluded the equal sharing principle and awarded the wife 40 per cent of the assets which was held to be a suitable departure from equality to reflect the agreement. The fact that the agreement excluded the sharing principle but still allowed the wife to make a claim based upon her reasonable needs was relevant as the Supreme Court had taken the view in *Radmacher* that it would be easiest to show that such agreements, which still allowed maintenance claims to be made, were not unfair.

In *V v V*[508] the parties entered into a pre-nuptial agreement which allowed the husband to retain all of the property that he had acquired prior to the marriage. The estimated value of this property was £1 million. The question before Charles J was whether the district judge had been correct to attach limited weight to this agreement on the grounds that it made no express provision for what should happen in the event of divorce, and made no provision for the parties' future children.

### Summary

Charles J noted that Radmacher 'necessitates a significant change to the approach to be adopted . . . to the impact of agreements between the parties in respect of their finances. At the heart of that significant change, is the need to recognise the weight that should now be given to autonomy, and thus to the choices made by the parties to a marriage . . . The new respect to be given to individual autonomy means that the fact of an agreement can alter what is a fair result and so found a different award to the one that would otherwise have been made. . .'[509]

---

[501] For detailed discussion, see Chapter 6.    [502] [2010] UKSC 42, at [195].    [503] Ibid, [128].
[504] Ibid, [129].    [505] Ibid.    [506] [2011] EWHC 2878 (Fam).    [507] Ibid, [34].
[508] [2011] EWHC 3230.    [509] Ibid, [36].

As such, notwithstanding the fact that the wife did not have legal advice prior to entering the agreement, it was found that both parties had intended the agreement to be effective and were aware, as intelligent people, of its obvious purpose.[510] Furthermore, the fact that there had been no valuation of the husband's assets did not detract from the significance of the agreement as it was found that the wife was indifferent to the precise value of the husband's property and thus there had been no material non-disclosure at the time the agreement was signed. On the question of whether there were any factors which made the agreement unfair, Charles J held that the mere fact that the wife was in the weaker bargaining position did not limit the effect of the agreement in this case. There was no evidence to suggest that the agreement was not one that was willingly and honestly entered into by both parties.[511] Thus, in the overall assessment of the award to be made, the agreement was an important factor to be weighed in the balance. The court therefore held that in the application of the section 25 exercise, in particular, 'when assessing the sharing principle and the impact of contributions, the marriage settlement provides a good and powerful reason for departing from an equal division of the assets that are now available'.[512]

An agreement which, if implemented, would leave one party in severe financial need might be considered by the court to be unfair. This can be seen in *Luckwell* v *Limata*[513] where the pre-nuptial agreement was overridden by the court in order to meet the husband's housing needs. In this case the parties had been married for 8 years and had three children. Prior to the marriage, the parties entered into a pre-nuptial agreement under which the husband agreed to make no claim on the wife's separate property, or gifts made to her by her family. During the marriage, subsequent agreements were made to the same effect and, on all occasions, each party received legal advice when signing them. On divorce, however, the husband applied for financial provision and the question turned on the weight to be given to the agreements. The court accepted that the agreements were a highly relevant circumstance of the case, having been entered into freely by a mature man who was given expert legal advice. There were no vitiating factors such as duress or non-disclosure.[514] However, the husband was in a 'predicament of real need' with no home, no current income, no capital, considerable debts, and no borrowing capacity[515]. As well as requiring accommodation for himself, he required appropriate accommodation for his three children to visit. Indeed, the court noted the importance, when achievable, of each of the two parents having at least adequate homes in which their children can visit them and stay.[516] The court, therefore, held that current and likely future need could outweigh the fact of an agreement in the overall circumstances of a particular case. The weakness or unfairness of the agreements in this case was that they provided nothing at all for the husband no matter how long the marriage or how great his need upon breakdown.[517] The judge, therefore, held that he must make some capital provision for the husband on the basis of his needs and in conjunction with his role as father, noting the damaging result of the children seeing their mother live in relative luxury, while their father lived in relative penury.[518] Thus, a relative modest award was made in the husband's favour to satisfy his financial needs, although this was less than the likely award in the absence of the agreements.[519]

There have been some examples of agreements that have failed on the basis that they were not fully and freely entered into by the parties. In *GS* v *L*[520] King J found that neither party had a full appreciation of the implications of the agreement which had been made primarily to address the

---

[510] Ibid, [48].        [511] Ibid, [64].        [512] Ibid, [73].        [513] [2014] EWHC 502 (Fam).

[514] Ibid, at [133].        [515] Ibid, at [139].

[516] The court cited *Cartwright* v *Cartwright* (1983) 4 FLR 463 and *M* v *B (Ancillary proceedings: lump sum)* [1998] 1 FLR 53 as authority for this proposition.

[517] [2014] EWHC 502, at [139].        [518] Ibid, at [144].

[519] The wife was ordered to provide £900,000 as a housing fund for the husband until all three children reached their majority. When the youngest child reached 22, that property would be sold and 45 per cent of the proceeds of sale would revert to the wife. The remainder would be used by the husband to fund an alternative property.

[520] [2011] EWHC 1759.

situation regarding the parties' finances in the event of the husband's death. The effect of the agreement was unclear and, as such, King J felt that little weight could be attached to it. No weight was attached to the agreement in *Kremen v Agrest (No 11) (Financial Remedy: Non-Disclosure: Post-Nuptial Agreement)*.[521] Not only was there no disclosure by the husband of the full extent of his wealth, but the wife had no independent legal advice and no understanding of the rights under English law that she was foregoing by the agreement. She did not freely enter into the agreement with a full appreciation of its implications, it was the product of pressure from her husband. Accordingly, her agreement was not an informed one.[522] Further, Mostyn J found that the signing of the agreement had been a charade and he was not convinced that the parties intended that the agreement would determine the outcome on divorce. On a more general note, Mostyn J suggested that it will be unusual for agreements to be given effect if the parties have not received legal advice:

> It seems to me that it will only be in an unusual case where it can be said that absent independent legal advice and full disclosure, a party can be taken to have freely entered into a marital agreement with a full appreciation of its implications . . . It would surely have to be shown that the spouse, like Mr Granatino, had a high degree of financial and legal sophistication in order to have a full appreciation of what legal rights he or she is signing away.

Thus, while the court in *V v V*[523] attached weight to the agreement even though it was made in the absence of legal advice, much will depend on all of the circumstances surrounding the making of the agreement and the general understanding of the parties about its implications.

## 9.4 Debate surrounding pre-nuptial agreements

The majority decision in *Granatino* goes some way to addressing the calls by many commentators for pre-nuptial agreements to be given greater weight in the regulation of the financial affairs of married couples.[524] Prior to *Granatino*, Stephen Cretney pointed to the 'remarkable anomaly' created by the fact that while marriage can be described as a partnership, English law did not 'allow husband and wife by contract (whether pre- or post-nuptial) to exercise the right, which it accords virtually all other partners, to make their own agreement as to the terms'.[525] Yet, a couple who are not married could enter into a binding cohabitation contract to regulate their financial and property affairs.[526] While it is sometimes said that pre-nuptial agreements undermine marriage, there is also an argument that attaching greater weight to pre-nuptial agreements may encourage people to marry, or more correctly, counter any disincentive to marry caused by the potential of court-imposed solutions particularly in big money cases. It is also the case that such agreements direct parties away from litigation, thus reducing legal costs and court time.

Pre-nuptial agreements are recognised in many other European countries and throughout the world.[527] Thus greater recognition of pre-nuptial agreements may bring the position in England and Wales more in line with international experience. It may reduce 'forum shopping' in relation

---

[521] [2012] EWHC 45.     [522] Ibid, [70].     [523] [2011] EWHC 3230.

[524] See eg S. Cretney, 'The Family and the Law—Status or Contract?' [2003] Child and Family Law Quarterly 403; B. Clark, 'Should Greater Prominence be Given to Pre-Nuptial Contracts in the Law of Ancillary Relief' [2004] Child and Family Law Quarterly 399; J. Morley, 'Enforceable Pre-Nuptial Agreements: Their Time Has Come' [2006] Family Law 772; see also Resolution, 'A More Certain Future—Recognition of Pre-Marital Agreements in England and Wales' (2004), arguing for binding pre-nuptials except in cases of significant injustice. It was accepted that defining 'significant injustice' may result in litigation, but that this was a small price to pay for the certainty of legally binding pre-nuptial agreements, para 7.7.

[525] S. Cretney, 'The Family and the Law—Status or Contract?' [2003] Child and Family Law Quarterly 403.

[526] *Sutton v Mischon De Reya and Gawor and Co* [2004] 1 FLR 837.

[527] For a detailed treatment, see J. Scherpe (ed), *Marital Agreements and Private Autonomy in Comparative Perspective* (Oxford: Hart, 2012) and K. Boele-Woelki, J. Miles, and J. M. Scherpe (eds), *The Future of Family Property in Europe* (Antwerp: Intersentia, 2011).

to international divorces. This is where one spouse who does not want to be bound by a pre-nuptial agreement entered into in another jurisdiction where it is binding, would seek to initiate divorce proceedings in the UK.[528] Indeed in *Crossley v Crossley*[529] Thorpe LJ observed that a strong argument for the codification of the law on pre-nuptials was to address the difficulties caused by the different approaches taken to divorce and financial matters across Europe. He said:

> [T]here is an obvious divide between the provisions of the civil law jurisdictions and the absence of any marital property tradition in the common law systems. Undoubtedly there would be some narrowing between this European divide if greater opportunity were given within our justice system for parties to contract in advance of marriage to make provision for the possibility of dissolution. The approach that Bennet J took in this case seems to me to accord with a developing view that pre-nuptial contracts are gaining in importance in a particularly fraught area that confronts so many parties separating and divorcing.[530]

The Court of Appeal had previously voiced its support for pre-nuptial agreements in *Charman v Charman*:[531]

> If, unlike the rest of Europe, the property consequences of divorce are to be regulated by the principles of needs, compensation and sharing, should not the parties to the marriage, or the projected marriage, have at the least the opportunity to order their own affairs otherwise by a nuptial contract?[532]

However, George, Harris, and Herring[533] have observed that arguments:

> should not blind us to the possibility that, in practice, giving pre-nuptial agreements greater recognition might not only fail to increase the certainty and simplicity of the law, reduce conflict and litigation, and lower costs, but, on the contrary, might cause greater legal uncertainty and complexity, and/or increase opportunities and incentives to litigate. It would also constrain the court's ability to impose, and the parties' incentives to agree, fair settlements.[534]

Making the parties' agreement binding inevitably leads to the question of how to build in safeguards to protect the economically vulnerable in relationships, or to prevent the enforcement of a contract in situations where circumstances have changed to make its terms unfair to one party.[535] Statutory force could be given to agreements alongside carefully drafted protective mechanisms to filter out agreements which are problematic due to some procedural or substantive unfairness. As early as 1998, the Home Office consultation document, *Supporting Families*, recommended that written pre-nuptial agreements should be binding subject to certain safeguards. There was a mixed response to the consultation document and no further action taken.

### 9.4.1 Law Commission Report on Matrimonial Property, Needs and Agreements

On 26 February 2014 the Law Commission published its long-awaited report on prenuptial agreements.[536] This Report is the culmination of a three-year project which began with the

---

[528] J. Morley, 'Enforceable Pre-Nuptial Agreements: Their Time Has Come' [2006] Family Law 772 at 775.
[529] [2007] EWCA Civ 1491.    [530] Ibid.    [531] [2007] EWCA Civ 503.    [532] Ibid, at [124].
[533] R. H. George, P. G. Harris, and J. Herring, 'Pre-Nuptial Agreements: For Better or For Worse?' [2009] Family Law 934.
[534] Ibid, 938.
[535] However, problems should not be overstated: Morley points out that '[n]one of the many common law jurisdictions that enforce prenuptial agreements have given the parties the freedom to create unconscionable or seriously unjust agreements . . . in every case the courts have retained full power to scrutinise prenuptial agreements to prevent injustice'. J. Morley, 'Enforceable Pre-Nuptial Agreements: Their Time Has Come' [2006] Family Law 772 at 773.
[536] Law Commission, *Matrimonial Property, Needs and Agreements* (Law Com No 343, 2014), http://lawcommission. justice.gov.uk/docs/lc343_matrimonial_property.pdf.

publication of a Consultation Paper in 2011, which dealt with marital property agreements.[537] This was followed by a supplementary paper which extended the remit of the project to include an examination of two additional areas of the law on financial provision: the definition of 'needs' in the post-divorce context, and the definition and treatment of non-matrimonial property.[538]

The Report, which includes a draft bill, recommends that couples be allowed to make legally binding pre- or post-nuptial agreements about the disposal of their assets in the event of divorce provided that the agreement meets certain criteria. This move to make qualifying nuptial agreements binding follows case law since 2008, which has begun to give more weight to such agreements.[539] This culminated in the decision of the Supreme Court in *Radmacher v Granatino*,[540] which ruled that provided that each party freely entered into the agreement and had a full appreciation of its implications, the court should give effect to nuptial agreements unless this would result in unfairness. These cases are discussed in Chapter 4. As the Law Commission noted, the courts have gone as far as they could 'in endorsing the validity of marital property agreements without an amendment of the statutory framework; only legislation can enable parties to enforce agreements without involving the courts' discretionary jurisdiction under the Matrimonial Causes Act 1973'.[541] In light of this, the Commission recommends that legislation be enacted to introduce 'qualifying nuptial agreements' (QNA). These would be a new form of contract, subject to requirements as to their formation including the provision of legal advice and financial disclosure.[542]

Under the proposals, 'qualifying' nuptial agreements must:

– meet the standard contractual criteria, that is, be absent of fraud, undue influence or mis-representation;

– be made by deed;

– be signed no less than 28 days before the marriage or civil partnership and contain a statement that the parties understand the nature of the agreement in that it will partially remove the court's discretion to make financial orders.

Further, the parties must have had independent legal advice and made full disclosure regarding their finances. The agreement will be binding provided that its terms meet the needs of the parties and any children. In particular, the QNA will not be able to fetter the court's power to make financial provision for children. Thus, qualifying agreements will not enable one or both parties to contract out of any responsibility to meet each other's financial needs.[543] According to the Commission:

> By ensuring that needs cannot be compromised by a qualifying nuptial agreement, we make it clear that an agreement which leaves a spouse or former spouse without reasonable provision for income, housing, and the other elements that family lawyers understand as "needs", will continue to be subject to the courts' control.[544]

Overall, the work of the Commission is to be applauded and the recommendation to make QNA's binding to be welcomed in order to imbue the law on financial provision with more certainty, to give parties greater autonomy over their financial affairs on divorce, and ultimately to lead to a reduction in costly litigation. However, making nuptial agreements binding should not be relied upon as the sole

---

[537] Law Commission, *Marital Property Agreements* (Consultation Paper No 198, 2011), http://lawcommission.justice.gov.uk/docs/cp198_Marital_Property_Agreements_Consultation.pdf.

[538] Law Commission, *Matrimonial Property, Needs and Agreements: A Supplementary Consultation Paper* (Consultation Paper No 208, 2012), http://lawcommission.justice.gov.uk/docs/cp208_matrimonial_property.pdf

[539] See *MacLeod v MacLeod* [2008] UKPC 64.     [540] [2010] UKSC 42.

[541] Law Commission, *Matrimonial Property, Needs and Agreements* (Law Com No 343, 2014), para 1.34.

[542] Ibid.

[543] This is also the approach under current law. See *Luckwell v Limata* [2014] EWHC 502 (Fam) for a recent example of a pre-nuptial agreement being overridden by the court in order to meet the husband's housing needs.

[544] Ibid, para 5.3.

or primary method of improving the law on financial provision. Reform in this area of the law is not solely about producing fair outcomes in individual cases, whether imposed by the court or reached between the parties themselves. Indeed, as Herring points out, the bases of financial provision on divorce have implications beyond constructing a fair settlement between the parties. Amongst a range of wider social and political interests, Herrings cites the 'symbolic value of childcare', noting that the message sent by the courts through the construction of financial orders on divorce will to some extent 'influence the perception of childcare (and the caring of dependants generally) in the wider society'.[545] Due to their symbolic importance, the rules which govern financial provision on divorce should be clear and principled because they send important social messages about the obligations created by being in a formalised relationship of a marriage or a civil partnership. That means that it is not enough to attempt to improve the operation of the law by giving statutory force to pre-nuptial contracts thus allowing parties to achieve certainty and predictability by making their own agreements. At the level of policy, an in-depth general review of the financial obligations created by marriage and civil partnership is long overdue in order to provide clearer answers as to why the *fact* of being married (or in a civil partnership) creates rights and responsibilities between the parties. Thus, the law on financial orders following divorce needs to be looked at by policy-makers to establish clear reasons for financial and property distribution on divorce and dissolution of civil partnerships.

# 10  Appeals and rehearings

## 10.1  The Barder test

A rigorous approach is taken to appeals against a court order or applications for a rehearing. An appeal must be lodged within days of the order being made and not the date from which the order is to be implemented, as must an application for a rehearing.[546] Appeals or a rehearing are occasionally allowed out of time, but only if the stringent conditions laid down by the House of Lords in *Barder v Caluori*[547] are satisfied. These are that:

 (i)  new events have occurred since the order was made;

 (ii)  these events invalidate the basis on which the order was made so that an appeal would be certain, or very likely, to succeed;

 (iii)  the new events have occurred within a relatively short time of the order being made;

 (iv)  the application for leave to appeal out of time has been made reasonably promptly; and

 (v)  the granting of leave does not prejudice third parties who have acquired interests in good faith and for value in the property which is the subject of the order.

Point (ii) is the most problematic aspect of the *Barder* criteria as it can be difficult to determine the assumption upon which an order has been made and assess whether this has been invalidated or falsified by subsequent events. The approach to be taken was neatly summed up by Smith LJ in *Williams v Lindley*:[548]

> the task of the judge considering the application for leave is, first, to identify the supervening event. He must then consider whether that event has invalidated the basis upon which the original order

---

[545]  J. Herring, 'Why Financial Orders on Divorce Should be Unfair' (2005) 19(2) International Journal of Law, Policy and the Family 218.

[546]  *B v B (Financial Provision: Leave to Apply)* [1994] 1 FLR 219.

[547]  [1987] 2 All ER 440. In *Power v Power* [1996] 3 FCR 338 the Court of Appeal stated that the same test should be adopted where there is an application for a rehearing; see too *B v B (Financial Provision: Leave to Apply)* [1994] 1 FLR 219. For a clear example of the application of the test see *Heard v Heard* [1995] 1 FLR 970.

[548]  [2005] EWCA Civ 103.

was made, so that an appeal would almost certainly succeed. The words 'so that', linking the invalidation of the basis of the original order with the prospects of success of an appeal, mean that the two must be causally related to each other. In my view, the judge should consider whether the supervening event is such that, if it had been foreseen at the time of the order, the order made would have been significantly different. If so, an appeal from the order would be almost certain to succeed.[549]

Lord Brandon in *Barder v Caluori* explained that this is a difficult question because it involves a conflict between two important principles: the principle that it is in the public interest that there should be finality to litigation, and the principle that justice required cases to be decided on the true facts and not on assumptions or estimates which were conclusively shown by later events to have been erroneous.[550] In *Thompson v Thompson*,[551] Mustill LJ, when applying the *Barder* principles, emphasised the severity of the requirements laid down by Lord Brandon. He said that the reviewing court should look in broad terms at the balance of the financial relationship created by the order under review, and ask itself how this balance had been affected by the new state of affairs. Broadly speaking, it should make no difference whether something had happened to alter the original evaluation of the parties' assets or liabilities, or whether an entirely new factor had come into play, such as the receipt of an unexpected legacy. The cause of the change should not have been foreseen[552] and taken into account when the order was made. However, Mustill LJ also expressed the view that the change should not have been brought about by the *conscious* fault of the person who sought to take advantage of it. He explained that 'merely to say that the applicant must not have brought the change on himself is not enough, for this would disqualify an applicant who had been ruined by an honest error of business judgment.'[553] Despite this concession, the judgment laid emphasis on the exceptional nature of the circumstances which had to be established before leave out of time would be granted, 'otherwise the whole basis of this essentially practical jurisdiction will be put out of joint'.[554] This means that it is only in an 'exceptionally small' number of cases that a court order will be revised.[555] In *Shaw v Shaw*[556] Thorpe LJ said that '[a]n appeal, albeit perhaps necessary to correct error or to redress an unfair result, is nevertheless a misfortune for the family in that it increases costs and extends the duration of conflict . . . The public interest in finality of litigation in this field must always be emphasised.'[557] Thus, as noted by Lawrence Collins LJ in *Dixon v Marchant*[558] 'the reported cases, with very few exceptions, apply the [*Barder* principle] strictly, and with good reason'.[559]

It was the death of one of the parties which led to the application to appeal out of time being allowed in *Barder v Caluori*. In this case a consent order was made, under which the husband was ordered to transfer the matrimonial home and its contents to the wife. The order had been agreed

---

[549] Ibid, [46].     [550] [1987] 2 All ER 440 at 451.     [551] [1991] 2 FR 530.

[552] See *Cornick v Cornick* [1994] 2 FLR 530; *S v S (Ancillary Relief: Consent Order)* [2002] 1 FLR 922.

[553] [1991] 2 FLR 530 at 538.

[554] The other key factor influencing the court was that the trial judge had found that the wife's appeal would be certain to succeed. Cf *Ritchie v Ritchie* [1996] 1 FLR 898 where the Court of Appeal held that the new events which had occurred, namely for the husband to accept redundancy and fail to pay the mortgage, could not invalidate the fundamental assumption upon which the order had been made and therefore the proposed appeal was neither certain nor very likely to succeed.

[555] *Shaw v Shaw* [2002] 2 FLR 1204 at [44].     [556] [2002] 2 FLR 1204.     [557] Ibid.

[558] [2008] 1 FLR 655 at [100].

[559] However, in cases where one party has been guilty of bad conduct such as fraud, misrepresentation, or non-disclosure, the courts are more willing to invoke the *Barder* principles: S. Hughes, 'Over the *Barder*line' [2008] Family Law 670 at 672. Moreover, in situations such as one party's non-disclosure of assets, that party cannot subsequently complain about the other party's delay in bringing an application to appeal out of time. The other party would have to make an application within a reasonable time from the non-disclosure coming to light and not from the date of the original order. See *Den Heyer v Newby* [2006] 1 FLR 1114 where Thorpe LJ said that 'the duty of promptitude on the applicant has to be measured in the context of the obligation that clearly rests on the respondent to furnish, if not detailed information, then at least the core information to enable the enquiry to be professionally evaluated', at [28].

on the tacit assumption that the wife and the two children would require a home for many years. Tragically, before the order had been executed the wife killed the two children of the family and committed suicide. The wife had devised her estate to her mother. Clearly, the assumption on which the order had been made had been totally invalidated. The husband's appeal against the order was therefore allowed despite the fact that it was out of time. Similarly in *Reid v Reid*[560] the wife, who was aged 74, died two months after the consent order was made. The husband's application to appeal out of time against the order was granted on the ground that the wife's death was a new event which was not reasonably foreseeable. Once it was accepted that the wife's death was a new event within the meaning of the *Barder* principles, the question then arose of what would have been the appropriate order at the time, had it been known that the wife had only two months to live. The court held that the severe contraction of the length of the wife's future needs would have led to a significantly different result and thus permission to appeal was given and a new order was substituted.

However, the premature death of one of the parties will not lead to an appeal out of time in all cases. In *Benson v Benson*[561] six months after a consent order was made the wife died from cancer. A compromise agreement was reached between the husband and those acting on behalf of the wife's estate under which part of the consent order would not be enforced. Meanwhile, the husband was also having business difficulties which worsened his financial position and he sought leave to appeal against the consent order, although he did not make this application until a year after his wife's death. Bracewell J was satisfied that the first three requirements in *Barder* were satisfied with respect to the wife's premature death. However, she rejected the husband's contention that his deteriorating financial circumstances amounted to a new event, as the potential seeds for disaster had been sown and were plain to the husband prior to him entering into the consent order. She further found that the delay in mounting the appeal had been lengthy and lacked the promptness which cases of this kind require, and that the reason was that the compromise arrangement was originally acceptable to the husband, and that it only became unpalatable at a later date. Bracewell J dismissed the husband's application on two grounds. Applying the principle in *Edgar v Edgar*[562] that an agreement which had been freely entered into should not be displaced unless there are compelling grounds, she held that the husband had reached an agreement after receiving both legal and financial advice, and therefore the principle applied. Moreover, by delaying so long he failed to satisfy the fourth test in *Barder* that an application for leave to appeal should be made reasonably promptly.

Appeals have occurred where orders have been made on the basis that property or business assets have a particular value, and where the actual value has proved to be considerably higher, as in *Thompson v Thompson*;[563] or considerably lower, as in *Heard v Heard*.[564] In *Cornick v Cornick*[565] Hale J (as she then was) distinguished between cases where an asset which was correctly valued at the date of the hearing changes value within a short time due to 'natural processes of price fluctuation', and those cases where either the asset was incorrectly valued at the date of the hearing or where, subsequent to the hearing, something unforeseen happened to alter the value of the asset. While the latter circumstances could possibly come within the *Barder* principles (provided the other conditions were satisfied) the 'natural processes of price fluctuation' would not. Thus, in

---

[560] [2003] EWHC 2878 (Fam).     [561] [1996] 1 FLR 692.

[562] [1980] 3 All ER 887, discussed in Section 8.1.

[563] [1991] 2 FLR 530. In this case the husband's business had been valued at £20,000 but was sold for £45,000 just five days after the time limit for appealing an order had expired. The Court of Appeal granted the wife leave to appeal out of time.

[564] [1995] 1 FLR 970. The main family asset, the matrimonial home, could only be sold at about half its estimated value, and since the intention had been that the husband would be able to rehouse himself out of the proceeds of sale this amounted to a new event invalidating the basis of the original order. The husband's delay in appealing could be explained and his appeal was therefore allowed and the case remitted.

[565] [1994] 2 FLR 530.

this case, the wife was awarded periodical payments and a lump sum payment which amounted to 51 per cent of the husband's capital assets. Shortly after the hearing the value of the husband's shares rose to such an extent that the lump sum payment now only represented 20 per cent of the capital assets. The wife sought leave to appeal out of time on the basis that the increase in the value of the shares was a new event which meant that the issue could be reopened. The court dismissed the application. The assets were correctly valued at the date of the hearing and there was nothing on the facts to require the court to disregard the principle that the natural processes of price fluctuation did not entitle the wife to the relief sought. Hale J (as she then was) said '[o]nce the couple are divorced and their capital divided, they cannot normally expect to profit from, anymore than they expect to lose by, later changes in the other's fortune.'[566]

To come within the *Barder* principles, it is clear that the new event or change in circumstances must have been unforeseeable at the time the order was made.[567] In *B v B*[568] the wife appealed out of time against a consent order on the basis that the matrimonial home which was valued at £1.25 million at the date of the hearing was subsequently sold by the husband for £1.6 million. The application was dismissed. The property rose in value due to the rising property market and as a result of the husband's refurbishment of the property, which cost over £60,000. The court held that even if the renovations and the rise in the property market had not been foreseen at the time the order was made, they were foreseeable. The rising property market was a matter of common knowledge and there was no reason to suppose that the husband, who was a property developer, would not have made clear his intention to refurbish the property if inquiry had been made of him.[569] The circumstances which caused the increase in the value of the property were foreseeable and, as such, the increase was not a new and supervening event within the *Barder* principles. Similarly in *Maskell v Maskell*[570] the Court of Appeal held that the husband's redundancy just two months after the order was made was not a supervening event. Rather, loss of employment was a foreseeable challenge that happened to hundreds of thousands of breadwinners.[571]

Another situation where the *Barder* principle has been successfully applied is the remarriage of the recipient spouse shortly after an order has been made. In *Wells v Wells*[572] six months after the husband was ordered to transfer his entire interest in the matrimonial home to his wife, the wife remarried and went to live with the children in the second husband's house. The husband was granted leave to appeal out of time on the ground that the wife's situation had fundamentally changed, and the whole basis of the order had been vitiated.[573] Similarly, in *Williams v Lindley*[574] the parties separated and the wife and one of the parties' two children went to live in the home of her employer. The wife denied that she was in a relationship with her employer and she sought a transfer of the husband's share in the matrimonial home to enable her to return there to live with the children. A consent order was made which provided for a 70:30 split in the equity in the home in her favour. Shortly afterwards, the wife married her employer and the husband applied to set aside the consent order. The Court of Appeal held that this was a 'plain case' for the grant of leave to appeal out of time.[575] The main foundation for the original order was the wife's urgent need to rehouse herself and her children. This foundation was destroyed within one month by her engagement and subsequent remarriage. However, this case was distinguished by the Court of Appeal in *Dixon v Marchant*.[576] In this case the parties divorced in 1993 and the husband was ordered to pay a lump sum plus periodical payments during the parties' joint lives or until the wife's remarriage or further order. In 2005 the husband sought a variation of the original order and a consent order was made in 2006 which capitalised the periodical payments into a lump sum payment of £125,000. During this time the husband believed that the wife was cohabiting with her long-term partner.

---

[566] Ibid.     [567] Ibid.     [568] [2007] EWHC 2472 (Fam).     [569] Ibid, [40].
[570] [2003] 1 FLR 1138.     [571] Ibid, [4].     [572] [1992] 2 FLR 66.
[573] The husband in *Chaudhuri v Chaudhuri* [1992] 2 FLR 73 failed when relying on similar facts because, crucially, the order appealed against contemplated the possibility of the wife remarrying.
[574] [2005] 2 FLR 710.     [575] Ibid, [24].     [576] [2008] EWCA Civ 11.

However, as part of the negotiations leading to this agreement, the wife indicated that she was not cohabiting and had no intention of either doing so or remarrying. Seven months after the consent order was made, the wife married the man with whom her husband had believed her to be cohabiting. The husband applied to have the consent order set aside. The main issue was whether the wife's remarriage was a new event which invalidated the basis and fundamental assumption upon which the consent order had been made. The Court of Appeal was divided on this question. The majority rejected the husband's application holding that the basis of the consent order was a straightforward capitalisation of the wife's periodical payments in order to achieve a clean break between the parties. As this was the core purpose of the order, the wife's remarriage was not a special factor on the facts of the case. While the husband had made inquiry about the wife's relationship with her future husband, this was to quell his suspicion that she was cohabiting with him. He was not, according to the court, protesting about nor seeking to protect himself from the risk of her remarriage.[577] Further, the wife's indication of her present situation during the negotiations leading to the consent order carried no implication of her future intention and thus the risk of remarriage was a risk that the husband had to bear.[578] Ward LJ pointed out that the capitalisation of the wife's periodical payments in the consent order carried risks for both parties. For the husband, there was the risk that the wife would remarry and in that event he would have been better off continuing to make maintenance payments as these would have ceased on her remarriage. For the wife, the risk was that the lump sum would be exhausted during her lifetime and thus she would have been better off preserving her rights to maintenance.[579] To succeed in his application, the husband had to show that there was a mutual assumption between the parties, and shared by the court, that for an indefinite period to be measured in years rather than months or weeks the wife would not remarry.[580] However, according to Ward LJ there was nothing in the agreement to suggest that the husband was given any right to claw back any part of the lump sum if the wife should remarry soon after the payment had been made.[581] Both *Wells v Wells*[582] and *Williams v Lindley*[583] were distinguished on the basis that the respective orders had been made to provide a roof over the heads of the wife and children and, in both cases, the wife's remarriage removed this need. In the present case, however, the reason for making the consent order was to capitalise the wife's periodical payments and thus her subsequent remarriage did not invalidate the basis upon which this order was made. Lawrence Collins LJ also dismissed the application noting that the facts of the case 'fall far below the necessary standard' to meet the *Barder* principle.[584] However, he based his judgment on the importance of achieving finality and emphasised that the application of the *Barder* principle is reserved for exceptional cases. Indeed, those cases where the principle was successfully invoked were cases in which 'justice cried out for a remedy'.[585] This, however, was not one of those cases. Wall LJ provided the dissenting judgment. In his view, the fundamental assumption behind the agreement was that the wife would not remarry. Relying upon *Williams v Lindley*,[586] he took the view that the fact of the wife's remarriage made 'the order not merely unsustainable, but—on its face—unjust'.[587]

This case confirms that in the public interest of finality in litigation, it is only in exceptional cases that new events will allow the court to revise a clean break order. The fact of the recipient's remarriage will not, by and of itself, constitute a *Barder* event where periodical payments have been capitalised. Indeed, Ward LJ noted that there is no reported case 'where remarriage as such is the one and only decisive event'.[588] In other cases (such as *Williams v Lindley*) where remarriage was relied upon, the purpose of the original order was obviated by the changing circumstances created by the remarriage and not by the remarriage itself. This case also reveals the uncertainty

---

[577] Ibid, [23].

[578] On this point the court relied upon *Smith v Smith* [1976] Fam 18 and *H v H (Family Provision: Remarriage)* [1975] Fam 19.

[579] [2008] EWCA Civ 11 at [24].     [580] Ibid, [25].     [581] Ibid, [26].     [582] [1992] 2 FLR 66.

[583] [2005] 2 FLR 710.     [584] [2008] EWCA Civ 11 at [100].     [585] Ibid, [95].     [586] Ibid, [70].

[587] Ibid, [34].     [588] Ibid, [20].

surrounding the application of the *Barder* criteria. The court was divided on whether the consent order was based on the assumption that the wife would not remarry. Zuckerman points out that 'the difference between situations in which justice cries out and those where no such cry is heard is largely a matter of degree and evaluation and liable to be influenced by the judge's moral views about the rights and wrongs of the couple'.[589] He suggests that a preferable solution to appealing out of time in these sorts of case is to use a provisional order subject to a change of circumstances:

> [R]ather than try to work out after the event what was and what was not a fundamental assumption, the court making the order should set out the circumstances that would justify an application for variation . . . this approach . . . would do no more than spell out the assumptions that the court already makes and it would have the added advantage that parties would have to work out more carefully what they want to achieve.[590]

Indeed, in *Dixon v Marchant*, the agreement to capitalise the husband's maintenance payments could have provided for the eventuality of the wife's remarriage within a specified time frame of the order being made thus allowing him to recoup some of his money on the occurrence of this event. Douglas notes that Ward LJ appears to have based his reasoning on the fact that the husband could have required such a clause within the agreement[591] which would have allowed him to claw back part of the lump sum and thus he would not have had to appeal out of time against the original order. Of course, an obvious problem with this approach, which requires eventualities to be written into capitalised maintenance agreements, is in securing the other party's agreement to it.

In *Myerson v Myerson*[592] the husband received a bundle of high-risk assets upon the order of the court but shortly after the making of the order the economy declined and the assets reduced to 14 per cent of their previous value. Thorpe LJ held that this was not a *Barder* event; the husband had agreed to the order and had known that his assets were subject to the natural process of price fluctuation.

## 10.2 **Variation**

Section 31 governs the variation of financial provision orders. Under section 31, the court has the power to vary or discharge an order or suspend or revive any provision contained within an order. However, this only applies to the following ancillary relief orders:[593]

   (i) maintenance pending suit or interim maintenance;

   (ii) periodical payments order (secured or unsecured);

   (iii) an order for the payment of a lump sum by instalments;

---

[589] A. Zuckerman, 'Finality of Litigation—Setting Aside a Final Judgment' (2008) 27(2) Civil Justice Quarterly 151 at 157.

[590] Ibid.

[591] A. Douglas, 'Comment on *Dixon v Marchant*' [2008] Family Law 306. Douglas cites *L v L* [2008] 1 FLR 26 as an example where a particular eventuality was built into a consent order. In this case a consent order included a clause that the husband would pay the wife an annual income of £75,000 should her earnings fall below that sum. Shortly afterwards when the wife gave up work and sought payment, the husband applied to have the consent order set aside on the ground, *inter alia*, that her lack of income was a *Barder* event. This argument was rejected by the court as the order had made specific provision for this eventuality even though it had happened sooner than expected. As noted by Douglas:

> the possibility of the wife's income reducing was expressly covered in the consent order. It was held, inter alia, that the husband could not therefore claim that her giving up work sooner than expected was a Barder 'event'—far from invalidating the basis of the order, it was the occurrence of an event for which the order itself made specific provision.

[592] [2009] EWCA Civ 282.     [593] MCA 1973, s 31(2).

(iv) any deferred order made by virtue of s 23(1)(c) (lump sums) which includes provision in respect of pension rights;

(v) an order for the sale of property;

(vi) a pension sharing order under s 24B which is made before the decree absolute.

Property adjustment orders and lump sum orders cannot be varied.[594] Once made, they are final orders and the only way in which they can be altered is for one party to appeal against the order or to seek to have it set aside. Periodical payment orders can, however, be varied upwards, downwards, or they can be terminated altogether. The court can also vary the period for which payments are to be made. The only exception to this is if the court has made an order under section 28(1A), which prevents the recipient of fixed-term periodical payments from applying under section 31 for an extension of the term specified in the order.

### 10.2.1 Timing of the application to vary

The court's variation powers under section 31 are unfettered[595] and apply with equal force to consent orders.[596] The applicant is not required to establish exceptional circumstances or a material change in circumstances before a variation order can be made, but the exercise of the discretion may, of course, be affected by that consideration.[597] One very important issue, however, relates to the timing of the application to vary. It is essential to ensure that an application to vary a limited term order is made before the order expires, for otherwise there will be no order in existence which is capable of being varied. In *T v T (Financial Provision)*[598] a periodical payments order had been made in favour of a wife which was expressed to take effect 'until such date as the wife shall remarry or until the husband retires or further order'. After the husband retired the wife applied to vary the order. It was conceded that the court would have had jurisdiction to extend the order to beyond the husband's retirement date had the wife made her application before the husband retired.[599] However, the court ruled that its jurisdiction had come to an end once the retirement took place. The addition of the words 'or further order' did not come to the wife's assistance because the Court of Appeal held that these words meant 'a further order in the meantime'. Thus, it is very important that an application to vary is made within good time of the original order coming to an end. Leaving it too late will mean the failure of the variation application because it falls into a time-limit trap.

This was illustrated by *G v G (Periodical Payments: Jurisdiction)*.[600] A consent order was made which contained the following terms: 'The respondent to pay or cause to be paid to the petitioner . . . periodical payments at the rate of £14,000 per annum . . . until the petitioner shall remarry, cohabit with another man for a period of 6 months . . . or until the child of the family, C, shall attain the age of 18 years whichever shall be sooner or until further order.' There was no direction given under section 28(1A) that the wife could not apply for an extension of the term specified in the order, so provided she made her application in time she could have obtained a variation of the order under section 31. However, the wife made her application to vary the original order one month after C reached her eighteenth birthday, one of the cut-off points specified in the consent order. Accordingly, the Court of Appeal ruled that the court had no jurisdiction to vary the original order because it had already expired. Interestingly, however, Ward LJ expressed the *obiter* view that 'it is essential not only that application be made but that an order be made before the expiration of the term'.[601] In other words, suggesting a more stringent test that not

---

[594] The instalments by which a lump sum order by instalments is to be paid can be varied.

[595] See Thorpe LJ in *Harris v Harris* [2001] 1 FCR 68.    [596] *B v B (Consent Order: Variation)* [1995] 1 FLR 9.

[597] *Flavell v Flavell* [1997] 1 FLR 353.    [598] [1988] 1 FLR 480.

[599] This concession was confirmed in *Richardson v Richardson* [1993] 4 All ER 673.

[600] [1997] 1 All ER 272.    [601] Ibid, 284.

only had the application to vary to be made before the time limit in a periodical payment order expired, but that the actual variation order had to be made before this date. However, the Court of Appeal did not follow this dictum in *Jones v Jones*.[602] In this case under the terms of a consent order the parties agreed that the husband would make periodical payments to the wife until 12 January 1998. No direction was made under section 28(1A) which prevented the wife from seeking to extend that term. On 8 January 1998, the wife applied for an extension and the application was granted in June 1998. On appeal the question that fell to be determined was whether after the original termination date of 12 January, the judge had jurisdiction to hear the wife's application. The Court of Appeal held that the judge did have jurisdiction to extend the order even though the application was determined after the period referred to in the consent order had expired. The crucial point was that the wife's application was made *before* the order expired. Thus, the court can vary or extend an order under section 31 provided that the application is made during the life of the order and it does not matter if the application is not determined after the specified term has expired.

### 10.2.2 Which factors must the court consider?

When exercising its powers under section 31 the court has regard to all the circumstances of the case, first consideration being given to the welfare of any child of the family under the age of 18.[603] The court also considers any change of circumstances in any of the matters to which the court had regard when the original order was made, although in *Flavell v Flavell*[604] the Court of Appeal held that the power of the court to vary orders was not dependent on exceptional circumstances or material change. While these are issues that can affect the exercise of the court's discretion, they are not a requirement of a successful application. The court must, however, consider the possibility of a clean break on a variation application. Under section 31(7)(a), the court must consider whether to vary a periodical payments order so that payments shall only be made for a period of time which will be sufficient, in the opinion of the court, to enable the recipient to adjust without undue hardship to the termination of the payments. So where a clean break has not been possible at the time of the original order, subsequent developments such as one party's increased capital, may make it possible at a later date.[605]

To achieve a clean break, the court has the power to capitalise a periodical payments order. This simply means that the court can substitute a periodical payments order with a capital order, such as a lump sum. This power is given by section 31(7A)–(7G) which were inserted into the MCA 1973 by the Family Law Act 1996.[606] Under these provisions, when discharging a periodical payments order or varying that order so that payments are to be made for a limited time only, the court has the power to make one or more of the following orders: a lump sum order; a property adjustment order; and a pension-sharing order. Further, the court can also direct that the payee is not entitled to make any further application for a periodical payments order or an extension of the order.[607] When the court is capitalising a periodical payments order, one important question concerns determining the quantum of the capital order. Is the court limited to a strict mathematical calculation of the capital equivalent of the ongoing periodical payments or can the court conduct a broader assessment which reopens how the couple's assets should be distributed? The Court of Appeal provided a very clear answer to this question in *Pearce v Pearce*.[608] When terminating one party's entitlement to future periodical payments, the function of the court is not to reopen capital

---

[602] [2000] 2 FCR 201.    [603] MCA 1973, s 31(7).    [604] [1997] 1 FLR 353.

[605] *Pearce v Pearce* [2003] 2 FLR 1144 at [39]. In a case where the payer has died, the court shall also consider the changed circumstances resulting from his/her death, s 31(7)(b).

[606] Family Law Act 1996, Sch 8, para 16. This followed the recommendation of the Law Commission in its Report, *Family Law: The Ground for Divorce* (Law Com No 192, 1990), para 6.10.

[607] Section 31(7B)(c).    [608] [2003] 2 FLR 1144.

claims but to substitute for the ongoing payments a capital order which compensates the payee and achieves the clean break.[609] The court said that:

> [t]here is simply no power or discretion to embark on further adjustment of capital to reflect the outcome of unwise or unfortunate investment on one side or prudent or lucky investment on the other.[610]

Thorpe LJ laid down the following approach to be taken by a judge faced with capitalising periodical payments: the judge should first determine what, if any, variation should be made in the order for periodical payments; second, fix the date when the new order will commence, and finally substitute a capital order, calculated in accordance with the Duxbury tables, for the periodical payments which are being terminated.[611] According to Thorpe LJ such an approach was necessary 'as a safeguard against the temptation to further adjust the capital division between the parties to reflect the factors which were not foreseen or which did not pertain at the date of the original division'.[612]

Section 31 confers on the court a 'broad discretion' to determine variation applications.[613] The question of when the court will vary a periodical payments order, either upwards or downwards or perhaps terminate it altogether, is an interesting one because it raises issues surrounding the legal obligation one has to a former spouse.

---

### Key case

This was the central issue in *North v North*[614] where the wife applied for an upwards variation of a nominal periodical payments order which had been in place for many years. The parties divorced after 14 years of marriage. They had two children who remained with the husband after the divorce. The financial order, which was made in 1981, made provision for a house for the wife and for the transfer of ground rents to her which provided her with an annual income. The order also contained provision for a nominal order of periodical payments to the wife at a rate of 5p per annum for the parties' joint lives, until the wife remarried or until further order. The wife did not attempt to find employment after the divorce and the husband had, on several occasions, helped her out financially. In 2000 the wife realised all her assets, worth some £328,000, and moved to Australia. She rented an apartment in one of the most expensive areas in Sydney Harbour and placed her money in various investments which incurred substantial losses. She returned to the UK and sought an upwards variation of the nominal periodical payments order made in 1981. Her assets at the time amounted to around £155,000 (after legal costs), which generated an income of £5,000. The husband's financial position meanwhile had improved significantly since the original order was made. His net assets were worth almost £5 million and he had an income of £60,000. In relation to the wife's application to vary the periodical payments upwards, the district judge found that her diminished financial circumstances were of her own making. However, he awarded her periodical payments of £16,500 per annum, capitalised into a lump sum of £202,000. The husband's appeal against the order was upheld by the Court of Appeal. This is an interesting case because it raised the thorny

---

[609] Ibid, [45]. In reaching the conclusion, the dicta of Charles J in *Cornick v Cornick (No 3)* [2001] 2 FLR 1240 at 1262–1264, were disapproved.

[610] [2003] 2 FLR 1144 at [36].

[611] Ibid, [37]. Thorpe LJ also said that, when determining what substitute order should be made, first consideration should be given to the option of carving out of the payer's pension funds a pension for the payee equivalent to the discharged periodical payments order.

[612] [2003] 2 FLR 1144 at [39].     [613] *North v North* [2007] EWCA Civ 760 at [31], *per* Thorpe LJ.

[614] [2007] EWCA Civ 760.

issue of whether the husband should bear any responsibility for his former wife's current financial position, over 25 years after the parties divorced. Given the findings of the district judge that the wife's financial circumstances were of her own making, in particular due to her lifestyle choices of opting not to work, moving to Australia, and making investments, and that the husband had acted generously and honourably, one could speculate that the court, rather than increasing the periodical payments, would have terminated them. However, the Court of Appeal distinguished between circumstances where assets were dissipated through financial mismanagement, extravagance, or irresponsibility, for which a former spouse would bear no responsibility, and where losses were incurred as a result of misfortune. In relation to the latter, the court did not rule out the possibility that, if so able, the payer be ordered to provide financial assistance in such circumstances. When determining an application under section 31, the court has unfettered discretion. Thorpe LJ made it clear, however, that the overarching objective is to achieve a fair result, which has two elements: 'the order must be fair to the applicant in need, and to the respondent who must pay'.[615] He continued:

> In any application under Section 31 the applicant's needs are likely to be the dominant or magnetic factor. But it does not follow that the respondent is inevitably responsible financially for any established needs. He is not an insurer against all hazards nor, when fairness is the measure, is he necessarily liable for needs created by the applicant's financial mismanagement, extravagance or irresponsibility. The prodigal former wife cannot hope to turn to a former husband in pursuit of a legal remedy, whatever may be her hope that he might out of charity come to her rescue.[616]

This meant that the wife's financial needs, which were created by her lifestyle choices (such as her failure to utilise her earning potential and her choice of a more hazardous future in Australia), were of her own making, and her husband could not be held responsible for them.[617] However, Thorpe LJ held that the losses incurred by her investments were in a different category. They were 'more the outcome of hazard and therefore to be characterised as misfortune rather than mismanagement'.[618] Thus the court held that the wife had an entitlement to a modest award, quantified at £3,000 per annum to be capitalised.[619]

So it seems that while a former spouse will not be obliged to meet the financial needs of the applicant which have been caused by his or her 'financial mismanagement, extravagance or irresponsibility', an award could be made to compensate for financial needs which were not self-created. As Merrigan points out, while the payee has a responsibility to 'manage the money she has as best she can', poor conduct which has a significant financial impact 'is a factor to reduce but not necessarily defeat the wife's claim for upward variation of maintenance'.[620] Thus much depends on the facts and circumstances of each individual case. However, will it always be clear whether financial losses are incurred by 'misfortune' rather than 'mismanagement'? It is unfortunate that the court did not take the opportunity to articulate clearly why the husband should bear some responsibility for his former wife's investment losses incurred by misfortune. Was this simply on the basis that she found herself in an unfortunate financial position, not all of her own making, and that as the husband had sufficient money to provide assistance he should, in the interests of fairness, be ordered to do so?[621] However, there has to be some rational ground upon which to base a legal

---

[615] Ibid, [32].     [616] Ibid.     [617] Ibid, [33].     [618] Ibid, [34].

[619] Indeed, it is clear that if an upwards variation is ordered, the court will strive to capitalise the order, should resources allow, and dismiss the periodical payments order.

[620] D. Merrigan, 'Variation of Nominal Periodical Payment Orders' [2007] Family Law 1009 at 1011.

[621] Of course, this will only be possible where a variation application is permitted and so is not an option where, eg, the court has made an order under s 28(1A).

obligation and appealing to one's sense of subjective fairness is simply not enough. One should remember that the wife's losses were incurred as a result of decisions made many years after the divorce. While these may have been unfortunate and not the fault of the wife, neither were they the fault of the husband whose obligations to the wife could have been regarded as extinguished after payment of the capital sum on the original order and his financial assistance over the years. Indeed, this was not a situation where a nominal order is made because one's obligation to a spouse could not be fulfilled on divorce. In those circumstances, the nominal order allows the court to revisit the issue should the payer's financial circumstances improve. In such situations, an upwards variation of the nominal order (capitalised if resources permit) may be entirely appropriate. But this will have been done to fulfil outstanding obligations created by the marriage. In *North*, however, this was not the case. By contrast, the husband was ordered to bear some responsibility for investment losses incurred by the wife, which had nothing to do with the marriage, or the wife's contributions to the family. This type of thinking is in contrast to other jurisprudence in the area of ancillary relief where, for example, property acquired or bonuses awarded after the parties' separation is generally unavailable in the financial settlement.[622] In other words, assets which are generated after separation or divorce are usually regarded as belonging to those to whom they have accrued. Similarly then, why are financial losses, which are incurred after the parties' separation or divorce, not regarded as being the sole responsibility of the one who incurs them. This, it is suggested, is a particularly strong argument on the facts of *North* where the losses were incurred many years after the parties had divorced.

In another unusual variation application, *Lauder v Lauder*,[623] the court had to decide whether to vary the parties' pre-*White* settlement which was made in 1988 to take account of the fact that the wife's earning capacity had been restricted by her contributions to the family in line with the 'compensation' strand in *Miller; McFarlane*. Given that the parties' settlement had been made long before this decision, the question was whether the wife could increase her award in line with the more generous interpretation of recent jurisprudence. The parties had been married for 24 years and had three children who were aged 20, 18, and 14 at the time of the divorce. The wife, who was aged 50 at the time of the divorce, was awarded periodical payments of £8,000 per annum which equated to 35 per cent of the husband's net income. The order also envisaged that the wife would receive two-thirds of the value of the matrimonial home. However, the couple agreed not to implement the order so that the wife and children could live in the matrimonial home. During this time, the husband paid for the upkeep of the home and supplemented the wife's income. The wife secured employment earning £23,500 by the date of her retirement at the age of 62. In 2003, the matrimonial home was sold. In line with the original order, the wife received £414,000 from the proceeds of sale, and the husband received some £314,000. By now the husband was worth in the region of £4.5 million and had a net income of £200,000. By contrast, the wife's income was £9,000. The wife applied for an upwards variation of the periodical payments order. At first instance, the district judge awarded her £40,000 per annum, capitalised at £500,000. On appeal, Baron J opined that the core issue was whether this figure was fair, noting that the decision was handed down before *Miller; McFarlane* and so it had to be considered how that decision impacted on this case.[624]

Baron J held that the proper approach was to apply the terms of the Act in light of the facts and to give proper consideration to the guidance given by the House of Lords in *Miller; McFarlane*.[625] Thus, on the variation application, the court had to interpret the wife's needs generously and consider whether compensation was required. In terms of her needs, Baron J held that the wife's needs had not been 'generously interpreted'. Drawing attention to the fact that the marriage had lasted 24 years, producing three children, and that the wife had continued to spend

---

[622] See Section 5.5.3.3.   [623] [2007] 2 FLR 802.   [624] Ibid, [42].   [625] Ibid, [57].

many years caring for the youngest child after the divorce, Baron J awarded the wife capital-ised periodical payments of £725,000. This award included an element of compensation for the wife's relationship-generated economic disadvantage.[626] Even though the wife had attempted to become self-sufficient after the divorce, she had a modest earning capacity which was a 'direct result of the marriage and the parties' decision that she should be a wife and mother'.[627] The court held that 'this requires proper compensation'.[628] The husband argued that the strength of this compensation claim was diminished because so many years had passed since the divorce in 1985. Baron J rejected this assertion:

> This wife, who suffered ill health during the course of the marriage, could never, after 24 years of marriage at the age of 50 years, be expected to earn substantial sums of money which would enable her to save sufficient to look to her own resources in old age. Her salary, at its zenith, was just over £23,000 per annum gross, that was about one tenth of the husband's net income. Her caring role within the family inevitably affected her ability to generate income or assets as she grew older. When this marriage came to an end she was past the age of being able to start a career anew.[629]

In addition, the fact that they did not implement the original order, an unusual decision which placed them in economic limbo, resulted in greater economic disadvantage to the wife. However, it is of note that the court held that the 'sharing' principle in *Miller; McFarlane* was not relevant. As made clear in *Pearce v Pearce*,[630] the court cannot reopen capital claims on a variation application even if the law had progressed to make the original order appear 'discriminatory and unfair'.[631] One is 'not entitled to a second bite of the capital cherry'[632] and thus in *Lauder* the court held that 'this application cannot be used as a basis to distribute capital by the back door' and thus no ele-ment of sharing was provided.[633]

The significance of this case lies in the fact that the guidance of the House of Lords in *Miller; McFarlane* on needs and compensation (but not equal sharing) applies not only to an original application for ancillary relief but also on an application for variation of an original order. This was confirmed by the President of the Family Division in *VB v JP*.[634] In this case the wife ap-plied for an increase in the amount of periodical payments awarded in 2002 on the basis that she was entitled to compensation for her lost earning potential. The court rejected the husband's assertion that compensation could not be considered on a claim for variation saying that the language of the House of Lords in *Miller; McFarlane* is 'of general application and extends where appropriate to consideration by the court of the overall fairness of an order made upon an ap-plication to vary a joint lives periodical payments order'.[635] The court held, therefore, that it was right to have regard to the wife's 'undoubted relationship generated disadvantage'[636] and found that there was a mutual decision between the parties that the wife would sacrifice her career for the 'role of mother and carer for a husband who was busy, worked long hours, and, despite his wish, could devote only a very minor part of his time to his "family life", given the demands of his job and his ability to pursue it successfully to the full as a result'.[637] By contrast to the wife's diminished earning capacity, the husband's career had progressed and his income had increased significantly since the original order was made. Although the wife had clearly suffered lost earn-ing potential and was thus entitled to compensation, this was difficult to quantify. However, because a clean break was not possible on the facts and the parties agreed that there was an in-definite continuing need for periodic maintenance, it was not necessary to quantify the element

---

[626] It is of note that Baron J did not quantify the wife's compensation as a separate element of the award but within an assessment of the wife's needs as 'generously interpreted'. See earlier Section 5.5.2 on compensation.
[627] [2007] 2 FLR 802 at [65].     [628] Ibid, [65].     [629] Ibid, [67].     [630] [2003] 2 FLR 1144.
[631] [2007] 2 FLR 802 at [21].     [632] Ibid.     [633] Ibid, [70].     [634] [2008] 1 FLR 742.
[635] Ibid, [64].     [636] Ibid, [66].     [637] Ibid, [38].

of compensation separately. Instead, it was considered as part of the assessment of the wife's needs generously assessed against the standard of living during the marriage and husband's increased income.

A contingency which is sometimes included in consent orders for periodical payments is that the order will cease if the wife should cohabit with another man for longer than a specified period. The risk to the wife of an order containing such a clause is that her new partner may not be in the position to maintain her himself. Although courts have clearly stated that cohabitation should not be equated with remarriage when a periodical payments order is made,[638] or when an application has been made in variation proceedings to discharge the order,[639] there seems to be nothing to prevent the inclusion of a clause of this type in a periodical payments order. The wife can apply for a variation of this (or any other) term before the cut-off date has been reached, provided that no direction to the contrary has been made under section 28(1A). But once the specified period of cohabitation has been fulfilled it seems that the order for periodical payments terminates automatically. Moreover, the order cannot be revived even if the cohabitation subsequently ceases, and there is a general rule against repeat applications being made for orders.[640]

It is suggested that orders containing a clause that periodical payments should cease automatically if a former wife should cohabit with another man should be avoided. Such provisions are the modern equivalent of the old *dum casta* orders, which at one time used to stipulate that the wife must remain 'chaste' if she wished her periodical payments to continue.[641] They are objectionable in that they may lead to snooping and may restrain the wife from forming an intimate relationship out of fear that she will lose her source of income from her ex-husband. Whereas cohabitation may provide good cause to apply for variation or termination of an order for periodical payments, for an order to terminate automatically in the event of the wife cohabiting, irrespective of her partner's income, could cause such a wife a great deal of financial hardship.[642]

## 11  Financial provision orders during the marriage

Before spouses even get to the stage of petitioning for divorce, their relationship may be breaking down in circumstances in which one spouse is failing to make reasonable financial provision for the other. In such cases, it is possible for an application to be made to the court for reasonable financial provision during the marriage, although such applications are not that common.[643]

Two pieces of legislation give courts the powers to address these circumstances. An application can be made to the magistrates' court under the Domestic Proceedings and Magistrates' Courts Act 1978 for an order to be made for periodical payments and/or a lump sum not exceeding £1,000.[644] Alternatively, the applicant can apply to a county court, or to the High Court, under section 27 of the MCA 1973, for an order for secured or unsecured periodical payments, and a lump sum, unlimited in amount. In either case, orders are limited to periodical payments or lump sums and no property adjustment order can be made. In either case, the applicant must establish that the respondent spouse has failed to provide him or her with reasonable maintenance.

---

[638] *Atkinson v Atkinson (No 2)* [1996] 1 FLR 51.      [639] *Atkinson v Atkinson* [1987] 3 All ER 849.

[640] Section 22A(3).      [641] Cf *Squire v Squire* [1905] P 4.

[642] See further on this issue, M. Hayes 'Cohabitation Clauses in Financial Provision and Property Adjustment Orders: Law, Policy and Justice' (1994) 110 LQR 124.

[643] J. Eekelaar, 'Post-Divorce Financial Obligations' in S. Katz, J. Eekelaar, and M. Maclean (eds), *Cross-Currents: Family Law and Policy in the United States and England* (Oxford: Oxford University Press, 2000), p 407.

[644] The order would be made under s 2. However, where the parties agree that a financial provision order should be made, the application should be brought under s 6.

**Key legislation**

Section 1 of the Domestic Proceedings and Magistrates' Courts Act 1978[645] provides:

> Either party to a marriage may apply to a magistrates' court for an order under section 2 of this Act on the ground that the other party to the marriage—
>
> (a) has failed to provide reasonable maintenance for the applicant; or
> (b) has failed to provide, or to make a proper contribution towards, reasonable maintenance for any child of the family; or
> (c) has behaved in such a way that the applicant cannot reasonably be expected to live with the respondent; or
> (d) has deserted the applicant.

In practice, it is unlikely that the respondent will litigate over whether he or she has wilfully neglected to maintain the applicant. Instead this ground is likely to be conceded and any contest will be over whether an order should be made in light of the parties' respective financial circumstances and, if so, how it should be quantified. In relation to failure to provide reasonable maintenance for the applicant, this is relatively easy to establish in a case where the applicant has no independent income, or only a limited income. Even where a respondent has no source of income from which he or she can pay their spouse maintenance, the ground of failure to provide reasonable maintenance can nonetheless be established. In such cases, the magistrates' courts can make nominal orders, for example for 10p per annum, in favour of an applicant.[646] The advantage of such a nominal order is that it recognises that spouses have a legal duty to maintain each other and it is an order which can be varied upwards should the respondent's circumstances subsequently improve.[647] Paragraph (b) has been rendered virtually obsolete because the Child Support Act 1991[648] in general prevents a court making orders for periodical payments in favour of a child.[649]

Where the grounds for making an order are established or conceded, the court, in deciding whether to exercise its powers and, if so, in what manner, must have regard to all the circumstances of the case, must give first consideration to the welfare while a minor of any child of the family, and have regard to the several matters which are listed in section 3. These are virtually the same matters as those to which a court must have regard in the exercise of financial provision and property adjustment powers on the grant of a decree of divorce, nullity, or judicial separation.[650] The differences are that, because the parties are still married, the clean break principle does not apply, since the spouses' mutual obligation to maintain one another continues, and of course there is no need to consider benefits which might be lost by reason of the marriage being terminated.

Proceedings may also be brought in the county court or the High Court for periodical payments and/or a lump sum on the grounds of failure to provide reasonable maintenance for a spouse, or a child of the family, under section 27 of the MCA 1973.[651] Under section 27, the court can make a secured periodical payments order and there is no limit on the amount which can be awarded as a lump sum.[652]

---

[645] The equivalent provisions for civil partners are contained in the Civil Partnership Act 2004, Sch 6.

[646] See eg *Chase v Chase* (1983) 13 Fam Law 21.

[647] The court can vary or revoke a periodical payments order under the Domestic Proceedings and Magistrates' Courts Act 1978, s 20.

[648] As amended by the Child Support, Pensions and Social Security Act 2000. See Chapter 6.

[649] Child Support Act 1991, s 8. On the Act, and financial and property provision for children generally, see Chapter 6.

[650] MCA 1973, s 25.

[651] The equivalent provisions for civil partners are contained in the Civil Partnership Act 2004, Sch 5, Pt 9.

[652] Although, just like the magistrates' court, the court cannot make a property adjustment order. In relation to children, the court's powers are similarly negated by the Child Support Act 1991, s 8.

# Discussion Questions

1. The decisions of the House of Lords in *White v White* and *Miller; McFarlane* completely transformed the guiding principles which apply when courts are considering financial orders following divorce. In pursuit of gender-based equality between the parties, the courts have introduced the default rule of equal sharing on divorce. To what extent do you agree with this statement? What issues do you think require further clarification?

2. As indicated, the courts have developed the principle of equality when considering financial orders following divorce. Is this principle sustainable in cases involving families of modest or very limited means?

3. When should non-matrimonial property be available for distribution in financial provision orders on divorce?

4. 'The court should give effect to a nuptial agreement that is freely entered into by each party with a full appreciation of its implications unless in the circumstances prevailing it would not be fair to hold the parties to the agreement' (*Radmacher v Granatino*). Critically analyse this statement.

# Further Reading

COOKE, E., '*Miller/McFarlane*: Law in Search of a Definition' [2007] Child and Family Law Quarterly 98

CRETNEY, S., 'The Family and the Law—Status or Contract?' [2003] Child and Family Law Quarterly 403

EEKELAAR, J. 'Post-Divorce Financial Obligations' in S. Katz, J. Eekelaar, and M. Maclean (eds), *Cross-Currents: Family Law and Policy in the United States and England* (Oxford: Oxford University Press, 2000)

EEKELAAR, J., 'Property and Financial Settlement on Divorce—Sharing and Compensating' [2006] 36 Family Law 754

FREEMAN, J., FRANCIS, V., CUNNIFF, P., and COVENEY, H., 'Guarding the Triple Crown: Pre-Nuptial Agreements in Three Jurisdictions' [2008] Family Law 239

GLENNON, L., 'Obligations between Adult Partners: Moving from Form to Function?' (2008) 22(1) International Journal of Law, Policy and the Family 22

GLENNON, L., 'The Limitations of Equality Discourses on the Contours of Intimate Obligations' in J. Wallbank, S. Choudhry, and J. Herring (eds), *Rights, Gender and Family Law* (Abingdon: Routledge, 2010)

JACKSON, E., WASOFF, F., MACLEAN, M., and DOBASH, R., 'Financial Support on Divorce: The Right Mixture of Rules and Discretion?' (1993) 7 International Journal of Law and the Family 230

KELLY, A., 'Rehabilitating Partnership Marriage as a Theory of Wealth Distribution at Divorce: In Recognition of a Shared Life' (2004) 19 Wisconsin Women's Law Journal 141

MILES, J., '*Charman v Charman (No 4)*—Making Sense of Need, Compensation and Equal Sharing after *Miller/McFarlane*' [2008] Child and Family Law Quarterly 378

MILES, J., 'Marriage and Divorce in the Supreme Court and the Law Commission: For love or money?' [2011] Modern Law Review 430

O'DONOVAN, K., 'Flirting with Academic Categorisations' [2005] 17 Child and Family Law Quarterly 415

SCHERPE, J. M., 'Fairness, Freedom and Foreign Elements—Marital Agreements in England and Wales after *Radmacher v Granatino*' [2011] Child and Family Law Quarterly 513

SCHERPE, J. M., *Marital Agreements and Private Autonomy in Comparative Perspective* (Oxford: Hart, 2012)

THOMPSON, S., '*Radmacher (formerly Granatino) v Granatino* [2010] UKSC 42' [2011] 33 Journal of Social Welfare and Family Law 61

Visit the Online Resource Centre at **www.oxfordtextbooks.co.uk/orc/gilmore_glennon5e/** for a range of further features including a detailed bibliography and self-test questions.

online
resource
centre

# 5

# Property disputes of unmarried cohabitants on relationship breakdown

## INTRODUCTION

Unmarried and unregistered cohabitants face a host of practical issues on relationship breakdown which are identical to those confronting spouses on divorce. Namely, how is one home to be shared between two persons who each have rights and needs? How is provision to be made for housing the children? Should one party continue to provide financial support to the other? However, at this point the similarity between married and unmarried couples ends. Although their problems are the same, the legal solutions are different. Spouses have the benefit of a statutory regime which takes regard of their married status and which allows courts to respond flexibly to their specific circumstances. A spouse who has no right to occupy the matrimonial home flowing from a proprietary interest, has a statutory right of occupation in the matrimonial home while married;[1] and where the marriage is ended by divorce, a separation order, or a nullity decree, the court has power to distribute the parties' full range of assets (including the family home, pensions, and income provision) to achieve a fair outcome.[2] It is therefore comparatively unusual nowadays for disputes between spouses relating to their rights in the home to be determined by the application of principles which are not specific to their marital status.[3]

There is no such statutory right of occupation or property adjustment regime available to unmarried or unregistered couples.[4] As we have seen, a cohabitant can apply under Part IV of the Family Law Act 1996 for an occupation order in relation to the family home but, if successful, this will only confer short-term occupancy rights.[5] Upon relationship breakdown, courts have no power to make an order about the house, or any other property, on the basis that an adjustment of the parties' respective rights would be fair and reasonable between them.[6] Instead the entitlement of unmarried partners to ownership of the family home is governed by the ordinary principles of law and equity. These are principles of general application which have not been designed specifically to deal with the financial consequences of relationship breakdown between cohabitants. As such, they are generally regarded as inadequate

---

[1] Family Law Act 1996, s 30. See Chapter 3.

[2] Matrimonial Causes Act 1973, Part II; Civil Partnership Act 2004, Sch 5.

[3] Where a third party has a claim on the property, the spouses' respective rights in the property take on a different significance, as in *Lloyds Bank plc v Rosset* [1991] 1 AC 107, which is discussed in Sections 1.2.1 and 1.2.2. A detailed account of third party claims on the property of spouses and cohabitants is beyond the scope of this book.

[4] Unmarried cohabitants are recognised in some legislative contexts where cohabitation for a period of time will confer certain rights and duties. For a discussion of the legal status of cohabitants, see A. Barlow and G. James, 'Regulating Marriage and Cohabitation in 21st Century Britain' (2004) 67(2) Modern Law Review 143. Unregistered same-sex cohabitants are in the same position as unmarried opposite-sex cohabitants. For ease of reference, however, this chapter will refer to unmarried cohabitants and this should be taken to include unregistered cohabitants.

[5] See Chapter 3.

[6] The courts have limited powers to make property-based orders for the benefit of any children under the Children Act 1989, Sch 1. See Section 2.7.

to resolve family property disputes, producing unfair outcomes in certain situations. That there are no specially designed family law principles to govern these situations has attracted considerable criticism from scholars and practitioners. While the Law Commission has made recommendations for reform,[7] there is still no sign of legislation to remedy the inadequacies of the current law. It remains the case that when the court is called upon to resolve a property dispute between unmarried cohabitants on relationship breakdown, the 'focus is on determining who *owns* what as a strict matter of property law, rather than to whom it *should* in fairness be given'.[8]

Before discussing these property law principles, it is worth highlighting the situations to which they apply. As already stated, the main 'domestic' situation which falls prey to the inadequacies of trust law is when unmarried couples separate and there is a dispute concerning ownership of the former family home. However, on some occasions, a spouse must also have recourse to these general principles. While disputes between spouses on divorce are resolved by the flexible and discretionary-based financial regime, if a spouse wishes to establish their interest in the family home *during* the marriage, the financial regime has no jurisdiction. Instead, ordinary property law principles will determine the matter. This is likely to arise when a dispute concerns the family home and a third party.[9] For example, if a third party creditor, such as a mortgagee, seeks possession of the home, another family member whether it be a spouse, civil partner, or cohabitant may seek an ownership interest in the home under ordinary trust principles in an attempt to defeat the third party's claim to possession. The question that we must now ask is: What are the ordinary property law principles which apply in these situations?

# 1  Ownership of the family home: property law principles

## 1.1  Establishing legal ownership

The starting point for determining the parties' respective rights in the family home is to look at the conveyance or other document of title which will establish who has *legal title* to the property. It may be alleged that the person with the legal title has made a gift of land to his or her partner. However, a basic rule of property law is that:

> all conveyances of land or of any interest therein are void for the purpose of conveying or creating a legal estate unless made by deed.[10]

Thus with regard to the legal estate there is certainty, and any informal written transaction designed to dispose of the legal estate is void.[11]

## 1.2  Establishing beneficial ownership

However, establishing the identity of the legal owner is not the end of the matter because the whereabouts of the beneficial ownership in the property must also be considered. The person who has the legal title may hold the property on trust for another person who will have a beneficial interest in

---

[7]  Law Commission, *Cohabitation: The Financial Consequences of Relationship Breakdown* (Law Com No 307, 2007).

[8]  Law Commission, *Cohabitation: The Financial Consequences of Relationship Breakdown, A Consultation Paper* (Law Com No 179, 2006), para 3.3 (emphasis added).

[9]  Such a dispute arose in *Lloyds Bank v Rosset* [1991] 1 AC 107.        [10]  Law of Property Act 1925, s 52(1).

[11]  See *Crago v Julian* [1992] 1 WLR 372 in which it was held that a deed is necessary even to assign an informal weekly tenancy. See also *Camden LBC v Alexandrou (No 2)* (1998) 30 HLR 534.

the property. It is here that the law becomes more complex because a trust may be created expressly (express trusts), or by implication (implied trusts).

### 1.2.1 Express trusts

---

#### Key legislation

Under section 53(1)(b) of the Law of Property Act 1925 an express trust of land must be in writing. The provision states that:

> a declaration of trust respecting land or any interest therein must be manifested and proved by some writing signed by some person who is able to declare such a trust or by his will.

---

Without such writing, any purported declaration of trust of land is unenforceable.[12] As such, an oral agreement that the legal owner is to hold the property on trust for his or her partner will not be sufficient to create an express trust. This is well illustrated in *Lloyds Bank v Rosset*.[13] The wife claimed a beneficial entitlement to share in the matrimonial home which had been conveyed into the sole name of her husband on the basis that this had been agreed between the parties. Responding to her claim, Lord Bridge said:

> Even if there had been the clearest oral agreement between Mr. and Mrs. Rosset that Mr. Rosset was to hold the property in trust for them both as tenants in common, this would, of course, have been ineffective since a valid declaration of trust by way of gift of a beneficial interest in land is required by section 53(1) of the Law of Property Act 1925 to be in writing.[14]

Sometimes there is an express declaration of beneficial entitlement in the conveyance which will specify how the beneficial interest in the property is to be split between the parties. Such an express declaration will, in the absence of fraud or mistake at the time of the transaction, conclusively determine the question of title between the parties.[15] This means that if the property is conveyed into the parties' joint names with an express declaration that it is to be held by them as beneficial joint tenants, each is entitled to a half share in the proceeds of sale of the property.[16]

### 1.2.2 Implied trusts

Problems surface, however, when there is no written declaration of trust. This is likely to arise in circumstances where the property was not jointly purchased by the parties. Say, for example, one person moves into their partner's house and they live together for many years in the property and raise a family together.[17] If the relationship breaks down the non-owner (ie, the person who

---

[12] The requirement of writing may not be enforced in a case of fraud, *Rochefoucauld v Boustead* [1897] 1 Ch 196.

[13] [1991] 1 AC 107.      [14] Ibid, 129.

[15] *Pettitt v Pettitt* [1969] 2 All ER 385 at 407 *per* Lord Upjohn. See also *Goodman v Gallant* [1986] 1 FLR 513 at 517 and 523. Baroness Hale suggested in *Stack v Dowden* [2007] UKHL 17 at [49] that an express declaration of trust can also be varied by subsequent agreement or affected by proprietary estoppel. While a subsequent declaration of trust which is in writing can vary an earlier express trust, it is doubtful that an oral agreement could vary an express trust. It has also been pointed out that while it is conceivable that an express trust could be varied by a subsequent proprietary estoppel, there is no direct authority for this proposition, A. Chandler, 'Express Declarations of Trust, Rectification and Rescissions: *Goodman v Gallant* Revisited' [2008] Family Law 1210.

[16] Of course, the express declaration of trust may specify that the parties are to share the beneficial interest in some other proportion.

[17] Research in 2001 showed that about one-quarter of cohabitants taking part in a large survey reported that they had moved into their partner's property at the start of the relationship, J. Haskey, 'Cohabiting Couples in Great Britain: Accommodation Sharing, Tenure and Property Ownership' (2001) 103 Population Trends 26. See G. Douglas, J. Pearce, and H. Woodward, Cardiff Law School Research Paper No 1, 'A Failure of Trust: Resolving Property Disputes on Cohabitation Breakdown' (2007), para 2.22.

simply moved in) may claim that it would be unconscionable to allow the other to retain the entire beneficial interest in the property. However, because there is no written declaration of trust falling within section 53(1)(b), the only way the non-owner will be able to establish an interest in the home is through the law of implied trusts which may arise, by implication, from the circumstances of the case.[18]

---

### Summary

The law of implied trusts enables equity to require the legal owner of land to hold the property on trust for another where it would be inequitable to allow him or her to deny the other a beneficial interest in the land. The broad determining principle is that equity will step in and impose a trust where not to do so would allow the legal owner to become unjustly enriched at the expense of the other.

---

However, while section 53(2) allows the creation of an implied trust in the absence of a formal declaration of trust, it does not specify how the courts should decide whether such a trust has, in fact, arisen. It is the courts themselves which have created the principles to determine whether an implied trust has been created. It is important to remember that these principles are not confined to family law cases. They are property law principles of universal application and are not specifically designed to resolve disputes relating to ownership of the family home.[19] The general nature of these principles has created tensions. Courts have struggled over the years to remain true to the doctrinal principles underpinning implied trusts while, at the same time, applying them in a way which takes account of the somewhat vague and haphazard way in which couples often deal with their financial and property affairs when they are living together in harmony. Thus there remains a considerable amount of uncertainty about the application of these general principles to family law cases. Recent case law has emphasised that judges must apply the technical requirements of ordinary property law principles and not impose their own idea of fairness between the parties.[20] However, as will be seen in this chapter, dicta from the same cases also suggest that the principles do apply in a slightly different way when being used to resolve disputes in the 'domestic' context, that is, concerning the family home.[21]

Implied trusts fall into two main categories: resulting trusts and constructive trusts. The following sections will highlight the core elements of each. It should be understood at the outset, however, that the resulting trust has much less significance in the resolution of domestic property disputes than in the past. The constructive trust is now the primary legal mechanism for determining the whereabouts of the beneficial interest in the property in the absence of an express declaration of trust.

## 1.3 The resulting trust

---

### Summary

A resulting trust will arise where the person whose name is not on the legal title to the property makes a direct financial contribution to its purchase price.

---

[18]  Under the Law of Property Act 1925, s 53(2), the lack of a written declaration of trust does not prevent the creation or operation of resulting, implied, or constructive trusts.

[19]  *Pettitt v Pettitt* [1970] AC 777; *Gissing v Gissing* [1971] 1 AC 886.

[20]  *Stack v Dowden* [2007] UKHL 17 at [61].          [21]  Ibid, [3], [14], [33], [42], [56], [60].

These direct payments to the acquisition of the property will entitle the contributor to a share in the property proportionate to the amount of their contribution. For example, if one person pays 20 per cent of the purchase price of a house, the law will presume that this was not a gift and, as such, they will acquire a 20 per cent share in the value of the property. This presumption can be rebutted by evidence that the contribution was made as a gift or a loan. It used to be the case that the presumption of resulting trust did not apply where a husband made a transfer of money or property to his wife or a father made such a transfer to his child. In these circumstances it was presumed that a gift was intended and the recipient wife or child would hold the property absolutely. This was known as the presumption of *advancement* and it was based on the historic duties imposed on husbands and fathers to maintain their wives and children. Given the changing contours of familial obligations where husbands and fathers no longer have a unilateral duty to support their wives and children financially, the presumption of advancement has been abolished by section 199 of the Equality Act 2010.[22]

The resulting trust doctrine has several limitations when applied in the domestic context to determine the parties' respective beneficial interests in the family home. First, only direct financial contributions to the acquisition of the property will give rise to a resulting trust and it is doubtful whether more indirect contributions such as the payment of household bills and domestic labour (housework and childcare) will suffice. Secondly, it seems that only initial contributions to the purchase price will generate a resulting trust, and not contributions made after the purchase.[23] Thirdly, the contributor's share in the property under the resulting trust analysis will only be proportionate to the amount of their contributions. However, following the House of Lords' decision in *Stack v Dowden*[24] it would appear that the resulting trust framework is now much less relevant in determining the whereabouts of the beneficial interest in the family home. The majority of the House of Lords stated that the resulting trust will no longer operate as a legal presumption in domestic cases[25] and in *Abbott v Abbott*[26] Baroness Hale confirmed that, in such cases, 'the constructive trust is generally the more appropriate tool of analysis'.[27]

## 1.4 **The constructive trust**

### Summary

A constructive trust will arise where there was a common intention (either express or implied) between the parties to share the beneficial ownership of the property, and the person claiming such a share has relied on this intention to his or her detriment.

This is known as the common intention constructive trust. While it is a more flexible legal tool than the resulting trust, particularly in the context of relationships where the parties may make a range of important financial and non-financial contributions to the family, it does have its problems. In particular, it is based on finding evidence (express or implied) of the parties' *common intention* to share ownership of the property. However, the problem is that parties to a romantic relationship may not discuss or even think about their expectations or intentions regarding ownership of the family home until the relationship breaks down and then, of course, the demise of the relationship

---

[22] See J. Glister, 'Section 199 of the Equality Act 2010: How Not to Abolish the Presumption of Advancement' [2010] Modern Law Review 807.

[23] *Curley v Parkes* [2004] EWCA Civ 1515.     [24] [2007] UKHL 17.

[25] *Stack v Dowden* [2007] UKHL 17 at [31] *per* Lord Hope, at [60] *per* Baroness Hale. Lord Neuberger dissented and considered that unequal contributions to the acquisition of the property gives rise to the presumption of a resulting trust, at [123]. He pointed out, of course, that this is just a presumption which can be rebutted by other evidence and thus replaced by a constructive trust.

[26] [2007] UKPC 53.     [27] Ibid, [4]. See also *Jones v Kernott* [2011] UKSC 53.

will give the parties a very different perspective about what they intended regarding the property. Retrospectively seeking to ascertain the parties' respective intentions about property ownership at the time of acquisition or any time thereafter is a somewhat fictitious exercise with clear evidential difficulties, but it is at the heart of the common intention constructive trust. In addition, there is a considerable amount of uncertainty about the type of conduct from which the court will infer that the parties had a common intention to share ownership of the property, and of the acts of reliance which will suffice to give rise to the constructive trust. Thus while the constructive trust gives the courts more leeway to consider a broader range of familial contributions when determining ownership of the family home, they still must adhere to its doctrinal requirements. Courts will not be able to impose a constructive trust just because it appears to be the correct thing to do on the facts or because justice requires it.

### 1.5  Distinguishing two situations

The law of implied trusts will have to step in to determine the whereabouts of the beneficial interests in the property in two main situations where the conveyance does not contain an express declaration of trust:

**Situation 1:** where the legal title to the property is in the *joint names* of the parties but the conveyance does not indicate how the beneficial interest is to be shared between them. We will call these 'joint names cases'. In this situation the crucial question is whether joint beneficial ownership is to be presumed. And, if so, can this be displaced by evidence that unequal beneficial ownership was intended?

**Situation 2:** where the property is conveyed into the *sole name* of one party, and there is no declaration of beneficial entitlement. We will call these 'sole name cases'. In this situation, equity will presume that the owner of the legal estate has the sole beneficial entitlement. In order to rebut this presumption and acquire a beneficial interest, the non-legal owner must establish that the legal owner holds the property as trustee for both parties in equal or unequal shares. The question which the courts have tried to answer is: how can this be done?

In both situations, the law of implied trusts (in particular, the common intention constructive trust) will resolve these issues and determine the respective entitlement of each party to the property. The following sections will take each situation in turn and discuss the legal principles to determine the whereabouts of the beneficial interests.

## 2  Joint names cases

To re-cap, in this situation the parties are joint legal owners of the property but there is no express declaration of the parties' beneficial entitlement. Which legal principles will determine how the beneficial interest is to be shared? That there are difficult issues regarding the quantification of the beneficial interest in such cases may seem to be surprising. One might assume that if property is held legally in the parties' joint names, then the beneficial interests will automatically, as a matter of logic, be shared equally between them. However, prior to the House of Lords' decision in *Stack v Dowden*, this was not the case. The whereabouts of the beneficial interest was determined by the application of ordinary trust principles and case law suggested that if one party had made a greater financial contribution to the purchase price of the property, they would, under the presumption of a resulting trust, receive a share of the beneficial interest which was proportionate to their contribution.[28] For example, if one person contributed 75 per cent of the purchase price of the property, this greater financial contribution would give them a 75 per cent share of the beneficial interest despite the fact that the property was held in the parties' joint names. However, this all changed

---

[28]  See *Walker v Hall* [1984] FLR 126; *Springette v Defoe* [1992] 2 FLR 388; *Huntingford v Hobbs* [1993] 1 FLR 736.

when the House of Lords in *Stack v Dowden*,[29] which was the first case concerning a property dispute between unmarried cohabitants to reach the House of Lords, set out a new set of principles to determine the quantification of the beneficial interests in joint names cases. The Supreme Court had the opportunity to consider the position once again in 2011 in *Jones v Kernott*.[30]

## 2.1 *Stack v Dowden*: the facts

> ### Key case
>
> The parties (an unmarried couple with four children) purchased a home in joint names. The purchase of the property was financed primarily by Ms Dowden who earned more than her partner, Mr Stack. In particular, it was funded by the sale of another property, which had been in Ms Dowden's sole name, plus savings in her sole name as well as a mortgage held in joint names. At the time of the purchase, the parties had already been living together for around ten years and had four children. Nine years later the relationship broke down and Mr Stack applied to the court for an order for sale of the property and an equal division of the proceeds. While the property was registered in joint names, there was no declaration of trust specifying how the beneficial interest was to be shared. The transfer deed simply included a clause which contained a declaration that the survivor of the parties could give a valid receipt for capital money arising from the sale of the property. In the Court of Appeal, Mr Stack was awarded just 35 per cent of the value of the property and he appealed to the House of Lords. The House of Lords upheld the decision of the Court of Appeal. All their Lordships reached the same outcome although Lord Neuberger dissented on the reasoning.

### 2.1.1 Was there an express trust?

The first issue that had to be decided was whether there was any evidence of an express trust. In particular, did the declaration in the transfer deed that the survivor of the parties could give a valid receipt for capital money received on the sale of the property amount to an express declaration of a beneficial joint tenancy? The House of Lords, confirming earlier case law,[31] held that it did not. Even though this 'valid receipt clause' could be consistent with the declaration of a beneficial joint tenancy (where, on the death of one party, the other automatically takes his or her share under the doctrine of survivorship), the court held that it could also be consistent with another form of property ownership.[32] As a result, there was *no express declaration of trust* and the whereabouts of the beneficial interest in the property had to be determined by ordinary trust principles.[33]

---

[29] [2007] UKHL 17.      [30] [2011] UKSC 53.

[31] *Harwood v Harwood* [1991 2 FLR 274; *Huntington v Hobbs* [1993] 1 FLR 736.

[32] [2007] UKHL 17 at [51] *per* Baroness Hale.

[33] It should be noted that a new form was introduced in 1998 for conveyances of registered land into joint names. Form TR1 contains a section for the transferees to declare whether they are to hold the property on trust for themselves as joint tenants, as tenants in common in equal shares, or in any other way (see J. Wilson, 'Tripping up on the TR1' [2006] Family Law 305). Completion of this part of the form will ensure that there is an express declaration of the beneficial interests which will be conclusive in the absence of fraud or mistake, *Goodman v Gallant* [1986] 1 FLR 513. However, as Baroness Hale made it clear in *Stack v Dowden*, completing this section of the form is not compulsory and non-completion does not affect the validity of the transfer, at [52] (see Editorial, 'Anything to Declare? Express declaration of trust on Land Registry form TR1: The Doubts Raised in *Stack v Dowden*' (2007) 71 Conveyance and Property Lawyer 364). As such, there will still be cases where registered land is transferred into joint names but there is no express declaration of the beneficial interests. Further problems lie in the fact that the language used in the form is not comprehensible to the lay person and so legal advice is usually required to ensure that the parties understand how to complete it. G. Douglas, J. Pearce, and H. Woodward, 'Cohabitants, Property and the Law: A Study of Injustice' (2009) 72(1) Modern Law Review 24 at 40–1.

### 2.1.2 The starting point presumption

**Summary**

The Lords confirmed that in all cases where there is no express declaration of the beneficial interests in the family home, the starting presumption is that *equity follows the law* and the beneficial interests will reflect the legal interests in the property.[34] This means that where there is joint legal ownership, the starting point is joint beneficial ownership.[35] As Baroness Hale made clear:

> at least in the domestic consumer context, a conveyance into joint names indicates both legal and beneficial joint tenancy, unless and until the contrary is proved.[36]

If one party wants a greater share, then the onus is on them to show that there was a common intention that the beneficial ownership was to be different from the legal ownership. Baroness Hale made it clear, however, that this is a very heavy burden to discharge in the domestic context and so 'is not a task to be lightly embarked upon'.[37] Applying this to the facts of the case, the property was in joint names and so the starting presumption was that the parties were to share the beneficial interests equally. If Ms Dowden wanted a greater share, then she had the onus of establishing that the property should be held in unequal beneficial shares. The obvious question is: In what circumstances will the court be persuaded that this is the case?

### 2.1.3 How to establish that the property is to be held in unequal shares?

There were two approaches open to the court. First, in line with previous case law, the Lords could have confirmed that the presumption of the resulting trust means that the parties' shares in the property mirror their respective financial contributions to its acquisition.[38] Alternatively, the court had the option of taking a broader approach by looking at all the relevant circumstances (and not just financial contributions) to ascertain the parties' common intention regarding the ownership of the property.[39] The majority of the court took the latter approach, making a distinction between the operation of trust principles in commercial situations and when applied to cases concerning the family home. Baroness Hale said that 'these days, the importance to be attached to who paid for what in a domestic context may be very different from its importance in other contexts or long ago'.[40] While the resulting trust operates as a legal presumption in commercial cases where the parties are dealing with each other at arm's length, the majority considered that this is not appropriate in the 'domestic consumer context' where the dispute concerns the family home.[41] In the words of Lord Hope:

> cohabiting couples are in a different kind of relationship. The place where they live together is their home. Living together is an exercise in give and take, mutual co-operation and compromise. Who pays for what in regard to the home has to be seen in the wider context of their overall relationship. A more practical, down-to-earth, fact-based approach is called for in their case.[42]

This is a significant point because it indicates the emergence of a different jurisprudence for domestic cases where the resulting trust will no longer operate as a legal presumption. It means that the presumption of joint beneficial ownership will not be rebutted by the mere fact that the parties have

---

[34] *Stack v Dowden* [2007] UKHL 17 at [33] *per* Lord Walker, at [54] *per* Baroness Hale.
[35] Ibid, [56] *per* Baroness Hale. The starting point when there is sole legal ownership is sole beneficial ownership.
[36] Ibid, [58].     [37] Ibid, [68].     [38] Unless, of course, a contrary intention could be shown.
[39] *Stack v Dowden* [2007] UKHL 17 at [59] *per* Baroness Hale.     [40] Ibid, [60].
[41] Lord Neuberger dissented on this reasoning and did not agree that different principles should apply in the domestic and commercial context, ibid, at [101]–[107].
[42] Ibid, [3].

made unequal financial contributions to the acquisition of the property. However, if the resulting trust does not apply, how are the parties' respective beneficial shares to be quantified when the home is in the parties' joint names? How is the presumption of joint and equal beneficial interests to be rebutted, if at all?

## Summary

The House of Lords made it clear in *Stack* that the presumption will only be rebutted if there is evidence that the parties had a shared intention to hold the property in unequal shares. If there is no evidence of an express agreement between the parties, the task of the court is to undertake a survey of the parties' whole course of dealing taking account of their conduct insofar as it throws light on the question of what they must 'be taken to have intended'.[43] Each case will be decided on its own facts and 'many more factors than financial contributions may be relevant to divining the parties' true intentions'.[44] According to Baroness Hale, these include:[45]

- any advice or discussions at the time of the transfer;
- the reasons why the home was acquired in the parties' joint names;
- the reasons why (if this is the case) the survivor was authorised to give a valid receipt for the capital moneys;
- the purpose for which the home was acquired;
- the nature of the parties' relationship;
- whether they have children for whom they had a responsibility to provide a home;
- how the purchase was financed, both initially and subsequently;
- how the parties arranged their finances;
- how the parties discharged the outgoings on the property and their other household expenses.

In addition, Baroness Hale considered that the parties' individual characteristics and personalities may also be relevant when ascertaining their intentions in relation to the property.[46] The majority took the view that cases where joint legal owners will be found to have intended that their beneficial interests should be different from their legal interests will be 'very unusual'.[47] As it turned out, however, *Stack v Dowden* was regarded as being one of these 'unusual' cases and the House of Lords held that Ms Dowden was able to rebut the presumption of joint beneficial ownership. Indeed, Baroness Hale said that there were 'many factors to which Ms Dowden can point to indicate that these parties did have a different common intention'.[48]

The first factor was that Ms Dowden contributed far more financially to the acquisition of the property than Mr Stack. There was evidence that Mr Stack had made some improvements to the parties' earlier property but it was not possible to quantify their value to the eventual sale price which was then put towards the purchase of the new property. Secondly, the parties did not pool their separate resources, even notionally, for the common good.[49] All of their finances and property, except for the house in question and an associated endowment policy, were kept strictly separate. Thirdly, both parties undertook separate responsibility for that part of the expenditure which they had agreed to pay and, significantly, the court found that it was Ms Dowden who undertook primary financial responsibility for the property. By contrast, it was implied that Mr Stack did not contribute as much as he could have done to the family's expenditure. Indeed, Probert concludes that Baroness Hale

---

[43] Ibid, [61] *per* Baroness Hale.   [44] Ibid, [69] *per* Baroness Hale.   [45] Ibid.
[46] Although it is very unclear how such subjective considerations would be applied.
[47] Ibid, [69].   [48] Ibid, [87].   [49] Ibid, [90].

strongly implied that Mr Stack simply did not pull his weight in contributing to the parties' finances, contributing only to the interest and premiums on the property while all other regular commitments were undertaken by Ms Dowden.[50] Taken together these factors, according to the court, made this a 'very unusual case'.[51] Baroness Hale said:

> there cannot be many unmarried couples who have lived together for as long as this, who have had four children together, and whose affairs have been kept as rigidly separate as this couple's affair were kept. This is all strongly indicative that they did not intend their shares, even in the property which was put into both their names, to be equal.[52]

As a result, the court held that Mr Stack was only entitled to a 35 per cent share in the beneficial interest. Lord Neuberger concurred in the result but dissented on the reasoning. His Lordship disagreed with the view that different principles should apply in domestic cases[53] and, as such, he applied ordinary resulting trust principles.[54] Under Lord Neuberger's analysis, Mr Stack was only entitled to a 35 per cent share of the beneficial interest in light of his financial contribution to the acquisition of the property.

This is a very important decision which has altered the way in which the beneficial interests in the family home will be determined in joint names cases. While it has provided some welcome clarification, particularly in laying down the starting presumption that equity follows the law, it has also come under criticism for leaving several questions unanswered. The important elements of the decision and some points of confusion arising from it are detailed in the following section. But at the outset it is worth nothing that Lord Neuberger, speaking extra-judicially, has expressed reservations at the majority's reasoning.[55] His Lordship outlined four main concerns. First, he questioned the assumption that unmarried couples intended to share the property as joint tenants in equity, speculating that one reason such couples do not marry is to keep their assets separate. Secondly, the application of a different set of rules to the domestic consumer context gives rise to the issue of which familial relationships, exactly, this refers to. Thirdly, under what circumstances will it be appropriate to depart from the presumption of joint beneficial ownership? Fourthly, he considered that the approach of the majority in *Stack*, in particular the search for what the parties must be taken to have intended, will encourage lengthy and costly legal disputes.

### 2.1.4 **Ascertaining the parties' common intention**

The core issue in *Stack* was the test adopted by the House of Lords for quantifying the parties' shares in joint names cases. The majority concluded that if there is no evidence of an express agreement between the parties, then the task of the court is to ascertain the parties' shared intention from their whole course of conduct. By contrast, in the earlier sole name case of *Oxley v Hiscock*,[56] Chadwick LJ considered that the court's task was to search for a fair outcome, noting that each party 'is entitled to that share which the court considers fair having regard to the whole course of dealing between them in relation to the property'.[57] In *Stack v Dowden*, Baroness Hale rejected this approach. She preferred the 'holistic' approach to quantification advocated by the Law Commission in its 2002 Discussion Paper, *Sharing Homes*, where they said that: there is much to be said for adopting what has been called a 'holistic approach' to quantification, undertaking a survey

---

[50] R. Probert, 'Equality in the Family Home' (2007) Feminist Legal Studies 341 at 347. *Stack v Dowden* [2007] UKHL 17 at [91] *per* Baroness Hale.

[51] *Stack v Dowden* [2007] UKHL 17 at [91] *per* Baroness Hale.     [52] Ibid, [92].     [53] Ibid, [107].

[54] Ibid, [110]–[116].

[55] Lord Neuberger, 'The Conspirators, the Tax Man, the Bill of Rights and a Bit About the Lovers', Chancery Bar Association Annual Lecture, 10 March 2008, available at http://www.chba.org.uk/library/seminar_notes/news4.

[56] [2004] EWCA Civ 546.     [57] Ibid, [69].

of the whole course of dealing between the parties and taking account of all conduct which throws light on the question what shares were intended.[58] Baroness Hale preferred this approach for two reasons.[59] First, it emphasises that the court's search is for the result which the parties must have intended. Secondly, this search cannot be abandoned in favour of the result which the court itself considers fair. Thus, Baroness Hale 're-asserted strongly' the need to find the parties' common intention in relation to the property.[60]

One could say that, in terms of finding the correct approach, Baroness Hale tried to steer a middle course. On the one hand, her Ladyship expressed disapproval of an approach which gives the court the power to impose its own sense of fairness but, on the other hand, she did not wish to adhere to strict resulting trust principles which would decide the issue solely on the basis of the parties' direct financial contributions to the acquisition of the property. Instead, she sought a middle ground which took a holistic approach to quantification but under the auspices of searching for the parties' true intentions in relation to be property.

---

### Talking point

However, *Stack* did not make clear whether the court can *impute* an intention to the parties which they did not in fact hold. The majority suggested that the parties' intention could be inferred, or even imputed, from their conduct in relation to the property.[61] There is a subtle but important distinction between *inferring* and *imputing* an intention. Lord Neuberger described the distinction as follows:

> An inferred intention is one which is objectively deduced to be the subjective actual intention of the parties, in the light of their actions and statements. An imputed intention is one which is attributed to the parties, even though no such actual intention can be deduced from their actions and statements, and even though they had no such intention. Imputation involves concluding what the parties would have intended, whereas inference involves concluding what they did intend.[62]

**Q.** Do you think that the difference between inferring an imputing an intention is merely a matter of linguistics? In other words, is it a distinction without a difference?

---

Piska observes that an imputed intention is not regarded as representing the parties' actual intentions at all. Rather, it is 'the court's estimation of what is fair'.[63] However, there is a contradiction here. Even though Baroness Hale said that the search was to ascertain the parties' shared intentions, actual, inferred, or *imputed*,[64] her Ladyship was clear that the court should not impose its own sense of fairness. However, if the court is permitted to impute an intention to the parties which they may never have had (which the majority appeared to suggest was permissible) then this, by implication, could import subjective notions of fairness as the court assigns an 'intention' to the parties based on its view of their mutual interaction. Does this mean, then, that the court can covertly impose its own sense of fairness by adopting the guise of searching for the parties' intentions,

---

[58] Law Commission, *Sharing Homes: A Discussion Paper* (Law Com No 278, 2002), para 4.27.

[59] *Stack v Dowden* [2007] UKHL 17 at [60]–[61].

[60] G. Battersby, 'Ownership of the Family Home: *Stack v Dowden* in the House of Lords' [2008] Child and Family Law Quarterly 255.

[61] Baroness Hale said that the 'search is to ascertain the parties' intentions, actual, inferred or imputed, with respect to the property in light of their whole course of conduct in relation to it', *Stack v Dowden* [2007] UKHL 17 at [60].

[62] Ibid, [126]. His Lordship accepted that the parties' intention may be inferred from their conduct but rejected the idea that a court can impute an intention to the parties. He said that the process of imputation would be a 'difficult, subjective and uncertain' exercise which is contrary to established principle, at [125]–[127].

[63] N. Piska, 'Intention, Fairness and the Presumption of Resulting Trust after *Stack v Dowden*' (2008) 71(1) Modern Law Review 114 at 127.

[64] *Stack v Dowden* [2007] UKHL 17 at [60] (emphasis added).

or more precisely, searching for what the parties must 'be taken to have intended'?[65] The Supreme Court has now had the opportunity to re-visit this issue in *Jones v Kernott*.[66]

### 2.1.5 Why were the facts of *Stack v Dowden* regarded as unusual?

The actual outcome of the case has attracted considerable criticism. In particular, commentators have posed the question of why the facts were regarded as being so unusual as to allow Ms Dowden to discharge the 'considerable burden' of rebutting the presumption of joint beneficial ownership.[67]

Despite the majority's rejection of the resulting trust framework under which the parties' financial contributions determine their respective beneficial entitlement in a strict arithmetical fashion, it was these contributions which emerged as the most important factor under the constructive trust analysis.[68] Baroness Hale said that the fact that Ms Dowden contributed far more to the acquisition of the property in relation to the initial purchase price and subsequent capital repayments of the mortgage, were factors to 'support an inference of an intention to share otherwise than equally'.[69] It is also worth pointing out that the same outcome was reached from the analyses of the majority, whose reasoning was based on the common intention constructive trust, and the dissenting speech of Lord Neuberger who applied the resulting trust. Thus, despite the sentiment of the majority who urged consideration of a range of factors from which to ascertain the parties' intentions, it is hard not to reach the conclusion that, at the end of the day, it was Ms Dowden's greater financial contribution which was the determining factor. Lord Neuberger (the dissenting voice in *Stack*) speaking extra-judicially has criticised this reasoning saying:

> If the presumption of equality is to be rebutted because the contributions are significantly different, it is a pretty useless presumption: the only time you need it, it isn't there.[70]

In addition, the court seemed to regard the couple's independent financial arrangements as unusual. However, empirical evidence suggests that independent money-management arrangements are not that uncommon among cohabiting couples and it has been observed that this 'would hardly mark *Stack* as an exceptional case'.[71]

Thus, the 'whole course of conduct' approach to quantification advocated by the majority was undermined in practice by the actual outcome of the case which placed considerable emphasis on the parties' financial contributions and money-management practices. Further, while Baroness Hale provided a non-exhaustive list of factors to be considered when ascertaining the parties' intentions, no further guidance was given on how they should be applied. Even though one factor in this list was the 'nature of the parties' relationship, it is clear from the court's reasoning that general familial characteristics had little relevance when determining the parties' intentions in relation to

---

[65] N. Piska, 'Intention, Fairness and the Presumption of Resulting Trust after *Stack v Dowden*' (2008) 71(1) Modern Law Review 114 at 128.

[66] [2011] UKSC 53, see Section 2.1.7.

[67] See eg M. Dixon, 'The Never-Ending Story—Co-ownership after *Stack v Dowden*' (2007) Conveyancer and Property Lawyer 456 at 460; W. Swadling, 'The Common Intention Constructive Trust in the House of Lords: An Opportunity Missed' (2007) Law Quarterly Review 511 at 515.

[68] As noted by Lord Walker, the facts which traditionally gave rise to a resulting trust (direct contributions to the purchase price) will be relevant when considering the full range of the parties' contributions, both direct and indirect, in the constructive trust analysis and the search for the parties' common intention, [2007] UKHL 17 at [31].

[69] Ibid, [89].

[70] Lord Neuberger, 'The Conspirators, the Tax Man, the Bill of Rights and a Bit About the Lovers', Chancery Bar Association Annual Lecture, 10 March 2008, para 15, available at http://www.chba.org.uk/library/seminar_notes/news4.

[71] R. Probert, 'Equality in the Family Home' (2007) Feminist Legal Studies 341 at 347. Probert cites C. Vogler, M. Brockmann, and R. Wiggins, 'Intimate Relationships and Changing Patterns of Money Management at the Beginning of the Twenty-First Century' (2006) 57(3) British Journal of Sociology 455–482. See also G. Douglas, J. Pearce, and H. Woodward, 'Cohabitants, Property and the Law: A Study of Injustice' (2009) 72(1) Modern Law Review 24–47.

the property. Indeed, Mr Stack was left with only 35 per cent of the property notwithstanding the fact that this was a very lengthy relationship which had produced four children. However, Baroness Hale ruled that the trial judge had erred in looking at the:

> parties' relationship rather than the matters which were particularly relevant to their intentions about this property. He found his conclusion on the length and nature of their relationship, which he repeatedly referred to as a partnership.[72]

According to Baroness Hale, these factors could not provide an adequate answer to the question of property ownership amounting to 'little more than saying that these people were in a relationship for 27 years and had four children together'.[73] Thus, it is clear that the only conduct from which inferences can be drawn in relation to the parties' intentions is conduct *relating to the property*. While the majority permitted, and indeed advocated, a consideration of the whole course of dealing between the parties, the wider contributions of the parties (beyond their financial contributions) and other relationship-based factors (such as the length of the relationship, whether the parties have children) had little bearing on the actual outcome of the case.

There was a great deal of uncertainty about the implications of *Stack v Dowden*. Several questions arose. In particular, what factual circumstances will lead a court to displace the presumption that the beneficial interest is to be shared equally in joint names cases? Would future courts follow the reasoning implicit in the actual outcome of *Stack*, that is, by attaching greater weight to the parties' respective financial contributions? Or, would courts follow the rhetoric of the speeches of the majority by looking at the whole course of dealing between the parties in relation to the property?[74] In short, how easy or difficult will it be to displace the starting presumption in joint names cases that equity follows the law and the beneficial interest is to be shared equally?

### 2.1.6 *Fowler v Barron*

The Court of Appeal had the opportunity to apply *Stack* in *Fowler v Barron*.[75] The parties had been in an unmarried relationship for 23 years and had two children. They bought a house in 1998 and made a conscious decision to put the property into joint names but did not receive legal advice about the consequences of doing so. Mr Barron, a retired fireman who was 30 years older than Miss Fowler, paid the deposit on the property and paid the balance of the purchase price out of the proceeds of sale of his flat where the parties had previously been living. The parties took a joint mortgage of £35,000 and Mr Barron paid the instalments. The parties never had a joint bank account and Mr Barron paid all of the direct costs associated with the property, such as the council tax and utilities bills. Miss Fowler worked for most of the duration of the relationship and spent her income on gifts, school expenses, clothing, holidays, and special occasions. The parties also had mutual wills, each leaving his or her interest in the property to the other on their death. While the property was held in the parties' joint legal names, the transfer document did not contain any declaration of trust stating how the beneficial interest was to be shared. In addition, there was no evidence of any discussion between them as to how the property was to be held. When the relationship broke down, the question arose as to the whereabouts of the beneficial interest. Mr Barron argued that in light of his much greater financial contributions to the acquisition of the property, he should receive more than a 50 per cent of the beneficial interest in it.

In light of the outcome in *Stack v Dowden*, one might think this an even more persuasive case for rebutting the presumption of joint beneficial ownership given that (unlike Mr Stack) Miss Fowler had made *no* financial contribution, either direct or indirect, to the purchase price of the property or to the mortgage repayments. However, the Court of Appeal distinguished *Stack v Dowden* and

---

72 [2007] UKHL 17 at [86].     73 Ibid.
74 R. Probert, 'Equality in the Family Home' (2007) Feminist Legal Studies 341 at 348.
75 [2008] EWCA Civ 377.

left Miss Fowler with a 50 per cent share in the property. In doing so, it put the rhetoric of the House of Lords into practice by holding that it was incorrect to concentrate on financial contributions instead of looking more broadly at the parties' whole course of conduct in relation to the property. This worked in favour of Miss Fowler.

In distinguishing *Stack v Dowden*, Arden LJ said that the facts of *Fowler v Barron* were 'different in many respects'.[76] First, the couple had executed mutual wills which indicated to the court that they each had a beneficial interest to leave to the other. Secondly, unlike the position in *Stack*, the parties in this case had no substantial assets other than the property. This led Arden LJ to decide that it was not reasonable to infer that the parties intended that Miss Fowler should have no share of the house if the relationship broke down leaving her potentially dependent on state benefits and housing support.[77] In addition, the court inferred from the couple's money-management arrangements that they treated their 'incomes and asset as one pool from which household expenses were paid'.[78] While they maintained separate bank accounts, it was this general pulling of resources for the good of the family that allowed Arden LJ to draw the inference that it made no difference to them who paid for what expense. There was no prior agreement between the parties as to who would pay for what and, taken with the evidence of the mutual wills, the inference was that 'the parties simply did not care about the respective size of each other's contributions'.[79] Thus, according to the Court of Appeal, Mr Barron had not discharged the onus of showing that there was a common intention that the parties would own the property in unequal shares. While Mr Barron gave evidence that when he put the property into the parties' joint names he only ever intended that Miss Fowler have a beneficial interest in the property in the event of his death, the court held that this could not be relied upon. It was only a secret intention on his part and was not a shared intention from which inferences could be drawn. Thus, the presumption of joint beneficial interest was not rebutted, notwithstanding the fact that Miss Fowler had made no financial contribution to the acquisition of the property.

This decision offered some clarification, in particular in determining when the 'default rule'[80] of joint beneficial ownership is rebutted. When ascertaining whether the parties had a shared intention to hold the property in unequal shares, the Court of Appeal said that the task is to:

> consider whether the facts as found are inconsistent with the inference of a common intention to share the property in equal shares to an extent sufficient to discharge the civil standard of proof on the person seeking to displace the presumption arising from a transfer into joint names.[81]

In other words, is there anything on the facts which is *inconsistent* with the presumption that the parties are to share the beneficial ownership equally? The parties' respective financial contributions to the acquisition of the property is just one factor for consideration and the mere fact that one party has contributed more than the other will not, by itself, rebut the presumption of equal beneficial shares.[82] In taking this approach, the Court of Appeal has allayed some of the concerns about the implications of *Stack*. It also illustrates just how questionable the actual outcome was in that case. Given the similarities between the two cases, one can ask why *Stack* was deemed to be a very unusual case which justified Mr Stack's share being limited to 35 per cent and yet there was 'nothing at all unusual' about *Fowler v Barron* to rebut the presumption of equal beneficial ownership. Both involved lengthy cohabiting relationships with children. We know that Mr Stack made a much smaller financial contribution to the acquisition of the property than his female partner,

---

[76] Ibid, [46].   [77] Ibid.   [78] Ibid.   [79] Ibid, [41] *per* Arden LJ.
[80] Ibid, [34].   [81] Ibid, [35] *per* Arden LJ.
[82] Arden LJ said that it was not the mere fact that the parties had made unequal contributions to the purchase price which allowed Ms Dowden to rebut the presumption of equal shares in *Stack v Dowden*. What mattered more was the 'inferences to be drawn as to their shared intentions to be gleaned from the evidence overall', ibid, [45]. The fact that they kept their financial affairs 'rigidly separate', did not pool their separate resources for the common good, and that Mr Stack did not contribute as much as he could have done to the family's finances made *Stack* an unusual case, ibid, [20] *per* Arden LJ.

although he did pay the mortgage interest and contributed towards paying off the capital. Outside this, the parties kept their finances separate. The facts of *Fowler v Barron* reveal a similar pattern. In fact, Miss Fowler made no direct or indirect financial contribution to the purchase price of the property or to any mortgage repayment. She kept her income separate but used it to contribute to family's general expenditure, and the parties did not have a joint bank account. So, what exactly made *Stack* an unusual case and *Fowler* not?

As indicated, the Court of Appeal put forward various reasons for distinguishing the two cases. However, none are particularly convincing. For example, the evidence of the mutual wills in *Fowler* was deemed to be important in giving rise to the inference that they intended that each should have an interest in the property. However, surely the only proper inference that can be drawn from the mutual wills is that, on death, each intended their interest in the property to pass to the other. It does not necessarily indicate that they intended, should the relationship break down, that the property be split equally between them.[83] Further, the inference that it was unlikely that the parties intended Miss Fowler to have no share of the house if the relationship broke down, leaving her potentially dependent on state benefits, is not fully explained. There is, of course, another contrast between the two cases which may have had some part to play in persuading the majority of the House of Lords that *Stack* was an exceptional case. The only feature of that case which marks it as unusual was the fact that it was the female partner who was the primary breadwinner and who contributed more financially to purchasing the family home than her male partner.[84] In addition, it was implied that Mr Stack did not contribute as much financially as he could have done.[85] By contrast, there was a much more conventional division of responsibility in *Fowler* where the male partner was the primary economic provider and both parties contributed what they could to the household expenses. One wonders, therefore, whether gender-based assumptions surrounding the conventional division of economic responsibility within families had some intuitive role to play in *Stack*. Indeed, Piska observes that 'with the exception that it was the woman who contributed more financially *Stack* was not an unusual case in the slightest'.[86]

Overall, the decision of the Court of Appeal in *Fowler v Barron* confirms the strength of the 'default rule' in joint names cases that the parties are presumed to hold the beneficial interest in equal shares, with a person who wishes to claim otherwise facing a very difficult task. Indeed, both the reasoning and the outcome of the case clearly confirm that parties can be equal beneficial owners of the property even if their financial contributions to the purchase price have been unequal. The Court of Appeal provided welcome clarification that in determining whether the presumption of joint beneficial ownership is rebutted, the court will consider whether the facts of the case are 'inconsistent with the inference of a common intention to share the property in equal shares'.[87] It seems that if there is 'cogent evidence'[88] that the parties maintain rigidly separate and independent finances and, most importantly, do not pool their resources for the common good then this may be sufficient to rebut the presumption of equal ownership in joint names cases. However, in the absence of such clear evidence, it seems that the presumption that the parties intended their beneficial interests to be equal will prevail.

[83] See N. Piska, 'Distinctions without a Difference? Explaining *Stack v Dowden*' (2008) Conveyancer and Property Lawyer 451 at 458–9. Piska points out that they may instead have intended a beneficial tenancy in common in unequal shares.

[84] This can be regarded as unusual because studies show that men continue to earn more than women, see Office for National Statistics, 2010 Annual Survey of Hours and Earnings (2011), available at www.ons.gov.uk/ons/rel/ashe/annual-survey-of-hours-and-earnings/2010-revised-results/index.html; C. Dobbs, 'Patterns of Pay: Results of the Annual Survey of Hours and Earnings 1997 to 2008' (2009) 3(3) Economic & Labour Market Review 24–32.

[85] [2007] UKHL 17 at [91] *per* Baroness Hale.

[86] N. Piska, 'Distinctions without a Difference? Explaining *Stack v Dowden*' (2008) Conveyancer and Property Lawyer 451 at 460.

[87] [2008] EWCA Civ 377 at [35] *per* Arden LJ.    [88] Ibid, [51] *per* Toulson LJ.

### 2.1.7 *Jones v Kernott*

---

## Key case

The Supreme Court has now had the opportunity to revisit the decision in *Stack* in *Jones v Kernott*.[89] The parties, Ms Jones and Mr Kernott, met in 1980 and five years later bought 39 Badger Hall Avenue in joint names for £30,000. The conveyance did not contain a declaration of trust. Ms Jones contributed £6,000 towards the purchase price and the balance was raised by way of a mortgage in their joint names. The parties shared the household expenses until October 1993 when Mr Kernott moved out of the property leaving Ms Jones and their children residing there. Ms Jones paid all the household expenses from that point on and Mr Kernott made no further contribution towards the acquisition of the property.

At some point, the parties cashed in a joint life insurance policy. Mr Kernott used his share of the proceeds as a deposit for a home of his own. In May 1996, he bought 114 Stanley Road. The judge at first instance had found that he was only able to afford this new home because he no longer contributed towards the cost of the Badger Hall property. This arrangement continued until 2006 when Mr Kernott indicated to Ms Jones that he wanted his share of the Badger Hall property which remained in the parties' joint names. In October 2007, Ms Jones applied for a declaration that she owned the entire beneficial interest in the Badger Hall property. At this time, the Badger Hall property was valued at £245,000. She claimed that since 1993, the parties' actions showed that their intentions with respect to the Badger Hall property had altered from the original intention to hold the beneficial interest jointly into unequal shares.

The judge at first instance accepted this contention, stating that he had to consider what was just and fair between the parties having regard to the whole course of dealing between them. He decided that Ms Jones was entitled to a 90 per cent share in the property. Mr Kernott appealed to the High Court where his appeal was dismissed.[90] An appeal to the Court of Appeal was allowed by a majority with Jacob LJ dissenting. Rix and Wall LJJ held that there was nothing to indicate that the parties' intentions had changed after their separation. Rix LJ held that *Stack v Dowden* was authority for the proposition that the courts could not impute an intention 'where none was expressly uttered or inferentially formed'.[91] Neither Rix nor Wall LJJ considered that there was sufficient evidence to infer a change in the parties' intentions in this case.

In the Supreme Court, their Lordships unanimously restored the judgment made at first instance and Ms Jones recovered 90 per cent of the proceeds of the disputed property.[92] However, the judges reached their decisions by different routes as they failed to agree on whether it was possible, on the facts of the case, to draw inferences as to a change over time in the parties' intentions regarding their shares in the disputed property. In their leading judgment, Lord Walker and Lady Hale (with whom Lord Collins agreed) held that there was no need for the court to impute an intention to the parties as it could be inferred from their conduct that their intention regarding ownership of the home had changed after separation. Post-1993, Ms Jones had paid the mortgage and all of the household expenses. In light of this, the majority ruled that it was logical to infer that the parties intended Mr Kernott's interest in the property to crystallise when he purchased his own house.[93] In reaching this conclusion, the court made it clear that the presumption of joint beneficial ownership in joint names cases can be displaced by showing that the parties had a different common intention as to the quantum of their respective shares in a property, either at the time of acquisition or at a later date. In other words, the parties' intentions as to shares can change over time and can be ambulatory in nature.[94] In terms of finding this common intention, the court confirmed that a broad-brush approach was to be taken with the court looking at the parties' whole course of dealing and not just at their financial contributions. Their Lordships took the view that courts should use their best efforts to infer the parties' actual intentions from their conduct and should not 'shrink from making

---

[89] [2011] UKSC 53.     [90] [2009] EWHC 1713 (Ch).     [91] [2010] EWCA Civ 578 at [77].
[92] [2011] UKSC 53.     [93] Ibid, [48].     [94] Ibid, [14].

findings on disputed evidence'.[95] However, even though the majority inferred the parties' intentions from their conduct, they suggested that if this had not been possible, the court must then consider what shares are fair. According to Lord Walker and Lady Hale, where it is not possible to ascertain by direct evidence or by inference what the parties' actual intention was as to the shares in which they would own the property, the court has to consider what shares are fair, having regard to the whole course of dealing between them in relation to the property.[96]

While the majority were able to infer from the parties' conduct that their intentions regarding their shares in the disputed property had changed, Lord Wilson and Lord Kerr felt that such inferences could not be drawn. Instead, Lord Wilson openly imputed an intention to the parties that the house was to be held in unequal proportions as determined by the county court judge, and Lord Kerr held that this was a fair outcome which should stand. This calls into question the legitimacy of openly imputing an intention to the parties which they may never have held to give effect to an outcome which the court considers fair. It is unfortunate that the court did not take the opportunity to clarify this issue, or to thrash out the consequences of the imputation process. Indeed, Lord Collins stated that in his view, in the present context, the differences between inference and imputation are 'largely terminological and conceptual and are likely to make no difference in practice'.[97] While Lord Walker and Lady Hale felt that the conceptual difference between inferring and imputing an intention was clear, they considered that the difference in practice may not be so great.[98] By contrast, Lord Kerr held that the divergence between inference and imputation might well produce a difference in practice.[99] While his Lordship questioned the aptness of imputation, he considered that it may not be practicable to discard it. He concluded that 'the court should anxiously examine the circumstances in order, where possible, to ascertain the parties' intention but it should not be reluctant to recognise, when it is appropriate to do so, that inference of an intention is not possible and that imputation of an intention is the only course to follow'.[100]

That there is a significant difference between inferring and imputing an intention has already been highlighted,[101] and for many commentators the latter is a step too far. For example, Bailey-Harris and Wilson[102] persuasively comment that rebutting the presumption of joint beneficial ownership arising from joint registration by anything other than evidence of actual intention is highly questionable. They lament the fact that Lord Kerr did not develop his scepticism regarding imputation further and take a critical view of the approach of the court saying that:

According to the Supreme Court, imputation is a process of last resort where there is no evidence of the parties' actual intention to hold the property otherwise than as equal owners in equity. But in that situation, surely the presumption should simply hold, since it is not rebutted by evidence? How can a presumption (and a fortiori one which is supposed to be strong) be rebutted not by evidence but by the court filling the black hole in the evidence by its own determination of what is fair? This is surely highly unconventional. What is the point of having a presumption at all, if it can be rebutted not only by evidence of the parties' actual contrary intention but also by the court's own determination of what is fair?[103]

Bailey-Harris and Wilson further speculate that such an approach will encourage litigation as it provides an 'incentive for joint registered owners in cases where there is no express declaration of trust to "have a go" at arguing in court that the interests are other than equal'.[104]

---

[95] R. Bailey-Harris and J. Wilson, '*Jones v Kernott*—Another Helping of the Witches Brew?', available at www.familylawweek.co.uk.

[96] [2011] UKSC 53 at [51], point 4.  [97] Ibid, [58] and [65].  [98] Ibid, [34].

[99] Ibid, [73]–[75].  [100] Ibid, [72].  [101] See Section 2.1.4.

[102] R. Bailey-Harris and J. Wilson, '*Jones v Kernott*—Another Helping of the Witches Brew?' available at http://www.familylawweek.co.uk.

[103] Ibid.  [104] Ibid.

It is hard to avoid the view that the distinction between imputing an intention based on what appears to be fair between the parties and inferring an intention from the parties' conduct is a flimsy one. This view is given further credence by the recent decision of the Court of Appeal in *Barnes* v *Phillips*.[105] In this case, the parties began a relationship in 1983 and had two children. They purchased a property together in 1996. The purchase price was approximately £135,000. They used £25,000 from their savings for the deposit and took out a joint repayment mortgage for the balance. The property was registered in their names as joint tenants. The respondent worked full-time as a nurse except when the children were very young when she worked part-time, and the appellant was a self-employed businessman. He paid the mortgage and some of the bills and the respondent paid the rest. The appellant, who also owned some rental properties in his sole name, ran into financial difficulties. The parties remortgaged their property in 2005, using the money to discharge to initial mortgage and to pay the appellant's debts. The parties separated shortly afterwards and the appellant moved out. He continued to make contributions towards the mortgage for over two years but by 2008 the respondent was paying the mortgage by herself. She also had almost entire financial responsibility for all the work and expenditure required on the property, and for the couple's two children.

The question before the court was whether there was a change of intention between the parties to hold the property in equal shares. The judge at first instance found that on the purchase of the property they were joint tenants in law and in equity because that was their intention. Both contributed equally to what was, in essence, a 'marriage without a wedding ceremony'. He found that there was no express agreement to vary the shares and he did not consider whether he could infer from the parties' conduct, an intention to vary their shares. Instead he simply found that he was entitled to impute an intention to the parties as to the size of their respective shares in the property based on fairness. He concluded that, on the facts, a fair division was 85 per cent/15 per cent in the respondent's favour. The appellant appealed on the ground, *inter alia*, that the judge had erred in law in that having found that there was no agreement by the parties to change their beneficial interests, it was simply not open to him to impute to them a common intention that their shares were unequal.

In the Court of Appeal, Lloyd LJ, giving the lead judgment with which Longmore LJ and Hayden J concurred, confirmed that, in line with *Jones* v *Kernott*, the proper approach in cases such as this is to, firstly, consider whether there was any express agreement to alter the parties' shares in the property. If such an agreement cannot be found, the question then is whether an intention to change their respective shares can be inferred from the parties' conduct. If an agreement to vary the size of the shares can be found, whether express or inferred, the question then turns to the size of those shares. Lloyd LJ confirmed that, in the present case, the judge at first instance had missed a 'critical step' in this process. He had moved directly from finding that there was no express agreement to vary the shares, to holding that he could impute an intention to the parties as to the size of their shares. However, imputation of intention is permissible only at the stage of ascertaining the shares in which the property was held following the demonstration of an actual intention to vary the shares in the property. In other words, one cannot impute an intention to vary the shares in the property in the first instance. Lloyd LJ found that it was, therefore, open to the court to consider whether a common intention to vary the shares could be inferred, noting that on the authority of *Jones* v *Kernott*, 'the scope for inference in this context is very extensive indeed'.[106]

On the facts of the case, the Court of Appeal drew the inference that the parties intended to alter their shares in the property and upheld that 85 per cent/15per cent division in the respondent's favour. Thus, the judge at first instance and the Court of Appeal reached the same outcome, but by different routes. While the judge at first instance had merely imputed an intention to the parties as to the size of their shares, the Court of Appeal clarified that such an imputation is not permissible at the stage of deciding whether to depart from equal division. The Court of Appeal, instead,

---

[105] [2015] EWCA Civ 1056.     [106] Ibid, at [30].

looked at the evidential features of the case to infer from the parties' conduct that they must have intended to alter their shares in the property.[107] This was based on the following facts: throughout the relationship, the appellant was carrying on business activities; he had three rental properties in his own name; the remortgage in 2005 was for his sole benefit and to pay off his debts; and he had the benefit of 25 per cent of the equity in the property when the property was remortgaged. In consequence, a common intention was to be inferred at that point to vary their interests in the property. This view was further supported by the fact that after January 2008, the appellant made no further contribution to the mortgage. It seems, therefore, that because the scope for drawing inferences regarding the parties' intentions from their conduct is wide, the distinction between inferring and imputing an intention remains blurred.

### 2.1.8 To which 'domestic' situations will the presumption of joint beneficial ownership apply?

Another question arising from *Stack* is the range of domestic relationships to which the presumption of joint beneficial ownership will apply. The presumption of a joint beneficial tenancy will only apply in the domestic context where the property which is in the parties' joint names is their home, and not where it was purchased as an investment (even if the owners are also family members). If the presumption does not apply, and if there is no express declaration of the beneficial interest, then the resulting trust will determine the parties' respective beneficial shares in the property.

---

**Key case**

This was made clear by the Court of Appeal in the post-*Stack* decision of *Laskar v Laskar*.[108] In this case, the mother purchased a council house at a discount under a right to buy scheme. In order to secure the mortgage, the property was transferred into the joint names of her and her daughter and both became jointly liable under it. The daughter also contributed a small amount of money towards the purchase price. The property was bought as an investment and shortly after the purchase it was rented out. The mother was solely responsible for the property and for the mortgage repayments which were funded from the rental income. When relations between the mother and daughter broke down, the daughter claimed that as the property was in the parties' joint names, there was a presumption at law that the beneficial ownership would be shared equally. The Court of Appeal held that this presumption did not apply because even though the parties were family members, the property was bought as an investment.[109] Instead, the parties' shares in the property were determined by resulting trust principles and thus the daughter received a 33 per cent interest in the property which reflected her contribution to its acquisition. It is worth noting that Lord Neuberger was of the view that even if the presumption of joint beneficial ownership applied, it would have been rebutted by several factors, in particular the fact that the parties maintained separate finances; that the property was purchased as an investment; that the mother had several other children which suggested that it was unlikely that she intended to benefit one over the others; that there was a disparity in the value of the parties' contributions to the purchase price; and that the daughter was a co-purchaser only because the mother could not afford the property on her own.[110]

---

However, this should not be taken to mean that the principles of *Stack v Dowden* only apply to cohabitants in a sexual relationship as opposed to other family members who share a property as a home. In *Adekunle v Ritchie*[111] a mother and her son (who was one of ten children) bought property

---

[107] Ibid, at [31].     [108] [2008] EWCA Civ 347.     [109] Ibid, [17] *per* Lord Neuberger.
[110] Ibid, [19]. See also *Geary v Rankine* [2012] EWCA Civ 555 which confirms that where the parties are business partners as well as domestic partners, the principles of the resulting trust are more appropriate.
[111] [2007] BPIR 1177.

jointly but there was no declaration of the beneficial interests. The property was purchased as a home for them both where they lived for some years before the mother's death. Judge Behrens held that the presumption of beneficial joint tenancy applied. However, the judge also suggested that it may be easier to rebut the presumption 'when one is not dealing with the situation of a couple living together'.[112] Indeed, although the presumption applied in this case it was rebutted on the facts and the son received only a one-third share in the property. The judge said that this was an unusual case where the evidence indicated that the parties did not intend their shares in the property to be equal.[113] In particular, attention was drawn to the following factors: the property was bought primarily to provide a home for the mother; the parties' finances were separate; the reason the property was put into joint names was because the mother was unable to fund the mortgage without assistance from her son; and the mother had nine other children with whom she was on good terms and there was no reason to think that she would have wanted the whole of her estate to pass to one son alone.[114] However, the fact that the property was conveyed into joint names, that the son was jointly liable under the mortgage, that he was occupying the property at the time of acquisition, and that he contributed to the mortgage led the judge to conclude that he was to have some beneficial interest in the property. A strict arithmetical calculation based on his financial contribution to the acquisition of the property would have given him no more than a 25 per cent share in the property. However, taking a holistic approach to quantification, the judge awarded him a one-third share.

## 2.2 **Sole name cases**

The second situation that we must consider is the 'sole name case'—where the property is conveyed into the sole name of one party (the legal owner), and the other person claims that they have a beneficial interest in it.

It is clear from *Stack v Dowden* that the starting point in all cases is that equity follows the law. There is thus an immediate difference between sole and joint names cases. In joint names cases, the law will presume that both parties have an equal beneficial interest in the property, although one party can try to rebut this in an attempt to receive a larger share. However, if the property is registered in the sole name of one party, it will be presumed that this person also holds the sole beneficial title.[115] The onus is on the person claiming that the beneficial ownership is different from the legal ownership to show that there was a common intention to hold the property in some other shares. This means that in sole ownership cases, the non-legal owner must establish that he or she has a beneficial interest in the first place, before showing exactly what that interest is.[116]

---

### Summary

There are thus two separate questions that have to be considered in sole name cases:[117]

- Applying the principles of the common intention constructive trust, can the non-legal owner establish that the legal title is held on trust for both parties?

- If he or she can, the court must then decide the size of this person's beneficial interest (the quantification issue).

---

[112] Ibid, [65].     [113] Ibid, [67].     [114] Ibid, [66].
[115] *Stack v Dowden* [2007] UKHL 17 at [56] *per* Baroness Hale.     [116] Ibid, [56] and [61].
[117] *Abbott v Abbott* [2007] UKPC 53 at [4] *per* Baroness Hale.

### 2.2.1 Establishing the existence of a beneficial interest

In order to *establish* a beneficial interest under a constructive trust, the non-legal owner must show that the parties had a common intention to share the ownership of the property. On top of this, the non-legal owner must also show that he or she acted to their detriment, or significantly altered their position, in reliance on this common intention.

#### 2.2.1.1 Common intention

The most difficult question is whether or not there was a common intention between the parties to share the property. It is important to be aware that the common intention must relate to sharing the *ownership* of the property and not just its *occupation* as a joint family home. In addition, an agreement to operate a business together is not tantamount to agreeing to share ownership of property. In *Geary v Rankine*[118] Mr Rankine purchased property in his own name to be run as a guesthouse for business purposes. He initially planned to have a manager in place to run the guesthouse but when that did not work out he ran it himself with help from his cohabitant, Ms Geary. When the parties separated, Ms Geary argued that a common intention constructive trust had arisen following acquisition, as a result of her work in the business, giving her a beneficial interest in the property. The Court of Appeal rejected this argument. Lewison LJ held that the burden of establishing such a trust was 'all the more difficult to discharge where, as here, the property was bought as an investment rather than as a home'.[119] In such circumstances, where the partners are business partners as well as domestic partners, the presumption of resulting trust may be more appropriate. Thus Ms Geary failed in her claim because as Lewison LJ pointed out, '. . . it is an impermissible leap to go from common intention that the parties would run a business together to a conclusion that it was their common intention that the property in which the business was run, and which was bought entirely with money provided by one of them, would belong to both of them.'[120]

The leading case on establishing the existence of a beneficial interest is *Lloyd's Bank v Rosset*.[121] Lord Bridge stated that common intention can be established in one of two ways. It can be evidenced from the oral statements exchanged between the parties (express common intention), or it can arise from the parties' conduct (inferred common intention). Before looking at these in turn, it is worth pointing out that while the court will consider the intention of the parties at the time of the acquisition of the property, it is now accepted that the parties' intention may change during the course of their relationship. For example, in *Aspden v Elvy*,[122] Mr Aspden bought a farm in his sole name in which he lived with his partner Ms Elvy. At this point he was entitled legally and beneficially to all of the property. Some time later he made a transfer of a barn on the farm to Ms Elvy. This was an outright gift and she became the absolute legal and beneficial owner of the property. Over the next two years, however, Mr Aspden spent money renovating the barn and carried out work on it which increased its value. The court held that in light of this work and the whole course of dealing between the parties, they must have had a common intention to share ownership of the property. Mr Aspden was awarded a 25 per cent share of the barn.

#### 2.2.1.2 Express common intention

A common intention can be established by evidence of express discussions between the parties (however informal) which show that they had an agreement, arrangement, or understanding to share the beneficial ownership of the property.

---

[118] [2012] EWCA Civ 555.  [119] Ibid, [18].  [120] Ibid, [22].
[121] [1991] 1 AC 107 at 133.  [122] [2012] EWHC 1387 (Ch).

---

### Talking point

Indeed, Lord Bridge said that the first question to be resolved is whether:

> there has at any time prior to the acquisition [of the property], or exceptionally at some later date, been any agreement, arrangement or understanding reached between [the parties] that the property is to be shared beneficially. The finding of an agreement or arrangement to share in this sense can only, I think, be based on evidence of express discussions between the partners, however imperfectly remembered and however imprecise their terms may have been.[123]

**Q.** Do you think it is realistic to expect couples to have such discussions about property ownership?

---

The emphasis on express discussions between the parties means that:

> the tenderest exchanges of a common law courtship may assume unforeseen significance many years later when they are brought under equity's microscope and subjected to an analysis under which many thousands of pounds of value may be liable to turn on fine questions as to whether the relevant words were spoken in earnest or in dalliance and with or without representational intent.[124]

Case law shows that the common intention which is evidenced by the parties' express discussions can be purely 'notional'.[125] There may be circumstances where one party held no intention to share the ownership of the property with their partner, but through their words and conduct (in particular, excuses made for not putting the property into joint names) led the other to believe that such an intention was held. Two cases where the court found evidence of an express common intention demonstrate this. In *Eves v Eves*[126] an unmarried couple, who had a child, decided to buy a house. The man provided the deposit and paid the mortgage. At the time of the purchase, the man told the woman that 'it was to be their house and a home for themselves and their children'. He said that as she was under 21 years of age, the property could not be put into their joint names but had to be in his name alone. He told her that, but for her age, it would have been purchased in joint names. In fact, he was being dishonest and all along he intended that the property should be his alone. However, the woman accepted his explanation. The house itself was in a very dilapidated condition and the woman carried out a great deal of work in the house and garden to make it habitable.[127] Subsequently the man left her and married someone else.[128] The Court of Appeal held that the man clearly led the woman to believe that she would have some undefined interest in the property. This allowed the court to find that there was an express common intention to share the ownership of the property. The woman's performance of manual labour in reliance upon this common intention was sufficient to constitute detrimental reliance, and the court imposed a constructive trust in her favour. She was awarded one-quarter of the equity of the property.[129]

---

[123] Ibid, 132. The agreement does not have to define the extent or size of each party's share (see *Oxley v Hiscock* [2004] EWCA Civ 546 at [37] and [40]). Quantification is an issue that only follows if a common intention to share is found between the parties.

[124] *Hammond v Mitchell* [1992] 2 All ER 109 at 121 *per* Waite J.

[125] G. Douglas, J. Pearce, and H. Woodward, Cardiff Law School Research Paper No 1, 'A Failure of Trust: Resolving Property Disputes on Cohabitation Breakdown' (2007), para 3.13. See also N. Glover and P. Todd, 'The Myth of Common Intention' (1996) Legal Studies 325.

[126] [1975] 3 All ER 768.

[127] This included painting and decorating, breaking up concrete in the garden, demolishing and rebuilding a shed, and preparing the garden for turfing.

[128] The women by then had given birth to their second child.

[129] *Eves v Eves* was distinguished in the recent case of *Curran v Collins* [2015] EWCA Civ 404. In this case, the property was in Mr Collins' sole name. His partner, Ms Curran, had raised with him why she was not a joint owner of the property and he provided an excuse on the basis of the cost of life insurance policies. In rejecting her claim that she had

Similarly, in *Grant v Edwards*[130] the house was conveyed into the sole name of the man because the woman was already married to someone else. Here, too, the man falsely led the woman to believe that her name was being excluded from the title deeds for good reason; he told her that if she were to be named as joint legal owner this might prejudice her position in the matrimonial proceedings between her and her husband. Subsequently the women made substantial indirect contributions towards the mortgage by applying her earnings towards the joint household expenses, without which the mortgage instalments could not have been paid by the man. The Court of Appeal held that the man's statement that the woman's name would be on the title deeds but for the matrimonial proceedings was sufficient to show the necessary common intention that the ownership should be shared.[131]

These cases, described by Lord Bridge in *Lloyds Bank v Rosset* as 'outstanding examples' of express common intention,[132] show that such an intention can be found even if one party did not actually hold the intention professed but led the other to believe that he or she did so. However, the Court of Appeal took a tougher line in *James v Thomas*,[133] refusing to find that the assurances made by the legal owner to the claimant established a common intention between them. In this case Miss James moved into a property which was registered in the sole name of her partner, Mr Thomas. Both parties carried out work on the property and whenever the parties discussed these improvements, Mr Thomas told her that they would 'benefit us both'. The court rejected the argument that this evidenced a common intention to share the beneficial ownership of the property, holding instead that this was simply intended to mean that the improvements would make their home more comfortable and would improve the quality of their life together. It was neither intended nor understood to be a promise of some proprietary interest either at the time the statement was made or in the future.[134] This was reinforced by Mr Thomas's unwillingness to put the property into joint names when asked to do so by Miss James. He also told her that she would be 'well provided for' in the event of his death. The court said that this was not a representation that she was to have a proprietary interest in the property during his lifetime. It was a representation of what would happen on his death based on the assumption that they would still be living together when that eventuality occurred.[135] This decision has been criticised as inconsistent with earlier case law.[136] Greer says:

> Ms James would have been more successful if Mr Thomas had simply lied to avoid putting the property into joint names, rather than evaded the issue, which seems to make a nonsense of the law.[137]

It seems, then, that if the legal owner makes an excuse for not putting the property into joint names this may be sufficient to allow the court to find an express common intention on the basis that the non-owner reasonably believed that such an intention existed. However, more general references to the couple's mutual well-being and quality of life will not, without more, evidence an express common intention regarding ownership of the property.

---

a beneficial interest in the property, Lewison LJ in the Court of Appeal distinguished *Eves* v *Eves* on the basis that the property in question was not being used as the family home and that, in *Eves*, there had been a positive assertion that the property would have been purchased in joint names had it not been for Ms Eves' age. The excuse here, by contrast, could not be taken to imply that the man considered that Ms Curran should be an owner of the property.

[130] [1986] 2 All ER 426.

[131] At one stage the man paid insurance moneys relating to the house into a savings account in the parties' joint names, which reinforced the evidence of how the parties intended the property to be shared, namely that each should be entitled to a half share. See also *Hammond v Mitchell* [1992] 2 All ER 109 where an express agreement between an unmarried couple was found after the man said to the woman, 'Don't worry about the future because when we are married [the house] will be half yours anyway and I'll always look after you and [our child].'

[132] [1991] 1 AC 107 at 133.    [133] [2007] EWCA Civ 1212.

[134] Ibid, [33].    [135] Ibid, [35].    [136] See eg *Hammond v Mitchell* [1992] 2 All ER 109.

[137] S. Greer, 'Back to the Bad Old Days?' (2008) 158 New Law Journal 174.

In the absence of a representation from one party to the other as in *Eves v Eves*, or a mutually held intention evidenced by express discussions between the parties, no express common intention will be found to exist. More often than not, this will be the case. While it would, of course, be sensible for cohabitants to discuss important financial and property-related matters either at the beginning, or during, their relationship, it is unsurprising that this tends not to happen.[138] Instead, couples will usually deal with each other on the basis of mutual trust and in the expectation that their 'relationship will endure'.[139] As has been pointed out: for a couple embarking on a serious relationship, discussion of the terms to apply at parting is almost a contradiction of the shared hopes that have brought them together.[140]

A related problem with finding an express common intention is that when a relationship breaks down, particularly when this is accompanied by feelings of hostility, the parties' respective memories about past discussions regarding the family home are likely to become selective and self-serving.[141] So, in many cases, there will be no clear and reliable evidence of an express agreement or understanding between the parties about how the property was to be shared between them.

### 2.2.1.3 Inferred common intention

Failure to establish an express agreement or arrangement between the parties regarding ownership of the property is not necessarily fatal to the non-legal owner's claim to a beneficial interest in it. Evidence relating to the parties' conduct may be sufficient to establish a constructive trust where the conduct is such that the court can infer that the parties both intended that the beneficial ownership of the property should be shared.[142] While the court can infer such an agreement from the parties' conduct, the Court of Appeal has made it clear that it cannot look at the case in the 'round' and impute such an intention to the parties based on what appears to be fair.[143] However, from what conduct will the court infer such a common intention? This has been one of the most controversial questions in family law.

---

**Key case**

In *Lloyds Bank v Rosset*,[144] Lord Bridge, speaking *obiter*, gave a very restrictive answer. He said that direct contributions to the purchase price were the *only* conduct from which such a common intention could be inferred:

> [D]irect contributions to the purchase price by the partner who is not the legal owner, whether initially or by payment of mortgage instalments, will readily justify the inference necessary for the creation of a constructive trust. But . . . it is at least extremely doubtful whether anything less will do.[145]

---

[138] See A. Barlow, C. Burgoyne, and J. Smithson, *The Living Together Campaign—An Investigation of its Impact on Legally Aware Cohabitants* (London: Ministry of Justice, 2007).

[139] *Midland Bank plc v Cooke* [1995] 2 FLR 915 at 927 *per* Waite LJ.      [140] Ibid.

[141] See the observations of Baroness Hale in *Stack v Dowden* [2007] UKHL 17 at [68].

[142] Even if it is clear that the parties neither discussed nor intended any agreement as to how the beneficial interest was to be shared, this does not prevent the court from inferring, on general equitable principles, that such an agreement existed, see *Midland Bank plc v Cooke* [1995] 4 All ER 562 at 574–5; and *Stack v Dowden* [2007] UKHL 17 at [25] where Lord Walker said that the House of Lords in *Lloyds Bank v Rosset* agreed that a ' "common intention" trust could be inferred even when there was no evidence of an actual agreement'. See *Abbott v Abbott* [2007] UKPC 53 at [5].

[143] *Capehorn v Harris* [2015] EWCA Civ 955. In this case the judge at first instance held that one partner's contribution to the couple's business was sufficient to impute an intention to the parties that he was to acquire a share in the property held in his partner's sole name. The Court of Appeal made it very clear, however, that in the absence of an express agreement between the parties to share the beneficial interest, such an agreement can only be inferred from the parties' conduct. While the Court of Appeal gave little guidance on the type of conduct which would justify such an inference, it made it very clear that the court is not entitled to impute an intention to the parties that they were to share the beneficial interest in the property. On the facts of the case, the court did not find the evidence to infer an agreement to share the ownership of the property in question.

[144] [1991] 1 AC 107.      [145] Ibid, 133 *per* Lord Bridge.

In *Lloyds Bank v Rosset* the issue to be resolved was whether Mrs Rosset had acquired a beneficial interest in the matrimonial home, a derelict farmhouse, which had been purchased in her husband's sole name and which she had helped to renovate. Mr Rosset had used the property as security for a bank loan without Mrs Rosset's knowledge and when he was unable to repay the loan the bank started proceedings for possession and sale of the property. Mrs Rosset resisted the bank's claim. She alleged that she had made a significant contribution to the acquisition of the property by the work she had personally undertaken in the course of its renovation. This included doing some painting and decorating, designing two rooms, coordinating work with the builders, and engaging in various other tasks connected with the house. She claimed that the parties had a common intention that she should share in the ownership of the property and that therefore she had a beneficial interest under a constructive trust.[146] The trial judge and the Court of Appeal were each satisfied that Mr and Mrs Rosset held the necessary common intention that she should have an interest in the property, that she had acted on the basis of that common intention to her detriment, and that therefore she had acquired a beneficial interest under a constructive trust. However, Lord Bridge, stating the unanimous opinion of the Law Lords, ruled that the two inferior courts had been wrong.

The House of Lords rejected Mrs Rosset's claim of a beneficial interest, holding that she could not establish the requisite common intention that ownership of the property be shared either by proving that the parties had informally agreed to this or by establishing conduct on her own part such that the court should infer an agreement. Lord Bridge emphasised that there must be a common intention to share *ownership* of the property, saying that:

> neither a common intention by spouses that a house is to be renovated as a 'joint venture' nor a common intention that the house is to be shared by the parents and children as the family home throws any light on their intentions with respect to the beneficial ownership of the property.[147]

In relation to Mrs Rosset's efforts in respect of the renovation of the property, from which the trial judge had drawn the inference of a common intention that she should have a beneficial interest, Lord Bridge said:

> By itself this activity, it seems to me, could not possibly justify any such inference. It was common ground that Mrs. Rosset was extremely anxious that the new matrimonial home should be ready for occupation before Christmas if possible. In these circumstances it would seem the most natural thing in the world for any wife, in the absence of her husband abroad, to spend all the time she could spare and to employ any skills she might have, such as the ability to decorate a room, in doing all she could to accelerate progress of the work quite irrespective of any expectation she might have of enjoying a beneficial interest in the property . . . On any view the monetary value of Mrs. Rosset's work expressed as a contribution to a property acquired at a cost exceeding £70,000 must have been so trifling as to be almost de minimis.[148]

Thus Lord Bridge not only took the view that this conduct could not justify the inference that there had been a common intention that Mrs Rosset should have a beneficial interest in the matrimonial home, he also characterised her contribution as so trifling that it was doubtful whether it amounted to sufficient detriment.

This restrictive view means that someone who makes no direct financial contribution towards the acquisition of the property, nor pays off any part of the mortgage instalments, but who makes other important financial and non-financial contributions (such as contributing towards the household bills, looking after the house, and taking care of the children) may not be able to establish a beneficial interest in the family home should the relationship break down.[149]

---

[146] She therefore claimed that she had an overriding interest under the Land Registration Act 1925, s 70(1)(g), which would prevail against the bank because she had been in actual occupation of the land on the date when the bank's charge was created. The 1925 Act has been repealed and replaced by the Land Registration Act 2002. The third party aspects of this and other cases are beyond the scope of this book.

[147] [1991] 1 AC 107 at 130.      [148] Ibid, 131.

[149] Unless, of course, there is evidence of an express common intention to share ownership of the property.

The clearest example of courts giving no monetary value to domestic labour is *Burns v Burns*.[150] In this case a woman lived with her male partner for 19 years in a property which was conveyed into the man's sole name. They were known as Mr and Mrs Burns and had two children. There was no express declaration that Mrs Burns should have a share in the beneficial ownership of the family home, nor had she made any direct financial contribution to its acquisition. She gave up her job to have the children and when she returned to work she used her income to contribute to the household expenses and to purchase clothes for the family. At no time did Mr Burns ask her to contribute to the household expenses in order to relieve the financial burden on him, and her purchases did not release his earnings to enable him to pay the mortgage. When the relationship broke down, Mrs Burns sought to establish a common intention that she should have a beneficial interest in the property on the grounds that she had brought up the children, carried out domestic tasks, redecorated the interior of the house, used her earnings to contribute towards the housekeeping expenses, and had bought fixtures and fittings and various consumer durables. Her claim was rejected by the Court of Appeal. There was no evidence of any express common intention that she was to have a share in the home. Further, as she had made no direct financial contribution to its acquisition, there was no conduct from which such a common intention could be inferred. The Court of Appeal held that none of her expenditure was referable to the acquisition of the property. It held that paying for chattels and decorating the property did not amount to evidence of a common intention that she should have an interest in the house.[151] Fox LJ said:

> [T]he mere fact that the parties live together and do the ordinary domestic tasks is, in my view, no indication at all that they thereby intended to alter the existing property rights of either of them.[152]

Thus Mrs Burns was denied any share in the property which had been the family home for 19 years. Mr Burns, on the other hand, was entitled to retain the entire beneficial interest in the property which Mrs Burns had cleaned, decorated, and otherwise looked after and in which she had laboured for his benefit as well as for the benefit of herself and the children. It has been observed that:

> the continuing criticism of this case lies in the failure of the law to call her partner to account for the benefits he had enjoyed during their relationship, simply because these were not valued in financial terms.[153]

While the Court of Appeal felt some sympathy for Mrs Burns' position, it held that it was not for the courts to attempt to remedy any inequity; this was a matter for Parliament. Unfortunately, there has been no such statutory reform and it has been left to the courts to continue to apply these principles to domestic cases. This restrictive approach has been heavily criticised as being too dependent on financial contributions, which works against a partner (usually the woman) who has made indirect financial contributions to the general household expenses, or has made wholly domestic contributions through looking after the home and raising children.

### 2.2.1.4 Are there signs of a more flexible jurisprudence?

The strict requirements laid down by Lord Bridge in *Rosset* certainly make it very difficult to establish a beneficial interest. Unfortunately, there is no evidence that the courts may be persuaded to take a more flexible approach to purely domestic labour. Thus, it remains the case that the economic sacrifices involved in carrying out purely domestic work and other non-financial contributions

---

[150] [1984] Ch 317.

[151] See too *Pettitt v Pettitt* [1969] 2 All ER 385 at 416 where Lord Diplock was dismissive of the notion that handiwork around the house by a husband should give rise to him acquiring a beneficial interest in the property owned by the wife.

[152] [1984] Ch 317 at 331.

[153] G. Douglas, J. Pearce, and H. Woodward, 'Cohabitants, Property and the Law: A Study of Injustice' (2009) 72(1) Modern Law Review 24 at 31.

which benefit the family will not, by themselves, give rise to an interest in the home. For Mrs Burns this meant that she 'had no financial remedy for the loss she sustained as a result of the time and efforts she had devoted to the family'.[154] However, there is some evidence of a more flexible approach being taken by some judges in relation to *indirect financial contributions*. That is, where one person contributes towards the general household expenses which enables their partner to pay the mortgage instalments. There is a very strong argument that such indirect contributions should give rise to a constructive trust. As the Law Commission has pointed out:

> In many cases, a couple will not engage in discussion, but agree to an ordering of the household finances such that one pays off the mortgage while the other pays the household bills.[155]

The Law Commission concluded that the payer of the bills should be given credit for their contribution and therefore such an indirect contribution to the mortgage should give rise to the common intention that the beneficial entitlement to the home be shared.[156] Indeed, others have pointed out that, under trust principles, there is no reason why indirect financial contributions should not give rise to a constructive trust:

> So long as the claimant has made an indirect contribution that is referable to the acquisition of the house, the requisite inference of an intention to share the property should apply, given that the contribution to joint household expenses has enabled the legal owner more easily to pay the mortgage instalments out of his (or her) own money.[157]

However, in *Rosset*, Lord Bridge appeared to rule out the possibility of a common intention being inferred from such *indirect* financial contributions when he said that 'it is at least extremely doubtful that anything less' than direct financial contributions would suffice. However, Nicholas Mostyn QC, sitting as deputy High Court judge in the first instance decision of *Le Foe v Le Foe*[158] thought otherwise. In this case, Mrs Le Foe had not made any direct contributions to the purchase of the family home, although she made substantial financial contributions to the family's day-to-day expenditure. Mostyn QC interpreted the speech of Lord Bridge in *Rosset* in a flexible manner. He suggested that Lord Bridge did not state the proposition that, in the absence of an agreement, *only* direct financial contributions would give rise to a constructive trust, in absolute terms. Rather, in his view, Lord Bridge was simply saying that it is only in exceptional cases that conduct other than direct contributions to the purchase price would give rise to a common intention to share the equity.[159] As a result, Mostyn QC inferred from the wife's indirect contributions to the mortgage, a common intention between the parties to share the property beneficially. In support of this view, he cited dicta from May LJ in *Burns v Burns*[160] and Lord Diplock in *Gissing v Gissing*,[161] who said:

> It may be no more than a matter of convenience which spouse pays particular household accounts, particularly when both are earning, and if the wife goes out to work and devotes part of her earnings or uses her private income to meet joint expenses of the household which would otherwise be met by the husband, so as to enable him to pay the mortgage instalments out of his moneys which would be consistent with and might be corroborative of an original common intention that she should share in the beneficial interest in the matrimonial home and that her payments of other household expenses were intended by both spouses to be treated as including a contribution by the wife to the purchase price of the matrimonial home.

---

[154] Law Commission, *Sharing Homes: A Discussion Paper* (Law Com No 278, 2002), para 5.17.
[155] Ibid, para 4.26.     [156] Ibid, para 4.27.
[157] M. Pawlowski, 'Beneficial Entitlement—No Longer Doing Justice' (2007) Conveyancer and Property Lawyer 354 at 361.
[158] [2001] 2 FLR 970.     [159] Ibid, [43].     [160] [1984] Ch 317.     [161] [1971 AC 886 at 907–8.

The majority of the House of Lords in *Stack v Dowden*[162] also appeared to support a more flexible interpretation of Lord Bridge's *obiter* comments in *Lloyds Bank v Rosset*, although unfortunately no reference was made to *Le Foe v Le Foe*. Lord Walker questioned whether Lord Bridge's narrow view of the contributions which give rise to a constructive trust was in line with earlier authorities, and he noted that this restrictive approach had attracted considerable academic criticism for producing injustice. He continued that 'the law has moved on, and your Lordships should move it a little more in the same direction'.[163] Unfortunately, as *Stack v Dowden* was a joint names case, these comments were merely *obiter*. Indeed, Baroness Hale noted that the question of what is required to *establish* a common intention 'does not concern us now', but she nonetheless accepted the view of the Law Commission that Lord Bridge had 'set the hurdle rather too high' in holding that only direct financial contributions will suffice as conduct from which to infer common intention.[164]

This view was reiterated by Baroness Hale in *Abbott v Abbott*.[165] Following the sentiments of her *obiter* comments in *Stack*, Baroness Hale said that in relation to the view of Lord Bridge that nothing less than direct contributions to the purchase price would give rise to the inference to share the beneficial interest, the 'law has undoubtedly moved on'.[166] However, her Ladyship did not specify in exactly what way and, once again, no reference was made to the decision of Mostyn J in *Le Foe*. Her Ladyship continued by citing from her speech in *Stack* where she said that:

> the law has indeed moved on in response to changing social and economic conditions. The search is to ascertain the parties' shared intentions, actual, inferred or imputed, with respect to the property in light of their whole course of conduct in relation to it.[167]

However, the exact implications of this observation for how 'the law has moved on' in relation to the conduct from which a common intention to share the beneficial interest can be inferred in sole name cases are very unclear. Was Baroness Hale suggesting that where there is no express agreement evidencing the parties' intention, the court will undertake a survey of the whole course of dealing between the parties in relation to the property, taking account of all conduct which throws light on the question of what shares were intended? Is this broad-brush approach, which up to now has only been applied when quantifying an already established beneficial interest, to be taken when ascertaining whether the parties intended to share the beneficial interest in a property that was conveyed into the name of one party only? Does this mean that, in line with *Le Foe v Le Foe*, a common intention to share ownership of the home can be inferred from indirect contributions to the general household expenses?

While comments in both *Stack* and *Abbott* suggest that this is the direction in which the law is moving, it would be premature to say that this is where it has now reached. It should be remembered that comments about the 'law moving on' in relation to *establishing* a beneficial interest were strictly *obiter* in both *Stack* and *Abbott*. *Stack* was a joint names case and in *Abbott* the wife already had a beneficial interest and so the issue for the court was in quantifying the size of her interest. One source of confusion is that there are two separate questions in these cases, and it is unclear to what extent the test for one applies to the other. The first question in sole name cases is whether there is a common intention to share the beneficial interest. The second question, which arises in both sole name and joint names cases, concerns the search for the parties' common intention regarding the quantification of an already established beneficial interest. The 'whole course of conduct test', which Baroness Hale approved in *Stack*, was adopted in relation to the second question on quantification. The issue is, to what extent does this test apply to the first question of *establishing*

---

[162] [2007] UKHL 17.     [163] Ibid, [26].     [164] Ibid, [63].

[165] [2007] UKPC 53 at [3]. It was accepted that the claimant had a beneficial interest in the property and so the issue for the Privy Council was the size of each parties' share.

[166] Ibid, [3] *per* Baroness Hale.

[167] Ibid, [6] citing *Stack v Dowden* [2007] UKHL 17 at [60] *per* Baroness Hale.

a beneficial interest in sole name cases? Despite the articulation of general sentiments about the law moving on, the speeches of the Lords in *Stack* and *Abbot* do not provide any guidance on how such a test would apply to this first question in sole name cases: that is, how a common intention to share could be inferred from the parties' whole course of conduct.[168] The matter is further complicated when one considers that Baroness Hale also said in *Abbott* that the law has moved on in relation to the question of 'quantifying an acknowledged beneficial interest'.[169] But what of the case where there is no acknowledged beneficial interest and the court is trying to ascertain whether the non-legal owner has *established* a beneficial interest from the parties' conduct? Despite the clear sentiments in both *Stack* and *Abbott* that the speech of Lord Bridge was too restrictive, there remains a considerable amount of uncertainty regarding whether and how the law has moved on in sole name cases when, in the absence of an express agreement between the parties, the court has to look at their conduct in order to infer a common intention to share the property beneficially.

### 2.2.1.5 An opportunity missed?

The Court of Appeal has addressed the implications of *Stack* for sole name cases. Unfortunately, in both a very restrictive view has been taken of the type of conduct from which a common intention can be inferred, thus failing to capitalise on the *obiter* remarks made in *Stack* and *Abbot* which suggested that Lord Bridge had set the bar too high.[170] In *James v Thomas*[171] an unmarried couple lived together for almost 15 years in a property which was in the man's sole name. Mr Thomas purchased the property a number of years before the parties had even met. Shortly afterwards, he and Miss James formed a relationship and she moved in with him but she did not financially contribute to the acquisition of the property. She did, however, work with Mr Thomas in his business as a building and drainage contractor without payment. She initially carried out manual labour but, after a number of years, focused on the bookkeeping and paperwork associated with the business on a part-time basis. Their household, living, and personal expenses were paid out of a bank account which was in the sole name of Mr Thomas, and this account also operated as a business account. After some time, the business was carried on as a partnership between the parties and the bank account was put into their joint names. They both carried out extensive renovations to the property, which were funded by the income generated by the business. When the relationship broke down, Miss James claimed that she had a beneficial interest in the property by way of a constructive trust or proprietary estoppel. The Court of Appeal rejected her claim.

It is significant that Mr Thomas had purchased the property before the parties met because the main issue was whether a common intention to share it could be formed *after* the property had been acquired. The court confirmed that, in principle, it could. The common intention necessary

---

[168] The Supreme Court did not offer any further clarification in *Jones v Kernott* [2011] UKSC 53 on the type of conduct from which the court can infer the parties' common intention to share beneficial ownership of the property in sole name cases. More recently, in *Geary v Rankine* [2012] EWCA Civ 555 the Court of Appeal made it clear that common intention could only be based on the parties' actual shared intentions, whether express or inferred from their conduct, at [21]. Unhelpfully, however, no indication was given as to the type of conduct from which common intention could be inferred. See also *Thompson v Hurst* [2012] EWCA Civ 1752 and *Capehorn v Harris* [2015] EWCA Civ 955 where the Court of Appeal made it clear that while the court can infer an agreement to share the beneficial interest from the parties' conduct, it cannot look at the case in the 'round' and impute such an intention to the parties based on what appears to be fair. It is only if such an agreement has been found, whether an express agreement or one what has been inferred, that the court may then impute an intention that each person is entitled to the share which it considers fair having regard to the whole course of dealing between the parties, at [17]. In other words, imputation is allowed in relation to quantification of the shares once an agreement has been found, but the court is not entitled to impute an intention to the parties on the first stage in the analysis, that is, in deciding whether an agreement to share can be found to exist. Once again, however, little guidance was given regarding the conduct from which the court could infer a common intention to share ownership of the property.

[169] *Abbott v Abbott* [2007] UKPC 53 at [19].

[170] See also *Frost v Clarke* [2008] EWHC 742 (Ch) and *Mirza v Mirza* [2009] EWHC 3 (Ch).

[171] [2007] EWCA Civ 1212.

to give rise to a constructive trust may be formed at any time before, during, or after the acquisition of the property.[172] The court also confirmed that the common intention regarding the beneficial interests in the property may be inferred from evidence of the parties' conduct during the whole course of their dealings in relation to the property.[173] While this seems promising, a sting in the tail was to follow. The Court of Appeal said that:

> in the absence of an express post-acquisition agreement, a court will be slow to infer from conduct alone that parties intended to vary existing beneficial interests at the time of acquisition.[174]

This unfortunately means that it will be very hard for a claimant to establish a common intention to share the beneficial interest from conduct which takes place *after* the property has been acquired. On the facts of the case, there was no express agreement between the parties and so the question was whether a common intention could be inferred from the parties' whole course of dealings in relation to the property. The real question was whether her contributions to the business, which helped to generate the income to pay off the mortgage, gave rise to the inference of a common intention to share the property. The court said it did not. Given that the couple's only source of income came from the business, the court thought that it was unsurprising that Miss James did all she could to ensure its success. Thus her contributions were 'wholly explicable on other grounds' and did not give rise to the inference that the parties had agreed, or reached a common understanding, that she was to have a share in the property.[175] As such, the Court of Appeal held that Miss James was not entitled to a beneficial interest.

In light of her contributions to the business, and the fact that it was the money generated by the business which paid off the mortgage as well as other household and personal expenses, this seems to be a very unfair outcome. Indeed, it is particularly harsh when one considers that, in his evidence, Mr Thomas conceded that in fairness Miss James was entitled to some interest in the property.[176] However, Chadwick LJ emphasised that this assessment is not about what was fair.[177] He said:

> Her interest in the property (if any) must be determined by applying principles of law and equity which (however inadequate to meet the circumstances in which parties live together in the twenty-first century) must now be taken as well-established. Unless she can bring herself within those principles, her claim . . . must fail.[178]

Unfortunately the court took a very restrictive view of the post-acquisition conduct from which a common intention could be inferred, flying in the face of the *obiter* views expressed in *Stack* and *Abbott* that the law had moved on. Looking at the reasoning of the court, it is very hard to see how the law has moved on at all. On the type of conduct which would suffice to establish a common intention, Chadwick LJ said:

> [A]lthough it is possible to envisage circumstances in which the fact that one party began to make contributions to capital repayments due under a mortgage might evidence an agreement that that party was to have a share in the property, the circumstances of this case are not of that nature.[179]

Thus, according to Chadwick LJ, capital repayments to the mortgage may evidence an agreement to share the property. This bears a striking resemblance to the suggestion of Lord Bridge in *Rosset* that direct contributions to the purchase price were required. While Chadwick LJ did not expressly say that nothing else would suffice, the restrictive nature of the language he used (it is *possible* that

---

[172] Ibid, [19].    [173] Ibid.    [174] Ibid, [24] *per* Chadwick LJ.
[175] Ibid, [27] *per* Chadwick LJ.    [176] Ibid, [37].    [177] Ibid, [38].
[178] Ibid, *per* Chadwick LJ.    [179] Ibid, [27].

such contributions *might* evidence an agreement) does not augur well for the argument that more indirect contributions (such as paying household bills) would be enough. The substantial contributions Miss James made to the business were not enough because they were explicable on other grounds. However, it is arguable that this was a strong case from which to infer from Miss James's substantial, unpaid, contributions to the business, a common intention to share the property:

> [T]his was not a case where a live-in-lover claims a share on the ground of paying for a new shag-pile rug, plasma television and a share of the gas, Sky Plus and other essential outgoings . . . This was a case where all apparent wealth . . . was the result of joint effort.[180]

This decision was relied upon in a subsequent Court of Appeal case. In *Morris v Morris*[181] the claimant who was married to Mr Morris, claimed a beneficial interest in the assets of a farming partnership, including the farm, which Mr Morris ran with his mother (who was now deceased). The mother had been the sole legal owner of the farm, and she granted a tenancy of the land year-on-year to the farming partnership. In the early years of the relationship, the claimant provided substantial assistance to the farming business without remuneration. She paid towards the construction of a riding school on the farm which she then ran herself. The riding school became very successful and she eventually incorporated a company and transferred the riding school business to it. When her relationship with Mr Morris broke down, the claimant moved out of the farmhouse and sought a beneficial interest in the farm premises. The trial judge awarded her a 25 per cent share on the basis that her contributions to the farming business and the riding school gave rise to a common intention between the parties (the claimant, her husband, and his mother) that she was to have a beneficial interest in the farm. The claimant had relied upon this to her detriment and thus a constructive trust was established in her favour. The Court of Appeal disagreed and drew a distinction between claiming a share in the business of the farming partnership and claiming a proprietary share in the farm itself. Sir Peter Gibson said:

> It is one thing to say that the claimant believed herself to be an integral part of a business conducted on particular land. It is another to find that the claimant has established an interest in the land itself.[182]

There was no express agreement or discussion between the parties, and neither Mr Morris nor his mother led the claimant to believe that she was to get an interest. The only hope the claimant had of establishing a constructive trust was for the court to infer a common intention from the parties' conduct.

In terms of the correct approach to be taken in these cases, Sir Peter Gibson recited the test from *Stack* that the task of the court is to ascertain the parties' shared intentions in relation to the property in light of their whole course of conduct. However, he then undermined the use of this test when the non-owner is trying to *establish* a beneficial interest in sole name cases. He pointed out that the 'whole course of conduct test' in *Stack* was directed at the second question relating to quantification after a common intention to share had already been established. In terms of the first question he said that:

> the authorities make clear that a common intention constructive trust based only on conduct will only be found in exceptional circumstances.[183]

He confirmed the view of Chadwick LJ in *James v Thomas*[184] that in the absence of an express post-acquisition agreement, a court will be slow to infer from conduct alone that parties intended

---

[180] A. Ralton, 'Establishing a Beneficial Share: *Rosset* Revisited' [2008] Family Law 424 at 426.
[181] [2008] EWCA Civ 257.     [182] Ibid, [16]. See also [49] *per* Pill LJ.
[183] Ibid, [23].     [184] [2007] EWCA Civ 1212.

to vary existing beneficial interests established at the time of acquisition.[185] In terms of the present case, the Court of Appeal concluded that the evidence was 'wholly inadequate' to establish a common intention. The claimant's work on the farm was not of such an exceptional nature as to lead to any inference that she must have acted in the belief that she was acquiring an interest. In addition, the development of the riding school, even though it did add to the capital value of the farm, was for her own financial benefit.[186]

Despite the *obiter* remarks in *Stack* about the law moving on, it remains the case that in the absence of an express agreement or direct financial contributions to the acquisition of the property, it remains very difficult for a non-legal owner to establish a beneficial interest. In light of the more recent decisions of the Court of Appeal, it seems that it is premature to speak of the 'demise of the direct contributions rule' for inferring a common intention to share the property.[187] Of course, it must be pointed out that in both *James v Thomas* and *Morris v Morris*, the property was acquired *before* the parties had even met. Not only did the claimants have to rely on post-acquisition conduct from which to infer a common intention, but they were relying on this conduct to establish a beneficial interest in a property which was not even acquired as the family home. What of a case where the parties are in a relationship and property is acquired in the sole name of one, but it was to be the family home for both of them? Would these circumstances persuade the court to take a more generous view of the conduct of the non-legal owner, which would justify the inference of a common intention to share? Would indirect financial contributions be enough then? Some think they might,[188] but dicta from the cases discussed suggest otherwise. The Court of Appeal has made it very clear that courts will be slow to infer from post-acquisition conduct that the parties intended to vary the beneficial interests that existed at the time of acquisition (in our example, in the sole name of one party). Ongoing domestic labour associated with running a household, and indirect financial contributions (such as paying bills), by their very nature, fall into the category of post-acquisition conduct. Given the reluctance to infer from such conduct alone that the parties intended to share the beneficial interest, there is nothing to suggest that the purpose for which the property was acquired would have a significant impact on this reasoning.

Indeed, the reasoning of the Court of Appeal may actually make it more difficult for a common intention to be inferred from indirect financial contributions. Let us recall that in *James v Thomas* the court rejected the claimant's argument that her indirect contributions evidenced an intention to share the property because her conduct was explicable on other grounds. However, this aspect of the court's reasoning is particularly worrying because it appears to set a very high threshold in relation to conduct from which an intention can be inferred. It suggests that one of the questions to be asked in relation to a person's indirect contributions (such as labour in a business without remuneration, paying bills, or contributing to the general household expenditure) is whether the contributions can be explained on another basis.[189] This does not bode well for the argument that such contributions give rise to an inference that the parties had agreed or reached a common understanding that the contributor was to receive a share of the property. Instead, it could readily be argued that these contributions were made for the general welfare of the family and to ensure the smooth running of the household and not out of any pecuniary self-interest.[190] The domestic context in which this issue arises works against one who makes indirect contributions because in

---

[185] [2008] EWCA Civ 257 at [19].      [186] Ibid, [26].

[187] Gardner speculates that, in light of *Stack v Dowden* and *Abbott v Abbott*, this rule (which suggests that common intention can only be inferred from direct contributions to the purchase price) may no longer exist, S. Gardner, 'Family Property Today' (2008) Law Quarterly Review 422 at 424 and 433.

[188] N. Piska, 'A Common Intention or a Rare Bird? Proprietary Interests, Personal Claims and Services Rendered by Lovers Post-Acquisition: *James v Thomas; Morris v Morris*' [2009] Child and Family Law Quarterly 104.

[189] That is, there was another reason for the contributor to make these contributions outside an agreement or common understanding between the parties that the contributor was to receive a share of the property.

[190] *James v Thomas* [2007] EWCA Civ 1212 at [36].

the cut and thrust of day-to-day family living it will generally be possible to find another reason why such contributions were made.

In this respect, a conundrum may be emerging. The majority in *Stack* thought that property law principles should apply in a slightly different (and more flexible) way when dealing with the family home.[191] In particular, the resulting trust no longer operates as a legal presumption because to restrict the size of a party's share in the beneficial interest to an amount proportionate to their direct financial contributions would ignore their whole course of conduct and overall contributions.[192] However, in another way, the domestic context may make some of the evidential hurdles harder to overcome. In particular, after *James v Thomas* it seems that to give rise to the inference of a common intention, the court must be persuaded that the conduct in question was performed by the claimant in the belief that she was getting an interest in the property.[193] If the conduct can be explained on other grounds, this may negate the finding of a common intention. However, in the domestic context, it may be relatively easy for a non-legal owner's contributions to be explained on the ground that her actions were for the benefit of the family rather than a pecuniary interest on her part to acquire a beneficial interest in the property.

### 2.2.1.6 *Improvements to the property*

Another type of indirect financial contribution to the property is where one party carries out substantial work on the property which adds value to it.

---

**Key legislation**

Under section 37 of the Matrimonial Proceedings and Property Act 1970, if a spouse, civil partner, or engaged person makes a substantial contribution in money or money's worth to the improvement of property in which their spouse, civil partner, or fiancé(e) has an interest, the contributions of the former will generate an interest in the property in their favour.

---

This is subject to any agreement which the parties may reach themselves. This provision does not apply to unmarried cohabitants. However, the majority in *Stack* suggested that improvements, such as manual labour, which add significant value to the property will generate an interest under a constructive trust. Lord Walker pointed out that as most homes are now bought with mortgage finance, 'buying a house does very often continue, in a real sense, throughout the period of its ownership'.[194] He opined that the law should recognise this by taking a wide view of what counts towards a contribution to the acquisition of the property. While he was sceptical about the value of alleged improvements that are really insignificant, there was support for the argument that improvements which added significant value to the property should be taken into account to create an interest in the property.[195]

### 2.2.1.7 *Detrimental reliance*

Establishing that there was a common intention (either express or implied) between the parties to share the ownership of the house will not, by itself, create a constructive trust.[196] On top of this the party claiming a beneficial interest must demonstrate that they significantly altered their position or acted to their detriment on the basis of the common intention. Direct contributions to the purchase price or mortgage instalments will constitute detrimental reliance. This means that if the

---

[191] *Stack v Dowden* [2007] UKHL 17 at [3], [14], [33], [42], [56], [60].     [192] Ibid, [31], [33], [60].

[193] This built on the reasoning of *Stack* where the court said that the conduct from which a common intention can be inferred must be conduct relating to the property.

[194] [2007] UKHL 17 at [34].     [195] Ibid, [12] *per* Lord Hope; [36] *per* Lord Walker, and [70] *per* Baroness Hale.

[196] See *Smith v Bottomley* [2013] EWCA Civ 953.

claimant makes a direct contribution to the purchase price of the property, these contributions will have a dual function. They will give rise to the requisite common intention and will also act as detriment to establish the constructive trust in the claimant's favour.

In the case of express common intention, however, it is unclear exactly what type of contributions will constitute detrimental reliance, and the extent to which there has to be a link between the common intention and the conduct relied upon as a detriment. It seems that what is required is conduct upon which the claimant 'could not reasonably have been expected to embark *unless* she was to have an interest in the house'.[197] In other words, if someone carries out activities which would have ordinarily been expected of them regardless of whether they were to obtain an interest in the house, then this may not be regarded as detrimental reliance. However, if someone's conduct goes beyond that which was expected of them, then a court is more likely to conclude that this constitutes detrimental reliance. For example, in *Eves v Eves*, the woman's manual labour on the property which included breaking up the concrete in the front garden and carrying the pieces to a skip and helping to demolish a shed and construct a new one, was detrimental reliance because the court inferred that she would not have carried out such work if she was not to have an interest in the property. In the words of Brightman J:

> I find it difficult to suppose that she would have been wielding the 14 lb. sledge hammer, breaking up the large area of concrete, filling the skip and doing the other things which were carried out when they moved in, except in pursuance of some expressed or implied arrangement and on the understanding that she was helping to improve a house in which she was to all practical intents and purposes promised that she had an interest.[198]

The court said that this work was 'much more than many wives would do' and had no difficulty in holding that this constituted detrimental reliance. However, it is by no means certain that a court will regard a person's 'ordinary' domestic labour (such as looking after the home, raising children, even paying household bills) as detrimental reliance and may instead view it as work which the claimant would have been doing in any event.[199] As the Law Commission observed:

> [I]f the applicant oversteps the boundary of what might be 'expected' of a partner, particularly in light of the applicant's gender, a finding of detrimental reliance is more likely.[200]

In *James v Thomas*, the question of detrimental reliance did not even arise because the claimant failed at the first hurdle of trying to establish a common intention. However, Chadwick LJ suggested that, in any event, she would not have been able to establish that her contributions amounted to detrimental reliance. He said that she had:

> worked in the business, and contributed her labour to the improvements to the property, because she and Mr Thomas were making their life together as man and wife. The [property] was their home: the business was their livelihood. It is a mistake to think that the motives which lead parties in such a relationship to act as they do are necessarily attributable to pecuniary self-interest.[201]

---

[197] *Grant v Edwards* [1986] Ch 638, *per* Nourse LJ (emphasis added).

[198] *Eves v Eves* [1975] 1 WLR 1338 at 1345.

[199] However, in *Grant v Edwards* [1986] Ch 638, Sir Nicolas Browne-Wilkinson V-C (as he then was) took a more liberal approach suggesting that detriment could be interpreted broadly as 'any act done by [the claimant] . . . to her detriment relating to the joint lives of the parties', at 657.

[200] Law Commission, *Cohabitation: The Financial Consequences of Relationship Breakdown* (Law Com No 307, 2007), para A.37.

[201] [2007] EWCA Civ 1212 at [36].

So the reasoning which may prevent the court from inferring the existence of a common intention where the performance of the conduct can be explained on other grounds, may also prevent the court from finding detrimental reliance.

## 2.3 **Quantification of the beneficial interest**

Once it is established that the claimant is to have a beneficial interest in the property, the next question is the size (quantum) of their interest. The first matter the court will look at is whether there was an actual agreement between the parties about the size of their respective shares. The Court of Appeal made it clear in *Crossley v Crossley*[202] that:

> where the parties have reached a consensus on the beneficial interests in the property, the court will give effect to it, unless there is very good reason for not doing so, such as subsequent renegotiation.

If there is no evidence of such an express agreement between the parties, the court will have to quantify their respective shares in the property. As confirmed by the House of Lords in *Stack v Dowden*, and the Supreme Court in *Jones v Kernott*,[203] it will do so by surveying the whole course of dealing between the parties taking account of all conduct which throws light on the question what shares were either intended or fair. This is the test to be used in both joint names and sole name cases.[204]

*Stack* marked a real turning point for joint names cases. Prior to *Stack*, resulting trust principles determined the size of the parties' shares.[205] However, for some time a more flexible approach to quantification had been taken in sole name cases.[206] In *Midland Bank plc v Cooke*[207] the matrimonial home had been conveyed into the sole name of the husband. The purchase price was provided by a mortgage, some of Mr Cooke's personal savings, and a gift from the husband's parents to the couple. As this was a joint gift, Mrs Cooke's share of it amounted to a 6.47 per cent contribution to the purchase price. She had therefore made a direct contribution to the acquisition of the property which established the necessary common intention. The question for the Court of Appeal was whether her share should be limited to the percentage of the purchase price which she contributed directly (ie, 6.47 per cent). The Court of Appeal answered this question with an unequivocal 'no'. Instead, Waite LJ said that where there is no express evidence of the parties' intentions, it is the duty of the judge to undertake a survey of the whole course of dealing between the parties. That scrutiny should relate to matters relevant to the parties' ownership and occupation of the property and their sharing of its burdens and advantages, and should not confine itself to the limited range of acts of direct contribution of the sort that were needed to found a beneficial interest in the first place. Instead, the court should take into consideration all conduct which threw light on what shares were intended. On the facts, although the wife had made no further financial contribution to the acquisition of the property, there was evidence that, in addition to bringing up the parties' three children, she had worked and paid household bills, and had undertaken liability under a second charge on the property for the benefit of the husband's business. This led Waite LJ to conclude that:

> [o]ne could hardly have a clearer example of a couple who had agreed to share everything equally; the profits of his business while it prospered, and the risks of indebtedness suffered through its

---

[202] [2005] EWCA Civ 1581 at [32] *per* Sir Peter Gibson. See also *Oxley v Hiscock* [2004] EWCA Civ 546 at [69].

[203] [2011] UKSC 53.

[204] *Abbott v Abbott* [2007] UKPC 53; *Holman v Howes* [2007] EWCA Civ 877. The Supreme Court made it clear in *Jones v Kernott* [2011] UKSC 53 that the approach to quantification is the same in sole name and joint names cases, at [52].

[205] See *Walker v Hall* [1984] FLR 126; *Springette v Defoe* [1992] 2 FLR 388; *Huntingford v Hobbs* [1993] 1 FLR 736.

[206] *Oxley v Hiscock* [2004] EWCA Civ 546; *Midland Bank plc v Cooke* [1995] 4 All ER 562; *Drake v Whipp* [1996] 1 FLR 826.

[207] [1995] 2 FLR 915.

failure; the upbringing of their children; the rewards of her own career as a teacher; and most relevantly, a home into which he put his savings and to which she was to give over the years the benefit
of the maintenance and improvement contribution.[208]

He added that when in addition the parties had taken on the commitment of marriage, the conclusion was inescapable that their presumed intention was to share the beneficial interest of the
property in equal shares.

In *Oxley v Hiscock*,[209] Chadwick LJ attempted to inject even more flexibility into the quantification exercise when he said that the task of the court was to determine what was a *fair outcome*
between the parties in light of their whole course of conduct in relation to the property. However,
this approach was rejected by the House of Lords in *Stack v Dowden* and Baroness Hale asserted
that the correct approach to quantification was a 'holistic' one where the court surveyed the whole
course of dealing between the parties, taking account of all conduct which threw light on the question of what shares were intended. While this was expressed in the context of a joint names case,
the same applies to sole name cases. This was confirmed by the Privy Council in *Abbott v Abbott*.[210]
This case concerned the divorce of a couple in Antigua. However, the law in Antigua and Barbuda
does not have a matrimonial finance regime and thus property disputes have to be resolved by
applying ordinary property and trust law principles. The wife claimed that she had a beneficial
interest in the former matrimonial home which was held in the husband's sole name. The property
was built on a plot of land which had been given to the couple by the husband's mother. The construction of the property was financed partly by a mortgage executed by the husband and by funds
provided by the husband's mother. The funds were paid into the couple's joint bank account. The
wife worked on and off during the marriage and all the couple's income went into their joint bank
account from which the mortgage instalments and insurance premiums were paid. The wife also
made herself jointly and severally liable for the mortgage. The husband accepted that the wife had
a beneficial interest in the home and thus the real question for the court was in quantifying the size
of her share.[211] The Court of Appeal held that the wife was only entitled to around an 8 per cent
share of the beneficial interest in the home, a percentage which reflected her direct contributions
to the mortgage instalments. The wife successfully appealed to the Privy Council where it was held
that she was entitled to a half share in the property.

The Privy Council confirmed that the constructive trust is 'the more appropriate tool of analysis
in most matrimonial cases'.[212] As such, the resulting trust did not operate as a legal presumption to
limit the wife's share to 8 per cent, which reflected her direct financial contribution to its acquisition. In this case the home was built on a plot of land given to the couple by the husband's mother
and further funds provided by the mother helped to finance the construction of the property. The
court recited the accepted principle that if a parent gives financial assistance to a newly married
couple to acquire their matrimonial home, the usual inference is that it was intended as a gift to
both of them rather than to one alone.[213] This inference of a joint gift was supported by the behaviour of the parties during the marriage. They organised their finances jointly and all of their

---

[208] Ibid, 928. The wife's contribution to the 'maintenance and improvement of the property' was through redecora-
tion, alterations, and improvements and repairs carried out with or without the assistance of contractors, whose bills
she paid.

[209] [2004] EWCA Civ 546.

[210] [2007] UKPC 53 at [6]. See also *Holman v Howes* [2007] EWCA Civ 877 where the Court of Appeal made it clear
that if it is accepted that both parties have a beneficial interest, then the same approach will be taken to quantification
and 'there need not necessarily be any difference according to whether the legal estate is in one or two names', at [28].
The Court of Appeal also made it clear that the only conduct that can be relied upon is conduct which evidences the
parties' *shared* intentions. The claimant's conduct in this case could not be relied upon because it was simply *unilateral*
conduct which had taken place after the property had been acquired.

[211] [2007] UKPC 53 at [19].    [212] Ibid, [4].

[213] Ibid, [17]. See *McHardy and Sons (A Firm) v Warren* [1994] 2 FLR 338 at 340; *Midland Bank plc v Cooke* [1995] 4
All ER 562 at 570.

income went into a joint bank account from which the mortgage was paid and for which they were jointly liable. The couple were married for almost 20 years and had children. The Privy Council confirmed that the task of the court was to survey the whole course of the parties' conduct in order to ascertain their shared intentions in relation to the property. Placing emphasis on the fact that the parties organised their finances jointly and undertook joint liability for the mortgage,[214] the court concluded that the wife was entitled to a half share.

It should be pointed out, however, that although the general approach to quantification is the same in both sole name and joint names cases, Baroness Hale did suggest in *Stack* that there were some differences.[215] First Baroness Hale said that in joint names cases, the 'fact' that the property has been registered in joint names must be taken into account. Her Ladyship continued:

> It will almost always have been a conscious decision to put the house into joint names . . . Committing oneself to spend large sums of money on a place to live is not normally done by accident or without giving it a moment's thought.[216]

In addition, Baroness Hale considered that:

> when a couple are joint owners of the home and jointly liable for the mortgage, the inferences to be drawn from who pays for what may be very different from the inferences to be drawn when only one is owner of the home. The arithmetical calculation of how much was paid by each is also likely to be less important.[217]

This suggests that who paid for what may be more relevant in sole name cases. However, in both *Midland Bank plc v Cooke* and *Abbott v Abbott*, which were both sole name cases, the court took a broad-brush approach to quantifying the parties' shares, looking at their whole course of conduct in relation to the property. For example, Mrs Cooke was able to establish that she had a beneficial interest after making a small contribution to the purchase price of the property. Once this hurdle was crossed, the court took a broad view of the parties' whole course of dealing and awarded her a half share of the property. It must be remembered, however, that in both of these cases the parties were married. It is entirely possible that a less generous approach would be taken in a sole name case where the parties are not married. There are a number of reasons for this. First, in *Stack*, Baroness Hale said that 'in the cohabitation context, mercenary considerations may be more to the fore than they would be in marriage'.[218] Indeed, in *Midland Bank v Cooke*, Waite LJ stated at the conclusion of his judgment that the fact that the parties were married was important in his determination that Mrs Cooke should receive a half share in the beneficial interest. If the case concerned an unmarried couple it is questionable whether he would have quantified a cohabitant's share so generously. Indeed, in *Mortgage Corporation v Shaire*[219] Neuberger J (as he then was) said that:

> the extent of the financial contribution is perhaps not as important an aspect as it was once thought to be. It may well carry more weight in a case where the parties are unmarried than where they were married.[220]

It is possible that there are enough hooks within these dicta to persuade the courts to prioritise the parties' financial contributions in sole name cases where the parties are unmarried. In addition, it must be remembered that when ascertaining the parties' intentions, the court is concerned with conduct *relating to the property*. More general relationship factors, such as how long the parties

---

[214] The court noted that this has always been regarded as a significant factor [2007] UKPC 53, [18] *per* Baroness Hale citing *Hyett v Stanley* [2003] EWCA Civ 942.

[215] As Lloyd LJ observed in *Holman v Howes* [2007] EWCA Civ 877 at [28].

[216] *Stack v Dowden* [2007] UKHL 17 at [66].

[217] Ibid, [69].     [218] Ibid.     [219] [2001] Ch 743.     [220] Ibid, 750.

lived together and whether they had children, are less important than factors which reveal the parties' approach to their financial affairs, such as whether they were economically interdependent. In *Abbott* the court placed considerable emphasis on the fact that the parties organised their finances jointly and undertook joint liability for the mortgage. The wife was awarded a half share in the property. However, it is by no means certain that the same outcome would have been reached if there had been no such evidence of financial solidarity but the parties had nevertheless lived a lengthy, emotionally interdependent life together as an *unmarried* couple. Thus, while the same general approach is taken to quantification in sole and joint names cases, it is possible that the courts will apply this in a more restrictive way in sole name cases where the parties are unmarried by paying more attention to the parties' financial contributions.

## 2.4 Proprietary estoppel

An alternative to establishing a constructive trust is for the claimant to make out a case of 'proprietary estoppel' in order to acquire a share in the property or to obtain some other remedy in relation to it. There are some overlaps between the theoretical bases of the constructive trust doctrine and proprietary estoppel, to the extent that there has been some debate about whether the doctrines should be assimilated. However, recent jurisprudence has emphasised the significant differences between the two, in particular in the nature of the relief available. Lord Hope said in *Stack v Dowden*[221] that he was:

> now rather less enthusiastic about the notion that proprietary estoppel and 'common interest' constructive trusts can or should be completely assimilated. Proprietary estoppel typically consists of asserting an equitable claim against the conscience of the 'true' owner. The claim is a 'mere equity'. It is to be satisfied by the minimum award necessary to do justice . . . which may sometimes lead to no more than a monetary award. A 'common intention' constructive trust, by contrast, is identifying the true beneficial owner or owners, and the size of their beneficial interests.

While establishing a constructive trust will give the claimant a beneficial interest in the property, making out a case of proprietary estoppel gives the court the discretion to grant whatever remedy is necessary to satisfy the equity. Thus 'the claimant who establishes a proprietary estoppel may do less well that the claimant who establishes a constructive trust'.[222]

The law relating to proprietary estoppel is complex. The doctrine lacks precise definition and it has been left to the courts to mould it through the development of case law. As noted recently, 'there is no definition of proprietary estoppel that is both comprehensive and uncontroversial (and many attempts at one have been neither).'[223] Given the complex nature of proprietary estoppel, it is important to look at case law to ascertain the central elements of the doctrine and the circumstances when it can be invoked.

### 2.4.1 What is proprietary estoppel?

Proprietary estoppel prevents the owner of land from insisting on his or her strict legal rights. It arises where the claimant is deliberately misled into believing, or mistakenly believes, that he or she has a present interest in property owned by another, or that he or she will be given such an interest in the future. The owner of the property must have assured, encouraged, or acquiesced in the claimant's wrongful or mistaken belief and the claimant, in reliance on this belief, must act to his or her detriment. If the owner then seeks to take unconscionable advantage of the claimant by denying him or her the right or benefit which had been expected, a proprietary estoppel may give

---

[221] [2007] UKHL 17 at [37] *per* Lord Hope.     [222] *Q v Q* [2008] EWHC 1874 at [113].
[223] S. Gardner, *An Introduction to Land Law* (2007), p 101: cited by Lord Walker in *Thorner v Major* [2009] UKHL 18.

rise to an equity to which the court will seek to give effect.[224] Recent case law has emphasised that although there are different elements to proprietary estoppel, a broad inquiry must be undertaken to see whether it arises on the facts of a particular case to prevent the unconscionable conduct of the legal owner.[225] In *Gillet v Holt*,[226] Walker LJ said that:

> the doctrine of proprietary estoppel cannot be treated as subdivided into three of four watertight compartments . . . the fundamental principle that equity is concerned to prevent unconscionable conduct permeates all the elements of the doctrine. In the end the court must look at the matter in the round.

Thus, while there are several elements to the doctrine (most notably an assurance or representation by the legal owner, and the non-owner's induced detrimental reliance) these elements are 'often intertwined' and will be considered as part of the court's broad inquiry into whether the legal owner's repudiation of the assurance was unconscionable or unfair in all the circumstances.[227]

### 2.4.2 Was there an assurance or representation by the owner?

To make out a case of proprietary estoppel, there must first be a representation or assurance by the owner that the claimant is to have some interest in the property. What type of assurance will suffice?[228] In *Thorner v Major*,[229] the House of Lords said that the relevant assurance must be 'clear enough'. Whether this is so depends on the facts and circumstances of each individual case. Indeed, the Lords said in *Thorner* that the meaning to be ascribed to one party's words depends on the 'factual context' in which they were made,[230] and it seems that the character of the individuals will also be relevant. This 'factual context' will help to determine how the statements were intended by their maker, how they were understood by the person to whom they were made, and whether such understanding and subsequent reliance were reasonable.[231] The assurance must also relate to some particular asset or property. As Sir Peter Gibson made clear in *Morris v Morris*:[232]

> it is well-established that the representation or assurance must be specific, such as would entitle the person to whom it was made reasonably to rely on it or change his or her position.

While the assurance must relate to an interest in specific property, the actual nature of that interest does not have to be specified.[233] However, more general assurances that the non-owner 'would never want for anything' or 'would be taken care of' will not be enough to found a proprietary

---

[224] *Re Basham (Deceased)* [1987] 1 All ER 405 at 410.

[225] *Gillet v Holt* [2001] Ch 210; *Jennings v Rice* [2002] EWCA Civ 159.

[226] *Gillet v Holt* [2001] Ch 210 at 225.     [227] Ibid.

[228] In *Yeoman's Row Management Ltd v Cobbe* [2008] UKHL 55 the House of Lords cast doubt on the extent to which statements made during commercial negotiations can found a claim of proprietary estoppel should one party subsequently renege on a mere 'gentleman's agreement' that had been reached between the parties. It was held that, in a commercial setting where a formal contract was expected to be formed, the parties cannot rely upon proprietary estoppel to protect their expectations arising from the negotiations. While the decision concerned a commercial case where 'the claimant is typically a business person with access to legal advice and what he or she is expecting to get is a *contract*', at [68] *per* Lord Walker (emphasis in original), one wonders what its impact would be on domestic cases. Indeed, some thought that this restrictive approach sounded the death knell for the doctrine of proprietary estoppel, see B. McFarlane and A. Robertson, 'The Death of Proprietary Estoppel' (2008) Lloyd's Maritime and Commercial Law Quarterly 449. This view, which was described by Lord Walker in *Thorner v Major* [2009] UKHL 18 at [31] as 'apocalyptic', was premature. In *Thorner v Major* [2009] UKHL 18, the House of Lords confirmed that the observations of the court in *Yeoman's Row Management Ltd v Cobbe* were not relevant in the domestic context. See *Yeoman's Row Management Ltd v Cobbe* [2008] UKHL 55 at [68] *per* Lord Walker.

[229] [2009] UKHL 18.     [230] Ibid, [80].     [231] Ibid.

[232] [2008] EWCA Civ 257 at [28]. In *Thorner v Major* [2009] UKHL 18, Lord Walker said that the assurances given to the claimant must relate to identified property owned (or perhaps about to be owned) by the defendant, at [61].

[233] *James v Thomas* [2007] EWCA Civ 1212 at [32].

estoppel.[234] These are simply general representations regarding the non-owner's well-being and because they do not relate to any specific property, they cannot be relied upon to found an estoppel claim. Indeed, words or conduct which lead the non-owner to harbour a mere expectation that he or she will be allowed to continue to live in the property will not be enough.[235] In *James v Thomas*,[236] the owner (Mr James) assured the non-owner that their joint work improving the property would benefit them both and that she would be provided for on his death. Chadwick LJ, in the Court of Appeal, held that these general statements were not 'intended or understood to be a promise of some proprietary interest, either present or in the future' and so were insufficient to found a claim based on proprietary estoppel.[237] Similarly in *Morris v Morris*,[238] the Court of Appeal found that there was no representation made to the claimant which led her to believe that she had an interest in the property in question. While Sir Peter Gibson considered that her partner had behaved badly after the parties had separated, this was not enough, by itself, to show that there had been unconscionable disadvantage for the purposes of establishing proprietary estoppel.[239]

### 2.4.3 Detrimental reliance

If an assurance or representation that the non-owner is to have an interest in the property has been made, the non-owner must rely upon this to his or her detriment. Detriment, for the purposes of proprietary estoppel, is not a 'narrow or technical concept' and, although it can, it does not have to consist of the expenditure of money.[240] A range of conduct, such as domestic labour, indirect financial contributions to the family's general expenditure, and foregoing paid employment, may constitute detrimental reliance as long as it is something substantial.[241] In *Gillett v Holt*,[242] the court said:

> [W]hether the detriment is sufficiently substantial is to be tested by whether it would be unjust or inequitable to allow the assurance to be disregarded.

A good example of proprietary estoppel is *Greasley v Cooke*.[243] Doris Cooke had lived all her adult life with the same family: living as man and wife with one brother, working in the house without payment, looking after a mentally ill member of the household, and remaining there after several members of the family had left or died. She had been encouraged by the family to believe that she could regard the property as her home for the rest of her life and she therefore did not ask for payment for her contributions. At the age of 62, she was told to leave the house by the one surviving brother. The trial judge held that her belief that she could remain in the house for as long as she lived had been induced by assurances given to her by family members, but that she had failed to prove that she had acted to her detriment in reliance on these assurances. The Court of Appeal held that it was to be presumed that she had acted on the faith of these assurances, and that it was up to those who wished to evict her to prove that she had not acted to her detriment or otherwise been prejudiced by remaining in the house, and they failed to do so. The Court of Appeal granted her a declaration that she was entitled to remain rent free in the house for the rest of her life.[244]

The owner's representation regarding the conferral of an interest in the property does not have to be the only reason for the non-owner's conduct, but it does have to be a factor. In *Wayling v Jones*[245] the plaintiff (as they were then called) lived with the deceased and acted as his companion for 16 years. He provided substantial help in running the deceased's business and, in return,

---

[234] *Lissimore v Downing* [2003] 2 FLR 308; *James v Thomas* [2007] EWCA Civ 1212 at [31]–[32].

[235] See N. Piska, 'A Common Intention or a Rare Bird? Proprietary Interests, Personal Claims and Services Rendered by Lovers Post-Acquisition: *James v Thomas; Morris v Morris*' [2009] Child and Family Law Quarterly 104.

[236] [2007] EWCA Civ 1212.      [237] Ibid, [33]–[34]. See also *Holman v Howes* [2007] EWCA Civ 877.

[238] [2008] EWCA Civ 257.      [239] Ibid, [29].      [240] *Gillet v Holt* [2001] Ch 210 at 232.

[241] Ibid.      [242] Ibid, 232.      [243] [1980] 3 All ER 710.

[244] See also *Re Basham (Deceased)* [1987] 1 All ER 405, where the plaintiff also worked without receiving payment.

[245] [1995] 2 FLR 1029.

received pocket money, living expenses, and an express promise that he would inherit the deceased's property, a hotel. On the deceased's death, the plaintiff argued that he was entitled to the value of the hotel as promised to him but the judge at first instance rejected this claim holding that the plaintiff had failed to prove that the detriment he had suffered (not receiving adequate wages and continuing to serve the deceased until his death) had been in reliance on his belief that he would inherit the deceased's property. Allowing the plaintiff's appeal and giving the judgment of the court, Balcombe LJ held that the following principles applied: first, there must be a sufficient link between the promises relied upon and the conduct which constituted detriment; secondly, the promises relied upon did not have to be the sole inducement for the conduct, it was sufficient if they were an inducement; and, thirdly, once it had been established that promises had been made, and that there had been conduct by the plaintiff of such a nature that an inducement could be inferred, then the burden of proof shifted to the defendant to establish that the plaintiff did not rely on the promises.[246]

Proprietary estoppel may therefore come to the assistance of a person who claims an interest in the home he or she shared with their partner in whose name the property is vested. An example of this is *Pascoe v Turner*.[247] After the breakdown of their relationship, Mr Pascoe told Mrs Turner, with whom he had been living for ten years, that the house and its contents were hers. However, no conveyance of the property was ever drawn up. Therefore, although there was evidence of intention by Mr Pascoe to make a gift of the house to Mrs Turner, it was an imperfect gift.[248] However, Mrs Turner, having been told that the house was hers, set about improving it and spent a substantial sum on the property. Mr Pascoe allowed this to happen and at no time suggested that she was putting her money and her labour into his house. Subsequently he brought proceedings for possession. The Court of Appeal held that Mr Pascoe had encouraged or acquiesced in the manner in which Mrs Turner had changed her position for the worse in the belief that the house was hers, and that she was thus able to establish proprietary estoppel. The court satisfied the equity arising in this case by transferring the house to Mrs Turner.[249] Thus, where a person has been assured that he or she will be able to remain in property owned by their partner, and where the former acts to his or her detriment in reliance on this assurance (eg by spending money on the property) equity may intervene to grant a remedy.

### 2.4.4 Conduct found insufficient to give rise to proprietary estoppel

In *Coombes v Smith*,[250] Mrs Coombes, a married woman, formed a relationship with Mr Smith, a married man, and had his child. Mr Smith bought a house intended for them both, but although Mrs Coombes left her husband and moved in, Mr Smith never did. He refused her requests to put the property in joint names, but reassured her that he would always look after her. He paid the bills and the mortgage and frequently visited her and their child. Mrs Coombes decorated the house on a number of occasions and tidied the garden. When their relationship eventually broke down, Mrs Coombes sought an order that Mr Smith transfer the property and its contents to her absolutely, or alternatively sought a declaration that he was bound to allow her to occupy the property and to use its contents for the rest of her life.

Mr Smith conceded that Mrs Coombes had an equity to remain in the property until their daughter reached 17, although he said that she had no entitlement to remain in the property after that time. The court upheld his claim and said that no proprietary estoppel had arisen. It held that

---

[246] The plaintiff was awarded the net proceeds of the sale of the hotel.     [247] [1979] 2 All ER 945.

[248] Law of Property Act 1925, s 52(1).

[249] In granting this remedy the court was clearly influenced by the fact that the court regarded Mr Pascoe as a man who would pursue his purpose of evicting Mrs Turner from the house by any legal means at his disposal, and that therefore Mrs Turner needed a remedy which would be effective to protect her against any future manifestations of Mr Pascoe's ruthlessness. It rejected the remedy of granting her a licence to live in the house for the rest of her life because she could not protect this right against a purchaser for value without notice.

[250] [1986] 1 WLR 808.

Mrs Coombes's belief that Mr Smith would always provide her with a roof over her head was quite different from a belief that she had the legal right to remain in the property against his wishes, and therefore she was unable to establish that she had acted under a mistaken belief that she had security of tenure. It distinguished *Pascoe v Turner*[251] on the grounds that there were no words of gift and there were no improvements made to the property in the mistaken belief that the property was hers.

The most significant feature of the judgment from the point of view of a person who claims that she has an entitlement to remain in her ex-partner's house, was the manner in which the court approached the assurance given by Mr Smith to Mrs Coombes that 'he would never see her without a roof over her head'. The court said that all of the statements relied upon by the plaintiff were made by the owner while the relationship was continuing and thus did not amount to an assurance of what would happen in the event of the relationship breaking down. The court further held that, even if Mrs Coombes had been led to believe that she had a right to remain in the property for the rest of her life, she had not behaved in a way which was detrimental to her or changed her position in reliance on Mr Smith's representation. It held that it would be wholly unreal to find that she had allowed herself to become pregnant in reliance on some mistaken belief as to her legal rights and, in any event, allowing oneself to become pregnant could not amount to detriment in the context of proprietary estoppel. Nor did any prejudice arise from her having redecorated the property, as this was done in the context of her continuing relationship with Mr Smith. Thus even if the court assumed the existence of the requisite mistaken belief about her legal rights, Mrs Coombes failed in her claim because she was unable to establish that she had acted in such a way as to give rise to an equity in her favour.

More recent case law has confirmed this view. Thus, if the owner of the property makes general assurances to his or her partner during the course of the relationship regarding their continued well-being, the court is unlikely to find that this equates to a representation regarding either the ownership or occupation of the family home should the relationship break down.[252] Similarly, as with the constructive trust, the court may be unwilling to find that the claimant has acted to his or her detriment in reliance on the owner's assurance if their conduct was carried out for some reason other than the claimant thought that he or she was acquiring an interest in the property. In *James v Thomas*,[253] for example, the claimant's activities in contributing to her partner's business and working to improve the property were explained by Chadwick LJ on the basis that the couple were making their joint life together as man and wife. He said:

> [T]he Cottage was their home: the business was their livelihood. It is a mistake to think that the motives which lead parties in such a relationship to act as they do are necessarily attributable to pecuniary self-interest.[254]

There is a realism in the court's view that assurances made by the owning party about property rights when an unmarried cohabiting relationship was happy were almost certainly not intended to have binding force when the relationship broke down. However, these cases also show that proprietary estoppel, like the constructive trust, cannot handle the economic fall-out of a relationship breakdown and the disadvantageous situation which one partner may find themselves in if he or she had not paid for, or financially contributed towards, the acquisition of the family home. The law relating to the acquisition of a beneficial interest in the family home, and the law of proprietary estoppel, are not truly part of family law; they are about property law and its amelioration by equity. It is persons who have been living in a family relationship who usually need to rely on equity at its most generous, but it has been seen that this generosity is limited by doctrines which have universal

---

[251] [1979] 2 All ER 945.  [252] *James v Thomas* [2007] EWCA Civ 1212; *Morris v Morris* [2008] EWCA Civ 257.
[253] [2007] EWCA Civ 1212.  [254] Ibid, [36].

application. Equity has a part to play in assisting the unmarried where there is unfairness, but this part is limited.

### 2.4.5 Satisfying the equity in a case of proprietary estoppel

If proprietary estoppel is made out, the court has discretion as to what remedy to provide in light of the assurances and the nature of the detrimental reliance.[255] When deciding what remedy to grant, the court will consider what is 'the minimum equity to do justice to the plaintiff'.[256] A wide-ranging number of remedies are available such as granting a licence to the claimant,[257] monetary compensation,[258] or conferring some sort of proprietary interest on the claimant.[259] However, case law has made it clear that there must be *proportionality* between the expectation of the claimant and the detriment that he or she has actually suffered:

> [T]he value of [the equity which arises] will depend upon all the circumstances including the expectation and detriment. The task of the court is to do justice. The most essential requirement is that there must be proportionality between the expectation and the detriment.[260]

In *Jennings v Rice*[261] the claimant began working for the deceased as a gardener in 1970. Over time he became her carer and from the late 1980s she stopped paying him for his services telling him instead that he would have the house and furniture on her death. During the last few years of her life, the claimant, at the deceased's request, spent nearly every night on a sofa in a sitting room of her house to provide her with security. However, when she died she did not leave a will and the claimant argued that he was entitled to the value of the house and furniture (worth £435,000) under the doctrine of proprietary estoppel. The Court of Appeal said that when deciding how to satisfy an equity based on proprietary estoppel, it was essential that there was proportionality between the claimant's expectation and the detriment suffered. While the claimant may have expected to receive the full value of the house, the Court of Appeal said that this would not be proportionate to the detriment which he had incurred. The court upheld the decision of the judge at first instance to award him £200,000 as the minimum necessary to satisfy his equity. Thus, the remedy will not necessarily meet the claimant's expectations in relation to what was promised and may simply compensate the claimant for the detriment which was incurred by reliance on the assurance or representation.

## 2.5 Orders under the Trusts of Land and Appointment of Trustees Act 1996

If the family home is co-owned by the parties but, upon relationship breakdown, they cannot reach agreement about whether the property should be sold and how the proceeds divided, or whether one party should continue living in the property (particularly where it is still a home to the parties' children) the provisions of the Trusts of Land and Appointment of Trustees Act 1996 (TOLATA) will apply. Where beneficial entitlement to land is shared, the TOLATA provides that it is held as a trust of land.

---

[255] Thus in *Re Basham (Deceased)* [1987] 1 All ER 405 the plaintiff had been encouraged to believe that she would inherit a cottage in return for caring for the deceased. Since the plaintiff had subordinated her own interests and wish to move away in reliance on this belief, it was held that she was entitled to inherit the cottage.

[256] *Crabb v Arun District Council* [1976] Ch 179 at 198.     [257] *Inwards v Baker* [1965] 2 QB 29.

[258] *Dodsworth v Dodsworth* (1973) 228 EG 1115.

[259] This could be a life interest (*Greasley v Cooke* [1980] 1 WLR 1306), a fee simple (*Pascoe v Turner* [1979] 1 WLR 431), or an easement (*Crabb v Arun District Council* [1976] Ch 179).

[260] *Jennings v Rice* [2002] EWCA Civ 159 at [36] *per* Aldous LJ; *Holman v Howes* [2007] EWCA Civ 877 at [40]. See A. Robertson, 'The Reliance Basis of Proprietary Estoppel Remedies' (2008) 72 Conveyancer and Property Lawyer 295–321.

[261] [2002] EWCA Civ 159.

---

**Key legislation**

Under section 14 of the TOLATA, any person who is a trustee of land, or who has an interest in property which is subject to a trust of land may apply to the court for an order to resolve the disputes concerning the occupation and sale of the property. The court has the power to make an order which relates to the exercise by the trustees of any of their functions, or it will declare the nature or extent of a person's interest in the property subject to the trust, and in either case the court may make any such order as it thinks fit.

---

This means that the court can order a sale of the property, or order that the sale be postponed. If the court orders that the sale is postponed and one partner is allowed to remain in occupation, that person may be ordered to pay compensation (occupation rent) to the excluded party during their period of occupation.[262]

It must be emphasised, however, that the TOLATA is not a property-adjustment regime similar to that available to govern the property disputes of divorcing spouses or civil partners who are dissolving their partnership.[263] Although under section 14 the court is empowered to make 'such order as it thinks fit', it cannot alter the parties' respective beneficial interests. If the property is in the sole name of one party and the non-owner fails to establish that he or she has a beneficial interest in the property under the application of ordinary trust principles, the court does not have the power under the TOLATA to confer any such interest on the non-owner. Thus the TOLATA operates within the strict confines of the parties' existing beneficial interests in the property and while it can determine the sale and occupation of the property, it cannot alter the parties' existing beneficial interests in it.

### 2.5.1 Criteria for determining applications made under the TOLATA

---

**Key legislation**

Section 15 of the TOLATA details the matters to which the court must have regard when determining an application. They include:

(a) the intentions of the person or persons (if any) who created the trust,
(b) the purposes for which the property subject to the trust is held,
(c) the welfare of any minor who occupies or might reasonably be expected to occupy any land subject to the trust as his home, and
(d) the interests of any secured creditor or beneficiary.

---

[262] TOLATA, s 13. These statutory provisions replace the old powers of equitable accounting where a beneficiary in occupation of the property would be ordered to pay an occupation rent to a beneficiary who was excluded from the property. However, the House of Lords pointed out in *Stack v Dowden* [2007] UKHL 17 that although the governing principles are now found in the TOLATA rather than under the old principles of equity, the results will usually be the same, at [94], *per* Baroness Hale and [150] *per* Lord Neuberger. In *Stack*, Mr Stack applied for occupation rent to compensate him for his exclusion from the property and to cover the cost of his alternative accommodation. His claim was rejected by the majority on the basis that the house was to be sold as soon as possible and thus he 'would not be kept out of his money for long', at [94]. See also *Wilcox v Tait* [2006] EWCA Civ 1867; *Murphy v Gooch* [2007] EWCA Civ 603; *Young v Lauretani* [2007] EWHC 1244 (Ch); *Rahnema v Rahbari* [2008] 2 P & CR DG5. See further E. Cooke, 'Accounting Payments: Please Can We Get the Maths Right?' [2007] Family Law 1024.

[263] This adjustive regime is found under the Matrimonial Causes Act 1973, Pt II; Civil Partnership Act 2004, Sch 5. See Chapter 4.

Section 15(2) further provides that where the application concerns the power of the trustees to exclude or restrict the right of a beneficiary to occupy the land,[264] the court must also have regard to the circumstances and wishes of each of the beneficiaries who is entitled to occupy the land.

How do the provisions of the Act affect the real difficulties faced by cohabitants when their relationship breaks down? Can the Act assist them when they are unhappy living together under the same roof? What are the implications for cohabitants who enjoy a shared beneficial entitlement as equitable joint tenants or tenants in common where one wishes to realise his or her beneficial share in the property and the other wishes to remain in occupation? The following sections will consider these questions.

### 2.5.2  Disputes over occupation of the property

Consider first a dispute between beneficially entitled cohabitants over occupation of the property. There is an overlap here with the powers of the courts to make occupation orders under the Family Law Act 1996, section 33.[265] It is suggested that a cohabitant would be ill-advised to apply for an order under section 14 of the TOLATA because the courts' powers under the Family Law Act 1996 are more extensive. Furthermore, under the Family Law Act 1996, the criteria guiding the courts' decision-making focus on matters such as the parties' respective resources, the likely effect of any order on the health, safety, or well-being of the parties and any relevant child, and, where significant harm is alleged, a balance of harm test is applied.[266] These welfare-orientated criteria are more appropriate to disputes over occupation of the family home than those contained in section 15 of the TOLATA. A cohabitant might well face difficulty in persuading a court to exclude his or her partner's right to occupy the family home under the Family Law Act 1996 because courts regard exclusion orders of this nature as draconian. However, he or she has more of a chance of success under that Act than under the TOLATA. The court's powers under section 14(1) only relate to the exercise by the trustees of any of their functions, and trustees may not unreasonably exclude or restrict entitlement to occupy the land.[267]

### 2.5.3  Disagreement over sale of the family home

It is where cohabitants cannot agree over whether the property should be retained or sold that the provisions of the TOLATA may come to their assistance. The 1996 Act repeals section 30 of the Law of Property Act 1925 (which governed the execution of the trust for sale), and the criteria in section 15 are aimed at consolidating and rationalising the approach previously adopted by the courts when applying section 30.[268] The framers of the Act did not intend to change the law on how the courts had exercised their powers under section 30. Rather, it was their intention to mirror the position which had been reached through the development of case law. Nevertheless, an important difference between the old law and the TOLATA is that cases prior to the Act which involved a trust for sale were decided against a background of a duty to sell. That duty no longer exists, meaning that courts enjoy greater flexibility when determining whether to postpone sale.[269] Another difference is the introduction of statutory criteria to guide the courts in the exercise of their discretion.[270] When the court is exercising its powers under the TOLATA and deciding whether to order or postpone the sale of the property, one important factor will be the underlying

---

[264] Section 13.      [265] Occupation orders are explained in Chapter 3.

[266] Family Law Act 1996, s 33(6), (7).

[267] TOLATA, s 13(2). The trustees must take account of the intentions of the person(s) who created the trust, the purposes for which the land is held, and the circumstances and wishes of the beneficiaries (s 13(4)).

[268] Following proposals for reform made in *Transfer of Land, Trusts of Land* (Law Com No 181, 1989). Section 30 provided: If the trustees for sale refuse to sell or to exercise any of [their] powers . . . , or any requisite consent cannot be obtained, any person may apply to the court for a vesting or other order for giving effect to the proposed transaction or for an order directing the trustees for sale to give effect thereto, and the court may make such order as it thinks fit.

[269] *Mortgage Corpn v Shaire* [2001] Ch 743 at 758 *per* Neuberger J (as he then was).

[270] Section 15. These criteria are given equal weight.

*purpose* of the trust. If the property was bought as a home for the couple but the parties' relationship has broken down, the court is likely to order sale because the purpose for which the property was acquired has come to an end.[271] However, where the purpose was to provide a home for the family and this has not been extinguished because children are still living in the property, then sale may be postponed whilst this purpose still exists.[272]

In situations where third parties have a financial interest in the proceedings or where one of the parties is bankrupt, the courts have wider concerns. Section 15(1)(d) of the TOLATA directs the court to consider 'the interests of any secured creditor of any beneficiary' when exercising its discretion. A trustee in bankruptcy has the duty to realise the debtor's assets for the benefit of the creditors, and this may involve seeking a sale of the family home under section 14 of the TOLATA. Case law has established that the rights of creditors will usually prevail over the rights of other family members living in the property even if it is still being used as the family home. An order for the sale of the home will be made unless there are exceptional circumstances, and the fact that family members, including children, face eviction which would cause them hardship does not amount to an exceptional circumstance which would either prevent sale or justify its postponement.[273] Nourse LJ said in the leading case of *Re Citro (A Bankrupt)* that while such circumstances engender:

> a natural sympathy in all who hear of them, [they] cannot be described as exceptional. They are the melancholy consequences of debt and improvidence with which every civilised society has been familiar.[274]

It seems that only circumstances which are inherently unusual will qualify as exceptional.[275] For example, cases where a sale has been postponed due to the presence of exceptional circumstances have related to a family member's illness.[276] However, even if there are exceptional circumstances, the court can still order sale of the property.[277]

In addition, section 335A(3) of the Insolvency Act 1986 provides that once a year has elapsed since the first vesting of the bankrupt's estate in a trustee, the court must assume, unless the circumstances of the case are exceptional, that the interests of the bankrupt's creditors outweigh all other considerations. In *Barca v Mears*[278] it was questioned whether this narrow construction of 'exceptional circumstances' under which the rights of creditors will usually prevail was compatible with the European Convention on Human Rights and the right to respect for private and family life under Article 8. The court did not reach a firm conclusion on the issue. However, subsequent cases have suggested that human rights considerations do not require any 'significant modification' to the approach currently taken when balancing the interests of the creditors, the bankrupt, and the bankrupt's family.[279] It seems that, until further clarification, the impact of human rights considerations on the law in this area remains a moot point.

### 2.6 Transfer of tenancies between cohabitants

Section 53 of and Schedule 7 to the Family Law Act 1996 introduced for the first time a form of property transfer order between unmarried cohabitants.[280] The power to transfer specified tenancies on

---

[271] *Jones v Challenger* [1960] 1 All ER 785.      [272] *Re Evers' Trust* [1980] 3 All ER 399.

[273] *Re Citro (A Bankrupt)* [1991] 1 FLR 71; *Dean v Stout (Trustee in Bankruptcy)* [2005] EWHC 3315 (Ch); *Barca v Mears* [2005] 2 FLR 1; *Donohue v Ingram* [2006] EWHC 282.

[274] [1991] 1 FLR 71 at 82.      [275] *Re Citro (A Bankrupt)* [1991] 1 FLR 71.

[276] *Re Bremner (A Bankrupt)* [1999] 1 LR 912; *Claughton v Charalambous* [1999] 1 FLR 740.

[277] *Dean v Stout* [2005] EWHC 3315 (Ch).

[278] [2004] EWHC 2170 (Ch). See also *Donohue v Ingram* [2006] EWHC 282 (Ch) and *Jackson v Bell* [2001] EWCA Civ 387.

[279] *Foyle v Turner* [2007] BPIR 43; *Turner v Avis* [2009] 1 FLR 74.

[280] A transfer of tenancy order can also be made between spouses on the granting of a decree of divorce, a decree of nullity, or a decree of judicial separation, or between civil partners when the court has the power to make a property adjustment order (Family Law Act 1996, Sch 7, para 2). Remarriage or the formation of a subsequent civil partnership

making divorce or separation orders, or a nullity decree, was re-enacted and extended to cohabitants where they separate. The legislation provides that where a cohabitant is entitled either solely or jointly with the other cohabitant to occupy a dwelling-house by virtue of a relevant tenancy,[281] and where the cohabitants cease to live together as husband and wife, the court may make an order transferring the tenancy from one to the other, provided that the dwelling-house was a home in which they lived together as husband and wife.[282] A relevant tenancy means:

(a) a protected tenancy or statutory tenancy within the meaning of the Rent Act 1977;

(b) a statutory tenancy within the meaning of the Rent (Agriculture) Act 1976;

(c) a secure tenancy within the meaning of section 79 of the Housing Act 1985; or

(d) an assured tenancy or assured agricultural occupancy within the meaning of Part 1 of the Housing Act 1988.

In determining whether to exercise its power to transfer the tenancy, the court must have regard to all the circumstances of the case including when and how the tenancy was granted or otherwise acquired, the housing needs and housing resources of the parties and any relevant child, their financial resources, and the likely effect of an order or the decision not to make an order on the health, safety, or well-being of the parties or any relevant child.[283] Where only one cohabitant is entitled to occupy the dwelling-house by virtue of the tenancy, the court, in addition, must take account of the conduct of the parties in relation to each other and otherwise, the nature of their relationship, the length of time during which they have lived together as husband and wife, whether there are or have been children who are children of both parties or for whom both parties have or have had parental responsibility, and the length of time that has elapsed since the parties ceased to live together.[284] The court must also consider the suitability of the parties as tenants[285] and the landlord must be given an opportunity to be heard.[286]

If a transfer order is made, the transferor can be compensated for his or her loss. The transferee may be directed by the court to make payments to the transferor.[287] The court, when deciding whether to make such an order, must have regard to the financial loss which would otherwise be suffered by the transferor, the parties' needs, their financial resources, and their financial obligations.[288] Such payments may be deferred or made in instalments but only where immediate payment of the sum by the transferee would cause the transferee greater financial hardship than any financial hardship to the transferor caused by postponement.[289] In addition, the court may direct that both cohabitants are to be jointly and severally liable to discharge or perform the liabilities and obligations in respect of the dwelling-house.[290] It may further direct that one cohabitant is to indemnify the

---

prevents a spouse or civil partner from applying for a transfer of tenancy order. However, the marriage of a cohabitant does not affect his or her right to apply for such an order.

[281] See *Gay v Sheeran* [1999] 3 All ER 795 which indicates that an order can only be made where the tenancy was held either solely by one cohabitant or jointly between the two cohabitants but not where the tenancy was held by a cohabitant and a third party.

[282] Schedule 7, paras 3 and 4.

[283] The housing needs and resources of the couple took priority in the court's decision in the recent case of *Guerroudj v Rymarczyk* [2015] EWCA Civ 743. In this case a couple lived together as joint tenants in local authority accommodation. The man suffered from back problems and, therefore, was entitled to employment and support allowance. When the parties' relationship broke down, both parties issued proceedings for a transfer of the tenancy in their sole name. The judge granted the tenancy to the woman on the grounds that if the man were made homeless, the local authority would be under a duty to rehouse him on a priority basis due to his disability. However, the woman would be likely to suffer a greater hardship if she lost the tenancy. The Court of Appeal dismissed the man's appeal holding that the judge was entitled to find that the man's medical problems had been the main reason for him being offered the tenancy in the first place, and therefore it was not unreasonable to conclude that he would once again be rehoused and treated as a priority.

[284] Schedule 7, para 5. These criteria are the same as those which the court must take into account when determining whether to make an occupation order under the Family Law Act 1996, ss 33 and 36; see Chapter 3.

[285] Family Law Act 1996, Sch 7, para 5(c).   [286] Ibid, para 14(1).   [287] Ibid, para 10(1).

[288] Ibid, para 10(4).   [289] Ibid, para 10(2), (5).   [290] Ibid, para 11(1).

other against payments made, or expenses incurred, in discharging or performing such liabilities and obligations.[291]

Research has shown that cohabiting couples are more likely to rent their home than married couples[292] and so, upon relationship breakdown, it is useful that courts have the power to transfer a relevant tenancy into the name of one party. Not only do they allow a tenancy in joint names to be transferred into the applicant's sole name, but they also confer power on the court to transfer a tenancy to one partner even where the other partner was the sole tenant. The criteria which guide the court, although different from the criteria which guide courts when making property adjustment orders between spouses and civil partners on divorce/dissolution,[293] nonetheless direct the court to engage in a similar exercise, namely to discover the nature and extent of the parties' resources and to balance their respective needs. However, there is little evidence to indicate how this power is exercised and how often it is used.[294] Further, even though, in comparative terms, cohabitants may rent more often than married couples, overall cohabitants are more likely to be owner-occupiers.[295] However, the property adjustment power under Schedule 7 to the Family Law Act 1996 only relates to certain residential tenancies in the social and private sector and does not apply to disputes concerning an owner-occupied family home. As we have seen, these disputes are resolved according to trust law principles which do not give the courts the discretionary power to consider welfare-based criteria and to resolve disputes in the interests of fairness.

## 2.7 Schedule 1 to the Children Act 1989

The only time settlements of property and property transfer orders can be made between cohabitants is under Schedule 1 to the Children Act 1989. However, these orders are of limited use because they can only be made for the benefit of the child where the couple have children and not in order to reach a fair outcome between the cohabitants themselves. Under these provisions, if an unmarried couple with a child separate, the court may order that the child and the primary carer are allowed to remain in the family home or that a property be purchased for their accommodation while the child is dependent. However, once the child has reached the age of majority or has ceased full-time education, the property will revert to its true owner and the court does not have the power to adjust the parties' strict property entitlements in the interests of fairness.[296] This is clearly of only short-term use to a person who has no ownership interest in the property but has been allowed to live there while caring for a child:

> [A]lthough a carer may be secure for the duration of the child's dependency, she is likely eventually to lose her home and, unless she has been able to establish a [beneficial] share . . . or has saved hard in the interim (or established a new relationship), be in the position of Mrs Burns with nowhere to go. This makes Schedule 1 a less attractive option than it might otherwise appear.[297]

---

[291] Ibid, para 11(2).

[292] Office for National Statistics, General Household Survey 2007 (2008), Table 4.10, available at http://www.ons.gov.uk/ons/rel/ghs/general-household-survey/2007-report/index.html.

[293] Matrimonial Causes Act 1973, Pt II; Civil Partnership Act 2004, Sch 5. See Chapter 4.

[294] See Law Commission, *Cohabitation: The Financial Consequences of Relationship Breakdown* (Law Com No 307, 2007), para A.66. Recent research suggests that many lawyers have no experience of an application to transfer a tenancy, G. Douglas, J. Pearce, and H. Woodward, Cardiff Law School Research Paper No 1, 'A Failure of Trust: Resolving Property Disputes on Cohabitation Breakdown' (2007), para 8.40.

[295] Office for National Statistics, *General Household Survey 2007* (2008), Table 4.10, available at http://www.ons.gov.uk/ons/rel/ghs/general-household-survey/2007-report/index.html.

[296] See *A v A (A Minor: Financial Provision)* [1994] 1 FLR 657; *T v S (Financial Provision for Children)* [1994] 2 FLR 883; *Re P (Child: Financial Provision)* [2003] EWCA Civ 837; *N v D* [2008] 1 FLR 1629. These provisions and relevant case law are discussed in more detail in Chapter 6.

[297] G. Douglas, J. Pearce, and H. Woodward, Cardiff Law School Research Paper No 1, 'A Failure of Trust: Resolving Property Disputes on Cohabitation Breakdown' (2007), para 3.46. See J. Tod and E. Cooke, 'Schedule 1 and the Need for Reform: *N v D*' [2008] Family Law 751.

Evidence suggests that this provision is not used that much,[298] that there are procedural difficulties surrounding its application,[299] and that it is only suitable where there are enough assets to fund two properties.[300]

## 2.8 **The need for reform**

As we have seen, when unmarried couples separate their property disputes are resolved by the application of ordinary trust law principles. It is generally accepted, however, that these principles, which are not specially designed for application to family law cases, are unsuitable. Under these principles, the courts cannot redistribute the parties' property to achieve a fair outcome between them but must instead search for the parties' shared intentions in relation to ownership (not occupation) of the property. By contrast, when spouses and civil partners end their relationship by divorce or dissolution, a specifically designed set of family law principles determines their post-relationship property and financial arrangements. Under these principles, the courts can redistribute property ownership unfettered by the restrictions inherent in trust law and can specifically take account of the contributions which each party has made to the welfare of the family. It has been said many times that the lack of a similar legal framework to govern the disputes of unmarried cohabitants on relationship breakdown remains one of the most urgent policy questions in family law. Many have argued that specially designed family law principles which are capable of taking the full range of the parties' contributions into account and assessing their prospective needs should be introduced to resolve these disputes. In 2007, the Law Commission recommended proposals to reform the law in this area but these have been shelved by the Government for the time being.

The following section will outline some deficiencies in the current law, before outlining the recommendations of the Law Commission and other policy-driven initiatives to reform the law which have, as yet, come to nothing.

### 2.8.1 **Arguments in favour of reform**

#### 2.8.1.1 *The search for the parties' shared intentions*

The constructive trust, which is now the primary legal mechanism to determine the parties' respective shares in the family home, is based on ascertaining the parties' shared intentions in relation to ownership of the property. However, more often than not, cohabitants will have given no thought to these issues during the relationship either due a reluctance to contemplate their relationship breaking down or perhaps because they do not appreciate the importance of articulating their intentions in this regard. Indeed, a large number of cohabitants falsely believe that once they have lived together for a period of time they have the same rights as married couples.[301] This failure to communicate gives rise to serious difficulties both in determining whether a trust arises and in quantifying the extent of the claiming party's beneficial interest. Furthermore, even if the parties have discussed the matter, there may be no clear and reliable evidence of their intentions. The court's task will then be to infer the parties' intention from their conduct.

It has been observed that this judicial search for the parties' common intention is an uncertain and artificial exercise which can give rise to illogical outcomes.[302] For example, as we have seen, a

---

[298] See S. Arthur, J. Lewis, M. Maclean, S. Finch, and R. Fitzgerald, 'Settling Up: Making Financial Arrangements after Divorce or Separation' (National Centre for Social Research, 2002); G. Douglas, J. Pearce, and H. Woodward, Cardiff Law School Research Paper No 1, 'A Failure of Trust: Resolving Property Disputes on Cohabitation Breakdown' (2007).

[299] Ibid, paras 7.28–7.30.     [300] Ibid, para 8.50.

[301] A. Barlow, C. Burgoyne, E. Clery, and J. Smithson, 'Cohabitation and the Law: Myths, Money and the Media' in A. Park et al (eds), *British Social Attitudes: The 24th Report* (London: Sage, 2008).

[302] Law Commission, *Sharing Homes: A Discussion Paper* (Law Com No 278, 2002), para 2.106; Law Commission, *Cohabitation: The Financial Consequences of Relationship Breakdown, A Consultation Paper* (Law Com No 179, 2006), Part 4.

common intention may be found where the legal owner lied about the reasons why the property was not put into joint names thus giving the impression that he or she intended to share ownership of the property when no such intention existed (such as in *Eves v Eves*[303]). By contrast, no common intention will be found by the legal owner's mere promises of future support to his or her partner (as in *James v Thomas*[304]). It also remains very unclear from what conduct the court will infer a common intention.

The core problem is that this doctrinal framework, which is fixated on the parties' intentions, is based on assumptions about the behaviour of cohabiting couples. However, empirical research casts doubt on the reliability of these assumptions. For example, the presumption that equity follows the law, which means that joint legal ownership will lead to the presumption of joint beneficial ownership, may not reflect the parties' actual intentions. As Lord Neuberger (dissenting) recognised in *Stack v Dowden*:[305]

> The property may be bought in joint names for reasons which cast no light on the parties' intentions with regard to beneficial ownership. It may be the solicitor's decision or assumption, the lender's preference for the security of two borrowers, or the happenstance of how the initial contact with the solicitor was made.

This view is confirmed by research which shows that couples who put their home into joint names did not tend to understand the consequences of their actions and did not appreciate that the property would then be owned equally.[306] This study also found that these couples typically showed little interest in the significance of sole or joint ownership. This was due to the fact that they simply did not understand the legal jargon associated with these concepts, and also when they were at the point of moving in together, they were generally unwilling to contemplate the relationship breaking down.[307]

In addition, the case law shows that when ascertaining the parties' shared intentions, the courts pay great attention to the way in which the parties organised their finances, asking questions such as whether the parties were financially interdependent; whether they had a joint bank account; and how responsibility for the household finances was shared. Such evidence will have significant consequences when determining the beneficial interests in the home because it gives the court a basis upon which to draw conclusions about the parties' intentions in relation to property ownership. For example, in *Stack*, the fact that the parties retained their financial independence led the court to conclude that this was an unusual case which meant that the presumption of joint beneficial ownership was rebutted. However, research has shown that the manner in which the parties organised their property and finances is not a reliable indicator of other aspects of their relationship, such as their commitment or their intentions regarding ownership of the family home.[308] For example, if a couple have separate bank accounts this does not necessarily indicate separate finances.[309] Once again, Lord Neuberger was cautious about drawing such conclusions in *Stack* and said:

> There is a substantial difference, in law, in commercial terms, in practice, and almost always in terms of value and importance, between the ownership of a home and the ownership of a bank account or, indeed, furniture, furnishings and other chattels.[310]

---

[303] [1975] 3 All ER 768.     [304] [2007] EWCA Civ 1212.     [305] [2007] UKHL 17 at [113].

[306] G. Douglas, J. Pearce, and H. Woodward, 'Cohabitants, Property and the Law: A Study of Injustice' (2009) 72(1) Modern Law Review 24 at 39.

[307] Ibid.

[308] Ibid, 37–8; A. Barlow, C. Burgoyne, and J. Smithson, *The Living Together Campaign—An Investigation of its Impact on Legally Aware Cohabitants* (London: Ministry of Justice, 2007), p 42.

[309] A. Barlow, C. Burgoyne, E. Clery, and J. Smithson, 'Cohabitation and the Law: Myths, Money and the Media' in A. Park et al (eds), *British Social Attitudes: The 24th Report* (London: Sage, 2008).

[310] *Stack v Dowden* [2007] UKHL 17 at [133]–[134].

### 2.8.1.2 Evidential problems

The search for the parties' shared intentions is made all the more artificial when one considers that the court is attempting, *retrospectively*, to ascertain these intentions. It should be borne in mind that this inquiry arises on relationship breakdown when the parties are in dispute about ownership of the property. This means that the parties' recollections of their past dealings are likely to be tainted by the breakdown and the probable ill-feeling associated with this, and it is unlikely that the parties will offer an unbiased account of their own intentions towards the property. As Baroness Hale pointed out:

> In family disputes, strong feelings are aroused when couples split up. These often lead the parties, honestly but mistakenly, to reinterpret the past in self-exculpatory or vengeful terms.[311]

Thus, it is very hard to obtain reliable evidence about the parties' actual intentions surrounding the property either when it was acquired or during the parties' relationship.

### 2.8.1.3 The law is unclear and open to interpretation

As the Law Commission has pointed out, the content of the law in this area is wholly dependent on the development of case law. The lack of a statutory framework to govern the financial and property disputes of unmarried cohabitants on relationship breakdown means that any change in the law is dependent on the right case coming along and reaching the Supreme Court,[312] and even then it is open to interpretation. For example, it remains very unclear whether common intention can now be inferred from indirect financial contributions. Thus, the law in this area is extremely complex and research has shown that many solicitors are uncomfortable in dealing with these cases.[313] This creates obvious difficulties when advising clients about the likely outcome of a legal dispute.

### 2.8.1.4 Property law principles can produce unfair outcomes

It has been pointed out that the current law is unfair, uncertain, and illogical.[314] One of the main problems is that property law principles do not give value to the contributions a partner makes to the welfare of the family, nor do they take any account of the economic sacrifices made by a partner who foregoes or limits a career in order to take care of the house and children.[315] In a sole name case, a common intention to share the property will not be inferred from domestic contributions and thus such contributions, by themselves, will not be sufficient to establish a constructive trust.[316] In addition, even if there is evidence of express common intention, the non-owner's performance of domestic contributions is unlikely to be sufficient to constitute detrimental reliance because they may be classed as contributions which he or she would have made in any event and not because it was thought that they would generate an interest in the property.[317] This assessment is probably correct in that such familial contributions are unlikely to have been made due to 'pecuniary self-interest'.[318] However, a different outcome would result if these contributions were considered within a remedial family law framework which had the flexibility to recognise their value to the welfare of the family as well as acknowledging the economic sacrifices associated with making these contributions. The doctrinal framework of the property law principles within which they are currently assessed is wholly inadequate because these principles require the contributions

---

[311] Ibid, [67].

[312] Law Commission, *Cohabitation: The Financial Consequences of Relationship Breakdown, A Consultation Paper* (Law Com No 179, 2006), para 5.100.

[313] G. Douglas, J. Pearce, and H. Woodward, 'Cohabitants, Property and the Law: A Study of Injustice' (2009) 72(1) Modern Law Review 24 at 41.

[314] Law Commission, *Cohabitation: The Financial Consequences of Relationship Breakdown, A Consultation Paper* (Law Com No 179, 2006), para 4.1.

[315] Ibid, para 4.5.     [316] *Burns v Burns* [1984] Ch 317.

[317] *James v Thomas* [2007] EWCA Civ 1212.     [318] Ibid, [36].

in question to evidence an intention to share ownership of the property and to constitute detrimental reliance, which insists that their performance is due to a belief that a proprietary interest would result. This led the Law Commission to conclude that:

> the current law can produce unfair outcomes for cohabitants, in particular for the primary carer of children who may experience significant economic disadvantage following separation.[319]

Indeed, empirical research has identified four situations where the current law can result in unfair outcomes.[320] As outlined earlier, the obvious situation is the 'Mrs Burns' scenario where a cohabitant fails to establish a beneficial interest in the family home, even after a lengthy relationship, because she has made no direct financial contribution to its acquisition. In the study, the disadvantaged non-owner was always the female partner who had cared for the children during a lengthy cohabitation.[321] Secondly, the researchers identified a 'newer category of injustice' where a home was owned by one partner before the cohabitation began but was then re-mortgaged and put into the joint names of the original owner and his or her new partner in order to demonstrate a higher joint income to cover an increase in mortgage payments. The subsequent transfer into joint names meant that the property was shared equally 'with no recognition of the partner's prior ownership'. Thirdly, unfairness can arise where one partner provided all or most of the money to purchase a property which was then put into joint names. The research revealed the fact that the property may have been put into joint names for a variety of reasons, such as lack of understanding of the legal position or an unwillingness to consider the possibility of the relationship breaking down. The researchers concluded that these instances of unfairness arise:

> from the mismatch between the result given by adherence to the legal title and the underlying reality of the situation. The . . . law as it currently stands may just as unfairly reward a party who has done little to deserve their share, as penalise a party who has done much but cannot quantify it in the terms required by the technicalities of the case-law.[322]

Finally, unfairness can arise where one party made a substantial contribution (financial and otherwise) to the relationship and to the home, but this did not result in any or a greater proprietary interest due to lack of evidence regarding the contribution or of the couple's common intention. An example of this is *James v Thomas*.[323]

### 2.8.1.5  The increase in cohabitation and public support for reform

The rate of unmarried cohabitation has consistently grown since the 1980s. Statistics show that in 2006 around one-quarter (25 per cent) of unmarried men and women between the ages of 16 and 59 were cohabiting.[324] By contrast, in 1986, only 11 per cent of unmarried men and 13 per cent of unmarried women were cohabiting.[325] While the rate of unmarried cohabitation has been on the

---

[319] Law Commission, *Cohabitation: The Financial Consequences of Relationship Breakdown* (Law Com No 307, 2007), para 2.13. See R. Tennant, J. Taylor, and J. Lewis, 'Separating from Cohabitation: Making Arrangements for Finances and Parenting', Department for Constitutional Affairs Research Report 7/2006 (London, DCA, 2006); G. Douglas, J. Pearce, and H. Woodward, Cardiff Law School Research Paper No 1, 'A Failure of Trust: Resolving Property Disputes on Cohabitation Breakdown' (2007).

[320] G. Douglas, J. Pearce, and H. Woodward, 'Cohabitants, Property and the Law: A Study of Injustice' (2009) 72(1) Modern Law Review 24 at 34–6.

[321] G. Douglas, J. Pearce, and H. Woodward, Cardiff Law School Research Paper No 1, 'A Failure of Trust: Resolving Property Disputes on Cohabitation Breakdown' (2007); G. Douglas, J. Pearce, and H. Woodward, 'Cohabitants, Property and the Law: A Study of Injustice' (2009) 72(1) Modern Law Review 24.

[322] G. Douglas, J. Pearce, and H. Woodward, 'Cohabitants, Property and the Law: A Study of Injustice' (2009) 72(1) Modern Law Review 24 at 32.

[323] [2007] EWCA Civ 1212.

[324] National Statistics, *Social Trends 2008* (London: Office for National Statistics, 2008), p 21.          [325] Ibid.

rise, the number of couples marrying is in decline and figures indicate that in 2007 the marriage rates in England and Wales fell to the lowest level since records began.[326]

Research also shows that public attitudes to unmarried cohabitation are positive and that there is public support for reform. In the 2000 British Social Attitudes Survey, 67 per cent of those surveyed thought that it was acceptable for a couple to live together without intending to get married, and only 27 per cent believed that married couples make better parents than unmarried ones.[327] This has led to the view that, in terms of social attitudes, the 'centrality of the formally married couple has diminished'.[328] Research has also revealed that the majority of people think that the law should treat cohabiting couples the same as married couples when relationships break down, especially where the couple have children.[329]

### 2.8.2 Arguments against reform

Despite the strength of the case for reform, some arguments have been made against reform:

#### 2.8.2.1 Respecting the choice of cohabitants not to marry or enter into a civil partnership

Some argue that as cohabitants choose not to marry or enter into a civil partnership, this should be respected and thus the law should not impose a regulatory regime to govern their affairs.[330] As Deech argues, 'there ought to be a corner of freedom for such couples to which they can escape and avoid family law'.[331] However, the notion of 'choice' in this context is not as straightforward as it may appear. One party may want to formalise the relationship through marriage or civil registration, but the other may not and so it cannot be assumed that the fact that the parties are cohabiting indicates a deliberate mutual choice to avoid relationship regulation. In addition, this argument is complicated by the fact that research has shown that the majority of unmarried cohabitants mistakenly believe that cohabitation for a period of time gives rise, under general law, to the same or similar legal rights as marriage. Known as the 'common law marriage myth',[332] this statistical evidence contradicts the simplistic argument that cohabitants deliberately avoid legal regulation because it shows that a large number of cohabitants falsely believe that such marital-like regulation will, in time, be conferred upon them.

#### 2.8.2.2 Educating cohabitants about their legal position is enough

The government's initial response to the 'common law marriage myth' was to attempt to educate cohabitants regarding their lack of rights and responsibilities and to encourage them to put agreements in place to govern their affairs. A public information campaign called the 'Living Together Campaign' (LTC) was set up to provide advice on the legal rights which cohabitants have. The LTC website also contains downloadable agreements which the parties can use to agree, in advance, the terms of their relationship and outcomes should the relationship break down. However, researchers discovered that by the end of the research project, very few individuals had actually taken these steps. There were a diverse range of reasons for this inaction, including situations when one partner

---

[326] See http://www.guardian.co.uk/news/datablog/2010/feb/11/marriage-rates-uk-data#data.

[327] A. Barlow, S. Duncan, G. James, and A. Park, 'Just a Piece of Paper? Marriage and Cohabitation in Britain' in A. Park, J. Curtice, K. Thomson, L. Jarvis, and C. Bromley (eds), *British Social Attitudes: The 18th Report* (London: Sage, 2001), pp 29–57.

[328] S. Duncan and M. Phillips, 'New Families? Tradition and Change in Modern Relationships' in A. Park et al (eds), *British Social Attitudes: The 24th Report* (London: Sage, 2008), p 25.

[329] A. Barlow, C. Burgoyne, E. Clery, and J. Smithson, 'Cohabitation and the Law: Myths, Money and the Media' in A. Park et al (eds), *British Social Attitudes: The 24th Report* (London: Sage, 2008).

[330] R. Deech, 'The Case against the Legal Recognition of Cohabitation' (1980) 29 International and Comparative Law Quarterly 480.

[331] Ibid, 483.

[332] In the 2008 British Social Attitudes Report, 53 per cent of unmarried cohabitants falsely believed that common law marriage exists, A. Barlow, C. Burgoyne, E. Clery, and J. Smithson, 'Cohabitation and the Law: Myths, Money and the Media' in A. Park et al (eds), *British Social Attitudes: The 24th Report* (London: Sage, 2008), pp 40–2.

to the relationship would not agree to action being taken or 'optimism bias' where the parties did not feel that they had to consider eventualities such as death or relationship breakdown.[333] Thus, this study shows that even cohabitants who are aware of their legal position do not tend to take immediate action to protect themselves which undermines the argument that merely educating cohabitants about their rights and duties under the current law is a sufficient response to the inadequacies of this law.

### 2.8.2.3 *The lack of commitment in cohabiting relationships*

Allied with the argument that cohabitants make a deliberate and mutual decision to avoid legal regulation, those who oppose giving greater legal rights to unmarried couples often point to statistical evidence which shows that cohabiting relationships tend to break down more often than marriage.[334] It is argued that as cohabitants do not display the same level of mutual commitment as spouses, they do not deserve the same level of family law regulation. However, it is too simplistic to make the argument that cohabiting couples lack commitment and consequently should be denied greater legal protection when the relationship breaks down. Indeed, research has shown that different levels of commitment can be found in the broad continuum of cohabiting relationships from the 'mutually committed' where the parties consider their relationship to be akin to marriage, to the more 'contingently committed' where parties do not presume that the relationship will endure.[335] In a recent research study, the relationships of unmarried cohabitants fell into four categories identified by the researchers:[336]

- *the ideologues*: cohabitants within this category were in long-term and committed relationships, but one or both partners had an ideological objection to marriage;
- *the romantics*: couples within this group saw marriage as a very serious commitment and while they expected to get married eventually, they viewed their cohabitation as a step towards this;
- *the pragmatists*: couples within this group were also mutually committed to the relationship but made decisions about whether to marry on legal or financial grounds;
- *the uneven couples*: couples within this group did not hold mutually compatible views about their relationship. One may have wanted to marry but the other partner did not, or one was more committed to the relationship than the other.

This research shows that cohabitants do not form a homogenous group upon which generalised assumptions can be made about their level of mutual commitment or their views on the desirability of legal regulation.

Furthermore, it is misleading to draw bright-line distinctions between the commitment involved in married and unmarried relationships when research shows that different levels of commitment and interdependencies can also be found in marriage.[337] It is also worth pointing out the irony involved in these arguments which focus on the more durable nature of marriage over unmarried relationships and thus to the different levels of commitment as a justification for privileging marriage. The statutory regime which gives the court the power to re-adjust the parties' property and

---

[333] A. Barlow, C. Burgoyne, and J. Smithson, *The Living Together Campaign—An Investigation of its Impact on Legally Aware Cohabitants* (London: Ministry of Justice, 2007), pp 33–6.

[334] Law Commission, *Cohabitation: The Financial Consequences of Relationship Breakdown, A Consultation Paper* (Law Com No 179, 2006), para 2.36, fn 67.

[335] C. Smart and P. Stevens, *Cohabitation Breakdown* (London: FPSC/Rowntree, 2000). See also G. Douglas, J. Pearce, and H. Woodward, Cardiff Law School Research Paper No 1, 'A Failure of Trust: Resolving Property Disputes on Cohabitation Breakdown' (2007), para 4.4.

[336] A. Barlow and J. Smithson, 'Legal Assumptions, Cohabitants Talk and the Rocky Road to Reform' [2010] Child and Family Law Quarterly 328.

[337] J. Eekelaar and M. Maclean, 'Marriage and the Moral Bases of Personal Relationships' (2004) 31(4) Journal of Law and Society 510; A. Barlow, S. Duncan, G. James, and A. Park, *Cohabitation, Marriage and the Law: Social Change and Legal Reform in the 21st Century* (Oxford: Hart, 2005).

finances on divorce/dissolution does not apply whilst the parties are still married or in a civil partnership. These redistributive powers are *only* available when the marriage or civil partnership has come to an end and when the parties' commitment has been breached either by mutual consent or the will of one spouse. This somewhat undermines the importance of marital commitment when justifying the distinction between married and unmarried relationships.

The relevance of the nature of the parties' commitment to the relationship must also be questioned, alongside consideration of the purpose of the law. If it is accepted that one important function of family law is to protect vulnerable family members, then it would seem that, regardless of the parties' commitment to the relationship, a regulatory regime is required to address the economic fall-out associated with the breakdown of a cohabiting relationship where one partner (and the children) may be left in a weak economic position as a result of the relationship. As Barlow observes:

> Arguably, those who are more likely to separate are in greater need of family law regulation to protect not only the weaker economic partner but more importantly the children of the relationship who are currently impoverished when their parents' relationship breaks down to a far greater extent than children of divorced parents.[338]

### 2.8.2.4 The fear of undermining marriage

There is a fear that extending the legal protection afforded to unmarried cohabitants would undermine marriage. This fear certainly impacts upon the political will to introduce legislation in this area as politicians are cautious about appearing to undermine this important social institution. However, research has shown that in countries where cohabiting couples have been given greater recognition and protection in law, there has been no negative impact on the marriage rates.[339] Furthermore, one could also ask why it is necessary to maintain the current law for unmarried cohabitants in order to support the institution of marriage. Indeed, the Law Commission has said that:

> the objective of promoting marriage does not require us to deny any remedy to individuals experiencing financial hardship at the end of a cohabiting relationship. The institution of marriage, and individual marriages, can be supported without perpetuating the hardship experienced by such individuals.[340]

Further, given the stark contrast between the two regimes in terms of providing financial relief on separation, unmarried cohabitation may be the preferred choice for the wealthier party in a relationship who wishes to protect his or her assets.[341] Maintaining the current law for unmarried cohabitants could therefore 'create a disincentive for one partner to marry'.[342]

---

[338] A. Barlow, 'Cohabitation Law Reform—Messages from Research' (2006) 14 Feminist Legal Studies 167 at 172.

[339] K. Kiernan, A. Barlow, and R. Merlo, 'Cohabitation Law Reform and its Impact on Marriage: Evidence from Australia and Europe' (2007) 63 International Family Law 71.

[340] Law Commission, *Cohabitation: The Financial Consequences of Relationship Breakdown, A Consultation Paper* (Law Com No 179, 2006), para 5.34; Law Commission, *Cohabitation: The Financial Consequences of Relationship Breakdown* (Law Com No 307, 2007), paras 2.36–2.45.

[341] Law Commission, *Cohabitation: The Financial Consequences of Relationship Breakdown, A Consultation Paper* (Law Com No 179, 2006), para 5.19, which cited B. Hale, 'Unmarried Couples and Family Law' (2004) 34 Family Law 419 at 422; A. Barlow, S. Duncan, G. James, and A. Park, *Cohabitation, Marriage and the Law: Social Change and Legal Reform in the 21st Century* (Oxford: Hart, 2005), p 109.

[342] Law Commission, *Cohabitation: The Financial Consequences of Relationship Breakdown, A Consultation Paper* (Law Com No 179, 2006), para 5.19.

### 2.8.3 **Reform initiatives**

Whether and how to replace trust law principles with a flexible family law regime to resolve the financial and property disputes between cohabitants on relationship breakdown is not a new question facing policy-makers. In 1995 Charles Harpum, then Law Commissioner for England and Wales, wrote: 'the law which regulates the rights and obligations of those who, in many disparate relationships (whether sexual or otherwise), share a home together but are not married is acknowledged to be thoroughly unsatisfactory by lawyers and non-lawyers alike . . . Homesharers are not denizens of some black hole of outlawry. Is it better for the law that regulates their affairs to be developed by legislation after an exhaustive consideration of the issues or should it continue to be left to the chances of litigation?'[343] Recommendations for reform have been made a number of times, none of which have reached the statute books.

#### 2.8.3.1 *The Law Society (2002)*

The Law Society reviewed the legal position of cohabitants in 2002 and produced recommendations for reform.[344] It drew attention to the fact that opt-in schemes where couples have to register their relationship formally in order to acquire legal protection do 'not provide for parties in long-term relationships where one party refuses to marry or register the relationship and, as a result, the other party has no financial rights on relationship breakdown'. In light of this, it recommended that cohabitants who had lived together for a continuous period of at least two years or who had a child together would be eligible to apply for financial relief on relationship breakdown.[345] The core objective of the proposals was to protect economically vulnerable cohabitants, especially those who may 'suffer financial disadvantage as a result of having shared their home, income and the upbringing of any children with another person'.[346] While the Society sought to improve the legal position of cohabitants on relationship breakdown, it did not seek to achieve the practical or symbolic assimilation of marriage and cohabitation. In terms of capital provision on separation, the Society recommended a less extensive and operationally distinct system from the financial provision system which applies on divorce.

The Society proposed that the court would have the power to make property adjustment orders and lump sum orders between eligible cohabitants on relationship breakdown. Each claim would be assessed according to the principle that fair account should be taken of any economic advantage derived by either party from contributions by the other, and of any economic disadvantages suffered by either party in the interests of the other or of the family. 'Contributions' included domestic labour such as maintaining or running the home or the family. The Society recommended that cohabitants would only be allowed to apply for maintenance for limited periods and only to provide resources to facilitate the recipient's retraining or to reflect capital payments which could not be made by way of a lump sum. As well as recommending financial relief between separating cohabitants, the proposals also included the conferral of rights for eligible cohabitants in other areas of law such as succession, tax, immigration, transfer of tenancies, and occupation of the home. The Society recommended that the current law relating to property disputes should continue to apply to cohabitants who were not eligible to apply under the scheme (ie, cohabitants who had lived together for less than two years and had no relevant children). These proposals were not acted upon but in the same year that they were published, the Law Commission published a much anticipated Discussion Paper on the property rights of home-sharers.

---

[343] C. Harpum, 'Cohabitation Consultation' [1995] 25 Family Law 657.

[344] Law Society, *Cohabitation: The Case for Clear Law. Proposals for Reform* (London: Representation and Law Reform Directorate, 2002).

[345] The report also recommended civil registration for same-sex couples, which has now been enacted in the Civil Partnership Act 2004.

[346] Law Society, *Cohabitation: the Case for Clear Law. Proposals for Reform* (London: Representation and Law Reform Directorate, 2002), para 12.

### 2.8.3.2 The Law Commission (2002)

The Law Commission embarked on a review of the property rights of home-sharers in 1994 and despite the intention to produce a consultation paper in 1996, it was not until July 2002 that a Discussion Paper was published.[347] This paper examined the property rights of those who shared a home, and included not only unmarried cohabitants but also 'friends, relatives and others who may be living together for reasons of companionship or care and support'.[348] The paper cited the well-known criticisms of the law in this area including the myth of searching for the parties' common intention and the confusion in case law about the types of contribution from which a common intention will be inferred. The Commission concluded that:

> The current requirements for establishing the existence of an interest under a trust are not ideally suited to the typical informality of those sharing a home. We feel that to demand proof of an intention to share the beneficial interest in the home can be somewhat unrealistic, as people do not tend to think about their home in such legalistic terms. The emphasis on financial input towards the acquisition of the home fails to recognise the realities of most cohabiting relationships. Finally, and importantly, the uncertainties in the present law can cause lengthy and costly litigation, wasting court time, public funding and the parties' own resources.[349]

The Commission then laid out a property-based model for reform under which home-sharers would acquire a proprietary interest in the home, behind a statutory trust, based on a range of contributions (both financial and non-financial) to the shared home. However, in the end the Commission did not recommend this proposal for the determination of shares in the home because it was not convinced that it could 'operate fairly and evenly across the diverse circumstances which are now to be encountered'.[350]

Ultimately the broad remit of the project which looked at the rights of home-sharers in the shared home, as opposed to just unmarried cohabitants, contributed to the defeat of the Commission as the Discussion Paper merely suggested the need for a relationship-based solution to the problem but did not offer any concrete proposals.

### 2.8.3.3 The Law Commission (2007)

By 2005, however, the legal position of unmarried cohabitants was on the political agenda and the Law Commission was tasked by the Department for Constitutional Affairs to conduct a review of cohabitation law and, in particular, the financial hardship suffered by cohabitants or their children on the termination of their relationship by breakdown or death. The impetus for this policy review came from the enactment of the Civil Partnership Act 2004. During the passage of this legislation through Parliament, concerns were raised about the legal position of unmarried/unregistered relationships and, in particular, the economic hardship suffered by cohabitants 'owing to the current lack of any coherent legal remedies addressing their financial and property disputes' on relationship breakdown.[351] It seems that the refusal to allow unmarried opposite-sex couples to register their relationship under the newly enacted civil partnerships scheme created the impression that same-sex couples were being given preferential treatment.[352] Thus, it became politically important to be seen to take steps to remedy the difficulties faced by unmarried opposite-sex couples on the termination of their relationships.

---

[347] Law Commission, *Sharing Homes: A Discussion Paper* (Law Com No 278, 2002).

[348] Ibid, Executive Summary, para 1.    [349] Ibid, para 2.11.    [350] Ibid, Executive Summary, para 15.

[351] Law Commission, *Cohabitation: The Financial Consequences of Relationship Breakdown* (Law Com No 307, 2007), para 1.18.

[352] See L. Glennon, 'Obligations Between Adult Partners: Moving from Form to Function?' (2008) 22(1) International Journal of Law, Policy and the Family 22.

The Law Commission published a Consultation Paper in 2006[353] and its final report, which contained recommendations for reform, was published in 2007.[354] Once again, the Commission was critical of the current law and concluded that:

> [t]he general law . . . is not equipped to provide a comprehensive solution to problems arising on separation, responding to the economic consequences of the parties' contributions to their relationship. Moreover, since it is limited to addressing the beneficial ownership of individual assets, the general law of property and trusts offers very little remedial flexibility.[355]

Given the inadequacy of the current law, which was described as complex, uncertain, expensive to rely on, and not designed for family circumstances,[356] the Law Commission recommended that the courts be given powers to adjust the parties' property rights on relationship breakdown in order to minimise the economic detriment one party may suffer as a result of a cohabiting relationship.

Under the proposals, financial relief upon separation would be available to eligible cohabitants who had not disapplied the statutory scheme[357] and who had made 'qualifying contributions to the relationship giving rise to certain enduring consequences at the point of separation'.[358] To be eligible to apply, cohabitants must have had a child together or have lived together for a specified number of years. The Commission recommended that the requisite period should be set by statute but suggested a period of between two and five years. Under the proposals, being eligible to apply for financial relief would not be enough to obtain an award. In order to obtain a remedy, applicants would have to prove that they had made *qualifying contributions* to the relationship which gave rise to a *retained benefit* in the hands of the respondent, or to their *economic disadvantage*. By contrast to the limited types of contributions which are recognised under the law of trusts, a qualifying contribution, for the purposes of the proposed statutory scheme, was defined as any financial or non-financial contribution which was made to the parties' shared life or to the welfare of members of their families. The scheme did not try to quantify, in financial terms, the value of these contributions to the family, but instead considered the lasting economic impact of these contributions on the parties.

Under the proposals, the court could grant financial relief to reverse any *retained benefit* which the respondent had acquired as a result of the relationship. This could take the form of capital, income, or earning capacity that had been acquired, retained, or enhanced. The court could also grant financial relief to share the *economic disadvantage* suffered by the applicant. An economic disadvantage is a present or future loss and could include a diminution in current savings as a result of expenditure or of earnings lost during the relationship, lost future earnings, or the future cost of paid childcare. Such economic disadvantage could arise, for example, where one party gave up work or worked part time in order to look after the family. However, the economic disadvantage claimed must be 'susceptible to proof of an actual loss on the balance of probabilities' and the applicant would also be under a duty to mitigate this loss.[359] It is important to note that, under the proposals, there must be a causal link between the contributions made by the applicant and the alleged benefit retained by the respondent or disadvantage suffered by the applicant.[360]

In granting financial relief, the court could make lump sums, property transfers, property settlements, orders for sale, and pension sharing orders. Awards under the scheme would be made on a

---

[353] Law Commission, *Cohabitation: The Financial Consequences of Relationship Breakdown, A Consultation Paper* (Law Com No 179, 2006).

[354] Law Commission, *Cohabitation: The Financial Consequences of Relationship Breakdown* (Law Com No 307, 2007).

[355] Ibid, para 2.16.     [356] Ibid, Executive Summary, para 1.4.     [357] Ibid, para 2.94.

[358] Ibid, Executive Summary, para 1.13.

[359] Ibid, para 4.62. The Law Commission make it clear that an applicant who claimed on the basis of incurred economic disadvantage would be expected to mitigate their loss by making the best of their existing resources and minimising their disadvantage as far as possible, ibid, para 4.63.

[360] Ibid, para 4.43.

clean break basis and, unlike the position on divorce and dissolution of a civil partnership, periodical payments would not generally be available. The Commission envisaged that the only situation where such payments could be made would be to meet the continuing childcare costs incurred by the applicant to enable him or her to take up employment. In deciding what order to make in order to reverse the retained benefit held by the respondent, or share the economic disadvantage suffered by the applicant, the court would have regard to the following list of 'discretionary factors', first consideration being given to the welfare of any child of both parties who had not attained the age of 18:

- the financial needs and obligations of both parties;
- the extent and nature of the financial resources which each party has or is likely to have in the foreseeable future;
- the welfare of any children who live with, or might reasonably be expected to live with, either party; and
- the conduct of each party (defined restrictively) but to include cases where a qualifying contribution was made despite the express disagreement of the other party.

While there is a discretionary element to this proposed scheme, it is very different to the discretionary-based financial provision system which applies to divorcing spouses or civil partners who are dissolving their partnership. The Commission rejected the extension of this system to cohabitants because:

> cohabitants have not given each other the legal commitment, or accepted the status, of marriage or civil partnership. We therefore believe that it is necessary to find a middle ground between, on the one hand, the law that currently applies to cohabitants and, on the other, the law that applies to spouses and civil partners on their separation.[361]

Thus, the objective of the proposed scheme for cohabitants was not to distribute the fruits of the parties' joint life together, nor to meet the financial needs of the applicant (unless they were caused by their contributions to the relationship). Instead, the objective of the scheme was to allow the court to make an order to ensure that the 'pluses and minuses of the relationship' were fairly shared between the couple.[362]

The Commission also attempted to find a balance between ensuring that the contributions and sacrifices made in an intimate relationship are fairly distributed between the parties on separation, whilst taking account of the 'importance of preserving individuals' freedom to conduct their private relationships on their own terms'.[363] Thus, to respect the autonomy of couples who wish to define the terms of their relationships themselves, the Commission recommended that couples should be allowed to opt-out of the statutory scheme leaving them free to make their own arrangements. To be valid, such an agreement would have to be in writing and signed by both parties. While the court would have the power to set such agreements aside, the Commission said that this should only be done if their enforcement would give rise to manifest unfairness.

However, in March 2008, the Justice Minister announced that 'for the time being' no further action would be taken in relation to the Law Commission's proposals. The decision on their implementation was postponed pending research into the cost and efficacy of provisions in Scotland (under the Family Law (Scotland) Act 2006) which gave rights to cohabitants similar to those proposed by the Law Commission.[364]

---

[361] Ibid, para 4.2.    [362] Ibid, Executive Summary, para 1.19.    [363] Ibid, para 2.93.
[364] Hansard, HC 6 March 2008, vol 472, col 123WS.

### 2.8.3.4 The Cohabitation Bill (2008)

In response to this impasse, Lord Lester of Herne Hill (backed by Resolution, which is an association of family lawyers) introduced a Private Member's Bill in the House of Lords on the rights of unmarried cohabitants. The Cohabitation Bill was introduced to the House of Lords on 11 December 2008 and had its second reading in March 2009. During its second reading, both the Government spokesperson and the Opposition spokesperson indicated that they did not support the Bill.

The Bill sought to establish a legal framework for financial provision on separation for unmarried and unregistered cohabitants.[365] Eligible cohabitants could apply for a financial settlement order on separation. To be eligible, cohabitants must have lived together as a couple for at least two years or have had a child together. The Bill provided that the court could make a financial settlement order on the parties' separation if, having regard to all the circumstances, the court considers that it is just and equitable to do so. The court could make the full range of orders that are available in the context of financial relief—that is: lump sum orders; periodical payments; transfer of property orders; property settlements; sale of property orders; and pension sharing orders. In determining an application, the Bill provided a range of matters to which the court to have regard, including:

- the welfare of any child (this is the first consideration);
- the nature of the commitment between the parties (including the degree of dependency or interdependency) and the duration of the relationship;
- the contributions each party has made to the relationship in financial terms or by caring for the relevant children or looking after the home;
- any economic advantage retained by either party as a result of the relationship;
- any economic disadvantage suffered by either party as a result of the relationship;
- the income, property, and resources of each party;
- the financial needs and obligations of the parties;
- the scope of each partner to obtain paid work, taking into account the cost of any childcare required to facilitate the primary caregiver's employment;
- any written agreement indicating the couple's intentions.

As with the Law Commission's proposals, there are some significant differences between this proposed system and the financial provision system which applies to divorcing spouses and civil partners who are dissolving their partnership. As Probert indicates, under the Cohabitation Bill the 'degree of commitment within the relationship is to be tested rather than assumed'.[366] In addition, the court's discretion under the Cohabitation Bill was limited by several underlying principles. First, there was no presumption that the parties should share equally in the property belonging to either or both of them. Secondly, the Bill provided that both parties should be self-supporting as soon as reasonably practicable. Finally, any award should not exceed the applicant's reasonable needs. While it would be possible for the court to make periodical payments in favour of an applicant, the maximum period for such payments would generally be three years unless a longer period was necessary to avoid the recipient's exceptional hardship caused by the cohabitation or to meet the costs of childcare to enable the primary carer to maintain gainful employment.

While this was a useful attempt to fill the void left by the Government's decision to delay progress on reform, the Bill was not without its problems. In particular, it is unclear exactly what a

---

[365] For a comparison between the recommendations of the Law Commission and the provisions of Lord Lester's Cohabitation Bill, see E. Hess, 'The Rights of Cohabitants: When and How Will the Law be Reformed' [2009] Family Law 405.

[366] R. Probert, 'The Cohabitation Bill' [2009] Family Law 150.

financial settlement order would be designed to achieve. As Probert points out, while equalising the economic impact of the relationship between the parties was the clear objective of the Law Commission's proposals, the economic advantages and disadvantages which flow from the cohabitation are just factors to be considered within Lord Lester's Cohabitation Bill. Probert wonders how the scheme would apply in different contexts. For example, take the situation where one party contributes to the purchase price of a property, which is registered in the sole name of the other. Under property law principles (which currently apply), the contributor would be entitled to a share under a trust. The Law Commission's scheme would also have generated a remedy because this contribution would constitute a retained benefit in the hands of the respondent, which the court would have to reverse. But under Lord Lester's Cohabitation Bill this was just one factor to be taken into account. Probert asks: 'given the principle that the award should not exceed the reasonable needs of the applicant, does this mean that contributions made by a self-supporting cohabitant will simply be disregarded?'[367] Given the Bill's lack of focus, it is unclear how its provisions would work in practice.

### 2.8.3.5 *The Cohabitation Rights Bill 2014–15*

A new Private Member's Bill, The Cohabitation Rights Bill 2014–15, was introduced into the House of Lords in 2014 by Liberal Democrat MP Lord Marks. The Bill received its second reading in the House of Lords on 12 December 2014 and, at the time of writing, was at the Committee stage, during which time its provisions will be subjected to greater scrutiny by the House. The Bill proposes to implement the recommendations of the Law Commission in 2007 by making provision for an 'opt-out' system that would automatically bring cohabiting couples (who had lived together as a couple for two or more years, or had a child together) within its remit unless they opted out. The Bill, amongst other things, seeks to provide a legal remedy in the situation where one party is left financially disadvantaged following the breakdown of an unmarried relationship. However, in the absence of Government support, this Bill is likely to be destined to the same fate as prior initiatives in this area.

It is clear, however, that reform is necessary. In a recent speech talking about family law reform, President of the Family Division Sir James Munby, said of the 'long-running problem of cohabitant's rights': 'if a marriage is terminated by divorce the court has the power to redistribute the matrimonial assets between the spouses. There is no such relief for cohabitants when their relationship breaks down, however long the relationship has lasted. This is an injustice which has been recognised as long as I have been in the law. Reform is desperately needed. The Law Commission has recommended reform. Thus far Governments have failed to act. Reform is inevitable. It is inconceivable that society will not right this injustice in due course. How many more women are to be condemned to injustice in the meantime?'[368] It is also worth pointing out that the financial provision system which governs financial provision on divorce and dissolution of civil partnerships is not without its problems as the courts continue to grapple with emerging principles in the application of their broad discretion.[369] One useful approach for reform may be to combine these debates at the level of policy. In a parliamentary debate, Lord Goodhart suggested such an approach when he said:

> [A]s the rights of cohabitees are necessarily linked at least indirectly to those of married couples and civil partners, would it not be a good idea to include in the Law Commission's review the rights arising on the dissolution of a marriage or civil partnership?[370]

---

[367] Ibid.
[368] President of the Family Division, The Family Justice Reforms, 29 April 2014, https://www.judiciary.gov.uk/wp-content/uploads/2014/05/family-justice-reforms-29042014.pdf.
[369] See Chapter 4.     [370] See Hansard, Lords Debates 6 June 2006, vol 682, col 1136, *per* Lord Goodhart.

Thus, it has been argued that the debates on married and unmarried couples should be considered as integrated policy issues as they raise similar questions concerning obligations within domestic relationships of varying duration and circumstance.[371] However, it is worth noting that all the policy considerations of the legal position of unmarried cohabitants have deliberately sought to distance their proposals from the financial provision system which applies on divorce and dissolution of civil partnerships in order to maintain the practical and ideological superiority of marriage (and now civil partnerships). Indeed, given the political imperative of being seen not to undermine marriage, it is likely that the economic consequences of married and unmarried relationships will continue to be seen as separate policy issues. In the context of cohabitation law, it seems that the objective of any reforming law will be to provide the 'basic protections'[372] or a 'safety net, no more and no less' to avoid unfairness on the termination of long-term cohabiting partnerships, particularly those involving children.[373] At the very least, however, this would be an improvement to the current outcomes generated by the ill-suited law of implied trusts.

## Discussion Questions

1. A cohabitant seeking a share of a beneficial interest in a property where they are not a legal owner is subject to the law of trusts. Explain what such a cohabitant would have to prove to claim a share of the property.

2. The law of trusts is ill-suited to resolving the property disputes of unmarried cohabitants on relationship breakdown. Giving reasons for your answer, discuss the extent to which you agree with this statement.

3. A cohabitant may not wish to marry or enter a civil partnership for a range of different reasons. Should the law of cohabitation be reformed at all?

## Further Reading

BARLOW, A. and JAMES, G., 'Regulating Marriage and Cohabitation in 21st Century Britain' (2004) 67(2) Modern Law Review 143

BARLOW, A. and SMITHSON, J., 'Legal Assumptions, Cohabitants' Talk and the Rocky Road to Reform' [2010] Child and Family Law Quarterly 328

BARLOW, A., BURGOYNE, C., CLERY, E., and SMITHSON, J., 'Cohabitation and the Law: Myths, Money and the Media' in A. Park et al (eds), *British Social Attitudes: The 24th Report* (London: Sage, 2008)

BATTERSBY, G., 'Ownership of the Family Home: *Stack v Dowden* in the House of Lords' [2008] Child and Family Law Quarterly 255

DOUGLAS, G., PEARCE, J., and WOODWARD, H., Cardiff Law School Research Paper No 1, '*A Failure of Trust: Resolving Property Disputes on Cohabitation Breakdown*' (2007)

GARDNER, S., 'Rethinking Family Property' (1993) 109 Law Quarterly Review 263

---

[371] L. Glennon, 'Obligations Between Adult Partners: Moving from Form to Function?' (2008) 22(1) International Journal of Law, Policy and the Family 22.

[372] The Cohabitation Bill 2008, cl 1.

[373] See Hansard, Lords Debates 6 June 2006, vol 682, col 1137, per Baroness Ashton of Upholland (Parliamentary Under-Secretary, Department for Constitutional Affairs).

GARDNER, S. and DAVIDSON, K., 'The Future of *Stack v Dowden*' (2011) 127 Law Quarterly Review 13

GARDNER, S., 'Problems in family property' (2013) 72 Cambridge Law Journal 301

GLOVER N. and TODD, P., 'The Myth of Common Intention' (1996) Legal Studies 325

PROBERT, R., 'The Cohabitation Bill' [2009] Family Law 150

 Visit the Online Resource Centre at **www.oxfordtextbooks.co.uk/orc/gilmore_glennon5e/**

**online**
**resource**
**centre** for a range of further features including a detailed bibliography and self-test questions.

# PART 2

# Child Family Law

6  Financial support for children ................................................................319

7  A child's parents: parentage, parenthood, and parental responsibility ...............345

8  Children's rights .............................................................................424

9  Private law disputes and issues in children cases .......................................455

10  Children needing services, care, and protection ........................................593

11  Adoption and special guardianship .....................................................700

# 6

# Financial support for children

## INTRODUCTION

When a child's parents are separated, an issue frequently arises as to the appropriate financial support which should be provided for the child by the parent with whom the child is not living (the non-resident parent). This issue is regulated by one or more of several statutes depending on the circumstances: the Child Support Act 1991 (CSA 1991), as amended; Schedule 1 to the Children Act 1989; the Matrimonial Causes Act 1973; and the Civil Partnership Act 2004. The applicability of the CSA 1991 in a particular case can limit to some extent the use of the other statutes mentioned, so it is convenient to begin our explanation of this area of law[1] with an account of the CSA 1991 and its background.

## 1 The Child Support Act 1991: background and recent reforms

### 1.1 Birth of the Child Support Act

Prior to 5 April 1993, the date on which the CSA 1991 came into force, parental disputes about child support were dealt with by the courts. While in theory this had the benefit of a judge's careful consideration of the individual circumstances of each case, it had proved problematic in practice: the amounts of court-ordered maintenance tended to be small and poorly enforced.

---

**Talking point**

There was a natural tendency for lawyers, acting in the interests of their clients, to try to maximise the availability of welfare benefits on family breakdown.[2] The impact of this on the public purse became more visible with increasing numbers of lone-parent families on welfare benefits, in part as a result of the increase in divorce following the Divorce Reform Act 1969. A change of approach was instigated by Prime Minister Margaret Thatcher, who thought it 'scandalous that only one in three children entitled to receive maintenance actually benefited from regular payments'.[3] Thatcher's intervention led to the

---

[1] This chapter provides an overview of the most important features. For detailed scholarly discussion of theory, law, and policy, see N. Wikeley, *Child Support Law and Policy* (Oxford: Hart, 2006).

[2] And see *Delaney v Delaney* [1990] 2 FLR 457. For a summary of the role of welfare benefits in child support, see A. Bainham and S. Gilmore, *Children – The Modern Law* (Bristol: Jordan Publishing, 2013), pp 451–60.

[3] M. Thatcher, *The Downing Street Years* (London: Harper Collins, 1995), p 630, quoted in S. Cretney, *Family Law in the Twentieth Century: A History* (Oxford: Oxford University Press, 2003), p 475. Thatcher's 'interest drove the project forward at a breath-taking pace': see M. Maclean with J. Kurczewski, *Making Family Law* (Oxford: Hart, 2011), p 45. The recommendations of an Interdepartmental Working Group led straight to a White Paper, DSS, *Children Come*

passing of the CSA 1991,[4] which sought to address the problems by establishing an administrative process for the assessment, collection, and enforcement of child maintenance. A body called the Child Support Agency was set up to carry out these functions, under the control of a Secretary of State.

**Q.** What might be the advantages or disadvantages of court-based and administrative systems of child support respectively?

In the case of parents who were on certain welfare benefits, the Act placed a duty on parents to authorise the Secretary of State to assess and collect child maintenance.

The Act aligned well with an increasing sensitivity to children's rights[5] and the idea of parental responsibility[6] and, as an initiative which both helped children and saved public money, commanded broad political appeal. Furthermore, the adoption of an administrative scheme could draw support from similar initiatives in other jurisdictions, notably the USA and Australia.[7]

## 1.2 **Problems**

From the outset, however, there was dissatisfaction with some of the detail of the implementation of the new policy.[8] The task of formulating how child support was to be calculated fell, with advice from the Treasury, to the Department of Social Security (DSS). This resulted in a complex, social security-style, mathematical formula for calculating child support maintenance. The formula was quite unlike the model in Australia, where child support was calculated by reference to a simple percentage of a parent's income in the previous year, ascertained from income tax records.[9] It produced in some cases what appeared to be disproportionately high assessments and there was little flexibility to accommodate exceptional circumstances. For example, little thought was given to the Act's impact on clean break financial settlements upon divorce prior to the Act.[10] There were also concerns about the Act's emphasis on legal parenthood,[11] and its failure to take sufficient account of the duties of social parenthood which some parents also had within newly constituted families.

*First: The Government's Proposals on the Maintenance of Children* (Cm 1263, 1990), omitting the usual public consultation by way of a Green Paper. Cf A. Garnham and E. Knights, *Putting the Treasury First* (London: Child Poverty Action Group, 1994), pp 84–92.

[4] For a look behind the scenes of the making of this legislation, see 'Prime Ministerial Intervention: The Child Support Act 1991' in M. Maclean with J. Kurczewski, *Making Family Law* (Oxford: Hart, 2011). The scheme had many of the hallmarks of Thatcherism: the 'natural' family as a site of social control and as a defence of freedom for the individual: see M. Maclean and J. Eekelaar, 'Child Support: The British Solution' (1993) 7 International Journal of Law and the Family 205.

[5] As illustrated by the *Gillick* case in 1986, see Ch 8. See J. Eekelaar, 'Families and Children: From Welfarism to Rights' in J. C. McCrudden and G. Chambers (eds), *Individual Rights and the Law in Britain* (Oxford, Oxford University Press, 1994).

[6] In, eg, the then recently enacted Children Act 1989.

[7] M. Maclean, 'The Making of the Child Support Act: Policy Making at the Intersection of Law and Social Policy' (1994) 21(4) Journal of Law and Society 505.

[8] See R. Collier, 'The Campaign Against the Child Support Act, Errant Fathers and Family Men' [1994] Family Law 384. See also C. Glendinning, K. Clarke, and G. Craig, 'Implementing the Child Support Act' (1996) 18(3) Journal of Social Welfare and Family Law 273–89; G. Gillespie 'Child Support—The Hand that Rocks the Cradle' [1996] Family Law 162.

[9] Such records were then not available in this jurisdiction. For comparison of developments in Australia and the UK since the late 1980s, see B. Fehlberg and M. Maclean 'Child Support Policy in Australia and the United Kingdom: Changing Priorities but a Similar Tough Deal for Children?' (2009) 23(1) International Journal of Law, Policy and the Family 1–24.

[10] Eg a father might transfer his whole interest in the matrimonial home to his former wife in return for not having to make periodical payments to her and their children. See eg *Crozier v Crozier* [1994] 1 FLR 126.

[11] For a critical examination of how the CSA 1991 constructed 'family', see A. Diduck, 'The Unmodified Family: The Child Support Act and the Construction of Legal Subjects' (1995) 22(4) Journal of Law and Society 527.

There was some evidence that the Act was 'failing to improve the financial situation of children', and that it was perceived (at least by some parents) as 'coercive and intrusive', and as providing little incentive to cooperate with the Child Support Agency.[12] Not surprisingly given the dissatisfaction, from its inception the Child Support Agency encountered difficulties enforcing and collecting child support maintenance.[13]

## 1.3 **Responding to criticism**

The Government responded to sustained criticism by enacting the Child Support Act 1995,[14] which introduced greater flexibility, with departures from the formula in prescribed circumstances ('departure directions', now known as 'variations').[15] However, problems with collection and enforcement persisted and further amendments were made. Part I of the Child Support, Pensions and Social Security Act 2000[16] strengthened the powers available to the Secretary of State to enforce payment of child support and introduced a new scheme for calculating child support maintenance. The calculation of child support was simplified so that in most cases the amount payable was a percentage of a non-resident parent's net income, depending on the number of dependent children (15 per cent for one child, 20 per cent for two children, and 25 per cent for three or more). Allowance for the cost of bringing up other 'relevant children' in the parent's household (eg a step-child) was also introduced. Overall, however, the complexity of the system had increased because there were now two schemes running in parallel.

## 1.4 **Loss of confidence and a review of the system**

Despite all these attempts to improve the system, by 2006 public confidence in the Child Support Agency had reached such a low that the then Prime Minister, Tony Blair, asked Sir David Henshaw to undertake a thoroughgoing review. Henshaw reported[17] that the Child Support Agency was not fit for purpose and that there were such negative perceptions of it that it should be replaced by a completely new body, called the Child Maintenance and Enforcement Commission (C-MEC), with increased powers of enforcement. This recommendation and other suggested amendments to the CSA 1991 were adopted by the Government.[18] They were enacted in the Child Maintenance and Other Payments Act 2008,[19] which has since been amended by the Welfare Reform Act 2012.[20] On

---

[12] D. Abbott, 'The Child Support Act 1991: The Lives of Parents With Care Living in Liverpool' (1996) 18(1) Journal of Social Welfare and Family Law 21.

[13] G. Davis, N. Wikeley, R. Young et al, *Child Support in Action* (Oxford: Hart, 1998).

[14] Preceded by a White Paper, *Improving Child Support* (Cm 2745, 1995). For criticism, see A. Horton, 'Improving Child Support—A Missed Opportunity' [1995] Child and Family Law Quarterly 26.

[15] CSA 1991, s 28F and Sch 4B, Pt 1. There was also a change of terminology, from 'absent parent' which was perceived by some as offensive, to 'non-resident parent': see J. Wallbank, 'The Campaign for Change of the Child Support Act 1991: Reconstructing the "Absent Father"' (1997) 6 Social and Legal Studies 191.

[16] Preceded by a Green Paper in July 1998, *Children First: A New Approach to Child Support* (Cm 3992, 1998) (see C. Barton, 'Third Time Lucky for Child Support?—The 1998 Green Paper' [1998] Family Law 668; N. Mostyn, 'The Green Paper on Child Support' [1999] Family Law 95), and a White Paper, *A New Contract for Welfare: Children's Rights and Parents' Responsibilities* (Cm 4349, 1999), on which see C. Barton, 'Child Support—Tony's Turn' [1999] Family Law 704. See also J. Pirrie, 'The Child Support, Pensions and Social Security Bill' [1999] Family Law 199.

[17] Sir David Henshaw's Report to the Secretary of State for Work and Pensions, *Recovering Child Support: Routes to Responsibility* (Cm 6894, July 2006).

[18] Department for Work and Pensions, *A New System of Child Maintenance* (Cm 6979, December 2006).

[19] For an account of the principal changes effected by the 2008 Act and the role of the new Commission, see N. Wikeley, 'Child Support: the Brave New World' [2008] Family Law 1024 and 'Child Support: Carrots and Sticks' [2008] Family Law 1102.

[20] See ss 136–142. For policy debate surrounding the proposed reforms of the Welfare Reform Bill that led to the 2012 Act, see DWP, *Strengthening Families, Promoting Parental Responsibility: The Future of Child Maintenance* (Cm 7990, 2011), available at www.dwp.gov.uk/docs/strengthening-families.pdf; DWP, *Government's Response to the*

1 August 2012, C-MEC was abolished and replaced with a new body called the Child Maintenance Service, in order to bring its functions more directly under the control and accountability of the Secretary of State within the Department for Work and Pensions.[21]

Perhaps the most significant change effected by the 2008 Act is that parents on welfare benefits are no longer compelled to pursue child maintenance through the Child Maintenance Service. The new policy is to encourage all parents, whether on welfare benefits or not, to make their own arrangements for child support and only to invoke the assistance of the Child Maintenance Service where agreement cannot be reached. Indeed, this policy has been underlined further by section 136 of the Welfare Reform Act 2012, which inserts a new provision into the CSA 1991,[22] providing that the Child Maintenance Service 'may take such steps as it considers appropriate to encourage the making and keeping of maintenance agreements' and, before accepting an application to it, may 'invite the applicant to consider with the [Service] whether it is possible to make such an agreement'.[23] Thus the new legislation represents an attempt to effect a significant general shift towards private ordering of child maintenance, and there has been a significant reduction in the number of applications under the CSA 1991.[24] It has been argued, however, that the legislation may have a differential impact as regards social class, those using the statutory system tending to be drawn from more vulnerable groups and, by contrast, wealthier families having more flexibility to set up their own voluntary arrangements.[25]

In addition, the 2008 Act introduced another formula for calculating child maintenance, this time based on percentages of historic gross income (as opposed to current net income under the 2000 Act's changes). Thus there are potentially now three possible schemes in place depending on when calculation of maintenance was requested, although the aim is that eventually all cases will be dealt with under the 2008 Act's scheme.

The new gross income scheme came into effect for a limited number of cases on 10 December 2012.[26] In due course, clients on the other schemes will be actively supported either to apply to the new scheme or to make a family-based arrangement.[27] It is envisaged that by around 2017 a single system of child maintenance will be in place.[28] In order to avoid an overcomplex exposition, this chapter discusses the scheme as implemented by the 2008 Act.

*Consultation on Strengthening Families, Promoting Parental Responsibility* (Cm 8130, 2011), available at www.dwp. gov.uk/docs/strengthening-families-response.pdf; Work and Pensions Select Committee, *The Government's Proposed Child Maintenance Reforms* (2011), available at www.publications.parliament.uk/pa/cm201012/cmselect/cmworpen/ 1047/104702.htm.

[21] Public Bodies (Child Maintenance and Enforcement Commission: Abolition and Transfer of Functions) Order 2012, made pursuant to the Public Bodies Act 2011.

[22] Section 9(2A).

[23] A new s 9A of the CSA 1991 (inserted by the Welfare Reform Act 2012, s 138) allows C-MEC to provide an indicative calculation of maintenance under the CSA 1991, thus providing some basis for privately agreeing an appropriate amount of maintenance.

[24] A reduction of approximately two-thirds of average monthly applications: see S. McKay, 'Child Support, Child Contact and Social Class', Chapter 9 in J. Wallbank and J. Herring (eds), *Vulnerabilities, Care and Family Law* (Abingdon: Routledge, 2014), pp 167–80, at p 169.

[25] S. McKay, 'Child Support, Child Contact and Social Class', Chapter 9 in J. Wallbank and J. Herring (eds), *Vulnerabilities, Care and Family Law* (Abingdon: Routledge, 2014), pp 167–80, at p 180.

[26] Child Maintenance and Other Payments Act 2008 (Commencement No 10 and Transitional Provisions) Order 2012 (SI 2012/3042). See D. Burrows, 'Child Support: The Start of the Gross Income Scheme' [2013] Family Law 208; and see also B. Carter, 'Child Support: 20 Years On' [2013] Family Law 1191.

[27] See www.childmaintenance.org/en/childsupport/timetable.html.

[28] C-MEC's view (ibid) that this would be achieved by 2015 was optimistic.

## 2 The Child Support Act 1991: the law

### 2.1 Parents and children to whom the Act applies

An important point to grasp right at the outset is that, unlike other statutes in this context, the CSA 1991 is only concerned with imposing liability for child support as between a child and his or her legal parent.[29]

#### 2.1.1 Parents

Parent is defined in section 54 as a 'person who is in law the father or mother of a child'.[30] For the purposes of the 1991 Act a parent must be habitually resident in the UK,[31] unless employed abroad by the civil service, armed forces, a UK company, or prescribed body.[32] Section 26(2) sets out certain cases in which it is assumed that a person is the parent of a child, for example where a child is adopted, where parents are parents pursuant to a parental order or other assisted-conception provisions of the Human Fertilisation and Embryology Acts, or where there has been a declaration of parentage, or the person concerned has been adjudged to be the child's parent in court proceedings. Where section 26(2) does not apply, it is possible for the parent with care to apply for a declaration of parentage, in which a direction for scientific testing can be made.[33]

#### 2.1.2 Child

Section 55(1) provides that, for the purposes of the Act, a person is a child if he has not attained the age of 16, or has not attained the age of 20 and satisfies conditions as may be prescribed. Under the previous legislation the conditions were that the person was receiving full-time education which is not advanced education (ie, below degree level).[34] A person is not a child if he or she is or has been married or in a civil partnership.[35]

### 2.2 Each parent's duty to maintain a qualifying child

Section 1(1) provides that 'each parent of a qualifying child is responsible for maintaining him'. Note that this statutory duty to maintain is not imposed in respect of every child, only those who qualify under the Act. Put simply, the Act only applies to children whose parents do not live with each other. Section 3 of the Act puts this more precisely, defining a 'qualifying child' by reference to the situation of the parents, who may be either a 'non-resident parent' or a 'parent with care'. A child is a qualifying child if one or both of his parents are in relation to him non-resident.[36] A non-resident parent is a parent not living in the same household with the child, where the child is living with 'a person with care'.[37] A person with care is the person with whom the child has his home; who usually provides day-to-day care for the child (whether exclusively or in conjunction with any other person); and who does not fall within a prescribed category of person.[38] Being a

---

[29] To be contrasted with the courts' residual powers to award financial provision for children, which can in certain circumstances be made against step-parents.

[30] See Chapter 7 for a detailed discussion of who in law a child's parent is, and see in this context *Re M (Child Support: Parentage)* [1997] 2 FLR 90.

[31] CSA 1991, s 44.      [32] Ibid, s 44(2A).

[33] See ibid, s 27. Fees for testing can be recovered, see s 27A. See further Chapter 7 for discussion of establishing legal parentage.

[34] See Child Support (Miscellaneous Amendments) (No 2) Regulations 2009 (SI 2009/2909).

[35] Section 55(2). This includes void marriages and civil partnerships.      [36] Section 3(1).

[37] Section 3(2). There may be more than one person with care: see s 3(5).

[38] CSA 1991, s 3(3). See Child Support (Miscellaneous Amendments) Regulations 1993 (SI 1993/913) and the Child Support (Maintenance Calculation Procedure) Regulations 2000 (SI 2001/157).

'parent with care' is not simply a matter of 'legal responsibility for the welfare of a child'. Rather, the meaning of 'day-to-day care' for the purposes of s 3(3)(b) carries practical connotations: the focus is on who is usually 'providing the hands-on care or the "immediate, short-term and mundane aspects of care". . . it is about who puts food on the table, washes the child's clothes, deals with the letters from school and reads a bedtime story'.[39]

## 2.3 Applications for a maintenance calculation and collection/ enforcement

A person with care[40] or a non-resident parent may apply under section 4 for a calculation of maintenance for the child under the provisions of the Act (known as a maintenance calculation).[41] A non-resident parent has a duty to make—and meets his or her responsibility under s 1(1) by making—any periodical payments determined in accordance with a maintenance calculation under the Act.[42] Such payments are called 'child support maintenance'.[43] Where a calculation has been made, C-MEC may arrange for the child support maintenance to be collected or the support obligation to be enforced if the parent applies for those services.[44]

No application can be made where there is in force: a written maintenance agreement made before 5 April 1993 (ie, before the CSA 1991 was first implemented);[45] or a maintenance order made before 3 March 2003;[46] or if a maintenance order made on or after the date 3 March 2003 is in force but has been so for less than the period of one year beginning with the date on which it was made.[47]

## 2.4 The maintenance calculation

The maintenance payable by a non-resident parent is calculated with reference to provisions in Schedule 1 to the Act. Payment of maintenance is calculated according to gross weekly income and is paid at four different rates depending on the non-resident parent's income: a basic, reduced, flat, or nil rate.

### 2.4.1 The basic rate

Where the non-resident parent's weekly income is £200 or more, the basic rate is applied.[48] The following percentage of the non-resident parent's gross weekly income is applied up to a ceiling of £800 weekly income:

- 12 per cent for one qualifying child;
- 16 per cent for two qualifying children;
- 19 per cent for three or more qualifying children.

---

[39] *GR v CMEC (CSM)* [2011] UKUT 101 (AAC), [2011] 2 FLR 962 (Upper Tribunal Judge Wikeley), at paras [48] and [49].

[40] Where there is more than one person with care, but all do not have parental responsibility for the qualifying child, only those with parental responsibility may apply: see s 5.

[41] Under s 4(1). As mentioned earlier in this chapter, s 6 of the Act, which used to compel use of the Child Support Agency by those who were on prescribed benefits, was repealed from 14 July 2008 by the Child Maintenance and Other Payments Act 2008.

[42] See s 1(2) and (3).     [43] CSA 1991, s 3(6).

[44] Ibid, s 4(2). Section 137 of the Welfare Reform Act 2012 inserts a new s 4(2A) providing that the Commission may only make arrangements under subs (2)(a) if—'(a) the non-resident parent agrees to the arrangements, or (b) the Commission is satisfied that without the arrangements child support maintenance is unlikely to be paid in accordance with the calculation.'

[45] Ibid, s 4(10)(a).

[46] Ibid. See the Child Support (Applications: Prescribed Date) Regulations 2003 (SI 2003/194), reg 10(1)(a).

[47] CSA 1991, s 4(10)(aa).     [48] Ibid, Sch 1, para 2.

For any gross weekly income above £800 up to £3,000,[49] the following percentages apply:

- 9 per cent for one qualifying child;
- 12 per cent for two qualifying children;
- 15 per cent for three or more qualifying children.

If the non-resident parent also has one or more relevant other children, gross weekly income used for these calculations is treated as reduced by the following percentage:

- 11 per cent where the non-resident parent has one relevant other child;
- 14 per cent where the non-resident parent has two relevant other children;
- 16 per cent where the non-resident parent has three or more relevant other children.[50]

Relevant other children are children other than qualifying children in respect of whom the non-resident parent or his or her partner receives child benefit.[51]

### 2.4.2 Reduced rate

A reduced rate (determined in accordance with regulations) is payable where the non-resident parent's income is less than £200 but more than £100, but the reduced rate may not be less than £7.

### 2.4.3 Flat rate

Where the non-resident parent's weekly income is £100 or less or he or she, or his or her partner, is receiving prescribed benefits or a pension, a flat rate of £7 is payable.

### 2.4.4 Nil rate

A nil rate is payable where the non-resident parent is of a prescribed description, or has a gross weekly income below £7.

### 2.4.5 Where the non-resident parent is maintaining another child under an arrangement

Where the non-resident parent has other non-qualifying children who are nevertheless maintained under a maintenance order or agreement, all of the maintained children are used to identify the appropriate rate within Schedule 1.[52] The amount calculated is divided by the total number of maintained children, and then multiplied by the number of qualifying children. Take the following example. A non-resident parent, living alone,[53] has weekly gross income of £400. He has three children, two of whom are maintained under a maintenance agreement and one of whom is a qualifying child for CSA purposes. The child support maintenance payable is one-third (19 per cent of £400), that is, £25.33. In this way the calculation recognises a higher percentage rate would apply if claims were being made under the Act for all the children, but at the same time recognises that the non-resident parent is already maintaining some of the children under other arrangements. Thus, he or she pays less than if the percentage relating to one qualifying child were simply applied, that is, 12 per cent of £400, which would be £48.

### 2.4.6 Apportionment

Sometimes a non-resident parent may have qualifying children who do not all live together, so that there is more than one person with care. In such cases, the amount payable to each person with care is calculated by apportioning the rate between the persons with care. The rate of maintenance

---

[49] Income over £3,000 is ignored for the purposes of Sch 1: Sch 1, para 10(3).   [50] Schedule 1, para 2(3).
[51] Under Pt IX of the Social Security Contributions and Benefits Act 1992: see CSA 1991, Sch 1, para 10C.
[52] Schedule 1, para 5A.
[53] To avoid additional complexity in calculation that would occur if he or she had other 'relevant children'.

liability is divided by the number of qualifying children, and shared among the persons with care according to the number of qualifying children in relation to whom each is a person with care.[54]

### 2.4.7  Reduction for shared care

If the overnight care of a qualifying child is, or is to be, shared between a non-resident parent and the person with care, in the case of the basic or reduced rates there is a decrease in maintenance payable according to the number of such nights which the Child Maintenance Service determines there to have been, or expects there to be, or both during a prescribed 12-month period. The amount of that decrease for one child is set out in Table 6.1 (although the amount payable can never fall below £7 per week).[55]

**Table 6.1**  Reduction for shared care

| Number of nights | Fraction to subtract |
| --- | --- |
| 52–103 | One-seventh |
| 104–155 | Two-sevenths |
| 156–174 | Three-sevenths |
| 175 or more | One-half[56] |

The flat rate is reduced to nil if a non-resident parent has care of the child for at least 52 nights in a prescribed 12-month period.[57] It should be emphasised that the reduction applies for *overnight* care. These provisions do not assist a non-resident parent who might incur considerable expenses in providing substantial daytime care of the child but who does not have the child sufficiently overnight to qualify for a reduction.[58] This is arguably unfair and, of course, the current scheme provides an obvious incentive for parents to argue about amounts of staying contact.[59]

### 2.4.8  Variations from the calculation

It is possible for either parent to apply to obtain a variation from the usual calculation in certain circumstances[60] under section 28F and Part 1 of Schedule 4B. The making of a variation is informed by the general principles that parents should be responsible for maintaining their children whenever they can afford to do so; and where a parent has more than one child, his obligation to maintain any one of them should be no less of an obligation than his obligation to maintain any other of them.[61] The Child Maintenance Service may agree to a variation if satisfied that the case is one which falls within one or more of the cases set out in Part I of Schedule 4B or in regulations made under that Part; and it is its opinion that, in all the circumstances of the case, it would be just and equitable to agree to a variation.[62] In considering whether it would be just and equitable in any case to agree to a variation, the Child Maintenance Service must have regard, in particular, to the welfare of any child likely to be affected if it did agree to a variation.[63]

---

[54]  Schedule 1, para 6.        [55]  Schedule 1, para 7(7).

[56]  If the fraction is one-half, the amount payable is further decreased by £7: see Sch 1, para 7(6).

[57]  Schedule 1, para 8(2).

[58]  See eg *R (Plumb) v Secretary of State for Work and Pensions* [2002] EWHC 1125 (Admin).

[59]  Although see *Re B (Contact: Child Support)* [2006] EWCA Civ 1574, [2007] 1 FLR 1949 (in deciding on contact, the court should not have regard to the impact of its determination upon a parent's liability to pay child support). For criticism, see S. Gilmore, '*Re B (Contact: Child Support)*—Horses and Carts: Contact and Child Support' [2007] Child and Family Law Quarterly 357.

[60]  CSA 1991, s 28A(1).        [61]  Ibid, s 28E.        [62]  Ibid, s 28F(1).

[63]  Ibid, s 28F(2), together with prescribed matters.

Schedule 4B sets out cases in which a departure direction may be given. First there is the category of prescribed special expenses, which include costs incurred in travelling to work, in maintaining contact with children, costs attributable to a long-term illness or disability of the applicant or of a dependant of the applicant, debts incurred for the family or members of the family before the non-resident parent became a non-resident parent in relation to a child, and costs incurred by a parent in supporting a child who is not his child but who is part of his family. A second category is property or capital transfers made prior to 5 April 1993 (date of implementation of the CSA 1991). There are also some additional cases, such as where a person's lifestyle is inconsistent with the level of his income, or housing or travel costs are unreasonably high.

## 2.5 **Enforcement**

The 1991 Act provides the Child Maintenance Service with wide powers of collection and enforcement. Section 31 enables it to order a non-resident parent's employers to deduct child support directly from earnings or from accounts. If this proves impossible or ineffective, the Service can apply to the magistrates' court for a liability order.[64] This can be enforced by levying distress or sale of the non-resident parent's goods,[65] or by a charging order or by means of a third party debt.[66] Where this fails, the applicant can apply for a warrant committing the non-resident parent to prison or disqualifying him or her from holding a driving licence.[67] The court is given power to decide which sanction is more appropriate in the circumstances and must do so. However, the 'right to liberty is such a fundamental human right that deprivation must always be an order of last resort' and 'the liable person is entitled to know why the option of disqualification was rejected and why imprisonment was preferred'.[68] Where the Child Maintenance Service has failed to recover maintenance by means of enforcement action and maintenance still remains payable and the Service is of the opinion that there has been wilful refusal or culpable neglect on the part of the person concerned, then it can apply for an order disqualifying the person from holding a driving licence or a UK passport.[69] The court must be satisfied of wilful refusal or culpable neglect.

In *R (On the Application of Kehoe) v Secretary of State for Work and Pensions*[70] the House of Lords held that this was a comprehensive scheme for enforcement of child support under the CSA 1991 by the Secretary of State and that the applicant in that case, Mrs Kehoe, did not have an individual right to pursue enforcement of child maintenance before the courts against her former husband. The European Court of Human Rights rejected Mrs Kehoe's claim that the CSA 1991 and the House of Lords' ruling violated her right under Article 6 of the European Convention.[71]

---

[64] Ibid, s 32M. A Court must proceed on the basis that a maintenance calculation has been lawfully and properly made and cannot question such calculation on an application for a liability order: see *Farley v Secretary of State for Work and Pensions and Another* [2006] UKHL 31 [2006] 2 FLR 1243.

[65] CSA 1991, s 35.     [66] Ibid, s 36.

[67] Ibid, s 39A. In order for s 39A to apply, the methods in ss 35 and 36 must actually have been invoked and 'the facts to be established are: (1) that a liability order has been made; (2) that the [Service] has sought to levy distress or to enforce under s 36; (3) that an amount remains unpaid and how much it is; (4) that the liable person has or had the means to pay it; and (5) that he has wilfully refused or culpably neglected to pay the outstanding sums': see *Karoonian v CMEC; Gibbons v CMEC* [2012] EWCA Civ 1379 [2013] 1 FLR 1121, at para [23]. The proceedings are criminal in nature, requiring proof of wilful refusal or culpable neglect, and the procedure must comply with Article 6 of the ECHR: see ibid.

[68] *Karoonian v CMEC; Gibbons v CMEC* [2012] EWCA Civ 1379 [2013] 1 FLR 1121, at para [29].

[69] CSA 1991, s 39B.

[70] [2005] UKHL 48. For a detailed account and criticism, see N. Wikeley, 'A Duty but Not a Right: Child Support after *R (Kehoe) v Secretary of State for Work and Pensions*' [2006] Child and Family Law Quarterly 287.

[71] *Kehoe v UK* [2008] ECHR 528, [2008] 2 FLR 1014.

## 3  The courts' residual role with respect to child maintenance

In order to give effect to the Child Support Act's policy of a general administrative scheme for calculation and collection of child support maintenance, it was necessary to limit the exercise of the courts' powers to make orders for maintenance which still exist in various statutes. Section 8(1) and (3) of the CSA 1991 read together provide that in any case where the Child Maintenance Service would have jurisdiction to make a maintenance calculation with respect to a qualifying child and a non-resident parent 'no court shall exercise any power which it would otherwise have to make, vary or revive any maintenance order[72] in relation to the child and non-resident parent concerned'.[73] In other words, as a general rule the courts' powers to make periodical payments are paralysed when the Child Maintenance Service has jurisdiction over child support maintenance.

However, there are some exceptions to the general rule which are set out in section 8 of the CSA itself.

### 3.1  Section 8(3A): Existing maintenance orders

Where there is a pre-March 2003 maintenance order and by reason of that order an application for a maintenance calculation is prevented,[74] the courts retain jurisdiction to vary the maintenance order. The courts also retain jurisdiction to vary a maintenance order which was made on or after 3 March 2003 provided no maintenance calculation has actually been made. Where the court makes a child maintenance order, 'the appropriate starting point should almost invariably be the amount arrived at by application of the Child Support Rules.'[75]

### 3.2  Section 8(5): Existing maintenance agreements

If there is a written agreement providing that a non-resident parent shall make or secure the making of periodical payments to or for the benefit of the child, a court has power to make a maintenance order which is, in all material respects, in the same terms as the agreement.

### 3.3  Section 8(6): A topping up order

As discussed earlier, only income up to £3,000 per week is used in the basic rate calculation of child support maintenance in Schedule 1 to the CSA 1991. That figure is likely to exhaust the available income of most non-resident parents. However, in the case of a very wealthy non-resident parent whose gross weekly income exceeds that figure,[76] the courts have jurisdiction to top-up the provision made under the CSA 1991 with court-ordered periodical payments, provided that there is a maintenance calculation in force with respect to the child.[77] The court must be satisfied that the circumstances of the case make it appropriate for the non-resident parent to make or secure the making of periodical payments under a maintenance order in addition to the child support maintenance

---

[72] By s 8(11) a 'maintenance order' means an order requiring the making or securing of periodical payments to or for the benefit of the child made under the MCA 1973, Pt II; the Domestic Proceedings and Magistrates' Courts Act 1978; the Matrimonial and Family Proceedings Act 1984, Pt III; the Children Act 1989, Sch 1; the Civil Partnership Act 2004, Sch 5, 6, or 7.

[73] Subsection (4) clarifies that subs (3) does not prevent a court from revoking a maintenance order.

[74] By s 4(10) or 7(10).

[75] See *GW v RW* [2003] 2 FLR 108, [74]; and *TW v TM (Minors) (Child Maintenance: Jurisdiction and Departure from Formula)* [2015] EWHC 3054 (Fam).

[76] Ie, exceeds the figure referred to in para 10(3) of Sch 1 (as it has effect from time to time pursuant to regulations made under para 10A(1)(b)). See s 8(6)(b).

[77] Section 8(6)(a). See S. Mahmood and C. Hallam, 'Schedule 1 and the CSA: Getting into the Top-up Zone' [2011] Family Law 266.

payable in accordance with the maintenance calculation.[78] In *Dickson v Rennie*[79] Holman J commented that it is:

> crystal clear from the scheme of the Act as a whole, and s 8(6) within it, that … to make a top-up order the relevant 'gross weekly income' for the purposes of s 8(6)(b) has to be the gross weekly income that has been assessed or calculated by the Secretary of State or the CMS. Quite clearly that subsection is, indeed, providing a 'top-up' jurisdiction; it is not providing some avenue of challenge or appeal to the calculation or assessment that has earlier been performed by the Secretary of State or the CMS.[80]

### 3.4 Section 8(7): Educational expenses

Section 8(7) provides that a court may make a maintenance order if:

(a) the child is, will be or (if the order were to be made) would be receiving instruction at an educational establishment or undergoing training for a trade, profession or vocation (whether or not while in gainful employment); and

(b) the order is made solely for the purposes of requiring the person making or securing the making of periodical payments fixed by the order to meet some or all of the expenses incurred in connection with the provision of the instruction or training.

### 3.5 Section 8(8): Expenses attributable to a child's disability

A court may make a maintenance order where a child is disabled[81] and 'the order is made solely for the purpose of requiring the person making or securing the making of periodical payments fixed by the order to meet some or all of any expenses attributable to the child's disability'.

### 3.6 Section 8(10): Orders against a person with care

Nothing in section 8 prevents a court from exercising any power which it has to make a maintenance order in relation to a child if the order is made against a person with care of the child.

---

**Key case**

In *C v F (Disabled Child: Maintenance Orders)*[82] the Court of Appeal held that the courts' powers under these exemptions were limited by the conditions imposed within each exemption. So in the case of a child under a disability, or in further or higher education, the order must be designed simply to meet expenses attributable to these circumstances. Thorpe LJ expressed the view, *obiter*, that the limits imposed by the CSA 1991 would continue to apply until the child reached an age when that Act no longer applied, and thereafter the broader provisions of Schedule 1 to the Children Act 1989 would prevail.[83] The court was clear, however, that the duration of any orders made by a court under the exemption provisions were not limited to the latest date for payments made under the CSA 1991. Such a restriction would undermine the purpose of some of the exemption provisions. For example, there is no reason why a maintenance agreement embodied in a court order should not provide for maintenance beyond the age of 16 even though the child is not receiving

---

[78] For an example, see *H v C* [2009] 2 FLR 1540, [2009] 2 FLR 1540.
[79] [2014] EWHC 4306 (Fam) [2015] 2 FLR 978.      [80] Ibid, [30].
[81] For this purpose a child is disabled if he is blind, deaf, or dumb or is substantially and permanently handicapped by illness, injury, mental disorder, or congenital deformity or such other disability as may be prescribed (s 8(9)).
[82] [1998] 2 FLR 1, CA.
[83] Ibid, 8, a view with which Butler-Sloss and Hutchinson LJJ were inclined to agree but expressed no firm conclusion.

> full-time education. Moreover, the courts' powers allow orders in respect of children in tertiary education and of children, including adult children, under a disability, and it would be absurd if an order had to come to an end when, for example, a child had just completed his or her first year at university.

There will, of course, be some situations where the restriction in section 8(1) and (3) of the CSA 1991 will simply not apply because the CSA 1991 is not applicable in the first place. An example is the case of a non-resident father who is not habitually resident in the UK within the meaning of the Act. The CSA 1991 does not apply because he is not a parent within the meaning of the Act and there would therefore be no restriction on use of court-ordered periodical payments should an application be made against him.[84]

Capital provision is unaffected by the CSA 1991, although in a case to which it applies, the power to make a lump sum award should be exercised only 'to meet the need of a child in respect of a particular item of capital expenditure'. Lump sums should not be used 'in such a way as to provide for the regular support of the child, which would ordinarily have been provided by an order for periodic payments',[85] since to do so would circumvent the policy in section 8(1) and (3) of the CSA 1991.

## 4  The courts' powers

Having clarified the relationship between the CSA 1991 and the courts' powers, we now turn to consider the various statutes under which court-based provision might be made. The High Court or county court has powers under the Matrimonial Causes Act 1973 to address financial support for children on or after a decree of divorce or nullity; and the Civil Partnership Act 2004 makes similar provision in the case of dissolution or annulment of a civil partnership.[86] Of these jurisdictions, only the Matrimonial Causes Act (MCA) 1973 will be considered in the following section in order to simplify the exposition, and also because the case law has been developed in relation to those provisions. Reference will be made only to 'marriage', but it should borne in mind throughout that the statutory framework is similar (and is likely to be applied similarly) in respect of the children of civil partners.

Later in this chapter we shall discuss another jurisdiction in Schedule 1 to the Children Act 1989 which is available to provide support for all children irrespective of their parents' marital status.[87] There is thus a choice of jurisdiction in the case of children whose parents are married. Where the parents' circumstances are such that the MCA 1973 would apply, however, there may be advantages in using those provisions. The MCA 1973 contains wider powers than those in Schedule 1 to the Children Act 1989, for example a power to order the sale of property.[88]

### 4.1  Matrimonial Causes Act 1973

Under Part II of the MCA 1973, on or after the grant of a decree of divorce or nullity the court has power to make various orders for financial provision or property adjustment to or for the benefit of a child of the family.

---

[84] See eg *A v A*, discussed in Section 4.7.5.

[85] *Phillips v Peace* [1996] 2 FLR 230 at 235B–D, *per* Johnson J. For comment, see J. A. Priest, 'Child Support and the Non-Standard Earner—Pass the Heineken, Please! *Phillips v Peace*' [1997] Child and Family Law Quarterly 63. See also on the distinction between a lump sum and a maintenance order as defined in the CSA 1991, s 8(11), and *AMS v Child Support Officer* [1998] 1 FLR 955. See further, J. Priest, 'Capital Settlements and the Child Support Act' [1998] Family Law 115 and 170.

[86] Civil Partnership Act 2004, Sch 5.          [87] Or civil partnership status.

[88] MCA 1973, s 24A. There are also wider powers relating to disclosure and preservation of assets.

**Key legislation**

Section 52 of the 1973 Act provides that child of the family in relation to the parties to a marriage, means:

(a) a child of both of those parties; and

(b) any other child, not being a child who is placed with those parties as foster parents by a local authority or voluntary organisation, who has been treated by both of those parties as a child of their family.

The concept of the child of the family recognises that a person who chooses to marry someone who already has children may take on responsibility for the children as well as for his spouse.[89] If the marriage ends, this responsibility may involve making financial and property provision for these children, although as we shall see it is tempered by the liability of anyone else to maintain the child. Before any obligation can be imposed, it must first be established that the non-parent has treated the child as a child of the family. This is a question of fact turning on evidence of how he or she behaved towards the child.[90] It is an objective test:[91] 'The independent outside observer has to look at the situation and say: "Does the evidence show that the child was treated as a member of the family?".'[92]

It is not possible to treat an unborn child as a child of the family, as a foetus is not a child.[93] Thus if a married couple live together during the woman's pregnancy but split up before the child is born, the child will not be a child of the family.[94] This will be so even though the husband may allow it to be thought he is the father of the child when he is not.[95] Where, however, a child lives in the same household with a step-parent for some considerable period of time it is almost inevitable that he or she will be treated as a child of the family.[96] By contrast, if the child has his home with other family members but merely visits his parent and step-parent, this does not make him a child of the family and the step-parent is not financially responsible for him if the marriage breaks down.[97] A child can be treated as a child of the family even where a husband has treated him as such in the mistaken belief that the child is his own child. In *W(RJ) v W(SJ)*[98] a husband was deceived by his wife about the paternity of their two children, and after the marriage broke down blood tests revealed that he was not the father. Park J held that both children had been treated as children of the family and that the husband's lack of knowledge of the facts relating to the children's paternity was immaterial to their status.

As discussed in Chapter 4, the welfare whilst a minor of any child of the family who has not attained the age of 18 will be the court's first consideration when considering financial orders for (former) spouses upon their divorce.[99] Providing support for any such children (eg by provision to the children's primary carer of a secure home) is likely to form an important part (and focus) of many financial relief packages. The power of the court to transfer property to a spouse

---

[89] However, note that the liability may be to children other than stepchildren, eg an orphaned relative who has lived with the parties and has been treated as a child of their family; or a foster child who was placed privately, who has been treated as a child of the family for some considerable time, and whose parents cannot support him financially.

[90] *M v M (Child of the Family)* (1981) 2 FLR 39, CA; *D v D (Child of the Family)* (1981) 2 FLR 93, CA; *W v W (Child of the Family)* [1984] FLR 796, CA; *Carron v Carron* [1984] FLR 805, CA; *Teeling v Teeling* [1984] FLR 808, CA.

[91] *D v D (Child of the Family)* (1981) 2 FLR 93 at 96.     [92] Ibid, 97.

[93] *A v A (Family: Unborn Child)* [1974] Fam 6 at 15F: 'A man cannot behave towards a child and therefore cannot treat a child as part of the family, unless the child has been born and is living', *per* Bagnall J.

[94] *A v A (Family: Unborn Child)* [1974] Fam 6.

[95] *M v M (Child of the Family)* (1981) 2 FLR 39, CA (couple split up before child's birth).

[96] See *Teeling v Teeling* [1984] FLR 808 (six-month period of cohabitation, discussed in Section 4.4).

[97] *D v D (Child of the Family)* (1981) 2 FLR 93.     [98] [1972] Fam 152.     [99] MCA 1973, s 25(1).

in his or her own right clearly provides greater flexibility surrounding provision for children. Here, however, we focus specifically on the orders which can be made to or for the benefit of the children.

## 4.2 Available orders

The available orders are set out in sections 23 and 24 of the MCA 1973, which will already be familiar to those conversant with the law relating to financial orders for spouses discussed in Chapter 4. Paragraphs (d), (e), and (f) of section 23 set out various financial provision orders that can be made to or for the benefit of a child of the family: periodical payments, secured periodical payments, and lump sums respectively. Under section 24 the court can order lump sums, transfers of property, and settlements of property to or for the benefit of such children.

## 4.3 Exercise of the court's discretion

The exercise of the court's discretion is guided by section 25(3) and (4).

---

### Key legislation

Section 25(3), which applies in all cases, sets out particular matters to which the court must have regard when making orders to or for the benefit of children. These are:

(a) the financial needs of the child;

(b) the income, earning capacity (if any), property and other financial resources of the child;

(c) any physical or mental disability of the child;

(d) the manner in which he was being and in which the parties to the marriage expected him to be educated or trained;

(e) the considerations mentioned in relation to the parties to the marriage in paragraphs (a), (b), (c) and (e) of subsection (2) above.

---

The considerations in section 25(2) in relation to the parties to the marriage mentioned in paragraph (e) are discussed in detail in Chapter 4. Put briefly, the court is required to consider the parties' resources, obligations, standard of living before the breakdown, and whether they have any physical or mental disability.

## 4.4 Maintenance of a child by a party who is not the child's parent

As regards the exercise of the courts' powers[100] in favour of a child who is not the child of that party, section 25(4) provides that the court must also have regard:

(a) to whether that party assumed any responsibility for the child's maintenance, and, if so, to the extent to which, and the basis upon which, that party assumed such responsibility and to the length of time for which that party discharged such responsibility;

(b) to whether in assuming and discharging such responsibility that party did so knowing that the child was not his or her own;

(c) to the liability of any other person to maintain the child.

---

[100] Under s 23(1)(d), (e), or (f), (2) or (4), 24, or 24A.

In *Teeling v Teeling*[101] a wife left her husband and had a child by another man. The husband and wife then got back together for only six months before the wife left again. The court found that the baby had been treated as a child of the family, but that the husband's best answer to a claim was to be found in section 25(4), commenting that 'if ever a case was *de minimis* so far as the assumption of any responsibility by this husband for this child was concerned, it is this case'.[102] The court is specifically required to consider the basis on which such a husband had assumed and discharged his financial responsibility for the child and whether he did so knowing that the child was not his own. Thus lack of knowledge on the part of a deceived husband is material to whether he should be ordered to make provision for a child who is a child of the family but not his own. In *W(RJ) v W(SJ)*,[103] the case of the husband who was deceived about the paternity of two children (mentioned earlier), it was implicit in the judgment that no order for financial provision would be made against the husband. The obligation of a person who has treated a child as a child of the family must also be considered with regard to the liability of any other person to maintain the child.

The court's power to make an order is not precluded by the fact of a legal parent's liability[104] and in an appropriate case the child could receive payments from both adults concerned. However, as we have seen, the CSA 1991 emphasises that the primary responsibility for child support remains with the legal parent regardless of the length of time for which a step-parent has been providing for the child. A step-parent who is pursued for child maintenance in the courts will therefore normally be well advised to insist that the applicant first seeks to obtain support for the child from his or her parent through the intervention of the Child Maintenance Service.

## 4.5 Duration of orders

In the first instance, periodical payments are not to extend beyond the child's seventeenth birthday,[105] unless the court considers that in the circumstances of the case the welfare of the child requires that it should extend to a later date.[106] In any event, the general rule is that periodical payments or secured periodical payments are not to extend beyond a child's 18th birthday.[107] Furthermore, no order for financial provision or for transfer of property is to be made in favour of a child who has attained the age of 18.[108]

The restrictions on making provision for a child over the age of 18 do not apply if it appears to the court that:

(a) the child is, or will be, or if an order were made . . . would be, receiving instruction at an educational establishment or undergoing training for a trade, profession or vocation, whether or not he is also, or will also be, in gainful employment; or

(b) there are special circumstances which justify the making of an order without complying with either or both of those provisions.[109]

## 4.6 Provision for children as dependants

The statute enables the courts to make financial provision for children 'as dependants, rather than as persons with an interest or a potential interest in the assets of the family'.[110] This has been said

---

[101] [1984] FLR 808.    [102] Ibid, 810.    [103] [1972] Fam 152.    [104] *Carron v Carron* [1984] FLR 805.
[105] Ie the birthday following attaining the upper limit of compulsory school age: s 29(2)(a).
[106] Section 29(2)(a).    [107] MCA 1973, s 29(2)(b).    [108] Ibid, s 29(1).
[109] Ibid, s 29(3). The fact that the child may be receiving a student award does not preclude the court making further provision: see *B v B (Adult Student: Liability to Support)* [1998] 1 FLR 373. See further T. Costley-White, 'Maintenance Liability for Students' [1999] Family Law 45.
[110] G. Miller, 'Capital Provision for Children' (1997) 1 Private Client Business 51. See also J. Miller, 'Children and Family Capital on Divorce' (1993) 5 Journal of Child Law 113.

by the Court of Appeal on several occasions. In *Chamberlain v Chamberlain*,[111] for example, the Court of Appeal held that a judge had erred in settling a house 'so that the beneficial interest, at the end of the day, became that of the children in equal shares'. The court observed that there were 'no circumstances to suggest that any of the children had special circumstances which required them to make demands on their parents after the completion of their full-time education'.[112] The court made clear that, provided the parents met their responsibilities to their children as dependants, the house, acquired by the work and resources of the parents, should revert to the parents.[113] In *Lilford (Lord) v Glynn*,[114] the Court of Appeal stated that the wealth of a parent did not amount to special circumstances, and held that the same principle applied even where the child's parent was a millionaire. The court held that it had not been right to order a child's father to settle funds to provide income to a child during the child's whole lifetime, observing:

> A father—even the richest father—ought not to be regarded as having 'financial obligations [or] responsibilities' to provide funds for the purposes of such settlements as are envisaged in this case on children who are under no disability and whose maintenance and education is secure.[115]

However, *Lilford (Lord) v Glynn*[116] was distinguished in *Tavoulareas v Tavoulareas*.[117] In that case neither parent was employed, being supported by their wealthy families. The trial judge ordered the husband to settle on the wife a lump sum of £250,000 to provide for housing for both the wife and their child, which sum would revert to the husband at the end of the child's dependency. The Court of Appeal substituted an order that the sum of £250,000 should be paid to trustees to hold the same for the benefit of the wife during the child's dependency for the purpose of providing them both with accommodation, but that at the conclusion of the child's dependency the reversion would be to the child. Thorpe LJ stated that this was an exceptional case where the reversion to the child was fully justified. Within these wealthy families there was a tradition of making capital provision to children upon attaining adulthood, and the outcome therefore reflected the traditions and convictions of those involved.[118]

The parties' capital had been derived from their respective families, and neither had made any contribution to the sum which would go into the settlement, and neither had a foreseeable need for that sum when the settlement came to an end.

While Thorpe LJ described this as an exceptional case, he also stated that 'in an infinite number of cases since [*Lilford (Lord) v Glynn*] settlements have been ordered during the dependency of a child or children and the court invariably chooses, at the conclusion of the dependency, whether the reversion should be for the settlor, for the parties in some shares, or to the child'.[119] This statement, or the outcome in *Tavoulareas*, is certainly not easy to reconcile with earlier Court of Appeal authorities, since the judgment in *Tavoulareas* does not explain satisfactorily how the award of the

---

[111] [1973] 1 WLR 1557.

[112] Ibid, 1564 *per* Scarman LJ. See also *Kiely v Kiely* [1988] 1 FLR 248, CA at 252B–C, *per* Booth J: 'the provisions of the 1973 Act make it clear that the statutory scheme is to enable the court to make proper financial provision for children as children or dependants'; and *Harnett v Harnett* [1973] Fam 156 at 161, *per* Bagnall J: 'In the vast majority of cases the financial position of a child of a subsisting marriage is simply to be afforded shelter, food and education according to the means of his parents.'

[113] Compare *Griffiths v Griffiths* [1984] Fam 70 where capital provision was appropriate because a parent had failed to meet responsibilities to a child.

[114] [1979] 1 WLR 78.     [115] Ibid, 85 *per* Orr LJ.

[116] *Lilford (Lord) v Glynn* [1979] 1 WLR 78, (1978) FLR Rep 427, [1979] 1 All ER 441, CA.

[117] [1998] 2 FLR 418.

[118] See at 429 *per* Thorpe LJ. Gilmore criticises the prominence given to the family tradition of passing property between generations and questions whether children from families which do not have such traditions should be treated any differently: S. Gilmore, 'Re P (Child)(Financial Provision)—Shoeboxes and Comical Shopping Trips—Child Support From the Affluent to Fabulously Rich' (2004) 16(1) Child and Family Law Quarterly 103.

[119] *Tavoulareas v Tavoulareas* [1998] 2 FLR 418 at 429.

reversion to the child absolutely on reaching adulthood related to needs of the child as a dependant during minority.[120] It also seems to be out of line with the decision of the Court of Appeal in *C v C (Financial Relief: Short Marriage)*.[121] The facts were equally unusual, if not more so. The parties had met when the wife was working as a high-class prostitute. They married, had a child, and separated. The husband, who was very wealthy, wanted any lump sum that he was required to pay to be settled on the wife for the purpose of providing her and the child with a home, and for that sum to revert to the child when the settlement came to an end. The trial judge refused to accede to this request for the reason that the wife should have more than a limited interest in the property. The Court of Appeal dismissed the husband's appeal on two grounds. It found that the trial judge had not been plainly wrong with regard to the needs of the wife; and it held that there was a long line of authorities from *Chamberlain v Chamberlain* to *Lilford (Lord) v Glynn* that the powers to make lump sum and settlement orders were not normally exercised to provide funds directly for the children.

## 4.7 Children Act 1989, section 15 and Schedule 1

If a child's parents are not married, the jurisdiction which will need to be used to make provision beyond that made under the CSA 1991 is contained in Schedule 1 to the Children Act 1989.[122] The provisions are similar to those under the MCA 1973, although there are some differences which are highlighted in the following sections.[123] The core provisions are in paragraphs 1 to 4. In brief, paragraph 1 sets out the available orders and who (apart from the child himself) can apply for them; paragraph 2 deals with applications by the child himself as an adult; paragraph 3 explains various matters relating to the duration of orders; and paragraph 4 sets out the criteria by which the court exercises its discretion.

### 4.7.1 Who can apply?

#### 4.7.1.1 Applications on behalf of the child

In most cases, the court will be exercising its powers under Schedule 1 in response to an application (although there are some circumstances in which the powers can be exercised even though no application has been made[124]). Those who can apply on behalf of the child are a parent, guardian, or special guardian of a child or any person who is named in a child arrangements order as a person with whom a child is to live.[125] The category of potential applicants is thus wider in some respects than under the MCA 1973. The provision which allows an application by a person in whose favour a child arrangements order is in force is an important one which comes to the assistance of relatives or friends of the child who have undertaken the burden of responsibility for caring for the child but do not have the means to support it. It seems likely that the power of the courts to make orders in favour of a person with a child arrangements order is not generally known. This is unfortunate because it might persuade relatives and others interested in the child

---

[120] See Gilmore (n 118) who also points out that the assumption of the child's dependency in *Tavoulareas* seems out of line with the policy adopted in claims under the Inheritance (Provision for Family and Dependants) Act 1975 (see eg Browne-Wilkinson J in *Re Dennis (Deceased)* [1981] 2 All ER 140 at 145: 'why should anybody else make provision for you if you are capable maintaining yourself?').

[121] [1997] 2 FLR 26.

[122] See generally, J. Bazley QC et al (One Garden Court Chambers), *Applications under Schedule 1 to the Children Act 1989* (Bristol: Family Law, 2010).

[123] For example, there is in the Children Act 1989 no provision equivalent to the part of s 25(2)(a) of the MCA 1973, requiring the court to have regard to any increase in earning capacity which it would be reasonable for a party to take steps to acquire; unlike s 25(1) of the MCA 1973, the Children Act 1989 does not treat a child's welfare as the 'first consideration'; and under the Children Act 1989, applications can be made by adult children: see Sch 1, para 2.

[124] Where a child is a ward of court or where a court is making, varying, or discharging a child arrangements or special guardianship order: see Sch 1, paras 1(6) and 1(7).

[125] Schedule 1, para 1(1). A person against whom an order is made can apply to vary or discharge an order: see Sch 1, para 1(4).

to look after the child where the parents are unable or unwilling to do so. Moreover, those who are already looking after a child on an informal basis in a case where parents are refusing, or failing, to contribute towards the costs of their child's upbringing would sometimes be well advised to apply for a child arrangements order so that they can obtain income, and possibly a capital contribution, towards the child's upkeep.

### 4.7.1.2  Applications by adult children

It is also possible for an adult child who is a trainee or student, or who can show special circumstances, to apply for his or her own provision pursuant to Schedule 1, paragraph 2. In order for provision to be made it must appear to the court:

(a) that the applicant is, will be or (if an order were made) would be receiving instruction at an educational establishment or undergoing training for a trade, profession or vocation, whether or not while in gainful employment; or

(b) that there are special circumstances which justify the making of an order.

In such cases the court's available powers are limited to making periodical payments or lump sum orders, and the orders can only be made against a parent[126] (not step-parents or others), and only where parents are not living in the same household as each other.[127] In what follows, we shall concentrate on the more usual case of applications on behalf of minor children.

### 4.7.2  Available orders

Schedule 1, paragraph 1(2) contains a range of powers to make financial provision or property adjustment to or for the benefit of a child.[128] The courts can require either or both of the child's parents to provide financially for the child by way of periodical payments, secured periodical payments,[129] lump sums,[130] or through the settlement[131] or transfer[132] of property.[133] The powers can be exercised at any time[134] although orders for transfer or settlement of property may be exercised only once against the same person in respect of the same child.[135] Whether the full range of orders is available, however, depends on which court is hearing the application. Applications under Schedule 1 can be to the High Court, a county court, or a magistrates' court. The High Court or a county court can make any of the available orders. However, the magistrates' court can only make periodical payments and/or lump sums[136] and lump sums in the magistrates' court shall not exceed £1,000.[137]

---

[126]  Schedule 1, para 2(2).

[127]  Schedule 1, para 2(4). An application may also not be made under para 2 if, immediately before the applicant reached the age of 16, a periodical payments order was in force with respect to him or her (Sch 1, para 2(3)).

[128]  In *CF v KM (Financial Provision for Child: Costs of Legal Proceedings)* [2010] EWHC 1754 (Fam), [2011] 1 FLR 208, Charles J held that an interim lump sum could be awarded for the benefit of the child in respect of the legal fees of Sch 1 proceedings. Charles J said that Bennett J's view in *W v J (Child: Variation of Financial Provision)* [2003] EWHC 2657 (Fam), [2004] 2 FLR 300 at paras [45]–[49] that the words 'for the benefit of the child' in para 1(2)(a) were not wide enough to cover moneys payable by one parent for the other's legal fees had been overtaken by subsequent case law. See also *A v A (Maintenance Pending Suit: Provision for Legal Fees)* [2001] 1 WLR 605, [2001] 1 FLR 377, and *PG v TW (No 1) (Child: Financial Provision: Legal Funding)* [2012] EWHC 1892 (Fam). On the approach to awarding legal costs in an appeal concerning Schedule 1 to the Children Act 1989, see *KS v ND (Schedule 1: Appeal: Costs)* [2013] EWHC 464 (Fam), [2013] 2 FLR 698 (costs should prima facie follow the event).

[129]  Schedule 1, para 1(2)(a) and (b). The orders may be for such term as may be specified in the order.

[130]  Schedule 1, para 1(2)(c).     [131]  Schedule 1, para 1(2)(d).     [132]  Schedule 1, para 1(2)(e).

[133]  To which either parent is entitled (either in possession or in reversion).

[134]  Schedule 1, para 1(3). Unlike, eg, under the MCA jurisdiction, where the order must be on or after divorce or annulment.

[135]  Schedule 1, para 1(5).     [136]  Schedule 1, para 1(1)(b).     [137]  Schedule 1, para 5(2).

### 4.7.3 Against whom can orders be made

Orders can be made against either or both of a child's parents as defined in Schedule 1, paragraph 16.[138] Parent includes any party to a marriage or civil partnership (whether subsisting or not) in relation to whom the child is a child of the family. Child of the family, in relation to parties to a marriage, or to two people who are civil partners of each other, means: (a) a child of both of them, and (b) any other child, other than a child placed with them as foster parents by a local authority or voluntary organisation, who has been treated by both of them as a child of their family.[139] So, in the same way as discussed in relation to the MCA 1973 earlier in this chapter, orders can be made not only against parents, but against step-parents and former step-parents, indeed against any person who is or was a party to a marriage or civil partnership where both parties to that relationship treated the child as part of that family (subject to the exceptions relating to certain foster parents).

In *T v B (Parental Responsibility: Financial Provision)*[140] a child had been raised for several years by a lesbian couple, the child's mother having conceived through anonymous sperm donation at a clinic. The couple's relationship had broken down and a shared residence order had been made conferring parental responsibility on the mother's former partner. The mother then sought orders under Schedule 1 to the Children Act 1989 against the former partner, and the question arose as to the meaning of 'parent' within Schedule 1. Moylan J held that the mother's former partner was a 'social and psychological parent',[141] but that the word 'parent' in Schedule 1 means legal parent.[142] Here the mother's former partner could not be a legal parent because the child had been born prior to enactment of the Human Fertilisation and Embryology Act 2008 which now confers legal parenthood in such a case; and Moylan J was clear that 'the mere obtaining of parental responsibility is clearly not intended to make someone a legal parent when they would not otherwise be such'.[143]

### 4.7.4 Duration of orders

Similar rules to those in the MCA 1973 apply with respect to the duration of orders.[144]

### 4.7.5 Exercise of the court's discretion

**Key legislation**

In deciding whether to exercise its powers under paragraph 1 or 2, and if so in what manner, paragraph 4(1) provides that the court must have regard to all the circumstances including—

(a) the income, earning capacity, property and other financial resources which each person mentioned in sub-paragraph (4) has or is likely to have in the foreseeable future;

---

[138] A court has power to make an order under Sch 1 notwithstanding the bankruptcy of the respondent, *Re G (Children Act 1989, Schedule 1)* [1996] 2 FLR 171. As Singer J said at 177:

It would be quite wrong . . . for the mother and, of course in particular the child, to be left with no order simply because a third party had got round to the exercise of their rights to obtain a bankruptcy order against the father.

[139] See Children Act 1989, s 105(1).     [140] [2010] EWHC 1444 (Fam), [2010] 2 FLR 1966.

[141] Ibid, [54].     [142] Ibid, [67]. See also *J v J (A Minor: Property Transfer)* [1993] 2 FLR 56 at 59.

[143] [2010] EWHC 1444 (Fam) at [63].

[144] Schedule 1, para 3(1) provides that periodical payments '. . . (a) shall not in the first instance extend beyond the child's seventeenth birthday unless the court thinks it right in the circumstances of the case to specify a later date; and (b) shall not in any event extend beyond the child's eighteenth birthday.'

Schedule 1, para 3(2) provides that '[p]aragraph (b) of sub-paragraph (1) shall not apply in the case of a child if it appears to the court that—

(a) the child is, or will be or (if an order were made without complying with that paragraph) would be receiving instruction at an educational establishment or undergoing training for a trade, profession or vocation, whether or not while in gainful employment; or

(b) there are special circumstances which justify the making of an order without complying with that paragraph.'

(b) the financial needs, obligations and responsibilities which each person mentioned in sub-paragraph (4) has or is likely to have in the foreseeable future;

(c) the financial needs of the child;

(d) the income, earning capacity (if any), property and other financial resources of the child;

(e) any physical or mental disability of the child;

(f) the manner in which the child was being, or was expected to be, educated or trained.

The persons mentioned in sub-paragraph (4) are any parent,[145] the applicant, and any other person in whose favour the court proposes to make the order. Unlike section 25(2)(c) of the MCA 1973 as applied to children's claims, by section 25(3)(e) of the MCA 1973, paragraph 4(1) of the Children Act 1989 does not include any reference to the standard of living enjoyed by the family before the breakdown of the marriage, although standard of living is clearly relevant to 'needs'. The omission no doubt recognises that unmarried parents may never have lived together as a family. In addition, the physical or mental disabilities of the parent are not expressly in issue under the Children Act 1989,[146] an omission which is not easy to understand.

Where the court is deciding whether to make an order against a person who is not the mother or the father of the child, additional considerations in paragraph 4(2) apply:

(a) whether that person has assumed responsibility for the maintenance of the child and, if so, the extent to which and basis on which he assumed that responsibility and the length of the period during which he met that responsibility;

(b) whether he did so knowing that the child was not his child;

(c) the liability of any other person to maintain the child.[147]

The principle of the paramountcy of the child's welfare in section 1 of the Children Act 1989 does not apply to orders for financial and property provision made under Schedule 1 to the Act. This is made plain in section 105 which states that a child's 'upbringing' does not include a child's maintenance. Neither is the child's welfare the first consideration as under section 25(1) of the MCA 1973. There is no reference to the child's welfare at all in Schedule 1, and the only guidance provided by the statute is the criteria in paragraph 4. In *K v K (Minors: Property Transfer)*[148] the trial judge ordered a father of four children to transfer his interest in a joint tenancy of the council house in which the family were living to the children's mother for the benefit of the children of the family.[149] When arriving at his decision, the judge treated the children's welfare as paramount and omitted to refer to the criteria then governing orders for children. In particular he did not take account of the father's nine years of accrued rights under the right to buy provisions of the Housing Act 1980, his ability to find and pay for other accommodation, and his very low income. The Court of Appeal ordered a retrial,[150] finding

---

[145]  In the case of an application under Sch 1, para 2 by an adult child, 'parent' is confined to the mother and father of the child, although in the case of a child who has a parent by virtue of s 42 or 43 of the Human Fertilisation and Embryology Act 2008, any reference in Sch 1, para 4, to the child's father is a reference to the woman who is a parent of the child by virtue of that section.

[146]  Unlike s 25(2)(e) of the MCA 1973, as applied by s 25(3)(e).

[147]  If the court makes such an order, it must record in the order that the order is made on the basis that the person against whom the order is made is not the child's father (see para 4(3)).

[148]  [1992] 2 All ER 727.

[149]  Under the Guardianship of Minors Act 1971, s 11B(2)(d). The power to order one unmarried cohabitant to transfer the tenancy in the family home to the other is found in the Family Law Act 1996, Sch 7.

[150]  Although the Court of Appeal ordered a retrial, it nonetheless accepted that such an order was for the benefit of the children and that it therefore fell within the court's powers under Sch 1. However, the willingness of the court to contemplate making a property transfer order for the benefit of children, as distinct from a settlement order with reversion to the settlor, seems to have been unique, and is probably limited to cases involving the transfer of a council or other tenancy.

that the judge had erred in principle in treating the child's welfare as paramount and failing to conduct this balancing exercise.

In *A v A (A Minor: Financial Provision)*[151] Ward J concluded that, notwithstanding any differences between the Children Act 1989 and the MCA 1973, the claims of children of married and unmarried parents should be dealt with similarly. He noted that the trend against making provision in favour of adult children who have ceased their full-time education is reinforced in the Children Act 1989 jurisdiction by paragraph 2 of Schedule 1, where, in the case of an application by an adult child, there is no power to make a property adjustment order.[152] In that case the father of one child of a family of three children was a multi-millionaire who was resident outside the jurisdiction. The mother applied for periodical payments and for an outright transfer of property either to herself for the benefit of the child, or to the child herself. Ward J awarded £20,000 per annum[153] for the child's maintenance, commenting that insofar as that sum indirectly benefited the child's half-sisters,[154] for whom the father was not financially responsible, it could be justified by reference to the child's welfare which, while not an express consideration under the statute, was one of the circumstances that his Lordship took into account.[155] Ward J included within that sum an allowance for the mother's care of the child, which, it had been established in *Haroutunian v Jennings*,[156] is not wrong in principle. Ward J quantified this allowance by reference to the cost of professional childcare, such as a nanny, or mother's help such as an *au pair*.[157]

Applying the same approach as under the 1973 Act jurisdiction, however, Ward J rejected the application for property transfer and ordered that the house owned by the father, in which the mother and the three children were living, should be settled on the child to terminate six months after she attained the age of 18, or completed full-time tertiary education, whichever was the later.[158] It was a term of the settlement that 'while A is under the control of her mother and thereafter for so long as A does not object, the mother shall have the right to occupy the property to the exclusion of the father and without paying rent therefor for the purpose of providing a home and care and support for A'. Arguably this was a rather legalistic and insensitive approach to a mother's role in caring for her child. Acceptance of the idea that a child should be entitled to object to her mother continuing to occupy the family home once the child reached the age when she was no longer under the control of her mother is at best surprising. It surely cannot be in the interests of a child that she should have this kind of power over her mother, and the order made had the potential to be extraordinarily damaging to the relationship between the child, her mother, and her siblings.

In *J v C (Child: Financial Provision)*[159] Hale J also held that the child's welfare, 'even if neither the paramount nor the first consideration, must be one of the relevant circumstances to be taken into account when assessing whether and how to order provision'.[160] In that case, after the breakdown of the (unmarried) parents' relationship, the father won £1.4 million on the National Lottery. The child, her mother, and her two half—sisters, lived in three-bedroom rented accommodation, supported by public funds. There was a dispute between the parties as to the nature of their relationship and whether the child was wanted. Hale J did not consider that 'any great weight should be attached' to those disputed circumstances,[161] and held that the child was 'entitled to be brought up

---

[151] [1994] 1 FLR 657.   [152] Ibid, 661.

[153] Because the father lived a 'precarious life' and was domiciled abroad, and thus a claim under the Inheritance (Provision for Family and Dependants) Act 1975 was not possible, the periodical payments were to be secured against the father's home in London.

[154] There is no jurisdiction to order sums of direct benefit to such children: see *Morgan v Hill* [2006] EWCA Civ 1602, [2007] 1 FLR 1480 at [38].

[155] Ward J commented ([1994] 1 FLR 657 at 667): 'Somewhat to my surprise and for reasons I cannot understand, welfare plays no express part in the considerations to which I have to have regard.'

[156] (1980) 1 FLR 62.   [157] [1994] 1 FLR 657 at 665H–666B.   [158] Ibid, 663.

[159] [1999] 1 FLR 152.   [160] Ibid, 156G.   [161] Ibid, 154B.

in circumstances which bear some sort of relationship with the father's current resources'.[162] It was to the child's benefit to be brought up with, and in similar circumstances to, her half-sisters. This required the purchase[163] of a four-bedroom property, together with reasonable furnishings and a motor car.

In *T v S (Financial Provision for Children)*[164] the parents and their five children had lived in considerable style, with a house in the country and a London flat, until the father was sentenced to two years' imprisonment for possession of cocaine.[165] Upon the mother's application under Schedule 1, the District Judge found the father an unsatisfactory witness who seemed unwilling to give accurate disclosure of his means. By then it seemed that there was only £36,000 left to support the children, which the judge held was to be used to purchase a family home, settled until the children reached 21 or completed their education, then to pass to the children in equal shares. On the father's appeal, Johnson J, following the case law approach in the MCA 1973 jurisdiction, held that the property should revert to the father, not the children. He rejected counsel's argument that the difficulty of establishing the father's resources should be seen as a special circumstance justifying provision for the children's beyond their education. Johnson J held that 'in its reference to special circumstances in relation to the duration of periodical payments, Parliament was intending the court ordinarily to look at special circumstances related to the children—such, for example, as some physical or other handicap'.[166] Johnson J commented: 'The sadness here is that, after a long and seemingly happy relationship, this mother of five children, never having been married to their father, has no rights against him of her own. She has no right to be supported by him in the short, still less the long term; no right in herself to have even a roof over her head.' As this case illustrates, an unmarried parent who brings up the children has no continuing claim for support and shelter in her declining years and can literally be turned out into the street once her mothering role has ended.[167]

---

### Key case

The leading decision on Schedule 1 to the Children Act 1989 is now *Re P (Child: Financial Provision)*[168] in which the Court of Appeal held that the decisions in *A v A (A Minor: Financial Provision)* and *J v C (Child: Financial Provision)* were 'unquestionably sound and should be clearly endorsed',[169] albeit with two qualifications. First, commenting on *A v A (A Minor: Financial Provision)*, Thorpe LJ, delivering the leading judgment, indicated that 'a more generous approach to the calculation of the mother's allowance is not only permissible but also realistic'.[170] The court suggested that quantification of such allowance should not be limited to the cost of a professional nanny, as this may not do full justice to a mother's role in providing 24-hour care for a child. Secondly, the court amplified Hale J's discussion, in *J v C (Child: Financial Provision)*,[171] of the role of welfare

---

[162] Ibid, 160A–B. See also *Haroutunian v Jennings* (1981) 1 FLR 62 at 65, where Sir George Baker P acknowledged a 'long historical precedent for accepting that a rich man will pay more than a poor man for the maintenance of his child, legitimate or illegitimate'.

[163] Therefore, where resources allow, making provision, as a matter of public policy, to reduce or eliminate the children's need to be supported by public funds.

[164] [1994] 2 FLR 883, *per* Johnson J.

[165] Found, together with £75,000, in a vacuum cleaner, following a police raid on the London flat.

[166] [1994] 2 FLR 883 at 889. See also, agreeing with this passage, Butler-Sloss LJ in *C v F (Disabled Child: Maintenance Orders)* [1998] 2 FLR 1 at 3F.

[167] For further comment on *T v S* and *A v A*, see E. Cooke, 'Children and Real Property—Trusts, Interests and Considerations' [1998] Family Law 349.

[168] [2003] EWCA Civ 837, [2003] 2 FLR 865. For commentary, see S. Gilmore 'Re P (Child) (Financial Provision)— Shoeboxes and Comical Shopping Trips—Child Support From the Affluent to Fabulously Rich' (2004) 16(1) Child and Family Law Quarterly 103.

[169] [2003] EWCA Civ 837, [2003] 2 FLR 865, [41].          [170] Ibid, [43].          [171] [1999] 1 FLR 152 at 156G.

by adding that 'welfare must be not just "one of the relevant circumstances" but, in the generality of cases, a constant influence on the discretionary outcome'.[172]

In *Re P* the child had been conceived towards the end of the parents' four-year, intermittent, sexual relationship. The father was a successful international businessman, who described himself as 'fabulously rich' and whose London home was valued at over £10 million. The mother's earnings and home were modest. In her application under Schedule 1, the mother sought a lump sum in the range of £1.2–2.3 million. The judge allowed £450,000 for provision of a home, with £30,000 to furnish the property, and £20,000 for a car, and annual periodical payments of £35,360. In reaching this conclusion the judge attached some importance to the fact that the father had no financial obligations to the child beyond her minority, and he did not therefore wish to create an expectation of luxury from which the child would need to adapt should the father then withdraw his support. The mother appealed, contending that the judge's ruling failed 'to reflect the scale of the father's fortune and expenditure'.[173]

Allowing the mother's appeal, the Court of Appeal offered a useful method by which a judge should determine a case similar to this. A judge's starting point should be 'to decide, at least generically, the home that the respondent must provide for the child', since it 'introduces some useful boundaries'.[174] The court confirmed that the usual provision would be a settlement with reversion to the settlor. The next step is to assess, in the light of the choice of home, the 'cost of furnishing and equipping the home and the cost of the family car'. The judge should then determine what 'the mother reasonably requires to fund her expenditure in maintaining the home and its contents and in meeting her other expenditure external to the home'.[175] Here Thorpe LJ emphasised that 'what is required is a broad commonsense assessment'.[176] The final step is to consider quantification of an allowance for the mother's care of the child. Here the court drew attention to the tension between the latter and the fact that the mother has no personal entitlement to funds from the father. Bodey J commented that 'it is not possible to reduce to words any formula for seeking to ensure that the above distinction is maintained',[177] and there will 'inevitably be numerous grey areas, where the need asserted is of no direct benefit to the child, but is (or is arguably) of legitimate indirect benefit in helping reasonably to sustain the mother's physical/emotional welfare'.[178] It is 'these fine (and largely insoluble) distinctions of fact and degree within the grey area of indirect benefit to the child' which justify 'a broad budgetary approach by the court in bigger money cases'.[179] Thorpe LJ explained the court's approach, as follows:

> the court must recognise the responsibility, and often the sacrifice, of the unmarried parent (generally the mother) who is to be the primary carer for the child, perhaps the exclusive carer if the absent parent disassociates from the child. In order to discharge this responsibility the carer must have control of a budget that reflects her position and the position of the father, both social and financial. On the one hand she should not be burdened with unnecessary financial anxiety or have to resort to parsimony when the other parent chooses to live lavishly. On the other hand whatever is provided is there to be spent at the expiration of the year for which it is provided. There can be no slack to enable the recipient to fund a pension or an endowment policy or otherwise to put money away for a rainy day. In some cases it may be appropriate for the court to expect the mother to keep

---

[172] [2003] EWCA Civ 837, [2003] 2 FLR 865 at para [44]. Thorpe LJ explained that this amplification was justified by reference to the purpose of the statutory exercise, which is: 'to ensure for the child of parents who have never married and who have become alienated and combative, support and also protection against adult irresponsibility and selfishness, at least insofar as money and property can achieve those ends' (ibid, [44]). Expressing it differently, but in an approach that may be indistinguishable in practice, Bodey J suggested that welfare was 'naturally a very relevant consideration as one of ". . . all the circumstances . . ." of the case' (ibid, [76]).

[173] [2003] EWCA Civ 837, [2003] 2 FLR 865 at para [20]. The judge's award of £450,000 for a home represented only 5 per cent of the cost of the father's own principal residence.

[174] Ibid, [45].

[175] Such as school fees, holidays, routine travel expenses, entertainment, presents, etc, ibid, [47].

[176] Ibid.    [177] Ibid, [80].    [178] Ibid, [81].    [179] Ibid, [82].

relatively detailed accounts of her outgoings and expenditure in the first and then in succeeding years of receipt.[180]

Applying this guidance to the facts, the court held that a budget of £1 million was realistic to provide a home for the child, with a further sum of £100,000 to finish, furnish, and equip such a property. The court also awarded annual periodical payments of £70,000, to include the cost of running the home. In reaching its more generous conclusions, it held that the judge had been wrong to allow the speculative risk that the father would withdraw or reduce support at the end of the child's minority to influence the determination of the application.[181]

In *Re S (Unmarried Parents: Financial Provisions)*[182] the Court of Appeal made clear that *Re P* should not be interpreted as setting a benchmark for assessment of quantum in future cases. In *Re S* there was a dispute as to quantum of a housing trust fund; the mother was seeking to remain in Kensington, London at a suggested cost of £1.6–2 million, while the father suggested more modest accommodation in Parsons Green/Fulham. In reaching a middle-ground figure of £800,000, Bennett J had regarded the quantum of the housing fund of £1 million in *Re P* as a benchmark and had scaled down that provision to reflect the disparity in wealth between the father in *Re P* and the father in this case. The Court of Appeal held that that was an erroneous fetter on the wide discretionary exercise required by Schedule 1.[183] In addition, Bennett J had been influenced by the mother's egocentricity and the fact that what motivated her to wish to live in Kensington was her own selfish need. The Court of Appeal was concerned that the judge had thereby been distracted from the real focus which should have been an appraisal of the daughter's needs and interests, which were distinct from the mother's and not tainted simply by association with the mother's.[184] The judge should have asked: what would be the consequence for the daughter if she lost the security of her familiar environment in Kensington?[185] The court indicated that this was 'a neat illustration of the advantages of ensuring separate representation for the child in some cases' brought under Schedule 1.[186]

In *Re C (Financial Provision)*[187] District Judge Million, sitting in the Family Division, explained that *Re P* did not establish a rule of law that housing provision must be by way of a settlement; the distinction made in *Re P* was between outright transfer and a settlement. The ruling in *Re P* did not preclude the possibility that provision might, in an appropriate case, be made by financing a rented property.[188] In *Re C* a mother and her 4-year-old boy had recently moved from abroad to London and the mother was seeking a variation to periodical payments in part to cover payment of rent on a flat they were occupying. The father, whose wealth was approximately £100 million, was willing to finance a suitable property through a trust (at a cost of approximately £2 million), because payment of rent would be 'dead money'. The mother preferred to rent because she did not wish to feel that her property was controlled by the father, wanted to retain more flexibility about where she could live in the future, and wished the boy to remain in a place with which he was familiar.[189] The judge held that on the facts the mother's objections did not provide a rational basis for rejecting a trust, as the father was content for the mother to have a choice as to the trustees, the trust document could include the ability to move home, and the child's familiarity with the home was over exaggerated.[190]

---

[180] Ibid, [48] and [49]. The last point was made once again at para [54] of the judgment: 'Again the father may be entitled to reasonably detailed accounts of expenditure so that he can be satisfied that, taking one year with another, all is spent to meet the needs for which it is provided and none goes to the personal or exclusive benefit of the mother.'

[181] Ibid, [68] and [95].    [182] [2006] EWCA Civ 479, [2006] 2 FLR 950.    [183] Ibid, [14].
[184] Ibid, [15].    [185] Ibid.    [186] Ibid, [17].    [187] [2007] 2 FLR 13.    [188] Ibid, [45].
[189] See at [46].    [190] See at [47]–[50].

The facts in *F v G (Child: Financial Provision)*[191] differed from *Re P* in that the couple had co-habited until the child was 2 years old. Singer J held that statements in *Re P*[192] endorsing the view expressed in *J v C* that the considerations as to the length and nature of the parents' relationship are generally of little if any relevance, had to be viewed in the context of the facts of that case. Singer J held in *F v G* that although 'standard of living' is not one of the specific considerations in paragraph 4(1) of Schedule 1, 'the extent to which the unit of primary carer and child have become accustomed to a particular level of lifestyle can impact legitimately on an evaluation of the child's needs, reasonably to be viewed against his or her history'.[193] His Lordship thus sought to mitigate the disparity between the father's spending power and the child's household by adopting a level of award which would enable the mother to provide 'a fabric of home life not too brutally remote from that which the father's hard work enables him to sustain'. In that case the father was worth £4.6 million. The mother had limited capital and a net salary of £37,000 per annum. Singer J awarded a housing fund of £900,000 and periodical payments to include a parent as carer element of £60,000 per annum. Singer J allocated to the mother's salary the cost of a nanny (approximately £24,000) as the mother's contribution to her and the child's lifestyle, and awarded a full parent as carer allowance from the father, thus allowing the mother to make her own decision about employment and whether a nanny were needed or not.[194]

### 4.7.6 The significance of a prior maintenance agreement

In some cases, a child's parents may have concluded a written agreement for financial provision for the child. Such an agreement does not prevent an application under Schedule 1 to the Children Act 1989. Indeed, Schedule 1, paragraph 10(3), provides that provisions of a maintenance agreement can be varied or revoked by the court upon application if the court is satisfied that the agreement does not contain proper financial arrangements with respect to the child. In *Morgan v Hill*[195] the Court of Appeal held that whether an application is made under paragraph 10(3) or under paragraph 1 of Schedule 1, the same approach applies. The pre-existing agreement is seen as the starting point of the court's assessment,[196] which if it is to be departed from must be either demonstrated to be unenforceable given the circumstances surrounding its creation or inadequate in its extent.[197]

## Discussion Questions

1. To what extent do you think that the Child Support Act 1991 has been successful in achieving Mrs Thatcher's goal of ensuring that children are supported by their parents?

2. Is the recent policy effected by the Child Maintenance and Other Payments Act 2008 encouraging parents to make their own agreements relating to child support a welcome improvement to the child support system?

3. When do the courts retain jurisdiction in relation to child support?

4. What principles guide the courts' exercise of discretion when making orders for financial provision for children? Is the courts' approach satisfactory?

---

[191] [2004] EWHC 1848 (Fam), [2005] 1 FLR 261 *per* Singer J.

[192] See [2003] EWCA Civ 837, [2003] 2 FLR 865, *per* Bodey J at [76].

[193] [2004] EWHC 1848 (Fam), [2005] 1 FLR 261 at [35]. See also *N v D* [2008] 1 FLR 1629.

[194] [2004] EWHC 1848 (Fam), [2005] 1 FLR 261 at [50]–[53].

[195] [2006] EWCA Civ 1602, [2007] 1 FLR 1480.    [196] Ibid, [33], [57], and [61]    [197] Ibid, [33].

# Further Reading

BAZLEY, J. et al (One Garden Court Chambers), *Applications under Schedule 1 to the Children Act 1989* (Bristol: Family Law, 2010)

COLLIER, R., 'The Campaign Against the Child Support Act, Errant Fathers and Family Men' [1994] Family Law 384

DIDUCK, A., 'The Unmodified Family: The Child Support Act and the Construction of Legal Subjects' (1995) 22(4) Journal of Law and Society 527

FEHLBERG, B. and MACLEAN, M., 'Child Support Policy in Australia and the United Kingdom: Changing Priorities but a Similar Tough Deal for Children?' (2009) 23(1) International Journal of Law, Policy and the Family 1–24

GILMORE, S., '*Re P (Child) (Financial Provision)*—Shoeboxes and Comical Shopping Trips—Child Support from the Affluent to Fabulously Rich' (2004) 16(1) Child and Family Law Quarterly 103

GLENDINNING, C., CLARKE, K., and CRAIG, G., 'Implementing the Child Support Act' (1996) 18(3) Journal of Social Welfare and Family Law 273–289

MACLEAN, M. and EEKELAAR, J., 'Child Support: The British Solution' (1993) 7 International Journal of Law and the Family 205

WIKELEY, N., 'A Duty But Not a Right: Child Support after *R (Kehoe) v Secretary of State for Work and Pensions*' [2006] Child and Family Law Quarterly 287

WIKELEY, N., *Child Support Law and Policy* (Oxford: Hart, 2006)

WIKELEY, N., 'Child Support: The Brave New World' [2008] Family Law 1024

WIKELEY, N., 'Child Support: Carrots and Sticks' [2008] Family Law 1102

Visit the Online Resource Centre at **www.oxfordtextbooks.co.uk/orc/gilmore_glennon5e/** for a range of further features including a detailed bibliography and self-test questions.

# 7

# A child's parents: parentage, parenthood, and parental responsibility

## INTRODUCTION

This chapter examines how English law answers the question, 'Who is a child's parent?'[1] The answer has become increasingly complex as the law has responded to social change and to scientific developments in artificial reproduction techniques.[2] The semen used to fertilise a woman's egg may have been donated by a man who is not her husband or partner, and the donor may be anonymous. Eggs, as well as semen, can be donated and this can result in a woman giving birth to a child which has grown from another woman's egg. The child's mother may be in a same-sex relationship or partnered with a transsexual person. The law has had to address questions such as: Who is a child's mother when a woman gives birth to a child conceived as a result of egg donation by another woman? Is the child to have two mothers? Can a female-to-male transsexual person become a child's father? Is a mother's same-sex partner to be recognised as her child's parent too? If so, in what sense? As this last question suggests, the law's response is also complicated by the fact that the notion of 'being a parent' has several different facets.

## 1  A child's parents

### 1.1  Different senses of 'parent': biological, social, and legal

Sometimes reference is made to a child's 'natural' parent.[3] This focuses on parenthood in a biological sense, recognising a person's genetic connection as a natural progenitor of the child and/or a person's[4] gestational contribution: bearing and delivering the child. It is also possible to talk of a social and psychological parent. This, as Baroness Hale has explained, describes a relationship developing

---

[1] A. Bainham, S. Day Sclater, and M. Richards (eds), *What is a Parent? A Socio-Legal Analysis* (Oxford: Hart, 1999). For a collection of papers, both philosophical and legal, see S. Gilmore (ed) *Parental Rights and Responsibilities* (Oxford: Routledge, 2016, forthcoming).

[2] See S. Sheldon, 'Fragmenting Fatherhood: The Regulation of Reproductive Technologies' (2005) 68(4) Modern Law Review 523–53 for discussion of the ability of reproductive technologies to disrupt and confuse our understandings of parenthood.

[3] See the discussion by Baroness Hale of Richmond in *Re G (Children) (Residence: Same-Sex Partner)* [2006] UKHL 43, [2006] 4 All ER 241 at [33]–[37].

[4] The word 'person' rather than 'woman' is chosen here because following enactment of the Gender Recognition Act 2004 it is possible for a man to give birth to a child. In the rest of this chapter, however, 'woman' is used, recognising the usual gender of a person giving birth to a child.

through the fulfilment of the child's psychological, and day-to-day physical, needs.[5] These two aspects of parenthood are succinctly captured by the ideas of a parent 'by being' and a parent 'by doing'.[6] Frequently, of course, the same person (usually the child's natural mother or father) will combine these aspects of parenthood. A third way in which parenthood can be understood (which is the focus of this chapter) is its legal sense: the person who, *in law*, is regarded as a child's parent. From among the various understandings of parenthood within a society, choices may be made as to who is to be regarded in law as a parent. For example, in English law a biological parent will not always be regarded in law as a parent, and a child's legal parent may sometimes be someone who is not biologically related to the child. Furthermore, a legal parent may not necessarily be the child's social and psychological parent. As this last example shows, the law must address not merely the question of who a child's parent is, but also the rights and responsibilities attending that status, and whether and how legal responsibility for a child's upbringing is to be allocated to those caring for a child.

## 1.2 Law's distinctions: parentage, parenthood, and parental responsibility

Andrew Bainham has usefully observed that the law's engagement with the question 'who is a parent?' involves three 'subtle, elusive, yet important distinctions' in terminology: 'parentage', 'parenthood', and 'parental responsibility'.[7] The term 'parentage' is concerned with the genetic connection between the child and the persons who provided the gametes which led to the child's conception.[8] 'Parentage' is thus a matter of fact, focusing on genetic truth or presumed genetic truth. As Bainham points out, keeping this concept distinct is important, particularly from the child's perspective, because it focuses attention on the child's interest in knowing his or her origins. By contrast, the term 'parenthood' conveys the idea of a status associated with the raising of a child, and the term 'legal parenthood' is concerned with who, *as a matter of law*, is recognised as a parent.

---

### Key legislation

The third term, 'parental responsibility' is defined in section 3 of the Children Act 1989 as 'all the rights, duties, powers, responsibilities and authority which by law a parent of a child has in relation to the child and his property'.

---

This status is allocated as a matter of law. As we shall see, some legal parents will have parental responsibility while others may not. Parental responsibility can also be conferred on someone who is not a legal parent, thus providing a person with the necessary legal status to carry out his or her social role of looking after a child. In *Re H-B (Contact)*[9] Sir James Munby P emphasised that:

parental responsibility is more, much more, than a mere lawyer's concept or a principle of law. It is a fundamentally important reflection of the realities of the human condition, of the very

---

[5] [2006] UKHL 43, [2006] 4 All ER 241 at [35]:

the relationship which develops through the child demanding and the parent providing for the child's needs, initially at the most basic level of feeding, nurturing, comforting and loving, and later at the more sophisticated level of guiding, socialising, educating and protecting.

[6] J. Masson, 'Parenting by Being; Parenting by Doing—In Search of Principles for Founding Families' in J. R. Spencer and A. Du Bois-Pedain (eds), *Freedom and Responsibility in Reproductive Choice* (Oxford: Oxford University Press, 2006), Ch 8.

[7] A. Bainham, 'Parentage, Parenthood and Parental Responsibility: Subtle, Elusive Yet Important Distinctions' in A. Bainham et al, *What is a Parent? A Socio-Legal Analysis* (Oxford: Hart, 1999), Ch 2.

[8] Shapiro prefers use of the term 'progenitor' because it does not automatically link that person with the term 'parent': see J. Shapiro, 'Changing Ways, New Technologies and the Devaluation of the Genetic Connection to Children' in M. Maclean (ed), *Family Law and Family Values* (Oxford: Hart, 2005), p 90.

[9] [2015] EWCA Civ 389, at [72].

essence of the relationship of parent and child. Parental responsibility exists outside and anterior to the law. Parental responsibility involves duties owed by the parent not just to the court. First and foremost, and even more importantly, parental responsibility involves duties owed by each parent to the child.

It is helpful to an understanding of the law to keep these three concepts distinct although, as we shall see, the law makes many connections between them. For example, in most cases parentage and legal parenthood coincide because the general rule in English law is that legal parenthood is attributed according to biological connection;[10] and there are also important links between legal parenthood and how parental responsibility is allocated or acquired: for example, all mothers are initially allocated parental responsibility for their children.

## 2 Parentage

### 2.1 The presumption of paternity in favour of the mother's husband

The common law established a presumption of fact that a child born or conceived during the mother's lawful marriage is her husband's child.[11] The presumption relates to children conceived prior to a marriage and born within marriage, and to children who are born within the normal gestation period after a marriage has ended by death or divorce.[12] The presumption was created at a time when society's expectation was that children would not be born outside wedlock, when birth outside marriage could bring significant legal disadvantages to the child, and when great importance was therefore attached to a child's so-called 'legitimate' birth within marriage. The presumption is known therefore as the presumption of legitimacy, and at one time the importance of this status meant that the presumption could only be rebutted to a high standard of proof. Nowadays, however, the legal disadvantages to children born outside marriage have largely been eradicated by the Family Law Reform Act 1987, and section 26 of the Family Law Reform Act 1969 provides that the presumption may be rebutted on the balance of probabilities, that is by evidence which shows that it is more probably true than not that the husband is not the father.

Where applicable, account will also need to be taken of the presumption of legitimacy in any case of disputed paternity. However, the importance of this presumption as a factor in deciding such cases has diminished over time and it is now probably of limited practical significance. In *Re H and A*[13] Thorpe LJ questioned 'the relevance of the presumption or the justification for its application' in that context, commenting:

> In the nineteenth century, when science had nothing to offer and illegitimacy was a social stigma as well as a depriver of rights, the presumption was a necessary tool, the use of which required no justification . . . But as science has hastened on and as more and more children are born out of marriage it seems to me that the paternity of any child is to be established by science and not by legal presumption or inference.

### 2.2 Where parentage is in issue: declarations of parentage

Where there is an issue or dispute as to a child's parentage, it may be necessary ultimately to resolve it in court proceedings.

---

[10] Whether actual or presumed. For criticism of automatic deference to biology, see J. G. Dwyer, *The Relationship Rights of Children* (New York: Cambridge University Press, 2006).

[11] *Banbury Peerage Case* [1803–13] All ER Rep 171, 1 Sim and St 153, 57 ER 62.

[12] *Gardner v Gardner* (1877) 2 App Cas 723.     [13] [2002] EWCA Civ 383, [2002] 2 FCR 469 at [30].

---

**Key legislation**

Section 55A(1) of the Family Law Act 1986 provides that 'any person[14] may apply to a court[15] for a declaration as to whether or not a person named in the application is or was the parent of another person so named'.[16]

---

The declaration is binding on all persons.[17] Where one of the persons named in the application is a child the court may refuse to hear the application if it considers that the determination of the application would not be in the best interests of the child.[18]

### 2.2.1 Proving paternity

Nowadays the usual method of proving parentage is by scientific evidence in the form of a DNA profile which can demonstrate to a degree of probability approaching certainty whether a person is the child's genetic parent or not.[19] Prior to the availability of DNA profiling, scientific testing would take the form of blood tests which could exclude the possibility that a man was a child's father or provide some probability that he was, but could not prove the same conclusively. In the past, therefore, there would be much greater emphasis than is the case now on other evidence, in the absence of scientific evidence, or supplementing it. This might consist of witness statements showing the alleged father's inclination and opportunity to have sexual intercourse with the mother at the relevant time (or indeed the lack of the same, and perhaps evidence of the mother's relationship with a different man). There might also be evidence after the birth, such as the mother entering (or failing to enter) the father's name on the register of births. In *Brierley v Brierley and Williams*[20] a husband petitioned for divorce on the basis of his wife's adultery, the evidence being the birth of a child at a time when the husband, who had been absent on military service in France during the First World War, could not have been the father. To prove the adultery the husband produced a registration of the child's birth, signed by the mother, which had left the father's name blank. McCardie J could see 'no reason to doubt that prima facie evidence may be furnished by the entry in the register or a certified copy'. Such circumstantial evidence is now unlikely to be crucial in most instances, but in cases where forensic testing is unavailable, for example where the alleged father has died and/or cannot be traced, evidence other than scientific evidence may still assume some importance, and indeed the presumption of legitimacy might still command the outcome. Where scientific evidence could assist, however, the court has a power in Part III of the Family Law Reform Act 1969 to direct scientific testing.

---

[14] In certain cases, the court must refuse to hear the application unless satisfied that the applicant has a sufficient personal interest in the determination of the application: see s 55A(3) and (4).

[15] High Court, a county court, or a magistrates' court.

[16] Either of the persons named must be domiciled in England and Wales or have been habitually resident in England and Wales for at least one year: see Family Law Act 1986, s 55A(2).

[17] It may be important, therefore, in the child's interests that an application for leave to appeal out of time is granted where a declaration has been made erroneously: see [2003] EWHC 2163 (Fam), [2004] 1 FLR 282 at [17].

[18] Family Law Act 1986, s 55A(5).

[19] For a discussion of DNA testing and kinship, see T. Freeman and M. Richards, 'DNA Testing and Kinship: Paternity, Genealogy and the Search for the "Truth" of our Genetic Origins' in F. Ebtehaj, B. Lindley, and M. Richards (eds), *Kinship Matters* (Oxford: Hart, 2006); for a discussion of the impact in the USA, see M. A. Rothstein, T. H. Murray, G. E. Kaebnick, and M. Anderlik Majunder (eds), *Genetic Ties and the Family. The Impact of Paternity Testing on Parents and Children* (Baltimore, MD: Johns Hopkins University Press, 2005). See also H. Draper and J. Ives, 'Paternity Testing: A Poor Test of Fatherhood' (2009) 31(4) Journal of Social Welfare and Family Law 407–18.

[20] [1918] P 257.

## 2.3 Directions for scientific testing under section 20 of the Family Law Reform Act 1969

### Key legislation

A court has a discretion to direct scientific testing to ascertain parentage under section 20 of the Family Law Reform Act 1969,[21] which provides:

(1) In any civil proceedings in which the parentage of any person falls to be determined, the court may, either of its own motion or on an application by any party to the proceedings, give a direction—

(a) for the use of scientific tests to ascertain whether such tests show that a party to the proceedings is or is not the father or mother of that person; and

(b) for the taking, within a period specified in the direction, of bodily samples from all or any of the following, namely, that person, any party who is alleged to be the father or mother of that person and any other party to the proceedings . . .[22]

It can be seen that the court cannot make a direction for scientific testing on a free-standing application under section 20.[23] The jurisdiction only arises where there are already civil proceedings before the court in which the parentage of a person falls to be determined. This would be the case, for example, where a formal application for a declaration of parentage has been made pursuant to section 55A of the Family Law Act 1986, although such an application is not essential.[24] The issue of parentage could be raised in other proceedings, as is sometimes the case when a man makes an application for a parental responsibility order or contact order and the child's mother claims that he is not the father and therefore not entitled to apply for the order.

### 2.3.1 Sufficient evidential basis to justify consideration of the application

The first question, upon any application under section 20, is whether there is sufficient evidential basis to justify serious consideration of the application.[25] This was the approach adopted by Hedley J in *Re D (Paternity)*[26] who concluded (and thus appeared to require) in that case that there were 'reasonable grounds for believing' that the applicant was the child's father, 'sufficient to warrant scientific testing'.[27] If such grounds exist, the court will then go on to consider whether to exercise its discretion.

### 2.3.2 The discretion to direct scientific testing

General guidance on the discretion to direct scientific testing was given in two cases heard together by the House of Lords in *S v S; W v Official Solicitor*.[28] The point of law to be resolved was whether a blood test could be ordered despite the fact that the child might not benefit from the outcome of

---

[21] Any direction for such testing should indicate that it is being made pursuant to s 20 and should specify the body which is to carry out the testing, which should be accredited by the Ministry of Justice: Family Law Reform Act 1969, s 20(1A), and see *Re F (Children) (DNA Evidence)* [2007] EWHC 3235 (Fam), [2008] 1 FLR 348 (Anthony Hayden QC). The manner of giving effect to a direction is regulated by s 22 of the 1969 Act and the Blood Tests (Evidence of Paternity) Regulations 1971 (SI 1971/1861), as amended.

[22] Where the proceedings consist of an application under s 55A or s 56 of the Family Law Act 1986, reference to a 'party to the proceedings' includes a reference to any party named in the application: see Family Law Reform Act 1969, s 20(2A).

[23] *Re E (Parental Responsibility: Blood Tests)* [1995] 1 FLR 392.

[24] *Re D (Paternity)* [2006] EWHC 3545 (Fam), [2007] 2 FLR 26, *per* Hedley J at [4].    [25] Ibid, [5].

[26] [2006] EWHC 3545 (Fam), [2007] 2 FLR 26.    [27] Ibid, [10].

[28] [1972] AC 24. For a detailed commentary, see A Bainham, 'Welfare, Truth and Justice: The Children of Extra-Marital Liaisons' in S. Gilmore, J. Herring, and R. Probert (eds), *Landmark Cases in Family Law* (Oxford: Hart, 2011), pp 113–34.

the test. The concern was that testing would risk the child's loss of the benefit of the presumption of legitimacy. The Official Solicitor argued that testing should not take place unless it could be shown to be in the child's best interests. Despite the similarity of their facts, the two cases had elicited different responses in the Court of Appeal. In *S v S*, a husband, who was petitioning for divorce on the ground of his wife's adultery, denied paternity of his wife's child. The Official Solicitor, representing the child, objected to testing. The Court of Appeal held that a test should be directed. In *W v Official Solicitor* a wife who had given birth to a child who was strikingly dissimilar to her older children who were conceived with the husband, confessed to adultery with a man who had now disappeared. In contrast to *S v S*, the husband's request for testing to ascertain the child's paternity was refused by the Court of Appeal. The House of Lords unanimously dismissed the first appeal and allowed the second, the outcome in each case being that testing was directed.

The case was decided in relation to the courts' jurisdiction to direct testing prior to implementation of Part III of the Family Law Reform Act 1969, although the principles expounded by the House of Lords are equally applicable to directions under the Act. Indeed, in *obiter* comments Lord Reid observed that it could not have been intended that the then soon to be implemented section 20(1) of the 1969 Act should confer upon the courts an unfettered discretion. That discretion was to be exercised according to principles settled by the superior courts.[29] His Lordship held that 'the court ought to permit a blood test of a young child to be taken unless satisfied that that would be against the child's interests'.[30] The House of Lords made clear, therefore, that the paramountcy of the child's welfare is *not* the governing principle. This is because, as Lord Hodson commented:

> the interests of other persons than the infant are involved in ordinary litigation. The infant needs protection but that is no justification for making his rights superior to those of others.[31]

Thus the interests of justice, as well as the interests of the child, are raised. Lord Hodson went on to observe that:

> The interests of justice in the abstract are best served by the ascertainment of the truth and there must be few cases where the interests of children can be shown to be best served by the suppression of truth.[32]

The House recognised, however, that there:

> may be a conflict between the interests of the child and the general requirements of justice. Justice requires that available evidence should not be suppressed but it may be against the interests of the child to produce it.[33]

The House held that a court's duty to protect children will not ordinarily provide a ground for refusing to direct forensic testing merely because, in revealing the truth, it might show that the child was not born in lawful wedlock. It explained that following the enactment of section 26 of the 1969 Act, which allows the presumption of legitimacy to be rebutted on the balance of probabilities, 'the

---

[29] 1972] AC 24 at 45.

[30] Ibid, p 45. See also Lord MacDermott at p 51: 'while the court should be alert to exercise its protective jurisdiction on behalf of an infant, it does not need to be satisfied before ordering a blood test that the outcome thereof will be for the benefit of the infant.'

[31] [1972] AC 24 at 58.

[32] Ibid, 57. See also Lord Morris' opinion, in which (at 55) he talked of the 'general desirability of arriving at the truth' which 'points to the further desirability of having the best evidence available'. He commented (at 56) that in most cases comparable to *S v S* 'the interests of the child are best served if the truth is ascertained'.

[33] Ibid, 44.

presumption of legitimacy now merely determines the onus of proof'[34] and 'public policy no longer requires that special protection should be given by the law to the status of legitimacy'.[35] The House added that while the child must be protected:

> it is not really protecting the child to ban a blood test on some vague and shadowy conjecture that it may turn out to be to its disadvantage: it may equally well turn out to be for its advantage or at least do no harm.[36]

Since this leading decision in *S v S; W v Official Solicitor*, examination of the interests at stake in this context has been refined by increased emphasis on human rights, in particular a person's 'identity rights'. The focus on the child's various interests has been sharpened by increased emphasis within English law upon children's rights. Before examining various examples of how the court has exercised its discretion under section 20, it is convenient first to explain the human rights context in which decisions must now be taken.

## 2.4 **Legal recognition of persons' interests in knowing genetic origins**

The law recognises a child's interest in knowing his or her genetic origins. It is specifically protected by Article 7 of the United Nations Convention on the Rights of the Child (UNCRC),[37] which provides that a child has, 'as far as possible, the right to know and be cared for by his or her parents'. In addition, the European Court of Human Rights has said that the right to respect for private life within Article 8(1) of the European Convention on Human Rights (ECHR):

> includes a person's physical and psychological integrity and can sometimes embrace aspects of an individual's physical and social identity. Respect for 'private life' must also comprise to a certain degree the right to establish relationships with other human beings.[38]

---

### Key case

In *Mikuliè v Croatia*[39] the Court added that there appears to be 'no reason why the notion of "private life" should be taken to exclude the determination of the legal relationship between a child . . . and her natural father'.[40] In that case a girl sought to establish in legal proceedings that a particular man was her father. After five years, the proceedings were still pending before an appellate court and the child alleged a breach of the right to a fair trial within Article 6(1) in that the proceedings were not concluded in a reasonable time. She further alleged that consequently there had been a breach of Article 8. The Court reiterated that 'particular diligence is required in cases concerning civil status and capacity'[41] and held that in all the circumstances Article 6(1) had been breached. In addition, the Court unanimously held that the Croatian courts' inefficiency had 'left the applicant in a state of prolonged uncertainty as to her personal identity', and failed to secure respect for her private life.[42]

The interest which a parent, or presumed parent, may have in establishing or disputing a child's parentage is also recognised. In a series of decisions,[43] the European Court of Human Rights has also

---

[34] Ibid, 41 *per* Lord Reid.    [35] Ibid, 43 *per* Lord Reid.    [36] Ibid, 45.
[37] New York, 20 November 1989; Treaty Series No 44 of 1992 (Cm 1976).
[38] *Mikulić v Croatia* (App no 53176/99) [2002] 1 FCR 720, para 53. See S. Besson, 'Enforcing the Child's Right to Know her Origins: Contrasting Approaches under the Convention on the Rights of the Child and the European Convention on Human Rights' (2007) 21(2) International Journal of Law, Policy and the Family 137.
[39] (App no 53176/99) [2002] 1 FCR 720.    [40] Ibid.    [41] Ibid, para 44.    [42] Ibid, para 66.
[43] *Tavli v Turkey* [2007] 1 FLR 1136, ECtHR; *Paulik v Slovakia* (App no 10699/05) [2007] 1 FLR 1090, ECtHR; *Shofman v Russia* (App no 74826/01) [2006] 1 FLR 680, ECtHR (no challenge possible because of expiry of one-year

found breaches of the Convention where fathers have not been afforded an opportunity to present DNA evidence to establish paternity, or to deny paternity where the law has presumed it. It has held that 'the situation in which a legal presumption is allowed to prevail over biological and social reality, without regard to both established facts and the wishes of those concerned and without actually benefiting anyone, is not compatible, even having regard to the margin of appreciation left to the State, with the obligation to secure effective "respect" for private and family life'.[44] In some cases, however, the margin of appreciation afforded to a state may mean that Article 8 is not breached if a parent is not permitted to establish his paternity. In *Kautzor v Germany*,[45] for example, the child was conceived during marriage but born after the spouses separated, and the husband had never seen the child. The mother's new partner had acknowledged paternity with the mother's consent. It was held that the state had a margin of appreciation in how it determined paternity and there was no infringement of the former husband's rights under Article 8 of the ECHR in not permitting him to challenge the mother's partner's paternity.

The decision in *Mikulić* was applied in domestic law in *Rose v Secretary of State for Health and Human Fertilisation and Embryology Authority*,[46] in which the claimants were both an adult and a child. Both had been born as a result of artificial insemination by anonymous donor sperm. They requested the Secretary of State to make available non-identifying information about sperm donors and to institute a voluntary contact register to facilitate contact between donors and their offspring where they wished to have it. The Secretary of State responded that a consultation paper would be published shortly and ministers would then consider the matter. The claimants sought judicial review of this response, arguing that their rights under Article 8 of the ECHR were engaged and that the state had positive obligations to comply with their requests. Scott Baker J found that Article 8 was engaged, holding that the concept of personal identity within Article 8 recognised by the European Court of Human Rights 'plainly includes the right to obtain information about a biological parent who will inevitably have contributed to the identity of his child'.[47] Following this decision, the Human Fertilisation and Embryology Authority (Disclosure of Donor Information) Regulations 2004 made provision regulating the disclosure of donor information (see Section 3.8.2).

There is, however, no absolute right to knowledge of origins, as demonstrated by the decision of the Grand Chamber of the European Court of Human Rights in *Odièvre v France*.[48] The case concerned the procedure permitted by French law (known as 'accouchement sous X') which allowed a mother to give birth anonymously, and prohibited subsequent disclosure of information identifying the mother. The policy underlying the French law was to protect the mother's health during pregnancy, to prevent abortions, and to avoid children being abandoned in other, possibly harmful, ways.[49] Ms Odièvre, whose mother had given birth anonymously under this law,

time limit); *Mizzi v Malta* (App no 2611/02) [2006] 1 FLR 1048, ECtHR (no mechanism to disavow parenthood arising from presumption of legitimacy despite scientific tests); *Rozanski v Poland* (App no 55339/00) [2006] 2 FCR 178. See A. Bainham, 'Truth Will Out: Paternity in Europe' [2007] Cambridge Law Journal 278.

[44] See also *Paulik v Slovakia* (App no 10699/05) [2007] 1 FLR 1090, ECtHR (breach of convention where no legal mechanism to disclaim legal paternity of 40-year-old 'daughter' who had no objection to the applicant disclaiming paternity on the basis of DNA tests which showed he was not her father: see esp paras [43], [44], and [47]); and *Tavli v Turkey* (App no 11449/02) [2007] 1 FLR 1136, ECtHR (breach of Art 8 where Turkish law did not permit admission of fresh DNA evidence to annul earlier decision as to applicant's paternity of his wife's child and to permit re-trial): 'domestic courts should interpret the existing legislation in the light of scientific progress and the social repercussions that follow' (at [36]).

[45] (App No 23338/09) [2012] 2 FLR 396.          [46] [2002] EWHC 1593 (Admin), QB, Scott Baker J.

[47] Ibid, [48].

[48] (App no 42326/98) [2002] 1 FCR 621, ECtHR (Grand Chamber). See E. Steiner, 'Desperately Seeking Mother— Anonymous Births in the European Court of Human Rights' (2003) 15(4) Child and Family Law Quarterly 425–48. See also the discussion of secret adoptions in Chapter 11.

[49] See N. Lefaucheur, 'The French "Tradition" of Anonymous Birth: The Lines of Argument' (2004) 18(3) International Journal of Law, Policy and the Family 319.

claimed that her inability to establish the identity of her mother breached Article 8 of the ECHR. The Court, distinguishing *Mikulić v Croatia*,[50] found by a majority of 10 to 7 no violation of the applicant's rights. The majority observed that Article 8 also applied to the mother, and the mother's interests, for example in remaining anonymous in order to protect her health by giving birth in appropriate medical conditions, were not easily reconciled with the applicant's interests.[51] The Court also recognised that the general interest was at stake, one of the aims of the legislation being respect for life, a higher ranking value guaranteed by the Convention.[52] In these circumstances, the Court found that France had not exceeded its margin of appreciation. There was a strong dissenting opinion, however, which did not accept the Court's distinguishing of earlier authorities. The minority pointed out that the Court's role is to examine whether a fair balance has been struck between the competing interests, and it is not a matter of determining which interest, in a given case, must take absolute precedence over others.[53] They observed that no balancing of interests was possible in this case since French law accepted the mother's decision as an absolute defence to requests for information.[54] Furthermore, there were no reliable data to show that there would be an increased risk of abortion or infanticide if the system of anonymous births were abolished.[55] As to the margin of appreciation afforded to France, the minority observed that 'no other legislative system is so weighted in favour of the protection of maternal anonymity',[56] and that the majority failed to take account of the consensus to be found in international instruments such as in Article 7 of the UNCRC. The minority was 'firmly of the opinion that the *right to an identity . . .* is within the inner core of the right to respect for one's private life' and accordingly 'the fairest scrutiny was called for when weighing up the competing interests'.[57]

Later decisions have adopted this view that there must be a very careful weighing of the competing interests against a person's interest in establishing his or her identity. In *Jäggi v Switzerland*[58] the Court found a violation of Article 8 where it was unconvinced by the Swiss authorities' reasons for refusing a 67-year-old man's request for DNA testing of the corpse of a man who, in 1939, had been declared his father. The Court observed:

> [T]he right to an identity, which includes the right to know one's parentage, is an integral part of the notion of private life. In such cases, particularly rigorous scrutiny is called for when weighing up the competing interests.

In line with the approach established by the European Court of Human Rights, Ryder J observed in *Lambeth London Borough v S, C, V and J (By His Guardian)*[59] that:

> [a] person's right to establish their identity is not absolute in the sense that there is no absolute right of access to genetic information. Access to genetic information may be controlled by the state, but if that control is to be lawful ie human rights compliant there has to be a mechanism that provides that any interference is only that which is lawful, necessary in a democratic society for the specified Art 8(2) purposes and proportionate.

In that case a boy, aged 7, was the subject of care proceedings. D, a man assumed to be the boy's father, had been unlawfully killed by the mother's husband. In the course of their investigation, the police obtained from a blood sample a DNA profile. In the care proceedings, the local authority's plan was to place the boy with D's mother (his paternal grandmother), which the child's mother resisted on the basis of her allegation that there was no genetic link between the child and D. The local

---

[50] (App no 53176/99) [2002] 1 FCR 720 and *Gaskin v UK* (App no 10454/83) (1989) 12 EHRR 36 (adult's claim for access to social services records regarding his upbringing in care).

[51] (App no 42326/98) [2002] 1 FCR 621, ECtHR (Grand Chamber), para 44.    [52] Ibid, para 45.

[53] Ibid, Dissenting Opinion, para 6.    [54] Ibid, para 7.    [55] Ibid, para 9.    [56] Ibid, para 13.

[57] Ibid, para 11.    [58] App no 58757/00, ECtHR.    [59] [2006] EWHC 326 (Fam), [2007] 1 FLR 152.

authority sought a direction that the DNA evidence held by the police be released in order to determine conclusively the child's paternity. Ryder J held that there was no power to order disclosure and dismissed the application. He held that the use of the sample was restricted to the purposes specified in section 64(1A) of the Police and Criminal Evidence Act 1984, which regulates the use of retained samples. To remain human rights-compliant that provision had to be construed strictly, and the prohibition on other uses was a proportionate interference having regard to the public policy which underpins the 1984 Act.[60] Similarly, in *Re X and Another v Z (Children) and Another*[61] the Court of Appeal, construing section 22 of the Police and Criminal Evidence Act 1984, held that DNA found at a crime scene cannot be used for purposes other than criminal law enforcement.

The increased focus on individual rights, together with scientific developments, has meant that if any general trend can be identified in the case law on section 20 of the Family Law Reform Act 1969, it has been towards ascertaining the truth by recognising parentage. However, the case law illustrates that the child's interests may occasionally demand that forensic testing does not take place.[62]

In *Re F (A Minor) (Blood Tests: Parental Rights)*[63] a child, E, was conceived at a time when her mother, Mrs F, was having sexual relations with both her husband (Mr F) and the applicant, Mr B. The relationship between Mrs F and Mr B ended before E's birth, and E had been brought up as a child of Mr and Mrs F's family. B had had no contact with E. Believing that he was her natural father, B applied for a parental responsibility order under section 4 of the Children Act 1989, and an order for contact under sections 8 and 10 of that Act. Those applications raised the issue of B's paternity, since the court only has jurisdiction under section 4 to make a parental responsibility order in favour of the child's father, and Mr B could only apply for a contact order (without leave of the court) if he was E's father. B applied in the proceedings, therefore, for a direction for testing to determine paternity. Judge Callman dismissed the application on the basis that the father's prospects of success in his applications for contact and parental responsibility were 'remote and unlikely', and it would thus be unfair to expose the child to the risk of losing the presumption of legitimacy.[64] The Court of Appeal upheld this decision. While finding that the judge had perhaps placed rather more emphasis on the presumption of legitimacy than is appropriate in modern circumstances, the court held that this did not detract from the general thrust of the judge's approach, with which it could find no error. The court agreed with the judge, commenting:

> If the probable outcome of [the] proceedings will be the same whoever may be the natural father of E., then there can be no point in exposing E. to the possible disadvantages of a blood test.

The Court of Appeal was unmoved by Mr B's argument that it was in E's interests to know the truth about her parentage, for example to allow her knowledge of her genetic make-up which might be relevant for the possible diagnosis, prevention, mitigation, or cure of some medical disorder. The court saw the chance that this 'might operate so as to harm E's interests' as 'infinitesimal when brought into balance against the harm that might be caused to her if B were able to proceed with his applications'.[65] In addition, Mr B's argument based on Article 7 of the UNCRC,[66] which provides that a child shall have 'as far as possible, the right to know and be cared for by his or her parents' was given short shrift. Balcombe LJ responded that in this case it was 'not in fact possible for E to be cared for by both her parents (if B is such)'.[67] The court commented:

> E's welfare depends for the foreseeable future primarily upon her relationship with her mother . . . Anything that may disturb that relationship or the stability of the family unit within

---

[60] Ibid, [44]–[46].    [61] [2015] EWCA Civ 34 (Master of the Rolls, McFarlane and Beatson LJJ).
[62] For discussion of the role of rights and welfare in this context, see J. Wallbank, 'The Role of Rights and Utility in Instituting a Child's Right to Know her Genetic History' (2004) 13 Social and Legal Studies 245–63.
[63] [1993] Fam 314, CA.    [64] Ibid, 319.    [65] Ibid, 320.    [66] Treaty Series No 44 of 1992 (Cm 1976).
[67] [1993] Fam 314 at 321.

which E has lived since her birth is likely to be detrimental to E's welfare, and unless that detriment is shown to be counter-balanced by other positive advantages to her which an order for the taking of blood tests could confer, then the judge's refusal to order blood tests was not merely an exercise of his discretion with which we can not interfere, but one with which in the circumstances of this case we agree.[68]

This decision may be criticised for placing 'very little weight on the value to E of knowing the truth about her parentage, as a benefit in its own right, quite detached from the potential value of a parent–child relationship with B'.[69] As Fortin argues, the court 'should have given greater weight to the psychological value to E of knowing the truth about her origins'.[70] She rightly points out that the link between the issue of testing and the outcome of the substantive applications was illogical, since it is 'perfectly possible for a court to decide that though it will not benefit a child ever to meet her natural parent, it is psychologically important for her to know the truth about her origins'.[71] In other words, the law might become more coherent if the issue of biological parentage were detached from the issue of the child's social relationships.[72]

Some of the difficulties with the Court of Appeal's approach in *Re F* received acknowledgement in *Re H (A Minor) (Blood Tests: Parental Rights)*,[73] which adopted a different emphasis. There a mother and her husband had two children together. The husband then had a vasectomy and for the following five years the couple continued to have sexual intercourse without conceiving a child. The marriage fell into difficulties and the mother began a sexual relationship with another man, the applicant. She fell pregnant at a time when she was having sexual relations with both her husband and the applicant. She believed, however, that the applicant was the baby's father, and involved him in her ante-natal care. The husband moved out of the matrimonial home, and initially there was an understanding that the applicant would move in. In preparation for this, the mother told her eldest child (then aged 13) about her pregnancy and plans, and that the baby's father was not her husband. The plans did not materialise, however, as the mother terminated the affair and was reconciled with her husband, who accepted the baby as his own. The applicant applied for a parental responsibility order and a contact order and, if paternity was denied, a direction for scientific testing. The judge made the direction and on appeal by the mother the Court of Appeal upheld the judge's decision.

In contrast to the court's approach in *Re F*, the Court of Appeal held that the paternity issue is 'entitled to consideration on its own'[74] as distinct from the parental responsibility and contact order proceedings. The 'outcome of the proceedings in which the paternity issue has been raised, in so far as it bears on the welfare of the child, must be taken into account' but whilst those proceedings 'are obviously factors which impinge on the child's welfare', they are 'not determinative' of the question whether there should be testing.[75] Ward LJ observed that there are two separate rights in Article 7 of the UNCRC, 'the one to know, and the other to be cared for by, one's parents', and that Balcombe LJ's judgment in *Re F* had concentrated on the child's right to be cared for.[76] In Ward

---

[68] Ibid. For another example, see *O v L (Blood Tests)* [1995] 2 FLR 930, CA, explained in the second edition of this book.

[69] J. Fortin, '*Re F*: "The Gooseberry Bush Approach"' (1994) 57 Modern Law Review 296 at 297.

[70] Ibid, 298.    [71] Ibid.

[72] Ibid, 306. See for a similar view, J. Eekelaar, 'Parenthood, Social Engineering and Rights' in D. Morgan and G. Douglas (eds), *Constituting Families: A Study in Governance* (Stuttgart: Steiner, 1994).

[73] [1997] Fam 89, CA. For comment see B. Gilbert, 'Paternity, Truth and the Interests of the Child—Some Problems of *Re H (Paternity: Blood Test)*' [1996] Child and Family Law Quarterly 361; A. Bainham, 'Vasectomies, Lovers and Disputed Offspring: Honesty is the Best Policy (Sometimes)' (1996) 55 Cambridge Law Journal 444–6.

[74] [1997] Fam 89 at 105.    [75] Ibid.

[76] See J. Fortin, '*Re F*: "The Gooseberry Bush Approach"' (1994) 57 Modern Law Review 296 at 305.

LJ's view (with which Neill LJ agreed) 'every child has a right to know the truth unless his welfare clearly justifies the cover up'.[77]

Ward LJ, while emphasising that, in cases which depend on the exercise of a discretion, it is seldom useful to draw factual similarities between cases, addressed counsel's submission that there was similarity between *Re F* and this case, but remained unpersuaded. The applicant here had a substantial claim to be the child's father as evidenced by the mother's belief that he was the father, and by her husband's vasectomy. Thus the claimant would have a good chance of establishing paternity irrespective of whether a direction was given. The judge had been correct, therefore, to make the direction to obtain the best evidence. Moreover, the truth could not be repressed forever as the eldest child was already aware of the paternity issue. As the court put it, better that the child should know the truth rather that 'a time-bomb ticking away'.[78]

In *Re T (Paternity: Ordering Blood Tests)*[79] a husband and wife, who had been unable to have a baby (it having been established that the husband had a low sperm count) agreed that the wife would have sexual intercourse with another man. The wife did so with the applicant and with three other men during a period when she was likely to conceive. The wife became pregnant and gave birth to a child, T, who was brought up by his mother and her husband. When the child was about 1 year old, the applicant had applied for parental responsibility and contact without success and the magistrates had refused to give a direction for DNA testing. At that time the child's paternity was put in the public domain by doubts and suspicions 'going round' a local school and by the applicant's behaviour. He proclaimed himself the father on citizens-band radio, attended the husband's workplace with a placard proclaiming the same, and put leaflets with the same message through local letterboxes. The applicant renewed his applications when T was aged 7, following the passing of the Human Rights Act 1998. Bodey J gave a direction for testing. In his Lordship's view this was not a situation in which tests would create a serious risk of de-stabilising the present family, and any such risk was outweighed by the risk of T learning of the suspicions about his paternity given that they were public knowledge. Bodey J explained that T 'has a right to respect for his private life (in the sense of having knowledge of his identity, which encompasses his true paternity)'. T also had a right to respect for his family life, which should not be put at risk except as held to be in T's interests. In addition, the mother and the husband had rights to respect for family life which should not be intruded upon, except as might be necessary to give effect to T's rights, or the applicant's (if he were to be found to have a right to respect for family life within Article 8).[80] Evaluating and balancing those various interests, Bodey J concluded:

> [T]he weightiest emerges clearly as being that of T, namely that he should have the possibility of knowing, perhaps with certainty, his true roots and identity. I find that any such interference as would occur to the right to respect for the family/private life of the mother and her husband, to be proportionate to the legitimate aim of providing T with the possibility of certainty as to his real paternity, a knowledge which would accompany him throughout his life.[81]

In *Re H and A (Children)*[82] the Court of Appeal made clear that the approaches taken in *Re H* and in *Re T* are not necessarily confined to cases with similar facts, namely when there is some doubt surrounding the procreative capacity of the husband concerned. In *Re H and A (Children)* Mrs R had a sexual relationship with Mr B for four years, during which time twins were conceived and

---

[77] [1997] Fam 89 at 106.     [78] Ibid, 108.     [79] [2001] 2 FLR 1190, FD (Bodey J).

[80] Bodey J suggested *obiter* that it was unlikely on the facts that the applicant could make out a successful case for existing 'family life'.

[81] *Re T (Paternity: Ordering Blood Tests)* [2001] 2 FLR 1190 at 1197–1198. See for other human rights analyses in this context, see Dame Elizabeth Butler-Sloss P in *Secretary of State for Work and Pensions v Jones* [2003] EWHC 2163 (Fam), [2004] 1 FLR 282 at [18] and Ryder J in *Lambeth London Borough v S, C, V and J (By His Guardian)* [2006] EWHC 326 (Fam), [2007] 1 FLR 152 at [29].

[82] [2002] EWCA Civ 383, [2002] 2 FCR 469.

born. Her husband, Mr R, remained in ignorance of his wife's adultery and accepted the twins as his own, taking over their primary care when his wife went out to work. Upon the breakdown of the adulterous relationship, Mr B sought contact and parental responsibility in respect of the children. For a year Mrs R managed to conceal the litigation from her husband while she challenged Mr B's paternity. Mr R became aware of the proceedings when he stumbled upon some court papers in his wife's handbag (here lies a lesson for every man!). Mr R subsequently gave evidence in the proceedings, stating that if Mr B were found to be the father he would be unable to continue to care for the children. Mr R stated that he was 99 per cent certain that he was the father. The judge dismissed the application for fear of the 'disastrous disintegrative effects' on the existing family of a finding that Mr B was the father. He distinguished the case from *Re H* and *Re T* on the basis that in this case the husband did not have a low sperm count nor had he had a vasectomy.[83] The Court of Appeal remitted the case for re-trial,[84] holding that the judge had erred in the balancing process. He had given too simplistic an emphasis to the strength of the marriage given the wife's continuing lack of candour about her relationship with Mr B.[85] He had also given insufficient weight to the possibility of the matter coming to the children's attention in the future, given the existence of gossip at the mother's workplace and the fact that Mr B had made known his convictions to his family and friends.[86] The Court of Appeal doubted whether the judge gave sufficient weight to the importance of certainty, and held that the factual differences between this case and others did not begin to:

> displace the points of principle to be drawn from the cases, first that the interests of justice are best served by the ascertainment of the truth and second that the court should be furnished with the best available science and not confined to such unsatisfactory alternatives as presumptions and inferences.[87]

### 2.4.1 Consent and the effect of a direction

Section 20(1) does not empower the court to *order* an adult to be tested;[88] all that it does in that context is to permit a direction for the use of tests to ascertain paternity.[89] Section 21(1) of the 1969 Act makes clear that, subject to provisions of that section, a person's consent is required to the taking of a bodily sample[90] in order to give effect to a direction under section 20. Section 21(4) provides, however, that a sample may be taken from a person who lacks capacity[91] to give his consent, if consent is given by the court, or certain persons authorised to consent on that person's behalf.[92] In respect of children, section 21(2), in line with section 8 of the 1969 Act, clarifies that the consent of a child aged 16 or over is as effective as if he or she were of full age. In the case of a child under 16 (not being such a person as is referred to in s 21(4)) a sample can be taken if the person who has care and control of the child consents, or if the court considers that it would be in the child's best interests for the sample to be taken.[93] A notable omission from section 21 is any reference to the ability of the competent child under 16 to consent to testing but a competent child under 16 could provide consent under the common law in *Gillick v West Norfolk and Wisbech AHA*.[94] The section implies, in line with the common law's approach to children's refusal of consent, that the child's

---

⁸³ Ibid, [16].     ⁸⁴ Ibid, [31].     ⁸⁵ Ibid, [26] and [27].     ⁸⁶ Ibid, [20].     ⁸⁷ Ibid, [29].

⁸⁸ See *S v S; W v Official Solicitor* [1972] AC 24 at 43 *per* Lord Reid, at 52 *per* Lord Morris of Borth-y-Gest, and at 57 *per* Lord Hodson.

⁸⁹ [1997] Fam 89, CA at 100D (discussion in context of direction for blood tests).

⁹⁰ Defined in the Family Law Reform Act 1969, s 25, as a 'sample of bodily fluid or bodily tissue taken for the purpose of scientific tests'.

⁹¹ Within the meaning of the Mental Capacity Act 2005.

⁹² Eg the donee of an enduring, or lasting, power of attorney, or a deputy appointed by the Court of Protection: see Family Law Reform Act 1969, s 21(4).

⁹³ Family Law Reform Act 1969, s 21(3).     ⁹⁴ [1986] AC 112.

refusal to be tested can be overridden by the child's carer,[95] and explicitly states that the sample can be taken if the court considers it would be in the child's best interests.

In *L v P (Paternity Test: Child's Objection)*[96] the question was whether a 15-year-old girl's objections to a paternity test should be respected. The applicant married the child's mother before the child's birth, accepted that he was the father, and his name was on the child's birth certificate. The couple divorced shortly thereafter, the applicant had little contact with the girl, and substantial arrears of child support accrued. The Child Support Agency sought to enforce the child support liability whereupon he applied under s 55A of the Family Law Act 1986 for a declaration that he was not the child's father and sought DNA testing. The girl objected on the basis, *inter alia*, that if the test revealed he was not her father, it would have serious implications for her relationship with her mother, who would be found to have lied to her throughout her childhood. The mother was not prepared to provide her consent on the child's behalf. Hedley J refused to give a direction for DNA testing. He saw the girl's objection as 'carefully thought-out and entirely proper',[97] and as 'rational and cogent', reflecting 'a degree of maturity and understanding which compels respect'.[98] Hedley J found that the girl was of 'sufficient understanding and intelligence to enable . . . her to understand fully what is proposed', as required by *Gillick* for her to be capable of consenting,[99] while also noting that that capacity did not give her the power to refuse.[100] In those circumstances, Hedley J concluded that it would be 'extremely difficult to impose an order under section 21(3)'.[101] Hedley J identified three reasons for his conclusion:[102] (1) the girl's objection was reasonable and one that ought to be respected; (2) the 'significant history of the father affirming his position as a parent'; and (3) the facts raised burdens which really made it impossible for the applicant to suggest seriously that he was not the girl's father.

In an earlier case, *Re D (Paternity)*,[103] Hedley J held that 'best interests' in section 21(3) 'must pay particular regard to the views of the child having regard to his age and understanding'.[104] In that case a child, T, was placed shortly after his birth with a woman who was assumed to be his paternal grandmother and brought up by her. Her son had been identified by T's teenage mother as his father and he had acknowledged his paternity. On T's 10th birthday, he was visited by a man (the applicant in the case) who had had a relationship with T's mother around the time of his conception. The applicant was accompanied by a friend, who tactlessly introduced the applicant to T as his real father. Shortly thereafter the applicant made applications for residence, contact, and parental responsibility in respect of T, in which the issue of T's paternity was raised. T had had a difficult childhood, experiencing educational and behavioural problems, and was described as 'a troubled and angry person'. T was adamant that he wanted nothing to do with the applicant and was 'deeply resistant to scientific testing'. Hedley J saw consent as integral to the workings of Part III of the 1969 Act and focused on whether a sample should be taken from T in his best interests pursuant to section 21(3) of the Family Law Reform Act 1969.

Hedley J found that T's opposition was his own view expressed at a 'highly emotive stage of his life', and was satisfied that while it was in T's best interests to know the truth sooner rather than later, it was not in T's interests to press the issue at this turbulent point his life. His Lordship thus

---

[95] A person who probably will, but may not necessarily, have parental responsibility within the meaning of the Children Act 1989, s 3. The statutory provisions do not sit easily with the comment of Lord Reid in *S v S; W v Official Solicitor* [1972] AC 24 at 45, that 'as soon as a child is able to understand these matters it would generally be unwise to subject it to this operation against its will'.

[96] [2011] EWHC 3399 (Fam), [2013] 1 FLR 578 Hedley J.     [97] Ibid, [23].

[98] Ibid, [26].     [99] Ibid, [21].

[100] However, see *Re P (Identity of Mother)* [2011] EWCA Civ 795, [2012] 1 FLR 351, where at [13] the Court of Appeal commented that it was not envisaged that a sample would be taken from the 15-year-old child concerned without her consent; but the court added that that 'does not leave the court powerless, or reliant on findings of fact based on the balance of probabilities. The statute is very clear that it is open to the court to draw an inference based on [the child's] refusal to provide a sample.'

[101] [2011] EWHC 3399 (Fam) at [26].     [102] Ibid, [28] and [29].

[103] [2006] EWHC 3545 (Fam), [2007] 2 FLR 26.     [104] Ibid, [24].

gave a direction that the applicant be tested, but stayed without limit of time a similar direction in relation to T, in the hope that T would be encouraged to think about the issue and if he eventually agreed to be tested the results could be made known to the applicant.

It should be noted therefore that the child's interests can be considered at two distinct stages, first under section 20, and if a direction is given then possibly again under section 21. There are different approaches to welfare at each stage and judges must take care not to confuse the two tests.[105]

### 2.4.2 Failure to comply with a direction

> **Key legislation**
>
> Section 23(1) of the Family Law Reform Act 1969 provides that:
>
> Where a court gives a direction under section 20 of this Act and any person fails to take any step required of him for the purpose of giving effect to the direction, the court may draw such inferences, if any, from that fact as appear proper in the circumstances.

Where paternity proceedings arise in relation to a child who is born to a married woman, and where consent to scientific testing is refused by one of the adults concerned, the legal position is made more complicated by the presumption of legitimacy. Section 23(2) separates the presumption of legitimacy from claiming relief in reliance on the presumption. In a case in which a party who is relying on the presumption refuses to be tested, or to allow the child to be tested, the court may dismiss the claim for relief even though there may be an absence of evidence to rebut the presumption. An example might be where a married woman alleges that a man other than her husband is the father of her child for child support purposes. Where the man denies paternity, but refuses to be tested, it seems that it would be possible for a court to order that the man should be liable to make child support payments, even though there is an absence of evidence to rebut the presumption of legitimacy. However, where a husband relies on the presumption of legitimacy and refuses to be tested, the inference will be drawn that he is not the father of the child.

### 2.4.3 Inferences to be drawn from a failure to comply with a direction

What inferences may a court properly draw from the refusal of a person to be tested in the face of the court's direction? This question arose in *Re A (A Minor) (Paternity: Refusal of Blood Test)*.[106] In that case, a mother was having a sexual relationship with three different men around the time of her child's conception. In the circumstances each could equally have been the child's father but the mother claimed child support maintenance against only one, Mr G, a 'prosperous businessman' who 'lived a luxurious life'.[107] A direction for testing to ascertain paternity was made in the proceedings but Mr G failed to cooperate. His argument was that he should not be put at risk of a finding of paternity when two other men were also 'in the frame' yet not similarly at risk. The judge dismissed the application, finding that he could not conclude on the balance of probabilities that Mr G was the father, and could not draw an inference from the failure to be tested that Mr G knew that he was the father. The Court of Appeal overturned the judge's decision, remitting the case for hearing of the level of maintenance that Mr G should pay. Waite LJ (Sir Ralph Gibson agreeing) held that the judge had fallen into error in so limiting his powers of inference under section 23(1) of the Family Law Reform Act 1969. The court explained that those powers are 'wholly at large and unconfined' and 'amply wide enough to extend to an inference drawn as to the very fact which is in issue in the proceedings, namely the child's actual paternity'.[108] In determining what inference

---

[105]  See eg *Re L (A Child)* [2009] EWCA Civ 1239, [2010] 2 FLR 188.      [106]  [1994] 2 FLR 463, CA.
[107]  Ibid, 470.      [108]  Ibid, 472.

should be drawn in the case, Waite LJ explained that genetic testing can now achieve certainty, and commented:

> Any man who is unsure of his own paternity and harbours the least doubt as to whether the child he is alleged to have fathered may be that of another man now has it within his power to set all doubt at rest by submitting to a test. It has ceased, therefore, to be possible for any man in such circumstances to be forced against his will to accept paternity of a child whom he does not believe to be his.
>
> Against that background of law and scientific advance, it seems to me to follow, both in justice and common sense, that if a mother makes a claim against one of the possible fathers, and he chooses to exercise his right not to submit to be tested, the inference that he is the father of the child should be virtually inescapable. He would certainly have to advance very clear and cogent reasons for this refusal to be tested—reasons which it would be just and fair and reasonable for him to be allowed to maintain.[109]

The court found the father's reason for refusal irrelevant. It held that the issue was one of evidence, not equity, and that the court 'should find proven forensically what G, by his refusal has prevented from being established scientifically'.[110]

Subsequently, courts have adopted a robust approach where one of the parties has refused to be tested and have taken full advantage of their entitlement to draw such inferences as appear proper.

In *Re G (Parentage: Blood Sample)*[111] Thorpe LJ added:

> The court must be astute to discern what are the real motivations behind the refusal. It should look critically at proffered explanation or justification. It should only uphold an explanation that is objectively valid, demonstrating rationality, logicality, and consistency. Anything less will usually lead to an adverse inference.[112]

In that case the applicant sought a contact order in respect of a child whom he believed he had conceived with his former wife. Several directions for testing were made in the proceedings after the mother put the applicant's paternity in issue by suggesting that she had had sexual intercourse with another man around the time of the child's conception. Despite the directions, the applicant refused to be tested. The applicant declared that he was 99.9 per cent certain that he was the child's father but was unwilling to undergo testing. This was because the child would be upset if she were to be told that he was not the father, and the mother would use that finding to thwart his contact. In the absence of scientific evidence the judge declared that the applicant was the child's father on the bases, *inter alia*, that he could not be satisfied that sexual intercourse had not taken place between the parties at the relevant time; that the applicant had been registered as the father on the child's birth certificate; and that the mother had only put the child's paternity in issue two and a half years after the child's birth. The Court of Appeal held that the judge had misdirected himself in not drawing an adverse inference against the father for his failure to undergo testing. The court noted the illogicality of the father's stance, and that his assessment of the probabilities was wrong: on the evidence he could have no better than a 50 per cent chance of being the father. While acknowledging that counsel was correct that the absence of scientific testing did not alter those probabilities, the court pointed out that the proper inference permitted by section 23 of the Family Law Reform Act 1969 was held in *Re A (A Minor) (Paternity: Refusal of Blood Test)*[113] to be a 'forensic inference', and commented:

> The forensic process is advanced by presenting the truth to the court. He who obstructs the truth will have the inference drawn against him. The inexorable advance of science cannot be ignored.[114]

---

[109] Ibid, 472–3.     [110] Ibid, 473.     [111] *Re G (Parentage: Blood Sample)* [1997] 1 FLR 360, CA.
[112] Ibid, 367.     [113] [1994] 2 FLR 463, CA.     [114] Ibid, 466–7.

In summary, therefore, except in respect of a child, the courts cannot compel the availability of necessary scientific evidence to ascertain paternity. They can merely direct such evidence be made available in the hope that the direction will be complied with. Where it is not, a proper inference (presumably that the refusal to comply is made to hide the truth) may be drawn. Indeed, it has been said that an inference could be drawn even where no direction has been given if there has been a failure to provide the best evidence, 'even if the inference is not as strong as when the court's direction is flouted'.[115]

## 2.5 Disclosure of parentage to children

As we have seen, the courts have increasingly taken the view that normally the truth about a child's parentage should emerge, and that attempts to obstruct this process should be met by the drawing of adverse inferences. In *Re D (Paternity)* Hedley J observed that this approach has obvious merits: 'truth . . . is easier to handle than fiction and also it is designed to avoid information coming to a young person's attention in a haphazard, unorganized and indeed sometimes malicious context'.[116]

However, concern has been expressed that the shift in the case law may be going too far too quickly in one direction.[117] There is a risk that the focus on ascertaining the truth is applied in practice almost as a blanket rule. Family dynamics vary from one household to another, particularly over an issue as sensitive as contested paternity. Directions for scientific tests may force disclosure at a time which may not fit in with the child's pace and sense of security, or may deliver a body blow to a recovering marriage which is still fragile with regard to the previous relationship which led to the child's birth. If forcing scientific testing on an unwilling married couple has a destructive effect on their personal relationship, or on the husband's relationship with the child, this may be more harmful to the child than giving him knowledge of the true facts during childhood. While some men may have no difficulty in treating another man's child as their own even where there is doubt about the child's paternity, other men may find it emotionally impossible to continue to respond to the child as their own where the fact of their non-paternity is established by incontrovertible evidence. Cultural factors may sometimes play a significant role in these responses.[118]

There is an argument, therefore, that while the courts should be aware of the benefits of truth and the child's interests in knowing his or her origins, they should also be able to respond flexibly to parentage disputes in a manner which is able to acknowledge the complexity of adult relationships, and which is perceptive of the family life of the particular child concerned.

Even where scientific testing has established that a man is the father of a child, it does not follow that the child will necessarily come to know of that paternity. In *J v C*[119] a child believed that his mother's long-term partner was his father, although in proceedings for contact by a man, J, DNA testing confirmed that J was the father. The proceedings were adjourned to determine whether the child's conception was forced, as the mother claimed, or consensual as J claimed. By the time of the hearing, the whereabouts of the father were unknown and the application was not pursued. The question arose, however, whether the court could, and should, of its own motion direct that the child be informed about his true father. Presuming that he had the necessary jurisdiction, Sumner J concluded that he should not do so in this case because of the mother's vulnerability to mental illness, explaining that the advantage of the child learning the truth was 'outweighed by the impact it would be likely to have on his mother and family upon whom he is so dependent'.[120] However,

---

[115] *Re H (A Minor) (Blood Tests: Parental Rights)* [1997] Fam 89 at 103.

[116] [2006] EWHC 3545 (Fam), [2007] 2 FLR 26 (Hedley J).

[117] J. Fortin, 'Children's Right to Know Their Origins—Too Far, Too Fast?' [2009] Child and Family Law Quarterly 336–55.

[118] See eg in the context of contact: *Re B (Contact: Stepfather's Opposition)* [1997] 2 FLR 579.

[119] [2006] EWHC 2837 (Fam), [2007] 1 FCR 365 (Sumner J).     [120] Ibid, [12].

his Lordship urged the family to take advice, commenting that for the boy to know sooner rather than later might be to his advantage, rather than waiting until 16 when the impact might be greater given the turmoil of puberty.[121]

# 3  Legal parenthood

## 3.1  Motherhood

Lord Simon of Glaisdale in the *Ampthill Peerage Case* stated that motherhood, although 'a legal relationship, is based on a fact, being proved demonstrably by parturition'.[122] These words do not equate giving birth with motherhood; they speak of proving motherhood. It could be argued therefore that, as a matter of the *common law*, the underlying basis for motherhood might be the genetic connection, as *evidenced by* parturition. Usually of course there is no issue because the woman carrying the child will also be the genetic mother. However, a woman can now give birth to a child to whom she is not genetically related, for example where an embryo is implanted in her which has been created with the egg of another woman. Is the woman who gave birth the mother of the child or is the woman who donated her egg the mother? Later in this chapter we shall explore the competing arguments in this situation. The law in statute, however, answers this question unequivocally.

---

### Key legislation

Section 33 of the Human Fertilisation and Embryology Act (HFEA) 2008 provides:

> The woman who is carrying or has carried a child as a result of the placing in her of an embryo or of sperm and eggs,[123] and no other woman, is to be treated as the mother of the child.[124]

---

An identical provision is to be found in section 27 of the HFEA 1990, which applies prior to implementation of the 2008 Act. Whichever provision applies, however, the law is clear that the woman who gives birth to a child is the child's mother whether or not the child is genetically related to her.

---

### Talking point

As Baroness Hale commented in *Re G (Children) (Residence: Same-Sex Partner)*:[125]

> While this may be partly for reasons of certainty and convenience, it also recognises a deeper truth: that the process of carrying a child and giving him birth (which may well be followed by breast-feeding for some months) brings with it, in the vast majority of cases, a very special relationship between mother and child, a relationship which is different from any other.[126]

**Q.** Are biological parents more special than social parents?

---

[121] Ibid, [14].      [122] [1977] AC 547 at 577.
[123] Whether this happened in the UK or elsewhere: see s 33(3).
[124] The provision does not apply to the extent that the child is treated by virtue of adoption as not being the woman's child: see s 33(2).
[125] [2006] 4 All ER 241.      [126] Ibid, [34].

## 3.2 **Fatherhood**

### 3.2.1 **The general rule**

The general rule in English law, subject to the provisions of the Human Fertilisation and Embryology Acts (discussed in the following sections), is that a child's father is the man whose sperm resulted in the child's conception. Unless a statutory provision applies to the contrary, the child's father will be his or her genetic father.[127] In most cases, therefore, the issue of who, in law, is the father of a child will simply be a question of the child's *parentage*.

### 3.2.2 **Assisted conception and fatherhood**

The fatherhood of a child conceived through assisted conception may be determined by one of three different statutes, depending upon the date of the child's conception: the Family Law Reform Act 1987, the HFEA 1990, or the HFEA 2008.

---

### Key legislation

Section 27 of the Family Law Reform Act 1987 was the first provision to regulate fatherhood in cases of assisted conception, and to recognise legal parenthood in a case where there was no blood relationship between the adult and child concerned.[128] It allowed fatherhood to be conferred on the mother's husband in a case of her artificial insemination by another man. It came into force on 4 April 1988 and provided:

(1) Where after the coming into force of this section a child is born in England and Wales as the result of the artificial insemination of a woman who—

    (a) was at the time of the insemination a party to a marriage (being a marriage which had not at that time been dissolved or annulled); and

    (b) was artificially inseminated with the semen of some person other than the other party to that marriage,

then, unless it is proved to the satisfaction of any court by which the matter has to be determined that the other party to that marriage did not consent to the insemination, the child shall be treated in law as the child of the parties to that marriage and shall not be treated as the child of any person other than the parties to that marriage.

---

The HFEA 1990, which was brought into force on 1 August 1991, introduced, in sections 27–9, new provisions regulating parenthood in light of scientific advances in assisted reproduction techniques.[129] As we have seen, the Act clarified who was to be the mother of a child in cases of egg donation. Section 28(2) of the 1990 Act adopted the same formula as section 27 of the Family Law Reform Act 1987 with respect to a woman's husband acquiring legal fatherhood, with some necessary re-wording to extend its substance beyond artificial insemination to other forms of assisted conception. Section 27 of the 1987 Act therefore became otiose for the future, and the 1990 Act provided[130] that it was not to have effect in relation to children carried as a result of artificial insemination after the commencement of relevant provisions of the 1990 Act. Section 27 of the Family Law Reform Act 1987 still remains applicable, however, to determining parenthood in the

---

[127] Illustrated by the *Leeds* case discussed in Section 3.7.

[128] Following a recommendation of the Law Commission in its *Report on Illegitimacy* (Law Com No 118, 1982), paras 12.1–12.27.

[129] The Act was preceded by the *Report of the Committee of Inquiry into Human Fertilisation and Embryology* (the Warnock Committee) (Cmnd 9314, 1984) and a White Paper, *Human Fertilisation and Embryology: A Framework for Legislation* (Cm 259, 1987).

[130] In s 49(4).

case of some children conceived through artificial insemination prior to implementation of sections 27–29 of the 1990 Act. Indeed, as we shall see later, the Court of Appeal had occasion to interpret and apply it as recently as 2006 in *J v C and Another*.[131]

The 1990 Act was groundbreaking in introducing (in s 28(3)) a provision which allowed the male partner of a woman, to whom she was not married, to become the legal father of a child to whom he was not genetically related, provided the couple were having treatment services together at a licensed clinic.

Part II of the HFEA 2008 sets out, in sections 33–48, a new scheme for determining parenthood in cases of assisted reproduction. Those provisions will apply only to children carried by women as a result of the placing in them of embryos or of sperm and eggs, or their artificial insemination (as the case may be) after their commencement,[132] and sections 27–29 of the 1990 Act do not have effect after that time.[133] The 2008 Act's provisions on parenthood were implemented on 6 April 2009, except for section 54 (parental orders), which was implemented on 6 April 2010. The new Act is the product of a public consultation[134] and pre-legislative scrutiny of a draft Bill.[135] In substance, many of the relevant sections of the new Act are re-enactments of provisions in the 1990 Act, sometimes with amendments to take account of problems which were highlighted by case law. The principal change to the law on parenthood effected by the 2008 Act is to extend to female civil partners provisions which formerly only applied to married couples, and to extend to female partners who are not civil partners those provisions which formerly applied only to heterosexual unmarried couples.

While it is the new Act which applies to children who are born now, the 1990 Act and its case law will remain important in determining the parenthood of children born before implementation of the 2008 Act. A knowledge of the 1990 Act and its case law is also likely to prove helpful in understanding the genesis of some of the 2008 provisions, and how the re-enacted provisions are likely to be interpreted. In what follows, we set out and explain relevant provisions of the 1990 Act and their case law, and then examine the changes effected by the 2008 Act.

### 3.3 **The Human Fertilisation and Embryology Act 1990**

The provision of assisted conception by clinics is regulated by the Human Fertilisation and Embryology Authority under the HFEA 1990 and a Code of Practice.[136] The Act sets out in section 13 conditions of licences for treatment, which include, in section 13(5), the requirement that '[a] woman shall not be provided with treatment services unless account has been taken of the welfare of any child who may be born as a result of the treatment (including the need of that child for supportive parenting), and of any other child who may be affected by the birth'. Section 13(5) was amended by the HFEA 2008 to remove what used to be a reference to the child's need for a father.[137] There are also restrictions on certain forms of treatment unless suitable counselling has

---

[131] [2006] EWCA Civ 551, [2007] Fam 1.   [132] HFEA 2008, s 57(1).   [133] Ibid, s 57(2).

[134] Department of Health, *Review of the Human Fertilisation and Embryology Act—A Public Consultation* (London: Department of Health, 2005).

[135] Human Tissue and Embryos (Draft) Bill (Cm 7087), which was based on a White Paper, *Review of the Human Fertilisation and Embryology Act: Proposals for Revised Legislation (including establishment of the Regulatory Authority for Tissue and Embryos)* (Cm 6989, December 2006). The Bill was scrutinised by the Joint Committee on the Human Tissue and Embryos (Draft) Bill Session 2006–07: see *Human Tissue and Embryos (Draft) Bill Volume 1: Report* HL Paper 169-I, HC Paper 630-I, published 1 August 2007.

[136] See HFEA 1990, s 25 and Code of Practice.

[137] For the arguments on this issue, see L. Smith, 'Clashing Symbols? Reconciling Support for Fathers and Fatherless Families After the Human Fertilisation and Embryology Act 2008' [2010] Child and Family Law Quarterly 46–70. See also G. Douglas, 'Assisted Reproduction and the Welfare of the Child' (1993) 46(2) Current Legal Problems 53–74; E. Blyth, 'The United Kingdom's Human Fertilisation and Embryology Act 1990 and the Welfare of the Child: A Critique' (1995) 3 International Journal of Children's Rights 417–38; E. Jackson, 'Conception and the Irrelevance of the Welfare Principle' (2002) 65 Modern Law Review 176–203.

been given.[138] The storage[139] and use of a person's genetic material are closely controlled by the requirement of written consent within Schedule 3 to the 1990 Act,[140] and a suitable opportunity for counselling must be given before consent is given.[141] Schedule 3, paragraph 5, makes clear that a person's gametes must not be used for the purposes of treatment services unless there is an effective Schedule 3 consent,[142] although this is not required where the gametes are being used for the person and another receiving treatment services together.[143] These provisions protect individual autonomy in the use of genetic material and consequently a person's wish whether to have a child. However, their application in some situations has led to 'hard cases'.

In *Evans v UK*[144] Natalie Evans was diagnosed with pre-cancerous ovaries and told that her ovaries would need to be removed. She was advised to harvest some of her eggs to secure the possibility of future IVF treatment, and also that there were higher prospects of successfully having a child if, instead of freezing her eggs, embryos created with her partner, J, were frozen. The couple were told that it was possible for either to withdraw his or her consent at any time before the embryos were implanted. But J reassured Ms Evans that they would not split up and that she did not need to consider the freezing of her eggs. They entered into the necessary consents by signing relevant forms. However, the relationship subsequently broke down, and J wrote to the clinic stating that the embryos should be destroyed.

Evans sought an injunction requiring J to restore his consent, and a declaration that J could not vary his earlier consent. She claimed that her rights under Articles 8, 12, and 14 of the ECHR were breached, and the embryos were entitled to protection under Article 2. These claims were denied by the Court of Appeal, and permission to appeal to the Lords was refused, so Evans took her case to the European Court of Human Rights and the case ultimately came before the Court's Grand Chamber. Unanimously the Court held that Article 2 was not violated. A majority held that Article 8 of the ECHR was engaged but that the Article 8 rights of J and Natalie Evans were each engaged and entirely irreconcilable. Either Evans would be denied parenthood or J would be forced into it. The Court also held that the case did not simply involve 'a conflict between individuals; the legislation in question also served a number of wider, public interests, in upholding the principle of the primacy of consent and promoting legal clarity and certainty.'[145] In addition, as there was no uniform approach in Europe the state had to be afforded a wide margin of appreciation,[146] and the absolute nature of the consent requirement was held not inconsistent with Article 8.[147] Similarly, there was no breach of Article 8 together with Article 14. The dissenting judges held that the bright-line consent rule precluded any balancing of the competing interests in the case and its application on the facts was disproportionate to the impact on the applicant in the circumstances and gave no weight to J's reassurances. Craig Lind, in a commentary on the case,[148] has argued that there should be less sympathy for J because 'people who have sexual relations (and even those who approach clinics for procreative help) take a risk of children emerging that they were not planning to have, however carefully they set out to protect themselves against that eventuality'.[149] He argues that the desire for genetic parenthood embedded (socially) within us 'should give rise to a more nuanced . . . public policy position than the one accepted in the legislation and by the courts in this case'.[150] Lind also makes the point that there may have been indirect discrimination, in the sense that it is much easier to store sperm than it is to store eggs, so Ms Evans was in a position that

---

[138] HFEA 1990, s 13(6) and Sch 3ZA, Pt 1.    [139] See Sch 3, para 8.

[140] Schedule 3, para 1. See eg *R v Human Fertilisation and Embryology Authority, ex p Blood* [1997] 2 All ER 687, CA (collection of husband's sperm while unconscious using electro-ejaculation was unlawful). See also *L v Human Fertilisation and Embryology Authority and Secretary of State* [2008] EWHC 2149 (Fam).

[141] Schedule 3, para 3.    [142] Ibid, para 5(1).    [143] Ibid, para 5(3).

[144] [2007] 2 FCR 5 (Grand Chamber, ECtHR).    [145] Ibid, para 74.

[146] Ibid, para 81.    [147] Ibid, para 89.

[148] C. Lind, 'Evans v United Kingdom—Judgments of Solomon: Power, Gender and Procreation' [2006] Child and Family Law Quarterly 576.

[149] Ibid, 583.    [150] Ibid, 587.

no man would ever be in. Lind thus argues for a more nuanced approach in such cases, allowing 'personalised justice, appropriately tailored to the human tragedies that can beset anyone's life'.[151]

### 3.4 Section 28: the legal but not biological father

Section 28(2) and (3) of the HFEA 1990 allow a man who is not genetically related to a child to become the child's legal father. Section 28(5) clarifies that those provisions do not apply 'to any child who, by virtue of the rules of common law, is treated as the legitimate child of the parties to a marriage'. So, in the case of a child born to a married woman, section 28 does not apply to make a man other than the woman's husband the child's father, or to make a child fatherless, unless and until the presumption of legitimacy is rebutted.

### 3.4.1 The mother's husband and assisted conception

---

**Key legislation**

Section 28(2) of the HFEA 1990 provides:

If—

    (a) at the time of the placing in her of the embryo or the sperm and eggs or of her insemination, the woman was a party to a marriage, and

    (b) the creation of the embryo carried by her was not brought about with the sperm of the other party to the marriage,

then, subject to subsection (5) below, the other party to the marriage shall be treated as the father of the child unless it is shown that he did not consent to the placing in her of the embryo or the sperm and eggs or to her insemination (as the case may be).

---

Section 28(2) applies whether or not the conception was assisted through a so-called self-help method of artificial insemination or with professional help. It also applies whether the assisted conception took place in the UK or elsewhere.[152] The word 'marriage' in section 28 means a marriage subsisting at the time, unless a judicial separation was then in force, and includes a void marriage if at the relevant time either or both of the parties reasonably believed that the marriage was valid.[153]

The subsection treats the mother's husband as the child's father 'unless it is shown that he did not consent'. The meaning of this phrase was considered *obiter* by McFarlane J in *Re G (Surrogacy: Foreign Domicile)*.[154] In that case a surrogate mother, Mrs J, who was artificially inseminated with the sperm of Mr G, remained married to her estranged husband, raising the possibility that her husband could be the father of the surrogate child who was now living with the commissioning parents, Mr G and his wife. It was contended that the absence of Mrs J's husband's consent to the procedure demonstrated that he did not consent. McFarlane J disagreed, observing that the words 'it is shown' require the court to be *satisfied* that the husband did not consent, and the absence of clear evidence of consent does not mean that it is shown that a person has not consented.[155] Mrs J's evidence, however, was that her husband was aware of her general intention to act as a surrogate mother and had no objection to her doing so, but was not aware of the particular

---

[151] Ibid, 592.    [152] HFEA 1990, s 28(8).

[153] Ibid, s 28(7). 'Void' in this context probably does not include a marriage which is void because the parties are not respectively male and female: see the discussion in Section 3.9 of *J v C and Another* [2006] EWCA Civ 551, [2007] Fam 1, a case on the similarly worded s 27 of the Family Law Reform Act 1987.

[154] [2007] EWHC 2814 (Fam), [2008] 1 FLR 1047 at [30]–[39].    [155] Ibid, [39].

surrogacy procedure which led to the child's conception. He was therefore not in a position either to consent or not consent to the particular arrangement. The husband failed to respond to correspondence requesting clarification. In the absence of further evidence from the husband and on the evidence presented, McFarlane J declared that it was shown that the husband did not consent to his wife's insemination.[156] It was also proved that the child was conceived as a result of the artificial insemination and, the presumption of legitimacy having been rebutted, therefore Mr G was in law the child's father.

### 3.4.2 Assisted conception and unmarried couples

> ### Key legislation
>
> Section 28(3) of the HFEA 1990 provides:
>
> (3) If no man is treated, by virtue of subsection (2) above, as the father of the child but—
>
> (a) the embryo or the sperm and eggs were placed in the woman, or she was artificially inseminated, in the course of treatment services provided for her and a man together by a person to whom a licence applies, and
>
> (b) the creation of the embryo carried by her was not brought about with the sperm of that man,
>
> then, subject to subsection (5) below, that man shall be treated as the father of the child.

It has been said that subsections (2) and (3) of section 28 are mutually exclusive.[157] Section 28(3) allows a man who is neither married to the child's mother nor genetically related to the child to become the child's legal parent.

### 3.4.3 Licensed treatment

Unlike section 28(2), this provision applies only to treatment services[158] by a person to whom a licence applies, that is clinics which are licensed by the Human Fertilisation and Embryology Authority. Section 28(3) does not, therefore, apply to treatment provided abroad. For this reason, in *U v W (Attorney General Intervening)*,[159] Wilson J held that twins born to a couple who received treatment by artificial insemination of the mother by donor sperm at a clinic in Rome were fatherless. Consequently, the mother's partner, from whom she was now estranged, had no duty to support the children under the Child Support Act 1991.[160]

### 3.4.4 In the course of treatment services provided for a woman and a man together

The requirement that treatment services are provided for the woman and man together does not require that there is any physical treatment of the man. In *U v V (Attorney General Intervening)*[161] Wilson J held that in the provision of treatment services with donor sperm what has to be demonstrated is that 'the doctor was responding to a request for that form of treatment made by the woman and the man as a couple'. In other words, there must be a 'joint enterprise', in the sense that the *services* are provided *for the man too*. It is clear that there can be no joint enterprise where a man's sperm is to be used after his death.[162]

---

[156] Ibid, [37].

[157] *Leeds Teaching Hospital NHS Trust v A and others* [2003] 1 FCR 599, [2003] EWHC 259 (QB).

[158] Defined in the HFEA 1990, s 2(1).    [159] [1998] Fam 29.

[160] It was held that the restriction of provision of services in another state of the EU did not breach Art 59 of the Treaty of Rome. The restriction could be justified on policy grounds.

[161] [1998] Fam 29.

[162] *R v Human Fertilisation and Embryology Authority, ex p Blood* [1997] 2 All ER 687, CA.

However, having treatment services together involves more than the man simply being present with the woman at the medical practitioner's premises and paying for the treatment. In *Re Q (Parental Order)*[163] Johnson J held in such circumstances that an unmarried woman who was acting as a surrogate mother to a married couple was not having treatment services with the husband. It seems, therefore, that the section envisages that the joint enterprise is one in which the couple treated are seeking to be parents of the resulting child together.[164]

In *Re R (IVF: Paternity of Child)*[165] the question was whether section 28(3) applied where a man had participated during much of the treatment provided, but had separated from the woman by the time the embryo which led to the child's birth was placed within her. The child's mother's partner, B, became infertile following treatment for testicular cancer and the couple sought treatment at a licensed clinic. The mother signed a consent form to IVF with donor sperm (matched to the physical characteristics of the mother and B), and B countersigned acknowledging that he and the mother were being treated together and he would be recognised as the legal father of any resulting child. Two embryos were placed in the mother, and the remaining embryos were frozen for future use. The mother and B then separated and the mother formed a new relationship with another man. The mother did not tell the clinic of the separation but continued to have treatment with some of the remaining embryos, which resulted in the birth of a baby girl. B knew nothing of this later treatment until he found out that the mother was pregnant. B applied for a parental responsibility order in respect of the child and the issue of whether he was the child's father arose in the proceedings. At first instance Hedley J found that B was the father. Laying emphasis on clarity, simplicity, and certainty, his Lordship held that the parties should be regarded as still in a joint enterprise until it was expressly ended by being brought to the attention of the clinic.[166] The Court of Appeal allowed the mother's appeal. Hale LJ (delivering the judgment of the court) said that conferring parenthood was a 'serious matter' and section 28(3) should 'only apply to those cases which clearly fall within the footprint of the statutory language'.[167] The Court of Appeal's analysis of the structure of section 28(2) and (3) revealed that both subsections saw the critical time for determining legal parenthood as the point at which the embryo or the sperm and eggs are placed in the woman. The court concluded:

> There must be a point in time when the question has to be judged. The simple answer is that the embryo must be placed in the mother at a time when treatment services are being provided for the woman and the man together.

Applying this approach to the facts, the couple had separated at the relevant time and thus B could not be the father pursuant to section 28(3). The child therefore had no legal father.

B's appeal to the House of Lords was dismissed.[168] Lord Walker of Gestingthorpe, with whom the rest of the Appellate Committee agreed, was content to adopt the Court of Appeal's reasoning as to the interpretation of section 28(3),[169] adding the observation that:

> important though certainty is, it is even more important that the very significant legal relationship of parenthood should not be based on a fiction (especially if the fiction involves a measure of deception by the mother).[170]

---

[163] [1996] 1 FLR 369.

[164] Although not a case on s 28(3), *Re B (Parentage)* [1996] 2 FLR 15 appears to suggest that the man and the woman need not necessarily be intimate partners, provided they are embarked upon a joint enterprise of producing a child for whom the man will be the parent.

[165] [2003] Fam 129, CA (Morritt V-C, Hale and Dyson LJJ).     [166] [2002] 2 FLR 843 at [10].

[167] Ibid, [20].     [168] *Re R (A Child) (IVF: Paternity)* [2005] UKHL 33, [2005] 2 AC 621.

[169] Ibid, [41].     [170] Ibid, [42].

His Lordship clarified, however, that this 'does not imply the view that no weight should be given to the perspective (or perception) of medical staff at the clinic'.[171] He explained:

> The clinic's perception is one element to be taken into account in answering the factual question which the Court of Appeal posed, following the language of section 28(3). The idea of providing treatment services to two people 'together' does involve a 'mental element' . . . and the perceptions of the medical staff at the clinic are part of that. But they cannot be the decisive element if they are based partly on deception, and if the rest of the evidence shows that at the material time there is no longer any 'joint enterprise' between the woman and her ex-partner.[172]

Where a person is treated as the father by virtue of section 28, no other person is to be treated as the father of the child,[173] and in general that person is treated as the father for all purposes.[174] The legal fatherhood conferred by section 28 is the same as that conferred on a biological father. In *Re CH (Contact: Parentage)*[175] a husband was the legal father of a child born to his wife by artificial insemination by donor sperm. The marriage broke down after an episode of drunken violence by the husband and the mother sought to deny the husband contact with the child. She argued that he should not be treated in the same way as a child's biological father. It was held that the same general approach to contact applied to all men who were regarded in law as the father of a child, irrespective of biological connection.

### 3.5 **The Human Fertilisation and Embryology Act 2008**

Section 28(2) and (3) of the HFEA 1990 is replicated, in its basic substance, by sections 35–38 of the HFEA 2008.[176] Section 35 adopts wording similar to section 28(2).[177] It should be clear that for either section 28(2) of the 1990 Act or section 35 of the 2008 Act to apply, the child must not be conceived by a donor's sperm during sexual intercourse. How the child was conceived was a matter of dispute in *M v F and H (Legal Paternity)*,[178] a case which also addressed *obiter* whether the husband could be said not to have consented to his wife's artificial insemination. In that case a wife, who was unable to conceive naturally with her husband, contacted a sperm donor, Mr F, who had advertised his services on a website. The wife misled the sperm donor that her husband supported her quest for donor insemination, when in fact he did not approve of it. Although the sperm donor met both the wife and husband, the husband's lack of approval was not communicated to the sperm donor. Subsequently, the wife conceived with sperm provided by the sperm donor and gave birth to a child. The husband and wife divorced. The mother alleged that the child had been conceived

---

[171] Ibid, [43]. As the House acknowledged, this point had been made by Craig Lind in a commentary on the Court of Appeal's decision: see C. Lind, '*In re R (Paternity of IVF Baby)*—Unmarried Paternity under the Human Fertilisation and Embryology Act 1990' [2003] Child and Family Law Quarterly 327 at 332–3.

[172] Lord Hope of Craighead had earlier observed that the Court of Appeal's 'simple approach' left open what he saw as the issue in the appeal, namely how it is to be determined whether the services were being provided for the woman and the man together (at [14] and [16]). In his Lordship's view the question should be determined in the light of all of the evidence, including the perspectives of client and clinic, neither of which has priority (at [19]).

[173] Section 28(4). Section 28(2) and (3) do not apply, however, to any child to the extent that the child is treated by virtue of adoption as not being the man's child: s 28(5).

[174] HFEA 1990, s 29(1). There is an exception where the child is conceived when the father is deceased. In such a case, which is discussed in Section 3.8.3, the father is only permitted to become the father for the purpose of registration on the child's birth certificate.

[175] [1996] 1 FLR 569.

[176] See J. McCandless and S. Sheldon, 'The Human Fertilisation and Embryology Act (2008) and the Tenacity of the Sexual Family Form' (2010) 72(2) Modern Law Review 175–207 for discussion of the 2008 Act's focus on the sexual family model and its resistance to the possibility that a child can have two 'mothers' or indeed two 'fathers'.

[177] For a recent dictum supporting the view that these provisions apply to unlicensed treatment, see *M v F and H (Legal Paternity)* [2013] EWHC 1901 (Fam) at [28].

[178] [2013] EWHC 1901 (Fam), Peter Jackson J.

through sexual intercourse with Mr F rather than artificial insemination (AI), which Mr F denied. She sought a declaration under s 55A of the Family Law Act 1986 that Mr F was the father and applied for financial provision under Schedule 1 to the Children Act 1989. Peter Jackson J found on the evidence that the child was conceived naturally and accordingly declared that Mr F was the biological and legal parent[179] as a matter of common law.[180] His Lordship went on to consider, *obiter*, the position under section 35 of the Human Fertilisation and Embryology Act 2008 with regard to consent had the child been conceived artificially. He found that the husband had acquiesced in the artificial insemination but that it had been shown that he did not consent. The husband's:

> failure to vocalize his objection or to have taken active steps to prevent the AI could only amount to consent if they were the outward signs of an inward consent. They cannot convert something short of consent into consent within the meaning of s 35 HFEA 2008. Nor does the reverse burden of proof dilute the meaning of consent itself. Insofar as this is in any way hard on Mr F, who could for a short while at the beginning have been forgiven for believing that he was going to be meeting a united couple, it should be borne in mind that he made no effort whatever to find out what [the husband] actually thought when they very briefly met.[181]

Peter Jackson J also rejected an argument that absence of consent had to be communicated to all those affected, commenting that that is 'not what the statute says and it would not be possible for absence of consent to be communicated to "all those affected" in many situations, including most obviously a situation in which the husband did not even know that the wife had embarked on AI'.[182]

The substance of section 28(3) of the 1990 Act appears in sections 36 and 37 of the new Act, but the wording of the new Act seeks to set out more precisely the circumstances in which the man and the woman will be receiving treatment services together, in order to deal with the difficulties that were presented in *Re R (A Child) (IVF: Paternity)*.[183] This is achieved by requiring that 'agreed fatherhood conditions', set out in section 37, are satisfied. The provisions are complex, and it is convenient to set them out in full.

---

### Key legislation

Section 36 provides:

> If no man is treated by virtue of section 35 as the father of the child and no woman is treated by virtue of section 42 as a parent of the child but—
>
> (a) the embryo or the sperm and eggs were placed in W, or W was artificially inseminated, in the course of treatment services provided in the United Kingdom by a person to whom a licence applies,
> (b) at the time when the embryo or the sperm and eggs were placed in W, or W was artificially inseminated, the agreed fatherhood conditions (as set out in section 37) were satisfied in relation to a man, in relation to treatment provided to W under the licence,
> (c) the man remained alive at that time, and
> (d) the creation of the embryo carried by W was not brought about with the man's sperm,
>
> then, subject to section 38(2) to (4), the man is to be treated as the father of the child.

---

[179] Ibid, [23].

[180] Ibid, [27], rejecting the argument that the 2008 Act is an exclusive code for determining parenthood which, if it did not apply, left the child fatherless.

[181] It should be noted that later in time the matter was not in doubt since there was a second meeting at which Mr F became aware that the husband was against artificial insemination.

[182] [2013] EWHC 1901 at [26].        [183] [2005] UKHL 33, [2005] 2 AC 621.

The 'agreed fatherhood conditions', are met in relation to a man (M) in relation to treatment provided to a woman (W) under licence if, but only if:

- (a) M has given the person responsible a notice stating that he consents to being treated as the father of any child resulting from treatment provided to W under the licence,

- (b) W has given the person responsible a notice stating that she consents to M being so treated,

- (c) neither M nor W has, since giving notice under paragraph (a) or (b), given the person responsible notice of the withdrawal of M's or W's consent to M being so treated,

- (d) W has not, since the giving of the notice under paragraph (b), given the person responsible—

    - (i) a further notice under that paragraph stating that she consents to another man being treated as the father of any resulting child, or

    - (ii) a notice under section 44(1)(b) stating that she consents to a woman being treated as a parent of any resulting child, and

- (e) W and M are not within prohibited degrees of relationship in relation to each other.

### 3.6 **Lesbian couples, assisted conception, and parenthood**

Sections 42–44 of the HFEA 2008 extend the substance of sections 35–37 of the 2008 Act to female same-sex couples. Section 42(1) applies in the case of a woman who is in a civil partnership at the time of treatment, and provides:

> If at the time of the placing in her of the embryo or the sperm and eggs or of her artificial insemination, W was a party to a civil partnership, then subject to section 45(2) to (4), the other party to the civil partnership is to be treated as a parent of the child unless it is shown that she did not consent to the placing in W of the embryo or the sperm and eggs or to her artificial insemination (as the case may be).

Sections 43 and 44 apply to a female couple who are not in a civil partnership but who are undergoing treatment services together. Section 43 is in similar terms to section 36, with necessary modifications to accommodate the fact that in this case the treatment is being provided to two women. Section 44 then sets out a series of 'female parenthood conditions' which must be fulfilled if the partner of the child's mother is to acquire legal parenthood. Again, the conditions are similar to those in section 37, with necessary modifications to accommodate the same-sex circumstances. The mother's partner who fulfils the conditions of sections 43 and 44 becomes the child's other legal parent.

The requirements that the treatment is carried out in accordance with the clinic's licence, and that consent is given under section 44 in accordance with the rules, are strict ones. In *AB v CD and the Z Fertility Clinic*[184] a woman had a cycle of treatment with donor sperm at a licensed clinic on 4 and 5 May 2009, shortly after section 44 of the Human Fertilisation and Embryology Act 2008 had been implemented. She wished to share legal parenthood with her female partner and on 5 May 2009 the couple signed forms purporting to give their bilateral agreement to the mother's partner becoming a legal parent of any child born as a result of the treatment. The treatment was successful and twins were born. Cobb J held, however, that the mother's partner was not a legal parent since the consent forms were neither signed nor submitted prior to the treatment on 4 May 2009,[185] and 'in any event were completed and submitted in breach of the clinic's licence obligations in that: (a) there was no offer of counselling to the parties on this issue; (b) the "consent" on the forms was not "informed consent" '. Even if the forms had been effective, the treatment itself was ineffective to confer legal

---

[184] [2013] EWHC 1418 (Fam), [2013] 2 FLR 1357, Cobb J.    [185] Ibid, [96].

parenthood, since the clinic failed to comply with other licence conditions[186] such that the treatment was not offered under the strict terms of the clinic's licence.

Following Cobb J's decision, an audit of the practices of licensed clinics was carried out which showed significant failings in several clinics with regard to use of relevant forms to record consent to legal parenthood and record keeping. Several cases in which children had been born following donor insemination but mistakes with regard to consent forms or record keeping had occurred, came before the courts. In *X v Y (St Bartholomew's Hospital Centre for Reproductive Medicine (CRM intervening))*[187] a man, X, the mother's partner, sought a declaration of parentage in respect of a child who had been born to the mother following their treatment together at a licensed clinic. However, the evidence of the mother's partner's consent, as required by section 37 of the HFEA 2008, was not on the clinic's file. Theis J found that the father had probably signed the necessary consent form but that it had subsequently been mislaid by the clinic. Her ladyship held that the breach of record keeping did not invalidate the clinic's licence so that the treatment was 'provided under a licence'.

Similar cases came before Sir James Munby P in *In the matter of HFEA 2008 (Cases A, B, C, D, E, F, G and H Declaration of Parentage)*.[188] Making declarations of parentage in seven cases, Munby P concluded[189] that, in principle, the court can act on parol evidence to establish that which cannot be found was in fact properly completed and signed before the treatment began; the court can correct mistakes by rectification or, in the case of an obvious mistake, by a process of construction. His lordship also concluded that 'what one is looking for is compliance with the substance, not slavish adherence to a form'. With what is surely a touch of humour on an otherwise serious point, he asked: 'Is parenthood to be denied by the triumph of form over substance? In my judgment, not.' So unlike the *obiter* comments of Cobb J in *AB v CD and the Z Fertility Clinic*, and in agreement with Theis J's reasoning in *X v Y*, Munby P concluded that treatment carried out with relevant consents, albeit not evidenced on the official forms, would still be treatment 'under licence' and could still confer legal parenthood.

### 3.7  Biology: the default position

Where a child is conceived by assisted conception but for some reason the requirements of the legislation are not fulfilled, then the child's father will be determined by biological connection, as illustrated in *Leeds Teaching Hospitals NHS Trust v A*.[190] In that case Mr and Mrs A, a white couple, consented to treatment under the HFEA 1990 whereby Mrs A was to be inseminated with her husband's sperm. Mr and Mrs B, a black couple, were also undergoing treatment at the same clinic and Mr B's sperm was erroneously injected into Mrs A's egg. The error became clear when twins of mixed heritage were born to Mrs A. It was agreed that Mr and Mrs A would raise the twins, but the question arose as to who was the legal father. It was clear that Mr A had not consented to his wife's treatment with Mr B's sperm, so section 28(2) could not apply to make Mr A the father. In addition, the clinic's error vitiated the concept of 'treatment together' in section 28(3).

In the absence of any person being the father within section 28, the fall-back position was the genetic connection between Mr B and the children, and Mr B was therefore the father. Mr and Mrs A's right to respect for family life was engaged, but any interference with it by declaring Mr B the father

---

[186] Ibid, paras [88] and [89]:

'(i) The clinic had not provided sufficient information to *both* parties to enable them to make informed decisions about parentage issues at the time of the treatment.

(ii) The clinic did not provide the parties with an opportunity to receive proper counselling about the step proposed prior to treatment.

(iii) Inadequate records have been kept of the treatment and the delivery of the WP/PP forms.'

[187] [2015] EWFC 13.    [188] [2015] EWHC 2602 (Fam).    [189] Ibid, at [63].

[190] *Leeds Teaching Hospital NHS Trust v A and others* [2003] EWHC 259 (QB), [2003] 1 FCR 599.

was justified and proportionate, since it preserved the truth about the personal identity of the twins, and there were mechanisms, for example adoption, by which Mr A could acquire security in respect of his relationship with the children.

## 3.8 **Persons not regarded in law as a parent**

There are situations in which the law expressly states that a person will not be regarded in law as a child's parent.

### 3.8.1 **Anonymous sperm donors**

Section 28(6)(a) of the HFEA 1990 provides that where sperm is used in accordance with consent required by Schedule 3, paragraph 5, then the sperm donor is not treated as the father. There is a similar provision in section 41(1) of the 2008 Act.

### 3.8.2 **Access to information about donors**

The Human Fertilisation and Embryology Authority (Disclosure of Donor Information) Regulations 2004 make provision regulating the disclosure of donor information.[191] The Human Fertilisation and Embryology Authority is required to keep a register of donor information, and under section 31ZA of the HFEA 1990 a person who has attained the age of 16 may make a request of the Authority for information about any donor to whom he or she may be genetically related,[192] and request whether there are other donor-conceived children of the donor (ie, genetic siblings of the applicant). The available information the Authority is required to supply about the donor is contained in the regulations. A range of information which is not capable of identifying the donor can be obtained at age 16: general physical characteristics such as sex, ethnic group, eye and skin colour; year of birth; medical history; religion, occupation, interests, and skills and why the donor provided sperm, eggs, or embryos; marital status, and whether the donor has children.[193] Under section 31ZA the Authority must supply information about the number of, sex, and birth year of genetic siblings. Upon reaching the age of 18, an applicant is also entitled to identifying information supplied by donors after 31 March 2005. The information includes the donor's name, date and place of birth, appearance, and last postal address.[194] At age 18, identifying information about donor-conceived genetic siblings can also be obtained, provided the siblings have consented to its release.[195] Identifying information is only provided in adulthood and there is no duty upon parents to disclose the fact that a child has been conceived as a result of donor insemination. It may be questioned therefore whether the law adequately protects the child's interests in obtaining information about biological origins during minority. As Andrew Bainham has observed, the current position may place a child born as a result of donor sperm to a mother and her heterosexual partner at a disadvantage compared with a similar child born to a mother and her lesbian partner since in the latter case the existence of the donor will eventually be obvious to the child.[196]

---

[191]  For discussion of this issue, see eg E. Blyth and A. Farrand, 'Anonymity in Donor-Assisted Conception and the UN Convention on the Rights of the Child' (2004) 12 International Journal of Children's Rights 89–104; C. Jones, 'The Identification of "Parents" and "Siblings": New Possibilities Under the Reformed Human Fertilisation and Embryology Act' in J. Herring, J. Wallbank, and S. Choudhry (eds), *Rights, Gender and Family Law* (Abingdon: Routledge-Cavendish, 2009), pp 219–38.

[192]  Under s 31ZC, the Authority may notify the donor that a request under s 31ZA(2)(a) has been made.

[193]  Regulation 2(2).

[194]  Regulation 2(3). The Authority may also keep a voluntary contact register of persons who wish to have contact: HFEA 1990, s 31ZF.

[195]  HFEA 1990, s 31ZE.

[196]  A. Bainham, 'Arguments about Parentage' (2008) 67(2) Cambridge Law Journal 322–51 at 336.

### 3.8.3 **Use of deceased man's sperm**

Section 28(6)(b) of the 1990 Act provides that where sperm, or an embryo created with a man's sperm, is used after a man's death, then the man is not to be treated for any purposes as the resulting child's father. A similar provision is found in section 41(2) of the 2008 Act.

However, the general rule is subject to an exception.[197] Where sperm is used, or an embryo placed in woman, after a man's death, in circumstances where, but for the death, he would have been the child's father, then the man can be the father for the purpose of enabling the man's particulars to be entered as those of the child's father in a register of live births but the man is to be treated in law as *not* being the father of the child for any other purpose.[198] In order for the provisions to apply, the man must have consented in writing to use after his death, and the child's mother must elect within 42 days of the birth to have the man registered on the birth certificate.

### 3.8.4 **Use of embryo after mother's partner's death**

A similar rule is now applied in the case of legal parenthood of a mother's same-sex partner.[199] If an embryo resulting in the mother's child is created when the mother is in a civil partnership, or in the course of licensed treatment with the mother's same-sex partner, and the partner dies before the embryo is implanted, then the partner can be the legal parent for the purpose of birth registration. The conditions of the partner's consent and the mother's election are the same as those discussed earlier in relation to fathers.

### 3.9 **Transsexual persons and parenthood**

As discussed in more detail in Chapter 1, the Gender Recognition Act 2004[200] now permits a transsexual person to acquire a new gender as a matter of law. An application must be made to a Gender Recognition Panel to obtain a Gender Recognition Certificate. The Act does not require the transsexual person to have had gender reassignment surgery but to provide evidence of gender dysphoria and make various statutory declarations. Unless a person's gender has been changed by this process, English law holds that a person's sex is determined by reference to biological criteria at birth.[201] Once the certificate is obtained, the newly acquired gender becomes that person's gender for all purposes, subject to certain provisions of the Gender Recognition Act 2004. A Gender Recognition Certificate does not have retrospective effect. Section 9(2) of the 2004 Act provides that the certificate does not affect things done or events occurring before the certificate; and section 12 specifically provides that the fact that a person's gender has become the acquired gender under the 2004 Act does not affect the status of the person as the father or mother of a child. So, for example, if a person gives birth to a child and then acquires a Gender Recognition Certificate changing her gender to male, the person will now be a man but will also remain the child's mother. It is also possible for a female-to-male transsexual person to become a father of a child through sections 35 and 36 of the HFEA 2008. A female-to-male transsexual person with a Gender Recognition Certificate can now validly marry a woman, and so it is possible that section 35 could apply to confer fatherhood on the transsexual person. As the woman's husband, he will be the father of any child conceived by assisted conception unless it is shown that he did not consent to the treatment. If not married, he could acquire fatherhood by undergoing treatment services together with a woman at a licensed clinic. Even if a female-to-male transsexual person does not have a Gender Recognition Certificate, 'he' (she as a matter of law) could still become a parent of the

---

[197] See HFEA 1990, s 28(5A)–(5I) and HFEA 2008, s 39.     [198] HFEA 1990, s 29(3B) and HFEA 2008, s 39.

[199] See HFEA 2008, s 46.

[200] For an outline of the Act's provisions, see S. Gilmore, 'The Gender Recognition Act 2004' [2004] Family Law 741.

[201] *Corbett v Corbett (Otherwise Ashley)* [1971] P 83.

child using sections 43 and 44 of the HFEA 2008 which confer parenthood on the female partner of the child's mother. 'He' would then be a parent, but not a father.

It is now possible as a matter of law for someone to be the mother of one child and the father of another. Furthermore, someone who is regarded in law as a man, but who has not undergone gender reassignment surgery and therefore still has female reproductive organs, could give birth to a child. To complicate matters further, that person may have been fertilised by a male-to-female transsexual person who similarly has not had surgery. Whether, in this situation, the person giving birth would be regarded as the mother or the father of the child has yet to arise for decision. These scenarios raise the possibility of male mothers and female fathers. It may not be long, however, before the courts are confronted with difficult cases like these.

In *J v C and Another*[202] Mr J and Mrs C went through a ceremony of marriage. Mr J was 30 and had been suffering from gender dysphoria. Although born as a female, Mr J had lived as a man since aged 17. The couple lived together for a number of years with the wife in ignorance of the true facts. In the process of a divorce she became aware from Mr J's birth certificate that 'he' was a woman and then sought a decree of nullity of marriage.

Two children had been conceived to the couple by artificial insemination by donor, one of whom, E, was still under 18. E was conceived prior to 1 August 1991 when the 1990 Act came into force, so the relevant statute which applied was section 27 of the Family Law Reform Act 1987. Mr J sought orders under section 8 of the Children Act 1989 in respect of E. By the time the case came to court, Mr J had obtained a Gender Recognition Certificate recognising his acquired male gender. The question arose as to whether he was the child's father so as not to require leave to make those applications (ie, did he fall within section 10(4) of the Children Act 1989?). It was contended for Mr J that the word 'marriage' in section 27 includes a void marriage[203] and therefore the provision applied to him.[204] The Court of Appeal observed, however, that section 27 talks of 'a party to a marriage' and 'the other party to the marriage' and concluded that this wording suggested that the parties referred to in section 27 must be respectively male and female. Presumably the same reasoning would be applied to relevant provisions of the Human Fertilisation and Embryology Acts.[205] Furthermore, Mr J's Gender Recognition Certificate did not affect that interpretation since the Gender Recognition Act 2004 makes clear, in section 9(2), that the certificate does not have retrospective effect. Accordingly the court concluded that Mr J is not and never was E's parent.

Prior to enactment of the Gender Recognition Act 2004, the European Court of Human Rights in *X, Y and Z v UK*[206] afforded the UK a wide margin of appreciation on the issue of legal recognition of transsexual parenthood. It found no violation of Article 8 of the ECHR where English law refused to register a female-to-male transsexual person as the father of a child born to 'his' female partner as a result of artificial insemination by donor. Since that time there has undoubtedly been increased legal recognition of transsexualism within states, and perhaps such a wide margin of appreciation could no longer be assumed. However, it seems unlikely that English law would be found to be in breach of the Convention in similar circumstances today following enactment of the Gender Recognition Act 2004.

---

[202] [2006] EWCA Civ 551.    [203] See s 27(2).

[204] Matrimonial Causes Act 1973, s 11(c), provides that a marriage is void if the parties are not respectively male and female.

[205] HFEA 2008, s 49, defines a marriage in s 35 to include a void marriage, provided either or both of the parties reasonably believed at the time that the marriage was valid. The definition of marriage in the HFEA 1990, s 28(2), is in the same terms.

[206] *X, Y and Z v UK* [1997] 2 FLR 892. See C. Lind, 'Perceptions of Sex in the Legal Determination of Fatherhood—*X, Y and Z v UK*' [1997] Child and Family Law Quarterly 401.

## 3.10 **Surrogacy and parental orders**

Occasionally, a woman may be willing to act as a surrogate mother[207] for a couple who are unable to have children. The Surrogacy Arrangements Act 1985 provides that no surrogacy arrangement[208] is enforceable by or against any of the persons making it.[209] Furthermore, negotiating a surrogacy arrangement on a commercial basis and advertising surrogacy are both illegal activities.[210] Otherwise, however, a surrogacy arrangement is not unlawful. If the commissioning couple are to become the child's parents they will need to adopt the child or apply for a parental order, 'an order providing for a child to be treated in law as the child of the applicants'.[211] The law on adoption is dealt with in detail in Chapter 11. Here we concentrate on the possibility of obtaining a parental order. The requirements for the making of a parental order were formerly contained in section 30 of the HFEA 1990. The HFEA 2008 repealed section 30 and the law on parental orders is now regulated by section 54 of the 2008 Act.[212] The conditions for making an order remain, in substance, similar to those under the 1990 Act, and the case law relating to section 30 is likely to remain useful in interpreting the new provision. Of course, any orders made under section 30 of the 1990 Act prior to the change in the law remain in force and are unaffected.

The main difference that the new legislation brings is a broadening of the categories of possible applicants. Under section 30 of the 1990 Act, it was possible to make an order only in favour of a married couple. Under the new legislation applicants may be either spouses, civil partners of each other, or 'two persons who are living as partners in an enduring family relationship and are not within prohibited degrees of relationship in relation to each other'.[213] It can be seen, therefore, that an application for a parental order can only be made by a couple. In *Re Z (A Child: Human Fertilisation and Embryology Act: Parental Order)*,[214] a child was conceived in Minnesota, USA, using the father's sperm and the egg of a third party which was implanted in a surrogate mother. A US court granted the father sole legal parenthood. The father subsequently brought the child to the UK and sought a parental order. Munby P held that the application failed in limine since 'as a single parent, as a sole applicant, the father cannot bring himself within section 54(1) of the 2008 Act.'[215] It was argued on the applicant's behalf that this is a discriminatory interference with a single person's rights to respect for private and family life contrary to Articles 8 and 14 of the ECHR[216] and that the provision should be read down pursuant to section 3 of the Human Rights Act 1998 in order to accommodate the applicant. Assuming for the purpose of judgment

---

[207] For a useful collection of essays on this topic, see R. Cook, S. Day Sclater, and F. Kaganas, *Surrogate Motherhood International Perspectives* (Oxford: Hart, 2003). For an account of the development of the law, see Hale LJ's judgment in *Briody v St Helen's and Knowsley Area Health Authority* [2001] EWCA Civ 1010, [2001] 2 FLR 1094. For criticism of the law, see K. Horsey and S. Sheldon, 'Still Hazy After All These Years: The Law Regulating Surrogacy' (2012) 20(1) Medical Law Review 67–89; and K. Horsey, 'Challenging Presumptions: Legal Parenthood and Surrogacy Arrangements' [2010] Child and Family Law Quarterly 449 (law should reflect pre-conception intentions, supporting the use of enforceable agreements).

[208] Defined in the Surrogacy Arrangements Act 1985, s 1.   [209] Ibid, s 1A.

[210] Ibid, ss 2 and 3. For cases in which solicitors breached the Surrogacy Arrangements Act 1985 by drafting an agreement for a fee, see *Re G and M (Parental Orders)* [2014] EWHC 1561 (Fam), and *JP v LP and Others (Surrogacy Arrangements: Wardship)* [2014] EWHC 595 (Fam). Indeed, giving legal recognition to any commercial element in surrogacy is viewed as contrary to public policy: see *Briody v St Helen's and Knowsley Area Health Authority* [2001] EWCA Civ 1010, [2001] 2 FLR 1094 (woman unable to claim cost of commercial surrogacy arrangement in California as part of damages against Health Authority for negligently causing her infertility).

[211] See HFEA 2008, s 54(1).

[212] Together with s 55, which makes supplementary provision. For an overview of the case law, see C. Fenton-Glynn, 'The regulation and recognition of surrogacy under English law: an overview of the case-law' [2015] CFLQ 83, arguing that the law is in urgent need of reform.

[213] HFEA 2008, s 54(2). For discussion of prohibited degrees of relationship, see Chapter 1.

[214] [2015] EWFC 73, Sir James Munby P.   [215] Ibid, at [39].

[216] Relying on *In re G (Adoption: Unmarried Couple)* [2008] UKHL 38, [2009] 1 AC 173, [8], [107], [132], for the view that being single is a 'status' within the meaning of Article 14 of the ECHR.

the correctness of the submissions on the ECHR,[217] his lordship rejected the claim, concluding that the 'principle that only two people—a couple—can apply for a parental order has been a clear and prominent feature of the legislation throughout'.[218] He saw this as supported by the very clear difference of policy drawn by Parliament between possible applicants for adoption and parental orders respectively, a necessary distinction based on principle which was evidenced in debate on the 2008 Act.[219] To construe the legislation as contended for, therefore, would not be compatible with its underlying thrust; on the contrary, 'it would be to ignore what is, as it has always been, a key feature of the scheme and scope of the legislation.'[220]

In deciding whether to make a parental order, the court must apply the child's welfare as the paramount consideration.[221] In order for an order to be made, the child must have been carried by a woman who is not one of the applicants, as a result of the placing in her of an embryo or sperm and eggs or her artificial insemination[222] and the gametes of at least one of the applicants must have been used to bring about the creation of the embryo. In other words, at least one of the applicants must be genetically related to the child.[223] In addition, the court must be satisfied of various conditions in section 54(3)–(8).

(i) The application for the order must be made within six months of the child's birth.[224] In the past, a number of high court judges had indicated that the six month time limit is not extendable.[225] In *JP v LP and Others (Surrogacy Arrangement: Wardship)*,[226] for example, Eleanor King J made the child a ward of court and made orders regulating parental responsibility,[227] having concluded that there is no provision to extend the time limit, and thus a parental order was not available. However, more recently, several cases have taken a different view. In *Re X (A Child) (Parental Order: Time Limit)*[228] Munby P permitted an application made two years and two

---

[217] But not deciding the matter, since these were 'issues which may yet need to be considered and ruled on if, as may be, the father decides to seek a declaration of incompatibility' (see [2015] EWFC 73, at [41]).

[218] [2015] EWFC 73, at [36].

[219] See eg, the statement of Dawn Primarolo, Minister of State, Department of Health, in the Public Bill Committee debate on clause 54 of the Bill in the House of Commons on 12 June 2008 (cols 248–49): 'adoption involves a child who already exists and whose parents are not able to keep the child, for whom new parents are sought…Surrogacy, however, involves agreeing to hand over a child even before conception. The Government are still of the view that the magnitude of that means that it is best dealt with by a couple. That is why we have made the arrangements that we have.'

[220] [2015] EWFC 73, at [37]. See also Theis J in *B v C (Surrogacy: Adoption)* [2015] EWFC 17 (Fam), at [20], who treated it as axiomatic that: 'A single person is…unable to apply for a parental order.'

[221] Adoption and Children Act 2002, s 1 (see Chapter 11), applies to applications under the HFEA 2008, s 54 with necessary modifications: see the Human Fertilisation and Embryology (Parental Orders) Regulations 2010 (SI 2010/985), reg 2, Sch 1.

[222] This applies whether the woman was in the UK or elsewhere at the relevant time: see HFEA s 54(10).

[223] The court is not precluded from disposing of an application by a couple where the genetically related parent dies prior to the application being determined by the court: *A v P (Surrogacy: Parental Order: Death of Application)* [2011] EWHC 1738 (Fam), [2012] 2 FLR 145.

[224] HFEA 2008, s 54(3). Within the period of six months beginning with the day on which the section came into force, couples who were not eligible to apply under the 1990 Act could apply for an order in respect of a child born before implementation of s 54: see s 54(11).

[225] See *Re X (Children) (Parental Order: Foreign Surrogacy)* (Hedley J), at [12] 'a non-extendable time limit'; *Re S (Parental Order)* [2009] EWHC 2977 (Fam), [2010] 1 FLR 1156 (Hedley J), at [9] 'the time limit … appears to be incapable of enlargement'; *J v G (Parental Orders)* [2013] EWHC 1432 (Fam), [2014] 1 FLR 297 (Theis J) at [30] 'no power vested in the court to extend that period'; *JP v LP and Others (Surrogacy Arrangement: Wardship)* [2014] EWHC 595 (Fam), [2015] 1 FLR 307 (Eleanor King J), at [29] 'There is no provision within the Act to provide for a discretionary extension to the statutory time limit and no one sought to argue that the court could, or should, whether by means of the use of its inherent jurisdiction or otherwise, seek to circumnavigate the mandatory provisions of the statute'; and *Re WT (Foreign Surrogacy)* [2014] EWHC 1303 (Theis J), at [42](3) that there is 'no power vested in the court to extend that period.'

[226] [2014] EWHC 595 (Fam).

[227] The commissioning father and mother, who had separated, were granted shared residence, and the surrogate mother was prohibited from exercising parental responsibility without the court's leave.

[228] [2014] EWHC 3135 (Fam), [2015] Fam 186, [2015] 1 FLR 349 (Sir James Munby P). For comment, see C. Fenton-Glynn, 'The Difficulty of Enforcing Surrogacy Arrangements' [2015] CLJ 34.

months after the child's birth. In that case, the commissioning parents, a married couple, had a child with the assistance of a surrogate mother in India. The child was conceived using an egg donated by a third party and the commissioning father's sperm. The couple returned to the UK with the child, but their relationship subsequently faltered and they separated. Only when the father issued an application for residence of the child did the commissioning parents become aware of the requirements of section 54, the court hearing the residence issue observing that they were not the child's parents in English law. The parents therefore applied out of time for a parental order. Munby P disagreed with the strict application of the time limit in earlier decisions, noting that Parliament identified no reason for the time limit and Parliamentary debates are silent as to any policy underpinning it. Turning to the statutory language, his lordship saw the question as whether Parliament can fairly be taken to have intended total invalidity of section 54 on failure to comply with the time limit.[229] This had to be assessed by reference to the guidance of Lord Penzance in *Howard v Bodington*:[230] 'having regard to and in the light of the statutory subject matter, the background, the purpose of the requirement (if known), its importance, its relation to the general object intended to be secured by the Act, and the actual or possible impact of non-compliance on the parties'. On a straightforward application of the principle in *Howard v Bodington*, his lordship concluded that the time period could be extended, commenting:

> Can Parliament really have intended that the gate should be barred forever if the application for a parental order is lodged even one day late? I cannot think so. Parliament has not explained its thinking, but given the transcendental importance of a parental order, with its consequences stretching many, many decades into the future, can it sensibly be thought that Parliament intended the difference between 6 months and 6 months and one day to be determinative and one day's delay to be fatal? I assume that Parliament intended a sensible result. Given the subject matter, given the consequences for the commissioning parents, never mind those for the child, to construe s 54(3) as barring forever an application made just one day late is not, in my judgment, sensible. It is the very antithesis of sensible; it is almost nonsensical.[231]

Munby P noted that 'any application for a parental order implicates both the child's right to 'family life' and also the child's right to 'private life'[232] and that the same conclusion is 'amply justified having regard to the Convention'.[233] He explained that every case will be fact specific and concluded on the facts of this case[234] that it should be allowed to proceed.[235]

Munby P's approach was followed by Theis J in *AB v CD (Surrogacy - Time Limit and Consent)*,[236] permitting an application two and a half years after the children's birth; and by Russell J in *D and G v ED and DD (Parental Order: Time Limit)*.[237] In the latter case the applicants had two children, aged 8 and 5, as a result of surrogacy arrangements in the USA. The couple brought the children to

---

[229]  As posed by Lord Steyn in *R v Soneji and Another* [2005] UKHL 49, [2006] 1 AC 340, at [52]: 'can Parliament fairly be taken to have intended total invalidity?'

[230]  (1877) 2 PD 203 and most recently re-stated by Sir Stanley Burnton in *Newbold and Others v Coal Authority* [2013] EWCA Civ 584, [2014] 1 WLR 1288.

[231]  [2014] EWHC 3135 (Fam), [2015] Fam 186, [2015] 1 FLR 349, at [55]. His lordship added that even if 'the underlying policy is that identified by Eleanor King J in *JP v LP and Others (Surrogacy Arrangement: Wardship)* [2014] EWHC 595 (Fam), [2015] 1 FLR 307, namely to provide for the speedy consensual regularisation of the legal parental status of a child's carers following a birth resulting from a surrogacy arrangement; that policy surely does not require s 54(3) to be read as meaning that any delay, however trivial, is to be fatal.'

[232]  [2014] EWHC 3135 (Fam), [2015] Fam 186, [2015] 1 FLR 349, at [61].          [233]  Ibid, at [58].

[234]  A 13 month delay between expiry of the six month period and knowledge of the provision.

[235]  [2014] EWHC 3135 (Fam), [2015] Fam 186, [2015] 1 FLR 349, at [65].

[236]  [2015] EWFC 12; and in *Re A and B (No 2) (Parental Order)* [2015] EWHC 2080.

[237]  [2015] EWHC 911 (Fam).

the UK, being initially unaware that court orders giving them parental status in California were ineffective in the UK. In 2013 they were advised to apply to adopt the children so as to give them parental status in English law. However, when *Re X* was decided during the proceedings, they applied for parental orders. Russell J recognised that the time elapsed since the births and the applications (8 years and 5 years 5 months) was much longer than in *Re X*. However, she saw 'no reason in law, particularly as there is no prejudice to any other party, why [she] should not assume a similar approach in respect of any discretion under s54(3) and apply the paramountcy of the welfare principle—unless the case is one of the clearest abuse of public policy.'[238] Russell J observed that a parental order provides a 'whole of life' identity as members of the Applicants' family, consistent with their US birth certificates and permits birth registration in the UK, whereas adoption implies 'a change of family and wrongly suggest that the children have had a disrupted rather than continuously secure identity within their family'. Thus the parental order 'better meets the children's 'lifelong' welfare, and involves a whole of life perspective extending, not just forward, but also retrospectively from birth until death'.[239] As she noted, 'Parliament provided for parental orders to be the legal remedy designed for surrogacy situations and it is a contrivance to use adoption as an alternative solution unless there is no other option within the court's discretion.'[240]

**(ii)** At the time of the application and the making of the order the child's home must be with the applicants. This does not specify that the child's or the applicants' home must be in the UK.[241] *Re X (A Child) (Parental Order: Time Limit)*[242] the commissioning parents were separated at the time the application was issued, but they were not divorced, and later reconciled. A further question arose therefore for the court in relation to s 54(4)(a): could it be said that the little boy's home was with them at the time of the application? Munby P concluded that albeit they lived in separate houses, the child's living arrangements were split between them and it could 'fairly be said that he lived with them.'[243] Even if that were not right, there existed family life between the commissioning parents and the boy and the statute could and should be read down to achieve this result.[244]

In *Re A and B (No 2) (Parental Order)* [2015] EWHC 2080 (Fam) the applicants, a married couple, entered into a surrogacy arrangement with an Indian clinic, the surrogate mother giving birth in 2011 to twins conceived with the commissioning father's sperm and donated eggs. However, the couple did not realise that they did not have legal parental status in England until 2014. At that time the marriage was in difficulties and they had separated. The children lived in the matrimonial home with the mother and the father in rented accommodation. He had regular contact with the children every Thursday and three weekends in four. In light of *Re X*, Theis J was satisfied, in the circumstances of this case (the parties having acted in good faith), that the application should proceed despite being issued more than six months after the children's birth.[245] Theis J also held that section 54(4) should be construed purposively so as to accommodate the circumstances of the case.[246] She agreed with counsel's submission that 'Parliament could not have intended that a designation as important as legal parenthood should be denied because the commissioning parents occupied separate physical homes, notwithstanding that the children enjoyed family life with them'.[247] Here, the couple remained married and committed to the children. Not to construe the legislation purposively would have 'detrimental long term consequences'[248] for the family and the children's welfare.[249] Theis J added: 'As in *Re X* I am satisfied that if I am not correct in that analysis

---

[238] Ibid, at [47].   [239] Ibid at [64].   [240] Ibid, at [68].

[241] *Re Q (Parental Order: Domicile)* [2014] EWHC 1307 (Fam), [2015] 1 FLR 704.

[242] [2014] EWHC 3135 (Fam), [2015] Fam 186, [2015] 1 FLR 349 (Sir James Munby P).   [243] Ibid, at [67].

[244] Ibid, at [68].   [245] Para [66].   [246] Para [70].

[247] Set out at [44], agreeing at [71]. As counsel pointed out, had 'the parental order application been made within six months of the children's birth the requirement under s 54(4)(a) would have been met. If the applicants separated shortly after the order is granted it does not vitiate the making of the parental order.'

[248] Para [72].   [249] Para [73].

the Convention applies, Article 8 is undoubtedly engaged, and the statute should be "read down" to achieve the same result'.[250]

**(iii)** Either or both of the applicants must be domiciled in the UK, Channel Islands, or Isle of Man.[251] In *Re Q (Parental Order: Domicile)*[252] Theis J observed that there 'is no requirement under s 54 of the HFEA 2008 that the applicant or that the child should be present in the jurisdiction. The court's jurisdiction to make a parental order rests solely on the requirement in s 54(4) (b) that at least one of the applicants has a domicile in a part of the UK, Channel Islands or the Isle of Man.'[253] Every person receives at birth a domicile of origin, no person can be without a domicile, nor have more than one domicile; and a person is, in general, domiciled in the country in which he is considered by English law to have his permanent home.[254] In *Re Q (Parental Order: Domicile)*[255] Theis J accepted that the key principles relating to domicile could be distilled as follows:

> i. a domicile of origin adheres unless the acquisition of a domicile of choice is proved to the required standard (balance of probabilities) by the person asserting such a change; ii. to acquire a domicile of choice there must be both 'animo et facto' i.e. a person must both reside in a new country and also form a sufficient intention to live permanently or indefinitely in that country; iii. acquisition of a domicile of choice is not to be lightly inferred; and iv. important factors which are relevant in considering whether a person has formed the necessary intention are whether they intend to return to live in their country of origin on the happening of a realistically foreseeable contingency, and whether they are resident in a country for a general or limited purpose.[256]

In *Re Q* a British wife and French husband, living in France, sought a parental order in respect of a child, Q, who had been born in the USA as a result of a surrogacy arrangement, and they had subsequently adopted the child there. The question arose as to whether the wife retained her domicile of origin. On the facts, Theis J found that the wife maintained connections with the UK and her residence in France was 'for a limited purpose, related to her relationship and subsequent marriage' and that she intended to return to live in this jurisdiction on the happening of a number of realistically foreseeable contingencies: upon her husband being able to leave his business; upon his retirement; to support Q's education here or upon her husband's death. Accordingly, the wife retained her domicile of origin and, despite the overseas adoption order,[257] Theis J held that a parental order, being most suited to surrogacy arrangements, met Q's lifelong welfare needs in this case. In *Re B-G (Parental Orders: Domicile)*[258] a child was born in England and Wales as a result of a surrogacy arrangement, whereby the child was carried by the sister of a man born in England and Wales, and the sperm provided by the man's South African husband. The couple lived in South Africa. Upon the couple's application for a parental order, Peter Jackson J held on the facts that,

---

[250] Para [76].

[251] A person is, in general, domiciled in the country in which he is considered by English law to have his permanent home. For the legal principles relating to domicile, see *Z and B v C (Parental Order: Domicile)* [2011] EWHC 3181 (Fam), [2012] 2 FLR 797 paras [13]–[17]; and see *Mark v Mark* [2005] UKHL 42, [2006] 1 AC 98. For a case in which the couple had sold their home and severed all ties with the United States and had lived in England for four years, thus acquiring a domicile of choice in England, see *Re A and B (Parental Order: Domicile)* [2013] EWHC 426 (Fam).

[252] [2014] EWHC 1307 (Fam), Theis J.        [253] Ibid, at para [20].

[254] *Z v B v C (Parental Order: Domicile)* [2011] EWHC 3181 (Fam), Theis J, at para 13.

[255] [2014] EWHC 1307 (Fam), Theis J. As set out in a number of cases (in particular, *Barlow Clowes International Ltd (In Liquidation) & Ors v Henwood* [2008] EWCA Civ 577 per Arden LJ at paragraph 8).

[256] [2014] EWHC 1307 (Fam), at paras [22] and [23].

[257] Which was not unlawful under section 83 of the Adoption and Children Act 2002 because the couple were not habitually resident in the UK at the time of the adoption. Section 83 prohibits foreign adoptions outside the framework of the Hague Adoption Convention 1993. See also *Re G and M (Parental Orders)* [2014] EWHC 1561 (Fam), Theis J.

[258] [2014] EWHC 444 (Fam), Peter Jackson J.

even if the British father was habitually resident in South Africa, he had not lost his domicile of origin in England and Wales. The couple had a common intention to return to the UK in the foreseeable future. Similarly in *Re A (A Child) (Parental Order: Surrogacy Arrangement*[259]), applying *Re Q (Parental Order: Domicile)*,[260] Theis J was satisfied that the commissioning father, who was born in England, but lived in Switzerland, France, and South Africa, and was seeking residence in Dubai, maintained UK domicile. The commissioning couple visited the UK regularly and planned to educate the children in the UK and eventually return to live here.[261] In *Re A and B (Parental Order: Domicile)*,[262] however, there was evidence establishing abandonment of the commissioning couple's respective domiciles of origin in Poland and the USA, their intention being to remain indefinitely in the UK, thus acquiring a domicile of choice.[263] Similarly, in *Re A and B (No 2) (Parental Order)*[264] A who was born in Uganda and B who was born in Kenya, both British Citizens, had acquired a domicile of choice in the UK: they had lived in the UK as children and adults and had never intended to reside elsewhere.[265]

In *Re G (Surrogacy: Foreign Domicile)*[266] McFarlane J pointed out, in relation to the same requirement in section 30(7) of the 1990 Act, that this provision is mandatory, and accordingly it is impossible for commissioning parents who are both not so domiciled to obtain a parental order.[267] His Lordship suggested that such arrangements were to be discouraged because of the likely legal complications. The case concerned a Turkish couple, Mr and Mrs G, who, with the help of a British surrogacy agency, Childlessness Overcome Through Surrogacy (COTS), engaged the services of Mrs J, a surrogate mother in England. Mrs J's egg was fertilised with Mr G's sperm and a child was born. Mr and Mrs G then applied for a parental order, during which proceedings it became apparent that Mr and Mrs G did not fulfil the domicile requirements. The resulting 'mess' required seven High Court hearings at a cost of £35,000 to the taxpayer, eventually resulting in an order under section 84(2) of the Adoption and Children Act 2002. This provision allows the court to grant parental responsibility to persons who the court is satisfied intend to adopt the child outside the British Islands.[268] McFarlane J was sufficiently concerned by the surrogacy agency's lack of awareness of the legal requirements 'to question whether some form of inspection or authorization should be required in order to improve the quality of advice' given, and sent a copy of his judgment to the relevant Minister of State for consideration.[269]

**(iv)** At the time of the making of the order both applicants must have attained the age of 18.[270]

**(v)** The court must be satisfied that the woman who carried the child and any other parent of the child (who is not one of the applicants) 'have freely, and with full understanding of what is involved, agreed unconditionally to the making of the order'.[271] This does not require the agreement of someone who cannot be found or who is incapable of giving agreement.[272] The agreement of the woman who carried the child is ineffective if it is given by her less than six weeks after the child's birth.[273] In *Re D and L (Surrogacy)*[274] male civil partners applied for a parental order in respect of twins who were born to a surrogate mother in India and with whom the men

---

[259] [2015] EWHC 1756.     [260] [2014] EWHC 1307 (Fam), [2015] 1 FLR 704.

[261] See also *AB v CD (Surrogacy—Time Limit and Consent)* [2015] EWFC 12 in which the commissioning couple had dual British and Australian, and retained domicile of origin despite having obtained Australian citizenship.

[262] [2013] EWHC 426 (Fam).

[263] See also *Z and B v C (Parental Oder: Domicile)* [2011] WEHC 3181 (Fam), [2012] 2 FLR 797, Theis J.

[264] [2015] EWHC 2080 (Fam)     [265] Ibid, at [50] and [78].

[266] [2007] EWHC 2814 (Fam), [2008] 1 FLR 1047.     [267] Ibid, [15].     [268] See ibid, [46]–[50].

[269] Ibid, [29]. See D. Howe, 'International Surrogacy—A Cautionary Tale' [2008] Family Law 60. See, for some of the problems, *Re X (children) (Parental Order: Foreign Surrogacy)* [2008] EWHC 3030 (Fam), [2009] Fam 71; L. Theis QC, 'A Trek Through the Thorn Forest' [2009] Family Law 239; and *Re K (Minors: Foreign Surrogacy)* [2010] EWHC 1180, and *Re IJ (A Child) (Overseas Surrogacy: Parental Order)* [2011] EWHC 921 (Fam), [2011] 2 FLR 646, and *J v G (Parental Orders)* [2013] EWHC 1432 (Fam) Theis J.

[270] HFEA 2008 s 54(5).     [271] Ibid, s 54(6).     [272] Ibid, s 54(7)     [273] Ibid.

[274] [2012] EWHC 2631 (Fam) [2013] 2 FLR 275, Baker J.

had communicated only indirectly through a clinic. The surrogate mother agreed to the surrogacy arrangement but the clinic failed to provide evidence of the mother's consent (at least six weeks after the birth) to the making of the parental order and the applicants were subsequently unable to trace the mother. Baker J held that in such a case 'the court must carefully scrutinise the evidence as to the efforts which have been taken to find her'[275] and it is 'only when all reasonable steps have been taken to locate her without success that a court is likely to dispense with the need for valid consent'.[276] The court can consider any consent given before the expiry of six weeks after the birth but the weight given to such consent is likely to be limited.[277] The child's welfare is the paramount consideration when deciding 'whether to make an order without the consent of the woman who gave birth in circumstances in which she cannot be found or is incapable of giving consent'.[278] Applying those points to the facts of the case, his Lordship concluded that the agreement of the surrogate mother was not required on the ground that she could not be found.[279] Baker J warned, however, that 'applicants and their advisers should learn the lessons of this case, and take steps to ensure that clear lines of communication with the surrogate are established before the birth to facilitate the giving of consent after the expiry of the 6-week period'.[280]

In *AB v CD (Surrogacy—Time Limit and Consent)*[281] a same-sex couple were seeking a parental order in respect of twins who had been born following a surrogacy arrangement in India. The surrogate mother had signed two affidavits, one confirming that she was divorced and another consenting to the surrogacy arrangement and to the fact that upon the birth the applicants would have equal parental responsibility for the children. Theis J found that there was insufficient evidence to show that the surrogate mother was divorced, but held that, if she was married, her husband was not the father of the children in English law under section 35 of the Human Fertilisation and Embryology Act 2008 as it was shown by his complete lack of involvement in the surrogacy arrangement that he 'did not consent' within the meaning of that provision. Theis J also held that section 54(6) was not satisfied as the affidavit did not show that the surrogate agreed that she would lose her parental status. However, by the time of the application, the surrogate could not be traced, despite considerable efforts to locate her, and, accordingly, Theis J concluded that her consent was not required.

(vi) The court must be satisfied that:

no money or other benefit (other than for expenses reasonably incurred) has been given or received by either of the applicants for or in consideration of—

(a) the making of the order,

(b) any agreement required by subsection (6),

(c) the handing over of the child to the applicants, or

(d) the making of arrangements with a view to the making of the order,

unless authorised by the court.[282]

The statute refers to payments made by the applicants, so it includes payments made, for example, to a surrogacy agency, as well as payment made to the surrogate mother.

The courts have held, in relation to a similar provision in the 1990 Act, that authorisation may be given retrospectively.[283] In *X (Children) (Parental Order: Foreign Surrogacy)*[284] Hedley J drew from the authorities that, in terms of the policy considerations, the court should 'pose itself three

---

[275] Ibid, [28].      [276] Ibid.      [277] Ibid, [29].

[278] Ibid, [30]. Baker J added that it would be wrong to utilise this provision as a means of avoiding the need to take all reasonable steps to obtain the woman's consent.

[279] Ibid, [34].      [280] Ibid, [35].      [281] [2015] EWFC 12.      [282] HFEA 2008 s 54(8).

[283] See *Re Q (A Minor) (Parental Order)* [1996] 1 FLR 369, Johnson J, and *In the Matter of C (A Child)* [2002] EWHC 157 (Fam).

[284] [2008] EWHC 3030 (Fam), [2009] Fam 71.

questions: (1) was the sum paid disproportionate to reasonable expenses? (2) Were the applicants acting in good faith and without "moral taint" in their dealings with the surrogate mother? (3) Were the applicants party to any attempt to defraud the authorities?'[285] In *Re S (Parental Order)*[286] his Lordship added that the court should be astute not to be involved in anything resembling payment for children, should ensure that commercial surrogacy is not used to circumvent childcare laws and to place children in unsuitable arrangements, and that money is not used to overbear the will of a surrogate.[287] However, the law now requires the child's welfare be not merely the first consideration (as it was in relation to section 30 of the 1990 Act) but the paramount consideration on an application under section 54,[288] and in *Re L (A Child) (Parental Order: Foreign Surrogacy)*[289] Hedley J commented that the effect of the change in the law must be to weigh the balance between public policy considerations and welfare decisively in favour of welfare and that 'it will only be in the clearest case of the abuse of public policy that the court will be able to withhold an order if otherwise welfare considerations support its making'.[290] So 'if it is desired to control commercial surrogacy arrangements, those controls need to operate before the court process is initiated i.e. at the border or even before'.[291] His Lordship emphasised, however, that 'notwithstanding the paramountcy of welfare, the court should continue carefully to scrutinise applications for authorisation under section 54(8) with a view to policing the public policy matters'.[292] In *Re WT (Foreign Surrogacy Arrangements)*[293] Theis J summarized the now well-established principles, as follows:[294]

(1) the question whether a sum paid is disproportionate to 'reasonable expenses' is a question of fact in each case. What the court will be considering is whether the sum is so low that it may unfairly exploit the surrogate mother, or so high that it may place undue pressure on her with the risk, in either scenario, that it may overbear her free will.

(2) the principle underpinning section 54(8), which must be respected by the court, is that it is contrary to public policy to sanction excessive payments that effectively amount to buying children from overseas.

(3) however . . . the decision whether to authorise payments retrospectively is a decision relating to a parental order and in making that decision, the court must regard the child's welfare as the paramount consideration.

(4) as a consequence it is difficult to imagine a set of circumstances in which, by the time an application for a parental order comes to court, the welfare of any child, particularly a foreign child, would not be gravely compromised by a refusal to make the order: As a result: 'it will only be in the clearest case of the abuse of public policy that the court will be able to withhold an order if otherwise welfare considerations support its making'.

(5) where the applicants for a parental order are acting in good faith and without 'moral taint' in their dealings with the surrogate mother, with no attempt to defraud the authorities, and the payments are not so disproportionate that the granting of parental orders would be an affront to public policy, it will ordinarily be appropriate for the court to exercise its discretion to give retrospective authorisation, having regard to the paramountcy of the child's lifelong welfare.

---

[285] Ibid, [21], drawing on *Re Adoption Application (Payments for Adoption)* [1987] Fam 81 and *In the Matter of C (A Child)* [2002] EWHC 157 (Fam).

[286] [2009] EWHC 2977, [2010] 1 FLR 1156.      [287] Ibid, [7].

[288] Human Fertilisation and Embryology (Parental Orders) Regulations 2010 (SI 2010/985), reg 2, Sch 1.

[289] [2010] EWHC 3146, [2011] Fam 106.      [290] Ibid, [10].      [291] Ibid.

[292] See also Sir Nicholas Wall P in *Re X and Y (Children: Foreign Surrogacy)* [2011] EWHC 3147 (Fam), endorsing Hedley J's approach.

[293] [2014] EWHC 1303 (Fam), [2015] 1 FLR 960, at para [35].

[294] Principles with which Sir James Munby P agreed, and cited, in *Re X (A Child) (Parental Order: Time Limit)* [2014] EWHC 3135 (Fam), [2015] Fam 186, [2015] 1 FLR 349, at [75] et seq.

An example of the conflict with which the courts are presented in this context is provided by *In the Matter of C (A Child)*.[295] In that case a couple, Mr and Mrs X, agreed to pay a surrogate mother, SM, expenses of £12,000, some of which was said to relate to loss of earnings. This was higher than the level of reasonable expenses recommended by COTS, which had assisted in bringing the parties together. SM duly gave birth to a child, C, who lived with Mr and Mrs X from birth, and Mr and Mrs X applied for a parental order. It transpired, however, that SM had been on income support, which she continued to claim, and thus some of the expenses claimed did not relate to loss of earnings. The issue for Wall J was whether in these circumstances he should authorise the payment retrospectively. In exercising his discretion, applying the degree of taint approach, Wall J weighed the following points:[296] (i) the sum paid was not disproportionate; (ii) Mr and Mrs X had not known that SM was on income support until after the pregnancy; (iii) Mr and Mrs X entered into the memorandum 'in good faith and without corrupt intent';[297] (iv) the responsibility for allegedly defrauding the Department of Social Security was SM's alone; and (v) it was manifestly in C's best interests to be brought up by Mr and Mrs X.

Having examined the courts' interpretation of section 54, it is difficult not to agree with Professor Gillian Douglas' comment that the courts are regularly having to apply the section 'in such a way that weaknesses, failings and omissions are sidestepped in order to arrive at the only sensible result compatible with the child's welfare needs'. As she observes, the ' law is frankly becoming an embarrassment and is surely in need of urgent reform to reflect the reality, which is that "commercial" surrogacy has now become an accepted way of creating a family.'[298] The cases also disclose the very different approaches to surrogacy which different jurisdictions take, and the need perhaps for a convention to regulate this issue internationally.[299]

Once an order is made under section 54, the child becomes the child of the applicants, and the woman who gave birth is no longer recognised as the mother. Such orders are intended to regulate legal parenthood permanently for the future and the occasions on which it will be possible to revoke such an order will be rare. In *G v G (Parental Order: Revocation)*[300] a parental order was made in favour of a husband and wife, but the couple separated shortly thereafter. The husband, who was biologically related to the child and had parental responsibility, became aware that at the time of the making of the order the wife had had an affair, that she believed the marriage to be over, and intended to bring up the child on her own. He sought to have the order set aside, arguing that he and the surrogate would not have proceeded in those circumstances. The husband also argued that the order had been made without following the correct procedure and hearing all the necessary evidence, including a Cafcass report. The case came before Hedley J who declined to revoke the order. His Lordship held that because a parental order, like adoption, confers status, 'there should, so far as is possible, be certainty and clarity and, therefore, the court in considering such an application should be guided by the authorities on revoking adoption orders'[301] and accordingly the 'bar is set very high'.[302] In light of those authorities, the circumstances of this case were not of the order to justify revocation, which, given that the wife was the only mother the child had known, would conduce against the child's welfare. Hedley J also concluded that the order would have been made had the judge considered the Cafcass report, and for that reason and for the reason of protecting the child's welfare he concluded that he should not set aside the order for the purpose of protecting the integrity of the court process.[303]

It should be noted that proceedings under section 54 are family proceedings for the purposes of the Children Act 1989, so a court could make an order under section 8 of that Act instead of or in addition to the section 54 order. In some cases, child arrangements orders have been made to

---

[295] [2002] EWHC 157 (Fam).        [296] Ibid, [34].        [297] Ibid, [20].        [298] [2015] Fam Law.

[299] See also C. Fenton-Glynn, 'The Regulation and Recognition of Surrogacy under English Law: An Overview of the Case-Law' [2015] CFLQ 83.

[300] [2012] EWHC 1979 (Fam), [2013] 1 FLR 286.        [301] Ibid, [43].

[302] Ibid. See the authorities on revocation of adoption in Chapter 11.        [303] [2013] 1 FLR 286, at [44].

regulate the parent/child relationships created by the surrogacy arrangement. In *H v S (Disputed Surrogacy Agreement)*[304] a dispute arose between the child's mother and a same-sex couple as to the parenting arrangements for a child whom one of the couple and mother had conceived other than through sexual intercourse. There was no question of a parental order as the mother did not consent. However, Russell J made a child arrangements order that the child live with the couple, having found that the pregnancy was contrived with the aim of the same-sex couple having a child, a matter acquiesced to by all parties at the time. Her ladyship was clear that the decision was not to uphold the agreement, but rather to decide on the child's living arrangements in the child's best interests, the decision on which fortunately coincided with the reality of the child's conception.[305]

In *Re P (Residence: Appeal)*,[306] in a desperate bid to have further children of her own, a woman deceived couples by holding herself out as a surrogate mother then telling them that she had miscarried. The father of one of the children found out about the deception and sought a residence order in respect of his child who was 18 months old. Coleridge J transferred residence to the biological father and his wife.

# 4 Making sense of the law on parenthood

## 4.1 Rationales for attributing parenthood

### 4.1.1 Biology

As we have seen, English law's default position on parenthood is to appeal to biological connection.[307] In favour of that approach is the fact that, at least in name, all children will have parents,[308] whereas a move away from that approach raises the possibility of increasing numbers of children who may only have a mother.[309] Legal recognition of gestational mothers not only acknowledges that in most cases there will also be a genetic connection between mother and child, but recognises the mother's physical involvement in producing the child, the importance of maternal bonding during gestation, and that relinquishing the child may have an adverse effect on the mother's psychological health. In addition, there are arguments that not to recognise the gestational mother risks her exploitation or commodification in surrogacy arrangements. Furthermore, as Rebecca Probert has observed, an appeal to gestation provides greater certainty, particularly in cases of surrogacy involving more than one commissioning couple (perhaps unbeknown to each other).[310]

### 4.1.2 Intent-based parenthood

Another approach is intent-based parenthood.[311] There are several examples of this approach in English law.[312] It might be argued that the law in section 28(6) of the HFEA 1990 and section 41 of the HFEA 2008, reflects a sperm donor's intention *not* to become a parent; and in cases of surrogacy arrangements or adoption, the commissioning couple or adoptive parents might be said to

---

[304] [2015] EWFC 36, Russell J.      [305] Ibid, at [125].

[306] *Re P (Residence: Appeal)* [2007] EWCA Civ 1053, [2008] 1 FLR 198.

[307] There are several components: genetic and gestational roles; biological features of the act of coitus; and biological factors (eg hormonal changes) affecting post-natal behaviour. M. Johnson, 'A Biomedical Perspective on Parenthood' in A. Bainham et al, *What is a Parent?* (Oxford: Hart, 1999), Ch 3.

[308] J. Shapiro, 'Changing Ways, New Technologies and the Devaluation of the Genetic Connection to Children' in M. Maclean (ed), *Family Law and Family Values* (Oxford: Hart, 2005), p 93.

[309] Ibid.

[310] R. Probert, 'Families, Assisted Reproduction and the Law' [2004] Child and Family Law Quarterly 273.

[311] For an argument in favour of intent-based parenthood in the context of an examination of English law, see T. Callus, 'A New Parenthood Paradigm for Twenty-First Century Family Law in England the Wales' (2012) 32(3) Legal Studies 347–68, discussed later.

[312] And in other jurisdictions: see eg the role of intention in addressing the competing claims of genetic and gestational parents in the Californian Supreme Court decision of *Johnson v Calvert* 5 Cal 4th 84, 851 P2d 776 (1993).

intend to become parents of the child. As Gillian Douglas points out, however, this basis of attributing parenthood is not unproblematic. It 'implies a preparedness to recognise the free alienability of parental responsibility', that is, the child as a form of property that can be transferred to others. She quite rightly asks: 'should lack of intention be a means of avoiding parenthood?'[313]

Arguing in favour of intent-based parenthood in the context of surrogacy arrangements, Hill[314] observes that the context in which the child is being conceived (eg through donation of sperm or egg) cannot be ignored and that, in such contexts, the arguments in favour of gestational mothers may not be so powerful. Expectations may affect feelings, both in respect of the impact of relinquishing the child and the bonding process. Hill also reminds us of bonding processes between a child and his or her adoptive parents, and that arguments about the psychological effects of relinquishing a child might also apply in favour of a commissioning couple in a surrogacy arrangement. A further argument in support an intent-based approach is that it avoids any gender stereotyping.[315]

### 4.1.3 Welfare

An appeal to the child's welfare is also sometimes evident in attributing parenthood. While adopters or those seeking a parental order may intend to be parents, the making of an adoption order or parental order is ultimately the decision of a court, applying the child's welfare as its paramount consideration. The view that children's welfare should be more widely the underlying basis for attributing parenthood has been advocated by Professor James Dwyer.[316] Focusing on children's relationship rights, Dwyer interrogates philosophically the approach in many jurisdictions whereby children are allocated to their natural parents without scrutiny of the parents' suitability. He argues, therefore, that in each case the child's welfare should be considered before allocating child and parent to each other. Apart from the obvious practical difficulties of implementing this approach, it risks imposing a state view about appropriate lifestyles and parenting.[317]

### 4.1.4 Responsibility/causation

As Rebecca Probert[318] points out, intent-based parenthood does not fit well with English law's treatment of a child conceived as a consequence of a 'one night stand', where the child is not necessarily intended. Probert suggests, therefore, that 'responsibility' in terms of causation may be a more appropriate underlying basis for attribution of parenthood in such cases.

### 4.1.5 Function

Another way of deciding whether someone is a parent is to look at parents' functions and examine who is performing those functions. Such an approach, as Shapiro points out, 'ensures a high degree of correspondence between those who are social parents and those who will gain legal recognition', but the analysis may be 'intrusive, time-consuming and expensive', and there is 'little consensus about what it means to act like a parent'.[319]

---

[313] G. Douglas, 'The Intention to be a Parent and the Making of Mothers' (1994) 57(4) Modern Law Review 636 at 640.

[314] J. Hill, 'What Does it Mean to be a "Parent"? The Claims of Biology as the Basis for Parental Rights' (1991) 66 New York University Law Review 353.

[315] M. Shultz, 'Reproductive Technology and Intent-Based Parenthood: An Opportunity for Gender Neutrality' (1990) Wisconsin Law Review 297.

[316] J. G. Dwyer, 'The Relationship Rights of Children' (New York: Cambridge University Press, 2006). For reviews, see S. Gilmore, 'The Relationship Rights of Children' (2008) 22(2) International Journal of Law, Policy and the Family 273; and C. Sawyer, 'Review Article: A Brave New World Order' [2007] Child and Family Law Quarterly 518.

[317] For criticism, see the review by S. Gilmore, 'The Relationship Rights of Children' (2008) 22(2) International Journal of Law, Policy and the Family 273 at 281; see also C. Sawyer, 'Review Article: A Brave New World Order' [2007] Child and Family Law Quarterly 518.

[318] R. Probert, 'Families, Assisted Reproduction and the Law' [2004] Child and Family Law Quarterly 273.

[319] J. Shapiro, 'Changing Ways, New Technologies and the Devaluation of the Genetic Connection to Children' in M. Maclean (ed), *Family Law and Family Values* (Oxford: Hart, 2005), p 92.

## 5 Criticism of the law

Emily Jackson is critical of the law's assumption that a child can only have two parents.[320] She argues that the law has been 'stymied by the principle of parental exclusivity', leading to law which is 'spectacularly confused and confusing',[321] and 'unable adequately to accommodate increasingly complex reproductive arrangements'.[322] Jackson contends that '[t]ransparency and descriptive accuracy' require 'a model of parenthood that is capable of accommodating its social and technical fragmentation'.[323] This, as she points out, would not necessarily mean an increase in the number of persons having parental responsibilities, for there could be in some cases an extension of 'symbolic recognition of parenthood' without necessarily conferring rights or duties upon such persons.[324] On Jackson's view, therefore, the current law need not necessarily deny legal recognition (as it does) to the genetic role of the egg donor or the gestational function of the surrogate mother who has given up her child to a commissioning couple.[325]

Similarly, Thérèse Callus[326] argues that the 'current reliance on only two parents, advocating biological truth in some circumstances and privileging social reality in others, results in a law which is neither just, certain or practical'.[327] Callus therefore argues for a new parenthood paradigm in which 'both social parent and biological progenitor be appropriately recognised'.[328] This, she argues, could 'be achieved by delegalizing parent*age* while privileging parent*hood*, thereby connecting legal and social parental responsibilities',[329] and 'using intention as the fundamental basis for the legal status of parenthood'.[330] There is the obvious difficulty of evidencing intention but, as Callus suggests, there could be a pre-birth declaration, or some adaptation of the use of parental orders, as currently in section 54 of the HFEA 2008.[331]

By contrast, Andrew Bainham has argued that there appears to be a form of 'status anxiety' among those caring for children. He identifies a pervasive concern 'that their status be improved and a strong desire to gain the full status associated with parenthood'.[332] He argues that 'caution is required in assuming too readily that what looks like a parent must be a parent'.[333]

Bainham is thus critical of the HFEA 2008 insofar as it extends the status of legal parenthood to a wider range of individuals who do not have any biological connection with the child. He argues that:

> while it may be appropriate to give to the lesbian partner and other social parents parental responsibility (depending on the extent to which the individual actually performs parenting functions), it is inappropriate to make that person the legal parent because this is to distort and misrepresent kinship.[334]

[320] E. Jackson, 'What is a Parent?' in A. Diduck and K. O'Donovan (eds), *Feminist Perspectives on Family Law* (Abingdon: Routledge-Cavendish, 2006), p 60.

[321] Ibid.    [322] Ibid, p 66.    [323] Ibid, p 74.    [324] Ibid, p 70.

[325] See also J. Wallbank, 'Too Many Mothers? Surrogacy, Kinship and the Welfare of the Child' [2002] Medical Law Review 271, arguing for focus on child's rights to a link with biological mother.

[326] T. Callus, 'A New Parenthood Paradigm for Twenty-First Century Family Law in England and Wales?' (2012) 32(3) Legal Studies 347.

[327] Ibid, p 355.    [328] Ibid, p 359.    [329] Ibid.

[330] Ibid, p 361. Parenthood would then also bestow parental responsibility.    [331] Ibid, pp 364–65.

[332] A. Bainham, 'Status Anxiety? The Rush for Family Recognition' in F. Ebtehaj, B. Lindley, and M. Richards (eds), *Kinship Matters* (Oxford: Hart, 2006), p 58.

[333] Ibid, p 61; and see A. Bainham, 'Birthrights? The Rights and Obligations Associated with the Birth of a Child' in J. Spencer and A. Pedain (eds), *Freedom and Responsibility in Reproductive Choice* (Oxford: Hart, 2006).

[334] A. Bainham, 'Arguments about Parentage' (2008) 67(2) Cambridge Law Journal 321–355 at 341. See also T. Callus, 'First 'Designer Babies, now À La Carte Parents' [2008] Family Law 143.

Illustrating the point, he observes that the lesbian parent's parents become grandparents, yet the sperm donor and his family drop entirely out of the 'parenthood' picture.[335] As Bainham observes, these developments contrast with the focus on ascertaining biological truth in the case law on establishing paternity.

## 6 Allocation of parental responsibility

Legal parenthood of itself carries with it certain important legal incidents, such as the duty to maintain a child.[336] However, in the Children Act 1989 there is a further concept, 'parental responsibility', defined for the purpose of the Act in section 3(1) as 'all the rights, duties, powers, responsibilities and authority which by law a parent of a child has in relation to the child and his property'.[337] If a person, including a parent, is to have these additional legal relations, he or she must have parental responsibility. The Children Act 1989 sets out who has parental responsibility and the means by which those who do not have it may acquire it.

English law distinguishes between married and unmarried parents in the allocation of parental responsibility.

---

**Key legislation**

Section 2(1) of the Children Act 1989 provides:

> Where a child's father and mother were married to each other at the time of his birth, they shall each hav e parental responsibility for the child.

In the case of unmarried parents, section 2(2) provides:

> Where a child's mother and father were not married to each other at the time of his birth—
>
> (a) the mother shall have parental responsibility for the child;
> (b) the father shall not have parental responsibility for the child, unless he acquires it in accordance with the provisions of this Act.

---

The words 'being married to each other at the time of the child's birth' in section 2(1) are extended[338] to include some relationships in which the parties clearly were not, as a matter of fact, married to each other at the time of the child's birth. Parents who are parties to a void marriage fall within section 2(1) provided that at the time of the child's conception, or the time of the marriage, if later, either or both of them reasonably believed that the marriage was valid.[339] This reasonable belief is presumed unless the contrary is shown.[340] This means that both parents enjoy parental responsibility if, for example, one of the parents was aged under 16 at the date of the marriage, provided either or both of them did not realise this. It means that a man who is already married to someone else, and who knowingly enters into a bigamous marriage, has parental responsibility for any child of that marriage if his 'wife' reasonably believed that their marriage was valid at one of the relevant times.

The phrase 'married to each other at the time of the child's birth' also applies to parents who marry after the child's birth.[341] The father acquires parental responsibility from the date of the marriage.

---

[335] Bainham, 'Arguments about Parentage'.     [336] Child Support Act 1991, s 1.

[337] See Children Act 1989, s 3(2) and (3).

[338] Section 2(3) stipulates that subs (1) must be read with s 1 of the Family Law Reform Act 1987, which in turn refers to s 1 of the Legitimacy Act 1976.

[339] Legitimacy Act 1976, s 1(1).     [340] Ibid, s 1(4).

[341] Family Law Reform Act 1987, s 1(3)(b), ie, a legitimated person within the meaning of the Legitimacy Act 1976, s 10.

Section 2(1) now also applies in the case of the child's mother and a female parent who acquires legal parenthood pursuant to section 42 or 43 of the HFEA 2008. Thus English law is extending what may be seen by some as the now dated and offensive concepts of legitimacy and illegitimacy, in contrast to several other jurisdictions in which such distinctions have been completely removed.[342]

In addition, the parents of adopted children are included within the definition of parents married to each other at the time of the child's birth.[343]

Finally, parents of any person who is otherwise treated in law as legitimate also fall within section 2(1).[344] This provision draws in those cases, usually where there is a foreign element, where a child is treated by law as a child of parents who are married at the time of the child's birth even though this is not factually the case.

All other parents are treated as parents who were not married to each other at the time of the child's birth. The combined effect of section 2(1) and (2) of the Children Act 1989 is that mothers always have parental responsibility, as do fathers who are married to the child's mother. By contrast, a father who is not married to the child's mother does not automatically obtain parental responsibility: he is thus treated differently in two ways—less favourably than the unmarried mother and less favourably than a father who is married to the mother. To understand this position, which on its face may seem unjustifiably discriminatory, it is necessary briefly to explain how the law has developed.

Historically, parental responsibility in respect of a child born out of wedlock vested solely in the mother.[345] The current law emerged from the Law Commission's examination of the status of illegitimacy in the late 1970s. Initially the Commission favoured complete abolition of the status of illegitimacy,[346] including any difference between fathers based on marital status. However, following consultation, the Commission changed its view,[347] explaining that its initial proposal had provoked 'serious anxiety' in a 'significant body of well-informed and experienced commentators',[348] many of whom suggested that parental rights should vest automatically 'only in a class of fathers defined so as to exclude the "unmeritorious"'.[349] The Commission concluded that it would be wrong to ignore the reported concerns where they could not be shown to be without foundation[350] and, being unable to define a class of unmeritorious fathers,[351] recommended that the unmarried father should not acquire parental rights automatically but should be entitled to seek a court order conferring parental rights and duties.[352]

Section 4 of the Family Law Reform Act 1987 was enacted, which enabled an unmarried father to obtain a status similar to a married father. The essence of that provision was re-enacted in section 4 of the Children Act 1989, with some changes to take account of the shift in terminology in that Act from parental rights and duties to 'parental responsibility', and the order is now known as a 'parental

---

[342] See, for criticism, A. Bainham, 'Is Legitimacy Legitimate?' [2009] Family Law 673.

[343] Family Law Reform Act 1987, s 1(3)(c).     [344] Ibid, s 1(3)(d).

[345] *Barnardo v McHugh* [1891] AC 388.

[346] Law Commision, *Illegitimacy* (Law Com WP No 74, 1979). See A. Bainham, 'The Illegitimacy Saga' in R. Probert and C. Barton (eds), *Fifty Years in Family Law Essays for Stephen Cretney* (Cambridge: Intersentia, 2012) and S. Cretney, *Family Law in the Twentieth Century: A History* (Oxford: Oxford University Press, 2003), Ch 15.

[347] Law Commission, *Illegitimacy* (Law Com No 118, 1982).

[348] Ibid, para 4.46.

[349] Ibid, para 4.27. For criticism of the Working Paper's conclusions, see M. Hayes (1980) 43 MLR 299, and see the concerns of the National Council for One-parent Families, cited in Law Com No 118, fn 91.

[350] Ibid, para 4.49. It might equally have been said that the onus should be on those asserting.

[351] Ibid, paras 4.28–4.43.

[352] Ibid, para 4.50. See also Law Commission, *Illegitimacy (Second Report)* (Law Com No 157, 1986), para 1.1. Law Commission, *Illegitimacy* (Law Com No 118, 1982), para 7.26. Compare the views of the Scottish Law Commission (Law Com No 135, 1992), paras 2.36–2.50 concluding that 'both parents of the child should have parental responsibilities and rights whether or not they are or have been married to each other'. See A. Bainham, 'Reforming Scottish Children Law—Sense from North of the Border' (1993) 5(1) Journal of Child Law 3 at 5–7.

responsibility order'.[353] Section 4 of the Children Act 1989 further strengthened the unmarried father's position with another mechanism for acquiring parental responsibility, namely a formal agreement between the mother and the father, known as a 'parental responsibility agreement'.[354]

In the late 1990s there was a further public consultation on the law on parental responsibility, issued by the Lord Chancellor's Department.[355] Its tone was sympathetic to unmarried fathers, explaining that discrimination against unmarried fathers is 'increasingly seen as unacceptable, in view of the large numbers of children who are born to unmarried parents, many of whom are likely to be in stable relationships'.[356] The Consultation Paper commented that it was 'clearly impossible to assume that most unmarried fathers are irresponsible or uninterested in their children, and do not deserve a legal role as parents'.[357] However, as Sheldon notes, 'it is equally unconvincing to assert that all unmarried fathers *are* assuming such a useful and positive role'.[358]

Following consultation,[359] a new provision was inserted[360] into section 4 of the Children Act 1989 conferring parental responsibility on a father through joint registration of the father's name on the child's birth certificate.[361] While welcomed by some, the amendment has been criticised by others for diluting the degree of commitment needed for fathers to acquire parental responsibility, for placing the onus on women to apply to revoke parental responsibility where problems arise, and for doing 'little to enhance and promote the relationships between children and their fathers in any practical way'.[362]

## 6.1 **Acquisition of parental responsibility by an unmarried father**

There are thus now three methods within section 4 of the Children Act 1989 by which an 'unmarried father' may acquire parental responsibility.

---

### Key legislation

Section 4, as amended, provides:

(1) Where a child's father and mother were not married to each other at the time of his birth, the father shall acquire parental responsibility for the child if—

    (a) he becomes registered as the child's father . . . ;

    (b) he and the child's mother make an agreement (a 'parental responsibility agreement') providing for him to have parental responsibility for the child; or

    (c) the court, on his application, orders that he shall have parental responsibility for the child.

---

[353] Now in Children Act 1989, s 4(1)(c).

[354] Now in ibid, s 4(1)(b).

[355] Lord Chancellor's Department, *1. Court Procedures for the Determination of Paternity, 2. The Law on Parental Responsibility for Unmarried Fathers* (March 1998). The Consultation Paper set out several options for reform.

[356] Law Com No 118, para 51. In 2000 almost 40 per cent of live births occurred outside marriage, 80 per cent of which were jointly registered, 75 per cent of which were to parents living at the same address: see (2002) 32 Social Trends 47.

[357] Law Com No 118, para 51.

[358] S. Sheldon, 'Unmarried Fathers And Parental Responsibility: A Case For Reform?' (2001) 9 Feminist Legal Studies 93 at 112.

[359] For an account of some of the responses to the consultation, see S. Sheldon, 'Unmarried Fathers And Parental Responsibility: A Case For Reform?' (2001) 9 Feminist Legal Studies 93.

[360] By the Adoption and Children Act 2002, s 111.

[361] Children Act 1989, s 4(1)(a). See D. Sharp, 'Parental Responsibility—Where Next?' [2001] Family Law 606 and J. Masson, 'The Impact of the Adoption and Children Act 2002 Part I—Parental Responsibility' [2003] Family Law 581. For criticism of the provision, see J. Wallbank, 'Clause 106 of the Adoption and Children Bill: Legislation for the "Good" Father?' (2002) 22(2) Legal Studies 276.

[362] Ibid, 278.

### 6.1.1 Section 4(1)(a): registration of father on child's birth certificate

Section 4(1)(a) of the Children Act 1989 provides that the father of a child will have parental responsibility if he is registered as the father on the child's birth certificate.

Its effect is not as extensive as might at first appear. First, the provision is not retrospective. Section 4(1)(a) was implemented on 1 December 2003 so acquisition of parental responsibility in this way only applies in respect of registrations on or after that date. Thus the father of a newly born child who is registered as the father now, is in a better position vis-à-vis parental responsibility than the man who was registered prior to 1 December 2003 and has cared for the child for many years. In addition, currently the registration of an unmarried father can only be effected with the mother's agreement (ie, jointly), or where the father has a court order which already recognises his legal parenthood.[363] In *AAA v ASH, Registrar General for England and Wales and the Secretary for Justice*[364] a father who had contracted an Islamic marriage with his child's mother which was not valid in English law attended alone to register his child's birth. Sir Christopher Sumner held that the father (being an unmarried father) had not registered in compliance with the relevant provisions and the 'registration' had not conferred parental responsibility. Schedule 6 to the Welfare Reform Act 2009[365] (which at the time of writing has yet to be implemented) inserts new sections 2A and 2B into the Births and Deaths Registration Act 1953 imposing a duty upon a mother to disclose information about a child's father, the scope of which will be prescribed by regulations. The mother is not required to provide the information if she declares that the child has no father,[366] the father has died, she does not know his identity or whereabouts, or the father lacks capacity within the meaning of the Mental Capacity Act 2005.[367] The mother also does not have to provide the information if she has reason to fear for her safety or that of the child if the father is contacted in relation to the registration of the birth.[368] Schedule 6 further introduces provisions whereby the alleged father can be contacted to acknowledge parentage,[369] or his parentage ascertained by scientific testing with consent,[370] and the fact that he is the father then registered. The effect of these provisions will be to reduce a mother's control over birth registration and thus over acquisition of parental responsibility.

However, currently section 4(1)(a) does little to improve the position of unmarried fathers where the mother is resistant to his involvement in decisions concerning the child's upbringing. The general effect of section 4(1)(a), however, is likely to be a gradual decrease in the proportion of unmarried fathers who do not have parental responsibility, resulting eventually in only a small proportion of fathers who will not have it.

---

[363] Registered means registered under any of paras (a), (b), and (c) of s 10(1) or under s 10A(1) of the Births and Deaths Registration Act 1953. Thus, registration on a child's birth certificate in another jurisdiction which confers parental responsibility in that jurisdiction will not suffice: see *Re S (Relocation: Parental Responsibility)* [2013] EWHC 1295 (Fam), [2013] 2 FLR 1453[2013] 2 FLR 1453 at [62] (birth certificate in Colombia conferred parental responsibility on step-father in Columbia but not in England and Wales). Re-registration by the Registrar General under s 14A does not confer parental responsibility on the father, because s 14A is not one of the enactments specified in the Children Act 1989, s 4(1A): see *M v F and H (Legal Paternity)* [2013] EWHC 1901 (Fam) at [31].

[364] [2009] EWHC 636 (Fam), [2010] 1 FLR 1.

[365] For the policy behind this provision, see Department for Work and Pensions, *Joint Birth Registration: Recording Responsibility* (Cm 7293, June 2008), and the preceding Green Paper *Joint Birth Registration: Promoting Parental Responsibility* (Cm 7160, 2007). For discussion, see S. Sheldon, 'From "Absent Objects of Blame" to "Fathers Who Want to Take Responsibility": Reforming Birth Registration Law' (2009) 31(4) Journal of Social Welfare and Family Law 373–389 (reflecting a genetic understanding of parent as actively engaged) and A. Bainham, 'What is the Point of Birth Registration?' [2008] Child and Family Law Quarterly 449.

[366] By virtue of the HFEA 2008, s 41.   [367] Births and Deaths Registration Act 1953, s 2B(3) and (4).

[368] Ibid.   [369] Ibid, s 2C. The father can also declare his parentage: see s 2D.

[370] Ibid, s 2E.

### 6.1.2 Section 4(1)(b): parental responsibility agreement

Section 4(1)(b) of the Children Act 1989 enables the unmarried father to acquire parental responsibility by agreement with the mother. The agreement must be made in accordance with regulations,[371] on the relevant set form,[372] signed and witnessed, and registered in the Principal Registry of the Family Division in London. The signatures must be witnessed by a lay justice or an officer of the court. It is important for parents to understand that, once made, the agreement cannot be revoked by the parties; it can only be ended by a court.

The making of a parental responsibility agreement is not itself an exercise of parental responsibility. In *Re X (Minors) (Care Proceedings: Parental Responsibility)*[373] a mother wished to share parental responsibility with the child's father. The child was in the care of the local authority and the local authority wanted, if possible, to prevent the father gaining parental responsibility. Wilson J held that a local authority's power under section 33(3)(b) of the Children Act 1989 to control the extent to which the parents of a child in its care may meet their parental responsibility, could not be exercised to prevent the child's mother from entering a parental responsibility agreement. Since the father was signing the agreement necessarily without parental responsibility, it would be paradoxical to conclude that in doing the same the mother was exercising her parental responsibility.[374] Furthermore, the local authority would not have been able to prevent the acquisition of parental responsibility through marriage, and a good reason ought to be shown for adopting a different result in the case of parental responsibility acquired by way of a parental responsibility agreement.[375]

There has been a low (some might say disappointing) uptake in the use of parental responsibility agreements.[376] The low uptake probably reflects at least two factors. There is evidence that many unmarried parents are unaware that the unmarried father lacks parental responsibility, especially when he is cohabiting with the mother, and also unaware of the possibility of making an agreement.[377] In addition, research by Pickford[378] identified the father's reluctance to broach with the mother the subject of making an agreement for fear that it may disrupt their relationship.

### 6.1.3 Section 4(1)(c): application for a parental responsibility order

If a father who desires parental responsibility has been unable to secure it in the ways discussed earlier (ie, with the mother's agreement), he will need to seek parental responsibility from a court. Usually he would do so by applying for a parental responsibility order (PRO) under section 4(1)(c) of the Children Act 1989.[379] The applicant for a PRO under section 4 of the Act must be the child's legal father,[380] and jurisdiction should not be founded upon a concession that the applicant is the child's father.[381] An application for a PRO is a discrete application which must be determined separately from other matters, such as contact between the parent and child.[382]

---

[371] Parental Responsibility Agreement Regulations 1991 (SI 1991/1478), as amended by the Parental Responsibility Agreement (Amendment) Regulations 2005 (SI 2005/2808) and the Parental Responsibility Agreement (Amendment) Regulations 2009 (SI 2009/2026) (in force 1 September 2009).

[372] Form C(PRA1).  [373] [2000] Fam 156.  [374] Ibid, 161.  [375] Ibid.

[376] Especially as no fee is imposed when the agreement is registered at the Principal Registry of the Family Division.

[377] R. Pickford, 'Unmarried Fathers and the Law' in A. Bainham, S. Day Sclater, and M. Richards (eds), *What is a Parent? A Socio-Legal Analysis* (Oxford: Hart, 1999); and see S. McRae, *Cohabiting Mothers, Changing Marriage and Motherhood* (London: Policy Studies Institute, 1993), pp 70–1.

[378] Pickford, 'Unmarried Fathers'.

[379] The child need not be living within the jurisdiction: see *Re S (Parental Responsibility: Jurisdiction)* [1998] 2 FLR 921.

[380] *R v Secretary of State for Social Security, ex p W* [1999] 2 FLR 604, FD, Johnson J, at 607D: 'there is no jurisdiction to make an order in favour of anyone who is not the father'. *Re S (Parental Responsibility: Jurisdiction)* [1998] 2 FLR 921.

[381] *Re D (A Child) (IVF Treatment)* [2001] 1 FLR 972, CA (Butler-Sloss P, Hale and Arden LJJ) *per* Arden LJ at [42]. See also Hale LJ at [36] and [37] and Butler-Sloss P at [10].

[382] See *Re W (Parental Responsibility Order: Inter-Relationship with Direct Contact)* [2013] EWCA Civ 335, [2013] 2 FLR 1337 at [6] and [11], and *Re H (A Child: Parental Responsibility)* [2002] EWCA Civ 542 (15 April 2002) at [14], both applying *Re C and V (Contact and Parental Responsibility)* [1998] 1 FLR 392, CA (contact and parental responsibility

### 6.1.3.1 The courts' general guidance

How do the courts decide such applications? The Court of Appeal has taken the view that there is no doubt that a father's acquisition of parental responsibility for a child is a matter with respect to the child's upbringing,[383] and that section 1(1) of the Children Act 1989 applies to the making of a PRO[384] and a court must treat the child's welfare as its paramount consideration. By section 1(2A), inserted by section 11 of the Children and Families Act 2014, a court is to presume, unless the contrary is shown, that involvement of the parent in the life of the child will further the child's welfare. The existing case law will now need to be read alongside this provision (which is discussed more fully in Chapter 9, section 5.11.5). Because the court is considering whether to make an order under the Children Act 1989, section 1(5) also applies: the court shall not make the order unless it is better for the child than making no order at all. Use of the checklist of matters bearing on a child's welfare in section 1(3), however, is not mandatory,[385] although factors within it, for example the child's ascertainable wishes and feelings,[386] may well be relevant. Within the confines of the relevant statutory criteria, the PRO is 'the subject of a discretion cast in the widest terms',[387] and the Court of Appeal has explained that:

> [i]n every case it is a matter of weighing in the balance the various factors in favour and against granting parental responsibility and deciding, on the facts of the individual case, whether an order for parental responsibility is in the interests of the child.[388]

The courts have provided guidance on how to approach a PRO application, but it is important not to lose sight of the court's wide discretion and its basic task as set out earlier. Guidance stems both from cases decided under section 4 of the Family Law Reform Act 1987 and from those decided under section 4 of the Children Act 1989, which replaced it. In *Re CB (A Minor) (Parental Responsibility Order)*[389] Waite J said that, in his view, Parliament intended to carry forward the case law decided under the 1987 Act.

The Court of Appeal has approached applications for a PRO from the perspective that prima facie it must be 'for the child's benefit or welfare that it has an absent parent sufficiently concerned and interested to want to have a parental responsibility order'.[390] The court has seen the order as potentially impacting positively on the child's welfare in two senses. First, it may promote a degree of father involvement which allows the father to contribute practically to the promotion of the child's welfare[391] and, secondly, the order itself may impact upon the child's self-esteem.

---

distinct questions to be addressed from different perspectives). See also *Re CB (A Minor) (Parental Responsibility Order)* [1993] 1 FLR 920, FD (Waite J).

[383] *In the Matter of Z (Children)* [2008] EWCA Civ 1556 at [13]. In fact, the courts have asserted this rather than reaching a reasoned conclusion on the matter, and the point is not beyond doubt. See for arguments to the contrary, S. Gilmore, 'Parental Responsibility and the Unmarried Father—A New Dimension to the Debate' [2003] Child and Family Law Quarterly 21, esp at 31–4.

[384] See eg *Re H (Parental Responsibility)* [1998] 1 FLR 855, CA.

[385] Children Act 1989, s 1(4), and *Re H and A (Minors)*, 19 January 1993, CA (Balcombe and Waite LJJ), Lexis-Nexis Professional.

[386] See eg *In the Matter of TB; A Community and Hospitals Trust*, Transcript GILF3498, 25 September 2001, Gillen J (High Court of Northern Ireland).

[387] *Re CB (A Minor) (Parental Responsibility Order)* [1993] 1 FLR 920, FD, Waite J at 922G.

[388] *Re P (Parental Responsibility)* [1998] 2 FLR 96 at 107F–G. See also Lord Woolf MR in *Re P (Parental Responsibility)* [1997] 2 FLR 722 at 728H: 'the judge had to weigh in the balance the various factors in favour and against granting parental responsibility.' And *Re H (Parental Responsibility)* [1998] 1 FLR 855, CA at 859H–860A *per* Butler-Sloss LJ: 'the duty in each case to take into account all the relevant circumstances and to decide whether the order proposed is in the best interests of the child.'

[389] [1993] 1 FLR 920, FD. Although the case law post-dates enactment of the Children Act 1989.

[390] *Re G (A Minor) (Parental Responsibility Order)* [1994] 1 FLR 504, CA at 508C.

[391] See *Re G (A Minor) (Parental Responsibility Order)* [1994] 1 FLR 504, CA.

---

**Talking point**

Ward LJ explained in *Re S (Parental Responsibility)*,[392] that a child's self-esteem is aided by a positive favourable image of an absent father. Therefore it is important to:

> ensure that the law confers upon a committed father that stamp of approval, lest the child grow up with some belief that he is in some way disqualified from fulfilling his role and that the reason for the disqualification is something inherent which will be inherited by the child, making her struggle to find her own identity all the more fraught.[393]

**Q.** Should parental responsibility therefore be conferred on a father even when a court concludes that he cannot exercise it, or exercise it appropriately?

---

The Court of Appeal has sought to provide guidance on the factors which are likely to indicate that the father's involvement will promote the child's welfare. In *Re H (Minors) (Local Authority: Parental Rights) (No 3)*,[394] Balcombe LJ, delivering the Court of Appeal's judgment, said:

> In considering whether to make an order . . . the court will have to take into account a number of factors, of which the following will undoubtedly be material (although there may well be others, as the list is not intended to be exhaustive):
>
> (1) the degree of commitment which the father has shown towards the child;
> (2) the degree of attachment which exists between the father and the child;[395] and
> (3) the reasons of the father for applying for the order.[396]

In *Re G (A Minor) (Parental Responsibility Order)*[397] his Lordship explained that where the *Re H* criteria are fulfilled, 'prima facie it would be for the welfare of the child that such an order should be made';[398] and in *Re Et (Parental Responsibility: Blood Tests)*[399] added that in such a case he 'would require to be convinced by cogent evidence that the child's welfare would be adversely affected by the making of such an order'.[400]

Later decisions have cautioned against the *Re H* criteria being elevated to the status of a statutory definition and have emphasised that they are 'subordinate to the welfare principle and therefore must not divert attention from other considerations which bear upon the child's welfare'.[401] As Ward LJ explained in *Re C and V (Contact and Parental Responsibility)*, they represent:

> some, though not all, of the factors which might be material in answering a much more general question as to whether [a] particular father shows genuine concern for the child and a genuine wish to assume the mantle of responsibility in law which nature has already thrust upon him.[402]

---

[392] [1995] 2 FLR 648, CA.

[393] Ibid, 657H. Said in *Re P (Parental Responsibility)* [1998] 2 FLR 96 at 107B, to reflect 'current psychiatric and socio-logical thinking'. The self-esteem argument will not always be relevant, eg in the case of a severely disabled child: see eg *Re M (Contact) (Parental Responsibility)* [2001] 2 FLR 342, FD (Black J).

[394] [1991] Fam 151.

[395] This appears to be a two-way process: see *Re B (A Minor)*, 17 October 1995, CA (Hale J and Russell LJ).

[396] Ibid, 158D, building on Ward J's judgment in *D v Hereford and Worcester County Council* [1991] Fam 14, [1991] 1 FLR 205, in which, as his Lordship later explained in *Re P (Parental Responsibility)* [1997] 2 FLR 722, CA at 724, he had 'ventured to put a test in the most general terms of whether or not the father had behaved, or would behave, with parental responsibility for the child'.

[397] [1994] 1 FLR 504, CA.       [398] Ibid, 508D. See also *Re P* [1998] 2 FLR 96, CA at 106B.

[399] [1995] 1 FLR 392, Saville and Mann LJJ agreeing.       [400] Ibid, 398G.

[401] *M v M (Parental Responsibility)* [1999] 2 FLR 737, FD, Wilson J at 743B–C.

[402] *Re C and V (Contact and Parental Responsibility)* [1998] 1 FLR 392 at 397G–H *per* Ward LJ.

However, Balcombe LJ's judgments have established the *Re H* criteria as highly significant factors in each case, and they are regarded as the 'starting point'[403] for considering an application.[404] In each case, therefore, the court considers the father's commitment to the child, the attachment between father and child (and vice versa), and the reasons for the application.

### 6.1.3.2 Commitment

A father's commitment can be demonstrated in various ways. Commitment (and attachment) might be demonstrated through contact with the child. In *Re J (Parental Responsibility)*,[405] for example, Stuart-White J focused on a father's contact with his 11-year-old child, concluding that contact five or six times in her lifetime did not demonstrate sufficient commitment to warrant the making of a PRO.

Commitment might also be shown through payment of maintenance.[406] While a failure to pay maintenance may evidence some lack of commitment, a deliberate failure to pay maintenance will not necessarily result in denial of a PRO. In *Re H (Parental Responsibility: Maintenance)*[407] the father had never missed contact with his children and had pursued applications to the court when contact had been denied by the mother. His application for parental responsibility was genuinely motivated and there was existing attachment between the father and his children. However, while the father had provided some clothing for the children, he obstinately refused to pay maintenance, claiming that it would be wrongly used by the mother to buy alcohol and cigarettes. Unimpressed by this attitude, the trial judge had adjourned the application for parental responsibility to enable the father to demonstrate his commitment to the children by assisting in their financial upkeep. The Court of Appeal held that, while the judge was rightly critical of the father for not providing financially for his children, he ought not to have used 'the weapon of withholding a parental responsibility order for the purpose of exacting from the father what may be regarded as his financial dues'. In doing so the judge had placed undue emphasis on the father's financial shortcomings at the expense of paying proper regard to the father's other merits, and had also been unmindful of the need to avoid delay. The decision is, of course, not uncontroversial. For some, the idea that a father should enjoy the rights associated with parental responsibility in circumstances where he has shown himself determined not to pay towards his child's support will be seen as divesting the notion of parental responsibility of any significant moral content and as giving an undesirable message to fathers about what having responsibility for a child entails.

### 6.1.3.3 Attachment

The second factor which the courts will look closely at is the degree of attachment between father and child (and vice versa). They have tended to apply this criterion quite rigidly. Where, however, the mother has unjustifiably prevented the father from establishing contact with the child, a rigid focus on attachment is arguably unduly harsh to the father.[408] It is suggested that in such cases the lack of attachment should be viewed in all the circumstances and given very little, if any, weight if the father is genuine and committed. A lack of attachment will not, however, necessarily result in dismissal of the father's application; the court sometimes adjourns the application to allow time to establish it.

---

[403] *Re H (Parental Responsibility)* [1998] 1 FLR 855, CA at 859H *per* Butler-Sloss LJ.

[404] They have been described as the 'most material considerations': see *Re S (A Minor) (Stay of Proceedings)* [1993] 2 FLR 912, CA at 917E.

[405] [1999] 1 FLR 784, FD (Stuart-White J).          [406] Ibid.          [407] [1996] 1 FLR 867, CA.

[408] See S. Gilmore, 'Parental Responsibility and the Unmarried Father—A New Dimension to the Debate' [2003] Child and Family Law Quarterly 21.

### 6.1.3.4 Reasons for applying

The third of the *Re H* criteria looks to whether the father has genuine, bona fide, reasons for applying. It does not require the father to have specific reasons for applying for parental responsibility; the purpose is to identify the father whose motives for wanting parental responsibility are improper. In *M v M (Parental Responsibility)*[409] Wilson J held that this criterion, and indeed the definition of parental responsibility in section 3 of the Children Act 1989, presupposes that a father is capable of reason. In declining to grant parental responsibility to a father who had a very low IQ (partly caused by a motorcycle accident) his Lordship held that it was not appropriate to grant parental responsibility to a father who did not have the mental ability to exercise it appropriately.

Apart from the exceptional case where a father is mentally incapable of exercising parental responsibility, 'an order is not precluded merely because parental rights may not in practice be exercisable'.[410] The inability to exercise some or all parental responsibilities might occur, for example, because the father is ill or in prison or the child is in the care of a local authority. In *Re C (Minors) (Parental Rights)*[411] Waite J (sitting in the Court of Appeal) explained that circumstances might arise when a father (perhaps through mental illness) had to 'step out of his children's lives altogether', but his parental responsibility does not become 'a dead letter or a mere paper title'. It has 'real and tangible value, not only as something he can cherish for the sake of his own peace of mind, but also as a status carrying with it rights in waiting'.[412] In that case, the unmarried parents of two children had parted and there was medical evidence to the effect that the mother's mental stability would be at risk if the father was allowed contact with the children. The court therefore determined that contact should be denied for the time being. However, in relation to the parental rights and duties order Waite J concluded that while the prospective enforceability of parental rights is a relevant consideration, there is nothing within the legislation to suggest that it should be an overriding consideration, and it could never be right to refuse a parental rights and duties order on the automatic ground that it would be vitiated by an inability to enforce it.[413]

### 6.1.3.5 The parental responsibility order generally characterised as designed to confer a status

The courts have viewed the PRO as 'designed not to do more than confer on the natural father the status of fatherhood which a father would have when married to the mother'.[414] Furthermore it has been said that 'on any view an order for parental responsibility gives the father no power to override the decision of the mother, who already has such responsibility: in the event of disagreement between them on a specific issue relating to the child, the court will have to resolve it'.[415]

### 6.1.3.6 Court should not focus unduly on how parental responsibility may be exercised

In *Re S (Parental Responsibility)*,[416] the Court of Appeal, emphasising that the purpose of a PRO is to confer status, held that when deciding whether to grant parental responsibility it is 'wrong to

---

[409] [1999] 2 FLR 737.

[410] *W v Ealing London Borough Council* [1993] 2 FLR 788, CA (Stephen Brown P, Simon Brown, and Peter Gibson LJJ) at 796C–D, drawing on *Re C (Minors) (Parental Rights)* [1992] 1 FLR 1, where the Court of Appeal held that whilst prospective enforceability of an order is a relevant factor, it is not an overriding one, and an order cannot be vitiated automatically because the powers conferred are not immediately exercisable.

[411] [1992] 1 FLR 1, CA.

[412] Ibid, 3G–4B. See also, *Re S (A Minor) (Stay of Proceedings)* [1993] 2 FLR 912, CA at 918A *per* Lloyd LJ: 'a matter to which the father may well attach importance for its own sake'.

[413] For another example, see *Re H (Minors) (Local Authority: Parental Rights) (No 3)* [1991] Fam 151, sub nom *Re H (Illegitimate Children: Father: Parental Rights) (No 2)* [1991] 1 FLR 214.

[414] *Re C and V (Contact and Parental Responsibility)* [1998] 1 FLR 392 at 397. For discussion of parental responsibility as a status, see J. Eekelaar, 'Parental Responsibility—A New Legal Status?' (1996) 112 LQR 233.

[415] *Re P (A Minor) (Parental Responsibility Order)* [1994] 1 FLR 578 at 584G–585D (the mother in that case had a residence order which meant that the father could not exercise parental responsibility inconsistently with that order: see the Children Act 1989, s 2(8)).

[416] *Re S (Parental Responsibility)* [1995] 2 FLR 648, CA.

place undue and therefore false emphasis on the rights and duties and the powers comprised in "parental responsibility" '.[417] It explained that the 'wide exercise of s 8 orders can control the abuse, if any, of the exercise of parental responsibility which is adverse to the welfare of the child'.[418] As Ward LJ put it in *Re C and V (Contact and Parental Responsibility):*[419]

> It is perfectly proper to inquire what reasons impelled the application, but, unless those reasons are demonstrably improper and wrong, the court should not on this application regulate how parental responsibility will in fact be exercised.[420]

The application of these principles is strikingly illustrated by the facts of *Re S (Parental Responsibility).*[421] In that case the father was acknowledged on the child's birth certificate and had cohabited with the mother in a committed relationship for four years. The parents' relationship broke down when the child was about one year old. The father continued to have regular contact with his daughter, from which the child benefited, and he contributed to the child's housing costs, maintenance, and nursery school fees, apart from a period of three months when he was out of work. About a year later the father was arrested and subsequently pleaded guilty to possession of obscene photographs of children that the authorities had intercepted in his post. The mother reacted by severing the contact, but the child became deeply distressed and her behaviour at school deteriorated. Consequently the mother allowed contact to be resumed, initially supervised, but over time the supervision was relaxed and eventually the child had staying contact with the father. Upon the father's application for a PRO, the judge, concerned by the father's conviction and his potential to interfere in the mother's care of the child, refused the application. The Court of Appeal allowed the father's appeal. Ward LJ, delivering the leading judgment, held that the judge 'rightly had regard to the fact of his conviction' but 'however disreputable the conviction, it was not one which demonstrably and directly affected the child in her day-to-day life' given the existing contact arrangements. The judge had failed to appreciate that the scope for the father to interfere was not material,[422] and had 'failed to appreciate the emphasis that Balcombe LJ placed upon children growing up in the knowledge that their father is committed enough to wish to have parental responsibility conferred upon him'. In Ward LJ's view, the father's commitment and the uncontroverted attachment and affection between father and child abundantly satisfied the requirements for the making of a PRO, and there had been no cogent reason, indeed little reason at all, for refusing the order. The decision is clearly a controversial one. For some, the idea that a father with this sort of conviction should be granted parental responsibility will be perceived as distasteful and wrong.[423]

The approach in *Re S* was also adopted by the Court of Appeal in *Re C and V (Contact and Parental Responsibility).*[424] In that case the child suffered with a medical problem which required the mother's experienced management of a tracheotomy tube in order to maintain the child's health. Upon the breakdown of the parents' relationship, the mother resisted the father's wish to maintain contact with his son and to acquire parental responsibility. The judge refused the father's application for a contact order. He was influenced by the court welfare officer's reluctant conclusion that attempts to enforce contact would be strongly resisted and prove highly stressful to the mother, which anxiety could have a detrimental impact on her capacity to care for the child. For similar reasons, the judge dismissed the father's application for a PRO. The Court of Appeal (Ward LJ again delivering the leading judgment) held that, while the judge had not been plainly wrong to deny contact, he had misdirected himself in applying the same reasoning to the PRO application. The judge had failed to make specific findings about the father's commitment.[425] The parents had

---

[417] Ibid, 657F.    [418] Ibid.    [419] [1998] 1 FLR 392.
[420] Ibid, 397.    [421] [1995] 2 FLR 648, CA.
[422] Especially as there was a paucity of evidence to justify that finding.
[423] F. Kaganas, 'Responsible or Feckless Fathers?—*Re S (Parental Responsibility)*' [1996] Child and Family Law Quarterly 165.
[424] [1998] 1 FLR 392, CA.    [425] Ibid, 397.

had a four-year relationship, the father had been present at the child's birth, during the relationship he had assisted in looking after the boy (including on occasions performing the suction necessary to clear his tube), and the court welfare officer reported that the father's concern for the child was genuine.[426] On those facts, the Court of Appeal had no difficulty finding that the father fulfilled the necessary tests to acquire parental responsibility, and the father's potential use of parental responsibility in the circumstances of this case was not a material factor.

In *Re P (Parental Responsibility)*[427] the Court of Appeal clarified further that while an order 'will not usually be refused simply because, through hostility to the child's mother or an excess of zeal, he may seek to exercise parental responsibility inappropriately', where:

> the father intends to use a parental responsibility order for improper or inappropriate ends to try to interfere with and possibly undermine the mother's care of the child, then clearly the court retains the discretion to refuse a parental responsibility order even if part of the father's likely abuse of the order can be contained by prohibited steps orders under s 8 of the Children Act 1989.[428]

Building on this, in *Re M (Parental Responsibility Order)*[429] Ryder LJ commented that:

> The status conferred by parental responsibility is an important legal recognition of the delicate balance between rights, duties, powers, responsibilities and authority that are the components of family and private life. It is integral to the concept of parental responsibility. It is not, however, a separate 'stand alone' factor, let alone a presumptive factor to be weighed alongside other *Re S (Parental Responsibility)* factors in the welfare consideration of whether a parental responsibility order should be made.[430]

In that case the father of an 11-year-old boy sought a parental responsibility order, being particularly concerned to have information about the child's education and access to medical information. The mother and boy opposed the applications, the boy not wishing his father to know where he was being educated because as a young boy he had been taken by the father from school overnight to a place unknown to his mother or the authorities. The father's application was refused and his appeal to the Court of Appeal dismissed. The Court of Appeal commented:

> In a circumstance where a father wants the very information that a young person wishes to deny him access to, and where that child is of an age and understanding to articulate his reasons, the court needs to be very anxious in its scrutiny. The judge scrutinised the evidence of the father and M and as a consequence was cautious. He was right to be. Having regard to the father's behaviours, the mother's vulnerabilities, and M's wishes it cannot be said that the judge was wrong in his evaluative judgment that it would be detrimental to M's welfare to allow the father to exercise even the limited aspects of parental responsibility that he identified.[431]

### 6.1.3.7 *Hedging the order and conditional orders*

As we have seen, a distinction is made between a parent with improper motives and one who may simply be overzealous in his desire to exercise parental responsibility. Hostility between the parties and/or lack of mutual respect, while clearly relevant insofar as it impacts upon the child's welfare, is not per se sufficient to deny a father parental responsibility.[432] Where there is a risk that the

---

[426] Ibid, 398.       [427] *Re P (Parental Responsibility)* [1998] 2 FLR 96.       [428] Ibid, 107–8.
[429] [2013] EWCA Civ 969 (Lloyd, Beatson, and Ryder LJJ).       [430] Ibid, [27].       [431] Ibid, [25].
[432] *Re D (A Minor)* [1995] 3 FCR 783, FD (Sir Stephen Brown P). See also *Re S (A Minor) (Parental Responsibility)* [1995] 3 FCR 564, FD (Sir Stephen Brown P) at 568B, criticising the welfare officer's 'undue reliance upon the difficult relationship between the parties as being a relevant factor to take into account'. See eg *Re M (Contact: Family Assistance: McKenzie Friend)* [1999] 1 FLR 75, CA (Ward and Roch LJJ) at 80E–F: commenting of the father that there

father may be overzealous, or where it is not felt to be appropriate for the father to exercise parental responsibility in a particular area of the child's life, these concerns may be addressed by way of undertakings from the father, by hedging the order with conditions, or indeed making the order conditional on the imposition of certain conditions.[433]

In *Re D (Contact and Parental Responsibility: Lesbian Mothers and Known Father)*[434] a lesbian couple, A and C, advertised for a man who would father a child. Mr B responded, and with A he fathered a girl, D. The lesbian couple's view was that Mr B would be acknowledged as D's father, but that he would play a minimal role in her life (eg contact once every three weeks or so). However, once the child was born, it became clear that Mr B envisaged a greater role in D's life. He sought parental responsibility, which the couple opposed.

They were concerned about Mr B's potential to interfere in their upbringing of the child. The concern was based upon Mr B's past behaviour. For example, D suffered from arthritis and the father wrote a letter to D's medical consultant which embarrassingly suggested that A and C had concerns about the treatment D was receiving. On another occasion, D was to attend a school open day on her 4th birthday, but B wanted to see her that day. Mr B had said that he would locate the school, and the mothers had been worried that he would turn up on the day and cause difficulties which might prejudice D's chance of getting a place at the school.

Black J was not convinced that it was appropriate simply to apply the existing principles to the novel facts of this case, and expert evidence was provided to the court by Dr Claire Sturge, Consultant Child and Adolescent Psychiatrist.[435] She advised that a third parent would be confusing for the child and her sense of security would be strongest if responsibility for her lay within the nuclear family. She suggested that the solution would be for the father to be officially recognised in some way, but not to be involved in the nitty-gritty of her daily life. Black J was concerned about Mr B's potential to interfere but in the end these concerns were eased by Mr B agreeing to be bound by undertakings not to interfere in matters of D's schooling and medical treatment. Black J granted a PRO, making clear that the order was made in reliance upon those restrictions.[436] Thus, by 'means of this more than usually detailed parental responsibility order' her Ladyship hoped that the respective statuses of the parties could properly be recognised.[437]

The courts' willingness to grant parental responsibility with one hand and then substantially control its exercise with the other, and the consequent characterisation of parental responsibility as a mere status, has led Helen Reece to comment that, at least in some cases, English law has seen a degrading of the concept of parental responsibility in recent years from the notion of 'parental authority' to 'nothing more than official approval'.[438]

### 6.1.3.8 Cases where the child particularly needs a father with parental responsibility

There may be features of a case which particularly suggest that the child needs another parent with parental responsibility and which therefore may make the granting of a PRO more likely.[439] An example is where the mother herself has acted irresponsibly. As Thorpe J commented in *S v R*, a case in which the whereabouts of the children were unknown as the mother had relocated without the

---

was 'no evidence whatever to suggest that he has behaved irresponsibly towards the children, however irresponsible he may have been to [the mother] as her partner'.

[433] It is not possible, however, to suspend a PRO. In *Re G (Parental Responsibility Order)* [2006] 2 FLR 1092, CA, the court overturned a judge's decision to grant a PRO suspended provided the mother supply information about the child's education and health. Hedley J observed that while this could be achieved by a raft of specific issue orders, to do so would be most unusual. Instead, the Court of Appeal adjourned the PRO application with liberty to restore, upon the mother's undertakings to provide information to the father about the child's education and health.

[434] [2006] 1 FCR 556, FD (Black J).     [435] Ibid, [24]–[28].

[436] Ibid, [91].     [437] Ibid, [93].

[438] H. Reece, 'The Degradation of Parental Responsibility' in R. Probert, S. Gilmore, and J. Herring (eds), *Responsible Parents and Parental Responsibility* (Oxford: Hart, 2009), p 102.

[439] *Re E (Parental Responsibility: Blood Tests)* [1995] 1 FLR 392 at 398H; *Re A (A Minor)* [1996] 1 FCR 5, FD (Thorpe J).

father's knowledge in breach of a contact order:[440] 'if the mother is going to behave irresponsibly in relation to her obligations there is all the more need for [the child] to be supported by another adult with parental responsibility.' Another reason might be where a mother is very ill[441] and it is helpful to confer parental responsibility to secure another parent with parental responsibility in the event of her likely death.[442]

### 6.1.3.9  When will a parental responsibility order be denied?

Most applications for parental responsibility orders are successful and it is relatively rare for parental responsibility to be completely denied. The Court of Appeal has explained that in such cases it is 'irresponsibility in the father's behaviour, or his abuse or likely abuse of parental responsibility which may disqualify him'.[443] A number of case law examples of such behaviours are discussed in the following sections.

### 6.1.3.9.1  Inappropriate use cases

One category of case in which parental responsibility is sometimes denied is where the father's motive for possessing parental responsibility appears to be improper; what have been termed[444] the 'inappropriate use' cases. *W v Ealing London Borough Council*[445] provides an example. The children were in the care of the local authority, and leave had been given to the authority to terminate contact between the children and their parents prior to placing the children with long-term foster parents with a view to their adoption. The children had been prepared for separation from their parents, and two possible adoptive families had been found, neither of whom wanted contact between the children and their mother and father to continue. In these circumstances Connell J dismissed the father's application for parental responsibility as introductions to the prospective adopters were imminent and to change the situation would have left the children in limbo or confused them. A further ground was that the father would not have been in any position to play any significant role in the future. Dismissing the father's appeal, the Court of Appeal found that the father's only reason for applying for a PRO was 'the hope that he might thereby thwart the making of an adoption order'[446] and held that in those circumstances Connell J had been entitled to refuse the order and thus eliminate that risk. The Court of Appeal pointed out that that approach is not inconsistent with earlier expressed principles, commenting:

> [T]he principle that an order is not precluded merely because parental rights may not in practice be exercisable is no authority for the converse proposition that an order must be made in such circumstances.[447]

Parental responsibility has also been denied where the father will seek to use parental responsibility to unsettle the mother and undermine her day-to-day care of the child. An example is provided by *Re M (Contact) (Parental Responsibility)*.[448] The case concerned a 17-year-old girl, KM, who suffered from cerebral palsy, functioned at the level of a six-month-old, and was totally dependent

---

[440] *S v R* [1993] 1 FCR 331, FD (Thorpe J).

[441] See eg *Re S (A Minor)*, 5 October 1994, CA (Neill LJ, Wilson J) (mother seriously ill with neuro-degenerative disorder).

[442] *Re W (A Minor)*, 16 March 1994, CA (Balcombe and Hobhouse LJJ); *Re D (Minors)*, 20 March 1995, CA (Butler-Sloss, Morritt, and Hutchison LJJ).

[443] *Re P (Parental Responsibility)* [1998] 2 FLR 96, at 108C–D.

[444] *Re M (Contact) (Parental Responsibility)* [2001] 2 FLR 342 (Black J).        [445] [1993] 2 FLR 788, CA.

[446] Ibid, 796C.

[447] At 796C–D. Indeed, it has been held that, where the father's use of parental responsibility is likely to be inappropriate, the existence of a care order is 'insufficient protection to merit the granting of a parental responsibility order without more': see *In the Matter of TB; A Community Hospitals Trust*, Transcript GILF3498, 29 September 2001, High Court of Northern Ireland (Gillen J).

[448] [2001] 2 FLR 342.

for all her needs. She was living with the mother and the mother's partner. Since the parents' separation, the father and his family had frequently complained to the authorities about the mother's care of KM. In addition, the family alleged that the mother's partner represented a risk of sexual abuse to her based on his previous trial (albeit acquittal) for the sexual assault of a 13-year-old girl. As a result of these tensions, there had been a series of angry confrontations between the families. Upon the father's application for a PRO, Black J found that to a significant extent the father's motivation was concern for KM and therefore she 'should start well-disposed to the father's application'. However, her Ladyship was concerned that the father would 'seek to misuse such an order as a "make weight" in future dealings with those in authority such as the police, social services, the school and doctors, about KM'. She was concerned that the father and the wider family misunderstood the nature of a PRO and saw it as providing some sort of right to intervene. She concluded therefore that there was a very real problem of potential misuse, which in the extreme circumstances of the case could not be prevented by hedging the order with safeguards in the form of restrictions on the exercise of parental responsibility. Accordingly her Ladyship held that it was not in KM's interests to grant parental responsibility where the father 'would be highly likely to misuse it to lend weight to future interference in her care, thus continuing the stress on the mother and potentially undermining her ability to care properly for KM'. KM required a settled existence free from stress, particularly in light of her special needs.

A further example of concern about a father's likely interference is provided by the case of *Re P (Parental Responsibility)*.[449] In that case there was a very substantial disparity in the parties' ages: the mother was 26 and the father 78. The judge found that they had met and began having sexual intercourse when the mother was just 15 years old, the father having convinced her that if she had sexual intercourse with him she would be saved from the devil. They subsequently cohabited and had a daughter together. They separated when the child was four years old and the father continued to have extensive contact. The contact ceased, however, and only resumed as supervised contact at a contact centre, when the mother became aware that the father was in possession of a number of photographs of pre-pubescent children in obscene or suggestive poses, some of whom were his grandchildren. A psychological report on the father disclosed that he had difficulties with sexual boundaries. In addition, the father was very critical of the mother's care of the child, on many occasions reporting to social services his concerns, which were found to be without foundation. He made a groundless allegation that the mother's new cohabitant was sexually abusing the child and he had taken a video of the child supposedly disclosing the same. The father indicated in evidence that he would use parental responsibility to monitor the child's health and schooling and to approve, or disapprove, of babysitters to ensure that they were not paedophiles. The judge's decision to deny parental responsibility because it would be used to undermine the mother's care of the children was upheld by the Court of Appeal. The judge did not base the denial of parental responsibility upon any potential risk of sexual abuse which the father might pose to the child. However, the Court of Appeal considered the matter *obiter*. The court commented that the issues of contact and parental responsibility are not wholly irrelevant to each other and if the judge had relied upon the fact that the father posed a sufficient risk to the child in the future to necessitate the indefinite supervision of his contact, she would have been entitled to deny parental responsibility on that basis too. The court indicated that the judge would have had to ask herself: 'whether a man who had no understanding of sexual boundaries and who posed a risk to his daughter such that his contact to her had to be supervised for the indefinite future, was fit to have parental responsibility to his child'.

A final, and more recent, example is provided by *Re B (Role of Biological Father)*,[450] which might be contrasted with *Re D (Contact and Parental Responsibility: Lesbian Mothers and Known*

[449]  [1998] 2 FLR 96, CA.

[450]  [2007] EWHC 1952 (Fam) [2008] 1 FLR 1015. See also *R v E and F (Female Parents: Known Father)* [2010] EWHC 417 (Fam), [2010] 2 FLR 383 and S. Blain and A. Worwood, 'Alternative Families and Changing Perceptions of Parenthood' [2011] Family Law 289.

*Father*),[451] discussed in Section 6.1.3.7. In *Re B* lesbian civil partners, CV and S, had a child conceived through insemination of CV with the sperm of S's brother, TJ. Three months into the pregnancy the lesbian partners became estranged from the donor father. The father asserted that it was intended that he have a real, albeit limited, role. The lesbian partners had envisaged a more distant relationship. TJ applied for parental responsibility and contact, which the lesbian partners resisted.

Hedley J made no order with respect to the PRO application. His Lordship was concerned that TJ would seek to exercise parental responsibility forcefully to assert his views, which would undermine the lesbian parents' status. In these circumstances, in contrast to the decision in *Re D (Contact and Parental Responsibility: Lesbian Mothers and Known Father)*,[452] Hedley J could see no benefit of a restricted grant of parental responsibility. His Lordship granted contact four times a year (on one occasion at a family gathering), the purpose of which was not to allow the development of status or a relationship which would threaten the autonomy of CV and S. Hedley J explained that the contact order was made merely:

> so that without artificiality [the child] can picture TJ as someone significant but not ordinarily important in his life yet someone with whom (in time and if he so wishes) he can explore the implications of the kind man who enabled him to be and he can ask questions to satisfy his own natural curiosity.[453]

Thus in this case parental responsibility was denied to preserve the lesbian couple's autonomy in light of the risk of the father's interference, although a contact order was used to preserve some link and the child's knowledge of his father. In a subsequent case,[454] Hedley J used the concepts of principal and secondary parenting to describe the intended respective roles of the child's mother and her female partner, and the child's father and his male partner. However, in *A v B and another (Contact: Alternative Families)*[455] the Court of Appeal cautioned against the use of such concepts,[456] and also expressed concerns about the practice of referring to the child's father as a donor, since it may misleadingly give the impression that the father is giving his child away.[457] The Court of Appeal eschewed giving further general guidance on how to address parenting disputes in cases involving 'alternative families', emphasising that each case is fact-specific.[458]

In *JB v KS and E (Contact: Parental Responsibility)*[459] Hayden J expressed the hope that the word donor 'becomes extinct, in this context, in the lexicon of the family law reports'. His lordship could not 'easily contemplate any factual circumstance where its use is anything other than belittling and disrespectful to all concerned, most importantly the child'.[460]

In that case, the parents, a woman, who described herself as a 'gay lady', and a heterosexual man, met via a website connecting men with women who want a child but not a relationship. The man provided sperm for the woman's impregnation over a period when she struggled to conceive and also suffered a miscarriage. The arrangement never crystallised into a strict and tightly controlled plan as to future parenting roles, but as a result of their shared struggle to conceive a child they developed a close, non-sexual relationship. Eventually the woman fell pregnant and gave birth to a son. The father presented the relationship with the mother to his family and friends as a conventional heterosexual relationship and had been unable to remedy this misrepresentation. The mother agreed that the father should have contact with the child and a relationship had developed

---

[451] [2006] 1 FCR 556, FD (Black J).        [452] Ibid.

[453] *Re B (Role of Biological Father)* [2007] EWHC 1952 (Fam), [2008] 1 FLR 1015[2008] 1 FLR 1015 at [29].

[454] *ML v RW* [2011] EWHC 2455 (Fam) at [16].

[455] [2012] EWCA Civ 285, [2012] 1 FCR 510. See for comment, A. Zanghellini, '*A v B and C* [2012] EWCA Civ 285—Heteronormativity, Poly-parenting, and the Homo-nuclear Family' [2012] Child and Family Law Quarterly 475.

[456] [2012] EWCA Civ 285, at [30].        [457] Ibid, [48] and [49].

[458] Ibid, [23] and [39]. For research on lesbian mothers' perspectives, see L. Smith, 'Is Three a Crowd? Lesbian Mothers' Perspectives on Parental Status in Law' [2006] Child and Family Law Quarterly 231–52.

[459] [2015] EWHC 180 (Fam) [2015] 2 FLR 1180.        [460] Ibid, at [40].

between father and son. The father was not initially registered on the birth certificate, although following a declaration of parentage the birth was re-registered with the father's name.[461] However, this did not have the effect of conferring parental responsibility on the father,[462] and he now sought a PRO in respect of the boy, who was by then 4 years old. Hayden J noted that the 'theme that runs through the law in this area is that each case has ultimately to be looked at on its own individual facts', neither the High Court nor Court of Appeal providing 'guidance as to how to approach welfare issues such as 'parental responsibility' and 'contact' in families where children are conceived by adult arrangement outside sexual intercourse.'[463] His lordship was clear 'that it would be entirely wrong to approach this case as if [the boy] had been born in the context of a loving heterosexual relationship and determine any of the issues from that premise. But there was a relationship, it was respectful, it was inevitably intimate and it was enduring. This was not a brief commercial encounter, far from it.'[464] Hayden J found a number of key features of the case which pointed compellingly to the making of a PRO, including the parents' lengthy relationship, their capacity for cooperation based on core mutual respect, the intended and established relationship between father and child, the parent's agreement that the mother would be the primary carer, the father's financial support of the child, and the guardian's support for the making of the order.[465]

Leanne Smith,[466] writing on the position of known 'donors' in lesbian parenting arrangements, identifies a paradox:

> Excluding known donors from legal recognition through a system which recognises only two parents validates and protects lesbian families but also reinforces the dyadic parenting norm based on heterosexual reproduction. Conversely, giving legal recognition to multiple persons undermines the dyadic norm but reasserts heteronormativity by elevating the importance of genetic parentage and fathers.[467]

Accordingly, she suggests a compromise which recognises the donor but situates him in an expected hierarchy of parental relationships which recognises the narratives of lesbian parenting.[468] This would, at least as a guideline or starting point for judges, provide some principle and predictability in decision making.

### 6.1.3.9.2 The father's previous behaviour

The second broad category of case when parental responsibility may be denied is where the father's previous behaviour demonstrates the inappropriateness of his being granted parental responsibility.

In some cases, the father may have physically harmed the mother or child. In *Re T (A Minor) (Parental Responsibility: Contact)*[469] the mother was violently assaulted by the father when she was six months pregnant, requiring hospital attendance, which brought the relationship to an end. The father assaulted the mother again when he visited her at work and, following a dispute, headbutted the mother when she had the 7-month-old child in her arms. In addition, the father refused to return the child following contact sessions, including on one occasion for a period of nine days. The Court of Appeal dismissed the father's appeal against Ewbank J's decision to deny him parental

---

[461] Under Births and Deaths Registration Act 1953, s 14A.

[462] Because section 14A of the Births and Deaths Registration Act 1953 is not one of the enactments named in section 4 of the Children Act 1989 as conferring parental responsibility by birth registration.

[463] [2015] EWHC 180 (Fam), [2015] 2 FLR 1180, at [34], citing the 'helpful exegesis of the case law set out in *Re G (Shared Residence Order: Biological Mother of Donor Egg)* [2014] EWCA Civ 336, [2014] 2 FLR 897, per Black LJ.

[464] [2015] EWHC 180 (Fam), [2015] 2 FLR 1180, at [35].   [465] Ibid, at [39].

[466] L. Smith, 'Tangling the Web of Legal Parenthood: Legal Responses to the Use of Known Donors in Lesbian Parenting Arrangements' (2013) 33(3) Legal Studies 355.

[467] Ibid, 378.   [468] Ibid, 379.   [469] [1993] 2 FLR 450, CA.

responsibility, expressing the view that it was 'clearly the right decision'[470] in a case of 'cruel and callous behaviour in respect of a young child, with no thought for her welfare'.[471]

*In Re H (Parental Responsibility)*[472] the parents' relationship had broken down and the child spent Friday nights with his father. On return from one such visit, the child was considerably distressed and had a severe bruise and a scratch on his face. Subsequent medical examination disclosed that the child had several disturbing bruises on other parts of his body, including on his chest and trunk, inner and outer part of the ear, along the shaft of his penis, and on his scrotum. The father denied that he had caused the injuries and he subsequently applied for contact and parental responsibility. The father could demonstrate commitment to the child, the child was attached to him, and he had genuine reasons for fostering the relationship, and since the child's injuries had been discovered the child had continued to enjoy excellent supervised contact with the father. The judge, however, concluded that contact should continue to be supervised, and held that on all the facts the father was not suitable to hold parental responsibility. He concluded that, contrary to the father's denial, the father had injured the child[473] and also found, with the support of expert evidence, that some of the child's injuries were characteristic of not just over chastisement or a moment of frustration or anger but connoted something more sinister, in the nature of deliberate cruelty and possibly sadistic abuse. The father's appeal to the Court of Appeal was dismissed. The court commented that 'the judge was fully justified in deciding that a man who behaved like that to his son and made no attempt to come to terms with what he had done, was not fit to have parental responsibility for the child' and explained that:

> the appropriateness of the order has to be considered on the particular facts of each individual case. If, reviewing all the circumstances, the judge considers that there are factors adverse to the father sufficient to tip the balance against the order proposed, it would not be right to make the order, even though the three [*Re H* criteria] can be shown by the father.[474]

A father might demonstrate irresponsibility in other ways. In *Re P (Parental Responsibility)*[475] the two children had been born when their father was serving a term of 15 years' imprisonment for robbery. The father played little or no part in the children's lives, apart from having contact with them during the time that he had been in prison. Having returned to the family on a home visit, he spent his time committing another robbery for which he was sentenced to a further term of 15 years' imprisonment. The judge declined to make a PRO. Refusing the father's appeal, the Court of Appeal held that the judge's decision could not be said to be plainly wrong. The court explained that a prisoner does not lose his personal rights when sentenced to imprisonment except insofar as his imprisonment makes this necessary, and is entitled to apply for parental responsibility. However, as Lord Woolf MR explained:

> If a parent behaves in a manner which he should appreciate can, and is likely to, result in his being sentenced for a long period of imprisonment, he should be taken to realise that this has a damaging effect on his children. It is an act of irresponsibility on his part towards his children. When, as here, you have a pattern of criminal conduct, the court is entitled to take into account as a relevant factor,

---

[470] Ibid, 457.     [471] Ibid, 456.     [472] [1998] 1 FLR 855, CA.

[473] In reaching this conclusion, the judge had evidence that the father had previously been cautioned by the police for striking another two-year-old child heavily in the face.

[474] [1998] 1 FLR 855, CA at 860.

[475] [1997] 2 FLR 722, CA. See also the obiter comments of Ward LJ at 726E–F, providing further examples of factors which could be weighed against a father as demonstrating that he had devalued his responsibility: a father who for selfish or misguided reasons chose to abandon his family to work abroad or broke up the family through reckless acts of drunkenness.

not a conclusive factor, that conduct in deciding whether or not it is appropriate to grant that parent parental responsibility.[476]

A mother's reaction to the father's previous behaviour can also be a reason for denying parental responsibility. In *Re L (Contact: Genuine Fear)*[477] the mother had an intense fear of the father, who when much younger had been a 'Hell's Angel' with a violent past. The mother's fear arose principally from her knowledge that previously the father had been convicted of stabbing his wife and her solicitor in the Royal Courts of Justice, and stabbing his wife's boyfriend on another occasion. At the time of the hearing, however, the father had not been convicted of any offence for 15 years. Because of the mother's phobia of the father (as the judge described it), the father only had indirect contact with the child. There was no contact at all with the mother and the father did not know where the child lived or went to school. In these circumstances, Bruce Blair QC, sitting as a Deputy High Court Judge, concluded[478] that, while parental responsibility can be regarded as 'a status carrying with it rights in waiting',[479] the chance of the father having any meaningful say in the child's life was 'wholly imaginary rather than real'. It would 'barely, in practice, confer a status' and would cause additional distress to the mother which could be communicated to the child. Accordingly, the judge made no order as to parental responsibility.

## 6.2 Should unmarried fathers be afforded equal treatment?

Should the law give parental responsibility automatically to all fathers irrespective of marital status? The debate surrounding this issue is a complex one, with several different strands.

### 6.2.1 Human rights arguments

In *Re Z (Children)*[480] the Court of Appeal held that it was inapt that a father's argument that the current law is discriminatory should be developed, 'the most obvious reason [being] that it has already been considered and rejected in the European Court of Human Rights in the case of *B v United Kingdom*'.[481] In *B v UK*[482] the unmarried parents of a child separated and the mother, who was Italian, relocated to Italy taking the child with her. The English courts held that the removal of the child from the jurisdiction was not unlawful as the mother had sole parental responsibility, and therefore the father's consent to removal was not required. Furthermore, his application to have the child returned was dismissed. The father complained of a breach of Articles 8 and 14 of the ECHR in that his right to respect for family life was not protected in the same way as a married father. The complaint was declared inadmissible on the basis of 'an objective and reasonable justification for the difference of treatment', namely the range of possible relationships between children and unmarried fathers which vary 'from ignorance and indifference to a close stable relationship indistinguishable from the conventional family-based unit'.[483]

However, the court's reasoning in *B v UK* was scant and several arguments can be mounted against it. First, there is no obvious link between marriage and the range of different unmarried fathers and thus it is very difficult to see the latter as an objective and reasonable justification for the use of the former to discriminate. The connection between parental responsibility and marriage might be defended on the basis of seeking to encourage parents to marry and thus to bring up children in a relationship which is regarded as generally more stable than cohabitation. However, marriage is not necessarily an indicator of the quality of a parent/child relationship. Furthermore, there is a difficulty for the man who wishes to marry but his partner does not. The Scottish Law

---

[476] Ibid, 728.  [477] [2002] 1 FLR 621, FD.  [478] Ibid, [49]–[53].

[479] See *Re C (Minors) (Parental Rights)* [1992] 1 FLR 1, CA.  [480] [2008] EWCA Civ 1556.

[481] Ibid, [15].  [482] [2000] 1 FLR 1.

[483] For a similar conclusion on the law in Scotland, see *McMichael v UK* (1995) 20 EHRR 205, and the excellent analysis by G. Branchflower, 'Parental Responsibility and Human Rights' [1999] Family Law 34.

Commission did not accept the link with marriage in this context, noting a situation, which it doubted was in line with current social thinking, whereby:

> a man who abandoned his wife when she was pregnant, and never saw his child, would have full parental responsibilities and rights, whereas a man who was cohabiting with the mother of his child and playing a full paternal role would have none.[484]

Furthermore, in *Marckx v Belgium*[485] the European Court of Human Rights held that Belgian law breached an unmarried mother's right to respect for family life in its requirement that she undergo a process of formal recognition as the child's mother and thus its failure to recognise a legal relationship between the mother and child from the moment of birth. It is difficult to see why the same reasoning should not apply in the case of a man whose paternity has been established, for example through DNA testing.[486] Moreover, the *Marckx* case made clear that its ruling was not dependent on a wish to take care of the child, as the Court commented that 'it may happen that also a married mother might not wish to bring up her child, and yet, as far as she is concerned, the birth alone will have created the bond of affiliation'.[487] In *Marckx* the Court also found that the child's Article 14 right to enjoy the rights under the Convention free from discrimination had been breached when taken in conjunction with Article 8. This presumably would afford a child of an unmarried father scope to argue that his or her human rights are breached by being treated differently from a similar child whose parents are married. As Andrew Bainham has pointed out, the European Court of Human Rights in *Johnston v Republic of Ireland*[488] appears to have recognised that 'parents and children have *mutual* rights to respect for their family life'.[489] He argues, therefore, that it follows that discrimination against the child represents discrimination against the father, and vice versa.[490]

### 6.2.2 Unmeritorious fathers and potentially negative exercise of parental responsibility

As the Strasbourg case law shows, the arguments against giving all fathers parental responsibility automatically have tended to focus on the fact that unmarried fathers inhabit a spectrum, and on the potentially negative exercise of parental responsibility[491] by some unmarried fathers.[492] However, this argument has been rendered very weak now by case law which indicates that parental responsibility does not give a father power to interfere in the resident parent's day-to-day care of the child, and which characterises parental responsibility as a status, and as one which can be

---

[484]  Scottish Law Commission, *Report on Family Law* (Scot Law Com No 135, 1992), para 2.36.

[485]  (1979–80) 2 EHRR 14. For detailed discussion of this case and its impact, see W. Pintens and J. M. Scherpe, 'The *Marckx* Case: A "Whole Code of Family Law"?' in S. Gilmore, J. Herring, and R. Probert (eds), *Landmark Cases in Family Law* (Oxford: Hart, 2011), p 155.

[486]  G. Branchflower, 'Parental Responsibility and Human Rights' [1999] Family Law 34; A. Bainham, 'When is a Parent Not a Parent? Reflections on the Unmarried Father and His Child in English Law' (1989) 3 International Journal of Law, Policy and the Family 208–39 at 212.

[487]  *Marckx* at para 39, a point made by Branchflower, 'Parental Responsibility and Human Rights'.

[488]  (1986) 9 EHRR 203.

[489]  A. Bainham, 'When is a Parent Not a Parent? Reflections on the Unmarried Father and His Child in English Law' (1989) 3 International Journal of Law, Policy and the Family 208–39 at 215.

[490]  Compare S. Sheldon, 'Unmarried Fathers and Parental Responsibility: A Case for Reform?' (2001) 9 Feminist Legal Studies 93 at 106–7.

[491]  Whether parental responsibility can be exercised negatively is debatable since at least in the view of the House of Lords in *Gillick v West Norfolk and Wisbech AHA* [1986] AC 112, parental rights exist for the benefit of the child and are exercisable only insofar as they are necessary for the child's protection.

[492]  Commentators have observed the English Law Commission's 'apparent willingness to equate the psychological needs of unmarried mothers with the best interests of their children': see A. Bainham, 'When is a Parent Not a Parent? Reflections on the Unmarried Father and His Child in English Law' (1989) 3 International Journal of Law, Policy and the Family 208–39 at 231. P. Townsend and A. Baker, 'Unmarried Fathers—Are We Ending Discrimination at Last?' (1998) 162(13) Justice of the Peace 236. See also Scottish Law Commission No 135, at para 2.40.

hedged with conditions that can degrade it to almost nothing.[493] Furthermore, as Wilson J pointed out in *Re P (A Minor) (Parental Responsibility Order)*[494] one does not need parental responsibility to cause disturbance if minded to do so.[495]

The Law Commission cited the dramatic example of a rapist automatically gaining parental responsibility,[496] which, while likely to elicit an emotive response, is a dubious example on which to draw to inform a general policy. As Barton has observed, drawing on Painter's research on the incidence of rape within marriage,[497] 'the vast majority of rapine children are legitimate'.[498] Furthermore, the rapist might be dealt with by way of an exception,[499] although the practical and emotional difficulties for the mother of proving such an exception should not be underestimated.

It might also be said that if the fact that a man is unmeritorious is a valid basis for denying a father rights in relation to his child, should that basis not apply to all fathers irrespective of marital status?[500] It could be argued that all parents should initially have parental responsibility, which should be revocable where it is inappropriate for the holder to have it.[501] The debate has centred, however, on the unmeritorious unmarried father, with little discussion of the potential also for unmeritorious mothers or unmeritorious married fathers. This prompts the question whether there is anything per se about motherhood or married fatherhood, which would justify different treatment of unmarried fathers.

### 6.2.3 Are unmarried fathers less worthy than mothers?

There are strong arguments in favour of according parental responsibility automatically to all mothers: the physical nurture of the child during pregnancy, and (usually) ensuing attachment, together with the fact that nature delivers the child into the mother's care. Moreover, as Sheldon points out, it is 'somewhat easier to generalise about unmarried mothers' in that 'most unmarried mothers *are* assuming an active parenting role'.[502] However, fathers can be heavily committed at the pre-natal stage and it is not only fathers' parenting abilities and commitments to their children that vary. Consider, for example, the case of a mother who abuses drugs and/or alcohol, damaging her foetus, and who is unable to care appropriately for her child.[503] She will still obtain parental responsibility automatically and cannot have it removed except by way of her child's adoption. Furthermore, as the child grows older, arguments about the mother's role in pregnancy must surely

---

[493] See H. Reece, 'The Degradation of Parental Responsibility' in R. Probert, S. Gilmore, and J. Herring (eds), *Responsible Parents and Parental Responsibility* (Oxford: Hart, 2009). Of course, the point cuts both ways: it might be said that if possession of parental responsibility makes little difference in practice, the unmarried father does not really need it.

[494] [1994] 1 FLR 578, FD (Wilson J).

[495] And as Eekelaar has pointed out, the father might equally be vulnerable to harassment on the part of the mother: J. Eekelaar, 'Second Thoughts on Illegitimacy Reform' [1985] Family Law 261.

[496] Described as an 'extreme and no doubt unrealistic example' (Law Com WP No 74, 1979, para 3.9).

[497] K. Painter, *Wife Rape, Marriage and the Law—Survey Report: Key Findings and Recommendations* (Manchester: Faculty of Economic and Social Studies, University of Manchester, 1991).

[498] C. Barton, 'Equal Responsibility for all Fathers?' (1998) 142(17) Solicitors Journal 401.

[499] Although the Law Commission concluded that, given the availability of abortion, such a man was likely to be 'statistically insignificant' so as not to merit special provision to exclude him as an unmeritorious father (para 4.30).

[500] See generally J. M. Scherpe, 'Establishing and Ending Parental Responsibility: A Comparative View' in R. Probert, S. Gilmore, and J. Herring (eds), *Responsible Parents and Parental Responsibility* (Oxford: Hart, 2009).

[501] See ibid for comparative discussion. See also H. Conway, 'Parental Responsibility and the Unmarried Father' (1996) 146 New Law Journal 782.

[502] S. Sheldon, 'Unmarried Fathers and Parental Responsibility: A Case For Reform?' (2001) 9 Feminist Legal Studies 93 at 112.

[503] It might also be said that except in the limited period and circumstances in which a lawful abortion is permitted, the mother's connection with the child during pregnancy is the imposed consequence of conception, rather than evidence of commitment to her child based on choice.

decline in significance, yet the discrimination against the unmarried father extends beyond the child's infancy, throughout the child's life.[504]

The debate about similarities or differences between mothers and fathers has been made more complex by the Gender Recognition Act 2004, which allows a person to change his or her gender. It is now possible for a person to be the mother of one child and the father of another. In such a case, the same unmarried person would have automatic parental responsibility *qua* mother in relation to one child, but *qua* father would have to acquire it in accordance with the provisions of the Children Act 1989. While, of course, this is simply the consequence of applying section 2 of the Children Act 1989 to an admittedly unusual case, there is perhaps something rather revealing about the fact that the law here treats the same person differently according to his or her gender.[505]

### 6.2.4 Should the law reflect social change and attitudes?

An argument in favour of according parental responsibility automatically to all fathers is based on social change as evidenced by statistics which show an increasing proportion of births outside marriage to parents in cohabiting relationships.[506] In England and Wales in 2007 there were 690,013 live births, of which 305,550 were outside marriage.[507] A further argument is based on the perceptions of such parents. Research by Ros Pickford[508] found that three-quarters of a random sample of unmarried fathers were unaware that there is a difference in legal status between unmarried and married fathers. Almost all 'expressed great surprise, and many were very annoyed or angry'[509] when informed that they did not have parental responsibility. The fathers' views of the law were based upon their assumption 'that marriage is not a relevant criterion for distinguishing fathers in terms of the legal rights' which 'derived from cultural beliefs such as in the existence of "common-law" marriage, or from their experience of other areas of law such as child support',[510] in which every father is liable to maintain his child.

Indeed it has been argued that if all fathers have financial support responsibilities to their children they should also be accorded other responsibilities.[511] By contrast, however, concerns have been expressed that linking child support and parental responsibility may commodify children.[512] In addition, it might be argued that mere biological connection should not found a duty of child support.[513]

---

[504] An observation made in a different context by the Constitutional Court of South Africa in *Fraser v Children's Court Pretoria North and Others* (CCT31/96) [1997] ZACC 1, 1996 (8) BCLR 1085, 1997 (2) SA 218.

[505] S. Gilmore, 'The Gender Recognition Act 2004' [2004] Family Law 741 at 744.

[506] The English Law Commission arguably attached excessive weight to parents' formal legal relationships when the tide was moving (and has been since) towards greater recognition of *de facto* relationships: see R. Ingleby, 'Law Commission No 118: Illegitimacy' (1984) Journal of Social Welfare Law 170–4. This may be attributable to the Commission's goal of not debasing the institution of marriage (para 4.39).

[507] *Review of the National Statistician on Births and Patterns of Family Building in England and Wales, 2007* (ONS, 2008).

[508] R. Pickford, *Fathers, Marriage and the Law* (London: Family Policy Studies Centre for the Joseph Rowntree Foundation, 1999); and for a discussion, see R. Pickford, 'Unmarried Fathers and the Law' in A. Bainham, S. Day Sclater, and M. Richards, *What is a Parent? A Socio-Legal Analysis* (Oxford: Hart, 1999), pp 143–59. See also I. Dey and F. Wasoff, 'Mixed Messages: Parental Responsibilities, Public Opinion and the Reforms of Family Law' (2006) 20 International Journal of Law, Policy and the Family 225, who report figures from the Scottish Social Attitudes Survey showing that, in 2004, 34 per cent of respondents said unmarried fathers had the same rights as married fathers (with 13 per cent 'don't knows').

[509] R. Pickford, 'Unmarried Fathers and the Law', p 149.     [510] Ibid, p 146.

[511] See, eg H. Conway, 'Parental Responsibility and the Unmarried Father' (1996) 146 New Law Journal 782.

[512] See S. Sheldon, 'Unmarried Fathers and Parental Responsibility: A Case for Reform?' (2001) 9 Feminist Legal Studies 93 at 107.

[513] Whether such a view is in children's general interests or would be politically acceptable is debatable.

### 6.2.5  Does the current law encourage irresponsibility?

It may also be argued that the perception of unmarried fathers as prima facie not worthy of parental responsibility does little to encourage them to play an active and responsible role in their children's lives.[514] Indeed, the real discrimination may lie in the fact that all mothers are required to accept their parental responsibility yet all fathers are not. As Bainham has pointed out, if the unmarried father represents a problem, it may be one of '*indifference* rather than interference'.[515] However, Sheldon has observed that the idea that granting parental responsibility will encourage more men to take responsibility for their children lacks empirical support, and comments that:

> On balance, it seems rather improbable that a status of which the vast majority of the population has remained demonstrably in ignorance, which accords limited advantages and which gives no right to contact with children is likely to have much influence on men's commitment towards parenting.[516]

### 6.2.6  Should parental responsibility follow active parenting?

Ruth Deech has argued that a father's claim to parental rights lies in his active involvement in the child's life,[517] making a distinction between the absent father (even one who cares *about* his child) and the father who cares *for* his child. She argues that only 'the father who offers the child a home to the best of his ability should have any authority over the child' and suggests that the question should be not be 'does the absent unmarried father have too few rights, but does he have too few responsibilities'.

---

**Talking point**

Deech argues that:

> Fatherhood that does not encompass a fair share of [the day-to-day practical parenting tasks] is an empty egotistical concept and has the consequences that the man does not know the child sufficiently well to be able sensibly to take decisions about education, religion, discipline, medical treatment, change of abode, adoption, marriage and property. Therefore the absent unmarried father, as contrasted with the cohabiting father, should not automatically be entitled to these rights.[518]

**Q.** Do you agree? Can this view be reconciled with Ward LJ's opinion that conferring parental responsibility aids the child's self-esteem?

---

She concedes, however, that criticism of absent fathers is 'to recognise, not to decry, the importance of a father's involvement',[519] and admits that her argument concerning parental involvement

---

[514] The Scottish Law Commission commented that the law 'may be seen as encouraging irresponsibility in some men' (at para 2.37). '[T]hat is no reason for the law to encourage and reinforce an irresponsible attitude' (at para 2.39).

[515] A. Bainham, 'When is a Parent Not a Parent? Reflections on the Unmarried Father and His Child in English Law' (1989) 3 International Journal of Law, Policy and the Family 208–39 at 231.

[516] S. Sheldon, 'Unmarried Fathers and Parental Responsibility: A Case for Reform?' (2001) 9 Feminist Legal Studies 93 at 108.

[517] R. Deech, 'The Unmarried Father and Human Rights' (1992) 4 Journal of Child Law 3. See also S. Sheldon, 'Unmarried Fathers and Parental Responsibility: A Case for Reform?' (2001) 9 Feminist Legal Studies 93 at 114–15; chapters by C. Smart and M. L. Fineman in C. Smart and S. Sevenhuijsen (eds), *Child Custody and the Politics of Gender* (London: Routledge, 1989); J. Wallbank, 'Clause 106 of the Adoption and Children Bill' (2002) Legal Studies 276 at 295.

[518] R. Deech, 'The Unmarried Father and Human Rights' (1992) 4 Journal of Child Law 3 at 8.

[519] Ibid, at 8.

could apply equally to the absent married father and the absent unmarried mother.[520] In contrast to Deech's position, however, it may be argued that cohabitation is not necessarily an indicator of commitment to a child. Indeed, in some situations the most committed thing a father might do is to withdraw from the family home. Furthermore, a father's absence from the home does not necessarily preclude his taking decisions if apprised of relevant facts/information. Undoubtedly, a caring parent's close involvement with the child could arguably obscure clear judgement whereas absence might produce a more detached (objective) decision.

### 6.2.7 The child's right to dual parenting?

Linked to this is an argument that focuses on the child's right to have the input of both parents. It might be argued, however, that providing another adult with decision-making powers in relation to the child does not necessarily promote the child's rights.[521]

### 6.2.8 The case law on parental responsibility orders

A further argument in favour of according parental responsibility automatically to all fathers relates to the case law on applications for a PRO. First, most applications are successful,[522] begging the question whether it would be more cost-effective to require mothers in the rare remaining cases to apply to divest a father of his parental responsibility. It might be argued, however, that such an approach ignores the issue of the delay which will occur while legal proceedings are taken, fails to give weight to the potential for disruption of the child's upbringing, and is also open to the more profound objection that it makes too many assumptions about the efficacy of legal proceedings in dealing with family conflict.

    Secondly, Gilmore, in a critical analysis of the case law,[523] has identified a number of anomalies and inconsistencies in the case law, and on occasions a rigid application of the *Re H* criteria, working to the injustice of some fathers (eg requiring proof of attachment in circumstances where the mother's behaviour has prevented attachment). In addition he has pointed out that the courts' requirement that the father demonstrate positive criteria such as commitment and attachment is out of line with the policy debate which informed the PRO, where the concern was not that fathers should have to show that they are meritorious, but that the unmeritorious father was excluded. Gilmore argues that this judicial failure to articulate clear, consistent, and just principles, which reflect the relevant policy background, may add further impetus to the call for allocation of parental responsibility to all fathers irrespective of marital status.

### 6.2.9 Certainty

Perhaps the strongest argument in favour of retaining the current position is certainty. Currently, there is documentary evidence that a holder of parental responsibility has parental responsibility: a marriage certificate; a birth certificate; or some court record of agreement or order. If all fathers had parental responsibility by reason of legal parenthood, the only way of knowing whether an unmarried father had parental responsibility would be to ascertain paternity.[524]

---

[520]  Deech (ibid) goes on to maintain that as long as marriage remains as a status, 'then a logical distinction has to remain between the unmarried father and the married father'. At this point her argument becomes difficult to defend, for it contends that a distinction should be maintained between parents based on marital status, but ultimately argues for a position which eschews such status as the criterion for attributing parental responsibility; and, while arguing for a non-discriminatory approach, it endorses the distinction between married and unmarried fathers, which discriminates in its general assumption that marital fathers *are*, and non-marital fathers *are not*, caring parents.

[521]  Ibid.

[522]  In 2010 there were 5,520 orders made in 5,980 disposals: see Ministry of Justice, *Judicial and Court Statistics 2010*, Table 2.4.

[523]  S. Gilmore, 'Parental Responsibility and the Unmarried Father—A New Dimension to the Debate' [2003] Child and Family Law Quarterly 21.

[524]  R. Pickford, 'Unmarried Fathers and the Law' in A. Bainham, S. Day Sclater, and M. Richards, *What is a Parent? A Socio-Legal Analysis* (Oxford: Hart, 1999), p 154.

### 6.2.10 The need for ongoing evaluation of the arguments

One final criticism that can be made of the law in this area relates to the manner of its incremental development. When the Lord Chancellor's Department consulted in 1998, the current legal position was taken as the starting point. While account was taken of social change, there was no attempt to re-evaluate the soundness or otherwise of the Law Commission's *arguments* in light of the subsequent views of the Scottish Law Commission, academic commentary, social change, or the developing case law on PROs. For example, the Law Commission's argument that automatic parental responsibility would discourage mothers from identifying the child's father is now dated, since the law now connects acquisition of parental responsibility to birth registration, and the law's new policy is that joint birth registration should be the norm.[525]

The increased methods by which the unmarried father can acquire parental responsibility and the declining proportion of fathers who consequently will not have it may have a dampening effect on any appetite for further change. In such a climate it is easy to lose sight of the fact that recent changes do not fully eradicate discrimination against unmarried fathers. The arguments are well known to commentators who have followed the law's development, and it is easy to portray this debate as a series of well-worn arguments both for and against the current position, which are fairly evenly balanced.[526] It is possible, however, that what has been missing from recent policy debate is ongoing *evaluation* of the arguments.

## 6.3 Acquisition of parental responsibility by a female parent

Section 4ZA of the Children Act 1989 provides that a parent (other than the child's mother) who acquires legal parenthood under section 43 of the HFEA 2008 may acquire parental responsibility in similar ways to the unmarried father, as discussed earlier: through birth registration,[527] a formal parental responsibility agreement, or a PRO. Whether the courts will adopt similar principles to those established in relation to unmarried fathers remains to be seen, although it is possible that a more liberal approach may be adopted, given that the female parent will necessarily have embarked upon a formal process to acquire legal parenthood.

## 6.4 Acquisition of parental responsibility by a step-parent

Section 4A of the Children Act 1989 provides a method by which a step-parent (defined as the spouse or civil partner[528] of the child's parent) can acquire parental responsibility. For the provision to apply, the child's parent (who is the step-parent's partner) must have parental responsibility for the child.[529] The parent and step-parent couple can agree that the step-parent shall have parental responsibility although if the child's other parent also has parental responsibility the agreement of both parents is required.[530] Such an agreement is a parental responsibility agreement in the same way as an agreement under section 4(1)(b), discussed in Section 6.1.2, and the same formalities apply in order to give effect to it. In addition, a court may, on the application of the step-parent, provide for the step-parent to have parental responsibility for the child.[531] In *Re R (Parental*

---

[525] Welfare Reform Act 2009, Sch 6; Department for Work and Pensions, *Joint Birth Registration: Recording Responsibility* (Cm 7293, June 2008), and the preceding Green Paper *Joint Birth Registration: Promoting Parental Responsibility* (Cm 7160).

[526] See eg J. Herring, *Family Law*, 4th edn (London: Pearson, 2009).

[527] There were 22 registrations in 2009 and 335 in 2010: 'Live Births in England and Wales by Characteristics of Mother 2010' (ONS, 2011).

[528] As amended by the Civil Partnership Act 2004, s 75(2).

[529] See *Re A and B (Parental Order: Domicile)* [2013] EWHC 426 (Fam) at [16], a case in which an order was erroneously made under s 4A because it failed to comply with the requirement that the parent have parental responsibility.

[530] Children Act 1989, s 4A(1)(a).     [531] Ibid, s 4A(1)(b).

*Responsibility)*[532] a child had been brought up by his mother and her husband for nearly three years, the husband believing the child to be his. However, it transpired that the child had been fathered by another man and the husband and the mother were now divorcing. The husband sought parental responsibility under section 4A(1)(b). Peter Jackson J declined the application holding that 'in normal circumstances the beneficiary of such an order will be a person who might be described as an incoming step-parent who wishes to bring up a child together with the parent with parental responsibility and will be centrally participating in the upbringing of the child in future', and that 'the other situations in which an order might be made are likely to be limited'.[533] His Lordship noted that it was only by chance that the power in section 4A existed at all, as it would not do so if the couple were already divorced.

## 6.5 **Further methods of acquiring parental responsibility**

So far we have been exploring the methods of acquiring parental responsibility which are reserved to a child's parent or step-parent. There are several other ways of acquiring parental responsibility which are open to a wider range of persons and which, in some cases, also provide additional methods by which a parent can acquire parental responsibility.

### 6.5.1 **Parental responsibility conferred by a child arrangements order**

A child arrangements order is an order in section 8 of the Children Act 1989, which *inter alia* allows the court to settle the arrangements as to the person or persons with whom a child lives. It makes sense that the person who is caring for the child should have all the rights, duties, powers, and authority which are seen as necessary to provide for a child's upbringing.

In the case of a successful application with respect to the child's living arrangements by the child's father, or a parent by virtue of section 43 of the HFEA 2008, section 12(1) provides that the order be accompanied by a PRO in that person's favour. Section 12(1A) provides that where such a person is named in the child arrangements order as a person with whom the child is to spend time or otherwise have contact, but not as a person with whom the child is to live, the court must decide whether it would be appropriate to make a PRO. In each case the PRO cannot be revoked during the currency of the child arrangements order[534] and even if the order is subsequently brought to an end the parent retains his or her PRO.

Section 12(2) and (2A) make similar provision to section 12(1) and (1A) with respect to applicants who are not parents. In such cases, the child arrangements order confers parental responsibility during the currency of the order. If the order is subsequently revoked parental responsibility is lost. Section 12(3) provides that the parental responsibility conferred by section 12(2) or section 12(2A) does not confer the right to agree, or refuse to agree, to the making of an adoption order or an order under section 84 of the Adoption and Children Act 2002, nor the right to appoint a guardian for the child.

The law relating to the application for, and making of, child arrangements orders is dealt with in detail in Chapter 9.

### 6.5.2 **Parental responsibility conferred in child protection proceedings**

Sometimes the parental care provided for a child may fall below that which can reasonably be expected, and the state may need to intervene to care and protect the child. Some of the court orders

---

[532]  [2011] EWHC 1535 (Fam), [2011] 2 FLR 1132.

[533]  See, however, also *Re S (Relocation: Parental Responsibility)* [2013] EWHC 1295 (Fam), [2013] 2 FLR 1453, [2013] 2 FLR 1453 at [63], reiterating this view, but also acknowledging that the power to confer parental responsibility is a flexible one and what is important is what is in the child's best interests for the future.

[534]  Children Act 1989, s 12(4).

which can be obtained in that context confer parental responsibility upon the applicant, usually the local authority (eg an emergency protection order or a care order).[535] These orders and their effects are discussed in detail in Chapter 10.

### 6.5.3 Adoption

When an adoption order is made under the Adoption and Children Act 2002, the legal parenthood and parental responsibility of the child's (previous) parents is extinguished and acquired by the adoptive parent or parents.[536] The law on adoption is discussed in more detail in Chapter 11.

### 6.5.4 Special guardianship

A means of providing some security in the relationship between a child and his or her substitute carer, without the full family transplant effect of adoption, is by way of a special guardianship order (SGO).[537] This order, which can be made in private law or public law proceedings, provides the successful applicant with a parental responsibility which may be exercised exclusively by the special guardian(s). The parental responsibility of others, while not extinguished, cannot be exercised while the SGO is in force, and some restrictions are placed on the ability of parents to apply to court in respect of the child. The law on special guardianship, including case law guidance on how the courts decide between the making of a SGO or an adoption order, is discussed in detail in Chapter 11.

### 6.5.5 Appointment of a guardian

In contrast to special guardianship, guardianship under section 5 of the Children Act 1989 is concerned with providing the child with a person with parental responsibility[538] in the event of the death of a person or persons who had parental responsibility for the child. A guardian may only be appointed in accordance with the provisions of section 5,[539] which provides that the appointment may be made by a court or by certain individuals.

A court may, by order, appoint a guardian for the child, either of its own motion in family proceedings or upon application by an individual.[540] The court can make the guardianship order if the child has no parent with parental responsibility for him or her, if the child's only or last surviving special guardian has died, or if the child's parent, guardian, or special guardian who was named in a child arrangements order as a person with whom the child was to live, has died while the order was in force.[541] Such an appointment may have an advantage over a child arrangements order in a case where a child has been orphaned, because a guardian obtains greater powers. The guardian can in turn appoint a guardian for the child, and the guardian's agreement to the child's adoption is required.

The individuals[542] who may appoint a guardian are a parent who has parental responsibility for the child, a child's guardian, or a child's special guardian. The appointment can be achieved in a relatively informal manner: it can be made by deed or will, but it is also sufficient if it is simply 'made in writing, is dated and is signed by the person[543] making the appointment'.[544]

---

[535] See ibid, ss 44(5) and 33.    [536] Adoption and Children Act 2002, ss 46 and 67.

[537] Children Act 1989, ss 14A–14F.

[538] By s 5(6), a person appointed as a guardian has parental responsibility for the child.

[539] Children Act 1989, s 5(13).

[540] Ibid, s 5(1) and (2). As noted earlier, a local authority cannot appoint a guardian.

[541] Ibid, s 5(1). Provided that any surviving parent did not also have that 'residence order' made in his or her favour: see ibid, s 5(9).

[542] Who may act alone or jointly: see ibid, s 5(10).

[543] Or signed at the direction of such person in the presence of two witnesses who each attest the signature.

[544] Children Act 1989, s 5(5). The appointment is not effective unless these requirements are fulfilled.

### 6.5.5.1 When does the individual's appointment of a guardian take effect?

A guardian's appointment does not take effect unless both parents with parental responsibility have died,[545] or unless, immediately before the death of the person making the appointment, a child arrangements order in favour of the deceased was still in force in which that person was named as a person with whom the child was to live,[546] and such an order was not also made in favour of a surviving parent,[547] or unless the person making the appointment was the child's only (or last surviving) special guardian.

The general policy, therefore, is that where the parents are living with the child together in harmony, appointment of a guardian should only take effect when both parents die. The effect is to preclude any sharing of parental responsibility with the guardian appointed by the deceased parent. It is an approach which might not necessarily be welcomed by all parents, given that the benefits and burdens of bringing up children are often easier to manage when the task is shared. The Law Commission, however, when recommending that the law be changed from the common law position under which the testamentary guardianship took effect from death, was influenced (perhaps unduly so) by the notion that the deceased spouse was seeking to rule the other from the grave.[548]

Where the parents are estranged, each may be less content with the notion that the surviving parent will have sole responsibility for the child's upbringing, and they may wish to appoint a guardian to have parental responsibility in conjunction with the survivor. This may be particularly likely where a parent anticipates his or her premature death and wants a relative to have care of his or her children; or where a parent has remarried and wants the new spouse to be the child's guardian. In such a case, the appointment will only take immediate effect if the deceased spouse had a sole child arrangements order dealing with the child's residence, prior to his or her death. In some cases the child may no longer be living with his parents, being cared for by a special guardian. In such a case, the law permits an only or last surviving special guardian to make an appointment which takes immediate effect upon his or her death. In such cases, parental responsibility is shared by the guardian with any surviving person who has parental responsibility.

Appointment of a guardian revokes any earlier appointment unless the intention is to appoint an additional guardian.[549] An appointment can also be revoked expressly in writing[550] or by deliberate destruction of the instrument which created it.[551] An appointment in favour of a spouse or civil partner is revoked by subsequent divorce/dissolution or annulment of that relationship unless the appointment shows a contrary intention.[552]

## 7 Duration of parental responsibility

Parental responsibility within the Children Act 1989 is defined *in relation to the child*. As 'child' is defined for the purpose of the Act as a person under the age of 18,[553] 'parental responsibility' within the meaning of the Children Act 1989 ends when a child attains 18. In the case of parental responsibility allocated automatically by operation of law, parental responsibility continues until the child's majority and cannot be removed except by way of adoption or a parental order. Parental responsibility conferred by an emergency protection order, SGO, care order, or on a non-parent by way of a child arrangements order, exists only during the currency of the order and will come to an end if, for example, the order is discharged or expires. Parental responsibility conferred by birth registration, parental responsibility agreement, or PRO only ceases if a court so orders[554] upon the

---

[545] Ibid, s 5(7)(a).    [546] Ibid, s 5(7)(b).    [547] Ibid, s 5(9).    [548] Law Com No 172, para 2.27.
[549] Children Act 1989, s 6(1).    [550] Ibid, s 6(2).    [551] Ibid, s 6(3).    [552] Ibid, s 6(3A) and (3B).
[553] Ibid, s 105.    [554] Ibid, ss 4(2A), 4ZA(5), and 4A(3).

application of any person who has parental responsibility for the child or, with leave of the court, of the child himself or herself.[555]

# 8 Removal of parental responsibility

Cases involving applications for the removal of parental responsibility are rare. In *Re P (Terminating Parental Responsibility)*[556] Singer J provided some guidance on their disposal which has been approved by the Court of Appeal. In that case the child had been admitted to hospital aged 9 weeks with a skull fracture which had left her permanently physically and mentally disabled. Evidence showed that she had also suffered rib and leg fractures at other times, suggesting systematic abuse over time. The child, who was two and a half at the time of the hearing, had been taken into care and was thriving with long-term foster parents. The father subsequently pleaded guilty to offences relating to the commission of the child's injuries and was in prison. At an earlier stage, however, when the father and mother maintained common cause that neither had caused the injuries, the mother entered into a parental responsibility agreement with the father. The mother later maintained that had she known that the father was the perpetrator she would not have done so.

Upon the mother's application to revoke the parental responsibility agreement, Singer J held that section 1(1) of the Children Act 1989 should apply to its determination in the same way that it applied to an application to grant parental responsibility. He considered it pertinent to consider what would have been the court's response had the father been applying for a PRO. His Lordship explained, however, that he started 'from the proposition that parental responsibility—both wanting to have it and its exercise—is a laudable desire which is to be encouraged rather than rebuffed' and postulated as a first principle 'that parental responsibility once obtained should not be terminated in the case of a non-marital father on less than solid grounds, with a presumption for continuance rather than for termination'.[557]

Revoking the parental responsibility agreement, Singer J could see no element of parental responsibility which the father could in the present or foreseeable circumstances exercise in a way which would benefit the child. In addition, its continuance had considerable potential ramifications for future adversity to the child: it would give a message to others that the father had not forfeited parental responsibility; it might undermine the mother's confidence in the stability of the child's placement; it could be unsettling for the foster parents; and it imposed an unrealistic demand on the local authority in requiring them to consider the father's potential exercise of parental responsibility when exercising their powers under the care order.

In *Re M (Minors)*[558] the Court of Appeal endorsed the principles enunciated by Singer J as 'exactly the appropriate way in which a judge should approach an application of this nature'. However, Hale J explained that rather than asking whether a PRO would have been made, the court's task might more relevantly be put as evaluating 'how he has gone about meeting that responsibility since the order was made and what benefit the children have derived from it or may be expected to derive from it in the future'. The case concerned a father's appeal against discharge of a PRO which had been made by consent. The Court of Appeal dismissed the appeal, holding that there had been strong evidence to discharge the order. The father had done everything he could to undermine the

---

[555] Ibid, ss 4(3) and (4), 4ZA(6) and (7), and 4A(3) and (4). Leave may only be granted if the court is satisfied that the child has sufficient understanding to make the proposed application.

[556] [1995] 1 FLR 1048, FD.

[557] Ibid, 1052. His Lordship added that it should not be allowed to become a weapon in the hands of the dissatisfied mother of the non-marital child: it should be used by the court as an appropriate step in the regulation of the child's life where the circumstances really do warrant it and not otherwise.

[558] Court of Appeal, 11 October 1995 (unreported) (Hale J and Pill LJ).

mother and make her life a misery and the children had not benefited from parental responsibility in the past, nor were they likely to in future.

The Court of Appeal decision in *Re M (Minors)* was not cited by the High Court in *CW v SG (Parental Responsibility: Consequential Orders)*,[559] in which Baker J removed parental responsibility from a father who had been convicted of sexual offences against two of the mother's children. However, Baker J endorsed the approach of Singer J in *Re P*, rejecting counsel's argument that the facts of the case could be distinguished from *Re P*. He also rejected an argument that section 4(2A) is incompatible with Articles 8 and 14 in that a married father in these circumstances could not have his parental responsibility revoked in this way.[560] The approach taken by Singer J and Baker J was also endorsed by Roderic Wood J in *Re A (Termination of Parental Responsibility)*[561] in removing parental responsibility from a father who had shown a lack of commitment to the child in the past,[562] and had subjected the mother to a 'prolonged and vicious assault'[563] for which he was imprisoned. The judge commented that:

> [t]o leave the father as a joint holder of parental responsibility would lead to the mother having perforce to have dealings with the father which would, on any objective view of the evidence, be intolerable to her, and which would more probably than not lead to a profound instability for her, with the inevitable consequences for the deterioration in the arrangements for the children as she sought to combat the seriously undermining effects upon her of such an intrusion.[564]

Baker J's decision in *CW v SG (Parental Responsibility: Consequential Orders)*[565] was upheld by the Court of Appeal in *Re D (A Child)*,[566] although the Court of Appeal made no reference to the earlier Court of Appeal decision in *Re M*. The Court of Appeal, like *Re M*, endorsed the paramountcy of the child's welfare as the guiding principle in revocation applications. The arguably uncritical use of the paramountcy principle in this context has been criticised.[567] Parental responsibility is not entirely child-centred, and an order removing parental responsibility is, in a sense, more draconian than a care order, where parental responsibility is merely shared with the local authority, albeit under the local authority's control. It may be therefore that simply focusing on the welfare of the child may not adequately, as a matter of process, protect the parent's interests in possessing parental responsibility.

In contrast to *Re P* and *Re M*, however, the court in *Re D* indicated that there is no presumption of continuance of parental responsibility. However, this difference in the authorities has perhaps now been overtaken by the implementation, since *Re D*, of the presumption of parental involvement in section 1(2A) of the Children Act 1989. This applies to revocation applications under section 4(2A), although it seems unlikely that it will have much impact on such applications. Where parental involvement is entirely inappropriate, section 1(6)(b) is likely to preclude the application of a presumption of involvement. If, by contrast, 'there is some evidence in the proceedings that the father could be involved in a way that would not put the child at risk of suffering harm, it is perhaps unlikely that revocation will represent a last resort, proportionate response.'[568]

## 9  The position of persons without parental responsibility

A person might have the care of a child while neither being a parent nor having parental responsibility within the meaning of section 3 of the Children Act 1989. What is the legal position of such a person? First, as Munby J pointed out in *R (G) v Nottingham City Council*[569] any person may

---

[559] [2013] EWHC 854 (Fam), [2013] 2 FLR 655.          [560] Ibid, [22].          [561] [2013] EWHC 2963 (Fam).
[562] Ibid, [29].          [563] Ibid, [7].          [564] Ibid, [27].          [565] [2013] EWHC 854 (Fam), [2013] 2 FLR 655.
[566] [2014] EWCA Civ 315. For critical comment, see S. Gilmore, 'Withdrawal of Parental Responsibility: Lost Authority and a Lost Opportunity' (2015) 78(6) *Modern Law Review* 1042.
[567] Ibid.          [568] Ibid.          [569] [2008] EWHC 152 (Admin), [2008] 1 FLR 1660, QBD.

intervene to prevent an actual or threatened criminal assault taking place, and a 'threat of immediate significant violence is enough, particularly if it involves a young child'.[570]

---

### Key legislation

Secondly, in some circumstances reliance might be placed on section 3(5) of the Children Act 1989, which provides:

A person who—

(a) does not have parental responsibility for a particular child; but

(b) has care of the child,

may (subject to the provisions of this Act) do what is reasonable in all the circumstances of the case for the purpose of safeguarding or promoting the child's welfare.

---

The scope of this broad provision turns on what view is taken of what it is reasonable to do in all the circumstances of a case. It is possible, for example, that reliance could be placed on section 3(5) by medical personnel to obtain consent to medical treatment from a child's carer where persons with parental responsibility cannot be contacted, at least in respect of orthodox forms of treatment. The reasonableness might turn on the seriousness of the medical condition, the complexity of the decision to consent and its impact, and whether treatment could be delayed to allow a parent to be contacted. It might be entirely reasonable to use section 3(5) to consent to a child's broken arm being set, where the child's parent is on an overnight flight and cannot be contacted by telephone. It might not be viewed as reasonable to consent in the same way to a limb amputation which could be delayed to the following day. In *R (G) v Nottingham City Council*[571] Munby J explained that there might also be 'circumstances in which a hospital could rely upon s 3(5) as justifying action taken in relation to a child in its medical care, despite the absence of parental consent and the absence of any court order' where medical intervention is 'required in order to preserve the child's life or to protect a child from irreversible harm in circumstances of such urgency that there is not even time to make an urgent telephone application to a judge'.[572] In such a situation the doctor could even act despite a parental refusal of consent if the parent is acting unreasonably or contrary to the child's best interests.[573]

Another context in which this question may arise is where the person with care forms the view that it would be against the interests of the child to return him to the care of a parent. For example, if parents returned home drunk and a babysitter formed the opinion that it would be unsafe to leave the child in the house with them, could she lawfully remove the child from the premises and take the child to her own home? It would seem desirable that the law should authorise such a properly motivated action, and section 3(5) would almost certainly cover this situation.

More difficult is the position when a child is being accommodated by a local authority under section 20 of the Children Act 1989, and a parent wishes immediately to remove his or her child from that accommodation. A local authority does not have parental responsibility for an accommodated child, and section 20(8) specifically states that any person who has parental responsibility may at any time remove the child from accommodation provided by the local authority under that section. Whether section 3(5) would allow a foster parent, or a person in charge of a children's home, to refuse to hand the child over in express disregard of section 20(8) has yet to be determined. It would seem desirable that section 3(5) should provide such persons with protection for a very short period, during which time, for example, steps are being taken to invoke police protection.

---

[570] Ibid, [21].     [571] Ibid.     [572] Ibid, [24].     [573] Ibid, [25].

## 10  The nature and scope of parental responsibility

### 10.1  The complexity of parental responsibilities

Section 3(4) of the Children Act 1989 makes clear that the fact that a person has, or does not have, parental responsibility for a child shall not affect any obligation which the parent may have in relation to the child (such as a statutory duty to maintain the child) or any rights which, in the event of the child's death, the parent (or any other person) may have in relation to the child's property. In this way English law is able to maintain a distinction between a parent and a parent who additionally has parental responsibility within the meaning of the Children Act 1989.[574] The suggestion in the definition of parental responsibility in section 3 of the Children Act 1989 that a person with parental responsibility has *all* the rights, duties, powers, responsibilities, and authority which by law a parent has in relation to a child is slightly misleading, however, as acquisition of parental responsibility does not confer all of the duties that parents owe to their children. First, as we have seen there may be some limitations on the content of parental responsibility depending on how it has been acquired. Secondly, the duty to make child support payments pursuant to the Child Support Act 1991 can only be imposed upon a child's parent.[575] Thirdly, the definition in section 3 of the Act refers to parental responsibility in relation to a child, who for the purpose of the Act is a person who has not attained 18 years.[576] Parental responsibility under the Children Act 1989 does not therefore include any duties which a parent might owe to an adult child.[577] A parent's responsibilities and the concept of parental responsibility are not, therefore, the same, and only a parent who has parental responsibility has the full complement of parental 'rights' and responsibilities.

The law is complicated further by the fact that, as John Eekelaar has observed,[578] there are rules relating to when parenthood and parental responsibility respectively are a necessary and/or sufficient condition of imposing a duty on a person, or for that person acting in matters relating to the child. Sometimes only a parent will have a duty: for example the duty to make child support payments pursuant to the Child Support Act 1991. Sometimes simply having parental responsibility will suffice—for example in the case of consenting to the child's marriage.[579] On occasions, however, it is necessary to be both a parent *and* to have parental responsibility, for example in order to consent to the child's adoption.[580] In yet other cases either being a parent *or* having parental responsibility will suffice. For example, under section 10(4) of the Children Act 1989. either a parent or a person with parental responsibility can apply for any order under section 8 of the Act without leave of the court. In some cases, however, the exercise of parental rights (eg the right to appoint a

---

[574] For the view that the difference is rather limited, see J. Eekelaar, 'Rethinking Parental Responsibility' [2001] Family Law 426. For criticism of Eekelaar's arguments, see S. Gilmore, J. Herring, and R. Probert (eds), 'Parental Responsibility—Law, Issues and Themes' in R. Probert, S. Gilmore, and J. Herring, *Responsible Parents and Parental Responsibility* (Oxford: Hart, 2009), Ch 1.

[575] The duty to maintain in the Child Support Act 1991, s 1, is owed in respect of a 'qualifying child', which definition requires the existence of a non-resident *parent*. While the courts see conferring parental responsibility as a matter with respect to the child's upbringing, to which Children Act 1989, s 1(1) applies, s 105(1) defines a child's upbringing as excluding his or her maintenance. See further, N. Wikeley, 'Financial Support for Children after Parental Separation: Parental Responsibility and Responsible Parenting' in R. Probert, S. Gilmore, and J. Herring (eds), *Responsible Parents and Parental Responsibilty* (Oxford: Hart, 2009).

[576] Children Act 1989, s 105(1).

[577] Eg the duty to maintain a child within the Child Support Act 1991 extends to adult children under 19 years who are receiving full-time education which is not advanced: s 55(1)(b). See also s 55(7) and (8) and the Child Support (Maintenance Calculation Procedure) Regulations 2000 (SI 2001/157) Sch 1, para 5(1) in relation to short-term provision to persons under 19 who have just left full-time education.

[578] J. Eekelaar, 'Rethinking Parental Responsibility' [2001] Family Law 426.

[579] See R. Probert, 'Parental Responsibility and Children's Partnership Choices' in R. Probert, S. Gilmore, and J. Herring, *Responsible Parents and Parental Responsibility* (Oxford: Hart, 2009).

[580] Adoption and Children Act 2002, ss 47 and 52(6).

guardian or to object to a child's adoption) requires that the parent has parental responsibility for the child within the meaning of the Children Act 1989.

## 10.2 Statutory guidance on the nature and exercise of parental responsibility in section 2 of the Children Act 1989

Section 2 of the Children Act 1989 provides some general statutory guidance on the nature and exercise of parental responsibility.

### 10.2.1 Parental responsibility may be shared

First, as will already be apparent, section 2(5) provides that more than one person (whether a parent or not) may have parental responsibility at the same time. Furthermore, section 2(6) makes clear that a person who has parental responsibility 'shall not cease to have that responsibility solely because some other person subsequently acquires parental responsibility for the child'.

### 10.2.2 Each holder of parental responsibility may act alone in meeting his or her parental responsibility

Section 2(7) of the Children Act 1989 provides that each holder of parental responsibility may act alone in meeting his parental responsibility. Section 2(7) clarifies, however, that this does affect the operation of any enactment which requires the consent of more than one person with parental responsibility. An example of such an enactment is section 13, which provides that where a child arrangements order is in force with respect to a child, the child's surname cannot be changed nor can the child be taken out of the jurisdiction for more than a month without the consent of all persons with parental responsibility. Section 2(8) further clarifies that the fact that a person has parental responsibility does not entitle him or her to act in any way which would be incompatible with an order made under the Act. So, for example, if a mother has a child arrangements order, it would not be possible for the father to exercise his parental responsibility to suggest that the child attend a school so far away from the mother's home that that decision would be incompatible with the order.

The courts have interpreted section 2(7), apparently contrary to its clear wording and the background to the provision, to mean that there is still a 'right to be consulted on schooling, serious medical problems and other important occurrences in the child's life'.[581] As John Eekelaar has observed,[582] this interpretation of section 2(7) places a difficulty in the way of according parental responsibility to all fathers, since it would sometimes place a very onerous duty upon the mother to trace, or even to identify, the father, causing delays in decision making about the child.

### 10.2.3 Parental responsibility cannot be surrendered or transferred

No doubt there is many a parent who has been tempted to say: 'Give me a break; have my parental responsibility for the day'. The law does not permit this; parental responsibility cannot be surrendered or transferred except by court order.[583] However, the law does permit a holder of parental responsibility to 'arrange for some or all of it to be met by one or more persons acting on his behalf'[584] as, for example, where a parent delegates the exercise of parental responsibility to a childminder.[585]

---

[581] *Re H (Parental Responsibility)* [1998] 1 FLR 855 at 859A *per* Butler-Sloss LJ. For specific examples of exceptions to s 2(7), see *Re G (Parental Responsibility: Education)* [1994] 2 FLR 964; *Re PC (Change of Surname)* [1997] 2 FLR 730; *Re J (Specific Issue Orders: Child's Religious Upbringing and Circumcision)* [2000] 1 FLR 571. For criticism, see J. Eekelaar, 'Do Parents have a Duty to Consult?' (1998) 114 LQR 337; J. Eekelaar, 'Rethinking Parental Responsibility' [2001] Family Law 426; and S. Maidment, 'Parental Responsibility—Is there a Duty to Consult?' [2001] Family Law 518.

[582] J. Eekelaar, 'Rethinking Parental Responsibility' [2001] Family Law 426–30.

[583] Children Act 1989, s 2(9).        [584] Ibid.

[585] The making of the arrangement does not affect any liability of the person making it which may arise from any failure to meet any part of his parental responsibility: see s 2(11).

## 10.3 **The content and scope of parental responsibility**

There is no definitive list of the 'rights, duties, powers, responsibility and authority' which constitute parental responsibility and, unlike some jurisdictions,[586] English law has not sought to define in statute the particular legal incidents attaching to parental responsibility. These must be found therefore in the common law and in particular statutory provisions.

The precise nature and content of parental responsibilities is likely to vary according to the particular aspect of parental responsibility concerned.[587] At a general level, however, the scope of parental responsibility is perhaps best understood as a sphere of liberty[588] within which those with parental responsibility are granted the primary responsibility for the child's upbringing free from outside interference.[589] Although section 3 refers to the holder having 'rights', it will rarely be the case that a parental right will be a claim-right in the sense that someone else has a correlative duty. For example, a mother might say 'I have a right to dress my child as I wish in expensive clothing', but it is clear that she does not have a right to do so in the sense that someone else has a corresponding duty to provide such clothing. She has a liberty to dress her child as she wishes, and others do not have a right to meddle in her decision. It can be seen that the word 'right' can be used rather loosely in different senses and it is important in this context to be clear about the sense in which it is used.

---

### Talking point

Where do the bounds of that sphere of liberty lie?[590] In *Gillick v West Norfolk and Wisbech Area Health Authority and Department of Health and Social Security*[591] (hereafter *Gillick*), Lord Fraser of Tullybelton said:

> parental rights to control a child do not exist for the benefit of the parent. They exist for the benefit of the child and they are justified only in so far as they enable the parent to perform his duties towards the child, and towards other children in the family.[592]

**Q.** Are parental rights entirely child-centred as this dictum suggests?

---

In that important decision (which is discussed in detail in Chapter 8) the House of Lords held that a doctor could prescribe contraceptive treatment for a girl under 16 years old without her parents' knowledge and consent provided the doctor was satisfied, *inter alia*, that it was in the child's best interests to do so without parental knowledge.

Lord Fraser's dictum, taken together with the overall ruling in the case, may suggest that parental discretion must be exercised in a child's best interests. This might suggest that parental rights

---

[586]  Eg in Scotland see the Children (Scotland) Act 1995, ss 1 and 2.

[587]  For an attempt to provide detailed accounts of the nature and content of some major areas of parental responsibility, see R. Probert, S. Gilmore, and J. Herring (eds), *Responsible Parents and Parental Responsibility* (Oxford: Hart, 2009).

[588]  Or Hohfeldian privileges. See W. N. Hohfeld, *Fundamental Legal Conceptions As Applied in Judicial Reasoning* (New Haven, CT: Yale University Press, 1919); and see *per* Lord Oliver of Aylmerton in *Re KD (A Minor) (Access: Principles)* [1988] 2 FLR 139 at 153.

[589]  *Parental* responsibility rather than *state* responsibility: see J. Eekelaar, 'Parental Responsibility: State of Nature or Nature of the State' [1991] Journal of Social Welfare and Family Law 37.

[590]  See generally B. M. Dickens, 'The Modern Function and Limits of Parental Rights' (1981) 97 LQR 462, and the discussion in A. Bainham, *Children, Parents and the State* (London: Sweet & Maxwell, 1988), p 48, and generally Ch 3; and S. Gilmore, 'The Limits of Parental Responsibility' in R. Probert, S. Gilmore, and J. Herring, *Responsible Parents and Parental Responsibility* (Oxford: Hart, 2009).

[591]  [1986] 1 AC 112.

[592]  Ibid, 170 D–E. See also *per* Lord Scarman: 'Parental rights are derived from parental duty and exist only so long as they are needed for the protection of the person and property of the child' (at 22).

are characterised as entirely 'child-centred'. However, as Andrew Bainham points out, welfare is 'so inherently vague a standard of behaviour'[593] that in day-to-day dealings with children this may translate (in the words of Bernard Dickens) to 'a parental discretion to employ control over children for purposes not violating children's interests, but equally not advancing their welfare or best interests'.[594] This allows recognition of what, it is submitted, is the better view of the nature of parental rights, namely that there are some aspects of parental discretion which are parent-centred.[595] Examples include a parent's choice over a child's religious upbringing (which may be protected to a greater degree than some other aspects of parental responsibility since it may be regarded as an aspect of a parent's rights to religious freedom)[596] or the choice of the child's home.[597] It may also be argued that there are parental interests which derive from the parent's investment of time and energy in parenting, that is, aspects of the parent's family life which should be respected independently.

### 10.3.1 Potential legal restrictions on the exercise of parental responsibility

In practice, therefore, the law permits parents discretion in matters of parental responsibility provided the discretion does not conflict with any parental legal duties, nor violate the child's interests in such a way that the law has declared unacceptable. *Legal* control of parental responsibility does not, therefore, preclude all parental harm to children. Several sources of potential legal restriction on the exercise of parental responsibility can be identified.[598] First, there are restrictions imposed by the criminal law. In particular, the extent to which a parent may use corporal punishment to discipline a child is limited by offences against the person,[599] although parents (and those acting *in loco parentis*) still have a defence of reasonable punishment to a charge of common assault.[600] Secondly, there are specific legal provisions in Parts IV and V of the Children Act 1989 which permit the state to intervene to protect and/or care for a child when the child is suffering or is at risk of suffering significant harm attributable to lack of reasonable parental care. Thirdly, it is possible for an individual to challenge aspects of the exercise of parental responsibility in private law proceedings. In deciding an issue with respect to the child's upbringing, a court is required to treat the child's welfare as its paramount consideration. Thus, it is possible that an exercise of parental responsibility could be overridden by the court on that basis, although a court may be reluctant to intervene on matters in respect of which there is room for reasonable disagreement.[601] A fourth potential restriction on the exercise of parental responsibility is the child's right to make his or her own decisions. The extent to which (if at all) English law recognises the child's autonomy interest as a restraint on parental responsibility is a complex issue,[602] which is discussed in detail in Chapter 8.

---

[593] A. Bainham, *Children, Parents and the State* (London: Sweet & Maxwell, 1988), p 59.

[594] B. M. Dickens, 'The Modern Function and Limits of Parental Rights' (1981) 97 LQR 462 at 464, cited in A. Bainham, *Children, Parents and the State* (London: Sweet & Maxwell, 1988), p 58.

[595] See A. McCall Smith, 'Is Anything Left of Parental Rights?' in E. Sutherland and A. McCall Smith (eds), *Family Rights: Family Law and Medical Advance* (Edinburgh: Edinburgh University Press, 1990) and A. Bainham, 'Is Anything Now Left of Parental Rights?' in R. Probert, S. Gilmore, and J. Herring (eds), *Responsible Parents and Parental Responsibility* (Oxford: Hart, 2009) (discussing the difference between parent-centred and child-centred parental rights—what Bainham terms the independence and priority theses).

[596] See R. Taylor, 'Parental Responsibility and Religion' in R. Probert, S. Gilmore, and J. Herring (eds), *Responsible Parents and Parental Responsibility* (Oxford: Hart, 2009).

[597] *Re E (Residence: Imposition of Conditions)* [1997] 2 FLR 638.

[598] See S. Gilmore, J. Herring, and R. Probert, 'Parental Responsibility: Law, Issues and Themes' in R. Probert, S. Gilmore, and J. Herring, *Responsible Parents and Parental Responsibility* (Oxford: Hart, 2009), esp pp 13–15.

[599] Under the Offences Against the Person Act 1861.

[600] Children and Young Persons Act 1933, s 1(7) and Children Act 2004, s 58. For a full account of the law, see S. Choudhry, 'Parental Responsibility and Corporal Punishment' in R. Probert, S. Gilmore, and J. Herring (eds), *Responsible Parents and Parental Responsibility* (Oxford: Hart, 2009), pp 165–83.

[601] See eg *Re W (Residence Order)* [1999] 1 FLR 869, CA where the issue was nudity in the home.

[602] See the discussion in S. Gilmore, 'The Limits of Parental Responsibility' in R. Probert, S. Gilmore, and J. Herring (eds), *Responsible Parents and Parental Responsibility* (Oxford: Hart, 2009).

Fifthly, it is possible that parents' powers are automatically qualified by a requirement of reasonableness, in the sense that a parent must not act unreasonably. The point has been made by Andrew Bainham,[603] by reference to some decisions in which courts have made *ex post facto* adjudications that a parent exceeded his lawful authority:[604] in *R v D*[605] the House of Lords upheld a father's conviction for kidnap of his 5-year-old son) and in *R v Rahman*[606] the Court of Appeal upheld a father's conviction for false imprisonment of his teenage daughter. In the former case, the unlawfulness of the father's act turned upon a presumed lack of consent on the part of the child, which may be equated with the reasonableness of the act. In the latter, the detention was in such circumstances 'as to take it out of the realm of reasonable discipline'.[607] The analysis suggests that in dealings with a child, a third party may need to have regard to the reasonableness of a parent's view.[608] However, other than in cases requiring confidentiality, cases of necessity, or requiring the child's very short-term protection, a third party would be wise to be cautious in overriding the perceived unreasonable views of a parent who has parental responsibility, without seeking court approval.[609]

## 11  The link with chapters that follow

We have now examined all the concepts associated with 'being a parent' in English law: parentage, parenthood, and parental responsibility. In the chapters that follow, we explore the various ways (discussed earlier) in which parental rights and responsibilities may be restricted. In Chapter 8 we explore the concept of children's rights, including the important debate concerning the scope of children's autonomy; in Chapter 9 we look at how the courts decide issues or disputes surrounding the exercise of parental responsibility in private law disputes; and in Chapter 10 we examine the role of the state in childcare and protection.

## Discussion Questions

1.  Do children have a right to know of their biological origins? Critically assess the courts' approach to establishing legal parentage; have they gone too far too fast?

2.  To what extent are (a) biological connection, (b) intention, and (c) a child's welfare important in attributing legal parenthood in English law? To what extent do you think these factors should be important? Is the law on parenthood coherent? Should it be?

3.  A father who has not married his child's mother does not automatically gain parental responsibility for the child. Discuss the policy behind this position, and assess the case for reform of the law on parental responsibility for 'unmarried fathers'.

4.  Assess the case law on parental responsibility orders. Should the courts adopt different principles in the case of so-called 'alternative families'?

## Further Reading

BAINHAM, A., 'Arguments about Parentage' (2008) 67(2) Cambridge Law Journal 321

BAINHAM, A., 'What is the Point of Birth Registration?' [2008] Child and Family Law Quarterly 449

BAINHAM, A., DAY CLATER, S., and RICHARDS, M. (eds), *What is a Parent? A Socio-Legal Analysis* (Oxford: Hart, 1999)

---

[603] A. Bainham, *Children, Parents and the State* (London: Sweet & Maxwell, 1988), pp 54–7.
[604] Ibid, p 56.   [605] [1984] AC 778.   [606] (1985) 81 Cr App R 349.
[607] A. Bainham, *Children, Parents and the State* (London: Sweet & Maxwell, 1988), pp 54–7.
[608] Ibid, p 57.   [609] See *Glass v UK* (App no 61827/00) [2004] 1 FLR 1019.

CALLUS, T., 'A New Parenthood Paradigm for Twenty-First Century Family Law in England the Wales' (2012) 32(3) Legal Studies 347–368

EEKELAAR, J., 'Rethinking Parental Responsibility' [2001] Family Law 426

FENTON-GLYNN, C., 'The Regulation and Recognition of Surrogacy Under English Law: An Overview of the Case-Law' [2015] Child and Family Law Quarterly 83

FORTIN, J, 'Children's Right to Know Their Origins—Too Far, Too Fast?' [2009] Child and Family Law Quarterly 336

GILMORE, S., 'Parental Responsibility and the Unmarried Father—A New Dimension to the Debate' [2003] Child and Family Law Quarterly 21

GILMORE, S., 'Withdrawal of Parental Responsibility: Lost Authority and a Lost Opportunity' (2015) 78(6) Modern Law Review 1042

HILL, J., 'What Does it Mean to be a "Parent"? The Claims of Biology as the Basis for Parental Rights' (1991) 66 New York University Law Review 353

HORSEY, K. and SHELDON, S., 'Still Hazy After All These Years: The Law Regulating Surrogacy' (2012) 20(1) Medical Law Review 67

JACKSON, E., 'What is a Parent?' in A. Diduck and K. O'Donovan (eds), *Feminist Perspectives on Family Law* (Abingdon: Routledge-Cavendish, 2006), pp 59–74

LOWE, N., 'The Meaning and Allocation of Parental Responsibility: A Common Lawyer's Perspective' (1997) 11(2) International Journal of Law, Policy and the Family 192

McCANDLESS, J. and SHELDON, S., 'The Human Fertilisation and Embryology Act (2008) and the Tenacity of the Sexual Family Form' (2010) 72(2) Modern Law Review 175

PROBERT, R., 'Families, Assisted Reproduction and the Law' [2004] Child and Family Law Quarterly 273

PROBERT, R., GILMORE, S., and HERRING, J. (eds), *Responsible Parents and Parental Responsibility* (Oxford: Hart, 2009)

SHELDON, S., 'From "Absent Objects of Blame" to "Fathers Who Want to Take Responsibility": Reforming Birth Registration Law' (2009) 31(4) Journal of Social Welfare and Family Law 373

SMITH, L., 'Is Three a Crowd? Lesbian Mothers' Perspectives on Parental Status in Law' [2006] Child and Family Law Quarterly 231

SMITH, L., 'Clashing Symbols? Reconciling Support for Fathers and Fatherless Families After the Human Fertilisation and Embryology Act 2008' [2010] Child and Family Law Quarterly 46

SMITH, L., 'Tangling the Web of Legal Parenthood: Legal Responses to the Use of Known Donors in Lesbian Parenting Arrangements' (2013) 33(3) Legal Studies 355–381

ZANGHELLINI, A., 'A v B and C [2012] EWCA Civ 285—Heteronormativity, Poly-parenting, and the Homo-nuclear Family' [2012] Child and Family Law Quarterly 475

 Visit the Online Resource Centre at **www.oxfordtextbooks.co.uk/orc/gilmore_glennon5e/**

**online resource centre** for a range of further features including a detailed bibliography and self-test questions.

# 8

# Children's rights

## INTRODUCTION

This chapter introduces some theoretical discussions concerning children's rights and examines some 'core' legal provisions and case law in which the issue of the legal protection of children's interests has been explored. Much of the chapter explores what is perhaps the most challenging question raised by children's rights in practice: the extent to which the law allows, and should allow, children to make their own decisions. Indeed, this chapter follows on directly from the last on parental responsibility because such rights are potentially one constraint on the exercise of parental responsibility.

## 1 Fundamental debates surrounding children's rights

Any discussion of children's rights is immediately complicated by the fact that the words 'children's rights'[1] can be understood in different senses. As Lucinda Ferguson observes, there is a difference between talking about rights for children as we might talk about rights for any human being, and talking about *children's* rights in the sense that makes them distinctive to children.[2] Furthermore, each of the words in the phrase 'children's rights' raises debate. What do we mean by a child? The concepts of child and childhood are not givens, but rather social constructs, with scope for competing visions of childhood, and complications for a vision of children's rights. There are also different conceptions of the concept of a right, with associated difficulties for accommodating children's rights.

### 1.1 Conceptions of a right: will theory v interest theory

The first difficulty is that theorists do not agree on the concept of a right.[3] There are two main theories of rights. The Interest Theory holds that rights derive from persons' interests. On this view, a person will have a right simply if that person's interest is sufficient ground for holding another to

---

[1] The following are good starting points into the literature: J. Fortin, *Children's Rights and the Developing Law*, 3rd edn (Cambridge: Cambridge University Press, 2009); D. Archard, *Children Rights and Childhood* (London: Routledge, 2004) and the works cited in his bibliographical essay at pp 231–42; M. D. A. Freeman, *The Moral Status of Children: Essays on the Rights of the Child* (The Hague: Martinus Nijhoff, 1997); P. Alston, S. Parker, and J. Seymour (eds), *Children, Rights and the Law* (Oxford: Clarendon Press, 1992); M. D. A. Freeman, *The Rights and the Wrongs of Children* (London: Frances Pinter, 1983); B. Franklin (ed), *The New Handbook of Children's Rights Comparative Policy and Practice* (London: Routledge, 2002); P. Alderson, *Young Children's Rights*, 2nd edn (London: Jessica Kingsley, 2008). For a detailed practitioner work, see A. MacDonald, *The Rights of the Child Law and Practice* (Bristol: Family Law, 2011).

[2] L. Ferguson, 'Not Merely Rights for Children but Children's Rights: The Theory Gap and the Assumption of the Importance of Children's Rights' (2013) 21 International Journal of Children's Rights 177–208.

[3] See eg, J. Waldron (ed), *Theories of Rights* (Oxford: Oxford University Press, 1984); M. H. Kramer, N.E. Simmonds, and H. Steiner, *A Debate Over Rights: Philosophical Enquiries* (Oxford: Oxford University Press, 1998).

be subject to a duty. By contrast, the Will Theory holds that one can only talk meaningfully about a person having a right if the person can waive, or exercise, enforcement of the right. In other words, while the Interest Theory protects a person's interests independently of his or her choices, the Will Theory draws a necessary connection between the idea of a person having a right and the exercise of the person's will with respect to the right. Of course, babies and very young children will not have the necessary knowledge or understanding to exercise their will in this way, so the will theory conceptually denies some children the very possibility of having rights. This point was made by the late Professor Neil MacCormick, who used the case of children's rights to test the appropriateness of general theories of rights.[4] MacCormick argued that the will theory should be rejected as a general theory because of its inability to accommodate fully the case of children's rights. In the case of children at least, the interest theory is more apposite. As Michael Freeman has put it: 'Children have interests to protect before they develop wills to assert, and others can complain on behalf of younger children when those interests are trampled on.'[5]

## 1.2 **Should children have rights?**

If it is accepted that children are capable of possessing rights, a further question arises as to whether children should be accorded (legal) rights. Several philosophical justifications for children's rights have been put forward. Michael Freeman has sought out a moral justification for children's rights based on the notion of autonomy. He argues that rights protect the integrity of a person in leading his or her life, based on a belief in equality and respect for autonomy. For Freeman, to 'believe in autonomy is to believe that anyone's autonomy is as morally significant as anyone else's'.[6] We should therefore respect a child's autonomy, treating the child as a person and as a right-holder[7] (although Freeman also acknowledges that children's autonomy must be seen in the context of their sometimes lesser abilities/capacities). By contrast, Katherine Federle is concerned that the justification for children's rights should not be tied to children's capacities or incapacities.[8] She argues that while the interest theory 'does not automatically exclude children from the class of rights-holders, it does define children's interests in terms of their incapacities'[9] and there is a tendency to empower adults to intervene in children's lives rather than empowering children.[10] The kinds of rights that Federle envisions are thus not premised upon capacity but upon power or more precisely, powerlessness. In other words, rights exist to remedy powerlessness and should flow downhill to the least powerful. Paternalistic justifications thus become unacceptable.

Another argument in favour of rights has been advanced by Martha Minow, who highlights the ability which rights may have to forge connection with others, by providing a procedural basis for communication.[11] The importance of rights in this sense may have particular resonance for children, providing them with an appropriate status for communication with adults.

---

[4] N. MacCormick, 'Children's Rights: A Test Case for Theories of Rights' in N. MacCormick, *Legal Right and Social Democracy* (Oxford: Clarendon Press, 1982). For analysis and criticism of the will theory, see also J. G. Dwyer, 'The Conceptual Possibility of Children Having Rights', appendix in *The Relationship Rights of Children* (Cambridge: Cambridge University Press, 2006).

[5] M. D. A. Freeman, 'Taking Children's Rights More Seriously' in P. Alston, S. Parker, and J. Seymour (eds), *Children, Rights and the Law* (Oxford: Clarendon Press, 1992), 52, at 58.

[6] Ibid, p 64.    [7] Ibid, p 65.

[8] K. H. Federle, 'On the Road to Reconceiving Rights for Children: A Post-Feminist Analysis of the Capacity Principle' (1993) De Paul Law Review 983; K. H. Federle, 'Rights Flow Downhill' (1994) 2 International Journal of Children's Rights 343; K. H. Federle, 'Looking Ahead: An Empowerment Perspective on the Rights of Children' (1995) 68(4) Temple Law Review 1585. Federle's treatment of power may require further refinement: see H. Lim and J. Roche, 'Feminism and Children's Rights' in J. Bridgeman and D. Monk (eds), *Feminist Perspectives on Child Law* (London: Cavendish, 2000), pp 238–41.

[9] K. H. Federle, 'Rights Flow Downhill' (1994) 2 International Journal of Children's Rights 343 at 354.

[10] Ibid, 365.

[11] M. Minow, 'Interpreting Rights: An Essay for Robert Cover' (1987) Yale Law Journal 1860.

While these may be justifications for rights for children, Ferguson suggests that the theoretical basis upon which children possess *children's rights* currently evades us. She argues that 'we do not currently have a child-centred theory of children's rights' nor 'good evidence that it benefits children to think of them in terms of legal children's rights'.[12]

Martin Guggenheim[13] is suspicious of the alleged child-centredness of children's rights and their use, observing from a US perspective how such rights are manipulated in legal disputes by adults to try to advance their own interests as against other adults. He argues that there should be more focus on adult obligations.[14]

Similarly, Onora O'Neill has argued[15] that if we care about children's lives we may have good reasons to focus on adults' obligations to children rather than appealing to children's fundamental rights.[16] O'Neill's preference for a focus on obligations is founded on her observation that there are some obligations, such as being kind and helping to develop others' capacities, which are imperfect obligations because the precise obligations and to whom they are owed are not specified. Consequently, such obligations have no allocated right-holders and therefore no counterpart set of rights. The analysis provides useful insights: that a shift to the idiom of rights risks excluding and neglecting some things that may matter to children[17] because such things drop out of the picture if, approaching from a right's perspective, no right-holder can be identified; and that 'rights-based approaches are incomplete in that they tell us nothing about what should be done when nobody has a right to its being done'.[18] Supporting her argument, O'Neill contends that children are unlike other oppressed groups claiming rights. Children are 'more fundamentally but less permanently powerless; their main remedy is to grow up'.[19]

Another argument sometimes made is that rights are not the most appropriate basis for regulating close personal relationships, such as the interactions of parent and child, and it is inappropriate for children to have rights within their family. As David Archard explains, there is a standpoint in this context 'that rights talk is morally impoverished and neglects an alternative ethical view of the world, in which the affectionate, caring interdependence which ideally characterises the parent–child relationship assumes an exemplary significance'.[20] Against these views, however, Michael Freeman has argued that criticism of rights as impoverished idealises adult–child relations and presents a myth of childhood as a golden age,[21] yet the realities of many children's lives are different. A child who is being abused within a family may well see greater value in having a 'public' right to claim protection. Freeman also doubts that children's dependency is quite as different from other oppressed groups as O'Neill suggests, in that childhood can be artificially prolonged and is determined by those in authority.[22] This brings us neatly to another difficulty encountered in the phrase 'children's rights', namely the meaning of 'child' and of 'childhood'.

---

[12] L. Ferguson, 'Not Merely Rights for Children but Children's Rights: The Theory Gap and the Assumption of the Importance of Children's Rights' (2013) 21 International Journal of Children's Rights 177–208.

[13] M. Guggenheim, *What's Wrong With Children's Rights* (Harvard University Press, 2005).

[14] For a succinct account of Guggenheim's thesis, see A. Bainham and S. Gilmore, *Children The Modern Law* (Family Law, Jordan Publishing, 2013), at pp 313–15.

[15] O. O'Neill, 'Children's Rights and Children's Lives' (1988) 98 Ethics 445–463, also published in P. Alston, S. Parker, and J. Seymour (eds), *Children, Rights and the Law* (Oxford: Clarendon Press, 1992).

[16] Ibid, p 39.      [17] Ibid, pp 35–6.      [18] Ibid, p 39.

[19] Ibid. For criticism of O'Neill's arguments, see eg T. D. Campbell, 'The Rights of the Minor: As Person, As Child, As Juvenile, As Future Adult' in Alston et al, *Children, Rights and the Law*, pp 12–16; M. D. A. Freeman, 'Taking Children's Rights More Seriously' in ibid, pp 56–61.

[20] D. Archard, *Children Rights and Childhood* (London: Routledge, 2004), p 112, and for criticism of the point, see pp 118–23.

[21] Freeman, (n 19), pp 55–6.      [22] Ibid, p 56.

## 1.3 **Children and childhoods**

Who is to be regarded as a child, and consequently the boundary between childhood and adulthood, is socially constructed by the laws of a particular society.[23]

### 1.3.1 **Debating the adult/child boundary**

The fact that childhood and adulthood are socially constructed raises profound questions as to whether such a distinction can be justified and, if so, as to the setting and 'policing' of the boundary. The boundary was challenged by child liberationist ideology in the 1960s and 1970s which, placing great emphasis on individual autonomy, proposed an extension of adults' rights to children (such as the right to live independently, the right to drive, and to have sex).[24] Although politically naïve, child liberationist ideology was important in highlighting the issue of children's rights.[25] More moderate versions of this perspective might now argue that children should not be discriminated against simply on the basis of their age.

An argument for having a boundary between adulthood and childhood derives from the fact that in the early stages of a person's life paternalism is essential for survival. If we accept this fundamental need, then removal of the adult/child distinction would be purchased at the, arguably unacceptable, price of opening the door generally to paternalism beyond childhood.[26] It might also be objected that the setting of any boundary is arbitrary but that objection, if pursued to its logical limit, is capable of supporting the conclusion that either everyone or no one stands in need of paternalistic protection.[27]

### 1.3.2 **Policing the adult/child boundary**

If we accept that a boundary is necessary and inevitably arbitrary, how is the boundary to be decided and policed? There will be some adults with lesser abilities than children and some children with greater abilities than some adults. But societies are also concerned with efficiency and may need to take account of factors such as administrative convenience. Choosing a particular age as the starting point for adulthood (or for deciding whether a child is prima facie competent to do certain things, such as drive a car or have sexual intercourse) is more convenient than having to assess in each individual case whether a person is so competent. The drawing of such lines, however, can render some results which, at first blush, may seem surprising. A striking example is provided by Jonathan Herring, who observes that a child aged 16 may lawfully have sexual intercourse with his or her MP, but cannot vote for him or her.[28] However, those two activities are clearly different (unless you have attended some rather unusual polling stations!). It is as well also to recall that the setting of any boundary is not simply a matter of empirical finding, but also of judgement. If children were enfranchised, arguably our view of the vote would change rather than our view of children.[29] Furthermore, once set, the boundary introduces a quantitative distinction between adults and children, which treats (or has treated) everyone equally, namely the amount of time allocated to acquire experience before adulthood.[30]

---

[23] See in England and Wales, Family Law Reform Act 1969, s 1.

[24] Eg R. Farson, *Birthrights* (London: Collier Macmillan, 1974) and J. Holt, *Escape from Childhood* (Harmondsworth: Penguin, 1975). For a cross-section of the diverse origins of this ideology, see P. Adams et al, *Children's Rights* (London: Longman, 1972) and for an overview, see D. Archard, *Children Rights and Childhood* (London: Routledge, 2004), Ch 5 and L. Fox Harding, *Perspectives in Child Care Policy* (London: Longman, 1997), Ch 5.

[25] M. D. A. Freeman, *The Rights and Wrongs of Children* (London: Frances Pinter, 1983).

[26] F. Schrag, 'The Child in the Moral Order' (1977) 52 Philosophy 167 at 176.

[27] R. Lindley, 'Teenagers and Other Children' in G. Scarre (ed), *Children, Parents and Politics* (New York: Cambridge University Press, 1989), p 78.

[28] J. Herring, *Family Law*, 5th edn (London: Longman, 2011), p 435.

[29] J. Hughes, 'Thinking about Children' in G. Scarre (ed), *Children, Parents and Politics* (New York: Cambridge University Press, 1989), p 48.

[30] G. Scarre, 'Children and Paternalism' (1980) 55 Philosophy 117.

## 1.4 Different childhoods

---

### Talking point

It is not just the law that socially constructs, nor only the boundaries of childhood that are socially constructed. The nature of childhood is contingent on matters such as the particular time, society, and culture in which the child lives.[31] Children may experience very different childhoods at different times[32] in different parts of the world.

**Q.** What implications does this have for children's rights?

---

For example, child labour has a very different meaning for a child in England (perhaps doing a paper round for pocket money) compared with a child living in a country where daily child labour is required for family survival. For the drafters of international conventions seeking to set out children's rights, there are evident tensions between striving for universal rights and recognising cultural pluralism.[33] We may need to exercise caution when talking in general terms about 'children's rights'.

### 1.4.1 Society's perceptions of children

The social construction of childhood has clear implications for how children are perceived within society. Given its juxtaposition with adulthood it would not be surprising that perhaps the dominant vision of childhood is as a vulnerable and dependent period, children as beings who need to be nurtured into adulthood. This dominant perception may render less visible children's potential to exercise autonomy,[34] or indeed the role of children as actors in society (eg as carers[35]).

A further, interesting, point made by Carole Smith[36] is that the childhood/adulthood distinction may offer some explanation for resistance to granting children the right to make their own decisions, particularly where those decisions might lead to irreparable harm or death. As Smith observes:

> we are not prepared to withdraw our protection or to abandon the legal distinction between children and adults. To do so would strike at the very heart of the adult-child relationship which enables adults to locate themselves emotionally, as being affectionate, caring, protective, and socially, as being responsible for moulding the next generation of citizens.[37]

---

[31]  See A. James, C. Jenks, and A. Prout, *Theorizing Childhood* (Cambridge: Polity Press, 1998); C. Jenks, *Childhood* (London: Routledge, 1996); A. James and A. Prout (eds), *Constructing and Reconstructing Childhood* (London: Falmer Press, 1997); P Ariès, *Centuries of Childhood: A Social History of Family Life* (London: Jonathan Cape, 1962).

[32]  See eg A. Wade, 'Being Responsible: "Good" Parents and Children's Autonomy' in J. Bridgeman, H. Keating, and C. Lind (eds), *Responsibility, Law and the Family* (Aldershot: Ashgate, 2008), p 211, comparing across generations parents' attitudes to children's freedom.

[33]  On which, see M. D. A. Freeman, 'Children's Rights and Cultural Pluralism' in *The Moral Status of Children* (The Hague: Martinus Nijhoff, 1997).

[34]  See the discussion in C. Smith, 'Children's Rights: Judicial Ambivalence and Social Resistance' (1997) 11 International Journal of Law, Policy and the Family 103, esp at 106–10.

[35]  See eg V. Morrow, 'Responsible Children and Children's Responsibilities? Sibling Caretaking and Babysitting by School-age Children' in J. Bridgeman, H. Keating, and C. Lind (eds), *Responsibility, Law and the Family* (Aldershot: Ashgate, 2008), p 105, and generally Part 2 of this book.

[36]  C. Smith, 'Children's Rights: Judicial Ambivalence and Social Resistance' (1997) 11 International Journal of Law, Policy and the Family 103.

[37]  Ibid, 135.

## 2  Categorising children's rights: the interests children might plausibly claim

If the category of 'child' and the possibility of children being right-holders are accepted, it remains to consider the various interests that children might plausibly claim. The word 'plausibly' here is carefully chosen. As John Eekelaar has pointed out, there is a difference between 'welfarism' (ie, actions motivated solely by the purpose of promoting another's welfare) and the idea of a person having a right, which is related to the perception that people make claims.[38] Eekelaar's purpose in making this point is not to suggest that very young (incompetent) children should be denied rights, but to emphasise that even in such cases it 'could never be enough to assert simply that an action will be in the child's welfare'. He argues that if we are to talk of a child's right in the context of such actions, we 'need to think how the action could be one which the child might plausibly want'.[39] In a seminal article on children's rights,[40] Eekelaar identified three general categories of interests that children might plausibly claim: basic, developmental, and autonomy interests. By these, he means the following:

- Basic interest

  Children's general physical, emotional, and intellectual care within the social capabilities of the child's immediate caregivers (as a minimal expectation).[41]

- Developmental interest

  Children's 'equal opportunity to maximise the resources available to them during their childhood (including their own inherent abilities) so as to minimize the degree to which they enter adult life affected by avoidable prejudices incurred during childhood. In short their capacities are to be developed to their best advantage.'[42]

- Autonomy interest

  Children's freedom to choose their own lifestyle and to enter social relations according to their own inclinations uncontrolled by the authority of the adult world, whether parents or institutions.[43]

The value of such categorisation is that it draws attention to the potential interaction of the various interests. The child's developmental interest is likely to be promoted by exercises of autonomy, perhaps especially if those exercises of autonomy are accompanied by mistakes from which a child learns. There is also, as Freeman points out, a false dichotomy between protecting children and protecting their other interests. As he explains, '[c]hildren who are not protected, whose welfare is not advanced, will not be able to exercise self-determination: on the other hand, a failure to recognise the personality of children is likely to result in an undermining of their protection with children reduced to objects of intervention'.[44] However, there are also occasions when the various interests can conflict.[45] An example, which will be picked up in discussion of case law later in this

---

[38] J. Eekelaar, 'The Importance of Thinking That Children Have Rights' in P. Alston, S. Parker, and J. Seymour (eds), *Children, Rights and the Law* (Oxford: Clarendon Press, 1992), p 221. Eekelaar adds that 'a claim simply that people should act to further my welfare as they define it is in reality to make no claim at all'. See also his discussion of isolating interests pertaining to the child, in 'The Emergence of Children's Rights' (1986) 6 Oxford Journal of Legal Studies 161 at 169.

[39] J. Eekelaar, 'The Importance of Thinking That Children Have Rights' in P. Alston et al, *Children, Rights and the Law*, p 230 (ie, via an hypothetical *process*). See also J. Eekelaar, 'The Interests of the Child and the Child's Wishes: The Role of Dynamic Self-Determinism' (1994) 8 International Journal of Law and the Family 42.

[40] J. Eekelaar 'The Emergence of Children's Rights' (1986) 6 Oxford Journal of Legal Studies 161.

[41] Ibid, 170.        [42] Ibid, 170.        [43] Ibid, 171.

[44] M. D. A. Freeman, 'Laws Conventions and Rights' (1993) 7(1) Children and Society 37 at 42.

[45] Eg, if we allow a young child to exercise his or her autonomy interest by walking in the middle of a motorway, the child's basic interest is likely soon to be compromised.

chapter, is the competent adolescent who wishes to refuse medical treatment where the refusal will lead to irreparable harm or death. The autonomy and basic interests are in stark conflict in such cases. Theorists have reflected on ways of addressing these types of conflict.

### 2.1 Eekelaar's future-oriented consent and Freeman's liberal paternalism

Eekelaar suggested that in seeking to reconcile a conflict between children's basic interests and their decisions, 'some kind of imaginative leap may be required' to 'guess what a child might retrospectively have wanted once it reaches a position of maturity'.[46] Eekelaar acknowledges that the values of the adult world may intrude but that is to be openly accepted, encouraging debate about them.[47] Eekelaar suggests that while some adults might not approve of the fact that their autonomy was thwarted in childhood so as not to leave them at a disadvantage as against other children in realising their life-chances in adulthood, it seems improbable that this would be a common view. Hence, he concludes that the autonomy interests may be ranked 'subordinate to the basic and developmental interests' but that 'where they may be exercised without threatening these two interests, the claim for their satisfaction must be high'.[48]

Michael Freeman, drawing on John Rawls's theory of justice,[49] reaches a similar view, his version of 'liberal paternalism'.[50] Put simply, Rawls posited general principles of justice, using as a starting point the idea that people would be ignorant of their own position within a society. Freeman observes that if the persons participating in this hypothetical social contract did not know whether or not they were children, it is probable that most would wish to mature to an independent adulthood. The participants would know of children's limited capacities and how the actions of those with limited capacities could limit the exercise of autonomy in the future as an adult. Thus, there would be acceptance of interventions which would preclude action or conduct which would frustrate the achievement of the goal of reaching an autonomous adulthood. Freeman would thus defend a version of paternalism to avoid such irrationality.

While these are useful methods of seeking to reconcile some of children's conflicting interests, one must perhaps be careful not to see children merely in terms of future adults. The point has been made by Tom Campbell, who classifies minors' interests in such a way as to highlight some interests which are distinctively children's. Campbell suggests thinking about the rights of the minor as person, as child, as juvenile, and as future adult. This recognises the interests that children may have in the here and now at different stages of their development, such as the right to play as a child for its own sake.[51]

## 3 Legal protection of children's interests

To what extent, if at all, are the various categories of interests identified by Eekelaar protected by English law? Children's basic interests in survival and avoidance of harm are protected by various child protection measures in Parts IV and V of the Children Act 1989, which are explored in detail in Chapter 10. Indirectly, children are also protected by the criminal law, both general offences and

---

[46] J. Eekelaar 'The Emergence of Children's Rights' (1986) 6 Oxford Journal of Legal Studies 161 at 170.

[47] Ibid.

[48] Ibid. See also J. Eekelaar, 'The Importance of Thinking That Children Have Rights' in P. Alston, S. Parker, and J. Seymour (eds), *Children, Rights and the Law* (Oxford: Clarendon Press, 1992), pp 230–1.

[49] J. Rawls, *A Theory of Justice* (Oxford: Oxford University Press, 1973).

[50] See M. D. A. Freeman, *The Rights and Wrongs of Children* (London: Frances Pinter, 1983) and M. D. A. Freeman, 'Taking Children's Rights More Seriously' in P. Alston, S. Parker, and J. Seymour (eds), *Children, Rights and the Law* (Oxford: Clarendon Press, 1992), pp 66–9.

[51] See T. D. Campbell, 'The Rights of the Minor: As Person, As Child, As Juvenile, As Future Adult' in P. Alston et al, *Children, Rights and the Law*, pp 21–2.

specific offences against children, such as sexual offences or child neglect. There is also a raft of legal provisions which seek to secure children's developmental interests through their education.[52] The extent to which the law recognises a child's autonomy interest is a matter of considerable debate, however, and will now be explored in some detail. In English law the issue of children's autonomy has been explored principally in the context of children's medical treatment.

## 3.1 **Recognition of children's autonomy interest?**

### 3.1.1 *Gillick v West Norfolk and Wisbech Area Health Authority*

---

**Key case**

The leading case is the House of Lords' decision in *Gillick v West Norfolk and Wisbech Area Health Authority and Department of Health and Social Security*.[53] The case arose out of Mrs Victoria Gillick's objection to a DHSS Memorandum of Guidance,[54] which advised that in exceptional circumstances a doctor could prescribe contraception to a girl under 16 without her parents' knowledge or consent. Having failed to receive an assurance from the West Norfolk and Wisbech Area Health Authority that her own children would not be so treated without her knowledge, Mrs Gillick sought a declaration in the High Court that the Memorandum gave advice which was unlawful. She was unsuccessful before Woolf J at first instance,[55] won a unanimous victory in the Court of Appeal,[56] but was ultimately defeated in the House of Lords by a majority of 3 to 2.[57]

---

Mrs Gillick's 'crusade',[58] which provoked considerable public debate,[59] was translated into three strands of legal argument. It was contended that a doctor could not lawfully prescribe contraceptives to a girl under 16 without parental consent because: (i) the girl could not consent to medical

---

[52]  Discussion of education law is beyond the scope of this book, but see A. Bainham, *Children The Modern Law*, 3rd edn (Bristol: Family Law, 2005), Ch 16.

[53]  [1986] 1 AC 112. For an assessment of the case's impact on children's rights, see J. Fortin, 'The *Gillick* Decision—Not Just a High-Water Mark' in S. Gilmore, J. Herring, and R. Probert, *Landmark Cases in Family Law* (Oxford: Hart, 2011). The case has attracted a lot of commentary: see G. Austin, 'Righting a Child's Right to Refuse Medical Treatment, Section 11 of the New Zealand Bill of Rights Act and the *Gillick* Competent Child' (1992) 7(4) Otago Law Review 578; A. Bainham, 'The Balance of Power in Family Decisions' (1986) 45(2) Cambridge Law Journal 262; A. Bainham, *Children, Parents and the State* (London: Sweet & Maxwell, 1988), Ch 3; S. de Cruz, 'Parents, Doctors and Children: The *Gillick* Case and Beyond' [1987] Journal of Social Welfare and Family Law 93; J. Devereux, 'The Capacity of a Child in Australia to Consent to Medical Treatment—*Gillick* Revisited?' (1991) 11(2) Oxford Journal of Legal Studies 283 at 289–94; J. Eekelaar, 'The Eclipse of Parental Rights' (1986) 102 LQR 4 and 'The Emergence of Children's Rights' (1986) 6 Oxford Journal of Legal Studies 161; M. Jones, 'Consent to Medical Treatment by Minors after *Gillick*' (1986) 2 Professional Negligence 41; I. Kennedy, 'The Doctor, the Pill and the 15-Year-Old Girl' in I. Kennedy, *Treat Me Right: Essays in Medical Law and Ethics* (Oxford: Oxford University Press, 1988) Ch 5; S. Lee, 'Towards a Jurisprudence of Consent' in J. Eekelaar and S. Ball (eds), *Oxford Essays in Jurisprudence* (Oxford: Oxford University Press, 1987), Ch 9; J. Montgomery, 'Children as Property?' (1988) 51 Modern Law Review 323; P. Parkinson, 'The *Gillick* Case—Just What has it Decided?' [1986] Family Law 11; G. L. Peiris, 'The *Gillick* Case: Parental Authority, Teenage Independence and Public Policy' [1987] Current Legal Problems 93; G. Williams, 'The *Gillick* Saga' [1985] New Law Journal 1156–8 and 1179–82.

[54]  HN(80)46, Section G (as revised). See [1986] 1 AC 112 at 179–80.     [55]  [1984] QB 581.

[56]  [1986] 1 AC 112, CA (Eveleigh, Fox, and Parker LJJ).

[57]  Lord Fraser of Tullybelton, Lord Scarman, and Lord Bridge of Harwich; Lord Brandon of Oakbrook and Lord Templeman dissenting. It has been observed that their Lordships' disagreement was 'largely, perhaps entirely, brought about by divergent views on policy': G. Williams, 'The *Gillick* Saga' [1985] New Law Journal 1156 at 1157 (eg Lord Brandon viewed the lawfulness of the activities countenanced by the Memorandum of Guidance as itself a matter of public policy, [1986] 1 AC 112 at 195 F–G).

[58]  As Lord Templeman referred to it: see [1986] 1 AC 112 at 206 G–H.

[59]  For an analysis of the public portrayal of the debate, drawing on newspaper coverage at the time, see S. Gilmore, 'The Limits of Parental Responsibility' in R. Probert, S. Gilmore, and J. Herring, *Responsible Parents and Parental Responsibility* (Oxford: Hart, 2009).

treatment;[60] (ii) to do so would infringe parental rights; and (iii) it would constitute the criminal offence of aiding unlawful sexual intercourse.[61] The narrow criminal law point found favour only in Lord Brandon's dissent and will not be examined further. The other two arguments have an important bearing on the legal relationship between parents and children and were considered in detail by the majority. Lord Fraser and Lord Scarman each delivered opinions on the substantive issues. Lord Scarman agreed with Lord Fraser, and Lord Bridge agreed with both opinions. It is proposed to examine the opinions in turn since, as we shall see, identifying what the case represents as a precedent is a complex issue.

### 3.1.2 Lord Fraser

Lord Fraser began his opinion by examining Mrs Gillick's contention that a child under 16 could not consent to medical treatment. Mrs Gillick had relied on several statutory provisions, in particular section 8 of the Family Law Reform Act 1969, which gave children who had attained the age of 16 years a statutory right to consent to medical treatment. Lord Fraser concluded that no statutory provision cited by counsel compelled that conclusion, and that section 8 of the 1969 Act had been enacted merely for the avoidance of doubt. In Lord Fraser's opinion, a girl under 16 could lawfully consent to contraceptive advice, examination, and treatment, provided 'she has sufficient understanding and intelligence to know what they involve'.[62]

Lord Fraser then examined Mrs Gillick's argument, supported by nineteenth-century authorities such as *In Re Agar-Ellis*,[63] that she had in law complete authority over her children and thus control over their medical treatment. Lord Fraser declared that the nineteenth-century authorities were an historical curiosity and no longer authoritative, and held as a matter of general principle that:

> parental rights to control a child do not exist for the benefit of the parent. They exist for the benefit of the child and they are justified only in so far as they enable the parent to perform his duties towards the child, and towards other children in the family.[64]

Rejecting also the view that the child's intellectual ability was irrelevant, he approved Lord Denning's opinion in *Hewer v Bryant*[65] that:

> the legal right of a parent to the custody of a child ends at the 18th birthday: and even up till then, it is a dwindling right which the courts will hesitate to enforce against the wishes of the child, and the more so the older he is. It starts with a right of control and ends with little more than advice.[66]

Lord Fraser explained that '[s]ocial customs change, and the law ought to, and does in fact, have regard to such changes when they are of major importance'.[67] Explaining perceptions of the parent/child relationship in the late twentieth century, he said:

> It is, in my view, contrary to the ordinary experience of mankind, at least in Western Europe . . . to say that a child or a young person remains in fact under the complete control of his parents until he attains the definite age of majority, now 18 in the United Kingdom, and that on attaining that age he suddenly acquires independence. In practice most wise parents relax their control gradually as the child develops and encourage him or her to become increasingly independent. Moreover the degree

---

[60] The position prior to *Gillick* was obscure. See P. D. G. Skegg, 'Consent to Medical Procedures on Minors' (1973) 36 Modern Law Review 370 and A. Samuels, 'Can a Minor (Under 16) Consent to a Medical Operation?' [1984] Family Law 30.

[61] Contrary to the Sexual Offences Act 1956, ss 5, 6, and 28(1).    [62] [1986] 1 AC 112 at 170A.

[63] (1883) 24 ChD 317.

[64] [1986] 1 AC 112 at 170D–E, supporting this view, if necessary, by reference to *Blackstone's Commentaries*, 17th edn (1830), vol 1, p 452.

[65] [1970] 1 QB 357.    [66] Ibid, 369.    [67] [1986] 1 AC 112 at 171F.

> of parental control actually exercised over a particular child does in practice vary considerably according to his understanding and intelligence and it would, in my opinion, be unrealistic for the courts not to recognise these facts.[68]

It is less clear, however, whether Lord Fraser translated this description of good practice in relation to children's evolving independence into legal principle. In Lord Fraser's opinion, once absolute parental rights were abandoned the solution in the appeal had to be found in the idea of the child's best interests. For Lord Fraser the 'only practicable course [was] to entrust the doctor with a discretion to act in accordance with his view of what is best in the interests of the girl who is his patient'.[69] He identified five conditions of which the doctor would need to be satisfied if he were to be justified in proceeding without a parent's consent or knowledge:

> (1) that the girl (although under 16 years of age) will understand his advice; (2) that he cannot persuade her to inform her parents or to allow him to inform the parents that she is seeking contraceptive advice; (3) that she is very likely to begin or to continue having sexual intercourse with or without contraceptive treatment; (4) that unless she receives contraceptive advice or treatment her physical or mental health or both are likely to suffer; (5) that her best interests require him to give her contraceptive advice, treatment or both without the parental consent.[70]

It should be noted that the condition in (5) is not simply that treatment be in the child's best interests, but that it be in the child's interests to have such treatment *without parental consent*.[71] Arguably, the guidelines show, in the context of medical practice with its special feature of patient confidentiality, how the doctor must negotiate parents' interests with children's interests in decision making: the doctor must ensure, in what is an extension[72] of his clinical judgement, that the parents' duty of protection can be safely abandoned.[73]

### 3.1.3 Lord Scarman

Lord Scarman agreed with Lord Fraser's opinion but felt that the importance of the case also necessitated his expressing his views in his own words. Drawing on similar authorities, he concluded that the underlying principle of the law, as exposed by Blackstone and acknowledged in the case law, is that 'parental right yields to the child's right to make his own decisions when he reaches a sufficient understanding and intelligence to be capable of making up his own mind on the matter requiring decision'.[74] Lord Scarman suggested that earlier 'age of discretion' cases, and specifically *R v Howes*,[75] may afford 'a clue to the true principle of the law'.[76] These cases were ones in which a father issued a writ of habeas corpus to secure the return of his child who had left home without consent. The courts would refuse an order if the child had attained an age of discretion. By analogy with the Abduction Acts, the first of which appeared in the sixteenth century, the age of discretion was set at 14 for boys and 16 for girls. In *R v Howes* Cockburn CJ rejected the argument that a girl could be emancipated from her father before the age of 16, pointing out that legal recognition of her precocity might risk her harm. Drawing on *R v Howes*, Lord Scarman explained that the principle

---

[68] Ibid, 171D–F.   [69] Ibid, 174B–C.   [70] Ibid, 174D–E.

[71] Cf G. Williams, 'The *Gillick* Saga' [1985] New Law Journal 1179–1182 at 1179, who in setting out what he terms Lord Fraser's five ethical precepts leaves out the words which refer to parental consent in ethical precept number five. Williams's omission is hardly surprising, however, since he views the parental rights issue in *Gillick* as a misdirection of judicial effort (at 1182).

[72] For detailed arguments supporting the view that Lord Fraser extends the doctor's role, see I. Kennedy, 'The Doctor, the Pill and the 15-Year-Old Girl' in I. Kennedy, *Treat me Right: Essays in Medical Law and Ethics* (Oxford: Oxford University Press, 1988), pp 94–5.

[73] Cf Kennedy, ibid, p 94, who suggests that Lord Fraser takes this view as a matter of public policy.

[74] [1986] 1 AC 112 at 186D.   [75] (1860) 3 E & E 332.   [76] [1986] 1 AC 112 at 183F.

underlying the habeas corpus cases was that 'an order would be refused if the child had *sufficient intelligence and understanding to make up his own mind*'[77] and continued:

> While it is unrealistic to treat a 16th century Act as a safe guide in the matter of a girl's discretion, . . . we can agree with Cockburn CJ as to the principle of the law—the attainment by a child of an age of sufficient discretion to exercise a *wise choice in his or her interests*.[78]

Applying these principles to the medical context of the case, Lord Scarman explained that:

> as a matter of law the parental right to determine whether or not their minor child below the age of 16 will have medical treatment terminates if and when the child achieves a sufficient understanding and intelligence to enable him or her to understand fully what is proposed. It will be a question of fact whether a child seeking advice has sufficient understanding of what is involved to give a consent valid in law.[79]

He went on to impose a stringent test for the child's capacity, going beyond mere understanding of the nature of the advice given. Lord Scarman explained that in the context of providing a girl with contraceptive advice and treatment:

> There are moral and family questions, especially her relationship with her parents; long-term problems associated with the emotional impact of pregnancy and its termination; and there are the risks to health of sexual intercourse at her age, risks which contraception may diminish but cannot eliminate. It follows that a doctor will have to satisfy himself that she is able to appraise these factors before he can safely proceed upon the basis that she has at law capacity to consent to contraceptive treatment.[80]

### 3.1.4 Lord Bridge of Harwich

Lord Bridge addressed a procedural point raised by the case, but otherwise simply agreed with both Lord Fraser and Lord Scarman on the substantive issue. Lord Bridge's failure to expand might be seen as rather unhelpful given the different emphases in the other two majority judgments. As we have seen, Lord Fraser took a welfare approach, whereas in Lord Scarman's opinion there is a much stronger focus on the child's capacities. These different approaches have led to the suggestion that the case may have no clear *ratio decidendi*.[81] The fact that Lord Bridge felt able to agree with both opinions, however, may suggest that he did not see the two other majority opinions as representing wholly inconsistent positions.[82]

## 3.2 Interpreting *Gillick*

Given the differences in the majority opinions, it is perhaps not surprising that academics have been divided in their assessment of the decision.[83] Undoubtedly *Gillick* is a 'landmark decision

---

[77] Ibid, 187D.

[78] Ibid, 187H–188A (emphasis added). Fortin argues that Lord Scarman's statement that the age of discretion was the attainment of 'sufficient discretion to enable him or her to exercise a *wise* choice' was merely a factual description of how the ages of discretion were chosen and did not suggest that he himself confined the notion of *Gillick* competence to those with a capacity for wisdom: see J. Fortin, 'The *Gillick* Decision—Not Just a High-Water Mark' in S. Gilmore, J. Herring, and R. Probert (eds), *Landmark Cases in Family Law* (Oxford: Hart, 2011), pp 206–7.

[79] [1986] 1 AC 112 at 188–9.      [80] Ibid, 189D.

[81] P. Parkinson, 'The *Gillick* Case—Just What has it Decided?' [1986] Family Law 11.

[82] The position is made even more interesting by Lord Templeman's dissenting opinion, which appeared to accept that a child might make his or her own decisions, but that having contraception under 16 was not one of them.

[83] J. Eekelaar, 'The Eclipse of Parental Rights' (1986) 102 LQR 4 and 'The Emergence of Children's Rights' (1986) 6 Oxford Journal of Legal Studies 161. Compare A. Bainham, 'The Balance of Power in Family Decisions' (1986) 45(2)

for children's rights'[84] emancipating children from nineteenth-century views of absolute parental authority, but whether it is a case about children's autonomy rights which accorded to children general rights to make their own decisions, as some have claimed,[85] is debatable. Within academic work, perhaps the most prominent and influential proponent of this view is John Eekelaar. Eekelaar focused on passages in Lord Scarman's opinion in which Lord Scarman referred to parental rights yielding[86] or terminating,[87] and observed that:

> [t]he significance of Lord Scarman's opinion with respect to children's autonomy interests cannot be over-rated. It follows from his reasoning that, where a child has reached capacity, there is no room for a parent to impose a contrary view, *even if this is more in accord with the child's best interests.* For its legal superiority to the child's decision can rest only on its status as a parental right. But this is extinguished when the child reaches full capacity.[88]

Eekelaar maintained that Lord Fraser should not be taken to have expressed a different view, pointing out that the part of Lord Fraser's opinion dealing with parental rights 'is placed firmly within the context of medical treatment, whereas Lord Scarman discusses parental rights on a general level'.[89]

Thus, in Eekelaar's view, *Gillick* involved a reconciliation of the autonomy interest with the basic and developmental interests 'through the empirical application of the concept of the acquisition of full capacity',[90] namely intellectual understanding supplemented by emotional maturity. It accorded to children a decision-making power which, once granted, could be exercised without adult restraint. He declared, therefore, that *Gillick* had conferred on children 'in wider measure than ever before, that most dangerous but most precious of rights: the right to make their own mistakes'.[91]

By contrast, another leading child law scholar, Andrew Bainham, suggests that *Gillick* 'represents a small but significant shift towards the thinking of the child liberationist school'[92] but that we should not 'equate this with a policy of legal autonomy or independence for children'.[93] For

---

Cambridge Law Journal 262 and S. Gilmore, 'The Limits of Parental Responsibility' in R. Probert, S. Gilmore, and J. Herring (eds), *Responsible Parents and Parental Responsibility* (Oxford: Hart, 2009). And for a defence of the children's rights interpretation of *Gillick*, see J. Fortin, 'The *Gillick* Decision—Not Just a High-Water Mark' in S. Gilmore, J. Herring, and R. Probert (eds), *Landmark Cases in Family Law* (Oxford: Hart, 2011).

[84] As the Children's Legal Centre described it at the time: see (1985) 22 Childright 11; and see Fortin in Gilmore et al, *Landmark Cases in Family Law*.

[85] This was the Children's Legal Centre's perception of its landmark status: 'the first legal judgment which unequivocally recognises the right of young people to make decisions about their lives and their bodies if they are old enough to have a mature appreciation of the issues and to make up their own minds' ((1985) 22 Childright, 16). And this approach was said to apply to 'every area of children's lives other than those regulated by statute'. Many suggestions for its future application soon emerged in the pages of *Childright*. For a summary, see 'Wider Implications of *Gillick*' (1986) 26 Childright 17. For a general discussion of the 'potentially far-reaching implications' of what was clearly perceived as a 'fundamental shift in legal doctrine', see S. M. Cretney, '*Gillick* and the Concept of Legal Capacity' (1989) 105 LQR 356.

[86] [1986] 1 AC 112 at 186D.          [87] Ibid, 188H.

[88] (1986) 6 Oxford Journal of Legal Studies 161 at 181. The case would thus apparently require a re-orientation of the court's approach to wardship and custody disputes on divorce (see J. Eekelaar, '*Gillick* in the Divorce Court' (1986) 136 New Law Journal 184), where welfare would now have to defer to the competent child's wishes.

[89] (1986) LQR at 6. Eekelaar also argued ((1986) LQR 7) that Lord Fraser's conditions (2) to (5) are matters for professional discipline only and have no reference to legal liability (see also J. Montgomery, 'Children as Property?' (1988) 51 Modern Law Review 323 at 339: 'they are obiter, and if they have force it is as the content of the doctor's duty of care in negligence'); A. Grubb, 'Contraceptive Advice and Medical Treatment for Children' [1986] Cambridge Law Journal 3 at 5. However, Silber J has since held that Lord Fraser's guidelines are legal conditions. Even if they were not legal conditions, the fact that they have no reference to legal liability does not mean that they can be entirely ignored.

[90] (1986) Oxford Journal of Legal Studies 161 at 181.

[91] Ibid, 182. It is a view that he thought may not ultimately find favour with the judiciary: J. Eekelaar, '*Gillick*: Further Limits on Parents' Rights to Punish' (1986) 28 Childright 9.

[92] A. Bainham, 'The Balance of Power in Family Decisions' (1986) 45(2) Cambridge Law Journal 262 at 275.

[93] Ibid.

Bainham, the majority speeches in *Gillick* 'support a participatory model of decision making, . . . according to parents *and* children qualified or relative autonomy'.[94]

One of the authors of this book, Stephen Gilmore, has questioned more directly whether Eekelaar's interpretation of *Gillick* is the most plausible.[95] He has argued that *Gillick* is essentially a case about children's *welfare* not their autonomy interests.[96] This is demonstrated in the public debate surrounding the litigation, counsel's arguments, and their Lordships' characterisation of the issues, all of which focused on resolving the potentially conflicting claims of doctors and parents to know what was in a child's best interests.[97] Indeed their Lordships had rejected an application by the Children's Legal Centre to make submissions or instruct counsel as *amicus curiae* on behalf of children in general.[98] These are reasons for some caution regarding a children's autonomy rights reading of *Gillick*.

Remember that Eekelaar focused heavily on parts of Lord Scarman's opinion, and then argued that Lord Fraser's focus on child welfare in the case should be seen as confined to the medical aspects of the case and not detract from Lord Scarman's general approach. By contrast, Gilmore points out that Lord Scarman agreed with Lord Fraser's opinion, and therefore Lord Scarman's opinion should be read in light of that agreement. Defending a children's autonomy rights reading of Lord Scarman's opinion, Jane Fortin[99] has countered that Lord Scarman's 'words of agreement with Lord Fraser's opinion were unsurprising, given their joint view that Mrs Gillick's application was unfounded' and that 'he clearly agreed with much of Lord Fraser's assessment of the preceding case law'.[100] However, it should be recalled that Lord Scarman agreed with Lord Fraser's *speech* not just the outcome and he did not qualify his agreement[101] so he should on the face of it be taken to have agreed with all of it.

Gilmore questions why Lord Fraser's welfare approach in the medical context should not be seen as *reflecting* their Lordships' earlier general conclusions as to the point at which parental right yields. He also points out that the fact that Lord Scarman drew on case law on the ages of discretion, the aim of which was to protect children, makes it difficult to conclude that Lord Scarman envisaged the law allowing children to make decisions that would lead to their irreparable harm. These arguments should be borne in mind when thinking about the difficult question of what was meant in *Gillick* by the point at which parental right yields to the child's right.

So what did *Gillick* establish as a matter of law? It would certainly be difficult to see *Gillick* as a binding precedent for the view that children have the right to make their own mistakes.[102] The most *Gillick* could represent as a binding precedent would be the child's power to consent to medical treatment offered without parental knowledge or consent because it is considered in the child's best interests to do so. At its most abstract, it endorses a child's power to accept someone else's bona fide, yet possibly mistaken, view of what is in a child's interests. Put simply, the 'reasoning of

---

[94] A. Bainham, *Children, Parents and the State* (London: Sweet & Maxwell, 1988), p 72.

[95] S. Gilmore, 'The Limits of Parental Responsibility' in R. Probert, S. Gilmore, and J. Herring, *Responsible Parents and Parental Responsibility* (Oxford: Hart, 2009); but compare J. Fortin, 'The *Gillick* Decision—Not Just a High-Water Mark' in S. Gilmore, J. Herring, and R. Probert (eds), *Landmark Cases in Family Law* (Oxford: Hart, 2011), p 199, who argues that many of the attempts to dilute the impact of Lord Scarman's views can be answered (see pp 206–8).

[96] S. Gilmore, 'The Limits of Parental Responsibility' in R. Probert, S. Gilmore, and J. Herring, *Responsible Parents and Parental Responsibility* (Oxford: Hart, 2009).

[97] See also Eekelaar's own comment: '[t]he public debate which surrounded the litigation tended to revolve around the competing claims of parents and doctors to determine children's interests' (1986) 6 Oxford Journal of Legal Studies 161 at 178.

[98] (1985) *Legal Action* 3. The DHSS consented but Mrs Gillick did not. No reasons were given by their Lordships.

[99] J. Fortin, 'The *Gillick* Decision—Not Just a High-Water Mark' in S. Gilmore, J. Herring, and R. Probert (eds), *Landmark Cases in Family Law* (Oxford: Hart, 2011) pp 199, 205–7.

[100] Ibid, p 206.

[101] Except by saying that the issues were so important that he wished to express his opinion in his own words.

[102] S. Gilmore, 'The Limits of Parental Responsibility' in R. Probert, S. Gilmore, and J. Herring, *Responsible Parents and Parental Responsibility* (Oxford: Hart, 2009).

Lords Fraser and Scarman was built upon a consideration of the best interests of the sexually active minor, not upon the right of the minor to be sexually active',[103] or indeed to demand contraceptive treatment.

That is not to say that the general principles articulated by Lord Scarman were not groundbreaking. As Fortin contends, in terms of *Gillick*'s landmark status 'it does not matter what the precise effects of the majority decision were'.[104] *Gillick* 'undeniably placed the idea of children's autonomy rights in the legal consciousness in a way which had not previously existed'.[105] It also undoubtedly had an influence on the Children Act 1989.[106] However, it is maintained that it is still important to distinguish between what it achieved as a matter of law and what it promised. Essentially what *Gillick* achieved was to create a climate of expectation that a child will be consulted, and his or her wishes and feelings will be taken into account, when any important decision is made in respect of his or her upbringing. What *Gillick* did *not* achieve was to create a rule that the wishes and feelings of a child will always prevail over the wishes and feelings of the persons with parental responsibility, even though the child has sufficient competence[107] to understand the full implications of the decision to be made. The opportunity to suggest the incorporation of such a rule in legislation was afforded during the massive review of child law which took place before the Children Act 1989 was enacted, but no suggestion for such a rule was made.

### 3.3 *Axon*: a human rights challenge to *Gillick*

---

**Key case**

Over 20 years after *Gillick* was decided, and following implementation of the Human Rights Act 1998, a human rights challenge was mounted to the approach in *Gillick* by Ms Sue Axon, in the context of abortion advice and treatment and an updated version of the relevant Guidance.[108] Ms Axon had had an abortion when she was younger, which had caused her personal difficulties, and she did not want her daughters to be offered such advice or treatment without her knowledge; she wanted the opportunity to give her daughters the benefit of her own experience. In judicial review proceedings[109] she sought a declaration that medical professionals are under no obligation to maintain confidentiality in relation to abortion advice and treatment unless disclosure might prejudice the child's physical or mental health. She

---

[103] S. Gilmore, J. Herring, and R. Probert, 'Introduction: Parental Responsibility—Law, Issues and Themes' in R. Probert, S. Gilmore, and J. Herring, *Responsible Parents and Parental Responsibility* (Oxford: Hart, 2009), p 4.

[104] J. Fortin, 'The *Gillick* Decision—Not Just a High-Water Mark' in S. Gilmore, J. Herring, and R. Probert (eds), *Landmark Cases in Family Law* (Oxford: Hart, 2011) p 199, at p 222.

[105] S. Gilmore, J. Herring, and R. Probert, 'Introduction: Parental Responsibility—Law, Issues and Themes' in R. Probert, S. Gilmore, and J. Herring, *Responsible Parents and Parental Responsibility* (Oxford: Hart, 2009), p 6. See H. Teff, *Reasonable Care, Legal Perspectives on the Doctor/Patient Relationship* (Oxford: Clarendon Press, 1994), p 152: undeniable that *Gillick* 'came to be seen as a symbolic milestone in the enfranchisement of children'.

[106] See eg children's rights to refuse assessment in ss 38(6), 43(8), and 44(7). However, see *South Glamorgan County Council v W and B* [1993] 1 FLR 574 in which the inherent jurisdiction was used to override the child's refusal, discussed in more detail in Chapter 10. See C. Lyon 'What's Happened to the Child's "Right" to Refuse?—*South Glamorgan County Council v. W and B*' (1994) 6(2) Journal of Child Law 84.

[107] For a discussion of problems with the notion of *Gillick* competence, see E. Cave, 'Goodbye *Gillick*? Problems with the Concept of Child Competence' (2014) 34(1) Legal Studies 103–22.

[108] Guidance for Doctors and other Health Professionals on the Provision of Advice and Treatment to Young People under 16 on Contraception, Sexual and Reproductive Health (29 July 2004), gateway reference No 3382. Relevant parts of the Guidance are set out at [2006] EWHC 37 (Admin), [2006] QB 539 at [22]–[24].

[109] *R (Axon) v Secretary of State for Health* [2006] EWHC 37 (Admin). For comment, see J. Bridgeman, 'Case Comment: Young People and Sexual Health: Whose Rights? Whose Responsibilities?' [2006] Medical Law Review 418; R. Taylor, 'Reversing the Retreat from *Gillick*? *R (Axon) v Secretary of State for Health*' [2007] Child and Family Law Quarterly 81.

also argued (and sought declarations to the effect) that the Guidance misrepresented *Gillick*, and failed to discharge the state's positive obligation to give practical and effective protection to her rights under Article 8(1) of the European Convention on Human Rights (ECHR). Silber J rejected her claims, holding that there was no such misrepresentation, and that the approach in *Gillick* 'was and is of general application to *all* forms of medical advice and treatment', including therefore abortion advice and treatment. Silber J clarified that Lord Fraser's guidelines are legal pre-conditions[110] and to be strictly observed. He also indicated that Lord Fraser's first condition, that the child understands the advice, was to be read in light of Lord Scarman's stringent test for capacity, and explained that 'all relevant matters' were included within the meaning of 'understanding'.[111]

Addressing Ms Axon's argument based on Article 8(1) of the ECHR, Silber J held that 'any right to family life on the part of a parent dwindles as their child gets older and is able to understand the consequence of different choices and then to make decisions relating to them'[112] and that 'this autonomy must undermine any article 8 rights of a parent to family life'.[113] Accordingly:

> parents do not have article 8 rights to be notified of any advice of a medical professional after the young person is able to look after himself or herself and make his or her own decisions.[114]

In reaching this conclusion, Silber J commented that 'the right of young people to make decisions about their own lives by themselves at the expense of the views of their parents has now become an increasingly important and accepted feature of family life'.[115] He saw this 'change in the landscape of family matters, in which rights of children are becoming increasingly important' as a reason for not retreating from the approach in *Gillick*.[116] He concluded that there was nothing in the Guidance which interferes with a parent's Article 8 rights since the medical professional must act in the child's best interests.[117] Alternatively, any infringement could be justified under Article 8(2). He held that the legislative objective (of reducing unwanted pregnancies and addressing sexually transmitted diseases) is sufficiently important to justify limiting parents' Article 8 rights; and Lord Fraser's guidelines were rationally connected to that objective and impaired freedom no more than necessary to achieve it.[118]

## 4 Children's rights in cases of refusal of medical treatment

*Gillick v West Norfolk and Wisbech Area Health Authority* was concerned with whether a competent child could *consent* to medical treatment, and whether such consent could be countermanded by a person with parental responsibility. In two subsequent decisions of the Court of Appeal, *Re R (A Minor) (Wardship: Consent to Treatment)*[119] and *Re W (A Minor) (Medical Treatment: Court's*

---

[110] *Axon* at [110] and [111].

[111] Ibid, [154]. See also the passage from Lord Scarman's opinion set out at n 80. [112] Ibid, [129].

[113] Ibid, [130]. [114] Ibid, [132].

[115] Citing as illustrations Arts 16(1) and 12(1) of the United Nations Convention on the Rights of the Child and the judgment of Thorpe LJ in *Mabon v Mabon* [2005] EWCA Civ 634, [2005] Fam 366.

[116] *Axon* at [80]. [117] Ibid, [134]. [118] Ibid, [150]–[152].

[119] [1992] Fam 11 (Lord Donaldson MR, Staughton and Farquharson LJJ), hereafter *Re R*. See A. Bainham, 'The Judge and the Competent Minor' (1992) 108 LQR 194; G. Douglas, 'The Retreat from *Gillick*' (1992) 55 Modern Law Review 569; P. Fennell, 'Informal Compulsion: The Psychiatric Treatment of Juveniles under Common Law' [1992] Journal of Social Welfare and Family Law 311; J. Masson, 'Adolescent Crisis and Parental Power' [1991] Family Law 528; J. Montgomery, 'Parents and Children in Dispute: Who Has the Final Word?' (1992) 4 Journal of Child Law 85; J. Murphy, 'Circumscribing the Autonomy of "*Gillick* Competent" Children' (1992) 43(1) Northern Ireland Legal Quarterly 60; S. Parker and J. Dewar [1992] Journal of Social Welfare and Family Law 143 (case commentary on *Re R*); R. Thornton, 'Multiple Keyholders—Wardship and Consent to Medical Treatment' [1992] Cambridge Law Journal 34; J. Urwin, '*Re R*: The Resurrection of Parental Powers?' (1992) 8 Professional Negligence 69.

*Jurisdiction)*,[120] and in a series of High Court judgments,[121] the tension between child autonomy and child protection has acquired a sharper practical focus, as the issue has switched to the validity of a child's *refusal* of consent in circumstances where a failure to undergo treatment might result in irreparable harm or death.

## 4.1 *Re R (a minor) (wardship: consent to treatment)*

In *Re R* a local authority initiated wardship proceedings in respect of a girl, R, aged 15 years 10 months, who had a history of family problems and psychiatric illness, characterised by violent and suicidal behaviour. R, who was the subject of an interim care order,[122] had been placed with the consent of the local authority, in an adolescent psychiatric unit, where the treatment regime included, when necessary, compulsory administration of anti-psychotic medication. The local authority initially consented to the administration of anti-psychotic medication. In one of her lucid periods, R refused her medication. A social worker, who had experience with cases involving persons who are mentally ill, then had a three-hour telephone conversation with R after which he decided that R sounded lucid and rational and he did not regard her as 'sectionable'.[123] The local authority therefore took the view that they could not give permission for R to have drugs administered against her will. The adolescent unit refused to care for R without a free hand in the administration of her medication, and the wardship application therefore sought leave for administration of the medication without R's consent.

The application came before Waite J who heard evidence from a consultant child psychiatrist, Dr R.[124] In a written report, Dr R concluded that when he had seen R five days before the hearing she had been 'of sufficient maturity and understanding to comprehend the treatment being recommended and was rational'. He cautioned, however, that should she not continue with treatment her more florid psychotic behaviour was likely to return and she might become a serious suicidal risk. In his oral evidence, Dr R explained that he was familiar with the decision in *Gillick*, which, in his view, required in R's case a consideration of 'whether, having regard to her development and maturity, she understands the nature of the implications of the treatment proposed', and concluded that when he had seen her, R was 'mature enough to understand the nature of the proposal'. Waite J, stating *obiter* that a judge in wardship could not override the refusal of a competent child, granted the local authority's application on the ground that R's mental condition precluded her from achieving such competence.

On appeal, James Munby QC for the Official Solicitor, acting as R's guardian ad litem, contended that Waite J was wrong as to R's competence, but was correct as to the powers of the judge in wardship. Relying on Lord Scarman's judgment in *Gillick*, he argued that parental rights to consent are terminated when a child achieves capacity to consent, and since the court in wardship steps into the parents' shoes the court is equally precluded from exercising its powers against the child's wishes.

The Court of Appeal rejected these arguments. It was by no means satisfied that R understood the implications of the treatment being withheld, as distinct from understanding what was proposed

---

[120] [1993] Fam 64 (Lord Donaldson MR, Balcombe and Nolan LJJ), hereafter *Re W*. See J. Eekelaar, 'White Coats or Flak Jackets? Doctors, Children and the Courts—Again' (1993) 109 LQR 182; H. Houghton-James, 'The Child's Right to Die' [1992] Family Law 550; N. Lowe and S. Juss, 'Medical Treatment—Pragmatism and the Search for Principle' (1993) 56 Modern Law Review 865; J. Masson, '*Re W*: Appealing from the Golden Cage' (1993) 5(1) Journal of Child Law 37; M. Mulholland, '*Re W (A Minor)*: Autonomy, Consent and the Anorexic Teenager' (1993) 9(1) Professional Negligence 21; R. Thornton, 'Minors and Medical Treatment—Who Decides?' [1993] Cambridge Law Journal 34.

[121] Discussed at Section 4.6.

[122] The case was decided pre-Children Act 1989, so the restrictions on the use of wardship in s 100 of that Act did not apply.

[123] That is, liable to be made the subject of an application under ss 2 and 3 of the Mental Health Act 1983.

[124] The summary of this evidence which follows is taken from *Re R* [1992] Fam 11 at 19–21.

to be done by way of treatment. The evidence had established that R's mental state fluctuated, so that even if, on a good day, she was capable of reaching the standard of competence required to meet the *Gillick* criteria, on other days she was not only *Gillick* incompetent, she was actually sectionable. Lord Donaldson MR ruled that 'no child in that situation can be regarded as "*Gillick* competent" . . . "*Gillick* competence" is a developmental concept and will not be lost or acquired on a day-to-day or week-to-week basis. In the case of mental disability, that disability must also be taken into account, particularly where it is fluctuating in effect.'[125] Farquharson LJ observed that '[t]he *Gillick* test is not apt to a situation where the understanding and capacity of the child varies from day to day according to the effect of her illness'.[126]

This sufficed to dispose of the case, but in response to a request from counsel for their Lordships to clarify the legal position, the court went further. It held that, in wardship, the child's wishes could be overridden irrespective of competence, the court's powers being wider than those of parents. Lord Donaldson alone made further *obiter* comments concerning the relationship between parents' and children's powers of consent, in a passage which bears extended citation:

> What Mr. Munby's argument overlooks is that Lord Scarman was discussing the parents' right '*to determine* whether or not their minor child below the age of 16 will have medical treatment' (my emphasis) and this is the 'parental right' to which he was referring at p. 186D. A right of determination is wider than a right to consent. The parents can only have a right of determination if *either* the child has no right to consent, that is, is not a keyholder, *or* the parents hold a master key which could nullify the child's consent. I do not understand Lord Scarman to be saying that, if a child was '*Gillick* competent', to adopt the convenient phrase used in argument, the parents ceased to have an independent right of consent as contrasted with ceasing to have a right of determination, that is, a veto. In a case in which the '*Gillick* competent' child refuses treatment, but the parents' consent, that consent *enables* treatment to be undertaken lawfully, but in no way determines that the child shall be so treated. In a case in which the positions are reversed, it is the child's consent which is the enabling factor and again the parents' refusal of consent is not determinative. If Lord Scarman intended to go further than this and to say that in the case of a '*Gillick* competent' child, a parent has no right either to consent or to refuse consent, his remarks were obiter, because the only question in issue was Mrs Gillick's alleged right of veto. Furthermore, I consider that they would have been wrong.[127]

Lord Donaldson's analysis, distinguishing between determination and consent, has been criticised by some commentators. Andrew Bainham has argued that if a doctor is faced with a conflict between parent and child and 'proceeds on the basis of the parent's view, he is in reality giving effect to a parental veto over the child's view, and thus the distinction between determination and consent falls apart'.[128] In similar vein, Gillian Douglas[129] views consent as part of the right to determine, not an alternative to it, illustrating her point by way of two examples: first, if I have the right to determine that my 1-year-old child is inoculated, then I have power to consent to the giving of an injection; secondly, if I do not have power to determine the length of a 15-year-old's hair, then I cannot have power to consent to its being cut against the child's wishes.

It seems, however, that Lord Donaldson was interpreting the word 'determine' differently, in the sense of an *exclusive* power to decide. Lord Donaldson would respond to Douglas's first example by

---

[125] [1992] Fam 11 at 25–26 *per* Lord Donaldson MR. The concept of 'competence' was subsequently developed in *Re C (Refusal of Medical Treatment)* [1994] 1 FLR 31 where Thorpe J ruled that the decision-making process should be approached in three stages: (i) comprehending and retaining treatment information; (ii) believing it; and (iii) weighing it in the balance to arrive at a choice. This test was applied in *A Metropolitan Borough Council v DB* [1997] 1 FLR 767 where the court ruled that a 17-year-old pregnant girl who was addicted to drugs, living in squalid conditions, and had a phobia against needles failed to satisfy each stage of the test. Compulsory medical treatment of the girl was therefore authorised.

[126] *Re R* [1992] Fam 11, at 32.       [127] [1992] Fam 11 at 23E–H.

[128] A. Bainham, 'The Judge and the Competent Minor' (1992) 108 LQR 194 at 198.

[129] G. Douglas, 'The Retreat from *Gillick*' (1992) 55 Modern Law Review 569 at 575.

pointing out that it is only because the child cannot consent that parental consent is determinative. To the second, presumably Lord Donaldson would say: 'Though the parent can consent to haircuts, she cannot be said to have a right to determine the issue of haircuts if she cannot prevent the child consenting to a particular haircut.' So the arguments here reduce to arguments over which of different possible meanings of the word 'determine' Lord Scarman used in *Gillick* and it was of course Lord Donaldson's job to interpret that word.

Lord Donaldson offered two principal arguments in support of his view that there can be concurrent consents in parent and child. First, he could not agree that, to avoid being sued in trespass, the law required a doctor 'to determine as a matter of law in whom the right of consent resided at the particular time in relation to the particular treatment'.[130] This, he felt, would place doctors in 'an intolerable dilemma' when, for example, there was a dispute between parents and a child nearing the age of 16.[131] This appeal to legal certainty seems out of step with the flexible approach of the Lords in *Gillick*.[132] Neither *Gillick* nor section 8 of the Family Law Reform Act 1969 seems directed at protecting doctors from litigation,[133] and it may be that 'it is no more difficult to determine the child's competence when the child is refusing'.[134] As Parker and Dewar have argued, consequentialist justifications appear to point the other way[135] since to place the doctor at some risk might operate as a presumption in favour of competence and of complying with the child's wishes.[136]

Lord Donaldson's second argument suggested that section 8 of the Family Law Reform Act 1969 was inconsistent with counsel's interpretation of Lord Scarman's speech.[137] So far as material, section 8 provides:

(1) The consent of a minor who has attained the age of 16 years to any . . . medical treatment, which in the absence of consent would constitute a trespass to the person, shall be as effective as it would be if he were of full age; and where a minor has by virtue of this section given an effective consent to any treatment it shall not be necessary to obtain any consent for it from his parent or guardian; . . .

(3) Nothing in this section shall be construed as making ineffective any consent which would have been effective if this section had not been enacted.

Lord Donaldson indicated that if parental power to consent was extinguished upon a child's acquisition of capacity to consent, then not only would it not be necessary to obtain a parent's consent as section 8(1) provides, it would be legally impossible. He further argued that section 8(3) 'would create problems since, if the section had not been enacted, a parent's consent would undoubtedly have been effective *as a consent*'.[138] These arguments are not without merit. Furthermore,

---

[130] [1992] Fam 11 at 24A–C.

[131] Ibid. Although also acknowledged by at least one commentator as a 'significant theoretical problem'. See J. Montgomery, 'Parents and Children in Dispute: Who Has the Final Word?' (1992) 4 Journal of Child Law 85 at 87.

[132] G. Austin, 'Righting a Child's Right to Refuse Medical Treatment, Section 11 of the New Zealand Bill of Rights Act and the *Gillick* Competent Child' (1992) 7(4) Otago Law Review 578 at 585. As Murphy observes, whilst the House of Lords held that parental rights exist for the benefit of the child, 'it is difficult to see why in *Re R* the Master of the Rolls held them to exist also for the benefit of the doctor': J. Murphy, 'Circumscribing the Autonomy of "*Gillick* Competent" Children' (1992) 43(1) Northern Ireland Legal Quarterly 60 at 62.

[133] R. Thornton, 'Multiple Keyholders—Wardship and Consent to Medical Treatment' [1992] Cambridge Law Journal 34 at 36.

[134] A. Grubb, 'Treatment Decisions: Keeping it in the Family' in A. Grubb (ed), *Choices and Decisions in Health Care* (Chichester: Wiley, 1993), p 63.

[135] S. Parker and J. Dewar, [1992] Journal of Social Welfare and Family Law 143 (case commentary on *Re R*) at 146–7.

[136] Ibid, 146.     [137] [1992] Fam 11 at 24F–G.

[138] Ibid, 24G–H. In *Re W* [1993] Fam 64 at 77, Lord Donaldson reiterated these arguments, where additionally he described s 8(3) as 'preserving the common law immediately before the Act, which undoubtedly gave parents a power to consent for all children up to the age of 21'.

as Gilmore and Herring have argued in a detailed analysis of the background to section 8,[139] its parliamentary history and the approach of the Latey Committee Report,[140] which recommended the provision, does not suggest that the intention was that parental powers of consent would be extinguished upon the child achieving capacity. While, as Eekelaar has observed, section 8(3) 'cannot be construed as imposing a restraint in perpetuity on the later development of the common law'[141] there does not seem to be any reason why the statute should not provide some indication, or confirmation, of the appropriate interpretation of the common law.[142]

To summarise, then, Lord Donaldson was clearly of the opinion that in a case where a '*Gillick* competent' child refuses treatment, but someone with parental responsibility consents, that treatment can lawfully be given to the child. He acknowledged that the child's refusal of consent will be a very important factor in the doctor's decision whether or not to treat, but held that it does not stop treatment going ahead if consent is obtained from another person with parental responsibility.

### 4.2 *Re W (a minor) (medical treatment: court's jurisdiction)*

Lord Donaldson's approach in *Re R* attracted considerable criticism and an opportunity to reconsider his approach was presented by the case of *Re W (A Minor) (Medical Treatment: Court's Jurisdiction)*.[143] A 16-year-old child, W, who was in the care of a local authority, developed anorexia nervosa and was admitted to an adolescent residential unit for treatment. Following a deterioration in W's condition, the local authority obtained leave to invoke the inherent jurisdiction of the High Court. By the time the case came to court the girl's weight had dropped to such a low level that, should she continue to lose weight for more than a few days, her capacity to have children in later life would be put seriously at risk, and a little later her life itself might be in danger. Contrary to W's wishes and the advice of her consultant, the local authority sought the court's permission to transfer W from her adolescent unit where she was consenting to treatment, to a unit specialising in eating disorders and to treat her there, if necessary without her consent. Thorpe J held[144] that W had sufficient understanding to make an informed decision but nevertheless that he had jurisdiction to authorise treatment and should do so in W's best interests.

W's case differed materially from *Re R* in two respects: she had attained the age of 16, and by section 8 of the Family Law Reform Act 1969 had a statutory power to consent to medical treatment; and had been adjudged competent. On appeal to the Court of Appeal, W contended that section 8 had provided her with an absolute right to determine whether or not she received medical treatment, and accordingly under the principle in *A v Liverpool City Council*[145] the court was precluded from accepting jurisdiction. The Court of Appeal rejected this interpretation of section 8,[146] and held that a judge exercising the inherent jurisdiction had power to override the wishes of a competent 16- or 17-year-old.

Lord Donaldson again ventured 'to doubt whether Lord Scarman meant more than that the *exclusive* right of the parents to consent to treatment terminated',[147] a doubt now shared by Balcombe LJ,[148] although Lord Donaldson now acknowledged that he 'may well be wrong'.[149] Despite this

---

[139] S. Gilmore and J. Herring, '"No" is the Hardest Word: Consent and Children's Autonomy' [2011] Child and Family Law Quarterly 3, esp at 17–19.

[140] *Report of the Committee on the Age of Majority* (Cmnd 3342, 1967).

[141] J. Eekelaar, 'The Emergence of Children's Rights' (1986) 6 Oxford Journal of Legal Studies 161 at 184.

[142] S. Gilmore and J. Herring, '"No" is the Hardest Word: Consent and Children's Autonomy' [2011] Child and Family Law Quarterly 3, esp at 19.

[143] [1993] Fam 64. See criticism of *Re R* at 75.       [144] *Re J (a Minor)*, The Times, 14 May 1992.

[145] [1982] AC 363.

[146] [1993] Fam 64 at 77B–C *per* Lord Donaldson MR, at 87H *per* Balcombe LJ, at 92E–H *per* Nolan LJ.

[147] Ibid, 76C.       [148] Ibid, 87E–F.

[149] Ibid. Several commentaries have addressed both *Re R* and *Re W*: J. Bridgeman, 'Old Enough to Know Best?' (1993) 13 Legal Studies 69; L. Edwards, 'The Right to Consent and the Right to Refuse; More Problems with Minors and Medical Consent' [1993] Juridical Review 52; A. Grubb, 'Treatment Decisions: Keeping it in the Family' in A. Grubb (ed), *Choices*

concession, however, he reiterated his view that there could be concurrent consents, although he now preferred the analogy of the legal flak-jacket (providing the doctor with a shield against a claim in battery) to his earlier keyholder analogy since keys are capable of both locking and unlocking.[150] Balcombe LJ agreed. Nolan LJ appeared to have some reservations about this point.

Lord Donaldson MR emphasised, however, that the wishes of a competent child were of the greatest clinical importance. In response to the 'hair-raising' possibility, which had been canvassed before him in argument, of abortions being carried out by doctors with the consent of parents on unwilling 16- and 17-year-olds, he was content to place reliance on medical ethics to act as a restraining influence in such cases. Balcombe LJ was also of the opinion that a doctor would not terminate the pregnancy of a mentally competent 16-year-old merely upon the consent of the child's parents. He added that it would seem inevitable that the matter would have to come before the court in such highly unlikely circumstances. Nolan LJ offered the child the strongest safeguard when he said:

> We are not directly concerned with cases in which the jurisdiction of the court has not been invoked, and in which accordingly the decision on treatment may depend upon the consent of the child or of the parent. I for my part would think it axiomatic, however, in order to avoid the risk of grave breaches of the law that in any case where time permitted, where major surgical or other procedures (such as an abortion) were proposed, and whereby the parents or those in loco parentis were prepared to give consent but the child (having sufficient understanding to make an informed decision) was not, the jurisdiction of the court should always be invoked.[151]

The court was united, however, in its view that a court has the power to override a minor's consent to medical treatment. With regard to the court's approach, Lord Donaldson indicated that 'good parenting involves giving minors as much rope as they can handle without an unacceptable risk that they will hang themselves' and that it was self-evident that the well-being, welfare, or interests of the minor:

> involves giving them the maximum degree of decision-making which is prudent. Prudence does not involve avoiding all risk, but it does involve avoiding taking risks which, if they eventuate, may have irreparable consequences or which are disproportionate to the benefits which could accrue from taking them.[152]

Balcombe LJ stressed that 'the judge should approach the exercise of the discretion with a predeliction to give effect to the child's wishes on the basis that prima facie that will be in his or her best interests'.[153] He added that W's wishes should have been respected 'unless there were very strong reasons for rejecting them'. Nolan LJ was certain that a court had not only the power, but also the inescapable responsibility, of deciding what should be done in W's case, guided by the welfare principle in section 1(1) of the Children Act 1989, and the checklist of matters in section 1(3) to which a court is required to have regard. However, he commented:

> I am very far from asserting any general rule that the court should prefer its own view of what is in the best interests of the child to those of the child itself. In considering the welfare of the child, the court must not only recognise but if necessary defend the right of the child, having sufficient understanding to make an informed decision, to make his or her own choice.[154]

---

*and Decisions in Health Care* (Chichester: Wiley, 1993), p 37; J. K. Mason, 'Master of the Balancers; Non-Voluntary Therapy under the Mantle of Lord Donaldson' [1993] Juridical Review 115; J. Murphy, 'W(h)ither Adolescent Autonomy?' [1992] Journal of Social Welfare and Family Law 529.

[150] Ibid, 78D–E.   [151] [1993] Fam 64 at 94.   [152] Ibid, 81.   [153] Ibid, 644.
[154] [1992] 4 All ER 627 at 648.

## 4.3 **Authorising the use of reasonable force**

In cases subsequent to *Re W,* judges have not hesitated, where necessary, to authorise the use of reasonable force[155] in order to ensure a child's treatment. In *Re C (Detention: Medical Treatment)*[156] a cautious and conscientious approach was taken by Wall J to ordering the detention of a minor (aged 16) against her will for the purpose of giving her medical treatment for anorexia nervosa. He held that in the exercise of the inherent jurisdiction of the court he had power to direct that the girl reside at a clinic, and to authorise the use of reasonable force (if necessary)[157] to detain her in the clinic. He also found that while he must have regard to the child's wishes and feelings, he could override these if they were not in her best interests, but that where the child had capacity to give or refuse consent, then the weight which the court should give to her wishes and feelings would increase. However, Wall J acknowledged that an order for the detention of a minor aged 16 against her will was a draconian remedy. In the instant case, because the girl's civil liberties were involved, he held that the order should be time-limited and have built into it stringent safeguards to protect the girl's interests, ensuring that she suffered the least distress and retained the greatest dignity.[158]

Despite their concern for the welfare of the children concerned, this and other rulings are none-theless open to criticism. By exercising the inherent jurisdiction of the High Court in those cases where the child is suffering from a mental illness or serious mental disturbance, judges are by-passing the protective measures which are built into the Mental Health Act 1983,[159] and they may as a result be exposing children to medical and behavioural regimes and treatment processes to which far more stringent safeguards apply where adults are involved.

### 4.3.1 **Is there a need to seek the authorisation of a court?**

In *Re K, W and H (Minors) (Medical Treatment)*.[160] Thorpe J said that applications for orders au-thorising medical treatment, made by a hospital in respect of three highly disturbed 15-year-old girls who might not wish to consent in the future to the emergency use of medication, had been misconceived and unnecessary. He ruled that the girls were not '*Gillick* competent' to make deci-sions about their own medical treatment but that, even if they were, it was clear that the law allowed treatment to be given provided that someone with parental responsibility had given consent. An alarming feature of this case was that the judge took the view that the law was 'perfectly clear in this field', and that 'where more than one person has the power to consent, only a refusal by all having that power will create a veto'.[161] He rejected the hospital's appraisal of the situation as being highly complex and confusing. Thorpe J's approach stands in some contrast to that of Nolan LJ set out earlier. It is suggested that Thorpe J's certain approach in *Re K, W and H (Minors)* coupled in that case with a finding that the girls did not have sufficient competence to instruct their own lawyers, despite the beliefs of their lawyers to the contrary, bodes ill for competent and incompe-tent children who are in conflict with persons with parental responsibility in relation to medical

---

[155] See generally, J. Fortin, 'Children's Rights and the Use of Physical Force' [2001] Child and Family Law Quarterly 243.

[156] [1997] 2 FLR 180. See P. de Cruz, 'Adolescent Autonomy, Detention for Medical Treatment and *Re C*' (1999) 62 Modern Law Review 595.

[157] See also *A Metropolitan Borough Council v DB* [1997] 1 FLR 767.

[158] Interestingly, Wall J took the view that the girl's 'best safeguard is legal representation and access to the court though her lawyers' and that any order should give her liberty to apply at short notice. In this way, Wall J gave open en-dorsement to the view that children, like adults, should be entitled to turn to the courts when their liberties are at stake.

[159] See J. Masson, '*Re W*: Appealing from the Golden Cage' (1993) 5(1) Journal of Child Law 37.

[160] [1993] 1 FLR 854. Even though at the time of his judgment the only ruling on parental consent and *Gillick* com-petence had been in *Re R (A Minor) (Wardship: Medical Treatment)*, on which only Lord Donaldson MR had expressed a concluded view. For commentary, see P. Bates, 'Children in Secure Psychiatric Units: *Re K, W and H*—"Out of Sight, Out of Mind"?' (1994) 6(3) Journal of Child Law 131.

[161] [1993] 1 FLR 854.

decisions.[162] It illustrates the dangers of translating reasoned judgments, in which various reservations are expressed, into a simplified rule of law. It is important, therefore, that some of the thinking of the judges in *Re W (A Minor) (Wardship: Medical Treatment)* about the weight to be given to the competent child's wishes in medical cases is not lost.

## 4.4 Criticism of *Re R* and *Re W*: the distinction between consent and refusal

Nigel Lowe and Satvinder Juss support the approach in *Re W* as one which consistently seeks to protect children by facilitating medical treatment easily when it is in a child's best interests, whilst at the same time protecting children from their own, and their parents', 'wrong-headed decisions'.[163] This reflects the view that:

> [t]he consequences of withholding consent to treatment are usually much more significant and potentially dangerous than simply giving consent—unless one believes that most treatments are either unnecessary or are likely to be more dangerous than the condition for which they were prescribed.[164]

However, as Gillian Douglas has pointed out, the position is not as straightforward as this suggests, since there may be more than one recognised medical view and thus a choice between treatments. Douglas also argues that a refusal of consent should be given greater weight because overriding it involves both 'intellectual and bodily' interference with a person's autonomy.[165]

Attention has also been drawn to alleged anomalies that *Re W* creates. Jo Bridgeman points to the 'strange position' of a 17-year-old mother, who has far more control over her child's medical treatment than her own, for whereas she can both consent and refuse consent to her child's medical treatment, the mother's refusal of consent can be overridden by her own parents.[166] Furthermore, Margaret Brazier makes the powerful point that:

> [i]n practical terms legal principles which result in a mother having no say as to whether her teenage daughter agrees to an abortion, no right even to know of the operation, but being able to require that same daughter to undergo abortion against her will, are odd in the extreme.[167]

In contrast to Lowe and Juss's viewpoint, therefore, many academic commentators have criticised *Re W* as entrenching in English law an illogical distinction between consent to and refusal of

---

[162] See also *South Glamorgan County Council v W and B* [1993] 1 FLR 574, which is discussed in Chapter 10. C. Bridge, 'Adolescents and Mental Disorder: Who Consents to Treatment?' (1997) 3 Medical Law International 51, suggests that differentiation should be made between three different categories of adolescent disturbance: the competent young person who refuses treatment that an adult may refuse; the rebellious teenager, whose refusal is triggered by simple teenage angst; and the mentally ill teenager, whose refusal is triggered by illness. She submits that adolescent autonomy needs to be more fully understood and the Mental Health Act 1983 more readily used in treating young people.

[163] N. Lowe and S. Juss, 'Medical Treatment—Pragmatism and the Search for Principle' (1993) 56 Modern Law Review 865 at 871–2.

[164] J. Pearce, 'Consent to Treatment During Childhood, The Assessment of Competence and Avoidance of Conflict' (1994) 165 British Journal of Psychiatry 713 at 713. See also Mason and McCall Smith, who observe that 'while consent involves acceptance of an experienced view, refusal rejects that experience–and does so from a position of limited understanding': J. K. Mason and R. A. McCall Smith, *Law and Medical Ethics* (London, 1999), p 160.

[165] G. Douglas, 'The Retreat from *Gillick*' (1992) 55 Modern Law Review 569 at 576.

[166] J. Bridgeman, 'Old Enough to Know Best?' (1993) 13 Legal Studies 69 at 80. It is possible to argue, however, that the 'strange position' encountered by the child mother in Bridgeman's example is not a consequence of legal inconsistency, but of the fact that unusually a 'child mother' falls into both categories of 'child' and 'mother'. The law consistently requires of a parent, whether adult or child, that powers of consent are exercised in the child's best interests. In any event, the alleged anomaly is more apparent than real since it seems inevitable that by the time the child is capable of exercising a choice to refuse medical treatment, the child's mother will be an adult.

[167] M. Brazier, *Medicine, Patients and the Law* (London: Penguin, 1992), p 346.

treatment.[168] It is a criticism supported by the admission of Balcombe LJ himself in *Re W* that '[i]n logic there can be no difference between an ability to consent to treatment and an ability to refuse treatment'.[169] Many commentators have found difficulty understanding how a child could be competent to consent yet lack capacity to refuse.[170] In a recent article, however, Stephen Gilmore and Jonathan Herring have sought to explain how in certain circumstances this is possible, and to offer a partial defence of Lord Donaldson's concurrent consents approach.[171] They argue that it is important to distinguish the following two ways of saying no to treatment:

(1) A 'rejection of proposed treatment'. Here the child is offered the option of consenting to a particular treatment. The child considers the proposed treatment and indicates that he or she does not consent to it; or, in other words, declines to provide consent to that particular treatment.

(2) A 'refusal of treatment'. Here the child has decided not to have any treatment whatsoever. It is not merely the patient's wish to decline particular treatment, but a decision to refuse all treatment, a conscious decision to incur the consequences of a total failure to treat.[172]

Gilmore and Herring maintain that these definitions carry at least two significant distinctions: first as to the capacity required of the child in each case; and, secondly, that they involve asking two different questions. Rejection of proposed treatment involves asking, 'do I assent or not to the treatment proposed?'; a refusal of treatment involves the question 'do I refuse all treatment, understanding all the consequences which ensue from that decision?' They draw from this analysis that:

> it does not necessarily follow from the fact that a child has capacity to consent (and/or capacity to decline consent) to certain specific treatment, X, that he or she will have capacity to refuse all treatment . . . the child considering whether or not to consent will not necessarily have addressed the 'refusal of treatment' question (not least because he or she may only have been told by the doctor about the proposed treatment). In a case in which the child has capacity to consent to X but does not fully understand the consequences of a total failure to treat, parental responsibility to consent is not fully extinguished by the child's capacity and it is necessary for a parent to have the power to consent to treatment, including, if necessary, treatment X.[173]

## 4.5 **The so-called 'retreat from** *Gillick'*

A popular, if not dominant, characterisation of the case law amongst academic lawyers, arising from the radical children's autonomy rights interpretation of *Gillick* and harsh criticism of the post-*Gillick* cases, *Re R* and *Re W*, is that the *Gillick* case represented a high-water mark for

---

[168] J. Bridgeman, 'Old Enough to Know Best?' (1993) 13 Legal Studies 69 at 80.

[169] [1993] Fam 64 at 88B–C.

[170] See discussion in S. Gilmore and J. Herring, '"No" is the Hardest Word: Consent and Children's Autonomy' [2011] Child and Family Law Quarterly 3.

[171] Ibid; and see also S. Gilmore and J. Herring, 'Children's Refusal of Medical Treatment: Could *Re W* be Distinguished?' [2011] Family Law 715.

[172] S. Gilmore and J. Herring, 'Children's Refusal of Medical Treatment: Could *Re W* be Distinguished?' [2011] Family Law 715. For criticism of these arguments see E. Cave and J. Wallbank, 'Minors' Capacity to Refuse Treatment: A Reply to Gilmore and Herring' [2012] Medical Law Review, arguing *inter alia* that the distinctions made by Gilmore and Herring are not workable in clinical practice since from 'a clinician's point of view, competence cannot always be judged in relation to specific treatment, but instead must relate to the decision'. For a response, see S. Gilmore and J. Herring, 'Children's Refusal of Treatment: The Debate Continues' [2012] Family Law 973. For a judicial view that consenting simply involves understanding what is proposed and no more, see *L v P (Paternity Test: Child's Objection)* [2011] EWHC 3399 (Fam), Hedley J.

[173] S. Gilmore and J. Herring, 'Children's Refusal of Medical Treatment: Could *Re W* be Distinguished?' [2011] Family Law 715, at 716. They go on to argue that *Re W* might be distinguished in a future case of a fully competent child on the basis that the girl in *Re W* was only shown to have capacity to consent and not to refuse all treatment.

children's autonomy rights, from which there has since been a recession.[174] However, as should be apparent from the foregoing account of the case law, whether or not there has been a retreat from *Gillick* rather depends upon one's interpretation of that case. The existence of a retreat from *Gillick* is complicated by two further factors. First, Lord Donaldson indicates explicitly on at least two occasions that his reasoning in *Re W* on the conflict between parent and minor is *obiter*.[175] Secondly, since *Gillick* only dealt with the issue of consent to medical treatment, it was perfectly permissible to distinguish *Gillick* on its facts and formulate a different rule in relation to refusal of consent. It is pertinent to recall the words of Lord Scarman himself in *Gillick* that the case was 'the beginning, not the conclusion, of a legal development in a field glimpsed by one or two judges in recent times . . . but not yet fully explored'.[176] It should not be overlooked that the decision in *Gillick* in part *acquires* its meaning from its application in *Re R* and *Re W*. Thus, as Hamilton has commented, it may be:

> incorrect to view *Re W* as a great step backwards in children's rights or as an emasculation of the *Gillick* principle; rather it constitutes a recognition that the autonomy granted in *Gillick* only applies to cases where a decision does not cause irreversible damage to health.[177]

These arguments reveal a rather complex picture concerning the existence, nature, and extent of any so-called retreat from *Gillick*.

## 4.6 **Will a child ever be considered sufficiently competent to refuse life-saving treatment?**

In *Re E (A Minor) (Wardship: Medical Treatment)*[178] a boy, A, who was a few months short of his 16th birthday, was being treated in hospital for leukaemia. He and his parents were Jehovah's Witnesses and for religious reasons they refused consent to the use of any blood transfusions. The replacement blood products were needed to replenish A's blood cells which were diminishing as a result of the drugs that were being administered to him. If the hospital continued to treat without transfusions A's prospects of remission were much diminished[179] and the state of his blood cells meant that there would be a risk within a day or so of a stroke or heart attack caused by internal bleeding. The hospital issued a summons in wardship seeking leave to treat A as appropriate, including with the

---

[174] Found perhaps most explicitly in Douglas's oft-cited commentary on *Re R*, proclaiming in its title 'the retreat from *Gillick*' (G. Douglas, 'The Retreat from *Gillick*' (1992) 55 Modern Law Review 569) but see also J. Bridgeman, 'Old Enough to Know Best?' (1993) 13 Legal Studies 69 at 80 ('leaps and bounds away from the approach in *Gillick*'); S. Cretney and J. Masson, *Principles of Family Law* (London: Sweet & Maxwell, 1997), pp 593–5; M. Freeman, *The Moral Status of Children: Essays on the Rights of the Child* (The Hague: Martinus Nijhoff, 1997), p 345 ('a false dawn'); C. Lyon and P. de Cruz, *Child Abuse*, 2nd edn (Bristol: Family Law, 1993), p 379 ('the already very marked retreat from the principles of the *Gillick* decision'); J. Roche, 'Children's Rights: In the Name of the Child' [1995] Journal of Social Welfare and Family Law 281 at 282. It is a view which has spread unquestioned to other disciplines: see eg V. Bell, 'Governing Childhood: Neo-Liberalism and the Law' (1993) 22(3) Economy and Society 390 (sociology); C. Smith, 'Children's Rights: Judicial Ambivalence and Social Resistance' (1997) 11 International Journal of Law, Policy and the Family 103 at 110–20 (social work); D. Dickenson and D. Jones, 'True Wishes: The Philosophy and Developmental Psychology of Children's Informed Consent' (1995) 2(4) Philosophy, Psychiatry and Psychology 287 at 291 (psychology): 'it seems *clear* that the English courts, through case-law, are swinging towards care and protection' (emphasis added), although there is little if any analysis of *Gillick* in the paper; J. Pearce, 'Consent to Treatment During Childhood, The Assessment of Competence and Avoidance of Conflict' (1994) 165 British Journal of Psychiatry 713 at 714 (child psychiatry); J. Pilcher, 'Contrary to *Gillick*: British Children and Sexual Rights since 1985' (1997) 5 International Journal of Children's Rights 299 (sociology).

[175] [1993] Fam 64 at 79E: 'that is not this case'; and at 76D–E: 'but even that is not the issue before this court. That is whether *the court* has such a power.'

[176] [1986] 1 AC 112 at 176C.     [177] C. Hamilton, 'Editorial' (1993) 5(1) Journal of Child Law 1.

[178] [1993] 1 FLR 386.

[179] Forty per cent to 50 per cent rather than possibly a 70 per cent chance if transfusions were administered.

transfusions. The application was granted by Ward J, who found that A was not of sufficient intelligence, understanding, and maturity to refuse. He commented:

> I find that A is a boy of sufficient intelligence to be able to take decisions about his own well-being, but I also find that there is a range of decisions of which some are outside his ability fully to grasp their implications. Impressed though I was by his obvious intelligence, by his calm discussion of the implications, by his assertion even that he would refuse well knowing that he may die as a result, in my judgment A does not have a full understanding of the whole implication of what the refusal of that treatment involves . . .
>
> I am quite satisfied that A does not have any sufficient comprehension of the pain he has yet to suffer, of the fear that he will be undergoing, of the distress not only occasioned by that fear but also—and importantly—the distress he will inevitably suffer as he, a loving son, helplessly watches his parents' and his family's distress. They are a close family, and they are a brave family, but I find that he has no realization of the full implications which lie before him as to the process of dying. He may have some concept of the fact that he will die, but as to the manner of his death and to the extent of his and his family's suffering I find he has not the ability to turn his mind to it nor the will to do so.[180]

Ward J added, however, that the child's competence to refuse is not the issue in wardship where the welfare of the child dominates the decision, and a judgement has to be taken objectively. He agreed that the court, 'exercising its prerogative of protection, should be very slow to allow an infant to martyr himself'. Ward J emphasised, however, that the child's wishes and feelings are an important factor in ascertaining the child's welfare and, having regard to the closeness of A's attaining 16, A's wishes and feelings were a very important matter, weighing very heavily in the scales.[181] But Ward J was also far from satisfied that at the age of 15 A's will was fully free,[182] and concluded that when balanced against the need for the chance to live a precious life, the decision to refuse transfusions was inimical to A's well-being.[183] However, despite the court's ruling, once A reached the age of 18, he exercised his right as an adult to refuse treatment and died.[184]

A similar case arose after the decisions in *Re R* and *Re W* in *Re S (A Minor) (Consent to Medical Treatment)*.[185] A 15½-year-old girl, S, had suffered since birth from the most serious form of thalassaemia.[186] Her treatment required monthly hospitalisation for blood transfusion and daily injections to her abdomen. Unlike *Re E*, therefore, this involved ongoing, long-term treatment rather than a one-off response to the development of an illness. When S was 10 years old, her mother began attending Jehovah's Witness meetings, although S's treatment continued with the consent of her father. When S was 15, however, she failed to attend one of her monthly appointments, indicating that she now refused blood as an adherent to the Jehovah's Witness faith. The social services department became concerned for S's welfare and sought use of the inherent jurisdiction[187] to

---

[180] [1993] 1 FLR 386 at 391.

[181] Ward J had rejected an argument based on s 8 of the Family Law Reform Act 1969 because A had not attained the age of 16. But the emphasis on the age of 16 here suggests that Ward J might have viewed s 8 as giving children aged 16 both the right to consent and refuse. As noted earlier in this chapter, however, that is a view not shared by the Court of Appeal in *Re W*.

[182] In that his volition had been 'conditioned by the very powerful expressions of faith to which all members of the creed adhere': see [1993] 1 FLR 386 at 393.

[183] [1993] 1 FLR 386 at 393.

[184] As reported by counsel, Mr Daniel, to Johnson J in a subsequent case *Re S (A Minor) (Consent to Medical Treatment)* [1994] 2 FLR 1065 at 1075.

[185] [1994] 2 FLR 1065.

[186] A condition in which the body cannot produce red blood cells which carry oxygen around the body, so transfusion is necessary for survival. There are also problems with extraction of iron from the body.

[187] It is not clear from the decision how this was possible and why leave to apply for a specific issue order was not pursued. There is no indication that the child was in care: see the Children Act 1989, ss 9 and 100.

permit the treatment. By the time the application came before the court, S had missed two monthly appointments and there was a risk that she could die within weeks. Johnson J granted the application. He noted the strong emphasis that had to be given to S's wishes and feelings, as required by *Re W*, but found on the facts that S was not competent. She was confused as to the facts surrounding her illness, fed up with her treatment and thus susceptible to influence from her mother[188] and other Jehovah's Witnesses, and she did not fully understand the implications of her decision. In similar vein to Ward J in *Re E*, Johnson J commented:

> It seems to me that an understanding that she will die is not enough. For her decision to carry weight she should have a greater understanding of the manner of death and pain and the distress.[189]

In *Re L (Medical Treatment: Gillick Competence)*[190] a 14-year-old girl sustained severe scalds to over half of her body when she fell into a hot bath, possibly because she had had an epileptic fit. In order to survive, she required surgery, which had an 80 per cent chance of success. The operations would require blood transfusions but the girl, who was described as mature for her age, expressed a strong and sincere wish as a Jehovah's Witness not to have blood products. If she did not have the treatment, however, she would suffer a particularly horrible death: gangrene would supervene, followed by a very distressing time. The surgeon concerned did not feel that it was appropriate to explore in detail with her the manner of her death. Sir Stephen Brown P found that the girl had led a sheltered life[191] and held that she was not *Gillick* competent in the context of all the necessary details which it would be appropriate for her to be able to form a view about. His Lordship had no hesitation in holding that it was in the girl's best interests to permit the operation and that that would have been the appropriate order even if she had been *Gillick* competent. Caroline Bridge is critical of the court's approach, commenting:

> The fact that she had not been told, by either her doctor or her family, of the distressing nature of her predicted death meant that L lacked vital information. Without it she could not properly understand her predicament and could not make a valid decision. She was, effectively, denied the ability to give informed consent. She was certainly denied an informed refusal. She was simply not informed about the risks (of gangrene, for example) yet an understanding of risk is integral to making a valid decision.[192]

In *Re M (Medical Treatment: Consent)*[193] a 15-year-old girl, M, suffered heart failure and was close to death unless she had a heart transplant. A few weeks earlier she had been a healthy active girl. While her mother consented, M refused to consent to the transplant. The hospital concerned sought authorisation to carry out the operation. Johnson J took great pains to ensure

---

[188] Johnson J had cited *Re T (An Adult) (Consent to Medical Treatment)* [1993] Fam 95, where the Court of Appeal drew attention to two important outside influences on patient decision making: the strength of will of the patient and the relationship of the persuader to the patient (eg the influence of parents on their children).

[189] [1994] 2 FLR 1065 at 1076.

[190] [1998] 2 FLR 810. See C. Bridge, 'Religious Beliefs and Teenage Refusal of Medical Treatment' (1999) 62 Modern Law Review 585–94.

[191] Ibid, 813, although, as Bridge points out (ibid, 590), 'quite how a more robust and worldly upbringing could equip a 14 year old to make life and death decisions more soundly is difficult to imagine'. See also ibid, 589, where Bridge comments:

> the High Court is suggesting that the concept of *belief* is one which can only be properly arrived at with the passage of time, that it is akin to the development of cognitive functioning and the demands of maturity, rationality, intelligence and understanding. It is suggested here that belief is alien to these attributes. Its existence or otherwise should not form part of the assessment of adolescent competence.

[192] Ibid, 591.

[193] [1999] 2 FLR 1097. See R. Huxtable, '*Re M (Medical Treatment: Consent)* Time to Remove the "Flak Jacket"' [2000] Child and Family Law Quarterly 83.

that the girl was represented at short notice. The Official Solicitor reported (following an interview with M) that she did not want someone else's heart as she would feel different, nor to take medication for the rest of her life. At the same time, however, she did not want to die. On this evidence the Official Solicitor submitted that while M was intelligent and her wishes should carry considerable weight, events had 'overtaken her so swiftly that she had not been able to come to terms with her situation'.[194] In those circumstances Johnson J held that making the order sought was in M's best interests.

In *Re P (Medical Treatment: Best Interests)*[195] a boy, John, aged 16 years 10 months, suffered from hypermobility syndrome, a condition in which blood vessels are fragile and susceptible to bleeding. He had been admitted to hospital with a suspected rupture of his aorta. He and his parents objected to any blood transfusion because of their religious beliefs as Jehovah's Witnesses. That crisis had passed and the hospital had not at that time sought to treat John with blood products because operating was felt to be too dangerous. However, the hospital sought leave to administer blood should John's situation should become immediately life-threatening in future, and if in the professional opinion of those treating John such treatment were needed. Johnson J made the order sought, with the additional proviso that blood would only be administered if no other treatment were possible. In passing, Johnson J commented that:

> there may be cases as a child approaches the age of 18 when his refusal would be determinative. A court will have to consider whether to override the wishes of a child approaching the age of majority when the likelihood is that all that will have been achieved will have been deferment of an inevitable death and for a matter only of months.[196]

In addition, he acknowledged that in the case of a young man of nearly 17 with established convictions, there were weighty reasons why the order should not be made.[197] However, he concluded that John's best interests would be met by making the order, 'looking at the interests of John in the widest possible sense—medical, religious, social, whatever they be'.[198]

### 4.6.1 Comment

In none of the decisions discussed earlier was the child concerned permitted to refuse medical treatment. While many may agree with the outcomes in the cases, some of the reasoning by which the decisions were reached is susceptible to criticism. The courts have set the level of children's competence to refuse at a very high level. Arguably, the standard is one that many adults would not fulfil if required to demonstrate it, and it has been suggested such a test is unfair to children.[199] Secondly, in some cases[200] children have been prevented in their own best interests from having all the necessary information to make an informed decision. This has allowed the court to sidestep the crucial issue of reconciling the child's welfare and autonomy interests. Thirdly, as Bridge has pointed out, the case law involving children's religious beliefs seems to suggest that 'the concept of *belief* is one which can only be properly arrived at with the passage of time, that it is akin to the development of cognitive functioning and the demands of maturity, rationality, intelligence and understanding'. Yet, as she points out, 'belief is alien to these attributes. Its existence or otherwise should not form part of the assessment of adolescent competence.'[201] A fourth criticism is that the courts examine the child's *Gillick* competence, yet then go on to declare that irrespective of that

---

[194] [1999] 2 FLR 1097 at 1100.     [195] [2003] EWHC 2327, [2004] 2 FLR 1117.     [196] Ibid, [9].

[197] Ibid, [11].     [198] Ibid, [12].

[199] D. Archard and M. Skivenes, 'Balancing a Child's Best Interests and a Child's Views' (2009) 17 International Journal of Children's Rights 1 at 10.

[200] *Re E (A Minor) (Wardship: Medical Treatment)* [1993] 1 FLR 386 and *Re L (Medical Treatment: Gillick Competence)* [1998] 2 FLR 810.

[201] C. Bridge 'Religious Beliefs and Teenage Refusal of Medical Treatment' (1999) 62 Modern Law Review 585 at 589.

assessment the outcome is dictated by the child's best interests. Why adopt a functional test of capacity unless it is to be used? Or, perhaps there is some force in Bridge's point:

> that judges should not go through the pretence of applying a functional test of capacity when the outcome of the young person's decision is not one that they, or probably society, would countenance. The law should openly declare that welfare reigns when grave decisions with momentous outcomes are considered and recognise that adolescent autonomy is, inevitably, circumscribed.[202]

Finally, it is notable that in none of the cases are children's rights under the ECHR articulated, including those which were decided after 'incorporation' of Convention rights into English law by the Human Rights Act (HRA) 1998.

This brings us neatly to the final section of this chapter, which examines the extent to which children's rights have been articulated and protected by the ECHR and the HRA 1998.[203]

## 5 Children and the European Convention on Human Rights

The ECHR protects all persons irrespective of age, so when Convention rights were directly protected in English law by the HRA 1998, clearly 'the notion of children being rights holders could no longer be treated by the courts merely as an abstract proposition'.[204] Section 6 of the HRA 1998 provides that it is unlawful for a court to act in a way which is incompatible with Convention rights. However, the ECHR was not designed to deal with some of the subtler human rights issues which emerge within family law and takes no account of the differences between adults and children. It lacks any guidance on reconciling children's and parents' interests; and it has a narrow focus on civil and political rights, omitting social and economic rights.[205] Jane Fortin also highlighted a danger that the Act might effect a change of legal principles in ways which might endanger rather than promote children's rights, for example through greater focus on adults' rights. Thus children's advisers would need to display ingenuity in interpreting the Convention to children's benefit.[206]

The Articles of the Convention perhaps most likely to be employed in family disputes are Article 2 (right to life), Article 3 (prohibition on inhuman or degrading treatment), Article 5 (right to liberty and security of person), Article 6 (right to a fair trial), and Article 8 (the right to respect for private and family life).[207] Their impact on the domestic law is discussed at appropriate points throughout this book.

In several academic articles since implementation of the HRA, Professor Fortin has examined the developing impact the Act has had on legal recognition of children's rights.[208] Her conclusion, like that of others,[209] is that there has been a rather patchy recognition of children's Convention

---

[202] Ibid, 594. See also M. Brazier and C. Bridge, 'Coercion or Caring: Analyzing Adolescent Autonomy' (1996) 16(1) Legal Studies 84–109.

[203] See generally S. Choudhry and J. Herring, *European Human Rights and Family Law* (Oxford: Hart, 2010), esp Ch 6; U. Kilkelly, *The Child and the European Convention on Human Rights* (Ashgate: Dartmouth, 1999).

[204] J. Fortin, 'The HRA's Impact on Litigation Involving Children and their Families' (1999) 11 Child and Family Law Quarterly 237 at 255.

[205] Ibid.      [206] Ibid, at 241.

[207] These Articles are highlighted by Fortin, ibid, who discusses some of the issues in which they have arisen.

[208] J. Fortin, 'Children's Rights: Are the Courts Now Taking Them More Seriously?' (2004) 15 Kings College Law Journal 253; J. Fortin, 'Accommodating Children's Rights in a Post Human Rights Act Era' (2006) 69 Modern Law Review 299; J. Fortin, 'A Decade of the HRA and its Impact on Children's Rights' [2011] Family Law 176.

[209] See eg D. Bonner, H. Fenwick, and S. Harris-Short, 'Judicial Approaches to the Human Rights Act' (2003) 52(3) International Comparative Law Quarterly 549: 'In many cases "judicial reasoning under the Human Rights Act" is most conspicuous by its absence. The attitude of many members of the family bench and the higher appeal Courts when called upon to apply the Convention rights to family law matters has been cautious and defensive—even openly hostile'; and S. Harris-Short, 'Family Law and the Human Rights Act 1998: Judicial Restraint or Revolution' (2005) 17(3) Child and Family Law Quarterly 329.

rights. In some areas, such as children's claims within the education system or in cases of young offenders' engagement with the youth justice system, there is a ready use of Convention rights. There have also been some notable uses of the Convention in cases in which children's freedoms are a focus for the court, or are obviously apparent from the issues. An example is provided by *Re Roddy (A Child) (Identification: Restrictions on Publication)*.[210] In that case a local authority had sought care proceedings in respect of a girl, Angela Roddy, who had become pregnant at the age of 12 by a boy, X, of a similar age. Her case came to public attention amidst controversy that the Catholic Church had allegedly paid her not to have an abortion. Angela's baby was also taken into care. The local authority obtained injunctions protecting from publication the identities of Angela and X. When she was aged 16 (and described as a mature and articulate young person), Angela applied to the court to have the injunction lifted to the extent that it would enable her to tell to the press her experiences of the care system. Munby J recognised that a child is as much entitled to the protection of the European Convention as anyone else[211] and that Angela had a right to freedom of expression within Article 10 of the ECHR and also that the right to respect for private life within Article 8 protected 'the right to share what would otherwise be private with others'.[212] Munby J concluded that Angela was 'of an age, and has sufficient understanding and maturity, to decide for herself whether that which is private, personal and intimate should remain private or whether it should be shared with the whole world'.[213] Referring to the judgments in *Re W*, Munby J commented:

> In my judgment (and I wish to emphasise this) it is the responsibility—it is the duty—of the court not merely to recognise but, as Nolan LJ said, to defend what, if I may respectfully say so, he correctly described as the right of the child who has sufficient understanding to make an informed decision, to make his or her own choice. This is not mere pragmatism, although as Nolan LJ pointed out, any other approach is likely to be both futile and counter-productive. It is also, as he said, a matter of principle. For, as Balcombe LJ recognised, the court must recognise the child's integrity as a human being. And we do not recognise Angela's dignity and integrity as a human being—we do not respect her rights under Arts 8 and 10—unless we acknowledge that it is for her to make her own choice, and not for her parents or a judge or any other public authority to seek to make the choice on her behalf.[214]

Another example is *R (Axon) v Secretary of State for Health*[215] discussed earlier in this chapter.

In the main, however, there has been rather limited engagement with the implications of the HRA 1998 in private law cases involving children. Section 1 of the Children Act 1989 provides that whenever a court determines a matter with respect to a child's upbringing, the child's welfare shall be the court's paramount (currently interpreted to mean the sole) consideration. As discussed in detail elsewhere in this book[216] there has been a failure to acknowledge the difference between the paramountcy principle (in which the child's welfare is the sole focus) and the requirements of the Convention (in which it is not, and the interests of others must also be considered). A notable exception to this blindness to the Convention in private law cases is the issue of a child's paternity, where the courts have been much more ready to articulate the various interests involved within Article 8.[217]

---

[210] [2003] EWHC 2927 (Fam), [2004] 2 FLR 949. See also *Mabon v Mabon* [2005] 3 WLR 460 and see J. Fortin, 'Children's Representation Through the Looking Glass' [2007] Family Law 500.

[211] [2003] EWHC 2927 (Fam), [2004] 2 FLR 949 at [37].      [212] Ibid, [35] and [36].      [213] Ibid, [56].

[214] Ibid, [57].      [215] [2006] EWHC 37 (Admin), [2006] 2 FLR 206.      [216] See Chapter 9.

[217] A point made by J. Fortin, 'Children's Rights: Are the Courts Now Taking Them More Seriously?' (2004) 15 King's College Law Journal 253 at 270. See Bodey J's decision in *Re T (Paternity: Ordering Blood Tests)* [2001] 2 FLR 1190, discussed in Chapter 7.

Children's rights under the Convention are seldom articulated in public law child protection cases either, where the focus has rather been on protection of parents' Article 8 rights against inappropriate state intervention in family life.[218]

Fortin suggests, convincingly, that the different approaches may in part be explained by procedural factors, and the judicial response may reflect the nature of the application.[219] In many children cases the issues are handled before the courts as disputes between parents, which risks ignoring or sidelining children's rights.[220] A striking example is *R (On the application of Williamson) v Secretary of State for Education and Employment*[221] in which parents who believed in the availability of corporal punishment in schools argued that the statutory ban on corporal punishment in schools[222] infringed their rights to religious freedom under Article 9 of the Convention. The argument was unsuccessful but, as Baroness Hale observed,[223] the case was clearly about children's rights yet there was a failure to put any case from the children's perspective.

## 6 Conclusion

The issue of children's rights raises many theoretical and practical debates. Particularly challenging issues are the extent to which English law does, and should, recognise a child's autonomy interest. As we have seen, the case law on these issues is not easy to navigate. The issues have been addressed by the courts in the context of children's medical treatment. Controversially, the courts have held that while a child can consent validly to medical treatment, his or her refusal of treatment might be overridden by parental consent.

This raises an important practical question: what might a 'Gillick competent' child do when medical or psychiatric treatment is authorised by persons with parental responsibility, but without the child's consent? It is suggested that he or she would be best advised to seek leave to apply either for a specific issue order, or for a prohibited steps order, under section 8 of the Children Act 1989, or that he or she should seek leave to make an application for the exercise by the High Court of its inherent jurisdiction. Similarly, where the child concerned is younger and unable to initiate proceedings, a relative or other interested third party anxious about the child's predicament could seek leave to invoke the jurisdiction of the courts. Court involvement would act as a safeguard to detect whether those exercising parental responsibility for the child were abusing their powers and whether any decisions made were giving paramountcy to the interests of the child. The availability and use of section 8 orders in a wide range of matters concerning the care and upbringing of children, and the inherent jurisdiction of the High Court, are each discussed in the next chapter.

## Discussion Questions

1. To what extent has English law recognised a child's right to make his or her own decisions?

2. Has there been a retreat from *Gillick*?

3. Do you agree with Lord Donaldson's judgments in *Re R* and *Re W*? Should the law allow a competent child to refuse life-saving medical treatment? Why or why not?

---

[218] See J. Masson, '*Protecting Children or Protecting Human Rights*' (2010 unpublished paper presented at Staffordshire University), cited in J. Fortin, 'A Decade of the HRA and its Impact on Children's Rights' [2011] Family Law 176 at 179.

[219] See, ibid, 180.

[220] J. Fortin, 'Children's Rights: Are the Courts Now Taking Them More Seriously?' (2004) 15 Kings College Law Journal 253.

[221] [2005] UKHL 15, [2005] AC 246.　　[222] Under the Education Act 1996, s 548.

[223] [2005] UKHL 15, [2005] AC 246 at [71].

# Further Reading

ALDERSON, P., *Young Children's Rights*, 2nd edn (London: Jessica Kingsley, 2008)

ALSTON, P., PARKER, S., and SEYMOUR, J. (eds), *Children, Rights and the Law* (Oxford: Clarendon Press, 1992)

ARCHARD, D., *Children Rights and Childhood* (London: Routledge, 2004)

BAINHAM, A., 'The Balance of Power in Family Decisions' (1986) 45(2) Cambridge Law Journal 262

BAINHAM, A., 'The Judge and the Competent Minor' (1992) 108 Law Quarterly Review 194

BRIDGEMAN, J., 'Old Enough to Know Best?' (1993) 13 Legal Studies 69

CAVE, E., 'Goodbye *Gillick*? Problems with the Concept of Child Competence' (2014) 34(1) Legal Studies 103–22

CAVE, E. and WALLBANK, J., 'Minors' Capacity to Refuse Treatment: A Reply to Gilmore and Herring' [2012] Medical Law Review 423

DOUGLAS, G., 'The Retreat from *Gillick*' (1992) 55 Modern Law Review 569

EEKELAAR, J., 'The Emergence of Children's Rights' (1986) 6 Oxford Journal of Legal Studies 161

EEKELAAR, J., 'White Coats or Flak Jackets? Doctors, Children and the Courts—Again' (1993) 109 LQR 182

FERGUSON, L., 'Not Merely Rights for Children but Children's Rights: The Theory Gap and the Assumption of the Importance of Children's Rights' (2013) 21 International Journal of Children's Rights 177–208.

FORTIN, J., *Children's Rights and the Developing Law*, 3rd edn (Cambridge: Cambridge University Press, 2009)

FORTIN, J., 'The *Gillick* Decision—Not Just A High-Water Mark' in S. Gilmore, J. Herring, and R. Probert (eds), *Landmark Cases in Family Law* (Oxford: Hart, 2011), pp 199–23

FRANKLIN, B. (ed), *The New Handbook of Children's Rights Comparative Policy and Practice* (London: Routledge, 2002)

FREEMAN, M. D. A., *The Rights and the Wrongs of Children* (London: Francis Pinter, 1983)

FREEMAN, M. D. A., *The Moral Status of Children: Essays on the Rights of the Child* (The Hague: Martinhus Nijhoff, 1997)

GILMORE, S., 'The Limits of Parental Responsibility' in R. Probert, S. Gilmore, and J. Herring, *Responsible Parents and Parental Responsibility* (Oxford: Hart, 2009)

GILMORE, S. and HERRING, J., '"No" is the Hardest Word: Consent and Children's Autonomy' [2011] Child and Family Law Quarterly 3

GILMORE, S. and HERRING, J., 'Children's Refusal of Treatment: The Debate Continues' [2012] Family Law 973

LOWE, N. and JUSS, S., 'Medical Treatment—Pragmatism and the Search for Principle' (1993) 56 Modern Law Review 865

ROCHE, J., 'Children's Rights: In the Name of the Child' [1995] Journal of Social Welfare and Family Law 281

Visit the Online Resource Centre at **www.oxfordtextbooks.co.uk/orc/gilmore_glennon5e/** for a range of further features including a detailed bibliography and self-test questions.

online
resource
centre

# 9

# Private law disputes and issues in children cases

## INTRODUCTION

As explained in Chapter 7, there may be several different persons with parental responsibility for a child and scope, therefore, on occasions for disagreement on matters concerning a child's upbringing. Disputes are perhaps most likely to occur on relationship breakdown, when heightened emotion and bitterness surrounding the break-up may make agreement difficult. The courts may then ultimately be charged with resolving the matter. They may be asked to decide, for example, with whom a child shall live, whether a parent and child should have contact, or some other specific issue, such as which school a child is to attend. In this chapter, we examine how the courts resolve such private disputes. Before examining the various orders at the courts' disposal and the courts' decisions in specific areas, it is convenient first to set out some general principles for deciding children cases which are contained in section 1 of the Children Act 1989.

## 1  The courts' focus on child welfare: background

In deciding matters with respect to a child's upbringing, the courts look to the welfare of the child concerned. The Court of Chancery introduced the child's interests as a justification for awarding care of a child to the child's mother in cases of dispute with the father.[1] A similar approach emerged in statute[2] and eventually, by section 1 of the Guardianship of Infants Act 1925, the child's welfare became the 'first and paramount' consideration in such cases. That provision, which meant that the parents' 'legal claims were to be ignored and the child's welfare was to prevail',[3] remained the law for many decades, being later consolidated with minor changes of terminology in section 1 of the Guardianship of Minors Act 1971. The ascendancy of child welfare in court decision making thus emerged as a by-product of a struggle to equalise the legal position of mothers and fathers. To this day, however, the paramountcy of the child's welfare remains the golden thread that runs through court decision making in children cases. It is now found in section 1 of the Children Act 1989.

---

[1]  See eg *De Manneville v De Manneville* (1804) 10 Ves 54 and *Wellesley v Duke of Beaufort* (1827) 2 Russ Rep 1. By the early 1890s, the child's welfare had become the 'dominant matter' in such determinations. See *R v Gyngall* [1893] 2 QB 232 and *Re McGrath* [1893] 1 Ch 143. For a general review of the emergence of the welfare principle, see J. C. Hall, 'The Waning of Parental Rights' (1972) 31 Cambridge Law 248–65.

[2]  The Guardianship of Infants Act 1886 provided that the child's welfare was to be a consideration for the court in custody disputes between parents.

[3]  [2006] 2 FLR 629 at 638 at [27] *per* Baroness Hale of Richmond.

## 1.1  Decision-making principles in section 1 of the Children Act 1989

### 1.1.1  The paramountcy principle

**Key legislation**

Section 1(1) of the Children Act 1989 provides:

> When a court determines any question with respect to
>
> (a) the upbringing of a child; or
>
> (b) the administration of the child's property or the application of any income arising from it,
>
> the child's welfare shall be the court's paramount consideration.

The general approach in section 1(1) is supplemented by further provisions in subsections (2)–(5). Before examining how the courts have interpreted and applied the paramountcy principle, it is convenient first to set out the scope of application of the paramountcy principle and the supplementary principles in section 1.

### 1.1.2  When does the paramountcy principle apply?

#### 1.1.2.1  Any proceedings

Section 1(1) applies to *any* relevant court determinations,[4] in all proceedings where the requirements of the subsection are fulfilled, for example the exercise of the High Court's inherent jurisdiction in matters with respect to a child's upbringing.

#### 1.1.2.2  Upbringing or administration of child's property

However, it is necessary in each case to ask whether the question is with respect to the administration of the child's property or to the child's upbringing.[5] Upbringing is defined in section 105 of the Children Act 1989 to include 'the care of the child but not his maintenance', but is otherwise left to the courts to interpret. In *Re Z (A Minor) (Freedom of Publication)*[6] Ward LJ acknowledged that it 'is not always easy to decide when a question of upbringing is being determined',[7] but explained that it is 'one which relates to how the child is being reared'.[8] In *Re X (A Child) (Injunctions Restraining Publication)*[9] Bracewell J added that:

> [t]he words 'reared' and 'upbringing' carry a meaning of the bringing up, care for, treatment, education, and instruction of the child by its parents or by those who are substitute parents. It involves a process where the parent is the subject and the child is the object, so that s 1(1) of the 1989 Act applies only to those actions of which the child is the object and not to those in which the child is the subject.[10]

#### 1.1.2.3  Child's welfare must be directly in issue

The child's welfare is paramount only if the child's upbringing falls to be 'decided as a matter directly in issue'.[11] As Ward LJ explained in *Re Z* (in the previous section), the child's upbringing must be the

---

[4]  Compare s 1(5) of the Children Act 1989, discussed in Section 1.4.

[5]  The courts have not always done so explicitly: an example is the issue of a child's name, which has been assumed to be a matter with respect to the child's upbringing.

[6]  [1997] Fam 1.      [7]  See [1997] Fam 1 at 28.      [8]  Ibid, 29.      [9]  [2001] 1 FCR 541.

[10]  Ibid, 546, respectfully agreeing with what she described as the careful analysis by Munby J in *Kelly v BBC* [2001] 1 All ER 323 at 348 et seq.

[11]  *Richards v Richards* [1984] AC 174 at 203, [1983] 2 All ER 807 at 815 (Lord Hailsham of St Marylebone LC).

'central issue'. For example, as explained in Chapter 7, it has been held that the paramountcy principle does not apply to the question whether scientific tests should be directed to determine paternity, since the interests of justice as well as the child's welfare are engaged on such applications.[12] Similarly, a child's welfare is not directly in issue where the question is whether the child's allegedly violent parent should be 'ousted' from the family home.[13]

### 1.1.2.4 Paramountcy must not be impliedly or expressly excluded by other provisions

The last example illustrates that the paramountcy principle also does not apply where another statutory provision expressly or impliedly excludes its operation. The aim of Part IV of the Family Law Act 1996 is to provide a comprehensive scheme for regulating occupation of the family home in cases of domestic violence, and the statute sets out specific criteria that must be applied in such cases. The implication is that Parliament intended those specific criteria to apply rather than the paramountcy principle. Similarly, it has been held that the paramountcy principle does not apply to Part III of the Children Act 1989, and in particular to a local authority's application to place a child in secure accommodation pursuant section 25 of the Act.[14] One of the grounds upon which a child can be so accommodated is that he is likely to injure other persons if he is kept in any other description of accommodation.[15] This requirement to consider danger to others is clearly incompatible with treating the child's welfare as paramount.[16]

Sometimes statutory provisions are explicit that the paramountcy principle does not apply (eg where the court is making orders for a child's maintenance),[17] or a statute may explicitly adopt a different emphasis on child welfare. For example, when making financial provision and property adjustment ancillary to divorce, a court must give *first* (not paramount) consideration to the welfare whilst a minor of any child of the family.[18]

### 1.1.2.5 Cases involving the welfare of more than one child

In a case involving more than one child the court will need to consider, as a matter of statutory construction, which child's upbringing is the one with respect to which the court is determining a question.[19] In *Birmingham City Council v H (A Minor)*[20] a 14-year-old girl, M, gave birth to a little boy, R. M, who had a history of absconding and volatile behaviour and was considered to be beyond parental control, was in secure accommodation. There was evidence that M's care of R had been inadequate and that she had on occasions treated him roughly. Connell J granted the local authority care orders in respect of both M and R. Within the care proceedings, M applied under section 34(3) of the Children Act 1989 for contact with her baby, and the local authority applied under section 34(4) for permission to refuse M contact with R. The evidence suggested that M might harm herself if she were prevented from having contact with her baby. However, there was also some evidence that contact might present a risk of physical harm to R, and if contact were to take place in secure accommodation, as proposed, it could prove distressing to both the child

---

[12] *S v S; W v Official Solicitor* [1970] 3 All ER 107.

[13] *Richards v Richards* [1984] AC 174, a decision under previous legislation, the Matrimonial Homes Act 1983. The relevant legislation is now in the Family Law Act 1996, Pt IV. See Chapter 3.

[14] *Re M (A Minor) (Secure Accommodation Order)* [1995] Fam 108.          [15] Children Act 1989, s 25(1)(b).

[16] *Re M (A Minor) (Secure Accommodation Order)* [1995] Fam 108, *per* Butler-Sloss LJ, Hoffmann LJ agreeing. Hoffmann LJ added a further reason: s 25 was derived from the Child Care Act 1980 which did not have a provision equivalent to s 1(1) of the Children Act 1989. The court also held that application of s 1(5) of the Children Act 1989 is incompatible with the duty in s 25 to make an order if the criteria are fulfilled. See Section 1.4 for discussion of s 1(5).

[17] The definition of upbringing in s 1 does not include the child's maintenance: see the Children Act 1989, s 105(1).

[18] Matrimonial Causes Act 1973, s 25(1).

[19] In the draft Bill suggested by the Law Commission in its Report No 172 (1988), prior to the enactment of the 1989 Act, it was provided that, when determining any question under the Act, the welfare of 'any child likely to be affected' should be the court's only concern. That provision was not adopted by Parliament.

[20] [1994] 2 AC 212.

and mother. Connell J held that R's welfare (and not M's) was paramount on these applications and granted the council permission to refuse contact. On M's appeal, the Court of Appeal set aside Connell J's order.[21] The Court of Appeal explained that the approach to contact is a matter of substantive law and should not depend upon the fact that procedurally M's application was made under section 34(3) in R's care proceedings rather than under section 34(2) in M's care proceedings. As it was impossible to treat the upbringing of both children as paramount, the issue of contact required a weighing in the balance of the respective interests of M and R.[22] Applying that approach, the court concluded that contact would be positively beneficial to M and, provided it was adequately monitored, should not be detrimental to R.[23]

On the local authority's appeal, the House of Lords unanimously held that the Court of Appeal had erred in law and restored Connell J's order. Lord Slynn, delivering the leading opinion, found the solution in the appeal through an analysis of the structure of section 34. His Lordship held that in the applications under section 34(3) and (4) R's welfare was paramount, and when the court had decided that it was appropriate to authorise the local authority to refuse contact, there could be no value in making an order under subsection (2) allowing contact between M (as a child, and whose welfare would be paramount) and a named person, her son R.[24] As Douglas points out, however, this is unconvincing since 'one could equally put things the other way round. If the mother had applied, as a child in care under section 34(2), and it had been decided that she should be allowed to have contact with her son, there would have been no point in making a refusal order under section 34(4).'[25] As Thornton observes, 'to point out that only one of two contradictory orders should be made does not answer the question of the basis upon which the court is to choose between them'.[26] It is submitted that overall this decision was a disappointing response to the problems raised in the appeal. The House failed to seize the opportunity to deliver a judgment of principle on how the courts should deal with cases involving children's conflicting interests.[27] However, the *Birmingham* case has been interpreted as putting in place a general approach to construction where the welfare of two children is implicated in a case.[28]

## 1.2 Section 1(2): 'delay likely to prejudice the child's welfare'

### Key legislation

Section 1(2) of the Children Act 1989 recognises the harm that delay in deciding a child's case can potentially cause to the child. It provides:

---

[21]  [1993] 1 FLR 883, CA.

[22]  The courts have subsequently acknowledged that in some exceptional cases, such as a decision to separate conjoined twins to preserve the life of one, there may be no alternative but to weigh the children's respective interests: see *Re A (Children) (Conjoined Twins: Surgical Separation)* [2001] Fam 147.

[23]  [1993] 1 FLR 883, 894.

[24]  A rather puzzling aspect of Lord Slynn's reasoning is the suggestion that such an order could be made in the family proceedings in question. The family proceedings in which the applications under s 34(3) and (4) were made were the proceedings under Pt IV of the Children Act 1989 in respect of R. In those family proceedings, where the child concerned is R, it is submitted that the word 'child' in s 34(2) would refer to R, not M.

[25]  G. Douglas, 'In Whose Best Interests?' (1994) LQR 379 at 381.

[26]  R. Thornton, 'Children and Children's Children: Whose Welfare is Paramount?' [1994] Cambridge Law Journal 41 at 43.

[27]  G. Douglas, 'In Whose Best Interests?' (1994) LQR 379 at 382.

[28]  See in relation to siblings *Re S (Contact: Application by Sibling)* [1998] 2 FLR 897, FD (Charles J), *Re F (Contact: Child in Care)* [1995] 1 FLR 510, FD (Wilson J), and *Re T and E (Proceedings: Conflicting Interests)* [1995] 1 FLR 581, FD (Wall J); and see *F v Leeds City Council* [1994] 2 FLR 60 at 63 (applied to the Children Act 1989, s 31).

> In any proceedings in which any question with respect to the upbringing of a child arises, the court shall have regard to the general principle that any delay in determining the question is likely to prejudice the welfare of the child.

The courts recognise, however, that a planned and purposeful delay may be warranted if it will ultimately achieve an outcome in the child's welfare. For example, more time may be required for an investigation to be completed[29] or to produce a report for the court[30] so that the court can take a fully informed decision.[31]

## 1.3 Section 1(2A): The presumption of parental involvement

The Family Justice Review recommended no change to the substantive law by which post-separation parenting disputes are dealt with.[32] However, contrary to that advice, the Government concluded that while reference to division of children's time should be avoided,[33] 'there should be a legislative statement of the importance of children having an ongoing relationship with both parents after family separation, where that is safe, and in the child's best interests'.[34] Following consultation[35] the Government's proposal was enacted by section 11 of the Children and Families Act 2014, which inserted a new presumption of parental involvement into section 1 of the Children Act 1989, as follows:

> (2A) A court, in the circumstances mentioned in subsection (4)(a) or (7), is as respects each parent within subsection (6)(a) to presume, unless the contrary is shown, that involvement of that parent in the life of the child concerned will further the child's welfare.'
> (2B) In subsection (2A) "involvement" means involvement of some kind, either direct or indirect, but not any particular division of a child's time.

Subsection (6) defines parent for the purpose of this provision, as follows:

> In subsection (2A) "parent" means parent of the child concerned; and, for the purposes of that subsection, a parent of the child concerned—
>
> (a) is within this paragraph if that parent can be involved in the child's life in a way that does not put the child at risk of suffering harm; and

---

[29] *C v Solihull MBC* [1993] 1 FLR 290 and see also *Hounslow LBC v A* [1993] 1 FLR 702 (delay required to complete local authority investigations).

[30] See *Re W (Welfare Reports)* [1995] 2 FLR 142, CA.

[31] In some cases, however, the inimical effect of delay may mean that it is not appropriate to make findings of fact on past allegations of abuse: see eg *Re W (Withdrawal of Allegations of Abuse)* [2012] EWCA Civ 1307.

[32] Family Justice Review Final Report (Ministry of Justice, November 2011), and see Ministry of Justice and Department for Education, The Government Response to the Family Justice Review: A System with Children and Families at its Heart (Cm 8273, February 2012), paras 59–64.

[33] In light of experiences of legislating in Australia: see Ministry of Justice and Department for Education, *The Government Response to the Family Justice Review: A System with Children and Families at its Heart* (Cm 8273, February 2012), para 62. For discussion of the Australian experience, see H. Rhoades, 'Legislating to Promote Children's Welfare and the Quest for Certainty' [2012] Child and Family Law Quarterly 158; B. Fehlberg, 'Legislating for Shared Parenting: How the Family Justice Review Got it Right' [2012] Family Law 709; B. Fehlberg, B. Smyth, M. Maclean, and C. Roberts, 'Legislating for Shared Time Parenting After Separation: A Research Review' (2011) 25(3) International Journal of Law, Policy and the Family 318.

[34] Ministry of Justice and Department for Education, The Government Response to the Family Justice Review: A System with Children and Families at its Heart (Cm 8273, February 2012), para 61.

[35] Department for Education and Ministry of Justice, *Co-operative Parenting Following Family Separation: Proposed Legislation on the Involvement of Both Parents in a Child's Life* (13 June 2012).

(b) is to be treated as being within paragraph (a) unless there is some evidence before the court in the particular proceedings to suggest that involvement of that parent in the child's life would put the child at risk of suffering harm whatever the form of the involvement.

This provison applies whenever the court is making or revoking a parental responsibility order, or making, varying, or discharging a contested section 8 order in favour of a parent,[36] and is discussed at relevant points in relation to those orders.

### 1.4  Section 1(3): the welfare checklist

Within the confines of section 1(1), the court is given a very wide discretion when deciding children's cases. The Children Act 1989 provides, in section 1(3)(a)–(g), a checklist of factors, most of which were derived from earlier case law and are widely accepted to be relevant to the promotion of a child's welfare, in order to exercise some control and structure over decision making, designed to achieve balanced decisions after the court has consciously weighed all the factors which it ought to take into account. As Baroness Hale explained in *Re G (Children) (Residence: Same-Sex Partner)*, 'in any difficult or finely balanced case . . . it is a great help to address each of the factors in the list, along with any others which may be relevant, so as to ensure that no particular feature of the case is given more weight than it should properly bear'.[37]

---

**Key legislation**

Section 1(3) provides:

In the circumstances mentioned in subsection (4), a court shall have regard in particular to—

(a) the ascertainable wishes and feelings of the child concerned (considered in the light of his age and understanding);
(b) his physical, emotional and educational needs;
(c) the likely effect on him of any change in his circumstances;
(d) his age, sex, background and any characteristics of his which the court considers relevant;
(e) any harm which he has suffered or is at risk of suffering;
(f) how capable each of his parents, and any other person in relation to whom the court considers the question to be relevant, is of meeting his needs;
(g) the range of powers available to the court under this Act in the proceedings in question.

---

Section 1(4) indicates that the checklist *must* be considered where a court is considering whether to make, vary, or discharge an order under section 8 of the Children Act 1989, and the making, variation, or discharge is opposed by any party to the proceedings. It must also be applied where the court is considering whether to make, vary, or discharge a special guardianship order[38] or an order under Part IV of the Act (ie, a care order or supervision order).[39]

Where all, or most, of the factors in the checklist point in one direction, the decision on what will best promote the child's welfare may be relatively straightforward, and indeed a court ruling is unlikely to be necessary. However, the complexity of children cases often means that the matters listed in the checklist pull in different directions. For example, the child's age may point to an order being made that she should live with her mother rather than an older relative but there may be evidence to suggest that the mother might cause the child to suffer harm. The court must then

---

[36] Children Act 1989, s 1(7).     [37] [2006] UKHL 43, [2006] 4 All ER 241 at [40].
[38] See Chapter 11.     [39] See Chapter 10.

determine whether the factor specified in paragraph (d) should be given greater weight than the factor specified in paragraph (e) and in this it must be guided by the factors in the other paragraphs, which again are likely to conflict and to point to different outcomes. Thus, opinion evidence may have been given that the child is likely to be badly affected by a change in her circumstances, which raises the considerations in paragraphs (b) and (c), but that if she were to remain with the mother it is unlikely that the mother could meet some of her needs, which raises paragraph (f).

## 1.5  **Section 1(5): No order unless better for the child**

### Key legislation

Section 1(5) of the Children Act 1989 provides:

> Where a court is considering whether or not to make one or more orders under this Act with respect to a child, it shall not make the order or any of the orders unless it considers that doing so would be better for the child than making no order at all.

Unlike the paramountcy principle, section 1(5) applies only when the court is making an order under the Children Act 1989. In *K v H (Child Maintenance)*[40] Sir Stephen Brown P held that section 1(1) sets the scene for the rest of section 1, and that section 1(5) is principally directed to orders relating to the upbringing of a child, the administration of a child's property, or the application of any income arising from it. His Lordship held therefore that section 1(5) does not apply to applications for financial provision for children under Schedule 1 to the Children Act 1989, since section 1(1) does not apply to such applications.

Section 1(5) derives from a recommendation of the Law Commission in its Report *Guardianship and Custody*.[41] The Commission was concerned about the practice prior to the Children Act 1989 whereby court orders were used in almost all divorce cases involving children.[42] The relationship between parents and children was formalised and characterised in legal language without much thought as to whether this was either desirable in the interests of children or wanted by their parents.[43] The courts' approach could be perceived by some as unnecessarily intrusive when parents were able to agree. Section 1(5) thus encapsulates the idea that court orders are designed to achieve a purpose and should not be granted automatically and without thought as to their consequences, but only where the court is satisfied that the order will improve matters for the child.

As the section puts it, the law's concern is to identify those cases where the proposed order will be better for the child than making no order. Sometimes section 1(5) has loosely been termed the 'no order principle', which risks associating the principle unduly with the idea of 'non-intervention'. As Andrew Bainham has observed, and as acknowledged in case law, the principle is more accurately paraphrased as the 'no *unnecessary* order principle'.[44] Munby J commented in *Re X and Y*[45] that section 1(5) at least 'requires that the court ought not to make unnecessary orders', for example 'if the parties can reach agreement between themselves'.[46] Many parents are able to make arrangements about their children, sometimes without assistance. Professional help may be useful in those

---

[40]  [1993] 2 FLR 61.        [41]  Law Com No 172 (1988).

[42]  See further J. Priest and J. Whybrow, *Custody Law in Practice in the Divorce and Domestic Courts*, supplement to Law Com WP No 96 (1986).

[43]  In court the following dialogue would be typical: 'The children are living with you Mrs Smith?' 'Yes.' 'They see their father regularly?' 'Yes.' 'You have no objection to Mr Smith having reasonable access to them?' 'No.' 'The court orders custody, care and control to Mrs Smith and reasonable access to Mr Smith.'

[44]  A. Bainham, 'Changing Families and Changing Concepts' (1998) Child and Family Law Quarterly 1.

[45]  [2001] 2 FCR 398.

[46]  Ibid, 417, citing by way of example the decision of Millett LJ in *Re T (Adoption: Contact)* [1995] 2 FLR 251 at 257–8.

cases where the parents initially cannot agree. Even where acceptable arrangements prove difficult to negotiate, a court order may not be necessary, although it may be advisable for the lawyers to incorporate the arrangements in a written agreement.

However, it does not follow that in every case in which a negotiated agreement is achieved an order will be unnecessary. To defer automatically to agreements would mean that the welfare principle had been 'hi-jacked by non-interventionism'[47] and, of course, some agreements may not promote a child's welfare.[48] As the Law Commission commented: 'in many, possibly most, uncontested cases an order is needed in the children's own interests, so as to confirm and give stability to the existing arrangements, to clarify the respective roles of the parents, to reassure the parent with whom the children will be living, and even to reassure the public authorities responsible for housing and income support that such arrangements have been made.'[49] In *Re G (Children)*[50] after protracted and difficult negotiations an agreement was struck whereby the father would receive his parental responsibility by consent in return for his agreeing that the mother should have the security of a residence order made in her favour in respect of the children. The District Judge, however, refused counsel's invitation to make the orders by consent. The judge took the view that section 1(5) dictated that there was a presumption against making an order and, as there was no longer any dispute about the matter, there was no good reason to upset that presumption. Allowing the mother's appeal, the Court of Appeal commented that the subsection:

> is perfectly clear. It does not . . . create a presumption one way or another. All it demands is that before the court makes any order it must ask the question: will it be better for the child to make the order than make no order at all? The section itself gives the test to be applied and the question to be asked. If judges in each case do just that then they cannot go wrong, it being axiomatic that every case is different, and each case will depend upon its own peculiar facts.[51]

The court identified three reasons why in this case the order should have been made: (i) in providing peace of mind to the mother it was an important factor producing stability in the children's lives; (ii) it was advantageous to the children in dissipating bitterness and mistrust between the parents; and (iii) in a case where an agreement has been carefully negotiated, a court should not be astute to go behind it; the court should have paid respect to the parents' views that an order would be beneficial to the management of the children's lives.

Section 1(5) has also been treated, particularly in the context of public law proceedings, as establishing the principle that the court should proceed from a 'non-interventionist' or 'least interventionist' approach.[52] In such cases section 1(5) may also have the desirable effect of promoting considered forward planning for children, in that persons seeking an order must normally explain to the court why an order is needed and what they will do with the order if it is granted. It will be seen in the following that courts may not make certain orders once a child has been placed in the care of a local authority. Hence, there may be all the more reason for a court to be satisfied, at the outset, that an order which vests major decision-making powers in a local authority will be better for the child than making no order at all.

---

[47] A. Bainham, 'The Privatisation of the Public Interest in Children' (1990) 53 Modern Law Review 206.

[48] See J. Craig, 'Everybody's Business: Applications for Contact Orders by Consent' [2007] Family Law 26.

[49] Law Com No 172 (1988), para 3.2. See eg *B v B (A Minor) (Residence Order)* [1992] 2 FLR 327 (appropriate to make a residence order in favour of a grandmother so that, amongst other matters, she had authority to consent to her grandchild going on school trips).

[50] [2005] EWCA Civ 1283, [2006] 1 FLR 771.      [51] Ibid, 774.

[52] See Law Com No 172 (1988), para 3.4. See also *B v B (A Minor) (Residence Order)* [1992] 2 FLR 327 at 328B 'state shall not intervene in the life of children and their families unless it is necessary to do so'; *Re DH (A Minor) (Child Abuse)* [1994] 1 FLR 679 at 707F *per* Wall J: courts where possible should 'seek to withdraw the shadow of litigation from parties' lives'; *Re O (Care or Supervision Order)* [1996] 2 FLR 755 at 760A *per* Hale J; see also *Oxfordshire County Council v L (Care or Supervision Order)* [1998] 1 FLR 70 at 74E: 'the less Draconian order was likely to be better for the child than the more Draconian or interventionist one.'

## 2 The meaning of 'welfare' and 'paramountcy'

In *Re G (Education: Religious Upbringing)*[53] Munby LJ[54] explained that:

> 'Welfare'[55]... extends to and embraces everything that relates to the child's development as a human being and to the child's present and future life as a human being. The judge must consider the child's welfare now, throughout the remainder of the child's minority and into and through adulthood ... How far into the future the judge must peer—and with modern life expectancy a judge dealing with a young child today may be looking to the twenty-second century—will depend upon the context and the nature of the issue.[56]

He cited and endorsed as still true today the view of Lindley LJ in *Re McGrath (Infants)*[57] that:

> the welfare of a child is not to be measured by money only, nor by physical comfort only. The word welfare must be taken in its widest sense. The moral and religious welfare of the child must be considered as well as its physical well-being. Nor can the ties of affection be disregarded.[58]

Evaluating a child's best interests thus involves:

> taking into account, where appropriate, a wide range of ethical, social, moral, religious, cultural, emotional and welfare considerations. Everything that conduces to a child's welfare and happiness or relates to the child's development and present and future life as a human being, including the child's familial, educational and social environment, and the child's social, cultural, ethnic and religious community, is potentially relevant and has, where appropriate, to be taken into account. The judge must adopt a holistic approach.[59]

His Lordship added that happiness 'is not pure hedonism. It can include such things as the cultivation of virtues and the achievement of worthwhile goals'[60] and that a 'child's relationships, both within and without the family, are always relevant to the child's interests; often they will be determinative'.[61] As Rachel Taylor has argued,[62] this 'ambitious approach to welfare is welcome for the breadth of consideration it gives to all aspects of the child's life and for its recognition of the centrality of relationships to children's well-being' but also sets up 'a daunting task for the judge' and highlights how indeterminate welfare decision-making can be.[63]

---

[53] [2012] EWCA Civ 123, [2013] 1 FLR 677. For comment, see R. Taylor, 'Secular Values and Sacred Rights: *Re G (Education: Religious Upbringing)*' [2013] Child and Family Law Quarterly 336; S. Johnson, 'Religion, Children and the Family Courts' [2013] Family Law 574; and J. Ecob and F. Iverson, 'An Orthodox Approach to Education' [2013] Family Law 56.

[54] Maurice Kay LJ and Sir Stephen Sedley agreeing.

[55] Which in this context is synonymous with 'well-being' and 'interests' (see Lord Hailsham LC in *Re B (A Minor) (Wardship: Sterilisation)* [1988] AC 199, at 202 (cited by Munby LJ [2012] EWCA Civ 123, [2013] 1 FLR 677 at [26]).

[56] [2012] EWCA Civ 123, [2013] 1 FLR 677 at [26].    [57] [1893] 1 Ch 143.

[58] Ibid, at 148, cited at [2012] EWCA Civ 123, [2013] 1 FLR 677 at [27].

[59] [2012] EWCA Civ 123, [2013] 1 FLR 677 at [27], citing Thorpe LJ's remark in *Re S (Adult Patient: Sterilisation)* [2001] Fam 15, at 30 that 'it would be undesirable and probably impossible to set bounds to what is relevant to a welfare determination'.

[60] [2012] EWCA Civ 123, [2013] 1 FLR 677 at [29], citing J. Herring and C. Foster 'Welfare Means Rationality, Virtue and Altruism' (2012) 32 *Legal Studies* 480 as presenting persuasive arguments in this context.

[61] [2012] EWCA Civ 123, [2013] 1 FLR 677 at [30].

[62] R. Taylor, 'Secular Values and Sacred Rights: *Re G (Education: Religious Upbringing)*' [2013] Child and Family Law Quarterly 336.

[63] Discussed further below.

In *Re G (Education: Religious Upbringing)*[64] the married parents of five children (including two girls) were part of the Chassidic community of ultra-Orthodox Jews. On the parents' separation the mother no longer wished to adhere to the strict observances of that community, wanted the children to live with her and have career and educational opportunities (such as attending university) which would not be available to them if they followed ultra-Orthodox practices. In upholding the judge's decision to grant residence of the children to the mother and to approve the mother's educational proposals, Munby LJ set out the task of the judge, acting as a 'judicial reasonable parent'.[65] Approaching things by reference to the views of reasonable parents on the proper treatment and methods of bringing up children, that task is: to 'recognise that equality of opportunity is a fundamental value of our society'; to 'foster, encourage and facilitate aspiration: both aspiration as a virtue in itself and, to the extent that it is practical and reasonable, the child's own aspirations'; and 'to maximise the child's opportunities in every sphere of life as they enter adulthood', the corollary of which is that 'the judge must be cautious about approving a regime which may have the effect of foreclosing or unduly limiting the child's ability to make such decisions in future'.[66] As Taylor points out, clarification of these values is welcome but involves 'a tension between the court's stated aim of neutrality and the imposition of majority standards that risk jeopardising that neutrality'.[67]

---

### Key case

The leading case on the meaning of the paramountcy principle is *J and Another v C and Others*.[68] The issue was whether a boy should be returned to the care of his natural parents in Spain or whether he should remain with his English foster parents with whom he had spent most of his childhood. The Spanish parents had come to England to improve their financial position. The families met when shortly after the child's birth the mother was found to be suffering from tuberculosis, and the foster parents looked after the child until the mother's discharge from hospital. The parents then returned with the child to Spain. However, they were living on low wages 'in what were virtually slum conditions'[69] and in the summer heat of Madrid the child's health rapidly deteriorated. At the parents' request, therefore, the child returned to England to stay with the foster parents. The parents were happy for this arrangement to continue while they sought to improve their financial position. They became concerned, however, when they received a tactless letter from the foster mother. This described how the boy (then 5 years old) had integrated with the foster family, had grown up as an English boy, and how it would be most disturbing for him to have to return to Madrid. The parents requested the child's return and Surrey County Council, in whose official care the child was, applied to have him made a ward of court. Ungoed-Thomas J, applying the child's welfare as the first and paramount consideration under section 1 of the Guardianship of Infants Act 1925, confirmed the wardship and committed the child's care to the foster parents. An appeal to the Court of Appeal was dismissed and the parents appealed to the House of Lords. There were considerable delays at each stage of the proceedings and by the time the case came before the House of Lords the child was 10½ years old. He had not seen his parents since he was 3 years old and had spent all but 27 months of his life with the foster parents. The parents were now living in suitable modern accommodation and their financial position was much improved.

---

[64] [2012] EWCA Civ 123, [2013] 1 FLR 677. For comment, see R. Taylor, 'Secular Values and Sacred Rights: *Re G (Education: Religious Upbringing)*' [2013] Child and Family Law Quarterly 336.

[65] See S. Johnson, 'Decisions, Decisions: Choice of School and the "Judicial Reasonable Parent"' [2013] Family Law 1003.

[66] Ibid, [80].

[67] R. Taylor, 'Secular Values and Sacred Rights: *Re G (Education: Religious Upbringing)*' [2013] Child and Family Law Quarterly 336.

[68] [1970] AC 668. See N. Lowe, '*J v C*: Placing The Child's Welfare Centre Stage' in S. Gilmore, J. Herring, and R. Probert (eds), *Landmark Cases in Family Law* (Oxford: Hart, 2011), Ch 3.

[69] [1970] AC 668 at 690.

> Dismissing the parents' appeal, the House clarified that the paramountcy principle was not confined to custody disputes as between parents,[70] and applied equally to a dispute between unimpeachable parents and a third party.[71]
>
> Lord MacDermott (with whom Lord Pearson expressly agreed) explained that the words 'shall regard the welfare of the infant as the first and paramount consideration':
>
> > mean more than that the child's welfare is to be treated as the top item in a list of items relevant to the matter in question. I think they connote a process whereby, when all the relevant facts, relationships, claims and wishes of parents, risks, choices and other circumstances are taken into account and weighed, the course to be followed will be that which is most in the interests of the child's welfare as that term has now to be understood. That is the first consideration because it is of first importance and the paramount consideration because it rules upon or determines the course to be followed.[72]

As the facts of *J v C*[73] illustrate, the principle that the child's welfare must be the court's paramount consideration sometimes exists uneasily alongside the idea that it is parents (usually) who enjoy parental responsibility and the right to bring up their own children. That social norm and the welfare principle may sometimes pull in different directions.

In *J v C* the House of Lords rejected the proposition that there was any presumption in favour of the natural parents of the child.[74] Lord MacDermott put their position in this way:

> In applying section 1, the rights and wishes of parents, whether unimpeachable or otherwise, must be assessed and weighed in their bearing on the welfare of the child in conjunction with all other factors relevant to that issue.
>
> While there is now no rule of law that the rights and wishes of unimpeachable parents must prevail over other considerations, such rights and wishes, recognised as they are by nature and society, can be capable of ministering to the total welfare of the child in a special way, and must therefore preponderate in many cases . . .[75]

In *Re KD (A Minor) (Ward: Termination of Access)*[76] the House of Lords was invited to reconsider Lord MacDermott's approach in light of the European Court of Human Rights' recognition that contact between a child and parent is a fundamental element of family life protected by Article 8 of the European Convention on Human Rights (ECHR).[77] A local authority had applied to terminate contact between a mother and her son so that they could place him for adoption. The boy had been separated from his mother since he was nine months old, and at the date of the decision giving rise to the appeal he had been with foster parents for two and a half years. There was 'only the most

---

[70] As suggested by the second limb of the section and by the preamble to the Act, which referred to equality between the sexes: Whereas Parliament by the Sex Disqualification (Removal) Act, 1919, and various other enactments, has sought to establish equality in law between the sexes, and it is expedient that this principle should obtain with respect to the guardianship of infants and the rights and responsibilities conferred thereby.

Disapproving *Re Carroll* [1931] 1 KB 317.

[71] [1970] AC 668 at 692 *per* Lord Guest and at 702 *per* Lord MacDermott.      [72] Ibid, 710–11.

[73] [1970] AC 668.

[74] And see *Re E-R (A Child)* [2015] EWCA Civ 405 (neither a presumption in favour of a parent, nor in favour of the status quo).

[75] [1970] AC 668, 715. Lord MacDermott also quoted FitzGibbon LJ in the Irish case of *Re O'Hara* [1900] 2 IR 232 at 240: In exercising the jurisdiction to control or to ignore the parental right the court must act cautiously, not as if it were a private person acting with regard to his own child, and acting in opposition to the parent only when judicially satisfied that the welfare of the child requires that the parental right should be suspended or superseded.

See also Lord Oliver of Aylmerton in *Re KD (A Minor) (Ward: Termination of Access)* [1988] AC 806 at 828.

[76] [1988] AC 806.      [77] Counsel cited in support *R v UK* (Case 6/1986/104/152), The Times, 9 July 1987.

shadowy possibility' of re-establishing the child with the mother.[78] The child had displayed signs of distress on access visits, and there was a risk that continued access would disturb the stability of his developing relationship with the foster parents. Granting the local authority's application, the judge concluded that contact provided no benefit to the boy and that he might suffer harm if it continued. On the mother's appeal, it was contended that the judge's exercise of discretion was flawed by an error in principle. Counsel submitted (based in part upon Article 8 of the ECHR) that a natural parent has a legal right to have contact with his or her child which must prevail where there is no positive evidence that contact will be damaging. It was said on the mother's behalf that the judge had merely concluded that the child *might* suffer harm, not that contact would be damaging. The House held that although the judge, in her use of the term 'might', had couched her findings in mild terms, her judgment effectively 'amounted to a finding that there was a present risk of harm from continued access'.[79] Since there had been a finding that continued contact was harmful, it was strictly unnecessary to express an opinion on counsel's primary contention regarding a parent's legal right of access. However, as the point had been fully argued, the House went on to consider, *obiter*, whether the welfare principle, as understood in *J v C*, applied to the termination of contact between a child and his parent or whether such an approach was inconsistent with Article 8 of the ECHR.

Lord Oliver, delivering an opinion with which the House unanimously agreed, could not discern any conflict between pronouncements of the European Court of Human Rights[80] and the principles laid down in *J v C*,[81] stating that:

> [s]uch conflict as exists is, I think, semantic only and lies in differing ways of giving expression to the single common concept that the natural bond and relationship between parent and child gives rise to universally recognised norms which ought not to be gratuitously interfered with and which, if interfered with at all, ought to be so only if the welfare of the child dictates.

Lord Oliver could see nothing in the jurisprudence of the European Court which contradicted or cast doubt on that decision or calls for reappraisal of it. His Lordship considered the debate to be 'one without content',[82] explaining:

> If the child's welfare dictates that there be access, it adds nothing to say that the parent has also a right to have it subject to considerations of the child's welfare. If the child's welfare dictates that there should be no access, then it is equally fruitless to ask whether that is because there is no right to access or because the right is overborne by considerations of the child's welfare.[83]

That the court's focus is solely on the child's welfare in matters concerning a child's upbringing was emphasised by the House of Lords in *Re B (A Minor) (Wardship: Sterilisation)*.[84] There the House was called upon to decide whether a 17-year-old girl with 'very limited intellectual development'[85] should be sterilised. The girl, who had the mental capacity of a 6-year-old child,[86] was showing signs of sexual awareness and drive. However, she did not understand the relationship between sexual intercourse and pregnancy. Because her menstrual cycle was irregular there was a risk that any pregnancy would only be discovered after an abortion would be possible. It was likely that any pregnancy would require a Caesarean section delivery and subsequently it would be difficult to prevent her from opening up the wound, preventing healing of the post-operative scar. The girl displayed no maternal feelings and there was no prospect of her caring for a child. The only feasible alternative to sterilisation to prevent pregnancy was use of the progesterone pill, although

---

[78] [1988] AC 806 at 829.     [79] Ibid, 820.     [80] In *R v UK* (Case 6/1986/104/152), The Times, 9 July 1987.
[81] [1970] AC 668.     [82] [1988] AC 806 at 827.
[83] Ibid, and see also *per* Lord Templeman to similar effect at 812.     [84] [1988] 1 AC 199.     [85] Ibid, 207.
[86] Ibid. Her ability to express herself was at the level of a 2-year-old.

its effectiveness was speculative.[87] The case had attracted media attention, with suggestions that it raised issues of eugenics and of sterilisation for social purposes. On behalf of the ward, counsel cited the decision of the Supreme Court of Canada in *In re Eve*[88] which had distinguished between sterilisation for 'therapeutic'[89] and 'non-therapeutic' purposes respectively, and had held that sterilisation should never be authorised for 'non-therapeutic' purposes. The House of Lords regarded this distinction as 'quite irrelevant to the correct application of the welfare principle'[90] which was the 'only consideration involved'.[91] As Lord Oliver of Aylmerton[92] explained:

> The primary and paramount consideration is only whether [measures taken] are for the welfare and benefit of this particular young woman situate as she is situate in this case.[93]

He went on to emphasise what the case was *not* about:

> [T]his case is not about sterilization for social purposes; it is not about eugenics; it is not about the convenience of those whose task it is to care for the ward or the anxieties of her family; and it involves no general principle of public policy.[94]

Following the House of Lords' guidance in *J v C* and *Re KD*, there were several Court of Appeal cases which gave expression to the position of parents in the application of the paramountcy principle in different ways, some making reference to a 'parental right'[95] and others not.[96] As Waite LJ commented in *Re W (A Minor) (Residence Order)*,[97] those authorities illustrated:

> the difficulty of finding, within the infinite variety of circumstances in which the welfare of a child may fall to be applied as the paramount consideration, some principle which does precise justice to the element in every child's welfare represented by the advantage of maintaining the ties of nature with its own parent.

In *Re W* the Court of Appeal suggested that the law was 'best and most succinctly expressed' by Lord Donaldson of Lymington in *Re H (A Minor) (Custody: Interim Care and Control)*[98] when he indicated that by use of the term 'parental right', all that was meant was that the welfare principle was to be applied with 'a strong supposition that, other things being equal, it is in the interests of the child that it shall remain with its natural parents. But that has to give way to particular needs in particular situations.'[99]

An opportunity for the House of Lords to clarify the position arose in *Re G (Children) (Residence: Same-Sex Partner)*.[100] The parties, CG and CW, had lived together in a lesbian relationship for seven years. With a view to the couple having a family, CG had given birth to two girls conceived using sperm from an anonymous donor. The couple's relationship broke down, however, and there was a dispute concerning CW's contact with the girls. CW eventually obtained a shared residence order, although the order provided that the children's time was to be spent primarily in

---

[87] There were concerns about the ability to administer the pill every day, and its reaction with anti-convulsant drugs that she would also be taking.

[88] 31 DLR (4th) 1.

[89] In the sense of treatment of some malfunction or disease. See [1988] 1 AC 199 at 211.

[90] Ibid, at 204 *per* Lord Hailsham of St Marylebone LC, with whom Lord Bridge of Harwich, Lord Templeman, and Lord Brandon of Oakbrook agreed. Lord Oliver of Aylmerton described it as 'entirely immaterial': see ibid at 211. See also Lord Bridge expressly at 205.

[91] Ibid, at 202 *per* Lord Hailsham LC.

[92] With whom Lord Bridge of Harwich, Lord Templeman, and Lord Brandon of Oakbrook expressly agreed.

[93] Ibid, 211.          [94] Ibid, 212.          [95] Eg *Re K (A Minor) (Custody)* [1990] 2 FLR 64, CA.

[96] Eg *Re W (A Minor) (Residence Order)* [1993] 2 FCR 589, CA.          [97] [1993] 2 FLR 625 at 639.

[98] [1991] 2 FLR 109, CA.          [99] Ibid, 113.

[100] [2006] UKHL 43, [2006] 4 All ER 241. The dispute between the parties in this case has continued after the House of Lords decision: see *Re G (Shared Residence)* [2012] EWCA Civ 1434, [2013] 1 FLR 1323[2013] 1 FLR 1323.

the mother's household. The mother had given evidence that she wished to relocate from her home in Leicester to Cornwall and, because of concern that the proposed move was in part designed to frustrate CW's contact, a condition of the mother's residence order was that she live in the Leicester area.[101] The mother defied this condition, relocating without telling CW, who had to issue applications under the Family Law Act 1986 to find the girls. Contact had been maintained since the children had been found. However, in light of this episode, CW applied for the residential arrangements to be changed so that the children's primary home would be with her. Bracewell J granted the application, reversing the times allocated to each home, because her Ladyship had no confidence that if CG remained the primary carer she would promote the children's close relationship with CW. The Court of Appeal dismissed the mother's appeal. However, a further appeal to the House of Lords was allowed. The case again raised the issue of principle of what weight is to be attached to the fact that one party, CG, was the natural and legal parent of the child and the other, CW, was not.

Baroness Hale delivered an opinion with which the rest of the Appellate Committee agreed. Her Ladyship set out the law in *J v C* and made brief reference to the principal Court of Appeal authorities, quoting in particular Lord Donaldson's formulation of the law in *Re H (A Minor) (Custody: Interim Care and Control)*.[102] Baroness Hale then said that the statutory position is plain, as expressed by Lord MacDermott in *J v* C: the welfare of the child 'rules upon or determines the course to be followed'; and she explained that there 'is no question of a parental right'.[103] She cited with approval the Law Commission's view in its Working Paper No 96,[104] which preceded the Children Act 1989, that '[t]he welfare test itself is well able to encompass any special contribution which natural parents can make to the emotional needs of their child'.

Baroness Hale went on to say that none of this means that the fact of parentage is irrelevant.[105] She explained that the position in English law is akin to that in Australian law as explained by Lindenmayer J in *Hodak v Newman*:[106]

> [T]he fact of parenthood is to be regarded as an important and significant factor in considering which proposals better advance the welfare of the child. Such fact does not, however, establish a presumption in favour of the natural parent, nor generate a preferential position in favour of the natural parent from which the court commences its decision making process.[107]

The House held that the Court of Appeal had allowed the unusual context of the case to distract them from these principles of universal application, and had failed to explore the important and significant factor that CG is the natural mother of the children in every sense of that term: genetic, gestational, and psychological.[108]

Lord Scott commented that 'mothers are special' and was unable to accept that the circumstances came even close to justifying the change of primary home from the mother to the partner.[109]

Lord Nicholls, in a speech with which Lord Rodger agreed, added that:

> [i]n reaching its decision the court should always have in mind that in the ordinary way the rearing of a child by his or her biological parent can be expected to be in the child's best interests . . . I decry any tendency to diminish this factor. A child should not be removed from the primary care of his or her biological parents without compelling reason. Where such a reason exists the judge should spell this out explicitly.[110]

---

[101] Such conditions are unusual. For further discussion, see Section 5.9.     [102] [1991] 2 FLR 109, CA.

[103] [2006] UKHL 43 at [31].     [104] *Review of Child Law: Custody* (Law Com WP No 96, 1986), para 6.22.

[105] [2006] UKHL 43, [2006] 4 All ER 241 at [31].

[106] (1993) 16 Fam LR 1, approved by the Full Court of the Family Court of Australia in *Rice v Miller* (1993) 16 Fam LR 970 and *Re Evelyn* [1998] Fam CA 55.

[107] [2006] UKHL 43, [2006] 4 All ER 241 at [27].     [108] Ibid, [44].

[109] Ibid, [3].     [110] Ibid, [2].

One might have thought that Baroness Hale's opinion in *Re G* would represent the last word on the meaning of the paramountcy principle. However, only three years later the Supreme Court was required to clarify the position in *Re B (A Child) (Residence)*,[111] in which Lord Nicholls' dictum appeared to have caused some confusion. The case concerned a boy, Harry, who was nearly 4 years old, who had lived with his maternal grandmother since birth because his parents had been incapable of caring for him in his early years. The father applied for a residence order in respect of Harry so that he could join the father's new family. In granting the grandmother a residence order with staying contact to both parents, the justices indicated that '*Re G* . . . stated that a child should not be removed from primary care of biological parents'. The Court of Appeal agreed with a judge's conclusion that the justices' decision was plainly wrong. However, the grandmother's appeal to the Supreme Court was allowed in a judgment of the whole court delivered by Lord Kerr. While the justices had misapprehended the real import of *Re G* they had nevertheless applied the child's welfare as paramount, carefully evaluating the evidence and weighing competing factors. The Supreme Court noted that the justices' misreading of *Re G* appeared to be an erroneous reliance upon Lord Nicholls's opinion and took the opportunity to clarify the opinions in *Re G*.

The Supreme Court indicated that the principal message from *Re G* was to give the final quietus to the notion that parental rights have any part to play in the assessment of where the best interests of a child lay. If, and insofar as that required reaffirmation, the Supreme Court underscored the point again, stating:

> All consideration of the importance of parenthood in private law disputes about residence must be firmly rooted in an examination of what is in the child's best interests. This is the paramount consideration. It is only as a contributor to the child's welfare that parenthood assumes any significance. In common with all other factors bearing on what is in the best interests of the child, it must be examined for its potential to fulfil that aim.[112]

The child's welfare 'must be the dominant and overriding factor that ultimately determines disputes about residence and contact and there can be no dilution of its importance by reference to extraneous matters'.[113]

The court pointed out that Lord Nicholls had been careful to qualify his statement that 'the rearing of a child by his or her biological parent can be expected to be in the child's best interests' with the words 'in the ordinary way'. He did not propound any general rule to the effect that a child should not be removed from the primary care of biological parents.[114] His opinion was set firmly in the context of his acknowledgement that the child's welfare is paramount. Lord Nicholls 'was doing no more than reflecting common experience that, in general, children tend to thrive when brought up by parents to whom they have been born'. The Supreme Court added, however, that 'many disputes about residence and contact do not follow the ordinary way' and therefore 'although one should keep in mind the common experience to which Lord Nicholls was referring, one must not be slow to recognise those cases where that common experience does not provide a reliable guide'.[115]

So where does this leave the law? The decisions in *Re G* and *Re B* have confirmed that in applying section 1(1) of the Children Act 1989 the child's welfare is the court's sole consideration and that any whittling down of the protection that principle affords to children should not be entertained. A clear message has been given that attempts to emphasise a parent's position should avoid references to a 'parental right'. It is striking, however, that this view has been reached without any reference to the Human Rights Act (HRA) 1998 and consideration of parents' (and others') rights to

---

[111] [2009] UKSC 5. See, for comment, K. Everett and L. Yeatman, 'Are Some Parents More Natural than Others?' [2010] Child and Family Law Quarterly 290, and A. Bainham, 'Rowing Back From *Re G*: Natural Parents in the Supreme Court' [2010] Family Law 394.

[112] [2009] UKSC 5, [37].        [113] Ibid, [34].        [114] See ibid, [34].        [115] Ibid, [35].

respect for family life in Article 8 of the ECHR. As discussed later in this chapter, this is one in a line of cases interpreting and applying the paramountcy principle which do not really engage with the question whether treating the child's welfare as the sole consideration can survive the enactment of the HRA 1998.

It is a pity that Baroness Hale in *Re G* did not engage more fully with the Court of Appeal's case law. It will be recalled that her Ladyship neither expressly approved nor disapproved any of the Court of Appeal tests. This leaves rather unclear the status of the earlier Court of Appeal authorities and their consistency or otherwise with pronouncements in the House of Lords/Supreme Court. For example, it is rather unclear whether Lord Donaldson's view that there is a 'strong supposition that, other things being equal, it is in the interests of the child that it shall remain with its natural parents' survives *Re G*. This depends on whether it can be reconciled with Lindenmayer J's view in *Hodak v Newman* (cited with approval by Baroness Hale as reflecting English law) that the fact of parenthood does not 'generate a preferential position in favour of the natural parent from which the court commences its decision making process'. It is clear that Lindenmayer J saw a 'preferential position' as distinct from, and additional to, a presumption. To what extent (if at all) is that very widely expressed restriction consistent with Lord Donaldson's approach and, indeed, Lord Nicholls's view that the court 'should always have in mind that in the ordinary way the rearing of a child by his or her biological parent can be expected to be in the child's best interests'?[116] The courts must now recognise the special way in which parenthood can minister to the child's welfare, yet not generate a preferential position in favour of the natural parent.

While the courts have explained that there is no parental right or preferential position for parents, the emphasis which the courts will place on the position of parents has probably not altered in substance. The focus of recent decisions has been on how expression is properly given to that emphasis: the courts have clarified that it is encompassed within the application of the welfare principle, in the view that parenthood is an 'important and significant factor' bearing on the question of which proposals better advance the child's welfare. Lord Nicholls's speech in *Re G* was not intended to detract from the paramountcy principle. His statements must be seen in the context of the application of section 1 of the Children Act 1989, as guidance seeking to ensure that the child's welfare is treated as paramount.

Each case will turn upon its own facts. However, it seems likely that the approach in earlier case law[117] that parents should not be prevented from caring for their child simply on the basis of a balancing exercise which concludes that substitute parents could offer the child a more advantageous style of upbringing will not alter.[118]

An illustration of how the parents' position is not easily displaced is provided by *Re M (Child's Upbringing)*,[119] which raised cross-cultural issues similar to those which arose in *J v C*. Great weight was placed by the trial judge and the Court of Appeal on the notion that a 10-year-old South African boy's development 'must be, in the last resort and profoundly, Zulu development and not Afrikaans or English development'.[120] The boy had been living in England with a South African woman and her family for about four years during which time he had only intermittent contact with his natural family. Expert evidence was given that abrupt separation from his 'psychological' family would cause him severe trauma. Nonetheless, the court ordered that he be returned to South Africa. Neill LJ justified this conclusion by asserting that the boy had a right to be reunited with his Zulu parents. Similarly, Ward LJ asserted that the child's roots were in South Africa and that he therefore ought to return to his family there.[121]

The court's characterisation of the child's right as the 'right to be brought up by the parents who gave birth to him' is interesting. The child certainly may not regard it as his 'right' to be

---

[116] [2006] UKHL 43 at [2].     [117] See the 2nd edition of this book.
[118] See eg *Re D (A Child) (Residence: Natural Parent)* [2000] 1 FCR 97, FD (Johnson J) and *Re K (A Minor) (Wardship: Adoption)* [1991] 1 FLR 57 (danger of social engineering recognised).
[119] [1996] 2 FCR 473. Contrast *Re H (A Minor: Custody)* [1990] 1 FLR 51.
[120] [1996] 2 FCR 473, 485.     [121] Ibid, 495.

brought up by his parents who, to him, may be strangers compared with his substitute parents whom he regards as his family. There appears to have been some recognition of this point in *Re H (A Child: Residence)*[122] in which the Court of Appeal commented that 'the biological parent may not always be the natural parent in the eyes of the child' and in cases where the child has been for long in the settled care of a non-parent, the court must arrive at its choice applying the statute.

## 3  Is section 1(1) of the Children Act 1989 compatible with the requirements of the Human Rights Act 1998?

The Supreme Court has confirmed the strong interpretation given to the word 'paramountcy' in section 1(1) of the Children Act 1989 in *J v C* and other House of Lords' decisions. Indeed the position has arguably been strengthened, with the added message that our Supreme Court justices should not contemplate any change 'which might have the effect of weakening the protection given to children under the present law'.[123] In reaching those decisions, however, there was no engagement at all with the question whether the paramountcy principle so interpreted is compatible with the requirements of the HRA 1998. This failure is not a new phenomenon. Several commentators have highlighted previous judicial failures (some might say instances of unwillingness) to engage fully with the issue, as evidenced by rather dubious reasoning in several cases in which the judiciary has asserted that the balancing of interests required under section 1(1) and (3) of the Children Act 1989 is the same as that required by Article 8 of the ECHR.[124] It has been suggested that any difference between the requirements of Article 8 of the ECHR and section 1 of the Children Act 1989 is merely semantic,[125] or that the paramountcy principle is recognised in the jurisprudence of the European Court of Human Rights.

In *Payne v Payne*[126] Thorpe LJ commented that 'the jurisprudence of the European Court of Human Rights inevitably recognises the paramountcy principle, albeit not expressed in the language of our domestic statute'[127] citing in support a statement in *Johansen v Norway*[128] that 'the court will attach particular importance to the best interests of the child, which . . . may override those of the parent.'[129] A similar view was taken in *Re S (Contact: Promoting Relationship with Absent Parent)*[130] citing in support the view of the European Court in *Yousef v The Netherlands*:

> that in judicial decisions where the rights under art 8 of parents and those of a child are at stake, the child's rights must be the paramount consideration. If any balancing of interests is necessary, the interests of the child must prevail (see *Elsholz v Germany* [2001] ECHR 25735/94 at para 52 and *TP and KM v UK* [2001] ECHR 28945/95 at para 72).[131]

However, as several commentators have cogently argued,[132] Article 8 of the ECHR and section 1 of the Children Act 1989 do not merely express the same thing in a different way and, even if

---

[122]  [2002] 3 FCR 277.

[123]  See *per* Baroness Hale of Richmond in *Re G (Children) (Residence: Same-Sex Partner)* [2006] UKHL 43 at [30].

[124]  *Payne v Payne* [2001] EWCA Civ 166, [2001] Fam 473; *Re H (Contact Order) (No 2)* [2002] 1 FLR 23; *Re B (Adoption: Natural Parent)* [2001] UKHL 70, [2002] 1 FLR 196; *Re KD (A Minor) (Ward: Terminating Access)* [1988] AC 806 at 825.

[125]  *Re KD (A Minor) (Ward: Terminating Access)* [1988] AC 806 at 825. See also *Re B (Adoption: Natural Parent)* [2001] UKHL 70, [2002] 1 FLR 196, discussed further in Chapter 11.

[126]  [2001] EWCA Civ 166, [2001] Fam 473, confirmed on several occasions: see Sections 5.14.1 et seq.

[127]  Ibid, [38].        [128]  (1996) 23 EHRR 33 at 72, para 78.

[129]  [2001] EWCA Civ 166, [2001] Fam 473 at [39].        [130]  [2004] EWCA Civ 18, [2004] 1 FLR 1279 at [15].

[131]  (App no 33711/96) (2003) 36 EHRR 20, at para 73.

[132]  J. Herring, 'The Human Rights Act and the Welfare Principle in Family Law: Conflicting or Complementary?' (1999) 11 Child and Family Law Quarterly 223; S. Harris-Short, 'Case Commentary: Putting the Child at the Heart of Adoption?—*Re B (Adoption: Natural Parent)*' (2002) 14(3) Child and Family Law Quarterly 325; D. Bonner, H. Fenwick, and S. Harris-Short, 'Judicial Approaches to the Human Rights Act' (2003) 52(3) International and Comparative Law Quarterly 549.

they do, their different processes are not without significance. As Jonathan Herring observes, the Convention requires the court to take into account the interests of parents which do not directly bear upon the child's welfare. There is also a qualitative difference between applying the welfare principle and Article 8: the former is a determination of *fact*, the latter a matter of *judgment*.[133] The ECHR requires a weighing of respective interests: an outcome (ie, respect for family life) is prescribed unless overridden by considerations specified in Article 8(2), and interference with a parent's right must be proportionate. The words represented by ellipsis and omitted from Thorpe LJ's quotation from *Johansen v Norway* in *Payne* are '*depending on their nature and seriousness*'. The quotation in full actually reads: 'the court will attach particular importance to the best interests of the child, which depending on their nature and seriousness may override those of the parent.'[134]

Thus, while the interests of the child may justify interference with the parent's right, they cannot do so automatically.[135] Reliance on *Yousef v The Netherlands* is also problematic since it is clear from the cases footnoted by the court that the word 'paramount' was not being used in the same sense as the domestic authorities.[136]

The better view, therefore, may be that some reformulation of the paramountcy principle is required in light of human rights jurisprudence. Choudhry and Fenwick have argued that the correct approach now requires what has been termed a 'parallel analysis'. In this process, the participants in any dispute start presumptively equal and interference with the Article 8(1) rights of each must be considered in accordance with the requirements of Article 8(2). The participants' rights are then weighed against each other in an ultimate balancing exercise, in which the child's welfare is privileged but not automatically decisive.[137] In the majority of cases the outcome will probably be the same whether one adopts the paramountcy principle or a parallel analysis. However, the process by which a decision is reached, in the sense of whether it accords respect to individuals' independent interests, is arguably important too. This point appears to be overlooked in the domestic case law.

There is thus considerable debate (and doubt) surrounding the correct interpretation of section 1(1) in light of the HRA 1998, and academic criticisms of the paramountcy principle have assumed a more pressing and practical significance. It is useful, perhaps, to think of the academic criticism as having two strands: the first examines welfare decision making per se; the second focuses on the elevation of the child welfare to the sole consideration.

## 4 Criticism of the welfare principle

### 4.1 'Welfare' as a decision-making criterion

In defence of the welfare principle, Herring has pointed to several of its virtues:[138]

> [It] focuses the court's attention on the person whose voice may be the quietest both literally and metaphorically and who has the least control over whether the issue arrives before the court or in the way it does. The child may also be the person with whom the court is least able to empathise.[139]

---

[133] Herring, 'The Human Rights Act'.     [134] *Payne v Payne* [2001] EWCA Civ 166, [2001] Fam 473 at [39].

[135] See D. Bonner, H. Fenwick, and S. Harris-Short, 'Judicial Approaches to the Human Rights Act' (2003) 52(3) International and Comparative Law Quarterly 549.

[136] Ibid, fn 154.

[137] S. Choudhry and H. Fenwick, 'Taking the Rights of Parents and Children Seriously: Confronting the Welfare Principle under the Human Rights Act' (2005) 25(3) Oxford Journal of Legal Studies 453.

[138] J. Herring, 'Farewell Welfare?' (2005) 27(2) Journal of Social Welfare and Family Law 159–71.

[139] J. Herring, 'The Human Rights Act and the Welfare Principle in Family Law: Conflicting or Complementary?' (1999) 11(3) Child and Family Law Quarterly 223.

In addition, it is 'probably one of the most accurately understood legal principles among the general public'[140] and, since child welfare is something about which parents are likely to agree at least in principle, it is a useful basis for achieving negotiated settlements.[141]

Two further important attractions of the 'welfare principle' are its flexibility and adaptability. Because it does not specify a particular outcome but merely guides in a very general way, it is flexible in its particular application to the facts of individual cases. Moreover, it can accommodate changes over time in 'accepted' notions of child welfare, following social change and new insights from research evidence. Of course, this feature of the principle means that court decisions in earlier times must be read cautiously.

Yet, these last-mentioned advantages are also viewed as a source of criticism of the principle. In 1975, Robert Mnookin drew attention to the indeterminacy of welfare decision making.[142] He illustrated the point with the example of a dispute concerning custody of a child. Should the child live with dad or with mum? Mnookin pointed out that, in order to answer this question in a rational way, it would be necessary to specify the possible outcomes for the child and then ascertain their probability. Thus, the decision-maker requires considerable information and must contend with various competing theories and bodies of knowledge about human behaviour. Therefore, it can be argued that the welfare principle makes predicting the outcome of a case (and consequently the ability to achieve a negotiated settlement) more difficult than if a clearer rule were applied. Furthermore, the flexible application of the welfare principle to children's individual circumstances may cause delay and be expensive.[143] These decision costs could be cut down by introducing a rule-based approach, such as a rule (or presumption) in a custody case in favour of the person who was the child's primary caretaker before breakdown of the parents' relationship, although the concomitant disadvantage of a rule is that it may lack sufficient flexibility in interpretation and application and lead to different cases being treated alike.[144]

A further criticism of the welfare principle is its potential lack of transparency. It may be unclear what factors have weighed heavily with the judge in reaching his or her decision and it is possible that, under the guise of the child's welfare, other values can be smuggled in. An example given by Helen Reece[145] is the attitude displayed in older case law in the 1980s, which stated that all things being equal it was better for children to be brought up with a father and a mother rather than by same-sex parents. Reece makes a powerful point that it is not just the child before the court who may be affected by such a ruling; it stigmatises as living in inferior environments all children who are living perfectly happily with same-sex parents.[146]

While the criticisms mentioned have force, they need also to be kept in some perspective. The problem of indeterminacy can sometimes be solved by drawing on a consensus, particularly as to what does not promote children's welfare.[147] If one parent has harmed the child and the other has not, it may be patently clear in whose favour a dispute about the child's sole residence should be

---

[140] J. Herring, 'Farewell Welfare?' (2005) 27(2) Journal of Social Welfare and Family Law 159 at 168.

[141] Ibid, 163.

[142] R. H. Mnookin, 'Child-Custody Adjudication: Judicial Functions in the Face of Indeterminacy' (1975) 39(3) Law and Contemporary Problems 226–293. See also S. Parker, 'The Best Interests of the Child—Principles and Problems' in P. Alston (ed), *The Best Interests of the Child: Reconciling Culture and Human Rights* (Oxford, Clarendon Press, 1994).

[143] As Herring points out this may be compounded by evidential difficulties of ascertaining what happened in private and at times of heightened emotion: 'Farewell Welfare?' (2005) 27(2) Journal of Social Welfare and Family Law 159 at 160.

[144] See C. Schneider, 'Discretion and Rules: A Lawyer's View' in K. Hawkins (ed), *The Uses of Discretion* (Oxford, Clarendon Press, 1992), on the relative benefits of discretion and rules.

[145] H. Reece, 'The Paramountcy Principle: Consensus or Construct?' (1996) 49 Current Legal Problems 267–304.

[146] See ibid and H. Reece, 'Subverting the Stigmatization Argument' (1996) 23(4) Journal of Law and Society 484–505.

[147] Although any consensus as to how welfare is promoted is itself contingent on a vast array of historical and political decisions relating to how we are governed, see S. Parker, 'The Best Interests of the Child—Principles and Problems' in P. Alston (ed), *The Best Interests of the Child: Reconciling Culture and Human Rights* (Oxford, Clarendon Press, 1994).

decided. Furthermore, as Herring observes, judges appear to be striving not to let their personal views influence their decisions, at least not overtly.[148] Case law indicates that the judicial focus is on the practical consequences for the child of parental behaviour and that the courts avoid making value judgements about parents' lifestyles, for example on matters such as religion and sexuality.

### 4.2 **Criticisms of the paramountcy of the child's welfare**

The second strand of criticism of section 1(1) of the Children Act 1989 relates to English law's elevation of child welfare to the paramount consideration.

Helen Reece[149] has pointed out that while the paramountcy principle commands a strong consensus of support its foundations are not strong on a rational argument. First, Reece makes the strong point that general arguments that children's welfare should be treated as paramount are somewhat undermined by the narrow scope of the application of the paramountcy principle, in that it only applies in court decision making.[150] If it is an appropriate approach to ordering the lives of children and parents, why does it not apply in all decisions or actions concerning children?[151] Reece also shows that a number of questionable assertions are commonly advanced to justify treating children's welfare as paramount, for example that children are vulnerable and need protection. As Reece observes, it is a fallacy that protection requires priority: it does not follow that in order to protect a child adequately his or her welfare must be the sole consideration. She illustrates the point with the example of a parent seeking to take three children of different ages safely across a road, during which the parent's attentions will not be directed solely to one child, nor solely to the children, in ensuring that the whole family crosses safely. As Reece and other commentators have argued, the paramountcy principle is unjust in its focus solely on the child, and falls foul of the Kantian ethic that persons are ends in themselves and not merely to be viewed as means to the promotion of others' welfare.[152]

## 5  **Section 8 orders**

### Key legislation

Section 8 of the Children Act 1989 contains orders (referred to as 'section 8 orders')[153] whose purpose is to deal flexibly with practical issues concerning a child's upbringing.[154] They are defined in section 8 as follows:

'child arrangements order' means an order regulating arrangements relating to any of the following -

(a) with whom a child is to live, spend time or otherwise have contact, and

(b) when a child is to live, spend time or otherwise have contact with any person

---

[148] J. Herring, 'Farewell Welfare?' (2005) 27(2) Journal of Social Welfare and Family Law 159 at 162.

[149] H. Reece, 'The Paramountcy Principle: Consensus or Construct? (1996) 49 Current Legal Problems 267–304.

[150] See for discussion, J. Herring, 'The Human Rights Act and the Welfare Principle in Family Law: Conflicting or Complementary?' (1999) 11(3) Child and Family Law Quarterly 223.

[151] The United Nations Convention on the Rights of the Child, Art 3 does not make the child's welfare paramount; it is merely the primary consideration.

[152] See eg J. Elster, 'Solomonic Judgments: Against the Best Interest of the Child' (1987) 54(1) University of Chicago Law Review 1–45. Elster argues that the child's welfare should be privileged whilst avoiding excessive harm to others. For a similar approach, see J. Eekelaar, 'Beyond the Welfare Principle' [2002] Child and Family Law Quarterly 237.

[153] The term 'section 8 order' is used in s 8 itself to describe the orders.

[154] See Ward LJ in *Re G (Residence: Restriction on Further Applications)* [2008] EWCA Civ 1468, [2009] 1 FLR 894, CA at [18], commenting in discussion of a residence order that it 'simply regulates a factual state of affairs'.

'a prohibited steps order' means an order that no step which could be taken by a parent in meeting his parental responsibility for a child, and which is of a kind specified in the order, shall be taken by any person without the consent of the court, and

'a specific issue order' means an order giving directions for the purpose of determining a specific question which has arisen, or which may arise, in connection with any aspect of parental responsibility for a child.

The child arrangements order was introduced by section 12 of the Children and Families Act 2014, replacing orders previously known as contact orders and residence orders. The change was recommended by the Family Justice Review as achieving a move away from what it saw as the loaded terms of contact and residence, which tended to emphasise the difference between the resident and non-resident parent on separation, and had been a source of contention. Since the existing case law has developed in relation to contact and residence orders, it is still important to be aware of their definitions. A residence order is 'an order settling the arrangements to be made as to the person with whom a child is to live' and a contact order is 'an order requiring the person with whom a child lives, or is to live, to allow the child to visit or stay with the person named in the order, or for that person and the child otherwise to have contact with each other'.

A specific issue order could be made in most of the situations which are covered by the meanings given to the other section 8 orders. However, section 9(5) of the Children Act 1989 provides that:

No court shall exercise its powers to make a specific issue or prohibited steps order—

(a) with a view to achieving a result which could be achieved by making a child arrangements order.

This ensures that child arrangements orders are defined consistently, and prevents them being substituted by specific issue or prohibited steps orders, particularly in uncontested cases, 'to achieve much the same practical results but without the same legal effects'.[155] As we shall see, in particular in the case of a child arrangements order dealing with the child's living arrangements significant legal consequences flow from the order.

## 5.1 Giving directions and imposing conditions on section 8 orders

### Key legislation

The flexibility of section 8 orders is enhanced by section 11(7), which provides:

(7) A section 8 order may—
    (a) contain directions about how it is to be carried into effect;
    (b) impose conditions which must be complied with by any person—
        (i) who is named in the order as a person with whom the child concerned is to live, spend time or otherwise have contact;
        (ii) who is a parent of the child concerned;
        (iii) who is not a parent of his but who has parental responsibility for him; or
        (iv) with whom the child is living,[156]
    and to whom the conditions are expressed to apply;

---

[155] *Review of Child Law: Guardianship and Custody* (Law Com No 172, 1988), para 4.19.
[156] There is no power to impose a condition on any other person: see *Re M (Judge's Discretion)* [2001] EWCA Civ 1428, [2002] 1 FLR 730.

(c) be made to have effect for a specified period, or contain provisions which are to have effect for a specified period;

(d) make such incidental, supplemental or consequential provision as the court thinks fit.

This provision 'confers a wide and comprehensive power to make orders which will be effective'.[157] However, section 11(7) supplements a section 8 order and it does not entitle the court to give directions and impose conditions which fall outside the scope of the main order. In *D v N (Contact Order: Conditions)*[158] a judge attached conditions to a defined contact order which included, *inter alia*, orders relating to the father obtaining a passport for the child, entering or telephoning the mother's place of work, entering premises owned by relatives of the mother and molesting these relatives, and removing the child from the mother. Sir Stephen Brown P held that these conditions were outside the powers of the court when adding conditions to a contact order. He stated that very great care should be exercised before what were in effect injunctive orders were brought under the umbrella of section 11(7) powers. The case law on section 11(7) is explored at various points later in this chapter in discussion of its use with particular section 8 orders.

## 5.2 The family assistance order

Section 16 of the Children Act 1989 provides a court with power to make a family assistance order[159] in any family proceedings in which the court could make an order under Part II of the Act. The order, which is usually made of the court's own motion, is 'intended to provide focused short-term help to a family to overcome the problems and conflicts associated with their parents' separation'.[160] The order may require a local authority to make an officer of the authority available,[161] 'to advise, assist and (where appropriate) befriend any person named in the order' or require a Children and Family Court Advisory and Support Service (Cafcass) officer (or Welsh family proceedings officer) to do the same. The persons who may be named in the order are: any parent, guardian, or special guardian of the child; any person with whom the child is living or who is named in a child arrangements order as a person with whom the child is to live, spend time or otherwise have contact; or the child concerned.[162] The order may direct such person(s) to 'take such steps as may be so specified with a view to enabling the officer concerned to be kept informed of the address of any person named in the order and to be allowed to visit any such person'. The order may be made on its own or (more usually) alongside the making of a section 8 order. In the latter case, the order 'may direct the officer concerned to report to the court on such matters relating to the section 8 order as the court may require (including the question whether the section 8 order ought to be varied or discharged)'.[163]

There are some constraints on the making of the order. It can only be made with the consent of every person named in the order (other than the child).[164] In the case of a direction to a local authority, the local authority must agree to the making of the order, or the child concerned must be, or will be, living in the local authority's area.[165] The order can have effect for a maximum period of 12 months[166] although it can be renewed.[167]

The making of a family assistance order clearly has resource implications for any local authority which is subject to the order. This is illustrated by the case of *Re C (Family Assistance Order)*.[168]

---

[157] *Re O (Contact: Imposition of Conditions)* [1995] 2 FLR 124, CA at 128.     [158] [1997] 2 FLR 797.

[159] See R. Little, 'In Practice: Family Assistance Orders: Rising to the Challenge' [2009] Family Law 435.

[160] Children Act 1989 Guidance and Regulations (2008), vol 1, para 2.67. See, however, *Re C (Family Assistance Order)* MC/CIV04/13, a case in the Magistrate's Court of the Falkland Islands, in which a similar provision was used to assist a young girl who had witnessed sexual abuse.

[161] Section 16(1).     [162] Section 16(2).     [163] Section 16(6).     [164] Section 16(3).

[165] Section 16(7).

[166] Section 16(5). The period was extended from six months by the Children and Adoption Act 2006, s 6(1), (4).

[167] See *Re E (Family Assistance Order)* [1999] 2 FLR 512, FD (Bennett J) discussed later in this section.

[168] [1996] 1 FLR 424, FD.

Johnson J had made a family assistance order with a view to a local authority assisting in re-establishing a boy's relationship with his mother. The boy had earlier applied for and been granted a residence order so that he could live with his aunt and uncle. The application had attracted considerable, and hurtful, press publicity, being an early case under the Children Act 1989 in which, as the press put it, a child had sought to 'divorce his parents'. Counsel for the local authority came back to court to tell Johnson J that the local authority simply did not have the resources to carry out the order. Johnson J saw no reason to question the local authority's opinion and was of the view that there was no remedy which would be appropriate or sensible. While an order directed to the director of social services, endorsed with a penal notice, could be made so that enforcement proceedings could ensue, that would be totally contrary to the best interests of the boy and the childcare system as a whole.[169]

*Re C* can be contrasted with *Re E (Family Assistance Order)*.[170] A mother was convicted of the manslaughter of her child's father and was detained in a psychiatric unit. The child, aged 6, was living with a paternal aunt. A local authority had been assisting in facilitating contact between the child and the mother (arranging and paying for some transport). The child moved from that local authority's area and the new local authority in whose area the child was living was reluctant to take on any role with respect to maintenance of contact because of its cost and resource implications. Bennett J explained that because the child was living in the local authority's area an order could be made against the new local authority even though it did not agree to the order. If such an order were made, the local authority would have to consider whether or not facilitating contact was to be part of the assistance they gave the child. However, his Lordship observed that 'under such an order it would be their duty to advise, assist and befriend' the child and the judge could not 'see that they could reasonably exclude providing facilities for [the child] to have supervised contact with her mother'. The question for the court, however, was whether it should exercise its discretion to make the order in the case of a reluctant authority. It was argued on behalf of the authority that a family assistance order should not be used to make long-term provision for a child in the way proposed. Making the order, Bennett J said that although generally speaking section 16 of the Children Act 1989 is aimed at the short term and the court will lean against simply making one family assistance order after another for a substantial period of time, there was nothing else in this case that the court could do under the Children Act to ensure that the child's contact with the mother continued, which everyone agreed was in the child's best interests.

## 5.3 **The courts' powers to make a section 8 order**

Section 10 of the Children Act 1989 sets out several situations in which the courts have power to make a section 8 order. The Act designates certain proceedings as 'family proceedings', and empowers a court to make a section 8 order 'in any family proceedings in which a question arises with respect to the welfare of any child'. The power can be exercised either upon an application[171] or of the court's 'own motion'.[172] Thus, where the court takes the view that a section 8 order would be in the child's best interests, it can make such an order even though no application for an order has been made.[173]

---

[169] See also *S v P (Contact Application: Family Assistance Order)* [1997] 2 FLR 277, FD (HHJ Callman) rejecting a suggestion that a local authority undertake duties to escort a child to visit his father in prison under the guise of a family assistance order (see esp at 279).

[170] [1999] 2 FLR 512, FD (Bennett J).

[171] Children Act 1989, s 10(1)(a).     [172] Ibid, s 10(1)(b).

[173] The order could be made even in favour of a person who would be ineligible to apply for an order: see *Gloucestershire County Council v P* [1999] 2 FLR 61; see also Children Act 1989 Guidance and Regulations (2008), vol 1, para 2.45.

'Family proceedings', for the purpose of the Children Act 1989, means any proceedings 'under the inherent jurisdiction of the High Court in relation to children'[174] or under any of the enactments listed under section 8(4). These enactments are:

- Parts I, II, and IV of the Children Act 1989;
- the Matrimonial Causes Act 1973;
- Schedule 5 to the Civil Partnership Act 2004;
- the Adoption and Children Act 2002;
- the Domestic Proceedings and Magistrates' Courts Act 1978;
- Schedule 6 to the Civil Partnership Act 2004;
- Part III of the Matrimonial and Family Proceedings Act 1984;
- the Family Law Act 1996;
- sections 11 and 12 of the Crime and Disorder Act 1998.

The availability of section 8 orders in family proceedings recognises that often an issue about a child arises in the context of other proceedings, and it would be wasteful of time and resources, and more stressful for the parties, if different proceedings had to be commenced to resolve inter-related family matters. The jurisdiction in family proceedings also allows a court to choose how best to respond to an application, since it is not limited to making the order which has been sought. For example, a court might decide that there is sufficient evidence to enable it to make a care order under section 31, but that the child's interests would better be served by making a residence order in favour of a concerned relative. Perhaps the most obvious example is divorce proceedings in which issues about the child's future residence and contact with a non-resident parent will invariably arise.[175] Section 41 of the Matrimonial Causes Act 1973, which enjoined a court to consider whether it should exercise its powers under the Children Act 1989 and provided that exceptionally the need to make arrangements for the children could delay decree absolute has been repealed by the Children and Families Act 2014, section 17.

A section 8 order may also be made upon a free-standing application under section 10(2) of the Act. For example, in the case of the separation of parents who are not married, there would be no divorce proceedings in which a section 8 order might be made. A parent could, however, make a free-standing application to the court for an order should a dispute arise about a child's upbringing. An application for a section 8 order is itself 'family proceedings' since it is made under Part II of the Children Act 1989, which is one of the enactments listed in section 8(4) of the Act (as listed earlier).

## 5.4  Who may apply for a section 8 order?

The law is mindful that section 8 orders can have a major impact on the life of a child and on those who have parental responsibility. Some applications might be wholly without merit, could waste valuable court time, and could divert attention and resources from those genuine cases in need of resolution. A balance is achieved by designating certain persons as entitled to apply for section 8 orders, and by allowing all other persons to apply only if the court is first prepared to give them leave. In addition, there are special rules which apply to children, local authorities, and local authority foster parents.

---

[174]  Children Act 1989, s 8(3).
[175]  Exceptionally, the need to make appropriate arrangements for the children may delay the making of a decree absolute: see s 41(2).

### 5.4.1 Persons entitled to apply for any section 8 order

Section 10(4) of the Children Act 1989 provides:

> The following persons are entitled to apply to the court for any section 8 order with respect to a child—
>
> (a) any parent, guardian or special guardian of the child;
> (aa) any person who by virtue of section 4A has parental responsibility for the child;
> (b) any person who is named, in a child arrangements order that is in force with respect to the child, as a person with whom the child is to live.

The entitlement of all parents to apply for any section 8 order recognises their prime position. It is also a provision which comes to the assistance of the unmarried father since entitlement to apply does not depend on possession of parental responsibility. Since parental responsibility may be shared, it is essential for holders of parental responsibility to have access to a court to resolve a dispute or issue by means of a section 8 order.

### 5.4.2 Persons entitled to apply for a child arrangements order

Section 10(5) identifies a privileged group of persons who are entitled to apply for a child arrangements order.

> (a) any party to a marriage (whether or not subsisting) in relation to whom the child is a child of the family;
> (aa) any civil partner in a civil partnership (whether or not subsisting) in relation to whom the child is a child of the family;
> (b) any person with whom the child has lived for a period of at least three years;
> (c) any person—
>    (i) in any case where a child arrangements order in force with respect to the child regulates arrangements relating to with whom the child is to live or when the child is to live with any person, has the consent of each of the persons in whose favour the order was made;
>    (ii) in any case where the child is in the care of a local authority, has the consent of that authority; or
>    (iii) in any other case, has the consent of each of those (if any) who have parental responsibility for the child.
> (d) any person who has parental responsibility for the child by virtue of provision made under section 12(2A).

The uniting characteristic which accords these persons special treatment is that to require them to seek the court's leave to apply would amount to a meaningless formality because it would almost invariably be granted.[176] Given the close relationships listed in section 10(5), it is curious that there is no entitlement to apply for a specific issue or prohibited steps order.

#### 5.4.2.1 Any party to a marriage or civil partnership in relation to whom a child is a child of the family

A person who is or has been a child's parent's spouse or civil partner (ie, a step-parent or former step-parent) is entitled to apply for a child arrangements order provided that he or she has treated the child as a child of their family.[177] Sometimes a husband may falsely believe that he is the father of his wife's child and not discover the true facts until after the marriage has broken down. In a case of this kind the child will nonetheless be a child of the family because he will have been treated as

---

[176] See Law Com No 172 (1988), para 4.45.       [177] As defined in s 105(1).

such, albeit on a mistaken basis.[178] Consequently, although not the father of the child, the husband will be entitled to apply for a child arrangements order.

### 5.4.2.2  Any person with whom the child has lived for a period of at least three years

Any person with whom the child has lived for a period of at least three years is entitled to apply for a child arrangements order.[179] Section 10(10) provides that the period of three years need not be continuous but must not have begun more than five years before, or ended more than three months before, the making of the application. This three-year provision recognises that it is in the interests of children that persons who have provided a child with a home over a considerable period of time are able to apply for an order, either to secure that position or to ensure that contact with the child is maintained. Furthermore, no one is able to pre-empt an application simply by removing the child, as there is the three-month period of grace within which proceedings can be commenced. Three years is an arbitrary period which may bear no relationship either to a child's sense of time or to the strength of his personal attachments. These will vary considerably according to the child's particular circumstances, and will be influenced by the child's age, personality, and stage of development. However, the chosen period seeks to strike a balance between recognising the importance of a child's attachments to persons other than parents, and not exposing parents to the threat of legal proceedings, and the fear of losing their children to substitute carers, without the preliminary safeguard of an application for leave.

### 5.4.2.3  Any person who has the necessary consents

Where a person is not entitled to apply under any of the provisions already discussed, he or she may still be entitled provided necessary consents have been obtained as detailed in section 10(5)(c). Where there are persons in whose favour a relevant child arrangements order was made, the consent of each is required in order to confer entitlement on an applicant. In such circumstances, others who share parental responsibility for the child have no power to give or withhold consent.

In a case where the child is in the care of a local authority, it is the consent of the authority which confers entitlement to apply.[180] In any other case, that is to say when there is no child arrangements order in force and the child is not in local authority care, a person is entitled to apply who has the consent of each of those (if any) who have parental responsibility for the child. Where there is no one with parental responsibility to provide consent, then a potential applicant clearly cannot obtain consent and, unless otherwise entitled to apply, would require the leave of the court.

### 5.4.2.4  Those acquiring parental responsibility under section 12(2A)

See discussion of section 12(2A) in Chapter 7, at section 6.5.1.

### 5.4.3  Relatives and foster parents: entitlement to apply for a child arrangements order regulating the child's residence

A local authority foster parent or a relative[181] of the child is entitled to apply for a child arrangements order with respect to the child's residence if the child has lived with the foster parent or relative for a period of at least one year immediately preceding the application.[182] If such persons have had the care of the child for less than one year, it would be necessary to examine whether the person could apply by reason of falling within section 10(5) of the Act. In the case of a local authority foster

---

[178]  *W (RJ) v W (SJ)* [1971] 3 All ER 303.      [179]  Section 10(5)(b).

[180]  Section 9(1) prohibits a court from making any section 8 order other than a 'residence order' with respect to a child in care, so in fact an application for a 'residence order' is the only one which can be made in relation to a child in care. See discussion at Section 5.6.1.

[181]  'Relative', in relation to a child, means a grandparent, brother, sister, uncle, or aunt (whether of the full blood or half blood or by marriage or civil partnership) or step-parent: see Children Act 1989, s 105.

[182]  Section 10(5A), (5B), and 5(C).

parent, where the child is being looked after by the local authority under a care order, he or she would need the consent of the local authority under section 10(5)(c)(ii) in order to be entitled to make an application for a child arrangements order. But where the child is an accommodated child (ie, looked after by the authority but not compulsorily in its care by way of a care order) then before the foster parent can be entitled to apply, he or she would either have to obtain the consent of each person with a relevant child arrangements order under section 10(5)(c)(i); or in any other case, the consent of each of those (if any) who have parental responsibility for the child under section 10(5)(c)(iii). Where the relationship between the foster parent(s) and the natural parent(s) is good, the provisions relating to the consent of persons with parental responsibility could be important if, shortly after placement of the child, a dispute arose between the child's parents and the local authority as to the most appropriate foster placement for the child. In a case of this kind, the parents might be willing to consent to the foster parents making an application for a child arrangements order despite objections from the local authority.

## 5.5  Leave to apply for a section 8 order

We have examined the limited class of persons who are entitled to apply for section 8 orders. However, the door of the court is not necessarily closed to non-entitled persons. Subject to some special rules, which apply to applications by local authorities and local authority foster parents, which will be discussed later, any person may seek the leave of the court to apply for any section 8 order either in family proceedings or on a free-standing application.[183] When deciding whether to grant leave the court must have regard to criteria in section 10(9) of the Children Act 1989, which are discussed in detail in the following section. The court must give reasons for its decision.[184]

Whether leave is granted to a non-entitled person is usually of crucial importance to that person. Often an applicant for leave has been excluded from the child's life by the persons who have parental responsibility or by plans for the child's future. Several such cases involve grandparents[185] and there have been calls in some quarters for grandparents to be included in the category of persons who can apply automatically for a section 8 order.[186] As Gillian Douglas has commented, striking a balance between 'enabling a grandparent to seek the court's help in securing his relationship with the grandchild, and on the other, preventing "interfering" grandparents or others from challenging parents' control over their children, is not an easy one'.[187] Examining the growing research evidence,[188] Douglas comments that the 'very wide range of grand-parenting styles and patterns

---

[183]  An alternative route to a hearing for a non-entitled person is to apply to be joined as a party to existing family proceedings. A party has the opportunity to adduce evidence and to make submissions with a view to persuading a court to exercise its own motion powers to make a section 8 order in his or her favour. In *G v Kirklees Metropolitan Borough Council* [1993] 1 FLR 805 Booth J stated that the criteria which apply to an application for leave are equally applicable to an application to be joined as a party.

[184]  *T v W (Contact: Reasons For Refusing Leave)* [1996] 2 FLR 473, FD (Connell J).

[185]  For consideration of the position before the Children Act 1989, see G. Douglas and N. V. Lowe, 'Grandparents and the Legal Process' (1990) Journal of Social Welfare Law 89.

[186]  For discussions of this debate, see C. Barton, '*Troxel et vir v Granville*—Grandparent Visitation Rights in the United States Supreme Court' [2001] Child and Family Law Quarterly 101; F. Kaganas and C. Piper, 'Grandparents and Contact: *"Rights v Welfare"* Revisited' (2001) 15 International Journal of Law, Policy and the Family 250.

[187]  G. Douglas, 'Case Commentary—*Re J (Leave To Issue Application For Residence Order)*—Recognising Grandparents' Concern or Controlling Their Interference?' [2003] Child and Family Law Quarterly 103. See for an example within case law of these tensions: *Re F and R (Section 8 Order: Grandparent's Application)* [1995] 1 FLR 524, FD (Cazalet J) in which the grandmother stated that she had a close relationship with her grandchildren, yet the parents maintained that she interfered and was not interested in seeing the children.

[188]  G. Dench and J. Ogg, *Grandparenting in Britain: A Baseline Study* (London: Institute of Community Studies, 2002) (found more likely to be maternal grandparents involved); G. Douglas and N. Ferguson, 'The Role of Grandparents in Divorced Families' (2003) 17 International Journal of Law, Policy and the Family 41 (showed variety in roles grandparents play); A. Richards, *Second Time Around—A Survey of Grandparents Raising their Grandchildren* (London: Family Rights Group, 2001) (may be cultural differences).

of family behaviour that develop across the three generations suggests that, for the moment, it is wise to be cautious about the reasons for grandparents' applications to seek orders, and to probe carefully the nature and quality of their relationship with the parents and grandchildren. This is precisely what section 10(9) allows the court to do.'[189]

### 5.5.1 The criteria on an application for leave

> **Key legislation**
>
> Section 10(9) of the Children Act 1989 provides:
>
> Where the person applying for leave to make an application for a section 8 order is not the child concerned, the court shall, in deciding whether or not to grant leave, have particular regard to—
> - (a) the nature of the proposed application for the section 8 order;
> - (b) the applicant's connection with the child;
> - (c) any risk there might be of that proposed application disrupting the child's life to such an extent that he would be harmed by it; and
> - (d) where the child is being looked after by a local authority—
>   - (i) the authority's plans for the child's future; and
>   - (ii) the wishes and feelings of the child's parents.

Notice first that this provision is concerned with applications for leave by persons other than the child concerned in the application. Applications by the child concerned are governed by section 10(8) of the Act which is discussed in Section 5.5.3.

In *Re A and others (Minors) (Residence Orders: Leave to Apply)*[190] the Court of Appeal ruled that the paramountcy principle in section 1(1) of the Children Act 1989 does not apply to an application for leave under section 10(9) since the court is not determining a question with respect to the upbringing of the child concerned[191] and some of the criteria in section 10(9) would be otiose if the whole matter were subject to the overriding provision of section 1(1).

For several years, the leading decision dictating the courts' approach to a leave application under section 10(9) was *Re M (Care: Contact: Grandmother's Application for Leave)*,[192] a case which was not directly concerned with section 10(9), but instead with section 34(3) of the Children Act 1989, which concerns applications for leave to apply for contact with a child who is in the care of the local authority. The leading decision now is *Re J (Leave to Issue Application for Residence Order)*,[193] which directly considered section 10(9). However, in order to understand fully the position following *Re J*, it is necessary briefly to refer to *Re M*.

The Court of Appeal recognised that section 10(9) did not directly govern applications for contact with a child in care,[194] but held that it would be anomalous if the court, in exercising its discretion under section 34, did not have in mind the criteria contained in section 10(9). The Court of Appeal thus imported into the task of exercising discretion under section 34(3) the four statutory criteria that Parliament had applied in section 10(9). In addition Ward LJ (with whom Butler-Sloss

---

[189] G. Douglas, 'Case Commentary—*Re J (Leave To Issue Application For Residence Order)*—Recognising Grandparents' Concern or Controlling Their Interference?' [2003] Child and Family Law Quarterly 103.

[190] [1992] Fam 182, [1992] 3 All ER 872.

[191] Citing *F v S (Adoption: Ward)* [1973] Fam 203, [1973] 1 All ER 722 in support.

[192] [1995] 2 FLR 86, CA.

[193] [2003] 1 FLR 114, CA. For a commentary on this decision and a stimulating discussion of the role of grandparents in children's lives, see G. Douglas, 'Case Commentary—*Re J (Leave To Issue Application For Residence Order)*—Recognising Grandparents' Concern or Controlling Their Interference?' [2003] Child and Family Law Quarterly 103.

[194] Because no court can make a section 8 order, other than a 'residence order', in respect of a child in the care of a local authority: see Children Act 1989, s 9(1).

and Simon Brown LJJ agreed) added a threefold test to be applied in exercise of the court's discretion, as follows:

> (1) If the application is frivolous or vexatious or otherwise an abuse of the process of the court, of course it will fail.
> (2) If the application for leave fails to disclose that there is any eventual real prospect of success, if those prospects of success are remote so that the application is obviously unsustainable, then it must also be dismissed . . .[195]
> (3) The applicant must satisfy the court that there is a serious issue to try and must present a good arguable case[196] . . .—is there a real issue which the applicant may reasonably ask the court to try and has he a case which is better than merely arguable yet not necessarily one which is shown to have a better-than-even chance, a fair chance, of success?[197]

In *Re J (Leave to Issue Application for Residence Order)*[198] a mother's history of psychiatric illness meant that she was unable to care for her child. The local authority considered placing the 18-month-old child with the maternal grandmother, Mrs J, who was aged 59, but concluded that bringing up the child would be too great a burden at that age. Mrs J therefore sought leave to apply for a residence order. The judge refused to grant leave and the grandmother appealed. Thorpe LJ (with whom Ferris J agreed) commented[199] that the statutory checklist in section 10(9) needs to be given its proper recognition and weight. He further observed that '[t]he statutory language is transparent. Nowhere does it import any obligation on the judge to carry out independently a review of future prospects.'[200] Thorpe LJ added[201] that, while the threefold test formulated by Ward LJ in *Re M* 'has the laudable purpose of excluding from the litigation exercise applications which are plainly hopeless', that guidance was given not directly in relation to the discharge of the judicial task under section 10(9). Thorpe LJ was 'anxious at the development of a practice that seems to substitute the test, "has the applicant satisfied the court that he or she has a good arguable case" for the test that Parliament applied in s 10(9)', an anxiety heightened by enactment of the HRA 1998 and rights under Articles 6 and 8 of the ECHR thereby protected in English law. The Court of Appeal concluded that:

> [w]hilst the decision in *Re M (Care: Contact: Grandmother's Application for Leave)* no doubt served a valuable purpose in its day and in relation to s 34(3) applications, it is important that trial judges should recognise the greater appreciation that has developed of the value of what grandparents have to offer, particularly to children of disabled parents. Judges should be careful not to dismiss such opportunities without full inquiry. That seems . . . to be the minimum essential protection of Arts 6 and 8 rights that Mrs J enjoys, given the very sad circumstances of the family.[202]

In *Re R (Adoption: Contact)*[203] Wall LJ said that he understood Thorpe LJ in *Re J* in essence to be disapproving the test devised by Ward LJ in *Re M*.[204] However, his Lordship went on usefully to clarify that *Re J* does not prohibit 'a broad assessment of the merits of a particular application'.[205]

---

[195] Citing *W v Ealing London Borough Council* [1993] 2 FLR 788, approving *Cheshire County Council v M* [1993] 1 FLR 463.

[196] The door of the court appears to have been opened even wider by Butler-Sloss LJ's statement (*obiter*) in *Re G (Child Case: Parental Involvement)* that the test for an application for leave was whether there was 'an arguable case'.

[197] [1995] 2 FLR 86 at 98.      [198] [2002] EWCA Civ 1364, [2003] 1 FLR 114, CA.

[199] Ibid, [17].      [200] Ibid, [14].      [201] Ibid, [18].

[202] Ibid, [19].      [203] [2005] EWCA Civ 1128, [2006] 1 FLR 373.

[204] Ibid, [41]. However, Thorpe LJ did not say so in terms; he merely observed that the guidance in *Re M* was not made directly in relation to s 10(9).

[205] Ibid, [46]. There are several dicta in the Court of Appeal which acknowledge that the merits are relevant on a leave application. See eg Wall LJ in *Re H (Leave to Apply for Residence Order)* [2008] 2 FLR 848 at [14] and Wilson LJ at [33].

What it prohibits 'is the determination of the application on the "no reasonable prospects of success" criterion'.[206]

In *Re H (Children)*[207] Thorpe LJ explained that:

> The whole purpose of the decision in *Re J* was to draw the attention of trial judges to the need to adopt a careful review of the s 10(9) criteria and not to replace those tests simply with a broad evaluation of the applicant's future prospects of success.

In *Re B (Paternal Grandmother: Joinder as Party)*[208] the Court of Appeal[209] explained that section 10(9) itself is not a test; it 'leaves the court to take into account all the material features of the case and merely highlights certain matters which are of particular relevance'.[210] Black LJ interpreted Thorpe LJ in *Re J* to mean that the merits were not irrelevant, in the sense that he would look for an arguable case but not something higher, and he was anxious to prevent the grant of leave hinging entirely on the merits.[211] Leave will not be granted if a case is not arguable.[212] Equally an arguable case may not necessarily be sufficient to entitle the grant of leave if outweighed by other factors in section 10(9).[213]

The recent authorities have usefully drawn attention to the need to ensure that any assessment of the merits of a case does not usurp careful attention to the criteria in section 10(9), to which we now turn.

### 5.5.1.1 The nature of the proposed application

The first factor, in paragraph (a) of the checklist in section 10(9), is the nature of the proposed application. In *Re R (Adoption: Contact)*,[214] a case in which a 17-year-old girl was applying for post-adoption contact with her younger half-sibling, Wall LJ observed that examining the nature of the proposed application may involve 'a consideration of the jurisprudence surrounding the circumstances in which such orders may or may not be made'.[215] In refusing leave in that case, the Court of Appeal commented that the judge was 'bound to have regard to the fact that, under the jurisprudence which has developed, contact orders in adoption proceedings are of themselves unusual'.[216] In *Re C (A Minor) (Adopted Child: Contact)*[217] the court was concerned to shield the adoptive parents from the unnecessary anxiety which might be caused by the child's natural mother's application for contact. It took the view that an application for leave by the mother could safely be refused without the adoptive parents' involvement. It therefore ruled that the Official Solicitor should be brought in as respondent in a case of this kind, his function being to represent the child's interests. Only if, having heard from the applicant and from the Official Solicitor and/or the local authority, the court was satisfied that the natural parent had made out a prima facie case for leave should notice be given to the adoptive parents. In this way the court would ensure that no application for leave was granted without the adoptive parents having first been given an opportunity to oppose it. The court refused the natural parent leave to apply for either a specific issue order, which would result in her learning the identity of the adoptive parents, or a contact order. It held that adoption orders are intended to be permanent and final, and that a fundamental question such as contact should not be subsequently reopened unless there is some fundamental change in circumstances.[218]

### 5.5.1.2 The applicant's connection with the child

Under section 10(9)(b) the court must consider the applicant's connection with the child. This criterion is often closely linked to the nature of the proposed application and is directed to

---

[206] [2005] EWCA Civ 1128, [2006] 1 FLR 373 at [46].
[207] [2003] EWCA Civ 369, [2003] All ER (D) 290 (Feb).     [208] [2012] 2 FLR 1358.
[209] Black LJ, with Laws LJ agreeing.     [210] [2012] 2 FLR 1358 at [39].     [211] Ibid, [47].
[212] Ibid, [48].     [213] Ibid, [49].     [214] [2005] EWCA Civ 1128, [2006] 1 FLR 373.
[215] Ibid, [50].     [216] Ibid, [45].     [217] [1993] 2 FLR 431.
[218] Ibid. See also *Re T (Adopted Children: Contact)* [1995] 2 FLR 792 and *X and Y v A Local Authority (Adoption: Procedure)* [2009] EWHC 47 (Fam) (McFarlane J), [2009] 2 FLR 984.

ascertaining whether the applicant can demonstrate a genuine relationship with, and a legitimate concern about, some matter relating to the child's upbringing. The word 'connection' is a broad one, embracing not merely any legal relationship between the child and the applicant but also *de facto* connections. In *Re G; Re Z (Children: Sperm Donors: Leave to Apply for Children Act Orders)*[219] Baker J granted leave to apply for contact orders in two cases in which men had respectively acted as a sperm donor in order to allow female civil partners to start a family. In each case, some contact between the donor and the child had ensued. Baker J commented that:

> the reforms implemented in ss 42, 45 and 48 of the Human Fertilisation and Embryology Act 2008, and the policy underpinning those reforms—to put lesbian couples and their children in exactly the same legal position as other types of parent and children—are relevant factors to be taken into account by the court, alongside all other relevant considerations, including the factors identified in s 10(9) of the Children Act. In some cases, the reforms, and the policy underpinning those reforms, will be decisive. Each case is, however, fact specific, and on the facts of these cases, having considered all submissions from all parties, I find that the most important factor is the connection that each applicant was allowed by the respondents to form with the child.[220]

A judge's exercise of discretion may be vitiated by a failure to give sufficient emphasis to the applicant's connection with the child. In *Re H (Leave to Apply for Residence Order)*[221] three half-siblings had been taken into care because of their mother's drug addiction. The second child, aged 9, had been adopted by a couple who wished to adopt the third child, aged 4, who had been freed for adoption and was living with foster carers. The second child's adoptive parents, Mr and Mrs A, also wanted to adopt the third child. Because of some concerns about their age, however, the local authority/adoption agency preferred a third, considerably younger, couple. Mr and Mrs A therefore applied to the court for leave to make an application for a residence order. The judge refused leave, having described Mr and Mrs A's connection with the third child as only indirect. The Court of Appeal allowed Mr and Mrs A's appeal, holding that the judge had erred in giving insufficient weight to (i) the fact that Mr and Mrs A are the legal parents of the third child's half-sibling; (ii) the principle that half-siblings should be brought up together wherever that is possible;[222] and (iii) the evidence that Mr and Mrs A were wholly capable of caring for the children.[223]

The fact that the applicant has close family ties with a child is of course not determinative, and it may not outweigh different considerations in the other paragraphs of section 10(9). In *Re A (A Minor) (Residence Order: Leave to Apply)*[224] a request was made by an aunt for leave to apply for a residence order in the course of care proceedings which were already underway. The trial court took the view, which was confirmed on appeal, that sufficient persons were already involved in the case, and that to join another would not be in the interests of the child because it would lead to delays and be disruptive.[225]

### 5.5.1.3 Any risk of disruption causing harm

The court is required under section 10(9)(c) to have particular regard to 'any risk there might be of the proposed application disrupting the child's life to such an extent that he would be

---

[219] [2013] EWHC 134 (Fam), [2013] 1 FLR 1334. See for discussion, N. Gamble, 'Lesbian Parents and Sperm Donors: *Re G and Re Z*' [2013] Family Law 1426.

[220] Ibid, [132]. See also *G v F (Shared Residence: Parental Responsibility)* [1998] 2 FLR 799, in which the applicant was the mother's former lesbian partner who had behaved towards the child as a joint parent. Bracewell J observed that the applicant's close connection with the child made this a clear case where leave should be granted.

[221] [2008] 2 FLR 848.

[222] See discussion in Section 5.7.2.     [223] [2008] 2 FLR 848 at [25].     [224] [1993] 1 FLR 425.

[225] See also *C v W (A Minor) (Contact: Leave to Apply)* [1998] 1 FCR 618 (father repeatedly failed to attend hearings; not in child's best interests to allow him to continue litigating).

harmed by it'. Indeed, it is regarded as a 'factor of crucial significance'.[226] 'Harm' for these purposes means ill-treatment or the impairment of health and development as defined by section
31(9) and (10) and section 105(1) of the Children Act 1989.[227] As the Court of Appeal in *Re M
(Care: Contact: Grandmother's Application for Leave)*[228] recognised, it follows from these definitions that a 'child's upset, unhappiness, confusion or anxiety, needs to be sufficiently severe before
it can amount to an impairment of emotional, social or behavioural development'.[229]

Secondly, as Wall LJ pointed out in *Re R (Adoption: Contact)*,[230] section 10(9)(c) 'refers to the risk
of disruption posed by the application, not by the outcome of the application'.[231] This point was
also stressed by Thorpe LJ in *Re H (Children)*,[232] explaining that it is 'a risk of what the trial of the
proposed application might do to disrupt the life of the child, not what the grant of that application
might do to disrupt the life of the child'.[233] So the question is not whether the applicant if granted
the application would prove to be a potentially disruptive factor in the child's life, it is whether the
applicant's litigation (during that process) would prove to be a disruptive factor.[234] As Ward LJ
commented in *Re M (Care: Contact: Grandmother's Application for Leave)*:[235]

> The very knowledge that litigation is pending can be sufficiently unsettling to be harmful; if leave
> is given, the process of investigating the merits of the application can be sufficiently disruptive if it
> involves the children in more interviews, psychiatric investigations and so forth. The stressfulness
> of litigation may impair the ability of those who have care of the child properly to discharge their
> responsibility to the child's detriment.[236]

### 5.5.1.4 *The local authority's plans for the child*

Under section 10(9)(d)(i), in a case where a child is being looked after by a local authority, a court is
required to have particular regard to the authority's plans for the child's future. In *Re A and others
(Minors) (Residence Orders: Leave to Apply)*[237] the Court of Appeal explained how a court should
approach a case where a local authority has plans for the child's future which are inconsistent with
the application for leave. It reasoned as follows: a local authority has a duty under section 22(3) to
safeguard and promote the welfare of any child in its care and:

> [a]ccordingly, the court should approach the application for leave on the basis that the authority's
> plans for the child's future are designed to safeguard and promote the child's welfare and that any
> departure from those plans might well 'disrupt the child's life to such an extent that he would be
> harmed by it'.[238]

This ruling highlights the dilemma faced by courts when a challenge is made to the way in which
a local authority is choosing to exercise its statutory powers, namely when it is proper for a court
to substitute its own judgment for the judgment of the authority about what decision will best promote the welfare of the child. *Re A and others (Minors) (Residence Orders: Leave to Apply)*[239] makes
clear that the decision whether or not to grant leave is one for a court, and the fact that a child is in
care does not detract from the court's decision-making function. However, the Court of Appeal

---

[226] *Re M (Care: Contact: Grandmother's Application for Leave)* [1995] 2 FLR 86 at 95. *A fortiori* where the child is in care.
[227] See *Re A and others (Minors) (Residence Orders: Leave to Apply)* [1992] Fam 182, [1992] 3 All ER 872.
[228] [1995] 2 FLR 86.      [229] Ibid, 96.      [230] [2005] EWCA Civ 1128, [2006] 1 FLR 373.
[231] Ibid, [55].      [232] [2003] EWCA Civ 369, [2003] All ER (D) 290 (Feb).      [233] Ibid, [26].
[234] Ibid. Contrast *Re A (A Minor) (Residence Order: Leave to Apply)* [1993] 1 FLR 425 in which Hollings J was 'satisfied that the right approach is to consider not just the effect of the application being made, which the child may not even
know of, but also what effect there might be of disrupting the child's life if the application succeeded' (at 428).
[235] [1995] 2 FLR 86.      [236] Ibid, 96.      [237] [1992] Fam 182.
[238] Ibid, 193.      [239] [1992] Fam 182.

ruled that a court must take as its starting point the notion that the local authority is under a statutory duty to promote the child's welfare, and *a fortiori* the authority's plans are therefore designed to advance the welfare of the child. Thus, the court created what appears to amount to an assumption in favour of not disrupting the authority's plans for the child, thus in practice requiring the applicant to provide arguments/evidence why the local authority's plans should be disrupted.

The phrase 'being looked after' by a local authority embraces both a child being provided with accommodation by the authority (ie, voluntarily) and one in care under a care order.[240] In relation to an accommodated child the authority does not have parental responsibility, and it could be somewhat anomalous to give significant weight to the local authority's plans for a child's future in circumstances when it does not have the power to implement these plans. It might therefore be maintained that less weight ought to be given to the authority's plans for an accommodated child than when the child is in care.

### 5.5.1.5 The wishes and feelings of the child's parents

In any case in which the local authority is looking after a child, section 10(9)(d)(ii) requires that the wishes and feelings of the child's parents be taken into account. It will be recalled that in *Re A and others (Minors) (Residence Orders: Leave to Apply)*[241] the Court of Appeal held that the judge had erred in applying the paramountcy principle to a leave application. The reason was that it would mean that the judge could not consider independently the mother's wishes and feelings. In that case, the mother was not even notified of the foster mother's application in respect of her four children in the care of a local authority. The Court of Appeal stated that by failing to give the mother notice the judge had deprived himself of information which was necessary for the proper exercise of his discretion.

### 5.5.2 Without notice applications for leave

A request for leave to apply for a section 8 order can be made without notice before a single magistrate or judge. However, the courts have been cautious regarding the hearing of without notice applications. The leave decision is important and while there may well be cases of urgency, or other circumstances, which make it right to grant leave without notice to the other side, in the ordinary case the interests of justice require that notice be given to parties who are likely to be affected if leave is granted, so that they can adduce evidence and make submissions.[242] In *Re W (Contact Application: Procedure)*[243] Wilson J stated that in almost all cases applications should be on notice, but gave an example from his experience of an exceptional type of case in which a without notice application might be made: where a mature teenage child has left home and seeks leave to apply for a residence order to secure his or her position in the home of another family member. In such a case the application might be granted and a short interim residence order put in place. In *Re SC (A Minor) (Leave to Seek Residence Order)*,[244] however, the court held that where the applicant for leave is a child, it is desirable that everyone with parental responsibility should be given notice of the application even though an application for leave can be made without notice. In *Nottinghamshire County Council v P*[245] the Court of Appeal stated that it was wholly inappropriate for a local authority to apply without notice before a single justice for leave to issue an application for a prohibited steps order. The court added that, in future, any such application should be transferred to the county court and that it should not be dealt with without notice.

### 5.5.3 The child concerned and leave

The Children Act 1989 recognises that in some instances children should be given the opportunity to initiate proceedings for a section 8 order on their own behalf. Children (as a category) do not fall

---

[240] Children Act 1989, s 23.      [241] [1992] Fam 182, [1992] 3 All ER 872.
[242] *Re M (Prohibited Steps Order: Application for Leave)* [1993] 1 FLR 275 at 278F–G *per* Johnson J.
[243] [2000] 1 FLR 263.      [244] [1994] 1 FLR 96.      [245] [1993] 3 All ER 815.

within the categories of persons who are entitled to apply for a section 8 order,[246] although a child is entitled to make a leave application. Applications by children for leave fall into two categories.

First there are cases in which the child applicant is also the child with respect to whom the court may make the section 8 order (ie, the child concerned). Such applications are subject to section 10(8) of the Children Act 1989, which provides:

> where the person applying for leave to make a section 8 application is the child concerned, the court may only grant leave if it is satisfied that he has sufficient understanding to make the proposed application for the section 8 order.[247]

A Practice Direction[248] provides that applications under section 10(8) of the Children Act 1989 must be heard in the High Court, and there have therefore been several reported first instance decisions concerning such applications. In *Re SC (A Minor) (Leave to Seek Residence Order)*[249] Booth J pointed out that a court has a discretion whether to grant leave even if it has been established under section 10(8) that the child has sufficient understanding to make the application and that it is right for the court to have regard to the likelihood of success of the proposed application, and to be satisfied that the child is not embarking on proceedings which are doomed to failure. Her Ladyship also clarified that, as the initial application for leave does not raise any question about the child's upbringing, the child's welfare is not the court's paramount consideration, a view which has been endorsed in subsequent decisions.[250] It has been said, however, that, although not paramount, the child's interests are 'very much at the centre of the court's thinking' on a leave application.[251]

In *Re SC (A Minor) (Leave to Seek Residence Order)*[252] a girl aged 14 years 8 months who had been in care for eight years and had had several failed foster placements, applied for leave to apply for a residence order to live with a friend, Mrs B. The local authority had earlier assessed Mrs B as a foster parent but had found her not to be suitable. The court recognised that in such a case, where the person with whom the child wishes to live may be unlikely to succeed on her own leave application, the child's application, to which the criteria in section 10(9) do not apply,[253] may provide a way of circumventing the more stringent criteria in section 10(9). However, the court did not think that that should prevent the child from being able to apply. On the facts Booth J granted leave.

In *Re C (A Minor) (Leave to Seek Section 8 Orders)*[254] a 15-year-old girl was seeking leave to apply for a residence order to live at the home of a friend and her family, and for a specific issue order to go on holiday with them to Bulgaria. In relation to the residence order, Johnson J took the view that there was no identifiable advantage in making a residence order at that time. He therefore adjourned the child's application for leave. In relation to the application for leave to apply for a specific issue order, he took the view that this was not the kind of issue which Parliament had envisaged as being litigated in a court when it allowed children to make applications for leave. Johnson

---

[246] Except in cases of variation of an order in which the child is named in the order (see s 10(6) and *Re W (Application for Leave: Whether Necessary)* [1996] 3 FCR 337).

[247] Much of the case law examining the level of understanding required of the child to pursue proceedings on his or her own has arisen in the context of the question of whether a child should be permitted to dispense with the services of a guardian ad litem during existing proceedings and be separately represented.

[248] Practice Direction Children Act 1989—Applications By Children [1993] 1 FLR 668.

[249] [1994] 1 FLR 96.

[250] *Re C (Residence: Child's Application for Leave)* [1995] 1 FLR 927, FD (Stuart-White J). There had earlier been a conflict in the authorities, but in *Re H (Residence Order: Child's Application for Leave)* [2000] 1 FLR 780 Johnson J agreed with Booth J's approach, resiling from the view he earlier expressed in *Re C (A Minor) (Leave to Seek Section 8 Orders)* [1994] 1 FLR 26.

[251] *Re C (Residence: Child's Application for Leave)* [1995] 1 FLR 927 at 929 *per* Stuart White J.

[252] [1994] 1 FLR 96.

[253] *Re C (A Minor) (Leave to Seek Section 8 Orders) per* Johnson J. See also Charles J in *Re S (A Minor) (Adopted Child: Contact)* [1999] Fam 283 at 291.

[254] [1994] 1 FLR 26.

J said that 'this jurisdiction is one which should be reserved for the resolution of matters of importance' and he did not consider that the question whether the child should go on a two-week holiday to Bulgaria was such a matter. He therefore refused the child's leave application.

In *Re C (Residence: Child's Application for Leave)*[255] an articulate 14-year-old girl, who was not content for her views to be put forward by a welfare officer, was seeking the leave of the court to apply for an order which, if granted, would enable her to live with her mother rather than her father. Granting the application, Stuart White J carefully applied the guidance in the earlier cases, finding that the child was of sufficient understanding to make the application, that it was impossible to say that the application could not succeed, and that the application concerned a 'matter of very considerable importance'.[256] A similar case, albeit with a contrasting outcome, is *Re H (Residence Order: Child's Application for Leave)*.[257] A very bright 12-year-old, whose intelligence was put on the 99th percentile for age and whose comprehension, social awareness, and abilities with respect to interpersonal relationships were 'very superior', applied for leave to apply for a residence order to live with his father upon his parents' divorce. The child's wish to live with the father was supported by the father. Johnson J concluded that the child had 'sufficient understanding' for the purpose of section 10(8) of the Children Act 1989. However, his Lordship refused the application on the basis that there was no argument or any cross-examination which could be addressed to the court on behalf of the child which would not in any event be addressed to the court on behalf of the father. There were disadvantages, such as the child seeing all the evidence in a case pending between parents and 'the spectre (a word [chosen] deliberately) of a mother being faced across a courtroom by solicitor or counsel acting on behalf of the child she bore'.[258]

In some cases a leave application may create a difficult practical problem, namely where is the child to live in the period between the application for leave and the hearing? The child may be living with a parent or other person, such as a step-parent, in circumstances of considerable animosity. An interim order temporarily to settle the arrangements as to the person with whom the child is to live would seem helpful, but it is doubtful whether one can be made at the leave to apply stage. The difficulty is that that step would interfere in a parent's parental responsibility on the basis of incomplete information and could be influential against the parent at trial. Therefore, where the child should live pending the hearing for leave raises some awkward questions of principle as well as the practical question of what should be done.

### 5.5.4 Where the child seeking leave is not the 'child concerned'

Where the child seeking leave is not 'the child concerned', the applicant child must satisfy the criteria in section 10(9) in the same way as any other applicant for leave. Moreover, in *Re S (Contact Application by Sibling)*[259] it was held that the court was not required to have exclusive regard to the criteria in section 10(9) where the case concerned an applicant child. The child's understanding remained a relevant consideration, as did the application's chances of success.

### 5.5.5 Restriction on leave applications by local authority foster parents

There is a restriction on leave applications by local authority foster parents. Section 9(3) of the Children Act 1989 provides:

> A person who is, or was at any time within the last six months, a local authority foster parent of a child may not apply for leave to apply for a section 8 order with respect to the child unless—
>
> (a) he has the consent of the authority;
> (b) he is a relative of the child; or
> (c) the child has lived with him for at least one year preceding the application.

---

[255] [1995] 1 FLR 927.    [256] Ibid.    [257] [2000] 1 FLR 780 (Johnson J).
[258] Ibid, 783.    [259] [1998] 2 FLR 897.

Why are local authority foster parents who require the court's leave singled out for special treatment? One of the many aims of the Children Act 1989 is to instil confidence in parents in state provision of social services for children in need and in care. Parents are encouraged to work in partnership with local authorities for the benefit of their children. Foster parents may often have more material possessions than a parent, and the opportunities afforded in the foster home to develop and enhance a child's physical, emotional, and educational progress may be superior to those that a parent is able to provide. These are all matters which are relevant to the application of the welfare principle which governs the determination of applications for section 8 orders. If a foster parent could apply like any other person for leave to apply for residence by way of a child arrangements order, a parent might be fearful of making temporary arrangements for his or her child with a local authority. This could rebound to the general disadvantage of children in need and in care, because parents might be tempted to make private arrangements for their children which are less appropriate to their child's needs, or they might become hostile to a foster placement simply because it appeared to be particularly well suited to their child's circumstances.

Unless a foster parent is a relative, or has looked after the child for at least one year, he or she must obtain the consent of the local authority to apply to the court for leave to apply for a section 8 order. Unless that consent is forthcoming, the foster parent is precluded from seeking a section 8 order. The consent provision is also there to reassure local authorities that they can develop their fostering services without losing control over the children.

In *Re P (A Minor) (Leave to Apply: Foster Parents)*[260] the question arose whether the local authority had the entitlement to give consent under section 9(3)(a) to a foster parent's application for leave to apply for a residence order, where the child was an accommodated child, and where the local authority therefore did not have parental responsibility for the child. It was argued that if a local authority were able to give consent under section 9(3), this would, in effect, allow the authority to circumvent the clear prohibition in section 9(2) that no application may be made by a local authority for a residence order or a contact order. Hale J dismissed this argument. She said that it was absolutely plain from the wording that the consent of the local authority accommodating the child was the consent which was needed. While this ruling was unremarkable on the point of law which it settled, the argument raised by counsel that this was a back-door way of allowing a local authority to apply for a residence order was uncomfortably close to the mark. However, it does expose an uncomfortable tension between the various policies which underpin different provisions in the Act. The ruling makes it clear that a local authority, where it takes the view that the welfare of the child requires that he should remain in the care of his foster parents, but where it also takes the view that it does not have sufficient grounds to satisfy the test for making a care order, can encourage the foster parents to make their own application for leave to apply for a residence order.[261] If a foster parent were to obtain residence by way of a child arrangements order, and if the local authority were to continue to make contributions towards the foster parents' costs of accommodating the child, and perhaps to continue to supervise the child on a voluntary basis too, the distinction between state intervention and private law applications would arguably become blurred to an unacceptable degree.

Section 9(3)(c) allows a local authority foster parent with whom the child has lived for at least one year to apply to a court for leave to apply for a section 8 order without first obtaining the consent of the local authority. The difference between that provision and section 10(5A) which entitles a local authority foster parent to apply for residence is that the entitlement in section 10(5A) arises where the child has been living with the foster parent for a period of at least one year *immediately*

---

[260] [1994] 2 FCR 1093.

[261] Which indeed was close to what happened in *Re P (A Minor) (Leave to Apply: Foster Parents)*. The local authority was also acting as an adoption agency in respect of the child. The parents, who were Orthodox Jews, objected to the foster parents as adoptive parents because they were not Orthodox Jews. The court granted the foster parents leave to apply for a residence order.

*preceding the application.* If the foster parent had had the child living with him or her for at least one year but had since ceased to look after the child, the foster parent would not be entitled to apply under section 10(5A). The foster parent would require leave (unless otherwise entitled) but would not be subject to the requirement of the local authority's consent since the child had lived with the foster parent for at least one year.

Once six months have elapsed since the foster parent last looked after the child, the foster parent is free to apply to the court for leave. Of course, the difficulty in overcoming the hurdle of the criteria in section 10(9) would almost certainly be accentuated by the lapse of time. However, a foster parent who was determined to apply for leave once the six months had elapsed might persuade the local authority to consent to her making a leave application at once. This would resolve the matter at an early stage and allow the child's future to be planned without the threat of future litigation.

## 5.6 Restrictions on applications for, and the use of, section 8 orders

Section 10(3) of the Children Act 1989 provides that section 10 is subject to the restrictions imposed by section 9.

### 5.6.1 In respect of a child in care

Section 9(1) provides that:

> [n]o court shall make any section 8 order, other than a child arrangements order to which subsection (6B) applies, with respect to a child who is in the care of a local authority.

This provision reflects an underlying policy within the Children Act 1989, that while the making of a care order is a decision for a court, once a local authority is entrusted via the care order with parental responsibility for the child, the courts should not supervise a local authority's day-to-day decision making with respect to the child. Thus, it is the local authority which can determine matters relating to the child's upbringing.[262] If courts were permitted to entertain applications for specific issue and prohibited steps orders in respect of a child in care this would give individuals the opportunity to challenge a local authority's exercise of parental responsibility. It would also give the courts power to dictate to local authorities how they should carry out their statutory powers and duties. That would conflict with the principle that the courts should not supervise, other than by judicial review, an area of discretion conferred on the local authority by Parliament.[263]

The exception in section 9(6B) is a child arrangements order relating only to the person with whom the child is to live, and/or when the child is to live with any person. Such an order not only settles the arrangements as to the person with whom the child is to live, it discharges a care order and brings to an end a local authority's parental responsibility for the child. Thus, such an order goes to the source of the local authority's powers and not to the manner in which they are being exercised.

### 5.6.2 A local authority may not apply for a child arrangements order

Section 9(2) provides that:

> [n]o application may be made by a local authority for a child arrangements order and no court shall make such an order in favour of a local authority.

Why is a local authority prohibited from seeking leave to apply for a child arrangements order, yet permitted to apply for leave to apply for a specific issue or prohibited steps order? Section 9(2) is directed at those cases where a local authority does not have a care order. Its aim is to prevent a local

---

[262] Except issues relating to contact (see Children Act 1989, s 34).
[263] *A v Liverpool City Council* [1981] 2 All ER 385.

authority from obtaining parental responsibility for a child otherwise than through making an application in care proceedings. A local authority may not apply for contact for similar reasons. Such an order could enable the authority to have enforceable contact with a child other than through obtaining a supervision order in an application brought in care proceedings.[264]

### 5.6.3  Where the child is 16 or over

Section 9(6) of the Children Act 1989 provides that no court is to make a section 8 order which is to have effect for a period which will end after the child has reached the age of 16 unless it is satisfied that the circumstances of the case are exceptional. A section 8 order ceases to have effect when the child reaches 16 'unless it is to have effect beyond that age by virtue of section 9(6)'.[265]

## 5.7  Child arrangements orders dealing with a child's residence

An application for an order regulating a child's residence commonly arises when the child's parents' relationship breaks down and the parents no longer live together. Each parent may wish to provide a home for the child. If the parents are unable to agree about the child's future living arrangements, it may ultimately fall to the court to decide the issue upon a contested application (or cross-applications) for a child arrangements order. Other persons, such as relatives or foster parents, may also be caught up in this type of dispute. In some cases it may be appropriate for more than one person to have residence, for example where two grandparents are looking after their grandchild. In such a case, where the persons concerned will live together in the same household, the order is known as joint residence. It is also possible for a residence order to be made in favour of two or more persons who do not live together in the same household. In that case the order is referred to as shared residence.

The case law on residence has been built upon the old order, the residence order, to which frequent reference is therefore necessary in what follows. A residence order is 'an order settling the arrangements to be made as to the person with whom a child is to live'. It is thus not directly concerned with *where* the child shall live in the sense of the location of the child's home; rather, it defines *the person(s) with whom the child shall live*. However, that is not to say that the issue of where the child will live is not relevant to the question of with whom the child shall live.[266] As Butler-Sloss LJ explained in *Re E (Residence: Imposition of Conditions)*:[267]

> The correct approach is to look at the issue of where the children will live as one of the relevant factors . . . If the case is finely balanced between the respective advantages and disadvantages of the parents, the proposals put forward by each parent will assume considerable importance.

Every case is different and must be decided upon its own unique facts.[268] The court will apply section 1(1) of the Children Act 1989, considering in particular the factors in the checklist in section 1(3) and weighing each in a balancing exercise aimed at ascertaining where the child's welfare lies and ultimately whether the application(s) should be granted or not. For example, the court is required to consider under paragraph (f) of the checklist how capable each of the child's parents

---

[264]  *F v Cambridgeshire County Council* [1995] 1 FLR 516 (wrong for a local authority to be made a party to contact proceedings, and it is not open to a local authority to invite a court to refuse to make a contact order).

[265]  Children Act 1989, s 91(10). See for example *Re H-B (Contact)* [2015] EWCA Civ 389, especially at [3].

[266]  For a recent case in which there was a dispute between the father and mother as to whether the mother was living with the children in her own home or with the children's grandparents, see *AMV v RM (Children: Judge's Visit to Private Home)* [2012] EWHC 3629 (Fam), [2013] 2 FLR 150 (in which the judge acted unlawfully by seeking to resolve the issue with her own visit to, and inspection of, the homes concerned).

[267]  [1997] 2 FLR 638, CA.

[268]  *Re H (Shared Residence: Parental Responsibility)* [1995] 2 FLR 883: 'each case will depend upon its own facts'; *Re T* [2009] EWCA Civ 388: 'every case is fact sensitive' (at [6]).

is of caring for the child and, under paragraph (g), any harm the child has suffered or is at risk of suffering. The fact that one parent is for some reason incapable of caring for the child appropriately may prove highly significant to the outcome.[269] Under these headings the court might also consider the extent to which a resident parent will facilitate contact with a non-resident parent. In *Re A (A Minor) (Custody)*[270] Butler-Sloss LJ said that the approach of a parent to contact is highly relevant to the determination of whether the child should live with him or her.[271] As we shall see later in this chapter, the courts are increasingly willing to use a change of residence (or at least the threat thereof) as a means of enforcing contact.

In many cases, however, each parent will be able to provide a reasonable standard of care for the child, and the decision about which parent will better provide for the child's welfare often turns on considerations in the checklist such as those relating to the child's physical, emotional, and educational needs (para (b)), and the child's age, sex, background, and any characteristics of his which the court considers relevant (para (d)). The court must also consider the ascertainable wishes and feelings of the child in light of his or her age and understanding (under para (a)). This too can be a powerful factor influencing the court's decision in a particular case, whether the wishes and feelings are evidenced by the statements of an articulate teenager or, for example, through a toddler's clinginess to a particular parent.

Of particular importance in residence disputes is paragraph (c), which directs a court to consider the likely effect on the child of any change in his circumstances. Of course, when parents part there is inevitably a change of circumstances for the children, though if one parent remains in the former family home with the children, he or she has a clear advantage under that head. Continuity is generally regarded as desirable for a child because it assists in giving a sense of security at a time when the child may feel vulnerable and threatened by the parents' separation. Bonds are likely to exist not only between the child and the parent with whom he is living, but also between the child and other members of the household, neighbours, friends, and companions at school. Thus, the parent who keeps the children in the immediacy of relationship breakdown is most likely, all other things being equal, to obtain a residence order. Parents seeking legal advice should be made fully aware of this bias towards the status quo. Even where a parent leaves the family home with the children, delays in litigation may mean that the new arrangements will have assumed some importance by the time of a court hearing. *Re B (Residence Order: Status Quo)*[272] illustrates the force of the status quo. The trial judge transferred residence from the father to the mother, taking the view that the child could only enjoy such contact if she was under the control of the mother. Allowing the father's appeal, the Court of Appeal agreed with counsel's submission that the judge was wrong to put speculative improvements in contact over continuity of care. The contact difficulties needed to be tackled but not by the drastic measure of upsetting the status quo, which in this case was of overwhelming importance for securing the child's future.

In addition to the statutory checklist structuring the court's exercise of discretion, the appellate courts have also developed guideline general principles to assist judges.

### 5.7.1 The relevance of the child's age and sex

In *Re W (A Minor) (Residence Order)*,[273] Lord Donaldson MR expressed the view that there is a rebuttable presumption of fact that the best interests of a baby are served by being with its mother.[274] In saying this his Lordship laid stress on the word 'baby' and indicated that different considerations apply in the case of a child. In *Re W* the mother initially agreed that her baby would be looked

---

[269] For a recent example of a case in which a father unsuccessfully sought a change of residence from the mother on the basis of the mother's alleged day-to-day mishandling of the children, see *Re C (Family Proceedings: Case Management)* [2012] EWCA Civ 1489, [2013] 1 FLR 1089. In an appropriate case, such allegations can be summarily dismissed by the judge. See ibid, [14].

[270] [1991] 2 FLR 394.    [271] Ibid, 400.    [272] [1998] 1 FLR 368.

[273] [1992] 2 FLR 332, CA.    [274] Ibid, 336.

after by the father, who duly collected the baby from the hospital shortly after the child's birth and was caring for the child. Shortly thereafter the mother changed her mind and sought the return of the child. A judge had ordered that the status quo be maintained pending the preparation of reports. Allowing the mother's appeal, the Court of Appeal substituted an interim residence order in her favour, Balcombe LJ commenting that 'it hardly requires saying that a baby of under four weeks old would normally be with his or her natural mother'. Agreeing with Balcombe LJ, Lord Donaldson added that it had not really been possible for a status quo to be established in the very short period of three weeks that the father had cared for the child.

Apart from this presumption of fact in the case of a baby, there is no presumption that one parent should be preferred to another parent at a particular age of the child or because of the child's sex. In *Re S (A Minor) (Custody)*[275] Butler-Sloss LJ explained that 'it is natural for young children to be with their mothers' but where there is a dispute 'it is a consideration but not a presumption'.[276] In *Re A (A Minor) (Custody)*[277] her Ladyship added that:

> [i]n cases where the child has remained throughout with the mother and is young, particularly when a baby or a toddler, the unbroken relationship of the mother and child is one which it would be very difficult to displace, unless the mother was unsuitable to care for the child.[278]

In *Re A (A Minor) (Custody)*[279] a mother left the matrimonial home with her 12-year-old daughter, leaving four of her children with the father, including a 6-year-old girl, K. Upon the mother's custody application, the judge, apparently starting from the proposition that girls naturally go with their mothers, awarded custody of K to the mother. At the time of the mother's application, the father had been caring for the girl (with the assistance of a full-time housekeeper and a girlfriend) for nearly 12 months. Allowing his appeal, the Court of Appeal held that the judge had applied the wrong test and also failed to take sufficient account of the status quo. Butler-Sloss LJ distinguished the situation where there has been a continuum of care by the mother (as described earlier) from one, as here, where the mother and child have been separated and she seeks the return of the child.

The approach in *Re S (A Minor) (Custody)* and *Re A (A Minor) (Custody)* was reflected in the House of Lords decision in *Brixey v Lynas*,[280] an appeal from Scotland in which the English case law was cited. In that case the parents, who were disputing the custody of a young child, were from very different backgrounds. As the House of Lords put it, the father was 'comfortably middle class, while the mother had had none of the educational and social advantages which he had had'. The child had been living with the mother when the Glasgow Sheriff Court granted custody to the father, taking the view that 'as a member of the father's family the child would have all the advantages of comfort, education and a strong and stable moral framework which they can offer'.[281] Allowing the mother's appeal, the Court of Session, First Division, found[282] that the sheriff had failed to take account of the important factor that during infancy the child's need for her mother is stronger than the need for a father. The Court of Session explained that this principle did not create any presumption in favour of the mother, nor rule of law, but reflected a generally recognised belief that a mother is ordinarily better able, for whatever reason, to minister to a very young child's needs than is a father. The father appealed to the House of Lords, contending *inter alia* that that approach amounted to a maternal preference and thus sexual prejudice. Dismissing the father's appeal, Lord Jauncey, in an opinion which had the full agreement of the House, commented that 'to ignore the fact that in normal circumstances, and I stress the word normal, a mother is better able than a father to fulfil

---

[275] [1991] 2 FLR 388, CA.

[276] Ibid, 390. See also *Re A (A Minor) Custody)* [1991] 2 FLR 394 at 400: 'There is no presumption which requires the mother, as mother, to be considered as the primary caretaker in preference to the father.'

[277] [1991] 2 FLR 394.    [278] Ibid, 400.    [279] Ibid.

[280] [1996] 2 FLR 499, HL (Sc).    [281] Ibid, 500.

[282] See *Brixey v Lynas*, 1994 SLT 847, and for comment see E. Sutherland, 'Mother knows best', 1994 SLT (News) 375.

the needs of a very young child is to ignore what is generally accepted to be reality'. He rejected the father's argument about sexual prejudice with the following words:

> To suggest that any recognition of the normal mother's natural ability to look after a very young child amounts to sexual discrimination is absurd. Nature has endowed men and women with very different attributes and it so happens that mothers are generally better fitted than fathers to provide for the needs of very young children. This is no more discriminatory than the fact that only women can give birth.[283] Every case must be considered on its own facts.[284]

Summarising the legal position, which can probably be taken also to reflect the House of Lords' view of the law of England and Wales, Lord Jauncey explained:

> [T]he advantage to a very young child of being with its mother is a consideration which must be taken into account in deciding where lie its best interests in custody proceedings in which the mother is involved. It is neither a presumption nor a principle but rather recognition of a widely held belief based on practical experience and the workings of nature. Its importance will vary according to the age of the child and to the other circumstances of each individual case such as whether the child has been living with or apart from the mother and whether she is or is not capable of providing proper care. Circumstances may be such that it has no importance at all. Furthermore it will always yield to other competing advantages which more effectively promote the welfare of the child. However, where a very young child has been with its mother since birth and there is no criticism of her ability to care for the child only the strongest competing advantages are likely to prevail.[285]

### 5.7.2 Young siblings should normally be brought up together

In *C v C (Minors: Custody)*[286] the Court of Appeal held that young siblings should, wherever possible, be brought up together in the same household, so that they may be an emotional support to each other following the family breakdown as they grow up. The children's mother moved out of the family home with the 7-year-old daughter, leaving their 4-year-old son with the father. She then obtained her own accommodation and applied for residence for both children. Noting that there was satisfactory contact between the boy and the mother, the judge made a split custody order confirming the existing arrangements. The Court of Appeal held that the judge had erred, and that a split order should not be made unless there were strong factors to warrant it.

In *B v B (Minors) (Custody, Care and Control)*[287] the High Court clarified that although it is desirable that siblings are brought up together, this factor is not of such importance always to override other factors in the balancing exercise, and particularly so where there is a large age gap between children. Upon the breakdown of the parents' relationship, the older two children (aged 10 and 9) lived with the father and the youngest (aged 2) with the mother. The older children wished to stay with their father and the youngest child was bonded with the mother. In those circumstances the status quo was confirmed by the court.

In a case in which there is a baby and a young child, the presumption of fact that the baby's best interests are best served by being with the mother, combined with the desirability of siblings being brought up together, will often lead to the conclusion that both children should be with the mother.

### 5.7.3 A parent's sexual orientation

There have been several cases in which the relevance of a parent's sexual orientation has been raised. The European Court of Human Rights in *Salgueiro da Silva Mouta v Portugal*[288] has held

---

[283] Of course, now following the Gender Recognition Act 2004 that is not wholly true.
[284] [1996] 2 FLR 499 at 504.     [285] Ibid, 505.     [286] [1988] 2 FLR 291, CA.
[287] See also *B v B (Residence Order: Restricting Applications)* [1991] 1 FLR 402, FD.
[288] *Salgueiro da Silva Mouta v Portugal* (App no 33290/96) [1999] ECHR, [2001] 1 FCR 653, ECtHR.

that, in the case of any relationship between a child and parent which constitutes family life within Article 8 of the ECHR, a decision regarding a child's residence in which a person's sexual orientation is of itself a decisive factor would constitute a breach of Articles 8 and 14 taken together. In *Salgueiro da Silva Mouta* a child's parents had divorced and the father was cohabiting in a homosexual relationship. The child's residence was initially with the mother. However, the mother failed to allow the father contact with the child,[289] and for that reason a court subsequently reversed the child's residence in favour of the father. The Lisbon Court of Appeal, however, allowed the mother's appeal against that decision, the majority commenting in the course of judgment that homosexuality 'is an abnormality and children should not grow up in the shadow of abnormal situations'.[290] The European Court of Human Rights unanimously found that the Lisbon court had made a distinction based on the father's sexuality which was not acceptable under the ECHR.

In light of this ruling, the leading domestic authority on this issue, the Court of Appeal decision in *C v C (A Minor) (Custody: Appeal)*[291] must be viewed with considerable caution, although it has never been overruled. In that case the court had to choose between parents of a 6-year-old girl who both clearly loved the child and could give her good physical care. The father had remarried and was living with his new wife; the mother was living with a lesbian partner. The trial judge gave the care of the child to the mother, holding that her lesbian relationship was not a matter to put into the balancing exercise since its impact on the child would be much the same whether she visited her mother from time to time or lived with her permanently. Allowing the father's appeal and remitting the case for a fresh hearing, the Court of Appeal ruled that the judge had been plainly wrong to engage in the balancing operation as if there were no lesbian relationship.

Glidewell LJ expressed the view that 'despite the vast changes over the past 30 years or so in the attitudes of our society generally to the institution of marriage, to sexual morality, and to homosexual relationships . . . a lesbian relationship between two adult women is an unusual background in which to bring up a child'. Balcombe LJ added that:

> [i]t is still the norm that children are brought up in a home with a father, mother and siblings (if any) and, other things being equal, such an upbringing is most likely to be conducive to their welfare. If, because the parents are divorced, such an upbringing is no longer possible, then a very material factor in considering where the child's welfare lies is which of the competing parents can offer the nearest approach to the norm.[292]

It is submitted that, in light of *Salgueiro da Silva Mouta* and the requirements of the HRA 1998, a domestic court would be highly unlikely to view this norm as a lawful justification for deciding a residence application in favour of a heterosexual parent rather than a homosexual parent. It should be noted that the assertions in *C v C* were made over 20 years ago[293] and must be viewed in light of increased social and legal recognition of same-sex relationships and parenting. By contrast with *C v C*, in *G v F (Shared Residence: Parental Responsibility)*[294] Bracewell J granted leave to apply for a shared residence order to the applicant who had formerly been in a lesbian relationship with the respondent, holding that sexual orientation is merely a background circumstance and that it would be 'entirely wrong . . . and unsustainable to seek, in any way, to reflect against the applicant by reason of the nature of her relationship with the respondent'.[295] It is submitted that the correct approach is as follows. As *C v C* makes clear that the parent's relationship (whether homosexual or heterosexual) cannot simply be ignored; it is one of the circumstances of the case. However, a parent's sexuality cannot be relevant per se, for to choose on that basis would be discriminatory; the nature of the parent's relationship is relevant only insofar as it impacts on the child's welfare.

---

[289] Facilitation of contact was not aided by the fact that the maternal grandparents were Jehovah's Witnesses and had strong religious objections to the father's homosexuality.

[290] [2001] 1 FCR 653 at 664 (para 14 of the judgment).    [291] [1991] 1 FLR 223.

[292] Ibid, 231.    [293] It was decided on 24 August 1990.    [294] [1998] 2 FLR 799.    [295] Ibid, 805.

### 5.7.4 **Religious beliefs and practices**

Sometimes a parent may object to the other parent's religious beliefs and/or practices, and fear the impact on the child of those beliefs.

In *Hoffmann v Austria*[296] the European Court of Human Rights held that to draw a distinction between parents in a custody dispute simply on the basis of one parent's religion is a violation of that parent's rights under Articles 8 and 14 of the ECHR taken together. In that case the parents of two children had been married as Roman Catholics, and Austrian legislation provided that during the marriage, in the absence of an agreement, 'neither parent may decide without the consent of the other that the child is to be brought up in a faith different from that shared by both parents at the time of their marriage'.[297] The mother had subsequently converted to the Jehovah's Witness faith and the parents divorced. In a dispute over custody of the children, the Austrian Supreme Court awarded custody of the children to the father. The court took account of the practical consequences of the religious convictions of the Jehovah's Witnesses, including their rejection of holidays such as Christmas and Easter, which are customarily celebrated by the majority of the Austrian population, their opposition to the administration of blood transfusions, and in general their position as a social minority living by its own distinctive rules.[298] The European Court of Human Rights commented that, depending on the circumstances of the case, those factors may be capable of tipping the scales in favour of one parent or the other. However, the Austrian court had also drawn on the said legislation in reaching its decision, noting that the mother was seeking to bring up the children in a religion other than that of the marriage. The European Court of Human Rights found that the Austrian Supreme Court had regarded the legislation as a decisive factor and had thus discriminated unlawfully simply on the basis of religion.[299]

The case can be compared with *Ismailova v Russia*[300] in which the parents married as Muslims and the mother converted to the Jehovah's Witness faith. Upon the parents' divorce the father sought and obtained custody of the couple's children, aged 7 and 4. In the course of granting residence to the father, the Russian courts noted that the mother and the children had been living in cramped conditions in a three-room flat with the maternal grandparents and the mother's three brothers. Jehovah's Witness meetings were held a few times a week at the flat and the children had been frightened by some of the things they had heard. For example, they had become frightened of rain and wind, being worried that a worldwide flood and earthquake would take place. The mother claimed a violation of Articles 8 and 14 of the ECHR in that she had been unlawfully discriminated against in the custody proceedings on the basis of her religion. The European Court of Human Rights found no violation, explaining that the domestic courts' decisions had not been based upon the mother's membership of the Jehovah's Witnesses but upon the impact of her religious practices upon the children's interests. Furthermore, this was only one aspect of the decision, which was also based on the children's financial, housing, and general living conditions.[301]

The English authorities have similarly drawn a distinction between religion and the effect of religious practices. They have seen as material such factors as indoctrination or isolation arising from religious practices.[302] In *Re T (Minors) (Custody: Religious Upbringing)*[303] the Court of Appeal made clear that it is not for the court to pass any judgment on the beliefs of the parents where they are socially acceptable and consistent with a decent and respectable life. This approach was given further endorsement in *Re G (Education: Religious Upbringing)*,[304] which was discussed in detail

---

[296] *Hoffmann v Austria* (App no 12875/87) [1993] ECHR 25, (1994) 17 EHRR 293, [1994] 1 FCR 193, ECtHR.

[297] Federal Act on the Religious Education of Children, art 2(2).     [298] *Hoffmann v Austria*, para 32.

[299] Ibid, para 33.     [300] [2008] 1 FLR 533.     [301] Ibid, [62].

[302] See eg *Re R (Residence: Religion)* [1993] 2 FLR 163 (father withdrawn from religious sect and thus affecting ability to have contact with child).

[303] (1981) 2 FLR 239. The case was decided in 1975.

[304] [2012] EWCA Civ 123, [2013] 1 FLR 677. For comment, see R. Taylor, 'Secular Values and Sacred Rights: *Re G (Education: Religious Upbringing)*' [2013] Child and Family Law Quarterly 336; S. Johnson, 'Religion, Children and the Family Courts' [2013] Family Law 574; and J. Ecob and F. Iverson, 'An Orthodox Approach to Education' [2013] Family Law 56.

earlier in this chapter. *Re T* concerned the custody of three children in wardship proceedings: two 15-year-old twin girls and their 8-year-old sister. The parents' marriage broke down as a result of the mother's interest in, and commitment to, the Jehovah's Witness faith. Evidence was given that Jehovah's Witnesses do not celebrate Christmas or birthdays and the life of that community became more important than the wider community. The judge regarded it of critical importance that if the mother were given custody the children would be withdrawn from ordinary family life, and was apprehensive of the children's possible alienation from the father.

A welfare report showed that the mother was bringing up the children as well adjusted, and the girls wanted to be with their mother. The judge awarded custody to the father. Allowing the mother's appeal, Scarman LJ commented that there was no reason why the mother should not espouse the beliefs and practices of the Jehovah's Witnesses for there was nothing immoral or socially obnoxious about them. The judge had given too much weight to the father's only complaint against the mother, namely her religious beliefs, and too little weight to the success of the mother in bringing up the children.

In *M v H (Education: Welfare)*[305] the child's residence was shared between the parents. The child lived for most of the time in Germany with the mother, who was a Jehovah's Witness, but spent considerable time also with the father in England, who was a Catholic. The question arose as to where the child should be educated, with consequent impact on the child's residence arrangements. Charles J decided that the child should be educated in England, supporting his decision with the view that thereby the likely social effects on the child of the mother's beliefs and practices as a Jehovah's Witness would have far less weight.[306]

Sometimes a parent's fears about the other parent's religious beliefs may have an impact upon the welfare of the child and this may need to be reflected in the court's order. An example, albeit in the context of a contact dispute, is *Wright v Wright*[307] where the mother's fear that the father would indoctrinate the child justified denial of the father's contact because the mother's emotional reaction if contact took place would be damaging to the child.

### 5.7.5 The child's background

A child's religious heritage is of course a relevant consideration on any application, being part of the child's background within section 1(3)(d) of the Children Act 1989, and an important factor where the child's religion is a powerful aspect of the family's way of life.[308] The weight given to the child's religion will vary according to the facts of each case.[309] Even where religious practices are not a source of concern, the child's religion may in some cases need to defer to other welfare considerations. In *Re P (Section 91(14) Guidelines) (Residence and Religious Heritage)*[310] a girl with Down's Syndrome was born to Orthodox Jewish parents (the father was a Rabbi) who were initially unable to care for her. From the age of 17 months, the child was placed with experienced foster parents who were non-practising Catholics. When the child was 8 years old the parents sought the return of their daughter. The judge concluded that the child should not be moved given her attachment to the foster parents. Upholding that decision, the Court of Appeal held that the 'undoubted importance for an Orthodox Jew of his religion which provides in itself a way of life which permeates all activities, is a factor to be put in the balancing exercise' but also noted that religious and cultural heritage could not be the overwhelming factor, nor displace the weighty welfare factors.[311] As noted earlier, in discussion of *Re G (Education: Religious Upbringing)*,[312] the judge's task will also be driven by seeking to achieve equality of opportunity, promoting aspiration, and the child's right to an open future.

---

[305] [2008] EWHC 324 (Fam), [2008] 1 FLR 1400.

[306] Ibid, [107]–[110]. The child would likely have a wider circle of friends and be able to celebrate birthdays and Christmas.

[307] (1981) 2 FLR 276.

[308] *Re P (Section 91(14) Guidelines) (Residence and Religious Heritage)* [1999] 2 FLR 573, CA.

[309] Ibid, 585.     [310] [1999] 2 FLR 573, CA.     [311] Ibid, 586.

[312] [2012] EWCA Civ 123, [2013] 1 FLR 677, [2013] 1 FLR 677.

## 5.8 **Shared residence**

Prior to enactment of the Children and Families Act 2014, section 11(4) of the Children Act 1989 provided:

> Where a residence order is made in favour of two or more persons who do not themselves all live together, the order may specify the periods during which the child is to live in the different households concerned.[313]

This provision followed a recommendation of the Law Commission which saw 'no reason why such orders should be actively discouraged given evidence from the USA that, where practicable, such arrangements could work well'.[314] It was never the expectation or intention that they would be a common form of order.[315] However, it was said that section 11(4) could 'be taken to be an encouragement to make more use of shared residence orders than hitherto'.[316] Section 11(4) has now been repealed by the 2014 Act, and the possibility of a child living in different households is accommodated within the definition of a child arrangements order. In what follows, however, we shall use the term 'shared residence' to refer to such child arrangements.

### 5.8.1 **On what bases can the court make a 'shared residence' order?**

> In *Re A (Joint Residence: Parental Responsibility)*[317] Sir Mark Potter P explained that there are three possible bases for making a shared residence order:
>
> (i) where it provides legal confirmation of the factual reality of a child's life;[318]
> (ii) where it is the means by which to confer parental responsibility on an individual who would otherwise not be able to apply for a free-standing parental responsibility order;[319]
> (iii) where, in a case where one party has the primary care of a child, it may be psychologically beneficial to the parents in emphasising the equality of their position and responsibilities.[320]

#### 5.8.1.1 *Reflecting the underlying reality of where the children live their lives*

A shared residence order is usually made where it 'provides legal confirmation of the factual reality of a child's life',[321] and it has been said that it 'is not intended to deal with issues of parental status';[322] the latter is recognised in 'parental responsibility' which gives an 'equal say in how the

---

[313] The subsection is 'permissive and its purpose is to direct the court's attention to the need, if it arises, to allocate the periods during which the child is "to live in the different households concerned" ': *Re H (A Child)* [2002] EWCA Civ 2005 at [33]. It is thus possible to make a shared residence order where persons in whose favour the order is made are living together in the same property (eg a house or flat), but not sharing households. See generally, S. Gilmore, 'Court Decision-Making in Shared Residence Order Cases—A Critical Examination' [2006] Child and Family Law Quarterly 478; S. Gilmore, 'Shared Residence: A Summary of the Courts' Guidance' [2010] Family Law 285; R. George and P. Harris, 'Parental Responsibility and Shared Residence Orders: Parliamentary Intentions and Judicial Interpretations' (2010) 22 Child and Family Law Quarterly 151; S. Harris-Short, 'Resisting the March Towards 50/50 Shared Residence. Rights, Welfare and Equality in Post-Separation Families' (2010) 22 Journal of Social Welfare and Family Law 257–274.

[314] Law Com No 172 (1988), para 4.12.

[315] '[P]artly because most children will still need the stability of a single home, and partly because in the cases where shared care is appropriate there is less likely to be a need for the court to make any order at all': see Children Act 1989 Guidance and Regulations (HMSO, 1991), vol 1: Court Orders, para 2.28 at p 10.

[316] *Re W (A Minor)*, CA (6 December 1993).

[317] [2008] EWCA Civ 867, [2008] 2 FLR 1593, CA.    [318] Ibid, [66].    [319] Ibid, [70].    [320] Ibid, [66].

[321] *Re A (Joint Residence: Parental Responsibility)* [2008] EWCA Civ 867, [2008] 2 FLR 1593, CA at [66] *per* Sir Mark Potter P.

[322] *Re H (Children)* [2009] EWCA Civ 902. See also *Re F (Children)* [2003] EWCA Civ 592 at [21].

children are to be brought up'.[323] A shared residence order will commonly reflect an arrangement whereby the child moves back and forth between the parents' respective households spending several days in each. However:

> The fact that the parents' homes are separated by a considerable distance does not preclude the possibility that the children's year will be divided between the homes of the two separated parents in such a way as to validate the making of a shared residence order.[324]

Furthermore, the children need not spend their time evenly, or more or less evenly, in the households concerned.[325] In *Re K (Shared Residence Order)*[326] the parents shared the child's time 40/60[327] in favour of the mother, and the father applied to increase this to 50/50 shared care reflected in a shared residence order. The judge, having concluded that the time should not be increased, refused to make a shared residence order. The Court of Appeal allowed the appeal with regard to the judge's refusal to reflect the arrangements in a shared residence order. Wilson LJ explained:

> [A] ruling in favour of an equal division of time and for a shared residence order, do not stand or fall together . . . the convenient course is . . . to rule first upon the optimum division of the child's time in his interests and then, in the light of that ruling, to proceed to consider whether the favoured division should be expressed as terms of a shared residence order or of a contact order.[328]

The material question, therefore, is whether the time spent with each parent can properly be characterised as shared residence. In *Re H (Children)*[329] Ward LJ explained that his:

> practical test is to postulate the question, ask the children, where do you live? If the answer is 'I live with my mummy but I go and stay with my daddy regularly', then you have the answer to your problem. That answer means a residence order with mummy and contact with daddy, but if the situation truly is such that the children say, 'Oh, we live with mummy for part of the time and with daddy for the other part of the time', then you have the justification for making a shared residence order.[330]

In other words: from the child's perspective, are the existing, or proposed, arrangements appropriately characterised as shared residence? At some point the child–parent contact will be such that it is better expressed in a contact order. In *Re W (Children) (Residence Order)*,[331] for example, Thorpe LJ held that it is:

> not open to a judge to make a shared residence order in circumstances such as this where the children sleep perhaps 320 days of the year with their mother and visit their father on a pattern of contact which, although regular and frequent, is at the lower end of what is conventionally ordered.[332]

---

[323] [2009] EWCA Civ 902 at [11]. Note, however, that a child arrangements order has an impact upon existing parental responsibility and a holder of residence will have greater rights than someone with parental responsibility who does not have a residence order: see discussion in Section 5.10.

[324] *Re F (Children) (Shared Residence Order)* [2003] EWCA Civ 592, [2003] 2 FLR 397 at [21].

[325] This was recognised in the Law Commission Report which preceded the Children Act 1989 (Law Commission, *Family Law: Review of Child Law* (Law Com No 172, 1988), para 4.12) and has been stated in several decisions: see *A v A (Shared Residence)* [2004] EWC 142 (Fam), [2004] 1 FLR 1195 at [115] *per* Wall J; *Re F (Shared Residence Order)* [2003] EWCA Civ 592, [2003] 2 FLR 347 at [10] and [34]; *Re W (Shared Residence Order)* [2009] EWCA Civ 370, [2009] 2 FLR 436, CA at [17].

[326] [2008] 2 FLR 380, CA.

[327] While common to express the shared time as a percentage, such statistics are 'usually only of limited value'. See *Re F (Shared Residence Order)* [2003] EWCA Civ 592, [2003] 2 FLR 397 at [30], and *Re W (Shared Residence Order)* [2009] EWCA Civ 370, [2009] 2 FLR 436, CA, at [17] *per* Wilson LJ.

[328] Ibid, [6].     [329] [2009] EWCA Civ 902, Moore-Bick LJ concurring.     [330] Ibid, [11].

[331] [2003] EWCA Civ 116.

[332] Ibid, [9], Chadwick LJ agreeing. Cf *Re W (Shared Residence Order)* [2009] EWCA Civ 370, [2009] 2 FLR 436, CA (shared residence made when father seeing child 25 per cent of the time).

### 5.8.1.2 Conferring parental responsibility where not otherwise possible

*Re A (Joint Residence: Parental Responsibility)* confirmed that a second basis for the making of a shared residence order is as a means of conferring parental responsibility 'on an individual who would otherwise not be able to apply for a free-standing parental responsibility order'.[333] A child had been brought up for two years on the erroneous assumption that the mother's cohabitant, A, was the child's father. Upon the breakdown of the adults' relationship the child continued to enjoy good contact with A, who represented his only father figure. The Court of Appeal upheld a shared residence order, which envisaged that the mother would remain the primary carer and was made principally to confer (by s 12(2) of the Children Act 1989) parental responsibility on A (who could not otherwise acquire it). The occasions on which a shared residence order will be needed to confer parental responsibility have been reduced by the increased free-standing methods by which parental responsibility can be acquired[334] However, such cases are still likely to arise.

In *Re G (Shared Residence Order: Biological Mother of Donor Egg)*[335] the appellant was the former lesbian partner of the respondent. During their relationship, the appellant donated eggs to the respondent, which were fertilised with the sperm of an anonymous donor, and the respondent gave birth to twins. After the couple's relationship broke down, the appellant used one of the remaining embryos to have a child of her own, and subsequently gave birth to a daughter, D. The children were thus full genetic siblings, being genetically related to the same donor father and the appellant. However, in law the respondent was the mother of the twins and the appellant the mother of D. The appellant was involved in the care of the twins and had contact, including staying contact upon the relationship breakdown. The appellant claimed to be both a genetic and psychological parent and sought a shared residence order in order to confer upon her parental responsibility for the twins. In refusing the order the judge thought it significant that the couple had not taken advantage of the provisions of the Human Fertilisation and Embryology Act 2008 to confer legal parenthood on the respondent in respect of D, and inferred that there was no intention to share parental responsibility for the children. The Court of Appeal allowed the appeal, Black LJ observing this did not necessarily follow since 'the relationship between the women was different by the time D was conceived.'[336] More significantly, the Court held that the judge had erred in failing to give weight to the fact of the appellant's biological connection with the children, there needing 'to be consideration given also to the appellant's importance as the children's genetic parent and as the mother of their full sibling, D, with whom they will form a relationship through contact'.[337] The court therefore remitted the case for re-hearing, albeit urging the mothers to seek agreement.

### 5.8.1.3 Can an order be made for the psychological benefit of a parent?

In *Re A (Joint Residence: Parental Responsibility)*[338] Sir Mark Potter P appeared to introduce a further distinct category of case in which the making of a shared residence order would be justified: 'where, in a case where one party has the primary care of a child, it may be psychologically beneficial to the *parents* in emphasising the equality of their position and responsibilities.'[339] However, it is submitted that this view is not consistent with the parliamentary intention behind residence orders,[340] finds no support in earlier authorities, nor is it consistent with the child focus

---

[333] *Re A (Joint Residence: Parental Responsibility)* [2008] EWCA Civ 867, [2008] 2 FLR 1593 at [70], drawing on *Re H (Shared Residence: Parental Responsibility)* [1995] 2 FLR 883.

[334] Eg Children Act 1989, ss 4ZA and 4A.   [335] [2014] EWCA Civ 336, [2014] 2 FLR 897.

[336] Ibid, at para [56].   [337] Ibid, at paras [52] and [53].   [338] [2008] 2 FLR 1593.

[339] Ibid, [66], Sir Robin Auld and Scott Baker LJ agreeing (emphasis added). His Lordship appeared to draw on a passage of Ward LJ's judgment in *Re H (Shared Residence: Parental Responsibility)* [1995] 2 FLR 883 at 889, which drew attention to the different psychological impact which residence and contact respectively may have. For criticism, see S. Gilmore, 'Shared Residence: A Summary of the Courts' Guidance' [2010] Family Law 285 (arguing this was a misreading of *Re H*, where the making of a shared residence order was firmly rooted in the psychological benefit to the *child* not the parent).

[340] See P. G. Harris and R. H. George, 'Parental Responsibility and Shared Residence Orders: Parliamentary Intentions and Judicial Interpretations' [2010] Child and Family Law Quarterly 151. See also A. Grand, 'In Practice: Disputes

required by section 1(1) of the Children Act 1989 as emphasised by the House of Lords in *Holmes-Moorhouse v Richmond-Upon-Thames LBC* (discussed in the next section).[341] Sir Mark Potter P's statement appears to be a misreading of some earlier authority which suggests that, in addition to reflecting the reality, a shared residence order may incidentally carry with it additional benefits. As Wall LJ commented in *Re P (Shared Residence Order)*:[342]

> Such an order emphasises the fact that both parents are equal in the eyes of the law and that they have equal duties and responsibilities as parents. The order can have the additional advantage of conveying the court's message that neither parent is in control and that the court expects parents to co-operate with each other for the benefit of their children.[343]

In *T v T (Shared Residence)*[344] a shared residence order had been made in favour of the child's mother and father, who, respectively, were living in same-sex relationships. The mother's partner, L, was not a party to the shared residence order although the judge had granted her parental responsibility. The mother and her partner argued that the shared residence order should not have been made and contended instead for a joint residence order in favour of the mother and her partner. The Court of Appeal held that the judge's exercise of discretion could not be criticised. However, it was submitted that, if the mother died, there would then be nothing to stop the father from asserting that the children should immediately go to live full time with him as the last surviving holder of a residence order. In light of that submission and the father's agreement to L being included in a shared residence order, the Court of Appeal made a shared residence order in favour of the mother, father, and L. Black LJ observed, however, that 'it cannot be anticipated that considerations relating to what may happen in the aftermath of an untimely death will regularly tip the balance in favour of a joint residence order in circumstances such as the present ones. In many cases, there will be a profusion of much more pressing factors that dictate another outcome.'[345]

### 5.8.2 Deciding whether it is appropriate to make a 'shared residence' order: general guidance

The starting point for considering the courts' approach to a shared residence order is the House of Lords' decision in *Holmes-Moorhouse v Richmond-Upon-Thames LBC*.[346] Unusually, this case did not concern a dispute between parents, but rather the impact of a shared residence order upon a housing authority's duties under the Housing Act 1996. Accordingly, the House was not provided with an opportunity fully to engage with earlier Court of Appeal authorities on shared residence. However, it made some important statements on the nature of shared residence and how shared residence applications should be approached.

A judge had ordered the father of four children to leave the rented family home and made a shared residence order that the children live with the father on alternate weeks and half of the school holidays. The court's order rendered the father homeless and a question arose for the housing authority as to whether, as the father claimed, he was a priority housing need within section 189(1) of the Housing Act 1996, being 'a person with whom dependent children . . . might reasonably be expected to reside'. The father argued that the shared residence order put him into this category. The relevant housing authority disagreed and ultimately appealed the matter to the House.

---

between Parents: Time for a New Order?' [2011] Family Law 74, suggesting that residence orders have become the new custody orders and that it is time for a newly worded order: a 'parental time order' which would deal only with time and avoid any references to parental status.

[341] [2009] UKHL 7, [2009] 1 FLR 904. See further, S. Gilmore, 'Shared Residence: A Summary of the Courts' Guidance' [2010] Family Law 285.

[342] [2005] EWCA Civ 1639, [2006] 2 FLR 347 at [22].

[343] Ibid, [22], repeated in *Re K (Shared Residence Order)* [2008] 2 FLR 380, CA, Buxton LJ agreeing.

[344] [2010] EWCA Civ 1366.     [345] Ibid, [47].     [346] [2009] UKHL 7, [2009] 1 FLR 904.

Lord Hoffmann delivered the leading opinion. He acknowledged that 'shared residence orders are not nowadays unusual'[347] but cautioned that a court 'should not make a shared residence order unless it appears reasonably likely that both parties will have accommodation in which the children can reside'.[348] The court's decision 'must be taken in the light of circumstances as they are or may reasonably expected to be'.[349]

Lord Hoffmann noted that the housing authority's decision imported wider considerations than those of a court making a shared residence order, and the fact that a court had made an order did not necessarily require the authority to provide the necessary accommodation. Indeed, in practice it would only be in exceptional circumstances that it would be reasonable to expect the authority to so conclude given that a substantial part of the property would remain empty half of the time.[350]

Baroness Hale of Richmond (with whom Lord Walker and Lord Neuberger expressly agreed) delivered a concurring opinion from a family lawyer's perspective, which Lord Hoffmann described as 'required reading by family judges dealing with residence orders'.[351] Her Ladyship emphasised that the court's focus in shared residence applications is the children, commenting that the application of the paramountcy principle in section 1(1) of the Children Act 1989 'means that it must choose from the available options the future which will be best for the children, not the future which will be best for the adults'.[352] In addition, her Ladyship emphasised the importance of considering the children's wishes and feelings, explaining that:

> these ought to be particularly important in shared residence cases, because it is the children who will have to divide their time between two homes and it is all too easy for the parents' wishes and feelings to predominate.[353]

Echoing Lord Hoffmann's opinion, Baroness Hale underlined the fact that:

> Family court orders are meant to provide practical solutions to the practical problems faced by separating families. They are not meant to be aspirational statements of what would be for the best in some ideal world which has little prospect of realisation. Ideally there may be many cases where it would be best for the children to have a home with each of their parents. But this is not always or even usually practicable.[354]

The Court of Appeal decisions on shared residence orders, still influenced by the pre-Children Act approach in *Riley v Riley*,[355] initially adopted a cautious approach, holding that they were only to be made in exceptional[356] or unusual[357] circumstances. However, a shift came in *D v D (Shared Residence Order)*.[358] In that case an arrangement had been settled for some time whereby the children spent 38 per cent of their time with their father. The children were doing well. There was a high level of animosity between the parents, however, and the judge was convinced that the mother was using her sole residence order as a weapon in her 'war' with the father. The judge therefore made a shared residence order with a view to diminishing the parental conflict. The mother appealed, contending, in light of the earlier authorities, that the making of a shared residence order required exceptional circumstances, or at least demonstration of a positive benefit to the children, none of which, it was alleged, existed so as to justify the judge's order.

---

[347] Ibid, [7]; and see the similar statement by Sir Mark Potter P in *Re A Joint Residence: Parental Responsibility)* [2008] EWCA Civ 867, [2008] 2 FLR 1593, CA at [66].

[348] [2009] UKHL 7, [2009] 1 FLR 904 at [8]      [349] Ibid.      [350] Ibid, [21].

[351] Ibid, [26].      [352] Ibid, [30].

[353] Ibid, [36]. See also *Re R (Residence: Shared Care: Children's Views)* [2005] EWCA Civ 542, [2006] 1 FLR 491.

[354] Ibid, [38].      [355] [1986] 2 FLR 429.

[356] *Re H (A Minor) (Shared Residence)* [1994] 1 FLR 717: 'it must be an order which would rarely be made and would depend upon exceptional circumstances.'

[357] *A v A (Minors) (Shared Residence Order)* [1994] 1 FLR 669, CA.      [358] [2001] 1 FLR 495, CA.

Hale LJ considered that there was a positive benefit to the children in making a shared residence order, and the judge's exercise of discretion was not open to challenge. Her Ladyship said that if 'it is either planned or has turned out that the children are spending substantial amounts of their time with each of their parents then . . . it may be an entirely appropriate order to make'. She added that she would not place 'any gloss on the legislative provisions, which are always subject to the paramount consideration of what is best for the children concerned'.[359] Dame Elizabeth Butler-Sloss P agreed that the earlier case law 'was unduly restrictive' and that the Court of Appeal 'should not impose restrictions upon the wording of the statute not actually found within the words of the section'.[360] In *Re W (Shared Residence Order)*[361] Wilson LJ helpfully confirmed that *D v D* now represents the better view.[362]

Building on *D v D (Shared Residence Order)*[363] the Court of Appeal has held that in such cases some justification for not making a shared residence order is required. In *Re A (Children) (Shared Residence)*,[364] for example, the Court of Appeal overturned a judge's refusal to make a shared residence order in favour of a mother who had a child staying with her four nights per week and half of the school holidays. The court held that the judge 'should have given the greatest weight to ensuring that the order duly reflected the realities, unless there were some counterbalancing welfare consideration that prevented that sensible outcome'.[365] In *Re P (Children) (Shared Residence Order)*[366] Wall LJ explained that the making of a shared residence order 'involves the exercise of a judicial discretion and does not automatically follow because children divide their time between their parents in proportions approaching equality', adding, however, that 'where that does happen . . . a shared residence order is most apt to describe what is actually happening on the ground; and . . . good reasons are required if a shared residence order is not to be made'.[367]

Lord Hoffmann's comment in *Holmes-Moorhouse* that 'shared residence orders are not nowadays unusual'[368] could be seen as offering some support at House of Lords level to this shift in the case law. However, it should also be recalled that Baroness Hale explained that shared residence orders are not usually practicable. Thus, while shared residence orders are not to be regarded as unusual orders, neither are they to be regarded as routinely of benefit to children. There is no reason to adopt a negative approach to shared residence, but its appropriateness in the individual case must be carefully considered applying the child's welfare as the paramount consideration.

Somewhat surprisingly, in light of the authorities, in *Re AR (A Child: Relocation)*[369] Mostyn J said that a shared residence order 'is nowadays the rule rather than the exception'. In one sense this is right; such orders are no longer exceptional. However, care must be taken in saying that they are the rule. In *T v T (Shared Residence)*[370] the Court of Appeal was clear that Mostyn J's statement 'is to go too far. Whether or not a joint or shared residence order is granted depends upon a determination of what is in the best interests of the child in the light of all the factors in the individual case.'[371] Furthermore, Sir Nicholas Wall P has stated extra-judicially that: 'if shared parenting orders as a concept are to become the norm, the initiative, in my view, must come from Parliament'.[372]

---

[359] Ibid, [32].

[360] Ibid, [39]. See S. Gilmore, 'Court Decision-Making in Shared Residence Order Cases: A Critical Examination' (2006) 18(4) Child and Family Law Quarterly 478–98 for difficulties with some of the reasoning in *D v D*.

[361] [2009] EWCA Civ 370, [2009] 2 FLR 436.

[362] Ibid, [13], citing [31]–[32] of Hale LJ's judgment in *D v D (Shared Residence Order)* [2001] 1 FLR 495. See also *Re C (A Child)* [2006] EWCA Civ 235 at [19]: 'the whole tenor of authority is against the identification of restricted circumstances in which shared residence orders may be made.'

[363] [2001] 1 FLR 495.          [364] [2002] EWCA Civ 1343, [2003] 3 FCR 656.

[365] Ibid, [10].          [366] [2005] EWCA Civ 1639, [2006] 1 FCR 309.          [367] Ibid, [22].

[368] [2009] UKHL 7, [2009] 1 FLR 904 at [7].          [369] [2010] EWHC 1346 (Fam), [2010] 2 FLR 1577.

[370] [2010] EWCA Civ 1366, CA.          [371] Ibid, [26].

[372] In an address to Families Need Fathers in September 2010, reported in Elizabeth Walsh, 'Newsline Extra: The Shape of Things to Come' [2010] Family Law 1232.

Alongside the courts' general approach, the courts have provided some guidance on the circumstances in which shared residence might be appropriate.

### 5.8.3 Proposed arrangements must be clear and not likely to cause the child confusion

In *A v A (Minors) (Shared Residence Order)*[373] the Court of Appeal held that it would be unlikely that a shared residence order would be made where there were:

> concrete issues still arising between the parties which had not been resolved, such as the amount of contact, whether it should be staying or visiting contact or another issue such as education, which were muddying the waters and which were creating difficulties between the parties which reflected the way in which the children were moving from one parent to the other in the contact period.[374]

### 5.8.4 Where parents are not capable of working in harmony

Parents' 'inability to work in harmony is not a reason for declining to make an order for shared residence'.[375] Nor is it, by itself, a reason for making a shared residence order.[376] However, there may be cases of deliberate and sustained marginalisation of one parent by the other, where the inability to work in harmony may sometimes provide a reason for making the order[377] in order to try to prevent such marginalisation by granting each party the same type of order.[378] There are also some cases in which parents, although granted contact:

> are nevertheless rightly refused shared residence on the basis that their motivation seems to be to strike at the other parent's role in the management of the child's life. In any application for an order for shared residence, the court should . . . be alert to discern such malign motivation.[379]

### 5.8.5 Should there be a presumption of shared residence?

How the law should respond to post-separation parenting disputes is controversial. Some argue on behalf of non-resident parents[380] that the usual award of residence to one parent and contact to the other should be supplanted with a norm of shared residence, or even automatic *equal* division of parenting time.[381] Should there be a presumption of shared residence in all cases?[382]

---

[373] [1994] 1 FLR 669.

[374] Ibid, 678. Compare *Re C (A Child)* [2006] EWCA Civ 235 at [21] (classic case for shared residence where child's school was close to both homes and child was happy, confident, and had a sense of belonging in each home).

[375] *Re W (Shared Residence Order)* [2009] EWCA Civ 370, [2009] 2 FLR 436.

[376] Ibid, [15], explaining Wall J's decision in *A v A (Shared Residence)* [2004] EWHC 142 (Fam), [2004] 1 FLR 1195 at [124].

[377] See eg *Re G (Residence: Same-Sex Partner)* [2006] UKHL 43, [2006] 2 FLR 629, HL.

[378] *Re W (Shared Residence Order)* [2009] EWCA Civ 370, [2009] 2 FLR 436.

[379] *Re K (Shared Residence Order)* [2008] 2 FLR 380, CA at [21] *per* Wilson LJ. *Re M (Children) (Residence Order)* [2004] EWCA Civ 1413 (order made unworkable by the father's domestic violence, rigidity, and failure to cooperate over arrangements for the children, and manipulation of the children by involving them in inappropriate discussions).

[380] Since most non-resident parents are fathers, the arguments have been publicised by fathers' rights organisations: see R. Collier, 'Fathers 4 Justice, Law and the New Politics of Fatherhood' (2005) 17 Child and Family Law Quarterly 511 and R. Collier and S. Sheldon (eds), *Fathers' Rights Activism and Law Reform in Comparative Perspective* (Oxford: Hart, 2006).

[381] H. Rhoades 'The Rise and Rise of Shared Parenting Laws: A Critical Reflection' (2002) 19 Canadian Journal of Family Law 75; H. Rhoades and S. B. Boyd, 'Reforming Custody Laws: A Comparative Study' (2004) 18(2) International Journal of Law, Policy and the Family 119.

[382] For debate, see S. Johnson, 'Shared Residence Orders: For and Against' [2009] Family Law 131 (arguing in favour of shared residence, and drawing attention to s 1(3)(g) of the Children Act which directs the court to consider, 'the range of powers available to the court in determining questions about children').

Research has not demonstrated any 'clear linear relationship between shared time and improving children's outcomes';[383] child well-being is most strongly connected to the quality of the post-separation parenting arrangement, although the amount of time a parent spends with the child is not irrelevant to quality. Shared residence can thus facilitate the opportunity for good quality parenting[384] from both parents in the normal setting of the parents' households. Furthermore, there are some studies that have reported positive outcomes for children in shared residence, and some studies comparing shared residence with other arrangements show modest comparative benefits of shared residence in some areas of child adjustment.[385] The evidence does not, therefore, suggest that a negative stance should be taken to shared residence.

However, reviews of research on the well-being of children in such arrangements would also caution against the introduction of a general presumption of shared residence.[386] If the parents of four children are to put in place a shared residence arrangement in which the children have their own permanent spaces in the parents' respective homes, the parents each require a home with sufficient accommodation for four children. Not surprisingly, research shows that parents who self-select such arrangements tend to be well educated and well resourced, perhaps with flexible work arrangements, and involvement in childcare when the relationship was intact.[387]

Successful arrangements also tend to involve cooperative, child-focused parents. These are not features typically exemplified by parents who are fighting over shared residence in the courts, and the research suggests that, in cases of high parental conflict, the courts should be particularly cautious about making a shared residence order.[388] In such situations, when the child is spending lengthy periods in each household, a child can become particularly caught between the parents' conflict, with consequent harmful effects on the child's well-being.

There is also some evidence from Australia that overnight 'shared care of children under four years of age had an independent and deleterious impact',[389] the repeated disruption of the child's care arguably causing stress and consequent developmental and behavioural problems.

---

[383] B. Fehlberg, B. Smyth, M. Maclean, and C. Roberts, 'Legislating for Shared Time Parenting After Separation: A Research Review' (2011) 25(3) International Journal of Law, Policy and the Family 318 at 321.

[384] Children benefit from authoritative parenting: see P. R. Amato and J. G. Gilbreth, 'Nonresident Fathers and Children's Well-Being: A Meta-Analysis' (1999) 61 Journal of Marriage and the Family 557.

[385] S. Gilmore, 'Contact/Shared Residence and Child Well-Being—Research Evidence and its Implications for Legal Decision Making' (2006) 20 International Journal of Law, Policy and the Family 344–65.

[386] For reviews and discussion of the research, see B. Fehlberg, B. Smyth, M. Maclean, and C. Roberts, 'Legislating for Shared Time Parenting After Separation: A Research Review' (2011) 25(3) International Journal of Law, Policy and the Family 318 at 321; L. Trinder, 'Shared Residence: A Review of Recent Research Evidence' [2010] Child and Family Law Quarterly 475; S. Gilmore, 'Shared Parenting: The Law and the Evidence (Part 2)' (2010) 20 Seen and Heard 21–35; S. Harris-Short, 'Resisting the March Towards 50/50 Shared Residence: Rights, Welfare and Equality in Post-Separation Families' (2010) 32(3) Journal of Social Welfare and Family Law 257–274, esp at 263 et seq; S. Gilmore, 'Contact/Shared Residence and Child Well-Being—Research Evidence and its Implications for Legal Decision Making' (2006) 20 International Journal of Law, Policy and the Family 344–65.

[387] See B. Fehlberg, B. Smyth, M. Maclean, and C. Roberts, 'Legislating for Shared Time Parenting After Separation: A Research Review' (2011) 25(3) International Journal of Law, Policy and the Family 318 at 322, and references cited therein.

[388] See J. McIntosh, B. Smyth, M. Kelaher, Y. Wells, and C. Long, *Post-Separation Parenting Arrangements and Developmental Outcomes for Infants and Children* (Victoria: Family Transitions for the Australian Government Attorney-General's Department, 2010). For discussion see J. McIntosh and R. Chisholm, 'Cautionary Notes on the Shared Care of Children in Conflicted Parental Separation' (2008) 14(1) Journal of Family Studies 37–52; J. McIntosh and R. Chisholm, 'Shared Care and Children's Best Interests in Conflicted Separation—A Cautionary Tale from Current Research' (2008) 20(1) Australian Family Lawyer 1; C. M. Buchanan, E. E. Maccoby, and S. M. Dornbusch, 'Caught Between Parents: Adolescents' Experience in Divorced Homes' (1991) 62(5) Child Development 1008; C. M. Buchanan, E. E. Maccoby, and S. M. Dornbusch, *Adolescents After Divorce* (Cambridge, MA: Harvard University Press, 1996).

[389] McIntosh et al, 'Cautionary Notes', 9.

In addition, some children can find shared residence burdensome,[390] for example having to carry their belongings to and fro between different homes and accommodating different rules/practices in each home. As the House of Lords acknowledged in *Holmes-Moorhouse*, it is very important to listen to the views of the children concerned since they are the ones who will have to live with the arrangement. Research from Norway by Skørten and Barlindhaug suggests that there is a danger that shared residence arrangements can be put in place by parents without consulting the children concerned.[391] Their analysis showed that particularly where the child had a highly educated father there was a danger of the child not being consulted. Very plausibly, Skørten and Barlindhaug argue that such well-educated fathers, who may be engaged in childcare as well as being breadwinners, may see their shared physical care of the child in terms of their right, which can undermine the child's say.[392]

As Sonia Harris-Short has pointed out,[393] in the UK such appeals to fairness, justice, and equality based on fathers' increasingly hands-on role in children's upbringing are not unproblematic, since empirical evidence on father involvement 'points very clearly to the wide gulf that exists between the rhetoric and the reality of parenting practices within the UK'.[394] She argues that the child's future interests should be firmly grounded in the realities of family life, since the pre-separation pattern of care is likely to be an important factor in the child's ability to adjust successfully within a post-separation shared care arrangement.[395] As Harris-Short notes, the debates are 'notably quiet as to whether the child's welfare similarly demands that he or she spends a substantial and significant amount of time with both parents when living within the intact family'.[396]

The recent experience of legislating to encourage shared-time parenting in Australia also suggests caution. The law there was changed in 2006 so that judges were to consider whether it would be in the best interests of a child and reasonably practicable to order equal time or substantial and significant time with both parents. The reforms led to a marked increase in court-ordered shared residence (paradoxically, the types of cases in which shared residence may be most risky[397]). The provisions were misunderstood as introducing a starting point of equal time, and discouraged mothers from disclosing family violence because they believed that this starting point meant there was no point in doing so.[398]

Having examined the evidence and the experience in Australia, the Family Justice Review[399] recommended no change to the law. However, the Government has recently indicated that, contrary to that advice, it intends to legislate with a form of words which will give emphasis to the idea that both parents should have a meaningful relationship with a child upon parental relationship breakdown.

---

[390] See eg the interviews with children reported in C. Smart, 'From Children's Shoes to Children's Voices' (2002) 40(3) Family Court Review 307–19, and the research in C. Smart, B. Neale, and A. Wade, *The Changing Experience of Childhood: Families and Divorce* (Cambridge: Polity Press, 2001).

[391] K. Skørten and R. Barlindhaug 'The Involvement of Children in Decisions about Shared Residence' (2007) 21 International Journal of Law, Policy and the Family 373–85.

[392] Ibid, 382.

[393] S. Harris-Short, 'Resisting the March Towards 50/50 Shared Residence: Rights, Welfare and Equality in Post-Separation Families' (2010) 32(3) Journal of Social Welfare and Family Law 257–74 at 266.

[394] Ibid, 268. See the analysis of the research at 267–8.   [395] Ibid, 270–1.

[396] S. Harris-Short, 'Building a House Upon Sand: Post-Separation Parenting, Shared Residence and Equality—Lessons from Sweden' [2011] Child and Family Law Quarterly 344 at 369, drawing on the experience in Sweden, on which see also A. Newnham, 'Shared Residence: Lessons from Sweden' [2011] Child and Family Law Quarterly 251.

[397] L. Trinder, 'Shared Residence: A Review of Recent Research Evidence' [2010] Child and Family Law Quarterly 475.

[398] See B. Fehlberg, B. Smyth, M. Maclean, and C. Roberts, 'Legislating for Shared Time Parenting After Separation: A Research Review' (2011) 25(3) International Journal of Law, Policy and the Family 236–30.

[399] *Family Justice Review Final Report* (Ministry of Justice, November 2011), and see Ministry of Justice and Department for Education, *The Government Response to the Family Justice Review: A System with Children and Families at its Heart* (Cm 8273, February 2012), paras 59–64.

## 5.9  **Attaching conditions to an order dealing with residence**

To what extent is it appropriate to attach a condition to an order dealing with a child's residence? The most common issue which arises in this context is whether the court can impose a condition limiting residence to a particular geographical location within the UK,[400] in other words, limiting the power of a parent to relocate within the jurisdiction. As we shall see later in this chapter, there is a large body of case law providing guidance on when a parent might be permitted to relocate outside the jurisdiction with a child. Until recently, the common view was that the authorities took a different approach in internal relocation cases, only preventing such relocation exceptionally. In *Re C (Internal Relocation)*,[401] however, Black LJ undertook a comprehensive review of the authorities. In several authorities the word 'exceptional' had been used to describe the likely incidence in which permission to relocate within the jurisdiction would be denied. Black LJ's analysis, however, disclosed an underlying 'central thread of welfare' running through the authorities and her ladyship did not therefore 'interpret the cases as imposing a supplementary requirement of exceptionality in internal relocation cases.'[402] Her ladyship commented:

> It is no doubt the case, as a matter of fact, that courts will be resistant to preventing a parent from exercising his or her choice as to where to live in the United Kingdom unless the child's welfare requires it, but that is not because of a rule that such a move can only be prevented in exceptional cases.[403]

It followed that 'Once welfare has been identified as the governing principle in internal relocation cases, there is no reason to differentiate between those cases and external relocation cases.'[404] Her ladyship was clear that there should not be a separate proportionality assessment; rather:

> matters should be approached as an analysis of the best interests of the child, whether the relocation is internal or external. Given the potential for the impact of the decision on the parents to affect the child as well, this necessarily involves a careful examination of the parents' wishes and their interests.

Vos LJ agreed, putting it as follows:

> In my judgment, parents who are staying behind will always be able, in some measure, to pray in aid their article 8 rights necessitating a consideration of the proportionality of any proposed interference with those rights. That consideration should be an essential part of the balancing exercise itself and should not be undertaken separately so as to disrupt a joined up decision-making process.[405]

Bodey J helpfully summarised the position, as follows:

a)  There is no difference in basic approach as between external relocation and internal relocation. The decision in either type of case hinges ultimately on the welfare of the child.
b)  The wishes, feelings and interests of the parents and the likely impact of the decision on each of them are of great importance, but in the context of evaluating and determining the welfare of the child.
c)  In either type of relocation case, external or internal, a Judge is likely to find helpful some or all of the considerations referred to in *Payne v Payne* [2001] 1 FLR 1052; but not as a prescriptive blueprint; rather and merely as a checklist of the sort of factors which will or may need to be weighed in the balance when determining which decision would better serve the welfare of the child.

Some of the earlier cases are discussed below by way of examples. However, any references to the term 'exceptional' now need to be interpreted in the light of Black LJ's judgment.

---

[400]  For research findings, see R. George and O. Cominetti, 'Domestic Relocation: Key Findings from the 2012 Study' [2013] Family Law 1573 finding 'a fairly linear relationship whereby more involvement by the non-moving parent reduced the likelihood of the relocation being allowed' (ibid, 1580).
[401]  [2015] EWCA Civ 1305.     [402]  Ibid, at [53].     [403]  Ibid.     [404]  Ibid, [54].     [405]  Ibid, at [84].

In *Re E (Residence: Imposition of Conditions)*[406] upon the breakdown of the parents' relationship, the mother, who was from Blackpool, proposed to relocate there with the children. The father, a Nigerian, wanted the children to remain in London close to his family, a view supported by the court welfare officer who felt strongly that the children fitted more easily into the multiracial and multicultural lifestyle of London. The Court of Appeal held that these circumstances were not exceptional and the judge had not been justified in adding a condition that the mother should reside in London in the former matrimonial home.

By contrast, in *Re H (Children: Residence Order: Condition)*[407] the circumstances were found to fall into the category of exceptional.[408] The mother had a problem with alcohol abuse which she was seeking to address, but had not yet achieved abstinence. The judge made a residence order to the father, but also prohibited the children's relocation with the father to Northern Ireland. The evidence showed that the proposed removal and the mother's consequent loss of contact with the children would be perceived by her as akin to a bereavement, the effect of which would be devastating, not only defeating her search for abstinence but capable of plunging her into accelerated alcoholic decline.[409] The Court of Appeal dismissed the father's appeal against the prohibited steps order, commenting that this was 'rightly classified as a highly exceptional case'.[410]

The circumstances were also exceptional in *Re S (A Child) (Residence Order: Condition) (No 2)*.[411] The mother wished to relocate with the child from London to Cornwall to live with her new partner. The child suffered from Down's Syndrome with associated medical problems. She was attached to the father and would find change in her routine difficult to manage. As Laws LJ succinctly summed up in upholding the judge's order preventing relocation:

> The combination of this little girl's disability and medical problems, the limits of her understanding, her foreshortened life expectancy, and the practicalities of travel between South London and Cornwall amply suffice to produce that result.[412]

*B v B (Residence: Condition Limiting Geographic Area)*[413] illustrates that the motive for relocation and the preparedness of the parent to facilitate contact following the move, may also be significant. In that case, the mother was hostile to the father and his contact with their 6-year-old child. She had made applications to relocate with the child to Australia to get away from the father and now wished to move from the South of England to Newcastle. The father wished the child to remain at school in the South of England. The High Court found that the mother could not be relied on to facilitate contact and that it was not in the child's interests to move in circumstances where the child's contact with the father would depend upon the mother ensuring that the child boarded an aeroplane for London. Viewing the circumstances of the case as exceptional, the court attached a condition to the mother's residence order providing that she was to live in an area bounded by the A4 to the north, the M25 to the west, and the A3 to the south and east until further order.

In *Re L (Shared Residence Order)*[414] the Court of Appeal held that the principles concerning imposition of conditions on a residence order apply in the same way to cases in which there are shared residence orders. Wall LJ explained[415] that a shared residence order must not be seen as an automatic bar to relocation or a trump card against relocation. There may be cases in which it is

---

[406] [1997] 2 FLR 638, CA.     [407] [2001] EWCA Civ 1338, [2001] 2 FLR 1277.

[408] In *Re B (Prohibited Steps Order)* [2007] EWCA Civ 1055, [2008] 1 FLR 613, CA Thorpe LJ acknowledged that he had not perhaps sufficiently clearly stated in *Re H* that the circumstances of the case clearly took the case into the exceptional category (at [7] and [8]).

[409] [2001] EWCA Civ 1338, [2001] 2 FLR 1277, [28].     [410] Ibid, [30].

[411] [2002] EWCA Civ 1795, [2002] 1 FCR 138.     [412] Ibid, [38].     [413] [2004] 2 FLR 979.

[414] [2009] EWCA Civ 20, [2009] 1 FLR 1157. See R. George, '*Re L (Internal Relocation: Shared Residence Order)* [2009] EWCA Civ 20, [2009] 1 FLR 1157' [2010] Journal of Social Welfare and Family Law 71.

[415] [2009] EWCA Civ 20, [2009] 1 FLR 1157 at [52].

determinative of welfare, yet there will be others where it will plainly be in the best interests of the child to relocate, notwithstanding the existence of a shared residence order.

Another issue which has arisen in relation to attaching conditions to an order is whether the courts can exercise control over the persons living with the child who is subject to a 'residence order'. The courts have been clear that there is no jurisdiction under the Children Act 1989 to oust a person from his or her home by way of a section 8 order,[416] and section 11(7) does not permit the court to attach conditions which have the effect of interfering with a clear right of occupation of property.[417] Nor does section 11(7) permit a court to make a child arrangements order to a parent containing either a condition that the children are not brought into contact with a partner, or a condition ordering her not to allow her partner to reside at her address.[418] It may in any event be unrealistic to put faith in the efficacy of such a protective measure to safeguard the children from harm. Only the residential parent would be under a duty to ensure that the condition was obeyed and no one would have a duty to inform the court where the condition was broken. Therefore, such a condition could be broken with impunity, possibly placing the child at risk, yet the inclusion of the condition might generate a false sense of security that the child was being properly protected. It is suggested, therefore, that the courts' cautious approach to conditions in section 8 orders is sensible. It strikes a proper balance between recognising that courts have extensive powers to make orders for the benefit of children and acknowledging that parents have a right to conduct their lives in the manner they choose.

### 5.10 The legal consequences of a child arrangements order with respect to the child's living arrangements

The legal consequences of a child arrangements order in which a person is named as a person with whom the child is to live are broadly: (i) that it confers parental responsibility on persons who would not otherwise have it; (ii) it diminishes the existing parental responsibility of the non-residential parent; and (iii) it discharges a care order.

### 5.10.1 Confers responsibilities and rights

The person who provides the child with a home will normally make most, or all, of the day-to-day decisions about the child's upbringing. Section 12(2) of the Children Act 1989 recognises this by providing that the holder of the order shall have parental responsibility for the child concerned while the order is in force.[419]

There is a further reason why a person who is caring for a child may wish to have an order. If the child is subsequently taken into local authority care, even though the order is discharged by the making of the care order, the status of having previously had residence could still prove important. Section 34 of the Children Act 1989 provides that a local authority shall allow the child reasonable contact with a person in whose favour a child arrangements order was in force immediately before the care order was made. It also entitles such a person to apply for a contact order under section 34 when there is a dispute with the local authority about what arrangements are reasonable. More generally, when a child is being looked after by a local authority it must involve any person with parental responsibility in decision making about the child.

### 5.10.2 Diminishes the parental responsibility of the non-residential parent

Section 8 orders are practical mechanisms for resolving issues or disputes; they are not supposed fundamentally to alter any existing parental responsibility. However, a child arrangements order

---

[416] *Re D (Prohibited Steps Order)* [1996] 2 FLR 273 at 278.     [417] Ibid, 279.

[418] *Re D (Residence: Imposition of Conditions)* [1996] 2 FLR 281.

[419] While an order must usually reflect the child's living arrangements, the courts have recognised that, exceptionally, an order may be used to confer parental responsibility on an individual where no other mechanism exists to achieve that result: see eg *Re H (Shared Residence: Parental Responsibility)* [1995] 2 FLR 883.

in which a person is named as the person with whom a child is to live undoubtedly does give some additional 'rights' to the residential parent, and does diminish the parental responsibility of the non-residential parent in various ways:

(i) Parental responsibility cannot be exercised in a way which is incompatible with the child arrangements order.[420]

(ii) It is normally the case that a person who takes, or sends, a child out of the UK without the consent of a parent with parental responsibility commits an offence.[421] However, such a person does not commit an offence where he has a relevant child arrangements order, and where he takes or sends the child from the UK for less than one month.[422] The aim of the one-month provision is to allow holidays abroad to be taken without prior consent or the court's approval.

(iii) Appointment of a guardian does not take effect when there is a surviving parent with parental responsibility unless the deceased parent had a child arrangements order.[423] It is only in the latter situation that the guardian shares parental responsibility with the surviving parent. This could expose the non-residential parent to forms of interference in the child's upbringing which he would not experience where no order had been made, and to that extent it may diminish his or her parental responsibility.

(iv) The normal rule that the consent of each parent with parental responsibility is needed to the marriage of their child aged under 18 is abrogated when such a child arrangements order is in force: only the consent of the person who has residence is needed.[424]

(v) A child arrangements order also affects who may confer entitlement to apply for a child arrangements order on a third party.[425]

(vi) As discussed in Chapter 10, a local authority may not provide accommodation for a child if any person with parental responsibility is willing and able to provide, or to arrange for accommodation to be provided, for the child.[426] Furthermore, any person with parental responsibility may remove the child at any time from local authority accommodation.[427] This rule does not apply when a child arrangements order with respect to the child's residence is in force.[428] Thus, for example, if parents divorce and no such order is made, the parent who does not have the day-to-day care of the child can prevent the child going into local authority accommodation, and can remove the child who is being accommodated at any time. But where there is an order and the residential parent wants the child to be accommodated, the local authority has a discretion as to whether to accommodate the child against the wishes of the non-residential parent. When the authority is insistent on accommodating the child, the remedy for the aggrieved parent is to apply for a child arrangements order.

### 5.10.3 Discharges a care order

When a child is the subject of a care order only a very limited class of persons are entitled to apply for the order to be discharged.[429] Fathers without parental responsibility, relatives, and other interested persons fall outside this class. However, section 91(1) of the Children Act 1989 provides that a child arrangements order discharges a care order. Thus, it may be possible for a relative, or other interested person, to take steps to bring a care order to an end by obtaining a child arrangements order. This is a vitally important provision where a relative wishes to look after a child but where a local authority refuses to place the child in the care of that relative.

---

[420] Children Act 1989, s 2(8).     [421] Child Abduction Act 1984, s 1.
[422] Children Act 1989, s 13.     [423] Ibid, s 5(7).
[424] Marriage Act 1949, s 3.     [425] Children Act 1989, s 10(5)(c).     [426] Ibid, s 20(7).
[427] Ibid, s 20(8).     [428] Ibid, s 20(9).
[429] Ibid, s 39(1): persons with parental responsibility, the child, or the local authority.

## 5.11  **Child arrangements concerning contact**

Most commonly when parents part, any child(ren) will be living with one parent and the so-called 'non-resident parent' will normally wish to continue to see them regularly. If post-separation contact is contested in principle, or if there is a dispute as to its nature and/or frequency, a court may need to consider the matter, and if necessary make a child arrangements order. Previously in this context such an order was known as a contact order, defined in section 8(1) of the Children Act 1989 as: 'an order requiring the person with whom a child lives, or is to live, to allow the child to visit or stay with the person named in the order, or for that person and the child otherwise to have contact with each other'.

As can be seen, the order provided for face-to-face contact between a person and the child, usually termed 'direct contact', and which could include overnight stays at the non-resident parent's home (known as 'staying contact').[430] Notice from the definition of a contact order that an order for direct contact placed an obligation upon the resident parent to allow contact;[431] the order was 'not directed at the child to submit to, still less to be forced into, visits or staying with the absent parent',[432] nor was any duty placed upon the person named in the order. In *Re LW (Children) (Enforcement and Committal: Contact); CPL v CH-W and others*[433] the Court of Appeal considered what was meant by the word 'allow' within the definition of a contact order in the context of an application to commit a father for breach of an order. The order stated that the father was to 'allow' contact and to make the child available. He had presented the child for the mother on the doorstep of his home but did no more, and contact did not take place because the child refused to go. Munby LJ said that 'to "allow" is to concede or to permit; to "make available" is to put at one's disposal or within one's reach. That was the father's obligation; no more and no less'.[434] The judge, however, had erroneously seen the father's obligation as to take steps within the exercise of his parental responsibility to ensure that contact took place. Munby LJ commented:

> The father may have been under a parental or moral obligation to do these things, but on the wording of these orders he was not, in my judgment, under any legal obligation such as to render him in breach of the orders for failing to do them, let alone for failing to achieve—to 'ensure'—that contact actually took place. Nor . . . was the father under a legally enforceable obligation to take such steps in the exercise of his parental discipline, guidance and encouragement as were reasonable in all the circumstances to ensure that contact took place.[435]

Like the child arrangements order, the definition of a contact order in section 8 of the Children Act 1989 also recognised that contact can be maintained with a child in a variety of ways other than (or in addition to) direct contact. In some situations, it may not be possible, or it may not be appropriate, for direct contact to take place. In these circumstances a court may order indirect contact, for example in a traditional way by means of letters, cards, presents for birthdays and Christmas, and telephone calls. The courts can be creative in embracing opportunities for indirect contact, and with advances in technology the options for maintaining indirect contact have increased through such mechanisms as texting, emailing, Skype, or Facetime video-calls over the internet, and social networking sites. In *Re B (Section 91(14) Order: Duration)*,[436] for example, the

---

[430]  In some cases, the issue of staying contact may require careful consideration with reference to expert opinion: see *Re C-G (Contact Order: Staying Contact with Father)* [2013] EWCA Civ 301, [2013] 2 FLR 1307 (child suffered from allergies; mother concerned about whether strict protective measures could be put in place in father's household during staying contact).

[431]  It follows that, in the case of direct contact, one 'cannot have a contact order without having first determined who the person is with whom a child lives': see *Re B (A Child: Contact)* [2001] EWCA Civ 1968 at [9]. See also *In the matter of S (A Child)* [2010] EWCA Civ 705: court only has power to make an order in the terms of the definition of a contact order.

[432]  *Re M (Minors)*, CA (26 January 2000).     [433]  [2010] EWCA Civ 1253, [2011] 1 FCR 78.

[434]  Ibid, [76].     [435]  Ibid.     [436]  [2003] EWCA Civ 1966, [2004] 1 FLR 871.

court sought to introduce contact between a child and father by the father, with the assistance of the local authority, making a video recording about his life.

In *Re O (Contact: Imposition of Conditions)*[437] the mother of a boy aged 2 was implacably opposed to the father's direct contact with him. The father therefore sought and was granted only indirect contact. The order provided that the mother was to: send to the father photographs of the child every three months; send the father copies of all reports pertaining to the child's progress at nursery or play group; inform the father and supply to him medical reports in the event of the child suffering a significant illness; and accept delivery of all cards and presents for the child via the postal system and read and show such deliveries to the child. The mother challenged the court's jurisdiction to impose these conditions upon her, citing in support the decision of Wall J in *Re M (A Minor) (Contact: Conditions)*.[438] In that case magistrates had directed a mother to write a letter every three months to the child's father, who was in prison, telling him about the progress of his child. They also ordered the mother to read letters from the father to the child. Wall J held that the magistrates had acted beyond their powers. He said that the effect of their order would have been to require the parents to have contact with each other, and that the court had no power to make such an order. Moreover, he was 'profoundly unhappy' about orders which required a parent to be proactive in facilitating contact such as reading communications to the child, and said that although the court may have had jurisdiction to give such a direction, nonetheless it should not have done so unless satisfied that the other parent consented, and was willing to undertake the task. He added that in the case of written communications any such order must also be subjected to the right of the resident parent to censor what is written if it is unsuitable for the child. He ruled that the direction was wrong in principle, and unwise on the facts, and therefore that it could not stand. The Court of Appeal in *Re O* rejected the mother's contentions, held that the judge's approach could not be faulted, and rejected Wall J's approach. Sir Thomas Bingham MR disagreed with the notion that an order should not be made otherwise than with the resident parent's consent because this was 'tantamount to saying that a mother's withholding of consent and expression of unwillingness to do something is enough to defeat the court's power to order that it should be done'.[439] Furthermore, his Lordship dissented from the view that the mother should be encouraged to think that she could only read what, in her judgement, should be read. He explained:

> [I]f an absent parent abuses the right of contact by writing inappropriate, offensive, insulting or obscene material, then there is a remedy to be exercised by curtailing such an order, and of course the [resident parent] need not read such material. But that is something quite different from saying that she enjoys any general right of deciding what should be read and what should not.[440]

The Master of the Rolls observed that the court 'has ample power to compel the mother to send photographs, medical reports and school reports in order to promote meaningful contact'.[441] Commenting robustly on the mutual obligations of parents to facilitate contact, he said:

> If the caring parent puts difficulties in the way of indirect contact by withholding presents or letters or failing to read letters to a child who cannot read, then such parents must understand that the court can compel compliance with its orders; it has sanctions available and no residence order is to be regarded as irrevocable. It is entirely reasonable that the parent with the care of the child should be obliged to report on the progress of the child to the absent parent.[442]

Agreeing, Swinton Thomas LJ was clear that the court 'can impose conditions which require positive steps to be taken by one parent or the other in order to facilitate the contact' and he gave

---

[437] [1995] 2 FLR 124, CA.    [438] [1994] 1 FLR 272.    [439] [1995] 2 FLR 124 at 131.
[440] Ibid, 132.    [441] Ibid, 132.    [442] Ibid, 130.

examples: a condition that the father must provide transport for the child or the mother is to be responsible for the expenses incurred in travel.

This robust defence of the efficacy of contact orders in the context of indirect contact stands in contrast to the outcome in the case of the direct contact order in *Re LW (Children) (Enforcement and Committal: Contact); CPL v CH-W and others*. That decision suggests that a direct contact order expressed baldly by reference to the order's definition in section 8 does not require positive steps to be taken beyond simply allowing the child to have contact. It may be, therefore, that practitioners will in future wish to use section 11(7) to impose conditions on direct contact orders so as to augment the resident parent's duties in respect of facilitating contact.

The case law leaves open the question of whether, and in what circumstances, a parent or other person can be ordered to take active steps to facilitate direct contact. In *Re M (A Minor) (Contact: Conditions)* the court was clear that there was power under section 11(7) to direct the residential parent to keep the other parent informed of the child's whereabouts as a necessary condition of contact taking place. In *Re O (Contact: Imposition of Conditions)* the Court of Appeal were certain that a mother must comply with an order to send photographs at regular intervals.[443] But these orders were a long way away from requiring the residential parent to take the child to visit the non-residential parent. Perhaps the solution lies in making this kind of cooperation a condition of making the order to that parent, thus squarely placing the burden of facilitating direct contact on the residential parent. However, the problem of enforcing the order[444] if the residential parent refused to cooperate would remain.

Occasionally it may be thought that contact should be informally supervised by a relative, or by the staff of an organisation which provides a setting for facilitating contact, usually known as a contact centre. These centres provide a particularly useful service where contact poses some risk to the child and must therefore be carefully observed, or where there is so much distrust and animosity between the parents that contact will only be possible if it takes place in a neutral setting.[445]

### 5.11.1  Contact a fundamental element of respect for family life

The existing relationship between a parent and child clearly attracts some legal protection. Article 9(3) of the United Nations Convention on the Rights of the Child[446] provides that:

> States Parties shall respect the right of the child who is separated from one or both parents to maintain personal relations and direct contact with both parents on a regular basis, except if it is contrary to the child's best interests.[447]

And the European Court of Human Rights has held on several occasions that:

> the mutual enjoyment by parent and child of each other's company constitutes a fundamental element of family life, even if the relationship between the parents has broken down, and domestic measures hindering such enjoyment amount to an interference with the right protected by Art 8 of the Convention.[448]

---

[443] Ibid, 133.     [444] Enforcement is discussed in detail below at Section 5.12.

[445] On which, see A. Perry and B. Rainey, 'Supervised, Supported and Indirect Contact Orders: Research Findings' (2007) 21 International Journal of Law, Policy and the Family 21; on the dangers of supervised contact, see C. Humphreys and C. Harrison, 'Squaring the Circle: Contact and Domestic Violence' [2003] Family Law 419.

[446] Adopted 20 November 1989, entered into force 2 September 1990, 1577 UNTS 3.

[447] See also United Nations Convention on the Rights of the Child, Arts 7, 8, and 18(1), which are usefully identified and discussed in A. Bainham, 'Contact as a Right and Obligation' in A. Bainham, B. Lindley, M. Richards, and L. Trinder (eds), *Children and Their Families: Contact, Rights and Welfare* (Oxford: Hart, 2003), p 62.

[448] *Johansen v Norway* (App no 17383/90) (1997) 23 EHRR 33 at para 52; *Bronda v Italy* (App no 22430/93) (2001) 33 EHRR 4 at para 51; *Elsholz v Germany* (App no 25735/94) (2002) 34 EHRR 58 at para 43; *Kosmopoulou v Greece* (App no 60457/00) [2004] 1 FLR 800 at [47].

As Article 8(2) makes clear, any interference must be 'in accordance with the law' and pursue legitimate aims within the meaning of Article 8(2), principally in this context the protection of the 'health or morals' and the 'rights and freedoms' of others, notably the child. Interference must also be 'necessary in a democratic society'. In determining whether a measure is so necessary, the court 'will consider whether, in the light of the case as a whole, the reasons adduced to justify this measure were relevant and sufficient for the purposes of Art 8, para 2'.[449] The review requires a fair balance to be struck between the interests of the child and parent.[450] It has been said, however, that 'consideration of what lies in the best interest of the child is of crucial importance in every case of this kind'[451] and that:

> particular importance must be attached to the best interests of the child which, depending on their nature and seriousness, may override those of the parent. In particular, the parent cannot be entitled under Art 8 of the Convention to have such measures taken as would harm the child's health and development.[452]

In *Re A (Intractable Contact Dispute: Human Rights Violations)*[453] a father, who was described as 'unimpeachable', sought contact when his daughter, M, was aged two, shortly after the breakdown of the parents' relationship. The ensuing litigation had lasted 12 years, and since 2006 alone there had been 82 court orders in proceedings involving seven judges and 10 Cafcass officers. The judge ordered no direct contact because of the teenage daughter's firm opposition to the court process and to further attempts to establish contact. The court agreed with the father's submission that there had been a systemic failure. Remitting the case for re-hearing, the court held that the proceedings as a whole had violated the procedural requirements within Article 8 of the ECHR and 'the result of this failure is that family life rights of M and her father to have an effective relationship with one another have been violated.' McFarlane LJ observed[454] that there will be a range of private law children orders which engage Art 8, and these certainly include 'no contact' orders or orders that deny direct contact. In such cases, in line with the Supreme Court's guidance in *Re B (A Child) (Care Proceedings: Threshold Criteria)*,[455] 'the trial judge's task is to comply with an obligation under s 6(1) of the Human Rights Act 1998 (HRA 1998) not to determine the application in a way which is incompatible with the Art 8 rights that are engaged.'[456]

### 5.11.2 The statutory presumption of parental involvement

As noted earlier in this chapter, section 1(2A) applies to any contested section 8 order application. Accordingly, it will be presumed in such cases that the parent's involvement in the child's life will further the child's welfare, unless, whatever the form of parental involvement, the child would be put at risk. There are likely to be very few such cases, so the presumption is likely to apply almost universally. For example, in a case involving domestic violence in which direct contact could not take place safely, but indirect contact would not put the child at risk, it would be presumed that involvement of the parent in the child's life will further the child's welfare. The convoluted drafting

---

[449] *Elsholz*, para 48.

[450] *Olsson v Sweden (No 2)* (App no 13441/87) (1994) 17 EHRR 134 at para 90; *Elsholz v Germany* (App no 25735/94) (2002) 34 EHRR 58 at para 50.

[451] *Elsholz*, para 48; *Hoppe v Germany* (App no 28422/95) [2003] 1 FLR 384.

[452] *Johansen v Norway* (App no 17383/90) (1997) 23 EHRR 33 at para 78; *Elsholz*, para 50; *Ignaccolo-Zenide v Romania* (App no 31679/96) (2001) 31 EHRR 7 at para 94; *Nuutinen v Finland* (App no 32842/96) (2002) 34 EHRR 15 at para 128; *Sahin v Germany* (App no 30943/96) [2003] 2 FLR 671 at [42]. For a summary of the Strasbourg jurisprudence, see *Re C (A Child) (Direct Contact: Suspension)* [2011] EWCA Civ 521 at [37]–[42], commenting at [43] that the 'domestic jurisprudence, if somewhat differently expressed, is to the same effect' (see at [44]–[47] for a partial anthology of the domestic authorities).

[453] [2013] EWCA Civ 1104, [2014] 1 FLR 1185.     [454] Ibid, at [42] and [43].

[455] [2013] UKSC 33, [2013] 1 WLR 1911, sub nom *Re B (Care Proceedings: Appeal)* [2013] 2 FLR 1075.

[456] [2013] EWCA Civ 1104, [2014] 1 FLR 1185, at [43]. See also *Re M (Contact Refusal: Appeal)* [2013] EWCA Civ 1147, at [15] per Macur LJ.

does not make absolutely clear, however, that the presumed involvement in such a case would be confined to an application for indirect contact, although that must be the common sense reading. While some will welcome this statutory recognition of the interests that parents have in maintaining involvement with their children, others may point out that the introduction of a presumption does not sit easily with the welfare principle, nor with the research evidence discussed below. Some will no doubt ask whether such a complex provision will provoke litigation, and question whether it is needed given that the courts already assume that parental involvement with children by way of contact or parental responsibility is beneficial unless the contrary is shown.[457]

### 5.11.3  The English courts' general approach to contact between a child and parent

In the case of a minor child[458] and parent, the domestic courts' general policy is that contact 'should be maintained wherever this is practical'.[459] There is, however, no automatic expectation that contact will be maintained or established in the case of persons other than parents. It has been said, for example, that contact between a child and step-parent is not presumed.[460] In the case of persons other than parents with whom the child may have a psychological link, the burden lies on the person who wishes to have contact to establish a case for making an order. The most usual situation in which a contact dispute arises, however, is between parents upon the breakdown of their relationship and it is on the guidance given by the courts in that context that we focus here.

In *Re O (Contact: Imposition of Conditions)*,[461] Sir Thomas Bingham MR provided a summary of the principles that apply in contact cases involving a parent, which has been described by a senior judge[462] as 'the definitive exposition' of the law.[463]

First of all Sir Thomas Bingham MR observed that overriding all else as provided in section 1(1) of the 1989 Act, the welfare of the child is the paramount consideration.[464] Of course, in a disputed application the checklist of factors in section 1(3) of the Children Act 1989 must be applied. Indeed in *Re M (Contact: Welfare Test)*,[465] Wilson J (sitting in the Court of Appeal) said that he found it helpful to cast the issues in a contact case into the framework of the checklist of considerations set out in section 1(3) of the Children Act 1989 and to ask:

> whether the fundamental emotional need of every child to have an enduring relationship with both his parents (s 1(3)(b)) is outweighed by the depth of harm which, in the light, inter alia, of his wishes and feelings (s 1(3)(a)), this child would be at risk of suffering (s 1(3)(e)) by virtue of a contact order.[466]

In *Re H (Contact Order (No 2))*[467] the Court of Appeal commented that:

> a proper application of the checklist in s 1(3) of the Children Act 1989 is equivalent to the balancing exercise required in the application of Art 8, which is then a useful cross-check to ensure that the

---

[457] For further discussion of this provision, and of the impact of other provisions of the Children and Families Act 2014, see A. Bainham and S. Gilmore, 'The English Children and Families Act 2014' (2015) 46 VUWLR 627.

[458] There is no assumption of contact between a parent and an adult child, even one under a disability: see *Re D-R (Adult: Contact)* [1999] 1 FLR 1161, CA.

[459] *Re B (A Minor) (Contact: Stepfather's Opposition)* [1997] 2 FLR 579. For an interesting recent analysis of the case law, arguing that the courts 'aim to change attitudes as well as conduct by attempting to manage the emotions that are thought to feed conflict', see F. Kaganas, 'Regulating Emotion: Judging Contact Disputes' [2011] Child and Family Law Quarterly 63.

[460] *Re H (A Minor) (Contact)* [1994] 2 FLR 776, CA.

[461] [1995] 2 FLR 124 at 128–30. For comment, see S. Jolly, 'Implacable Hostility, Contact, and the Limits of Law' (1995) 7 Child and Family Law Quarterly 228.

[462] Wall J as he then was, currently the President of the Family Division.

[463] In *Re P (Contact: Supervision)* [1996] 2 FLR 314 at 328.

[464] His Lordship added that: 'It cannot be emphasised too strongly that the court is concerned with the interests of the mother and the father only insofar as they bear on the welfare of the child.'

[465] [1995] 1 FLR 274, CA.     [466] Ibid.     [467] [2002] 1 FLR 22.

order proposed is in accordance with the law, necessary for the protection of the rights and free-doms of others and proportionate.

Secondly, in *Re O* the Master of the Rolls explained that:

[w]here parents of a child are separated and the child is in the day-to-day care of one of them, it is almost always in the interests of the child that he or she should have contact with the other parent. The reason for this scarcely needs spelling out. It is, of course, that the separation of parents involves a loss to the child, and it is desirable that that loss should so far as possible be made good by contact with the non-custodial parent, that is the parent in whose day-to-day care the child is not.[468]

His Lordship drew on *Re H (Minors) (Access)*,[469] in which it was stated that the question was whether there are any cogent reasons why a parent should be denied contact with his children, and that it is necessary to balance the risk of possible temporary upset against the long-term benefits which will accrue from maintaining contact.[470]

The third principle identified by Sir Thomas Bingham MR was that 'the court has power to en-force orders for contact, which it should not hesitate to exercise where it judges that it will overall promote the welfare of the child to do so'.

Fourthly, the Master of the Rolls acknowledged that cases unhappily and infrequently, but occa-sionally, arise in which a court is compelled to conclude that in existing circumstances an order for immediate direct contact should not be ordered. It is convenient to explain this in Section 5.11.6.4 on implacable hostility.

Fifthly, his Lordship observed that 'in cases in which, for whatever reason, direct contact cannot for the time being be ordered, it is ordinarily highly desirable that there should be indirect contact'.

In *In re L (A Child) (Contact: Domestic Violence) In re V (A Child) In re M (A Child) In re H (Children)*[471] (hereafter *Re LVMH*), Dame Elizabeth Butler-Sloss P respectfully agreed with Sir Thomas Bingham's review of the leading authorities on contact and his restatement of the main principles.[472] Her Ladyship emphasised again the court's duty to apply section 1(1) of the Children Act 1989 having regard to all the circumstances. Thorpe LJ, in agreeing with Butler-Sloss P's judg-ment, similarly endorsed that approach and the law as set out in *Re O*. Thorpe LJ went on, however, in a judgment with which Waller LJ agreed, to make further comments about the courts' general approach to contact. Thorpe LJ observed that the language of the judges in explaining the basis of decision making in relation to contact has shifted over the years,[473] in judgments sometimes reflective of the social attitudes and assumptions of their time.[474] He noted that contact had been described as a parental right,[475] the child's right,[476] and that judicial statements about how applica-tions for contact should be determined have also used the term 'presumption'[477] or 'principle'.

Thorpe LJ saw difficulty with the language of rights in this context, recognising that the word 'right' is a confusing word, particularly if used loosely.[478] The word is often used by lawyers in a

---

[468] *Re O* [1995] 2 FLR 124, CA at 128, drawing upon Balcombe LJ's judgment in *Re H (Minors) (Access)* [1992] 1 FLR 148, CA at 152 and Latey J's judgment in *M v M (Child: Access)* [1973] 2 All ER 81, DC.

[469] [1992] 1 FLR 148, CA at 152.

[470] Ibid 153, a view described in *Re J (A Minor) (Contact)* [1994] 1 FLR 729 as well established, and followed in many cases.

[471] [2001] Fam 260, CA.      [472] Ibid, 274.      [473] Ibid, 291.      [474] Ibid, 294.

[475] See eg *S v S* [1962] 1 WLR 445 at 448 *per* Willmer LJ.

[476] See eg *M v M (Child: Access)* [1973] 2 All ER 81 at 85, *per* Wrangham J; *A v L (Contact)* [1998] 1 FLR 361 at 365, Holman J describing contact as 'a fundamental right of a child'.

[477] See S. Gilmore, 'Disputing Contact: Challenging Some Assumptions' [2008] Child and Family Law Quarterly 285 for an account of judicial use of the term 'presumption' in the context of contact applications.

[478] See the observation of Ormrod LJ in *A v C* [1985] FLR 445 at 455, and of Lord Oliver of Aylmerton in *Re KD (A Minor) (Ward: Termination of Access)* [1988] AC 806, both cited by Thorpe LJ.

strong sense of a claim-right, with a correlative duty imposed upon another which ensures that the claim is fulfilled. Because the issue of court-ordered contact is always subject to the child's welfare it is not possible always to say that there is a duty to uphold contact and thus that there is a claim right to contact.

Thorpe LJ was also wary of the use of presumptions in the context of deciding contact applications, highlighting that a presumption alters the burden of proof and the consequent danger 'that the identification of a presumption will inhibit or distort the rigorous search for the welfare solution' or 'be used as an aid to determination when the individual advocate or judge feels either undecided or overwhelmed'.[479] While acknowledging that the distinction may be fine, Thorpe LJ preferred the term 'assumption', commenting that: 'it perhaps more accurately reflects the base of knowledge and experience from which the court embarks upon its application of the welfare principle in each disputed contact application.'[480]

In reaching this conclusion, Thorpe LJ relied on a general psychiatric report, compiled by Dr Claire Sturge and Dr Danya Glaser, known as the Sturge/Glaser report, and which he saw as fully identifying 'the benefits which children derive from continuing contact with the absent parent'.

His Lordship doubted 'that sufficient distinction had been made in the authorities between cases in which contact is sought in order to maintain an existing relationship, to revive a dormant relationship or to create a non-existent relationship', and commented:

> The judicial assumption that to order contact would be to promote welfare should surely wane across that spectrum. I would not assume the benefit with unquestioning confidence where a child has developed over its early years without any knowledge of its father, particularly if over those crucially formative years a psychological attachment to an alternative father has been achieved.[481]

Thorpe LJ's view of the role of presumptions now needs to be read together with section 1(2A) of the Children Act 1989, which introduces, in certain circumstances when the court is making a section 8 order, a presumption that parental involvement will further the child's welfare.

### 5.11.3.1 Summary

The case law, with reference to both the domestic authorities and those of the ECHR, was usefully brought together and summarised in *Re C (Direct Contact: Suspension)*,[482] as follows:

- Contact between parent and child is a fundamental element of family life and is almost always in the interests of the child.
- Contact between parent and child is to be terminated only in exceptional circumstances, where there are cogent reasons for doing so and when there is no alternative. Contact is to be terminated only if it will be detrimental to the child's welfare.
- There is a positive obligation on the State, and therefore on the judge, to take measures to maintain and to reconstitute the relationship between parent and child, in short, to maintain or restore contact. The judge has a positive duty to attempt to promote contact. The judge must grapple with all the available alternatives before abandoning hope of achieving some contact.[483] He must be careful not to come to a premature decision, for contact is to be stopped only as a last resort and only once it has become clear that the child will not benefit from continuing the attempt.[484]
- The court should take both a medium-term and long-term view and not accord excessive weight to what appear likely to be short-term or transient problems.

---

[479] *Re LVMH* [2001] Fam 260, CA at 295.     [480] Ibid, 295.     [481] Ibid, 294–5.

[482] [2011] EWCA Civ 521, [2011] 2 FLR 912.

[483] *Re P (Children)* [2008] EWCA Civ 1431, [2009] 1 FLR 1056 at [38].

[484] *Re S (Contact: Promoting Relationship with Absent Parent)* [2004] EWCA Civ 18, [2004] 1 FLR 1279 at [32].

- The key question, which requires 'stricter scrutiny', is whether the judge has taken all necessary steps to facilitate contact as can reasonably be demanded in the circumstances of the particular case.

- All that said, at the end of the day the welfare of the child is paramount; 'the child's interest must have precedence over any other consideration'.

### 5.11.4 Is there a right of contact?

Andrew Bainham has suggested that the international conventions recognise a right of contact as between parent and child.[485] He recognises that the protection afforded is not absolute, and therefore describes the right as a fundamental presumption 'which may be rebutted—but only for good reason'.[486] However, Stephen Gilmore has questioned whether it is helpful to talk of a right if the term 'presumption' is needed to describe it. As he points out, a right and a presumption are different things.[487] Gilmore argues that the right protected in Article 8 is a right to respect for family life, and only one (albeit fundamental) element of that right is respect for contact. There are other aspects of family life which may require respect, such as remaining free from a risk of domestic violence.[488]

### 5.11.5 Should there be an assumption in favour of contact?

It will be recalled that in reaching the conclusion that the benefits of contact should be assumed, Thorpe LJ in *Re LVMH*[489] relied on the Sturge/Glaser psychiatric report which he saw as fully identifying 'the benefits which children derive from continuing contact with the absent parent'. However, the Sturge/Glaser report emphasises that cases are fact-sensitive and identifies a range of benefits and detriments of contact which may or may not apply depending on the facts. As Dr Sturge has explained, the true position is that the report fully identifies the benefits which children derive from continuing contact with the absent parent *when certain conditions are met*.[490]

Reviews of the research evidence on the connection between contact arrangements and child well-being show that it is not contact per se but the quality of contact that is important to children's well-being.[491] There is a range of factors potentially impacting on the relationship between child well-being and post-separation parenting arrangements, such as the quality of the parents' relationship and the personalities of those involved.[492] As Stephen Gilmore has argued, the complexity revealed by the research 'does not advocate a form of legal decision-making which relies on generalisations'.[493] Furthermore, given the deleterious effects of conflict on child

---

[485] A. Bainham, 'Contact as a Right and Obligation' in A. Bainham, B. Lindley, M. Richards, and L. Trinder (eds), *Children and Their Families: Contact, Rights and Welfare* (Oxford: Hart, 2003).

[486] Ibid, p 75.

[487] S. Gilmore, 'Disputing Contact: Challenging some Assumptions' [2008] Child and Family Law Quarterly 285.

[488] As discussed later, the domestic case law rejects the use of the term 'right' in this context.

[489] [2001] Fam 260, CA.

[490] Correspondence with S. Gilmore, as discussed in S. Gilmore, 'Disputing Contact: Challenging Some Assumptions' [2008] Child and Family Law Quarterly 285.

[491] S. Gilmore, 'Contact/Shared Residence and Child Well-Being: Research Evidence and its Implications for Legal Decision-Making' (2006) 20 International Journal of Law, Policy and the Family 344 at 358.

[492] For the perspectives of adults who experienced parental separation in their youth, see J. Fortin, J. Hunt, and L. Scanlan, *Taking a Longer View of Contact: The perspectives of young adults who experienced parental separation in their youth* (Nuffield Foundation, Sussex Law School, 2012). For reviews of research, see eg J. Dunn, 'Annotation: Children's Relationships with their Nonresident Fathers' (2004) 45(4) Journal of Child Psychology and Psychiatry 659; S. Gilmore, 'Contact/Shared Residence and Child Well-Being: Research Evidence and its Implications for Legal Decision-Making' (2006) 20 International Journal of Law, Policy and the Family 344; J. Hunt, *Researching Contact* (London: National Council for One Parent Families, 2003).

[493] S. Gilmore, 'Contact/Shared Residence and Child Well-Being: Research Evidence and its Implications for Legal Decision-Making' (2006) 20 International Journal of Law, Policy and the Family 344 at 358–9. See also J. Hunt with C. Roberts, *Child Contact with Non-Resident Parents*, Family Policy Briefing 3 (Oxford: University of Oxford, 2004).

well-being,[494] the adoption of a presumption (or indeed an assumption) in favour of contact seems particularly contraindicated in disputed contact cases, with their profile of high conflict demonstrated in recent research.[495]

### 5.11.6  Difficult cases in which contact might be denied

Given the courts' approach to contact set out earlier, it is not surprising that denial of contact is rare. What are the circumstances in which contact might be denied?

#### 5.11.6.1  Contact in cases of child abuse or risk of child abuse

Since each case must be decided upon its facts, the courts have been reluctant to subscribe to general principles that there should be no contact in specified circumstances. There is thus no principle that direct contact will be denied even where the applicant has abused a child,[496] however serious the abuse.[497] Abuse is, however, in every case 'an extremely important factor to be taken into account',[498] and on the facts of a particular case can constitute a justification for denying contact.[499] The source of any allegation may need to be disclosed to avoid a compromise of a fair trial and breach of the rights to respect for family life of the parties,[500] and any allegations 'should be speedily investigated and resolved, not left to fester unresolved and a continuing source of friction and dispute' and once findings have been made 'everybody must thereafter approach the case on the basis of the facts as judicially found'.[501] The magnitude of the distress suffered by the non-abusing parent when sexual or other abuse is discovered or alleged, and the impact any contact order will have will be relevant to the court's decision. An anxious and distressed residential parent, who is fearful for her child's safety, may be unable to give an abused child the balanced and calm care which such a child needs.

In *L v L (Child Abuse: Access)*,[502] contact was ordered despite the father's sexual abuse of his daughter. The evidence disclosed a close bond between father and child; the child had benefited from contact and was socially well adjusted, showing no signs of disturbance from the abuse. The child's welfare could be safeguarded by supervision of contact and undertakings not to question the child about the abuse. However, the Court of Appeal has also pointed out[503] that limited contact

---

[494]  See G. T. Harold and M. Murch, 'Inter-Parental Conflict and Children's Adaptation to Separation and Divorce: Theory, Research and Implications for Family Law, Practice and Policy' [2005] Child and Family Law Quarterly 185.

[495]  S. Gilmore, 'Contact/Shared Residence and Child Well-Being: Research Evidence and its Implications for Legal Decision-Making' (2006) 20 International Journal of Law, Policy and the Family 344 at 359. See eg A. Buchanan, J. Hunt, H. Bretherton, and V. Bream, *Families in Conflict: Perspectives of Children and Parents on the Family Court Welfare Service* (Bristol: Policy Press, 2001); L. Trinder, J. Connolly, J. Kellett, and C. Notley, *A Profile of Applicants and Respondents in Contact Cases in Essex*, DCA Research Series 1/05 (2004); A. Perry and B. Rainey, 'Supervised, Supported and Indirect Contact Orders: Research Findings' (2007) 21 International Journal of Law, Policy and the Family 21 at 29.

[496]  The abused child may not necessarily be the child who is the subject of the application: see for an example *P v B* [2003] EWHC 327 (Fam).

[497]  *H v H (Child Abuse: Access)* [1989] 1 FLR 212, CA; *L v L (Child Abuse: Access)* [1989] 2 FLR 16, CA; *Re E-L (A Child) (Contact)* [2003] EWCA Civ 1947 at [8]: 'There is simply no principle or practice that would justify an inevitable conclusion for the termination of direct contact from the bare finding of past inappropriate sexual conduct.'

[498]  *H v H* [1989] 1 FLR 212, CA at 219.

[499]  Eg *Re R (A Minor) (Child Abuse: Access)* [1988] 1 FLR 206, CA. Where contact is denied with one child in a household because of abuse, then according to Fox LJ in *S v S (Child Abuse: Access)* [1988] 1 FLR 213, CA, contact should be denied to all the children since an order which distinguished between the children would be destructive of family cohesion and likely to cause tensions in the household. Where a court has not made any finding about alleged sexual abuse, it should be careful not to impugn a parent's character by what it says: see *Sanchez Cardenas v Norway* (App no 12148/03) [2007] ECHR 763.

[500]  *Re A (Sexual Abuse: Disclosure)* [2012] UKSC 60, [2013] 1 FLR 948 (privacy rights of woman with fragile mental health not sufficient justification for not ordering disclosure where she alleged that a child's father had committed sexual abuse). See [2013] Family Law 158.

[501]  *Re D (Intractable Contact Dispute: Publicity)* [2004] 1 FLR 1226 at [54].     [502]  [1989] 2 FLR 16, CA.

[503]  *R (A Minor) (Child Abuse: Access)* [1988] 1 FLR 206, CA and *S v S (Child Abuse: Access)* [1988] 1 FLR 213, CA.

under supervised conditions has the disadvantage that it may take place infrequently and in artificial surroundings. Furthermore, at some stage a child is likely to enquire why contact is taking place under these conditions and, if given the true answer, this could lead to difficulties. However, the Court of Appeal has indicated that there is no reason in principle why direct contact should not be ordered even in a case in which there is a need for long-term supervision.

In *Re S (Child Arrangements Order: Effect of Long-Term Supervised Contact on Welfare)*[504] the father appealed the judge's decision to grant him only indirect contact with his 7 year-old daughter by way of letters, cards and gifts. The father had been convicted of an offence concerning the downloading of photographs of young teenagers, sentenced to 30 months imprisonment and placed on the Sex Offenders Register. The father did not accept that he was properly convicted but accepted that as a consequence of that conviction, any contact had to be supervised indefinitely. A risk assessment concluded that while the father was a significant risk of sexual abuse to older female minors, the risk to the child was small. The Cafcass officer's recommendation was for supervised contact. The judge rejected this recommendation, appearing to indicate that long-term supervised contact was wrong in principle, and that reintroducing direct contact would be disturbing to the mother and child. The Court of Appeal upheld the appeal, remitting the case for rehearing. King LJ commented:

> there is no general proposition that there should be no direct contact if the welfare of the child in question requires that contact to be supervised over a long period of time … The reality is that, with ever decreasing resources and the closure of contact centres, long-term supervision will rarely be a realistic option in private law cases such as this; that does not mean however that in an appropriate case such a route should not be deployed as a means of allowing a child to continue to have a relationship with her absent parent.[505]

Her ladyship was clear that neither the fact that the reintroduction of contact may be unsettling for the child and resident parent, nor the inconvenience or interference to a parent's newly formed family life as a side effect of facilitating regular contact, is a cogent reason for denying contact. 'Only in the most extreme circumstances will "disturbance" to either child or parent merit a child arrangement order which does not provide for a child to see its absent parent.'[506] In this case, all the evidence was that the risk to the daughter was minimal and would be managed by supervision.

### 5.11.6.2 Contact in the context of domestic violence

The Children Act 1989 defines harm so as to include impairment of health or development 'suffered from seeing or hearing the ill-treatment of another'.[507] The dangers of domestic violence for children are well documented.[508] Some research demonstrates a correlation between domestic violence and child abuse,[509] and shows that some children witnessing domestic violence may experience psychological harm.[510] There is a risk that contact can be used as an opportunity for ongoing abuse and control of a former partner and may be associated with the risk of emotional

---

[504] [2015] EWCA Civ 689 (Etherton, Bean and King LJJ).

[505] Ibid, at paras [22] and [23].      [506] Ibid, at [30].

[507] Children Act 1989, s 31 as amended by s 120 of the Adoption and Children Act 2002.

[508] For an overview of the effects of domestic violence, see O. Mills, 'Effects of Domestic Violence on Children' [2008] Family Law 165; M. Hester and L. Radford *Domestic Violence and Child Contact Arrangements in England and Denmark* (Bristol: Policy Press, 1996); C. Humphreys and R. K. Thiara 'Neither Justice Nor Protection: Women's Experiences of Post-separation Violence' (2003) 25(3) Journal of Social Welfare and Family Law 195.

[509] M. Hester 'One Step Forward and Three Steps Back? Children, Abuse and Parental Contact in Denmark' (2002) Child and Family Law Quarterly 267; L. Bowker, M. Arbitell, and J. McFerron, 'On the Relationship Between Wife Beating and Child Abuse' in K. Yllo and M. Bograd (eds), *Feminist Perspectives on Wife Abuse* (London: Sage, 1989).

[510] M. Hester, C. Pearson, and N. Harwin *Making an Impact: Children and Domestic Violence* (London: Jessica Kingsley, 2000). Children's reactions vary: see C. McGee, *Childhood Experiences of Domestic Violence* (London: Jessica Kingsley, 2000).

manipulation of the child within contact.[511] In light of this evidence, some commentators have called for a presumption against contact where domestic violence is proved,[512] as in New Zealand, where such an approach is contained within legislation.[513]

The issue attracted considerable policy debate in the 1990s. There emerged a concern that the courts' general approach to ordering contact was obscuring a proper consideration of the dangers of doing so in cases involving domestic violence.[514] In a study of county court practice in 1996 and 1997, Bailey-Harris et al[515] found that there was in practice a strong rebuttable presumption in favour of ordering contact,[516] the effect of which was to downplay the genuine and rationally based concerns of resident parents, and erroneously to characterise such parents as unjustifiably hostile to contact.[517] The research concluded that 'the presumption in favour of contact has achieved such force that it virtually amounts to a rule yielding to a different outcome only in very exceptional circumstances',[518] and that research on domestic violence 'appears to have had little impact in practice on attitudes of judges and legal practitioners'.[519]

In 1999, the Lord Chancellor's Department issued on behalf of the Children Act Sub-Committee of the Lord Chancellor's Advisory Board on Family Law (CASC) a consultation paper on contact and domestic violence, the responses to which confirmed a widespread problem.[520] CASC's subsequent Report[521] recommended 'Good Practice Guidelines', in the form of a Practice Direction, heightening judicial awareness of the impact of domestic violence and the need for fact-finding in such cases.[522]

Shortly before the Report was published, the issue of contact and domestic violence came before the Court of Appeal in four consolidated appeals, Re LVMH.[523] The Court of Appeal was given advance sight of the CASC Report and took the opportunity to incorporate a summary of the CASC guidelines into its judgments. The court also had the benefit of an expert psychiatric report on the subject of contact and domestic violence (known as the Sturge/Glaser report).[524] This report

---

[511] J. Pryor and B. Rodgers, *Children in Changing Families: Life After Parental* Separation (Oxford: Blackwell, 2001), p 207.

[512] M. Kaye, 'Domestic Violence, Residence and Contact' (1996) 8 Child and Family Law Quarterly 285; M. Fineman, 'Domestic Violence, Custody and Visitation' (2002) 36 Family Law Quarterly 211.

[513] Domestic Violence Act 1995 (New Zealand).

[514] R. Bailey-Harris, J. Barron, and J. Pearce, 'From Utility to Rights? The Presumption of Contact in Practice' (1999) 13 International Journal of Law, Policy and the Family 111 at 129.

[515] R. Bailey-Harris, J. Barron, J. Pearce, and G. Davis, *Monitoring Private Law Applications Under the Children Act 1989* (London: Nuffield Foundation, 1998).

[516] R. Bailey-Harris, J. Barron, and J. Pearce, 'From Utility to Rights? The Presumption of Contact in Practice' (1999) 13 International Journal of Law, Policy and the Family 111.

[517] J. Wallbank, 'Castigating Mothers: The Judicial Response to "Wilful" Women in Disputes Over Paternal Contact in English Law' (1998) 20(4) Journal of Social Welfare and Family Law 357; C. Smart and B. Neale, 'Arguments Against Virtue—Must Contact Be Enforced?' (1997) 27 Family Law 332.

[518] R. Bailey-Harris, J. Barron, and J. Pearce, 'From Utility to Rights? The Presumption of Contact in Practice' (1999) 13 International Journal of Law, Policy and the Family 111, at 126.

[519] Ibid, 129.

[520] Although there had been some signs of a changing judicial attitude within case law: see R. Bailey-Harris, 'Contact—Challenging Conventional Wisdom?' (2001) 13(4) Child and Family Law Quarterly 361; F. Kaganas and S. Day Sclater, 'Contact and Domestic Violence—The Winds of Change' [2000] Family Law 630.

[521] Advisory Board on Family Law Children Act Sub-Committee, *A Report to the Lord Chancellor on the Question of Parental Contact in Cases Where There Is Domestic Violence* (Lord Chancellor's Department, 2000).

[522] Ibid, para 1.5, appendix 2 and para 3.6.4. The Sub-Committee was not persuaded of the 'need to move immediately to legislation', ibid, para 1.8. Opinion was divided on this point: see para 3.5. In the view of the Sub-Committee, the law, properly understood, contained all the necessary mechanisms for dealing with domestic violence in this context, ibid, para 1.5, appendix 2 and para 3.6.4.

[523] [2001] Fam 260, CA. For comment see F. Kaganas, '*Re L (Contact: Domestic Violence); Re V (Contact: Domestic Violence); Re M (Contact: Domestic Violence); Re H (Contact: Domestic Violence)*: Contact and Domestic Violence' (2000) 12 Child and Family Law Quarterly 311.

[524] C. Sturge and D. Glaser, 'Contact and Domestic Violence—The Experts' Court Report' (2000) 30 Family Law 615.

identified various advantages and disadvantages of contact depending on the circumstances, emphasised that the focus must be on the particular child and circumstances, and suggested that there should be an assumption against contact in cases of proven domestic violence. The Court of Appeal was thus provided with a perfect opportunity to offer general guidance on the approach to contact in cases of domestic violence.

Dame Elizabeth Butler-Sloss P acknowledged that the courts' general approach to contact may 'sometimes have discouraged sufficient attention being paid to the adverse effects on children living in the household where violence has occurred' and advised[525] that family judges and magistrates 'need to have a heightened awareness of the existence of and consequences (some long-term) on children of exposure to domestic violence'. The court gave guidance on how allegations of domestic violence should be addressed:

Where allegations of violence material to the outcome of a case are made 'those allegations must be adjudicated upon and found proved or not proved.'

The court 'should consider the conduct of both parties towards each other and towards the children, the effect on the children and on the residential parent, and the motivation of the parent seeking contact. Is it a desire to promote the best interests of the child or a means to continue violence and/or intimidation or harassment of the other parent?'

'In cases of serious[526] domestic violence, the ability of the offending parent to recognise his or her past conduct, to be aware of the need for change and to make genuine efforts to do so, will be likely to be an important consideration'; assertions, 'without evidence to back it up, may well not be sufficient.'[527]

However, noting that domestic violence comes in many forms, and contrary to the advice given in the Sturge/Glaser report, the Court of Appeal confirmed the view expressed in earlier case law,[528] that 'as a matter of principle, domestic violence of itself cannot constitute a bar to contact'[529] and there is 'no presumption that, on proof of domestic violence, the offending parent has to surmount a prima facie barrier of no contact'.[530] Thorpe LJ, agreeing with Dame Elizabeth Butler-Sloss P's judgment, said that this would risk creating 'an excessive concentration on past history and an over-reflection of physical abuse within the determination of individual cases'.[531] He agreed with Waller LJ's succinct summary that:

---

### Talking point

[D]omestic violence is not to be elevated to some special category; it is one highly material factor amongst many which may offset the assumption in favour of contact when the difficult balancing exercise is carried out by the judge applying the welfare principle and the welfare checklist, s 1(1) and (3) of the Children Act 1989.[532]

**Q.** Do you agree? Should there be a presumption against contact in cases of *very serious* domestic violence?

---

[525] [2001] Fam 260, CA at 272–3.

[526] This reference to serious violence appears in Butler-Sloss P's summary; earlier she referred to cases of *proved* domestic violence.

[527] Here Butler-Sloss P explained that Wall J in *Re M (Contact: Violent Parent)* [1999] 2 FLR 321 at 333 suggested that 'often in cases where domestic violence had been found, too little weight had been given to the need for the father to change' and 'that the father should demonstrate that he was a fit person to exercise contact and should show a track record of proper behaviour.'

[528] Eg *Re H (Leave to Apply for Residence Order)* [2008] 2 FLR 848.

[529] *Re H (Contact: Domestic Violence)* [1998] 2 FLR 42, CA; *Re L V M H* [2001] Fam 260, CA.        [530] Ibid, 273.

[531] Ibid, 300.        [532] Ibid, 301.

It can be argued that the court's considering only a presumption in which the basic facts include any type of domestic violence meant that the conclusion against use of a presumption became almost inevitable. The approach fails to distinguish between, for example, levels of seriousness of the domestic violence or whether the violence is likely to be repeated or not.[533]

The filtering down of the guidance in *Re LVMH* to trial courts appears to have been patchy,[534] and in *Re H (Contact: Domestic Violence)*[535] the Court of Appeal made clear that the guidelines in this seminal decision must be followed and that it was wholly unacceptable for the judge in that case to have made only a passing 'incomplete and highly selective' reference to it.[536]

In *Re C (Domestic Violence: Fact-Finding Hearing)*[537] Thorpe LJ commented that the judgments in *Re LVMH* 'had a wide impact and perhaps the members of this court gave insufficient attention to the burden that they were placing on judges'.[538] Accordingly there is now a Practice Direction which makes clear that it is a matter of discretion for the judge to order a fact-finding preliminary hearing and a judge does not have to provided he gives reasons for declining so to do.[539] The Practice Direction 12J *Child Arrangements and Contact Orders: Domestic Violence and Harm*,[540] provides detailed practice guidance on dealing with any case in which a question arises about residence or contact and in which it is alleged, or there is otherwise reason to suppose, that the child or a party has experienced domestic violence perpetrated by another party or that there is a risk of such violence. This provides for initial screening of cases by Cafcass and if there is a domestic violence issue then the court may give directions about the conduct of the hearing and for written evidence to be filed by the parties before the hearing.[541] Where a fact-finding hearing is necessary,[542] the hearings should be conducted by the same judge or, in the magistrates' court, by at least the same chairperson of the justices.[543]

---

[533] J. Herring, 'Connecting Contact: Contact in a Private Law Context' in A. Bainham, B. Lindley, M. Richards, and L. Trinder (eds), *Children and Their Families: Contact, Rights and Welfare* (Oxford: Hart, 2003), p 105.

[534] As acknowledged by the Government: see HM Government, *Parental Separation: Children's Needs and Parents' Responsibilities* (Cm 6273, 2004), para 48.

[535] [2005] EWCA Civ 1404, [2006] 1 FLR 943.

[536] Ibid, [76]. See also *Re K and S (Children) (Contact: Domestic Violence)* [2005] EWCA Civ 1660, [2006] 1 FCR 316 in which the Court of Appeal found difficulty understanding how over four years since its pronouncements its guidance could be overlooked, and found this a 'most serious deficiency in the trial process' (at [27]). See, however, *Re F (A Child) (Contact Order)* [2001] 1 FCR 422, CA (requiring the father to demonstrate that he was fit to have contact was not justified).

[537] [2009] EWCA Civ 994, [2010] 1 FLR 1728.

[538] Ibid, [14]. See Hedley J's comments in *S v S (Interim Contact)* [2009] EWHC 1575 (Fam), [2009] 2 FLR 1586 at 1587 to 1588 as to the pressures increases in requests for fact-finding hearings were placing on the judiciary.

[539] See eg *Re C (Domestic Violence: Fact-Finding Hearing)* [2009] EWCA Civ 994, [2010] 1 FLR 1728 (judge correctly declined fact-finding hearing given that the issues had already been determined in criminal proceedings).

[540] Supplementing Family Procedure Rules Part 12, and formerly set out at [2009] 2 FLR 1400, reissuing in revised form Practice Direction: Residence and Contact Orders: Domestic Violence and Harm [2008] 2 FLR 103 to reflect the decision of the House of Lords in *Re B (Care Proceedings: Standard of Proof)* [2008] UKHL 35, [2009] 1 AC 11.

[541] [2009] 2 FLR 1400 at [8]. Where there is a need for special arrangements to secure the safety of any party or child attending any hearing, the court shall ensure that appropriate arrangements are made for the hearing and for all subsequent hearings (at [9]).

[542] See also President's Guidance in Relation to Split Hearings [2010] 2 FLR 1897. In an appropriate case, costs of the hearing might be recovered: see *Re J (Costs of Fact-Finding Hearing)* [2009] EWCA Civ 1350, [2010] 1 FLR 1893 (mother entitled to costs where allegations proved and none alleged shown to be untrue).

[543] [2009] 2 FLR 1400 at [15]. Compare *M v A (Contact: Domestic Violence)* [2002] 2 FLR 921: where magistrates hold fact-finding hearing, the final hearing should be heard by the same bench (at [19] and [20]). A fact-finding hearing should not be abandoned before hearing all the evidence: *Re Z (Unsupervised Contact: Allegations of Domestic Violence)* [2009] EWCA Civ 430, [2009] 2 FLR 877 (judge abandoned fact-finding hearing after incident in which mother attacked father's partner in the court precinct). See also *Re FH (Dispensing with Fact-Finding Hearing)* [2008] EWCA Civ 1249, [2009] 1 FLR 349, CA (in context of care proceedings). Furthermore, a submission of no case to answer is inappropriate on a fact-finding hearing in Children Act proceedings as the judge sits in a quasi-inquisitorial role: *Re R (Family Proceedings: No Case to Answer)* [2009] EWCA Civ 1619, [2009] 2 FLR 83.

Where there are findings of domestic violence, the court 'should only make an order for contact if it can be satisfied that the physical and emotional safety of the child and the parent with whom the child is living can, as far as possible, be secured before during and after contact'.[544] If the court nevertheless considers that direct contact is in the child's best interests it should in particular consider[545] whether or not contact should be supervised, whether to impose a condition such as that the party in whose favour the order is made should seek treatment,[546] whether the contact should be for a specified period, and whether the order should be reviewed. If so, the court should set a date for review. The court should 'always make clear how its findings on the issue of domestic violence have influenced its decision'.[547] Recent research[548] suggests that the Practice Direction has had 'little or no impact on the incidence of fact-finding hearings'[549] and is not working as intended.[550]

In *Re A (Supervised Contact Order: Assessment of Impact of Domestic Violence)*[551] the mother of a three year-old girl, R, sought to overturn a judge's decision to order weekly supervised contact with the father, and to replace it with indirect contact only. The judge had made findings of fact that the mother had been raped and sexually assaulted by the father during their marriage, and that she had been physically assaulted on some occasions by his throwing books at her in anger. The mother was suffering from post-traumatic stress disorder and believed (erroneously as the judge found) that her life and her daughter's life were in danger from the father. On appeal the mother contended that the judge had minimised the impact of the domestic violence and had failed to refer to relevant authority and the practice direction. The Court of Appeal dismissed the appeal. It held that, while 'it is wise for some express reference to be made, at least, to PD12J in the judgment or record of decision',[552] in this case 'notwithstanding the lack of any express reference to those provisions, the judge conducted his analysis in a manner which was fully compatible with those requirements.'[553] The Court of Appeal endorsed the judge's 'justified and sensible observation to the effect that the findings made do not establish that the father presents as any sexual or physical risk to R or as a continuing physical risk to the mother.'[554] The Court commented:

> Fortunately, these allegations are indeed "low level" when compared to those cases with which the Family Court is well familiar involving a sustained course of significant personal violence driven by an all-controlling and dominant partner. In the present case the level of physical contact is minimal, no injuries are reported, the incidents seemingly arose out of short-lived anger or frustration … with no indication that the father is an individual who deliberately and regularly resorts to serious violence in order to dominate and control his partner.[555]

While it may be difficult to argue with the outcome in the context of supervised contact, nevertheless some may feel that the overall context of the domestic violence and its impact upon the mother were somewhat missed.

Even in a case involving domestic violence, the court will need carefully to consider the proportionality of its order. In *Re M (Contact Refusal: Appeal)*[556] a mother 'escaped' with three boys aged 7, 5, and 3 to a women's refuge, having been the victim of significant domestic violence over a prolonged period from the father, who had several personality disorders and criminal convictions for violence.

---

[544] [2009] 2 FLR 1400 at [26]. The Practice Direction sets out at [27] particular matters which the court should consider.

[545] Ibid, [28].     [546] Subject to necessary consents.     [547] [2009] 2 FLR 1400 at [30].

[548] R. Hunter and A. Barnett, 'Fact-finding Hearings and the Implementation of Practice Direction 12J' [2013] Family Law 431 (623 responses from judges, lawyers, Cafcass officers, and others).

[549] Ibid, 432.

[550] Ibid, 436. The authors suggest that the difficulties are both cultural and material (ie, a culture shift has not been fully achieved together with severe resource limitations).

[551] [2015] EWCA Civ 486.

[552] Ibid, at [49].     [553] Ibid, at [56].     [554] Ibid, at [58].     [555] Ibid, at [41].

[556] [2013] EWCA Civ 1147.

Allowing the father's appeal against the judge's refusal to order direct contact, Macur LJ explained that such an order is draconian and 'can only be lawful within the meaning of Art 8(2) of the Convention if the order for no direct contact is necessary in a democratic society for the protection of the right of the mother, and consequently the minor children in her care, to grow up free from harm'.[557] Her ladyship was not convinced that the order was 'proportionate to the legitimate end which the judge pursued in ensuring the viability and stable placement of the children with their mother'.[558]

### 5.11.6.3 Children's wishes and feelings

Sometimes a child may find existing contact unsatisfying or otherwise problematic, or the idea of proposed contact may be distressing for the child. In such circumstances, where appropriate, the child's wishes and feelings concerning the contact may constitute a powerful reason for denying or discontinuing contact.[559] In *Re C (Contact: No Order for Contact)*[560] Connell J upheld the decision of justices to cease all contact between a father and an 8-year-old boy. Initially there had been direct contact between the boy and his father but this ceased following the boy's allegation of sexual abuse by the father's new stepson. The boy told his school that he would kill himself because of unhappiness about contact and, when indirect contact was attempted by letters and cards, he had destroyed the father's communications. Connell J acknowledged that ordinarily an order for indirect contact should be made, but the circumstances in this case were not ordinary and the justices' decision was open to them on the facts.

The child may have concerns about the parent's behaviour during contact, but where the behaviour stems from the parent's personality/characteristics, account must be taken of the child's need to know and accept the parent as he or she is. It has been said that children:

> have to know the parents that they have. It is generally not considered to be in the best interests of children to wish that they had different parents from those that they have. The more that they know the parents, the healthier their approach is likely to be.[561]

In *Re B (Minors: Access)*,[562] for example, a father was described as genuinely fond of his two children (aged 12 and 11) but socially awkward and prone to exhibit eccentric and even bizarre behaviour, which was capable of baffling and distressing them. For example, the children had complained that while they were in a field the father got out his cigarette lighter and tried to set fire to some of the grass where they were sitting. There was another occurrence when one of the children had been embarrassed by being given a children's bible by the father, which was wrapped up in a piece of newspaper with a photograph of a nude woman on it. The children also found visits to their father lacking stimulus, and had no desire to see him. The Court of Appeal held, however, that the children's interests required 'that they should have the opportunity of gradually understanding those attributes in their father'.[563] The court thus ordered limited contact which, whilst avoiding 'the distress involved in over-frequent contact', would 'prevent the father from becoming an unknown quantity in the children's minds, elevated, perhaps through absence, to a status inviting fear or fantasy in crucial teenage years'.[564]

In *Re F (Minors) (Denial of Contact)*,[565] however, a judge held that two boys aged 12 and 9 should not have the reality of their father's transsexualism 'forced on them at all costs'.[566] The children had difficulty making a connection between the father they had in the past and their father in his new gender and were 'steadfast in their present wish not to see their father'.

---

[557] Ibid, at [24].     [558] Ibid.

[559] For the view that within post-separation parenting debates there is an emerging image of the autonomous responsible child and increasing account taken of children's wishes, see F. Kaganas and A. Diduck, 'Incomplete Citizens: Changing Images of Post-Separation Children' (2004) 67 Modern Law Review 959.

[560] [2000] 2 FLR 723 (Fam).

[561] *Re L (Minors)*, CA (10 June 1998).     [562] [1992] 1 FLR 140, CA.     [563] Ibid, 146.     [564] Ibid.

[565] [1993] 2 FLR 677, CA. See also *Re J (Minors)*, CA (2 October 1997) and cf *Re L (Contact: Transsexual Applicant)* [1995] 2 FLR 438 (Fam).

[566] [1993] 2 FLR 677, CA at 683.

A psychiatrist gave evidence that contact was 'preferable but without the boys having to be forced', and the judge was not prepared to coerce the boys into having contact. The Court of Appeal upheld the judge's decision, declaring that he 'quite rightly gave the views of the boys very considerable weight'.[567]

Although the courts may be able to uphold a child's wishes not to have contact, and indeed thwart a child's wish to have contact,[568] they recognise that, at least in the case of teenage children, it may be impossible and counterproductive to force the child to have contact where he or she does not want it.[569] In *Re S (Contact: Children's Views)* it was recognised that children aged 16, 14, and 12 are 'entitled to have their views on contact respected' and that an alternative to ordering contact was to listen to the children, to try persuasion, and to try to provide opportunities for negotiation.[570]

In *Re G (Intractable Contact Dispute)*[571] HHJ Bellamy noted that:

> In high conflict cases involving older children, before making an order the court should consider, in light of what is known about the parents, the child and the family dynamics, whether there is a realistic possibility that the order contemplated is practical and workable and whether, in the event of non-compliance, there is a realistic possibility of it being successfully enforced.[572]

In *Re A (Intractable Contact Dispute: Human Rights Violations)*[573]direct contact was denied to a father because of his teenage daughter's recently expressed wish not to have contact. However, in the past she had agreed to contact. McFarlane LJ commented that:

> It is plainly right for judges to make their evaluation of a child's welfare based upon the current situation, but in analysing that situation they must bring to bear such evidence that may be relevant from what has transpired in the past. Here the situation was not straight-forward and did not simply involve a young person who has consistently expressed her view contrary to contact.[574]

### 5.11.6.3.1 *Parental alienation*

Where a child's 'attitudes are or may be shaped by the influences of others, the child's wishes and the child's understanding are to be considered in that light'.[575] There are several reported decisions involving a parent who has imbued the children with a negative attitude to the other parent,[576] in some cases to the extent of falsely persuading a child that the other parent has abused the child,[577] or coaching the child to make such allegations.[578] A judge must sufficiently address the origins of a child's alienation from a parent and must make sufficient findings on that issue.[579] Some commentators have suggested that there is a particular syndrome associated with this type of behaviour, which has been termed 'parental alienation syndrome'. However, this characterisation of the problem as a syndrome has been cogently criticised in academic commentary[580] and is not recognised

---

[567] Ibid, 684.

[568] *Re H (Minors)*, CA (3 December 1999) (child's wishes overridden by expert opinion).

[569] Ibid; *Re R (A Minor)*, CA (12 March 1998). [570] [2002] EWHC 540 (Fam), [2002] 1 FLR 1156 at 1170.

[571] [2013] EWHC B16 (Fam). [572] Ibid, at para [100].

[573] [2013] EWCA Civ 1104, [2014] 1 FLR 1185. [574] Ibid, at [74].

[575] *Re M (Minors)*, CA (26 January 2000). By contrast, a child's wish to have contact, expressed in the face of parental loyalty, may be given considerable weight: see *P v B* [2003] EWHC 327 (Fam) at [43].

[576] See eg *P v P* [2003] EWHC 151 (Fam), and cf *Re O (Contact: Withdrawal of Application)* [2003] EWHC 3031 (Fam), [2004] 1 FLR 1258 at [93] (allegation made but not upheld).

[577] *Re M (Intractable Contact Dispute: Interim Care Order)* [2003] EWHC 1024 (Fam), [2003] 2 FLR 636.

[578] *V v V (Children) (Contact: Implacable Hostility)* [2004] EWHC 1215 (Fam), [2004] 2 FLR 851.

[579] *Re T (A Child: Contact)* [2002] EWCA Civ 1736, [2003] 1 FLR 531 (cause of child's sudden and adamant refusal to stay with the father not adequately investigated).

[580] C. S. Bruch, 'Parental Alienation Syndrome and Alienated Children—Getting it Wrong in Child Custody Cases' (2002) 14(4) Child and Family Law Quarterly 381.

in English law.[581] It has been said that the behaviour is better characterised as an aspect of a parent's implacable hostility to contact.[582]

### 5.11.6.4  *Parent's implacable hostility*

Where contact is accompanied by negative feelings about the arrangements (eg tension, anger, or tears on the part of the resident parent), there is likely to be a conflict for the child in that the child may wish to avoid precipitating those emotions. The courts recognise that in such circumstances ordering contact may sometimes do more harm than good.

In *Re B (A Minor) (Access)*[583] it was accepted that 'implacable hostility' to contact could constitute an exception to the courts' general principle that a child should grow up in the knowledge of both his parents. The exception applied where 'to enforce, impose or seek to enforce or seek to impose access is going to have adverse effects on the child and injure it'.[584] Therefore, it may be that in some cases 'the welfare of the child requires the court to inflict injustice upon a parent with whom the child is not resident'.[585]

In *Re D (A Minor) (Contact: Mother's Hostility)*,[586] Waite LJ described this point as now 'well settled'.[587] In that case the mother left the father when she was six months pregnant, alleging that he treated her with violence, drank excessively, and had brought into the household another woman. Following the break-up the father appeared at the mother's home at night, on occasions causing a disturbance, and delivered her clothes back to her in a slashed condition. There followed injunction proceedings at which the father appeared with 12 associates and caused such intimidation to the mother's family that they had to leave the court by a private exit. A year after the child's birth, the father sought contact, claiming to be a reformed character. The judge dismissed the contact application on the basis that, while the father might be reformed, the indelible impression his behaviour had left on the mother meant that it would be injurious to the child to force the mother to allow contact. The father's appeal was dismissed. Waite LJ saw:

> no reason to think that the judge fell into any error of principle in deciding, as he clearly did on the plain interpretation of his judgment, that the mother's present attitude towards contact puts D at serious risk of major emotional harm if she were to be compelled to accept a degree of contact to the natural father against her will.[588]

In *Re O (Contact: Imposition of Conditions)* Sir Thomas Bingham MR drew attention to this use of the words 'serious risk of major emotional harm' and added that:

> [t]he court should not at all readily accept that the child's welfare will be injured by direct contact. Judging that question the court should take a medium-term and long-term view of the child's development and not accord excessive weight to what appear likely to be short-term or transient problems.[589]

---

[581]  *Re O (Contact: Withdrawal of Application)* [1995] 2 FLR 124, CA at [92].

[582]  C. Sturge and D. Glaser, 'Contact and Domestic Violence—The Experts' Court Report' (2000) 30 Family Law 615 at 622: the essential and important difference is that the Parental Alienation Syndrome assumes a cause (seen as misguided or malign on the part of the resident parent) which leads to a prescribed intervention whereas the concept (which no one claims to be a 'syndrome') is simply a statement aimed at the understanding of particular situations but for which a range of explanations is possible and for which there is no single and prescribed solution, this depending on the nature and individuality of each case.

[583]  [1984] FLR 648, CA.        [584]  Ibid, 649. See also *Re BC (A Minor) (Access)* [1985] FLR 639, CA.

[585]  *Re J (A Minor) (Contact)* [1994] 1 FLR 729, CA at 736.        [586]  [1993] 2 FLR 1, CA.        [587]  Ibid, 7.

[588]  Ibid.        [589]  [1995] 2 FLR 124, CA.

In *Re D (Contact: Reasons for Refusal)*,[590] Hale J, giving judgment in the Court of Appeal, reviewed the authorities and concluded that in a case of implacable hostility:

> the court will be very slow indeed to reach the conclusion that contact will be harmful to the child. It may eventually have to reach that conclusion but it will want to be satisfied that there is indeed a serious risk of major emotional harm before doing so.[591]

Waite LJ's reference in *Re D (A Minor) (Contact: Mother's Hostility)*[592] to 'a serious risk of major emotional harm' was descriptive of the judge's findings in that case. Interestingly, however, Hale J's summary of the law appears to elevate the absence of error of principle on the facts of *Re D (A Minor) (Contact: Mother's Hostility)* to the status of a principle based on the facts of that case. The criterion adopted by the Court of Appeal in *Re O (Contact: Imposition of Conditions)* when discussing *Re D (A Minor) (Contact: Mother's Hostility)*,[593] in line with earlier case law, is simply injury to the child's welfare.[594]

In each case the impact on the child of the resident parent's implacable hostility will need to be weighed against the medium or long-term benefits to the child of contact. The conclusion may not always be that the child's overall welfare will not be promoted by contact,[595] but in some cases the impact of the hostility may be determinative.[596]

However, parental hostility to contact is viewed as 'a very unattractive argument to place before a court'[597] and should never of itself be a reason for not ordering contact.[598] The Court of Appeal is anxious that there should not be 'a selfish parents' charter'.[599]

### 5.11.6.5 Genuine fear

In *Re D (Contact: Reasons for Refusal)*,[600] the Court of Appeal was anxious to ensure that the phrase 'implacable hostility' is not wrongly used. Hale J indicated that the term 'implacable hostility' is properly applied in cases where there is hostility and also no good reason can be discerned either for the hostility or for the opposition to contact. Hale J observed that it is 'rather different in the cases where the judge or the court finds that the mother's fears, not only for herself but also for the child, are genuine and rationally held'.

In *Re K (Contact: Mother's Anxiety)*,[601] for example, the father of a 5-year-old boy had been violent to the mother on several occasions and on one occasion had ransacked the mother's home leaving it 'virtually devoid of furnishing and any kind of domestic equipment'.[602] In addition, when the child was not yet 2 years old, he had been kidnapped in brutal circumstances by his father and the paternal grandfather, who had entered the mother's home at 3.30 a.m. and had torn the child away from her.[603] After the father was released from prison, having served a sentence of imprisonment for the kidnapping, he sought and was awarded supervised contact three times a year. After

---

[590] [1997] 2 FLR 48, CA.   [591] Ibid, 53. See also *Re P (Contact: Discretion)* [1998] 2 FLR 696 (Fam).
[592] [1993] 2 FLR 1, CA.   [593] Ibid.
[594] Eg there does not seem to be any reason why implacable hostility should not be a reason for denying contact where the mother's reaction to contact produces anxieties which would impact upon her ability to manage her child's medical treatment with consequent impact upon the child's physical well-being. The relevance of a child's physical illness and of the impact of proposed contact upon a parent's ability to care for a child has been acknowledged in other cases: see *Re H (A Child: Parental Responsibility)* [2002] EWCA Civ 542 and *Re C and V (Contact and Parental Responsibility)* 1998] 1 FLR 392.
[595] See eg *Re E (A Minor: Access)* [1987] 1 FLR 368.
[596] See eg *Re J (A Minor) (Contact)* [1994] 1 FLR 729 (10 year-old child's experience of contact arrangements associated with acrimony, recrimination, and family upset, telling court welfare officer that he did not wish to see his father again).
[597] *Re H (A Minor) (Contact)* [1994] 2 FLR 776, CA at 783.
[598] See *Re W (A Minor) (Contact)* [1994] 2 FLR 441 (abdication of judicial responsibility to decline to make contact order simply on the basis that the mother would not obey it).
[599] *Re H (A Minor) (Contact)* [1994] 2 FLR 776 at 782.   [600] [1997] 2 FLR 48, CA.
[601] [1999] 2 FLR 703.   [602] Ibid, 709.   [603] Ibid, 708–9.

two contact sessions, which had gone well and which the child had enjoyed, the mother applied to vary the contact order to indirect contact in light of the stress the contact caused her. As a result of her experiences with the father, the mother experienced a real and uncontrollable stress and anxiety about the child's direct contact with the father, which became palpable and was conveyed to the child. In the circumstances, Wall J ordered indirect contact only, finding that direct contact would expose the child, via the mother's reaction, to insupportable stress, placing the child in a fraught emotional state in which his loyalties would be torn, ultimately resulting in severe emotional harm.[604]

Provided the resident parent's fears are genuine, they need not necessarily be rationally held.[605] In *Re L (Contact: Genuine Fear)*[606] the father of a 7-year-old boy had treated the mother with violence during the relationship. During his early adult life he had been a 'Hell's Angel' and professional 'biker' with strong right-wing tendencies. In the 1980s he was sentenced to five years' imprisonment for causing grievous bodily harm with intent when he stabbed both his former wife and her solicitor in the precincts of the Royal Courts of Justice and then subsequently stabbed the mother's boyfriend in a separate incident. He had also been convicted on another occasion of possession of a shotgun without a certificate. This, his last criminal conviction, had occurred some 15 years prior to the hearing. The parents had split up when the child was 4 and the mother was living at an address unknown to the father, for fear that he would seek revenge upon her for leaving him. In denying the father direct contact, the judge found that the mother had a phobia of the father. Although not based on rational thinking,[607] it was genuine and intense such that the child would suffer marked emotional harm if an order for direct contact were made and the child were exposed to its emotional effect upon the mother, which would be profound and possibly destabilising.[608]

As *Re H (Contact Order) (No 2)*[609] illustrates, the effect of contact upon the primary carer's health may be the most important factor bearing upon the child's welfare, even where contact might take place safely. In that case, the father of two children, aged 9 and 5, suffered from Huntington's disease, a progressive neurodegenerative disorder, which had adverse effects on his mood and personality. On one occasion, during staying contact with the children, the father took the children out in his car. Concealed from the children, he had with him petrol and sleeping pills. He telephoned the mother and members of his own family, announcing that he intended to take his own life and the children's lives too. Fortunately, a member of the public became alarmed at the father's behaviour, called the police, and the children were saved. As a result of this incident the mother opposed direct contact, although she was content to facilitate indirect contact. Wall J found that contact which was properly supervised, and preceded by a careful assessment of the father's mood, could take place without the children coming to harm. However, nothing could reassure the mother (who was suffering from acute post-traumatic stress disorder) about the children's safety when in the presence of their father. She was aware that the father had been trained in the Special Air Service (SAS) and that he had the knowledge and strength to kill the children should his mood change suddenly. For example, she was concerned that if the children were sitting on the father's lap he could break their necks in an instant. Wall J found that there was 'a real risk—indeed a likelihood—of the mother suffering a nervous breakdown if an order for face-to-face contact between the children and their father [was] imposed on her'.[610] He concluded that the most important factor in an assessment of the children's welfare in this case was 'the need to protect and promote the mental and physical health of the children's primary carer'. It was especially important that the mother was healthy

---

[604] Ibid, 715. See also *Re J (Refusal of Contact)* [2012] EWCA Civ 720, [2013] 2 FLR 1042 (no order for contact upheld by Court of Appeal where father was physically and emotionally abusive and made threats to abduct the child).

[605] See *Re M (Contact: Family Assistance: McKenzie Friend)* [1999] 1 FLR 75, CA and *Re P (Contact: Discretion)* [1998] 2 FLR 696 (Fam).

[606] [2002] 1 FLR 621.

[607] In light of the facts set out earlier, this conclusion of the judge is perhaps one with which not everyone might agree.

[608] [2002] 1 FLR 621, [42].      [609] [2002] 1 FLR 22, FD (Wall J).      [610] Ibid, [45].

because of the degeneration in the father's health and his reduced life expectancy. Wall J thus made no order on the application for contact, holding that it was for the mother to decide on appropriate contact.[611]

The cases disclose a tension between the principle that risk of harm must be based upon facts proved on the balance of probabilities and a person's erroneously held view, which as a fact itself may impact on the child's welfare.

### 5.11.6.6 Step-parent opposition and the risk of destabilising the child's present family unit

Where a parent has formed a secure family unit with another partner, and particularly when the partner has acted as the child's parent in circumstances in which the child is unaware of his or her natural parent, there can sometimes be a risk that an application for contact by the child's other parent will destabilise the mother's new family unit. This may sometimes arise because the new partner is hostile to any proposed contact.

The courts recognise that in such situations the child's welfare may sometimes dictate that contact must be denied. In *Re B (Contact: Stepfather's Opposition)*[612] the parents of a child split up shortly after the child's birth. The mother remarried and the only father figure the child had known was the stepfather. When the child was 9 years old the father sought contact. The stepfather, who was a Sikh, was implacably opposed to contact and was threatening to reject the mother as well as the child. As a matter of the stepfather's cultural background it was simply not acceptable to him that there could be two father figures involved in the child's life. Recognising the genuineness with which those feelings were held, the court took the view that the serious harm that the break-up of the family would cause the child outweighed the real injustice to the father and therefore ruled that the interests of the child must prevail. However, the court hoped that the stepfather might in the future come to a different view.[613] The outcome chimes with the statement of Thorpe LJ in *Re LVMH* that he would not assume the benefit of contact with unquestioning confidence 'where a child has developed over its early years without any knowledge of its father, particularly if over those crucially formative years a psychological attachment to an alternative father has been achieved.'[614]

## 5.12 Facilitation and enforcement of child arrangements

In *Re W (Direct Contact)*,[615] McFarlane LJ explained that facilitating contact is one of the duties comprised in parental responsibility and where 'there are significant difficulties in the way of establishing safe and beneficial contact, the parents share the primary responsibility of addressing those difficulties'[616] and therefore 'the courts are entitled to look to each parent to use their best endeavours to deliver what their child needs, hard or burdensome or downright tough though that may be.'[617]

This view was endorsed and emphasized by the Court of Appeal in *Re H-B (Contact)*.[618] In that case, a father appealed orders in relation to his daughters aged 16 and 14 refusing him direct contact. The appeal was opposed by the mother and both girls. Contact had been disputed for over six years following an incident during which the father's new wife pushed one of the girls onto a sofa leading to some

---

[611] See also *Re A (A Child) (Contact: Sexual Abuse)* [2002] EWCA Civ 1595 at [24] (recognising the need to address a mother's fears, even where findings of fact did not support the mother's viewpoint. In that case the court ordered supervised contact to allay a mother's fears that the father had sexually abused the children, despite a judge's conclusion that sexual abuse had not taken place).

[612] [1997] 2 FLR 579, CA.

[613] See also *Re H (A Minor) (Parental Responsibility)* [1993] 1 FLR 484, CA (stepfather of a 2-year-old boy wrote to the natural father saying that his marriage to the mother would be put at risk if the father continued to have contact with the child. The court therefore refused contact on the ground that the child's welfare would not be served if he lost his present home and security because his mother's marriage broke down).

[614] [2000] Fam 260 at 294–5.

[615] [2012] EWCA Civ 999, [2013] 1 FLR 494 (Tomlinson and Rix LJJ agreeing).    [616] Ibid, [77].

[617] Ibid, [76].    [618] [2015] EWCA Civ 389.

minor bruising. Subsequently allegations were made against the father of sexual abuse and of hitting them. These allegations, whose source was identified as the mother, were rejected at a fact-finding hearing. The Court of Appeal acknowledged that sometimes 'family cases present problems that regrettably the courts cannot solve despite all their endeavours' and indicated that the parents would do well to read the postscript to McFarlane LJ's judgment in *Re W (Direct Contact)*.[619] As Vos LJ put it: 'It is part of the mother's parental responsibility to do all in her power to persuade her children to develop good relationships with their father, because that is in their best interests.' Munby P was also clear that 'the child's refusal cannot as such be a justification for parental failure'.[620] He commented:

> what one can reasonably demand – not merely as a matter of law but also and much more fundamentally as a matter of natural parental obligation – is that the parent, by argument, persuasion, cajolement, blandishments, inducements, sanctions (for example, 'grounding' or the confiscation of mobile phones, computers or other electronic equipment) or threats falling short of brute force,[621] or by a combination of them, does their level best to ensure compliance. That is what one would expect of a parent whose rebellious teenage child is foolishly refusing to do GCSEs or A-Levels or 'dropping out' into a life of drug-fuelled crime. Why should we expect any less of a parent whose rebellious teenage child is refusing to see her father?[622]

However, parental obduracy may continue despite the fact that a court order has been made. Cases of this kind are extremely difficult for practitioners to handle and for courts to manage. How the courts have dealt with such situations in the past has attracted criticism and policy debate. In March 2001, CASC issued another consultation paper, on the subject of facilitation and enforcement of contact.[623] It was followed by a report to the Lord Chancellor entitled *Making Contact Work*.[624] The consultation and report were prompted in part by parents' concerns that orders were easily flouted, and that the courts seemed reluctant or powerless to enforce them. The report identified a court process, which was too slow,[625] unpredictable,[626] and adversarial,[627] with sometimes a lack of judicial continuity in case management.[628] Improved court procedures were recommended, and the President of the Family Division subsequently published a Private Law Programme to improve the management of private family law cases[629] (which has since been revised to take account of subsequent developments).[630] CASC also concluded that the current powers of enforcement of contact orders were 'seriously deficient' and that legislation was required to provide a more flexible range of options.[631] Most of CASC's recommendations were carried forward by the Government,[632] which introduced new measures to facilitate contact and

---

[619]  Ibid, [61] and [62].     [620]  Ibid, [75].

[621]  See *Cambra v Jones* [2014] EWHC 2264 (Fam), at [20] and [25].     [622]  [2015] EWCA Civ 389, [76].

[623]  *Making Contact Work: A Consultation Paper from the Children Act Sub-Committee of the Lord Chancellor's Advisory Board on Family Law (CASC) on the Facilitation and Enforcement of Contact* (Lord Chancellor's Department, 2001).

[624]  *Making Contact Work: A Report to the Lord Chancellor on the Facilitation of Arrangements for Contact Between Children and their Non-Residential Parents and the Enforcement of Court Orders for Contact* (Lord Chancellor's Department, 2002).

[625]  Ibid, para 10.37 (eg delay caused by obtaining reports, see para 10.40).     [626]  Ibid, para 10.38.

[627]  Ibid, para 10.39. See also paras 10.14 and 10.11 for a list of specific problems identified.

[628]  Ibid, para 10.38. Similar concerns about the inadequacy of the system were subsequently expressed by the judiciary: see eg *V v V (Children) (Contact: Implacable Hostility)* [2004] EWHC 1215 (Fam), [2004] 2 FLR 851 at [7]–[12]; *Re D (Intractable Contact Dispute: Publicity)* [2004] EWHC 727, [2004] 1 FLR 1226.

[629]  See www.dca.gov.uk/family/plpguide.pdf.

[630]  Practice Direction: Revised Private Law Programme [2010] 2 FLR 717.

[631]  See *Making Contact Work*, para 14.55 for the detail. For criticism, see J. Eekelaar, 'Contact—Over the Limit' (2002) 32 Family Law 271.

[632]  *Government's Response to the Report of the Children Act Sub-Committee of the Lord Chancellor's Advisory Board on Family Law 'Making Contact Work'* (2002); Department for Constitutional Affairs and Department for Education and Skills, *The Government's Response to the Children Act Sub-Committee (CASC) Report: 'Making Contact Work'* (2004); HM Government, *Parental Separation: Children's Needs and Parents' Responsibilities* (Cm 6273, 2004).

enforce contact orders,[633] enacted in the Children and Adoption Act 2006. A survey conducted by the Office of National Statistics (ONS)[634] showed that most parents managed to reach their own agreements on post-separation contact, and that only about 10 per cent of children did not have any contact with a non-resident parent. So the Government's aim was to encourage more parents to agree contact arrangements,[635] whilst also providing more sophisticated mechanisms for facilitation and enforcement of contact for the more difficult cases.[636] As a whole, a changing role for Cafcass was envisaged, reducing resources spent on report writing to enable greater focus on provision of conciliation and support services.

### 5.12.1 Facilitating child arrangements

Section 16(4A) of the Children Act 1989 was one of several provisions inserted into that Act by the Children and Adoption Act 2006[637] to increase the courts' powers to facilitate contact. It provides that if the court makes a family assistance order with respect to a child and the order is to be in force at the same time as contact provision contained in a child arrangements order, the family assistance order may direct the officer concerned to give advice and assistance as regards establishing, improving, and maintaining contact to such of the persons named in the order as may be specified in the order.

Part 1 of the Children and Adoption Act 2006 also inserted into the Children Act 1989 sections 11A–11P, which supplement existing measures for facilitating and enforcing contact.

#### 5.12.1.1 Activity directions and conditions

Section 11A of the Act allows a court to make an activity direction whenever a court is considering whether to make a child arrangements order or considering failure to comply with provision in such an order.[638] The direction can only be made when there is a dispute about contact.[639] An activity direction is a direction requiring an individual who is a party to the proceedings to take part in an activity that would, in the court's opinion, help to establish, maintain or improve the involvement in the life of the child concerned of that individual, or another individual who is a party to the proceedings.[640] Note, therefore, that an activity direction may only be imposed on a very limited category of person, a party to the proceedings, and is made at the stage when the court is considering whether to make, vary, or discharge an order. An activity direction cannot be made when the court is finally disposing of the proceedings.[641] The direction specifies the

---

[633] Children and Adoption Bill 2005, 2005–06 HL-96 54/1, which was preceded by the Draft Children (Contact) and Adoption Bill (Cm 6462, 2005). For comment, see J. Masson and C. Humphreys, 'Facilitating and Enforcing Contact: the Bill and the Ten Per Cent' (2005) 35 Family Law 548. See House of Commons and House of Lords Joint Committee on the Draft Children (Contact) and Adoption Bill 'Draft Children (Contact) and Adoption Bill Volume 1: Report' (2004–05) HC 400-I, HL 100-I.

[634] A. Blackwell and F. Dawe, 'Non-Resident Parent Contact' (London: Department for Constitutional Affairs, 2003).

[635] HM Government, *Parental Separation: Children's Needs and Parents' Responsibilities* (Cm 6273, 2004), para 10.

[636] Research revealed the complexity of contact disputes, and that the courts' approach to decision making did not correlate with some of the factors parents regarded as important (such as blame for the breakdown of a relationship, or non-payment of child support): C. Smart, V. May, A. Wade, and C Furniss, *Residence and Contact Disputes in Court Volume 1*, Research Series 6/03 (London: Department for Constitutional Affairs, 2003), esp ch 6. The Government also had regard to existing research: see HM Government, *Children's Needs, Parents' Responsibilities: Supporting Evidence for Consultation Paper*.

[637] Inserted by the Children and Adoption Act 2006, s 6(1), (3).

[638] Children Act 1989, s 11A(1), (1A), (2A), and (2B). This includes varying or discharging a child arrangements order. Activity directions do not apply to contact orders in adoption proceedings. Such contact orders are excepted orders under the Act: see s 11B(4) and (5).

[639] Ibid, s 11B(1).      [640] Ibid, s 11A(3).      [641] Ibid, s 11A(7).

activity and the person providing the activity.[642] Section 11A(5) explains that the activities include, in particular:

(a) programmes, classes and counselling or guidance sessions of a kind that—
  (i) may assist a person as regards establishing, maintaining or improving involvement in a child's life;
  (ii) may, by addressing a person's violent behaviour, enable or facilitate involvement in a child's life;
(b) sessions in which information or advice is given as regards making or operating arrangements for involvement in a child's life, including making arrangements by means of mediation.[643]

In considering whether to make an activity direction, the welfare of the child concerned is the court's paramount consideration.[644]

An activity direction is to be contrasted with an activity *condition* under section 11C of the Act,[645] which may be imposed when the court actually makes (or varies) a child arrangements order. This can also require an individual to take part in an activity that would help to establish, maintain or improve the involvement in the life of the child concerned of that individual, or another individual who is a party to the proceedings.[646] However, it can be imposed on a wider range of individuals than just the parties. Section 11C(3) provides that the condition can be imposed on a person if he or she is:

(a) for the purposes of the child arrangements order so made or varied, the person with whom the child concerned lives or is to live;
(b) the person whose contact with the child concerned is provided for in that order; or
(c) a person upon whom that order imposes a condition under section 11(7)(b).

There are some limitations on what may be ordered by way of an activity direction or condition. No individual may be required to undergo medical or psychiatric examination, assessment, or treatment or to take part in mediation.[647] In addition, no direction or condition can be made in respect of a child, unless the child is the parent of the child concerned in the proceedings.[648] Activity directions and conditions can only be imposed on persons who are habitually resident in England and Wales.[649]

Before making an activity direction or condition, the court must satisfy itself of the following matters in section 11E(2)–(4):

(2) The first matter is that the activity proposed to be specified is appropriate in the circumstances of the case.
(3) The second matter is that the person proposed to be specified as the provider of the activity is suitable to provide the activity.
(4) The third matter is that the activity proposed to be specified is provided in a place to which the individual who would be subject to the direction (or the condition) can reasonably be expected to travel.

The court must obtain and consider information about the individual who would be subject to the direction or the condition and the likely effect of the direction or the condition on him.[650] This

---

[642] Ibid, s 11A(4).
[643] Section 11F(1) provides that the 'Secretary of State may by regulations make provision authorising him to make payments to assist individuals who are subject to activity directions or conditions in paying relevant charges or fees'.
[644] Children Act 1989, s 11A(9).
[645] Again specifying the activity and the person providing it: see ibid s 11C(4).      [646] Ibid, s 11C(2).
[647] Ibid, s 11A(6).      [648] Ibid, s 11B(2) and s 11D(1).      [649] Ibid, s 11B(7) and s 11D(3).
[650] Ibid, s 11E(5).

may in particular include information as to 'any conflict with the individual's religious beliefs' and 'any interference with the times (if any) at which he normally works or attends an educational establishment'.[651]

### 5.12.1.2 Monitoring contact and shared residence arrangements

Section 11G of the Children Act 1989 provides that upon making an activity direction or condition, the court may request a Cafcass officer or Welsh family proceedings officer to 'monitor, or arrange for the monitoring of, the individual's compliance with the direction (or the condition); and to report to the court on any failure by the individual to comply with the direction (or the condition). It is the officer's duty to comply with the request'.[652] Section 11H provides for similar monitoring of, and reporting on, an individual's compliance with a child arrangements order.[653] The monitoring cannot exceed a period of 12 months.[654] The request for monitoring can be made at any time during the course of the proceedings.[655] The section applies to an individual if the child arrangements order:

(a) provides for the child concerned to live with different persons at different times and names the individual as one of those persons;

(b) imposes requirements on the individual with regard to the child concerned spending time or otherwise having contact with some other person;

(c) names the individual as a person with whom the child concerned is to spend time or otherwise have contact; or

(d) imposes a condition under section 11(7)(b) on the individual.[656]

Paragraph (b) is a curious provision. It allows the monitoring of compliance with contact of a person who is not a resident parent, yet no legal duty of compliance is imposed on such a person.

### 5.12.1.3 Warning notices

Section 11I provides that where the court makes (or varies) a child arrangements order, it is to attach to the contact order (or the order varying the contact order) a notice warning of the consequences of failing to comply with the order.[657] The warning notice is important, not only in bringing attention to the consequences of breach, but also because, as we shall see, it is a pre-condition to the making of an enforcement order under section 11J of the Children Act 1989.

### 5.12.2 Enforcement of child arrangements

In *Glaser v UK*[658] the European Court of Human Rights made clear that there is an obligation on States to take measures to reunite parents and children but it is not an absolute obligation. While national authorities must do their utmost, any obligation to apply coercion must be limited since the interests/ rights of all concerned must be taken into account, and more particularly the best interests of the child. The key consideration is whether authorities have taken all necessary steps as can be reasonably demanded in the special circumstances of each case. In that case, a mother did not comply with a contact order made in 1993. She relocated to Scotland without the father's knowledge. He eventually located the children with the assistance of the English court and he brought successful proceedings in

---

[651] Ibid, s 11E(6).     [652] Ibid, s 11G(3).

[653] Again, the contact order is defined to exclude an excepted order, ibid, s 11H(10) 'within the meaning given by section 11B(4))'.

[654] Ibid, s 11H(6).     [655] Ibid, s 11H(5).

[656] Ibid, s 11H(3). The court may order any individual falling within subs (3) to take such steps as may be specified in the order with a view to enabling the Cafcass officer or Welsh family proceedings officer to comply with the court's request for monitoring: see s 11H(8).

[657] See S. Evans, 'To Warn or Not To Warn: Contact Enforcement' [2009] Family Law 530.

[658] [2001] 1 FLR 153.

Scotland for enforcement of the English contact order. Contact was finally re-established in 2000. The father claimed a breach of Articles 8 and 6 of the ECHR. Finding no violation, the Court observed that the applicant's difficulties flowed from the unilateral actions of the mother and the authorities could not have reasonably undertaken any more coercive step at any point.

The reason the duty to reunite is not absolute is that in some circumstances enforcing contact may be more harmful than the loss of contact to the child. As Butler-Sloss P commented in *Re S (Contact: Promoting Relationship with Absent Parent)*:[659]

---

### Talking point

There is a limit beyond which the court should not strive to promote contact and the court has the overriding obligation to put the welfare of the child at the forefront and above the rights of either parent.

**Q.** Do you agree? What about in cases in which in principle contact would benefit the child but for the mother's implacable hostility? Does giving up seeking to promote contact give the right message in such a case?

---

*Re O (Contact: Withdrawal of Application)*[660] provides an illustration of a case in which it was felt that the issue of contact should not be pushed further. The father wrongly believed that the mother was alienating his 12-year-old son. In fact the boy found frequent weekend staying contact with his father disruptive of his social life and the father's telephone calls on other occasions excessive. The father was described as rigid in his attitude and was relentlessly pursuing contact. Because of the difficulties with contact, the father applied to withdraw his application for contact. Wall J made clear that the court will go to great lengths before terminating contact[661] and that if there had been any prospect of repairing the relationship between the father and the child he would not have allowed the father to withdraw his application.[662] However, his Lordship was clear that there was no prospect of change in the father's attitude and no reasonable prospect of meaningful contact and he allowed the father to withdraw the application. Similarly, in *Re J-M (Contact Proceedings: Balance of Harm)*[663] the Court of Appeal upheld the decision of a judge who was faced with a 13 year-old boy who was described as 'sensitive but battle-weary',[664] and 'had not the slightest wish to have a relationship with [his father] and who, having had correspondence from [the father] which demeaned his family, did not wish, for understandable reasons, even to continue to receive letters from him'.[665] The judge concluded that there was no reasonable prospect of observed contact being possible, and that without the adolescent's support and cooperation, direct contact could not be pursued further.[666]

However, care must be taken to ensure that the conclusion that contact cannot be made to work is not reached prematurely. All possible attempts to facilitate contact must be tried before an order denying contact is made. As Christopher Clarke LJ pointed out in *Re R (No Order for Contact: Appeal)*[667] an order which precludes all contact and contains no provision which might encourage contact 'is rightly described as Draconian'.[668] In that case the father, described as a

---

[659] [2004] EWCA Civ 18, [2004] 1 FLR 1279 at [28].
[660] [2003] EWHC 3031 (Fam), [2004] 1 FLR 1258.
[661] Ibid, [89].     [662] Ibid, [88].     [663] [2014] EWCA Civ 434 (Maurice Kay, Black and Lewison LJJ).
[664] Ibid, at para [45].     [665] Ibid at para [39].
[666] Ibid, at para [42]. See also *Re W (Contact Dispute) (No 2)* [2014] EWCA Civ 401 in which the father's appeal against the judge's refusal to pursue direct contact further was dismissed. Black LJ commented, at [29]: 'it is not always possible to find out reliably, or at all, what the root cause of feelings is and there are very often a number of factors in play. There has already been a considerable amount of expert input into the children's lives without a firm "diagnosis" being arrived at. The judge's decision, supported by the guardian, was that the time had come when it was not in the children's interests to pursue matters further and I do not think he can be said to have been wrong.'
[667] [2014] EWCA Civ 1664 (Christopher Clarke, Patten and Macur LJJ).     [668] Ibid, at para [18].

decent man, had direct contact with his daughter from birth until she was three and a half. There was then a gap of seven years before indirect contact restarted. The indirect contact was not well received by the girl, and the judge made an order of no contact. Allowing the father's appeal, the Court held that the judge had not 'grappled with available alternatives, particularly when he did not have before him any evidence of the steps that could or might be taken to promote contact' and thus the court was not driven 'to conclude that the child would not benefit from continuing the attempt at contact, or that it had reached the position of last resort, or that there was no alternative other than the making of the order that was made.'[669] The Court remitted the case 'to enable the reintroduction of the child to the father in direct supervised contact on up to three occasions, and thereafter reports of such meetings to be filed.'[670]

The court will need to consider the child's long-term best interests. In *Re S (Contact: Promoting Relationship with Absent Parent)*[671] the parents were initially on good terms upon the breakdown of their relationship and the father had contact with their child. There was then an allegation of domestic violence and the parents' relationship deteriorated. The Recorder found that the mother was primarily responsible for the failure of contact and that she had no intention of making it work. In light of this conclusion, the Recorder made an order for indirect contact only. The Court of Appeal allowed the father's appeal, ordering a child psychiatric report, and commenting that it is:

> most important that the attempt to promote contact should not be abandoned until it was clear that the child would not benefit from continuing the attempt.[672]

In the case like this, of a child under 7 and a genuinely motivated father, the decision to abandon the hope of direct contact was premature; the problems should have been explored.

Similarly, in *Re M (Contact: Long-Term Best Interests)*[673] the Court of Appeal concluded that there was a need to continue to pursue the possibility of contact to prevent long-term harm to the children. In that case, the non-resident parent was the mother of two children aged 15 and 13. The mother suffered from a psychiatric illness and when the younger child was just 2 years old she had picked him up by the side of his head. The social services department was involved and the parents' marriage broke down. The mother had contact until an incident when the mother was refused contact and attempted physically to take the child. The father and his wife referred to this incident as an 'abduction' and since that time (some eight years previously) the mother had not had contact. The children subsequently refused to have contact with the mother out of fear of the mother. The judge ordered a two-year moratorium on direct contact, during which time it was hoped that the mother might re-establish a relationship through indirect contact. However, during that time the father did not encourage the children with regard to contact and they remained unaware of the mother's communications. The children expressed the view that they did not want contact with their mother. In these circumstances the judge made a more limited order for indirect contact by way of progress reports and photographs to the mother. The mother's appeal was allowed. The judge had been plainly wrong. While the wishes of teenage children ordinarily carry great weight, the children's understanding had been corrupted by the malignancy of the views they had been force-fed by the father. The case was to be transferred to the High Court to consider whether the children should be separately represented and an expert's opinion was required. Scott Baker LJ commented:

> Where, as in this case, the court has the picture that a parent is seeking, without good reason, to eliminate the other parent from the child's, or children's lives, the court should not stand by and take no positive action. Justice to the children and the deprived parent . . . require the court to leave no stone unturned that might resolve the situation and prevent long-term harm to the children.

---

[669] Ibid, at para [21].  [670] Ibid, at para [22].  [671] [2004] EWCA Civ 18, [2004] 1 FLR 1279.
[672] Ibid.  [673] [2006] 1 FLR 627, CA.

There may also come a time when it is right for legal proceedings to cease and for an attempt at therapy. In *Re Q (A Child)*[674] a 7 year-old boy was emotionally traumatised by a long-running dispute about contact with his father, the mother being hostile to contact and making false allegations against the father. The judge's order to cease the proceedings and to effect therapeutic intervention for the child was upheld by the Court of Appeal. The Court commented that the judge 'was engaging with an, albeit non-judicial, method which he hoped might prove effective where merely judicial methods had failed.'[675] The terms of his order indicated that he contemplated a future role for the court, and the Court of Appeal rejected the complaint that there had been a breach of either Article 6 or Article 8 of the ECHR.

If a court concludes that there is a case for enforcing contact, further welfare considerations may arise concerning the impact of the enforcement measures upon the child. There are various measures which can be adopted.

### 5.12.2.1 Committal

One option for enforcing contact is for the non-resident parent to make an application to commit an obdurate parent to prison for contempt in failing to obey the court's order. This presents a court with an extremely difficult dilemma: on the one hand, there is a legitimate view that a parent cannot be permitted to continue to flout the court's orders with impunity; on the other hand, in many cases an order committing the resident parent to prison is likely to cause harm to the child. In *Churchard v Churchard* Ormrod LJ, in a judgment with which Brandon LJ agreed, was firmly of the view that such applications were futile and damaging, and should not be made, observing that '[t]he court is only concerned with the welfare of the children and ought not to trouble itself too much about its own dignity'.[676]

This approach was doubted by Ward LJ, with whom Beldam LJ agreed, in *A v N (Committal: Refusal of Contact)*.[677] Whilst the court accepted that the child's welfare was a material consideration on an application to commit, it rejected the submission that the child's welfare was the paramount consideration.[678] In *Re F (Contact: Enforcement)*[679] Hale J, acknowledging the correctness of this approach, observed, however, that 'if a court is to put enforcement above the risk of harm to the child, it must be very clear indeed about the correctness of the orders it is seeking to enforce'.

In *A v N* the mother had 'flagrantly set herself upon a course of collision with the court's order' and had been given 'endless opportunities to comply' and the judge had 'bent over backwards to accommodate her'. Eventually the judge's patience ran out and he put into effect a suspended order committing the mother to prison for 42 days. Dismissing the mother's appeal, Ward LJ said:

> In my judgment, it is time that it is realised that against the wisdom of the observations of Ormrod LJ is to be balanced the consideration that orders of the court are made to be obeyed. They are not made for any other reason . . . it is perhaps appropriate that the message goes out in loud and clear terms that there does come a limit to the tolerance of the court to see its orders flouted by mothers even if they have to care for their young children. If she goes to prison it is her fault, not the fault of the judge . . . The Children Act 1989 makes it [the judge's] duty . . . to determine what is in the child's best interests. He, not this mother, has to decide whether contact will promote this child's welfare . . . He did not commit this mother to preserve his own dignity. He was concerned to preserve the due administration of justice which depends on orders of the court being obeyed.[680]

---

[674] [2015] EWCA Civ 991 (Sir James Munby P, Underhill LJ and Hildyard J).       [675] Ibid, at para [29].
[676] [1984] FLR 635 at 638.       [677] [1997] 1 FLR 533.       [678] Ibid, 540.       [679] [1998] 1 FLR 691.
[680] [1997] 1 FLR 533, 541–2. See also Beldam LJ to like effect at 542.

Subsequent case law has echoed these sentiments,[681] and the shift in the case law was summed up in *B v S*[682] by Wilson LJ, with whom Ward LJ agreed, when he said:

> The days are long gone when mothers can assume that their role as carers of children protects them from being sentenced to immediate terms of imprisonment for clear, repeated and deliberate breaches of contact orders.[683]

However, the courts have still accepted that this sanction should be used sparingly in children cases. As the Court of Appeal acknowledged in *Re S (Minors: Access)*:[684]

> it is a rare case—although I would not go so far as to say it can never happen—that the welfare of the child requires that the custodial parent be sent to prison for refusing to give the other parent access.[685]

In *Re LW (Children) (Enforcement and Committal: Contact); CPL v CH-W and others*[686] Munby LJ agreed with the common trope that committal is or ought to be a last resort. However, his Lordship went on to caution that that handy aphorism should not be misunderstood, explaining:

> Committal should not be used unless it is a proportionate response to the problem nor if some less drastic remedy will provide an adequate solution. But this does not mean that one has to wait unduly before having resort to committal, let alone waiting so long that the moment has passed and the situation has become irretrievable . . . on occasions, the understandable reluctance to resort to such a drastic remedy as committal means that when recourse to it is first proposed it is too late for committal, whereas a willingness to grasp the nettle by making a committal order at an earlier stage might have ended up making all the difference . . . The threat, or if need be the actual implementation, of a very short period of imprisonment—just a day or two—may at an earlier stage of the proceedings achieve more than the threat of a longer sentence at a much later stage in the process. I do not suggest this as a panacea—this is an area in which there is no panacea—but it is something which, I suggest, is worth keeping in mind.[687]

In *Re A (Intractable Contact Dispute: Human Rights Violations)*[688] McFarlane LJ endorsed this approach in *Re LW* and commented:

> The first time that a judge should give serious consideration to whether or not he or she will, if called upon, be prepared to enforce a contact order should be before the order is made and not only after a breach has occurred. Such forward thinking should be part of the judge's overall strategy for the case. If a directive contact order is called for, then, on making it, the judge should be clear, at least in his or her own mind, that, upon breach, enforcement may well follow. If, on the facts of the case, enforcement is not to be contemplated, then an alternative judicial strategy not involving a directive court order (and which might in an extreme case include a change of residence or, at the other extreme, dismissing the application for contact) must be developed.[689]

Proceedings for committal are a criminal charge for the purposes of Article 6 of the ECHR.[690] It follows that the burden of proving guilt, to the criminal standard of proof, lies on the person

---

[681] See eg *Re S (Contact Dispute: Committal)* [2004] EWCA Civ 1790, [2005] 1 FLR 812 at [14].

[682] [2009] EWCA Civ 548.

[683] Ibid, [16]. See also *Re LW (Children) (Enforcement and Committal: Contact); CPL v CH-W and others* [2010] EWCA Civ 1253 at [96]: 'Committal is—has to be—an essential weapon in the court's armoury'.

[684] [1990] 2 FLR 166.   [685] Ibid, 170.   [686] [2010] EWCA Civ 1253, [2011] 1 FLR 1095.

[687] Ibid, [108]. For earlier views on the potential usefulness of short prison sentences, see *Re M (Intractable Contact Dispute: Interim Care Orders)* [2003] EWHC 1024 (Fam), [2003] 2 FLR 636 at [117] and *Re D (Intractable Contact Dispute: Publicity)* [2004] EWHC 727 (Fam), [2004] 1 FLR 1226 at [57].

[688] [2013] EWCA Civ 1104, [2014] 1 FLR 1185.   [689] Ibid, at [61].

[690] The implications of Art 6 are usefully highlighted in *Hammerton v Hammerton* [2007] EWCA Civ 248, [2007] 2 FLR 1133, esp at [9].

seeking committal; the defendant is entitled to be represented;[691] and the defendant has a right against self-incrimination[692] and is not obliged to give evidence. A Practice Direction[693] seeks to ensure that committal proceedings in family proceedings safeguard the defendant's rights. Procedural irregularities which fail to protect the defendant's rights will lead to a committal order being overturned.[694]

Contempt of court 'involves a contumelious, that is to say a deliberate, disobedience to the order'.[695] It is necessary, therefore, that the order is clear on its face as to what those affected by the order are required to do or abstain from doing.[696]

### 5.12.2.2 The use of the child's residence arrangements to enforce contact provision

As Sir Thomas Bingham MR pointed out in *Re O (Contact: Imposition of Conditions)*[697] 'no residence order is to be regarded as irrevocable'[698] although 'orders transferring children from one parent to another are very rare and usually only taken as a matter of last resort'.[699] More recently the Court of Appeal has endorsed the propriety in an appropriate case of making a suspended residence order, providing for a future transfer of residence upon a further failure to comply with any conditions imposed. In *Re A (Suspended Residence Order)*[700] the judge found that the father had sexually abused the mother's daughter from a previous relationship, although he had not abused his own two sons. Contact had been ordered between the father and the boys but the mother, who believed that the father had also abused them, resisted contact and the father had not seen his sons (who were by then 8 and 11) for two years. The paternal grandparents made an application for a residence order with a view to effecting a reintroduction of the boys to their father. Coleridge J took the view that a transfer of residence would not be as harmful, in the long term, as the boys being 'continually and unrelentingly exposed to their mother's false beliefs combined with her unremitting hostility to the paternal family undiluted by contact'. He therefore made the requested residence order but suspended it provided the mother complied with a defined contact order. The mother's appeal against this order was dismissed by the Court of Appeal.[701] The mother subsequently failed to comply with the order and Coleridge J was forced to implement his threat. The mother's further appeal to the Court of Appeal against the transfer of residence to the grandparents was dismissed.[702] Although the suspended order was not, of itself, effective in this case, it seems likely that this type of order will prove an attractive, and probably an effective, option in other cases.[703]

---

[691] See ECHR, Art 6(3)(c), and *Re K (Contact: Committal Order)* [2002] EWCA Civ 1559, [2003] 1 FLR 277 at [21] and [23]; *Benham v UK* (1996) 22 EHRR 293 at 324; and *Re G (Contempt: Committal)* [2003] EWCA Civ 489, [2003] 1 WLR 2051, [2003] 2 FLR 58 at [22]. The obligation to afford a defendant representation imposed by virtue of ECHR, Art 6(3)(c) is not, however, unlimited (see *Re K* at [34] *per* Mance LJ (as he then was)).

[692] See *Re G (Contempt: Committal)* [2003] EWCA Civ 489, [2003] 1 WLR 2051, [2003] 2 FLR 58 at [22] and, eg, *Saunders v UK* (1996) 23 EHRR 313 and *R v Mushtaq* [2005] UKHL 25, [2005] 1 WLR 1513 at [53].

[693] Practice Direction (Family Proceedings: Committal) [2001] 1 WLR 1253, *sub nom* President's Direction: (Committal Applications and Proceedings in which a Committal Order may be made) [2001] 1 FLR 949.

[694] As Wall LJ explained in *Hammerton v Hammerton* [2007] EWCA Civ 248, [2007] 2 FLR 1133 at [35]: 'Provided the contemnor has had a fair trial and the order has been made on valid grounds, the existence of a defect in the committal application or in the order served will not result in it being set aside except insofar as the interests of justice require that to be done.' See *M v P (Contempt: Committal); Butler v Butler* [1993] Fam 167, [1993] 1 FLR 773 and *Rayden & Jackson on Divorce and Family Matters*, 18th rev edn (London: LexisNexis UK, 2005), vol 1(1), para 30.23.

[695] *Re A (Abduction: Contempt)* [2008] EWCA Civ 1138, [2009] 1 WLR 1482, [2009] 1 FLR 1 at [6].

[696] *Re S-C (Contempt)* [2010] EWCA Civ 21, [2010] 1 FLR 1478 at [17]. See *Re LW (Children) (Enforcement and Committal: Contact); CPL v CH-W and others* [2010] EWCA Civ 1253 as to what must be proved.

[697] [1995] 2 FLR 124, CA.        [698] Ibid, 130.

[699] *Re R (A Child)* [2009] EWCA Civ 1316 at [4] *per* Wall LJ.

[700] [2009] EWHC 1576 (Fam), [2010] 1 FLR 1679.        [701] *Re D (Children)* [2009] EWCA Civ 1551.

[702] *Re D (Children)* [2010] EWCA Civ 496.

[703] In *Re M (Contact)* [2012] EWHC 1948 (Fam), [2013] 1 FLR 1403, Peter Jackson J, in an apparently intractable case, ordered periods of staying contact and a transfer of residence should contact fail to take place.

In an appropriate case,[704] however, an order may be made for an immediate transfer of residence to address failure of contact.[705] In *Re S (Transfer of Residence)*[706] an immediate transfer of residence was made despite the child's objections. A boy aged 11 had been the subject of contact proceedings between his parents since he was one year old and had not seen his father for the last three years. The mother was implacably opposed to contact, and the child's expressed view that he did not wish to see his father, was said to be the product of parental alienation. Despite the boy's wishes to the contrary, therefore, the judge made an order for transfer of residence, having greater confidence in the father's ability to meet the child's overall needs.[707] In *Re A (Residence Order)*[708] the Court of Appeal indicated that if such an order is made there should be a narrow opportunity for the current resident parent to approach the Court of Appeal for relief, for example by stay of the order to the next working day.

### 5.12.2.3 The use of a section 37 direction

In some intractable contact disputes the children concerned may be suffering significant harm as a result of a parent's behaviour. Such cases will probably be relatively rare but, where the circumstances warrant it,[709] the judge has the option of giving a direction to a local authority pursuant to section 37 of the Children Act 1989 to investigate the child's circumstances. In *Re M (Intractable Contact Dispute: Interim Care Orders)*[710] the mother had succeeded in alienating two children from their father and paternal grandparents, by doing her best to instil in the children the false belief that they had been sexually abused by their father, and that one of the children had been physically maltreated and sexually abused by the grandparents. The court found that the allegations were false, and that actually the children were suffering significant emotional harm as a result of the behaviour of the mother who lacked all insight into the damage she was causing the children. In the circumstances, Wall J gave a section 37 direction.[711] The local authority, having investigated, sought and obtained an interim care order and the children were removed from the mother to foster parents where they could begin a process of reintroduction to the father and his family, free from the mother's control. The case was finally disposed of by making a residence order in favour of the father combined with a supervision order in favour of the local authority for two years, with contact between the children and the mother to be in the discretion of the local authority. Wall J made clear, however, that section 37 is 'a well-focused tool, to be used only when the case fits its criteria'.[712] There must therefore be reasonable grounds for believing that the child concerned is suffering or is likely to suffer significant harm. The action contemplated by the direction must be in the child's best interests, and thought through; there must be 'a coherent care plan of which temporary or permanent removal of the child from the resident parent is an integral part'.[713]

---

[704] The respondent must be given an opportunity to answer the case against him or her: see *Re B (Case Management)* [2012] EWCA Civ 1742, [2013] 1 FLR 963.

[705] See *per* Munby LJ in *Re LW (Children) (Enforcement and Committal: Contact); CPL v CH-W and others*, CA (4 November 2010).

[706] [2010] EWHC 192 (Fam), [2010] 1 FLR 1785.

[707] See also *Re C (Residence Order)* [2007] EWCA Civ 866, [2008] 1 FLR 211 (transfer ordered where mother had new baby and committal to prison not appropriate).

[708] [2007] EWCA Civ 899.

[709] For a series of cases in which Cobb J had to consider, over time, whether state intervention was warranted, see *Re A and B (Contact) (No 4)* [2015] EWHC 2839 (Fam), Cobb J (children 'weapons and victims of the battle between the parents'); *Re A and B (Children) (No 3)* [2015] EWHC 818 (Fam), Cobb J (making a 12 month supervision order in favour of local authority and order under s 91(14) Children Act 1989); *Re A and B (Contact) (No 2)* [2013] EWHC 4150 (Fam) Cobb J (refusing to make interim care order, value in placing responsibility for facilitating contact on parents rather than local authority); *Re A and B (Contact) (No 1)* [2013] EWHC 2305 Cobb J) (directing child psychiatrist's assessment of children's emotional well-being).

[710] [2003] EWHC 1024 (Fam), [2003] 2 FLR 636.

[711] Note that when a court gives a s 37 direction, it also has power to make an interim care order under s 38(1)(b) of the Children Act 1989, but immediate making of such an order was not felt to be necessary.

[712] [2003] EWHC 1024 (Fam), [2003] 2 FLR 636 at [8].     [713] Ibid, [11].

The reasons for the direction should be clearly spelled out. The children should be separately represented[714] and preferably the section 37 report should be supported by professional or expert advice.[715]

### 5.12.2.4 Enforcement orders

Section 11J of the Children Act 1989 provides a new mechanism for enforcing a contact order, known as an enforcement order. Section 11J(2) provides:

> If the court is satisfied beyond reasonable doubt that a person has failed to comply with the child arrangements order, it may make an order (an 'enforcement order') imposing on the person an unpaid work requirement.[716]

The order cannot be made unless the court is satisfied that the person concerned was given a warning notice under section 11I or was informed of the terms of such notice prior to the failure.[717]

There is a defence in section 11J(3) of 'reasonable excuse'. This provides that the court 'may not make an enforcement order if it is satisfied that the person had a reasonable excuse for failing to comply with the child arrangements order', the proof of which lies on the person claiming to have had a reasonable excuse, and the standard of proof is the balance of probabilities.[718] It is necessary to keep the question of reasonable excuse entirely separate and distinct from the logically prior question of breach.[719] There will be no breach where it is beyond the defendant's power to comply, for example 'when contact is prevented or delayed by unforeseen and insuperable transport or weather problems'.[720] However, reasonable excuse arises where, although it was within the power of the defendant to comply, he has a reasonable excuse for not doing so, for example where it is necessary to take the child to a doctor rather than going to contact.

An enforcement order can only be made upon an application; the court cannot under this provision enforce the order of its own motion. Those who can apply are: (i) the person with whom the child concerned lives or is to live; (ii) the person whose contact with the child concerned is provided for in the child arrangements order; (iii) any individual subject to a condition under section 11(7)(b) or a contact activity condition imposed by the child arrangements order; or (iv) the child concerned.[721] In the case of a child applicant, the child must obtain the leave of the court before making such an application,[722] which may be granted only if the court is satisfied that he or she has sufficient understanding to make the proposed application.[723]

---

[714] The definition of 'specified proceedings' (s 41(6)(b)) includes private law proceedings for child arrangements orders in which the court has given a direction under s 37(1) and has made or is considering whether to make an interim care order. In these circumstances a children's guardian must be appointed under s 41(1) unless the court is satisfied that it is not necessary to do so in order to safeguard the children's interests (see [2003] 2 FLR 636, [9] and see Ibid, [15]–[16]).

[715] Ibid, [17].

[716] Subject to the restrictions in the Children Act 1989 ss 11K and 11L: see s 11J(8). Section 11K(4) provides that a 'court may not make an enforcement order against a person unless the person is habitually resident in England and Wales; and an enforcement order ceases to have effect if the person subject to the order ceases to be habitually resident in England and Wales'. Section 11K(2) provides that a court 'may not make an enforcement order against a person in respect of any failure to comply with a child arrangements order occurring before the person attained the age of 18'. More than one enforcement order in relation to the same person on the same occasion can be made: see s 11J(10).

[717] Children Act 1989, 11K(1).     [718] Ibid, 11J(4).

[719] *Re LW (Children) (Enforcement and Committal: Contact); CPL v CH-W and others* [2010] EWCA Civ 1253, [2011] 1 FLR 1095.

[720] Ibid, [40] *per* Munby LJ, adding 'one thinks of the sudden and unexpected grounding of the nation's airlines by volcanic ash'.

[721] Children Act 1989, s 11J(5).     [722] Ibid, s 11J(6).     [723] Ibid, s 11J(7).

Before making the order, which may be a suspended order,[724] the court must be satisfied that:

> (a)  making the enforcement order proposed is necessary to secure the person's compliance with the child arrangements order or any child arrangements order that has effect in its place;
> (b)  the likely effect on the person of the enforcement order proposed to be made is proportionate to the seriousness of the breach.[725]

The court must also be satisfied that 'provision for the person to work under an unpaid work requirement imposed by an enforcement order can be made in the local justice area in which the person in breach resides or will reside'.[726] The court must obtain and consider information about the person and the likely effect of the enforcement order on him,[727] including any conflict with the person's religious beliefs; and any interference with the times (if any) at which he normally works or attends an educational establishment.[728]

The court must also 'take into account the welfare of the child who is the subject of the child arrangements order'.[729]

Where the court makes an enforcement order, it is to attach to the order a notice warning of the consequences of failing to comply with the order,[730] and the court is to ask a Cafcass officer or Welsh family proceedings officer to monitor and report on compliance with the order.[731]

### 5.12.2.5  Compensation for financial loss

Section 11O(2) of the Children Act 1989 provides that if the court is satisfied that an individual has failed to comply with a provision of a child arrangements order and another person (as defined by the section) has suffered financial loss by reason of the breach, it may make an order requiring the individual in breach to pay the person compensation in respect of his financial loss.[732] Unlike in the case of an enforcement order, the breach need only be proved to the civil standard (balance of probabilities).[733] The order can only be made on an application by the person who claims to have suffered financial loss. Those who may claim compensation are the person with whom the child concerned lives or is to live; the person whose contact with the child concerned is provided for in the child arrangements order; an individual subject to a condition under section 11(7)(b) or an activity condition imposed by the child arrangements order; or the child concerned.[734]

An order can only be made if prior to the breach the individual was given a copy of, or was otherwise informed of the terms of, a notice under section 11I relating to the order.[735] There is also a defence that the court is satisfied that the individual in breach had a reasonable excuse for failing to comply with the particular provision of the child arrangements order,[736] the burden of proof as to which lies on the individual claiming to have had a reasonable excuse.[737] The amount of compensation is to be determined by the court, but may not exceed the amount of the applicant's financial loss.[738] In determining the amount of compensation payable by the individual in breach, the court must take into account the individual's financial circumstances[739] and the welfare of the child concerned.[740] An amount ordered to be paid as compensation may be recovered by the applicant as a civil debt.[741]

---

[724]  Ibid, s 11J(9).    [725]  Ibid, s 11L(1).    [726]  Ibid, s 11L(2).

[727]  Ibid, s 11L(3).    [728]  Ibid, s 11L(4).    [729]  Ibid, s 11L(7).    [730]  Ibid, s 11N.

[731]  Ibid, s 11M. Schedule A1, Pt 1 makes provision as regards an unpaid work requirement, and Pt 2 makes provision in relation to the revocation and amendment of enforcement orders and failure to comply with such orders.

[732]  A court may not require an individual to pay compensation in respect of a failure by him to comply with a contact order where the failure occurred before the individual attained the age of 18: see ibid, s 11P.

[733]  See *Re LW (Children) (Enforcement and Committal: Contact); CPL v CH-W and others* [2010] EWCA Civ 1253, [2011] 1 FLR 1095 at [38].

[734]  As in the case of the child's application for an enforcement order, where the person proposing to apply for an order is the child concerned, the child must obtain the leave of the court, which may grant leave to the child concerned only if it is satisfied that he or she has sufficient understanding to make the proposed application (see s 11O(7) and (8)).

[735]  Children Act 1989, s 11P.    [736]  Ibid, s 11O(3).    [737]  Ibid, s 11O(4).    [738]  Ibid, s 11O(9).

[739]  Ibid, s 11O(10).    [740]  Ibid, s 11O(14).    [741]  Ibid, s 11O(11).

*5.12.2.6  Recent policy debate and research*

The Government has recently mooted the idea of further sanctions to enforce contact, such as curfew orders or the withholding of passports and driving licences. Following consultation,[742] however, it has decided against this approach and the focus instead will be on returning cases swiftly to court. Thought is also being given to extending powers of committal to magistrates and district judges, and to new contact activity or parent education programmes directed specifically at contact enforcement. Recent research has shown that 'most enforcement cases are about mutual conflict, risk and child refusal rather than implacable hostility' and that the 'existing sanctions are adequate if pursued robustly with the appropriate case'.[743]

## 5.13  Prohibited steps order

A prohibited steps order means:

> an order that no step which could be taken by a parent in meeting his parental responsibility for a child, and which is of the kind specified in the order, shall be taken by any person without the consent of the court.

This order is limited to controlling areas of parental responsibility which a parent could exercise. In *Croydon London Borough Council v A*[744] it was held that the trial court had been plainly wrong to make an order that the parents could not have contact with each other, as contact between parents has nothing to do with the exercise of parental responsibility. Similarly, a prohibited steps order cannot be used as a means to oust a parent from the home.[745] Nor may such an order be made where its purpose is to prevent a father from staying overnight at the matrimonial home at the conclusion of contact with his children.[746] Such use of a prohibited steps order would amount to the importation by the back door of an occupation order, which is governed by Part IV of the Family Law Act 1996.[747]

While the order is limited to aspects of parental responsibility, it can be used to control the behaviour of 'any person' towards a child, including therefore persons who do not have parental responsibility. Thus in *Re M (A Child) (Prohibited Steps Order: Appeal)*[748] a father sought a prohibited steps order preventing the child's stepfather from looking after a baby alone. The father's concern was that the stepfather was over 70 years old, suffered from angina, and might have a heart attack while caring for the child.

### 5.13.1  Can a prohibited steps order be used to prevent contact?

It will be recalled that section 9(5)(a) of the Children Act 1989 provides that a prohibited steps order cannot be made with a view to achieving a result which could be achieved by making a child arrangements order. If it is also recalled that in *Nottinghamshire County Council v P*[749] it was held that the term 'contact order' includes an order for no contact, the result of section 9(5)(a) is that a prohibited steps order cannot be made where it would be a disguised form of a 'no contact' order.

In *Re H (Prohibited Steps Order)*[750] the trial judge made a prohibited steps order against the mother (with whom the children were residing) to prevent the children from having contact with the abuser of one child. He declined to make a prohibited steps order against the abuser on the

---

[742] Ministry of Justice, *Co-operative Parenting Following Family Separation: Proposals on Enforcing Court-Ordered Child Arrangements: Summary of Consultation Responses and the Government's Response* (TSO, February 2013).

[743] L. Trinder, A. MacLeod, J. Pearce, and H. Woodward, 'Enforcing Child Contact Orders: Are the Family Courts Getting it Right?' [2013] Family Law 1145.

[744] [1992] Fam 169, CA.        [745] *Nottinghamshire County Council v P* [1993] 2 FLR 134.

[746] *Re D (Prohibited Steps Order)* [1996] 2 FLR 273.        [747] See Chapter 3.

[748] [2002] All ER (D) 401 (Nov).        [749] [1993] 2 FLR 134.        [750] [1995] 1 FLR 638.

ground that he had no jurisdiction as the abuser was not a party to the proceedings. The Court of Appeal held that the judge was in error in making a prohibited steps order against the mother because this directly contravened section 9(5); a prohibited steps order against the mother would achieve the same result as a contact order requiring the mother not to allow contact with the abuser, and could be enforced in the same way. However, a prohibited steps order which required the abuser not to seek contact with the children did not contravene section 9(5) and such an order could and should be made.[751]

### 5.13.2 Preventing removal

Removal of children from the UK without the consent of all those with parental responsibility is a criminal offence,[752] but parents and others may either not be aware of this or they may be prepared to break the criminal law. In addition, section 13 of the Children Act 1989 provides that a person named in a child arrangements order as a person with whom the child is to live can take or send the child out of the UK for a period of less than one month without either the consent of all those with parental responsibility or the court's leave.[753] In some situations any removal from the jurisdiction could expose the child to the risk of being taken permanently abroad and a prohibited steps order may therefore be necessary to obviate this risk.[754] Certainly it is advisable that such an order is sought by a person with parental responsibility where there is a perceived risk of the child being taken overseas without consent, for once a child has been taken from the country there may be difficulties securing the child's return. A person without parental responsibility, such as an unmarried father or other close relative, may be particularly well advised to apply for a prohibited steps order preventing removal from the jurisdiction, for such persons have no right to prevent a child being taken abroad. Where they enjoy a close relationship with the child, a court could well be persuaded to prohibit the child's removal unless those with parental responsibility first gained the permission of the court.[755]

A prohibited steps order might also be used to prohibit a child's relocation within the UK[756] although, as we have seen, an order restricting a resident parent's movements within the UK will only be made exceptionally.

## 5.14 Specific issue order

A specific issue order means:

> an order giving directions for the purpose of determining a specific question which has arisen, or which may arise, in connection with any aspect of parental responsibility for a child.[757]

The order will normally resolve a dispute about an aspect of parental responsibility. However, there need not necessarily be an issue between the parties. In *Re HG (Specific Issue Order: Sterilisation)*[758] a girl aged nearly 18 had severe epilepsy and a form of chromosomal deficiency which meant that she was an infant in terms of abilities. She lived in a school which meant she was likely at some time to be at risk of sexual relationships leading to pregnancy. The contraceptive pill was not suitable because of

---

[751] The court confirmed that it had this power despite the fact that the abuser was not a party to the proceedings. See ibid at 642, for discussion of the procedural difficulties which might arise in such without notice proceedings, and the court's suggested solution to them. See also M. Roberts, 'Ousting Abusers—Children Act 1989 or Inherent Jurisdiction? *Re H (Prohibited Steps Orders)*' (1995) 7 Child and Family Law Quarterly 243.

[752] Child Abduction Act 1984, s 1.    [753] See also ibid, s 1(4).

[754] See e.g., *Re P (Prohibited Steps Order: Removal from Jurisdiction)* [2013] EWCA Civ 1869.

[755] See *Re WB (Residence Orders)* [1995] 2 FLR 1023.

[756] See *Re B (Prohibited Steps Order)* [2007] EWCA Civ 1055, [2008] 1 FLR 613 in which, however, the order was not granted.

[757] See S. Gilmore, 'The Nature, Scope and Use of the Specific Issue Order' [2004] Child and Family Law Quarterly 367.

[758] [1993] 1 FLR 587, FD.

her epilepsy. It was accepted by all that it would be disastrous for the girl if she were to become pregnant because she would not be capable of understanding what was happening to her. Her parents wished to raise the question whether their daughter could be sterilised by making an application as the child's next friend[759] for a specific issue order. The case thus raised the question whether a specific issue order could be made when there was no issue (or dispute) between the persons having parental responsibility. It was held that the fact that a 'question has to be answered is what gives rise to the issue, not that there are protagonists on either side of the debate.'[760]

The issue which the order addresses must be one 'in connection with any aspect of parental responsibility for a child'. In *Re HG* the court had been confronted with an argument that, since the non-therapeutic sterilisation of a child required court approval,[761] the question of whether a child should be sterilised could not be one in connection with an aspect of parental responsibility. Thus, as the argument went, a specific issue order could not be made to sanction the operation. Peter Singer QC (sitting as Deputy High Court Judge) opined that it would be contrary to the philosophy of the Children Act 1989 if the definition of a specific issue order and of parental responsibility in section 3 of the Children Act 1989 were approached too restrictively. He held that the fact that a High Court judge must rule on sterilisation did not take from the parents their responsibility for forming their own conclusion and to take the necessary steps to implement that conclusion. Indeed, the court suggested that it may be one of the responsibilities of parenthood to bring the issue of sterilisation before a judge.

Clearly, however, there will be some issues which affect a child but which are outside the scope of the order, as illustrated by *Re J (Specific Issue Order: Leave to Apply)*.[762] In that case a child claimed to be a 'child in need' for the purposes of section 17 of the Children Act 1989. He sought leave to apply for a specific issue order which would deem him to be such a child. Wall J ruled that, as a matter of statutory construction, it was clear that it was the intention of Parliament that the exercise of a local authority's powers and duties under Part III of the Act should not be subject to judicial scrutiny or control except by means of judicial review. Accordingly, a specific issue order was inapposite to determine the question whether or not the applicant was a child in need. Moreover, the decision whether a child was a child in need was not a specific question which arose 'in connection with any aspect of parental responsibility'. Such a question must relate to the application of the exercise of parental responsibility to particular facts.[763]

A specific issue order may be of particular value to a parent in a situation where the child has his home elsewhere. The parent in charge of the day-to-day care of the child will make most decisions about the child's upbringing, but the other parent still retains an interest in these decisions and, where they are in dispute, the issue can be placed before a court and the court asked to decide. The order may also be of value to a third party who wishes to challenge a decision of a person with parental responsibility. In *Re F (Specific Issue: Child Interview)*[764] a father was accused of assaulting the mother of two children and had been committed for trial. His solicitor wished to interview the children because they may have witnessed the alleged assault. The mother, who had sole parental responsibility for the children, refused to consent to the interview taking place. Dismissing the mother's appeal against

---

[759] The Children Act 1989, s 10(7) entitles any person who falls within a category of persons prescribed by rules of court to apply for a section 8 order, and rules of court provide that a person under a disability may begin and prosecute proceedings by her next friend, in this case the parents. The parents could, of course, have made their own application for a specific issue order; however they were not entitled to legal aid to make an application themselves and legal proceedings in the High Court are very expensive. On the other hand, they could obtain legal aid to bring proceedings on behalf of their child. The court found this approach to be acceptable.

[760] *Re HG (Specific Issue Order: Sterilisation)* [1993] 1 FLR 587 (Peter Singer QC, sitting as a deputy High Court judge) at 595D–E.

[761] See *Re B (A Minor) (Wardship: Sterilisation)* [1988] AC 199.     [762] [1995] 1 FLR 669.

[763] *Re HG* and *Re J* are not easy to reconcile: see S. Gilmore, 'The Nature, Scope and Use of the Specific Issue Order' [2004] Child and Family Law Quarterly 367.

[764] [1995] 1 FLR 819.

the granting of a specific issue order permitting the solicitor to interview the children, the Court of Appeal held that the interview would be an ordeal which the boys would want to be spared if possible, but that that consideration had to be weighed against the advantages of securing a fair trial.

The specific issue order has been used across a range of issues[765] such as medical treatment/surgical intervention,[766] disputes surrounding children's education,[767] and disclosure of information.[768] Two particularly prominent issues, upon which we now focus, are relocation from the jurisdiction and disputes concerning a child's name.

### 5.14.1 Authorising the child's removal from the jurisdiction

The question of a child's removal from the jurisdiction[769] is an issue which arises relatively frequently before the courts[770] and has attracted a large body of case law.[771] Relocation disputes may be a growing phenomenon, arising from increases in family breakdown, greater international mobility, and changes in dating patterns (eg couples meeting over the internet).[772] The fact that cases tend to come before the courts is prompted by at least two factors. First, in many cases this is likely to be a contentious issue: if a child is taken out of the jurisdiction it is almost inevitable that the child will be unable to enjoy regular contact with the other parent, especially where the child is young. Secondly, the Child Abduction Act 1984 provides that it is a criminal offence for a person to take or send a child out of the UK without 'the appropriate consent'.[773] This safeguard means that before such removal is lawful, either all persons with parental responsibility for the child must have consented to the child's removal or the leave of the court must first have been obtained. Section 13(1)(b) of the Children Act 1989 reinforces this safeguard by providing that:

> Where a child arrangements order to which subsection (4) applies is in force with respect to a child, no person may—
> . . . (b) remove [the child] from the United Kingdom;
> without either the written consent of every person who has parental responsibility for the child or the leave of the court.

---

[765] See S. Gilmore, 'The Nature, Scope and Use of the Specific Issue Order' [2004] Child and Family Law Quarterly 367.

[766] See eg, *F (Mother) v F (Father)* [2013] EWHC 2638 (Fam), (a dispute between parents about MMR inoculation, where children aged 15 and 11 were refusing treatment). See Emma Cave, 'Adolescent Refusal of MMR Inoculation: *F (Mother v F (Father)* (2014) 77(4) *Modern Law Review* 630, arguing that the children's rights should be no less significant because the dispute is between parents; and see also *Re C (Welfare of Child: Immunisation)* [2003] EWHC 1376 (Fam), [2003] 2 FLR 1054, affirmed by the Court of Appeal in *Re B (A Child) (Immunisation)* [2003] EWCA Civ 1148, [2003] 2 FLR 1095; *Re C (HIV Test)* [1999] 2 FLR 1004, upholding Wilson J's decision in *Re C (A Child) (HIV Testing)* [2000] Fam 48; *Re R (A Minor) (Blood Transfusion)* [1993] 2 FLR 757 (Booth J); *Re J (Specific Issue Order: Child's Religious Upbringing and Circumcision)* [2000] 1 FLR 571.

[767] *Re A (Specific Issue Order: Parental Dispute)* [2001] 1 FLR 121; *Re Z (A Child) (Specific Issue Order: Religious Education)* [2002] EWCA Civ 501.

[768] Eg *Re K (Specific Issue Order)* [1999] 2 FLR 280 and *Re F (Specific Issue: Child Interview)* [1995] 1 FLR 819, discussed earlier in this section.

[769] For a discussion of the 'relocation' issue in law, policy, and practice, see R. George, *Relocation Disputes: Law and Practice in England and New Zealand* (Oxford: Hart Publishing, 2014). For a practical guide to the law, see R. George, F. Judd QC, D. Garrido, and A. Worwood, *Relocation A Practical Guide* (Bristol: Jordan Publishing Ltd, 2013).

[770] See Thorpe LJ's comment in *Re G (Leave to Remove)* [2007] EWCA Civ 1497, [2008] 1 FLR 1587 at [18] that the volume of such applications for permission to appeal and hearings is not inconsiderable. For an account of how judges at first instance decided cases, see R. George, 'How do judges decide international relocation cases?' [2015] Child and Family Law Quarterly 377.

[771] For useful accounts of the case law see M. Hayes, 'Relocation Cases: Is the Court of Appeal Applying the Correct Principles?' [2006] Child and Family Law Quarterly 351 and R. George, 'The Shifting Law: Relocation Disputes in New Zealand and England' (2009) 12 Otago Law Review 107.

[772] P. Parkinson, J. Cashmore, and J. Single, 'The Need for Reality Testing in Relocation Cases' (2010) 44(1) Family Law Quarterly 1–34 at 2–3.

[773] Defined in s 1(3). The Act is discussed in more detail in what follows.

Of course families commonly travel abroad for holidays, and the stringent nature of this provision could prove very disruptive and inconvenient for the parent with whom the child is living. Section 13(2) therefore contains some amelioration by providing that a person named in a child arrangements order as a person with whom the child is to live may take the child out of the jurisdiction for a period of up to one month without first obtaining such consents or the court's leave.[774]

In the event that a parent is resisting the other's long-term (permanent) relocation with the child, the court's authorisation will need to be sought. This can be achieved by seeking a specific issue order or, if there is a relevant child arrangements order in force, by seeking leave pursuant to section 13 of the Children Act 1989.[775]

### 5.14.1.1 Payne v Payne: *general guidance*

The leading decision is *Payne v Payne*,[776] in which the Court of Appeal held that the implementation of the HRA 1998 did 'not necessitate a revision of the fundamental approach to relocation applications' in decisions over the preceding 30 years deriving from *Poel v Poel*.[777] Reviewing those decisions, the court concluded that:

> relocation cases have been consistently decided upon the application of the following two propositions: (a) the welfare of the child is the paramount consideration; and (b) refusing the primary carer's reasonable proposals for the relocation of her family life is likely to impact detrimentally on the welfare of her dependent children. Therefore her application to relocate will be granted unless the court concludes that it is incompatible with the welfare of the children.[778]

The court emphasised that 'in most relocation cases the most crucial assessment and finding for the judge is likely to be the effect of the refusal of the application on the mother's future psychological and emotional stability';[779] and in 'any evaluation of the welfare of the child as the paramount consideration great weight must be given to this factor'.[780] The court explained, however, that there is no presumption that the reasonable proposals of the custodial parent should receive endorsement,[781] since this would be to risk breaching the respondent's rights under Articles 8 and 6 of the ECHR.[782] In order to 'guard against the risk of too perfunctory an investigation resulting from too ready an assumption that the mother's proposals are necessarily compatible with the child's welfare', however, the court suggested, at paragraph [40], the following approach:

> (a) Pose the question: is the mother's application genuine in the sense that it is not motivated by some selfish desire to exclude the father from the child's life? Then ask is the mother's application realistic, by which I mean founded on practical proposals both well researched and investigated? If the application fails either of these tests refusal will inevitably follow. (b) If however the application passes these tests then there must be a careful appraisal of the father's opposition: is it motivated by

---

[774] Children Act 1989, s 13(3). Also, when making the child arrangements order the court may grant the leave required by s 13(1)(b), either generally or for specified purposes.

[775] There is some rather sterile debate in the case law as to whether a specific issue order can be sought where a residence order is in force or whether in such a case the appropriate route is to apply for leave under s 13. See S. Gilmore, 'The Nature, Scope and Use of the Specific Issue Order' [2004] Child and Family Law Quarterly 367 and R. George, 'Changing Names, Changing Places: Reconsidering Section 13 of the Children Act 1989' [2008] Family Law 1121.

[776] [2001] Fam 473. For commentary, see A. Perry, 'Case Commentary: Leave to Remove Children from the Jurisdiction: *Payne v Payne*' [2001] Child and Family Law Quarterly 455; A. Bainham, 'Taking Children Abroad: Human Rights, Welfare and the Courts' [2001] Cambridge Law Journal 489.

[777] [1970] 1 WLR 1469. For a detailed assessment of this case, see R. Taylor, '*Poels* Apart: Fixed Principles and Shifting Values in Relocation Law' in S. Gilmore, J. Herring, and R. Probert, *Landmark Cases in Family Law* (Oxford: Hart, 2011). The court's reasoning in *Poel* was followed and developed in a line of pre-Children Act 1989 case law: see eg *Nash v Nash* [1973] 2 All ER 704; *Chamberlain v De La Mare* (1982) 4 FLR 434; *Lonslow v Hennig* [1986] 2 FLR 378; *Belton v Belton* [1987] 2 FLR 343; *Re F (A Ward) (Leave to Remove Ward Out of the Jurisdiction)* [1988] 2 FLR 116.

[778] [2001] Fam 473 at [26].     [779] Ibid, [26].     [780] Ibid, [41].     [781] Ibid, [40].     [782] Ibid.

genuine concern for the future of the child's welfare or is it driven by some ulterior motive? What would be the extent of the detriment to him and his future relationship with the child were the application granted? To what extent would that be offset by extension of the child's relationships with the maternal family and homeland? (c) What would be the impact on the mother, either as the single parent or as a new wife, of a refusal of her realistic proposal? (d) The outcome of the second and third appraisals must then be brought into an overriding review of the child's welfare as the paramount consideration, directed by the statutory checklist insofar as appropriate.

At paragraph [41], Thorpe LJ added:

In suggesting such a discipline I would not wish to be thought to have diminished the importance that this court has consistently attached to the emotional and psychological wellbeing of the primary carer. In any evaluation of the welfare of the child as the paramount consideration great weight must be given to this factor.

In *Re B (Leave to Remove: Impact of Refusal)*[783] the court emphasised the importance of paragraph [41] and that it is as much a part of the discipline set out as if it had been expressed in paragraph [40](c). The approach in paragraphs [40] and [41] are commonly referred to as the *Payne* discipline.

Butler-Sloss P in *Payne* agreed with Thorpe LJ. She went on to emphasise that all relevant factors need to be considered, including the following matters which, although not exclusive of other important matters which arise in an individual case, should be kept at the forefront of the judge's mind:[784]

(a)  The welfare of the child is always paramount.
(b)  There is no presumption created by section 13(1)(b) in favour of the applicant parent.
(c)  The reasonable proposals of the parent with a residence order wishing to live abroad carry great weight.
(d)  Consequently the proposals have to be scrutinised with care and the court needs to be satisfied that there is a genuine motivation for the move and not the intention to bring contact between the child and the other parent to an end.
(e)  The effect upon the applicant parent and the new family of the child of a refusal of leave is very important.
(f)  The effect upon the child of the denial of contact with the other parent and in some cases his family is very important.
(g)  The opportunity for continuing contact between the child and the parent left behind may be very significant.[785]

In *Re B (Children) (Removal from Jurisdiction); Re S (A Child) (Removal from Jurisdiction)*[786] the Court of Appeal offered the following extension to subparagraph (c) of paragraph [40] of the judgment in *Payne* (see the earlier quotation): 'Where the mother cares for the child or proposes to care for the child within a new family, the impact of refusal on the new family and the stepfather or prospective stepfather must also be carefully evaluated.' In those cases two mothers successfully appealed against refusal of leave to relocate.[787] In *Re B* the mother of two children, aged 10 and

[783] [2004] EWCA Civ 956, [2005] 2 FLR 239 at [14].

[784] *Payne v Payne* [2001] Fam 473 at [85].

[785] In *Re D (Leave to Remove: Appeal)* [2010] EWCA Civ 50, [2010] 2 FLR 1605 Wall LJ observed (at [18]) that 'the best summary of the approach which judges are required to take to these difficult decisions is contained in the judgment of the President, Dame Elizabeth Butler-Sloss in *Payne v Payne* at paras [85] to [88]'.

[786] [2003] EWCA Civ 1149, [2003] 2 FLR 1043. See also on the significance of re-marriage, *Re H (Application to Remove from the Jurisdiction)* [1998] 1 FLR 848.

[787] The cases were heard consecutively but the Court of Appeal gave judgment on them together.

6 years, who had divorced the children's father, wished to relocate to South Africa to be with her new partner, an affluent South African businessman who needed to live in South Africa to run his business interests there. In *Re S* the facts were similar. The mother of a 6-year-old child had formed a relationship with a man from the Philippines who had a right to live in Western Australia. They were soon to marry and she wished to relocate to Perth to live with him. He had a good salary there in a rather specialised job as a facial surgeon's clinical assistant. Overturning the judges' respective decisions, the Court of Appeal held that in each case insufficient weight had been given to the welfare as a whole of the new family. Thorpe LJ explained that the Court of Appeal had previously indicated that interference with reasonable decisions, particularly of step-parents, is something the court should undertake with considerable hesitation if the children are to continue to live with that step-parent.[788] His Lordship added:

> The mother's attachment and commitment to a man whose employment requires him to live in another jurisdiction may be a decisive factor in the determination of a relocation application. That does not entail putting the needs and interests of an adult before the welfare of the children. Rather the welfare of the children cannot be achieved unless the new family has the ordinary opportunity to pursue its goals and to make its choices without unreasonable restriction . . .
>
> That consideration applies with greater force in the case where the child's stepfather is a foreign national. There, as well as work, all his history, his family ties and his loyalties pull in the same direction. If the court frustrates that natural emigration it jeopardises the prospects of the new family's survival or blights its potential for fulfilment and happiness. That is manifestly contrary to the welfare of any child of that family. That is a reality which the court determining an application for relocation simply has to recognise.[789]

### 5.14.1.2 *The scope of* Payne

In *Re B (Leave to Remove: Impact of Refusal)*[790] Thorpe LJ explained that the principles set out in *Payne* apply generally to all applications by a primary carer. The court rejected counsel's submission that different principles might apply in a case in which, unlike in *Payne*, the relocation could be regarded as a 'lifestyle choice'.[791] There may, however, be some rare cases the facts of which are so unusual that it may not be apt to apply the discipline in *Payne* or aspects of it. In *Re J (Leave to Remove: Urgent Case)*[792] there were cross-applications for residence orders by the parents of two children aged 14 and 11. The children were living with their Bulgarian father and had expressed strong views that they did not wish to see their mother. The father went bankrupt and his home had burnt to the ground. He wished urgently to return to Bulgaria where he had been offered a job. The paternal grandparents had been supporting the father financially and had been paying the children's school fees but they too were proposing to relocate, selling their home to buy a property in Bulgaria. The judge allowed the relocation and the mother appealed contending that the father had not established that practical arrangements for the children's home and school had been made. The Court of Appeal held that the judge had been correct in the unusual circumstances to recognise 'the extraordinary and driving consideration that a sound future for the family could

---

[788]  *Chamberlain v De la Mare* (1983) 4 FLR 434 at 443H *per* Ormrod LJ and see also Griffiths LJ at 445, as endorsed by Butler-Sloss P in *Payne v Payne* at [73].

[789]  *Re B (Children) (Removal from Jurisdiction); Re S (A Child) (Removal from Jurisdiction)* [2003] EWCA Civ 1149, [2003] 2 FLR 1043 at [8] and [12].

[790]  [2004] EWCA Civ 956, [2005] 2 FLR 239 at [14].

[791]  See also Charles J's deprecation of the development of sub-classes of case in *Re C (Permission to Remove from Jurisdiction)* [2003] EWHC 596 (Fam), [2003] 1 FLR 1066 at [24](2) which was cited by Thorpe LJ.

[792]  [2006] EWCA Civ 1897, [2007] 1 FLR 2033, CA.

only be achieved by the father recovering an earning capacity in some other economy'.[793] Thorpe LJ commented:

> The judge ultimately had to decide between a mother's proposal for a residence order to be implemented in this jurisdiction and a father's residence order application to be implemented in another state. In those circumstances the discipline suggested in paras [40] and [41] of my judgment in *Payne v Payne* hardly applies.[794]

### 5.14.1.3 Does Payne *apply in shared residence cases?*

In *Re Y (Leave to Remove From Jurisdiction)*[795] Hedley J expressed the view that in a shared residence case the guidance in *Payne* should not be applied and that the court should simply apply section 1(1) and (3) of the Children Act 1989.[796] This approach was endorsed by Thorpe LJ in *K v K (Relocation: Shared Care Arrangement)*.[797] Thorpe LJ emphasised that what is significant is not simply the label of shared residence but the substance of:

> the practical arrangements for sharing the burden of care between two equally committed carers. Where each is providing a more or less equal proportion and one seeks to relocate externally then . . . the approach . . . in paragraph 40 in *Payne v. Payne* should not be utilised. The judge should rather exercise his discretion to grant or refuse by applying the statutory checklist in section 1(3) of the Children Act 1989.[798]

However, Black LJ indicated that she 'would not put *Payne* so completely to one side' in cases of shared care. She did not see '*Re Y* as representative of a different line of authority from *Payne*', but rather 'as a decision within the framework of which *Payne* is part', exemplifying 'how the weight attached to the relevant factors alters depending upon the facts of the case'.[799] Her Ladyship was concerned that cases should not get bogged down with preliminary skirmishes over the label to be applied to a child's arrangements or with arguments about whether a case is 'a *Payne* case' or a '*Re Y* case'. Moore-Bick LJ agreed with Thorpe LJ that the judge had failed to give sufficient consideration to authority subsequent to *Payne*[800] but appeared to go no further.

In *Re F (Child: International Relocation)*,[801] however, the Court of Appeal interpreted Moore-Bick LJ's judgment as agreeing with Black LJ, which it therefore saw as representing the majority view. It could be argued that this is a somewhat strained interpretation of Moore-Bick LJ's judgment,[802] but the court was clearly keen to endorse Black LJ's viewpoint, commenting: 'The last thing that this very difficult area of family law requires is satellite jurisprudence generating an ever-more detailed classification of supposedly different types of relocation case.'[803] This is a strong point and there may be some value in a set of guidelines which apply universally to all types of cases.[804] However, whether the decision in *Payne* provides the correct universal guidelines is questionable, especially since Thorpe LJ himself does not believe that the Payne guidance should be applied to a shared residence case.[805]

---

[793] Ibid, [28].     [794] Ibid, [27].     [795] [2004] 2 FLR 330.     [796] Ibid, [14]–[16].

[797] [2011] EWCA Civ 793, [2011] 2 FLR at [35]. For commentary, see R. George, 'Reviewing Relocation? *Re W (Relocation: Removal Outside Jurisdiction)* [2011] EWCA Civ 345 and *K v K (Relocation: Shared Care Arrangement)* [2011] EWCA Civ 793' [2012] Child and Family Law Quarterly 110.

[798] Ibid, [57].     [799] Ibid, [144].     [800] Ibid, [87].     [801] [2012] EWCA Civ 1364, [2013] 1 FLR 645.

[802] For criticism of the case generally and this interpretation, see R. George, 'International Relocation, Care Arrangements and Case Taxonomy' [2012] Family Law 1478.

[803] [2012] EWCA Civ 1364, [2013] 1 FLR 645 at [60].

[804] For this argument and a suggested set of flexible guidelines, see R. George, *Relocation Disputes Law and Practice in England and New Zealand* (Oxford: Hart Publishing, 2014).

[805] The point is made by R. George, 'International Relocation, Care Arrangements and Case Taxonomy' [2012] Family Law 1478 at 1482.

*Re F* was neither a case of a primary carer wishing to relocate, nor a shared residence case; rather it was a case of a mother wishing to change the child's primary care with the father in England to primary care with her in Spain where she already lived. The Court of Appeal held that the judge had not erred in referring to *Payne v Payne* in so far as anything in that case might be material.

Following *Re F*, therefore, *Payne* will apply in both primary care and shared care cases. As Rob George has pointed out, however, the position is complicated by the fact that in neither *K v K* nor *Re F* was the Court of Appeal's judgment in *Re C and M (Children)*[806] cited. That case, which was arguably a binding authority, held that the approach in *Poel v Poel* (as endorsed in *Payne*) does not apply to shared residence cases.[807]

### 5.14.2 Criticism, and clarification, of *Payne*

*Payne v Payne* has attracted considerable criticism from judges, practitioners, and academics.[808] It may be argued that the heavy emphasis on the emotional reaction of the primary carer represents an illegitimate gloss on the purity of the paramountcy principle,[809] or indeed on the process of fairly weighing the interests in the case. Through an analysis of case law applying *Payne*, Mary Hayes argued that the approach in *Payne* had fettered the complex balancing approach required by the welfare checklist and that following *Payne* there emerged an increasingly rigid body of precedent which disempowered trial judges and undermined and devalued the emphasis that might otherwise be placed upon the unique features of each case.[810] As Hayes pointed out, the effect of *Payne* is that the judge does not start his or her investigation with an open mind and the series of questions set out by Thorpe LJ is not balanced. While the judge must give emphasis to the primary carer's reactions, the judge is not instructed to have any preconceptions when carrying out an assessment of the detriment to the other parent. Furthermore, there is no reference to the impact on the latter's family.[811]

In *Re H (Leave to Remove)*,[812] Wilson LJ rightly cautioned that 'one must beware of endorsing a parody' of *Payne*, stressing that:

---

[806]  [1999] EWCA Civ 2039.

[807]  See R. George, 'Reviewing Relocation? *Re W (Relocation: Removal Outside Jurisdiction)* [2011] EWCA Civ 345 and *K v K (Relocation: Shared Care Arrangement)* [2011] EWCA Civ 793' [2012] Child and Family Law Quarterly 110.

[808]  See eg M. Hayes, 'Relocation Cases: Is the Court of Appeal Applying the Correct Principles?' [2006] Child and Family Law Quarterly 351; J. Herring and R. Taylor, 'Relocating Relocation' [2006] Child and Family Law Quarterly 517; P. Pressdee, 'Relocation, Relocation, Relocation: Rigorous Scrutiny Revisited' [2008] Family Law 220; C. Geekie, 'Relocation and Shared Residence: One Route or Two?' [2008] Family Law 446; R. George, 'The Shifting Law: Relocation Disputes in New Zealand and England' (2009) 12 Otago Law Review 107; M. Freeman, *Relocation: The Reunite Research* (London: Reunite, 2009); F. Judd and R. George, 'International Relocation: Do We Stand Alone?' [2010] Family Law 63.

[809]  See *Re AR (A Child: Relocation)* [2010] EWHC 1346 (Fam), [2010] 2 FLR 1577 at [8] *per* Mostyn J.

[810]  M. Hayes, 'Relocation Cases: Is the Court of Appeal Applying the Correct Principles?' [2006] Child and Family Law Quarterly 351. R. H. George, 'Reassessing Relocation: A Comparative Analysis of Legal Approaches to Disputes Over Family Migration After Parental Separation in England and New Zealand', DPhil Thesis, University of Oxford (2010), p 100 observes that of 23 international relocation judgments from the Court of Appeal since 1999, only four ended with relocation being refused; by contrast, 13 of the 23 cases were refused by the trial judges. As Judd and George have commented, in the current relocation climate it is hard to envisage a case in which granted relocation will be overturned on appeal (citing pre-*Payne* examples of *M v M (Removal from Jurisdiction)* [1993] 1 FCR 5 and *M v M (Minors) (Removal from Jurisdiction)* [1992] 2 FLR 303 (re-trial)): 'International Relocation: Do We Stand Alone?' [2010] Family Law 63. See also Chadwick LJ's criticism in *Re C (Leave to Remove from Jurisdiction)* of the degree of critical analysis to which Thorpe LJ subjected a trial judgment; and generally on this point in the context of international child abduction: *Re J (Child Returned Abroad: Convention Rights)* [2005] UKHL 40, [2005] 2 FLR 802. See, however, the recent case *Re S (Relocation: Interests of Siblings)* [2011] EWCA Civ 454, [2011] 2 FLR 678, where the Court of Appeal overturned a judge's decision to grant leave to relocate, albeit on unusual facts.

[811]  Hayes also notes that the discipline contains no indication that the wishes and feelings of the children are important.

[812]  [2010] EWCA Civ 915, [2010] 2 FLR 1875.

[b]oth Thorpe LJ, at para 26(a), and Dame Elizabeth Butler-Sloss P, at para 85(a), stressed that, in the determination of applications for permission to relocate, the welfare of the child was the paramount consideration. It is only against the subsidiary guidance to be collected from *Payne* that criticisms can perhaps more easily be levelled.[813]

As we shall see in the case law discussed below at 5.14.3, however, the *Payne* discipline has regularly been applied in practice in deciding cases.

There is some evidence that the concerns are shared by some practitioners. Robert George's interviews with 22 practitioners[814] revealed *Payne* as a 'coherent and well-understood approach to relocation disputes, but one which divides practitioners and causes significant discomfort for many who work with it'.[815] In *Re D (Leave to Remove: Appeal)*,[816] Wall LJ acknowledged the considerable criticism of *Payne* and that 'there is a perfectly respectable argument for the proposition that it places too great an emphasis on the wishes and feelings of the relocating parent, and ignores or relegates the harm done to children by a permanent breach of the relationship which children have with the left behind parent'.[817] His Lordship considered that that would in the right case constitute a 'compelling reason' for an appeal to be heard by the Supreme Court.[818] In *Re AR (A Child: Relocation)*[819] Mostyn J called for an urgent review of the ideology of *Poel/Payne* by the Supreme Court, commenting that the impact on the primary carer 'deserves its own berth and as such deserves its due weight, no more, no less'.[820] 'The problem with the attribution of great weight to this particular factor is that, paradoxically, it appears to penalise selflessness and virtue, while rewarding selfishness and uncontrolled emotion.'[821] His Lordship pointed out that 'the one word that is missing from *Payne* is, in fact, *sacrifice*'.[822] Mostyn J added[823] that the very obvious and critically important right of a child to have the meaningful participation of both of his parents in his upbringing (as protected by Art 8 of the ECHR) is sometimes 'lost in the relocation cases'. Jonathan Herring and Rachel Taylor have also called attention to the fact that there is a failure in relocation disputes to analyse the various interests of the child and the parties as arguably required by Article 8 of the ECHR.[824]

The point made by Mostyn J about 'sacrifice' is a powerful one. Against a focus on personal autonomy in this context, it could be said that parental responsibility requires parents and step-parents to negate their own wishes and feelings. A man who marries a woman who already has children knows that she has responsibilities to those children, and that they may have a father with whom they have a relationship which ought to be maintained. To feel bitter,

---

[813] Ibid, [21].     [814] Seven judges, seven barristers, five solicitors, and three court welfare officers.

[815] R. H. George, 'Reassessing Relocation: A Comparative Analysis of Legal Approaches to Disputes Over Family Migration After Parental Separation in England and New Zealand', DPhil Thesis, University of Oxford (2010), p 201. Some attractive features of *Payne* were also highlighted: it ensures that the court looks to medium/long-term welfare of the child, provides some certainty as to the process by which the court decides, and some clarity as to the information the court would require in evidence. There may be a gender split (at p 221) with women preferring *Payne*.

[816] [2010] EWCA Civ 50, [2010] 2 FLR 1605.

[817] Ibid, [33]. In *Re H (Leave to Remove)* [2010] EWCA Civ 915, [2010] 2 FLR 1875 (discussed in note 752) Wilson LJ (at [23]) questioned the use of the word 'ignores' in this quotation, but agreed that contact with the non-resident parent is relegated.

[818] Ibid, [34].     [819] [2010] EWHC 1346 (Fam), [2010] 2 FLR 1577.

[820] Reiterating some points he had made as counsel in *Re G (Leave to Remove)* [2007] EWCA Civ 1497, [2008] 1 FLR 1587.

[821] Ibid, [12]. See the endorsement of this paradox by Eleanor King J in *J v S* [2010] EWHC 2098 (Fam) at [96].

[822] *Re AR (A Child: Relocation)* [2010] EWHC 1346 (Fam), [2010] 2 FLR 1577 at [8]. However, compare Robert George who observes that this is an adult-centred analysis and that the issue is not about whether the parent is 'stoical' or 'uncontrolled', but about what effect her state of mind may have on the child: see R. George, 'The International Relocation Debate' [2012] Journal of Social Welfare and Family Law 141.

[823] [2010] EWHC 1346 (Fam), [2010] 2 FLR 1577 at [53].

[824] J. Herring and R. Taylor, 'Relocating Relocation' [2006] Child and Family Law Quarterly 517.

frustrated, and resentful about an inability to relocate may be a natural response, but these are arguably also self-indulgent emotions and ones which should not be placed at the forefront of the court's approach. It could be said that restrictions on mobility should simply be regarded as one of the burdens of bringing up children, and recognition that the parental responsibility of the natural parents is shared throughout the children's minority. Childhood passes rapidly, and when the children are old enough to express an informed opinion they can be asked whether the benefits of visiting a loved parent outweigh the opportunities offered by moving to a new country.

Despite the criticism, in *Re W (Relocation: Removal Outside Jurisdiction)*[825] Wall P indicated[826] that undue prominence has been accorded to his statements in *Re D (Leave to Remove: Appeal)*[827] and described *Payne* as 'not only the latest leading case on "relocation" in the English jurisprudence, but also a reserved decision of this court and binding on us'.[828] Reviewing that decision, he concluded that:

> the decision falls to be taken on what the court perceives to be in the best interests of the children concerned. Their welfare is our paramount consideration. The court must also apply the criteria and guidance set out in *Payne v Payne*.[829]

Lloyd LJ was slightly more circumspect in endorsing *Payne* as binding, noting only that trial judges had regarded it as so.[830] Elias LJ added (at para [156]): '*Payne* is binding, to the extent at least that guiding principles can be said to bind a court.' In *K v K (Relocation: Shared Care Arrangement)*[831] Moore-Bick LJ, having referred to *Re W*, accepted that *Payne* is binding but added that 'it is binding in the true sense only for its ratio decidendi'.[832] He observed that 'the only principle of law enunciated in *Payne v Payne* is that the welfare of the child is paramount; all the rest is guidance'.[833] And added that:

> where this court gives guidance on the proper approach to take in resolving any particular kind of dispute, judges at all levels must pay heed to that guidance and depart from it only after careful deliberation and when it is clear that the particular circumstances of the case require them to do so in order to give effect to fundamental principles.[834]

As Black LJ put it, the guidance:

> must be heeded for all the reasons that Moore-Bick LJ gives but as guidance not as rigid principle or so as to dictate a particular outcome in a sphere of law where the facts of individual cases are so infinitely variable.[835]

---

[825] [2011] EWCA Civ 345, [2011] 2 FLR 409.      [826] *Re W* [2011] EWCA Civ 345, [2011] 2 FLR 409 at [128].
[827] [2010] EWCA Civ 50, [2010] 2 FLR 1605.
[828] [2011] EWCA Civ 345, [2011] 2 FLR 409 at [13]. Interestingly, however, in March 2010 Thorpe LJ, as the Head of International Family Justice in England and Wales, at an International Judicial Conference on Cross-Border Family Relocation in Washington DC signed the Washington Declaration on International Family Relocation, with a view to harmonising the approach to relocation across States (see [2010] 2 International Family Law 211). The Declaration, which has no force of law, sets out a number of factors relevant to decisions on international relocation but, significantly, does not place emphasis on the emotional impact of refusal. Indeed as Wilson LJ observed in *Re H (Leave to Remove)* [2010] EWCA Civ 915, [2010] 2 FLR 1875 at [27], it may place insufficient weight on that factor. For discussion of the Washington Declaration and subsequent international developments, see R. George, 'The International Relocation Debate' [2012] Journal of Social Welfare and Family Law 141.
[829] *Re W* [2011] EWCA Civ 345, [2011] 2 FLR 409, [23].      [830] Ibid, [148].      [831] [2011] EWCA Civ 793.
[832] Ibid, [86]. See S. Gilmore, 'The *Payne* Saga: Precedent and Family Law Cases' [2011] Family Law 970.
[833] [2011] EWCA Civ 793 and see also, ibid, at [141] *per* Black LJ.      [834] Ibid, [86].      [835] Ibid, [142].

In *Re F (Child: International Relocation)*,[836] discussed earlier, the court underlined again, that:

> [t]he focus from beginning to end must be on the child's best interests. The child's welfare is paramount. Every case must be determined having regard to the 'welfare checklist', though of course also having regard, where relevant and helpful, to such guidance as may have been given by this court.[837]

In *Re F (A Child) (International Relocation Cases)*,[838] the father of a 12 year-old girl appealed against permission granted to the child's mother under section 13 of the Children Act 1989 to remove the girl permanently to Germany. Allowing the appeal, and directing a re-hearing before a different judge, Ryder LJ (with whom Christopher Clarke and McFarlane LJJ agreed) concluded that the judge had not engaged in 'an holistic evaluative analysis'.[839] Rather, the judge had allowed herself to be deflected from a welfare analysis by too great a focus on the *Payne* discipline. In particular, the judge failed to 'take account of any erosion in the quality of the relationship between father and daughter if L were to move to live in Germany.' The court was clear that:

> Selective or partial legal citation from *Payne* without any wider legal analysis is likely to be regarded as an error of law. In particular, a judgment that not only focuses solely on *Payne*, but also compounds that error by only referring to the four point "discipline" set out by Thorpe LJ at para 40 of his judgment in *Payne* is likely to be wholly wrong. There are no quick fixes to be had in these important and complicated cases.[840]

Summarising, Christopher Clarke LJ explained that it is necessary for the court:

> to consider the proposals both of the father and of the mother in the light of, inter alia, the welfare check list … and having regard to the interests of the parties, and most important of all, of the child. Such consideration needs to be directed at each of the proposals taken as a whole. The court also needs to compare the rival proposals against each other since a proposal, or a feature of a proposal, which may seem inappropriate, looked at on its own, may take on a different complexion when weighed against the alternative; and vice versa.[841]

Ryder LJ was firmly of the view that this is simply to apply the existing approach in *K v K (Children: Permanent Removal from Jurisdiction)*[842] and *Re F (A Child) (Relocation)*.[843] However, he added that:

> in the decade or more since *Payne* it would seem odd indeed for this court to use guidance which out of the context which was intended is redolent with gender based assumptions as to the role and relationships of parents with a child. Likewise, the absence of any emphasis on the child's wishes and feelings or to take the question one step back, the child's participation in the decision making process, is stark.[844]

---

[836] [2012] EWCA Civ 1364, [2013] 1 FLR 645.

[837] Ibid, [61]. High Court decisions since *Re F* show a strong emphasis on applying the welfare principle and checklist to the individual facts of cases, as seeing *Payne* merely as guidance not binding principle: see e.g., *Re TC and JC (Children: Relocation)* [2013] EWHC 292 (Fam), [2013] 2 FLR 484 (Mostyn J) at [11] for a useful summary of the approach now commanded by the authorities; *S v T (Permission to Relocate to Russia)* [2012] EWHC 4023 (Fam), [2013] 2 FLR 457 (Hedley J) at [5]; *Re L (Relocation: Shared Residence)* [2012] EWHC 3069 (Fam), [2013] 1 FLR 777 (Stephen Bellamy QC, sitting as a Judge of the High Court). However, the influence of the Payne discipline in the Court of Appeal can, it seems, still be strong: see *Re E (Relocation: Removal From the Jurisdiction)* [2012] EWCA Civ 1893, [2013] 2 FLR 290 (Thorpe, Moore-Bick, and Etherton LJJ).

[838] [2015] EWCA Civ 882. For comment, see E. Devereux and R. George 'Alas poor *Payne*, I knew him …': an interpretation of the Court of Appeal's decision in *Re F (International Relocation Cases)*' [2015] Fam Law 1232, and S. Gilmore, 'Less of the 'P' discipline and More of the 'H' word – putting *Payne* in its place! *Re F (A Child) (International Relocation Cases)* [2015] EWCA Civ 882' (2016) *Journal of Social Welfare and Family Law* (forthcoming).

[839] [2015] EWCA Civ 882, [4].     [840] Ibid, [27].     [841] Ibid, [43].

[842] [2011] EWCA Civ 793, [2012] Fam 134.     [843] [2012] EWCA Civ 1364, [2013] 1 FLR 645.

[844] [2015] EWCA Civ 882.

Ryder LJ added that 'international relocation cases engage arts 6 and 8 of the European Convention for the Protection of Human Rights and Fundamental Freedoms 1950 [ECHR]'[845] This requires that 'parents' plans be scrutinised and evaluated by reference to the proportionality of the same' because of the likelihood of the severance of the relationship between the child and one of her parents. The court has to ensure that 'the preferred option represents a proportionate interference in the art 8 ECHR rights of those involved'. Ryder LJ was clear, however, that it would 'not be every private law application that requires a proportionality evaluation, most of which would be 'adequately protected by the domestic statutory regime'.[846] How this proportionality point is to work in the context of the paramountcy of the child's welfare, however, is difficult to follow. It is also unclear why a test of proportionality is to apply in some cases and not others.[847] McFarlane LJ was more circumspect on this point, commenting that 'whatever the issue before the court, the task is the same; the court must weigh up all of the relevant factors, look at the case as a whole, and determine the course that best meets the need to afford paramount consideration to the child's welfare.'[848] The court's holistic approach, and its recognition of *Payne*'s inappropriate gender-based assumptions and failure expressly to focus on the wishes and feelings of children are welcome developments. However, as the court makes clear, the *Payne* guidance will still need to be considered in appropriate cases. The courts' interpretation of that guidance is considered below.

### 5.14.3  Applying the *Payne* discipline

*5.14.3.1  Are the applicant's proposals genuine and realistic?*

The court must be satisfied that the relocating parent's proposals are genuine and realistic. However, in *Re F and H (Children: Relocation)*[849] the Court of Appeal explained that:

> the bar as to practicalities that must be jumped by the relocation applicant is set at a wide variety of heights depending on the facts and circumstances of the case.[850]

In that case, a Texan mother of two girls aged 11 and 5 wished to relocate with her children back to Texas after six years in England. Although the mother failed to provide any clear information about the school that the little girls would attend in Texas and as to the mother's employment or earning capacity,[851] the judge permitted the relocation, commenting that the mother was resourceful and would ensure that the children were appropriately cared for and educated. The Court of Appeal held that the judge had not erred, holding that the 'bar is set particularly low where the primary carer is returning to the completely familiar home life after such a brief absence'.[852]

Provided they are realistic, the applicant's proposals need not necessarily be supported by detailed evidence. In *Re G (Removal from Jurisdiction)*[853] a mother who had obtained an international diploma in anatomy, physiology, and massage, intended to relocate with her 5-year-old twins from Yorkshire to Argentina, to work as a complementary therapist. The judge was suspicious of the potential of her qualifications, and of such a practice. The Court of Appeal doubted the validity

---

[845] Ibid, [31] and [32], citing *Glaser v United Kingdom* (Case No 32346/96) (2000) 33 EHRR 1.

[846] Ibid, [32].

[847] See S. Gilmore, 'Less of the 'P' discipline and More of the 'H' word – putting *Payne* in its place! *Re F (A Child) (International Relocation Cases)* [2015] EWCA Civ 882' (2016) *Journal of Social Welfare and Family Law* (forthcoming): 'as a matter of practical application of a proportionality test one might say that it becomes more material and significant a protection the greater the impact of a disproportionate decision. But that really ought not to go to whether proportionality is considered, but rather to a different matter, namely the extent to which proportionality may tax the mind of the court in the individual case, depending upon its complexity and importance.'

[848] [2015] EWCA Civ 882, [50].     [849] [2007] EWCA Civ 692, [2008] 2 FLR 1667[correct? yes].

[850] Ibid, [9].

[851] Especially since the contact regime that had been put in place required the mother to be absent from work for eight weeks a year.

[852] [2007] EWCA Civ 692, [2008] 2 FLR 1667 at [9].     [853] [2005] EWCA Civ 170, [2005] 2 FLR 166.

of the judge's conclusion that the mother had fallen short by producing no evidence of business conditions or of demand for her services or of her ability to provide them on a commercial basis.[854] However, leave may be refused where the applicant's proposals are ill thought out. In *K v K (A Minor) (Removal from Jurisdiction)*[855] a mother, who was born in the USA, applied to take the child of the marriage, who was nearly four, to the USA where the mother proposed to pursue post-graduate education. Refusing leave, Thorpe J found that she had paid insufficient attention to the practicalities of pursuing postgraduate studies in the USA. He also found that the mother had an underlying resilience which would enable her to cope with refusal and that the continuation of the relationship between the child and her father was of very great importance.[856]

### 5.14.3.2 *Detriment to the non-relocating parent*

As part of the discipline in *Payne*, the court must ask: what would be the extent of the detriment to the parent who opposes relocation and his or her future relationship with the child were the application granted? In some cases, the child's relationship with the respondent parent has proved material to the outcome. However, it seems to be rare in the more recent reported decisions for this factor to be material to the outcome.[857] As Mostyn J commented in *Re AR (Relocation)*, the Court of Appeal's approach in *Payne* has a tendency to bring about 'the almost invariable success of the application, save in those cases where it is demonstrably irrational, absurd or malevolent'.[858] *Re B (Leave to Remove)*[859] is a relatively rare example in recent years of a reported decision in which leave has been denied. The Court of Appeal upheld a judge's decision to refuse a mother's application for relocation, despite the fact that the mother had had a reactive depression to the family break-up which would be exacerbated by a refusal, because the effect of relocation would be to alienate the children from their father. *Re AR* itself is another example where a child's contact with the father proved an important factor bearing on the child's overall welfare, albeit in the more unusual situation of a shared care arrangement. The father was English and the mother French. The mother and child had previously lived in France but she had returned to London for postgraduate study, during which time the father, who had care of the child 40 per cent of the time, had established a close relationship with the child. The mother sought leave to remove the child to France again upon the completion of her course. Mostyn J refused leave and made a shared residence order, albeit with the mother as the principal carer.

In *J v S (Leave to Remove)*[860] Eleanor King J also highlighted the significance of the child's existing attachments, commenting:

> It is important that no court dealing with these cases shrinks from examining what the children involved will lose if the application is granted. For my part, I do not subscribe to the view that email and Skype are tolerable substitutes for [informal direct contact] . . . Often, even on the most restrictive application of the *Payne* discipline, the loss of frequent informal contact between father and child will be considered to be too high a price to pay to satisfying a primary carer's desire to relocate. In such circumstances even the knowledge that the mother will be bitterly disappointed and resentful will not drive a court to the conclusion that the children's interests lie in allowing relocation.[861]

---

[854] See also *Re M-K (A Child) (Relocation Outside the Jurisdiction)* [2006] EWCA Civ 1013, [2007] 1 FLR 432 (mother wishing to relocate to Brazil merely had a law degree but claimed to be an advocate, although she had an offer to work in her uncle's law firm—the judge focused unduly on the mother's description of her qualifications as affecting her credibility, with which she was given no fair opportunity to deal).

[855] [1992] 2 FLR 98.

[856] See also *M v A (Wardship: Removal from Jurisdiction)* [1993] 2 FLR 715 (mother's plans to relocate to Canada were ill thought out and failed to accommodate the needs and wishes of children aged 12 and 9) and *M v M (Minors) (Jurisdiction)* [1993] Family Law 396 (Israeli mother refused leave to take her children permanently to Israel because they did not want to be uprooted from their father, schools, and the UK).

[857] For an earlier example, see *Tyler v Tyler* [1989] 2 FLR 158.    [858] Ibid, [7].

[859] [2008] EWCA Civ 1034, [2008] 2 FLR 2059.    [860] [2010] EWHC 2098 (Fam), [2011] 1 FLR 1694.

[861] Ibid, [99].

However, on the facts her Ladyship concluded that a Japanese mother should be allowed to relocate back to Japan. The mother suffered with a long-term gastrointestinal illness associated with stress and depression and she would suffer long-term ill health and distress in the event that she was not able to return to Japan. This would be harmful to the welfare of the children, who were aware of the mother's fragile emotional state. In addition, the court was satisfied that the mother would not seek to minimise the strength of and the importance of the relationship between the father and the children.

In reaching her conclusion, Eleanor King J observed[862] that in conducting the balancing exercise she was bound by the discipline of *Payne*, not limited to the questions set out by Thorpe LJ, but also with the judgment of Butler-Sloss P at the forefront of her mind. *Payne* is thus considered only under the umbrella of the paramountcy rule and using the welfare checklist as a tool to assist, whilst always bearing in mind the Article 8 rights of the children. Her Ladyship, while recognising that Thorpe LJ's judgment[863] in *Payne* still resonated strongly and was highly material to the case before her, unhesitatingly agreed with counsel's submission that the court:

> must be careful not to allow itself to become confined in a strait-jacket, with the series of questions presenting the only test . . . Care must be taken to ensure that the question of the impact of refusal of the mother is but one component of an assessment of the best interests of the boys and not the only feature.[864]

### 5.14.3.3 *Impact of refusal on the applicant in its effect on child welfare*

As noted, the impact of refusal on the applicant is a powerful factor. However, it is not essential for the relocating parent to demonstrate a negative emotional impact of refusal in order to be successful. In *Re W (A Child) (Removal from Jurisdiction)*[865] the mother suffered with mental health problems, as a result of which she was permitted only indirect contact with her child who lived with the father. The father wished to relocate with his new wife to Australia where his brother lived, a desire which he had had for several years and which he made known to the mother during their relationship some five years earlier. The judge regarded the only impediment to the relocation as the possibility of reviving direct contact with the mother. In the context of the mother's illness, the judge regarded this as an unrealistic prospect and did not regard the disbenefit to the child of relocating as high. Even though the father had not given evidence of the impact of a refusal upon him, the Court of Appeal held that the judge's decision was a balanced exercise of discretion and could not be said to be flawed.

### 5.14.3.4 *Impact of removal on the child's welfare*

The court is concerned with the impact of the removal on the welfare of the child primarily as a minor, not as an adult. This point was made in *Re A (Leave to Remove: Cultural and Religious Considerations)*[866] in which the child's father raised cultural and religious considerations as arguments against the removal. Resisting the relocation to Holland (the mother's husband's homeland), the father argued that it would deny the boy the benefit of his father's guidance on the Muslim faith and he would have no prospect of succeeding to the mantle of head of the family in adulthood, which brought status and benefits within the family. McFarlane J observed that this was a matter relating to the child's life as an adult and, although not irrelevant, the court's 'primary task is to give paramount consideration to Y's upbringing as a child'.[867] He concluded that the balance was strongly in favour of the relocation. The father's religious guidance of the child could be achieved through contact.

---

[862] Ibid, [82].    [863] Especially *Payne* [2001] EWCA Civ 166, [2001] Fam 473 at [31].
[864] [2010] EWHC 2098 (Fam) at [81].    [865] [2005] EWCA Civ 1614, [2006] 1 FCR 346.
[866] [2006] EWHC 421 (Fam), [2006] 2 FLR 572.    [867] Ibid, [40].

### 5.14.4 **Relocation debate and research**

Recent research[868] has shown that in England and Wales approximately two-thirds of applications to relocate are successful, but that a wide range of factors influences the success of an individual case.[869]

The issue of relocation is hotly debated[870] in the academic literature, with two broad factions, one emphasising the importance of supporting the primary caretaker relationship, and the other focusing on the importance to the child of maintaining a relationship with both parents.[871] There is, however, a paucity of empirical evidence concerning the impact of relocation on parents and children.[872]

A study in England was undertaken for the child abduction charity Reunite[873] by Professor Marilyn Freeman,[874] who carried out a series of semi-structured interviews with 36 parents who were involved in 34 relocation cases between 1999 and 2009. The interviewees were 25 fathers, 23 of whom resisted relocation, and 11 mothers all of whom sought relocation. In 22 of the 34 cases (nearly 65 per cent) relocation was granted. The interviews revealed several themes. Post-relocation contact was difficult to maintain, both practically and because of the cost of staying in touch, and could be easily thwarted from a distance. There were also concerns that outcomes after relocation were not monitored. Many interviewees were concerned that Cafcass officers' objectivity seemed compromised by the prevailing approach of the courts. A majority of interviewees urged a more child-centric approach, with appointment of a guardian to protect the child's interests and a more scientific approach to the impact of relocation on the child. The left-behind parents, who comprised the majority within this study, spoke of the devastation the relocation had brought to their lives, although there was also some evidence of such emotional difficulties caused to parents who were thwarted in their wish to relocate. The research provides an important insight into the very real impact of relocation, particularly for left-behind parents. However, as Judd and George observe,[875] it would be difficult to draw broad conclusions from it as to how relocation law should be developed.

---

[868] R. George and O. Cominetti, 'International Relocation: Key Findings from the 2012 Study' [2013] Family Law 1430, and see also R. George and O. Cominetti, 'International Relocation in English Law: Thorpe LJ's Discipline and its Application' [2013] International Family Law 149.

[869] Such as pre-relocation child care arrangements, destination, reasons for application and opposing it, court location, type of judge, whether client is represented: see [2013] Family Law 1430 at 1431.

[870] See for a cross-section of perspectives: C. Bruch and J. Bowermaster, 'The Relocation of Children and Custodial Parents: Public Policy, Past and Present' (1995) 30 Family Law Quarterly 245; J. Kelly and M. Lamb, 'Developmental Issues in Relocation Cases Involving Young Children: When, Whether, and How?' (2003) 17 Journal of Family Psychology 193; C. Bruch, 'Sound Research or Wishful Thinking in Child Custody Case? Lessons from Relocation Law' (2006) 40 Family Law Quarterly 281; P. Stahl and L. Drozd (eds), *Relocation Issues in Child Custody Cases* (Binghamton, NY: Haworth Press, 2006); W. Austin, 'Relocation, Research, and Forensic Evaluation, Part I: Effects of Residential Mobility on Children of Divorce' (2008) 46 Family Court Review 137; see also articles in (2011) 23(2) Child and Family Law Quarterly.

[871] See the discussion in J. Herring and R. Taylor, 'Relocating Relocation' [2006] Child and Family Law Quarterly 517 at 519–22, who conclude: with so little agreement between researchers, the evidence to date is not capable of founding a general theory of harm to the child in relocation cases nor of providing conclusive support for a presumption either for or against relocation. At best the research evidence tells us that we should be aware of the potential harm to the child both due to any diminution in the quality of parenting of the resident parent and loss of contact with the non-resident parent.

[872] See N. Taylor, M. Gollop, and M. Henaghan, *Relocation Following Parental Separation: The Welfare and Best Interests of Children Research Report* (Centre for Research on Children and Families and Faculty of Law, University of Otago, Dunedin, June 2010) for an excellent account of the existing empirical research on relocation following parental separation (at Ch 3), and an extensive bibliography of relevant literature; see also the review of research by N. Taylor and M. Freeman, 'International Research Evidence on Relocation: Past, Present and Future' (2010) 44(3) Family Law Quarterly 317–339 and B. Horsfall and R. Kaspiew, 'Relocation in Separated and Non-Separated Families: Equivocal Evidence from the Social Science Literature' (2010) 24 Australian Journal of Family Law 34. See C. Bruch, 'Sound Research or Wishful Thinking in Child Custody Case? Lessons from Relocation Law' (2006) 40 Family Law Quarterly 281 for a critical account of some of the literature.

[873] See www.reunite.org.

[874] M. Freeman, 'Relocation: The Reunite Research Project' [2010] International Family Law 161.

[875] F. Judd and R. George, 'International Relocation: Do We Stand Alone?' [2010] Family Law 63 at 66, referencing C. O'Flinn, 'Back in the Fold' (2009) 159 New Law Journal 1416.

There have also been recent studies in other jurisdictions, for example in Australia and New Zealand. A prospective longitudinal study of relocation disputes is being carried out by Professor Parkinson and colleagues at the University of Sydney.[876] In a reported phase of the study, 80 parents,[877] 40 men (all opposing relocation) and 40 women (all but one relocating) in 71 cases[878] were interviewed at two points 18 months apart. The study cautions that the fact that contact is ordered does not mean that it will occur or do so with anticipated frequency. The study suggested that 'distant relocations may impose financial burdens on parents which may make the planned levels of contact unsustainable in the long-term'.[879] There was also evidence in some cases of difficulties arising over contact which, particularly in overseas relocations, was difficult to enforce and of concerns about the burden of travel on young children. Parkinson et al suggest that judges should 'reality test' any proposed contact and may need to ask whether the relocation would still be in the child's best interests if the proposed contact did not take place.[880] A similar study has been carried out in New Zealand by Taylor, Gollop, and Henaghan[881] interviewing 114 parents and 44 children in 100 families. The study has highlighted the diversity and complexity of relocation disputes,[882] revealing many different relocation sequences. Another study by Behrens, Smyth, and Kaspiew[883] carried out in-depth interviews with 38 separated parents (27 fathers and 11 mothers) involved in contested relocation proceedings in Australia[884] and found that the largest group of cases involved families in which the relocation dispute was only one source of conflict. For most of such cases, poor or abusive inter-parental relationships continued after relocation. This suggests that a court's consideration of the likely outcomes following the relocation dispute may need to take account of these wider issues. The difficulty of comparing international research should be noted, however, because different countries take quite different approaches to relocation disputes.[885]

### 5.14.5 Change of a child's surname

Another issue which has attracted a considerable amount of case law[886] is what surname a child should bear.[887] The leading authority is the House of Lords' decision in *Dawson v Wearmouth*.[888] The relationship between the unmarried parents of a baby boy called Alexander broke down within

---

[876] Reported in P. Parkinson, J. Cashmore, and J. Single, 'The Need for Reality Testing in Relocation Cases' (2010) 44(1) Family Law Quarterly 1–34. The Hon Richard Chisholm is also one of the researchers.

[877] And 19 children.     [878] Ten of these involved relocations to other countries.

[879] Parkinson et al, 'The Need for Reality Testing in Relocation Cases', at 33.     [880] Ibid, 34.

[881] N. Taylor, M. Gollop, and M. Henaghan, *Relocation Following Parental Separation: The Welfare and Best Interests of Children Research Report* (Centre for Research on Children and Families and Faculty of Law, University of Otago, Dunedin, June 2010). See also M. Henaghan, 'Relocation Cases—The Rhetoric and the Reality of a Child's Best Interests—A View from the Bottom of the World' [2011] Child and Family Law Quarterly 226.

[882] See N. Taylor, M. Gollop, and M. Henaghan, 'Relocation Following Parental Separation in New Zealand: Complexity and Diversity' [2010] International Family Law 97.

[883] R. Kaspiew, J. Behrens, and B. Smyth, *Relocation Disputes in Separated Families Prior to the 2006 Reforms: An Empirical Study* (2011) 86 Family Matters 70 (Australian Institute of Family Studies journal).

[884] From 2002 to 2005.

[885] See R. George, 'Practitioners' Views on Children's Welfare in Relocation Disputes: Comparing Approaches in England and New Zealand' [2011] Child and Family Law Quarterly 178 on how the differences might play out in practice, and R. George, 'The International Relocation Debate' [2012] Journal of Social Welfare and Family Law 141 for an overview of the different approaches and discussion of the possibility of harmonisation.

[886] For useful accounts of the case law, see A. R. Bond, 'Reconstructing Families—Changing Children's Surnames' [1998] Child and Family Law Quarterly 17; M. Hayes, '*Dawson v Wearmouth*: What's in a Name? A Child by Any Other Name is Surely Just as Sweet?' [1999] Child and Family Law Quarterly 423; and N. Gosden, 'Children's Surnames—How Satisfactory is the Current Law?' [2003] Family Law 186.

[887] See J. Herring, 'The Shaming of Naming: Parental Rights and Responsibilities in the Naming of Children' in R. Probert, S. Gilmore, and J. Herring (eds), *Responsible Parents and Parental Responsibility* (Oxford: Hart, 2009). In the context of a child in care, see the Children Act 1989, s 33(7) and *Re S (Change of Surname)* [1999] 1 FLR 672; in the context of special guardianship, see *Re L (Special Guardianship: Surname)* [2007] EWCA Civ 196, [2007] 2 FLR 50.

[888] [1999] 2 AC 308. See M. Hayes, '*Dawson v Wearmouth*: What's in a Name?'.

three weeks of the child's birth. Shortly thereafter, the mother, without consulting the father, registered Alexander with the surname Wearmouth. This was the name of her former husband, by whom she had two children bearing that surname, and whose name she had retained. Alexander's father, Mr Dawson, sought a specific issue order to change the child's surname to his. The trial judge, who approached the matter as if it had come before him before the child's birth was registered, directed that Alexander be known by the surname Dawson. On the mother's appeal, the Court of Appeal held that the judge had erred in principle. The court explained that the surname which appears on a child's birth certificate cannot be altered and consequently 'as a matter of principle registration is a profound matter'. The court held that registration is thus a 'major factor to be taken into account in the exercise of the court's discretion'.[889] Exercising its discretion afresh, the court held that the connection the mother and Alexander's half-siblings had to the name Wearmouth meant that that was a 'perfectly natural and logical choice for her to make' and could not be justly criticised as alien merely because it was also the name of the mother's ex-husband. The court went on to say that those factors, 'coupled with the all-important fact already stressed that this was the child's duly registered name' were 'very powerful factors in the mother's favour' which could 'only be displaced by strong countervailing considerations'.[890]

Mr Dawson appealed to the House of Lords contending, *inter alia*, that the Court of Appeal gave too much emphasis to registration. The appeal was dismissed. Lord Mackay, delivering the House's opinion, observed that the facts of this case could be distinguished from one in which there had been substantial usage of a father's name. He held that the correct approach is to apply section 1(1)[891] and (5) of the Children Act 1989, 'and not make an order for the change of name unless there is some evidence that this would lead to an improvement from the point of view of the welfare of the child'.[892] Lord Mackay held that on a fair reading, the Court of Appeal was not suggesting that the registration was conclusive of the issue, but that circumstances justifying the change would be required and that there were no such circumstances of sufficient strength to do so in this case.

Lord Jauncey, while not formally dissenting, commented on two matters. First, he did not accept that registration is necessarily a major factor in every case, the weight given to which must always depend upon the surrounding circumstances as they affect the welfare of the child. Secondly, his Lordship observed that a child's surname at birth is 'not simply a name plucked out of the air'; rather, normally the child is given the father's surname as a biological label, demonstrating the child's connection with the father and telling 'the world at large that the blood of the name flows in its veins'. Lord Jauncey considered that in a case such as this the court should have regard to the importance of maintaining a paternal link; the very real possibility that the mother might remarry and take a new husband's surname; and the fact that the child may wonder why he or she bears a name which is that of neither of the parents but rather that of a man with whom the child has no connection and whom it may never have seen. Lord Jauncey was left in doubt as to whether the Court of Appeal gave proper weight to these important matters in exercising their discretion.

Lord Hobhouse commented that the child's registered name represents the status quo and provides an important part of the background against which the court has to assess what will be in the interests of the child's welfare. He added that it is 'not without importance', 'has practical implications', and, 'other things being equal, it is in the long-term interests of the child that the name by which he is known should also be the name which appears on his birth certificate'. Lord Hobhouse expressed disapproval of how the Court of Appeal had expressed itself. He made clear

---

[889] [1998] Fam 75 at 82.     [890] Ibid, 83.

[891] See also Ward LJ in *Re C (Change of Surname)* 1998] 2 FLR 656 at 660 to the effect that change of a child's surname is a matter with respect to a child's upbringing.

[892] [1999] 2 AC 308 at 320–1. Lord Hobhouse of Woodborough said that the applicant 'has to make out a positive case in accordance with section 1 of the Act that it is in the interests of the child that the order should be made. If he fails to make out that *positive* case, his application will fail' (at 326).

that registration is a relevant and, maybe, important factor in assessing where the balance of advantage for the child's welfare lies but should not be treated as an 'all-important' factor which requires to be 'displaced by strong countervailing considerations', adding:

> Each case depends upon its own facts . . . . the registered surname is a relevant factor which must be taken into account and may, in certain cases, like any other relevant factor make the difference between whether an order is made or not.[893]

*Dawson v Wearmouth* was applied in *Re A (Change of Name)*[894] on similar facts and the same outcome was reached, although the process by which the Court of Appeal reached its decision raises some interesting issues. The parents of a child were Somalis. Within three months of her divorce, the mother conceived the child by a new partner (the father). The mother registered the child in the name of her former husband. The father was successful before the judge at first instance in obtaining a change of the name to that which the father claimed was required by the Somali custom of patrilineal naming. On the mother's appeal, the Court of Appeal received expert evidence on Somali cultural practices with regard to the naming of children and relevant Muslim law. Fatal to the father's case was that the evidence showed that the name for which the father was contending would not be the name in accordance with Somali custom for patrilineal naming. Instead, it showed that where, as here, the mother conceived in such proximity to her divorce, Muslim law provided that the child was regarded as the legitimate child of the mother's former husband and registered accordingly. In light of these findings the Court of Appeal held that there was no justification for changing the name and the judge had been wrong. Chadwick LJ commented that it would not be right 'without very good reason, to deny the child the benefit of a fiction which is conferred by custom and practice within a community for whom . . . illegitimacy is regarded as a much more serious stigma than divorce'.[895] This comment is interesting, as the court appears to recognise as a basis for its decision a cultural practice which adopts a view which Parliament has sought to eradicate from the laws of England and Wales. English law no longer regards illegitimacy as a stigma. The fact that the court sought out, and placed emphasis upon, the evidence of cultural practices in this case is also interesting, particularly when compared with *Dawson v Wearmouth*, in which the father's argument concerning the custom of patrilineal naming appeared only to strike a chord with Lord Jauncey. As Hale LJ observed in *Re R (Surname: Using Both Parents')*,[896] Lord Jauncey's view in *Dawson v Wearmouth* was a minority view. Her Ladyship added respectfully 'that the majority view was more consistent with the modern law'[897] and that it was:

> a matter of great sadness . . . that it is so often assumed, and even sometimes argued, that fathers need that outward and visible link in order to retain their relationship with, and commitment to, their child. That should not be the case. It is a poor sort of parent whose interest in and commitment to his child depends upon that child bearing his name. After all, that is a privilege which is not enjoyed by many mothers, even if they are not living with the child. They have to depend upon other more substantial things.[898]

The Court of Appeal's approach in *Re A* does not sit easily alongside *Dawson*. One wonders what the Court of Appeal's ruling in *Re A* would have been had all the expert evidence supported the father's case. Would that cultural context have justified an outcome different from Mr Dawson's case? The case law raises some obvious but important questions: can it be right that cultural considerations are given emphasis in one case and not the other, in relation to one culture and not another?

---

[893] Ibid, 328–9.    [894] [2003] EWCA Civ 56, [2003] 2 FLR 1.    [895] Ibid, [20].
[896] [2001] EWCA Civ 1344, [2001] 2 FLR 1358, CA.    [897] Ibid, [13].    [898] Ibid, [18].

As *Dawson v Wearmouth* makes clear, the status quo is clearly a factor for the court to consider. The court will wish to consider not only the registered surname but also the current legal and *de facto* position regarding the child's use of surname. Any changes of circumstances of the child since the original registration may be relevant. There may have been changes of name since registration, and the history regarding the child's surname is likely to be relevant. The reasons for any previous or proposed change will also be considered.

Reasons 'based on the fact that the child's name is or is not the same as the parent making the application do not generally carry much weight'.[899] One must be careful, however, how this is understood. Insofar as this is seen as a problem for the parent it is of little account.[900] So reasons such as the convenience of medical or school records are likely to be of little weight.[901] However, it has been said that the case law is not to be read as meaning 'that considerations of confusion, anxiety and embarrassment for the child were of little account'.[902] As we saw in the cases discussed earlier, the impact a name has may depend upon the facts and circumstances of the particular case. However, the courts have taken the view that, given the number of births outside marriage, generally there is no reason to suppose that a child will be 'embarrassed or particularly unusual in being registered at . . . school in a different name from the current surname of her mother'.[903] As Wilson J observed in *Re B (Change of Surname)*:[904]

> In these days of such frequent divorce and remarriage, of such frequent cohabitation outside marriage, and indeed increasingly of preservation of different surnames even within marriage, there is, in my view, no opprobrium nowadays upon a child who carries a surname different from that of the adults in his home.[905]

The lawfulness of any change of name may need to be considered in light of the Court of Appeal's view in *Dawson v Wearmouth* that a dispute about a child's surname 'must be referred to the court for determination whether or not there is a residence order in force and whoever has or has not parental responsibility'.[906]

*Re C (Change of Surname)*[907] held that where a surname has been lawfully changed[908] and is subsequently challenged, the correct approach is to look at whether the change has been in the child's interests.

The security of the foundation of a parent's name may be a relevant factor. In *Re R (Surname: Using Both Parents')*[909] the mother, who was intending to relocate to Spain, unilaterally had begun calling her child by the name of her own stepfather, which the mother had adopted since the child's birth. The judge ordered the change of name on the basis that it was in the child's interests to be brought up within a family with one name. On the father's appeal, Thorpe LJ commented that the relatively insecure foundation of the proposed name militated against change to that name.[910] This was a name which the maternal grandmother used informally but not for all formal purposes. Thorpe LJ pointed out that whether it was a name that the mother would bear in the long term was 'obviously an open question'.[911] Applying *Dawson v Wearmouth*, the Court of Appeal held that the judge had been wrong to order a change of surname, there being no evidence that a change would be in the

---

[899] *Re W (A Child) (Illegitimate Child: Change of Surname); Re A (A Child); Re B (Children)* [2001] Fam 1, CA at [9].

[900] *Re R (Surname: Using Both Parents')* [2001] EWCA Civ 1344, [2001] 2 FLR 1358 at [16].

[901] *Re T (Change of Surname)* [1998] 2 FLR 620 at 624A.

[902] *Re R (Surname: Using Both Parents')* [2001] EWCA Civ 1344, [2001] 2 FLR 1358 at [16].

[903] *Note: Re F (Child: Surname)* [1993] 2 FLR 837 at 838E *per* Ralph Gibson LJ.        [904] [1996] 1 FLR 791.

[905] Ibid, 795.

[906] [1998] 2 FLR 656 at 662–3. See Ward LJ at 664 endorsing the view that an order should be sought if there is a dispute.

[907] Ibid.

[908] On the facts of the case that conclusion might be doubted given that *Dawson v Wearmouth* was merely clarifying the existing legal position.

[909] [2001] EWCA Civ 1344, [2001] 2 FLR 1358, CA.        [910] Ibid, [8].        [911] Ibid.

child's interests. The court drew attention to the fact that it is customary in Spain for children to take two surnames, one from the paternal family and one from the maternal family. Hale LJ commented that 'parents and courts should be much more prepared to contemplate the use of both surnames in an appropriate case, because that is to recognise the importance of both parents'. The court thus urged the parents 'to consider the good sense of imitating Spanish custom'.[912]

A parent's change of name may be relevant. In *Re C (Change of Surname)*[913] the children, aged 8 and 7, had originally been known by their mother's maiden name. When the parents parted the father obtained a residence order and he subsequently caused the children to be known by his surname (not realising that he was prohibited from making this change). Proceedings were issued and the father was granted leave to cause the children to be known by his surname. The mother sought leave to appeal. She did not seek to prevent the daily use by the children of their father's name, but she did want them to retain her name for official purposes. Refusing the mother's application, the Court of Appeal noted that the mother had since married, had taken her husband's surname, and no longer used her maiden name. Therefore, although the stamp of parenthood reflected by a surname should not lightly be erased, retention of the mother's maiden name would not significantly assist in preserving the link between her and her children.

The child's wishes and feelings may prove important to the outcome in a particular case. In *Re PC (Change of Surname)*[914] Holman J said of children aged 12½ and 10 that 'it would be wrong of me even to contemplate trying to effect any reversal of the position which has now been reached without knowing their wishes and feelings and degree of understanding'. However, in *Re B (Change of Surname)*[915] the Court of Appeal confirmed the trial judge's refusal to permit a mother's application for the names of three teenage children to be changed to that of their stepfather despite the fact that they strongly wished this. The children were extremely hostile towards their father and to seeing him,[916] and contact had not taken place for five years. Since their mother's remarriage, the children had been known informally by their stepfather's surname, although formal records (such as school reports) bore their father's surname. The children reported that this situation was a source of embarrassment. Wilson J remarked that 'orders nowadays which run flatly counter to the wishes of normal children aged 16, 14 and 12 are virtually unknown to family law'.[917] However, his Lordship went on to draw a distinction between an application by the children's mother to lift an existing prohibition on change of name and imposing an order on the children in the teeth of their opposition.[918] He pointed out that the order did not oblige the children to do anything which they were refusing to do and that they could not be prevented from informally using their stepfather's name. However, he asserted that only the father's name should be recorded on formal documents and that the order prevented the mother from causing the children to be known by a new surname. He concluded that the grant of leave:

> would have sent out a wholly inappropriate message to the children, namely that the court agreed with them that their father was of the past, not of the present. Save following adoption, a father, while he lives, is always of the present.[919]

Despite this reasoning, which emanated from the basic principle that it is of fundamental importance for every child to have an enduring relationship with both parents, the decision sits uneasily with Lord Scarman's opinion in *Gillick v West Norfolk and Wisbech Area Health Authority*.[920] In light of that

---

[912]  Ibid, [12] *per* Thorpe LJ, echoed by Hale LJ at [20].     [913]  [1998] 1 FLR 549.

[914]  [1997] 2 FLR 730, FD.     [915]  [1996] 1 FLR 791, CA.

[916]  As demonstrated by their practice of destroying birthday and Christmas cards the father had sent, their refusal to travel on local buses in case the father, who was a bus driver, was driving, and their habit of referring to the father as 'him at Blyth'.

[917]  [1996] 1 FLR 791, 794.

[918]  Ibid, 794–5. The prohibition had been automatically imposed upon the making of a custody order to the mother at divorce.

[919]  Ibid, 795–6.     [920]  [1986] AC 112.

decision, was it right that the court should take the view that it had an unfettered right to impose its own view of welfare on competent adolescent children in order to prevent them from choosing the name by which they wished to be known formally? Adolescent children are usually very certain that they know their own minds, know what is good for them, and know what will cause them harm. It may be that the children's decision in *Re B (Change of Surname)* was mistaken, and that they would come to regret it. But their choice was relatively harmless (in the sense that it would not lead them positively to suffer harm in the same way that, say, refusal of medical treatment might). If there was ever a situation, therefore, to which the principles in *Gillick* ought to apply, this was it. Having said that, this was undoubtedly a difficult case and Wilson J's anxiety that to agree to the change of name would be interpreted by the child as an endorsement of the children's negative opinion of the father is understandable. However, that might have been handled by carefully giving reasons for the court's decision. Against the court's approach is the danger that, when the determined adolescent's wishes are thwarted, resulting resentment may be counterproductive to fostering good interpersonal relationships with the father. However, on the facts of the case, perhaps the relationships could not have got any worse.

The parents' marital status is also a factor. In *Re W (A Child) (Illegitimate Child: Change of Surname); Re A (A Child); Re B (Children)*[921] Butler-Sloss LJ, having provided a useful summary of the House of Lords decision in *Dawson v Wearmouth*, added:

> In the case of a child whose parents were married to each other, the fact of the marriage is important[922] and I would suggest that there would have to be strong reasons to change the name from the father's surname if the child was so registered . . . Where the child's parents were not married to each other, the mother has control over registration. Consequently on an application to change the surname of the child, the degree of commitment of the father to the child, the quality of contact, if it occurs, between father and child, the existence or absence of parental responsibility are all relevant factors to take into account.[923]

*Re A (A Child)* and *Re B (Children)*[924] illustrate some circumstances in which a change from the father's registered name may be warranted. In *Re A (A Child)* a boy, aged 10, had exactly the same name as his father, who was described as 'a notorious criminal'. The father had been sentenced to 21 years' imprisonment for offences of violence and the earliest he would be released from prison would be when the boy was 17. The parents had divorced and the mother sought a specific issue order to change the boy's name to her maiden name. The district judge made the order, having found that the mother had a genuine, deep-seated fear that, because of the father's notoriety, the boy was at real risk of harm from being taunted, victimised, or the subject of attack if his identity became known within the locality to which she had recently moved. The district judge's order was overturned by a circuit judge and the mother appealed to the Court of Appeal, which restored the district judge's decision.[925] In *Re B (Children)* the father of two young girls had been convicted of two offences of indecent assault of a 17-year-old girl and had pleaded guilty to indecent assault of

---

[921] [2001] Fam 1, CA.

[922] Compare *Re C (Change of Surname)* [1998] 2 FLR 656 at 660C–D: 'The judge's reference to finding more merit in the father's case had he not declined to marry the mother is an irrelevant consideration'.

[923] [2001] Fam 1, CA at 7G. See eg *Re P (Parental Responsibility)* [1997] 2 FLR 722, CA, discussed in Chapter 7. The children's father had been denied a parental responsibility order because of his irresponsibility in committing an offence of robbery while on home leave from prison. As part of a fresh start in a new town, the children were using the mother's maiden name, by which the children were now known at school. Ward LJ agreed with counsel that the fact that the father had failed in his application for parental responsibility much reduced his prospects of success on his application for change of name.

[924] [2001] Fam 1, CA.

[925] See also *AB v BB and Children (Through their Children's Guardian)* [2013] EWHC 227 (Fam) in which the mother feared the father, who had been cautioned for child cruelty and imprisoned for assault occasioning actual bodily harm to the mother. Theis J made an order for indirect contact by way of the father's letters delivered via Cafcass, and permitting a change of surname to prevent the father finding out where the family resided. See also in a public law context, *Re M, T, P, K and B (Care: Change of Name)* [2000] 2 FLR 645 (where the children were frightened their family would locate them).

his 11-year-old niece. The mother applied to change the children's surnames to her own name. The judge made the requested order in light of the peripheral part the father was likely to play in the future life of the two girls, which was upheld by the Court of Appeal.

Another case in which it was held to be necessary to permit a change of name is *Re S (Change of Names: Cultural Factors)*.[926] The mother was a Muslim who, at the age of 17 had eloped with a 22-year-old Sikh man to marry at Gretna Green. The couple subsequently had a child, who was 3 years old at the hearing. There were considerable tensions between the parents' respective religions and cultures and the mother's actions had been attended by great shame and anger on the part of her family, which had disowned her. The parents' relationship broke down and the mother became reconciled with her family and wished to move back to her original community. The mother wished to make a fresh start, eliminating the father from her life. The child had recognisably Sikh names and the mother applied to change the child's names so that he was not stamped within the Muslim community as a Sikh and she was not stamped as the 'slag' who had a relationship with a Sikh.[927] There was expert evidence to the effect that in order for the mother and child to be able to integrate into the community the child would need to be known by Muslim names. Wilson J therefore ordered that the child should have Muslim names for use on a day-to-day basis, but that the child should retain his Sikh names formally (eg for the purpose of obtaining a passport) in order to maintain his connection with that part of his family and cultural background.

### 5.15  **Restricting applications for section 8 orders under section 91(14)**

The court has power to prevent applications without the prior leave of the court. This may be achieved by exercising the inherent jurisdiction of the High Court[928] or a statutory power within section 91(14) of the Children Act 1989. This provides:

> On disposing of any application for an order under this Act, the court may (whether or not it makes any other order in response to the application) order that no application for an order under this Act of any specified kind may be made with respect to the child concerned by any person named in the order without leave of the court.

As Waite LJ observed in *B v B (Residence Order: Restricting Applications)*,[929] section 91(14), tucked away amongst 17 subsections which are largely administrative in character:

> represents a substantial interference with the fundamental principle of public policy enshrined in our unwritten constitution that all citizens enjoy a right of unrestricted access to the Queen's courts.

In *Re P (A Minor) (Residence Order: Child's Welfare)*,[930] however, Butler-Sloss LJ explained that it is only 'a partial restriction', which does not breach Article 6 of the ECHR, in that it merely prohibits an immediate inter partes hearing. The purpose of the bar is to prevent issues relating to a child's upbringing being the subject of constant, disruptive, unnecessary, and often highly contentious litigation.[931] It thereby protects the other parties and the child from being drawn into the proposed proceedings unless or until a court has ruled that the application should be allowed to proceed.[932] An order made under section 91(14) should do nothing to prevent a meritorious application.

---

[926] [2001] 2 FLR 1005 (Wilson J). See S. Jivraj and D. Herman, 'It is Difficult for a White Judge to Understand: Orientalism, Racialisation, and Christianity in English Child Welfare Cases' [2009] Child and Family Law Quarterly 283.
[927] [2001] 2 FLR 1005 at 1008.     [928] See eg *Re H (Child Orders: Restricting Applications)* [1991] FCR 896.
[929] [1997] 1 FLR 139 at 146.
[930] [2000] Fam 15, *sub nom Re P (Section 91(14) Guidelines) (Residence and Religious Heritage)* [1999] 2 FLR 573.
[931] See eg *Re N (Section 91(14) Order)* [1996] 1 FLR 356.     [932] [2000] Fam 15 at 38.

Notice that section 91(14) requires that the court specify the order(s) to which it is to apply[933] and that it only applies to orders under the Children Act 1989.[934] An absolute prohibition on making any application to the court 'would have to be made under the inherent jurisdiction of the court'.[935] In *Stringer v Stringer*[936] the Court of Appeal held that it is not permissible to attach any conditions to a section 91(14) order except those allowed by the section itself, that is relating to the type of relief to which it is to apply and its duration. The court was concerned that attaching conditions could have the effect, in a case in which the condition might not be achievable, of imposing an absolute bar on applying to the court which was not the purpose of section 91(14).[937] The court overturned a judge's order to the extent that it required a psychological or psychiatric report indicating that the father had engaged in treatment before the father was allowed to apply for leave. While no such condition can be attached to a section 91(14) order, the Court of Appeal observed that it is plainly permissible for a judge to tell a litigant that unless he or she addresses a particular issue and can show that he or she has addressed it, any application for permission to apply is unlikely to succeed.[938] Thus a non-binding incentive for change can be given.

An application for a section 91(14) order should usually be issued in advance on notice and be supported by evidence.[939] There may, however, be cases which require an exception to that approach. For example, the need for an order may only become apparent during the hearing,[940] whether upon a party's application or arising on the court's own initiative. In *Re C (Litigant in Person: Section 91(14) Order)*[941] Wall LJ said that it is of the utmost importance that parties or those affected by the order, particularly if they are litigants in person, should '(a) understand that such an application is being made, or that consideration is being given to making a s 91(14) order; (b) understand the meaning and effect of such an order; and (c) have a proper opportunity to make submissions to the court in answer to the application or to the suggestion that a s 91(14) order be made.'[942] A proper opportunity for a litigant in person to understand the effect of the order and to respond to it may require an adjournment for the application to be made on notice in writing.[943]

In *Re P (A Minor) (Residence Order: Child's Welfare)*[944] Butler-Sloss LJ, reviewing earlier authorities, provided useful guidance, in the context of section 91(14) orders, on the power to restrict access to the court.[945] In order to illustrate her Ladyship's guidance by reference to other case law and to deal with subsequent case law developments, it is convenient to deal with the guidance under two subheadings: (i) when section 91(14) orders may be made and (ii) the duration of orders.

---

[933] Thus it is wrong to make an order at large without specifying the orders to which it applied.

[934] *Re M (Education: Section 91(14) Order)* [2007] EWCA Civ 1550, [2008] 2 FLR 404.

[935] Butler-Sloss LJ in *Re P (A Minor) (Residence Order: Child's Welfare)*, citing *Re R (Residence: Contact: Restricting Applications)* [1998] 1 FLR 749 at 760 *per* Wilson J.

[936] [2006] EWCA Civ 1617, [2007] 1 FLR 1532.

[937] The court's reasoning on this point was provided in its judgment on the application for permission to appeal which preceded the appeal: see *Re S (Permission to Seek Relief)* [2006] EWCA Civ 1190, [2007] 1 FLR 482 at [73]–[75].

[938] *Stringer v Stringer* [2006] EWCA Civ 1617, [2007] 1 FLR 1532 at [10].

[939] See *Re C-J (Section 91(14) Order)* [2006] EWHC 1491 (Fam), [2006] 2 FLR 1213 at [19]; *Re S (Permission to Seek Relief)* [2006] EWCA Civ 1190, [2007] 1 FLR 482 at [91]; *Re C (Litigant in Person: Section 91(14) Order)* [2009] EWCA Civ 674, [2009] 2 FLR 1461 at [13].

[940] *Re S (Permission to Seek Relief)* [2006] EWCA Civ 1190, [2007] 1 FLR 482 at [91].

[941] [2009] EWCA Civ 674, [2009] 2 FLR 1461.

[942] Ibid, [13]. For an example of an order made in breach of the guidance in *Re C (Litigant in Person: Section 91(14) Order)* [2009] EWCA Civ 674, [2009] 2 FLR 1461, see *Re A (Contact: Section 91(14))* [2009] EWCA Civ 1548, [2010] 2 FLR 151, in which Wilson LJ commented at [17], that 'this court spends a surprising and unfortunate amount of its time in reversing orders under s 91(14) made on the inappropriately summary basis here exemplified'.

[943] *Re C (Litigant in Person: Section 91(14) Order)* [2009] EWCA Civ 674, [2009] 2 FLR 1461 at [13].

[944] [2000] Fam 15.

[945] The guidelines apply also to restrictions made under the inherent jurisdiction: see *Harris v Harris; Attorney-General v Harris* [2001] 2 FLR 895, FD.

### 5.15.1 When may section 91(14) orders be made?

In *Re P (A Minor) (Residence Order: Child's Welfare)*[946] Butler-Sloss LJ explained that the power to restrict applications involves an exercise of discretion in which the court must weigh all the relevant circumstances, treating the child's welfare as the paramount consideration.[947] An 'important consideration is that to impose a restriction is a statutory intrusion into the right of a party to bring proceedings before the court and to be heard in matters affecting his/her child.' Accordingly:

> The power is therefore to be used with great care and sparingly, the exception and not the rule . . . It is generally to be seen as a useful weapon of last resort in cases of repeated and unreasonable applications.

*Re R (Residence: Contact: Restricting Applications)*[948] graphically illustrates the frequency with which some parents may seek to bring proceedings under section 8 of the Children Act 1989. Between 1993 and 1996 a father had made no fewer than 18 applications for orders—15 to review contact arrangements with his child and three for residence. When hearing the father's latest application, the judge refused to make a residence order and made an order under section 91(14) restricting his right to bring further applications before the court. Dismissing the father's appeal against this restriction, the Court of Appeal held that when exercising its discretion to make an order under section 91(14), the best interests of the child must be weighed against the applicant's fundamental freedom of access to the courts without going through an initial screening process. The court found that this particular father was committed to his child and had steadily built up a relationship with him. It acknowledged that a section 91(14) order was a substantial interference with the applicant's fundamental right to raise issues affecting his child's welfare before a court, but it ruled that such a right had to be exercised consistently with the welfare of the child. In this regard, a court had to take account of the emotional effect on the residential parent of frequent applications to change a child's residence. As Wilson J said, 'nothing can raise the temperature of a family dispute more than an ill-considered, unfounded application for a residence order . . . Even worse can be the effect of a residence application when the applicant expresses himself or herself in intemperate and bilious terms.'[949]

Where the child's welfare dictates, the court can also make an order under section 91(14) where there is no past history of making unreasonable applications.[950] In such cases 'the court will need to be satisfied first that the facts go beyond the commonly encountered need for a time to settle to a regime ordered by the court and the all too common situation where there is animosity between the adults in dispute or between the local authority and the family and, secondly, that there is a serious risk that, without the imposition of the restriction, the child or the primary carers will be subject to unacceptable strain'.[951] For example, in *Re F (Restrictions on Applications)*[952] the mother had obtained an injunction under Part IV of the Family Law Act 1996 restraining the father from violence, threats of violence, from harassment, from communication except via solicitors, and from approaching within 100 metres of the mother's home. In light of the Cafcass officer's recommendation that face-to-face contact would 'alarm and unsettle the children', the father withdrew his application for contact. The judge added a direction that the father should not be permitted to apply without leave for a period of two-and-a-half years. Drawing attention to the guidance in *Re P*, the Court of Appeal held that the absence of repeated applications did not make the order wrong in principle; the judge had been entitled to take into account the history of the case from its inception and to protect the children's welfare in the way he had.[953]

---

[946] [2000] Fam 15.     [947] That is, s 91(14) is to be read together with s 1(1) of the Children Act 1989.

[948] [1998] 1 FLR 749.     [949] Ibid, 759.

[950] *Re F (Children) (Restriction on Applications)* [2005] EWCA Civ 499, [2005] 2 FLR 950.

[951] *Re P (A Minor) (Residence Order: Child's Welfare)* [2000] Fam 15. See also *B v B (Residence Order: Restricting Applications)* [1997] 1 FLR 139 at 145, citing *Re H (Child Orders: Restricting Applications)* [1991] FCR 896 at 899.

[952] [2005] EWCA Civ 499, [2005] 2 FLR 950.

[953] See also *Re J (A Child) (Restriction on Applications)* [2007] EWCA Civ 906, [2008] 1 FLR 369.

However, it is not appropriate to make a section 91(14) order simply to achieve 'breathing space'.[954] In *Re G (Residence: Restriction on Further Applications)*[955] the Court of Appeal over-turned an order made on that basis. The father sought shared residence but was awarded instead generous contact. The judge, taking the view that the father was entrenched in his wish for 50/50 shared care, imposed a section 91(14) restriction. The Court of Appeal pointed out that the father's applications had been reasonable, there was no evidence of harm to the child, nor had the mother reached 'saturation point' so that she was suffering in a way which impacted adversely on the child's welfare. The court said that the breathing space should be achieved simply by giving the order time to work itself out.[956]

### 5.15.2 Duration of a section 91(14) order

In *Re P (A Minor) (Residence Order: Child's Welfare)*[957] Butler-Sloss LJ explained that a restriction may be imposed with or without limitation of time. Unless revoked, the latter type of order will run until it ceases upon the child attaining 18 years of age.[958] In *Re S (Permission to Seek Relief)*[959] the Court of Appeal added that such an order (or indeed orders expressed to last until a child is 16) should be 'the exception rather than the rule' and 'the reasons for making them should be fully and carefully set out'.[960] Of course, all section 91(14) orders are exceptional, so as Wilson LJ pointed out in *Re J (A Child) (Restriction on Applications)*,[961] this means only that along the spectrum of exceptional cases 'orders of such duration should be made only in respect of cases at the egregious end, which merit the strongest degree of forensic protection for the child from further ill-founded conflict'.[962] This is because in the majority of cases the use of section 91(14) is still part of the court's 'over-arching strategy, which is to preserve and foster relationships wherever possible'.[963] Although there may be a minority of cases in which the court has reached the end of the road, in most cases, therefore, the court will need carefully to consider whether the duration of the order is compatible with its objective of restoring the parent/child relationship.[964]

As Butler-Sloss P explained in *Re P*:

> The degree of restriction should be proportionate to the harm it is intended to avoid. Therefore the court imposing the restriction should carefully consider the extent of the restriction to be imposed and specify, where appropriate, the type of application to be restrained and the duration of the order.[965]

As Wilson J observed in the Court of Appeal in *Re R (Residence: Contact: Restricting Applications)*[966] the setting of a term to the order is not without its potential difficulties. For example, apart from the difficulty in forecasting what would be the appropriate length of time before the applicant's rights revived, an order of fixed duration almost invites a fresh application at the expiry of the specified term.

In *Re B (Section 91(14) Order: Duration)*[967] a father applied for direct contact with his 9-year-old daughter, with whom he had not had contact for three years, and then only for four periods of

---

[954] *Re G (Residence: Restriction on Further Applications)* [2008] EWCA Civ 1468, [2009] 1 FLR 894. See also *Re C-J (Section 91(14) Order)* [2006] EWHC 1491 (Fam), [2006] 2 FLR 1213, FD (Coleridge J) and *B v B (Residence Order: Restricting Applications)* [1997] 1 FLR 139, CA—not to be used because the judge feels that 'the dust should be allowed to settle and a quietus be imposed on the family differences' (at 146 *per* Waite LJ).

[955] [2008] EWCA Civ 1468, [2009] 1 FLR 894.

[956] *Re G (Residence: Restriction on Further Applications)* [2008] EWCA Civ 1468, [2009] 1 FLR 894 at [14].

[957] [2000] Fam 15.

[958] See s 93(13) and *Re J (A Child) Restriction on Applications)* [2008] 1 FLR 369 at [16].

[959] [2006] EWCA Civ 1190, [2007] 1 FLR 482.    [960] Ibid, [85].

[961] [2007] EWCA Civ 906, [2008] 1 FLR 369.    [962] Ibid, [17].

[963] [2006] EWCA Civ 1190, [2007] 1 FLR 482 at [90].

[964] *Re B (Section 91(14) Order: Duration)* [2004] 1 FLR 871 at [16].    [965] [2000] Fam 15 at 38.

[966] [1998] 1 FLR 749.    [967] [2004] 1 FLR 871.

supervised contact. The judge made an order for indirect contact, which included the local authority's assistance in preparing a video about him and his life to show the daughter. The judge then added a direction under section 91(14) that there should be no further applications for the remainder of the child's minority because of the risk of emotional damage to the child. Allowing an appeal against that order, the Court of Appeal held that the objective of the court to restore the relationship was 'best achieved by limiting the s 91(14) prohibition to any application for direct contact and by setting the moratorium at a 2-year duration to enable the bespoke solution of video contact to be given a fair chance to shift attitudes and inhibitions'.[968] Similarly, in *Re D (A Child)*[969] it was held to be wrong in principle to impose a section 91(14) order for a period of five years where the consequence of doing so would make it very difficult for the father to seek contact once that period had expired. The order would be replaced by an order for a period of two years, permitting the father to maintain indirect contact during that period.

The circumstances of a particular case may, however, warrant an order which is imposed to last until the child's majority. In *Re J (A Child) (Restriction on Applications)*[970] the parents of a 12½-year-old severely autistic boy had been involved in a forensic struggle over him on and off for his whole life, initially in private law proceedings and latterly in care proceedings. A care order had been made because the mother's volatility and distress in dealing with the child's special difficulties made it inappropriate for him to be in her home. The local authority placed the child with the father. The mother sought to discharge the care order and during the hearing made several statements that she would never accept the care order. In those circumstances, Munby J made an order under section 91(14), to run for five and a half years until the child reached his majority, that the mother should not be permitted to apply to discharge the care order. This was upheld by the Court of Appeal.

### 5.15.3 Leave applications where a section 91(14) restriction exists

When a court is determining whether to grant an application for leave to apply for the section 91(14) restriction to be lifted, or for leave to proceed notwithstanding the bar, what factors should influence the court's discretion? In *Re A (Application for Leave)*[971] the Court of Appeal held that a Recorder had been wrong to apply the criteria in section 10(9) of the Children Act 1989 to such an application. One reason given by the court was that very often the person who has been barred by section 91(14) will be an applicant who would otherwise be entitled to apply for a section 8 order under section 10(4) or (5) of the Children Act 1989. In such cases it would not seem right to apply the section 10(9) leave criteria, which include the applicant's connection with the child. Thorpe LJ held therefore that permission for leave to apply in the context of a section 91(14) bar is a distinct application and his Lordship favoured 'the simplest of tests': 'Does this application demonstrate that there is any need for renewed judicial investigation? If yes, then leave should be granted.'[972] In *Re P (A Minor) (Residence Order: Child's Welfare)*[973] Butler-Sloss LJ expressed the approach slightly differently: 'the applicant must persuade the judge that he has an arguable case with some chance of success'.[974] In *Re S (Permission to Seek Relief)*,[975] however, the Court of Appeal saw no inconsistency in those respective approaches, which were seen as complementing each other: a judge will not 'see a need for renewed judicial investigation into an application which he does not think sets out an arguable case'.[976] The court went on to say that where a section 91(14) order has been imposed because of particular conduct, that conduct must have been addressed if the application for permission to apply is to warrant a renewed judicial investigation or to present an arguable case.[977]

---

[968] Ibid, [16]. See also *Radovanovic v Austria* (App no 42703/98) (2005) 41 EHRR 6, EtCHR.
[969] [2010] EWCA Civ 470.      [970] [2007] EWCA Civ 906, [2008] 1 FLR 369.
[971] [1998] 1 FLR 1.     [972] Ibid, 4.     [973] [2000] Fam 15.
[974] Ibid, 38. See also *Re G (Child Case: Parental Involvement)* [1996] 1 FLR 857, CA.
[975] [2006] EWCA Civ 1190, [2007] 1 FLR 482.     [976] Ibid, [78].     [977] Ibid, [79].

There are statements in *Re N (Section 91(14) Order)*[978] and in *Re A (Application for Leave)*[979] that an application for permission to apply should be determined inter partes. However, in *Re S (Permission to Seek Relief)*[980] the Court of Appeal said that it is open to a judge in certain sensitive circumstances[981] to direct that in the first instance an application is not to be served on the other party and be considered by the judge on the papers,[982] although an applicant for permission to appeal should not be denied an oral hearing if he or she seeks one.[983]

### 5.16 Local authority applications for section 8 orders

A local authority may seek a court's leave to apply for a specific issue or prohibited steps order.[984] This affords local authorities the opportunity to seek a court's assistance in making a ruling on one aspect of the exercise of parental responsibility, without otherwise interfering in the day-to-day control exercised by parents, and others, over a child's upbringing. This raises questions about which proceedings are the most appropriate when a local authority is the applicant. Should it apply under the public law provisions in Parts IV and V of the Children Act 1989 or for a specific issue order?[985]

In *Nottinghamshire County Council v P*[986] the Court of Appeal held that a local authority which believed a child to be at risk of suffering significant harm should proceed by way of an application for a care or supervision order and not use the private law provisions. This ruling means that where a local authority takes the view that it is safe to leave a child with one parent, but that the other parent presents a serious risk to the child, the local authority must seek to persuade the caring parent to apply for orders which will be effective to protect the child. This is likely to mean orders under section 8 and under legislation which permits a court to restrict a parent's access to the home.[987] Where the caring parent refuses, or is too frightened, to take such action, the local authority then has no alternative but to apply for an order in care proceedings.[988] Where a local authority will not take such steps, it appears that a court is powerless to direct it to do so.

The choice of which proceedings are appropriate will depend on the nature of the local authority's concerns about the child. It has been said that where a child's parents are 'caring, committed and capable and where only one issue arises for decision, albeit one of the gravest significance' to the child's welfare, it is wholly inappropriate for a court to make even an interim care order.[989] Such single issues have tended to arise in cases in which all persons with parental responsibility are refusing to agree to a child receiving medical treatment because the treatment runs counter to the parents' most profound and sincerely held beliefs. Usually it will be the local authority which will initiate legal proceedings on behalf of the child because it is under a statutory duty to intervene when a child is at risk of significant harm. In *Re R (A Minor) (Blood Transfusion)*[990] the issue to be resolved was whether a child should have a blood transfusion. Booth J ruled that a local authority should make an application for leave to apply for a specific issue order where such an application is possible[991] and where there is no need for any other public law order to safeguard the child's welfare. It was held that such cases should be determined, wherever possible, by a High Court judge.

---

[978] [1996] 1 FLR 356.      [979] [1998] 1 FLR 1 at 3E–F.      [980] [2006] EWCA Civ 1190, [2007] 1 FLR 482.

[981] Eg in the case of a fragile resident parent who may be adversely affected by the application which may be unmeritorious or unlikely to succeed.

[982] [2006] EWCA Civ 1190, [2007] 1 FLR 482 at [94].      [983] Ibid, [95].

[984] Except when it already has a care order, and the Children Act 1989, s 9(1) therefore applies.

[985] Or, indeed, for leave to apply to invoke the inherent jurisdiction of the High Court, discussed in Section 7.

[986] [1993] 2 FLR 134.      [987] See Family Law Act 1996, Pt IV, discussed in Chapter 3.

[988] An exclusion requirement could be attached to an emergency protection order or interim care order, thus preserving the child's residence with the parent who is not a risk to the child: see further Chapter 10.

[989] *Re O (A Minor) (Medical Treatment)* [1993] 2 FLR 149.      [990] [1993] 2 FLR 757.

[991] Sometimes, for example when a child is in care, it will not be possible to obtain a specific issue order: see Children Act 1989, s 9 and the discussion in Section 7.

Where a child is already the subject of a care order or interim care order, the local authority already has parental responsibility for the child and could exercise parental responsibility to consent to treatment.[992] However, the courts have taken the view that where such a decision is to be made against the strongly held beliefs of the child's parents, it should be made by a High Court judge.[993] If the child is in the care of a local authority a court is prevented by section 9(1) of the Children Act 1989 from making any section 8 order other than a residence arrangements order. Consequently, a specific issue order cannot be made in relation to a child in care. This was the position confronting the High Court in *Re O (A Minor) (Medical Treatment)*.[994] The parents who were Jehovah's Witnesses were refusing to authorise blood transfusions for their gravely ill child. A family proceedings court made an emergency protection order in ex parte proceedings followed by an interim care order, and the case was then transferred for hearing to the High Court. Johnson J was asked to express a view about the most appropriate legal framework in which such decisions should be made. He agreed with counsel, who had been unanimous in rejecting all proceedings governed by the Children Act 1989, and ruled that the inherent jurisdiction of the High Court was the only appropriate route in the circumstances.[995] In such a case a local authority should make an application under section 100(3) of the Children Act 1989 for leave to invoke the exercise of the court's inherent jurisdiction. We explain this jurisdiction in the final section of this chapter, at Section 7.

## 6 International child abduction

Earlier in the chapter we explored the courts' approach to granting permission for a parent to relocate from the jurisdiction. In some cases, however, children are removed from the jurisdiction without the necessary lawful authority and in circumstances which disrupt their attachment to the left-behind parent.[996] Not surprisingly, research shows that for some children parental child abduction can have significant negative effects on their emotional well-being and relationships throughout their life.[997] Most international abductions (about 70 per cent) are by mothers as the primary carer of the child, rather than cases of a non-resident parent snatching a child,[998] and in general abduction appears to be a growing problem.[999] When will removal of a child be unlawful?

---

[992] An emergency protection order made under the Children Act 1989, s 44, also confers limited parental responsibility on the local authority, and this can be exercised insofar as necessary to safeguard the child's welfare.

[993] Eg *Re R (A Minor) (Blood Transfusion)* [1993] 2 FLR 757 and *Re O (A Minor) (Medical Treatment)* [1993] 2 FLR 149.

[994] [1993] 2 FLR 149.

[995] Recall that the proceedings are family proceedings, and the High Court is entitled to make any section 8 order when exercising its inherent jurisdiction.

[996] See generally, R. Schuz, *The Hague Child Abduction Convention A Critical Analysis* (Oxford: Hart Publishing, 2013); T. Kruger, *International Child Abduction The Inadequacies of the Law* (Oxford: Hart Publishing, 2011); K. Trimmings, *Child Abduction Within the European Union* (Oxford: Hart Publishing, 2013). Other titles, albeit now somewhat dated, are P. Beaumont and P. McEleavy, *The Hague Convention on International Child Abduction* (Oxford: Oxford University Press, 1999) and A.-M. Hutchinson and H Setright, *International Parental Child Abduction* (2nd edn, Bristol: Jordan Publishing, 2003). Reunite, the leading non-governmental organisation dealing with child abduction in this jurisdiction, has a website with lots of useful information: see www.reunite.org.

[997] See M. Freeman, *International Child Abduction—The Effects* (Reunite, 2006).

[998] See N. V. Lowe, *A Statistical Analysis of Applications Made in 2008 Under the Hague Convention of 25 October 1980 on the Civil Aspects of International Child Abduction* (Hague Conference on Private International Law, 2011). See also *Re E (Children) (Abduction: Custody Appeal)* [2011] UKSC 27, [2011] 2 FLR 758 at [6], *per* Baroness Hale.

[999] For evidence of increasing numbers of applications to courts for return of children, see N. V. Lowe, *A Statistical Analysis of Applications Made in 2008 Under the Hague Convention of 25 October 1980 on the Civil Aspects of International Child Abduction* (Hague Conference on Private International Law, 2011). Comparing data of 2003 and 2008 surveys there has been a 44 per cent increase in the total number of applications made under the Convention with a 45 per cent increase in return applications.

## 6.1  A criminal offence: the Child Abduction Act 1984

Under s 1 of the Child Abduction Act 1984 it is an offence for anyone 'connected with a child'[1000] to take or send a child under the age of 16 years out of the UK without the consent of each person who is the child's mother, father (if he has parental responsibility), guardian, special guardian, anyone named in a child arrangements order as a person with whom the child is to live, or the leave of the court. Section 1(5) provides that the offence is not committed if the child is taken or sent:

(a)  . . . in the belief that the other person—
   (i)  has consented; or
   (ii)  would consent if he was aware of all the relevant circumstances; or
(b)  he has taken all reasonable steps to communicate with the other person but has been unable to communicate with him; or
(c)  the other person has unreasonably refused to consent.

There is also an exception where a child arrangements order is in force—which permits a person named in a child arrangements order as a person with whom the child is to live to remove a child for a period of up to one month.[1001]

## 6.2  Preventing abduction

A police officer has power to arrest anyone he or she reasonably suspects of attempting to take a child out of the UK unlawfully. If satisfied that the risk of removal is real and imminent, ie, within 48 hours,[1002] the police will inform the Border Agency that the child is at risk through its 'All Ports Warning System', with a view to preventing the child's removal. Unlawful removal might also be deterred by a prohibited steps order prohibiting removal,[1003] or by making the child a ward of court, or by way of orders for the control of passports, such as for their surrender or preventing their issue.[1004]

## 6.3  Recovery of abducted children

If prevention is not successful, the wronged parent may need to take legal steps to recover the child. The principal Convention dealing with international child abduction is the Hague Convention on the Civil Aspects of International Child Abduction ('the Hague Convention') which at the time of writing has 90 contracting States.[1005] The Convention seeks to regulate the return of children abducted to States which are parties to the Convention. It was implemented in the UK by the Child Abduction and Custody Act 1985. In relation to States of the European Union (except for

---

[1000]  Section 1(2) provides that: '[a] person is connected with a child for the purposes of this section if—

(a)  he is a parent of the child; or
(b)  in the case of a child whose parents were not married to each other at the time of his birth, there are reasonable grounds for believing that he is the father of the child; or
(c)  he is a guardian of the child; or
(ca)  he is a special guardian of the child; or
(d)  he is a person named in a child arrangements order as a person with whom the child will live is in force with respect to the child; or
(e)  he has custody of the child.'

[1001]  Children Act 1989, s 13(2).

[1002]  *Practice Direction (Child: Removal from Jurisdiction)* [1986] 1 All ER 983, [1986] 2 FLR 89 and Home Office Circular 21/1986.

[1003]  See eg *Re D (A Minor) (Child: Removal from Jurisdiction)* [1992] 1 All ER 892.

[1004]  For discussion of the scope of these powers, see *Re B (A Child: Evidence: Passport Order)* [2014] EWCA Civ 843, [2015] 1 FLR 871.

[1005]  See the Hague Conference on Private International Law website, at www.hcch.net/.

Denmark) the text of the Hague Convention is applied in a slightly modified form by a European Union Regulation,[1006] known as the Brussels II bis Regulation. The Brussels Regulation is concerned with rules of jurisdiction on matters relating to parental responsibility and Article 11 deals explicitly with child abduction. The modifications are highlighted at appropriate points in the discussion of the Hague Convention which follows.

The Child Abduction and Custody Act 1985 also implemented the European Convention on Recognition and Enforcement of Decisions concerning Custody of Children and Restoration of Custody of Children. This European Convention (known as the 'Luxembourg' Convention) applies only as between certain European States, and is concerned with the reciprocal enforcement of court orders concerning custody through a process of registering the original order in a court of the Contracting State[1007] to which the child has been removed. The court of that State thereby acquires powers of enforcement of the order,[1008] enabling return of the child.[1009] The European Convention has, however, now largely been superseded in practice by the Hague Convention and the Brussels Regulation, on which we focus next.

## 6.4 **The Hague Convention on the Civil Aspects of International Child Abduction**

An object of the Hague Convention is 'to secure the prompt return of children wrongfully removed to or retained in any Contracting State'.[1010] It is concerned to ensure that any dispute as to a child's care is determined in the place with which the child has currently most connection, and that the alleged abductor is denied any tactical advantage from the abduction.[1011] Indeed, the Contracting State to which the child has been removed or in which it has been retained shall not decide on the merits of rights of custody until it has been determined that the child is not to be returned under this Convention.[1012]

The Convention applies in relation to any child under the age of 16 years who was habitually resident in one Contracting State,[1013] and has been wrongfully removed to or retained in another Contracting State. The crucial first question, therefore, is what the child's habitual residence was *immediately before* the alleged wrongful removal or retention.

---

[1006]  Council Regulation (EC) No 2201/2003 of 27 November 2003 Concerning Jurisdiction and the Recognition and Enforcement of Judgments in Matrimonial Matters and in Matters of Parental Responsibility (2003) OJ L 338/1.

[1007]  There are limited circumstances in which a court may refuse to register an order for procedural irregularity or 'where it is found by reason of a change of circumstances including the passage of time but not including a mere change in the residence of the child after an improper removal, the effects of the original decision are manifestly no longer in accordance with the welfare of the child'. See Articles 9 and 10, and for examples, *Re M (Child Abduction) (European Convention)* [1994] 1 FLR 551 and *Re L (Abduction: European Convention: Access)* [1999] 2 FLR 1089.

[1008]  Child Abduction and Custody Act 1985, s 18.

[1009]  There is a similar process for recognising and enforcing orders as between jurisdictions within the United Kingdom under the Family Law Act 1986. See s 25, and for the background, Law Com Report No 138 *Custody of Children—Jurisdiction and Enforcement within the United Kingdom* (1984).

[1010]  Article 1; a further object is 'to ensure that rights of custody and of access under the law of one Contracting State are effectively respected in the other Contracting States'. For an account of the objects and workings of the Convention, see Elisa Pérez-Vera, *Explanatory Report on the 1980 Hague Child Abduction Convention* (HCCH, 1982).

[1011]  See Baroness Hale in *Re M (Abduction: Zimbabwe)* [2007] UKHL 55, [2008] 1 FLR 251: the message should go out to abductors that there are no safe havens amongst the Contracting States.

[1012]  Or unless an application under the Convention is not lodged within a reasonable time. See Article 16. A decision concerning the return of the child shall not be taken to be a determination on the merits of any custody issue: see Article 19. Failure to make a return order may in some circumstances constitute a breach of Article 8 of the ECHR, both procedurally and in its positive rights: see *RS v Poland (Application No 73777/09)* [2015] 2 FLR 848, ECtHR; *GS v Georgia (Application No 2361/13)* [2015] 2 FLR 647, ECtHR; and *Ferrari v Romania (Application No 1714/10)* [2015] 2 FLR 303, EctHR.

[1013]  Article 4.

## 6.4.1 Habitual residence

In *A v A and another (Children: Habitual Residence) (Reunite International Child Abduction Centre and others intervening)*[1014] the Supreme Court stated that it is highly desirable that the English and Welsh courts' approach to habitual residence should be the same as that of the Court of Justice of the European Union (CJEU),[1015] and that the Court of Justice's interpretation was to be preferred in so far as there was any difference between it and the approach of the domestic courts.[1016] The Supreme Court cited cases in which the CJEU had provided guidance. In *Proceedings brought by A* the CJEU had held that habitual residence:

> corresponds to the place which reflects some degree of integration by the child in a social and family environment. To that end, in particular the duration, regularity, conditions and reasons for the stay on the territory of a member state and the family's move to that state, the child's nationality, the place and conditions of attendance at school, linguistic knowledge and the family and social relationships of the child in that state must be taken into consideration. It is for the national court to establish the habitual residence of the child, taking account of all the circumstances specific to each individual case.[1017]

In *Mercredi v Chaffe*[1018] the CJEU added that:

> where the situation concerned is that of an infant who has been staying with her mother only a few days in a member state—other than that of her habitual residence—to which she has been removed, the factors which must be taken into consideration include, first, the duration, regularity, conditions and reasons for the stay in the territory of that member state and for the mother's move to that state and second, with particular reference to the child's age, the mother's geographic and family origins and the family and social connections which the mother and child have with that member state.

The CJEU also stated that:

> in order to determine where a child is habitually resident, *in addition to the physical presence of the child* in a member state, other factors must also make it clear that that presence is not in any way temporary or intermittent.[1019]

Earlier domestic authority had pointed out that habitual residence is 'primarily a question of fact to be determined by reference to all the relevant circumstances' and 'not to be treated as a term of art nor is it a legal concept in the sense of a set of pre-determined rules designed to produce a particular legal result in given circumstances',[1020] and that a child 'does not automatically take the habitual residence of its parents or custodial parent'.[1021]

---

[1014] [2013] UKSC 60, [2013] 3 WLR 761, on appeal from *ZA and PA v NA (Abduction: Habitual Residence)* [2012] EWCA Civ 1369, [2013] 1 FLR 1041.

[1015] [2013] UKSC 60, [2013] 3 WLR 761, [35].

[1016] [2013] UKSC 60 at [54].     [1017] (Case C-523/07) [2010] Fam 42.

[1018] Case C-497/10 PPU, [2012] Fam 22.     [1019] Ibid, para 49.

[1020] See *Re J (A Minor) (Abduction: Custody Rights)* [1990] 2 AC 562; and *Re S (A Minor) (Custody: Habitual Residence)* [1997] 4 All ER 251, and see the useful summaries of earlier authorities in *ZA and PA v NA (Abduction: Habitual Residence)* [2012] EWCA Civ 1396, [2013] 1 FLR 1041 at [47], and *Re P-J (Abduction: Habitual Residence: Consent)* [2009] EWCA Civ 588, [2009] 2 FLR 1051 at [24] et seq.

[1021] See e.g., *Re M (Abduction: Habitual Residence)* [1996] 1 FLR 887, CA at 891. Lord Brandon of Oakbrook's statement in *In re J (A Minor) (Abduction: Custody Rights)* [1990] 2 AC 562, that a young child in the sole lawful custody of his mother will necessarily have the same habitual residence as she does, is to be regarded as a helpful generalisation of fact, which will usually but not invariably be true, rather than a proposition of law: see *A v A and another (Children: Habitual Residence) (Reunite International Child Abduction Centre and others intervening)* [2013] UKSC 60, [2013] 3 WLR 761 at paras 44 and 73.

However, the approach of the CJEU makes clear that determination of habitual residence involves a factual determination *focusing on the child's situation*.[1022] In light of that approach, the Supreme Court questioned whether it was necessary to maintain the previously established rule in English law,[1023] that where both parents have equal status in relation to the child one parent could not unilaterally change the habitual residence of a child. The court commented that while this discourages child abductions, if not carefully qualified it is capable of leading to absurd results.[1024]

The question for the Supreme Court in *A v A* was whether habitual residence in a country requires the person in question to have been at some time physically present there. A mother, while pregnant, had taken her children to Pakistan on holiday to see their father. She was held against her will, and gave birth in Pakistan. She eventually escaped, albeit without the children, and obtained orders for the children's return. The Court of Appeal[1025] ruled that the acquisition of habitual residence in a country requires the child to be physically present there and consequently the order in respect of the youngest child had been made without jurisdiction. On the mother's appeal to the Supreme Court, an alternative basis for jurisdiction, namely the child's British nationality, was also raised.

Applying the CJEU test, the majority of the Supreme Court[1026] concluded that an approach which holds that presence in a country is a necessary pre-cursor to habitual residence accords most closely with the child's situation, rather than an approach which focuses on the relationship between the child and the primary carer. However, the CJEU's position was not entirely clear and to dispose of the case on this basis would require clarification from the CJEU.[1027] However, that was not necessary since the case might be resolved using the inherent jurisdiction, which could be exercised (albeit usually only exceptionally)[1028] on the basis of the child's British nationality.[1029] The court therefore allowed the appeal, remitting the case back to the High Court for determination of whether on the facts the inherent jurisdiction should be exercised to order the child's return. The Supreme Court's comments on the CJEU test for habitual residence are therefore merely *obiter*, but they clearly indicate the Supreme Court's view as to the correct test to be applied.

In *In re B (A Child)*[1030] the Supreme Court considered the circumstances in which a child may lose habitual residence. The Court had to consider whether a longstanding domestic analysis of those circumstances, which was heavily dependent on parental intention, is consonant with the modern international concept of habitual residence.[1031] The case concerned a seven- year-old girl, B, who had been conceived by donor sperm at a licensed hospital, at the joint request of the child's mother (the respondent) and her lesbian partner (the appellant). The treatment took place prior to implementation of the Human Fertilisation and Embryology Act 2008, which meant that the mother's partner did not become a legal parent of B, and she never acquired parental responsibility for B. However,

---

[1022] For discussion of different approaches, see R. Schuz, 'Habitual Residence of Children under the Hague Child Abduction Convention: Theory and Practice' [2001] Child and Family Law Quarterly 1.

[1023] *In re S (Minors) (Child Abduction: Wrongful Retention)* [1994] Fam 70, approved by the Court of Appeal in *Re M (Abduction: Habitual Residence)* [1996] 1 FLR 887.

[1024] Citing E. M. Clive, 'The Concept of Habitual Residence' [1997] Juridical Review 137 at 145.

[1025] Rimer and Patten LJJ, Thorpe LJ dissenting.

[1026] Lord Hughes dissenting. He concluded that the youngest child, like his siblings, is 'a member of a family unit which is firmly based in England and when born into it he was like the rest of its members habitually resident there' (at [93]) observing: 'If current physical presence is not essential, then so also can habitual residence exist without any physical presence yet having occurred, at least if it has only been prevented by some kind of unexpected force majeure' (at [92])

[1027] [2013] UKSC 60, [2013] 3 WLR 761, [58].

[1028] See for example in the context of forced marriage, *Re B; RB v FB and MA (Forced Marriage: Wardship: Jurisdiction)* [2008] 2 FLR 1624 (Hogg J). See the comments of Thorpe LJ in *Al Habtoor v Fotheringham* [2001] 1 FLR 951 at [42], and of McFarlane LJ in *Re N (Abduction: Appeal)* [2013] 1 FLR 457 at [29].

[1029] [2013] UKSC 60, [2013] 3 WLR 761, [60]. The jurisdiction exists in so far as it has not been taken away by provisions of the Family Law Act 1986.

[1030] [2016] UKSC 4.     [1031] Ibid, [32].

the mother and her partner were, in practice, joint parents of the child, until their relationship broke down. Thereafter, the mother progressively reduced the level of the appellant's contact with B. On 3 February 2014, the mother, who is of Pakistani origin, removed B to Pakistan without the appellant's knowledge. However, on 13 February 2014, the appellant issued applications under the Children Act 1989 for 'shared residence' or contact with B. On learning that B had been taken abroad, the appellant sought, alternatively, exercise of the inherent jurisdiction of the High Court in relation to B, as a British subject, in order to return her to England. This was not a case of child abduction as the removal of B to Pakistan was lawful, the mother being the sole holder of parental responsibility for B. However, whether the English court had jurisdiction to make the Children Act orders sought by the appellant depended on whether the child was still habitually resident in England. Hogg J and the Court of Appeal held that the child had lost habitual residence in England and there was no jurisdiction to make the Children Act orders. As Lord Wilson noted in the Supreme Court, this view meant that by the clandestine removal of B to Pakistan, the mother had placed B's interests beyond all judicial oversight, and this was something that demanded the Supreme Court's close scrutiny.[1032] The Supreme Court, by a majority of three to two,[1033] held that statements made by Lord Brandon in *In re J (A Minor) (Abduction: Custody Rights)*[1034] which suggested that a parent's intention to leave the jurisdiction would result in a loss of habitual residence should no longer be regarded as correct. That approach 'afforded to parental intention a dispositive effect inconsistent with the child-focussed European concept now adopted in England and Wales'.[1035] Instead, the court was of the view that habitual residence usually acts like a see-saw: 'in the expectation that, when a child gains a new habitual residence, he loses his old one'. By way of guidance, Lord Wilson of Culworth (who gave the leading majority judgment) set out 'some expectations which the fact-finder may well find to be unfulfilled in the case before him':[1036]

(a) the deeper the child's integration in the old state, probably the less fast his achievement of the requisite degree of integration in the new state;

(b) the greater the amount of adult pre-planning of the move, including pre-arrangements for the child's day-to-day life in the new state, probably the faster his achievement of that requisite degree; and

(c) were all the central members of the child's life in the old state to have moved with him, probably the faster his achievement of it and, conversely, were any of them to have remained behind and thus to represent for him a continuing link with the old state, probably the less fast his achievement of it.[1037]

Applying this approach to the facts,[1038] the Supreme Court concluded that on 13 February B retained habitual residence in England and accordingly the court had jurisdiction under the Children Act 1989. This conclusion meant that it was not necessary to consider the court's possible use of the inherent jurisdiction. However, Lady Hale and Lord Toulson, in a joint judgment agreeing with Lord Wilson's judgment, made clear that in such cases:

The real question is whether the circumstances are such that this British child requires that protection. For our part, we do not consider that the inherent jurisdiction is to be confined by a classification which limits its exercise to 'cases which are at the extreme end of the spectrum'.[1039]

---

[1032] Ibid, [26].

[1033] Lord Wilson, Lady Hale and Lord Toulson; Lord Sumption and Lord Clarke dissenting.

[1034] [1990] 2 AC 562, at 578-579: 'A person may cease to be habitually resident in country A in a single day if he or she leaves it with a settled intention not to return to it but to take up long-term residence in country B instead.'

[1035] [2016] UKSC 4, [47].     [1036] Ibid, [46].     [1037] Ibid.

[1038] At [2016] UKSC 4, [49] and [50], Lord Wilson weighs the various factors going to whether or not the child had disengaged from the jurisdiction.

[1039] [2016] UKSC 4, [60].

It is not necessary for a person to remain continuously in a particular country in order to retain habitual residence; thus a temporary or intermittent absence such as a holiday or a short educational visit will not bring to an end habitual residence.[1040] Nor, it seems, will enforced physical presence in a new jurisdiction be capable of changing a person's habitual residence.[1041] The wrongful removal of a child will not bring about a change of habitual residence.[1042]

In *Re L (A Child) (Custody: Habitual Residence) (Reunite International Child Abduction Centre intervening)*[1043] a mother brought her child to England from Texas where, under the terms of a court order she had the right to determine the child's place of residence. The court order in Texas was subsequently overturned on appeal there, giving the father in Texas exclusive right to decide the child's residence. The father applied for the child's return under the Hague Convention and, alternatively, pursuant to Article 18 of the Convention, under the court's inherent jurisdiction. This was resisted by the mother, and ultimately the case reached the Supreme Court on the father's appeal. The Supreme Court held that the English 'rule' against unilateral changes could not apply in such circumstances since the move was permitted by the initial order of the US court.[1044] Applying the approach to habitual residence in *A v A* (earlier) the court held that the child became integrated into a social and family environment during the 11½ months in which he lived in England before the US Court of Appeals' judgment and his habitual residence was then in England.[1045] There was thus no wrongful removal to or retention in England. However, Article 18 of the Hague Convention makes clear that the provisions on return of children in the Convention 'do not limit the power of a judicial or administrative authority to order the return of the child at any time'. By reason of the child's habitual residence, the court had jurisdiction under the inherent jurisdiction and exercised it to return the child forthwith, seeing as crucial the fact that this was 'a Texan child who is currently being denied a proper opportunity to develop a relationship with his father and with his country of birth'.[1046]

In *In re LC (Children)*[1047] the Supreme Court considered the role of a child's state of mind on the question of the child's habitual residence. In that case, on the breakdown of the parents' relationship, the Spanish mother, who had been living in England with the children's English father, took their four children to reside in Spain. After five months in Spain, the children returned to England for what was agreed to be no more than a holiday with the father, but the children were not returned. The mother sought the summary return of the children under the Hague Convention, which was resisted by the father because he disputed that the children had been habitually resident in Spain on the date of alleged retention in England, and alternatively contended that the older children objected to being returned. The judge found that the children had been habitually resident in Spain and that the retention was wrongful. He also found that the oldest child, T, who was aged 12 years nine months, objected to return and had attained the requisite age and maturity, but the judge decided not to exercise his discretion to decline to order T's return to Spain. On the father's appeal, the Court of Appeal held that the judge had erred in exercising his discretion but upheld the judge's finding as to habitual residence. The father appealed further to the Supreme Court on the issue of habitual residence, contending *inter alia* that the court had failed to take account of statements made by the three older

---

[1040] *Re M (Abduction: Habitual Residence)* [1996] 1 FLR 887, CA at 895, and see for example *Re P-J (Abduction: Habitual Residence: Consent)* [2009] EWCA Civ 588, [2009] 2 FLR 1051.

[1041] See *DT v LBT (Abduction: Domestic Abuse)* [2010] EWHC 3177, [2011] 1 FLR 1215 (although not so finding on the facts of the case. The mother alleged emotional, sexual, and physical abuse at the hands of the husband, and that she was bullied her into moving to Italy with the children. The mother's will had not been overborne and the children's habitual residence was Italy).

[1042] *Re J (A Minor) (Abduction: Custody Rights)* [1990] 2 AC 562, *per* Lord Donaldson MR and *Re N (Abduction: Habitual Residence)* [2000] 2 FLR 899.

[1043] [2013] UKSC 75, [2013] 3 WLR 1597.    [1044] Ibid, [25].    [1045] Ibid, [26] and [27].

[1046] Ibid, [36] and [38].

[1047] [2014] UKSC 1. For comment, see S. Gilmore and J. Herring, 'Listening to Children - Whatever' [2014] Law Quarterly Review, 531.

children to the Cafcass officer that they never considered Spain to be their home.[1048] Lord Wilson (with whom Lord Toulson and Lord Hodge agreed), commented that where a child 'goes lawfully to reside with a parent in a state in which that parent is habitually resident, it will no doubt be highly unusual for that child not to acquire habitual residence there too'.[1049] However:

> where the child is older, in particular one who is an adolescent or who should be treated as an adolescent because she (or he) has the maturity of an adolescent, and perhaps also where (to take the facts of this case) the older child's residence with the parent proves to be of short duration, the inquiry into her integration in the new environment must encompass more than the surface features of her life there.[1050]

The majority was clear that it is the state of mind of an *adolescent* child that may affect whether residence is habitual, not that of younger children. Accordingly, T's views were seen as relevant to whether she was integrated to some degree in a social and family environment in Spain, and the case was remitted for fresh consideration of the issue.[1051] A minority of the court, Lady Hale (with whom Lord Sumption agreed) was of the view that the 'logic which makes an adolescent's state of mind relevant applies equally to the younger children, although of course the answer to the factual question may be different in their case'.[1052] Making a strong point, Lady Hale observed:

> It would be wrong to overlay these essentially factual questions with a rule that the perceptions of younger children are irrelevant, just as it was to overlay them with a rule (rejected in *A v A*) that a child automatically shares the habitual residence of the parent with whom he is living.[1053]

The court went on to hold, in any event, that the proper course was to set aside the decision on habitual residence also in respect of the younger children so that the issue could be considered in relation to all four children together.[1054]

In *AR v RN (Habitual Residence)*[1055] the Supreme Court once again examined the issue of a child's habitual residence, in the context of what was initially intended to be a temporary relocation. The French father and British/Canadian mother agreed that the mother and children would relocate from France to Scotland, where the maternal grandparents lived, for 12 months during the mother's maternity leave. However, when the mother discovered the father's infidelity, she remained in Scotland and the father sought return of the children under the Hague Convention. Dismissing the father's appeal from an Extra Division of the Inner House of the Court of Session, the Supreme Court held that the Extra Division had been correct to conclude that the children were habitually resident in Scotland. The Court was clear that the Lord Ordinary, at first instance, had erred in suggesting that the absence of a joint parental intention to live permanently in Scotland was a decisive factor in deciding whether the children's habitual residence had changed.[1056] The Supreme Court unanimously made clear that a joint move is not required, and 'there is no "rule" that one parent cannot unilaterally change the habitual residence of a child.'[1057] In addition, the Court held that it is 'the stability of the residence that is important, not whether it is of a permanent character', and there is 'no requirement that the child should have been resident in the country in question for a particular period of time'.[1058]

---

[1048] See [2014] UKSC 1, [26] for an account of the children's views.

[1049] Ibid, [37]. Lady Hale observed at [64] that 'it is not a question of the parents' determining the habitual residence of their children. It is a question of the impact of the parental decisions about where they and the children will live upon the factual question of where the children habitually reside.'

[1050] Ibid.     [1051] Ibid [39] and [41].     [1052] Ibid, [58].     [1053] Ibid, [61].

[1054] Ibid, [43]. See *Re LC (Habitual Residence: Grave Risk of Harm)* [2014] EWFC 8 (Fam), [2015] 1 FLR 1019, Roderic Wood J (dismissing mother's application for return of the children—none had lost their habitual residence in England, or alternatively the defences of grave risk and children's objections were made out).

[1055] [2015] UKSC 35, [2015] 2 FLR 503.     [1056] Ibid, [21].     [1057] Ibid, [17].     [1058] Ibid, [16].

In *Re D (Habitual Residence: Consent and Acquiescence)*[1059] Pauffley J considered the issue of habitual residence in the context of an informal surrogacy arrangement. The mother, who lived in Germany, gave birth to a child conceived naturally under an arrangement whereby the father and his wife, who lived in England, would be the child's primary carers. After the birth, the father's wife lived with the mother and was the child's primary carer. The child then moved to the couple's home country, England, and the child thereafter lived with the couple in England. The mother applied under the Hague Convention for the child's return. Dismissing the mother's application, Pauffley J held on the facts that the child was only ever part of the husband and wife's family and at all times had remained habitually resident in England, the child's environment being centred on them.

### 6.4.2 Wrongful removal or retention: breach of rights of custody

Once habitual residence prior to removal has been established, the next question is whether there has been a wrongful removal or retention under the law of habitual residence. By Article 3 of the Hague Convention the removal or the retention of a child is to be considered wrongful where

a)  it is in breach of rights of custody attributed to a person, an institution or any other body, either jointly or alone, under the law of the State in which the child was habitually resident immediately before the removal or retention; and

b)  at the time of removal or retention those rights were actually exercised, either jointly or alone, or would have been so exercised but for the removal or retention.[1060]

Article 5 provides that ' "rights of custody" shall include rights relating to the care of the person of the child and, in particular, the right to determine the child's place of residence'. In *Re H (A Minor) (Abduction: Rights of Custody)*[1061] an unmarried father's application for guardianship was before an Irish court when the mother removed the child to England, and the father sought summary return of the child under the Convention. The House of Lords held that a court was a 'body' within the meaning of Article 3, and that at the relevant time the Irish court had the right to determine the child's place of residence and accordingly had 'rights of custody'. Similarly in *Re D (Abduction: Rights of Custody)*[1062] the House of Lords held that an individual's right of veto amounts to 'rights of custody' within the meaning of Article 5(a).

Where there is a court order the position will usually be clear as to whether rights have been breached.[1063] It has been held that breach of a shared care arrangement can be a wrongful retention of the child.[1064] In the case of a father with no parental responsibility who does not have a court order in his favour, he will usually have no custody rights capable of being breached,[1065] even if as a matter of fact he has been sharing the care of the child with the mother.[1066] Where there is no court order but joint parental responsibility, the wrongfulness of a removal will be determined according

---

[1059]  [2015] EWHC 1562.

[1060]  Article 3 also provides that the rights of custody mentioned in sub-paragraph a) above, 'may arise in particular by operation of law or by reason of a judicial or administrative decision, or by reason of an agreement having legal effect under the law of that State'.

[1061]  [2000] 2 AC 291, [2000] 1 FLR 374. See also *X County Council v B (Abduction: Rights of Custody in the Court)* [2009] EWHC 2635 (Fam) (court seised of application in care proceedings when parents absconded to Ireland—held that removal was in breach of court's custody rights).

[1062]  [2006] UKHL 51, [2007] 1 FLR 961, [2007] 1 FLR 961 at [37].

[1063]  However, for the complexities that might arise, see C. S. Bruch, 'Child Abduction and the English Courts' in A. Bainham, D. S. Pearl, and R. Pickford (eds), *Frontiers of Family Law* (2nd edn, John Wiley & Sons, 1995), p 55.

[1064]  *K v L (Child Abduction: Declaration)* [2012] EWHC 1234 (Fam), [2013] 1 FLR 998, confirming the academic view expressed by C. S. Bruch, 'Child Abduction and the English Courts' in A. Bainham, D. S. Pearl, and R. Pickford (eds), *Frontiers of Family Law* (2nd edn, John Wiley & Sons, 1995), p 55.

[1065]  *Re J (A Minor) (Abduction: Custody Rights)* [1990] 2 AC 562.

[1066]  *Re C (Child Abduction) (Unmarried Father: Rights of Custody)* [2003] 1 FLR 252. See also *S v H (Abduction: Access Rights)* [1997] 1 FLR 971.

to the Child Abduction Act 1984. As we have seen, this may turn on whether the defences in section 1(5) of the Child Abduction Act 1984 apply, including in some cases the question of reasonableness. Where the father has exclusive care of the child, however, he might be found to have prospects of obtaining a residence order and inchoate rights of custody for the purposes of the Convention.[1067]

In *Re K (Abduction: Inchoate Rights)*[1068] the Supreme Court considered whether the term 'rights of custody' is to be interpreted literally as a reference to legally recognised rights, or whether, purposively interpreted, it could embrace a wider category of 'inchoate rights', the existence of which would have been legally recognised had the question arisen before the removal or retention in question.[1069] The case concerned a 9 year-old boy, Karl, who was born in 2005 in Lithuania. In 2006 his mother moved to Northern Ireland, leaving the boy with his maternal grandparents. The mother had formally delegated Karl's care to the grandmother, and the grandmother's status as temporary carer was officially recognised (e.g. for child benefits) by their local administration. In 2012, the mother returned to Lithuania where she informed the Children's Rights Division of the City Administration that she would take her son into her own care, and the temporary care was terminated. However, the Children's Rights Division remained involved with the family, actively managing the dispute between the mother and the grandparents as to Karl's future welfare. The mother then removed the child to Northern Ireland in what the Supreme Court described as 'a shocking episode of which any mother should be deeply ashamed', the child having to 'to leave behind his country, his home, his toys and his clothes, his school and many other activities, and the grandparents with whom he had lived all his life'.[1070] The grandparents sought Karl's return, claiming that he was wrongfully retained in Northern Ireland. This raised the issue of whether the removal or retention was in breach of the grandmother's rights of custody.

The Supreme Court[1071] held that the Convention should be construed purposively to include persons with inchoate rights, defined consistently with the purpose of the Convention, as follows:

> (a) they must be undertaking the responsibilities, and thus enjoying the concomitant rights and powers, entailed in the primary care of the child ... (b) they must not be sharing those responsibilities with the person or persons having a legally recognised right to determine where the child shall live and how he shall be brought up ... (c) that person or persons must have either abandoned the child or delegated his primary care to them; (d) there must be some form of legal or official recognition of their position in the country of habitual residence. This is to distinguish those whose care of the child is lawful from those whose care is not lawful ... and (e) there must be every reason to believe that, were they to seek the protection of the courts of that country, the status quo would be preserved for the time being, so that the long-term future of the child could be determined in those courts in accordance with his best interests, and not by the pre-emptive strike of abduction.

The Court concluded on the facts that the grandmother's status constituted 'rights of custody', and that the Court was obliged to order the child's return.

### 6.4.2.1 *Article 15: seeking a determination on whether or not the removal or retention was wrongful within the meaning of Article 3 of the Convention*

Under Article 15 a determination can be sought from the authorities of the State of the child's habitual residence on whether the removal is wrongful in Convention terms. In *Re D (Abduction: Rights of Custody)*[1072] the House of Lords held that usually considerable weight

---

[1067] *Re F (Abduction: Unmarried Father: Sole Carer)* [2003] 1 FLR 839. See also *Re B (A Minor) (Abduction)* [1994] 2 FLR 249.

[1068] [2014] UKSC 29, [2014] 2 FLR 629.     [1069] Ibid, [3].     [1070] Ibid, [7].

[1071] Lord Wilson dissenting.     [1072] [2006] UKHL 51, [2007] 1 FLR 961.

should be attached to that authoritative decision[1073] which should only be questioned 'if its characterisation of the parent's rights is clearly out of line with the international understanding of the Convention's terms'.[1074]

### 6.4.3 Invoking the assistance of the Convention

Each Contracting State has a Central Authority[1075] to discharge the duties which are imposed by the Convention. The Central Authorities are required to cooperate with each other.[1076] Any person, institution, or other body claiming that a child has been removed or retained in breach of custody rights may apply either to the Central Authority of the child's habitual residence or to the Central Authority of any other Contracting State for assistance in securing the return of the child.[1077] The judicial or administrative authorities of Contracting States must act expeditiously in proceedings for the return of children.[1078] Under the Brussels II Revised Regulation, the court 'shall, except where exceptional circumstances make this impossible, issue its judgment no later than six weeks after the application is lodged'.[1079] The Hague Convention also states that if the judicial or administrative authority concerned has not reached a decision within six weeks from the date of commencement of the proceedings, the applicant or the Central Authority of the requested State has the right to request a statement of the reasons for the delay.

As noted earlier, cases under the Hague Convention are summary proceedings, and in England are heard and decided on the basis of written evidence, with the use of oral evidence rarely permitted.[1080]

In *Neulinger and Shuruk v Switzerland*[1081] the European Court of Human Rights found a violation of Article 8 of the ECHR in an abduction case where there was a failure to engage in an in-depth consideration of the Article 8 interests involved and this caused some consternation concerning potential tension between the summary nature of Hague Convention proceedings and the requirements of Article 8 of the ECHR. In *Re E (Children) (Abduction: Custody Appeal)*[1082] the Supreme Court sought therefore to clarify the decision in *Neulinger*. The Supreme Court explained that it was significant that in *Neulinger* there had been a considerable delay since the abduction, and that the violation in *Neulinger* arose, not from the proper application of the Hague Convention, but from the failure to take account of Article 8 interests in the context of that delay. The Supreme Court commented:

> The Hague Convention is designed to strike a fair balance between those two interests. If it is correctly applied it is most unlikely that there will be any breach of Art 8 or other European Convention rights unless other factors supervene. *Neulinger* does not require a departure from the normal summary process, provided that the decision is not arbitrary or mechanical.[1083]

---

[1073] Lord Brown of Eaton-under-Heywood went further to say that such determinations should be treated 'almost invariably as conclusive' (at [83]).

[1074] As may have been the case in *Hunter v Murrow (Abduction: Rights of Custody)* [2005] EWCA Civ 976, [2005] 2 FLR 1119.

[1075] In England and Wales the Central Authority is the Lord Chancellor, who delegates this role to the International Child Abduction and Contact Unit within the office of the Official Solicitor.

[1076] Article 7.     [1077] Article 8.

[1078] Article 11. In England in 2011 only 33 per cent of applications under the Brussels Regulation were disposed of within six weeks, and only 26 per cent of applications under the Convention overall. (Study by Victoria Stephens and Nigel Lowe, Nuffield Foundation.)

[1079] Article 11.3 of the Regulation.

[1080] See *Re K (Abduction: Case Management)* [2010] EWCA Civ 1546, [2011] 1 FLR 1268 and *Re E (Children) (Abduction: Custody Appeal)* [2011] UKSC 27, [2011] 2 FLR 758.

[1081] (App no 41615/07) [2011] 1 FLR 122, ECHR.     [1082] [2011] UKSC 27, [2011] 2 FLR 758.

[1083] Ibid, [52]. Indeed, the President of the Strasbourg court had acknowledged extra-judicially that the case 'does not therefore signal a change of direction' and that the case needed to be seen in the context of its facts. In a paper given at the Franco-British-Irish colloquium on family law on 14 May 2011.

In *Re S (A Child) (Abduction: Rights of Custody)*,[1084] the Supreme Court, being concerned that the view in *Neulinger* had been repeated by the ECtHR in *X v Latvia*,[1085] reiterated its:[1086]

> conviction . . . that neither the Hague Convention nor, surely, Art 8 of the European Convention requires the court which determines an application under the former to conduct an in-depth examination of the sort described. Indeed it would be entirely inappropriate.

### 6.4.4 When should the child's return be ordered?

#### 6.4.4.1 The general rules of return in Article 12

Article 12 provides that if an application is brought within 12 months of the wrongful removal, the court 'shall order the return of the child forthwith'.

Even where the proceedings have been commenced after a period of one year since removal, the court 'shall also order the return of the child, unless it is demonstrated that the child is now settled in its new environment'. In *Re M (Abduction: Zimbabwe)*[1087] the House of Lords held that Article 12 'does envisage that a settled child might nevertheless be returned within the Convention procedures'[1088] but was clear that it 'is wrong to import any test of exceptionality into the exercise of discretion under the Hague Convention. The circumstances in which return may be refused are themselves exceptions to the general rule. That in itself is sufficient exceptionality. It is neither necessary nor desirable to import an additional gloss into the Convention.'[1089] The House observed that the object of securing a swift return to the country of origin cannot be met in a settlement case, so the policy of the Convention would not necessarily point towards a return in such cases.[1090] The mother, a failed asylum-seeker, had brought two girls, who were now 13 and 10, from Zimbabwe in 2005. The family remained in the UK because of a moratorium on the return of failed asylum-seekers to Zimbabwe and the children were settled. The House held that there were powerful considerations on the facts of this case pointing to the merits of the case being determined in England rather than Zimbabwe.[1091]

#### 6.4.4.2 Article 13 exceptions

Article 12 is subject to a number of limited exceptions set out in Article 13, although, even where one of these is established, the court retains its discretion to order a return under Article 18. Article 13 provides that the requested State is not bound to order the return of the child if the person, institution, or other body which opposes its return establishes that

> a) the person, institution or other body having the care of the person of the child was not actually exercising the custody rights at the time of removal or retention, or had consented to or subsequently acquiesced in the removal or retention; or
>
> b) there is a grave risk that his or her return would expose the child to physical or psychological harm or otherwise place the child in an intolerable situation.
>
> The judicial or administrative authority may also refuse to order the return of the child if it finds that the child objects to being returned and has attained an age and degree of maturity at which it is appropriate to take account of its views.

---

[1084] [2012] UKSC 10, [2012] 2 FLR 442 at [34].     [1085] (App no 27853/09) [2012] 1 FLR 860.

[1086] [2012] UKSC 10, [2012] 2 FLR 442 at [34].     [1087] [2007] UKHL 55, [2008] 1 FLR 251.

[1088] Ibid, [31]. For criticism, see R. Schuz, 'In Search of a Settled Interpretation of Article 12(2) of the Hague Child Abduction Convention' [2008] Child and Family Law Quarterly 64.

[1089] [2008] 1 FLR 251 [40].     [1090] Ibid, [47].

[1091] See, for a case in which the judge failed to apply *Zimbabwe: Re O (Abduction: Settlement)* [2011] EWCA Civ 128, and compare with the *Zimbabwe* case *Re F (Abduction: Removal Outside Jurisdiction)* [2008] EWCA Civ 842 (children not settled where mother was a failed asylum seeker who was to be deported).

### 6.4.4.2.1 Consent or acquiescence: Article 13a

Under Article 13a the court may refuse to return a child where 'the person, institution or other body having care of the person of a child was not actually exercising the custody rights at the time of removal or retention, or had consented to or subsequently acquiesced in the removal or retention'. In *Re P-J (Abduction: Habitual Residence: Consent)*[1092] Ward LJ summarised the authorities on consent as follows:

> (1) Consent to the removal of the child must be clear and unequivocal; (2) Consent can be given to the removal at some future but unspecified time or upon the happening of some future event; (3) Such advance consent must, however, still be operative and in force at the time of the actual removal; (4) The happening of the future event must be reasonably capable of ascertainment. The condition must not have been expressed in terms which are too vague or uncertain for both parties to know whether the condition will be fulfilled. Fulfilment of the condition must not depend on the subjective determination of one party . . . The event must be objectively verifiable; (5) Consent, or the lack of it, must be viewed in the context of the realities of family life, or more precisely, in the context of the realities of the disintegration of family life. It is not to be viewed in the context of nor governed by the law of contract; (6) Consequently consent can be withdrawn at any time before actual removal. If it is, the proper course is for any dispute about removal to be resolved by the courts of the country of habitual residence before the child is removed; (7) The burden of proving the consent rests on him or her who asserts it; (8) The inquiry is inevitably fact specific and the facts and circumstances will vary infinitely from case to case; (9) The ultimate question is a simple one even if a multitude of facts bear upon the answer. It is simply this: had the other parent clearly and unequivocally consented to the removal?

In *Re H (Minors) (Abduction: Acquiescence)*[1093] the House of Lords held that the 'question whether the wronged parent has "acquiesced" in the removal or retention of the child depends upon his actual state of mind'. However, the 'subjective intention of the wronged parent is a question of fact for the trial judge to determine in all the circumstances of the case, the burden of proof being on the abducting parent'.[1094] Thus the intention can be inferred from any visible acts. In that case, the mother brought the children to England from Israel without the consent of the father, who, being an Orthodox Jew, pursued the matter initially through the Rabbinical court in Israel. Only when that process proved unsuccessful did he act under the Hague Convention. The House held that the father's actions were not clearly and unequivocally inconsistent with his pursuit of his summary remedy under the Convention and that he had not acquiesced.

Acquiescence can be either passive or active and, as noted previously, will need to be determined on the facts, in the circumstances of each case. For example, a willingness to enter negotiations with the abducting parent about the child's future,[1095] or attempting a reconciliation with the abducting parent[1096] has been held not to amount to acquiescence, whereas in a case of removal to England, a decision to attempt to settle in England and seek an order for contact in the English court was held to be acquiescence.[1097]

### 6.4.4.2.2 Grave risk of harm or intolerable situation: Article 13b

The court may also, under Article 13b, refuse to order the child's return where 'there is a grave risk that his or her return would expose the child to physical or psychological harm or otherwise

---

[1092] [2009] EWCA Civ 588, [2009] 2 FLR 1051 (consent can be conditional or for a limited time).
[1093] [1997] 1 FLR 872.     [1094] Ibid at 884.     [1095] *Re I (Abduction: Acquiescence)* [1999] 1 FLR 778.
[1096] *Re W (Abduction: Acquiescence: Children's Objections)* [2010] EWHC 332, [2010] 2 FLR 1150.
[1097] *Re B (Abduction: Acquiescence)* [1999] 2 FLR 818.

place the child in an intolerable situation'.[1098] In *Re E (Children) (Abduction: Custody Appeal)*[1099] the Supreme Court made clear that these words 'are quite plain and need no further elaboration or "gloss" '.[1100] The court explained that the words 'physical or psychological harm' are not qualified, but that they:

> gain colour from the alternative 'or *otherwise*' placed 'in an intolerable situation' (emphasis supplied). . . ' "Intolerable" is a strong word, but when applied to a child must mean "a situation which this particular child in these particular circumstances should not be expected to tolerate" '.[1101]

The court also clarified that the source of the risk is irrelevant and thus the risk could be based on a parent's subjective perception[1102] of events leading to a mental illness, which could have intolerable consequences for the child.

In a case to which the Brussels II Revised Regulation applies, Article 11.4 of the Regulation provides that a 'court cannot refuse to return a child on the basis of Article 13b of the 1980 Hague Convention if it is established that adequate arrangements have been made to secure the protection of the child after his or her return'. The Supreme Court pointed out that in such a case, where 'there are disputed allegations which can neither be tried nor objectively verified, the focus of the inquiry is bound to be on the sufficiency of any protective measures which can be put in place to reduce the risk. The clearer the need for protection, the more effective the measures will have to be.'[1103]

Whether grave risk of harm is established will depend on the particular facts of each case. The defence has succeeded where there has been substantial domestic abuse giving rise to a wholly understandable fear of returning,[1104] for example, where the mother had been shot by a hired gunman.[1105] In other cases, grave risk has not been made out, for example where the risk was said to arise from the general terrorist threat in Israel,[1106] or where, despite a risk that the mother's psychological state might deteriorate, there would be no serious impairment of her ability to care for the child.[1107]

### 6.4.4.2.3 *The child's wishes*

Article 13 of the Hague Convention also provides that the child's return may be refused where the court 'finds that the child objects to being returned and has attained an age and degree of maturity at which it is appropriate to take account of its views'.[1108] The threshold for taking account

---

[1098] Article 13(b). For some discussion of the scope of Art 13, see J. Caldwell, 'Child Welfare Defences in Child Abduction Cases—Some Recent Developments' [2001] Child and Family Law Quarterly 121.

[1099] [2011] UKSC 27, [2011] 2 FLR 758.  [1100] Ibid, [31].  [1101] Ibid, [34].

[1102] See also, confirming this subjective approach: *Re S (A Child) (Abduction: Rights of Custody)* [2012] UKSC 10, [2012] 2 FLR 442 at [34].

[1103] Ibid, [52]. For a case in which adequate arrangements to prevent grave risk of harm were put in place, see *Re K (Abduction: Case Management)* [2010] EWCA Civ 1546, [2011] 1 FLR 1268.

[1104] See *DT v LBT (Abduction: Domestic Abuse)* [2010] EWHC 3177 (Fam), [2011] 1 FLR 1215.

[1105] *Re D (Article 13b: Non-Return)* [2006] EWCA Civ 146, [2006] 2 FLR 305. See also *Klentzeris v Klentzeris* [2007] EWCA Civ 533, [2007] 2 FLR 996 (child had panic attack when recounting events in country of habitual residence—return refused). See also as examples, *Re F (Child Abduction: Risk if Returned)* [1995] 2 FLR 31 and *Re G (Abduction: Psychological Harm)* [1995] 1 FLR 64. See also *Re M (Abduction: Psychological Harm)* [1997] 2 FLR 690.

[1106] *Re S (Abduction: Custody Rights)* [2002] EWCA Civ 908.

[1107] *C v B (Abduction: Grave Risk)* [2005] EWHC 2988 (Fam). See also *Re W (Abduction: Domestic Violence)* [2004] EWHC 1247 (Fam), [2004] 2 FLR 499 (alleged abuse of child not sufficient).

[1108] See for an assessment, P. McEleavy, 'Evaluating the Views of Abducted Children: Trends in appellate case-law' [2008] Child and Family Law Quarterly 230.

of the child's views is fairly low.[1109] It has been said that this 'defence' involves addressing three questions:

> The first question to be considered is whether or not the objections to return are made out.[1110] The second is whether the age and maturity of the child are such that it is appropriate for the court to take account of those objections (unless that is so, the defence cannot be established). Assuming a positive finding in that respect, the court moves to the third question, whether or not it should exercise its discretion in favour of retention or return.[1111]

In *Re M (Republic of Ireland) (Child's Objections) (Joinder of Children as Parties to Appeal)*[1112] the Court of Appeal considered the first, gateway stage, regarding consideration of a child's objections. The case concerned an Irish father, British mother, and four children aged 17, 13, 11, and 6. The mother wrongfully removed the children to England, and the father issued proceedings under the Hague Convention. The children voiced fears and distress concerning the father's domestic violence. The judge, however, did not accept these statements as constituting objections in Hague Convention terms and made a return order. The mother and the two older children appealed. The Court of Appeal set aside the return order, holding that the judge had been wrong to conclude that the children were not objecting. The court took the opportunity to re-examine the Court of Appeal's approach, in particular the complex and technical approach of Ward LJ in *Re T (Abduction: Child's Objections to Return)*.[1113] The Court held that the approach in *Re T* should be abandoned as unhelpful and as potentially robbing the discretionary stage of its proper role. Instead the court should adopt a straightforward and robust examination of whether the simple terms of the Hague Convention were satisfied,[1114] an approach which was consistent with the House of Lords' approach in *Re M (Children) (Abduction: Rights of Custody)*[1115] and with the views of Wilson LJ in *Re W (Abduction: Child's Objections)*[1116] that the phrase 'to take account' in Article 13 'means no more than what is says.'[1117] Black LJ usefully summarised some features of the law which are well established: whether the child objects is a matter of fact; there is no fixed age below which a child's objections will not be taken into account; there must be objections, not anything less; the objection must be to returning to the country of habitual residence; and objections are not determinative.[1118]

In exercising its discretion, the court 'must balance the nature and strength of the child's objections against both the Convention considerations (obviously including comity and respect for the judicial processes in the requesting state) and also general welfare considerations'.[1119] The width of discretion was emphasized in *Re S (Habitual Residence and Child's Objections)*.[1120] The Court of Appeal rejected counsel's argument in this case that this stage is confined to considering which

---

[1109] See eg *Re W (Abduction: Child's Objections)* [2010] EWCA Civ 520, [2010] 2 FLR 1165 at [22] (taking into account the views of a six-year-old child). A child with learning difficulties may still articulate objections sufficiently rationally and intelligently: see *B v B (Abduction: Child with Learning Difficulties)* [2011] EWHC 2300 (14-year-old child with Asperger's Syndrome).

[1110] In *Re D (Abduction: Child's Objections)* [2011] EWCA Civ 1294, for example, the child's objection to returning to France that he was racially abused at a school in France was not made out, in that he had been attending another school prior to the abduction, at which he had not had problems.

[1111] *Re M (Abduction: Child's Objections)* [2007] EWCA Civ 260, [2007] 2 FLR 72 at [60].

[1112] [2015] EWCA Civ 26, [2015] 2 FLR 1074. See for an example, *SP v EB and KP* [2014] EWHC 3964 (Fam) in which Mostyn J refused to make a return order, returning a 14 year-old girl to Malta. He accepted that she was of a sufficient age and maturity to voice an objection that was capable of being taken into account, expressing a sound, reasoned and mature objection, namely that her society of friends and education would be considerably disrupted.

[1113] [2000] 2 FLR 192.     [1114] See also *Re U-B (Abduction: Objections to Return)* [2015] EWCA Civ 60.

[1115] [2007] UKHL 55, [2008] 1 FLR 251.     [1116] [2010] EWCA Civ 520, [2010] 2 FLR 1165, at [22].

[1117] Ibid, at [22]. See [2015] EWCA Civ 26, [2015] 2 FLR 1074, at [48].

[1118] [2015] EWCA Civ 26, [2015] 2 FLR 1074, at [35] et seq.

[1119] *Zaffino v Zaffino (Abduction: Children's Views)* [2005] EWCA Civ 1012, [2006] 1 FLR 410 at [19], *per* Thorpe LJ. See also *per* Wall LJ at [30]–[31].

[1120] [2015] EWCA Civ 2, [2015] 2 FLR 1338.

was the right forum for the necessary welfare proceedings. While there must not be a full-blown welfare inquiry at this stage, the discretion is at large to consider any material set against Hague Convention considerations. In *Re S* a Brazilian mother relocated from England to Brazil with two children, upon her separation from the English father. The children were now 10 and 12. After a holiday in England the 12 year-old girl wished to stay with her father in England and refused to return to Brazil. The judge at first instance held that she had not become habitually resident in Brazil because she was unhappy there and missed her father and therefore there had been no wrongful retention. The mother appealed. The Court of Appeal overturned the court's conclusion on habitual residence, holding that the girl had been habitually resident in Brazil despite any nagging doubts she had about living there. However, the court dismissed the mother's appeal, concluding that there had been ample material relating to the child's objections to return to justify a decision not to return the child.

Of course, in order to take account of the child's views, the child must be heard.[1121] Article 11.2 of the Brussels II Revised Regulation reverses the burden in relation to hearing the child, providing:

> When applying articles 12 and 13 of the 1980 Hague Convention, it shall be ensured that the child is given the opportunity to be heard during the proceedings unless this appears inappropriate having regard to his or her age or degree of maturity.

In *Re D (Abduction: Rights of Custody)*[1122] Baroness Hale suggested that while strictly this only applies to cases within the European Union, the principle is:

> of universal application and consistent with our international obligations under Art 12 of the United Nations Convention on the Rights of the Child 1989. It applies, not only when a 'defence' under Art 13 has been raised, but also in any case in which the court is being asked to apply Art 12 and direct the summary return of the child—in effect in every Hague Convention case. It erects a presumption that the child will be heard unless this appears inappropriate.[1123]

The child can be heard in various ways, but authority now suggests the desirability of a face-to-face meeting between judge and children in appropriate cases.[1124]

### 6.4.4.2.4  Violation of human rights and fundamental freedoms

A final defence, in Article 20, is that the child's return under the provisions of Article 12 may be refused if this would not be permitted by the fundamental principles of the requested State relating to the protection of human rights and fundamental freedoms.

## 6.5  Non-Convention countries

The options for a parent of a child abducted to a non-Convention country[1125] are more limited. The parent might seek extradition of the abductor, if an extradition treaty exists between the two countries concerned, or pursue civil proceedings in the country to which the child has been taken. In the case of children taken to England, an application must be brought in the High Court in

---

[1121]  See e.g., *Re S (Abduction: Hearing the Child)* [2014] EWCA Civ 1557, [2015] 2 FLR 588, at [28]: case remitted for failure to comply with the obligation to consider whether and how to hear the child.

[1122]  [2006] UKHL 51, [2007] 1 FLR 961.    [1123]  Ibid, [58].

[1124]  *Re J (Abduction: Children's Objections)* [2011] EWCA Civ 1448, [2012] 1 FLR 457 at [33]. See for examples *JPC v SLW and SMW (Abduction)* [2007] EWHC 1349 (Fam), [2007] 2 FLR 900, *De L v H* [2009] EWHC 3074 (Fam), [2010] 1 FLR 1229, and *Re G (Abduction: Children's Objections)* [2010] EWCA Civ 1232, [2011] 1 FLR 1645 at [15].

[1125]  See H. Setright, 'Removals to and from Non-Convention Countries—The Perspective of Courts in England and Wales' [2000] International Family Law 125.

wardship or under the inherent jurisdiction. The English court, while liable to act in the spirit of the Convention,[1126] is bound to apply the paramountcy of the child's welfare, which in the context of decisions about a return to another jurisdiction may require a culturally sensitive application in which cultural factors and the child's well-being as understood in this jurisdiction may well be in tension.[1127]

## 7  The inherent jurisdiction of the High Court

The inherent jurisdiction of the High Court in children cases dates back to feudal times. Its origins lie in the duty of the sovereign, as *parens patriae*, to take care of vulnerable subjects.[1128] One way of seeking the High Court's use of its inherent jurisdiction is by making a child a ward of court.[1129] A child becomes a ward as soon as an application in wardship is made, that is to say the jurisdiction takes effect even before any order is made, and no important step in the child's life can be taken without the court's leave.[1130] At the hearing, if the wardship is not discharged, the High Court takes control over the child's upbringing but will then delegate powers to make decisions to the persons who are responsible for looking after the child. The difference between asking the High Court to exercise its inherent jurisdiction and warding a child is that the court, when exercising its inherent jurisdiction, simply adjudicates on a particular aspect of the child's welfare; it does not place the child under the long-term control of the court.

There are rules in section 100 of the Children Act 1989 restricting a local authority's use of wardship and the inherent jurisdiction,[1131] which are discussed in the next section. However, nothing in the 1989 Act prevents others who have a genuine interest in the upbringing of a child from warding the child, or from otherwise asking the High Court to exercise its inherent jurisdiction to deal with a specific issue which has arisen. However, to use the jurisdiction when other remedies under the Children Act 1989 are denied, or have been used and exhausted, would turn the inherent jurisdiction into an alternative code for resolving disputes about children, with its own body of case law separate and distinct from cases decided under the Act. This would seriously undermine the Act and its associated procedures.

The inherent jurisdiction is therefore usually used to fill any gaps where otherwise there may be no jurisdiction to intervene. An example is provided by *Re X (A Minor) (Adoption Details: Disclosure)*.[1132] Under the Adoption Act then in force,[1133] the Registrar-General had a mandatory duty to keep a register of adopted children and had to allow any person to search the index and to have a certified copy of any entry. The fear in this case was that the birth mother, who was an aggressive and violent woman, of whom the child was terrified, would discover the child's whereabouts if she had access to this information. The Court of Appeal ruled that the High Court could order that the Registrar-General should not reveal details of the adoption recorded on the register

---

[1126]  *Re J (A Child) (Custody Rights: Jurisdiction)* [2006] 1 AC 80, paras 26–7, and cases cited therein.

[1127]  See for examples of the courts approach: *Re F (Minor: Abduction: Jurisdiction)* [1991] Fam 25; *Re P (A Minor) (Child Abduction: Non-Convention Country)* [1997] 1 FLR 780; *Re JA (Child Abduction: Non-Convention Country)* [1998] 1 FLR 231; *Re E (Abduction: Non-Convention Country)* [1999] 2 FLR 642; *B v El-B (Abduction: Sharia Law: Welfare of Child)* [2003] 1 FLR 811.

[1128]  See J. Seymour, 'Parens Patriae and Wardship Powers: Their Nature and Origins' (1994) 14 Oxford Journal of Legal Studies 159.

[1129]  See generally, and for its use especially prior to the Children Act 1989, N. Lowe and R. White, *Wards of Court*, 2nd edn (London: Barry Rose, 1986).

[1130]  See *Re S (Infants)* [1967] 1 All ER 202 at 209 *per* Cross J.

[1131]  See M. Parry, 'The Children Act 1989: Local Authorities, Wardship and the Revival of the Inherent Jurisdiction' [1992] Journal of Social Welfare and Family Law 212.

[1132]  [1994] 2 FLR 45.

[1133]  Adoption Act 1976, now superseded by the Adoption and Children Act 2002: see Chapter 11.

to any person without the leave of the court. Another need for the use of wardship arose where a contract for surrogate parenthood was involved, and where there appeared to be a need to throw a ring of care around the child, but where care proceedings were inappropriate.[1134]

## 7.1 **The Inherent jurisdiction and local authorities**

Historically, local authorities could invite the High Court to exercise its inherent jurisdiction in wardship to make up for apparent deficiencies in the statutory child protection framework. Wardship was used to safeguard children when other procedures and remedies were unavailable or had failed. In return, the local authority relinquished some of its control over a child to the court, and, before it took any important step in the child's life which related to his upbringing, it was required to refer the matter back to the court. Section 100 of the Children Act 1989 makes plain that it is no longer open to local authorities to ask the High Court to exercise the inherent jurisdiction as an alternative to taking proceedings under the Act. Section 100(2) provides that no court shall exercise the inherent jurisdiction to put a child in care, under local authority supervision, or into local authority accommodation. Nor may the jurisdiction be used for the purpose of conferring on any local authority the power to determine any question which has arisen, or which may arise, in connection with any aspect of parental responsibility for the child.[1135] In *Devon County Council v S*,[1136] Thorpe J drew a distinction between a local authority seeking to have protective powers conferred upon it through resort to the inherent jurisdiction, which is prohibited by section 100(2)(d), and a local authority inviting the court to exercise its inherent powers to make an order which does not give any powers to the local authority. The local authority could invite the court to exercise its own powers under the inherent jurisdiction where the purpose of the order was to prevent an abuser from having contact with children living at home with their mother.

The High Court may only grant a local authority leave to apply for the exercise of the court's inherent jurisdiction if it is satisfied both that the desired result cannot be achieved by any other order for which the local authority is entitled to apply and that there is reasonable cause to believe that if the court's inherent jurisdiction is not exercised the child is likely to suffer significant harm.[1137]

The reason for this restriction on the High Court's powers is that if a local authority could invoke the inherent jurisdiction, or make a child a ward of court, whenever it wished to do so, this could enable the authority to obtain parental responsibility for a child other than by satisfying the threshold test for care proceedings.[1138] The threshold test lays down a minimum standard which, if established, allows a court to authorise a child's placement in the care of a local authority. It is a universal standard applicable in all cases to all local authorities and the structure of the Children Act 1989 makes it absolutely clear that the test cannot be circumvented.

However, when a child is in the care of a local authority, sometimes a specific question may arise in connection with an aspect of the authority's parental responsibility where it takes the view that a court should be the decision-maker rather than itself. Examples might be where a child in care is seeking an abortion against her parents' wishes;[1139] where sterilisation is believed to be in a child's best interests;[1140] where a '*Gillick* competent' child is refusing consent to medical treatment;[1141] or where a child and his parents are refusing to consent to medical treatment on religious or other grounds.[1142] The strict legal position is that because the local authority has

---

[1134]  *Re C (A Minor) (Wardship: Surrogacy)* [1985] FLR 846. See for another example *D v N (Contact Order: Conditions)* [1997] 2 FLR 797.

[1135]  Children Act 1989, s 100(2).        [1136]  [1994] 1 FLR 355.        [1137]  Children Act 1989, s 100(4) and (5).

[1138]  Ibid, s 31(2).        [1139]  Eg *Re B (Wardship: Abortion)* [1991] 2 FLR 426.

[1140]  The sterilisation of a minor in virtually all cases requires the prior sanction of a High Court judge: Practice Note [1990] 2 FLR 530; *Re B (A Minor) (Wardship: Sterilisation)* [1987] 2 FLR 314.

[1141]  Eg *Re W (A Minor) (Medical Treatment)* [1992] 4 All ER 627. See Chapter 8.

[1142]  Eg *Re B (A Minor) (Wardship: Medical Treatment)* (1982) 3 FLR 717, FD.

parental responsibility it has the right to give the requisite consents to the medical treatment which is in issue. But these questions raise sensitive and controversial moral dilemmas, and it may be thought that a court, rather than the local authority, ought to be the final decision-maker. Because a local authority with care of a child cannot apply for a specific issue order in relation to that child, the local authority may properly turn to the High Court's inherent jurisdiction for assistance.

What is the position where a parent or a third party wishes to invoke the inherent jurisdiction in order to challenge a decision made by a local authority in the exercise of their parental responsibility? By placing a prohibition on specific issue orders being made in respect of children in care, section 9(1) of the Children Act 1989 makes it plain that Parliament did not intend that parents, or others, should be able to bring proceedings under the Act to challenge any of the many day-to-day decisions made by local authorities with respect to the children for whom they are responsible. Similarly it was recognised by the House of Lords in *A v Liverpool City Council*[1143] as a fundamental principle of law that the High Court will not exercise its inherent jurisdiction where this would interfere with the discretionary powers which Parliament has clearly given to local authorities.

Where, by contrast, the issue to be resolved does not involve an exercise of parental responsibility by the local authority, the High Court may be able to intervene. In *Re M (Care: Leave to Interview Child)*[1144] a solicitor acting for a father in criminal proceedings wished to interview the father's two sons for the purpose of preparing his defence. The boys were the subject of interim care orders, and while the local authority did not object to them being interviewed, there was disagreement about the conditions under which the interview should be carried out. The issue for the court was whether it could intervene under its inherent jurisdiction, or whether the decision was one for the local authority alone. Hale J held that local authorities have the same powers as parents when exercising their parental responsibility. These powers are not unlimited, and they may not be exercised in ways which infringe the rights of others. Here justice required that the father, who faced very serious charges, should be permitted properly to prepare his defence. The court had powers under its inherent jurisdiction to determine how the solicitor should interview the children and it would exercise these powers whether or not the local authority agreed.

How local authorities, which have special responsibilities towards children in need and children suffering, or likely to suffer, significant harm, have responded to the child care and protection framework, and how courts have approached child care and protection cases, are both considered in the next chapter.

## Discussion Questions

1. What is meant by 'welfare' in section 1(1) of the Children Act 1989? Should the paramountcy principle be abandoned? If so, what, if anything, could replace it?

2. Is shared residence the norm upon parental separation? Should it be?

3. Is there a right of contact between a non-resident parent and child in English law?

4. Should the courts assume that contact between a non-resident parent and a child is beneficial?

---

[1143] [1981] 2 All ER 385.      [1144] [1995] 1 FLR 825.

5. In cases of dispute, the relocation of a parent to a different country requires a difficult decision for a court between a parent wishing to start a new life and the parent left behind. Critically evaluate the English courts' approach.

## Further Reading

BAINHAM, A., 'Contact as a Right and Obligation' in A. Bainham, B. Lindley, M. Richards, and L. Trinder (eds), *Children and Their Families: Contact, Rights and Welfare* (Oxford: Hart, 2003), p 62

BAINHAM A. and GILMORE, S., 'The English Children and Families Act 2014' (2015) 46 VUWLR 627.

CHOUDHRY, S. and FENWICK, H., 'Taking the Rights of Parents and Children Seriously: Confronting the Welfare Principle under the Human Rights Act' (2005) 25(3) Oxford Journal of Legal Studies 453

COLLIER, R. and SHELDON, S. (eds), *Fathers' Rights Activism and Law Reform in Comparative Perspective* (Oxford: Hart, 2006)

EEKELAAR, J., 'Beyond the Welfare Principle' [2002] Child and Family Law Quarterly 237

FEHLBERG, B., SMYTH, B., MACLEAN, M., and ROBERTS, C., 'Legislating for Shared Time Parenting After Separation: A Research Review' (2011) 25(3) International Journal of Law, Policy and the Family 318

GEORGE, R., 'The International Relocation Debate' [2012] Journal of Social Welfare and Family Law 141

GEORGE, R., 'How do Judges Decide International Relocation Cases?' [2015] Child and Family Law Quarterly 377.

GEORGE, R. and COMINETTI, O., 'International Relocation: Key Findings from the 2012 Study' [2013] Family Law 1430

GILMORE, S., 'The Nature, Scope and Use of the Specific Issue Order' [2004] Child and Family Law Quarterly 367

GILMORE, S., 'Contact/Shared Residence and Child Well-Being—Research Evidence and its Implications for Legal Decision Making' (2006) 20 International Journal of Law, Policy and the Family 344

GILMORE, S., 'Court Decision-Making in Shared Residence Order Cases—A Critical Examination' [2006] Child and Family Law Quarterly 478

GILMORE, S., 'Disputing Contact: Challenging Some Assumptions' [2008] Child and Family Law Quarterly 285

GILMORE, S., 'Shared Residence: A Summary of the Courts' Guidance' [2010] Family Law 285

HARRIS, P. G. and GEORGE, R. H., 'Parental Responsibility and Shared Residence Orders: Parliamentary Intentions and Judicial Interpretations' [2010] Child and Family Law Quarterly 151

HARRIS-SHORT, S., 'Resisting the March Towards 50/50 Shared Residence. Rights, Welfare and Equality in Post-Separation Families' (2010) 32 Journal of Social Welfare and Family Law 257–74

HERRING, J., 'The Human Rights Act and the Welfare Principle in Family Law: Conflicting or Complementary?' (1999) 11 Child and Family Law Quarterly 223

HERRING, J., 'Farewell Welfare?' (2005) 27(2) Journal of Social Welfare and Family Law 159

HERRING, J. and FOSTER C., 'Welfare Means Rationality, Virtue and Altruism' (2012) 32 Legal Studies 480

KAGANAS, F., 'Regulating Emotion: Judging Contact Disputes' [2011] Child and Family Law Quarterly 63

LOWE, N., '*J v C*: Placing The Child's Welfare Centre Stage' in S. Gilmore, J. Herring, and R. Probert (eds), *Landmark Cases in Family Law* (Oxford: Hart, 2011), pp 27–45

Perry, A. and Rainey, B., 'Supervised, Supported and Indirect Contact Orders: Research Findings' (2007) 21 International Journal of Law, Policy and the Family 21

Reece, H., 'The Paramountcy Principle: Consensus or Construct?' (1996) 49 Current Legal Problems 267

Sturge, C. and Glaser, D., 'Contact and Domestic Violence—The Experts' Court Report' (2000) 30 Family Law 615

Trinder, L., 'Shared Residence: A Review of Recent Research Evidence' [2010] Child and Family Law Quarterly 475

Visit the Online Resource Centre at **www.oxfordtextbooks.co.uk/orc/gilmore_glennon5e/** for a range of further features including a detailed bibliography and self-test questions.

**online resource centre**

# Children needing services, care, and protection

## INTRODUCTION: A LIBERAL STANDARD

The care and protection of children is in most cases a natural parental instinct and will be perceived by parents as their moral duty.[1] However, if analysed philosophically, the moral duty arguably falls on a society as a whole.[2] How the care and protection of children are achieved in a particular society is a matter of political choice. The state could, for example, adopt a form of licensed parenthood,[3] checking on parenting abilities prior to allocating parents to children, although this would, in many cases, present obvious difficulties in predicting future parenting abilities. An even more extreme method would be to adopt a collectivist approach to children's care and upbringing, with the state directly concerned in all children's upbringing. Recognising the danger in this approach of indoctrination and social engineering, however, the law places value on the upbringing of children within families. As Baroness Hale explained in *Re B (Care Proceedings: Standard of Proof)*:[4]

> Families in all their subversive variety are the breeding ground of diversity and individuality. In a free and democratic society we value diversity and individuality. Hence the family is given special protection in all the modern human rights instruments including the European Convention on Human Rights (Article 8), the International Covenant on Civil and Political Rights (Article 23) and throughout the United Nations Convention on the Rights of the Child. As McReynolds J famously said in *Pierce v Society of Sisters* (1925) 268 US 510, 535, 'The child is not the mere creature of the State'.[5]

Of course, with this view in mind a society could simply defer to parental care within individual families.[6] But experience shows that sometimes individuals with parental responsibility for a child may be unable properly to fulfil their parental responsibilities without some assistance from the state, or there may be a need for the state to intervene in family life[7] to protect a child or to provide alternative care for the

---

[1] See C. Barton and G. Douglas, *Law and Parenthood* (London: Butterworths, 1995), Ch 2.

[2] Based on a general moral duty to promote human flourishing: see J. Eekelaar, 'Are Parents Morally Obliged to Care for Their Children?' (1991) 11(3) Oxford Journal of Legal Studies 340.

[3] See eg H. LaFollette, 'Licensing Parents' (1980) 9 Philosophy and Public Affairs 182; C. P. Mangel, 'Licensing Parents: How Feasible?' (1988) 22 Family Law Quarterly 17; J. C. Westman, *Licensing Parents: Can We Prevent Child Abuse and Neglect?* (Cambridge, MA: Perseus Books, 1994); M. Freeman, 'The Right to Responsible Parents' in J. Bridgeman, H. Keating, and C. Lind (eds), *Responsibility, Law and the Family* (Aldershot: Ashgate, 2008); J. G. Dwyer, *The Relationship Rights of Children* (New York: Cambridge University Press, 2006).

[4] [2008] UKHL 35, [2009] 1 AC 11.    [5] Ibid, [20].

[6] For a view approaching this, see J. Goldstein, A. Freud, and A. Solnit, *Before the Best Interests of the Child* (New York: Free Press, 1979), p 9: the child's need for safety within the confines of the family must be met by law through its recognition of family privacy as the barrier to state intrusion upon parental autonomy in childrearing.

[7] On one view, the notion that there is a private sphere of family life into which the state intervenes is a myth: see F. E. Olsen, 'The Myth of State Intervention in the Family' (1984–85) 18 University of Michigan Journal of Law Reform

child. Recognising the benefits of family life, but also the need to safeguard and promote the welfare of children, English law thus takes a middle ground, adopting a so-called 'liberal standard'.[8] This presumes that the upbringing of children within families is desirable and that the state does not intrude unless there is consent or stated conditions for state intervention are fulfilled. As we shall see, this approach requires the law to identify the point at, and basis upon, which the state is entitled to intervene.[9] In this chapter we seek to explain how English law expresses this liberal standard of state intervention in family life.

The relevant law is principally set out in the Children Act 1989, which repealed earlier legislation and radically altered the law on child care and child protection.[10] In order to understand the current law, it is helpful briefly to consider some of the deficiencies in the previous law and the various factors which influenced the change.

# 1 Background

## 1.1 The inadequacies of the previous law

The law on child care and protection prior to the Children Act 1989 had developed piecemeal along three main strands[11] and was unsatisfactory in several respects.[12] One strand was the law relating to the care of children who were orphaned or whose parents were otherwise unable to care for them, which manifested itself perhaps most memorably in the nineteenth-century workhouses, as depicted in Charles Dickens' novel, *Oliver Twist*.[13] The modern version of this provision, prior to the Children Act 1989, emerged in the Children Act 1948,[14] later consolidated in the Child Care

---

835–64 at 837: 'Because the state is deeply implicated in the formation and functioning of families, it is nonsense to talk about whether the state does or does not intervene in the family'; criticised by L. D. Houlgate, 'What is Legal Intervention in the Family? Family Law and Family Privacy' (1998) 17 Law and Philosophy 141–58 (because nothing can count as non-intervention, the conclusion that there is no such thing as non-intervention is logically empty).

   [8] D. Archard, *Children: Rights and Childhood*, 2nd edn (London: Routledge, 2004).

   [9] In thinking about state intervention in terms of explicit interventions to protect and care for children, sight should not be lost of the more subtle ways in which the state's policies exercise 'governance' over families through, eg, the education system and health advice/monitoring. As Archard explains, a 'therapeutic medical model stipulates a norm of familial "health" which, by means of professionals, insinuates into the "private" life of families' (D. Archard, ibid, 155). See J. Donzelot, *The Policing of Families: Welfare versus the State* (London: Hutchinson, 1980), drawing on the work/methodology of Michel Foucault.

   [10] For excellent detailed accounts of the law and policy in this area, see eg L. Hoyano and C. Keenan, *Child Abuse Law and Policy Across Boundaries* (Oxford: Oxford University Press, 2007); C. Lyon, *Child Abuse* (Bristol: Family Law, 2006 reprint). For critique of child protection systems, see B. Lonne, N. Parton, J. Thomson, and M. Harries, *Reforming Child Protection* (Abingdon: Routledge, 2009).

   [11] For an account, see R. Dingwall, J. Eekelaar, and T. Murray, *The Protection of Children: State Intervention and Family Life* (Oxford: Basil Blackwell, 1983), Ch 1. For background, see S. Cretney, *Family Law in the Twentieth Century—A History* (Oxford: Oxford University Press, 2003), Ch 20; J. Masson, 'From Curtis to Waterhouse: State Care and Child Protection in the UK 1945–2000' in S. Katz, J. Eekelaar, and M. Maclean (eds), *Cross-Currents: Family Law Policy in the US and England* (Oxford: Oxford University Press, 2000), Ch 26 (p 565); B. Hale et al, *The Family, Law and Society: Cases and Materials*, 5th edn (Oxford: Oxford University Press, 2005),Ch 11, esp pp 530 et seq; N. Parton, *The Politics of Child Abuse* (Basingstoke: Macmillan, 1985) N. Parton, *Governing the Family* (Basingstoke: Macmillan, 1991).

   [12] See M. Hayes, 'Removing Children from their Families—Law and Policy Before the Children Act 1989' in G. Douglas and N. Lowe (eds), *The Continuing Evolution of Family Law* (Bristol: Jordan Publishing, 2009).

   [13] The tone for the law was set as early as the Poor Relief Act of 1601, 43 Eliz c 2.

   [14] Preceded by the Monckton Report (Cmd 6636, 1945) the *Report of the Care of Children Committee* (Cmd 6922, 1946) (The Curtis Committee); S. Cretney, 'The State as a Parent: The Children Act 1948 in Retrospect' in *Law, Law Reform and the Family* (Oxford: Clarendon Press, 1998), ch 9; S. Cretney, 'The Children Act 1948—Lessons For Today?' [1997] Child and Family Law Quarterly 359; and S. Cretney, 'The State as a Parent: The Children Act 1948 in Retrospect' (1998) 114 LQR 419–59.

Act 1980. Under those provisions a local authority could assume parental rights and duties in respect of a child in its care administratively, simply by passing a council resolution.[15]

A second strand of law allowed an application to be made to a court for a care order committing a child into the care of a local authority. Section 1 of the Children and Young Persons Act 1969 provided that a child who was in need of care and control could be taken into care on various grounds, for example a child who was ill-treated or neglected or one who had committed an offence. The merging within the grounds of children who were victims of neglect and delinquent children who were viewed as a threat to society arose out of increasing concerns in the 1960s about childhood delinquency and a policy decision to deal with such children where possible by providing alternative care rather than through the penal system.[16] Importantly, this meant that the grounds for making a care order made no explicit reference to a lack of reasonable parental care because that criterion was not relevant in the case of the juvenile offender where the focus was on commission of an offence. Consequently, prior to the Children Act 1989, parents were not parties in care proceedings. There were also problems with shorter-term child protection measures. A local authority could obtain a 'place of safety order'[17] to remove a child immediately to its care for 28 days. Parents had no right to challenge the order or the local authority's decisions regarding access to the child.

The third strand was the use of the inherent jurisdiction of the High Court to place a child in care. Instead of applying for a care order, local authorities would issue a summons in wardship and then ask the judge to commit the child into the care of the local authority. Thus, the statutory grounds in the Children and Young Persons Act 1969 could be bypassed, and a child could be placed in care simply by applying the child's welfare as the first and paramount consideration. There was in this process no threshold barrier to state intervention and, in theory at least, a child could be placed in care simply on the basis that the child would fare better with substitute carers than with his or her parents.[18]

The law was clearly complex, lacking overall coherence, and in need of rationalisation. The need for change was recognised in 1984 by a House of Commons Committee,[19] and consequently an Interdepartmental Working Group was set up to review the law. Its report entitled the *Review of Child Care Law*[20] formed the core of the new philosophy and framework for state intervention in family life within the public law provisions of the Children Act 1989. The ensuing legislation sought to retain positive features of earlier legislation, such as the philosophy of providing support for children and families within the Children Act 1948. At the same time, however, it sought to deal with the various criticisms which have been highlighted by distinguishing more clearly between voluntary and compulsory intervention in family life, ensuring that there was only one route into local authority care when a threshold for state intervention had been passed; and to ensure that the interests of parents (and children) were appropriately protected.[21]

The relevant legislation is in Parts III, IV, and V of the Children Act 1989 and associated Schedules. Part III contains various provisions which facilitate local authorities' working in partnership with parents to safeguard and promote the welfare of children in their area; Part IV provides the legal

---

[15] Child Care Act 1980, s 3.

[16] J. Eekelaar, R. Dingwall, and T. Murray, 'Victims or Threats? Children in Care Proceedings' (1982) 4(2) Journal of Social Welfare and Family Law 68–82.

[17] Children and Young Persons Act 1969, s 28.

[18] M. Hayes, 'Removing Children from their Families—Law and Policy Before the Children Act 1989' in G. Douglas and N. Lowe (eds), *The Continuing Evolution of Family Law* (Bristol: Jordan Publishing, 2009), pp 99–101.

[19] Short Report, Social Services Committee (London: HMSO, 1984) (HC 360).

[20] DHSS, *Review of Child Care Law: Report to Ministers of an Inter-Departmental Working Party* (London: HMSO, 1985).

[21] Neatly summarised in the White Paper that preceded the Act: see Secretary of State for Social Services, *The Law on Child Care and Family Services* (Cm 62, 1987). Not surprisingly, the Act discloses a number of different perspectives: see L. Fox-Harding, 'The Children Act in Context: Four Perspectives on Child Care Law and Policy' (1991) 13 Journal of Social Welfare and Family Law 179.

framework for compulsory intervention by way of care or supervision of children; and Part V addresses investigation and emergency protection. The Act is supplemented, of course, by a lot of subordinate legislation and also by Guidance.[22]

The changes were also influenced by research,[23] which showed that, in general, there was precipitate intervention and overuse of emergency intervention, a picture graphically illustrated by the Cleveland Child Abuse Inquiry.[24] Over 200 children in the north-east of England were taken from their parents by social workers based on disputed allegations of sexual abuse founded on medical diagnoses by two paediatricians. The inquiry found that social workers had deferred unduly to the medical diagnosis, rather than considering it against the full family context. Magistrates had then effectively 'rubber-stamped' the applications for emergency orders. The inquiry highlighted the need for greater protection of parents' and children's rights. Seeking to address those concerns, the law now gives competent children the right to refuse medical assessments, has reduced the time children can be kept away from home following emergency intervention, and ensures contact between parent and child during this period.[25] In contrast to the picture painted by research and by the Cleveland affair, other inquiry reports into the deaths of children highlighted failures to intervene and deficiencies in practice.[26] Of particular influence on the law was the inquiry into the death of Kimberley Carlile.[27] Kimberley, aged 4, was killed by her stepfather, Nigel Hall, after a visiting social worker was refused access to the family home. This highlighted the need for clearer legal provisions on gaining access to children in cases of suspected abuse.

### 1.2  Ongoing practice concerns: the Climbié Report and the Children Act 2004

Following implementation of the Children Act 1989, further concerns were expressed about the workings of the child protection system in practice, most notably with regard to inter-agency communication. Lord Laming's inquiry into the death of Victoria Climbié[28] found that she suffered appalling abuse at the hands of her great aunt and the great aunt's partner, and remained unprotected despite the fact that she was known to 'four social services departments, two child protection teams of the Metropolitan Police Service (MPS), a specialist centre managed by the NSPCC, and she was admitted to two different hospitals because of suspected deliberate harm.'[29] The report recommended structural changes to the child protection system, which led to the Children Act 2004.

---

[22] See the various updated volumes of *The Children Act 1989 Guidance and Regulations*, available from the Department for Children Schools and Families, at www.education.gov.uk.

[23] J. Packman, *Who Needs Care? Social Work Decisions About Children* (Oxford: Blackwell, 1986).

[24] Secretary of State for Social Services, *Report of the Inquiry into Child Abuse in Cleveland* (Cmnd 412, 1988). See N. Parton, 'Sexual Abuse, the Cleveland Affair and the Private Family' in N. Parton, *Governing the Family* (Basingstoke: Macmillan, 1991).

[25] A Government-commissioned programme of research into child protection was initiated following the Cleveland Inquiry Report. A summary of the findings of 20 studies from that research programme was published in 1995: Department of Health, *Child Protection: Messages from Research* (London: HMSO, 1995), for a critique see C. Wattam, 'The Social Construction of Child Abuse for Practical Policy Purposes—A Review of Child Protection: Messages from Research' (1996) 8 Child and Family Law Quarterly 189. See also D. Gough, *Child Abuse Interventions: A Review of the Research Literature* (London: HMSO, 1993).

[26] N. Parton and N. Martin, 'Public Inquiries, Legalism and Child Care in England and Wales' (1989) 3 International Journal of Law and the Family 21–39.

[27] London Borough of Greenwich, *A Child in Mind: Protection of Children in a Responsible Society: Report of the Commission of Inquiry into the Circumstances Surrounding the Death of Kimberley Carlile* (1987).

[28] Lord Laming, *The Victoria Climbié Inquiry: Report of an Inquiry by Lord Laming* (Cm 5730, January 2003). See H. Conway, 'The Laming Inquiry—Victoria Climbié's Legacy' [2002] Family Law 755.

[29] Laming, *The Victoria Climbié Inquiry*, Summary Report, p 3.

## 1.3 **The Children Act 2004**

The Children Act 2004 was enacted with a view to ensuring that all organisations that work with children 'share a commitment to safeguard and promote their welfare' that is underpinned by statutory duties,[30] and that there are in place appropriate strategies to achieve the same. The relevant provisions of the 2004 Act are found in Part 2, which is concerned with children's services. First, the law seeks to give out the clear message that everyone who is professionally involved with children and young people shares responsibility for safeguarding and promoting their welfare. Local authorities that are children's services authorities,[31] headed by a Director of Children's Services, have specific statutory duties aimed at safeguarding and promoting children's welfare.[32] Section 11 of the Children Act 2004 requires various other bodies to ensure that their services and functions are discharged with regard to the need to safeguard and promote the welfare of children: for example, National Health Services;[33] the police, probation, and prison services; youth offending teams; and secure training centres.[34] Other statutes respectively place similar duties on those carrying out education functions,[35] on the Children and Family Court Advisory and Support Service (Cafcass),[36] and on the UK Border Agency.[37]

While each of these agencies has its own duties, the law also seeks to bring together relevant agencies to cooperate on the strategy for safeguarding and promoting children's welfare. Section 10 of the Children Act 2004 requires each local authority in England to make arrangements to promote cooperation between the authority and its relevant partners (as defined in s 10(4))[38] and such other persons or bodies as the authority considers appropriate.[39] The arrangements are to be made with a view to improving the well-being of children in the authority's area so far as relating to: physical and mental health and emotional, social, and economic well-being; protection from harm and neglect; and education, training, and recreation.[40] The relevant partners have a duty to cooperate with the local authority in making the arrangements.[41] So section 10 is the legal foundation for what are called Children's Trusts (ie, the bringing together of the local authority and its relevant partners with a view to cooperating regarding children's well-being in the area). By section 9A of the Children Act 2004, the Secretary of State can now set targets for safeguarding and promoting the welfare of children in a local authority's area.

Section 13 of the 2004 Act requires each children's services authority to establish a Local Safeguarding Children Board,[42] the objective of which is to coordinate and ensure the effectiveness of what is done by the organisations on the Board for the purposes of safeguarding and promoting the welfare of children in the relevant local authority's area.[43]

---

[30] Appendix 1.

[31] A metropolitan district council; district councils where there is no county council, a London Borough Council, the Common Council of the City of London, the Council of the Isles of Scilly.

[32] Children Act 2004, s 18.

[33] Primary care trusts, NHS trusts, NHS foundation trusts, strategic health authorities, designated special health authorities.

[34] See Children Act 2004, s 11(1) for the full list of persons/bodies to whom the section applies.

[35] See Education Act 2002, ss 175 and 157 and regulations; Children Act 1989, s 87 (accommodation at independent schools); Child Care Act 2006, s 40 (duty in respect of Early Years Foundation Stage).

[36] Criminal Justice and Court Services Act 2000.

[37] Borders, Citizenship and Immigration Act 2009, s 55.

[38] These include health, education, police, and probation services amongst others. The full list of relevant partners is set out in s 10(4).

[39] Being persons or bodies of any nature who exercise functions or are engaged in activities in relation to children in the authority's area.

[40] Section 10(3) provides that: '[i]n making arrangements under this section a [local authority] in England must have regard to the importance of parents and other persons caring for children in improving the well-being of children'.

[41] Children Act 2004, s 10(5).

[42] See Children Act 2004, ss 13–16 and the Local Safeguarding Children Boards Regulations 2006 (SI 2006/90) (made under s 13(2)); Local Safeguarding Children Boards (Amendment) Regulations 2010 (SI 2010/622) (made under s 13(4)).

[43] See Children Act 2004, s 14.

The legislation is supplemented by guidance on inter-agency cooperation, *Working Together to Safeguard Children*,[44] and on how social work assessments are to be carried out.[45]

## 2  Part III of the Children Act 1989

Part III of the Children Act 1989 is concerned with the duty of every local authority to provide support for children and their families. It recognises that families sometimes require help in bringing up children. A large body of regulations and guidance has been issued which provides further detail on how this Part (and other Parts) of the Act should be implemented.[46]

In carrying out its functions under Part III, the local authority can call on the support of other agencies, any local authority, local housing authority, health authorities,[47] or any other authorised person.[48] Under section 27 an authority whose help is so requested 'shall' comply with the request 'if it is compatible with their own statutory or other duties and obligations and does not unduly prejudice the discharge of any of their functions'.[49]

In *R v Northavon District Council, ex p Smith*,[50] a housing authority decided that the applicant and his wife were homeless and in priority need because they had five children, but that they had become homeless intentionally within section 60(1) of the Housing Act 1985. The housing authority therefore declined to provide accommodation in response to a request made under section 27 by the social services department. The House of Lords ruled that section 27 did not enable a local authority to require a housing authority to exercise its powers to provide housing. Instead it imposed a duty of cooperation between social services and housing authorities, both of which had together to do the best they could to carry out their respective responsibilities for children and housing.

Fundamental to the thinking in Part III of the Children Act 1989 is the principle that it is normally in the best interests of children to be brought up by their own families, and the expectation is that a local authority will, where possible, work in partnership with parents.[51] Part III seeks to facilitate this process by setting out the duty of every local authority to provide services for children in need and powers to provide services for other children.

---

### Key legislation

Section 17, the opening provision, states that:

(1) It shall be the general duty of every local authority...

  (a) to safeguard and promote the welfare of children within their area who are in need; and

  (b) so far as is consistent with that duty, to promote the upbringing of such children by their families, by providing a range and level of services appropriate to those children's needs.

---

[44] See HM Government, *Working Together to Safeguard Children: A Guide to Inter-Agency Working to Safeguard and Promote the Welfare of Children* (HM Government, March 2013), issued pursuant to the Local Authority Social Services Act 1970, s 7, and with which local authorities must therefore comply in carrying out their social services functions.

[45] Department of Health, *Framework for the Assessment of Children in Need and Their Families* (London: HMSO, 2000).

[46] Some details concerning the provision of services under Pt III, the regulation of child-minding, private foster care, community homes, and voluntary homes are beyond the scope of this book. For greater detail, see updated volumes of *The Children Act 1989 Guidance and Regulations*, available from the Department for Children Schools and Families at www.education.gov.uk. See too, M. D. A. Freeman, *Children, Their Families and the Law* (Basingstoke: Macmillan, 1992).

[47] Any local health board, special health authority, primary care trust, NHS trust, or NHS foundation trust.

[48] Children Act 1989, s 27(1).      [49] Ibid, s 27(2).      [50] [1994] 2 FLR 671, HL.

[51] See particularly Department of Health, *The Challenge of Partnership in Child Protection: Practice Guide* (London: HMSO, 1995); F. Kaganas, M. King, and C. Piper (eds), *Legislating for Harmony—Partnerships under the Children Act 1989* (London: Jessica Kingsley, 1996).

For the purpose of facilitating the discharge of the general duty in section 17, further provisions are set out in Part I of Schedule 2 to the Act. These are discussed in more detail later. For the moment, however, we need to examine the scope of section 17.

## 2.1 **Who are 'children in need'?**

Section 17(10) provides that a child shall be taken to be in need if:

(a) he is unlikely to achieve or maintain, or to have the opportunity of achieving or maintaining, a reasonable standard of health or development without the provision for him of services by a local authority under this Part;

(b) his health or development is likely to be significantly impaired, or further impaired, without the provision for him of such services; or

(c) he is disabled,

and 'family', in relation to such a child, includes any person who has parental responsibility for the child and any other person with whom he has been living.[52]

Section 17(11) explains what is meant by 'disabled', 'development', and 'health'. It provides:

For the purposes of this Part, a child is disabled if he is blind, deaf or dumb or suffers from mental disorder of any kind or is substantially and permanently handicapped by illness, injury or congenital deformity or such other disability as may be prescribed; and in this Part—

'development' means physical, intellectual, emotional, social or behavioural development; and 'health' means physical or mental health.

Thus it can be seen that the definition of a child in need focuses both on a child who is disabled and on a child who is at risk of impaired health or development unless preventive steps are taken. These steps may include not only the provision of services for the child himself but also their provision for any member of his family, if they are provided with a view to safeguarding or promoting the child's welfare.[53] Before determining what (if any) services to provide for a particular child in need, a local authority shall, so far as is reasonably practicable and consistent with the child's welfare:

(a) ascertain the child's wishes and feelings regarding the provision of those services; and

(b) give due consideration (having regard to his age and understanding) to such wishes and feelings of the child as they have been able to ascertain.[54]

There is power within section 17(6) to give assistance in kind or in cash. Under section 17A and regulations there is power to make direct payments[55] to assist a person with parental responsibility for a disabled child, a disabled person with parental responsibility for a child, or a disabled child aged 16 or 17.

Where a local authority fails to provide a service for a child in need which it 'shall' provide, it will be in breach of its statutory duty. However, evaluative judgement or discretion is also built into many of the duties within Part III and Schedule 2; often the provision made must either be

---

[52] Schedule 2, para 1 provides that a local authority must 'take reasonable steps to identify the extent to which there are children in need within their area' and para 2 provides that the local authority must keep a register of disabled children.

[53] Section 17(3).   [54] Section 17(4A).

[55] See Community Care, Services for Carers and Children's Services (Direct Payments) (Wales) Regulations 2004 (SI 2004/1748); Community Care, Services for Carers and Children's Services (Direct Payments) (England) Regulations 2009 (SI 2009/1887).

'reasonable' or 'as is appropriate'. Because local authority social services departments are under a duty not only to provide services for children in need in their area but also for other needy members of the community, and because they are operating with limited budgets, standards of reasonableness and appropriateness may sometimes be low.[56]

The nature of the duty in section 17(1) was explored by the House of Lords in three conjoined appeals, *R (G) v Barnet London Borough Council; R (W) v Lambeth London Borough Council; R (A) v Lambeth London Borough Council*.[57] In each case the claimants were single parent mothers. In the *Barnet* case, G, a Dutch national of Somali origin, came to England with her son to look for the child's father. She claimed that she left the Netherlands because she was ostracised by the Somali community on account of her son's illegitimacy. G did not qualify for income support or housing provision in England. The relevant local authority, Barnet LBC, said that if the mother refused to return to the Netherlands, it would place the child with foster parents but would not provide the mother with accommodation. In the second case, W was intentionally homeless. The local authority took the view that, should the need arise, accommodation could be arranged for her two children alone.[58] The third case concerned A, two of whose three children were autistic. She claimed that the accommodation the local authority had provided was not suitable for her children's needs. The children had severe learning difficulties and required constant supervision. The family had been housed in a ground-floor two-bedroom flat, with no enclosed garden or play area, very close to a road which presented a danger to the children should they run out of the front door or climb out of a ground-floor window. In each case the children were 'in need' (because of disability or the parents' homelessness). In each case, it was argued that the effect of section 17(1) of the Children Act 1989 was that the respondent local authorities owed a duty to each individual child in need to provide that child with residential accommodation to enable the child to live with his or her mother if an assessment showed that that was required to meet the children's needs. However, the House of Lords, by a majority of 3 to 2,[59] held that section 17(1) is a general 'framework' duty 'owed to the local population and did not result in a mandatory duty to meet the assessed needs of every individual child regardless of resources'.[60] This interpretation was supported by the wording of section 17, for example its reference to a 'general duty',[61] particularly when contrasted with the more specific duties set out in Schedule 2 to the Act.[62] To read the section as imposing the duty contended for, would have had the effect of 'turning the social services department of the local authority into another kind of housing department'.[63]

## 2.2 Provision of services: Schedule 2 to the Children Act 1989

### 2.2.1 Services for children in need living with their families

Schedule 2 supplements section 17, providing that local authorities 'shall make such provision as they consider appropriate' for the following services: advice, guidance and counselling; occupational, social, cultural, or recreational activities; home help; assistance with travelling; or to

---

[56] Hence the frequent complaint that the principles in Pt III are excellent but that the resources to implement them have not been provided. See eg *R v Royal Borough of Kingston upon Thames, ex p T* [1994] 1 FLR 798, where the local authority were unable to accommodate two Vietnamese sisters together, partly because of resource constraints.

[57] [2003] UKHL 57, [2004] 2 AC 208.

[58] Under the Children Act 1989, s 20, which is discussed in detail in Section 2.3.

[59] Lord Hope of Craighead, Lord Scott of Foscote, and Lord Millett; Lord Nicholls of Birkenhead and Lord Steyn dissenting.

[60] See [2003] UKHL 57, [2004] 2 AC 208 [85] and [91] *per* Lord Hope of Craighead; the quoted description of the effect of the decision is that of Baroness Hale of Richmond in *R (G) v Southwark London Borough Council* [2009] UKHL 26, [2009] 2 FLR 380 at [23].

[61] [2003] UKHL 57 [107]–[109] *per* Lord Millett.       [62] See eg ibid at [119] *per* Lord Scott of Foscote.

[63] Ibid at [93] *per* Lord Hope of Craighead.

enable the child concerned and his family to have a holiday.[64] Local authorities are also required to provide family centres within their area[65] where the child, his parents, any person with parental responsibility, and any other person who is looking after him may attend for occupational, social, cultural, or recreational activities; advice, guidance, and counselling; and where such a person may be provided with accommodation while he is receiving such advice, guidance, or counselling.[66] In relation to disabled children, paragraph 6 of Schedule 2 provides that every local authority shall provide services designed to minimise the effect on disabled children within its area of their disabilities; and to give such children the opportunity to lead lives which are as normal as possible; and to assist individuals who provide care for such children to continue to do so, or to do so more effectively, by giving them breaks from caring. Under section 18, a local authority 'shall' provide day care for pre-school children in need as is appropriate; it 'may' provide such care for other children.

### 2.2.2 Avoiding the need for compulsory intervention

Several provisions within Schedule 2 to the Act are concerned with providing services to avoid the need for compulsory intervention in the family. Schedule 2, paragraph 4(1) provides that every local authority 'shall take reasonable steps, through the provision of services under Part III of this Act, to prevent children within their area suffering ill-treatment or neglect'. More specifically, paragraph 5 provides that where it appears that a child is suffering, or is likely to suffer, ill-treatment at the hands of another person who is living on the same premises, the local authority 'may' assist that person to obtain alternative accommodation, and such assistance may include the provision of cash. Even where there may be serious concerns about a child, paragraph 7 provides that a local authority shall take reasonable steps designed to reduce the need to bring proceedings for a care or supervision order or other legal proceedings with respect to children.

### 2.2.3 Keeping families together

As we have seen, the guiding principle behind the duty to provide services to children in need is to promote the upbringing of children by their families. With that principle in mind, paragraph 10 of Schedule 2 provides that where any child who is in need and whom the relevant local authority are not looking after is living apart from his family, they shall take such steps as are reasonably practicable to enable him to live with his family or to promote contact between him and his family. The duty applies if, in the local authority's opinion, it is necessary to do so in order to safeguard or promote the child's welfare. This provision envisages a situation such as where the family home has burnt down or been flooded and parents and children are respectively being accommodated by different relatives in separate homes. In such a situation the local authority may become under a duty so far as reasonably practicable to keep the family together.

Sometimes it may not be possible to keep children and their families together and a child may need instead to live away from home. In certain circumstances a local authority may have a duty under section 20 of the Children Act 1989 to provide accommodation for children.[67]

## 2.3 Provision of accommodation for children

Local authorities have a general duty to take steps, so far as reasonably practicable, to secure sufficient appropriate accommodation for the children whom the local authority may need to look after.[68] Like section 17, this is a duty to children in need in general.

---

[64] Schedule 2, para 8.    [65] Not merely children in need.

[66] Schedule 2, para 9; qualified by 'as they consider appropriate'.

[67] In such a case there is a duty under para 8A of Sch 2 to promote contact between each accommodated child and that child's family.

[68] Children Act 1989, s 22G.

---

### Key legislation

In addition, section 20(1) of the Children Act 1989 provides:

> Every local authority shall provide accommodation for any child in need within their area who appears to them to require accommodation as a result of—
>
> (a) there being no person who has parental responsibility for him;
>
> (b) his being lost or having been abandoned; or
>
> (c) the person who has been caring for him being prevented (whether or not permanently, and for whatever reason) from providing him with suitable accommodation or care.

---

Section 20(6) of the Children Act 1989 specifically provides that:

> Before providing accommodation under this section, a local authority shall, so far as is reasonably practicable and consistent with the child's welfare—
>
> (a) ascertain the child's wishes and feelings regarding the provision of accommodation; and
>
> (b) give due consideration (having regard to his age and understanding) to such wishes and feelings of the child as they have been able to ascertain.

Unlike the duty in section 17 of the Children Act 1989, this duty is owed to individual children. In *R (G) v Southwark London Borough Council*[69] (the facts of which are discussed later in this chapter), the House of Lords indicated that applying section 20(1) 'involves an evaluative judgment on some matters but not a discretion'.[70] Baroness Hale of Richmond, who delivered the leading opinion, set out the following series of questions which must be considered when deciding whether section 20 applies.[71]

(1) Is the applicant a child?

The first question is whether the local authority is dealing with a child. In most cases it will be clear from a person's birth certificate or other formal documentation that a person is under 18 and therefore a child for the purpose of the Children Act 1989, as defined in section 105(1) of the Act. However, with increasing numbers of young persons seeking asylum in England and Wales and arriving without such documentation, and requiring accommodation, sometimes an issue can arise as to whether a person is a child for the purpose of section 20. Such questions arose in *R (On the application of A) v Croydon London Borough Council; R (On the application of M) v Lambeth London Borough Council*.[72] The Supreme Court held that the term 'child' within the Children Act 1989 is 'defined in wholly objective terms'[73] and is not simply a matter of a local authority's opinion as to whether a person is a child.[74] In other words, it is a jurisdictional fact going to the operation of the Children Act 1989. If there is a dispute, therefore, ultimately it will be a court which will be responsible for deciding that question of fact.

(2) Is the applicant a child 'in need'?

By contrast, whether a child is 'in need' within the meaning of the Act is a question of judgement to be left to the relevant local authority. The local authority's judgement can only be interfered with

---

[69] [2009] UKHL 26, [2009] 2 FLR 380.     [70] Ibid, [31].

[71] Ibid, [28]. Her Ladyship acknowledged that the series of questions was adopted from Ward LJ's judgment in *R (A) v Croydon London Borough Council; R (M) v Lambeth London Borough Council* [2008] EWCA Civ 1445, [2009] 1 FLR 1324 at [75].

[72] [2009] UKSC 8, [2009] 3 FCR 607.     [73] Ibid, [32].

[74] This view was supported by ss 25 and 46 of the Children Act 1989, which permit the keeping of a child in secure accommodation and police protection respectively. These provisions would not apply to an adult whatever the relevant authorities believed to be a person's age. See [2009] UKSC 8, [2009] 3 FCR 607 at [17]–[19].

on the principle set out in *Associated Provincial Picture Houses Ltd v Wednesbury Corp*[75] (ie, if no local authority could rationally have reached that conclusion). In most cases in which a child is without a home, he or she is likely to be 'in need'.[76] However, as Baroness Hale pointed out in *R (G) v Southwark London Borough Council*[77] there may be rare instances where such a child is not in need: for example, a child whose home has been temporarily damaged by fire or flood who can afford hotel accommodation.

(3) Is the child within the local authority's area?

(4) Does he or she appear to the local authority to require accommodation?

(5) Is the need the result of the various factors set out in section 20(1)(a)–(c)?

The child's situation must fall within one of the paragraphs within section 20(1). An example of the use of section 20(1) might be where a single parent mother is taken ill and admitted to hospital and thus prevented from looking after her child. However, section 20(1) would not apply, for example, where a child has been living independently for some time and may lose his or her accommodation.[78] The words 'being prevented from providing him with suitable accommodation or care' in section 20(1)(c) have been given a wide construction, so that children do not suffer from the shortcomings of their parents or carers.[79] As Lord Hope of Craighead commented in *R (G) v Barnet London Borough Council; R (W) v Lambeth London Borough Council; R (A) v Lambeth London Borough Council*[80] the words 'for whatever reason' indicate that the widest possible scope must be given to this provision. So this paragraph would embrace a child who has been excluded from home by a parent or a situation where a parent is intentionally homeless.[81]

(6) What are the child's wishes and feelings regarding the provision of accommodation?

(7) And the linked question: having regard to the child's age and understanding, what due consideration is to be given to those wishes and feelings?

In *R (G) v Southwark London Borough Council*[82] Baroness Hale of Richmond made clear that 'there is nothing in s 20 which allows the local authority to force their services upon older and competent children who do not want them.'[83] Her Ladyship had commented in the earlier case *R(M) v Hammersmith and Fulham London Borough Council*[84] that:

> there may well be cases in which there is a choice between s 17 and s 20, where the wishes of the child, at least of an older child who is fully informed of the consequences of the choices before her, may determine the matter. It is most unlikely that s 20 was intended to operate compulsorily against a child who is competent to decide for herself. The whole object of the 1989 Act was to draw a clear distinction between voluntary and compulsory powers and to require that compulsion could only be used after due process of law.[85]

---

[75] [1948] 1 KB 223, CA.

[76] See *R v Northavon District Council, ex p Smith* [1994] 2 AC 402, [1994] 2 FLR 671 at 406 and 672 respectively *per* Lord Templeman; and see *per* Lord Nicholls of Birkenhead in *R (G) v Barnet London Borough Council; R (W) v Lambeth London Borough Council; R (A) v Lambeth London Borough Council* [2003] UKHL 57, [2004] 1 FLR 454 at [19]: 'A child without accommodation is a child in need.'

[77] [2009] UKHL 26, [2009] 2 FLR 380 at [28](2).

[78] The example was given by Baroness Hale at [2009] UKHL 26, [2009] 2 FLR 380 at [28](5).

[79] Ibid, [28](5).    [80] [2003] UKHL 57, [2004] 2 AC 208, [2003] 3 WLR 1194, [2004] 1 FLR 454 at [100].

[81] *R (G) v Barnet London Borough Council; R (W) v Lambeth London Borough Council; R (A) v Lambeth London Borough Council* [2003] UKHL 57, [2004] 1 FLR 454 at [24]; see also *Attorney-General ex rel Tilley v Wandsworth London Borough Council* [1981] 1 WLR 854, *sub nom Attorney-General ex rel Tilley v London Borough of Wandsworth* (1981) 1 FLR 377.

[82] [2009] UKHL 26, [2009] 2 FLR 380 at [28](6).    [83] As supported by s 20(11) discussed later.

[84] [2008] UKHL 14, [2008] 1 FLR 1384.    [85] Ibid, [43].

## 2.4 **Ways in which the child can be accommodated**

The ways in which a child may be accommodated are set out in section 22C of the Children Act 1989. This provides that unless it would not be consistent with the child's welfare or would not be reasonably practicable,[86] the child should be placed with a parent or someone who has parental responsibility.[87] Otherwise the child's placement can be with a relative or friend, a local authority foster parent, or in a children's home.[88] The local authority must give preference to placing the child with a relative or friend.[89] So far as reasonably practicable it must place the child within its area[90] and ensure the placement allows the child to live near home, does not disrupt the child's education or training, allows the child to live with any siblings, and that if the child is disabled the accommodation is suitable to the child's needs.[91] It will be recalled that in the cases *R (G) v Barnet London Borough Council; R (W) v Lambeth London Borough Council; R (A) v Lambeth London Borough Council*[92] which were discussed earlier in relation to section 17 of the Children Act 1989, the mothers of the children concerned were arguing that they should be provided with accommodation together with their children. It was argued on the appellants' behalf that the duty to accommodate children if possible with a parent meant that the local authority had a duty also to provide accommodation for the mothers concerned. The House of Lords rejected this view, indicating that such provisions are concerned with placement, not housing, and assume that a parent of the child already has accommodation which the child might share.[93]

## 2.5 **The status of a 'looked after' child**

For children who are in need in the circumstances of section 20(1), the provision of accommodation is of obvious practical benefit to the child. However, being a child accommodated by the local authority can bring with it a status which is of wider benefit. Section 22 of the Children Act 1989 defines a category of children referred to as 'looked after by the local authority' and to whom certain duties are owed. The category includes both a child who is in the care of the local authority[94] (under a care order) and for whom the local authority therefore has parental responsibility, *and* a child who has been provided with accommodation by a local authority exercising its social services functions (in particular those under the Children Act 1989)[95] provided that the local authority has done so for a continuous period of more than 24 hours.[96] Section 22 excludes from this definition accommodation provided under section 17 of the Children Act 1989, so accommodation provided under that section does not give rise to the status of being looked after.[97]

A local authority has several duties in relation to 'looked after' children. There is a duty to safeguard and promote the child's welfare,[98] including in particular a duty to promote the child's educational achievement;[99] and to make such use of services available for children cared for by their own parents as appears to the authority reasonable in his case.[100] In addition, there is a duty to maintain the child 'in other respects apart from the provision of accommodation'.[101] These duties mean that, 'although the local authority do not have "parental responsibility" for a child who is accommodated under s 20, they are nevertheless replacing to some extent the role played by a

---

[86] Section 22C(4).

[87] Including in the case of a child in care, a person who had parental responsibility for the child under a child arrangements order prior to the care order being made: s 22B(3).

[88] Registered under the Care Standards Act 2000, Pt 2.   [89] Children Act 1989, s 22C(7).

[90] Ibid, s 22C(9).   [91] Ibid, s 22C(8).

[92] [2003] UKHL 57, [2004] 2 AC 208, [2003] 3 WLR 1194, [2004] 1 FLR 454.   [93] Ibid, [38].

[94] The local authority has a duty to provide accommodation for a child in its care: see s 22A.

[95] Children Act 1989, s 22(1).   [96] Ibid, s 22(2).

[97] Ibid, s 22(1)(b). Similarly, provision of accommodation under s 23B and s 24B.   [98] Ibid, s 22(1)(a).

[99] Ibid, s 22(3A).

[100] The emphasis on keeping families together whilst at the same time safeguarding and promoting the child's welfare can again be seen in this provision.

[101] Ibid, s 22B.

parent in the child's life, and are expected to look after the child in all the ways that a good parent would'.[102] Before making any decision with respect to a child whom it is looking after, or proposing to look after, a local authority shall, so far as is reasonably practicable, ascertain the wishes and feelings of the child, the child's parents, any person who has parental responsibility for the child, and any other person whose wishes and feelings the authority considers to be relevant, regarding the matter to be decided.[103] In the case of the child, in making any decision the local authority must give due consideration to the wishes and feelings ascertained, having regard to his or her age and understanding. In addition, the local authority must give due consideration to the child's religious persuasion, racial origin, and cultural and linguistic background.[104]

Schedule 2, paragraph 19A provides that it is 'the duty of the local authority looking after a child to advise, assist and befriend him with a view to promoting his welfare when they have ceased to look after him'. The fact that a child is, or has been, accommodated by the local authority can in some circumstances bring into effect further duties which are owed when the child has ceased to be looked after. There are different categories of children to whom additional duties are owed.

### 2.5.1 An 'eligible child'

The first category is known as an 'eligible child' as defined in Schedule 2, paragraph 19B. An eligible child is aged 16 or 17 who has been looked after by a local authority for 13 weeks, or periods amounting in all to 13 weeks, which began after he reached the age of 14 and ended after he reached the age of 16.[105] In such a case the local authority must arrange for the child to have a personal adviser,[106] and prepare what is called a pathway plan[107] and keep it under regular review.[108]

### 2.5.2 A 'relevant child'

A second category of child is a 'relevant child', as defined in section 23A of the Children Act 1989. A relevant child is a child who is aged 16 or 17 and who is not being looked after by any local authority and who, before last ceasing to be looked after, was an eligible child (as defined in the previous section). In such a case, the authority which last looked after the child (known as the responsible authority) has certain functions in relation to the child which are set out in section 23B. It must take reasonable steps to keep in touch with a 'relevant child', appoint a personal adviser and carry out an assessment, and prepare a pathway plan if one has not already been prepared. The authority has a duty to safeguard and promote the child's welfare and, unless it is satisfied that his welfare does not require it, to support the child by maintaining him and providing suitable accommodation and support,[109] which may be in cash.[110]

### 2.5.3 'Former relevant children'

Once a person reaches the age of 18 he or she is no longer a child and, of course, also no longer falls within the definitions of an eligible or relevant child. However, in defined circumstances some persons who were formerly looked after by a local authority will be owed duties by the authority into their early adult life. There is a further category of children known as 'former relevant children' to whom such duties are owed. They are any person who was being looked after by a local authority when the child attained the age of 18 and who immediately before ceasing to be looked after was an eligible child; or any person who has been a relevant child for the purposes of section 23A (and would be one if he were under 18). The local authority has a duty to take reasonable steps

---

[102] *Per* Baroness Hale of Richmond in *R (M) v Hammersmith and Fulham London Borough Council* [2008] UKHL 14, [2008] 1 FLR 1384 at [20].

[103] Children Act 1989 s 22(4).    [104] Ibid, s 22(5).

[105] Children Act 1989, Sch 2, para 19B(2)(b) and Care Planning, Placement and Case Review (England) Regulations 2010 (SI 2010/959), reg 40. The rules are modified in the case of a series of short-term placements, see reg 48.

[106] Children Act 1989, Schedule 2, para 19C.    [107] Ibid, para 19B(4).    [108] Ibid, para 19B(5).

[109] Ibid, s 23B(8).    [110] Ibid , s 23B(9).

to keep in touch with a former relevant child,[111] to continue the appointment of his or her personal adviser, and to keep the pathway plan under review. There is also a duty to give assistance as set out in section 24B(1) and (2), or other assistance, as the child's welfare and educational or training needs require it. These duties always subsist until the former relevant child reaches the age of 21.[112] However, if the former relevant child's pathway plan sets out a programme of education or training which extends beyond his 21st birthday, then the assistance of the kind referred to in section 24B(2), to the extent that his welfare and his educational or training needs require it, continues for as long as the former relevant child is pursuing the programme.[113] The local authority has a duty to pay an amount of money to such a person who is pursuing higher education.[114] Even in a case where these duties have ceased, duties in respect of the former relevant child's education may be resurrected provided he or she is under 25 and informs the authority that he or she is pursuing or wishes to pursue a programme of education.[115] Again, the local authority has duties to appoint a personal adviser and to prepare a pathway plan. In addition, there is a duty to assist by contributing to living expenses incurred in connection with the programme and by making a grant to meet educational expenses.[116]

As can be seen, a local authority's decision to accommodate a child pursuant to section 20 of the Children Act 1989 can have significant long-term resource implications for the local authority, which may be required to provide assistance to a person into his or her mid-twenties. There is a big difference between those duties and the duty which a local housing authority owes to a young homeless person, even if in priority need. It would not be surprising, therefore, if some local authorities took steps to avoid incurring duties under section 20.[117] In *R (M) v Hammersmith and Fulham London Borough Council*[118] the House of Lords made clear that a deliberate policy to avoid responsibilities under the 1989 Act by shifting them onto a housing department, while understandable, would be unlawful.[119] *R (M) v Hammersmith and Fulham London Borough Council*[120] concerned a teenager, M, with troubling behaviour who had been excluded from school at 14 and had never returned. She had become involved with the criminal justice system, with court cases pending. M presented to the local authority housing department with a letter written by her mother, who had an inoperable stomach tumour, saying that M, who was then 16, could no longer stay in her home because she had broken every rule that had been laid down. The local housing authority acted to provide M with accommodation pursuant to its interim duty under section 188(1) of the Housing Act 1996. That duty applies if the local housing authority 'have reason to believe that an applicant may be homeless, eligible for assistance and have a priority need'. The relevant provision in M's case dealing with priority need was article 3 of the Homelessness (Priority Need for Accommodation) (England) Order 2002, which defines persons aged 16 or 17 as in priority need. However, the Order specifically excepts relevant children under section 23A of the Children Act 1989 or children to whom a local authority owe a duty to provide accommodation under section 20 of the Children Act 1989. 'Thus, in the longer term, the Children Act duties supersede the Housing Act duties.'[121] Although there was official Guidance[122] which recommended a joint assessment of children aged 16 or 17 and advised that in cases of uncertainty about whether section 20 applied, a housing authority should contact the relevant social services authority, at no stage did the local housing authority refer the matter to the local authority children's services department.

M was housed in a succession of temporary placements in bed and breakfast hotel accommodation and in a hostel, from which she was evicted. Thereafter she lived with her sister, who had a baby, in one-bedroom accommodation not suitable for three people. Subsequently, M was sentenced for

---

[111]  Ibid, s 23C(2).        [112]  Ibid, s 23C(6).        [113]  Ibid, s 23C(7).        [114]  Ibis, s 23C(5A).

[115]  Ibid, s 23CA(1), inserted by Children and Young Persons Act 2008, s 22(2).        [116]  Ibis, s 23CA(5).

[117]  See the comment of Baroness Hale of Richmond in *R (M) v Hammersmith and Fulham London Borough Council* [2008] UKHL 14, [2008] 1 FLR 1384 at [24].

[118]  [2008] UKHL 14, [2008] 1 FLR 1384.        [119]  Ibid, [33].        [120]  Ibid.        [121]  Ibid, [15].

[122]  *Homelessness Code of Guidance for Local Authorities* (Office of the Deputy Prime Minister, 2002), para 8.37.

various offences, which included a four-month detention and training order. While in custody, M found out that she was pregnant and reached the age of 18. Proceedings for judicial review were issued on M's behalf while she was in custody, in order to try to secure accommodation for her upon her release. If M had been accommodated by the local authority under section 20 prior to her custody, she would of course be a recipient of the various duties discussed earlier. M's case ultimately reached the House of Lords on her appeal, where her argument was that the local authority had in fact been acting under section 20 of the Children Act 1989 when they thought they were acting under section 188 of the 1996 Act. The House of Lords dismissed the appeal, holding that no duty under section 20 had arisen since M's situation had never been drawn to the attention of the local social services authority. This outcome has been criticised by Jenny Driscoll and Kathryn Hollingsworth,[123] who observe that it could be argued that the housing department acted ultra vires by failing to have regard to the Code of Guidance, given that that was mandated by statute,[124] and referral to the social services authority was crucial to securing M's rights under the Children Act. Driscoll and Hollingsworth argue that there should be a legal duty to consider referral.

The reverse situation occurred in *R (G) v Southwark London Borough Council*.[125] A mother had excluded her 17-year-old son, A, from her home and he was 'sofa surfing' (sleeping on friends' sofas or in cars). He consulted solicitors and was advised to present at the children's services department of the local authority asking for urgent assessment of his needs under section 17 of the Children Act 1989 and for accommodation under section 20(1). A detailed assessment was carried out, identifying his housing and educational needs and revealing that he may be involved in gang activity. The local authority took the view that section 20 was 'not appropriate' and that his needs could be provided merely through provision of housing and other support. Judicial review proceedings were commenced challenging the local authority's decision which ultimately reached the House of Lords on A's appeal. The House of Lords unanimously allowed the appeal. A's circumstances fell within section 20(1), that duty had arisen, and the local authority 'were not entitled to "side-step" it by giving the accommodation a different label'.[126] The result was that A was accommodated by the local authority, became an eligible child within the meaning of paragraph 19B(2) of Schedule 2 to the Act, and, upon reaching 18, a 'former relevant child' within the meaning of section 23C(1), with all the attendant responsibilities attaching to the local authority.

## 2.6 Representations and complaints relating to Part III

Under section 26(3) of the Children Act 1989, local authorities are required to establish procedures for considering representations, including complaints, about how they are discharging their functions under Part III of the Children Act 1989.[127] Those entitled to use the procedures are any child being looked after by the local authority, a child in need, the child's parent, any other person who has parental responsibility for the child, any local authority foster parent, and 'such other person

---

[123] J. Driscoll and K. Hollingsworth, 'Accommodating Children in Need: *R (M) v Hammersmith and Fulham London Borough Council*' [2008] Child and Family Law Quarterly 522.

[124] The guidance was issued pursuant to s 182 of the Housing Act 1996, which provides that local authorities 'shall have regard to such guidance'.

[125] [2009] UKHL 26, [2009] 2 FLR 380.

[126] Ibid, [28]. For earlier case law in which there were similar labelling issues, giving a similar message: see *H, Barhanu and B v Wandsworth Hackney and Islington LBC* [2007] EWHC 1082 (Admin), [2007] 2 FLR 822; *R (L) v Nottinghamshire County Council* [2007] EWHC 2364 (Admin), [2007] All ER (D) 158 (Sept); *London Borough of Southwark v D sub nom R (On the Application of D) v A Local Authority* [2007] EWCA Civ 182, [2007] 1 FLR 2181, [2007] Family Law 701; *R (S) v Sutton London Borough Council* [2007] EWCA Civ 790, (2007) 10 CCLR 625.

[127] These include complaints about day care, services to support children within the family home, accommodation of a child, after care, and decisions relating to the placement of a child or the handling of a child's case. Section 24D of the Children Act 1989 also requires establishment of a similar procedure for the purpose of considering representations by a relevant child for the purposes of s 23A or a young person falling within s 23C, a person qualifying for advice and assistance, or a person falling within s 24B(2), about the discharge of functions in relation to him.

as the authority considers has a sufficient interest in the child's welfare to warrant his representations being considered by them'.[128] The duty under section 26(3) also applies in respect of persons using the local authority's adoption and special guardianship services.[129] Section 26A provides that every local authority shall make arrangements for the provision of assistance to children who make or intend to make representations under section 26,[130] including assistance by way of representation.[131]

The procedures established under section 26 must be publicised.[132] Regulations set out the way in which they should operate and each authority must use the regulations as the basis for the creation of their own procedure.[133]

A complainant must usually make his representations about a matter no later than one year after the grounds to make the representations arose.[134] The procedure has three stages. The first stage is local resolution of the complaint under regulation 14.[135] The local authority must consider and try to resolve the representations as soon as is reasonably practicable, usually within ten working days.[136] Where, however, the matter is not resolved, the complainant or, where one has been appointed, his advocate may request orally or in writing that the representations be investigated by the local authority together with an independent person, under regulation 17.[137] The response must be notified within 25 working days. If there is dissatisfaction with this outcome, the complainant can request that the matter be considered by a review panel[138] in accordance with regulation 19, which must meet within 30 days of the request. The panel consists of three independent persons,[139] one of whom will chair the panel. Within five days of meeting, the panel must produce recommendations. Within 15 working days of receiving the panel's recommendations the local authority must, together with the independent person appointed under regulation 17, consider the recommendations and determine (i) how the authority will respond to them; and (ii) what they propose to do in the light of them, and send to the complainant its response and proposals, along with information about making a complaint to a Local Commissioner.[140]

This procedure goes some way towards mitigating the limited role of the courts in supervising how local authorities carry out their statutory duties to children in need, children being accommodated, and children in care. The courts have no involvement with children in need and accommodated children, and later in this chapter it will be seen that once a care order is made, the court's role comes to an end and it has no jurisdiction to intervene in how the local authority is looking after a child. It is therefore crucial that a person with a grievance about a child's treatment by the local authority should have somewhere to turn and that there should be at least some independent element in the conduct of an inquiry into that grievance. It should also be stressed that one purpose behind the establishment of this procedure was to give children being looked after by local authorities an avenue for making complaints about the care they are receiving. Tragically, some children, particularly those in residential care, are victims of abuse from the very people with whom they have been placed to protect them from harm. Although the procedures set up by section 26 are

---

[128] Section 26(3).     [129] Section 26(3B) and (3C).     [130] Section 26A(1).     [131] Section 26A(2).

[132] Section 26(8). For interesting research about the variable nature of this publicity, see C. Williams and H. Jordan, 'Factors Relating to Publicity Surrounding the Complaints Procedure under the Children Act 1989' (1996) 8 Child and Family Law Quarterly 337.

[133] Children Act 1989 Representations Procedure (England) Regulations 2006 (SI 2006/1738). For Wales the procedure is set out in SI 2005/3365. References hereafter are to the English regulations.

[134] Ibid, reg 9(1). The local authority may still consider the representation if it would not be reasonable to expect the complainant to have made the representations within the time limit; and it is still possible to consider the representations effectively and fairly.

[135] Unless the complainant and the local authority agree that the representations should not be so considered, see reg 14(1).

[136] The period can be extended in the case of a complex representation.     [137] Reg 15(2).     [138] Reg 18.

[139] The independent person appointed in accordance with regulation 17 may not be a member of the panel, reg 19(3).

[140] Reg 20.

not designed to investigate allegations of child abuse, it is one method open to children to bring what is happening to them to the attention of others in the local authority. Where the complaints procedure is fully pursued and where the panel make recommendations then normally the local authority must abide by those recommendations unless it has substantial reasons for not doing so, and its failure to do so may be actionable in judicial review.[141]

The complaints procedure must first be exhausted before any proceedings for judicial review can be pursued. Another remedy might be to pursue a claim for breach of a Convention right under the Human Rights Act 1998.

## 2.7 **The voluntary nature of 'accommodation'**

The philosophy of Part III of the Children Act 1989 is to encourage local authorities to work in partnership with parents and persons with parental responsibility, and to promote mutual confidence and trust. The thinking is that parents and others should be able to turn to local authorities for positive help and support in bringing up their children, and that they should not have cause to fear that they may lose their children into state care if they take advantage of the services provided. Such fear may be very real in a case where a person with parental responsibility is encouraged to agree to his child being accommodated under section 20, because he or she thereby, as a matter of fact, loses a measure of control over the child's upbringing. Reassurance is provided by subsections (7) and (8), which together make clear that accommodation under section 20 may only be provided, or continue to be provided, if the persons with parental responsibility for the child do not object.

---

### Key legislation

Section 20(7) provides that:

A local authority may not provide accommodation under this section for any child if any person who—

(a) has parental responsibility for him; and

(b) is willing and able to—

  (i) provide accommodation for him; or

  (ii) arrange for accommodation to be provided for him, objects.

---

It can be seen that on its face section 20(7) does not require a local authority to obtain the consent of persons with parental responsibility before a child is received into accommodation. Such a provision would prove unworkable in some cases for the practical reason that it may not always be possible to contact such persons. However, where such a person is contactable, consent should be sought. In *Coventry City Council v C, B, CA and CH*[142] Hedley J gave guidance on how section 20 should operate. He stated that every 'social worker obtaining such a consent is under a personal duty (the outcome of which may not be dictated to them by others) to be satisfied that the person giving the consent does not lack the capacity to do so'.[143] If the person lacks capacity, no attempt to obtain consent should be made. If the person has capacity, the social worker 'must be satisfied that the consent is fully informed'.[144] In the *Coventry* case, a mother's consent had been inappropriately sought shortly after she had given birth and when she was under the influence of morphine for pain relief. Where there is a positive objection from a person with parental responsibility, the local

---

[141] *R v Avon County Council, ex p M* [1994] 2 FLR 1006.    [142] [2012] EWHC 2190 (Fam), [2013] 2 FLR 987.
[143] Ibid, [46].    [144] Ibid.

authority may not accommodate the child where the objecting person can make his or her own arrangements for the child.

The voluntary nature of accommodation is further underlined by section 20(8) which provides that in a case in which a child has been accommodated: 'Any person who has parental responsibility for a child may at any time remove the child from accommodation provided by or on behalf of the local authority under this section.'

In *Re N (Children) (Adoption: Jurisdiction)*[145] Sir James Munby P drew attention to several cases in which judicial concerns had been expressed about the use of section 20,[146] and indicated that the misuse and abuse of section 20 is a denial of the fundamental rights of both the parent and the child which will no longer be tolerated.[147] The cases highlighted four problems: (1) the failure to obtain informed consent from the parents at the outset; (2) deficiencies in the content and recording of section 20 agreements, including evidencing the parent's agreement; (3) such agreements lasting for too long; and (4) the seeming reluctance of local authorities to return the child to the parent(s) immediately upon a withdrawal of parental consent.

Munby P indicated that where 'the child's parent is known and in contact with the local authority, the local authority requires the consent of the parent'[148] and 'the use of section 20 'must not be compulsion in disguise'[149] nor 'mere "submission in the face of asserted State authority"'.[150] In *Newcastle City Council v WM and Others*,[151] for example, Cobb J concluded that the children, whose young mother was functioning in the learning disability range with an IQ of 61 and not in a position to care for any of them, had been accommodated unlawfully.[152] The local authority had failed to adhere to the guidance of Hedley J in *Coventry City Council v C, B, CA and CH.*

Secondly, 'a prudent local authority will surely always wish to ensure that an alleged parental consent in such a case is properly recorded in writing and evidenced by the parent's signature.'[153] In addition the agreement must be drafted appropriately. For example, in *Re W (Children)*[154] the agreement was described as 'almost comical in the manner in which it apparently proclaims that it has been entered into under something approaching duress.'[155]

The third problem, arrangements being allowed to continue for far too long, was apparent in *Re N* itself, the children having been accommodated for eight months prior to the local authority issuing care proceedings. Munby P commented that section 20 may 'have a proper role to play as a short-term measure pending the commencement of care proceedings, but the use of section 20 as a prelude to care proceedings for a period as long as here is a misuse by the local authority of its statutory powers.'[156] As Keehan J noted in *Northamptonshire County Council v AS and Ors*,[157] the

---

[145] [2015] EWCA Civ 1112.

[146] For examples, see *Re P (A Child: Use of S.20 CA 1989)* [2014] EWFC 775, *Re N (Children)* [2015] EWFC 37, *Medway Council v A and ors (Learning Disability: Foster Placement)* [2015] EWFC B66, *Gloucestershire County Council v M and C* [2015] EWFC B147, *Gloucestershire County Council v S* [2015] EWFC B149, *Re AS (Unlawful Removal of a Child)* [2015] EWFC B150, *Medway Council v M and T (By Her Children's Guardian)* [2015] EWFC B164, *Re CB (A Child)* [2015] EWCA Civ 888, [86], *Williams and anor v London Borough of Hackney* [2015] EWHC 2629 (QB), Sir Robert Francis QC (sitting as a High Court Judge); *Leicester City Council v S & Ors* [2014] EWHC 1575 (Fam), Moylan J.

[147] *Re N (Children) (Adoption: Jurisdiction)* [2015] EWCA Civ 1112, at [171].

[148] [2015] EWCA Civ 1112, at [163], citing *Re W (Children)* [2014] EWCA Civ 1065, at [34].

[149] [2015] EWCA Civ 1112, at [163], citing Hedley J in *Coventry City Council v C, B, CA and CH* [2012] EWHC 2190 (Fam), [2013] 2 FLR 987, at [27].

[150] [2015] EWCA Civ 1112, at [163]. See *R (G) v Nottingham City Council and Nottingham University Hospital* [2008] EWHC 400 (Admin), [2008] 1 FLR 1668, para 61, and *Coventry City Council v C, B, CA and CH* [2012] EWHC 2190 (Fam), [2013] 2 FLR 987, at [44].

[151] [2015] EWFC 42.     [152] Ibid, at [46].     [153] [2015] EWCA Civ 1112, at [166].     [154] [2014] EWCA Civ 1065,

[155] Ibid, at [41], per Tomlinson LJ. See for criticism of another agreement, *Williams and anor v London Borough of Hackney* [2015] EWHC 2629 (QB), at [65].

[156] [2015] EWCA Civ 1112, [157]. See also *Re A (A Child), Darlington Borough Council v M* [2015] EWFC 11, [100]: 'There is, I fear, far too much misuse and abuse of section 20 and this can no longer be tolerated.'

[157] [2015] EWHC 199 (Fam), at [37].

accommodated child will not have the benefit of an independent children's guardian to represent and safeguard his interests and the court is deprived of its ability to control planning for the child. Similarly, in *Medway Council v M, F and G (By her Children's Guardian)*,[158] a case in which there had been an allegation of non-accidental injury to a baby, G, which was withdrawn as there were uncertainties in the medical evidence, Theis J was concerned about a delay of 12 weeks between the parents attending the hospital and the local authority issuing proceedings. The parents indicated that they had little choice but to sign a section 20 agreement for the local authority to accommodate G on her discharge from hospital, whilst further medical opinion was sought. This meant that the parents did not have effective access to legal advice, and there was no framework for them to be involved in the further medical investigations being sought. Theis J commented[159] that there should be:

> great caution in using section 20 agreements in cases where complex medical evidence may become involved. Parents faced with that situation may consider they have little choice but to agree to section 20; they have no, or limited, access to legal advice and if they don't agree they risk being regarded by the LA as being "uncooperative".

Fourthly, Munby P was clear that section 20(8) means what it says, commenting:

> A local authority which fails to permit a parent to remove a child in circumstances within section 20(8) acts unlawfully, exposes itself to proceedings at the suit of the parent and may even be guilty of a criminal offence. A parent in that position could bring a claim against the local authority for judicial review or, indeed, seek an immediate writ of habeas corpus against the local authority. I should add that I am exceedingly sceptical as to whether a parent can lawfully contract out of section 20(8) in advance, as by agreeing with the local authority to give a specified period of notice before exercising their section 20(8) right.[160]

The voluntary nature of accommodation was made clear in *R v Tameside Metropolitan Borough Council, ex parte J*.[161] In that case a 13-year-old girl with multiple severe disabilities, autistic tendencies, and challenging behaviour had lived with her parents until she was 9 when the parents could no longer cope. The girl was thereafter accommodated by the local authority under section 20 and placed at a residential home for disabled children which was near the parents' home and also near the school that she attended. The local authority subsequently suggested that she be moved to live with foster parents, a move to which the parents objected. Despite the parents' objections, the local authority began to initiate contact between the child and the proposed foster parents with a view to the move. The child, acting by her mother as litigation friend, sought permission to apply for judicial review of the local authority's decision. Granting permission, Scott Baker J explained that the 'unspoken word in Pt III of the 1989 Act is co-operation—co-operation between the parents and the local authority to work together in the best interests of the child'.[162] A local authority accommodating a child is 'able to exercise mundane day-to-day powers of management' but a 'mere power of management cannot override the wishes of the parent with parental responsibility'.[163] His Lordship held that the general duty of a local authority to safeguard and promote the welfare of children within its area who are in need[164] does not entitle a local authority to accommodate a child in a (foster) placement against the wishes of those with parental responsibility.[165] Equally, his Lordship made clear that the parents cannot dictate where the local authority must accommodate the child. If there is

---

[158] [2014] EWHC 308 (Fam), Theis J.    [159] Ibid, at [11].    [160] [2015] EWCA Civ 1112, at [169].

[161] [2000] 1 FCR 173.    [162] Ibid, 180.

[163] Ibid, recognising that the 'distinction between management decisions and decisions which ultimately require the consent of those with parental responsibility may not always be an easy one to define' (at 181).

[164] Under Children Act 1989, s 17.    [165] [2000] 1 FCR 173 at 183.

an impasse, the local authority must ask whether there is a risk of significant harm to the child if its view does not prevail and if so it may be necessary for the local authority to invoke its compulsory powers of intervention. If the parents unreasonably refuse all the local authority has to offer then the local authority can argue that it has discharged its duty. Scott Baker J was of the view that in such a situation if the parents were unable to accommodate the child, 'then the significant harm threshold is likely to be crossed and the ultimate answer may be a care order'.[166] As we shall see later in this chapter, even when a care order is made, those with parental responsibility retain it and any overriding of parental responsibility will need to have regard to the right to respect for private and family life within Article 8 of the European Convention on Human Rights (ECHR).

In light of his survey in *Re N (Children) (Adoption: Jurisdiction)*[167] of the problematic use of section 20, Munby P added the following guidance to that already provided by Hedley J:

> i) Wherever possible the agreement of a parent to the accommodation of their child under section 20 should be properly recorded in writing and evidenced by the parent's signature; ii) The written document should be clear and precise as to its terms, drafted in simple and straight-forward language that the particular parent can readily understand; iii) The written document should spell out, following the language of section 20(8), that the parent can "remove the child" from the local authority accommodation "at any time"; iv) The written document should not seek to impose any fetters on the exercise of the parent's right under section 20(8); v) Where the parent is not fluent in English, the written document should be translated into the parent's own language and the parent should sign the foreign language text, adding, in the parent's language, words to the effect that 'I have read this document and I agree to its terms.[168]

In practice, however, even with these safeguards, parents may not feel able to remove a child, relying on section 20(8), for fear of inviting compulsory intervention; and it is noteworthy that in practice parents of accommodated children may be in a weaker position in relation to contact with their child, because there is no specific statutory duty imposed on a local authority to promote reasonable contact when a child is merely accommodated.[169]

### 2.7.1 The position of the father who does not have parental responsibility

Section 20(7) refers to persons with parental responsibility. A father who is not married to his child's mother is in a vulnerable position if he has not acquired parental responsibility. He has no enforceable right to object to his child being accommodated and he is not entitled to remove his child from accommodation at any time. However, his position is not entirely bleak. The general duty of a local authority is to promote the upbringing of children by their families[170] and a local authority is not required to receive the child into accommodation when a family member is offering to look after the child. In a case where the child is already being accommodated, the local authority can bring the accommodation arrangement to an end, or where it continues to accommodate the child, the local authority 'shall' make arrangements to enable an accommodated child to live with a parent unless that would not be reasonably practicable or consistent with his welfare. Thus, an unmarried father who does not have parental responsibility should only find himself in conflict with the local authority when placement with him appears to the authority to be against the interests of the child. Where the father objects to the authority's approach, his remedy would be to apply for a child arrangements order. In determining the merits of his application, the court would give paramount consideration to the welfare of the child, but presumably in a case in which the parent could offer appropriate care the court would give considerable weight to the fact that a

---

[166] Ibid, 181.    [167] [2015] EWCA Civ 1112.    [168] Ibid, at [170].

[169] A. Bainham, 'Swimming against the Tide: Challenging Contact Arrangements in the Public Law' [2015] Fam Law 1356, at 1359.

[170] Children Act 1989, s 17(1), discussed in Section 2.1.

parent was offering to provide a home for a child in a case where the alternative offered was foster care or accommodation in a residential home.

## 2.8 Some qualifications to the voluntary nature of 'accommodation'

Section 20(7) and (8) do not apply where a residence arrangements order is in place nor when the High Court's inherent jurisdiction has settled the child's carer; nor when the child concerned is 16 or over.

### 2.8.1 Where there is a child arrangements order settling the child's residence, or a person has the child's care by virtue of the High Court's inherent jurisdiction

A parent with parental responsibility is placed in a similar position to the unmarried father discussed earlier, where there is an order settling the arrangements as to the person with whom the child is to live in favour of another person. Section 20(9) provides that:

> Subsections (7) and (8) do not apply while any person—
>
> (a) who is named in a child arrangements order as a person with whom the child is to live; or
> (b) who has care of the child by virtue of an order made in the exercise of the High Court's inherent jurisdiction with respect to children,
>
> agrees to the child being looked after in accommodation provided by or on behalf of the local authority.

Where more than one person has the benefit of a residence arrangements order, all such persons must agree to the child being accommodated.[171]

The thinking lying behind subsection (9) is that it is the voice of the person who has had the benefit of the child's residence which should prevail in dealings with the local authority. Where there has been an estrangement between parents, between parents and others, or where some other reason has led to such a child arrangements order being made, a court must have decided that it is better for the child to make that order than not to make an order.[172] The thinking is that it is normally in the interests of the child that the person with the child arrangements order should be able to make arrangements about where the child will live, including placing him with a local authority, in spite of the objections of a parent or other person with parental responsibility.[173]

### 2.8.2 Where the child is 16

Another exception to the voluntary principle is where a child who has reached the age of 16 agrees to being accommodated. Section 20(11) provides that in these circumstances subsections (7) and (8) do not apply. Subsection (11) is an important example of how the law has moved towards allowing a child to determine his own upbringing in the face of objections from a parent or other person with parental responsibility. It assumes that a child of 16 is old enough, and has reached a sufficient level of understanding, to make an informed choice about where he wishes to live. In many cases this will be correct. The thinking is that a child of 16 is approaching full adulthood so that he or she should be entitled to leave home and to seek assistance from a local authority in obtaining properly regulated accommodation.[174] Where already accommodated, the child should

---

[171] Section 20(10).

[172] Section 1(5): see Chapter 9; or the High Court has intervened in the exercise of its inherent jurisdiction.

[173] For criticism, see A. Bainham *Children the New Law* (Bristol: Family Law, 1990), para 4.26.

[174] The local authority must accommodate a child aged 16 who is in need and whose welfare 'is likely to be seriously prejudiced if they do not provide him with accommodation' (s 20(3)). It may accommodate any child aged between 16 and 21 where to do so would 'safeguard or promote his welfare' (s 20(5)) and see *Re T (Accommodation by Local Authority)* [1995] 1 FLR 15 where a local authority's decision to refuse formally to accommodate a 17-year-old child was quashed in proceedings for judicial review.

be entitled to remain with the persons with whom he or she has been living in the face of parental objection. Subsection (11) also assists the local authority, because it need not consider instituting care proceedings to assist the mature child in a case where the persons with parental responsibility refuse to agree to the child being accommodated.

The disadvantage of subsection (11) is that it may sometimes place parents and others with parental responsibility in an intolerable position in a case where they do not wish the child to be accommodated. The fact that a child chooses to put himself into, or to remain in, local authority accommodation may be a matter of very great concern to them. Children being looked after by a local authority come from a variety of backgrounds, some of which are very disturbed. An accommodated child who comes from a 'good home' may live on premises where he or she associates with children who have been involved in prostitution, drug abuse, and various types of crime. The child's desire to remain in accommodation may be because these alternative forms of lifestyle seem attractive at an age which is notoriously associated with rebellion against parental norms. While those charged with the duty of looking after older accommodated children make every effort to ensure that such children are not involved in unhealthy, dangerous, and criminal forms of activity, there may be little they can do to prevent a determined child from becoming so involved. Local authorities do not have the power to restrict the liberty of delinquent children whom they are looking after, for more than 72 hours in any period of 28 consecutive days,[175] unless given specific authority to do so by a court.[176]

It would seem that the obvious solution would be for the persons with parental responsibility to apply for a residence arrangements order as this would have the effect of overriding the child's decision to be accommodated. However, such persons are normally powerless to obtain a residence order once a child is 16. Section 9(7) provides that a court shall not make any section 8 order with respect to a child who has reached the age of 16 unless it is satisfied that the circumstances of the case are exceptional. It is suggested that a person with parental responsibility should either seek to persuade a court to treat the case as exceptional or should seek the leave of the High Court to invoke the exercise of the inherent jurisdiction. Once decision-making power had been taken from the child and placed in the court, the court's decision would be determined by the view it took of the child's best interests, in relation to which the child's wishes and feelings would be but one element.

### 2.8.3 Accommodated children who need care or protection

Accommodation may be used by a local authority as an alternative to bringing care proceedings in a case where there are concerns and fears about the manner in which a child is being looked after.[177] While the voluntary nature of accommodation arrangements made under section 20 is in keeping with the partnership philosophy of the Act, in some cases subsections (7) and (8) may be difficult to reconcile with a local authority's child protection duties.

Some of the tensions in such cases can be addressed by careful forward planning between the local authority and the persons with parental responsibility. This type of planning enables the local authority and persons with parental responsibility to agree in advance about any problems which might arise through the strict enforcement of rights under section 20(8). For example, a parent might be prepared to agree that the best interests of a child are not normally served by a precipitate and unplanned removal from accommodation, and that at least a brief period of notice is normally better for the child.

The advantage of this type of formal planning between a local authority and persons with parental responsibility is that it reinforces the philosophy that local authorities, parents, and others

---

[175] Children (Secure Accommodation) Regulations 1991 (SI 1991/1505), reg 10(1).

[176] The Children Act 1989, s 25, enables a court to make a secure accommodation order on specified grounds for a maximum period of three months.

[177] The care provided is regulated by the Care Planning, Placement and Case Review (England) Regulations 2010 (SI 2010/959).

should work together in partnership and that each should trust the other. In this regard, warning parents and others in a written agreement that precipitate removal might lead to an application for an emergency protection order is honestly to reflect the reality. It tells them in no uncertain terms that a 'voluntary' arrangement might be transformed into a compulsory arrangement if their cooperation is withdrawn. Injecting this note of realism into accommodation arrangements may better promote the child's sense of security with his current carers, and the child can be reassured that his wishes and feelings will be taken into account before there is any sudden change of plan.

The disadvantage of agreements of this kind is that terms which require persons with parental responsibility to give a period of notice before removing a child from accommodation undermine the principle that the arrangement is voluntary. Parliament was insistent that no notice period should be included in section 20(8) in the face of very great pressure to include at least a brief period.[178] Local authorities are in a much stronger position than parents when suggesting what terms should be included, and they are likely to tell parents what the arrangements will be, however much this is couched in the language of mutual agreement. There is a risk that written accommodation agreements will take on a spurious authority in the eyes of those who are party to them, so that local authorities may feel that they can 'contract out' of the law's provisions, and parents and others may feel 'bound' by the terms and not be aware of their rights under section 20(8).

Research by Judith Masson indicates that in practice the boundary between voluntariness and coercion may be blurred.[179] Reflecting an obvious tension between risk assessment and working in partnership, Masson found that agreements between parents and the local authority were not always freely negotiated:

> Rather, they were conditions imposed on parents, which allowed the social services department to conclude that the issue of the children's care could remain a matter determined by the department and need not be brought before a court.[180]

This *de facto* compulsion does not carry with it the safeguards of formal compulsory intervention. Furthermore, the failure to comply with an agreement was then sometimes seen as a reason, and further ground, for compulsory intervention.

### 2.8.4 **No compulsory removal without court sanction**

Except in the case of police protection, a court order is required if a child is to be compulsorily removed from parental care. Astonishingly, the need to make this rather obvious point judicially arose in *R (G) Nottingham City Council*.[181] An 18-year-old woman who had been in local authority care and had a troubled history, including alcohol/drug abuse and self-harm, was about to deliver her child in hospital. Following a child protection meeting, the local authority intended to apply for an interim care order in respect of the baby immediately upon birth. Details of the plan were sent to all hospitals in the region. A 'birth plan' was prepared for the hospital medical staff by the Nottingham City NHS Primary Care Trust, which referred to the child protection meeting and indicated that the child was to be removed at birth. The plan made no reference, however, to the need first for a court order authorising removal. Two hours after the birth, the hospital staff, in accordance with the birth plan and express instructions from a social worker,[182] removed the baby

---

[178] House of Commons Debate, Standing Committee B, 18 May 1989, cols 137–54; House of Lords, Official Report, 20 December 1988, col 1335.

[179] J. Masson, 'Police Protection—Protecting Whom?' (2002) Journal of Social Welfare and Family Law 157; J. Masson, 'Emergency Intervention to Protect Children: Using and Avoiding Legal Controls' [2005] Child and Family Law Quarterly 75.

[180] Masson, 'Emergency Intervention to Protect Children', 82.

[181] [2008] EWHC 152 (Admin), [2008] 1 FLR 1660.

[182] This latter fact emerged in subsequent proceedings: see *R (G) v Nottingham City Council and Nottingham University Hospital* [2008] EWHC 400, [2008] 1 FLR 1668, QBD at [44].

from his mother to a different room in the hospital. In judicial review proceedings before Munby J,[183] counsel for the mother applied for an immediate order that the mother and her son be reunited since the removal was done without legal authority and in breach of the rights of the mother and the baby under Article 8 of the ECHR. Munby J ordered that, provided there was no lawful authority to remove the child, the NHS Hospital Trust was to take steps forthwith to reunite the mother and baby. They were reunited within minutes of the order being made.

It had been submitted on behalf of the local authority that the birth plan was a plan to accommodate K within the meaning of section 20 of the Children Act 1989.[184] The argument was founded on nothing more than the assertion that the mother knew and understood the details of the birth plan and that she did not raise objection to it nor to the removal of her newborn baby.[185] Munby J stated that these submissions were 'as divorced from legal substance' as they were remote from the emotional and hormonal realities of the woman's condition.[186] He continued:

> I am not suggesting that consent to the accommodation of a child in accordance with s 20 is required by law to be in writing—though, that said, a prudent local authority would surely always wish to ensure that an alleged parental consent in such a case is properly recorded in writing and evidenced by the parent's signature. Nor am I disputing that there may be cases where a child has in fact, and without parental objection, been accommodated by a local authority for such a period as might entitle a court to infer that the parent had in fact consented.[187]

However:

> To equate helpless acquiescence with consent when a parent is confronted in circumstances such as this with the misuse (or perhaps on another occasion the misrepresentation) of non-existent authority by an agent of the State is, in my judgment, both unprincipled and, indeed, fraught with potential danger.[188]

Munby J made clear what he considered ought to be obvious, namely that 'social workers have no power to remove children from their parents unless they have first obtained judicial sanction for what they are proposing to do'[189] and also emphasised that 'the powers conferred on the police by s 46 are *not* given to either local authorities or social workers'.[190] He added that 'the same goes, of course, for a hospital and its medical staff'[191] and that 'no baby, no child, can be removed simply as the result of a decision taken by officials in some room'.[192]

### 2.8.5 Qualifications

His Lordship clarified, however, that this is subject to two qualifications. First, a person is entitled to intervene 'in order to prevent an actual or threatened criminal assault taking place'.[193] Secondly, section 3(5) of the Children Act 1989 provides that 'a person who has care of a child may (subject to the provisions of the Children Act 1989) do what is reasonable in all the circumstances of the

---

[183] There were already judicial review proceedings before the court in respect of the woman, challenging a pathway plan for her under the leaving care legislation (discussed in Section 2.5). *R (G) v Nottingham City Council and Nottingham University Hospital* [2008] EWHC 400, [2008] 1 FLR 1668, QBD.

[184] Ibid, [48].     [185] Ibid, [51].     [186] Ibid, [52].     [187] Ibid, [53].

[188] Ibid, [55]. See also the guidance provided by Hedley J in *Coventry City Council v C, B, CA and CH* [2012] EWHC 2190 (Fam), [2013] 2 FLR 987[2013] 2 FLR 987 (discussed earlier).

[189] [2008] 1 FLR 1660, [17]. The sanction could be 'either an emergency protection order in accordance with s 44 of the Children Act 1989 or an interim care order in accordance with s 38 of the Act or perhaps, in an exceptional case (and subject to s 100 of the Act), a wardship order made by a judge of the Family Division of the High Court'.

[190] [2008] 1 FLR 1660, [15].

[191] Ibid, [17].     [192] Ibid, [18].

[193] Ibid, [21], adding that: '[a]ny threat of immediate significant violence is enough, particularly if it involves a young child'.

case for the purpose of safeguarding or promoting the child's welfare'.[194] This, or the doctrine of necessity, would for example allow medical care in order to protect a child from irreversible harm or death in circumstances of such urgency that other lawful authorisation could not be invoked.[195] In such situations, as Munby J explained, 'Law, medical ethics and common sense march hand in hand'.[196] In the *Nottingham* case, neither of the qualifications applied.

However, they might be relied on if a parent sought to remove a child from local authority accommodation in circumstances where the child would be at risk. A local authority might also be protected for a brief period by its general duty to safeguard and promote the welfare of a looked after child. There are overwhelming policy reasons why the local authority should not be compelled to hand the child over immediately, for the child might suffer the feared significant harm which will form the basis of an application for the emergency protection order. This reasoning is assisted by the Court of Appeal's ruling in *F v Wirral Metropolitan Borough Council*[197] that there is no separate tort of interference with parental rights. If a local authority were to be sued for retaining a child in breach of section 20(8), the plaintiff would have the burden of establishing that a tort had been committed against the *child*, and not against the person with parental responsibility. A separate possibility for speedy intervention might be, as Munby J also notes, to involve the police.

## 3 Significant harm: the threshold for compulsory intervention

With the intention of drawing a clear distinction between voluntary and compulsory interventions in family life, the Children Act 1989 establishes a threshold for compulsory intervention in family life based on the concept of 'significant harm'. As we shall see, the standard of proof with regard to this threshold criterion[198] varies according to the nature of the intervention.

### Key legislation

'Harm' is defined in section 31(9) to mean:

ill-treatment or the impairment of health or development including, for example, impairment suffered from seeing or hearing the ill-treatment of another;

'development' means physical, intellectual, emotional, social or behavioural development;
'health' means physical or mental health; and
'ill-treatment' includes sexual abuse and forms of ill-treatment which are not physical.

The definition of harm is thus very wide and covers all types of conceivable harm to the child. It specifically recognises the deleterious effects on child well-being of exposure to (domestic) violence[199] and includes impairment of a child's emotional development[200] as well as physical development.

---

[194] Ibid, [23].  [195] Ibid, [25].  [196] Ibid, [26].

[197] [1991] 2 All ER 648; for a useful comment see A. Bainham (1990) 3 Journal of Child Law 3.

[198] As it has come to be known: see [1993] 1 FLR 257 at 261 *per* Booth J.

[199] The definition now includes seeing or hearing domestic violence. See Social Services Inspectorate and Department of Health, *Domestic Violence and Social Care* (London: HMSO, 1995); P. Parkinson and C. Humphries, 'Children who Witness Domestic Violence: The Implications for Child Protection' (1998) 10 Child and Family Law Quarterly 147.

[200] For a case in which a care order was made because of significant emotional harm to the child arising from the parents' ongoing conflict over the care of the child, see *A City Council v M, F and C (By Her Children's Guardian)* [2013] 1 FLR 517 (HHJ Cleary).

An example of a case involving emotional abuse is *London Borough of Tower Hamlets v B*.[201] This is one of several cases that have come before the courts recently involving young women who have 'been either radicalised or exposed to extreme ideology promulgated by those subscribing to the values of the self-styled Islamic State'[202] and have been 'seduced, by a belief that travelling to Syria to become what is known as 'Jihadi brides' is somehow romantic and honourable both to them and to their families.'[203] An intelligent, ambitious 16-year-old woman, B, was intercepted by the Metropolitan Police Service Counter Terrorism Command aboard a flight, by which, she admitted, she intended to travel to Syria to join so-called Islamic State. In other cases, attempts to contain the risk of flight to Islamic State had been achieved through electronic tagging,[204] and B suggested that her case could be managed in the same way and by removing her access to the internet. B's parents 'professed their willingness to engage' and 'were eloquent and fulsome in their assurances'. However, this was shown to be a 'farrago of sophisticated dishonesty' when, following a subsequent search of the family home, members of the family were arrested on suspicion of the commission of offences under the Terrorism Act 2000. Hayden J had 'no hesitation in concluding that B has been subjected to serious emotional harm',[205] requiring her removal from the family home. Tagging could not protect her from this psychological and emotional harm; only a safe and neutral environment could.[206]

For the state to be entitled to intervene compulsorily, the harm must be 'significant'. This requirement means that not all falling off in standards of parenting causing harm to the child will permit state intervention.

In *Humberside County Council v B*[207] Booth J accepted,[208] indeed found 'very apt and helpful', counsel's submission that significant should be defined 'in accordance with dictionary definitions, first as being harm that the court should consider was either considerable or noteworthy or important' and 'as harm which the court should take into account in considering a child's future'.[209] In *Re L (Care: Threshold Criteria)*[210] Hedley J cautioned that it 'would be unwise to a degree to attempt an all embracing definition of significant harm . . . Significant harm is fact specific and must retain the breadth of meaning that human fallibility may require of it'.[211] Whether or not a child is suffering significant harm must therefore be seen in the context of all the circumstances of the case and in relation to the particular child with whom the court is concerned. A child may be exceptionally vulnerable in one way or another. In *Humberside County Council v B*[212] Booth J cited an example given in argument by counsel of a child who suffers from brittle bones, in whose case 'a push or a slap might be of great significance, whereas in the case of a child who does not so suffer it may be a minimal incident'.[213] But of course this cuts both ways: it is possible on this view that the impact of ill-treatment or other types of unacceptable parenting on a resilient child who is able to withstand the treatment or behaviour, may fall outside the scope of the meaning of 'significant harm' where the harm is not considerable, noteworthy, or important. However, where the standards of parenting of those who are looking after the child show no sign of being capable of change, so that the

---

[201] [2015] EWHC 2491 (Fam).

[202] Per Hayden J in *London Borough of Tower Hamlets v B* [2015] EWHC 2491 (Fam), at para [4].

[203] Ibid, at para [5].

[204] *Re X (Children) and Y (Children) (No 1)* [2015] EWHC 2265 (Fam), *Re X (Children) and Re Y (Children) (No 2)* [2015] EWHC 2358 (Fam), and see M. Downs, 'Is preventing violent extremism a facet of child protection?' [2015] Fam Law 1167.

[205] *London Borough of Tower Hamlets v B* [2015] EWHC 2491, at [28]     [206] Ibid, at [32].

[207] [1993] 1 FLR 257.     [208] Ibid, 265.     [209] Ibid, 263.     [210] [2007] 1 FLR 2050 at [51].

[211] The point, that the 'categories of abuse' should not be closed may perhaps be illustrated by a recent case in which the mother of three children caused her eldest adopted daughter to be artificially inseminated in order to provide the mother with another child: see *A Council v M and Others (No 1) (Fact-finding; Adoptive Child; Artificial Insemination)* [2012] EWHC 4241 (Fam); *A Council v M and Others (No 2) (Welfare; Adoptive Children; Artificial Insemination)* [2013] 2 FLR 1261.

[212] [1993] 1 FLR 257.     [213] Ibid, 263.

child will sustain the effects of poor parenting continued over a considerable period of time, it is suggested that such a child might be one whom a local authority should take steps to protect on the basis that he is 'likely' to suffer significant harm, because the harm he is presently suffering is likely to become 'considerable, noteworthy, or important'.

The inclusion of likely harm as a basis for taking child protection action allows for intervention before any actual harm is suffered.[214] Where a child is not presently suffering significant harm, it may be even more difficult for the local authority to determine when it is appropriate to intervene on the basis that a child is 'likely' to suffer significant harm. Professionals who engage in child protection work are aware that some parents and other carers may have little appreciation of the vulnerability of babies and small children to suffering significant harm. In the case of babie,s a shaking which is relatively mild by adult standards may lead to disastrous consequences such as brain damage, impairment of sight, or even death.[215] A parent with learning difficulties may not be able to be trusted always to test that the water in which a child is bathed is of the correct tempera-ture, yet for a child to be scalded may be fatal or it may have permanent serious consequences for the child's appearance, health, and development. When setting standards, and evaluating the risk of harm occurring to a child, the question to be resolved is: when should the parents and others be allowed the opportunity to demonstrate whether it is safe for the child to remain in their care, and when is it proper to intervene to prevent predicted harm from occurring?

## 3.1 Health or development: comparison with similar child

### Key legislation

Some assistance on the meaning of significant harm is provided by section 31(10), which provides:

Where the question of whether harm suffered by a child is significant turns on the child's health or development, his health or development shall be compared with that which could reasonably be expected of a similar child.[216]

In *Re O (A Minor) (Care Order: Education: Procedure)*[217] the meaning of 'significant harm', in the context of a child's intellectual, emotional, social, and behavioural development was considered, and parallels were drawn with a similar child. *Re O* concerned a 15-year-old girl who had been truanting from school for three years. Considerable efforts had been made by the local education authority to secure the girl's attendance at school, but to no avail. The main thrust of the local au-thority's application for a care order, which was supported by the guardian ad litem, was that if the girl's absenteeism was not arrested, it would have a profound effect on her ability to cope in adult life. Although there was anxiety about her intellectual and educational development,[218] the real concern related to her emotional and social development. It was said that her refusal to go to school

---

[214] Eg *F v Leeds City Council* [1994] 2 FLR 60 where the court found that the mother's dangerously egocentric behav-iour posed an unacceptable risk to her child. See also *Re A (A Minor) (Care Proceedings)* [1993] 1 FCR 824 where three children had already been removed from their mother. When a fourth child was born, the local authority immediately obtained an emergency protection order and commenced care proceedings on the basis of likely significant harm.

[215] For discussion of such cases and difficulties with expert opinion evidence in that context, see J. Bettle and J. Herring, 'Shaken Babies and Care Proceedings' [2011] Family Law 1370.

[216] For criticism of the similar child concept, see M. D. A. Freeman, 'Care After 1991' in D. Freestone (ed), *Children and the Law* (Hull: Hull University Press, 1990). Cf A. Bainham, 'Care after 1991—A Reply' (1993) 3 Journal of Child Law 99.

[217] [1992] 2 FLR 7.

[218] The evidence was that the girl had in fact acquired educational skills so that, in comparative terms, she was of about average ability.

'will have a major impact on her self-esteem, her self-confidence and her perception of herself . . . it will also seriously impair her ability to relate to peers and adults in a more formal way. This will inhibit [the girl's] development because school is, of course, not only about intellectual learning, it also provides young people with necessary social and relationship skills.'[219]

On appeal from magistrates who made a care order, Ewbank J ruled that it had been entirely open to the magistrates to come to the view that the girl's intellectual and social development was suffering, and was likely to suffer, significant harm. He said 'if a child does not go to school and is missing her education, it is not difficult to draw the conclusion that, if she had gone to school and had not truanted, she would have improved her intellectual and social development'. With regard to the comparison to be made with a similar child he said 'in the context of this type of case, "similar child" means a child of equivalent intellectual and social development, who has gone to school, and not merely an average child who may or may not be at school'.[220] Ewbank J therefore confirmed the care order, and the care plan that the girl should go to a children's home and should be taken to school from there until a pattern of attendance had been achieved, when consideration would be given to sending her home.[221]

Presumably the meaning of 'similar' in this context needs to take account of environmental, social, and cultural characteristics of the child. It seems that a similar child is a child with similar attributes, that is, a child of the same age, sex, and ethnic origin. Where a child has learning difficulties, he should be compared with a child with similar learning difficulties. Where the child was born prematurely, the child's achievement of developmental milestones should be compared with those achieved by other premature babies. Where the child has a spurt in growth in weight and height if put into hospital or foster care, and comparison is made with a similar child, the question to be asked is would a similar child demonstrate such a growth spurt under these conditions. Where such a child would not, the question then arises whether the first child has been malnourished or otherwise treated in an abusive manner which has led to his or her failing to grow and put on weight, or whether there is some organic cause for the condition.

More contentious is the question of how far a disadvantaged child should be compared to a similar disadvantaged child, or how far he should be compared with a child who has benefited from greater material, social, and intellectual advantages. An example might be of children living in deprived circumstances in an inner city area. It might be expected that some such children will be poorly clothed, have few toys or books, be fed on a diet which is not very healthy, and not receive much intellectual stimulus from those who are caring for them. It is suggested that it could probably be maintained that a child who is looked after in this way is being treated in no worse a manner than many other children living in deprived circumstances, and that the standard of care he is receiving amounts to good enough parenting in the light of his background. However, it is suggested that deprivation and relative poverty do not provide a reasonable excuse for a child being dressed in filthy clothing, for complete lack of attention to personal hygiene, for not seeking medical attention when the child is ill, and for no interest being taken in his intellectual and emotional development. Decision-makers must, of course, take account of poverty, but where one or more of these conditions applies to a child, then it seems proper to conclude that the level of care has fallen below the minimum standard which is acceptable.

In *Re L (Care: Threshold Criteria)*[222] Hedley J explained that for harm to be significant 'it is clear that it must be something unusual; at least something more than the commonplace human failure

---

[219] [1992] 2 FLR 7 at 11–12.     [220] Ibid, 12.

[221] See J. Fortin, 'Significant Harm Revisited' (1993) 5 Journal of Child Law 151, who argues that the facts did not justify removing a child from her parents, that it was wrong to use removal into state care to deal with a child's lack of self-esteem and self-confidence, and that an application for an education supervision order would have been the appropriate response. See too R. White (1992) 142 New Law Journal 396.

[222] [2007] 1 FLR 2050 at [51].

or inadequacy'. Hedley J observed that as a matter of policy it is 'recognised in law, that children are best brought up within natural families'[223] and that it follows inexorably that:

---

### Talking point

Society must be willing to tolerate very diverse standards of parenting, including the eccentric, the barely adequate, and the inconsistent. It follows too that children will inevitably have both very different experiences of parenting and very unequal consequences flowing from it. It means that some children will experience disadvantage and harm, while others flourish in atmospheres of loving security and emotional stability. These are the consequences of our fallible humanity and it is not the provenance of the state to spare children all the consequences of defective parenting. In any event, it simply could not be done.[224]

**Q.** Do you agree? Does male circumcision carried out for non-medical reasons constitute significant harm? (See discussion below).

---

Similarly, in *Re K; A Local Authority v N and Others*[225] Munby J commented[226] that:

> the court must always be sensitive to the cultural, social and religious circumstances of the particular child and family. And the court should, I think, be slow to find that parents only recently or comparatively recently arrived from a foreign country—particularly a country where standards and expectations may be more or less different, sometimes very different indeed, from those with which they are familiar—have fallen short of an acceptable standard of parenting if in truth they have done nothing wrong by the standards of their own community.[227]

The passages from the judgments of Hedley J and Munby J were endorsed by Ward LJ in *Re MA (Care Threshold)*,[228] who observed that, given the underlying philosophy of the Act, 'the harm must . . . be significant enough to justify the intervention of the State and disturb the autonomy of the parents to bring up their children by themselves in the way they choose'.[229] The citation and endorsement of the passages in *Re L* and *Re K* (set out in the preceding paragraphs) in the context of the decision in *Re MA*, however, has been a matter of concern for some commentators. That was a case in which there was no suggestion that the parents were claiming any cultural justification for the alleged ill-treatment of their children. As Hayes et al comment:

> any reference to the value placed by society on 'diversity and individuality' cannot be used to justify child cruelty or exposing young children to the risk of significant harm. Our developed laws of child protection are rooted in the protection of the rights and freedoms of all children within our society.[230]

---

[223] Citing in support Lord Templeman in *Re KD (A Minor: Ward) (Termination of Access)* [1988] AC 806 at 812: The best person to bring up a child is the natural parent. It matters not whether the parent is wise or foolish, rich or poor, educated or illiterate, provided the child's moral and physical health are not in danger. Public authorities cannot improve on nature.

[224] [2007] 1 FLR 2050 at [50].      [225] [2005] EWHC 2956 (Fam), [2007] 1 FLR 399.

[226] In the context of considering the threshold for making a care order pursuant to s 31 of the Children Act 1989.

[227] [2005] EWHC 2956 (Fam), [2007] 1 FLR 399 at [26].

[228] [2009] EWCA Civ 853, [2010] 1 FLR 431 at [51]. For commentary on this case, see H. Keating, 'Re MA: The Significance of Harm' [2011] Child and Family Law Quarterly 115 and J. Hayes, M. Hayes, and J. Williams, ' "Shocking" Abuse Followed by a "Staggering Ruling": *Re MA (Care Threshold)*' [2010] Family Law 166.

[229] [2009] EWCA Civ 853, [2010] 1 FLR 431 at [54].

[230] J. Hayes, M. Hayes, and J. Williams, ' "Shocking" Abuse Followed by a "Staggering Ruling": *Re MA (Care Threshold)*' [2010] Family Law 166. However, research does not suggest that a change to the threshold is required: see J. Brophy et al, *Significant Harm: Child Protection Litigation in a Multi-Cultural Setting* (London: Department for Constitutional Affairs, 2003) (examining cultural context in care proceedings and not recommending any change to the threshold

The interface between culture and significant harm was also explored in *Re B and G (Care Proceedings: FGM) (No 2)*.[231] This was the first case in which the issue of female genital mutilation (FGM)[232] has been raised in the context of considering 'significant harm' within care proceedings. Munby P found on the medical evidence that the allegation that the girl had suffered FGM was not made out. However, his lordship took the opportunity to address several wider issues which were raised by FGM, including whether there exists any valid distinction in this context between FGM and male circumcision. Munby P concluded that 'FGM in any form will suffice to establish "threshold" in accordance with section 31 of the Children Act 1989; male circumcision without more will not.'[233] His lordship was of the view that 'both involve significant harm',[234] although whereas 'it can never be reasonable parenting to inflict any form of FGM on a child', society and family law 'are prepared to tolerate non-therapeutic male circumcision performed for religious or even for purely cultural or conventional reasons'.[235] Munby P observed that FGM has no basis in any religion, nor medical justification, whereas male circumcision is often performed for religious reasons and is seen by some as providing hygienic or prophylactic benefits.[236] Accordingly male circumcision will not establish the threshold in section 31 since, although it will be significant harm, it will not be attributable to the care given to the child not being what it would reasonable for a parent to give.

One can readily understand this distinction as a pragmatic response to ensuring that longstanding cultural and religious acceptance of the practice of male circumcision is not caught by section 31. However, his lordship's conclusion that male circumcision represents 'significant harm' leads, in this context (and possibly by analogy, in others) to the unfortunate conclusion that it can be not unreasonable for parents deliberately to inflict significant harm upon their children.[237] Moreover, surely the reference to reasonable parental care in the threshold is not to justify deliberate infliction of significant harm by reference to practices which are considered as reasonable by some sectors of society. Rather, it is to ensure that significant harm is not caught by the threshold where, for example, that harm has been caused entirely accidentally, without any neglect on the part of the parents.

Munby P went on to highlight that difficult issues are likely to arise in FGM cases at the stage of making a welfare evaluation as to the future. For example, if FGM is proved as the only threshold factor in relation to one girl in a family, there will a basis for concluding likely significant harm to any female siblings, yet 'there will be no statutory basis for care proceedings in relation to any male sibling(s)'.[238] This raises difficult questions: 'Is her welfare best served by separating her permanently from her parents at the price of severing the sibling bond? Or is it best served by preserving the family unit?'[239] His lordship was clear that the law has an important role to play in preventing

---

criteria); J. Brophy, J. Jhutti-Johal, and C. Owen, 'Assessing and Documenting Child Ill-Treatment in Ethnic Minority Households' [2003] Family Law 756: no 'single issue' cases where allegations of significant harm to a child rested unequivocally on behaviours/attitudes defended as culturally acceptable by a parent but that professionals argued were unacceptable within western European assessments of ill-treatment.

[231] [2015] EWFC 3, Sir James Munby P. For comment, see J. Hayes QC, 'Protecting child victims of Female Genital Mutilation' [2015] Fam Law 282.

[232] The World Health Organisation (WHO) lists the following four categories: Type I: Clitoridectomy. Partial or total removal of the clitoris and in rare cases only the prepuce (the fold of skin surrounding the clitoris); Type II: Excision. Partial or total removal of the clitoris and labia minora with or without removal of the labia majora; Type III: Infibulation. Narrowing of the vaginal opening through the creation of a covering seal. The seal is formed by cutting and repositioning the labia minora or majora with or without removal of the clitoris; and Type IV: Other. All other harmful procedures to the genitals for non-medical reasons, for example pricking, piercing, incising, scraping and cauterizing the genital area.

[233] [2015] EWFC 3, at [73]. Section 31 requires proof of significant harm attributable to the care given to the child not being what it would be reasonable to expect a parent to give. See section 8 below.

[234] Ibid.    [235] Ibid, at [72].    [236] Ibid.

[237] As John Hayes QC observes, the characterisation of male circumcision as constituting significant harm could found an argument based on equality of treatment, in the sense that both sexes should similarly be protected from significant harm: J. Hayes QC, 'Protecting child victims of Female Genital Mutilation' [2015] Fam Law 282, at 289.

[238] [2015] EWFC 3, at [76].

[239] Ibid. Munby P added 'that local authorities and judges are probably well advised not to jump too readily to the conclusion that proven FGM should lead to adoption' (at [77]).

FGM, and the 'the inherent jurisdiction, as well as all the other jurisdictions of the High Court and the Family Court, must be as vigorously mobilised in the prevention of FGM as they have hitherto been in relation to forced marriage.[240]

## 4 Investigation

### 4.1 Investigating whether a child is suffering, or is likely to suffer, significant harm

A local authority have a duty in section 47 of the Children Act 1989 to investigate cases in which it is suspected that a child may be suffering or likely to suffer significant harm.[241]

---

**Key legislation**

Section 47(1) provides:

Where a local authority—

(a) are informed that a child who lives, or is found, in their area—
   (i) is the subject of an emergency protection order; or
   (ii) is in police protection; . . .
(b) have reasonable cause to suspect that a child who lives, or is found, in their area is suffering, or is likely to suffer, significant harm,

the authority shall make, or cause to be made, such enquiries as they consider necessary to enable them to decide whether they should take any action to safeguard or promote the child's welfare.

---

There is an identical duty where the local authority itself has obtained an emergency protection order with respect to a child.[242] The duty in section 47(1)(b) is triggered when the local authority has *reasonable cause to suspect* that a child is suffering, or is likely to suffer, significant harm. In *R (S) v Swindon Borough Council and another*[243] Scott Baker J commented that:

the threshold is quite low. This is hardly surprising as [the local authority's] obligation is to investigate ie make enquiries with a view to deciding whether to take any action to safeguard or promote the child's welfare.[244]

In that case, the claimant was a widower with three children, who had begun a relationship with a woman who had a daughter, K, then aged 9. The claimant was found not guilty on seven

---

[240] Ibid, at [78].

[241] For a case in which a local authority's failure properly to carry out duties under sections 17 and 47 in assessing risk to children from a sex-offender in the children's local community was held to be unlawful in judicial review proceedings, see *ET, BT and CT v Islington Borough Council* [2013] EWCA Civ 323. In *D v D (County Court Jurisdiction: Injunctions)* [1993] 2 FLR 802, the Court of Appeal ruled that the trial judge did not have jurisdiction to issue a direction which had the effect of inhibiting a local authority from carrying out its investigative function in response to a suspicion of child abuse in proceedings brought by parents for residence orders. Whether a High Court judge has such power was doubted, but left open: ibid, 811.

[242] Section 47(2).

[243] [2001] EWHC (Admin) 334, [2001] 3 FCR 702. See also *Gogay v Hertfordshire County Council* [2001] 1 FLR 280, CA at [49]: 'a s 47 investigation does not generally infringe the legal rights of anyone involved. It merely imposes on the local authority a duty to carry the investigation far enough to reach a conclusion' (employee should not be suspended simply because there is a s 47 investigation).

[244] [2001] 3 FCR 702 at [36].

charges of the indecent assault of K over an 18-month period. He had subsequently formed a relationship with a Mrs X, who had two daughters aged 11 and 7. The claimant and Mrs X wished to set up home together with their respective children and the claimant therefore wrote to Swindon Borough Council asking what social services intended to do. Mr X (the father of Mrs X's children) approached his local social services department expressing concern about his children's contact with the claimant. The local authorities concerned (the defendants in the case) took the view that K's allegations were to be believed and that the claimant could pose a risk to children, particularly children other than his own living in the same household, and therefore some consideration would need to be given to a plan to protect the children. The claimant applied for judicial review of those decisions, contending that the defendants had to be satisfied of the likelihood of significant harm before intervening. Scott Baker J dismissed the claim and, having drawn attention to the precise wording of section 47, observed that there was nothing at the criminal trial which ought to have led the defendants to the conclusion that what K had said was so unlikely to be true that they no longer had any reasonable cause to suspect the likelihood of significant harm. His Lordship explained that, although a local authority would 'no doubt look carefully at the result of a criminal trial and any matters of significance that emerged in the course of it', the fact of an acquittal does 'not prevent a local authority from forming a view which is adverse to the acquitted person',[245] and 'the various statutory duties under the 1989 Act must, if they are in play, be discharged'.[246]

Enquiries under section 47 are in particular directed towards establishing three things: whether the authority should make any application to the court, or exercise any of their other powers under the Children Act 1989 with respect to the child; whether it would be in the best interests of a child who is the subject of emergency protection to be in local authority accommodation; and whether, in the case of a child who has been taken into police protection, it would be in the child's best interests for the local authority to ask for an application to be made for an emergency protection order under section 46(7).[247]

Once the duty to make enquiries is in place, several other duties follow, or may follow depending on the circumstances. By section 47(4) the local authority is under a duty to take such steps as are reasonably practicable to obtain access to the child 'unless they are satisfied that they already have sufficient information with respect to him'. Section 47(6) follows up this provision by providing that where, in the course of the section 47 enquiries, any officer of the local authority concerned[248] is refused access to the child concerned or is denied information as to his whereabouts, 'the authority shall apply for an emergency protection order, a child assessment order, a care order or a supervision order with respect to the child unless they are satisfied that his welfare can be satisfactorily safeguarded without their doing so'.

Section 47(9) emphasises the importance of inter-agency cooperation by placing a duty on specified persons (listed in s 47(11))[249] to assist the local authority in conducting its enquiries unless it would be unreasonable in all the circumstances of the case.[250] Of course, the value of different agencies working together in the early detection and prevention of child abuse is emphasised in the guidance issued under the Act. The conduct of an investigation under section 47 requires not only the cooperation of other agencies, but also the cooperation of persons with parental responsibility for the child. Section 47 does not give a local authority any coercive powers

---

[245] Ibid, [37].　　[246] Ibid, [37].　　[247] Section 47(3).

[248] Or any person authorised by the authority to act on its behalf in connection with those enquiries.

[249] The persons specified are any local authority, any local housing authority, health authorities, and any other person authorised by the Secretary of State. Surprisingly, and arguably wrongly, the police are omitted from this list. See further E. Birchall and C. Hallett, *Working Together in Child Protection* (London: HMSO, 1995); C. Hallett, *Inter-Agency Coordination in Child Protection* (London: HMSO, 1995).

[250] Section 47(10).

and nothing in section 47 empowers a local authority to enter premises, despite the fact that one of its duties when conducting its investigation is to take such steps as are reasonably practicable to obtain access to the child.[251] Rather, the local authority is reliant on the person who has care of the child allowing them to see the child. However, cooperation from such a person may be forthcoming when the local authority's duty under section 47(6) is explained to him or her. It is suggested that only rarely should a local authority be satisfied that a child's welfare can be satisfactorily safeguarded without applying for a court order when the local authority has not actually seen, and (where appropriate) talked to, the child. It is a dangerously optimistic reaction to a suspicion of abuse which has not been properly investigated. Tragically, several children who have died at the hands of those looking after them are those children to whom social workers and others have not insisted on having proper access.[252]

If, at the conclusion of their enquiries, the local authority decides not to apply for a court order in respect of the child, it must decide whether it is appropriate to review the case at a later date and, if so, set a date for the review.[253] If a local authority concludes that it should take action to safeguard or promote the child's welfare it shall take that action (so far as it is both within its power and reasonably practicable for it to do so).[254] However, there may be no need for legal intervention even where significant harm is discovered. Where parents and other persons caring for the child are willing to work with social workers and other professionals in addressing the concerns which have arisen, it may be decided that the child can be adequately protected if he or she remains at home while work with the family is attempted.

## 4.2 Child assessment orders

Where access to a child is denied, or where information is denied as to the child's whereabouts, the local authority must apply for a court order unless it is satisfied that the child's welfare can otherwise be satisfactorily safeguarded. Normally the most appropriate response in such cases is to apply for an emergency protection order (discussed in Section 5). Sometimes, however, even when access to a child is obtained, persons with parental responsibility or those caring for a child may prevent a proper assessment from taking place by refusing to allow the child to be medically, or otherwise, examined. Where an assessment of the child is being frustrated in this way, the most appropriate response might be for a local authority or the NSPCC to apply for a child assessment order[255] under section 43 of the Children Act 1989. The effect of this order is to place any person who is in a position to produce the child under a duty to produce him to the persons named in the order, and to comply with the court's directions.[256] Only a local authority or an authorised person[257] can apply for a child assessment order.

---

[251] Section 47(4).

[252] For a classic and horrific recent example, see *Birmingham City Council v AG and A* [2009] EWHC 3720 (Fam), [2010] 2 FLR 580 (child starved to death after social worker failed to gain access to child's household). See also *A Child in Mind: The Report on the Death of Kimberley Carlile* (Greenwich London Borough Council, 1987). See too *A Child in Trust: Report on the Death of Jasmine Beckford* (London Borough of Brent, 1988); *Whose Child: Report on the Death of Tyra Henry* (London Borough of Greenwich, 1987); see Department of Health and Social Security, *Child Abuse: A Study of Inquiry Reports 1973–1981* (London: HMSO, 1982), Department of Health, *Child Abuse: A Study of Inquiry Reports 1980–89* (London: HMSO, 1991).

[253] Section 47(7).      [254] Section 47(8).

[255] That is the title given to an order under s 43 of the Children Act 1989: see s 43(2). For a general evaluation of the child assessment order, see R. Lavery, 'The Child Assessment Order—A Reassessment' (1996) 8 Child and Family Law Quarterly 41. See also G. Mitchell, 'The Child Assessment Order—A Breach of Principle?' [1991] XIII(I) Liverpool Law Review 53.

[256] Section 43(6); this person may not, of course, be a person with parental responsibility.

[257] Ie, a person authorised for the purpose of s 31 of the Children Act 1989 (currently only the NSPCC), see s 43(13).

## Key legislation

Section 43(1) provides that a child assessment order may be made if, but only if, the court is satisfied that:

(a) the applicant has reasonable cause to suspect that the child is suffering, or is likely to suffer, significant harm;

(b) an assessment of the child's health or development, or the way in which he has been treated, is required to enable the applicant to determine whether or not the child is suffering, or is likely to suffer, significant harm; and

(c) it is unlikely that such an assessment will be made, or be satisfactory, in the absence of an order under this section.

The standard of proof which must be satisfied is thus one of reasonable cause for suspicion only, and accordingly the type of intervention allowed is strictly limited. The order must specify the date on which the assessment is to begin and gives the local authority a time-limited period as specified in the order, up to a maximum of seven days from that date, in which to discover whether there is any real foundation to its suspicion.[258] The court takes control over the type of assessment which should take place, and may give such directions as it thinks fit. The order authorises any person carrying out an assessment to do so in accordance with the terms of the order.[259] Those carrying out the assessment are limited as to where the assessment is carried out: a child may only be kept away from home where this is in accordance with directions specified in the order; where it is necessary for the purposes of the assessment; and where it is for such period, or periods, as may be specified in the order.[260] Where a child is to be kept away from home, the court must give directions about contact arrangements.[261] The voice of the child may also be determinative in a case of this kind. A child who has sufficient understanding to make an informed decision may refuse to submit to a medical, psychiatric, or other assessment.[262]

It is up to the court to determine how far a child assessment order can be used as a 'fishing expedition' to discover whether the suspicion that the child is suffering, or is likely to suffer, significant harm is soundly based. It is not clear to what extent it would be appropriate for the court to be very specific in the type of assessment it authorises, and to what extent it can leave this to the discretion of the local authority. Very little use has been made of the child assessment order and there does not appear to be any reported case law directly in relation to this order.[263] It seems that the court is expected to be cautious about authorising removal of the child from the home. A fine balance must be struck between taking the steps which are needed to discover whether or not the local authority's decisions can be verified and causing unnecessary distress and anxiety to a child and his or her parents in a case where there is nothing untoward happening. The caution surrounding the structure of child assessment orders can be partly explained by the crisis which occurred in Cleveland in the period immediately preceding the passing of the Children Act 1989.[264]

It is important to appreciate that a child assessment order is not the appropriate order in a case in which a child requires emergency protection. Section 43(4) provides that no court shall make a child assessment order if it is satisfied that there are grounds for making an emergency protection

---

[258] Section 43(5).     [259] Section 43(6) and (7).     [260] Section 43(9).

[261] Section 43(10).     [262] Section 43(8).

[263] There is information which suggests that social workers are unhappy about the alienating effect of such an order, and consider that there is no need for an order where parents can be persuaded to cooperate, see J. Dickens, 'Assessment and the Control of Social Work: Analysis of Reasons for the Non-Use of the Child Assessment Order' [1993] Journal of Social Welfare and Family Law 88.

[264] *Report of the Inquiry into Child Abuse in Cleveland 1987* (Cm 412, 1988). For an account of the effect of the Cleveland Inquiry on the work of those involved with child sexual abuse, see A. Bentovim, *Cleveland 10 Years On—A Mental Health Perspective* [1998] Family Law 153–7, 202–7, and 267–9.

order and that it ought to make such an order rather than a child assessment order. This provision is designed to obviate the risk of children being left in a position of immediate danger because the wrong proceedings have been commenced. For the same reason, a court may treat an application for a child assessment order as an application for an emergency protection order.[265]

## 4.3 **The power of a court to direct a section 37 investigation in family proceedings**

One of the times when the welfare of a child may come under scrutiny is when an application is made to a court in family proceedings. Sometimes the evidence may give rise to concern, or even alarm, and the court may take the view that the position of a child should be further investigated. One response is to request a welfare report under section 7. Where there is serious concern about the upbringing of a child, such that the court takes the view that it may be appropriate to make a care or supervision order with respect to him, section 37 provides that the court may direct a local authority to undertake an investigation of the child's circumstances. In responding to this direction, and when undertaking its investigation, the local authority must consider whether it should apply for a care or supervision order, provide services or assistance for the child or his family, or take any other action with respect to the child. Because it is the court which is instigating the inquiry, it may wish to specify particular matters which it would like the local authority to look into.[266]

Where a local authority undertakes an investigation under a direction given under section 37 and decides not to apply for a care or supervision order, it must give the court its reasons. It must also inform the court of any service or assistance which it has provided, or intends to provide, for the child and his family, and of any other action which it has taken, or proposes to take, in relation to the child. However, it was held in *Nottinghamshire County Council v P*[267] that a court has no power to direct the local authority to initiate care proceedings where it is not satisfied with the authority's reasons for failing to do so. *Nottinghamshire County Council v P* is an example of a case where possession of the final decision-making power was crucial to the outcome. On the one hand, the trial judge and the Court of Appeal were in no doubt that a care order was necessary to prevent the children from suffering further significant harm; on the other hand, the local authority was obdurate in its refusal to pursue an application for a care order. The decision-making power lay with the local authority and, as Sir Stephen Brown P said, 'if a local authority doggedly resists taking the steps which are appropriate to the case of children at risk of suffering significant harm it appears that the court is powerless'.[268] Where, during the course of its section 37 investigation, the local authority uncovers matters which lead it to believe that a child is being abused, it can, of course, take steps to protect the child by making an application in care proceedings.

## 4.4 **Local authority responses to significant harm**

Determining which is the most effective response to a discovery that a child is suffering, or is likely to suffer, significant harm is not easy for local authorities. Detailed guidance on the procedures to be adopted by the local authority children's social care department and other relevant agencies in fulfilment of the local authority's duties to safeguard children is set out in *Working Together to Safeguard Children: A Guide to Inter-Agency Working to Safeguard and Promote the Welfare of Children*.[269] In outline, the procedures are as follows. Within one working day of receipt of a referral, a local authority social worker should decide on the type of response required: immediate protection and urgent action; an assessment under section 17 of the Children Act 1989 because the

---

[265] Section 43(3).   [266] See eg *Re H (A Minor) (Section 37 Direction)* [1993] 2 FLR 541.
[267] [1993] 2 FLR 134.   [268] Ibid, 148.   [269] HM Government, March 2013.

child is in need; or enquiries under section 47 because there is reasonable cause to suspect that the child is suffering, or likely to suffer, significant harm. If a section 47 investigation is required, it is preceded by a strategy discussion. The investigation consists of a core assessment in accordance with local protocols, led by a social worker, with contributions from other relevant professionals. This should take no more than 45 working days. If at any stage emergency action is required, it should be taken. If concerns are substantiated a child protection conference will be convened by the social work manager.[270] The purpose is to 'bring together and analyse, in an inter-agency setting, all relevant information and plan how best to safeguard and promote the welfare of the child'. If the conclusion is that the child is likely to suffer significant harm in the future, the decision will be to provide inter-agency help and intervention through a formal child protection plan.[271] The conference will formulate an outline child protection plan, under which the local authority or the NSPCC carry statutory responsibility for the child's welfare. Ongoing assessment by a core group of professionals feeds in to refinement of the child protection plan. A child protection review conference is held within three months of the initial child protection conference and further reviews at intervals of not more than six months for as long as the child remains the subject of the child protection plan. At these various stages the local authority will be considering whether concerns about significant harm remain and what if any measures, including legal measures, need to be implemented.

During these processes, the priority must be to ensure that the child is adequately protected. In compliance with Article 3 of the ECHR a local authority has a duty to prevent inhuman and degrading treatment of which it has knowledge or ought to have knowledge. In *Z and Others v UK*[272] a violation was found where a local authority took little action for several years in respect of children about whom there were serious concerns. The children had suffered psychological damage and neglect which should have been prevented.

## 5 Emergency protection orders

Sometimes there will be concern about the child's situation of such urgency that immediate steps to protect the child may be justified.[273] In these circumstances, an application can, and indeed should, be made under section 44 of the Children Act 1989 for an emergency protection order (EPO).

### 5.1 What is an emergency protection order?

An EPO operates as a direction to any person who is in the position to do so to comply with a request to produce the child. In addition, it authorises either the child's removal to accommodation provided by the applicant or the prevention of his removal from any hospital or other place in which he is currently being accommodated.[274] It is an offence intentionally to obstruct a person exercising these powers.[275] An EPO also gives the applicant parental responsibility for the child.[276] Clearly an order which authorises, for example, the sudden removal of a child from his home, sometimes without any prior warning, and gives parental responsibility to a third party is a powerful order with potential for traumatic effects on a child, his parents, and wider family, who may all become shocked, angry, or distressed when an EPO is obtained. The law therefore imposes tight control over when an EPO may be granted. The government guidance issued prior to the

---

[270] Within 15 days of the latest strategy discussion.

[271] In 2011, there were 42,700 children for whom child protection issues were recorded (18,700 for neglect, 12,100 for emotional abuse, 4,500 physical abuse, 2,300 sexual abuse, and 5,000 multiple categories) (figures from the NSPCC).

[272] [2000] 2 FLR 603.

[273] See J. Masson et al, *Protecting Powers: Emergency Intervention for Children's Protection* (Chichester: Wiley, 2007).

[274] Section 44(4).     [275] Section 44(15).     [276] Section 44(4)(c).

introduction of the Children Act 1989 states that the purpose of an EPO 'is to enable the child in a genuine emergency to be removed from where he is or be kept where he is, if and only if this is what is necessary to provide immediate short-term protection'.[277] In *Re X (Emergency Protection Orders)*[278] McFarlane J stressed the words 'genuine emergency' and 'only what is necessary to provide immediate short-term protection'.[279]

There is further tight control over the duration of the order and the powers which may be exercised in relation to the child while an order is in force. The order can be made initially for up to eight days, and then renewed once for up to a further seven days[280] but only where the court has reasonable cause to believe that the child is likely to suffer significant harm if the order is not extended. The fact that the order can initially be made for eight days does not mean that it should automatically be made for eight days. The court should consider the appropriate duration of the order in the circumstances of the case.

Section 44(5)(a) provides that the powers to remove the child or prevent the child's removal shall only be exercised 'in order to safeguard the welfare of the child'. Furthermore, if those powers are exercised, section 44(10) provides that if it appears that it is safe for the child to be returned, or allowed to be removed from the place in question, the applicant for the EPO shall return the child[281] or (as the case may be) allow him to be removed. Section 44(12) provides, however, that the applicant 'may again exercise his powers with respect to the child (at any time while the emergency protection order remains in force) if it appears to him that a change in the circumstances of the case makes it necessary for him to do so'.

Section 44(5)(b) provides that the person in whose favour the order is made 'shall take, and shall only take, such action in meeting his parental responsibility for the child as is reasonably required to safeguard or promote the welfare of the child (having regard in particular to the duration of the order)'. Thus, the parental responsibility conferred by an EPO is a very limited form. It is submitted, for example, that the parental responsibility conferred would not give the applicant power to authorise any major medical or psychiatric treatment without the agreement of a parent or other person with parental responsibility, unless the child is in urgent need of such treatment.

It is submitted, however, that the applicant would have parental responsibility to permit the child to be examined, or otherwise assessed, provided it is exercised to promote the child's welfare. An assessment or examination may be viewed as promoting the child's welfare as without the assessment/examination it may not be possible to establish whether the child is indeed suffering, or likely to suffer, significant harm, and to what that harm is attributable. However, the applicant's powers in this regard are subject to section 44(6)(b) which provides that when the court makes an EPO (or at any time during its currency)[282] it may give various directions as it considers appropriate with respect to the medical or psychiatric examination or other assessment of the child including a direction to the effect that there should be no such examination or assessment of the child, or no such examination or assessment unless the court directs otherwise.[283] The child may, if he is of sufficient understanding to make an informed decision, refuse to submit to the examination or other assessment.[284] Again, these provisions address concerns which were identified in the Cleveland inquiry[285] in 1988.

The court may also give directions with respect to the contact which is, or is not, to be allowed between the child and any named person.[286] Subject to such directions, the applicant must allow the child reasonable contact[287] with his parents or any person who has parental responsibility for

---

[277] *Children Act 1989—Guidance and Regulations* (London: HMSO, 1991), vol 1, p 51.
[278] [2006] EWHC 510 (Fam), [2006] 2 FLR 701.     [279] Ibid, [63].
[280] Children Act 1989, s 45(1), (5), and (6).
[281] Section 44(11) provides that this should be to the person from whose care he was removed; or if that is not reasonably practicable, a parent of his, any person who is not a parent of his but who has parental responsibility for him, or such other person as the applicant (with the agreement of the court) considers appropriate.
[282] Section 44(9).     [283] Section 44(8).     [284] Section 44(7).
[285] *Report of the Inquiry into Child Abuse in Cleveland 1987* (Cm 412, 1988).     [286] Section 44(6)(a).
[287] Section 44(13).

him, and various other persons closely connected to the child, as listed in section 44(13).[288] This provision reflects the assumption which permeates the Act that maintaining contact between a child and his parents, and others who have parental responsibility for him, is normally in the best interests of the child and must, therefore, be permitted unless a court authorises otherwise. Such contact may not, in the applicant's opinion, be in the interests of the child, and it is important that the applicant draws this to the attention of the court where he believes this to be the case.

## 5.2 The grounds for making an emergency protection order

Unlike a child assessment order, an EPO can be made without notice. Indeed, in some cases it is essential to do so, for if the person caring for the child were to be alerted in advance to the fact that an application for an order was being made, this could expose the child to an even greater risk of suffering significant harm.[289]

---

### Key legislation

The grounds for making an EPO are set out in section 44(1), which provides:

> Where any person ('the applicant') applies to the court for an order to be made under this section with respect to a child, the court may make the order if, but only if, it is satisfied that—
>
> (a) there is reasonable cause to believe that the child is likely to suffer significant harm if—
>   (i) he is not removed to accommodation provided by or on behalf of the applicant; or
>   (ii) he does not remain in the place in which he is then being accommodated;
> (b) in the case of an application made by a local authority—
>   (i) enquiries are being made with respect to the child under section 47(1)(b); and
>   (ii) those enquiries are being frustrated by access to the child being unreasonably refused to a person authorised to seek access and that the applicant has reasonable cause to believe that access to the child is required as a matter of urgency . . .[290]

---

Unlike the child assessment order, *any person* can apply for an emergency protection order via section 44(1)(a), although the 'frustrated access' grounds in section 44(1)(b) and (c) are open only to a local authority and the NSPCC respectively. Paragraph (a) requires that the court has reasonable cause to believe that the child is likely to suffer significant harm unless an EPO is made. In seeking to establish this ground, the applicant can put any information before the court, and the court can take it into account regardless of any enactment or rule of law which would otherwise prevent it from doing so, provided that, in the opinion of the court, it is relevant to the application.[291] The applicant must further persuade the court that there is a causative link between the harm being likely to occur and the child being removed from, or remaining in, his present accommodation. Thus, for example, if the child is reasonably

---

[288] The other categories are: any person with whom he was living immediately before the making of the order; any person named in a child arrangements order as a person with whom the child is to spend time or otherwise have contact; any person who is allowed to have contact with the child by virtue of an order under s 34; any person acting on behalf of any of those persons.

[289] Judith Masson's study of the use of EPOs found variations in the use of 'without notice' applications within different areas. In some areas there were quite high proportions (eg in one area just under 50 per cent of applications), and in areas where the courts were more reluctant to hear applications without notice, 'on notice' applications were much more likely to be preceded by police protection (in one area, in 53 per cent of cases): see J. Masson, 'Emergency Intervention to Protect Children: Using and Avoiding Legal Controls' [2005] Child and Family Law Quarterly 75.

[290] Paragraph (c) makes similar, but not identical, provisions in the case of enquiries made by an authorised person, presently only the NSPCC.

[291] Section 45(7).

believed to have suffered a serious non-accidental injury, but if the person who is suspected of having injured the child has been remanded in custody pending a criminal trial, and the person presently caring for him is not implicated in the abuse in any way, it is suggested that it is most unlikely there are grounds for making an EPO. On the other hand, where the alleged abuser has moved out of the home, but where there is uncertainty about where he is living, or whether he will stay away from the child, there may be grounds for an order being made. Where the alleged abuser is still in the home, or intends to discharge the child from hospital, there are likely to be very clear grounds for making the order.

Paragraph (b) is aimed at those cases where a local authority is making section 47 enquiries about the child in order to decide what action they should take to safeguard or promote his welfare.[292] In conducting such enquiries, the local authority must normally obtain access to the child.[293] This provision reflects the findings made in various enquiries which have been conducted into cases where child protection procedures have failed to protect children from being killed as a result of ill-treatment and neglect. These enquiries have emphasised that it is usually imperative that access is obtained to a child where there is a suspicion that he or she is suffering, or is likely to suffer, significant harm.[294] Unless the child is seen, and in the case of a young child physically examined for signs of injuries, ill-treatment, or neglect, and where appropriate (for example in the case of an older child) spoken to in private as well, it may be very easy for a parent to conceal significant harm to the child from a concerned professional. It should be noted that, when an application is made under section 44(1)(b), a court is empowered to make an EPO on the basis that the applicant has reasonable cause to *suspect* that the child is suffering, or is likely to suffer, significant harm[295] and has reasonable cause to believe that access to the child is urgently required. This is a lesser standard than the requirement that the court should have reasonable cause to *believe* that such harm is likely to occur, which must be proved in relation to applications made under section 44(1)(a). Clearly, where access is being refused, it may be impossible for the applicant to obtain the evidence to substantiate a belief, and therefore a reasonable suspicion provides an adequate basis for an order being made when taken together with access being unreasonably refused.[296]

---

### Key case

In *X Council v B (Emergency Protection Order)*[297] Munby J gave guidance on the use of the EPO jurisdiction. In that case a family had endured significant levels of stress as a result of their children's illnesses. The local authority became concerned at the mother's histrionic reaction to the situation, her alleged mismanagement of the children's medication, and failure to engage appropriately with medical services and offered therapies. When the mother was unwilling to discuss the matter at a strategy meeting, the local authority obtained without notice EPOs, each lasting for eight days, and the three younger children were taken into foster care. The local authority subsequently obtained interim care orders but the issues were satisfactorily resolved through negotiation. Accordingly, the case came before Munby J on the local authority's application to withdraw its application for care orders. Leave was granted. However, Munby J was concerned by some aspects of the way in which the children had entered care via the EPO. While his Lordship considered that the without notice application could be justified because of the possibility that the mother might administer medication and thus thwart the local authority's investigation, he was concerned that the order had been made to last for more than 24 or 48 hours, the time necessary to carry out tests, and that the children

---

[292] On s 47 generally, see Section 4.1.   [293] Section 47(4).

[294] See particularly, *A Child in Mind: The Report on the Death of Kimberley Carlile* (Greenwich London Borough Council, 1987).

[295] As this is the wording of s 47(1)(b) under which the enquiry was initiated.

[296] Section 44(3) provides that any person seeking access to a child in connection with enquiries shall, on being asked to do so, produce some duly authenticated document as evidence that he is such a person.

[297] [2004] EWHC 2015 (Fam), [2005] 1 FLR 341 (Munby J).

had been removed to foster care. His Lordship therefore took an opportunity to explain the human rights context in which the EPO jurisdiction operates. He acknowledged that 'there are cases where the need for such highly intrusive emergency intervention is imperatively demanded'[298] and that, in principle, the European Court of Human Rights has recognised that emergency removal of children is entirely compatible with the ECHR, including in cases of without notice applications.[299] He observed, however, that an EPO is 'a terrible and drastic remedy'[300] and that the European Court had stressed, in the context of the removal of a newborn baby, that such an order is a 'draconian' and 'extremely harsh' measure, requiring 'exceptional justification' and 'extraordinary compelling reasons'.[301] In his Lordship's view these principles should equally apply to cases of the removal of older children, who, unlike the newborn, will be conscious of what is happening to them in circumstances which may be frightening and/or distressing to the children.[302]

Munby J said that it is important that both the local authority and justices approach every application for an EPO 'with an anxious awareness of the extreme gravity of the relief being sought and a scrupulous regard for the European Convention rights of both the child and the parents'.[303] The Strasbourg jurisprudence, as recognised by the Court of Appeal, repeatedly emphasised that intervention 'must be proportionate to the legitimate aim of protecting the welfare and interests of the child'.[304] Munby J observed that this proportionality was all the more necessary in the context of interim care orders or EPOs 'when there have as yet been no adverse findings against the parent(s)'.[305] Citing *Haase v Germany* at paragraphs [90]–[95], his Lordship drew particular attention to the fact that the test is one of 'necessity' and there is a requirement that there be 'imminent danger'.[306] At paragraph [57] of his judgment, Munby J provided a useful summary of the important points. The essential points (adapting Munby J's words) were:

(1) An EPO should not be made unless the Family Proceedings Court (FPC) is satisfied that it is both necessary and proportionate and that no other less radical form of order will achieve the essential end of promoting the welfare of the child. Separation is only to be contemplated if immediate separation is essential to secure the child's safety: 'imminent danger' must be 'actually established'.

(2) Any order must provide for the least interventionist solution consistent with the preservation of the child's immediate safety.

(3) No EPO should be made for any longer than is absolutely necessary to protect the child.

(4) The evidence in support of the application for an EPO must be full, detailed, precise, and compelling.[307] Unparticularised generalities will not suffice. The sources of hearsay evidence must be identified. Expressions of opinion must be supported by detailed evidence and properly articulated reasoning.

(5) Save in wholly exceptional cases, parents must be given adequate prior notice of the date, time, and place of any application by a local authority for an EPO. They must also be given proper notice of the evidence the local authority is relying upon.

(6) There must be compelling reasons for a without notice application which will normally be appropriate only if the case is genuinely one of emergency or other great urgency or if there are compelling reasons to believe that the child's welfare will be compromised if the parents are alerted in advance to what is going on. In such a case there is a duty to make the fullest and most candid and frank disclosure of all the relevant factual and legal matters known to them.

---

[298] Ibid, [35], citing from his judgment in *Re M (Care Proceedings: Judicial Review)* [2003] EWHC 850 (Admin), [2003] 2 FLR 171 at [40].

[299] *K and T v Finland* (2000) 31 EHRR 484, [2000] 2 FLR 79, [2001] 2 FLR 707; *P, C and S v UK* (2002) 35 EHRR 31, [2002] 2 FLR 631; *Venema v Netherlands* [2003] 1 FLR 552; *Covezzi and Morselli v Italy* (2003) 38 EHRR 28; and *Haase v Germany* [2004] 2 FLR 39.

[300] [2004] EWHC 2015 (Fam), [2005] 1 FLR 341 at [34].          [301] Ibid.          [302] Ibid.          [303] Ibid, [41].

[304] See *Re O (Supervision Order)* [2001] EWCA Civ 16, [2001] 1 FLR 923 at [28]; *Re B (Care: Interference with Family Life)* [2003] 2 FLR 813 at [34]; *Re O (Care or Supervision Order)* at 760; *Oxfordshire County Council v L (Care or Supervision Order)* [1998] 1 FLR 70 at 74.

[305] *X Council v B* [2004] EWHC 2015 (Fam), [2005] 1 FLR 341 at [44].          [306] See ibid, [46].

[307] For criticism, see J. Masson, 'Emergency Protection Good Practice and Human Rights' [2004] Family Law 882.

(7) The FPC must 'keep a note of the substance of the oral evidence' and must also record in writing not merely its reasons but also any findings of fact.

(8) Parents against whom an EPO is made without notice are entitled to be given, if they ask, proper information as to what happened at the hearing and to be told, if they ask: (i) exactly what documents, bundles, or other evidential materials were lodged with the FPC either before or during the course of the hearing; and (ii) what legal authorities were cited to the FPC.

(9) The local authority, even after it has obtained an EPO, is under an obligation to consider less drastic alternatives to emergency removal (see s 44(5)).

(10) Section 44(10)(a) and (11)(a) impose on the local authority a continuing duty to exercise exceptional diligence in keeping the case under review day by day so as to ensure that parent and child are separated for no longer than is necessary to secure the child's safety.

(11) Arrangements for contact must be driven by the needs of the family, not stunted by lack of resources.

In *Re X (Emergency Protection Orders)*[308] McFarlane J agreed with each and every one of the observations in paragraph [57] of Munby J's judgment, indicating that they should be required reading for every magistrate and justices' clerk involved in an EPO application.[309] His Lordship advised that the key points made by Munby J in *X Council v B* should be copied and made available to the justices hearing an EPO on each occasion such an application is made and it is the duty of the applicant for an EPO to ensure that the *X Council v B* guidance is brought to the court's attention.

McFarlane J added that the hearing ought to be tape-recorded or a verbatim note taken, and that 'unless there is a very good reason to the contrary, the parents should always be given a full account of the material submitted to the court, the evidence given at the hearing, the submissions made to support the application and the justices' reasons whether the parents ask for this information or not'.[310] In *Re X*, a child was on the Child Protection Register in the category of 'emotional harm' and social workers had concerns about the mother's personality. Within two hours of a case conference, which had concluded that low-level intervention by way of a psychiatric assessment of the child's mother and a psychological assessment of the child should proceed, the local authority without notice obtained an EPO. The application was prompted by the fact that the mother had presented with the child at a local hospital for a check up as the child was complaining of abdominal pain. A nurse had contacted the social services department reporting that the mother was insisting on the child seeing a doctor despite the fact that a triage nurse had assessed the child and considered that there was no problem. Several elements of the social work team manager's evidence in support of the EPO application were misleading, incomplete, or wrong, presenting a seriously distorted picture to the bench. For example, the nurse's account became inflated to the fact that the mother was demanding further investigations and *treatment*, and the court was also told that the mother was suffering from fabricated or induced illness syndrome[311] despite the fact that this had never been professionally diagnosed. McFarlane J made clear that this 'is not a diagnosis that can be made by social workers acting alone, it is a matter that requires skilled medical appraisal'[312] and must be approached with care and caution in accordance with guidance. His Lordship considered that the processes by which the EPO was obtained were badly flawed.[313] The central errors were that there was no emergency, no imminent danger of harm that justified X's removal, the local authority testimony was partial, inaccurate, and misleading, and

---

[308] [2006] EWHC 510 (Fam), [2006] 2 FLR 701.     [309] Ibid, [65].     [310] Ibid, [66].

[311] Fabricating or inducing illness in her child. See for a full discussion of the child protection implication of this problem: Department for Education and Skills, *Safeguarding Children in Whom Illness is Fabricated or Induced* (London: TSO, 2008).

[312] [2006] EWHC 510 (Fam), [2006] 2 FLR 701 at [67].

[313] *Re X* [2006] EWHC 510 (Fam), [2006] 2 FLR 701 at [71].

the application was made against legal advice. McFarlane J indicated that a local authority lawyer in such circumstances must consider him/herself under a duty to present the case and to ensure that it is presented fairly and that the bench is fully aware of the legal context.[314] Evidence given to the justices should come from the best available source. Where there has been a case conference with respect to the child, the most recent case conference minutes should be produced to the court.[315]

The manner in which the case had been heard was also found wanting. The magistrates had fitted the case round a busy list rather than making separate appropriate time for it and had not separately considered the issue of whether a without notice application could be justified. They had also failed to give full reasons for their decision. McFarlane J gave the following additional guidance on types of cases which will rarely warrant an EPO:[316]

> mere lack of information or a need for assessment can never of themselves establish the existence of a genuine emergency sufficient to justify an EPO. The proper course in such a case is to consider application for a child assessment order or issuing s 31 proceedings and seeking the court's directions under s 38(6) for assessment . . .
>
>     cases of emotional abuse will rarely, if ever, warrant an EPO, let alone an application without notice . . .
>
>     cases of sexual abuse where the allegations are inchoate and non-specific, and where there is no evidence of immediate risk of harm to the child, will rarely warrant an EPO . . .
>
>     cases of fabricated or induced illness, where there is no medical evidence of immediate risk of direct physical harm to the child, will rarely warrant an EPO . . .
>
>     justices faced with an EPO application in a case of emotional abuse, non-specific allegations of sexual abuse and/or fabricated or induced illness, should actively consider refusing the EPO application on the basis that the local authority should then issue an application for an interim care order.

## 5.3  Including an exclusion requirement in an emergency protection order

Sometimes a preferable response to removal of the child is for action to be taken against the person who is alleged to be endangering him or her. Section 44A(1)[317] provides that the court may include an exclusion requirement in an EPO provided that the conditions in section 44A(2) are satisfied. An exclusion requirement can require the person concerned to leave a dwelling-house in which he is living with the child, prohibit the person entering it, and exclude the person from a defined area in which the relevant dwelling-house is situated.[318]

In essence the conditions require the court to be satisfied that if a person is excluded from the house where the child lives there is reasonable cause to believe that, in the case of an order made under section 44(1)(a), the child will not be likely to suffer significant harm even though not removed, or in the case of an order made on the grounds mentioned in paragraph (b) or (c) of section 44(1), that the enquiries referred to in those paragraphs will cease to be frustrated.[319] The court must also ensure that another person living in the same house consents to the exclusion order and is able and willing to give to the child the care which it would be reasonable to expect a parent to give him. The reason why an exclusion requirement is in addition to, rather than an alternative to, an EPO is to give the local authority the power immediately to remove the child where the cooperation of the person caring for the child is withdrawn or the exclusion requirement is otherwise broken.

The attraction of using an exclusion requirement is much stronger where the applicant can be confident that it will be backed up by strong enforcement powers. This is recognised in the

---

[314]  Ibid, [88].      [315]  Ibid, [101].      [316]  Ibid, [101].
[317]  Inserted, together with s 44B by the Family Law Act 1996, s 52, Sch 6, para 3.
[318]  Section 44A(3).      [319]  Including, where appropriate, a defined area around the house (s 44A(3)).

legislation. A power of arrest may be attached to an exclusion requirement.[320] This permits a police officer to arrest without warrant any person whom he has reasonable cause to believe to be in breach of the requirement.[321] Consequently, any breach of the order should lead to the arrest of the person excluded and this should avoid the necessity to remove the child, except in those cases where the person caring for the child has colluded in the breach. If the applicant removes the child from the house to other accommodation for more than 24 hours the exclusion requirement ceases to have effect.[322]

Under section 44B a court may accept an undertaking from the relevant person in any case where it has power to include an exclusion requirement in the EPO, but a power of arrest may not be added to an undertaking.[323] The undertaking is enforceable as if it were an order of the court.[324]

### 5.4 Executing the emergency protection order: the assistance of the police and health care professionals

When making an EPO the court may direct that the applicant, on exercising any powers conferred by the order, be accompanied by a medical practitioner, nurse, or midwife, if he so chooses.[325] This provision may assist in preventing removal of a child from the home in a case where fears about his health and safety prove to be unfounded. Section 44(5)(a) provides that the applicant shall only exercise the power to remove, or to prevent the removal of, the child in order to safeguard the welfare of the child. In a case where a doctor is willing to accompany the applicant (who will normally be a social worker) to the child's home, a medical examination of the child in the home might sometimes reveal that there is nothing to give rise to concern that the child is suffering, or is likely to suffer, significant harm. In such a case, the child should be left where he is. In a case where the child has been removed or retained under an EPO, and where it appears to the applicant that it is safe to return the child, or to allow him to be removed, the child must be returned or his removal must be allowed.[326]

Sometimes an applicant for an EPO may be unsure of the child's whereabouts or be denied entry to premises where he suspects the child to be. Sometimes he may have reasonable cause to believe that there is another child on the premises with respect to whom an EPO ought to be made. In cases of this kind, the applicant should apply for orders under section 48(3) and (4) which authorise him to enter premises and search for the children concerned. However, such orders do not authorise the applicant to break into premises by force; where force is needed the police must be involved and a warrant obtained under section 48(9).[327] In difficult cases, particularly where it is anticipated that those looking after the child will respond to being served with an EPO with violence, police involvement is likely to be an added feature of the implementation of the order.

### 5.5 Applying to discharge an emergency protection order

The child, a parent, anyone with parental responsibility for the child, or any person with whom the child was living immediately before the making of the order may apply for the EPO to be discharged.[328] However, this provision does not apply in a case where such a person was given at least one day's clear notice of the hearing at which the order was made, and was present at that hearing.[329] Allowing the order to be challenged gives some measure of safeguard to the

---

[320]  Section 44A(5).      [321]  Section 44A(8).      [322]  Section 44A(10).

[323]  Section 44B. Undertakings are permitted despite a firm recommendation to the contrary by the Law Commission, see *Domestic Violence and Occupation of the Family Home* (Law Com No 207, 1992), para 6.15.

[324]  Section 44B(3)(a).      [325]  Section 45(12).      [326]  Section 44(10).

[327]  See too the Police and Criminal Evidence Act 1984, s 17(1)(e), which authorises the police to enter premises without a warrant where there is an immediate risk to life or limb.

[328]  Section 45(8).

[329]  Section 45(11); also, an application to discharge cannot be made where the order has been extended under s 45(5).

interests of those persons affected by a without notice application; whereas those persons who had the opportunity to attend the hearing, and did attend, are not further entitled to challenge the order.

## 5.6 Challenging the making of, or refusal to make, an emergency protection order

Section 45(10) provides that no appeal may be made against the making of, or refusal to make, an EPO or against any direction given by the court in connection with such an order. In *Essex County Council v F*,[330] Douglas Brown J held that section 45(10) allows no scope for the use of the appellate process, and he ruled that if magistrates act unreasonably in refusing to make an order the only possible remedy is in proceedings brought in judicial review. But, of course, judicial review proceedings are totally impracticable in an emergency situation; they are not designed to provide speedy relief.[331] Douglas Brown J arrived at his ruling in *Essex County Council v F* with considerable regret because the facts 'cried out for the intervention of the court'; however, he took the view that the words of the statute gave him no alternative.[332]

It is suggested that the combined effect of section 45(10) and the ruling in *Essex County Council v F* is particularly alarming when it is recalled that applications for an EPO are often heard by a single magistrate. It cannot be acceptable that nothing further can be done to protect a child in a case where, as in the *Essex* case, the court's decision is plainly wrong. In that case, the mother promised the local authority that she would not remove the child from her foster parents until the hearing of the application in care proceedings, which would come before the court a few days later. However, other mothers might not be so compliant, and the fact that the child was secure in the *Essex* case may have lulled the judge into a false sense of security. It is the precedent force of *Essex County Council v F* in relation to other cases which makes the decision so disturbing. A child could be put in grave danger by the wrongful refusal of a court to make an EPO. He might even be badly injured or killed. It cannot be acceptable that the courts are apparently powerless to protect a child in circumstances of this kind.

It is therefore necessary to search for possible solutions and to consider what might be done if a case of this kind arose again. One possibility might be for the local authority to make a fresh application for an EPO to a judge, probably a High Court judge. Where a child's safety is gravely at risk, a judge might find that he has the power to make the order requested. There is no actual precedent which prevents the judge from making such an order, and he would be likely to be very aware of his own personal responsibility for any possible tragic outcome of his refusal to do so.

Another possibility might be to make an application for leave to invoke the inherent jurisdiction of the High Court. Section 100(4) allows use of the court's inherent jurisdiction where the court is satisfied that the result which the authority wishes to achieve could not be achieved through the making of any order other than in the exercise of the court's inherent jurisdiction. The local authority might thus rely on section 100(4) and ask the court to make an order placing the child in the care of an individual (but not, of course, an order which placed the child in the care of the local authority, or in local authority accommodation, as this is prohibited by section 100(2)). The court might, for example, order that the child be kept in hospital or live with a relative or friend of the family or possibly even with the local authority foster parents with whom he has been living, but only in their personal capacity and not as agents of the local authority.

---

[330] [1993] 1 FLR 847.

[331] On the possibility of the use of judicial review, see Munby J in *X Council v B* [2004] EWHC 2015 (Fam) at [40].

[332] See also the concerns of Johnson J in *Re P (Emergency Protection Order)* [1996] 1 FLR 482.

# 6 Police protection: Children Act 1989, section 46

The police have their own separate powers to remove children to suitable accommodation and to keep them there, or to prevent the child's removal from hospital or any other place. A police constable may exercise these powers where he has reasonable cause to believe that the child would otherwise be likely to suffer significant harm.[333] Section 46, together with Home Office Circular 017/2008, provides a code of guidance on how the police should exercise their powers, and how they should inform the parents and liaise with the local authority once they have taken the child into police protection. No child may be kept in police protection for more than 72 hours.[334] However, while a child is being kept in police protection, a designated officer may apply on behalf of the appropriate authority for an EPO to be made under section 44 with respect to the child.[335]

In *Langley v Liverpool City Council*[336] the Court of Appeal considered the relationship between an EPO and the use of police protection. All of the Langley family were profoundly deaf, apart from one of their four children, Callum, aged 4. The father also had Usher's Syndrome, which meant that he had tunnel vision and night blindness. He was registered blind. Despite this disability the father persisted in driving his car with the children, which was a matter of great concern to the local authority. The local authority became aware that Mr Langley had driven with Callum and the two older children from Liverpool to Derby where the older children were to be assessed for several days at the Royal School for the Deaf. The local authority obtained an EPO in respect of these three children and foster parents were alerted. By the time the EPO had been obtained, the parents and Callum had returned by car to Liverpool, although the local authority could not locate the whereabouts of the family who were not at home. Later the same evening, the social worker asked the police to assist in finding the family and they were finally located at home. On locating the family, the police officer concerned spoke to a member of the social work emergency duty team, who indicated that they wanted Callum to be taken into care. The police officer decided to remove Callum to foster care. The following day the social workers executed the EPO in respect of the other two children by removing them from the school. In claims by the parents, a judge found against the police and the council that the children's removals were unlawful, and the police and the council appealed to the Court of Appeal. The judge had held that, if an EPO is in force, the police cannot invoke section 46, and the only part that the police can play is by assisting, authorised by a warrant under section 48(9). The Court of Appeal disagreed with this analysis, holding that there 'is nothing in the language of the Act which compels the conclusion that s 46 cannot be invoked where an EPO is in force'.[337] However, the court held that 'discretionary statutory powers must be exercised to promote the policy and objects of the statute'[338] and that 'the statutory scheme clearly accords primacy to s 44'.[339] The court therefore held that 'where a police officer knows that an EPO is in force, he should not exercise the power of removing a child under s 46, unless there are compelling reasons to do so'.[340] The court explained that: '(i) removal of children should usually be effected pursuant to an EPO; and (ii) s 46 should be invoked only where it is not practicable to execute an EPO. In deciding whether it is practicable to

---

[333] Section 46(1).    [334] Section 46(6).    [335] Section 46(7).

[336] [2005] EWCA Civ 1173, [2006] 1 FLR 342. See also *Kiam v Crown Prosecution Service* [2014] EWHC 1606 (Admin).

[337] [2005] EWCA Civ 1173, [2006] 1 FLR 342, [30].

[338] Ibid, [33], citing *Padfield and Others v Minister of Agriculture, Fisheries and Food and Others* [1968] AC 997 at 1030C.

[339] *Langley* [2005] EWCA Civ 1173, [2006] 1 FLR 342 at [38]. At [37] the court pointed to a number of important differences between the s 44 and s 46 regimes. They include the following. First, the court can give directions with respect to contact, examinations, and assessments. This is a valuable power not available to the police. Secondly, an EPO gives the applicant parental responsibility, whereas while a child is being kept in police protection under s 46 neither the constable nor the designated officer has parental responsibility. Thirdly, no child can be kept in police protection for more than 72 hours, whereas an EPO may have effect for a period not exceeding 8 days (s 45(1)), and this period may be extended by up to 7 days (s 45(5)).

[340] Ibid, [36].

execute an EPO, the police must always have regard to the paramount need to protect children from significant harm.[341] The court held on the facts that there had been no compelling reason to use section 46; the police officer should have requested the emergency duty team to execute the EPO. Accordingly the police were liable for the unlawful removal of Callum, and the council had also acted unlawfully in 'ordering' Callum's removal.

*Langley* was applied in *A v East Sussex County Council and Chief Constable of Sussex Police*.[342] A baby was admitted to hospital after the mother alerted the emergency services to the fact that the child had stopped breathing. Two days later the medical staff thought the child fit for discharge. However, the mother, who had suffered post-natal depression and who was described as an anxious mother, had reported two further incidents of the child stopping breathing, although no one else had witnessed these events and no explanation could be found. The consultant doctor was concerned that this might be a case of factitious illness and that it was not safe for the child to go home without professional supervision. The mother was uncooperative, indicating that she wished to take the child home with only family supervision, and on one occasion 'kicked off' threatening to take the child home. The child was removed into foster care using the power of police protection in section 46. The mother subsequently agreed to go with the child to a mother and baby unit and following a positive assessment the mother and baby were allowed to go home. Proceedings were discontinued. The mother then brought a claim under section 7 of the Human Rights Act 1998 against the police and East Sussex County Council, the issue being whether the actions of the respondents were lawful and proportionate. The judge dismissed the claim and the mother's appeal to the Court of Appeal was dismissed. The Court of Appeal held that in the circumstances the judge had been entitled to reach the view that the respondents' actions were lawful. Applying *Langley v Liverpool City Council*,[343] the court held that on the facts as honestly and reasonably believed by the respondents at the time it had not been practicable to execute an EPO. Given the consultant's opinion regarding the child's safety, the fact that there was no agreement that the mother would not exercise her otherwise lawful right to remove the child, and the fact that the social services and police would not necessarily be able to keep track of her once she left, section 46 was required urgently to avert potential danger to the child. Hedley J (with whom Jackson and Carnwath LJJ agreed) commented:

> Sadly the experiences of the appellant simply illustrate the truth that viable child protection procedures in any society will sometimes inflict what turns out to have been unnecessary distress on families. That does not make them or the exercise of them thereby unlawful.[344]

In *Re D (Unborn Baby)*[345] the question arose as to whether it was lawful for the local authority to conceal from a pregnant mother and her partner its plan to remove the child immediately upon birth by way of police protection under section 46 of the Children Act 1989. The mother was in prison as a result of an assault against her own child. On an occasion of supervised contact, she had blindfolded and gagged the child before threatening her with a knife over a period of 15 minutes. Since arriving in prison, the mother had attempted suicide and had made worrying statements that her children would be better off dead than in the care of the local authority. She had been described by a psychologist as 'an emotionally desperate woman' who 'remains likely to engage in impulsive acts when frustrated and angry'. In these circumstances, the local authority had real concerns that she might lash out at her child if she were aware that the child was to be removed shortly after birth. As the child was not yet born, the court did not have any powers under the Children Act 1989 nor could the court exercise its inherent jurisdiction.[346] The local authority therefore sought declaratory relief,[347]

---

[341] Ibid, [40].     [342] [2010] EWCA Civ 743, [2010] 2 FLR 1596.
[343] [2005] EWCA Civ 1173, [2006] 1 FLR 342.     [344] [2010] EWCA Civ 743 at [21].
[345] [2009] EWHC 446 (Fam), [2009] 2 FLR 313.
[346] See *Re F (In Utero) (Wardship)* [1988] Fam 122, [1988] 2 FLR 307.
[347] On which see *Re F (Mental Patient: Sterilisation)* [1990] 2 AC 1, [1989] 2 FLR 376.

declaring that its proposed future course of conduct would be lawful. Munby J held that the same principles that apply regarding the necessity and proportionality of state intervention in family life applied to the question before him.[348] The test is therefore: 'Is the step which the local authority is proposing to take, that is, the step of not involving the parents in its planning and not communicating to the parents its plan for immediate removal at birth, something which is justified by "the overriding necessity of the interests of the child" or something which is "essential to secure [the child's] safety"?'[349]

Munby J had no hesitation in concluding that in the circumstances 'the very stringent test' for the local authority lawfully to take this 'very drastic and highly unusual step' was 'more than adequately met'.[350] His Lordship emphasised, however, that it will only be in very unusual and exceptional cases that a local authority will be so justified.[351]

Judith Masson's study of police protection[352] found that one of the main categories of use was in response to requests by social workers out of hours, for example in the case of emergency duty teams lacking court work experience. The prior existence of police protection then tended to reinforce the local authority's case on a subsequent application for an EPO. In light of her findings, Masson rightly questions whether these practices surrounding emergency intervention adequately secure accountability and protect parents' rights.[353]

## 7 Interim care and supervision orders

Where the local authority concludes that the only way to provide the child with the protection needed is for it either to share parental responsibility with his or her parents or to have the power formally to supervise the child's upbringing, it must bring an application for a care order or supervision order. Research shows that care proceedings are not brought without good reason.[354] Most cases contain multiple allegations of parenting failures, in respect of parents who have multiple vulnerability factors (eg alcohol/drug abuse, mental health problems, chaotic lifestyles).[355]

---

### Key legislation

Section 31(2) of the Children Act 1989 provides:

A court may only make a care order or supervision order if it is satisfied—

(a) that the child concerned is suffering, or is likely to suffer, significant harm; and

(b) that the harm, or likelihood of harm, is attributable to—

(i) the care given to the child, or likely to be given to him if the order were not made, not being what it would be reasonable to expect a parent to give to him; or

(ii) the child's being beyond parental control.

---

[348] [2009] EWHC 446 (Fam), [2009] 2 FLR 313 at [11].    [349] Ibid.    [350] Ibid, [15] and [23].

[351] His Lordship was of the view that the factual situation was rather different from that in *P, C and S v UK* (App no 56547/00) (2002) 35 EHRR 31, [2002] 2 FLR 631, ECtHR in which a risk of poisoning to the child could be more easily controlled on the birth of the child. See [26].

[352] J. Masson, 'Police Protection—Protecting Whom?' (2002) Journal of Social Welfare and Family Law 157.

[353] J. Masson, 'Emergency Intervention to Protect Children: Using and Avoiding Legal Controls' [2005] Child and Family Law Quarterly 75 at 94–6. Dame Margaret Booth, *Delay in Public Law Children Act Cases—Second Report* (1996), found that in some areas police protection powers, rather than EPOs, were used when the crisis arose out of hours: at para 8.15.

[354] J. Masson, J. Pearce, and K. Bader with O. Joyner, J. Marsden, and D. Westlake, *Care Profiling Study* (Ministry of Justice, March 2008).

[355] J. Brophy, *Research Review: Child care proceedings under the Children Act 1989*, DCA Research Series 5/06 (May 2006).

When an application is first made in care proceedings it would be most unusual for either the local authority, or the other parties to the proceedings, to be in a position fully to present their case. Moreover, the court will wish to have an independent investigation of the child's circumstances. Meanwhile arrangements must be made about where the child will live and with whom he may have contact. Sometimes the local authority will be satisfied that the child can be protected from harm if he remains living at home pending the final hearing of their application. It may, for example, be able to persuade the person whom it alleges is causing significant harm to the child to move away from the premises.[356] Sometimes a relative or friend of the child will offer to look after him and this may give the child the protection needed. In a case of this kind it may be appropriate to make a child arrangements order with respect to the child's living arrangements, in which case section 38(3) provides that the court must make an interim supervision order unless satisfied that the child's welfare will be satisfactorily safeguarded without such an order being made. Sometimes the local authority will offer to accommodate the child under section 20, and his parents, and any others with parental responsibility, may be willing to comply with this arrangement. It is where voluntary arrangements of this nature cannot be agreed, or where the local authority takes the view that it will not give the child sufficient protection, or where the local authority takes the view that it needs to have parental responsibility for the child during the period preceding the final hearing, that it is likely to make an application for an interim order.

Section 38(1) provides that where in any proceedings for a care order or supervision order[357] the proceedings are adjourned, the court may make an interim care order or an interim supervision order. There is also power to make an interim order where the court gives a direction under section 37(1) that the local authority should investigate the child's circumstances.

### 7.1 Duration of interim orders and renewal

Section 38 makes provision for various time limits to be imposed when an interim order is made.[358] The temporary nature of an interim order allows the court to maintain a degree of control over the steps taken by the local authority in the interim period. Issues can be raised about how the local authority is exercising its parental responsibility under the order each time an application is made for the renewal of the order. Where the court is dissatisfied with action taken by the local authority it can refuse to make a further interim order.[359] In *Re G (Minors) (Interim Care Order)*,[360] Waite LJ commented that:

> the clear intention to be inferred from s 38 of the Act [is] that Parliament intended the regime of an interim care order to operate as a tightly run procedure closely monitored by the court and affording to all parties an opportunity of frequent review as events unfold during the currency of the order. That purpose would be frustrated if a practice were to be allowed to grow up under which renewals of interim care orders were sought routinely by local authorities without any attempt to keep the court up to date with progress, or granted by the court perfunctorily without any of the inquiries necessary to eliminate the risk of essential disclosure being lost through administrative lethargy.

In *Re B (Interim Care Orders: Renewal)*[361] Black J held that the court has a discretion to control its procedure and evidence on an application for renewal of an interim care order. In that case a local

---

[356] It may assist that person to obtain alternative accommodation under Sch 2, para 5. It may also assist a parent to bring proceedings under Pt IV of the Family Law Act 1996 for an occupation order excluding a spouse, partner, or other 'associated person' from the home; see Chapter 3. See also the possibility of an exclusion requirement in s 38A, discussed in Section 7.6.

[357] But not in an application to extend a supervision order: see *Re A (Supervision Order: Extension)* [1995] 1 FLR 335.

[358] As amended by the Children and Families Act 2014, s 14.

[359] See *Re G (Minors) (Interim Care Order)* [1993] 2 FLR 839, CA.          [360] Ibid.

[361] [2001] 2 FLR 1217, FD.

authority had obtained an interim care order in respect of a boy, aged 9. The boy was home schooled and the local authority had concerns that, although bright and intellectually ahead of many of his peer group, he was emotionally and socially immature and would benefit from mixing with peers at school. The mother was strongly opposed to the local authority's intervention and the case came before a District Judge on the fourth contested application for renewal of the interim care order in six months. On this fourth occasion, the District Judge refused to have a fully contested hearing and limited counsel for the mother's submissions to any change of circumstances. On appeal, the mother contended that her rights under Article 6 of the ECHR and her procedural rights under Article 8 had been breached by the District Judge's approach. Black J dismissed the appeal, holding that while there is clearly no rule to the effect that no renewal application can be fully contested unless a change of circumstances is shown, a judge's discretion can be exercised in an appropriate case (such as this) to concentrate upon changes of circumstance.[362]

## 7.2 Interim care and supervision orders: the threshold

An application for an interim care or supervision order 'must be approached in two stages'.[363] The first stage is the threshold contained in section 38(2) of the Children Act 1989, which provides that a court shall not make an interim care order or an interim supervision order unless it is satisfied that there are *reasonable grounds for believing* that the circumstances with respect to the child are as mentioned in section 31(2). This means that the court does not have to be satisfied in fact that the grounds exist but simply that there are reasonable grounds for believing that they do.[364] Thus, evidence which might not be sufficient to satisfy the court at a final hearing may be acceptable to discharge the lower standard for an interim care order. An interim care order can be made despite the fact that a parent, relative, or other person who has not caused the child to suffer, and is not likely to cause the child to suffer, significant harm is offering to look after the child pending the final hearing.[365]

## 7.3 Deciding whether or not to grant the order and whether immediate removal is necessary

If the threshold is passed, the court must then go on to consider as a discrete issue whether or not to grant the order. This is a question to which section 1 of the Children Act 1989 applies, which must be applied having regard to the purpose of an interim order, which is to 'establish a holding position pending a full hearing'.[366] As the Court of Appeal put it in *Re G (Minors) (Interim Care Order)*,[367] the 'making of an interim care order is an essentially impartial step, favouring neither one side nor the other, and affording no one, least of all the local authority in whose favour it is made, an opportunity for tactical or adventitious advantage'.[368] Thorpe LJ explained in *Re LA (Care: Chronic Neglect)*[369] that 'the decision taken by the court on an interim care order application must necessarily be limited to issues that cannot await the fixture and must not extend to issues that are being

---

[362] Ibid, 1223–4. See at 1224 where the factors that are likely to be important are highlighted.

[363] *Re GR (Care Order)* [2010] EWCA Civ 871, [2011] 1 FLR 669 at [33].

[364] *Re B (A Minor) (Care Order: Criteria)* [1993] 1 FLR 815 (Douglas Brown J).

[365] *Re M (A Minor) (Care Order: Threshold Conditions)* discussed in Section 8.2 in detail.

[366] *Re GR (Care Order)* [2010] EWCA Civ 871, [2011] 1 FLR 669 at [35]. If the court has found that both parents are potential perpetrators of harm to the child concerned, the court should not differentiate between the parents in the orders made at the interim stage: see *Re D (Interim Care Order)* [2011] EWCA Civ 1743, [2013] 1 FLR 173.

[367] [1993] 2 FLR 839, CA.

[368] Ibid, 845. It was common ground in *Re G* that the threshold criteria in s 31 were fulfilled, and the court pointed out that in such a case the making of an interim care order is a neutral method of preserving the status quo. See the apparent endorsement of this decision in *Re B (Care Proceedings: Interim Care Order)* [2009] EWCA Civ 1254, [2010] 1 FLR 1211 at [52] and [53]. See also *per* Baroness Hale of Richmond in *Re G (Interim Care Order: Residential Assessment)* [2006] 1 AC 576 at [57]: 'This does not pre-judge the eventual outcome of the case'.

[369] [2009] EWCA Civ 822, [2010] 1 FLR 80.

prepared for determination at that fixture'.[370] An application for an interim order is not a trial run for the final hearing, and the courts have ruled that evidence, and the cross-examination of witnesses, should be restricted to the issues which are essential at the interim stage.[371]

A local authority may wish, by way of an interim care order, to remove a child from home and place a child with another parent,[372] a relative, or a foster carer, or continue an existing removal which began under an EPO. The courts have provided guidance on how to approach applications for interim care orders in such cases. In *Re LA (Care: Chronic Neglect)*[373] Thorpe LJ extracted from earlier Court of Appeal authorities[374] the proposition that 'separation is only to be ordered if the child's safety demands immediate separation'.[375] Thus, for example, in *Re K and H*[376] the Court of Appeal had so held in setting aside orders which removed children from their father's care because of concerns that he was facing serious criminal charges for drug offences. The facts did not disclose a need for immediate separation.

Thorpe LJ's analysis of the authorities was endorsed by Wall LJ in *Re B (Care Proceedings: Interim Care Order)*.[377] The case concerned a boy aged 6 and a girl aged 2. The boy was found on a visit to his home to be living in such alarming conditions that he was immediately removed under police protection and the parents were arrested on suspicion of child cruelty or wilful neglect. The boy was being kept in a filthy, poorly furnished bedroom, possibly in darkness, with no toys. These conditions were in marked contrast to the conditions in which the younger sister lived. She had 'a nicely decorated, furnished bedroom replete with appropriate toys'.[378] Subsequently, interim care orders were sought in respect of both children. The judge refused to make an order in respect of the girl. On appeal, the Court of Appeal found that the judge had directed himself immaculately by asking the following question: 'whether the continued removal of [the girl] from the care of her parents is proportionate to the risk of harm to which she will be exposed if she is allowed to return to her parents' care?' However, the judge's conclusion had seriously understated the treatment of the boy and was plainly wrong. Wall LJ found that there was abundant material from which to conclude that the child's safety, 'using that word in a broad sense to include her psychological welfare', did require interim protection.[379] In *Re GR (Care Order)*[380] the Court of Appeal invited particular attention to Wall LJ's definition of 'safety', commenting that the concept of safety is not confined to physical safety and includes the child's emotional safety or psychological welfare.[381] In *Re B (Interim Care Order)*[382] the Court of Appeal said that the test enunciated by the trial judge, which was approved in *Re B (Care Proceedings: Interim Care Order)*,[383] 'is one which can be universally applied'.[384]

*Re B (Interim Care Order)* provides an example of a case in which the test in *Re LA* was plainly met.[385] In that case there was a long history of domestic violence between the parents and the local

---

[370] Ibid, [7], drawing on *Re H (A Child) (Interim Order)* [2002] EWCA Civ 1932, [2003] 1 FCR 350 at [38] and [39].

[371] *Hampshire County Council v S* [1993] 1 FLR 559; *Re W (A Minor) (Interim Care Order)* [1994] 2 FLR 892.

[372] The placement could be outside the jurisdiction with permission granted under Sch 2, para 19 of the Children Act 1989. See *Islington London Borough Council v EV* [2010] EWHC 3240 (Fam), [2011] 1 FLR 1681 (assessment of four-year-old boy's placement with Turkish father in Turkey following mother's mental illness).

[373] [2009] EWCA Civ 822, [2010] 1 FLR 80.

[374] *Re H (A Child) (Interim Order)* [2002] EWCA Civ 1932, [2003] 1 FCR 350 at [39] and *Re K and H* [2006] EWCA Civ 1898, [2007] 1 FLR 2043 at [16].

[375] In *Re L (Care Proceedings: Removal of Child)* [2008] 1 FLR 575, Ryder J sought to articulate the test by reference to the following words: 'an imminent risk of really serious harm ie whether the risk to [the child's] safety demands immediate separation'. However, the words 'imminent risk of really serious harm' had apparently caused some confusion and Thorpe LJ in *Re LA (Care: Chronic Neglect)* took the opportunity to reassert the test as traditionally understood.

[376] [2006] EWCA Civ 1898, [2007] 1 FLR 2043.    [377] [2009] EWCA Civ 1254, [2010] 1 FLR 1211.

[378] The judge's description, cited at [22] of the Court of Appeal's judgment.

[379] [2009] EWCA Civ 1254, [2010] 1 FLR 1211 at [56].    [380] [2010] EWCA Civ 871, [2011] 1 FLR 669.

[381] Ibid, [42].    [382] [2010] EWCA Civ 324, [2010] 2 FLR 283.

[383] [2009] EWCA Civ 1254, [2010] 1 FLR 1211.    [384] [2010] EWCA Civ 324, [2010] 2 FLR 283 at [21].

[385] Ibid, [19]. See also *Re L (Interim Care Order: Extended Family)* [2013] EWCA Civ 179, [2013] 2 FLR 302 (immediate removal from grandmother's home required in order to prevent the grandmother removing the child and refusing

authority sought interim care orders to remove two children, aged 9 and 11, to foster care pending the local authority's assessment of the mother's ability to disengage from the father and to parent the children appropriately on her own. The Court of Appeal held that the judge had been correct to make the orders, there being an abundance of evidence that the exercise could only safely be attempted if the children were not living with the mother.[386]

Similarly, in *Re T (Interim Care Order: Removal of Children Where No Immediate Emergency)*,[387] the Court of Appeal upheld a judge's removal of children aged 4 and 5 from the care of their grandparents at the interim stage because of their current inability to deal with the children's disturbed behaviour, while not ruling them out in the long-term as carers. The court held that the judge had correctly applied *Re LA*. The children were profoundly emotionally and psychologically damaged by their previous experiences, and the paternal grandparents, despite their best endeavours, were not meeting the children's need for enhanced parenting. It was no longer in the children's interests to be exposed to further deterioration in their emotional wellbeing.[388]

By contrast, in *Re F (Care Proceedings: Interim Care Order)*[389] the test in *Re LA* was not satisfied. In that case a mother gave birth to twins. Her four older children had been taken into care, one within the previous year. It was common ground that the parents were competent to deliver good enough standards of care to the children in the interim.

However, the judge, placing emphasis on the history, made interim care orders removing the children from the parents on the basis that the children were at risk of emotional harm. Thorpe LJ held that the orders should be set aside: the judge had wrongly strayed into matters which fell to be addressed at the final hearing and her conclusion on the facts did 'not begin to meet the high threshold set by the authorities'.[390] Hedley J agreed, adding that while the child's welfare is the paramount consideration, fairness to parents is a matter that should be in the mind of the court at every stage of the proceedings. His Lordship observed that it 'can hardly be in the welfare of a child for the parents not to be given a fair opportunity for that child to be able to be brought up by them rather than by strangers'.[391] Sir Nicholas Wall P agreed with both judgments, observing that the same conclusion would have been reached had the trial judge correctly applied the test in *Re B*: in his Lordship's view, it 'would not have been a proportionate exercise of discretion to remove a child in the circumstances of this case'.[392] That is not to say that emotional harm can never justify an interim care order.[393]

In *Re M (Interim Care Order: Removal)*[394] the Court of Appeal made clear that a judge must consider the risk to the child from removal as well as the risks alleged by the local authority. In that case, R, the youngest of four children, aged 2, was removed under an interim care order to foster care, although the local authority had been unable to implement interim care orders in respect of the three older children, who absconded home and were living with the parents. The local authority's concerns related to domestic violence. The court saw the short-term risk to the child from the domestic violence over a four-month period awaiting trial as a relatively insignificant one of being caught in some physical crossfire given that there was no evidence of anything of that sort happening in the past. It also saw the continuation of the order as difficult to defend given that the judge had allowed the older children, who were at greater risk from the domestic violence, to remain at home.[395] The court also found that the judge had failed to put in the balance risk of harm to R of short-term emotional harm of deprivation of her parents, siblings, and home.[396] The court

---

to disclose the child's whereabouts, a case in which the judge did not expressly refer to the test in *Re LA (Care: Chronic Neglect)* [2009] EWCA Civ 822, [2010] 1 FLR 80 but the judgment showed that the child's immediate protection was the primary concern: see especially at [66]–[70]).

[386] [2010] EWCA Civ 324, [2010] 2 FLR 283 at [13].     [387] [2015] EWCA Civ 453.     [388] Ibid, at [29].

[389] [2010] EWCA Civ 826, [2010] 2 FLR 1455.     [390] Ibid, [23].     [391] Ibid, [29].     [392] Ibid, [32].

[393] See eg *Re A (Children) (Interim Care Order)* [2001] 3 FCR 402 (emotional abuse from failure to protect children from local community's influence over children giving evidence against their father in criminal proceedings).

[394] [2005] EWCA Civ 1594, [2006] 1 FLR 1043.     [395] Ibid, [25].     [396] Ibid, [23] and [24].

concluded that 'the very high standard that must be established to justify the continuing removal of a child from home' had not been made good and set aside the order.

Similarly, in *Re B (Refusal to Grant Interim Order)*[397] the Court of Appeal held that a judge had been plainly right not to remove children at the interim stage. There were concerns about the chaotic home in which the children's needs were neglected, the children's mothers'[398] lack of sexual inhibition, and failure to comply with an agreement with the local authority to inform them of male visitors to the home. The Court of Appeal held that the facts were amply sufficient to fulfil section 38(2), but that in relation to the additional and separate question of removal, the neglect and risk of sexual abuse did not provide sufficient justification for immediate removal.

There have been concerns that the test for making an interim care order is in some cases too high. Darren Howe[399] expresses concern that chronic situations (such as the domestic violence situation in *Re M (Interim Care Order: Removal)*[400] discussed earlier) and long-term neglect cases sit uncomfortably with the current test for interim removal and children in such situations are unlikely to be protected. He comments that 'we should not be leaving children in neglectful situations for months on end' pending final hearings. Andrew Bainham has highlighted the opposite problem: that, in some circumstances, in practice the bar may be set too low and interim care orders are being made too readily by lower courts.[401] Bainham's concern is with a prevalent practice whereby parents neither consent to nor oppose the making of the first interim care order. Of particular concern is the fact that in many cases the parents' position is unlikely to represent a true lack of opposition because of various pressures (eg the perception of the need to cooperate to achieve reunification with the child, and a wish to avoid an interim court ruling on the threshold criteria). The reason for the local authority's application will usually be that it will want parental responsibility and to have a more secure basis to promote the child's welfare during the care proceedings. However, Bainham points out that, in contrast to the Court of Appeal's characterisation of interim care orders as 'neutral' holding orders, this is not a credible view from the perspective of parents. Bainham argues that to achieve the local authority's aims without the juggernaut of care starting to roll by way of an interim care order, a solution might be to extend availability of the parental responsibility orders and agreements to local authorities, provided they have already instituted care proceedings. Alternatively, he argues, it might be possible to introduce a new, intermediate order, with new nomenclature which avoids at the interim stage the pejorative connotations which entering care has for many parents.

## 7.4 Interim care orders and assessment

In the period between first making an application in care proceedings and the final hearing, a local authority will normally wish to carry out a careful assessment of the child, his parents, his siblings, and others, such as relatives, who are important persons in his or her life. The purpose of this assessment is to give the local authority a clearer idea about the nature of the harm which the child is suffering, or is likely to suffer, and to whom it can be attributed. The local authority also needs to give close attention to whether a care or supervision order is the most appropriate response to the child's circumstances, and to decide on the arrangements it wishes to make for the future care of the child should it obtain a care order. Where the local authority has been granted an interim care order it will have parental responsibility for the child and thus will have the necessary powers in relation to the child to enable it to carry out a proper assessment. Indeed, as we have seen, this may well be one of the reasons why the local authority has sought an interim care order. The general

---

[397] [2012] EWCA Civ 1275, [2013] 2 FLR 153.

[398] The mothers were themselves mother and daughter, each living with their own child in the same household.

[399] D. Howe, 'Removal of Children at Interim Hearings: Is the Test Now Set Too High?' [2009] Family Law 320.

[400] [2005] EWCA Civ 1594, [2006] 1 FLR 1043.

[401] A. Bainham, 'Interim Care Orders: Is the Bar Set Too Low?' [2011] Family Law 374.

principle is that where a court makes a care order, be it an interim order or a final order, it loses its powers over the child's upbringing and gives control to the local authority.[402] A care order is a 'care order' whether the order made is interim or final[403] and a court cannot normally attach conditions or give directions about where the child shall live once a care order has been made.[404] However, one exception to this principle is to be found in section 38(6) and (7) of the Children Act 1989, which empower the courts to exercise a large measure of control over the assessment process despite the fact that an interim care order is in force.

Section 38(6) provides:

> Where the court makes an interim care order, or interim supervision order, it may give such directions (if any) as it considers appropriate with regard to the medical or psychiatric examination or other assessment of the child;[405] but if the child is of sufficient understanding to make an informed decision he may refuse to submit to the examination or other assessment.

Section 38(7) provides:

> A direction under subsection (6) may be to the effect that there is to be—
>
> (a) no such examination or assessment; or
> (b) no such examination or assessment unless the court directs otherwise.

These directions may be given when the interim order is made, or at any time when it is in force, and an application may be made at any time for a direction to be varied.[406] Subsection (6) reflects the need of the court to obtain information and guidance from doctors, social workers, and others about the child and his circumstances in order to assist it to determine whether the threshold test has been crossed, and to decide what order, if any, to make.

Section 38(7A) provides that:

> A direction under subsection (6) to the effect that there is to be a medical or psychiatric examination or other assessment of the child may be given only if the court is of the opinion that the examination or other assessment is necessary to assist the court to resolve the proceedings justly.

The court is to have regard to particular factors in section 38(7B) when deciding whether to give a direction.[407]

---

[402] This principle stems from the pre-Children Act 1989 ruling of the House of Lords in *A v Liverpool City Council* [1982] AC 363; and see M. Hayes, 'The Proper Role of Courts in Child Care Cases' (1996) 8 Child and Family Law Quarterly 201. For a different view, see J. Dewar, 'The Courts and Local Authority Autonomy' (1995) 7 Child and Family Law Quarterly 15.

[403] Section 31(11).

[404] *Re T (A Minor) (Care Order: Conditions)* [1994] 2 FLR 243; *Re L (Interim Care Order: Power of Court)* [1996] 2 FLR 742.

[405] In *Re W (Assessment of Child)* 1998] 2 FLR 130 the Court of Appeal held that the power in s 38(6) is wide enough to direct that an assessment be undertaken by a named individual although the court recognised that its jurisdiction is limited by the fact that it cannot compel an individual who is either unable or unwilling to carry out the assessment. The court commented that it should not encourage applications naming individuals and that if it is intended to name an individual the court should ascertain in advance that the individual is willing to act. The court suggested that a better practice might be to direct that the assessment be carried out by a 'suitably qualified individual' as in *Berkshire County Council v C and Others* [1993] Fam 203, [1993] 1 FLR 569, [1993] 2 WLR 475, FD.

[406] Section 38(8).

[407] '(a) any impact which any examination or other assessment would be likely to have on the welfare of the child, and any other impact which giving the direction would be likely to have on the welfare of the child, (b) the issues with which the examination or other assessment would assist the court, (c) the questions which the examination or other assessment would enable the court to answer, (d) the evidence otherwise available, (e) the impact which the direction would be likely to have on the timetable, duration and conduct of the proceedings, (f) the cost of the examination or

A local authority must comply with a direction under section 38(6) or (7).[408]

The scope of the court's powers under section 38(6) and their inter-relationship with the powers of the local authority at the interim stages of a child protection case were considered by the House of Lords in *Re C (Interim Care Order: Residential Assessment).*[409] C had suffered very serious and unexplained injuries while being looked after by his parents. An interim care order was made and C was placed with foster parents. C's parents, who were immature, lacked family support, and had a difficult relationship with each other; nonetheless, they had extensive contact with C and showed progress in caring for him. A clinical psychologist and the guardian ad litem, were firmly of the view that a proper evaluation of the parents' ability to care for C should be carried out before a final order was made, and that such an evaluation could only be carried out by means of an in-depth assessment at a residential unit. Hogg J ordered that the residential assessment take place, rejecting the local authority's submission that the court had no jurisdiction under section 38(6) to make such an order. The Court of Appeal reluctantly allowed the authority's appeal and gave leave to appeal to the House of Lords.

The point of construction for the House of Lords was whether the Court of Appeal had been correct to take a narrow view of the words 'other assessment of the child' in section 38(6) and to rule that they had to be construed as *ejusdem generis* with the words 'medical or psychiatric examination'. Their Lordships held that this narrow construction was wrong, that the words were wide enough to embrace a joint assessment of the child and his parents together. Accordingly, they ruled that Hogg J did have jurisdiction to order a residential assessment.[410] Lord Browne-Wilkinson, who delivered the sole speech, pointed out that the interaction between a child and his parents and others looking after him is an essential element in making any assessment of the child.[411] He stated that section 38(6) should be construed purposively so as to give effect to the underlying intentions of Parliament, namely to enable the court to obtain the information necessary for its own decision.[412]

The House of Lords had another occasion to consider section 38(6) in *Re G (A Minor) (Interim Care Order: Residential Assessment).*[413] In that case the mother's second child had died from a non-accidental injury in circumstances in which a judge was unable to decide which of the parents had caused the injuries. The mother's first child, by another man, was protected by being placed with his father. The mother then formed a more promising relationship with another man and they had a girl, Ellie. After a period of assessment of the mother's ability to address the issues surrounding the death of her second child, Johnson J held that he had no power under section 38(6) to direct

---

other assessment, and (g) any matters prescribed by Family Procedure Rules.' On the meaning of 'necessary', see *Re TG (Care Proceedings: Case Management: Expert Evidence)* [2013] EWCA Civ 5, [2013] 1 FLR 1250, [30] and *In re H-L (A Child) (Care Proceedings: Expert Evidence)* [2013] EWCA Civ 655, [2014] 1 WLR 1160, [2013] 2 FLR 1434, [3].

[408] *Re O (Minors) (Medical Examination)* [1993] 1 FLR 860. The local authority were unsuccessful in their appeal against a direction from justices that the children concerned should be tested to discover whether they were HIV positive.

[409] [1997] 1 FLR 1. For further discussion, see C. Smith, 'Judicial Power and Local Authority Discretion—The Contested Frontier' (1997) 9 Child and Family Law Quarterly 243.

[410] Their Lordships accepted that orders under s 38(6) have significant cost implications but held that this was not a reason for refusing to make an order, rather it was a matter the court should take into account when exercising its discretion. In *Re W (Assessment of Child)* [1998] 2 FLR 130, the Court of Appeal commented that local authority resources, both human and financial, and legal aid funds should all be borne in mind. Consequently, such applications should not be encouraged. See too, *Berkshire County Council v C* [1993] 1 FLR 569; *Re M (Residential Assessment Directions)* [1998] 2 FLR 371.

[411] The court has no power to order the parents to take part in any assessment against their wishes.

[412] '[T]he court is to have such powers to override the views of the local authority as are necessary to enable the court to discharge properly its function of deciding whether or not to accede to the local authority's application to take the child away from its parents by obtaining a care order' [1997] 1 FLR 1 at 7. Their Lordships acknowledged that assessments had financial implications and that account of these should be taken by the court.

[413] [2006] 1 AC 576.

at the local authority's expense a further period of psychotherapy for the mother because it fell on the side of therapy rather than assessment. The Court of Appeal allowed an appeal, holding that the essential question was not one of distinguishing between therapy and assessment but whether what is sought can broadly be classified as assessment to enable the court to obtain the information necessary for its decision. On appeal to the House of Lords, the issue was whether, on the true construction of section 38(6), the Court of Appeal had correctly identified the essential question for the court. The House of Lords allowed the appeal. Baroness Hale of Richmond delivered the leading opinion, with which there was unanimous agreement. Examining the legislative history of section 38(6) and (7) she concluded that the purpose of the provisions is 'not only to enable the court to obtain the information it needs, but also to enable the court to control the information-gathering activities of others'.[414] The emphasis is always on 'information obtaining' and there is nothing in the Act which permits a court to order the provision of services to anyone[415] and it 'cannot be a proper use of the court's powers under section 38(6) to seek to bring about change'.[416] The House concluded that what is directed under section 38(6) must be:

> an examination or assessment of the child, including where appropriate her relationship with her parents, the risk that her parents may present to her, and the ways in which those risks may be avoided or managed, all with a view to enabling the court to make the decisions which it has to make under the Act with the minimum of delay. Any services which are provided for the child and his family must be ancillary to that end. They must not be an end in themselves.[417]

Baroness Hale preferred to express no concluded view on the issue of whether or not the court has power to direct the local authority or any of the parties to fund the assessment.[418] But on the assumption that it does, her Ladyship said that the cost of any proposed assessment must be relevant to the court's decision.[419]

While Baroness Hale noted in the course of her opinion that the issue of the distinction between assessment and treatment had arisen in cases after *Re C*, her Ladyship did not directly address that issue. However, Lord Scott of Foscote (with whom Lord Mance agreed) examined those authorities.

Lord Scott agreed with Holman J's analysis in *Re M (Residential Assessment Directions)*.[420] In that case Holman J directed that a residential assessment take place, but limited the assessment period to the first eight weeks of the proposed programme because thereafter it shifted to treatment rather than assessment.[421] After referring to Lord Browne-Wilkinson's conclusions in *Re C*, Holman J concluded that the courts' powers:

> are limited to a process that can properly be characterized as 'assessment' rather than 'treatment', although no doubt all treatment is accompanied by a continuing process of assessment. And they are limited to a process which bona fide involves the participation of the child as an integral part of what is being assessed.[422]

---

[414] Ibid, [64].   [415] Ibid, [65].   [416] Ibid, [67].   [417] Ibid, [69].

[418] See, however, Lord Scott of Foscote's account of the position of the Legal Services Commission, at [20]–[23].

[419] On which see Holman J [1998] 2 FLR 371 at 382: the assessment should not be contrary to the best interests of the child, should be 'necessary' to enable the court to reach a proper decision and should not make unreasonable demands of a local authority. Contrast Hobhouse LJ in *Re B (Psychiatric Therapy for Parents)* [1999] 1 FLR 701 (paramountcy of child's welfare and cost relevant).

[420] [1998] 2 FLR 371.

[421] His Lordship commented that the words in s 38(6) are 'limited to a process that can properly be characterised as "assessment" rather than "treatment" ' and 'to a process which bona fide involves the participation of the child as an integral part of what is being assessed'.

[422] See also *Re B (Psychiatric Therapy for Parents)* [1999] 1 FLR 701.

Lord Scott also agreed with the analysis of Thorpe and Simon Brown LJJ in *Re D (Jurisdiction: Programme of Assessment or Therapy)*.[423] There it was held that a 'programme for assessment can encompass within it an element of therapy or treatment' but if 'the programme is essentially one for treatment rather than one for assessment it . . . must be held to be outside the court's powers to order'.[424] A judge had ordered a six-month residential assessment of a mother who was drug dependent. This involved the treatment of her underlying emotional and psychological disorder by a psychotherapist independent of the residential unit and the treatment of her drug addiction by that unit. The mother's capacity to relate to her baby was not substantially in question, although her care of the baby would be closely supervised and assessed during her stay. The Court of Appeal allowed the local authority's appeal, finding that the proposed programme clearly fell outside the limits of any programme which as a matter of fact and degree could properly be characterised as one primarily designed for the purpose of assessment rather than treatment. The programme's 'therapeutic component was altogether too prominent, its length altogether too long'.[425]

Lord Scott disagreed, however, with the conclusion of the Court of Appeal in *Re B (Interim Care Order: Directions)*.[426] There the court gave a direction that a mother and child be assessed at a mother and baby unit where the focus was on improving parents' childcare skills. Lord Scott was of the view that 'an assessment of the success of the programme in improving the parenting skills of the parents could not . . . be described as "an examination or assessment of the child" '. An assessment of mother/child attachment can be regarded as an assessment of the child, whereas assessment of the mother's ability to respond to professional concerns cannot.

Having reviewed the authorities, Lord Scott concluded that in *Re G* 'the main purpose of the proposed programme was therapy for the mother in order to give her the opportunity of change so as to become a safe and acceptable carer for Ellie'.[427] In his Lordship's view this purpose did not fall within section 38(6) 'notwithstanding that the results of the programme would be valuable and influential in enabling the court to decide whether a care order in respect of Ellie should be made and that if the purpose were to be achieved it would very greatly benefit Ellie'.[428]

Lord Clyde also recognised the distinction as a matter of language between assessment and treatment but commented that:

> without engaging in the terminological distinction it should be enough to recognise that the jurisdiction of the court is confined to obtaining information about the current state of affairs, including perhaps a forecast of what future progress might be possible, and does not extend to a continuing survey of the effects of treatment.[429]

In cases in which there are professional recommendations both of assessment and therapy, there will need to be careful consideration therefore of the precise nature of that which is being ordered under section 38(6) as distinct from interventions otherwise taking place. In *Re L and H (Residential Assessment)*[430] a mother had a history of struggling to care for her children. Her first child was cared for by the maternal grandmother, the second and third had been adopted outside the family, and the fourth child was in foster care following emergency protection. A comprehensive report of a consultant clinical psychologist prepared in the course of care proceedings relating to the fourth child recommended a residential parenting assessment to assess the mother's parenting ability and the ability of the parents' relationship to withstand the stresses of parenting. The psychologist also recommended that the mother and her partner would benefit from concurrent therapeutic interventions (in the form of cognitive behavioural therapy and couple therapy). Before the hearing, the mother's fifth child, M, was born and was joined to the care proceedings. The mother's application

---

[423] [1999] 2 FLR 632, reiterating the approach in *Re B* [1999] 1 FLR 701.
[424] [1999] 2 FLR 632 at 641 *per* Simon Brown LJ and at 637–9 *per* Thorpe LJ.
[425] At 641 *per* Simon Brown LJ.     [426] [2002] 1 FLR 545.     [427] [2006] 1 AC 576 at [14].
[428] Ibid.     [429] Ibid, [31].     [430] [2007] EWCA Civ 213, [2007] 1 FLR 1370.

for a section 38(6) assessment in line with the psychologist's recommendation was rejected by the judge on the grounds that it involved a therapeutic element and was concerned with the parents' relationship not with the child. The Court of Appeal allowed the mother's appeal and ordered assessment. The judge had misinterpreted the nature of the recommended assessment which did not contain therapeutic interventions. The therapeutic interventions were to take place concurrently, organised by others.[431] The proposed assessment in this case was on all fours with that in *Re C*.[432] The Court of Appeal was left with the feeling that the denial of an assessment to the parents was unfair and stressed that 'the hearing of the proceedings should be fair (or, to put the matter in the language of the European Convention, Art 6 compliant) and that the court should have before it all the relevant evidence necessary for the decision'.[433] The court acknowledged that there would be some cases in which professional advice might be unanimous that an assessment would serve no useful purpose (eg a parent who had been found to have grievously harmed a child but was still in denial about it or a parent who refused to acknowledge that a convicted paedophile was a danger to her children). However, where as in this case there was powerful, well-reasoned, objective, and balanced professional evidence that an assessment was worthwhile, that was a 'a powerful pointer to the propriety of such an order'.[434]

As these cases illustrate, section 38(6) assessments tend to be thought of in terms of residential assessments in institutional settings. However, in *Re A (Residential Assessment)*[435] Munby J made clear that it 'applies to any "examination" (medical or psychiatric) or any "assessment", whether short or long, and in whatever setting'.[436] His Lordship held, contrary to a local authority's contention, that justices had not erred in directing an assessment of a child whilst living at the home of her paternal aunt and great-grandmother. The aunt had a conviction which in the local authority's opinion would disqualify her under the relevant fostering regulations,[437] and contended therefore that the effect of the direction was to put in place an unregulated placement. Munby J pointed out that the House of Lords in *Re C* made clear that a direction which specified the venue at which a residential assessment was to take place did not wrongly interfere with the local authority's power under the Children Act 1989 to determine a child's place of residence under a care order, including an interim care order. In their Lordships' opinion, the power is concerned with a child's placement not his assessment. Munby J held that to accept the local authority's argument would be to read into section 38(6) restrictions which are not there.[438] Any concern that it was a placement unregulated by statute could be met by the fact that it was a placement regulated by the court, in that the court was satisfied that it was a safe and suitable placement. Against such an approach, however, is the fact that in some cases the court's order requires a local authority on which it is conferring parental responsibility to act against its better judgement and to take risks with which it disagrees. In such circumstances there may be an argument that the court should take its own steps to secure the safety of the child during the assessment period, for example by making an interim residence order (which could contain conditions and directions) coupled with an interim supervision order.[439]

---

[431] Ibid, [32].    [432] Ibid, [76].

[433] Ibid, [85]. See for another example *Re K (Care Order)* [2007] EWCA Civ 697, [2007] 2 FLR 1066 (two-day assessment ordered to avoid jeopardising 'the essential requirement of fairness to the mother in seeking to resist the care order'—see at [7]).

[434] Ibid, [88] and [91]. There is, of course, no question of a parent having a right to a further assessment. The court must ask whether a further assessment will assist the judge in reaching the right conclusion: see *Re J (Residential Assessment: Rights of Audience)* [2009] EWCA Civ 1210, [2010] 1 FLR 1290 at [10].

[435] [2009] EWHC 865 (Fam), [2009] 2 FLR 443 (Munby J).

[436] Ibid, [59]. The point became an academic one in the case but Munby J agreed to deliver a judgment on this matter of pubic interest since he had heard full argument.

[437] Fostering Services (Wales) Regulations 2003 (SI 2003/237), reg 38(2).

[438] [2009] EWHC 865 (Fam), [2009] 2 FLR 443 at [63].

[439] In *Re T (A Minor) (Care Order: Conditions)* [1994] 2 FLR 423 at 435 it was acknowledged by Nourse LJ that a placement at home could be achieved in this fashion.

## 7.5 **The child's right to refuse to be assessed**

Section 38(7) was included in the Act partly in response to matters raised in the Cleveland inquiry.[440] The report revealed that children who were suspected of having been sexually abused were subjected to repeated medical examinations and prolonged interviews which caused them a considerable degree of distress. Additional safeguards for the child appear in the final words of section 38(6) which provide that where a child is of sufficient understanding to make an informed decision he may refuse to submit to a medical or psychiatric examination or other assessment. However, the scope of this safeguard for the child has been limited by the ruling in *South Glamorgan County Council v W and B*[441] that the inherent jurisdiction can be used to override it. A girl refused to comply with the court's direction and the court found that she was competent to make an informed decision. The court then gave leave to the local authority to bring proceedings to invoke the exercise of the court's inherent jurisdiction to authorise that the child be assessed and treated without her consent. Leave was granted because the court was satisfied that the result which the local authority wished to achieve could not be achieved through the making of any order made otherwise than in the exercise of the court's inherent jurisdiction, and for which the local authority were entitled to apply. It therefore fulfilled the requirements of section 100(5) of the Children Act 1989. It was put to the court that the court's power under the inherent jurisdiction to override in a proper case the wishes of a child, and to give consent for medical treatment, had been abrogated by section 100. This view was rejected by the court on the grounds that the court had always been able to override the wishes of a competent child, and that it would require very clear words in a statute to take that right away.

There were compelling reasons why the child in *South Glamorgan County Council v W and B* should receive psychiatric assessment and treatment, and it is easy to appreciate why the court was determined to override her refusal. However, the difficulty with the ruling is that Parliament had specifically legislated, in section 38(6), that a child with sufficient competence could refuse to comply with a direction from a court that she undergo such an assessment. Thus Parliament appeared deliberately to have circumscribed the powers of a court in the face of a refusal from the child. The ruling in *South Glamorgan County Council v W and B* allowed the inherent jurisdiction to be used to give powers to the court which were denied it by statute.

## 7.6 **Interim care orders and excluding the alleged abuser from the home**

In the same way that an exclusion requirement can be added to an EPO (see the discussions of sections 44A and 44B in Section 5.3), section 38A provides that an exclusion requirement can be attached to[442] an interim care order[443] provided that the conditions in section 38A(2) are satisfied. These conditions are:

---

### Key legislation

(a) that there is reasonable cause to believe that, if a person ('the relevant person') is excluded from a dwelling house in which the child lives, the child will cease to suffer, or cease to be likely to suffer, significant harm, and

(b) that another person living in the house (whether a parent of the child or some other person)—

    (i) is able and willing to give the child the care which it would be reasonable to expect a parent to give to him, and

    (ii) consents to the inclusion of the exclusion requirement.

---

[440] *Report of the Inquiry into Child Abuse in Cleveland 1987* (Cm 412, 1988).    [441] [1993] 1 FLR 574.

[442] An exclusion requirement can only be made as an addition to, and not as an alternative to, an interim care order.

[443] Sections 38A and 38B were inserted by the Family Law Act 1996, s 52, Sch 6, para 1. For further discussion, see *Domestic Violence and Occupation of the Family Home* (Law Com No 207, 1992), paras 6.15–6.22.

The court may attach a power of arrest to an exclusion requirement[444] and a police constable may arrest without warrant any person whom he has reasonable cause to believe to be in breach of the requirement.[445] Section 38B allows for exclusion from the home to be regulated by undertakings rather than a court order.

## 7.7 The role of the children's guardian

Unless there is someone who has the duty to be the voice of the child, and who has a duty to safeguard the child's interests before the court, there is a risk that the child's perspective will be inadequately represented. Because care proceedings can often involve babies and young children who lack the capacity properly to instruct a lawyer, the normal safeguards afforded by separate legal representation do not assist the child to any great extent. A lawyer has only limited opportunities to make a close and independent investigation into the circumstances surrounding a child client's case, and he or she is likely therefore to feel obliged to support the local authority's perception of the case unless instructions are received from someone who has the authority to make enquiries and to represent the child's position. A children's guardian is such a person.[446] The need for children's guardians (formerly referred to as guardians ad litem) and the dangers inherent in an unopposed application being allowed to proceed without any separate investigation being conducted on behalf of the child, were graphically illustrated by the tragic circumstances of the death of Maria Colwell[447] following the discharge of her care order and her return to her mother and stepfather. At that time no one had the duty to give an account of Maria's wishes and feelings to the court, and no one had the duty to make an assessment, independent of the one made by the local authority, of whether Maria's mother and stepfather might ill-treat her, or otherwise cause her harm, were she to be returned to their care. Following the Colwell case, guardians were introduced, initially in respect of unopposed applications to discharge a care order, but gradually their use has been extended to other proceedings. Section 41 of the Children Act 1989 now provides a list of specified proceedings in which a court must appoint a children's guardian unless satisfied that it is not necessary to do so in order to safeguard the child's interests.[448] A failure to appoint a guardian where the case for the child's interests being separately represented is clear may leave a court open to successful judicial review.[449]

A children's guardian appointed in specified proceedings will be a Cafcass officer or Welsh family proceedings officer.[450] They are trained and experienced in social work. Section 41(2) of the Children Act 1989 provides that they shall be appointed in accordance with rules of court;[451] and be under a duty to safeguard the interests of the child in the manner prescribed by such rules.[452] The

---

[444] Section 38A(5).    [445] Section 38A(8).

[446] See www.nagalro.com for further information on the role of children's guardians.

[447] *Report of the Committee of Inquiry into the Care and Supervision provided in relation to Maria Colwell* (London: HMSO, 1974) (Chairman: T. G. Field-Fisher QC).

[448] Section 41(1) and (6): on an application to make or discharge a care order including when the court is considering making a child arrangements order with respect to the living arrangements of a child who is the subject of a care order; on an application to make, vary, or discharge a supervision order; when a direction has been made in family proceedings and the court has made, or is thinking of making, an interim care order; when an application is made with respect to contact with a child in care; in respect of any proceedings brought under Pt V; on an appeal in relation to any of the above proceedings, and an appeal in relation to s 34 of the Children Act 1989 (contact with a child in care). The list of specified proceedings does not include an application for an education supervision order under s 36 of the Act. See *Essex County Council v B* [1993] 1 FLR 866.

[449] *R v Pontlottyn Juvenile Court, ex p R* [1990] FCR 900.

[450] As set out in Children Act 1989, s 41 and Family Procedure Rules, r 16.17. See the functions of the services set out in Criminal Justice and Court Services Act 2000, s 12 and Children Act 2004, s 35.

[451] Section 41(2)(a). See Family Procedure Rules, rr 16.3 and 12.6 on the appointment of a children's guardian in specified proceedings.

[452] Section 41(2)(b)

relevant rules are set out in Part 16 of the Family Procedure Rules 2010, supplemented by Practice Direction 16A—Representation of Children, and rule 16.20(5) provides that the children's guardian's duties must be exercised in accordance with the Practice Direction. The children's guardian must 'act on behalf of the child upon the hearing of any application in proceedings with the duty of safeguarding the interests of the child',[453] and 'must also provide the court with such other assistance as it may require'.[454] In doing so the guardian must have regard to the principle in section 1(2) (that delay will normally be prejudicial to the child's welfare) and the matters in section 1(3) of the Children Act 1989 (the so-called welfare checklist). The children's guardian's duties are set out in Part 3 of Practice Direction 16A.

The guardian must appoint and instruct a solicitor to represent the child,[455] attend all directions, appointments, and hearings unless excused from so doing, and advise the court on various specified matters, such as the child's wishes and the child's level of understanding.[456] The guardian is responsible for serving and accepting service of documents on behalf of the child. Occasionally, the child may wish to give instructions to a solicitor which conflict with those of the guardian. This is most likely to arise where the guardian forms the view that it would be in the interests of the child if a care order were made and the child does not want to go into care. In such a case, provided that the solicitor is satisfied that the child is able, having regard to his understanding, to give instructions on his own behalf, the rules provide that the solicitor must conduct the case in accordance with the instructions received from the child.[457] The guardian will nonetheless continue to investigate the case on behalf of the child, and must perform all his or her duties set out in the rules and Practice Direction other than his or her duty to appoint a solicitor for the child.[458] These provisions are an example of how the law seeks to balance giving due weight to the child's right to be respected as an individual, and to have access to the type of legal safeguards which are given to adults, and the concern of the law to ensure that the welfare of children is afforded proper protection in proceedings designed to secure their safety and well-being.

The Practice Direction states that the guardian must carry out such investigations as may be necessary to carry out his or her duties, and in particular must contact or seek to interview such persons as he or she thinks appropriate or as the court directs.[459] The guardian must also obtain such professional assistance, such as a report from an expert, which he or she thinks appropriate, or which the court directs the guardian to obtain.[460] The guardian has a right to inspect and take copies of any local authority records[461] and adoption agency records,[462] and where he or she thinks that they may assist in the determination of the case, they must be brought to the attention of the court.[463] Following investigations, the children's guardian must, unless the court directs otherwise, file a written report advising on the interests of the child for the final hearing.[464] The parents and other parties must have the opportunity to read the report in advance of the hearing. This is particularly important where the guardian is supporting the local authority's application for a care order, for the persons affected are entitled to know details of the case which is being made against

---

[453] Family Procedure Rules, r 16.20(1).  [454] Ibid, r 16.20(2).

[455] Ibid, r 6.2, unless a solicitor has already been appointed or the children's guardian is authorised to and intends to have conduct of the proceedings on behalf of the child (r 6.3). The court has power to appoint a solicitor for the child (see Children Act 1989, s 41(3)). For guidance to solicitors on acting in the absence of a guardian, see the Law Society Practice Note: Acting in the Absence of a Children's Guardian [2010] 1 FLR 1632.

[456] Practice Direction 16A, 6.6.

[457] See *Re H (A Minor) (Care Proceedings: Child's Wishes)* [1993] 1 FLR 440; *Re P (Representation)* [1996] 1 FLR 486.

[458] See *Re M (Minors) (Care Proceedings: Child's Wishes)* [1994] 1 FLR 749 where Wall J laid down guidelines to be followed where the views of the guardian ad litem conflict with those of the child.

[459] Practice Direction 16A, 6.1(a).  [460] Ibid, 6.1(b).  [461] Children Act 1989, s 42.

[462] Adoption and Children Act 2002, s 103.

[463] Practice Direction 16A, 6.10. Where the local authority's care plan is adoption, the guardian has the right to see the case record in relation to the prospective adopters even though this is normally confidential: *Re T (A Minor) (Guardian ad Litem: Case Record)* [1994] 1 FLR 632.

[464] Practice Direction 16A, 6.8(a).

them, so that they can prepare their own case properly. Once the court has made its decision, the guardian has the responsibility (where appropriate) to convey the court's decision in a manner appropriate to the child's age and understanding.

# 8  The final hearing in care proceedings

## 8.1  **The threshold test**

At the final hearing the court must be satisfied, on the balance of probabilities, that the threshold test in section 31(2) has been made out before it has jurisdiction[465] to make either a care order or a supervision order. It is convenient to set this out again:

> A court may only make a care order or a supervision order if it is satisfied—
> (a)  that the child is suffering, or is likely to suffer, significant harm; and
> (b)  that the harm, or likelihood of harm, is attributable to—
>   (i)  the care given to the child, or likely to be given to him if the order were not made, not being what it would be reasonable to expect a parent to give to him; or
>   (ii)  the child's being beyond parental control.

In *Re B (A Child)*[466] the Supreme Court observed that the decision whether the threshold is fulfilled involves a value judgement,[467] an appraisal,[468] or an evaluation.[469] The court is not exercising a discretion. Thus on an appeal against a finding that the threshold is crossed, the question for the court is simply whether the judge's decision was wrong.[470]

In *Newham London Borough v AG*,[471] Sir Stephen Brown P issued a warning against courts taking a too legalistic approach to the analysis of the language of section 31(2). He said 'of course, the words of the statute must be considered, but I do not believe that Parliament meant them to be unduly restrictive when the evidence clearly indicates that a certain course should be taken in order to protect the child'.[472] As we shall see, however, the wording of section 31(2) has generated much case law, including several House of Lords/Supreme Court decisions.

The threshold test has several elements. It will be satisfied where it is shown that the child 'is suffering' significant harm or where it is shown that he or she is 'likely to suffer' such harm. In either case it must be shown that the significant harm is attributable either to a lack of reasonable parental care or to the child's being beyond parental control. The local authority 'must prove that there is the necessary link between the facts upon which it relies and its case on 'threshold'; it must

---

[465]  Article 8 of Brussels IIA provides that 'The courts of a Member State shall have jurisdiction in matters of parental responsibility over a child who is habitually resident in that Member State at the time the court is seised'. Care proceedings are caught by this provision so that in every care case where there is a European dimension, there must be an inquiry at the outset as to where the child is habitually resident. See *Re N (Children)* [2016] UKSC 15.

[466]  [2013] UKSC 33.

[467]  *In re B (A Child)* [2013] UKSC 33 at para 199 (Lady Hale), at para 44 (Lord Wilson), and para 56 (Lord Neuberger). See also Ward LJ in *Re MA (Care: Threshold)* [2010] 1 FLR 431 at para 56, and Black LJ in the Court of Appeal in *In re B* [2012] EWCA Civ 1475 at para 9.

[468]  *In re B (A Child)* [2013] UKSC 33 at para 109 (Lord Kerr).

[469]  Ibid, para 56, per Lord Neuberger, citing Clarke LJ in *Assicurazioni Generali SpA v Arab Insurance Group* [2003] 1 WLR 577 at paras 16 and 17, which was cited with approval by the House of Lords in *Datec Electronics Holdings Ltd v United Parcels Service Ltd* [2007] 1 WLR 1325 at para 46.

[470]  [2013] UKSC 33 at para 44 (Lord Wilson), para 56 (Lord Neuberger), para 139 (Lord Clarke), and paras 110 and 113 (Lord Kerr).

[471]  [1993] 1 FLR 281.          [472]  Ibid, 289.

demonstrate why certain facts, if proved, justify the conclusion that the child has suffered or is at risk of suffering significant harm of the type asserted by the local authority.[473]

Each part of the test will now be analysed.

## 8.2 'Is suffering significant harm'

The words of the threshold test relating to the child suffering significant harm are expressed in the present tense. It must be shown that the child 'is suffering' significant harm.

Before a final application is made in care proceedings there is always some considerable lapse of time between the commencement of the case and the final hearing while enquiries are made on behalf of the child by the child's guardian. By the time of the final hearing, when full evidence is given to substantiate the allegation that the child is suffering, or is likely to suffer, significant harm, protective steps will already have been taken. Indeed the child may be positively thriving in his new environment and clearly not so suffering in a literal sense. Difficult questions about the proper interpretation of section 31(2) have consequently arisen in cases where a relative, or other person, is offering to care for the child, and where there is no evidence to suggest that the child would positively come to harm if cared for by that person. Such cases not only give rise to awkward questions about the proper meaning of the language of section 31(2), they also raise fundamental issues of social policy, and go to the root of child protection practices and procedures. Essentially they pose the question 'when is it right for the state to be allowed to impose its own view on what would be best for the child when this view is at variance with the sincerely held wishes of members of the child's family?'[474]

---

### Key case

*Re M (A Minor) (Care Order: Threshold Conditions)*[475] concerned a two-year-old child. His parents were married and he had three half-siblings. In October 1991, when M was four months old, his father murdered his mother[476] in a very brutal manner in the presence of all the children. The police immediately obtained a place of safety order in respect of all the children.[477] After a week the three half-siblings went to live with Mrs W, the mother's maternal cousin, and in August 1992 she obtained a residence order which gave her parental responsibility for them.[478] However Mrs W, who was a lady in her mid-fifties, felt unable to care for M because he was so young and because of the special needs of the older children. M was therefore accommodated by the local authority and placed with a short-term foster mother. In May 1992 the local

---

[473] *Re A (A Child)* [2015] EWFC 11, approved by the Court of Appeal in *Re J (A Child)* [2015] EWCA Civ 222.

[474] This is a dilemma to which social workers and other professionals are constantly exposed when discussing a child's future at a child protection case conference.

[475] [1994] 3 All ER 298.

[476] Guidance in such cases was provided in *Birmingham City Council v AB and Others* [2014] EWHC 3090 (Fam) at [71]: 'the local authority must commence a care application as a matter of urgency, the threshold criteria being plainly met . . . as the local authority needs at once to have parental responsibility as no one else will have it save for the murderer . . . Second, the case should immediately be transferred to the High Court . . . Third, the local authority must do what it can to promote bereavement counselling for the children. Fourth, the local authority must bear in mind the children will have inevitable therapeutic needs and an appropriate psychiatric report should be engaged to examine these. Fifth, if the local authority is to place or leave the bereaved children with a close family member the local authority must as a matter of course urgently properly assess the family member who may himself or herself be suffering from loss arising from the killing and who may have difficulties in their own life and need careful evaluation.' See also *Re A and B (One Parent Killed by the Other)* [2011] 1 FLR 783. The perpetrator's family should not necessarily be discounted as future carers of the child. The view in this case that the threshold will always be met where one parent has killed the other is probably too broadly expressed.

[477] Under the Children and Young Persons Act 1969, s 28, now repealed.

[478] Children Act 1989, ss 8 and 12(2), and see Chapter 9.

authority applied for a care order in respect of M. Members of the father's family and Mrs W separately applied for residence orders, but before the final hearing the paternal relatives had discontinued their application. The final hearing was not until February 1993. Mrs W, who had managed to care for the older children, now felt able to care for M. The local authority were of the opinion that Mrs W could now also care for M. They therefore supported her application and were no longer pursuing their application for a care order. However, M's guardian ad litem recommended that a care order be made with a view to M being adopted outside the family.[479] The question therefore arose whether the grounds for making a care order had been made out and, if they had, whether such an order should be made in light of the suggestion that the child should be adopted.[480]

Bracewell J found that the threshold conditions for making a care order had been established and that the child's interests would be best served by a care order being made with a view to his adoption. Mrs W appealed, supported by the local authority.[481] The Court of Appeal disapproved Bracewell J's interpretation of the wording of the statute, holding that the words 'is suffering or is likely to suffer' in the present tense were not fulfilled at the date of disposal (ie, at the final hearing); it also disagreed with her judgment for reasons of social policy. Balcombe LJ, who gave the judgment of the court, said that the facts of *Re M* were analogous with a case where a child's parents have both been killed in a motor accident, but where relatives offer to care for the child, and said that for it to be open to a court to say that the second threshold condition was satisfied on facts of this kind would amount to a form of 'social engineering'.[482]

The House of Lords reversed the decision of the Court of Appeal and restored the care order which had been made by Bracewell J.[483] The House condemned the Court of Appeal's apparent pre-occupation with whether the present tense drafting of the statute was satisfied at the date of the final hearing. Rather, Lord Mackay LC ruled that:

> Where, at the time the application is to be disposed of, there are in place arrangements for the protection of the child by the local authority on an interim basis which protection has been continuously in place for some time, the relevant date with respect to which the court must be satisfied is the date at which the local authority initiated the procedure for protection under the Act from which these arrangements followed. If after a local authority had initiated protective arrangements the need for these had terminated, because the child's welfare had been satisfactorily provided for otherwise, in any subsequent proceedings it would not be possible to found jurisdiction on the situation at the time of the initiation of these arrangements. It is permissible only to look back from the date of disposal to the date of initiation of protection as a result of which local authority arrangements had been continuously in place thereafter to the date of disposal.[484]

---

[479] The father, who had by now been sentenced to life imprisonment for murder, supported the guardian ad litem's recommendation.

[480] A difficult feature in analysing this case is that the local authority were not seeking a care order, and although the court could make a care order on the recommendation of the guardian ad litem, she could not impose her view on the local authority on what should happen to the child if the care order was made.

[481] One of the many curious features of this case is that once a care order is made it is up to the local authority, and not the court, to decide about the child's future upbringing. Therefore the local authority could have chosen to disregard the judge's opinion that the child should be placed for adoption and have placed the child in the care of Mrs W, thus obviating the necessity for an appeal. However, for reasons which are not explained, the local authority appears to have conceded its decision-making powers to the court, and to have treated Bracewell J's view that adoption would best promote the welfare of the child as a ruling which was binding upon it.

[482] [1994] 1 All ER 424 at 432.

[483] Somewhat curiously, the appeal to the House of Lords was pursued not by the child's guardian ad litem but by the father. It is suggested that it was wrong for anyone other than the child to have been allowed to pursue the appeal. It is suggested that the fact that the father took the same view of the child's interests as the guardian ad litem should have been treated as irrelevant. It was a classic situation where the court should have assumed that there might at some stage be a conflict of interest between parent and child.

[484] [1994] 3 All ER 298, 305.

Thus, where there has been a continuum of protective measures between the first initiation of proceedings and the final hearing, the fact that the child is being currently well cared for does not preclude the making of a care order. Lord Mackay endorsed the view that the point of time at which the court has to consider whether a continuing situation exists is at the moment in time immediately before the process of protection is first put into motion.[485]

It was accepted by most commentators that the House of Lords' ruling on this point was in accordance with the purpose of the legislation, and that it struck the correct balance between giving respect to the rights of families to make provision for children who are suffering, or at risk of suffering, significant harm, and allowing local authority and court involvement with such children.[486]

*Re L (Care: Threshold Criteria)*[487] illustrates how the temporal dimension of the threshold criteria, as explained in *Re M*, applies. Care proceedings were brought in respect of two children, aged 11 and 7, whose parents had learning disabilities. The family first came to the local authority's attention when the elder child was sexually assaulted by a man whom the father knew to be a sex offender and allowed to stay in the family home. The offender was imprisoned and, after working with the family on preventing such risks in the future, the local authority closed its file. Two years later the local authority became involved again because of concerns about domestic violence and an allegation that one of the children had been beaten with a belt. The case was remitted by the Court of Appeal for rehearing (ultimately by Hedley J). Both the Court of Appeal[488] and Hedley J[489] held that it would be impermissible to rely on the historic matter of the sexual assault to address the question in the present whether the children are suffering significant harm. However, it would be going too far to say that it could not figure in an assessment of whether the children were then likely to suffer significant harm. As Hedley J put it, the court 'cannot, as a matter of law, close its mind to matters that have happened in the past . . . What it can do is take account of the extent to which anybody else regarded those matters as potentially of significant harm in considering whether or not to take it into account itself.'[490] Here it was clear that the local authority had closed its case on the sexual offender issue and did not consider it of any future significance.

The House of Lords' interpretation of the relevant date for proving the threshold criteria raises the question of whether evidence which emerges between the relevant date and the date of the hearing can be used. In *Re G (Children) (Care Order: Evidence)*[491] the Court of Appeal clarified that information acquired after the relevant date as to the state of affairs at the relevant date can be taken into account. Hale LJ offered the following obvious examples: 'further medical evidence about the injuries which promoted removal, new complaints by the child about other forms of abuse within the home or admissions made by the parents'.[492] However, later events cannot be relied upon unless they are capable of showing what the position was at the relevant time. For example, the inability of the parents to care for the child as a result of a complete collapse or mental illness brought on by the stress of the proceedings could not be relied on in the existing proceedings.[493]

Once the jurisdiction point had been resolved in *Re M (A Minor) (Care Order: Threshold Conditions)*[494] the House of Lords had to consider whether to confirm the residence order to Mrs W, or restore the care order made by Bracewell J. By the time the appeal reached the House of Lords the child had been living for several months with Mrs W and, because he was thriving in her care,

---

[485] This approach applies to both limbs of s 31(2)(a) of the Children Act 1989 (ie, also to 'is likely to suffer significant harm'): see *Southwark London Borough Council v B* [1999] 1 FCR 550, FD (Charles J).

[486] M. Hayes (1995) 58 Modern Law Review 878; A. Bainham (1994) 53 Cambridge Law Journal 458; J. Whybrow (1994) 6 Journal of Child Law 177. For a contrary view, see J. Masson (1994) 6 Journal of Child Law 170.

[487] [2007] 1 FLR 2050 (Hedley J). The case had been remitted by the Court of Appeal for rehearing: see *Re L (Children) (Care Proceedings: Significant Harm)* [2006] EWCA Civ 1282, [2007] 1 FLR 1068.

[488] *Re L (Children) (Care Proceedings: Significant Harm)* [2006] EWCA Civ 1282, [2007] 1 FLR 1068 at [13] *per* Wilson LJ.

[489] [2007] 1 FLR 2050 at [34] and [35].      [490] Ibid, [35].

[491] [2001] EWCA Civ 968, [2001] 2 FCR 757.      [492] Ibid, [13] and [22].

[493] An example given by Hale LJ, ibid, [14].      [494] [1994] 3 All ER 298.

all parties were agreed that there was no question of the child being taken from her at that time and placed for adoption. Somewhat astonishingly, however, their Lordships restored the care order. Lord Mackay gave as his reason for so doing that there was a possibility in the longer term of difficulties and the care order would enable the local authority to monitor the progress of the child. Also, a care order would give them the power to determine the extent to which the father should be allowed to meet his parental responsibility for the child.[495] Lord Templeman said that a care order would have the advantage for Mrs W that it would enable her to turn to the local authority for advice and help if necessary. He also expressed the view that it would have the advantage for the child that the local authority would be able to monitor his progress and intervene with speed if anything went wrong.

It is regrettable that there was virtually no discussion in the House of Lords of the important and controversial social policy issues raised by the case. No attempt was made to deal with Balcombe LJ's telling analogy with a case where a child's parents have been killed in a motor accident. No comparison was made between the results which would be produced by the competing interpretations of section 31(2).[496] At no stage did their Lordships address the question of fundamental difficulty posed by Bracewell J's ruling, namely when is it a proper application of the welfare principle to make an order which will result in a child being adopted when a relative is offering to care for him. It is suggested that the ruling was unsatisfactory with respect to their Lordships' approach to the choice of orders available. The justification given by Lords Mackay and Templeman for making a care order was an untenable application of the welfare principle. The statement that a care order would enable Mrs W to turn to the local authority for help and advice was undoubtedly correct. But such help and advice would almost certainly have been forthcoming in any event and, even if it were not, surely its desirability cannot justify permitting the state to take over parental responsibility? In relation to the court's continuing concerns about the child, these could adequately have been alleviated by making a residence order to Mrs W, possibly with conditions attached, and coupling it with a supervision order. The supervisor would have been charged with the duty to advise, assist, and befriend the child,[497] which would inevitably have involved giving help and advice to the child's carer. Moreover it was Mrs W, not the local authority, who would have responsibility for making the day-to-day decisions about the child's upbringing, but the House of Lords was expecting her to carry out this function without the benefit of a residence order and without the parental responsibility which such an order confers. The statement that a care order would enable the local authority to determine the extent to which the father should meet his parental responsibility for the child does not bear close examination. He was serving a life sentence for murder and had been recommended for deportation on his release. Thus, he would have no part to play in the child's life in the foreseeable future, if at all. Also, the child's siblings similarly needed protection from the father exercising parental responsibility at some time in the future, but it would have been inconceivable that anyone could have successfully pleaded that this would justify making a care order in respect of them too. Any problems could clearly have been dealt with by orders under section 8.[498]

### 8.3 'Or is likely to suffer significant harm'

The inclusion of 'likely' significant harm within the threshold test allows for an order to be made where the court finds that the child is at risk of such harm even where no significant harm to the

---

[495] Under s 33(3)(b).

[496] Eg where significant harm is caused by one parent at a time when the other parent is absent from the home, and where the local authority take steps to protect the child during that parent's absence, on his return the absent parent would not be able to claim that the court has no jurisdiction to make a care order. The local authority would be able to overcome the threshold test and the absent parent would be in the same position as Mrs W.

[497] Section 35(1).

[498] For further commentary, see M. Hayes, 'Care by the Family or Care by the State?' (1995) 58 Modern Law Review 878.

child has yet occured. In *Re H (A Minor) (Section 37 Direction)*,[499] Scott Baker J ventured the opinion that when looking at the likelihood of significant harm, the court is not limited to looking at the present and the immediate future. He said 'if a court concludes that a parent, or a carer, is likely to be unable to meet the emotional needs of a child in the future—even if years hence—my view is that the condition in section 31(2) would probably be met'.[500]

## 8.4 Proving actual or likely significant harm

---

### Key case

The leading decision on what is required in order to prove the threshold criteria is *Re H and Others (Minors) Sexual Abuse: Standard of Proof)*.[501] Four girls aged 15, 13, 8, and 2 were living with their mother and Mr R, who was the father of the younger two children and stepfather of the older two. The eldest girl, D, alleged that Mr R had sexually abused her from the age of 7 or 8. Mr R was charged with having raped D, although acquitted on all counts. Relying on the different standard of proof in civil proceedings, the local authority nevertheless instituted care proceedings in respect of the three younger daughters on the ground that they were likely to suffer significant harm.[502] The local authority's case was based solely on the alleged sexual abuse of D. The trial judge concluded that he could not be sure 'to the requisite high standard of proof' that D's allegations were true. He therefore found that the threshold criteria were not made out in respect of the younger children. However, he added: 'This is far from saying that I am satisfied the child's complaints are untrue . . . If it were relevant, I would be prepared to hold that there is a real possibility that her statement and her evidence are true.' The local authority's appeal (ultimately to the House of Lords) against the judge's finding that the threshold was not crossed, was dismissed by a majority of 3 to 2. Lord Nicholls of Birkenhead gave the speech for the majority, with which Lords Goff and Mustill agreed; Lords Lloyd and Browne-Wilkinson dissented.

---

### 8.4.1 Meaning of 'likely'

Their Lordships were unanimous that 'likely' in the context of the threshold test did not mean more likely than not.[503] They ruled that for the purposes of section 31(2)(a) 'likely' is being used 'in the sense of a real possibility, a possibility that cannot sensibly be ignored having regard to the nature and gravity of the feared harm in the particular case'.[504] As Lord Nicholls of Birkenhead explained, if the word 'likely' were given the meaning 'more likely than not' it would have the effect of preventing courts from making care and supervision orders in cases in which it was as likely as not that the child would suffer significant harm, as well as in cases in which the court was satisfied that there was a real possibility of significant harm to the child in the future.[505]

---

[499] [1993] 2 FLR 541.

[500] He did not need to resolve the question because no application had been made for a care or supervision order. The case concerned an application by a lesbian couple for a residence order in respect of a baby girl. Scott Baker J ordered the local authority to undertake an investigation under s 37(1).

[501] [1996] AC 563. For further comment, see M. Hayes, 'Reconciling Protection for Children with Justice for Parents' (1997) 17 Legal Studies 1; I. Hemingway and C. Williams, '*Re M and R: Re H and R*' [1997] Family Law 740; C. Keenan, 'Finding that a Child is at Risk from Sexual Abuse: *Re H (Minors) (Sexual Abuse: Standard of Proof*' (1997) 60 Modern Law Review 857; H. Keating, 'Shifting Standards in the House of Lords—*Re H and Others (Minors) (Sexual Abuse: Standard of Proof)*' (1996) 8 Child and Family Law Quarterly 157.

[502] The eldest daughter was being accommodated by the local authority with the agreement of her parents.

[503] See Lord Browne-Wilkinson [1996] AC 563 at 572 and at 576 *per* Lord Lloyd of Berwick.

[504] [1996] AC 563 at 565 *per* Lord Nicholls, approving *Newham London Borough Council v AG* [1993] 1 FLR 281. Lord Nicholls said that by parity of reasoning the word likely also bore the same meaning in ss 43, 44, 46, and 31(2)(b) ('care given to the child or "likely" to be given him').

[505] For an example of a Recorder getting the test wrong, see *Re R (Care Order: Threshold Criteria)* [2009] EWCA Civ 942, [2010] 1 FLR 673.

In *Re B (A Child)*,[506] Lady Hale provided further guidance on the meaning of 'likely' within section 31.[507] She explained that the reason for the adoption of 'likely' in the sense of 'real possibility' is that 'some harm is so catastrophic that even a relatively small degree of likelihood should be sufficient to justify the state in intervening to protect the child before it happens', the corollary of which is 'the less serious the harm, the more likely it has to be'.[508] Lady Hale added that the Act 'does not set limits upon when the harm may be likely to occur and clearly the court is entitled to look to the medium and longer term as well as to the child's immediate future'.[509] She added that:

> where harm has not yet been suffered, the court must consider the degree of likelihood that it will be suffered in the future. This will entail considering the degree of likelihood that the parents' future behaviour will amount to a lack of reasonable parental care. It will also entail considering the relationship between the significance of the harm feared and the likelihood that it will occur. Simply to state that there is a 'risk' is not enough. The court has to be satisfied, by relevant and sufficient evidence, that the harm is likely.[510]

## 8.4.2 Evidence establishing significant harm or likely significant harm

There must be facts, proved to the court's satisfaction if disputed, on which the court can properly conclude that the child is suffering harm.[511] An alleged but non-proven fact is not a fact for this purpose. Similarly with the second limb: there must be facts from which the court can properly conclude there is a real possibility that the child will suffer harm in the future.[512] Lord Nicholls offered three reasons: the word 'satisfied' in section 31(2) is the 'language of proof, not suspicion';[513] otherwise, the effect would be to reverse the burden of proof; and it would be odd if unproven facts which could not show that the child is suffering harm could nonetheless be used to infer future harm. In an important passage, however, Lord Nicholls went on to place this conclusion in context 'by noting, and emphasising, the width of the range of facts which may be relevant when the court is considering the threshold conditions'. He said:

> The range of facts which may properly be taken into account is infinite. Facts include the history of members of the family, the state of relationships within a family, proposed changes within the membership of a family, parental attitudes, and omissions which might not reasonably have been expected, just as much as actual physical assaults. They include threats, and abnormal behaviour by a child, and unsatisfactory parental responses to complaints or allegations. And facts, which are minor or even trivial if considered in isolation, when taken together may suffice to satisfy the court of the likelihood of future harm. The court will attach to all the relevant facts the appropriate weight when coming to an overall conclusion on the crucial issue.[514]

Lord Nicholls also stressed that that it is 'open to a court to conclude there is a real possibility that the child will suffer harm in the future although harm in the past has not been established'. He observed that there will be cases where, although alleged maltreatment itself is not proved, the evidence establishes a combination of profoundly worrying features affecting the care of the child, on the basis of which facts it would be open to a court to find a likelihood of significant harm. He concluded, however, that in this case there was only one relevant fact in issue, namely whether Mr R had

---

[506] [2013] UKSC 33. See J. Doughty, 'Re B (A Child) (Care Order) (2013) UKSC 33' (2013) 35(4) Journal of Social Welfare and Family Law 491–501.

[507] [2013] UKSC 33 at paras 188 and 189 *per* Lady Hale, which had the apparent approval of Lord Neuberger at para 56 and Lord Wilson at para 26.

[508] Ibid, 188.     [509] Ibid,189.     [510] Ibid, 193, *per* Lady Hale, citing *In re J* [2013] 2 WLR 649.

[511] There may be a breach of Article 8 of the ECHR if, in the case of alleged physical abuse, there is no objective evidence. See eg *BB and FB v Germany* (App nos 18734/09 and 9424/11) [2013] 2 FLR 847 (German court relied solely on children's statements alleging abuse, later found to be untruthful).

[512] [1996] AC 563 at 590.     [513] Ibid.     [514] [1996] AC 563 at 591.

sexually abused D.[515] Lord Nicholls (for the majority) held, therefore, that once the trial judge had been unable to find on the balance of probabilities that D had been abused there was no evidence upon which he could infer that the younger girls were likely to suffer significant harm. The judge's suspicions or lingering doubts could not form a proper basis for concluding that likely significant harm had been established.

The dissenting Law Lords took a different view as to what was open to the judge. Lord Lloyd expressed the opinion that evidence which is insufficient to establish the truth of an allegation to a required standard of proof nevertheless remains evidence in the case. It need not be disregarded. The trial judge's conclusion that there was a real possibility that the evidence of D was true was a finding based on her evidence coupled with a number of other 'micro' facts which supported her account. It was not a mere suspicion that Mr R was an abuser, it was a finding of risk based on facts. Therefore, it was open to the judge to find that the younger daughters were likely to suffer significant harm.[516] Lord Browne-Wilkinson, agreeing with Lord Lloyd's reasoning, illustrated the point by way of a striking example:[517]

> Say that in 1940 those responsible for giving air-raid warnings had received five unconfirmed sightings of approaching aircraft which might be enemy bombers. They could not, on balance of probabilities, have reached a conclusion that any one of those sightings was of an enemy aircraft: nor could they logically have put together five non-proven sightings so as to be satisfied that enemy aircraft were in fact approaching. But their task was not simply to decide whether enemy aircraft were approaching but whether there was a risk of an air-raid. The facts relevant to the assessment of such risk were the reports that unconfirmed sightings had been made, not the truth of such reports. They could well, on the basis of those unconfirmed reports, have been satisfied that there was a real possibility of an air-raid and given warning accordingly.

Lord Browne-Wilkinson also identified a number of what he called micro facts which fell short of proving that D had been abused, but which were nevertheless established as facts and from which it might be inferred that there was a real possibility of harm to the younger children.[518]

There seems to be nothing in these dissenting opinions with which Lord Nicholls would disagree as a matter of general principle.[519] Where the majority and minority part company is in their respective views of the relevance of the so-called micro facts in the unusual circumstances of this case which had been fought solely on the basis that the eldest girl, D, had been sexually abused. While the minority would have held that the micro facts were still relevant, the majority took the view that those facts 'lead nowhere relevant in this case if they do not lead to the conclusion that [D] was abused'.[520]

In *Re B (Children) (Care Proceedings: Standard of Proof) (Cafcass Intervening)*[521] the House of Lords re-visited its decision in *Re H*. The facts were similar to *Re H* in that among the matters in

---

[515] Such cases will be relatively rare, but see *Re P (A Minor) (Care: Evidence)* [1994] 2 FLR 751 and *Re P (Sexual Abuse: Standard of Proof)* [1996] 2 FLR 333. For an example of where a local authority failed to prove that the children had been sexually abused but where there was substantial other evidence of significant harm to the children, see *Re G and R (Child Sexual Abuse: Standard of Proof)* [1995] 2 FLR 867.

[516] For further analysis of difficulties of proof in child protection cases, see M. Hayes, 'Reconciling Protection of Children With Justice for Parents' [1997] 17 Legal Studies 1.

[517] [1996] AC 563 at 572–3.

[518] Eg that D had been consistent in her story from the time of her first complaint; that her statement was full and detailed; that there were opportunities for such abuse by Mr R and that he had been lying in denying that he had ever been alone either with D or with any of the other children; that one of the younger children had made statements which indicated that she had witnessed 'inappropriate' behaviour between Mr R and D; that the mother suspected that something had been going on between Mr R and D.

[519] Assuming that the evidence to which Lord Lloyd refers and the sightings (as opposed to what exactly was being sighted) in Lord Browne-Wilkinson's example are facts established on the balance of probabilities.

[520] [1996] AC 563 at 592.

[521] [2008] UKHL 35, [2009] AC 11. For commentary, see J. Hayes, 'Farewell to the Cogent Evidence Test: *Re B*' [2008] Family Law 859; H. Keating, 'Suspicions, Sitting on the Fence and Standards of Proof' [2009] Child and Family Law Quarterly 230.

dispute was whether Mr B, the father of a nine-year-old girl and a six-year-old boy, had sexually abused their 16-year-old stepsister, R. Charles J was unable to decide whether the sexual abuse had occurred and reasoned as follows: 'I am unable to conclude that there is no real possibility that Mr B sexually abused R as she asserts or substantially as she asserts and I have therefore concluded that there is a real possibility that he did.'[522] The House of Lords pointed out that the law operates a binary system in which facts in issue are either proved or not[523] and that it was not open to a judge to sit on the fence as Charles J had done. However, Charles J's reasoning squarely raised once again the principle of whether a likelihood of significant harm could be inferred from a real possibility that facts existed (in other words from suspicions). The children's guardian[524] invited the House to depart from its reasoning in *Re H* and to uphold Charles J's conclusion. The House unhesitatingly declined that invitation, stating that Lord Nicholls's reasons 'remain thoroughly convincing'.[525] Baroness Hale explained that:

---

### Talking point

The threshold is there to protect both the children and their parents from unjustified intervention in their lives. It would provide no protection at all if it could be established on the basis of unsubstantiated suspicions: that is, where a judge cannot say that there is no real possibility that abuse took place, so concludes that there is a real possibility that it did. In other words, the alleged perpetrator would have to prove that it did not.

**Q.** Should the same reasoning apply in a case in which a child has been harmed by one of two possible perpetrators but it is not clear which? (Discussed below at 8.6.1.2).

---

The House pointed out that it is difficult to see how reasons for interference with a child's right to respect for family life could be 'relevant and sufficient' as required by the European Court of Human Rights[526] if unproven allegations are the only basis for inferring that the child is at risk of harm.

### 8.4.3 The use of expert evidence

In many cases the judge will be assisted by medical or other expert evidence in deciding whether the threshold criteria are fulfilled.[527] It is common, for example, in cases in which it is alleged that a parent is abusing drugs, for hair strand testing to be carried out to assess drug use.[528] In rule 25.1 of the Family Procedure Rules the test which the court must apply when deciding whether to permit instruction of expert opinion is whether it is 'necessary to assist the court to resolve the proceedings' and the meaning of 'necessary' lies somewhere between 'indispensable' and 'useful',[529]

---

[522] Cited at [2008] UKHL 35, [2009] AC 11 at [30].

[523] See [2008] UKHL 35, [2009] AC 11 at [20] *per* Lord Hoffmann and at [31] and [32] *per* Baroness Hale of Richmond.

[524] With the support of the local authority and the child's mother.

[525] [2008] UKHL 35, [2009] AC 11 at [54].

[526] Citing for example *K and T v Finland* (2000) 31 EHRR 484; *Scozzari and Giunta v Italy* (2000) 35 EHRR 243; and *Kutzner v Germany* (2002) 35 EHRR 653.

[527] It is possible for the expert evidence to be provided by a clinician who is treating, or has treated, the child provided the therapeutic relationship is not wholly incompatible with an issue before the court: see *O-M, GM (and KM) v The Local Authority, LO and EM* [2009] EWCA Civ 1405, [2010] 2 FLR 58. Eg a clinician who is treating a child for sexual abuse on the basis that the abuse happened, would not be capable of giving expert opinion on whether it did occur.

[528] For a case in which the court declined to give general guidance, see *Bristol City Council v A and A and Others* [2012] EWHC 2548 (Fam), [2013] 2 FLR 1153 (Baker J).

[529] For a case in which expert evidence was crucial in highlighting a possible medical cause for alleged injury based on the possibility that the children were suffering from Ehlers-Danlos syndrome, see *Devon County Council v EB and Others* [2013] EWHC 968 (Fam). Even when such expert opinion is accepted, the judge will still need to consider

'reasonable' or 'desirable'.[530] Section 13 of the Children and Families Act 2014 effectively puts this test on a statutory footing, and introduces tight controls on expert evidence, by providing that experts may only be instructed and expert evidence used with the permission of the court. This is part of a strategy to address unnecessary delays in proceedings.

In *Re U (Serious Injury: Standard of Proof); Re B*[531] the Court of Appeal made clear that a local authority should not refrain from proceedings or discontinue proceedings simply because there is substantial disagreement between experts. That is because in care proceedings the judge 'invariably surveys a wide canvas, including detailed history of the parents' lives, their relationship and their interaction with professionals. There will be many contributions to this context, family members, neighbours, health records, as well as observation of professionals such as social workers, health visitors and children's guardian.' A case must be decided on the totality of the evidence and each piece of information needs 'to be weighed and assessed in the context of all the other pieces of information'.[532] However, where there is undisputed expert opinion evidence, 'the judge ought not to reject it without sound and articulated reason'.[533] Similarly, if a judge prefers the evidence of one expert over another, he or she must have a sound basis, and provide a reasoned explanation, for doing so.[534]

Cases in which there is a series of unexplained episodes of harm to a child which are not capable of medical explanation, or where there is disagreement between medical experts as to the possible causes, can be particularly difficult for the courts. Some such cases have been the subject of criminal prosecutions of parents. For example, in *R v Cannings*,[535] three of the defendant's four children died in early infancy and she was convicted of the murder of two of them. The conviction was quashed because there was no evidence other than the children's breathing having stopped and a serious disagreement among experts as to the cause. Fresh evidence of hereditary factors indicating a possible genetic cause was admitted. The court concluded that a natural cause could not be excluded as a reasonably possible explanation. The court took the opportunity to give guidance on inferences to be drawn from the evidence in such cases. In *Re U (Serious Injury: Standard of Proof); Re B*[536] the Court of Appeal held that the following considerations emphasised in *R v Cannings* are of direct application in care proceedings.[537]

(i) The cause of an injury or an episode that cannot be explained scientifically remains equivocal.[538]

(ii) Recurrence is not in itself probative.

(iii) Particular caution is necessary in any case where the medical experts disagree, one opinion declining to exclude a reasonable possibility of natural cause.

---

whether that finding is material on the facts. In *A Local Authority and NB* [2013] EWHC 4100 (Fam) Parker J dismissed the relevance of a finding of Ehlers-Danlos syndrome as it could not affect a central feature of the case, namely hypoxic ischemic injury.

[530] *Re H-L (Expert Evidence: Test for Permission)* [2013] EWCA Civ 655, [2013] 2 FLR 1434, [2013] 2 FLR 1434; and also *Re TG (Care Proceedings: Case Management: Expert Evidence)* [2013] EWCA Civ 5, [2013] 1 FLR 1250.

[531] [2004] EWCA Civ 567, [2004] 2 FLR 263.

[532] *Leeds City Council v YX and ZX (Assessment of Sexual Abuse)* [2008] EWHC 802 (Fam) at [106] *per* Holman J (medical evidence apparently diagnostic of sexual abuse had to be assessed in context of child's express denial that abuse occurred: care order application dismissed). See also *Lancashire County Council v D and E* [2008] EWHC 832 (Fam) (Charles J) (a judge is entitled to reject a plausible account, even where backed by medical documentation, and such an approach does not result in a reversal of the burden of proof): see *Re M (Fact-Finding Hearing: Burden of Proof)* [2008] EWCA Civ 1261, [2009] 1 FLR 1177 (mother's well-documented unstable knees rejected as reason for fall and consequent injury to baby).

[533] *Re D (Care Order: Evidence)* [2010] EWCA Civ 1000, [2011] 1 FLR 447 at [24].

[534] See *Re M-W (Care Proceedings: Expert Evidence)* [2010] EWCA Civ 12, [2010] 2 FLR 46 at [39] and [43].

[535] [2004] EWCA Crim 1, [2004] 1 All ER 725 (judge entitled to prefer factual evidence of witnesses over expert's psychological profile.)

[536] [2004] EWCA Civ 567, [2004] 2 FLR 263.          [537] Ibid, [23].

[538] And see *Re M (Fact-Finding Hearing: Injuries to Skull)* [2012] EWCA Civ 1710, [2013] 2 FLR 322 (parents are not to be found to be responsible for a child's injuries where the injuries are inexplicable by reference to expert medical evidence unless a reasoned justification is provided by the judge).

(iv) The court must always be on guard against the over-dogmatic expert, the expert whose reputation or *amour propre* is at stake, or the expert who has developed a scientific prejudice.

(v) The judge in care proceedings must never forget that today's medical certainty may be discarded by the next generation of experts or that scientific research will throw light into corners that are at present dark.[539]

The application of some of these principles is neatly illustrated by one of the cases heard in *Re U (Serious Injury: Standard of Proof); Re B.*[540] In *Re B* the mother of a disabled child was a paediatric nurse. The child was being treated on the hospital wards where the mother worked. The child suffered 11 episodes of potentially life-threatening rigor in six days, at times when the mother was nearby. All six experts agreed that infection was the most likely cause of the child's rigors, but only two opined that deliberate introduction of infection via a cannula attached to the child was the most likely cause. The latter view rested partly on the foundation that science had no other explanation. Bracewell J[541] concluded that the threshold criteria were made out having regard to the frequency and severity of the rigors without medical explanation, together with other circumstantial evidence.[542] The mother had a history of self-harm and depression and had admitted feeling panicky and physically ill in the presence of the child. She was present at the relevant times and had the relevant knowledge to interfere with the cannula. The Court of Appeal held that the judge's conclusions from the expert evidence and her treatment of the frequency of rigors as in some way probative were wrong, although ultimately Bracewell J's decision was upheld as the Court of Appeal concluded that the circumstantial evidence alone entitled her to so find.

As *Re B* illustrates, a parent's personality may be an important factor in the judge's assessment. However, the Court of Appeal has cautioned against undue reliance on personality (or psychometric) testing in assessing the credibility of a party or witness, and has stated that such testing does not ordinarily have any place in care cases. It is the task of the judge, not the expert, to assess credibility.[543]

In *Hertfordshire County Council v H*[544] a young mother had mental health problems and had attempted suicide. Her baby underwent two life-threatening events, although three experts could not say that the episodes had been caused by trauma. Parker J granted the local authority's application for permission to withdraw the proceedings, concluding that the mother's mental health difficulties could not 'prove what is otherwise unprovable'[545] and that withdrawal was in the child's interests.[546]

Where a non-accidental injury to a child has been proved and there is more than one child in the same household it will be highly unusual for that finding of harm not to justify the inference that protection of the other child(ren) is required. If the court is not to find the threshold met in respect of an uninjured child, the judge must give a full and reasoned explanation of why that

---

[539] Ibid. See also comments of Ryder J in *Lancashire County Council v R* [2008] EWHC 2959 (Fam), [2010] 1 FLR 387 at [52]–[55].

[540] [2004] EWCA Civ 567, [2004] 2 FLR 263.

[541] [2002] EWHC 20 (Fam), [2004] 2 FLR 200.

[542] See also *Re B (Non-Accidental Injury)* [2002] EWCA Civ 752, [2002] 2 FLR 1133 at [25] (a judge would fail in his primary protective function if he acceded to a submission that just because a doctor could not give a confident diagnosis, therefore there was no risk of harm).

[543] *Re S (Care: Parenting Skills: Personality Tests)* [2004] EWCA Civ 1029, [2005] 2 FLR 658 at [57] *per* Ward LJ, at [66] *per* Arden LJ, and at [71] *per* Scott Baker LJ. See also the concerns expressed in *Re L (Children) (Care Proceedings: Significant Harm)* [2006] EWCA Civ 1282, [2007] 1 FLR 1068.

[544] [2013] EWHC 4049 (Fam).    [545] Ibid, at [15].

[546] Applying *London Borough of Southwark v B* [1993] 2 FLR 559, CA; and compare *S (a Child) v Nottingham City Council and Others* [2013] EWCA Civ, where the local authority was not permitted to withdraw, there remaining a welfare question of how the child was to be protected from the risk of further non-accidental injury.

view has been reached. The Court of Appeal so held in *Re K (Care: Threshold Criteria)*[547] where the judge had found that one or other of the parents of two children aged six and one had suffocated the one-year-old, yet the judge had not found the threshold fulfilled in respect of the six-year-old. The Court of Appeal held that it was inadequate for the judge simply to say that the discrete episode of violence to the baby could be compartmentalised as not affecting the older child.[548]

## 8.5 **The burden and standard of proof in care proceedings**

In addition to examining the legal issues already mentioned, the House of Lords in *Re H and Others (Minors) (Sexual Abuse: Standard of Proof)*,[549] took the opportunity to explain the burden and standard of proof in care proceedings. Lord Nicholls of Birkenhead explained that the burden of establishing the threshold criteria lies on the applicant. The criteria 'must be affirmatively established to the satisfaction of the court'.[550] All their Lordships agreed that the standard of proof which applies to the threshold test is the ordinary civil standard of balance of probability.[551] As Lord Nicholls explained, the balance of probability standard means that 'a court is satisfied an event occurred if the court considers that, on the evidence, the occurrence of the event was more likely than not'. However, their Lordships differed on whether any further gloss should be placed on this test. The majority took the view that a generous degree of flexibility is built into the preponderance of probability standard and sought to explain this. Lord Nicholls therefore added that when assessing the probabilities 'the court will have in mind as a factor, to whatever extent is appropriate in the particular case, that the more serious the allegation the less likely it is that the event occurred and, hence, the stronger should be the evidence before the court concludes that the allegation is established on the balance of probability'.[552] He emphasised that this does not mean that the standard of proof is higher than the balance of probabilities;[553] rather 'it means only that the inherent probability or improbability of an event is itself a matter to be taken into account when weighing the probabilities and deciding whether, on balance, the event occurred. The more improbable the event, the stronger must be the evidence that it did occur before, on the balance of probability, its occurrence will be established'.[554] His Lordship said that this had been expressed neatly by Ungoed-Thomas J in *Re Dellow's Will Trusts*[555] in the following words: 'The more serious the allegation the more cogent is the evidence required to overcome the unlikelihood of what is alleged and thus to prove it'.[556] Lord Nicholls added that this approach provided a method of dealing with the instinctive feeling that even in civil proceedings a court should be more sure before finding serious allegations proved than when deciding less serious or trivial matters.

Lord Lloyd, in his dissenting speech, expressed the opinion that the standard of proof under section 31(2)[557] ought to be the simple balance of probability however serious the allegations involved. In reaching this conclusion, his Lordship was influenced by the fact that section 31(2)

---

[547] [2005] EWCA Civ 1226, [2006] 2 FLR 868.     [548] Ibid, [40] and [42].

[549] [1996] AC 563. For further comment, see M. Hayes, 'Reconciling Protection for Children with Justice for Parents' (1997) 17 Legal Studies 1; I. Hemingway and C. Williams, '*Re M and R: Re H and R*' [1997] Family Law 740; C. Keenan, 'Finding that a Child is at Risk from Sexual Abuse: *Re H (Minors) (Sexual Abuse: Standard of Proof)*' (1997) 60 Modern Law Review 857; H. Keating, 'Shifting Standards in the House of Lords—*Re H and Others (Minors) (Sexual Abuse: Standard of Proof)*' [1996] Child and Family Law Quarterly 157.

[550] [1996] AC 563 at 586.     [551] Ibid, 586 and 587.     [552] Ibid, 586.

[553] Indeed, he expressly rejected a so-called third standard of proof, somewhere between the criminal standard and simple balance of probabilities: see [1996] AC 563 at 587.

[554] Ibid, 586.     [555] [1964] 1 WLR 451 at 455.

[556] Adding that this substantially accords with the approach adopted by Morris LJ in *Hornal v Neuberger Products Ltd* [1957] 1 QB 247 at 266. On this test, see J. R. Spencer, 'Evidence in Child Abuse Cases: Too High a Price for Too High a Standard?' (1994) 6 Journal of Child Law 160.

[557] His Lordship confined his comments to s 31(2). In the absence of argument he was not prepared to endorse the wider view, expressed by Millett LJ in the Court of Appeal, that the standard in all civil cases should be the simple balance of probabilities.

merely represents a threshold and by no means dictates that a care order will be made. However, Lord Lloyd was concerned that unless the threshold criteria are met the local authority can do nothing to protect the child however grave the anticipated injury to the child, or however serious the apprehended consequences, adding:

> This seems to me to be a strong argument in favour of making the threshold test lower rather than higher. It would be a bizarre result if the more serious the anticipated injury, whether physical or sexual, the more difficult it became for the local authority to satisfy the initial burden of proof, and thereby ultimately, if the welfare test is satisfied, secure protection for the child.[558]

Furthermore, Lord Lloyd did not find helpful the majority's gloss about the cogency of the evidence needed to tip the balance of probabilities, and was concerned that 'there is a danger that the repeated use of the words will harden into a formula, which, like other formulas (especially those based on a metaphor) may lead to misunderstanding'.[559]

Baroness Hale of Richmond later observed in *Re B (Children) (Care Proceedings: Standard of Proof) (Cafcass Intervening)*[560] that 'Lord Lloyd's prediction proved only too correct'.[561] Despite the care with which Lord Nicholls sought to explain that the standard of proof is the balance of probabilities, his 'nuanced explanation left room for the nostrum, "the more serious the allegation, the more cogent the evidence needed to prove it", to take hold'. In addition, more confusion was created when in *R (McCann) v Crown Court at Manchester*[562] Lord Steyn cited Lord Nicholls's approach in *Re H (Minors) (Sexual Abuse: Standard of Proof)*[563] in support of there being in some cases a 'heightened civil standard' of proof.[564]

In *Re B (Children) (Care Proceedings: Standard of Proof) (Cafcass Intervening)*,[565] therefore, the House of Lords agreed that, in light of the difficulties that misinterpretation of Lord Nicholls's gloss had seemingly caused, it was time to 'loosen its grip and give it its quietus'.[566] Indeed, the House went further and announced 'loud and clear' that the standard of proof in care proceedings 'is the simple balance of probabilities, neither more nor less'.[567] Baroness Hale explained that the consequences of care proceedings are serious either way and:

> Neither the seriousness of the allegation nor the seriousness of the consequences should make any difference to the standard of proof to be applied in determining the facts. The inherent probabilities are simply something to be taken into account, where relevant, in deciding where the truth lies.[568]

As to the seriousness of any allegation, her Ladyship pointed out that:

> there is no logical or necessary connection between seriousness and probability. Some seriously harmful behaviour, such as murder, is sufficiently rare to be inherently improbable in most circumstances. Even then there are circumstances, such as a body with its throat cut and no weapon to

---

[558] [1996] AC 563 at 577.     [559] Ibid, 578.

[560] [2008] UKHL 35, [2009] AC 11.     [561] Ibid, [64].     [562] [2003] 1 AC 787.

[563] [1996] AC 563 at 586D–H.

[564] *R (McCann) v Crown Court at Manchester* [2003] 1 AC 787 at [37]. As Baroness Hale observed in *Re B*, Lord Nicholls's suggestion that the court should be 'more sure' in relation to serious allegations could be read as suggesting a higher standard than the simple preponderance of probabilities (see [2008] UKHL 35, [2009] AC 11 at [62]). See also the ambiguity in Lord Bingham of Cornhill's opinion in *B v Chief Constable of the Avon and Somerset Constabulary* [2001] 1 WLR 340. The dicta in *McCann* and *B v Chief Constable* were applied in care proceedings by Bodey J in *Re ET (Serious Injuries: Standard of Proof) (Note)* [2003] 2 FLR 1205, until the Court of Appeal corrected the position in *Re U (A Child) (Department for Education and Skills intervening)* [2005] Fam 134 at [13]. The developments in the case law on standard of proof are explored by Lord Hoffmann at [2008] UKHL 35, [2009] AC 11 at [5]–[12].

[565] [2008] UKHL 35, [2009] AC 11.     [566] Ibid, [64].     [567] Ibid, [70].

[568] Ibid. Lord Hoffmann stated that having regard to the inherent probabilities was a matter required by common sense not law (see at [15]).

hand, where it is not at all improbable. Other seriously harmful behaviour, such as alcohol or drug abuse, is regrettably all too common and not at all improbable.[569]

Baroness Hale also emphasised that the context in which allegations are made is important, commenting:

> Nor are serious allegations made in a vacuum. Consider the famous example of the animal seen in Regent's Park. If it is seen outside the zoo on a stretch of greensward regularly used for walking dogs, then of course it is more likely to be a dog than a lion. If it is seen in the zoo next to the lions' enclosure when the door is open, then it may well be more likely to be a lion than a dog.[570]

What do these dicta mean when translated to the child abuse context of the cases? The fact that an allegation of child abuse is a serious allegation does not affect the standard of proof. It is necessary in all cases simply to show that the allegation is more probably true than not. As to the inherent probabilities, the fact that, looking to the general population, it is unlikely that a stepfather is sexually abusing his stepdaughter is simply something to be taken into account, where relevant, in deciding where the truth lies. The difficulty may be in knowing when the inherent (general) probabilities are to be regarded as relevant or, even if relevant, how they are to be taken into account. For example, to what extent, if at all, is the general improbability of a stepfather having sexually abused his stepdaughter to be regarded as relevant in a particular case? There is an argument that once an allegation of sexual abuse has been made the relevant sample has shifted from the general population to stepdaughters who have made an allegation of serious abuse against a stepfather. While the position in the general population has a bearing on the likelihood (in general) of a parent being wrongly accused, once an allegation is made, arguably the more pertinent probability relates to the likelihood of a child making a false allegation.[571] It is submitted that the courts will need to think carefully in individual cases about the relevance of general inherent probabilities. In some cases, the issue of relevance will be more clear-cut than in others: for example, if there is evidence that a baby has suffered a non-accidental injury in unknown circumstances, the fact that such non-accidental injuries are relatively rare in the general population is clearly neither here nor there.

## 8.6 Harm attributable to care not being what it would be reasonable to expect a parent to give

### Key legislation

The second limb of section 31(2), in (b), requires proof that:

> . . . the harm, or likelihood of harm, is attributable to—
>
> (i) the care given to the child, or likely to be given to him if the order were not made, not being what it would be reasonable to expect a parent to give to him.

The phrase 'attributable to' connotes a causal connection between the harm or likelihood of harm and the care given or likely to be given, but the connection 'need not be that of a sole or dominant or direct cause and effect: a contributory causal connection suffices'.[572] So, for example, if a parent

---

[569] Ibid, [72].     [570] Ibid.

[571] H. Keating, 'Shifting Standards in the House of Lords—*Re H and Others (Minors) (Sexual Abuse: Standard of Proof)*' [1996] Child and Family Law Quarterly 157.

[572] *Lancashire County Council v B* [2002] 2 AC 147 at 162, echoing Donaldson J in *Walsh v Rother District Council* [1978] ICR 1216 at 1220.

entrusts a child to the care of another without checking that person's suitability and the third party injures the child, the harm may be regarded as attributable to the inadequate care of the parent as well as to the actions of the third party.[573] By contrast, section 31(2)(b) would not be fulfilled where a child is harmed in the circumstances of a 'one-off temporary entrustment of the child to a person reasonably believed by the parents to be suitable'.[574] However, if the parent is unsuitable to care for the child, the threshold may be fulfilled even though the parent has entrusted the child's care to others who are looking after the child appropriately. In *H v Trafford Borough Council*[575] the mother, who engaged in prostitution and was addicted to drugs, asked neighbours to babysit for her baby and then disappeared for six weeks. Although the mother reappeared briefly, she disappeared again and the following year she indicated that she did not now wish to resume care of her child. The local authority decided to commence care proceedings even though the child was being properly looked after by the neighbours. Wall J held that there should not be a narrow construction of section 31 which would prevent intervention to protect such a child. The magistrates were entitled to find that the child would be likely to suffer significant harm as the mother could have reclaimed the child at any time, thus exposing the child to the dangers of her lifestyle.

It has been said that where a child has suffered injuries, it is not open to a local authority simply to use the fact of those injuries as a basis for submitting that the threshold criteria are reached and that the parents are responsible. In *CL v East Riding Yorkshire Council, MB and BL (A Child)*[576] a father tripped and fell while carrying a seven-week-old baby and the baby struck his head on the floor suffering a skull fracture and brain injury. The judge found the threshold fulfilled on the basis that the child had suffered this serious injury while in the care of the parents.[577] The Court of Appeal held that the judge had been wrong to do so. The court commented that 'a child may receive serious accidental injuries whilst in the care of his or her parents, even where those parents are both conscientious and competent' and such injuries do not fall within section 31(2) of the Children Act 1989. The court held that that provision, 'translated into everyday language and experience' means that a local authority 'must prove that an injury is non-accidental'.[578] The occurrence of the injuries, by itself, was not sufficient to satisfy the threshold. This decision suggests that a child might not be protected from a very accident-prone or careless parent.[579] Yet, it may legitimately be asked whether a child who has suffered significant harm attributable to several accidental injuries at the hands of his or her parents is receiving care which it would be reasonable to expect a parent to give.[580]

### 8.6.1 Care must fall below an objectively acceptable level

The care given or likely to be given 'must fall below an objectively acceptable level'.[581] The focus is not on the care it would be reasonable to expect the actual child's parent or carer to give, but on what it would be reasonable to expect 'a parent' to give to the child. Furthermore, 'an absence of a

---

[573] The example was given by Lord Nicholls of Birkenhead in *Lancashire County Council v B* [2002] 2 AC 147 at 162.

[574] Ibid, 165.     [575] [1997] 3 FCR 113.     [576] [2006] EWCA Civ 49, [2006] 2 FLR 24.

[577] A further feature of the case was that the parents did not immediately summon an ambulance, and the judge found that the parents had failed to protect the child after the injury. This was not criticised on appeal. On failure to protect, see also *Re W (Care: Threshold Criteria)* [2007] EWCA Civ 102, [2007] 2 FLR 98 (mother could not be said to have failed to protect her child where there was no finding that the child's father, a sex offender, had sexually abused the child. A risk of future harm could also not be established on the basis of her former relationship with the father, as there was no evidence that she was likely to forge another relationship with a child abuser).

[578] [2006] EWCA Civ 49 at [52]. See also *Re J (Care Proceedings: Injuries)* [2009] 2 FLR 99, FD (Hogg J).

[579] For an example of a case in which an injury caused by the father's carelessness did not suffice to fulfil the threshold, see *Sutton v Gray and Others No 1* [2012] EWHC 2604 (Fam), [2013] 1 FLR 833 (Hogg J) (burn to seven-week-old baby placed too close to electric radiator).

[580] Cf the similar approach of HHJ Bryant at first instance in *Re B (Fact-Finding Hearing: Evidence)* [2008] EWCA Civ 1547, [2009] 2 FLR 14, described by the Court of Appeal (at [6]) as 'singular to himself'. HHJ Bryant declined to approach the issue on what the Court of Appeal said was 'a commonplace basis: were these injuries accidental or non-accidental?'

[581] *Lancashire County Council v B* [2002] 2 AC 147 at 162.

reasonable standard of parental care need not imply that the parents are at fault'.[582] As Hughes LJ observed in *Re D (Care Order: Evidence)*[583] if it were otherwise, 'the protection afforded to children would be very limited indeed, if not entirely illusory. It would in effect then be limited to protection against the parent who was fully able to provide proper care but either chose not to do so or neglected through fault to do so. That is not the meaning of s 31(2). It is abundantly clear that a parent may unhappily fail to provide reasonable care even though he is doing his incompetent best.'[584] If the threshold did not adopt an objective test, it would mean that a child could not be protected from persons with serious physical incapacities, serious or unpredictable mental illness, or (severe) learning disabilities.[585]

### 8.6.1.1 Parents with learning disabilities

The Court of Appeal has made clear that, in cases involving parents with learning disabilities, a care order is never made simply on the basis of the parent's learning disability.[586] To do so would be impermissible social engineering.[587] Equally, however, the court has observed that there is no issue of discrimination in this context in judging a learning disabled parent by the standards expected of a non-disabled parent.[588]

Although the objective nature of the test is easily stated and defended, cases involving learning disabled parents raise difficult questions in practice concerning the human rights of such individuals[589] and the extent to which they should be supported in parenting tasks,[590] and in proceedings before the court.[591] In *Kutzner v Germany*[592] the German authorities removed parental responsibility from the learning disabled parents of two children. The European Court of Human Rights found in the circumstances a breach of parents' rights to respect for family life as guaranteed by Article 8 of the ECHR. The Court commented that it was 'questionable whether the domestic administrative and judicial authorities [had] given sufficient consideration to additional measures of support as an alternative to what is by far the most extreme measure, namely separating the children from their parents'.[593] Clearly this raises an issue for any court about whether a care order is a proportionate response in the context of available support which could be provided to the child's parent(s). But it also potentially raises an issue with respect to the threshold criteria. Is the question whether the significant harm is attributable to 'the care given to the child not being what it would be reasonable to expect a parent to give' to be viewed in light of the provision of available support to a parent? Hedley J thought so in *LBH (A Local Authority) v KJ and IH*[594] in the slightly different context of a parent's care of a severely disabled child. His Lordship commented that parents do not expose themselves to compulsory state intervention in family life simply on the

---

[582] Ibid.  [583] [2010] EWCA Civ 1000, [2011] 1 FLR 447.

[584] Ibid, [35], and see also *Lancashire County Council v B* [2002] 2 AC 147 at 162; and for an example, see *Re G and A (Care Order: Freeing Order: Parents with a Learning Disability)* [2006] NI Fam 8 (parents' lack of insight would require 24-hour support which was impractical).

[585] See A. Bond, *Care Proceedings and Learning Disabled Parents: A Handbook for Family Lawyers* (Bristol: Jordan Publishing, 2011) for definitions, a useful overview of research evidence on parents with learning disabilities, and discussion of the relevant law, policy, and guidance.

[586] *Re L (Children) (Care Proceedings: Significant Harm)* [2006] EWCA Civ 1282, [2007] 1 FLR 1068 at [52].

[587] Ibid, [49].

[588] *Re D (A Child) (Care Order: Evidence)* [2010] EWCA Civ 1000, [2011] 1 FLR 447. Note, however, Munby J's suggestion in *Re G (Care: Challenge To Local Authority's Decision)* [2003] EWHC 551 (Fam), [2003] 2 FLR 42 at [59] that a local authority may have to work harder to fulfil its duty to ensure such parents understand the local authority's concerns.

[589] See eg United Nations Convention on the Rights of Persons with Disabilities, particularly in this context Art 23(2).

[590] See Department of Health and Department for Education and Skills, *Good Practice Guidance on Working with Parents with a Learning Disability* (London: TSO, 2007).

[591] On which, see *RP and Others v UK* (App no 38245/08), [2013] 1 FLR 744 (representation of disabled parent in care proceedings by the Official Solicitor was not a breach of Article 6 of the ECHR).

[592] (App no 46544/99) [2003] 1 FCR 249.  [593] Ibid, [75].

[594] [2007] EWHC 2798 (sitting in the Barnet County Court).

ground that the child's needs are beyond their capacities however assiduously they devote themselves to the care of the child (except where a child is beyond parental control).[595] He was also of the view that neither can it:

> be the case that a local authority can fail to put in the support properly required to enable a child to be cared for at home (absent expert evidence that a child could never be cared for at home because of disability whatever reasonable support was provided) and then use that failure as grounds for compulsory intervention under Part IV of the Act . . . each would involve a violation of Article 8(1) (as all such interventions on the face of it necessarily must) and that such violation in those circumstances would not be justifiable under Article 8(2).[596]

He added:

> a parent cannot be said to be responsible for a falling below the standard of 'reasonable care' if the public authorities cannot or do not provide what would be reasonably necessary to support that parent.

It has been suggested that the same reasoning could be applied to the support which might reasonably be provided to enable a learning disabled parent to parent his or her child appropriately.[597] However, the analogy with *LBH (A Local Authority) v KJ and IH*[598] is an uneasy one. Hedley J's concern in *LBH* is that parenting should not be found wanting in circumstances where 'a parent' (ie, parents generally) would not cope without support. By contrast, if the same approach is extended to learning disabled parents the emphasis is not on what could be expected of a 'a parent' generally; instead the focus is on what could reasonably be expected of the particular learning disabled parent with available support.

Nevertheless, in *Kent County Council v A mother and others*[599] Baker J commented that it is now recognised that people with a learning disability 'need to be supported and enabled to lead their lives as full members of the community' resulting in 'a wider acceptance that people with learning disability may, in many cases, with assistance, be able to bring up children successfully.' In *Re A (Care Proceedings: Learning Disabled Parent)*[600] Baker J was faced with a case in which the danger of not providing such assistance was apparent. A baby suffered injuries which were possibly attributable in part to the father's imperfect understanding of risks associated with his handling of the baby. The father had a learning disability but no one took steps to obtain assistance for him in caring for the baby. Baker J commented that the injury might have been avoided, and 'plainly more needs to be done in other cases to identify and address such risks at an earlier stage'.[601]

In cases involving disabled parents, any substantive or procedural issues arising from the disability will need to be identified at an early stage. It may be necessary to take steps to ensure that evidence can be taken appropriately from the disabled person. In *Re C (Care Proceedings: Parents with Disabilities)*[602] McFarlane LJ explained that it is crucial that professionals understand the possible need for 'interpretation'[603] of a disabled person's evidence. For example, in the context of deafness, appropriate communication might be facilitated by a relay interpreter, that is, a deaf person who acts as an "intermediary" (from a deaf perspective), providing 'cultural brokerage' between the qualified sign language interpreter and the deaf person.[604]

---

[595] Ibid, [20].     [596] Ibid, [21].

[597] See A. Bond, *Care Proceedings and Learning Disabled Parents: A Handbook for Family Lawyers* (Bristol: Jordan Publishing, 2011), pp 61–2.

[598] [2007] EWHC 2798 (sitting in the Barnet County Court).     [599] [2011] EWHC 402 Fam), at [132].

[600] [2013] EWHC 3502 (Fam).     [601] Ibid, at [82].     [602] [2014] EWCA Civ 128.

[603] As opposed to mere 'translation'.

[604] [2014] EWCA Civ 128, at [18]. See R Handa and S Tyler, '"Let's See How We Get On" Or the Need for Regulated Provision of Registered Witness Intermediaries in Family Proceedings' [2014] Fam Law 75.

*8.6.1.2 Unknown perpetrator cases*

---

### Key case

A particular difficulty in interpreting section 31(2)(b) arises where a child suffers a non-accidental injury but it is not possible to identify the perpetrator, for example when a child is being looked after by more than one person, sometimes in more than one household, and it is unclear when, and by whom, the child has suffered the injury. The issue came before the House of Lords in *Lancashire County Council v B*.[605] A paid childminder, who had a child of her own (child B) looked after a baby girl, child A, while A's parents were at work. Otherwise, A's parents looked after her. After this arrangement had been in place for two months, A, who was then 7 months old, was found to have sustained serious non-accidental head injuries. The local authority applied for care orders in respect of A and B (who was only a month older than A), relying exclusively on the injury sustained to A. The judge found that the injuries to A had been inflicted by a member of household A or household B[606] but not both, but was unable to say which of A's mother, A's father, or B's mother was the perpetrator. The judge was of the view that, having so found, the threshold criteria could not be fulfilled and he dismissed the care applications.[607] On the local authority's appeal, the Court of Appeal dismissed the appeal in respect of B, applying the approach to the standard of proof required by *Re H*. The court explained that since it had not been established as a matter of fact that B's mother had harmed A, there was no factual basis (as opposed to suspicion) from which the inference could be drawn that B was at risk in his household.[608] There was no appeal in respect of B. However, the Court of Appeal allowed the appeal in respect of A, and A's case subsequently came before the House of Lords on A's parents' appeal. The House of Lords dismissed the appeal, holding that the threshold was fulfilled. The House could not believe that Parliament intended the threshold criteria to operate so as to preclude protection of a child injured in the circumstances of A's case.[609] Lord Nicholls of Birkenhead, delivering an opinion with which there was unanimous agreement, held that the phrase 'care given to the child' normally refers primarily to the care given to the child by a parent or parents or other primary carers. However, the matter stands differently in a case in which the child's care is shared between primary carers and other carers and the court is unable to distinguish between the care given by those respective carers. Lord Nicholls said that in such a case 'the phrase "care given to the child" is apt to embrace not merely the care given by the parents or other primary carers; it is apt to embrace the care given by any of the carers'.[610] The House recognised that this interpretation meant that parents who were wholly innocent will face the possibility of losing their child but the factor outweighing all others is 'the prospect that an unidentified, and unidentifiable, carer may inflict further injury on a child he or she has already severely damaged'.[611]

---

This reasoning would similarly apply in a case in which a child has been injured in the care of both parents and it is not possible to establish which parent has caused the first child to suffer significant harm. Indeed in *Re CB and JB (Care Proceedings: Guidelines)*[612] Wall J ruled on such facts that the threshold was fulfilled. In that case the child who had been harmed had a sibling and Wall J went further to hold that a finding that the first child's injuries must have been caused by either the mother or the father gave rise to a real possibility, a possibility which could not sensibly be ignored, that the unharmed sibling would also suffer significant harm were he to be left in the care of both

---

[605] [2002] 2 AC 147.     [606] The judge excluded B's father as a possible perpetrator.

[607] The judge applied a dictum of Wall J in *Re G (A Minor) (Care Order: Threshold Conditions)* [1995] Fam 16 at 20, which suggested that the lack of care must be shown to be attributable to the parents.

[608] For criticism of the Court of Appeal's approach, see J. Hayes, 'The Threshold Test and the Unknown Perpetrator' [2000] Family Law 260.

[609] 2002] 2 AC 147 at 165.     [610] Ibid, 166.     [611] Ibid, 167.     [612] [1998] 2 FLR 211.

or either of his parents.[613] However, the latter ruling cannot now stand with the Court of Appeal decision in the *Lancashire* case, and with subsequent higher authority on this point. In *Re S-B (Children) (Care Proceedings: Standard of Proof)*,[614] Lady Hale applied the same approach as the Court of Appeal in the *Lancashire* case in a case involving siblings. In *Re S-B* a child, Jason, suffered non-accidental bruising when aged 4 weeks. The parents separated and the mother subsequently gave birth to another child, William. Care proceedings were brought in respect of William because of what had happened to Jason. The trial judge was unable to decide which of Jason's parents was responsible for the injuries, but found the threshold crossed in respect of William on the basis that there was a real possibility that the mother had injured Jason. The principal issue in the case was whether the judge had applied the correct standard of proof to the question of identifying the perpetrator of Jason's injury, and the case was remitted for re-hearing on the basis of the judge's error on that point. Baroness Hale added at paragraph [49] of her judgment that the judge's approach in relation to William was not permissible since *Re H* made clear that the finding of a real possibility of future harm had to be based upon findings of fact made on the balance of probabilities. Some commentators found this statement of principle worrying and suggested that it was not consistent with earlier authority.[615] As the dictum was arguably merely *obiter* there was doubt as to its status.

---

### Key case

An opportunity to address the issue directly came in *Re J (Care Proceedings: Possible Perpetrators)*.[616] In that case the local authority issued care proceedings in respect of three children, aged 7, 6, and 3 years who had been living in a family unit with parents, JJ and DJ.[617] The local authority became concerned for the welfare of the children because of the circumstances surrounding the death of JJ's first child, T-L, aged 3 weeks. In care proceedings in respect of JJ's second child, who was eventually adopted outside the family, a judge had found that T-L had suffered 'multiple fractures to her ribs, caused on at least two occasions, bruising to her left jaw, right side of her face, left shoulder and left inner elbow, all caused non-accidentally, and serious and untreated nappy rash. She had died as a result of asphyxia caused either by a deliberate act or by SW [T-L's father] taking her to bed with him and JJ leaving her in SW's care.'[618] Both of T-L's parents colluded to hide the truth so that the judge was unable to identify who the perpetrator was.

The local authority bringing the proceedings in *Re J* did not see JJ's collusion with SW as relevant now, given that JJ was living with her new partner, DJ, about whom there were no concerns relating to child protection.[619] The local authority relied solely upon the fact that JJ was a possible perpetrator of harm to

---

[613] As Wall J said (at 220): 'the argument to the contrary . . . strikes at the whole philosophy of child protection embodied in the Children Act 1989'.

[614] [2009] UKSC 178, [2010] 1 AC 678. See Ian Goldrein QC, 'There is Only So Much Juice in an Orange: *Re SB*' [2010] Family Law 196; J. Hayes, 'Ensuring Equal Protection for Siblings' [2010] Family Law 505. *Re CB and JB* was cited to the Supreme Court but was not referred to in the judgment.

[615] The reasoning in *Re S-B* was cited by the Court of Appeal in *Re F (Interim Care Order)* [2011] EWCA Civ 258, [2011] 2 FLR 856. For strong criticism, see M. Hayes, 'Why Didn't the Courts Protect this Child? *Re SB and Re F*' [2012] Family Law 169.

[616] [2013] UKSC 9, [2013] 1 FLR 1373.

[617] It is convenient to refer to DJ and JJ as 'the parents', although the youngest child was the child of JJ and her former partner and the other children were DJ's children from a previous relationship. DJ and JJ had subsequently married and had a child together, born in December 2011, who was not a subject of the care proceedings.

[618] [2013] UKSC 9, [2013] 1 FLR 1373 at [8].

[619] In the Supreme Court, Lord Wilson was 'not at all sure that such findings become irrelevant just because the mother is now living with another partner . . . for no doubt the child will continue to need protection from a variety of situations and from persons other than the new partner. More widely, such findings raise grave concerns about that mother's entire capacity for responsible care; and, if marshalled by a local authority as the factual foundation for the crossing of the threshold, they would need most carefully to be weighed against such evidence as indicated an improvement in her capacity for responsible care as at the relevant date' ([2013] UKSC 9, [2013] 1 FLR 1373 at [70]).

the baby.[620] The judge and the Court of Appeal,[621] effectively bound by Baroness Hale's ruling in paragraph [49] of *Re S-B* and earlier Court of Appeal cases, held that the threshold could not be fulfilled on that sole basis. In the Court of Appeal, however, McFarlane LJ opined that Lord Nicholls' opinions in the earlier House of Lords cases 'indicated a different approach between cases where absolutely no past harm had been proved, and those where past harm is established but the identity of the actual perpetrator cannot be proved on the balance of probabilities'.[622] The Court of Appeal thus saw a pressing need for the issue to be determined by the Supreme Court[623] and gave permission to appeal.

In the Supreme Court, Lady Hale, with whom a majority of the court agreed,[624] concluded that there is no inconsistency between paragraph [49] of *Re S-B* [2010] 1 AC 678 and any of the earlier House of Lords authorities, with which it was entirely consistent in principle, and *Re S-B* should be followed as a correct statement of the law.[625]

The local authority, citing the approach to uncertain perpetrators in *Lancashire County Council v B*[626] and *Re O*,[627] contended that inclusion in a pool of possible perpetrators should similarly be taken into account for the purpose of the likelihood criterion in section 31(2)(a).[628] Her Ladyship's response was that the *Lancashire* case was about section 31(2)(b), not (a),[629] and that there is 'nothing in *Re O* to cast doubt upon the necessity for founding a prediction of future harm upon a proven factual basis'.[630] One of the reasons that Lady Hale gave for her interpretation of the threshold was that there must be a clearly established objective basis for state interference, as required by Article 8 of the ECHR, which reasonable suspicion cannot supply.[631] This issue was subsequently clarified by the Supreme Court in *Re B (A Child)*.[632] The court explained that no interference with Article 8 occurs:

---

[620] The test for whether a person is a possible perpetrator is set out in *North Yorkshire County Council v SA* [2003] 2 FLR 849: 'is there a likelihood or real possibility that A or B or C was the perpetrator or a perpetrator of the inflicted injuries?' Where a court investigates a pool of possible perpetrators, the court must analyse the evidence and give reasons for a person's inclusion in, or exclusion from, the pool: see *S and Others (By their Children's Guardian) v Nottingham City Council and Others* [2013] EWCA Civ 771. The conclusion on the finding of possible perpetration must itself be properly reasoned: see *Re M (Fact-Finding Hearing: Burden of Proof)* [2012] EWCA Civ 1580, [2013] 2 FLR 874 at [16] and [17] (judge wrong to reason as follows: absent a parental explanation there was no satisfactory benign explanation, ergo there had to be a malevolent explanation). For a case in which a judge changed her mind after judgment but prior to sealing an order, see *Re L-B (Reversal of Judgment)* [2013] UKSC 8 (judge initially identified perpetrator and on further reflection found herself unable to do so).

[621] *Re J (Children) (Care Proceedings: Threshold Criteria)* [2012] EWCA Civ 380, [2012] 2 FLR 842 (McFarlane LJ, Lord Judge CJ, and Lord Neuberger of Abbotsbury MR).

[622] *Re J (Children) (Care Proceedings: Threshold Criteria)* [2012] EWCA Civ 380, [2012] 2 FLR 842 at [128].

[623] Ibid, [131].

[624] Lord Hope, Lord Reed, Lord Carnwath, and Lord Clarke. Lord Sumption agreed in part.

[625] [2013] UKSC 9 at [43]. Lady Hale also rejected Wall J's *obiter* conclusion in *Re B (Minors) (Care Proceedings: Practice)* [1999] 1 WLR 238 at 248 that a finding that there was a real likelihood that a mother caused harm to her baby could found the conclusion that there was a real likelihood that she would cause harm to a twin sibling. This, Lady Hale said, failed 'to distinguish between the degree of likelihood required by the word "likely" and the factual findings required to satisfy the court of that likelihood, a distinction which was clearly drawn by the House of Lords in the later case of *Re B* [2009] AC 11' ([2013] UKSC 9, [2013] 1 FLR 1373 at [21]). Later in her judgment, Lady Hale stated that it was in the context of discussion of section 31(2)(b) that Lord Nicholls in the *Lancashire* case 'referred with apparent approval to what Wall J had said in *Re B (Minors) (Care Proceedings: Practice)* [1999] 1 WLR 238, 248' (see [2013] UKSC 9, [2013] 1 FLR 1373 at [30]).

[626] [2000] 2 AC 147.

[627] [2003] UKHL 18, [2004] 1 AC 523, [2003] 1 FLR 1169. For comment, see M. Hayes, '*Re O and N; Re B*—Uncertain Evidence and Risk-taking in Child Protection Cases' [2004] Child and Family Law Quarterly 63.

[628] See [2013] UKSC 9, [2013] 1 FLR 1373 at [24] and [33].     [629] [2013] UKSC 9, [2013] 1 FLR 1373 at [25].

[630] [2013] UKSC 9, [2013] 1 FLR 1373 at [33].

[631] Ibid, [44]. A majority of the court saw room for argument as to whether Article 8 'is engaged by a provision which merely confers upon the court the jurisdiction' and 'merely opens the way to the possibility that an order may be made'. Ibid, [97], citing Lord Clyde in *Lancashire County Council v B* [2000] 2 AC 147 at 170.

[632] [2013] UKSC 33.

> when a judge concludes that the threshold is crossed. The interference occurs only if, at the welfare stage, the judge proceeds to make a care or supervision order; and it is that order which must therefore fall foul of article 8.[633]

It is clear therefore that one of Lady Hale's reasons for ruling as she did in *Re J* has since been overturned.

Lady Hale was clear that there is no suggestion that 'the fact that a previous child has been injured or even killed while in the same household as the parent should be ignored'; such a fact 'normally comes associated with innumerable other facts which may be relevant to the prediction of future harm to another child'[634] and which 'must be set alongside other facts'.[635] As she explained:

> There may, or may not, be a multitude of established facts from which such a likelihood can be established. There is no substitute for a careful, individualised assessment of where those facts take one. But *In re S-B* is authority for the proposition that a real possibility that this parent has harmed a child in the past is not, by itself, sufficient to establish the likelihood that she will cause harm to another child in the future.

Lord Hope also delivered a judgment which expressed a majority view,[636] explaining that if the possible perpetrators are still together, possible perpetration 'will be relevant, and may on its own be sufficient, to show that the threshold has been crossed'.[637] He declined to say that it would no longer be relevant if the parties have separated:

> first because it is information which invites further inquiry as to whether the subsequent child is likely to suffer harm while in the care of X; and, second, because, in combination with other facts and circumstances that the inquiry reveals about X's attitude or behaviour, it may help to show that this threshold has been crossed. It may have a bearing on the weight of the evidence when looked at as a whole, including an assessment of the balance of probabilities.[638]

For Lord Hope the crucial point was that 'it will not on its own be sufficient' and 'cannot, and must not, be treated on its own as a finding of fact that it was X who caused or contributed to the injuries'.[639]

Lord Wilson, concurring in the disposal, concluded that the mother's consignment to a pool of possible perpetrators of the injuries to T-L was *irrelevant* to whether the three subject children are

---

[633] *In re B (A Child)* [2013] UKSC 33 at para 29, *per* Lord Wilson. See also, agreeing, Lord Neuberger at para 62, Lady Hale at para 186, and Lord Clarke at para 134. Lord Kerr at para 129, tended to agree. Lady Hale added, however, that 'the reason why the threshold is crossed forms part of the court's reasons for making the order, and these must be "relevant and sufficient" '.

[634] Such as facts arising from the following questions, set out at [2013] UKSC 9, [2013] 1 FLR 1373 at [52]: 'How many injuries were there? When and how were they caused? On how many occasions were they inflicted? How obvious will they have been? Was the child in pain or unable to use his limbs? Would any ordinary parent have noticed this? Was there a delay in seeking medical attention? Was there concealment from or active deception of the authorities? What do those facts tell us about the child care capacities of the parent with whom we are concerned?'

[635] Such as those arising from the following questions, set out at [2013] UKSC 9, [2013] 1 FLR 1373 at [53]: 'What were the household circumstances at the time? Did drink and/or drugs feature? Was there violence between the adults? How have things changed since? Has this parent left the old relationship? Has she entered a new one? Is it different? What does this combination of facts tell us about the likelihood of harm to any of the individual children with whom the court is now concerned? Does what happened several years ago to a tiny baby in very different circumstances enable us to predict the likelihood of significant harm to much older children in a completely new household?'

[636] Lord Reed, Lord Carnwath, and Lord Clarke expressly agreed with his judgment.

[637] *Re J* [2013] UKSC 9, [2013] 1 FLR 1373 at [87].     [638] Ibid.

[639] Ibid, [88], adding: 'A prediction of future harm based on what has happened in the past will only be justified if one can link what has happened in the past directly and unequivocally with the person in the new family unit in whose care the subsequent child is living or will now live.'

likely to suffer significant harm, whether as a fact alone or taken together with other facts. In this latter respect, Lord Wilson's judgment (with which on this point Lord Sumption agreed) dissented from the majority. Lord Wilson held that, as a matter of logic, in order to draw the inference of likely harm in the new family unit it would be necessary to prove that the mother actually perpetrated the harm to the baby.[640] In Lord Wilson's opinion, the 'harm and the person's responsibility for it are the two planks on which any conclusion about likelihood must rest and they must be equally sturdy.[641]

The ruling in *Re J* has provoked considerable controversy. Some commentators have been highly critical of the reasoning in *Re J* and its implications,[642] while others support the decision. Those who oppose the decision argue that the Supreme Court adopted rather formal, unconvincing reasons for not engaging with the reasoning in the earlier House of Lords' decisions on uncertain perpetrators, and misinterpreted those decisions in the court's focus on logic and consistency, and application of *Re H* as an unbending rule. Especially in light of the decision in the *Lancashire* case, arguably the court was not bound to apply the approach in *Re H* to the facts of *Re J* which, given the proven past harm to another child, were qualitatively different. It can be argued that, by contrast with the Supreme Court's approach, the earlier authorities were concerned with seeking out an interpretation consistent with the policy consideration which weighed most heavily with the House of Lords, namely child protection, even though it was appreciated that an injustice might be done to the parents concerned.[643] The earlier authorities also emphasised that fulfilment of the threshold criteria merely empowers the court to consider the child's welfare in all the circumstances and, where necessary, put in place some proportionate intervention to protect the child concerned. It by no means follows that a care order would be made, or indeed if one were made that the child would be removed from the parent thereunder. The ruling in *Re J*, however, means that a local authority cannot even obtain a supervision order to monitor the child's welfare.

Critics of *Re J* are clearly concerned that the decision may place some children at risk of significant harm. They point to the fact that if two possible perpetrators of harm resulting in the death of a baby split up and each is living with a baby in a new family unit, neither child can be protected according to the ruling in *Re J*, and yet it would seem clear that at least one of the children is at risk.[644] The risk in an uncertain perpetrator case does not disappear simply because the parents separate.[645]

By contrast, supporters of the decision see it as providing the correct bulwark against unwarranted state intervention in family life.[646] The concern is that, if the Supreme Court had not ruled as it did, a possible perpetrator might never be free in future to start afresh in a new family unit without a risk of state intervention. It has been suggested that one possible solution to this might be to introduce a lower statutory threshold for the making of a supervision order.

The issues raised by *Re J* have been hotly debated in the House of Lords with regard to an amendment to the Children and Families Bill,[647] which would have permitted a judge to find likely harm from the sole fact of possible perpetration of proven harm to another child.[648] The amendment was laid by Lord Lloyd of Berwick[649] who, it will be recalled, was one of the dissenting judges in *Re H*.

---

[640] A majority of the court agreed with Lord Wilson on this point.  [641] Ibid, [74].

[642] S. Gilmore, '*Re J (Care Proceedings: Past Possible Perpetrators in a New Family Unit)* [2013] UKSC 9: Bulwarks and Logic—the blood which runs through the veins of law—but how much will be spilled in future?' [2013] Child and Family Law Quarterly 215; M. Hayes, 'The Supreme Court's Failure to Protect Vulnerable Children: *Re J (Children)*' [2013] Family Law 1015; J. Hayes, 'The Judge's Dilemma: *Re J*' [2014] Family Law 91.

[643] Ibid.     [644] See Gilmore, '*Re J (Care Proceedings)*' at 232–3.

[645] J. Hayes, 'The Judge's Dilemma: *Re J*' [2014] Family Law 91.

[646] See A. Bainham, 'Suspicious Minds: Protecting Children in the Face of Uncertainty' (2013) 72 Cambridge Law Journal 266.

[647] Amendment 16, Hansard HL, 17 Dec 2013, cols 1160 et seq (Report Stage).

[648] One of the authors, Stephen Gilmore, must declare an interest as a drafter of the initial amendment and as having campaigned, with Professor Mary Hayes (original author of this book), for Parliament to debate this issue.

[649] Lord Brown of Eaton-under-Heywood added his name to the amendment at Report Stage of the Bill.

The provision divided the opinion of legal members of the Lords (former Law Lords and Supreme Court justices). In debate at Report Stage, Lord Hope (who presided in *Re J* and had recently retired from the Supreme Court), opposed the amendment principally because, as drafted, it was too stark and went too far in its reference to 'sole fact' without any reference to the context of a particular case. However, Lord Hope acknowledged that there was a problem, and it was suggested that Lord Lloyd and other interested members of the Lords might wish to seek to agree a more acceptable wording of the amendment for debate at 3rd Reading.[650] Apparently Lords Lloyd and Hope agreed a draft amendment but the Government would not support it,[651] and the issue was not therefore pressed.

It is clear therefore that any conclusion that a person is a perpetrator of harm to a child must have a factual foundation which identifies the perpetrator. In *Re A-C; Re A (Fact-Finding: Possible Perpetrators)*[652] the Court of Appeal overturned a judge's finding that the father was the perpetrator. The evidence of the toxic and volatile relationship within the family unit was more than sufficient to support a theory that it was the father who behaved in a momentary and unpremeditated manner in injuring the child. However, equally, it supported a conclusion that it was the mother who was the sole perpetrator. There was a failure therefore to identify 'some established fact or facts upon which a reasonable inference that it was the father who did the deed could be based.'[653]

### 8.6.1.3 Orphans and abandoned children

Difficult questions as to whether a child can be said to be suffering significant harm attributable to lack of reasonable parental care and whether a care order can be made have arisen in cases in which children are orphaned or abandoned. In *Birmingham City Council v D; Birmingham City Council v M*[654] these questions arose with respect to children from two different families who were orphans, accommodated by the local authority, with no family members available to be appointed as their guardians. The local authority argued that the absence of parental responsibility in any person imperilled the children because they would not be fully empowered to deal with crises and emergencies, and that therefore the children were at risk of suffering significant harm. The application was resisted by the children's guardians ad litem, who said that the needs of orphans were addressed by the accommodation provisions in the Act.[655] Thorpe J rejected the local authority's application for the following reason:

> section 31 is plainly designed to protect families from invasive care orders unless there is a manifest need evidenced by a perceptible risk of significant harm . . . in these cases the local authority does not seek to invade, but to protect and compensate children who have been bereft of parental support. I have every sympathy with the local authority's motives and their aims, but I must construe section 31 sensibly and realistically. If there is some shortcoming in the statutory framework it is not for me to remedy the deficiency by a strained construction of section 31, particularly in the light of the opposition of the guardians ad litem.[656]

This illustrates that even where the proposals made by a local authority are entirely well meaning, and arguably in the child's best interests, they cannot be authorised by a court unless the grounds for an order are first established. Here Thorpe J took the view that the language of the relevant provision prevented the court from intervening, even had it wished to do so.

In *Re SH (Care Order: Orphan)*[657] the court was faced with a similar situation: an eleven-year-old boy was being accommodated by the local authority; he was an orphan and no member of his extended family was prepared to care for him. However, the facts differed in one vital respect. The

---

[650] On 5 February 2014.  [651] Copy of correspondence with S. Gilmore (author).
[652] [2013] EWCA Civ 1321.  [653] Ibid, at [32].
[654] [1994] 2 FLR 502 (Thorpe J).  [655] Sections 20, 22, and 23.
[656] [1994] 2 FLR 502 at 504–505.  [657] [1995] 1 FLR 746.

boy was accommodated by the local authority following allegations of sexual abuse by his father, in which the mother and a half-sister were also implicated. While the child was accommodated, his mother and father died in quick succession. The local authority continued to look after the boy, and two months after he became an orphan, the local authority sought a care order. Hollis J held that the threshold criteria could be fulfilled applying *Re M (A Minor) (Care Order: Threshold Conditions).*[658] There was evidence that the child was suffering significant harm when the local authority first took steps to rescue him and on that basis counsel conceded that the threshold could be fulfilled at the date of the hearing. It may be doubted whether that concession was correctly made. Lord Mackay in *Re M* made clear that jurisdiction can only be founded at an earlier date where protective measures are continuously in place to the date of disposal, and cannot be so founded where the need for protection has terminated prior to that date. It is submitted that the House of Lords did not just mean that, following intervention, there must be continuous accommodation of the child to the date of disposal. For the House of Lords' approach to make sense, surely the protective measures referred to must be those that were put in place to avoid the harm which is relied upon at the hearing to fulfil the threshold. Once the parents were dead, the need to protect the children from sexual abuse ceased. From that point, the boy, although continuing to be accommodated, was accommodated for a different reason, because he was orphaned.

However, having accepted that the threshold was crossed, Hollis J went on to consider whether a care order should be made. At this stage, the fact that no one had parental responsibility for the child was influential on Hollis J. When giving his reasons for concluding that a care order was in the child's best interests, he said that although the local authority had extensive powers under Part III of the Children Act 1989 it did not have the powers it might need when caring for the boy. Moreover, the guardianship provisions in section 5 were not apt to cover the situation because they were designed to confer guardianship upon an individual, not on an artificial individual such as the director of social services.

In the case of an orphaned child, whether the threshold test can be established appears, therefore, to turn on the court's view of the child's total situation. Being an orphan is not enough to overcome the threshold test, but where the fact of being an orphan is linked to other facts together they may provide sufficient evidence to establish that the child is suffering, or is likely to suffer, significant harm.[659]

Cazalet J applied similar reasoning to an abandoned child in *Re M (Care Order: Parental Responsibility).*[660] He held that the threshold test was established in the case of a baby who had been abandoned when only a few days old on the steps of a health centre. While there was a good chance, therefore, that the child would be found, Cazalet J reasoned that the fact of abandonment, with all the risks it entailed, meant the child was suffering significant harm immediately before he was found. Furthermore, and importantly, he held it was likely that the child would suffer significant harm in view of the fact that he would grow up having no knowledge of his background. Such lack of knowledge would probably cause him to have distressing fantasies about his origins and he would be deprived of a sense of belonging. Upon medical examination the child had been found to be developmentally delayed and to have some bone abnormalities. Cazalet J concluded that the child's future required firm and positive decisions which may have to be taken by the local authority at short notice and that it should therefore have parental responsibility with a view to implementing its care plan, which was to place the child for adoption.

In *London Borough of Hillingdon v AO*[661] a Nigerian childless couple claimed they had been duped into thinking the woman had given birth in Lagos. When the parents and child returned to the UK, DNA testing revealed the child was not related to the couple. In care proceedings, Hogg J

---

[658] [1994] 2 AC 424, which approved *Northamptonshire County Council v S* [1993] Fam 136, [1992] 3 WLR 1010.

[659] The Children Act Advisory Committee recommended that the position of children for whom no one has parental responsibility is in urgent need of review, CAAC Report 1994/5, p 32.

[660] [1996] 2 FLR 84.     [661] [2014] EWHC 75 (Fam) Hogg J.

accepted the parents' claim that 'there was a process, a charade in which they were unknowing players, in which they were deceived'.[662] The local authority had failed to make out a case against the parents. However, Hogg J found that the threshold criteria had 'clearly been crossed in circumstances and at the hands of persons unknown',[663] resulting in the child being effectively an orphan, with no one in this country with parental responsibility for her, and no information about her background.

## 8.7 **The harm is attributable to the child's being beyond parental control**

Occasionally a child may be suffering, or be likely to suffer, significant harm not because of a failure of reasonable parental care, but because he is beyond parental control.[664] Examples might be where a child has become addicted to drugs or is sexually promiscuous, but no doubt there are many other situations in which parents become powerless to influence the child's behaviour. An example arose in *M v Birmingham City Council*[665] where Stuart-White J held that the words 'beyond parental control' are 'a substantial expression capable of describing a state of affairs in the past, in the present or in the future according to the context in which it falls to be applied' and assumed, without deciding the point, that parental control refers to 'the parent of the child in question and not to parents, or reasonable parents, in general'.[666] In *Re K (Post-Adoption Placement Breakdown)*[667] a 15-year-old girl, who had been adopted at age 6 because of sexual and physical abuse prior to placement, presented extremely challenging behaviour to her adoptive parents, frequently absconding from home. The girl was diagnosed as suffering from an attachment disorder. In care proceedings, HHJ Bellamy, sitting as a judge of the High Court, found the girl to be beyond parental control, holding that 'even if a child is likely to suffer significant harm as a direct result of a disorder which affects that child's behaviour, if the consequent behaviour is such that a parent is unable to control the child then the child's being beyond parental control is, at the very least, a contributory cause of the likelihood of future harm'.[668]

It is suggested that those initiating care proceedings, and courts when determining an application brought in care proceedings, should be wary of improper reliance being placed on the beyond control provision. Where parents, or others, have truly tried their best to make reasonable arrangements for the child's upbringing it is right that they should not be stigmatised as causing the child to suffer, or to be likely to suffer, significant harm because the care they have given the child, or are likely to give the child, is not what it would be reasonable to expect a parent to give to him. However, it is equally stigmatising for the child to be found to be beyond parental control in a case where the fault lies with those who have brought him up. Such a finding is likely to influence the arrangements which are made about how the child will be looked after if a care order is made, or the types of activities in which the child will be required to take part if a supervision order is made. Justice to a child requires that he should only be labelled as beyond control where there is cogent evidence to support this allegation. Where a child is badly behaved, or otherwise apparently out of control, it may be comparatively easy to prove that the child is bringing harm upon himself. It may be far harder to prove wrongdoing or other failure by a parent which has led to the child coming to harm, or to be likely to come to harm. It seems likely that there is a risk that the attribution to the child of the cause of harm to the child, rather than the parent, might sometimes be selected as the basis for bringing proceedings, or making an order, because it is easier to prove. However, just

---

[662] Ibid, at [84].    [663] Ibid, at [85].    [664] Section 31(2)(b)(ii).

[665] [1994] 2 FLR 141. The child, aged 13, was very seriously disturbed and behaving in an uncontrollable fashion, such that she was posing a serious risk to herself and those around her.

[666] Ibid, 147.    [667] [2013] 1 FLR 1.

[668] Ibid, [149]. The judge cited at [152] of his judgment an unreported decision of the Court of Appeal, *L (A Minor)*, 18 March 1997, in which the court had indicated that fault is immaterial and it is not a matter of apportioning blame. The focus is on the fact of the child's being beyond parental control.

as it is wrong to label a parent as having caused his child to come to harm unless there is evidence to substantiate this, so too it is wrong to label a child as being beyond parental control if the true cause of his coming to harm is because his parents, or others, have failed to give him reasonable parental care.

## 8.8  The welfare question in care proceedings

Once established, the threshold criteria allow the court to make a care order or a supervision order. But proof of the grounds is permissive only. It by no means follows that those orders will always be in the child's best interests. Whether an order is made and, if so which, must be considered applying the child's welfare as the paramount consideration (section 1 of the Children Act 1989).[669] The checklist in section 1(3) must also be applied,[670] and the court must be satisfied that the making of an order is better for the child than making no order at all.[671]

The court's response must be a proportionate one. Although, as we have seen, the rights in the ECHR are not engaged at the threshold stage, they come into play at the welfare stage, and guidance was provided by the Supreme Court in *Re B (A Child)*.[672] The court must consider Convention rights when deciding whether to make the substantive order.[673] In *Re B (A Child)* a judge had made a care order and placed for adoption a three-year-old girl, Amelia, who had been removed from her parents at birth. The parents had maintained contact with Amelia and there was a warm, loving relationship with the parents. However, the mother had a dysfunctional upbringing and suffered from a somatisation disorder, and the father had a long criminal record. The evidence showed the parents were 'fundamentally dishonest, manipulative and antagonistic towards professionals'[674] and yet expert opinion indicated that placement with the parents could only happen pursuant to a programme of multi-disciplinary monitoring and support which would require honest cooperation. The judge concluded that the parents did not have the capacity to engage with professionals and that the only viable option for Amelia's future care was adoption. The Court of Appeal dismissed the parents' appeal, but was concerned[675] that the threshold was arguably barely crossed and yet the order was the most extreme that could be made.

On further appeal, the Supreme Court found on the facts that the threshold had been fulfilled[676] and by a majority (Lady Hale dissenting) upheld the judge's order on the basis that he had concluded on the evidence that it was 'the only viable option'. Lord Neuberger explained that 'the defective parenting that Amelia would undergo if she remained with her parents fell outside the wide spectrum of the acceptable "very diverse standards"[677] such as would justify the state stepping in'.[678] In reaching its conclusion the court emphasised that any order must be proportionate bearing in mind the requirements of Article 8 of the ECHR and that a care order in the circumstances of this case should only be made 'where nothing else will do'.

This approach applies equally to 'lesser forms of intervention'[679] (ie, lesser than adoption). In *Re G (A Child)*[680] the Court of Appeal held that where there is a choice of options, a judge must undertake a 'global, holistic evaluation of each of the options'.[681] In that case the Court of Appeal held

---

[669] Sometimes this is referred to as the welfare *stage*. However, the House of Lords has commented that there are not two stages in care proceedings: see *Re B (Children) (Sexual Abuse: Standard of Proof)* [2008] UKHL 35 at [74].

[670] It is mandatory in applications under Pt IV of the Children Act 1989: see s 1(4).        [671] Section 1(5).

[672] [2013] UKSC 33.        [673] See Ibid, at para 62 (Lord Neuberger).        [674] Ibid, para 19.

[675] See [2012] EWCA Civ 1475 at para 147, Lewison LJ, and at para 150, Rix LJ.

[676] See *per* Lord Wilson at para 48, Lord Kerr at paras 131–2, Lord Neuberger at para 64, and Lady Hale at paras 206–14 (with hesitation).

[677] Quoting Hedley J in *Re L (Care: Threshold Criteria)* [2007] 1 FLR 2050, 2063.

[678] *In re B (A Child)* [2013] UKSC 33 at para 69.

[679] *Re G (A Child)* [2013] EWCA Civ 965 at [32]. The significance of *Re B* (n 623) was also emphasised by Black LJ in *Re P (A Child)* [2013] EWCA Civ 963 at [102], and by the court (Lord Dyson MR, Sir James Munby P, and Black LJ) in *Re B-S (Children)* [2013] EWCA Civ 1146, [2014] 1 FLR 1035.

[680] [2013] EWCA Civ 965 (McFarlane LJ, Davis and Longmore LJJ agreeing).        [681] Ibid, [51].

that the judge had erred when he ruled out the prospect of the child being placed with the mother and thus concluded, without further consideration, that the only viable option was long-term fostering under a care order. He had failed to consider why permanent separation of mother and child was 'necessary' on the basis that it was the 'last resort' and 'nothing else will do'.

In *Re W (Care Proceedings: Functions of Court and Local Authority)*[682] the Court of Appeal explained that the local authority is required to set out the range of services that are available in respect of each placement option and under each of the orders which the court can impose.[683] It may be convenient for that to be put into the form of the section 31A care plan in the alternative.[684] The court then undertakes a welfare analysis of each option, evaluates those options relative to each other, and considers which orders are proportionate and necessary, if any.[685]

The Court of Appeal decision in *Re R (Adoption)*[686] makes clear that only realistic options for a child's future care need be considered in the welfare balancing exercise. In *Re M (A Child: Long-Term Fostering)*[687] the Court of Appeal was clear this will depend on the facts, with certain options 'readily discarded as not realistically possible', others perhaps 'just about possible but not in the child's interests, and yet others 'possible but it may be contrary to the interests of the child to pursue them.'[688] In addition, this process requires 'a careful eye to the realities of a child's life'[689] including all the possible consequences of delay.[690] In some cases this may need to be set against the claim that a parenting assessment, which will occasion delay, is required. In *Re S (Parenting Assessment)*[691] Munby P suggested the following questions in deciding whether the timescale for assessment of a parent could be extended in the child's interests, namely (i) is there solid, evidence-based reason to believe that the parent is committed to making the necessary changes; (ii) maintaining that commitment; and (iii) making the necessary changes within the child's timescale? In *London Borough of Wandsworth v W*,[692] for example, the mother of a five-year-old boy, who had a long history of drug abuse, wished to come off drugs and claimed she needed 18–24 months' psychotherapy. Eleanor King J found, in those circumstances, the child's interests were not met in light of an appropriate timescale for him.[693] An assessment must also be in furtherance of a realistic option for the child. In *London Borough of Tower Hamlets v D, E and F*[694] a baby aged four months had died and two children aged two and four had suffered extreme neglect for which the mother was awaiting sentence. Hayden J refused to authorise an independent social worker to travel to Somaliland to assess the father, as the father's proposal that the children live with him there did not accord with the availability of therapeutic support they required.[695]

In *Re Y (Care Proceedings: Proportionality Evaluation)*[696] the Court of Appeal commented that cases in which there is only one realistic option will be relatively rare.[697] Indeed that case presented 'a classic circumstance in which a proportionality evaluation may make a difference'.[698] The parents appealed the making of care orders in respect of their daughters aged 10 and 5. The father was imprisoned for violence to the mother and children and when, upon his release, the parents resumed cohabitation the local authority sought a care order. Thereafter the mother divorced the father and he had gone to live in The Gambia. The trial judge made the orders, finding that the

---

[682] [2013] EWCA Civ 1227.     [683] Ibid, at [100].     [684] Ibid, at [101].     [685] Ibid, at [100].
[686] [2014] EWCA civ 1625, [2015] 1 FLR 715.     [687] [2014] EWCA Civ 1406.     [688] Ibid, at [31].
[689] Ibid, at [30].     [690] Ibid, at [33].     [691] [2014] 2 FLR 575.     [692] [2014] EWHC 3682 (Fam).
[693] For a case in which adjournment was refused because of delay occasioned by immigration difficulties in permitting the mother to travel to the UK to be assessed, see *Re S (Care Order: Immigration)* [2014] EWHC 529 (Fam).
[694] [2014] EWHC 3901 (Fam).
[695] See by contrast *Re Z (A Child: Independent Social Work Asssessment* [2014] EWHC 729 (Fam) where the local authority's assessment of the father fell short of the required standard, and the father's application for an assessment was granted. Robust case management must not supersede fairness. See *Re S-W (Care Proceedings: Case Management Hearing)* [2015] EWCA Civ 27 (judge wrong to make final care orders at a Case Management Hearing; only rarely would that be appropriate).
[696] [2014] EWCA Civ 1553.     [697] See eg *Re S (Care Order: Appeal)* [2013] EWCA Civ 1835.
[698] [2014] EWCA civ 1553, at para [30].

mother was likely to reconcile with the father and place the children at risk. Allowing the appeal and substituting a child arrangements order in favour of the mother with a supervision order, with supervised contact to the father, the court explained that the 'critical question to be asked is not whether the negative aspect, namely the risk of breach of trust, caused the option to be unrealistic, but whether the negative aspects and the positive aspects of the mother's care and the availability of protective factors taken together made the option unrealistic.'[699]

In *Re S (Care Proceedings: Evaluation of Grandmother)*[700] the Court of Appeal commented that caution was required in ruling out before the hearing the only family member putting herself forward. There is a danger that such an approach may lead to linear reasoning. In that case a grandmother sought a special guardianship order in respect of a two-year-old child who had spent many months in her care. The local authority subsequently concluded that the grandmother was not the best person to have care of the child and the local authority's care plan was for adoption. The judge gave directions for hearing the local authority's care plan. The grandmother's appeal was allowed, the Court of Appeal setting aside the judge's order that care by the grandmother was not a realistic option.

In respect of any appeal against the court's ultimate decision at the welfare stage, an appellate court is not required by the Human Rights Act 1998 to assess the question of proportionality for itself *de novo*.[701] An appellate court should not interfere with a judge's decision on proportionality unless it decides that that conclusion is wrong.[702] The appellate court's duty to review the proportionality of the order does not mean it has to decide the case if it is more appropriate to remit it for rehearing.[703] However, a re-hearing 'should only occur where it is established to be necessary on the particular facts of the case and there is no alternative, less burdensome process available to the appellate court.'[704]

## 8.9  Delay likely to be prejudicial: sections 1(2) and 32

The principle in section 1(2) of the Children Act 1989, that delay is likely to be prejudicial to a child's welfare, applies of course to proceedings in Part IV of the Act. The court is required by section 32 to draw up a timetable with a view to expediting matters. Delay in care proceedings was a concern identified by the Family Justice Review. It cited statistics to show that such cases take an average of 61 weeks in care centres and 48 weeks in Family Proceedings Courts, and that 20,000 children were waiting for a decision in public law cases.[705] In response, the Government agreed to adopt measures to improve management of public law cases and tackle delay.[706]

---

[699]  At para [26]. Similarly, in *Re R (Care Proceedings: Welfare Analysis of Changed Circumstances)* [2014] EWCA Civ 597 the judge made care orders largely because the mother's new husband had a conviction for a sexual offence against a young girl and he had admitted an affair with a 15-year-old niece. However, the judge had failed to make any finding as to whether the mother was still associating with the husband, whom she had divorced, and the judge had also failed sufficiently to consider less draconian outcomes that might have been possible. See also *Re M (Guardian's Appeal from Care Proceedings)* [2014] EWCA Civ 226 (care order was not seen as the last resort, but instead the judge's order of residence to the mother with supervision was upheld).

[700]  [2015] EWCA Civ 325.

[701]  *In re B (A Child)* [2013] UKSC 33 at para 36 (Lord Wilson), para 83 (Lord Neuberger), para 136 (Lord Clarke); Lady Hale (paras 204–205) and Lord Kerr (paras 116–127) dissented on this point.

[702]  Lord Neuberger was concerned that otherwise the appellate court will have some sort of half-way house role between review and reconsideration: see para 89.

[703]  *Re B (Care Proceedings: Proportionality Evaluation)* [2014] EWCA Civ 565, at [53] and [54].

[704]  *Re H-C (Care Proceedings: Appeal from Care Order)* [2014] EWCA Civ 536, per McFarlane LJ at [38]. For an example of the appellate court substituting its own decision, see *Re V (Long-Term Fostering or Adoption* [2013] EWCA Civ 913, [2014] 1 FLR 1009.

[705]  See Family Justice Review Final Report at para 3.2. www.gov.uk/government/publications/family-justice-review-final-report.

[706]  Ministry of Justice and Department for Education, *The Government Response to the Family Justice Review: A System with Children and Families at its Heart* (Cm 8273, February 2012), especially at paras 54 and 55. The changes will work in tandem with child protection practice reforms: see Department for Education, The Munro Review of Child Protection: Final Report—A Child-Centred System (Cm 8062), July 2011.

The Family Justice Review saw the growth in the use of experts as a major contributor to unacceptable delay and recommended that primary legislation should assert that expert testimony be commissioned only where necessary to resolve the case, and that the legislation should reinforce that in commissioning an expert's report regard must be had to the impact of delay on the welfare of the child. The Family Justice Review also recommended that the current time-consuming requirement to renew interim care or supervision orders after eight weeks and thereafter every four weeks should be amended. As we have already seen, the Children and Families Act 2014 contains legislation regulating the use of expert opinion evidence,[707] and amending section 38(2) of the Children Act 1989.[708]

The Family Justice Review concluded that, in addition to addressing these specific issues, a firm approach was needed to address in general the difficulty of delay, and recommended that the Government should legislate to set a time limit on care proceedings of six months, with extensions only by exception. Section 14 of the Children and Families Act 2014 amends section 32 of the Children Act to provide that the timetable for disposing of an application should seek to do so within 26 weeks beginning with the day on which the application was issued. The Act provides that an extension may only be granted if 'necessary to enable the court to resolve the proceedings justly',[709] and extensions are 'not to be granted routinely and are to be seen as requiring specific justification'.[710] In deciding whether to grant an extension, the court will have to consider the impact on 'the welfare of the child to whom the application relates'.[711] Each separate extension is to be no more than eight weeks.[712]

## 8.10 Issues surrounding application of the checklist in care proceedings

When the court is deciding which, if any, order to make in an application under Part IV of the Children Act 1989, consideration of the checklist in section 1(3) is mandatory. We discuss in what follows certain particular issues which have arisen with regard to application of the checklist in this context.

### 8.10.1 Proof of harm in section 1(3)(e)

Paragraph (e) of the welfare checklist directs the court to have regard to 'any harm which [the child] has suffered or is at risk of suffering'. Thus, harm must be considered both at the threshold and welfare stages. Several issues have arisen for the courts on this provision.

#### 8.10.1.1 Unknown perpetrators at the disposal stage

In *Re O and another (Minors) (Care: Preliminary Hearing); Re B (A Minor)*[713] the House of Lords considered how the welfare stage of proceedings should be approached in unknown perpetrator cases following its earlier ruling in the *Lancashire County Council* cases (discussed in Section 8.6.1.2). The appeals in *Re O* and *Re B* arose from the different approach which the Court of Appeal had adopted in each case. In *Re B* a one-year-old child had been killed in the care of his parents in circumstances in which neither could be exonerated as the perpetrator. The parents subsequently split up. In care proceedings in respect of the child's six-year-old elder sibling, the Court of Appeal held that a judge cannot in these circumstances disregard the risk that the mother presents as a primary carer for the child. In *Re O* a six-month-old child suffered a skull fracture and neither parent could be exculpated. The parents parted when the child was admitted to hospital, the father was subsequently imprisoned, and the mother thereafter gave birth to the couple's second child. The local authority sought care orders in respect of both children. By contrast with *Re B*, the Court of Appeal held that a judge should proceed on the basis that the first child was not injured by her mother and the mother

---

[707] Section 13.    [708] Section 14(4).    [709] Section 14(5).    [710] Section 14(7).
[711] Section 14(6).    [712] Section 14(8).    [713] [2003] UKHL 18, [2004] 1 AC 523.

presented no risk to the children. Lord Nicholls of Birkenhead, delivering the House of Lords' decision, concluded that the approach in *Re O*:

> would be a self-defeating interpretation of the legislation. It would mean that, in 'uncertain perpetrator' cases, the court decides that the threshold criteria are satisfied but then lacks the ability to proceed in a sensible way in the best interests of the child. The preferable interpretation of the legislation is that in such cases the court is able to proceed at the welfare stage on the footing that each of the possible perpetrators is, indeed, just that: a possible perpetrator.[714]

However, his Lordship added that the 'importance to be attached to that possibility, as to every feature of the case, necessarily depends on the circumstances'.[715]

### 8.10.1.2 *Other cases of unproved allegations*

Another question the courts have had to address is how section 1(3)(e) is to be applied in a case in which the threshold criteria are proved on one ground such as neglect, but not on another. To what extent (if at all) can the court take into account at the welfare stage the possibility that the non-proven allegation may be true? The Court of Appeal considered the issue in *Re M and R (Child Abuse: Evidence)*[716] in light of the House of Lords' decision in *Re H (Minors) (Sexual Abuse: Standard of Proof)*.[717] In *Re M and R* the threshold test had been passed because the children had been emotionally abused. However, the trial judge declined to make a final care order because although there was a real possibility that sexual abuse had occurred, the judge ruled that the evidence of sexual abuse was not sufficient to prove the allegations to the requisite standard.[718] The local authority appealed, supported by the guardian ad litem. The question of law was whether the judge's conclusion that there was a real possibility that sexual abuse had occurred could be taken into consideration when the court was considering what order (if any) to make, and it was asserted on behalf of the child that there was sufficient evidence of sexual abuse for the purposes of section 1(3)(e). The Court of Appeal held that where there is a dispute at the welfare stage of the proceedings over whether the child has suffered, or is at risk of suffering, significant harm the court must apply the same reasoning as in *Re H*. It must reach a conclusion based on facts, not on suspicion or doubts.[719] In *Re P (Sexual Abuse: Standard of Proof)*[720] the Court of Appeal adopted the same approach to section 1(3)(e) in private law proceedings. These points did not call for decision in the House of Lords in *Re O and another (Minors) (Care: Preliminary Hearing); Re B (A Minor)*.[721] However, Lord Nicholls reviewed the authorities and found attractive the conclusions of the Court of Appeal in both cases.[722]

### 8.10.2 **The range of orders at the court's disposal: section 1(3)(g)**

Within the checklist, section 1(3)(g) specifically requires the court to have regard to the range of possible orders at its disposal. The court may conclude that a care order should be made or it may decide that a supervision order will afford the child sufficient protection against suffering further significant harm. The courts' approach to choosing between these orders is discussed later in the text once the legal effects of each of the orders have been considered. In some cases, however, neither order may be deemed appropriate. In some cases the court may determine that no useful purpose will be served by the local authority continuing to have involvement with the child, and that it is better for the child if no order at all is made. Sometimes a different order, for example a residence arrangements order, may be thought to be the most appropriate response, particularly

---

[714]  Ibid, [28].     [715]  Ibid, [31].     [716]  [1996] 2 FLR 195.     [717]  [1996] AC 563.

[718]  Despite the unanimous opinion evidence of three consultant psychiatrists that two children of the family had probably been abused.

[719]  [1996] 2 FLR 195, see Butler-Sloss LJ at 203. For a critique, see I. Hemingway and C. Williams, 'Re M and R: Re H and R' [1997] Family Law 740; contra see D. Bedingfield, *The Child in Need* (Bristol: Family Law, 1998), p 343.

[720]  [1996] 2 FLR 333, CA.     [721]  [2003] UKHL 18, [2004] 1 AC 523.     [722]  Ibid, [45].

where a relative is offering to look after the child. A residence arrangements order can be made subject to conditions or it could be coupled with a supervision order where this seems necessary for the purpose of protecting the child.[723] A family assistance order may be a helpful adjunct to a residence order, particularly where there may be difficulties about contact arrangements with the child.[724] A prohibited steps order might suffice, for example where the child may be protected by prohibiting a specified person from having any contact with the child.

Even when parties to the proceedings agree about which order is most suitable, the decision is nonetheless one for the court to make. The parties might, for example, all agree that the threshold for care is established but that the child can be adequately protected by a supervision order. The court, on the other hand, might be unhappy with this arrangement, and take the view that a care order is the only order which will properly safeguard the child from suffering further significant harm. In these circumstances it should make a care order. However, there must in general be cogent and strong reasons to force a more draconian order upon the local authority than that for which it has asked, and it is wrong to make a care order simply to encourage or oblige a local authority to fulfil its statutory duties towards children in need.[725] Similarly, the court can, of course, refuse to make a care order even though the local authority's application is supported by the children's guardian. However, where a court departs from a recommendation made by the guardian it must give particularly full and clear reasons for reaching a different decision.[726]

## 9 The local authority's care plan and respective roles of the local authority and court

The local authority is required by section 31A of the Children Act 1989 to prepare a care plan setting out the local authority's plan for the child's future care, keep the plan under review, and revise it if necessary.[727]

The adequacy and appropriateness of the care plan will be important factors in the court's decision whether to make a care order. That crucial decision, with its long-term implications, is the responsibility of the court. With the exception of the issue of contact between the child and individuals which is regulated by section 34 of the Children Act 1989,[728] the court cannot monitor implementation of the care plan once a care order is made.[729] The court cannot attach any conditions to a care order, or ask the guardian to report back on how the order is working, for this would amount to an attempt to regulate the manner in which a local authority exercise its powers under the order.[730] The court will only become involved in further litigation about the child where an application is made which would have the effect of discharging the care order[731] or where an application is made for a contact order under section 34. Thus, once the order is made, parental responsibility lies with the local authority

---

[723] See *Re DH (A Minor) (Child Abuse)* [1994] 1 FLR 679; *Re FS (Child Abuse: Evidence)* [1996] 2 FLR 158.

[724] See *Leeds City Council v C* [1993] 1 FLR 269.

[725] *Oxfordshire City Council v L (Care or Supervision Order)* [1998] 1 FLR 70.

[726] *S v Oxfordshire County Council* [1993] 1 FLR 452; *Leicestershire County Council v G* [1994] 2 FLR 329.

[727] See Care Planning, Placement and Case Review (England) Regulations 2010 (SI 2010/959) and the Fostering Services (England) Regulations 2011 (SI 2011/581) for the prescribed information and the manner in which it is to be presented. *Re J (Care: Care Plan)* [1994] 1 FLR 253; *Re K (Care Proceedings: Care Plan)* [2007] EWHC 393 (Fam).

[728] Discussed further in Section 14.

[729] See *Re S (Minors) (Care Order: Implementation of Care Plan); Re W (Minors) (Care Order: Adequacy of Care Plan)* [2002] 2 AC 291.

[730] *Kent County Council v C* [1993] 1 FLR 308; *Re B (A Minor) (Care Order: Review)* [1993] 1 FLR 421; *Re T (A Minor) (Care Order: Conditions)* [1994] 2 FLR 423.

[731] As when a direct application is made to discharge the care order under s 39; or where an application is made for a residence order (now a child arrangements order) which, if made, would have the effect of discharging the care order (s 91(1)).

and effectively all decision-making powers about the child are henceforth vested in the local authority and taken from the court.[732] The court, therefore, needs to have a clear idea of the nature of the local authority's plans for the child before it transfers decision-making powers to the authority.[733]

In *Re J (Minors) (Care: Care Plan)*[734] Wall J said that, wherever possible, evidence to support the care plan should be provided, though he acknowledged that the extent and nature of the evidence will vary from case to case, and that the local authority may have been inhibited from formulating long-term plans until sure of obtaining a care order.[735]

The court 'cannot dictate to the local authority what the care plan is to say'[736] and 'if it seeks to alter the local authority's care plan, must achieve its objective by persuasion rather than by compulsion'.[737] The point at which the court passes responsibility to the local authority is a matter of discretion,[738] and 'one for fine judgment, reflecting sensitivity, realism and an appropriate degree of judicial understanding of what can and cannot sensibly be expected of the local authority'.[739] Where the court disagrees with the care plan, one possibility is to make an interim care order to afford the local authority time to reconsider. However, an interim order 'is to be used for its intended purpose and not to be extended to providing a continuing control over the actions of the local authority',[740] although in an appropriate case the court can properly require the local authority to reconsider its care plan more than once.[741]

Ultimately, however, the court's role is limited to deciding whether an order should be made or not. As Nourse LJ explained in *Re T (A Minor) (Care Order: Conditions)*:[742]

> it is the duty of any court hearing an application for a care order carefully to scrutinise the local authority's care plan. If it does not agree with the care plan, it can refuse to make a care order . . . The cases in which it is appropriate to take such a course will no doubt be rare.[743]

In such cases, however, the court may ultimately be faced with the dilemma that, while it does not agree with the care plan, failure to make a care order will mean that unsuitable parents retain unfettered parental responsibility for a child. This was illustrated in stark form in *Re S and D (Children: Powers of Court)*[744] where the judge was in the unenviable position of disagreeing with the local authority's plan to place the children at home because he was convinced that it would place the children at grave risk of suffering further significant harm.[745] He therefore purported to protect the children through coupling a supervision order with private law orders designed to prevent the children's removal from

---

[732] Once a care order is made it lasts until the child reaches 18 unless it is brought to an end earlier by order of a court (s 91(12)).

[733] This sometimes gives rise to the question whether the court is in a position to make a final order or whether it should make an interim order: see Section 7.

[734] *Re J (Minors) (Care: Care Plan)* [1994] 1 FLR 253.

[735] Eg they are unlikely to arrange a potential adoption placement until certain that they will obtain a care order, but they could give the court some idea of how easy such an arrangement would be to make.

[736] *Re L (Care Proceedings: Human Rights Claims)* [2003] EWHC 665 (Fam), [2003] 2 FLR 160 at [11].

[737] *Re K (Care Proceedings: Care Plan)* [2008] 1 FLR 6 at [15].

[738] See eg Butler-Sloss LJ in *Re L (Sexual Abuse: Standard of Proof)* [1996] 1 FLR 116 at 124 and *Re R (Care Proceedings: Adjournment)* [1998] 2 FLR 390 at 399.

[739] *Re K (Care Proceedings: Care Plan)* [2008] 1 FLR 6 at [16].

[740] *Re L (Sexual Abuse: Standard of Proof)* [1996] 1 FLR 116 at 125. See also *per* Hale LJ in *Re W and B; Re W (Care Plan)* [2001] EWCA Civ 757, [2001] 2 FLR 582 at [67].

[741] *Re K (Care Proceedings: Care Plan)* [2008] 1 FLR 6 at [18]. See eg *Re X; Barnet London Borough Council v Y and X* [2006] 2 FLR 998.

[742] [1994] 2 FLR 423.

[743] Ibid, 429, drawing on Wall J's judgment in *Re J (Minors) (Care: Care Plan)* [1994] 1 FLR 253 at 257–62. See also *per* Butler-Sloss LJ in *Re L (Sexual Abuse: Standard of Proof)* [1996] 1 FLR 116 at 126.

[744] [1995] 2 FLR 456. For another example, see *R (Care Proceedings: Adjournment)* [1998] 2 FLR 390.

[745] There was overwhelming evidence that the mother could not provide an adequate standard of parenting and a suggestion that she was suffering from Munchausen's syndrome by proxy.

their foster parents, but in this regard he acted outside his powers.[746] Balcombe LJ, when asked to provide guidance to other courts faced with a similar dilemma, gave the unequivocal response that, regrettably, the judge has no alternative but to choose between the lesser of two evils:

> He may make a care order knowing that the local authority will then act in a way which he considers to be undesirable; or he may make no care order, which will often, as here, leave an unsuitable parent with parental responsibility for the children.[747]

Another aspect of the Family Justice Review's concern about delay in public law proceedings was that the courts had progressively extended their scrutiny of local authority care plans[748] for children and recommended that courts should avoid over-scrutiny and focus on core issues. Section 15 of the Children and Families Act 2014 substitutes new provisions of section 31 to seek to achieve this, as follows:

> (3A) A court deciding whether to make a care order—
>   (a) is required to consider the permanence provisions of the section 31A plan for the child concerned, but
>   (b) is not required to consider the remainder of the section 31A plan, subject to section 34(11).
> (3B) For the purposes of subsection (3A), the permanence provisions of a section 31A plan are such of the plan's provisions setting out the long-term plan for the upbringing of the child concerned as provide for any of the following—
>   (a) the child to live with any parent of the child's or with any other member of, or any friend of, the child's family;
>   (b) adoption;
>   (c) long-term care not within paragraph (a) or (b).

## 9.1 Reviewing implementation of the care plan

The House of Lords in *Re S (Minors) (Care Order: Implementation of Care Plan); Re W (Minors) (Care Order: Adequacy of Care Plan)*[749] recognised that in the case of a young child who is the subject of a care order who would not have the capacity to initiate further proceedings before the court, the absence of a mechanism for reviewing the implementation of a care plan might breach the child's human rights. For that reason, an amendment was made to section 26 of the Children Act 1989, together with regulations, to ensure that care plans are kept under review. Independent reviewing officers are employed to monitor the process and are able to refer appropriate cases to Cafcass. Cafcass officers are then able to initiate proceedings on the child's behalf under section 7 of the Human Rights Act 1998 or by way of judicial review.

# 10 The legal effect of a care order

When a care order is made, the local authority gains parental responsibility for the child, which is shared with persons who already have parental responsibility.[750] However, there are some statutory

[746] The Court of Appeal held that the orders were in breach of ss 9(5) and 100(2)(b).

[747] [1995] 2 FLR 456 at 463. For a similar example of local authority obduracy, see *Nottinghamshire County Council v P* [1993] 3 All ER 815.

[748] Ministry of Justice and Department for Education, *The Government Response to the Family Justice Review: A System with Children and Families at its Heart* (Cm 8273, February 2012), para 50.

[749] [2002] 2 AC 291.

[750] Children Act 1989, s 33. Unless the care order has discharged the order which originally conferred parental responsibility. A residence arrangements order is discharged when a care order is made so any parental responsibility

limits imposed on the parental responsibility conferred on the local authority. Section 33(6)(a) provides that an authority is not permitted to 'cause the child to be brought up in any religious persuasion other than that in which he would have been brought up if the order had not been made'.[751] In *Re A and D (Local Authority: Religious Upbringing)*[752] a Muslim father of a child who had been placed under a care order with maternal grandparents who were Catholics, contended that this provision means that a local authority must ensure that the child is brought up in the religion to which he 'belonged' at the time of the making of the care order. Rejecting this contention, Baker J drew attention to the fact that the nature of a child's religious persuasion, and parental control over it, evolves as the child matures.[753] He also pointed out that either or both parents might change religion after a care order is made. Indeed, in this case the child's mother, who had been a convert to Islam, had reconverted to Catholicism. In light of these observations, his Lordship held that 'the subtle and careful language used in s 33(6)(a) requires an equally subtle and careful interpretation, rather than the inflexible, and . . . unworkable, interpretation for which the father contends'.[754] He held that the local authority's duty under section 33(6)(a), like all its statutory duties under the Children Act 1989, is subject to its overriding duty under section 17(1) and section 22(3) to safeguard and promote the child's welfare.[755] The local authority must have regard to any parent's change of religion and, as the child develops and makes his own choices, must respect the child's personal autonomy and freedom of conscience, provided again that by doing so it is safeguarding his welfare. The court rejected the father's claims that section 33(6)(a) and his rights under Articles 8 and 9 of the ECHR had been infringed. The local authority was entitled, and correct, to adopt its policy of trying to ensure that the child was bought up with an understanding of his mixed and varied heritage, and given the opportunity to develop his own thinking, and was demonstrating a proportionate empathy with the different belief systems in the family.

A local authority also do not have the right to agree or refuse to agree to the making of an adoption order, or an order under section 84 of the Adoption and Children Act 2002, with respect to the child[756] or the right to appoint a guardian for the child.[757] While a care order is in force, no person may cause the child to be known by a new surname or remove him or her from the UK, without either the written consent of every person who has parental responsibility for the child or the leave of the court.[758]

Section 33(3)(b) goes on to state that the local authority has the power to determine the extent to which a parent, guardian, special guardian, or a person who has parental responsibility for the child by way of section 4A of the Children Act 1989, may meet his or her parental responsibility for the child. Thus, it can be seen that the local authority and others with parental responsibility are not equal holders of parental responsibility: decision making has been firmly vested by statute in the local authority. However, the local authority's power of control is not an unfettered one. It cannot be exercised unless the local authority is satisfied that it is necessary to safeguard or promote the child's welfare. It is also subject to any right, power, duty, or authority which persons mentioned in section 33(3)(b) have in relation to the child and his or her property by virtue of any other enactment. Furthermore, a parent who has care of the child subject to the care order remains entitled to do whatever is reasonable in the circumstances to safeguard or promote the child's welfare.[759]

It will be recalled that a child who is subject to a care order is a 'looked after' child under Part III of the Children Act 1989, so the duties in sections 22 to 22G (discussed earlier) in relation to

---

which is conferred only while the residence order is in force would be ended. Parental responsibility is not lost solely because some other person subsequently acquires it (s 2(6)). A useful analysis of the Children Act 1989, s 33 is provided by Baker J in *Re A and D (Local Authority: Religious Upbringing)* [2010] EWHC 2503 (Fam), [2011] 1 FLR 615 at [70] et seq.

[751] Section 33(6)(a).   [752] [2010] EWHC 2503 (Fam), [2011] 1 FLR 615.   [753] Ibid, [73].
[754] Ibid, [74].   [755] Ibid, [75].   [756] Section 33(6)(b)(ii).   [757] Section 33(6)(b) (iii).
[758] Section 33(7). See *Re S (A Minor) (Change of Surname)* [1999] 1 FCR 304 (court granting leave to a 15-year-old *Gillick* competent girl to change her surname to that of her maternal aunt and uncle, with whom she was living under a care order).
[759] Section 33(5).

placement, and consultation about the placement, apply. It is possible for a child to be placed at home with his parents despite being in the care of the local authority. Clearly, where it was the parents who caused, or failed to protect, the child from suffering, or being likely to suffer, significant harm, safeguards are needed to ensure the safety of the child when this arrangement is made. There are special regulations about such placements which require the local authority to be sure that the placement of the child is the most suitable way of performing its duty to safeguard and promote the child's welfare, to make regular visits and to review the placement as necessary.[760]

While, as we have seen, the court does not retain any supervisory jurisdiction over a care plan when exercising its jurisdiction under the Children Act 1989 or in wardship, the court's power to intervene in judicial review proceedings or when exercising its jurisdiction under the Human Rights Act 1998 remains. A local authority must therefore continue to be mindful of its human rights obligations when exercising powers under a care order.

In *Re G (Care: Challenge to Local Authority's Decision)*[761] a care order had been made, approving a care plan to rehabilitate children with their parents. Two years later, at a meeting to which the parents were not invited, the local authority decided to alter the plan and to remove the children because of increasing concerns. The local authority eventually reverted to its original plan of rehabilitation, and the case came before Munby J on an application for leave to withdraw the proceedings. In the course of granting leave, however, his Lordship took the opportunity to emphasise that Article 8 of the ECHR provides not only substantive protection but also significant procedural safeguards[762] and 'guarantees fairness in the decision-making process at *all* stages of child protection'[763] including when the local authority is implementing its care plan. Munby J stated that:

> [t]he fact that a local authority has parental responsibility for children pursuant to s 33(3)(a) of the Children Act 1989 does not entitle it to take decisions about those children without reference to, or over the heads of, the children's parents. A local authority, even if clothed with the authority of a care order, is not entitled to make significant changes in the care plan, or to change the arrangements under which the children are living, let alone to remove the children from home if they are living with their parents, without properly involving the parents in the decision-making process and without giving the parents a proper opportunity to make their case before a decision is made.[764]

## 11 Supervision orders

A supervision order places a child under the supervision of a designated local authority,[765] initially for a period of one year.[766] The order ceases after that period unless extended for such period(s) as the court may specify,[767] although it may not be extended to run beyond the end of the period of three years beginning with the date on which it was made.[768] The general duties of the supervisor

---

[760] Care Planning, Placement and Case Review (England) Regulations 2010 (SI 2010/959).

[761] [2003] EWHC 551 (Fam), [2003] 2 FLR 42.     [762] Ibid, [30].

[763] Ibid, [35], citing *Re L (Care: Assessment: Fair Trial)* [2002] EWHC 1379 (Fam), [2002] 2 FLR 730 at [88].

[764] [2003] EWHC 551 (Fam), [2003] 2 FLR 42 at [43]. See also *R (H) v Kingston Upon Hull City Council* [2013] EWHC 388 (Admin) in which the failure to consult on change of placement was challenged successfully in judicial review proceedings even though an interim care order was in place. See also *Re M (Care: Challenging Decisions by Local Authority)* [2001] 2 FLR 1300, FD.

[765] As defined in s 31(8). The order can be imposed upon any local authority in whose area the child is, or will, live but in other cases requires the local authority's agreement: see Sch 3, para 9(1).

[766] Schedule 3, para 6(1). The making of the order brings to an end any earlier supervision order or care order: see Sch 3, para 10.

[767] Schedule 3, para 6(3).

[768] Schedule 3, para 6(4). It is not possible to substitute a care order on an application to extend a supervision order: see *Re A (Supervision Order: Extension)* [1995] 1 FLR 335, CA.

are set out in section 35 of the Children Act 1989, and further detailed provisions are found in Parts I and II of Schedule 3.

Section 35 provides that it is the duty of the supervisor to advise, assist, and befriend the supervised child and to take such steps as are reasonably necessary to give effect to the order.[769] Furthermore, where the order is not wholly complied with, or where it appears no longer to be necessary, the supervisor must consider whether an application should be made to vary or discharge the order.[770] So compliance with the order cannot be directly enforced but clearly if the supervisor becomes anxious that supervision is not enough to protect the child from suffering significant harm, he or she should approach the court again for its reconsideration of the appropriate form of protection for the child. In an emergency, steps should be taken to obtain an emergency protection order.

The provisions within Schedule 3 enable a highly structured supervision order to be made which may afford the child adequate protection. A supervision order can be supplemented and strengthened by giving the supervisor additional powers. The order may require the supervised child to comply with directions given from time to time by the supervisor which require the child to do all or any of the following: live at a particular place; present to a person or persons at specified places and times; and participate in specified activities.[771] There is no power to give directions in respect of medical or psychiatric treatment or examination.[772] The directions can be given to the child without the child's consent, although in the case of an older child, the child's willingness to comply with such directions may be a relevant practical consideration as to whether the order is appropriate.[773] The order may also require the child to submit to medical or psychiatric examination and treatment.[774] In addition, the order can require the child to keep the supervisor informed of his or her address and allow the supervisor to visit.[775] Similarly, a 'responsible person', meaning any person who has parental responsibility for the child and any other person with whom the child is living,[776] can be required to inform as to the child's address (if known) and, if living with the child, required to allow the supervisor reasonable contact with the child.[777]

In many cases, the child will be too young to control his own upbringing in any way and to express a view on the directions and requirements imposed. Directions are likely to include such matters as that the child should go to a day nursery, attend a clinic, and go to a family centre on specified days. In such cases, cooperation from the persons looking after the child is normally essential if the supervision order is to work. Consequently, there is power, with the consent of a responsible person, to impose further obligations on that person,[778] to ensure that the supervised child complies with the directions imposed and any examination or treatment ordered. The order may also include a requirement that the responsible person complies with any directions given by the supervisor that he attends at certain places for the purpose of taking part in specified activities.

But even where the responsible person consents, the supervisor has no powers to secure direct compliance with the obligations. The supervisor's only 'sanction' in the case of non-cooperation is to consider seeking variation or discharge of the order.[779] It is, therefore, entirely inappropriate for a supervision order to be made where it is the court's intention that the local authority should be able to control the situation.[780]

In *Re H (Supervision Order)*,[781] the children concerned were living with their mother and having contact with their father. He had served a sentence of imprisonment for sexual assaults on his

---

[769] Section 35(1)(a) and (b).     [770] Section 35(1)(c).     [771] Schedule 3, para 2(1).

[772] Schedule 3, para 2(3).

[773] This may be particularly relevant where the significant harm is attributable to the child's being beyond parental control.

[774] The usual proviso about the competent child agreeing to such examination or treatment applies: Sch 3, paras 4(4) and 5(5).

[775] Schedule 3, para 8(1).     [776] Schedule 3, para 1.     [777] Schedule 3, para 8(2).

[778] Schedule 3, para 3.

[779] Section 35.     [780] *Re R and G (Minors) (Interim Care or Supervision Orders)* [1994] 1 FLR 793.

[781] [1994] 2 FLR 979.

stepchild. He was anxious to receive treatment for his behaviour and therefore readily agreed to attend at a specialist clinic. It was agreed by all parties, and by the court, that a supervision order was appropriate. But the mother, father, and guardian ad litem sought an order under Schedule 3 that the local authority should direct the father to attend a particular course of treatment at the clinic. The local authority contended that the court had no power to make such a direction. Bracewell J upheld the local authority's contention. She drew a contrast between the power of the court to direct that the child submit to a medical or psychiatric examination or treatment, and its powers to make orders in respect of a responsible person. She held that requirements as to treatment of the child are wholly the responsibility of the court, and must be specified in the order itself. However, she held that the imposition of obligations on a responsible person fell into a wholly different category, namely that such directions are solely a matter for the supervisor, and that it is not open to the court to order the local authority to give any such directions. Clearly, if a court were entitled to impose such an obligation on a local authority, this would amount to a form of court control over local authority expenditure. Services provided by clinics of this kind are an expensive resource, and therefore it is for the local authority, rather than the court, to decide whether use should be made of such services as part of the authority's child protection strategy.

In *Re M (A Minor) (No 2) (Appeal)*[782] Ward J justified declining to make a supervision order on the ground that confidence between the parents and the local authority had been 'irredeemably destroyed'. He reached this conclusion despite having found that the mother, by failing to obtain medical attention for the child, had caused the child to suffer, and to be likely to suffer, significant harm, and that the child was dangerously ill by the time she was taken to hospital. Against these findings, the issue of confidence between the parents and the local authority seems slight. Unless the local authority is authorised to make regular checks on a child's progress, there are real dangers that the child may slip through the net of child protection procedures. There is clear authority for the proposition that it is appropriate for a court to make a care order even though parties, the guardian, and the court itself all agree that the child should not be removed from his parents; and even where the local authority only wishes and proposes that there should be a supervision order.[783]

## 12  Deciding between a care order or supervision order

In most cases in which it is acknowledged that longer term protection of a child is required, the court will be deciding whether that protection is more appropriately afforded by way of a care order or a supervision order.[784] In *Re S (J) (A Minor) (Care or Supervision Order)*[785] HHJ Coningsby QC, sitting as a Family Division judge, pointed out that there is a tendency to look at those orders under the same umbrella because the statutory criteria for making them are the same. Where the local authority's plan is to place the child in the day-to-day care of a parent, the difference between the orders, at least superficially, is likely to be least visible.[786] However, HHJ Coningsby QC engaged in a careful analysis of the essential features of each order in that context,[787] and cautioned that supervision 'should not in any sense be seen as a sort of watered-down version of care'.[788] He

---

[782] [1994] 1 FLR 59. For critical commentary, see J. R. Spencer, 'Evidence in Child Abuse Cases: Too High a Price for Too High a Standard?' (1994) 6 Journal of Child Law 160, and the editorial by M. Hayes in the same issue.

[783] *Re B (Care or Supervision Order)* [1996] 2 FLR 693.

[784] See G. Brasse, 'Supervision or Care Orders?' [1997] Family Law 351.      [785] [1993] 2 FLR 919, FD.

[786] It has been argued that there is a need for a third, intermediate, order in such situations (a protected parental placement order), a supervision order with conditions attached and power to remove the child for 72 hours where a condition is breached: see A. A. Gillespie, 'Establishing a Third Order in Care Proceedings' [2000] Child and Family Law Quarterly 239.

[787] See especially 947–51.

[788] *Re S (J) (A Minor) (Care or Supervision Order)* [1993] 2 FLR 919 at 950 *per* Judge Coningsby QC; see too *Leicestershire County Council v G* [1994] 2 FLR 329.

observed that the concept of parental responsibility is at the heart of the difference. If granted a care order, the local authority has parental responsibility and 'the whip hand as far as control is concerned'.[789] In addition, a duty is imposed on the local authority to safeguard and promote the child's welfare.[790] If the child is placed at home with parents,[791] the placement is subject to the Care Planning, Placement and Case Review (England) Regulations 2010,[792] which impose duties on the local authority to monitor the welfare of the child in the placement by way of regular visits,[793] and to review the placement if the visit reveals that the placement may not be safeguarding the child's interests.[794] By contrast, parental responsibility and the obligation to safeguard the child's welfare do not pass to the local authority under a supervision order; they remain with the parent(s). Unlike a care order, a supervision order is also time limited (up to three years where extended). Finally, and importantly, the supervision order 'has less teeth than the care order' since, apart from the supervisor's access to the child (which can be enforced by a warrant under s 102), its provisions cannot be directly enforced, and breaches can only be evidence in further proceedings.[795]

So how is the court to choose between these different orders? First, the chosen order must be a proportionate response. A care order rather than a supervision order should be made only if the stronger order is necessary for the proper protection of the child.[796] In *Re O (Care or Supervision Order)*[797] Hale J stated that it was accepted by all parties that the court should begin with a preference for the less interventionist rather than the more interventionist approach and that this should be considered to be in the better interests of the child unless there are cogent reasons to the contrary;[798] and her Ladyship acknowledged that 'one must always beware an over-authoritarian or Draconian approach which has not been demonstrated to be necessary in the best interests of the children in the particular case yet'.[799] In that case there were long-standing concerns about the health and development of six children, who for the foreseeable future were to remain living with their parents. The parents had demonstrated some improvement and the local authority had intensified its involvement with the family. The sole issue was whether the children's welfare would be better served by a supervision order, sought by the local authority, or a care order, as argued by the children's guardian. The justices made a care order. Substituting a supervision order as more appropriate on the facts of the case, Hale J found that, as well as erring in the process of balancing relevant evidence, the justices had gone straight to the more draconian order without fully considering the effect of a supervision order. They had also failed to consider the case in the context of all of the local authority's duties under Part III of the Children Act 1989. The choice of order is linked to these duties to provide services to prevent children in their area suffering ill-treatment or neglect and to reduce the need to take proceedings for care or supervision orders, and Hale J emphasised that Parliament intended that these services should be offered.[800]

It has been said that an appropriate general approach is for the court to consider 'whether, in the light of gravity of the case as a whole, the local authority ought to have imposed upon it the extra duties'[801] which a care order brings. The need to put in place an appropriate level of protection is likely to be the decisive factor in any case. In *Re D (A Minor) (Care or Supervision Order)*[802] a father

---

[789] *Re S(J) (A Minor) (Care or Supervision Order)* [1993] 2 FLR 919 at 948.  [790] Children Act 1989, s 22.

[791] It is not wrong in law to make a care order where it is proposed to leave a child in the day-to-day care of parents: see *Re T (A Minor) (Care or Supervision Order)* [1994] 1 FLR 103 at 105–106, citing *M v Westminster City Council* [1985] FLR 325.

[792] SI 2010/959.  [793] Ibid, reg 28.  [794] Ibid, reg 30.

[795] See *Croydon London Borough Council v A (No 3)* [1992] 2 FLR 350. See also *per* Bracewell J in *Re T (A Minor) (Care or Supervision Order)* [1994] 1 FLR 103 at 106.

[796] *Re W (A Minor) (Interim Care Order)* [1994] 2 FLR 892; *Oxfordshire County Council v L (Care or Supervision Order)* [1998] 1 FLR 70.

[797] [1996] 2 FLR 755.  [798] Ibid, 760.  [799] Ibid, 763.

[800] For a similar case substituting a supervision order, see *Oxfordshire County Council v L (Care or Supervision Order)* [1998] 1 FLR 70.

[801] *Re S(J) (A Minor) (Care or Supervision Order)* [1993] 2 FLR 919 at 957.  [802] [1993] 2 FLR 423.

had been convicted of cruelty to a 2-month-old baby who had died from a fractured skull and other injuries.[803] A decade later he set up home with another woman and had another child. The local authority sought a supervision order in respect of the child, taking the view that the child was thriving and a care order would undermine working cooperatively with the parents. Ewbank J held that the child's protection was the decisive factor and the local authority's views were not an appropriate reason to make a supervision order where it would not afford the child sufficient protection.[804]

In some cases, the extent to which the order allows a quick response may be a major factor influencing the court. In *S (J) (A Minor) (Care or Supervision Order)*,[805] for example, the judge concluded that 'this is a case where things could occur so rapidly and so dangerously that the care order procedure is needed'.[806] While the local authority may, of course, apply for an EPO, it may be in the interests of the child that the authority should not have first to take this step before intervening. A care order may also act as an incentive to parents to comply with the care plan because they know that non-compliance may lead to their child being taken from them.[807] Such strong pressure cannot be exerted where a supervision order is in place.

In weighing the relative merits of a care order or a supervision order, a judge must properly advert to the difference between the two orders.[808] In *Re V (Care or Supervision Order)*[809] the judge had misunderstood the nature of a supervision order. A 16-year-old boy, S, who suffered with spastic quadriplegia and learning disabilities, was withdrawn from a special school by his mother. The father took a different view, agreeing with professional opinion that S's attendance at the school was beneficial. The local authority became concerned that S was regressing and sought a care order. The judge declined to make a care order for fear that it would put great strain on the parents' marriage. Instead, he made a supervision order subject to a condition that S continue to attend the school. The Court of Appeal held that the judge had erred, in that the 'concept of a supervision order subject to conditions cannot be fitted into the framework of the Children Act legislation'.[810] While the judge had been correct to give weight to the impact of the order on the parents' relationship, the impact of loss of school attendance on the child's welfare (which prevailed) was more significant, and a care order was required to ensure the child's attendance. It was particularly important on the facts that a care order be made because the boy was only three weeks off his 17th birthday, by which time neither order could be made.[811]

A care order can be made where the local authority is merely seeking a supervision order,[812] although Hale J commented in *Re O (Care or Supervision Order)*[813] that 'if the court is to impose upon the authority an order other than that for which it asks, there should be very cogent reasons indeed to do so'.[814] In *Re C (Care or Supervision Order)*,[815] for example, Sir Stephen Brown P upheld the decision of justices to make a care order (in respect of a six-month-old baby whose seven siblings had all been taken into care), where the local authority was merely seeking a supervision order.[816]

---

[803] The father was acquitted of the baby's murder. A four-year-old child had also suffered injury in the household.

[804] See esp [1993] 2 FLR 423, at 429.     [805] [1993] 2 FLR 919, FD.

[806] *Re S(J) (A Minor) (Care or Supervision Order)* [1993] 2 FLR 919 at 953. See also *Re R and G (Minors) (Interim Care or Supervision Orders)* [1994] 1 FLR 793, in which the justices apparently misunderstood the nature of a supervision order in thinking that the local authority could thereby force children to attend a family centre against their parents' wishes.

[807] See eg Bracewell J's comment in *Re T (A Minor) (Care or Supervision Order)* [1994] 1 FLR 103, CA at 107, that the judge 'was justified in reaching the conclusion that the existence of a care order would concentrate the minds of the parents on their responsibilities'.

[808] *Re S (Care or Supervision Order)* [1996] 1 FLR 753 at 759 *per* Beldam LJ.

[809] *Re V (Care or Supervision Order)* [1996] 1 FLR 776, CA.

[810] Ibid, 785. See also *Re S (Care or Supervision Order)* [1996] 1 FLR 753 where a judge erroneously attached conditions to a supervision order to try to protect a child from sexual abuse.

[811] Children Act 1989, s 31(3).

[812] Ibid, s 31(5).     [813] [1996] 2 FLR 755.     [814] Ibid, 759.     [815] [1999] 2 FLR 621.

[816] It is possible, however, that Sir Stephen Brown P questioned the emphasis in Hale J's judgment in *Re O*, following up her words quoted earlier with a comment that 'in point of fact' the case before him came down to the question of discretion: ibid, 624.

By contrast with these cases in which care orders were made, two cases provide further illustrations of circumstances in which a supervision order might be appropriate. In *Re B (Care or Supervision Order)*[817] the father of six children had absconded when due to stand trial for indecent assault of one of his daughters, and the children were living with the mother under a residence order which prohibited the children's contact with the father. Holman J found that the children's pressing needs were to be closely monitored and to undertake work with child protection professionals. His Lordship took into account as relevant, although not decisive, the social worker's view that the mother and children would react unfavourably to a care order, thus undermining the relationship of trust established with the social worker. Similarly in *Re C (Care or Supervision Order)*[818] a child was injured when the mother left him in the care of his father, whom the mother knew to be violent. The father was imprisoned and the child was living with the mother. Sumner J found that in the circumstances the risk to the child from the mother (eg setting up home with another violent man) was very low, and a supervision order represented a proportionate response.[819]

## 13  Discharge of care orders

Care orders may be discharged on the application of any person who has parental responsibility for the child, the child himself or the local authority.[820] There is no obligation on the applicant to satisfy the court that the threshold requirements no longer apply. The court has a discretionary jurisdiction from the outset and the welfare principle and welfare checklist apply.[821] Where, after hearing from the applicant, the court feels that the application stands no realistic prospect of success it is entitled to exercise its discretion and stop the case without hearing all the evidence.[822]

The requirement in section 1(3)(e) that the court shall have regard to any harm which the child has suffered or is at risk of suffering, therefore normally takes on a particular significance in discharge cases. The relevant time at which the risk must be considered is the risk current at the date of the discharge hearing.[823] In *Re S (Discharge of Care Order)*,[824] the Court of Appeal acknowledged that there are rare instances where justice to both children and adults requires the court which is hearing the discharge application to question not merely the relevance but also the soundness of the findings of fact made in the original proceedings. Although this amounts to a relaxation of the ordinary rules of issue estoppel, the court explained that such willingness 'does not originate from laxity or benevolence but from recognition that where children are concerned there is liable to be an infinite variety of circumstances whose proper consideration in the best interests of the child is not to be trammelled by the arbitrary imposition of procedural rules'.[825]

A judge is entitled to take into account the continuing effect, or lack of effect, of the care order.[826] In *Re C (Care: Discharge of Care Order)*[827] the Court of Appeal upheld a judge's decision to discharge a care order where the local authority could not give proper effect to it because

---

[817] [1996] 2 FLR 693.     [818] [2001] 2 FLR 466.

[819] Ibid, [52]. See also *Re O (Care Order: Discharge of Care Order)* [1999] 2 FLR 119 (discharging care order and making supervision order) and *Surrey County Council v S* [2014] EWCA Civ 601 (supervision order preferred to a care order in a case of neglect).

[820] Section 39(1). The child does not first require the leave of the court to make an application (unlike the position in private proceedings under s 10): *Re A (Care: Discharge Application by Child)* [1995] 1 FLR 599.

[821] See *Re S (Discharge of Care Order)* [1995] 2 FLR 639 at 643 *per* Waite LJ.

[822] *Re S and P (Discharge of Care Order)* [1995] 2 FLR 782.

[823] *Re S (Discharge of Care Order)* [1995] 2 FLR 639.     [824] [1995] 2 FLR 639.

[825] Ibid, 646.     [826] *Re C (Care: Discharge of Care Order)* [2009] EWCA Civ 955, [2010] 1 FLR 774.

[827] Ibid.

a 15-year-old boy repeatedly absconded to his mother's home, and thus the effect of the care order was to set up conflict.[828] However, it will be recalled that the point at which a child leaves care is relevant to the local authority's duties to provide ongoing support under the leaving care provisions, and the Court of Appeal added that the order's lack of effect 'needed to be balanced against the potential advantages under the leaving care provisions of preserving an empty husk of a care order'.[829]

## 14 Contact with a child in care

### Key legislation

Paragraph 15(1) of Schedule 2 positively promotes the maintenance of contact by providing that:

> Where a child is being looked after by a local authority, the authority shall, unless it is not reasonably practicable or consistent with his welfare, endeavour to promote contact between the child and—
>
> (a) his parents;
> (b) any person who is not a parent of his but who has parental responsibility for him; and
> (c) any relative, friend or other person connected with him.

Other provisions in the Children Act 1989 reinforce this general principle: local authorities are required to make efforts to secure that a child is accommodated near his home; parents and persons with parental responsibility should be told where the child is living;[830] and it is recognised that parents, relatives, and friends of a child in care may be too poor to afford the travelling costs involved in visiting the child, and the local authority has a discretion to make payments towards defraying these and other expenses.[831]

At the time when an application is made for a final care order, the local authority's attitude towards contact between the child and his parents will normally form part of its care plan for the child. Section 34(11) provides that before making a care order the court must consider the contact arrangements which the local authority has made, or proposes to make, and must invite the parties to the proceedings to comment on those arrangements.[832] The court is empowered at this stage[833] to make any order it thinks appropriate in relation to contact, either on application[834] or in the exercise its own motion powers.[835] However, in many cases an order will not be necessary.[836]

---

[828] Discharge applications can cause particular problems where it is clear that the local authority's care plan is not working, yet it cannot be said that the parents have improved sufficiently for it to be safe to return the child to their care, see G. Posner, 'Applications to Discharge Care Orders' [1998] Family Law 623.

[829] *Re C (Care: Discharge of Care Order)* [2009] EWCA Civ 955, [2010] 1 FLR 774 at [22]. On the facts of the case the leaving care provisions did not apply because the child had been living with his mother: see Children (Leaving Care) (England) Regulations 2001, reg 4(5). However, the court indicated that for a local authority to seek discharge in order to avoid the effect of the leaving care provisions would be an improper ground: see *Re C* at [31].

[830] Unless, in the case of a child in care, this would prejudice the child's welfare: Sch 2, para 15(2), (3), and (4).

[831] Schedule 2, para 16.

[832] See Department of Health and Social Services Inspectorate, *Contact Orders Study: A Study of Local Authority Decision Making around Contact Applications under Section 34* (London: HMSO, 1994).

[833] Section 34(10).

[834] Eg under s 34(2) or (3).

[835] Section 34(5). In *Re S (A Minor) (Care: Contact Order)* [1994] 2 FLR 222 at 226 Sir Francis Purchas commented that 'it must be extremely rare that a judge would wish to do so'.

[836] See *Re L (Minors) (Care Proceedings: Contact)* [1998] 3 FCR 339 at 347 *per* Wilson J.

This is because the law takes as its starting point the rule that a child must be allowed to have reasonable contact with his parents and other important persons in his life even though he has been removed from their care.[837] Contact is normally therefore a matter to be arranged by agreement between the local authority, the child, the parents, and other interested persons. Indeed, in the public law, applications for contact orders with a child in care were made in only 2 per cent of cases and for orders refusing contact in 3 per cent, and the court made orders in only 1 per cent of such cases.[838]

---

### Key legislation

Section 34(1) provides:

> Where a child is in the care of a local authority, the authority shall (subject to the provisions of this section) allow the child reasonable contact with—
>
> > (a)  his parents;
> > (b)  any guardian or special guardian of his;
> > (ba)  any person who by virtue of section 4A has parental responsibility for him;
> > (c)  where there was a child arrangements order in force with respect to the child immediately before the care order was made, any person named in the child arrangements order as a person with whom the child was to live; and
> > (d)  where, immediately before the care order was made a person had care of the child by virtue of an order made in the exercise of the High Court's inherent jurisdiction with respect to children, that person.

---

In this context, therefore, contact at the discretion of the local authority means 'reasonable contact'.[839] In *Re P (Minors) (Contact with Children in Care)*,[840] Ewbank J stated that 'reasonable' implies contact which has been agreed between the local authority and the parents or, if there is no such agreement, contact which is objectively reasonable. Clearly, what is reasonable will vary according to the particular circumstances,[841] and in some cases the evidence may justify quite restricted contact as reasonable.[842] It is unclear, however, whether reasonable contact in this context can be said to embrace merely indirect contact.[843]

---

[837]  Section 34(1). By contrast, where, unusually, parents of a child in care are refusing to have anything to do with him they cannot be compelled to have contact with him. Where parents are preventing a child in care from having contact with siblings, the child may seek the leave of the court to apply for a contact order under s 8. See *Re F (Contact: Child in Care)* [1995] 1 FLR 510.

[838]  D Cassidy and S Davey, Ministry of Justice Research Summary 5/11, *Family Justice Children's Proceedings – Review of Public and Private Law Cases Files in England & Wales*, 2011, cited in A. Bainham 'Swimming against the tide: challenging contact arrangements in the public law' [2015] Fam Law 1356.

[839]  Cf *L v London Borough of Bromley* [1998] 1 FLR 709: order that contact should be at the discretion of the local authority made in relation to a person who falls within s 34(1) means that the local authority must allow and arrange reasonable contact between the child and that person, and it is not inapt for the court to indicate the frequency which it has in mind.

[840]  [1993] 2 FLR 156.

[841]  On the facts of *Re P* two-and-a-half hours unsupervised contact per month was said to be reasonable, unless the children requested more contact.

[842]  See eg *Re C (Care: Contact)* [2009] EWCA Civ 959, [2010] 1 FLR 895, where the Court of Appeal upheld a care plan which restricted contact between a mother, who had been the sole carer of two children aged 9 and 7, to four times per year, which was justified by reference to expert evidence (see at [56]).

[843]  See the discussion in A.Bainham, 'Swimming against the Tide: Challenging Contact Arrangements in the Public Law' [2015] Fam Law 1356.

## 14.1 Regulating contact with a child in care in cases of disagreement

Where the local authority and the parents, or other specified persons, cannot agree on contact arrangements, an application can be made under section 34 for the court to determine the matter,[844] and a section 34 order is enforceable by committal proceedings should, for example, a foster parent be hostile to a parent's contact with a child.[845] Under section 34(2), the local authority or the child may apply to the court to make such order as it considers appropriate with respect to the contact which is allowed between the child and any named person. However, the effect of section 34(8) and the Care Planning, Placement and Case Review (England) Regulations 2010[846] is that the local authority can depart from the order with the agreement of the person in whose favour the order is made, provided that any child, being of sufficient age and understanding, also agrees.[847]

Under section 34(3), any person mentioned in section 34(1)(a)–(d) is similarly entitled to apply for a contact order.[848] Any other person who is aggrieved about the amount of contact may apply for a contact order provided that the court first gives leave.[849]

The Children Act 1989 does not contain specific criteria for determining whether an application for leave under section 34 should be granted. Detailed guidance on how this vacuum should be filled was given in *Re M (Care: Contact: Grandmother's Application for Leave)*.[850] Ward LJ stated that while it is clear that section 10(9), which deals with leave to apply for section 8 orders, does not govern contact with a child in care, it is equally clear that it could be anomalous were the court not to take account of the factors specified in section 10(9) when exercising its discretion to grant leave.[851]

## 14.2 Authorising the local authority to deny contact

In *Re B (Minors) (Care: Contact: Local Authority's Plans)*[852] Butler-Sloss LJ said that it is clear that the discretion to refuse to allow contact, or otherwise to determine what contact is reasonable, is firmly vested in the courts and not in the local authority.[853] She said that the proposals of the local authority, based on their appreciation of the best interests of the child, must command the greatest respect and consideration from the court, but that the duty to decide is in the court. Consequently, 'the court may have the task of requiring the local authority to justify their long-term plans to the extent only that those plans exclude contact between parent and child'. It is for the court to determine whether such a plan is in the best interests of the child.[854]

---

[844] For a full discussion of the difficulties in obtaining contact between parent and child in public law proceedings, and the view that there is a culture against making contact orders in public law proceedings, including placement and adoption proceedings, see Bainham, ibid.

[845] See *Re P-B (Contact: Committal)* [2009] 2 FLR 66, CA. Exceptionally a penal order might be attached.

[846] SI 2010/959.      [847] See ibid, reg 8(4).

[848] Section 34(3)(a). Where a court in earlier proceedings has made an order authorising that there should be no contact between a child and his parent, if an application is later made under s 34 a court is entitled to act robustly and to dismiss the application without hearing oral evidence: *Cheshire County Council v M* [1993] 1 FLR 463.

[849] Section 34(3)(b). As such persons are not entitled to contact within s 34(1), an order that their contact should be at the discretion of the local authority means only that the authority should endeavour to promote it unless it is not practicable or consistent with the welfare of the child (Sch 2, para 15(1)(c)); see *L v London Borough of Bromley* [1998] 1 FLR 709.

[850] [1995] 2 FLR 86. See discussion in Chapter 9, Section 5.5.

[851] Eg a court might be faced with an application by a grandparent for leave to apply for a residence order in relation to a child in care, or alternatively a contact order. For the first application, she would need leave of the court under s 10(9); for the second under s 34(3).

[852] [1993] 1 FLR 543.

[853] Butler-Sloss LJ said that her own earlier judgment in *Re S (A Minor) (Access Application)* [1991] 1 FLR 161 should be read 'with considerable caution'.

[854] Where the nature and extent of contact is an integral part of the local authority's care plan it is not permissible for a judge to adjourn proceedings for future consideration of what is reasonable contact since the judge would be 'straying into the forbidden territory of supervising the administration of the local authority's arrangements for rehabilitation': *Re S (A Minor) (Care: Contact Order)* [1994] 2 FLR 222 at 226 *per* Simon Brown LJ.

Section 34(6) empowers the local authority to refuse to allow the contact that would otherwise be required by virtue of section 34(1) if satisfied that: it is necessary to do so in order to safeguard or promote the child's welfare; the refusal is decided upon as a matter of urgency; and it does not last for more than seven days. Section 34(4) provides that upon the application of the local authority or the child the court may make an order authorising the authority to refuse to allow contact between the child and a named person within section 34(1). Although section 34 does not actually say so in terms, the implication of section 34(4) and (6) when read together is that, outside the exception in subsection (6), court authorisation for denial of contact is required.[855] Where the court authorises refusal, the local authority is in control over when contact is actually brought to an end. The authority may determine whether, for example, contact should be gradually phased out, whether there should be a final 'goodbye' visit, or whether contact should terminate forthwith. Section 34(6A) provides that where the local authority is authorised to refuse contact, paragraph 15(1) of schedule 2 no longer requires the local authority to endeavour to promote such contact.

Authorising the termination of contact is a draconian decision and one which courts will not make lightly.[856] In *Re E (A Minor) (Care Order: Contact)*[857] Simon Brown LJ recognised that 'although the value of contact may be limited by the parent's inadequacy, it may still be of fundamental importance to the long-term welfare of the child, unless of course it can be seen that in a given case it will inevitably disturb the child's care'.[858] He set out four reasons why contact may still be of importance:

> first, in giving the child the security of knowing that his parents love him and are interested in his welfare; secondly, by avoiding any damaging sense of loss to the child in seeing himself abandoned by his parents; thirdly, by enabling the child to commit himself to the substitute family with the seal of approval of the natural parents; and, fourthly, by giving the child the necessary sense of family and personal identity.[859]

In some cases, however, a local authority may decide to abandon any attempt to rehabilitate the child with his or her family because of the danger a parent presents to the child, and adoption may be their long-term plan for the child. In such a case, a court might also conclude that no further contact would be appropriate, for example because the parent could play no appropriate future role or would perhaps undermine the child's placement.[860] In a less clear-cut case the question of denial of contact may arise in the context of deciding whether the rehabilitation of the child with his family should be attempted when balancing the prospects of success against the fact that delay in determining a question about the child's upbringing is likely to prejudice the welfare of the child.[861]

Even where it is believed that the child needs the security of a settled placement away from the parents, the difficulty is to know how much time and effort should be given to exploring

---

[855] See *per* Butler-Sloss LJ in *Re B (Minors) (Care: Contact: Local Authority's Plans)* [1993] 1 FLR 543 at 547: 'a presumption of continuing reasonable contact . . . unless or until a court order under s 34(4)'.

[856] See Thorpe LJ in *Re H (Termination of Contact)* [2005] 2 FLR 408 at [11]: 'The function of the judge in upholding the Parliamentary intention of s 34 and in granting s 34(4) orders restrictively and stringently is an important one.' The judge must be careful not to pre-judge the issue at an interim stage: see *Re H-T (Contact: Sexual Abuse)* [2012] EWCA Civ 1215, [2013] EWCA Civ 1215.

[857] [1994] 1 FLR 146.

[858] *Re E (A Minor) (Care Order: Contact)* [1994] 1 FLR 146, CA at 154 *per* Simon Brown LJ.

[859] Ibid, 154–5.

[860] See eg *Birmingham City Council v H* in which Connell J authorised the local authority to terminate contact, having concluded that it was very unlikely that the 15-year-old mother, whose behaviour towards her child had caused anxiety, would make significant progress in her ability to care for the child.

[861] Section 1(2).

arrangements with potential for the parents continued contact with a child before an order authorising termination of contact.[862] In *Re E (A Minor) (Care Order: Contact)*[863] a local authority sought permission to refuse contact between children and parents in light of its plan to place the child for closed adoption. Expert evidence had been given that the children would benefit from contact and that the parents would not undermine an alternative open placement. The local authority had not yet investigated the possibility of finding suitable prospective adopters who would accept a degree of face-to-face contact with the parents. The judge granted the local authority's application, being of the view that he should not make an order incompatible with the local authority's plans unless the children's welfare dictated otherwise. The Court of Appeal held that the judge had failed to apply the correct test, as set out in *Re B*, and that had the judge done so he must inevitably have recognised that it was premature to authorise termination of contact in the circumstances.[864]

Denial of contact will be authorised where the child's safety demands it. In *Re K (Contact)*[865] a fight broke out between parents at a supervised contact session and the mother threw her baby for 18 inches to the supervisor. Munby J authorised refusal of contact until a case management conference when more stringent conditions for supervised contact might be put in place.

The courts also recognise that contact must not be allowed to destabilise or endanger the local authority's plans for a child. As Thorpe J said in *Re N (Minors) (Care Orders: Termination of Parental Contact)*[866] 'it is always tempting to keep doors open against possible developments in an uncertain future, but the future must be surveyed in terms of probabilities and not low possibilities'. The three children concerned had suffered very severe significant harm at the hands of their parents, and as a consequence had special needs and would be difficult to place with long-term foster or adoptive parents. Thorpe J found that the search for a permanent new family would be made more difficult if the children continued to have a relationship with their parents in the interim. He therefore concluded that the need for an order authorising the refusal of contact had been plainly established.[867]

However, an order under section 34(4) must not be made merely in anticipation of its future use. In *Re L (Sexual Abuse: Standard of Proof)*[868] a judge made a care order, taking the view that there was still a possibility of rehabilitating the mother with the children. He nevertheless terminated contact,[869] his motive being to save the local authority the necessity of making a further application to the court should the authority wish to bring contact to an end. The Court of Appeal held that the judge had been wrong to hand over prematurely to the local authority the residual responsibility for contact arrangements which should still have vested in the court.

An order authorising a local authority to terminate contact is not a final order, and an application may be made under section 34(9) for the order to be discharged.[870] On such an application the child's welfare is paramount. The burden is on the applicant to show that there has

---

[862] See *L v London Borough of Bromley* [1998] 1 FLR 709 allowing an appeal from justices who had failed to take account of the unlikelihood of finding adopters who could tolerate a high level of contact.

[863] [1994] 1 FLR 146.

[864] See also *Re S (Care: Parental Contact)* [2004] EWCA civ 1397, [2005] 1 FLR 469 (order inappropriate where also a finding that contact will be beneficial).

[865] [2008] 2 FLR 581.     [866] [1994] 2 FCR 1101 at 1107.

[867] See also *Re SW (A Minor) (Care Proceedings)* [1993] 2 FLR 609 in which Booth J held that the justices were correct to exercise their own motion powers to order no contact between a child and his mother in circumstances where there was no realistic chance that the child would return to live with her, where the local authority's plan was to find a permanent substitute family for the child, and where the children's guardian supported this plan.

[868] [1996] 1 FLR 116.

[869] The local authority had not sought a section 34(4) order; it was made at the request of the guardian ad litem.

[870] Section 34(9). The only express statutory restriction on making any kind of section 34 order is that provided by s 91(17).

been some material change in circumstances and that the application is not a disguised form of appeal.[871]

In *Re W (A Child) (Parental Contact: Prohibition)*[872] the Court of Appeal held that section 34 'does not create a prohibitory jurisdiction',[873] so the court cannot prohibit contact which the local authority consider advantageous to the child's welfare.[874]

To summarise, a court has the power to authorise a local authority to terminate contact with the persons specified in section 34(1), either on an application made by the local authority or in the exercise of its own motion powers. However, the court cannot compel the authority to do so. Similarly, where the court makes an order under section 34(2) regulating contact arrangements between the child and a specified person, these can only be altered by the local authority where the person affected by the contact order agrees, and an order of the court can be overridden where such an agreement is made.

In the next chapter, we examine the law on adoption, which may be one of the local authority's options for long-term substitute care of a child who requires protection.

## Discussion Questions

1. To what extent, if at all, should the notion of 'significant harm' take account of cultural factors?

2. Explain the approach to proof of the threshold criteria in section 31(2) of the Children Act 1989 following *Re H* [1996] AC 563 and *Re B (Children)* [2009] AC 11. Do you think the approach to proof of likely harm adequately protects children? How does the approach of the dissenting judges in *Re H* differ?

3. Is the decision in *Re J* [2013] UKSC 33 compatible with Lord Nicholls' opinions in *Lancashire County Council v B* [2002] AC 147, and *Re O and another; Re B* [2004] 1 AC 523?

4. Does the law on child protection strike an appropriate balance between the role of the courts and that of local authorities?

## Further Reading

BAINHAM, A., 'Interim Care Orders: Is the Bar Set Too Low?' [2011] Family Law 374

BAINHAM, A., 'Suspicious Minds: Protecting Children in the Face of Uncertainty' (2013) *72* Cambridge Law Journal 266.

BAINHAM, A., 'Swimming against the Tide: Challenging Contact Arrangements in the Public Law' [2015] Fam Law 1356.

BETTLE, J. and HERRING, J., 'Shaken Babies and Care Proceedings' [2011] Family Law 1370

CONWAY, H., 'The Laming Inquiry—Victoria Climbie's Legacy' [2002] Family Law 755

CRETNEY, S., *Family Law in the Twentieth Century—A History* (Oxford: Oxford University Press, 2003), Ch 20

---

[871] *Re T (Termination of Contact: Discharge of Order)* [1997] 1 FLR 517.    [872] [2000] Fam 130.
[873] Ibid, 138.
[874] Cf the Court of Appeal's view in *Re D and H (Care: Termination of Contact)* [1997] 1 FLR 841 that s 34(2) should not be used to phase out contact against the local authority's view. Even if such a jurisdiction existed, as Ewbank J held in *Kent County Council v C* [1993] 1 FLR 308, it would be foolish to exercise it because the effect of Children Act 1989, s 34(8) and the Contact with Children Regulations 1991 (SI 1991/891), reg 3, is that an order can be departed from by agreement.

DOUGHTY, J., 'Re B (A Child) (Care Order) (2013) UKSC 33' (2013) *35*(4) Journal of Social Welfare and Family Law 491–501

EEKELAAR, J., 'Are Parents Morally Obliged to Care for Their Children?' (1991) *11*(3) Oxford Journal of Legal Studies 340

FREEMAN, M., 'The Right to Responsible Parents' in J. Bridgeman, H. Keating, and C. Lind, *Responsibility, Law and the Family* (Aldershot: Ashgate, 2008), pp 21–40

GILLESPIE, A. A., 'Establishing a Third Order in Care Proceedings' [2000] Child and Family Law Quarterly 239

GILMORE, S., '*Re J (Care Proceedings: Past Possible Perpetrators in a New Family Unit)* [2013] UKSC 9: Bulwarks and logic—the blood which runs through the veins of law—but how much will be spilled in future?' [2013] Child and Family Law Quarterly 215

HALE, B. et al, *The Family, Law and Society: Cases and Materials*, 5th edn (Oxford: Oxford University Press, 2005), Ch 11 (for historical material). See also generally the 6th edn, 2009, Ch 11

HAYES, J., 'Ensuring Equal Protection for Siblings' [2010] Family Law 505

HAYES, J., 'Protecting Child Victims of Female Genital Mutilation' [2015] Fam Law 282

HAYES, J., HAYES, M., and WILLIAMS, J., '"Shocking" Abuse Followed by a "Staggering Ruling": *Re MA (Care Threshold)*' [2010] Family Law 166

HAYES, M., 'Removing Children from their Families—Law and Policy Before the Children Act 1989' in G. Douglas and N. Lowe (eds), *The Continuing Evolution of Family Law* (Bristol: Jordan Publishing, 2009)

HAYES, M., 'The Supreme Court's Failure to Protect Vulnerable Children: *Re J (Children)*' [2013] Family Law 1015

HOWE, D., 'Removal of Children at Interim Hearings: Is the Test Now Set Too High?' [2009] Family Law 320

KEATING, H., 'Suspicions, Sitting on the Fence and Standards of Proof' [2009] Child and Family Law Quarterly 230

KEATING, H., '*Re MA*: The Significance of Harm' [2011] Child and Family Law Quarterly 115

LONNE, B., PARTON, N., THOMSON, J., and HARRIES, M., *Reforming Child Protection* (Abindgon: Routledge, 2009)

LORD LAMING, *The Victoria Climbié Inquiry: Report of an Inquiry by Lord Laming* (Cm 5730, January 2003)

MASSON, J., 'From Curtis to Waterhouse: State Care and Child Protection in the UK 1945–2000' in S. Katz, J. Eekelaar, and M. Maclean (eds), *Cross-Currents: Family Law Policy in the US and England* (Oxford: Oxford University Press, 2000), pp 565–88

MASSON, J., 'Police Protection—Protecting Whom?' (2002) *24*(2) Journal of Social Welfare and Family Law 157

MASSON, J., 'Emergency Intervention to Protect Children: Using and Avoiding Legal Controls' [2005] Child and Family Law Quarterly 75

PARTON, N., *The Politics of Child Abuse* (Basingstoke: Macmillan, 1985)

PARTON, N., *Governing the Family* (Basingstoke: Macmillan, 1991)

Visit the Online Resource Centre at **www.oxfordtextbooks.co.uk/orc/gilmore_glennon5e/**

online
resource
centre

for a range of further features including a detailed bibliography and self-test questions.

# 11

# Adoption and special guardianship

## INTRODUCTION

This chapter explores two methods by which a child who is unable to live with his or her parents may be provided with a suitable long-term secure alternative family placement: adoption and special guardianship.

## 1 Adoption

Adoption in English law[1] is effected by the making of an adoption order under the Adoption and Children Act (ACA) 2002. It achieves an 'almost "total legal transplant" of a child from one family to another'.[2] The child is treated as if born to the adoptive parent(s) and the parental responsibility of the birth parents is extinguished.[3] The practice of adoption has a long history, although the legal regulation of adoption is relatively recent, the first English statute regulating adoption being the Adoption of Children Act 1926. The early legislation and the idea of adoption as a total legal transplant were developed in relation to a traditional model of adoption as 'a young unmarried mother giving up her healthy new born baby, reluctantly but voluntarily, to a married couple who are unable to have children of their own'.[4] In the inter-war period adoption was seen as a method of dealing discreetly with births of illegitimate children and, in the decades following the Second World War, as largely a service for infertile couples.[5] However, baby adoptions peaked in 1968, followed by a rapid decline reflecting increased availability of contraception and abortion, and a decline in the stigmas accompanying lone motherhood and illegitimacy.[6] The law has since been developed in several statutes,[7] as the law has sought to respond to social change and various policy shifts with regard to adoption.[8] As well as its use in relation to babies, adoption has also been used to cement the

---

[1] For international perspectives, see K. O'Halloran, *The Politics of Adoption: International Perspectives on Law, Policy and Practice*, 2nd edn (Vienna: Springer, 2009).

[2] *Re P (Adoption: Unmarried Couple)* [2008] UKHL 38.

[3] See ACA 2002, ss 46 and 67, discussed in detail in Sections 7.

[4] *Re P (Adoption: Unmarried Couple)* [2008] UKHL 38 at [89].

[5] See J. Lewis, 'Adoption: The Nature of Policy Shifts in England and Wales, 1972–2002' (2004) 18(2) International Journal of Law, Policy and the Family 235 at 238.

[6] Ibid. Lewis cites figures showing that in 1975, 4,548 babies under one year old (21 per cent) were adopted, which had declined by 1999 to merely 196 (5 per cent).

[7] For the history, see S. Cretney, *Family Law in the Twentieth Century—A History* (Oxford: Oxford University Press), Ch 17; N. V. Lowe, 'English Adoption Law: Past, Present and Future' in S. Katz, J. Eekelaar, and M. Maclean (eds), *Cross-Currents: Family Law and Policy in the US and England* (Oxford: Oxford University Press, 2000), Ch 14; and I. Dey, 'Adapting Adoption: A Case of Closet Politics?' (2005) 19(3) International Journal of Law, Policy and the Family 289.

[8] See J. Lewis, 'Adoption: The Nature of Policy Shifts in England and Wales, 1972–2002' (2004) 18(2) International Journal of Law, Policy and the Family 235; C. Bridge, 'Adoption Law: A Balance of Interests' in J. Herring (ed), *Family Law: Issues, Debates, Policy* (Cullompton: Willan, 2001).

relationship between a child and step-parent 'when an unmarried, widowed or divorced mother married'[9] and step-parent adoption increased following reform of divorce law and the ensuing rise in the divorce rate. As explained in Chapter 7, parents can now share parental responsibility with a step-parent, under section 4A of the Children Act 1989, without displacing the parents' role and, while circumstances still exist in which step-parent adoptions may be appropriate, their number has also declined.

By contrast, a third category of adoptions, namely of children who are looked after by the state and are in need of a new family, is increasing.[10] In the 1970s, following enactment of the Children Act 1975, adoption was aligned with local authority childcare professional services and increasingly seen as part of the state childcare system.[11] Given the shortcomings for children of life spent in local authority care, adoption came to be seen as a favourable method of achieving permanency for children who could not be rehabilitated with their parents. In contrast to the traditional model of adoption, which provided a family with a child, this form of adoption was concerned with providing a family for the child. These types of adoptions require adoptive parents who can meet the additional challenges which such adoptions present. As Baroness Hale has commented:

> Apart from the particular parenting problems these children might present, there might also be the stress of a contested adoption if the birth parents did not agree and a need for continued contact of some sort between the child and her birth family.[12]

Unsurprisingly, the rate of disruption of placement in the case of older children adopted out of care is greater than for children placed as babies.[13] As Nigel Lowe[14] has pointed out, the adoption of children from state care does not fit well with the model of the child as a one-off gift/donation to a family, characteristic of the traditional form of adoption. Lowe argues that a contract/services model better fits adoptions of children from state care: the adopters are providing a service to the local authority and the birth parents in bringing up the adoptive children and, given the on-going challenges as noted earlier, there should be adequate on-going provision of post-adoption support to adopters in this role.

It was against this changing face of adoption that the current law of adoption, in the ACA 2002,[15] was enacted; indeed, as we shall see, it was arguably seen as the solution to some of

---

[9] *Re P* [2008] UKHL 38 at [90].

[10] In 2000, prior to enactment of the current legislation, there were 2,700 adoptions of looked after children, accounting for more than half of adoptions that year: see I. Dey, 'Adapting Adoption: A Case of Closet Politics?' (2005) 19(3) International Journal of Law, Policy and the Family 289.

[11] Following recommendations of the Houghton Committee, *Report of the Departmental Committee on the Adoption of Children* (Cmnd 5107, 1972).

[12] *Re P* [2008] UKHL 38 at [91].

[13] See eg C. Dance and A. Rushton, 'Predictors of Outcome for Unrelated Adoptive Placements made During Middle Childhood' (2005) 10 Child and Family Social Work 269. Disruptions for adolescents are even higher: see eg D. Howe, D. Shemmings, and J. Feast, 'Age at Placement and Adult Adopted People's Experience of Being Adopted' (2001) 6 Child and Family Social Work 337. Success in baby adoptions is quite usual: see J. Castle, C. Beckett, and C. Groothues, 'Infant Adoption in England: A Longitudinal Account of Social and Cognitive Progress' (2000) 24 Adoption and Fostering 26. See also the discussion by S. Harris-Short in the context of recent reforms seeking to promote adoption as the best outcome for children in public law proceedings: 'Holding onto the Past? Adoption, Birth Parents and the Law in the Twenty-First Century' in R. Probert and C. Barton (eds), *Fifty Years in Family Law: Essays for Stephen Cretney* (Cambridge: Intersentia, 2012), p 147.

[14] N. Lowe, 'The Changing Face of Adoption—The Gift/Donation Model versus the Contract/Services Model' [1997] Child and Family Law Quarterly 371.

[15] On which, see generally in detail, C. Bridge and H. Swindells QC, *Adoption: The Modern Law* (Bristol: Family Law, 2003). For a brief overview, see D. Cullen, 'The Adoption and Children Act 2002' [2003] Family Law 235 and S. Mahmood, 'Adoption and Children Act 2002: Where Are We So Far?' [2004] Family Law 449.

the problems of the childcare system.[16] The Act is the product of two reviews of the law, one which began in the early 1990s and one in 2000. The law on adoption was not examined in the various reviews of child law in the run-up to enactment of the Children Act 1989. However, a similar process reviewing adoption law began shortly thereafter, in 1992, with a consultation document[17] produced by an interdepartmental working group.[18] A White Paper followed[19] and a Draft Bill[20] was published in 1996. However, the Bill was shelved following a change of government. Adoption reform gained further impetus some four years later when the Waterhouse Inquiry into the abuse of children in care homes in North Wales identified the drift of children in care as an issue.[21] The then Prime Minister, Tony Blair, led a review[22] of childcare policy and practice to see whether local authorities might be encouraged to make more use of adoption to achieve permanent new families for children. The review identified a problem with the low number of children adopted out of care each year (only 4 per cent of looked after children) and with the length of time children remained in care before a suitable adoptive home was found. In 1999 the average length of time a child had spent in care before an adoption order was made was two years and 10 months.[23] As Sonia Harris-Short neatly summarised, the message emerging from the review was: 'too many children are in care for too long; these children need a family who can meet their needs on a permanent basis; adoption can provide such a family; adoption law, therefore, needs to be reformed to achieve "more adoptions more quickly".'[24] A subsequent White Paper[25] recommended changes in practice, including setting time limits and targets for social workers. It also promised a change in the law. The Government's fast-track adoption approach was not universally admired. Harris-Short described the proposals as misconceived and not radical enough in their failure to target appropriate adopters for children in care, commenting:

> Imposing time-limits and target figures on battle weary social workers is not going to have the dramatic effect the Government is hoping for. The fundamental problem . . . is that the majority of potential adoptive parents still seem to expect 'trouble-free babies' and not older children with 'challenging backgrounds and complex needs'. There are, therefore, not enough babies to satisfy the demands of adopters and not enough adopters to satisfy the demands of children in need. It is unrealistic to expect that by simply telling child care professionals to do 'more of the same, more quickly', this fundamental difficulty is going to disappear.[26]

---

[16] J. Lewis, 'Adoption: The Nature of Policy Shifts in England and Wales, 1972–2002' (2004) 18(2) International Journal of Law, Policy and the Family 235. For background to the Act, see C. Bridge, 'Adoption Law: A Balance of Interests' in J. Herring (ed), *Family Law: Issues, Debates, Policy* (Cullompton: Willan, 2001).

[17] Department of Health and Welsh Office, Report to Ministers of the Interdepartmental Working Group, *Review of Adoption Law* (London: HMSO, 1992).

[18] Comprising the family law team of the Law Commission and members of relevant government departments.

[19] Department of Health and Welsh Office, Home Office, Lord Chancellor's Department, *Adoption: The Future* (Cm 2288, 1993).

[20] Department of Health and Welsh Office, *Adoption: A Service for Children, Draft Bill* (1996).

[21] Sir Ronald Waterhouse (Waterhouse Inquiry), *Lost in Care—Report of the Tribunal of Inquiry into the Abuse of Children in the Former County Council Areas of Gwynedd and Clwyd since 1974* (London: TSO, 2000).

[22] HM Government, Performance and Innovation Unit, *Prime Minister's Review: Adoption: Issued for Consultation* (London: TSO, July 2000). See C. Barton, 'Adoption: The Prime Minister's Review' [2000] Family Law 731.

[23] HM Government, Performance and Innovation Unit, *Prime Minister's Review of Adoption* (London: TSO, 2000), p 13.

[24] S. Harris-Short, 'The Adoption and Children Bill—A Fast Track to Failure?' [2001] Child and Family Law Quarterly 405. Harris-Short also indicated that it was probably fair to add 'as cheaply as possible'.

[25] Department of Health, *Adoption: A New Approach: A White Paper* (Cm 5017, 2000). On the extent to which the 2002 Act met the aims of the Paper, see D. Cullen, 'Adoption—A (Fairly) New Approach' [2005] Child and Family Law Quarterly 475.

[26] S. Harris-Short, 'The Adoption and Children Bill—A Fast Track to Failure?' [2001] Child and Family Law Quarterly 405.

Nevertheless, a Bill which resembled in structure the 1996 Draft Bill was introduced into Parliament,[27] and eventually became the ACA 2002. As the Bill passed through Parliament, a particularly hotly debated issue related to who is eligible to adopt.[28] At that time, only a joint adoption by a married couple or adoption by a single person was permitted. Neither the Bill as originally presented, nor the various preceding reviews,[29] advocated any broadening of the eligibility criteria.

---

### Talking point

Amendments made in the House of Commons to allow unmarried couples, including same-sex couples, to adopt were initially resisted by the House of Lords. The issue of allowing same-sex couples to adopt was particularly hard fought but eventually the amendments were passed.[30] The Government sought to diffuse opposition by emphasising that extension of the eligibility criteria constituted a pragmatic reform to avoid delay in adoptions and serve the welfare of children who needed to be adopted, although no doubt the 'real' issue was the law's compliance with human rights requirements. The Houses' Joint Committee on Human Rights expressed the view that 'a blanket ban on unmarried couples becoming eligible to adopt children would amount to unjustifiable discrimination on the ground of marital status, violating article 14 combined with article 8'.[31] As Ian Dey has argued, the Government's approach was arguably a case of 'closet politics', which denied a full airing of the issue of same-sex adoption in principle. Dey argues that this 'strategy failed to challenge popular prejudices; indeed, by implying that only the interests of children matter, it tacitly legitimated them'.[32]

**Q.** Do the reasons why reforms come about matter if ultimately the reform is achieved? Why or why not?

---

The strategy was successful, however, in achieving a desired outcome which was consistent with the overall policy focus of ensuring that more children are adopted more speedily from care and provided with permanent homes at less cost to the state than if they remained in state care.

With a view to addressing the overarching policy aim, the 2002 Act had four main objectives. As explained by Wall LJ in *Re F (Placement Order)*:[33] 'The first was to simplify the process. The second was to enable a crucial element of the decision-making process to be undertaken at an earlier stage. The third was to shift the emphasis to a concentration on the welfare of the child; and the fourth was to avoid delay.'[34] To these ends, the Act provides the legal framework for adoption services maintained by local authorities, and places the responsibility for placement of children for adoption in the hands of adoption agencies. The adoption process has two main stages. In the first, the child is placed for adoption, either by consent of the parents or by a 'placement order' after certain conditions are

---

[27] An Adoption and Children Bill went through most of its stages in the House of Commons in 2001 but was lost when the 2001 General Election was called. The same Bill was introduced in the 2001–02 session. See C. Barton, 'Adoption and Children Bill—Don't Let Them Out of Your Sight' [2001] Family Law 431 and S. Harris-Short, 'The Adoption and Children Bill—A Fast Track to Failure?' [2001] Child and Family Law Quarterly 405.

[28] See the useful account of the debates by Baroness Hale in *Re P* [2008] UKHL 38 at [93]–[98].

[29] See Department of Health and Welsh Office, Report to Ministers of the Interdepartmental Working Group, *Review of Adoption Law* (London: HMSO, 1992), paras 26.10–26.14; Department of Health and Welsh Office, Home Office, Lord Chancellor's Department, *Adoption: The Future* (Cm 2288, 1993), para 4.40, endorsing the 'the general preference of authorities, adoption agencies and their staffs for adoption by married couples'; the 2000 Review and White Paper contained no discussion of the issue.

[30] For an account of the debate, see I. Dey, 'Adapting Adoption: A Case of Closet Politics?' (2005) 19(3) International Journal of Law, Policy and the Family 289.

[31] 24th Report of the Session 2001–02, *Adoption and Children Bill: as amended by the House of Lords on Report*, HL Paper 177 (28 October 2002), para 25.

[32] I. Dey, 'Adapting Adoption: A Case of Closet Politics?' (2005) 19(3) International Journal of Law, Policy and the Family 289 at 307; see also A. Marshall, 'Comedy of Adoption—When is a Parent not a Parent?' [2003] Family Law 840.

[33] [2008] EWCA Civ 439, [2008] 2 FLR 550.     [34] Ibid, [72].

fulfilled and a court has decided that parental consent may be dispensed with. The Act introduces the paramountcy of the child's welfare as the criterion for all decisions relating to adoption and, as we shall see later in this chapter, that approach is particularly controversial as a criterion for dispensing with parental consent. The second stage of the adoption process involves an application to the court by prospective adopters for an adoption order. Certain conditions must be fulfilled before an application may be made, for example that the child has had his or her home with the adopter(s) for a certain period of time (which depends on the type of adoption). Further conditions must be complied with before an adoption order may be made. In many cases consent to the child's adoption will have been obtained much earlier in the adoption process at the placement stage, thus ensuring that the child's adoption is not thwarted at the last minute, although in limited circumstances, the adoption application may be opposed. Before making an order, the court is required to consider post-adoption contact between the child and his or her birth parent(s) or other relatives. In what follows, we explain the central features of the Act and how they have been interpreted in case law.

## 2  The adoption service

The Act places a duty upon each local authority to maintain services which collectively are referred to as 'the Adoption Service'.[35] The Service is to be designed to meet the needs, in relation to adoption, of:

(a)  children who may be adopted, their parents and guardians,

(b)  persons wishing to adopt a child, and

(c)  adopted persons, their parents, natural parents and former guardians.

The local authority must provide facilities for arranging the adoption of children and providing adoption support services.[36] At the request of the persons listed, a local authority is under a duty to carry out an assessment of that person's needs for adoption support services.[37]

The Act provides that certain functions relating to adoption are to be carried out by adoption agencies. An adoption agency can either be a local authority or a registered adoption society,[38] that is, an adoption society registered under Part 2 of the Care Standards Act 2000.[39] The Act and secondary legislation provide for the regulation of adoption agencies' functions in relation to adoption,[40] and how and by whom they are managed.[41] Provision is also made for independent review of the decisions of adoption agencies.[42]

## 3  Decision making in relation to adoption

### 3.1  The welfare principle

Section 1 of the ACA 2002 sets out some considerations which apply 'whenever a court or adoption agency is coming to a decision relating to the adoption of a child'.[43] Section 1 is similar to, but not exactly the same as, section 1 of the Children Act 1989. By section 1(2) of the ACA 2002 the paramount consideration of the court *or adoption agency* must be the child's welfare *throughout his life*.

---

[35]  ACA 2002, s 2(1).     [36]  Ibid, s 3(2).

[37]  Ibid, s 4; and see Adoption Support Services Regulations 2005 (SI 2005/691). See also ACA 2002, s 8 for the meaning of an adoption support agency.

[38]  ACA 2002, s 2(1).     [39]  Ibid, s 2(2).

[40]  Ibid, s 9, and see Adoption Agencies Regulations 2005 (SI 2005/389).     [41]  ACA 2002, s 10.

[42]  Ibid, s 12, and see Independent Review of Determinations (Adoption and Fostering) Regulations 2009 (SI 2009/395).

[43]  ACA 2002, s 1(1). See s 1(7) for assistance on the meaning of 'coming to a decision relating to the adoption of a child'.

Therefore, unlike section 1 of the Children Act 1989, section 1(2) of the ACA 2002 is not confined to court decision making.

## 3.2 Delay likely to prejudice child's welfare

By section 1(3) the court or adoption agency 'must at all times bear in mind that, in general, any delay in coming to the decision is likely to prejudice the child's welfare'. A considerable focus of recent policy debate on adoption has been on tackling delay in the adoption process.[44] The recent re-focus on adoption followed a campaign by the *Times* newspaper, which commissioned a report by Martin Narey.[45] Narey was subsequently appointed a ministerial advisor on adoption and has been influential on recent reforms. In March 2012 the Government published *An Action Plan for Adoption: Tackling Delay*,[46] which commented that 'all but a small handful of local authorities fail on average to meet the timescales that statutory guidance sets out for the different parts of the assessment process' with 'huge variation between local authorities' and that many 'fall short by a significant margin, with the very slowest local authorities taking an average of nearly three years for a child to go from entering care to being placed for adoption'.[47] The Government aims to tackle the problem by recruiting a greater number of prospective adopters,[48] and by speeding up processes.[49]

The Government has set out and will monitor performance thresholds once the court has formally decided that adoption is the best option: a minimal expectation of matching a child to a family within seven months,[50] and adoption within 21 months.[51] Part I of the Children and Families Act 2014[52] introduces several changes to the law to speed up the adoption process. These include, *inter alia*, requiring local authorities to consider concurrent fostering and adoption planning for children by placing children in foster placements which have the possibility of becoming an adoption placement,[53] and allowing children for whom a local authority in England are considering adoption (not just those who are suitable) to appear in the Adoption and Children Act Register which can be searched by prospective adopters.[54]

## 3.3 The welfare checklist

### Key legislation

There follows in section 1(4) a checklist of matters to which (among others) the court or adoption agency must have regard:

(a) the child's ascertainable wishes and feelings regarding the decision (considered in the light of the child's age and understanding);

(b) the child's particular needs;

---

[44] On the implications of delay, see: J. Selwyn, W. Sturgess, D. Quinton, and C. Baxter, *Costs and Outcomes of Non-infant Adoptions* (British Association for Adoption and Fostering, 2006), and H. Ward, R. Brown, and D. Westlake, *Safeguarding Babies and Very Young Children from Abuse and Neglect* (London: Jessica Kingsley Publishers, 2012).

[45] The Narey Report on adoption: a blueprint for Britain's lost children, *The Times*, 5 July 2011.

[46] Department for Education, *An Action Plan for Adoption: Tackling Delay* (March 2012).

[47] Ibid, para 96.

[48] Ibid, para 17. In April 2013 the Government launched a national gateway to advice and information on adoption known as First4Adoption.

[49] Streamlining the processes for second time adopters or for approved foster parents; requiring 'swifter use of the national Adoption Register in order to find the right adopters for a child wherever they might live'; and encouraging 'all local authorities to seek to place children with their potential adopters in anticipation of the court's placement order'.

[50] To be reduced to four months in due course.    [51] To be reduced to 14 months in due course.

[52] Following Department of Education, *Further Action on Adoption* (2013).    [53] Section 2.

[54] Section 7.

(c) the likely effect on the child (throughout his life) of having ceased to be a member of the original family and become an adopted person;

(d) the child's age, sex, background and any of the child's characteristics which the court or agency considers relevant;

(e) any harm (within the meaning of the Children Act 1989 (c 41)) which the child has suffered or is at risk of suffering;

(f) the relationship[55] which the child has with relatives,[56] and with any other person in relation to whom the court or agency considers the relationship to be relevant, including—

  (i) the likelihood of any such relationship continuing and the value to the child of its doing so,[57]

  (ii) the ability and willingness of any of the child's relatives, or of any such person, to provide the child with a secure environment in which the child can develop, and otherwise to meet the child's needs,

  (iii) the wishes and feelings of any of the child's relatives, or of any such person, regarding the child.

## 3.4 **The child's religion, origin, and background**

By section 1(5) an adoption agency, in placing a child for adoption, 'must give due consideration to the child's religious persuasion, racial origin and cultural and linguistic background'. Section 3 of the Children and Families Act 2014 repeals section 1(5) in so far as it applies to England (but not Wales) following a recommendation to 'legislate to reduce the number of adoptions delayed in order to achieve a perfect or near ethnic match between adoptive parents and the adoptive child'.[58]

## 3.5 **The range of powers available**

The court or adoption agency must also always consider the whole range of powers available to it in the child's case.[59]

## 3.6 **The no order principle**

The final principle in section 1 is the 'no order principle': the court must not make any order unless it would be better for the child than not doing so.[60]

---

[55] The term 'relationship' here is not confined to legal relationships: see s 1(8).

[56] The term 'relative' includes the child's mother or father: see s 1(8).

[57] In *Re M'P-P (Adoption Proceedings: Value to be Placed on Status Quo)* [2015] EWCA Civ 584, McFarlane LJ remitted a case for re-hearing, the judge having failed to engage 'in any real way with the effect on the children of moving them from the care of their primary, and only, attachment figure or with the value to them of maintaining that relationship'. (at [51]) His lordship noted that the relative importance of attachment/status quo arguments as against those relating to placement in the family will turn on the facts of a particular case, but less had been said in recent case law about the former, which will be of importance in some cases. (at [47]).

[58] See Department for Education, *An Action Plan for Adoption: Tackling Delay* (March 2012), having regard to research evidence: see J. Selwyn et al, *Pathways to Permanence for Black, Asian and Mixed Ethnicity Children* (British Association for Adoption and Fostering, 2010); Evan B. Donaldson Institute, *Finding Families for African American Children* (2009) www.adoptioninstitute.org; D. Quinton, *Matching In Adoptions From Care: A Conceptual And Research Review* (British Association for Adoption and Fostering, 2012).

[59] ACA 2002, s 1(6).    [60] Ibid.

### 3.7 **Section 1 of the Adoption and Children Act 2002 and Article 8 of the ECHR**

In *YC v United Kingdom*[61] the European Court of Human Rights (ECtHR) found no violation of Article 8 of the European Convention on Human Rights (ECHR) in circumstances in which a child was taken into care and an order placing the child for adoption made. In the course of giving judgment, the court commented:

> The identification of the child's best interests and the assessment of the overall proportionality of any given measure will require courts to weigh a number of factors in the balance. The court has not previously set out an exhaustive list of such factors, which may vary depending on the circumstances of the case in question. However, it observes that the considerations listed in s 1 of the 2002 Act . . . broadly reflect the various elements inherent in assessing the necessity under Art 8 of a measure placing a child for adoption. In particular, it considers that in seeking to identify the best interests of a child and in assessing the necessity of any proposed measure in the context of placement proceedings, the domestic court must demonstrate that it has had regard to, inter alia, the age, maturity and ascertained wishes of the child, the likely effect on the child of ceasing to be a member of his original family and the relationship the child has with relatives.[62]

As Sir James Munby P explained in *Re C (Adoption Proceedings: Change of Circumstances)*,[63] 'a judge who properly applies s 1 of the 2002 Act . . . will thereby normally also be complying with the requirements of Art 8'.

## 4 Adoption agencies' role in assessing suitable adoptions

The role of an adoption agency, with regard to particular children and potential adopters, is to decide whether a child is suitable for adoption, whether prospective adopters are in general suitable, and whether a proposed placement of a particular child with prospective adopters should be approved. The Adoption Agencies Regulations 2005 provide that an adoption agency must have one or more adoption panels[64] whose job it is to advise the agency in relation to adoption decisions. Each panel must comprise an independent Chair of the Panel and a minimum of three other persons, at least one of whom must be a registered social worker with at least three years' relevant post-qualification experience.[65]

Where an agency is considering adoption for a child, the agency is under a duty to open a case file relating to a child's adoption, in which is recorded relevant information/documents, such as records of proceedings, decisions, relevant consent, court orders etc.[66] The agency must, so far as reasonably practicable, provide counselling for, and ascertain the wishes and feelings of, the child[67] and parents.[68] The agency is required to obtain information on the child as specified in Schedule 1 to the Regulations, and must arrange for the child to be medically examined and a report obtained,[69] including, so far as is reasonably practicable, information about the child's family and the health of parents and siblings.[70] A report, known as the child's permanence report, containing the information which has been compiled, is then passed, with other relevant reports, to the adoption panel for its consideration.[71] The panel then considers whether the child should be placed for adoption and

---

[61] (App no 4547/10), [2012] 2 FLR 332.     [62] Ibid, [35].
[63] [2013] EWCA Civ 431, [2013] 2 FLR 139, [2013] 2 FLR 1393 at [41].
[64] Adoption Agencies Regulations 2005, reg 4.     [65] Ibid, regs 3 and 6.     [66] Ibid, reg 12.
[67] Ibid, reg 13.     [68] Ibid, reg 14.     [69] Ibid, reg 15.     [70] Ibid, reg 16.
[71] Ibid, reg 17. The adoption agency must obtain, so far as is reasonably practicable, any other relevant information which may be requested by the adoption panel and send that information to the panel (reg 17(3)).

makes a recommendation to the agency.[72] The agency must then come to a decision, taking into account the recommendation of the panel.

The agency is under a duty to carry out a similar process with regard to considering a prospective adopter's suitability to adopt a child, compiling a range of information for a case file.[73] The agency must arrange for police checks to be carried out, and a person cannot be considered as suitable to adopt if convicted or cautioned for specified offences.[74] As noted earlier, the law now permits adoption by an unmarried couple, including same-sex adopters. However, this fact may not of itself ensure that unmarried couples, and perhaps particularly same-sex adopters, will be on a level playing field with married couples in the adoption process. Indeed, work by Emma Hitchings and Tracey Sagar[75] reporting on interviews with a small sample of social workers working in the field of adoption, suggested that same-sex adopters might be more likely to be offered very damaged children, children who had proved difficult to place with others. There may also still be an expectation that same-sex couples should adopt distinct role differentiation as in many heterosexual relationships so as apparently not to confuse the adopted child. The law is clear, however, that it would be unlawful to discriminate against prospective adopters solely on the basis of marital status[76] or sexuality.[77]

The agency is under a duty to provide prospective adopters with preparation for adoption.[78] A prospective adopter's report is compiled by the agency[79] and sent to the adoption panel, which makes recommendations as to the prospective adopters' suitability.[80] The adoption agency is charged with the duty of making the decision as to the suitability of an adopter, taking account of the recommendation of the panel. The Suitability of Adopters Regulations 2005 set out the range of information which the agency must consider in reaching a decision about the suitability of adopters.[81] In determining the suitability of a couple to adopt a child, the agency must have proper regard to the need for stability and permanence in their relationship. If the adopter is deemed unsuitable, the decision must be given in writing, with reasons. If the prospective adopter is dissatisfied with the decision, he or she can apply to have it reviewed by an independent review panel.[82]

The next stage is matching the child with prospective adopters. Again, the agency is under duties to compile information regarding proposed placement (a placement report) which together with other relevant reports is put before the panel for recommendation.[83] The adoption panel makes a recommendation[84] which the agency is under a duty to consider when making its decision.[85] If the placement is approved and the prospective adopters wish to proceed, the agency must send the prospective adopters a placement plan before the child is placed, and notify the prospective adopters' general medical practitioner and the local authority of the placement.[86]

### 4.1 Can information about adoption be withheld from the child's father and other relatives?

As noted earlier, the adoption agency is under a duty to compile considerable information about the child as set out in Schedule 1 to the Adoption Agencies Regulations 2005, including information, as

---

[72] Ibid, reg 18.     [73] Ibid, reg 22.     [74] Ibid, reg 23.

[75] E. Hitchings and T. Sagar, 'The Adoption and Children Act 2002: A Level Playing Field for Same-Sex Adopters?' [2002] Child and Family Law Quarterly 60.

[76] *Re P* [2008] UKHL 38.

[77] *EB v France* (App no 43546/02) [2008] 1 FLR 850, ECtHR. For comment on this case, see I. Curry-Sumner, '*EB v France*: A Missed Opportunity?' [2009] Child and Family Law Quarterly 356. Note also the Equality Act 2010, ss 12 and 29.

[78] Adoption Agencies Regulations 2005, reg 24.     [79] Ibid, reg 25.     [80] Ibid, reg 26.

[81] SI 2005/1712, and see ACA 2002, s 45.

[82] ACA 2002, s 12, and see Independent Review of Determinations (Adoption and Fostering) Regulations 2009 (SI 2009/395).

[83] Adoption Agencies Regulations 2005, reg 31.     [84] Ibid, reg 32.     [85] Ibid, reg 33.

[86] Ibid, reg 35.

required by regulation 16, about the child's parents and relatives in Schedule 1, paragraph 3. However, cases sometimes arise in which the mother of a child wishes to give up her child for adoption without the father's knowledge or without informing her own family. The mother may even refuse to disclose who the father is. To what extent should the mother's wish for confidentiality be respected in such cases? Is the agency still required to collect the information specified in the regulations? In *Re L (Adoption: Contacting Natural Father)*[87] the mother of a girl had concealed her pregnancy from her family, left hospital two hours after the birth without seeing her baby, and requested that the baby be adopted. The mother maintained that she was unable (or as professionals suspected, unwilling) to disclose the father's identity. She was also adamant that her own family should not be informed of the child's birth. The local authority, with whom the child was accommodated, sought leave to invoke the inherent jurisdiction of the High Court for orders that it need not take further steps to identify the child's father nor inform or consult members of the maternal family concerning the intended adoption. Munby J held that respecting the mother's wishes was lawful[88] and made the orders sought. However, he took the view that a further attempt should be made to obtain information from the mother about the father, and directed that the mother disclose details about the father. The mother subsequently told the judge from the well of the court (ie, not in the witness box under oath) that she was unable to provide further information and Munby J concluded that no further steps could sensibly be undertaken. While his Lordship was of the view that the court had the necessary power under the inherent jurisdiction to order the mother to disclose the father's identity, he found deeply unattractive,[89] and smacking too much of the Inquisition to be tolerable,[90] the idea that the mother should be cross-examined in order to compel her to reveal the father's name. It would, in his Lordship's view, be wrong to coerce the mother in this way.[91]

Where the identity of the child's father is known, a question may still arise as to whether he should be told of the child's existence and any plans for adoption. If a father does not have parental responsibility, his consent to adoption is not required. Under the rules of court, a local authority is able to ask the High Court for directions on the need to give a father who does not have parental responsibility notice of the intention to place a child for adoption. The court has power to direct that a father be joined as a party to adoption proceedings. Equally, however, the child can be placed for adoption and an adoption order made without notice to a father who does not have parental responsibility. The authorities on whether a father should be told of proceedings with respect to his child have arisen similarly in the context of care proceedings and adoption proceedings.

In *Re A (Father: Knowledge of Child's Birth)*[92] the Court of Appeal dismissed a mother's appeal against Mostyn J's refusal of a declaration that the mother's husband (the child's father) not be told of the child's birth. The parents, who were in their forties with grown-up children, had been granted asylum from Afghanistan where the father and his family had suffered terribly at the hands of the Taliban.[93] As a result of his experiences, the father suffered mental health problems and was prone to unpredictable, frightening behaviour, including domestic violence. The mother's pregnancy was identified after it was possible for her to have an abortion, and she concealed the pregnancy and birth from the father and her son, although her daughters were aware of it. The mother feared the father's reaction to knowledge of the baby. However, the expert evidence did not support the mother's case that knowledge of the child would be adverse to the father's equilibrium.[94]

---

[87] [2007] EWHC 1771 (Fam), [2008] 1 FLR 1079.

[88] Ibid, [11], drawing on Holman J's judgment in *Z County Council v R* [2001] 1 FLR 365 at 367.

[89] *Re L*, [2007] EWHC 1771 (Fam), [2008] 1 FLR 1079, [38].     [90] Ibid, [40].     [91] Ibid, [41].

[92] [2011] EWCA Civ 273, [2011] 2 FLR 123.

[93] Relatives had been murdered and the father himself had been kidnapped and beaten up.

[94] [2011] EWCA Civ 273, [2011] 2 FLR 123 at [16].

Black LJ (with whom Longmore LJ agreed) reviewed earlier authorities and concluded that the thrust of the case law[95] was that 'the court will not be persuaded to sanction the withholding of information about the existence of a child from that child's parent or to dispense with service on him of proceedings relating to the child in anything other than exceptional circumstances where there are . . . strong countervailing factors'.[96] Accordingly, Mostyn J had been correct to conclude that the evidence was 'so deficient as to be incapable of satisfying any test of exceptionality'[97] and the father should not be denied knowledge of the child's existence.

As Munby J indicated in *Re L (Adoption: Contacting Natural Father)*,[98] however, 'every case is different and has to be decided having regard to its own unique circumstances'.[99] In *Re X (Care: Notice of Proceedings)*[100] the father was the brother-in-law of the mother, a 17-year-old Bangladeshi girl. The issue was whether the father, who did not know of the child's birth, should be served with notice of care proceedings. If the relationship between the mother and father became known in their community, the overall effect would be a catastrophic destruction of the family. Stuart-White J decided that the father should not be given notice. In *Re H; Re G (Adoption: Consultation of Unmarried Fathers)*[101] Butler-Sloss P gave further examples of countervailing circumstances, such as rape or other serious domestic violence that placed the mother at serious physical risk.[102] However, in *Re A (Father: Knowledge of Child's Birth)*[103] the Court of Appeal made clear that the authorities 'do not impose a requirement of significant physical risk'.[104]

---

### Key case

In *Re C (A Child) (Adoption: Duty of Local Authority)*[105] the court approached the matter 'from a slightly different angle'.[106] There an unmarried mother concealed her pregnancy from her family and placed her baby for adoption at birth. The child had been conceived as a result of a 'one-night stand'. The mother was opposed to the local authority making enquiries to see if any of the child's birth family would be suitable carers. The mother did not think that either of her divorced parents could care for the child, nor was there evidence that her siblings could do so. The judge held that the local authority was under a duty to inform itself of as much of the child's background as it was able and gave directions accordingly. On appeal, the Court of Appeal held that the judge had been wrong in principle and set aside his exercise of discretion. Arden LJ delivered the leading judgment, with which Thorpe LJ expressly agreed. Lawrence Collins LJ delivered a separate short judgment concurring in the result.

Arden LJ approached the case as a matter of statutory construction, holding that section 1 of the 2002 Act applied. Her Ladyship held, therefore, that there is no duty to make enquiries which are not in the

---

[95] For a review of some of the case law, see A. Bainham, 'Can We Protect Children and Protect Their Rights?' [2002] Family Law 279.

[96] [2011] EWCA Civ 273, [2011] 2 FLR 123 at [37]. See also *Re H and G (Adoption: Consultation of Unmarried Fathers)* [2001] 1 FLR 745 at [48]; *Re C (Adoption: Disclosure to Father)* [2005] EWHC 3385 (Fam), [2006] 2 FLR 589 at [17] ('very compelling reasons'); *Birmingham City Council v S, R and A* [2006] EWHC 3065 (Fam), [2007] 1 FLR 1223 at [73] ('cogent and compelling grounds').

[97] [2011] EWCA Civ 273, [2011] 2 FLR 123, [17].      [98] [2007] EWHC 1771 (Fam), [2008] 1 FLR 1079.

[99] Ibid, [25].      [100] [1996] 1 FLR 186.      [101] [2001] 1 FLR 745 at [48].

[102] See also *Z County Council v R* [2001] 1 FLR 365 (relatives suffering illness which made it impossible for them to care for the child).

[103] [2011] EWCA Civ 273, [2011] 2 FLR 123.

[104] Ibid, [45]. Insofar as there may have been statements inconsistent with that view in Mostyn J's judgment (about which there was doubt), those statements were overruled.

[105] [2007] EWCA Civ 1206, [2008] Fam 54. For comment, see B. Sloan, '*Re C (A Child) (Adoption: Duty of Local Authority)*—Welfare and the Rights of the Birth Family in "Fast Track" Adoption Cases' [2009] Child and Family Law Quarterly 87.

[106] As Black LJ put it in *Re A (Father: Knowledge of Child's Birth)* [2011] EWCA Civ 273, [2011] 2 FLR 123.

interests of the child to make, and enquiries 'are not in the interests of the child simply because they will provide more information about the child's background'.[107] The question for the court in this case was who would look after the child on a long-term basis applying the child's welfare as paramount, and the fact that the judge considered that the child would benefit from knowledge of her father in adult life was not sufficient to animate the exercise of discretion.[108]

Arden LJ commented:

> I do not consider that this court should require a preference to be given as a matter of policy to the natural family of a child. Section 1 [of the 2002 Act] does not impose any such policy. Rather, it requires the interests of the child to be considered. That must mean the child as an individual. In some cases, the birth tie will be very important, especially where the child is of an age to understand what is happening or where there are ethnic or cultural or religious reasons for keeping the child in the birth family. Where a child has never lived with her birth family, and is too young to understand what is going on, that argument must be weaker. In my judgment, in a case such as this, it is (absent any application by any member of the family, which succeeds) overtaken by the need to find the child a permanent home as soon as that can be done.

In this case the child was 4 months old and making attachments to the foster parents. In those circumstances, exercising the discretion afresh, the Court of Appeal found that the overriding need was to find the child a permanent home before the bond with the foster parents developed further.[109] The court's approach has been criticised for adopting a narrow interpretation of welfare which unduly emphasises permanence and the avoidance of delay criterion in the statute over other welfare factors, particularly as the requirement to examine the child's welfare throughout his or her life suggests a careful and broad assessment of welfare considerations.[110] In *Re A (Father: Knowledge of Child's Birth)*[111] the court commented that there is no reason to suppose that the court in *Re C* was contemplating a radical departure from the earlier authorities (discussed earlier), observing that Arden LJ in *Re C* clearly recognised that the circumstances in which a father would remain in ignorance about the child would be exceptional.[112]

The court in *Re C* also examined the human rights context under the European Convention on Human Rights (ECHR) to the situation presented. The right to respect for family life in Article 8 presupposes the existence of family life.[113] In the case of a father and a child born out of wedlock, whether family life exists within the meaning of Article 8 will depend on the circumstances, including the nature of the relationship between the natural parents and the demonstrable interest in and commitment by the natural father to the child both before and after the birth.[114] It can be established, therefore, where there are sufficiently close *de facto* family ties, for example arising through cohabitation.[115] However, family life may be established in the case of a potential

---

[107] [2007] EWCA Civ 1206, [2008] Fam 54 at [3].      [108] Ibid, [21].

[109] Ibid, [56] *per* Lawrence Collins LJ.

[110] B. Sloan, '*Re C (A Child) (Adoption: Duty of Local Authority)*—Welfare and the Rights of the Birth Family in "Fast Track" Adoption Cases' [2009] Child and Family Law Quarterly 87.

[111] [2011] EWCA Civ 273, [2011] 2 FLR 123 (Black LJ at [40], Longmore LJ agreeing).

[112] See *Re C* [2007] EWCA Civ 1206, [2008] Fam 54 at [24].

[113] See eg *Marckx v Belgium* (1979) 2 EHRR 330 at para 31; *Johnson v UK* (1999) 27 EHRR 296 at [62]. Arden LJ also held that near relatives, particularly grandparents, automatically have an Art 8 right to respect for family life (citing *Marckx v Belgium* (1979) 2 EHRR 330 at [45]; see *Re C* at [31] *per* Arden LJ and at [53] *per* Lawrence Collins LJ. This is a doubtful statement since, as several commentators have pointed out, *Marckx* suggests that family life could include ties between grandparents and grandchildren, but this does not mean that it arises simply by reason of formal kinship links. See B. Sloan, '*Re C (A Child) (Adoption: Duty of Local Authority)*—Welfare and the Rights of the Birth Family in "Fast Track" Adoption Cases' [2009] Child and Family Law Quarterly 87.

[114] See *Rozanski v Poland* (App no 55339/00) [2006] 2 FLR 1163.

[115] It need not involve cohabitation: see *Söderbäck v Sweden*: family life where only small amount of contact between father and daughter.

relationship, although the father must have had some relationship with the mother and expressed his commitment to the child in some way, even if there was no cohabitation.[116] Moreover, in *Pini v Romania*[117] the Strasbourg Court stated that intended family life may, in some circumstances, be enough to establish a right to respect for one's family life. Arden LJ concluded that in the circumstances of the case before her, the father had no Article 8 right which could be violated by adoption of the child without his knowledge. Lawrence Collins LJ observed that even if Article 8 were engaged, it would be difficult to envisage a situation in which there could be an interference with the exercise of that right where the father does not know (or care) about the existence of the child. Furthermore, his Lordship was of the view that the protection of the rights of the mother and child would plainly justify the interference with any such right.[118]

## 5  Rules relating to parental consent in adoption cases

Parental consent (and where necessary dispensing with it) plays an important role at various stages of the adoption process. It is convenient at the outset of our discussion of the legal framework for adoption, to set out some rules of interpretation which apply when there is a reference in the Act to any parent or guardian of a child giving or withdrawing consent to the placement of a child for adoption, or consent to the making of an adoption order (including a future adoption order).[119] The rules are set out in section 52.

Section 52(3) provides that consent given by the mother to the making of an adoption order is ineffective if it is given less than six weeks after the child's birth. Where consent can be validly given, section 52(5) makes clear that what is meant is 'consent given unconditionally and with full understanding of what is involved; but a person may consent to adoption without knowing the identity of the persons in whose favour the order will be made'.

Section 52 also clarifies whose consent is required. By section 52(6) 'parent' means a parent with parental responsibility. Furthermore, section 52(9) and (10) provide that if the child has been placed under section 19 with the consent of one parent, and at a later time the other parent of the child acquires parental responsibility for the child, the other parent is to be treated as having given consent at the earlier time in the same terms as the parent who consented. In such circumstances, even though an unmarried father may have acquired parental responsibility and may refuse consent to the making of an adoption order, his refusal would be ineffective to prevent the adoption.

## 6  Placement for adoption

The first stage in the legal process of adoption is placement of the child. Section 18 of the ACA 2002 authorises an adoption agency to place a child for adoption provided the agency is satisfied that the child ought to be placed for adoption.[120] A child under 6 weeks old may be lawfully placed with a prospective adopter provided the agency has obtained the written consent of the parents.[121] In the case of a child who is aged 6 weeks or over, the agency may only place the child with parental consent given under section 19 of the Act, or pursuant to a court order known as a placement order, under section 21.

---

[116] *Nylund v Finland* (App no 27110/95) (unreported) 29 June 1999; cf *G v Netherlands* (App no 16944/90) (1993) 16 EHRR CD 38; see *Re C* at [31]. See also *Görgülü v Germany* (family life where significant relationship ending before father aware of pregnancy).

[117] (2005) 40 EHRR 132, [2005] 2 FLR 596 at [143] although holding that there was no family life in the case of persons who had obtained adoption orders but had not had care of the children concerned, the Court indicated that the requirement for *de facto* ties 'does not mean that all intended family life falls entirely outside the ambit of Art. 8'.

[118] *Re C* at [55].      [119] See s 52(2).      [120] Section 18(2).

[121] Adoption Agencies Regulations 2005, reg 35.

## 6.1 Meaning of 'placing a child for adoption'

Placing a child for adoption is defined in section 18(5) of the Act as placing a child for adoption with prospective adopters and includes, where the child is already living with persons, leaving the child with them as prospective adopters.[122] In *Coventry City Council v O (Adoption)*[123] the Court of Appeal[124] held that 'a child is not "placed" for adoption until he begins to live with the proposed adopters or, if he is already living with them in their capacity as foster carers, when the adoption agency formally allows him to continue to live with them in their fresh capacity as prospective adopters'.[125] This the court saw as the natural construction of the verb 'place'.[126] The court thus overruled Coulson J's ruling in *R (W) v Brent London Borough Council*[127] that placement had occurred when a local authority resolved to place a child with identified adopters (ie, the date of ratification of the placement). It should also be noted that section 18(5) refers to placement with 'prospective adopters', not merely 'potential adopters'.[128] It is important to be clear precisely when a child is or is not placed for adoption because various legal incidents flow from being placed.

## 6.2 Placement by agency with parental consent (S 19)

> **Key legislation**
>
> Section 19(1) provides:
>
> Where an adoption agency is satisfied that each parent or guardian of a child has consented to the child—
>
> (a) being placed for adoption with prospective adopters identified in the consent, or
>
> (b) being placed for adoption with any prospective adopters who may be chosen by the agency,
>
> and has not withdrawn the consent, the agency is authorised to place the child for adoption accordingly.

Under section 20(1), a parent or guardian who consents to the child being placed for adoption may at the same or any subsequent time consent to the making of a future adoption order. Notice can also be given to the adoption agency that the person consenting does not wish to be informed of an application for an adoption order.[129]

Consent given under sections 19 and 20 has momentous consequences for the future of child and parent,[130] and there can come a point when the consent cannot be withdrawn. Section 52(4)

---

[122] However, see s 44(8):

Where—

(a) a local authority have placed a child with any persons otherwise than as prospective adopters, and

(b) the persons give notice of intention to adopt,

the authority are not to be treated as leaving the child with them as prospective adopters for the purposes of section 18(1)(b).

[123] [2011] EWCA Civ 729, [2011] 2 FLR 936.

[124] Lord Wilson of Culworth, Lord Neuberger of Abbotsbury, and Dame Janet Smith DBE.

[125] [2011] EWCA Civ 729, [2011] 2 FLR 936 at [44].

[126] See also the Adoption Agencies Regulations 2005, reg 35(2), cited by the court, which requires an adoption agency to send to a prospective adopter with whom it has decided to place a child an 'adoption placement plan' which, by para 3 of Sch 5, must identify the '[d]ate on which it is proposed to place the child for adoption with the prospective adopter'.

[127] [2010] EWHC 175 (Admin), [2010] 1 FLR 1914.

[128] For the distinction, see *Re S (Placement Order: Revocation)* [2008] EWCA Civ 1333, [2009] 1 FLR 503, which is discussed further in Section 6.7.

[129] Section 20(4).

[130] The effects of consent to placement are explored in more detail in Section 6.6. For a summary, see Eleanor King J in *A Local Authority v GC and Others* [2008] EWHC 2555 (Fam) at [21].

provides that withdrawal of any consent to the placement of a child for adoption, or of any consent given under section 20, is ineffective if it is given after an application for an adoption order is made. At that stage the adoption process is too far down the line to permit withdrawal of consent. Given these effects of sections 19 and 20, section 52 also specifies that consent under those provisions must be given in a form prescribed by rules,[131] and must be withdrawn in a form prescribed by rules, or alternatively in the case of withdrawal simply by giving notice to the agency.[132]

In *A Local Authority v GC and others*[133] the parents signed forms when a child was only four weeks old consenting to placement for adoption with prospective adopters under section 19, and purportedly giving advance consent to adoption under section 20. On a subsequent application to adopt the child, the justices' clerk noticed that the consent to adoption had been obtained before the child attained 6 weeks of age. The case came before Eleanor King J on the issue of whether the consent to placement was effective despite the fact that the child was under 6 weeks at the time. Her Ladyship noted that under section 18 placement of a child when aged under six weeks is an exception to the rule that placement can only take place pursuant to section 19 or 21 of the 2002 Act. (Regulation 35 of the Adoption Agencies Regulations 2005 provides that a child may be placed when still under 6 weeks provided there is a written agreement with the child's parent.) It was not necessary therefore for Eleanor King J to decide whether on the facts of the case there had been an effective section 19 placement, since, as her Ladyship found, the written consent meant that the child had been placed pursuant to a written agreement as required by the regulations and accordingly was an authorised placement. However, she stated that good practice and common sense suggest that section 19 consents should be obtained after the child attains the age of 6 weeks. Her Ladyship went on to hold that consent to placement when a child is under 6 weeks old cannot be relied on as a basis for making an adoption order,[134] since the law positively requires that the mother's consent to adoption is valid only once the child has attained the age of 6 weeks.[135] Therefore, as the child's parents were now no longer consenting to the child's adoption, the court needed to be satisfied that parental consent should be dispensed with.[136]

It is possible to make an early permanence placement with foster parents who have been approved for adoption. Such a placement where progression towards adoption is the anticipated outcome, is now on a statutory footing under section 22C(9B)(c) of the Children Act 1989. However, it is important for foster parents to appreciate that such placements may not always lead to adoption. This happened in *Re T (A Child) (Early Permanence Placement)*[137] where the child was placed with foster parents the day after his birth, but the local authority abandoned its plan for adoption in favour of support for a special guardianship order in favour of the paternal grandparents. The judge, however, joined the foster parents as parties to the existing care proceedings and gave them leave to apply for adoption. The Court of Appeal held that, in line with longstanding authority, it had been wrong to join the foster parents as parties. Munby P commented that the 'care judge is concerned at most with consideration of adoption in principle, not with evaluating the merits of particular proposed adopters' and explained that there is 'a very real risk that if, in a case such as this, the forensic process is allowed to become in effect a dispute between the prospective adopters and the birth family, the court will be diverted into an illegitimate inquiry as to which placement will be better for the child.'[138]

---

[131] Section 52(7).    [132] Section 52(8).

[133] [2008] EWHC 2555 (Fam), [2009] 1 FLR 299.    [134] Ibid, [34].

[135] See s 52, in accordance with the European Convention on the Adoption of Children 1967.

[136] See s 47(4).    [137] [2015] EWCA CIv 983.    [138] Ibid, [50].

## 6.3 **Placement orders**

A child can also be placed with prospective adopters pursuant to a 'placement order' under section 21 of the Act. This is a court order authorising a local authority to place a child for adoption with prospective adopters chosen by the authority.[139] This permits adoption without the consent of the child's parents, and even against the objection of the parents.[140]

---

### Key legislation

Under section 22(1) a local authority is under a duty to apply for a placement order if:

(a) the child is placed for adoption by them or is being provided with accommodation by them,

(b) no adoption agency is authorised to place the child for adoption,

(c) the child has no parent or guardian or the authority consider that the conditions in section 31(2) of the 1989 Act are met, and

(d) the authority are satisfied that the child ought to be placed for adoption.

---

Note that the wording is 'ought to be placed' rather than 'will be placed', and it has been held that a local authority can be satisfied that the child ought to be placed for adoption within the meaning of section 22(1)(d) 'even though it recognises the reality that a search for adoptive parents may be unsuccessful and that, if it is, the alternative plan will have to be for long-term fostering'.[141] In other words, there is 'no objection in principle to dual planning in appropriate cases'.[142]

### 6.3.1 **Placement order must be preceded by the correct procedure**

An application for a placement order must be preceded by compliance with the regulations which set out the procedure by which the agency must reach its decision whether the child should be placed for adoption. The framework laid down by Parliament cannot be bypassed or short-circuited.[143] If a judge becomes aware of a material irregularity in that procedure, the proceedings should be adjourned to allow the adoption agency to consider the matter in accordance with the regulations. The hearing before the judge cannot rectify those procedural difficulties.[144] In *Re B (Placement Order)*[145] there was a failure on the part of the local authority to provide the adoption agency panel with relevant expert reports in breach of the 2002 Act and the Adoption Agencies (Wales) Regulations 2005.[146] The Court of Appeal set out guidance,[147] the essence of which was that 'panel members should be made fully and properly aware of all the available material relevant to their decision'.[148]

---

[139] Section 21(1). Once a placement order is made, the local authority will need to make ongoing efforts to place the child in a suitable family. See *A and S v Lancashire County Council* [2013] 2 FLR 803 for a case in which the rights of two children under Art 3, 6, and 8 of the ECHR were breached through failure to place them. The children had been accommodated by the local authority when aged 2 years and 6 months respectively and freed for adoption, and at ages 16 and 14 were still not placed.

[140] In *Re D (A Child)* [2014] EWHC 3388 (Fam), at [35], Mostyn J noted that 'only three out of 28 European Union countries allow forced or non-consensual adoption.' However, compare C Fenton-Glynn, *Adoption without Consent* (European Parliament Policy Department C, 2015) who shows that every EU jurisdiction has such a mechanism.

[141] *Re P (Placement Orders: Parental Consent)* [2008] EWCA Civ 535, [2008] 2 FLR 625 at [137].        [142] Ibid.

[143] *Re B (Placement Order)* [2008] EWCA Civ 835, [2008] 2 FLR 1404 at [70]; and see also at [99]: 'the Regulations are there to be honoured and obeyed in their entirety'.

[144] Contrast *Re P-B* [2006] EWCA Civ 1016, where the agency's failure to fulfil its statutory duty was undiscovered until after the making of the placement order.

[145] [2008] EWCA Civ 835, [2008] 2 FLR 1404.

[146] SI 2005/1313.        [147] [2008] EWCA Civ 835, [2008] 2 FLR 1404 at [81].        [148] Ibid, [84].

### 6.3.2 Conditions for making a placement order

The court may not make a placement order in respect of a child unless the child is subject to a care order, or the court is satisfied that the conditions for making a care order are satisfied, or the child has no parent or guardian. In other words, the state may only intervene to place the child for adoption if there has at some stage been a finding that the child is suffering or likely to suffer significant harm attributable to a want of reasonable parental care or the child is orphaned. In addition, in any case in which a parent or guardian is still living, the court must be satisfied that each parent or guardian has consented to the child being placed for adoption with any prospective adopters who may be chosen by the local authority and has not withdrawn consent,[149] or that the parent's or guardian's consent should be dispensed with.

### 6.3.3 Dispensing with consent

> **Key legislation**
>
> Section 52(1) provides that:
>
> > The court cannot dispense with the consent of any parent or guardian of a child to the child being placed for adoption or to the making of an adoption order in respect of the child unless the court is satisfied that—
> >
> > (a) the parent or guardian cannot be found or lacks capacity (within the meaning of the Mental Capacity Act 2005) to give consent, or
> > (b) the welfare of the child requires the consent to be dispensed with.[150]

In *Re P (Placement Orders: Parental Consent)*[151] the Court of Appeal commented that the best guidance it could give to judges approaching the question of dispensation under section 52(1)(b) is 'to apply the statutory language with care to the facts of the particular case'.[152] The court held that deciding whether or not to dispense with parental consent to a placement order is a decision relating to the adoption of a child, and accordingly section 1(2) of the 2002 Act requires the court to treat 'the child's welfare throughout his life' as its 'paramount consideration'.[153] The court went on to give 'paramount' in this context the same meaning as in Lord MacDermott's famous dictum in *J v C*,[154] namely that the child's welfare 'rules upon and determines the course to be followed'. However, the court added that welfare in the context of adoption means welfare determined having regard to the matters set out in section 1(4) of the 2002 Act, which provides a far wider checklist of factors than that provided in section 1(3) of the Children Act 1989.[155] The court highlighted that the focus on the child's welfare 'throughout his life' emphasises that adoption has lifelong implications, and therefore a judge exercising his powers under section 52(1)(b) 'has to be satisfied that the child's welfare now, throughout the rest of his childhood, into adulthood and indeed throughout his life, requires that he or she be adopted'.[156] This is reinforced by section 1(4)(c), which specifically directs attention to the consequences for the child 'throughout his life'—and by section 1(4)(f). Thus, a judge must address the question in section 52(1)(b) whether 'the welfare of the child requires the consent to be dispensed with', and answer it by reference to section 1 of the 2002 Act, and in particular by a careful consideration of all the matters identified in section 1(4).[157] There is

---

[149] Section 21(3)(a).
[150] On the previous law, see s 16(2)(b) of the Adoption Act 1976, *Re W (An Infant)* [1971] 2 All ER 49, [1971] AC 682, and Lord Wilberforce's parent '(hypothetically) endowed with mind and temperament capable of making reasonable decisions'—see *Re D (Adoption: Parent's Consent)* [1977] 1 All ER 145 at 130, [1977] AC 602 at 625.
[151] [2008] EWCA Civ 535, [2008] 2 FLR 625.     [152] Ibid, [117].     [153] Ibid, [114].
[154] [1969] 1 All ER 788 at 821, [1970] AC 668 at 711.     [155] [2008] EWCA Civ 535, [2008] 2 FLR 625 at [115].
[156] Ibid, [128]. For an example, see *Re Q (Adoption)* [2011] EWCA Civ 1610.     [157] *Re P* ibid, [116].

therefore no so-called 'enhanced welfare test' in adoption cases as compared with other situations in which children's welfare is paramount. The vital difference is simply between the wording of section 1 of the 1989 Act and section 1 of the 2002 Act.[158]

The court commented that 'the word "requires" in s 52(1)(b) is a perfectly ordinary English word',[159] adding, however, that the word takes its colour from the statutory context in which it is used. Here the context is that of determining whether the child's welfare requires *adoption* rather than something short of adoption.[160] The court emphasised that the judge must 'be aware of the importance to the child of the decision being taken' adding that there 'is, perhaps, no more important or far-reaching decision for a child than to be adopted by strangers'.[161] It held that the Strasbourg jurisprudence also provides the context in which the word 'requires' is used, and the word was chosen as best conveying the essence of the Strasbourg jurisprudence.[162] Reviewing the main principles on state interference with the rights of children and parents under Article 8 of the ECHR (which will usually be engaged in this context),[163] the court explained that any interference must be in accordance with the law, pursue a legitimate aim, and be necessary in a democratic society (implying the existence of a 'pressing social need').[164] Intervention must represent a proportionate response to achieving the legitimate aim (in this context, protection of the child's welfare). The court stated that in assessing what is proportionate the judge must always bear in mind that adoption without parental consent is the most extreme interference with family life, and therefore cogent justification must exist.[165] Thus, the court held that, viewed from the perspective of the Strasbourg jurisprudence, the word 'requires' has 'the connotation of the imperative, what is demanded rather than what is merely optional or reasonable or desirable'.[166] The court emphasised the 'need for care, sensitivity and intellectual rigour on the part of judges hearing applications for placement orders'.[167] The judge must not apply section 1(4) simply as a mantra, nor act as a rubber stamp; the 'underlying facts, properly analysed, must support the judicial conclusion'.[168]

The court's approach here is a valiant attempt, within the constraints of the paramountcy principle as interpreted by the House of Lords/Supreme Court, to place emphasis on the child's interest in the birth family not being disintegrated by adoption. Despite the ruling in *YC v United Kingdom*[169] that a judge who applies section 1 of the 2002 Act normally complies with the requirements of Article 8 of the ECHR, there are strong arguments that the paramountcy principle, as interpreted by the House of Lords/Supreme Court, is not consistent with the requirements of the ECHR and Strasbourg jurisprudence which requires separate articulation of the Article 8 interests of the child and parents concerned.[170] The divergence between the paramountcy principle and Article 8 'encompasses both the reasoning process each requires and the substantive outcomes likely to be produced'.[171] Despite acknowledgement during the review of adoption law in the early 1990s that 'the permanent legal severance of the relationship between child and birth parents should be justified by clear and significant advantage to the child compared with less permanent options',[172] the paramountcy principle was introduced into adoption law with little justification other than seeking consistency with the approach in the Children Act 1989.[173] This change troubled commentators

---

[158] Ibid, [127].　　[159] Ibid.　　[160] Ibid, [126].　　[161] Ibid, [116].　　[162] Ibid, [125].

[163] Ibid, [119].

[164] See the discussion, ibid, at [119]–[124], citing *Re C and B (Children) (Care Order: Future Harm)* [2000] 2 FCR 614 at [33]; *Haase v Germany* [2005] 3 FCR 666 at [93]; *Re O (A Child) (Supervision Order: Future Harm)* [2001] EWCA Civ 16, [2001] 1 FCR 289 at [28]; *Re B (Children) (Care: Interference with Family Life)* [2003] EWCA Civ 786, [2004] 1 FCR 463 at [34]; *Re O (Minors) (Care or Supervision Order)* [1997] 2 FCR 17 at 22; *Johansen v Norway* (1996) 23 EHRR 33 at [78].

[165] See [2008] EWCA Civ 535, [2008] 2 FLR 625 at [124].　　[166] Ibid, [125].　　[167] Ibid, [132].

[168] Ibid, [131].　　[169] (App no 4547/10) [2012] 2 FLR 332[2012] 2 FLR 332.

[170] See in the context of adoption reform, S. Choudhry, 'The Adoption and Children Act 2002, the Welfare Principle and the Human Rights Act 1998—A Missed Opportunity?' [2003] Child and Family Law Quarterly 119.

[171] Ibid.　　[172] *Adoption the Future* (Cm 2288, 1993), p 263.

[173] *Adoption: A New Approach* (Cm 5017, 2000), paras 2.11 and 4.14.

even prior to enactment of the Act.[174] It has been suggested that if the same welfare test is used for whether an order should be made as well as for dispensing with consent, then the latter becomes a foregone conclusion and there is also a risk of social engineering,[175] although it has also been observed that there may be cases in which it is in the child's interests to be adopted, but not in the child's interests to be adopted without parental consent.[176]

As discussed in *Re B (A Child)*[177] if an adoption order is to be made in care proceedings, the order must be proportionate in the sense that 'nothing else will do' (see Chapter 10 at 8.8). In *Re B-S (Children)*[178] the Court of Appeal expressed real concern about sloppy practice with regard to evidence in adoption applications and poorly reasoned judgments.[179] The court insisted that judgments be adequately reasoned, the judicial task being 'to evaluate *all* the options, undertaking a global, holistic[180] and . . . multi-faceted evaluation of the child's welfare which takes into account *all* the negatives and the positives, *all* the pros and cons, of *each* option'.[181] The court explained:

> We do not envisage that proper compliance with what we are demanding, which may well impose a more onerous burden on practitioners and judges, will conflict with the requirement, soon to be imposed by statute, that care cases are to be concluded within a maximum of 26 weeks. Critical to the success of the reforms is robust judicial case management from the outset of every care case. Case management judges must be astute to ensure that the directions they give are apt to the task and also to ensure that their directions are complied with. Never is this more important than in cases where the local authority's plan envisages adoption. If, despite all, the court does not have the kind of evidence we have identified, and is therefore not properly equipped to decide these issues, then an adjournment must be directed, even if this takes the case over 26 weeks. Where the proposal before the court is for non-consensual adoption, the issues are too grave, the stakes for all are too high, for the outcome to be determined by rigorous adherence to an inflexible timetable and justice thereby potentially denied.[182]

In *Re R (Adoption)*[183] the Court of Appeal emphasised that *Re B-S*[184] 'was not intended to change and has not changed the law',[185] nor was it 'intended to erode or otherwise place a gloss upon the statutory requirements'; rather it was aimed 'precisely at discharging the court's statutory

---

[174] E. Cooke, 'Dispensing with Parental Consent to Adoption—A Choice of Welfare Tests' [1997] Child and Family Law Quarterly 259.

[175] S. Harris-Short, 'The Adoption and Children Bill—A Fast Track to Failure?' [2001] Child and Family Law Quarterly 405.

[176] E. Cooke, 'Dispensing with Parental Consent to Adoption—A Choice of Welfare Tests' [1997] Child and Family Law Quarterly 259.

[177] [2013] UKSC 33.

[178] [2013] EWCA Civ 1146. For a detailed account of the development of the case law post *Re B*, see B. Sloan, 'Adoption decisions in England: *Re B (A Child) (Care Proceedings: Appeal)* and beyond' (2015) 37(4) *Journal of Social Welfare and Family Law* 437–57. See also J. Doughty, 'Myths and misunderstanding in adoption law and policy' [2015] CFLQ 331.

[179] [2013] EWCA Civ 1146, [30], and citing by way of recent examples four cases: *Re V (Children)* [2013] EWCA Civ 913 (judgment of Black LJ); *Re S, K v The London Borough of Brent* [2013] EWCA Civ 926 (Ryder LJ); *Re P (A Child)* [2013] EWCA Civ 963 (Black LJ); and *Re G (A Child)* [2013] EWCA Civ 965 (McFarlane LJ).

[180] As explained by McFarlane LJ in *Re G (A Child)* [2013] EWCA Civ 965 at [49] et seq. See [2013] EWCA Civ 1146 at [41]–[46].

[181] [2013] EWCA Civ 1146 at [44]; and see also *Re C (Appeal from Care and Placement Orders)* [2013] EWCA Civ 1257. For a recent case in which the judge failed to 'engage the essence of Re B-S', see *Re S (Children)* [2014] EWCA Civ 135.

[182] [2013] EWCA Civ 1146 at [49].

[183] [2014] EWCA Civ 1625. For articles highlighting the tensions in current statutory requirements and case law guidance, see B. Sloan, 'Adoption decisions in England: *Re B (A Child) (Care Proceedings: Appeal)* and beyond' (2015) 37(4) *Journal of Social Welfare and Family Law* 437–57 and J. Doughty, 'Myths and misunderstanding in adoption law and policy' [2015] CFLQ 331.

[184] As amplified in *Re M-H (A Child)* [2014] EWCA Civ 1396, *Re M (A Child: Long-term Foster care)* [2014] EWCA Civ 1406, *CM v Blackburn with Darwen Borough Council* [2014] EWCA Civ 1479, and *Re Y (Children)* [2014] EWCA Civ 1553.

[185] [2014] EWCA Civ 1625, [44]. See also *CM v Blackburn with Darwen Borough Council* [2014] EWCA Civ 1479, at [33].

duty'.[186] It was 'primarily directed to practice', expressing concern about the 'inadequacy of the analysis and reasoning put forward in support of the case for adoption.'[187] The Court of Appeal endorsed Ryder LJ's helpful illumination of the nature of the judicial exercise required by *Re B-S*, as follows:

> The process of deductive reasoning involves the identification of whether there are realistic[188] options to be compared. If there are, a welfare evaluation is required.[189] That is an exercise which compares the benefits and detriments of each realistic option, one against the other, by reference to the section 1(3) welfare factors. The court identifies the option that is in the best interests of the children and then undertakes a proportionality evaluation to ask itself the question whether the interference in family life involved by that best interests option is justified.[190]

'Nothing else will do' does not therefore mean that everything else has to be considered. The Court of Appeal in *Re R* explained that:

> *Re B-S* does not require the further forensic pursuit of options which, having been properly evaluated, typically at an early stage in the proceedings, can legitimately be discarded[191] as not being realistic. *Re B-S* does not require that every conceivable option on the spectrum that runs between 'no order' and 'adoption' has to be canvassed and bottomed out with reasons in the evidence and judgment in every single case. Full consideration is required only with respect to those options which are 'realistically possible'. [192]

In *CM v Blackburn with Darwen Borough Council*,[193] the Court of Appeal held that the Court of Appeal decision in *Re B-S* does not preclude dual planning. The process of deductive reasoning, as described above, 'does not require there to be no other realistic option on the table, even less so no other option or that there is only one possible course for the child.'[194]

In *Re M-H (Placement Order: Correct Test to Dispense with Consent)*[195] the mother of a six-year old child had a history of drug problems and of living with violent men. She agreed that she could not care for her daughter but favoured a foster care arrangement rather than adoption. An expert recommended adoption, and the mother appealed arguing that the judge had merely accepted the expert opinion rather than applying the correct test 'nothing else will do'. Dismissing the appeal Macur LJ explained that just because fostering may provide a back-up it does not follow that adoption is not necessary, and accordingly 'the fact that there is another credible option worthy of examination will not mean that the test of "nothing else will do" automatically

---

[186] [2014] EWCA Civ 1625, [55].     [187] Ibid, [56].

[188] See *Re Y* [2014] EWCA Civ 1553, [28]: 'Realistic is an ordinary English word. It needs no definition or analysis to be applied to the identification of options in a case.'

[189] In comparatively rare cases of only one realistic option, it will not be required: see *Re S (A Child)* [2013] EWCA Civ 1835, [45]–[46].

[190] *Re Y (Children)* [2014] EWCA Civ 1553. [24]: and see the fuller description in *CM v Blackburn with Darwen Borough Council* [2014] EWCA Civ 1479, at [33].

[191] This 'demands an appropriate degree of rigour, in particular if there is dispute as to whether or not a particular option is or is not realistic. But *Re B-S* does not require that every stone has to be uncovered and the ground exhaustively examined before coming to a conclusion that a particular option is not realistic.' (*Re R (Adoption)* [2014] EWCA civ 1625, at [65]).

[192] *Re R (Adoption)* [2014] EWCA Civ 1625, at [59]; and see *Re LRP (A Child) (Care Proceedings: Placement Order)* [2013] EWHC 3974 (Fam),[40], Pauffley J: 'the focus should be upon the sensible and practical possibilities rather than every potential outcome, however far-fetched.' (Pauffley J); *Re HA (A Child)* [2013] EWHC 3634 (Fam), [28], Baker J: 'rigorous analysis and comparison of the realistic options for the child's future . . . does not require a court in every case to set out in tabular format the arguments for and against every conceivable option. Such a course would tend to obscure, rather than enlighten, the reasoning process.'

[193] [2014] EWCA Civ 1479.     [194] Ibid, at [34].     [195] [2014] EWCA Civ 1396.

bites.'[196] This recognises that placement orders are made in anticipation of finding adoptive parents and there will often be a contingency plan for long-term fostering.[197]

An example of a case relying on section 52(1)(a) is *Re K and Another v FY and Another*.[198] A married couple applied to adopt a young man, C, now aged nine and a half, who had lived with them, effectively, for his whole life. They presented a statutory declaration made by a person purporting to be the child's mother, a woman of Asian origin, stating that it was in C's best interests to stay in the UK with a view to adoption. Holman J was not willing to treat this document as satisfying the Act's requirements concerning consent, nor dispense with consent on the basis of the child's welfare; rather it was 'more appropriate to focus on the reality of this particular case, which is that neither the mother nor the father, whoever he may be, of this child can now be found.'[199]

### 6.3.4  Child must be suitable for placement

For an order to be made, it must be possible to say at the time of making the order that the order is in a child's best interests. In *Re T (Placement Order)*[200] a judge made care orders and placement orders in respect of boys aged 7 and 5, who had suffered neglect and inappropriate parenting by their parents, both of whom had significant learning disabilities. The boys were described by two experienced independent social workers as the most damaged and needy they had ever encountered in their work. The local authority's long-term plan was for the children to be adopted. However, it was proposed first to place the children with specialist therapeutic foster parents for six months and possibly a year, so as to help the children to learn how to form secure attachments. The children's father challenged the placement orders. Allowing his appeal and setting aside the placement orders, the Court of Appeal explained that, while mere uncertainty as to whether adoption will actually follow is not a reason for not making a placement order,[201] in this unusual case it was not simply a matter of potential difficulty of placement; rather the boys were not yet suitable for placement for adoption.[202] It had, therefore, not yet been possible to say that adoption was actually in the boys' best interests and the placement order was premature.[203]

## 6.4  Consequences of a placement order

The effect of a placement order is that certain orders under the Children Act 1989 cease to have effect, and certain orders under that Act can no longer be made, or in some cases applications are restricted by a leave requirement. On the making of a placement order, any order mentioned in section 8(1) of the Children Act 1989 and any supervision order ceases to have effect,[204] and no court can make a prohibited steps order, specific issue order, supervision order, or child assessment order in respect of the child.[205] No child arrangements order with respect to the child's living arrangements or special guardianship order may be made unless leave of the court has been obtained under section 29(4) and (5) respectively, or the applicant has obtained leave under section 47 to oppose an adoption order. An existing care order does not cease to exist, but does not have effect at any time when the placement order is in force.[206] These effects of a placement order are intended to ensure that (with limited exceptions) the adoption agency and prospective adopter are in control of the child's future day-to-day welfare pending a court decision concerning adoption, without the risk of interference from others via court orders. An exception is made where the applicant has been granted leave under relevant provisions to apply for a child arrangements order or special guardianship order. Another exception is that an application for contact provision under section 8 of the Children Act 1989 is still permitted, as contact is ultimately under court control, and it may be that in future such an application will be heard alongside an application for an adoption order. Apart from such a

---

[196]  Ibid, [9].     [197]  Ibid, [10].     [198]  [2014] EWHC 3111 (Fam), Holman J.     [199]  Ibid, [15].
[200]  [2008] EWCA Civ 248, [2008] 1 FLR 1721.     [201]  Ibid, [17].     [202]  Ibid, [18].     [203]  Ibid.
[204]  ACA 2002, s 29(2).     [205]  Ibid, s 29(3).     [206]  Ibid, s 29(1).

case,[207] where a placement order is in force, applications relating to contact with the child concerned are regulated by sections 26 and 27 of the ACA 2002 not the Children Act 1989.

## 6.5 Placement and contact

On an adoption agency being authorised to place a child for adoption, or placing a child for adoption who is less than 6 weeks old, any contact provision in a child arrangements order under section 8 of the Children Act 1989 or any order under section 34 of the Children Act 1989 ceases to have effect,[208] and no application can be made for contact under the 1989 Act. Instead, contact becomes regulated by sections 26 and 27 of the 2002 Act. Section 27(4) provides that before making a placement order the court must consider the arrangements which the adoption agency has made, or proposes to make, for allowing any person contact with the child, and invite the parties to the proceedings to comment on those arrangements. Section 26(2) provides for the making of a contact order 'requiring the person with whom the child lives, or is to live, to allow the child to visit or stay with the person named in the order, or for the person named in the order and the child otherwise to have contact with each other'. The court can make a contact order of its own initiative when making a placement order,[209] or an application for an order under this section may be made by:

(a) the child or the agency;

(b) any parent, guardian or relative;

(c) any person in whose favour there was provision for contact which ceased to have effect by virtue of section 26(1);

(d) if a child arrangements order was in force immediately before the adoption agency was authorised to place the child for adoption or (as the case may be) placed the child for adoption at a time when he was less than 6 weeks old, any person named in the order as a person with whom the child was to live;

(e) if a person had care of the child immediately before that time by virtue of an order made in the exercise of the High Court's inherent jurisdiction with respect to children, that person;

(f) any person who has obtained the court's leave to make the application.

An order under section 26 may provide for contact on any conditions the court considers appropriate.[210] The courts' approach to on-going contact in adoption cases is discussed further later in this chapter.

## 6.6 Effect of placement or authorisation to place

Where a child is placed for adoption or an agency is authorised to place a child under section 19, or a placement order is in force in respect of a child, the agency concerned has parental responsibility for the child and, while the child is placed with prospective adopters, they too have parental responsibility.[211] However, in such circumstances, a person may not cause the child to be known by a new surname or remove the child from the UK (except for a period of less than one month by a person who provides the child's home[212]), unless the court gives leave[213] or each parent or guardian of the child gives written consent.[214] Where a child is placed for adoption

---

[207] See ibid, s 26(5).

[208] Ibid, s 26(1) and (6). Any contact activity direction (see Children Act 1989, s 11A) relating to contact with the child is also discharged.

[209] ACA 2002, s 26(4).    [210] Ibid, s 27(5).    [211] Ibid, s 25.    [212] Ibid, s 28(4).

[213] See, for example, *Kent County Council v PA-K and IA (A Child)* [2013] EWHC 578 (Fam) (Pauffley J) (permission granted for one-year period).

[214] ACA 2002, s 28(2) and (3).

under section 19 or an adoption agency is authorised to place a child for adoption under that section, a parent or guardian of the child may not apply for a child arrangements order, and a guardian may not apply for a special guardianship order, unless an application for an adoption order has been made and the parent or guardian has obtained the court's leave to oppose the adoption order.[215]

Where a child is placed for adoption, there is authorisation to place, or a local authority is seeking a placement order, the stability of the child's current home placement (whether placed with prospective adopters or accommodated by the local authority) is protected to some extent by prohibitions on the child's removal. Where a child is placed for adoption by an adoption agency, or accommodated by an agency which is authorised to place the child, no person other than the agency is allowed to remove the child from the placement or accommodation.[216] Similarly, where a child is accommodated by a local authority and the authority has applied for a placement order which has not yet been disposed of, the child may only be removed from accommodation by the local authority or by a person who has the leave of the court.[217]

These general prohibitions on removal of a child are subject to sections 31–33 which provide for the child to be returned following a period of notice. If a parent or guardian informs the agency that he or she wishes the child to be returned and the child is accommodated but not placed for adoption, the agency must return the child within seven days beginning with the request. If the child is placed otherwise than under section 19 (eg as a baby under 6 weeks old), then the agency must give notice of the parents' request to the prospective adopters, who similarly must return the child within seven days, whereupon the agency must return the child to the parents.[218] In the case of a child who is placed pursuant to section 19 and consent to placement has been withdrawn, the same procedure applies except that the time frame for return of the child is 14 days, not seven.[219] None of these requirements to return the child applies, however, if an application for a placement order is, or has been, made and has not been disposed of.[220] If a child is placed for adoption and an application for a placement order fails, prospective adopters must return the child to the local authority on a date determined by the court.[221] In each of the cases mentioned, a failure on the part of prospective adopters to return the child as required constitutes a criminal offence.

Where a child is placed for adoption by an adoption agency, and the agency is of the opinion that the child should not remain with the prospective adopters, it may give notice to the prospective adopters to return the child within seven days.[222] However, if an application for an adoption order has been made, the adopters are not required to return the child unless the court so orders. In *RY v Southend Borough Council*[223] the Council sought, under section 35(2) of the ACA 2002, return of the child placed for adoption. The child, who suffered from cerebral palsy, had been placed with RY, a young woman who was also disabled, having been diagnosed with Ehlers Danlos Syndrome, Asperger's Syndrome, and joint problems which had necessitated her using a wheelchair. There was some suggestion that some of these health difficulties might have a psychological component, and the judge expressed concern that there had not been a full evaluation of RY's ability to cope with the child's needs as the child grew up. Of particular concern, however, were RY's interactions with health and social care professionals, obstructing rather than facilitating the child's care, her over-reporting of medical symptoms, too-frequent medical interventions, and calling for increased medical intervention contrary to professional opinion. Hayden J returned the child to the local authority, concluding that RY's emotional and psychological issues presented a risk of harm to the child so real and serious with consequences potentially so grave as to be wholly inimical to her welfare.

---

[215] Ibid, s 28(1).     [216] Ibid, s 30(1) and (3).     [217] Ibid, s 30(2).
[218] Ibid, s 31.     [219] Ibid, s 32.     [220] Ibid, s 31(2) and (3).     [221] Ibid, s 33.
[222] Under ACA 2002, s 35.     [223] [2015] EWHC 2509 (Fam), Hayden J.

## 6.7 **Duration, and revocation, of a placement order**

Once made, the placement order remains in force until an adoption order is made in respect of the child, or the child reaches the age of 18, marries, or forms a civil partnership, or the placement order is revoked under section 24 of the Act. The court may revoke a placement order if, on an application for an adoption order, it determines not to make the adoption order.[224] In addition, it may revoke the placement order on the application of any person. An important effect of making an application for revocation is to be found in section 24(5) of the Act. It provides that where such an application has been made and not disposed of and the child has not yet been placed for adoption by the authority, the child may not without the court's leave be placed for adoption under the placement order.

While any person may apply for revocation, section 24(2) places some restrictions on applications. It provides that:

> an application may not be made by a person other than the child or the local authority authorised by the order to place the child for adoption unless—
>
> (a) the court has given leave to apply, and
> (b) the child is not placed for adoption by the authority.

As paragraph (b) makes clear, an application for leave to revoke a placement order can only be made at a time when the child is not already placed for adoption. As provided in section 18(5), this means placed with prospective adopters. In *Re S (Placement Order: Revocation)*[225] a mother applied for leave to revoke a placement order, contending that her change of circumstances meant she could now safely care for her child. The local authority's plan for the child was adoption, and the child was placed with a foster carer who, while not making a specific commitment to adopt, had not precluded the possibility of her family adopting the child. In these circumstances the judge held that the child was placed with potential adopters and the leave application was precluded by section 24(2)(b). The Court of Appeal allowed the mother's appeal and remitted the case to the judge for rehearing. The court held that the statute required placement with prospective adopters, not merely potential adopters. The court pointed out that the word 'prospective' is defined 'as an adjective attributive of a person expected or expecting to be something particular in the future; alternatively, as something likely to happen at a future date. "Potential", by contrast, is defined as an adjective having or showing the capacity to become or develop into something in the future.'[226] The court made clear that placement for adoption only takes place once the child in question is matched to prospective adopters. Here only the first stage in the adoption process had been completed, namely whether adoption was in the child's best interests. The foster carer had not been approved in principle, let alone matched, as a prospective adopter for the child.[227] The foster carer had no more than the potential to emerge at a later stage as a prospective adopter.[228]

Section 24(2)(b) proved crucial in *Re F (Placement Order)*.[229] In that case, a girl, who was just under 2 years old at the date of the Court of Appeal's judgment, had been conceived following a casual relationship between her parents. The father, who had initially been unaware that he was the father, was served with care proceedings in respect of the child in which the local authority's plan was for the child's adoption. However, the father was hospitalised with a heart attack and took no part in the proceedings. The local authority was granted a placement order. Some months thereafter, after consulting solicitors, the father applied for leave to revoke the placement order under section 24(2). The solicitors sent the local authority a fax informing them of the father's application and asking the authority to confirm by return fax that the child had not yet been placed. There was no response to the fax. The authority convened an informal strategy meeting and, on the day before the hearing of the father's application, the local authority placed the child with prospective adopters. At the hearing, the local authority then

---

[224] ACA 2002, s 24(4).   [225] [2008] EWCA Civ 1333, [2009] 1 FLR 503.   [226] Ibid, [7].
[227] Ibid, [8].   [228] Ibid, [9].   [229] [2008] EWCA Civ 439, [2008] 2 FLR 550.

simply relied on section 24(2)(b) and the judge reluctantly agreed that in the circumstances no application to revoke could be made and therefore leave could not be granted. The father appealed, arguing that respect for his human rights required that words should be read into section 24(5) pursuant to section 3 of the Human Rights Act 1998 so that the prohibition in that subsection on placing a child when an application to revoke a placement order has been made should also apply when an application for leave to apply to revoke a placement order has been made. In this way, the local authority would have been prevented from placing the child once the father made his application for leave.

The Court of Appeal, by a majority,[230] dismissed the father's appeal, holding that it was impossible to read section 24(5) as contended for by the father. Indeed, section 24(5), read as part of the whole scheme for adoption under the 2002 Act, was 'human rights compliant'.[231] The majority reached this conclusion with regret, not because of any doubts about the law but because of the conduct of the local authority adoption agency in this case.[232] Wall LJ commented that the 'disgraceful conduct of the agency in this case is an example of the worst kind of sharp practice',[233] which demonstrated 'a profound if not total misunderstanding of its functions under the 2002 Act'.[234] It was 'an abuse of power, and wholly unacceptable'.[235] Wall LJ suggested[236] that were such behaviour to be repeated it could be the subject of an application for judicial review, and his Lordship could see no reason why the Administrative Court should not declare unlawful such a decision. The decision to place the child for adoption could be quashed. Directions could be given for hearing the application for leave to revoke, and in the meantime an injunction could be put in place restraining the local authority from placing the child for adoption. Wall LJ went on to indicate what should have happened in this case as a matter of good practice.[237] Either the father's solicitors should have sought an undertaking from the local authority that the child would not be placed pending the hearing of the father's application or, in the absence of such an undertaking, should have sought an injunction in similar terms. Alternatively, the local authority should have replied, explained that its plans to place the child were at an advanced stage, and then sought leave of the court to place the child.

Section 24(3) provides that the court 'cannot give leave under subsection (2)(a) unless satisfied that there has been a change in circumstances since the order was made'.

In *Re T (Application to Revoke Placement Orders: Change in Circumstances)*[238] the court considered the meaning of 'change of circumstances' within section 24 of the ACA 2002.[239] A judge made care and placement orders because of the risk of emotional abuse to children resulting from the parents' abusive relationship, and the father sought to revoke the orders. His case was that the parents were now divorced and he was in a new relationship. In addition, there had been distress exhibited by the children about their sibling contact being terminated to facilitate placement in an adoptive family. The judge had focused only on the father's change of circumstances. The Court of Appeal allowed the appeal, explaining that any changes pleaded must be 'relevant to the circumstances of the case' but are not limited to changes of the parents' circumstances. The judge was wrong on the facts not to find any change of circumstances, and should have considered the change in the children's circumstances since the placement order too.[240] The Court added that the:

> relevance of any change should be set against the finding or threshold upon which the original orders were made so that the test is not set too high. This will vary from case to case but in this case the threshold was at the lower end of the scale and the test should reflect that; it should be proportionate to the facts of this case.[241]

[230]  Wall and Wilson LJJ; Thorpe LJ dissenting.
[231]  [2008] EWCA Civ 439, [2008] 2 FLR 550 at [63] *per* Wall LJ, Wilson LJ agreeing.
[232]  [2008] EWCA Civ 439, [2008] 2 FLR 550 at [1].
[233]  Ibid, [93]. Indeed, the worst his Lordship had ever encountered in a career spanning nearly 40 years (see at [78]).
[234]  Ibid, [39].      [235]  Ibid, [44].      [236]  Ibid, [94].      [237]  See, ibid, [97] et seq.
[238]  [2014] EWCA Civ 1369.
[239]  See also *Re R (Appeal from Placement Order: Change of Circumstances)* [2013] EWCA Civ 1240.
[240]  [2014] EWCA Civ 1369, [44] and [51].      [241]  Ibid, [60].

Here the judge had set the test too high, in failing to set the change of circumstances against the principal concern which had been the continuing parents' relationship, and not considering the father's new relationship against the context of the threshold criteria, which had been fulfilled primarily on the basis of future risk to the children.[242]

In *M v Warwickshire County Council*[243] two children were taken into care because their mother abused alcohol and crack cocaine, rendering her incapable of looking after them appropriately. Care orders and placement orders had been made in respect of the children. However, the mother had since achieved significant improvements in her life and was applying for leave to revoke the placement orders. She had abstained from drugs, was no longer abusing alcohol, kept the home in a fit state, and had managed to hold down a part-time job. The judge found that there was a change of circumstances and that once he had so found he was obliged to grant leave. On appeal by the local authority, the Court of Appeal held that the judge had been right on these facts to find a change of circumstances, but had erred in granting leave automatically, since the grant of leave involves an exercise of discretion.[244] The court went on to provide guidance on what should be a court's general approach to exercising discretion under section 24(3). The court explained that section 1(7) of the 2002 Act makes clear that section 1 of that Act does not apply to an application for leave to revoke a placement order under section 24(2).[245] Thus the child's welfare is not the paramount consideration on an application for leave to revoke a placement order, although the court made clear that it is still, of course, a factor in the exercise of discretion. The court was of the view that, as in the case of many other leave applications in areas of family law, the court should ask whether the applicant would have a real prospect of success.[246] However, the court made clear that the prospect of success can only be a relevant factor to the exercise of discretion; 'it cannot be written in stone that the prospect of success has to be real'.[247] In other words, the court was merely commending those words as 'a reasonable working assumption, likely to be apt to the vast majority of applications'.[248] The Court of Appeal, in the words of Wilson LJ, went on to explain the overall correct approach, highlighting the relationship between child welfare and prospect of success:

> on establishment of a change in circumstances, a discretion arises in which the welfare of the child and the prospect of success should both be weighed . . . the requisite analysis of the prospect of success will almost always include the requisite analysis of the welfare of the child. For, were there to be a real prospect that an applicant would persuade the court that a child's welfare would best be served by revocation of the placement order, it would surely almost always serve the child's welfare for the applicant to be given leave to seek to do so. Conversely, were there not to be any such real prospect, it is hard to conceive that it would serve the welfare of the child for the application for leave to be granted. But I hesitate to suggest that analysis of welfare will always be satisfactorily subsumed within an analysis of prospect.[249]

In *M v Warwickshire County Council*, by the time the mother made her application for leave to revoke, the children had been in long-term foster care for three years, over half of their lives. In difficult circumstances, the children had eventually been well matched to proposed adopters.[250] The Court of Appeal noted that the only realistic aspiration that the mother would have at a revocation hearing would be an adjournment pending a full professional assessment of her parenting capacity, and the present adopters might not be relied on to tolerate the ensuing delay. In all the circumstances, the Court of Appeal held that the mother's application for leave must be refused.

---

[242] Ibid, [61].    [243] [2007] EWCA Civ 1084, [2008] 1 FLR 1093.    [244] Ibid, [30].
[245] Ibid, [22].    [246] Ibid, [27].    [247] Ibid.    [248] Ibid.    [249] Ibid, [29].
[250] Finding adopters had not proved easy apparently because of the children's ethnicity, the fact that one of them had cerebral palsy, and the father of the other child had been diagnosed with paranoid schizophrenia.

### 6.7.1 Revocation even when child will not be returned to parents

As *NS-H v Kingston Upon Hull City Council and MC*[251] demonstrates, occasionally it will be proper for a court to grant parental leave to revoke a placement order notwithstanding the absence of any real prospect that a court would find it to be in the interest of the child to return to live with the parent.[252] In that case a young boy, who had very low weight for his age, was taken into care and a placement order was also made. However, he continued to fail to thrive when living with foster parents and the local authority changed its care plan. The authority now intended to move him to new foster parents, and accepted that an adoptive home could only be found once he began to thrive. The child's mother sought leave to apply to revoke the placement order. There was no question in this case of the boy returning to live with his mother as it had been found that his initial failure to thrive was the result of the mother's defective attachment to the boy and her own past eating disorder, which had led to her mishandling of his feeding. The Court of Appeal overturned the judge's refusal to grant leave, holding that, applying the correct test (in the *Warwickshire* case, as set out earlier) the judge could only have concluded that leave should be granted.[253]

## 7 Applications to adopt

Following placement, the next step in the adoption process is for the prospective adopter(s) to make an application to adopt the child. The effect of making the application is that the child may not be placed with any other prospective adopter until the application is disposed of.[254] The Act defines who may adopt and be adopted, and thus the nature of an adoption application, and also sets out certain preliminaries which must be complied with before the application may be made.

### 7.1 Who may adopt?

An application for an adoption order may be made by a couple or by one person.[255] Each adopter must have been habitually resident in a part of the British Islands for a period of not less than one year ending with the date of the application.[256] In addition, the individual applicant, or at least one member of a couple, must be domiciled in a part of the British Islands.[257] The basis of the court's jurisdiction to make an adoption order is thus the domicile or habitual residence of the adoptive parents.[258] However, there is 'no limitation, whether by reference to nationality, domicile or habitual residence, upon the children who can be adopted or the natural parent(s) whose consent can be dispensed with pursuant to the 2002 Act'.[259] Thus the court can make an adoption order irrespective of the nationality, domicile, habitual residence, or presence within the jurisdiction of the natural parent(s), applying English law.[260] Whereas in the case of care proceedings, jurisdiction is founded on the habitual residence of the child, 'this is not so in the case of adoption or placement order proceedings under the 2002 Act.'[261]

---

[251] [2008] EWCA Civ 493, [2008] 2 FLR 918, CA.     [252] Ibid, [1].

[253] See at [27]. The court added, at [31], that in exercising discretion the court should guard against an opportunistic attempt to use an application for improper, collateral purposes.

[254] ACA 2002, s 18(4).     [255] Ibid, s 49.     [256] Ibid, s 49(3).     [257] Ibid, s 49(2).

[258] See ACA 2002, s 49, and *Re N (Children) (Adoption: Jurisdiction)* [2015] EWCA Civ 1112, [77].

[259] Ibid,[74], on which, see H. Markham 'Is it right to apply English adoption law to non-English Children – *Re CB*' [2015] Fam Law 1385.

[260] [2015] EWCA Civ 1112, [92].

[261] Article 1(3)(b) of BIIA provides that BIIA: 'shall not apply to . . . decisions on adoption, measures preparatory to adoption, or the annulment or revocation of adoption.' See *Re N (Children) (Adoption: Jurisdiction)* [2015] EWCA Civ 1112, at [74].

### 7.1.1 **Adoption by a couple**

An adoption order may be made on the application of a couple under section 50 of the 2002 Act. With one exception, both of the couple must have attained the age of 21 years. Where one of the couple is the mother or the father of the person to be adopted the age requirement is less stringent. An application can be made provided the parent has attained the age of 18 years and the other person of the couple has attained the age of 21 years.[262]

#### 7.1.1.1 *Meaning of couple*

For the purpose of the 2002 Act, section 144(4) defines a couple as:

(a) a married couple; or

(aa) two people who are civil partners of each other; or

(b) two people (whether of different sexes or the same sex) living as partners in an enduring family relationship.

Section 145(5) provides that the definition in section 144(4)(b) does not include two people one of whom is the other's parent, grandparent, sister, brother, aunt, or uncle, in each case whether of the full blood or half blood. The list of excluded relationships in section 144(5) includes such relationships as would exist but for adoption, and also a child's relationship with his or her adoptive, or former adoptive, parents, but no other adoptive relationships.[263]

The definition is silent as to whether the couple must live at the same address. This issue arose in *Re T and M (Adoption)*.[264] In that case, two women who were a couple each separately adopted a child while living in Nicaragua. The separate adoptions were necessary because Nicaragua did not permit adoption by a same-sex couple. One of the women was Nicaraguan and adopted a child, C, who was a member of her extended family, while the other woman, who was from the USA, adopted a child, J, from an orphanage. The women and the children came to live in the UK. However, J's previous experiences of abandonment by her parents led to difficulties in her relationship with the Nicaraguan woman (J's adoptive mother's partner). This led the women to set up two separate households close to each other, although they remained a couple and saw each other daily. J lived in one household with her adoptive mother, and C moved between the households in a shared residence arrangement. The couple then applied to adopt C as a couple and Hedley J (having first recognised at common law the validity of the Nicaraguan adoption order in respect of C) was required to consider whether the women were a couple, notwithstanding the fact that they were living in separate properties. Hedley J held that the words 'living as partners in an enduring family relationship' were 'no doubt chosen so as not to require the residence of both in the same property', which he did not see as unusual given that many a parent has had to work abroad leaving the rest of the family at home. He held that what is required is 'first, an unambiguous intention to create and maintain family life, and secondly, a factual matrix consistent with that intention',[265] adding that that 'is clearly a question of fact and degree in each case'.[266] Applying that approach, his Lordship found on the facts that the parties were within the ambit of section 144(4)(b) and thus entitled to make a joint application to adopt, since they lived in a committed and exclusive relationship and spent significant time as a unit of four, consistent with the background to the case and the shared-care arrangement.[267]

In *Re WM (Adoption: Non-Patrial)*,[268] a case under the former legislation (the Adoption Act 1976), Johnson J was required to consider whether an adoption order could be made in favour of a married couple who had separated. His Lordship made the order, noting that there was no specific provision in the legislation which prevented an order being made in favour of a separated couple.

---

[262] ACA 2002, s 50(1).     [263] Ibid, s 144(6).
[264] [2010] EWHC 964 (Fam), [2011] 1 FLR 1487 (Hedley J).     [265] Ibid, [16].
[266] Ibid.     [267] Ibid, [17].     [268] [1997] 1 FLR 132, FD.

In *Re CC (Adoption Application: Separated Applicants)*[269] Moylan J, having noted Johnson J's decision in *Re WM*,[270] made a joint adoption order despite the fact that the prospective adopters had separated, having found that they continued to parent the child cooperatively.

In *Re WM* Johnson J noted that the 1976 Act, with which he was concerned, provided (as does the 2002 Act—see discussion at Section 7.3.2) that an adoption order could not be made unless there had been sufficient opportunities to view the couple with the child in the home environment. However, in this case the social worker concerned had had sufficient opportunity to do so prior to the separation. Johnson J suggested, however, that had that not been the case it would seem that that provision would have proved a bar to making the order. The same reasoning would presumably apply to the similar provision under the 2002 Act.

### 7.1.2 Adoption by one person

An application to adopt can be made by one person under section 51 of the 2002 Act. In such a case, the applicant must have attained the age of 21 years and must fall into one of the following categories:

(1) The person is not married or a civil partner.[271]

(2) The court is satisfied that the person is the partner of a parent of the person to be adopted.[272] For the purposes of the 2002 Act, a person is the partner of a child's parent if the person and the parent are a couple but the person is not the child's parent.[273]

(3) The person is married or a civil partner, but the court is satisfied that:

   (a) 'the person's spouse or civil partner (as the case may be) cannot be found,

   (b) the spouses or civil partners have separated and are living apart, and the separation is likely to be permanent, or

   (c) the person's spouse or civil partner is by reason of ill-health, whether physical or mental, incapable of making an application for an adoption order.'[274]

An example of an application under section 51(1) of the ACA 2002 by a single person is provided by the extraordinary facts of *B v C (Surrogacy: Adoption)*.[275] A young unmarried man, B, in his 20s, conceived a child with the assistance of a licensed fertility clinic. Unusually, however, his sperm fertilised a donor egg, and the resultant embryo was then implanted in his own mother who, with her husband's agreement, acted as a surrogate for her son. On the day of the child's birth B's solicitors wrote to the Local Authority notifying them of his intention to issue an adoption application. The child, now aged 7 months, was living with B under a child arrangements order, and he sought an adoption order. Theis J analysed the resultant legal complexity as follows. The circumstances of the child's conception and birth resulted in the mother and her husband being the legal parents of the child, pursuant to sections 33 and 35 of the Human Fertilisation and Embryology Act 2008 respectively, and of course B and the child whom B had fathered biologically were therefore siblings. Placement for adoption with B was not unlawful as he was a legal brother of the child. However, since he was not a parent of the child he required leave to apply for the order. Theis J granted leave, and ultimately the adoption order, all parties and the local authority being satisfied that adoption would satisfy the life-long welfare interests of the child. By reason of the adoption order, therefore, the child's brother became his father, and his parents became his grandparents.

---

[269] [2013] EWHC 4815 (Fam).

[270] Also citing *Re C (Foreign Adoption: Natural Mother's Consent: Service)* [2006] 1 FLR 318, Bodey J.

[271] ACA 2002, s 51(1).     [272] Ibid, s 51(2).     [273] Ibid, s 50(7).

[274] See ibid, s 51(3) in relation to a married person, and s 51(3A) for the corresponding provision in relation to a civil partner.

[275] [2015] EWFC 17 (Fam).

In the case of an application by a partner of the child's parent (under section 51(2)), section 67(3)(a) provides that the adopted person 'is to be treated in law as not being the child of any person other than the adopter and the other one of the couple'. In *Re P (Step-parent Adoption)*[276] the mother's male partner, with whom the mother and children had lived for the previous seven years, applied to adopt two children, D and A, aged 14 and 12 respectively. The children had different fathers, each of whom was Polish, as was the mother. D's father had had little or no contact since D was two years old when his parents separated. The mother and A's father had divorced in 2005 and last contact between A and her father was when she was three years old. The mother had relocated from Poland to the UK and met the stepfather soon after her arrival. The adoption application was made with the full consent of the children's mother.

Mc Farlane LJ commented that the statutory scheme 'makes no distinction between a step-parent adoption order and any other adoption order.'[277] However, his lordship noted that the European Court of Human Rights in *Söderbäck v Sweden*[278] had distinguished between compulsory adoption of a child outside the family and step-parent adoption, the context of which differ significantly.[279] In *Söderbäck* a step-father sought to adopt a six-year-old girl, with whom he had lived since she was a baby. The father, who had had very limited contact with the girl, challenged an adoption order that had been made by the Swedish authorities. The ECtHR held that the adoption order was not disproportionate given the father's limited contact and the purpose of the order, to consolidate and formalise the child's existing family ties, and commented that the order:

> does not concern the severance of links between a mother and a child taken into public care but, rather, of links between a natural father and a child who had been in the care of her mother since she was born. Nor does it concern a parent who had had custody of the child or who in any other capacity had assumed the care of the child.[280]

McFarlane LJ held that the English court should recognise this distinction, and adopt the guidance of the ECtHR in *Söderbäck*[281] as to proportionality in step-parent adoption cases. Accordingly, factors that are likely to make it more likely that adoption is a proportionate measure are: where the parent has not had the child's care or asserted parental responsibility, had infrequent or no contact, and where there is an established family unit which includes the step-parent, which has existed for a significant period.[282] The Court of Appeal held that, given the fathers' lack of active involvement in their respective child's life over many years, the geographical separation, the children's long-established family ties with the step-father, and the children's strong wish to be adopted, an adoption order should have been made. The judge had 'failed to engage with the benefit that adoption would bring by marrying up the legal relationships with the 'de facto' relationships as they had become established within this small family unit.'[283]

### 7.1.3 Adoption by the child's mother or father

Special considerations apply on an application by the mother or father of the person to be adopted. Such an application may not be made unless the court is satisfied that:

(a) the other natural parent is dead or cannot be found,

(b) . . . there is no other parent,[284] or

(c) there is some other reason justifying the child's being adopted by the applicant alone.[285]

---

[276] [2014] EWCA Civ 1174.      [277] Ibid, [11].      [278] [1999] 1 FLR 250.      [279] [2014] EWCA Civ 1174, at [31].
[280] [1999] 1 FLR 250.      [281] [2014] EWCA Civ 1174, [48].      [282] Ibid.      [283] Ibid, at [67].
[284] By virtue of assisted conception provisions under the Human Fertilisation and Embryology Acts as specified in subs (5). The provisions are—(a) section 28 of the Human Fertilisation and Embryology Act 1990 (disregarding subsections (5A) to (5I) of that section), or (b) sections 34 to 47 of the Human Fertilisation and Embryology Act 2008 (disregarding sections 39, 40 and 46 of that Act).
[285] ACA 2002, s 51(4).

Where the court makes an adoption order on such an application, the court must record that it is satisfied as to the fact mentioned in paragraph (a) or (b) or, in the case of paragraph (c), record the reason.[286]

In *Re B (A Minor) (Natural Parent)*[287] the House of Lords considered a provision in section 15(3) of the Adoption Act 1976 which was in similar terms. In that case an adoption order was sought in respect of a 3-year-old girl by one of her natural parents (the father), with the consent of the child's mother. The mother had had a brief relationship with the father and initially he was unaware of the mother's pregnancy and the birth of his daughter. The mother gave up the child for adoption at birth. Purely by chance, the local authority became aware of the father's whereabouts, and when contacted by them he expressed his desire to look after the child.[288] The child had been placed with the father and he had since looked after her successfully. There was no issue as to whether the father should continue to care for his daughter; the issue was whether he should become her sole adoptive parent, the legal effect of which would be to remove the mother's legal parenthood and parental responsibility so that the child would have no maternal relations. The father was anxious that the mother might marry and wish to take over the care of the child in the future. His case was that the mother's continuing status as a parent with parental responsibility would perpetuate insecurity for him and that this would potentially affect the child's stability. Bracewell J made the adoption order.[289] However, the Court of Appeal reversed her decision,[290] holding that section 15(3) was to be interpreted to require that 'that there be some reason, comparable to the death, disappearance or anonymous sperm donation of the other natural parent, "justifying" his or her exclusion, not only from parental responsibility for but also from the whole life and lineage of the child'.[291] On the father's appeal, the House of Lords restored Bracewell J's order, holding that the Court of Appeal's interpretation had been unduly restrictive.[292] The House could see no reason to place this unexpressed limitation on the section[293] since there may be other situations when the welfare of the child justifies the exclusion of a natural parent, such as abandonment or persistent neglect or ill-treatment of the child.[294] The House recognised that 'permanent exclusion of the child's mother from the life of the child is a drastic and detrimental consequence of adoption so far as the child is concerned' and that the circumstances in which such an order will be justified are likely to be exceptional,[295] but added that how 'serious this loss is likely to be depends on the circumstances of the case'.[296] The House was of the view that 'all that is required, is that the reason, whatever it be, must be sufficient to justify the exclusion of the other parent'.[297] The court explained that the reason must be sufficient to outweigh the adverse consequences such an order may have by reason of the exclusion of one parent from the child's life. Consent of the excluded parent is not of itself a sufficient reason, but it is a factor to be taken into account. Its weight will depend on the circumstances. Whether any particular reason satisfies this test depends on the circumstances.[298]

The House held that it could not be said that Bracewell J had been plainly wrong to conclude that the child's best interests required the adoption order even though this would have the consequence of excluding the mother. According to the House, the judge's approach identified the pressing social need for adoption (the need to safeguard and promote the child's welfare) and represented the court's considered view on proportionality so as to fulfil the requirements of Article 8 of the ECHR.

---

[286] Ibid.

[287] [2001] UKHL 70, [2002] 1 FLR 196. See S. Harris-Short, '*Re B (Adoption: Natural Parent)* Putting the Child at the Heart of Adoption?' [2002] Child and Family Law Quarterly 325; A. Bainham, 'Unintentional Parenthood: The Case of the Reluctant Mother' [2002] Cambridge Law Journal 288.

[288] Upon the father being located, the mother had registered the father on the child's birth certificate and had entered into a parental responsibility agreement with him.

[289] *B v P (Adoption by Unmarried Father)* [2000] 2 FLR 717.

[290] *Re B (Adoption by One Natural Parent to Exclusion of Other)* [2001] 1 FLR 589 (Dame Elizabeth Butler-Sloss P and Potter and Hale LJJ).

[291] Ibid, [34].    [292] [2001] UKHL 70, [2002] 1 FLR 196 at [24].    [293] Ibid.    [294] Ibid, [23].
[295] Ibid, [27].    [296] Ibid, [22].    [297] Ibid, [24].    [298] Ibid, [24].

## 7.2 **Who may be adopted?**

An adoption order may not be made in relation to a person who has attained the age of 19 years[299] nor in relation to a person who is or has been married[300] or a civil partner.[301] Furthermore, an application for an adoption order may only be made if the person to be adopted has not attained the age of 18 years on the date of the application.[302] So an adoption order can be made in respect of a person at any time before his or her 19th birthday, provided the application was made while that person was still a minor. An adoption order may be made even if the child to be adopted is already an adopted child.[303]

## 7.3 **Preliminaries to adoption**

There are certain preliminaries which must be complied with before an adoption application may be made.

### 7.3.1 **Child must live with the adopter(s)**

First, an application may not be made unless the child has lived with the adopter(s) for a specified period of time. The precise period depends on the type of adoption. The rules are set out in section 42.

(i) If the child was placed for adoption by an adoption agency or in pursuance of an order of the High Court, or the applicant is a parent of the child, 'the child must have had his home with the applicant or, in the case of an application by a couple, with one or both of them at all times during the period of *ten weeks* preceding the application'[304]

(ii) If the applicant or one of the applicants is the partner of a parent of the child, 'the child must have had his home with the applicant or, as the case may be, applicants at all times during the period of *six months* preceding the application'[305]

(iii) If the applicants are local authority foster parents, then 'the child must have had his home with the applicants at all times during the period of *one year* preceding the application'[306]

(iv) In any other case, 'the child must have had his home with the applicant or, in the case of an application by a couple, with one or both of them for not less than *three years* (whether continuous or not) during the period of five years preceding the application'.[307]

#### 7.3.1.1 *Leave to make the adoption application where conditions in section 42(4) and (5) not fulfilled*

In the last two cases mentioned (points (iii) and (iv) above), the conditions do not prevent an application being made if the court gives leave to make it under section 42(6). In *ASB and KBS v MQS (Secretary of State for the Home Department Intervening)*[308] a 15-year-old boy was brought from Pakistan to England by his mother on a six-month visitor's visa, which could not be extended. The mother returned to Pakistan, leaving the child with his uncle and aunt. The child had remained after expiry of the visa and had spent over two years with the aunt and uncle who now wanted to adopt the boy. There was a genuine relationship of parent and child between the applicants and the boy, he had settled at school, and had a network of friends. As the boy had not had his home with

---

[299] ACA 2002, s 47(9).     [300] Ibid, s 47(8).     [301] Ibid, s 47(8A).

[302] Ibid, s 49(4).     [303] Ibid, s 46(5).

[304] Ibid, s 42(2), emphasis added. The requirement under s 42(2)(a) can be fulfilled in a placement abroad: see *Re A (Adoption: Removal)* [2009] EWCA Civ 41, [2010] Fam 9; *ECC (The Local Authority) v SM* [2010] EWHC 1694 (Fam), [2011] 1 FLR 234 at [13] *per* Hedley J.

[305] ACA 2002, s 42(3), emphasis added.     [306] Ibid, s 42(4), emphasis added.

[307] Ibid, s 42(5), emphasis added.

[308] [2009] EWHC 2491 (Fam) (Bennett J); and see on almost identical facts, *Re MW (Leave to Apply for Adoption)* [2014] EWHC 385 (Fam).

the couple for not less than three years during the five years preceding the application, leave to apply was required, pursuant to section 42(6).

In *Re A; Coventry County Council v CC and A*[309] the Court of Appeal had applied to section 42(6) the approach to a leave application as set out in *M v Warwickshire County Council*[310] in respect of an application under section 24(2), that is, the child's welfare and whether the application had a real prospect of success were both relevant considerations. Applying that approach,[311] Bennett J granted leave, finding that the immigration matters were not sufficient to persuade him to refuse leave.[312] However, Bennett J accepted that Lord Hoffmann's statement in *Re B (Adoption Order: Nationality)*[313] (a case on the Adoption Act 1976), that the court will not make an adoption order when adopters merely wish to assist the child to acquire a right of abode, applied also to applications under the 2002 Act.[314] Bennett J cautioned that it remained the court's obligation to be on its guard against misuse of adoption proceedings in that way.[315] His Lordship commented that:

> such action is most unlikely to (indeed I would go so far as to say, cannot) be in the child's best interests. For the proposed adopters would have proved to have been irresponsible, indeed thoroughly devious if not dishonest and thus not acting in the child's best interests in a fundamental respect. Thus such behaviour ought to preclude the child being committed, indeed committed irrevocably, by adoption to the care of such applicants.[316]

### 7.3.2 Sufficient opportunities to see the child in the home environment

Under section 42(7), an adoption order may not be made unless the court is satisfied that sufficient opportunities to see the child with the applicant or, in the case of an application by a couple, both of them together in the home environment have been given to the adoption agency concerned or, in any other case, to the local authority within whose area the home is. In *Re A (Adoption: Removal)*[317] the Court of Appeal held that the word 'home' is not geographically defined[318] and that in the case of a foreign adoption the more comfortable meaning for home environment is the adopters' home abroad.[319]

### 7.3.3 Adoption agency must submit report

Where an application for an adoption order relates to a child placed for adoption by an adoption agency, the agency must submit to the court a report on the suitability of the applicants and on any other matters relevant to the operation of section 1, and assist the court in any manner the court directs.[320]

### 7.3.4 Child not placed by adoption agency: notice of intention to adopt and report

Where proposed adopters wish to adopt a child who is not placed for adoption with them by an adoption agency, an adoption order may not be made unless the proposed adopters have given notice to the appropriate local authority of their intention to apply for the adoption order.[321] The notice must be given not more than two years, or less than three months, before the date on which the application for the adoption order is made.[322] Where leave to make an application to adopt would be required, notice may not be given until leave has been obtained.[323] On receipt of the notice of intention to adopt, the local authority 'must arrange for the investigation of the matter and submit to the court a report of the investigation', which in particular must 'so far as practicable, include the suitability of the proposed adopters and any other matters relevant to the operation of section 1 in relation to the application'.[324]

---

[309] [2007] EWCA Civ 1383, [2008] 1 FLR 959.  [310] [2007] EWCA Civ 1084, [2008] 1 FLR 1093.
[311] Ibid, [45] and [46].  [312] Ibid, [43] and [46].  [313] [1999] 2 AC 136 at 141.
[314] [2007] EWCA Civ 1084, [2008] 1 FLR 1093at [38].  [315] Ibid, [35].  [316] Ibid, [38].
[317] [2009] EWCA Civ 41, [2010] Fam 9.  [318] Ibid, [60].  [319] Ibid, [65].  [320] ACA 2002, s 43.
[321] Ibid, s 44(1) and (2).  [322] Ibid, s 44(3).  [323] Ibid, s 44(4).  [324] Ibid, s 44(5) and (6).

## 7.4  **Conditions for making an adoption order**

Where a child has a parent or guardian, an adoption order may not be made unless one of certain conditions set out in section 47 is fulfilled. The first condition, set out in section 47(2), is that, in the case of each parent or guardian of the child, the court is satisfied:

(a)  that the parent or guardian consents to the making of the adoption order;

(b)  that the parent or guardian has consented under section 20 (and has not withdrawn the consent) and does not oppose the making of the adoption order; or

(c)  that the parent's or guardian's consent should be dispensed with.[325]

The second condition, set out in section 47(4), is that:

(a)  the child has been placed for adoption by an adoption agency with the prospective adopters in whose favour the order is proposed to be made;

(b)  either—

  (i)  the child was placed for adoption with the consent of each parent or guardian and the consent of the mother was given when the child was at least six weeks old, or

  (ii)  the child was placed for adoption under a placement order; and

(c)  no parent or guardian opposes the making of the adoption order.

## 7.5  **Court's leave required to oppose making of adoption order**

Section 47(3) and (5) provide with regard to the first and second conditions respectively that a parent or guardian may not oppose the making of an adoption order without the court's leave. Section 47(7) provides that the court 'cannot give leave under subsection (3) or (5) unless satisfied that there has been a change in circumstances since the consent of the parent or guardian was given or, as the case may be, the placement order was made'.

It has been said that this process is 'not a re-run of the original placement application but an adjunct of the adoption process'.[326] In *Re W (Adoption Order: Set Aside and Leave to Oppose)*[327] the Court of Appeal said that it cannot be too strongly emphasised that an application for permission to oppose an adoption application 'is an absolute last ditch opportunity and it will only be in exceptionally rare circumstances that permission will be granted after the making of the care order, the making of the placement order, the placement of the child, and the issue of the adoption order application'.[328]

However, in *Re B-S (Children)*[329] the Court of Appeal commented that 'use of the phrase "exceptionally rare circumstances" carries with it far too great a potential for misunderstanding, misapplication and indeed injustice for safety'[330] and 'runs the risk—a very real and wholly unacceptable risk—of rendering section 47(5) nugatory and its protections illusory'. The court observed that if section 47(5) is to provide a real remedy the facts that the court has made both a care order and a placement order and that the child is now living with the prospective adopter, even in combination, cannot of themselves justify the refusal of leave. Rather, as the court explained:[331]

the judge must consider very carefully indeed whether the child's welfare really does necessitate the refusal of leave. The judge must keep at the forefront of his mind the teaching of *Re B*, in particular that adoption is the 'last resort' and only permissible if 'nothing else will do' and that, as

---

[325]  Ibid, s 47(2).    [326]  *Re D (Adoption: Leave to Oppose)* [2015] EWCA Civ 703, [32].

[327]  [2010] EWCA Civ 1535, [2011] 1 FLR 2153.

[328]  Ibid, [17]. Also *Re C (A Child)* [2013] EWCA Civ 431 at [29]–[30].

[329]  [2013] EWCA Civ 1146.    [330]  [2013] EWCA Civ 1146 at [70].    [331]  Ibid, [74].

> Lord Neuberger emphasised, the child's interests include being brought up by the parents or wider family unless the overriding requirements of the child's welfare make that not possible. That said, the child's welfare is paramount.

The court must assess the pros and cons of each option, but:

> As a general proposition, the greater the change in circumstances (assuming, of course, that the change is positive) and the more solid the parent's grounds for seeking leave to oppose, the more cogent and compelling the arguments based on the child's welfare must be if leave to oppose is to be refused.

The court added that:

> [t]he mere fact that the child has been placed with prospective adopters cannot be determinative, nor can the mere passage of time. On the other hand, the older the child and the longer the child has been placed the greater the adverse impacts of disturbing the arrangements are likely to be.

The judge must always bear in mind that what is paramount in every adoption case is the welfare of the child 'throughout his life'. The adverse impact on the prospective adopters must not be trivialised in its impact upon a child but also judges must be careful not to give it too much weight.

The applicant who wishes successfully to oppose an adoption application has three fences to jump:

> The first is to establish the necessary change of circumstances. The second is then to satisfy the court that, in the exercise of discretion, it would be right to grant permission. The third and final stage would of course be to persuade the court at the opposed hearing to refuse the adoption order and to reverse the direction in which the child's life has travelled since the inception of the original public law care proceedings.[332]

### 7.5.1 Change of circumstances

In *Re M (Adoption: Leave to Oppose)*[333] a child had been made the subject of a care order after a finding that she had sustained ten fractures non-accidentally. The parents subsequently obtained a report from an expert in the USA, which suggested that the child suffered from a metabolic bone disorder which made her susceptible to fractures. In subsequent adoption proceedings the parents of the child sought leave to oppose the making of an adoption order on the basis of new evidence contained in the report. Her Honour Judge Newton, sitting as a judge of the High Court, held that this new evidence, even taken at its highest, was not capable of being a change of circumstances within the meaning of section 47(7).[334] Even if the fresh evidence were accepted it could not amount to a change of circumstances since the findings in the care proceedings had not been overturned. The fresh evidence was a matter for the Court of Appeal on an appeal against the care order, not a matter for the adoption court.[335]

### 7.5.2 Exercising discretion on the application for leave

In *Re P (A Child) (Adoption: Leave Provisions)*[336] Ward LJ explained that:

> the question of leave falls to be decided by the application of s 1 of the 2002 Act to the facts of the case. The paramount consideration of the court must be the child's welfare throughout his or her life.[337]

---

[332] *Re W (Adoption Order: Set Aside and Leave to Oppose)* [2010] EWCA Civ 1535, [2011] 1 FLR 2153 at [18] *per* Thorpe LJ.
[333] [2010] 1 FLR 238 (HHJ Newton sitting as judge of the High Court).
[334] Ibid, [25].     [335] Ibid, [32].     [336] [2007] EWCA Civ 616, [2007] 2 FLR 1069.     [337] Ibid, [55].

Section 47 is thus a rare case where the paramountcy of the child's welfare applies to a leave application. In *Re W (Adoption Order: Set Aside and Leave to Oppose)*[338] the Court of Appeal gave guidance on exercising its broad discretion whether or not to grant permission under section 47(5).[339] Thorpe LJ, while acknowledging that each case must depend upon its particular facts, said that the 'judge must have great regard to impact of the grant of permission on the child within the context of the adoptive family'.[340] His Lordship suggested that if the facts are such that opposition to the adoption order would have a profoundly upsetting effect on the adopters and the child, such a consequence should not be contemplated unless the applicant 'demonstrates prospects of success that are not just fanciful and not just measureable'; in Thorpe LJ's opinion, with which other members of the court agreed, the prospects of success 'should have substance' or 'solidity'.[341] In *Re W*, a boy, aged five years ten months at the date of the appeal, had been removed from his mother's care when he was two years old because of her drug addiction and consequent inability to care for him. He was subsequently placed for adoption under a placement order when he was four. An adoption order was subsequently made without the mother being informed of the proceedings. The mother, who had liberated herself from her drug dependency, sought to set aside the adoption order and for permission to oppose the adoption application. Holman J set aside the order and allowed the mother permission to oppose. The Court of Appeal, applying the approach set out, allowed the adopters' appeal, finding that the judge had under-weighed the very powerful current imperatives in favour of adoption and overvalued the much more speculative aspects of the future.[342] The mother's recovery had simply come too late.

Each case will depend upon its facts, but an example of a case in which a father's application was successful is *Re LG (Adoption: Leave to Oppose)*.[343] The father had been ashamed to tell his family of his baby, of whose existence the paternal family had no knowledge during the currency of the care proceedings. However, the father was granted leave to oppose an adoption application under section 47(5) in respect of the child, and was granted permission to instruct an independent social worker to establish the suitability of members of his paternal family to care for the child. The assessments were positive, concluding with a recommendation that the paternal grandfather be granted a special guardianship order, a course which was supported by the local authority and guardian. Similarly, in *A and B v Rotherham Metropolitan Borough Council and Others*,[344] Holman J dismissed an adoption application and revoked a placement order in respect of a child who was placed with 'perfect adopters'. The child was of mixed race, and a paternal aunt, who was black, became a possible carer, and was assessed as entirely suitable. Holman J concluded that the 'unquantifiable but potentially considerable advantage of a move to the aunt' was 'the bridge to the paternal original family'.[345]

## 7.6 **Effect of an adoption order**

An adoption order is an order made by the court on an application under section 50 or 51.[346] The order gives parental responsibility for the child to the adopters or adopter.[347] It also operates to extinguish 'the parental responsibility which any person other than the adopters or adopter has for the adopted child immediately before the making of the order',[348] although it 'does not affect parental responsibility so far as it relates to any period before the making of the order'.[349] The adoption order also extinguishes 'any duty arising by virtue of an agreement[350] or an order of a court

---

[338] [2010] EWCA Civ 1535, [2011] 1 FLR 2153.   [339] Ibid, [20].   [340] Ibid.   [341] Ibid.
[342] Ibid, [25].   [343] [2015] EWFC 52.   [344] [2014] EWFC 47.
[345] Ibid, at [95].   [346] ACA 2002, s 46(1).   [347] Ibid.   [348] Ibid, s 46(2).   [349] Ibid, s 46(3)(a).
[350] Subject to, ibid, subs (4) which provides that subs (2)(d) does not apply to a duty arising by virtue of an agreement:

   (a)  which constitutes a trust, or
   (b)  which expressly provides that the duty is not to be extinguished by the making of an adoption order.

to make payments, so far as the payments are in respect of the adopted child's maintenance or upbringing for any period after the making of the adoption order'.[351]

### 7.6.1  Status conferred by adoption

As from the date of the adoption[352] an adopted person is to be treated in law as if born as the child of the adopters or adopter,[353] is the legitimate child of the adopters or adopter and, if adopted by a couple or one of a couple under section 51(2), is to be treated as the child of the relationship of the couple in question.[354] The adopted person is to be treated in law as not being the child of any person other than the adopters or adopter.[355]

The rules are adapted differently to the case of an order made on an application under section 51(2) by the partner of a parent of the adopted child. In such a case the order does not affect the parental responsibility of that parent or any duties with respect to child maintenance.[356] The adopted child is treated in law as not being the child of any person other than the adopter and the other one of the couple.[357]

The status conferred by adoption 'applies for the interpretation of enactments or instruments passed or made before as well as after the adoption, and so applies subject to any contrary indication . . . and has effect as respects things done, or events occurring, on or after the adoption'.[358] However, the status conferred by adoption does not apply for the purpose of the prohibited degrees of relationship for marriage or civil partnership,[359] nor for the purpose of sexual offences in sections 64 and 65 of the Sexual Offences Act 2003 (sex with an adult relative).[360] It also does not apply for the purpose of the British Nationality Act 1981, the Immigration Act 1971, or any other provision of law which determines British citizenship or the status of a British National (Overseas).[361]

The Act indicates that the relationship established by the adoption order may be described as an adoptive relationship and the adopter(s) as the child's adoptive mother/father/parent as the case may be.[362]

### 7.7  Setting aside an adoption order

As the outlined provisions show, adoption is the process whereby a child becomes a permanent and full member of a new family, and is treated as if born to the adopters.[363] Adoption orders are perceived 'as final, and as putting the adoptive parents fully in control'.[364] Thus, the imposition of conditions on adoption orders will be very rare.[365] In *Re S (A Minor) (Adoption: Blood Transfusion)*,[366] for example, the prospective adopters were Jehovah's Witnesses and they indicated that they could not consent to the child having a blood transfusion should one become necessary. The Court of Appeal held that it had been wrong for the judge to impose a condition of the adoption that the adoptive parents give an undertaking obliging them to involve the High Court if the contingency arose. The courts recognise the impact that not respecting the peculiar finality of adoption orders might have on the integrity of the adoption system and on prospective adopters coming forward to adopt. It will be very rare that an adoption order will be set aside.

---

[351] Ibid, s 46(2)(d).    [352] Ibid, s 67(5).    [353] Ibid, s 67(1).    [354] Ibid, s 67(2).

[355] Ibid, s 67(3). This is subject to subs (4) which provides:

> In the case of a person adopted by one of the person's natural parents as sole adoptive parent, subsection (3)(b) has no effect as respects entitlement to property depending on relationship to that parent, or as respects anything else depending on that relationship.

[356] Ie, the duties as mentioned in s 46(2)(d).    [357] ACA 2002, s 67(3).    [358] Ibid, s 67(6).

[359] Ibid, s 74(1)(a).    [360] Ibid, s 74(1)(b).    [361] Ibid, s 74(2).    [362] See ibid, s 68.

[363] Ibid, s 67, and see *per* Wall LJ in *Webster v Norfolk County Council and the Children (By their Children's Guardian)* [2009] EWCA Civ 59, [2009] 1 FLR 1378 at [145].

[364] Ibid, [146].    [365] *Re S (A Minor) (Adoption: Blood Transfusion)* [1995] 2 FCR 177, CA.    [366] Ibid.

The courts have set aside adoption orders in some cases where there has been a procedural ir-regularity involving a denial of natural justice,[367] such as when a parent has not been informed of an application for an adoption order. In *Re B (Adoption: Jurisdiction to Set Aside)*[368] Sir Thomas Bingham MR added that he would have 'little hesitation in holding that the court could set aside an adoption order which was shown to have been obtained by fraud'.[369] Otherwise, however, the courts have been very strict in their refusal to allow adoption orders to be challenged, except by way of appeal,[370] even where there has been a very clear and fundamental error which causes (some-times extreme) hardship. A powerful example is provided by the Scottish Court of Session case of *J v J and C's Tutor*.[371] In that case a couple adopted a child whom they believed to be healthy but later found out that the child had a severe brain injury.[372] The Scottish Court of Session unanimously held that it was no ground for revocation of the adoption order. That case was cited with apparent approval by Sir Thomas Bingham MR in *Re B (Adoption: Jurisdiction to Set Aside)*,[373] who com-mented that any discrepancy in English and Scottish authority on the issue of setting aside an adoption order was undesirable. In *Re B* the appellant, a man in his mid-thirties, had been adopted when he was three months old by an orthodox Jewish couple and brought up a Jew, but he later found out that his natural father was a Muslim Arab from Kuwait. As Simon Brown LJ put it, it 'is difficult to imagine a more ill-starred adoption placement'.[374] The appellant had wished to settle in Israel but had been suspected of being an Arab spy and had been asked to leave, and he also was not accepted in Kuwait. His adoptive parents were deceased and he now sought to set aside the adop-tion order. The Court of Appeal, albeit with sympathy for the appellant, unanimously dismissed the appeal, holding that the circumstances of the case provided no basis for setting aside the order. In so holding, the Court of Appeal recognised the strong policy considerations against doing so. Simon Brown LJ commented:

> Exceptional though this case undoubtedly is and strong though [the appellant's] grievance, more important still is the integrity of the adoption system; its inviolability must be the ultimate imperative.[375]

These public policy considerations mean that an adoption order will not necessarily be set aside even where natural parents have suffered a serious injustice in losing their children to adoption.[376] In *Webster v Norfolk County Council and the Children (By Their Children's Guardian)*[377] three of Mr and Mrs Webster's children were taken into care and adopted by strangers, following findings in care proceedings that their two-year-old child had suffered non-accidental injuries resulting in six fractures. The child had a feeding problem and on the advice of their doctor the parents had been feeding the child soya milk only. The child's diet was rejected by the experts in the case as a cause of

---

[367] See this characterisation of the case law in *Re B (Adoption: Jurisdiction to Set Aside)* [1995] Fam 239 at 245H and 252F. See for examples *Re F(R) (An Infant)* [1970] 1 QB 385; *Re RA (Minors)* (1974) 4 Fam Law 182; and *Re F (Infants) (Adoption Order: Validity)* [1977] Fam 165. And see *Re K (Adoption and Wardship)* [1997] 2 FLR 221 (child adopted from Bosnia despite having a guardian in Bosnia and members of the child's family were incarcerated in concentration camps in the fomer Yugoslavia).

[368] [1995] Fam 239.    [369] Ibid, 252G.

[370] For a recent example, see also *Re T (Adoption Order)* [2012] EWCA Civ 191, [2013] 1 FLR 360, in which the case was remitted for rehearing because of procedural irregularities, including the fact that the mother who was unrepre-sented did not have access to the Guardian's report.

[371] 1948 SC 636.

[372] For a recent case in which Baker J refused a local authority's application in care proceedings under s 38(6) of the Children Act 1989 for genetic testing of children prior to adoption in order to ascertain whether they had inherited Huntington's disease, see *Re Y and Z (Care Proceedings: Genetic Testing)* [2013] EWHC 953 (Fam), [2013] 2 FLR 249.

[373] [1995] Fam 239.    [374] Ibid, 249E.    [375] Ibid, 251E.

[376] *Webster v Norfolk County Council and the Children (By Their Children's Guardian)* [2009] EWCA Civ 59, [2009] 1 FLR 1378 at [148].

[377] [2009] EWCA Civ 59, [2009] 1 FLR 1378.

the fractures. Care proceedings were subsequently brought in respect of a fourth child born to the couple. Those proceedings were withdrawn, however, when fresh expert evidence showed that the older child's fractures had not been caused through abuse, but by a rare case of scurvy as a result of the diet. Nearly three years after the older children had been adopted, Mr and Mrs Webster sought leave to appeal out of time, to adduce the fresh evidence, and ultimately to have the adoptions set aside. The Court of Appeal unanimously dismissed the application, holding that it was far too late to seek to disturb the orders, having regard to the social importance of not undermining the irrevocability of adoption orders, and to the interests of the children, who by then had been settled with the adoptive parents for four years.[378]

A case which was viewed by the Court of Appeal as wholly exceptional, and in which leave to appeal out of time was granted and an appeal against an adoption order was successful, is *Re M (Minors) (Adoption)*.[379] In that case, a father who was leaving the country to live in the USA agreed to his two daughters' adoption by their mother and stepfather, with whom the girls were then living. However, the mother had terminal cancer and died three months later. The father's consent to adoption was given in ignorance of the mother's illness. He had since remarried and the children wished to live with him and his new wife, and the stepfather also agreed that that was the best course for the children. The Court of Appeal set aside the adoption order, holding that ignorance of the mother's illness vitiated his consent. The court made clear that it was in no way setting a precedent for any related set of facts in some other case. Moreover, in *Re B (Adoption: Jurisdiction to Set Aside)*[380] the Court of Appeal held that there were some important points of distinction between *Re M* and the case before it: the mistake in *Re B* as to religion or ethnicity could not vitiate consent; *Re M* was a case of permission to appeal out of time following a very short period of time rather than an application to set aside; it was a case involving minor children (rather than an adult) and the outcome was demanded by their best interests; and no injustice would result to any party as all were agreed as to the correctness of the eventual outcome.[381]

Similarly, in *PK v Mr and Mrs K*,[382] Pauffley J held that the case before her was within the highly exceptional range of cases such that she should exercise discretion to revoke an adoption order.[383] PK was adopted by Mr and Mrs K when she was about four years old. Two years later, she was sent to live with members of Mr and Mrs K's extended family in Ghana, where, PK claimed, she was subjected to significant abuse by members of the family. PK returned to England as a teenager, and in wardship proceedings her biological mother, with whom she was reunited, was granted care and control. The adoptive parents raised no objections to the mother's care of PK, and appeared to have relinquished responsibility for her, and played no part in the application to revoke the adoption order. Pauffley held that 'against the background described, there would be emotionally harmful consequences for PK if she were to remain the adopted child of Mr and Mrs K.'[384]

Another decision in which permission to appeal was not granted is *Re PW (Adoption)*.[385] In that case, a 69-year-old woman, who was orphaned aged 17 and adopted by the parents of her closest friend, applied for permission to appeal out of time 51 years after the order had been made. She claimed that she had been pressurised by the adoptive parents (now deceased) and that she had not felt able to gainsay their wishes. Parker J dismissed the application, finding that there was no procedural irregularity. Her Ladyship observed that adoption is supposed to create an irrevocable change of status, with significant legal consequences such as rights of intestacy, and therefore 'the longer it lasts, the harder it is to challenge'.[386]

---

[378] See also *Re W (Inherent Jurisdiction: Permission Application: Revocation of Adoption Order)* [2013] 2 FLR 1609, Bodey J (local authority's application to revoke adoption order in respect of a 12-year-old girl, adopted age four, whose placement had broken down and whose adoptive parents no longer wanted contact; judge refused application, being concerned that to do so would revive the natural parents' parental responsibility, and instead made the girl subject of a care order).

[379] [1991] 1 FLR 458.    [380] [1995] Fam 239.    [381] Ibid, 247.

[382] [2015] EWHC 2316 (Fam), Pauffley J.    [383] Ibid, [14].

[384] Ibid, [26], adding at [27]: 'The only advantage of a refusal of the application to revoke the adoption order would be the public policy considerations in upholding a validly made adoption order.'

[385] [2013] 1 FLR 96 (Parker J).    [386] Ibid, [36].

## 7.8 **Openness in adoption and on-going contact**

Over time, probably reflecting the changing landscape of those adopted, there has been a movement towards greater openness in adoptions.[387] As Lindley points out the term 'open adoption' 'encompasses a very broad range of circumstances and arrangements'.[388] It ranges from the idea of adoptive parents being open with their children by telling them about their adoption,[389] through so-called letterbox contact with the child's natural family by way of letters, cards, presents, photographs etc, to face-to-face contact with the child's natural parents and/or other relatives. One aspect of increasing openness surrounding adoption is the facility which adopted persons now have in adulthood to obtain information about their birth families.

### 7.8.1 **Access to information**

The 2002 Act makes provision for an adoption contact register to allow adoptees and relatives the opportunity to indicate that they would like contact.[390] The Act also makes provision for the disclosure of information to adopted persons. The disclosure is in most cases in the hands of the adoption agency concerned. The Act and regulations prescribe the information that must be kept relating to a person's adoption.[391] The information must be kept secure and for at least 100 years.[392] Certain information is regarded as 'protected information' as defined in section 57 of the Act. This is information which identifies or enables a person to be identified, information which would enable the adopted person to obtain a certified copy of the record of his birth, or information about an entry relating to the adopted person in the Adoption Contact Register.[393] Section 57 provides that such information may only be disclosed to a person by the agency in pursuance of the group of sections 56–65 of the Act. It is an offence to disclose such information in contravention of this provision.[394] An adopted person who has attained the age of 18 years has the right, at his request, to receive from the appropriate adoption agency any information which would enable him to obtain a certified copy of the record of his birth, unless the High Court orders otherwise.[395] The High Court may make such an order, on an application by the appropriate adoption agency, if satisfied that the circumstances are exceptional. An example of an exceptional case is provided by the case of *R v Registrar General, ex p Smith*.[396] In that case, the appellant was a patient in a secure mental hospital following conviction for murder of a stranger and manslaughter of his prison cellmate while under the psychotic belief that the cellmate was his adoptive mother. The court held that the Registrar-General had not acted unlawfully in denying the appellant access to a copy of his birth certificate for the reason that his natural mother might thereby be endangered.

The adult adopted person is also entitled to receive any prescribed information which the agency was required to disclose to the adopters.[397] Section 61 of the Act provides that if a person applies for

---

[387]   See J. Eekelaar, 'Contact and the Adoption Reform' in A. Bainham, B. Lindley, M. Richards, and L. Trinder (eds), *Children and Their Families: Contact, Rights and Welfare* (Oxford: Hart); C. Bridge, 'Adoption and Contact: The Value of Openness' [1994] Journal of Child Law 147; D. Casey and A. Gibberd, 'Adoption and Contact' [2000] Family Law 39; and C. Smith and J. Logan, 'Adoptive Parenthood as a "Legal Fiction"—Its Consequences for Direct Post-Adoption Contact' [2002] Child and Family Law Quarterly 281.

[388]   B. Lindley, 'Open Adoption—Is the Door Ajar?' [1997] Child and Family Law Quarterly 115.

[389]   Referred to by some as communicative openness as opposed to structural openness: see eg E. Neil, 'Post-Adoption Contact and Openness in Adoptive Parents' Minds: Consequences for Children's Development' (2009) 39 British Journal of Social Work 303.

[390]   ACA 2002, s 80, and see J. Haskey and E. Errington, 'Adoptees and Relatives Who Wish to Contact One Another: The Adoption Contact Register' (2001) 104 Population Trends 18.

[391]   ACA 2002, s 56, and Disclosure of Adoption Information (Post-Commencement Adoptions) Regulations 2005 (SI 2005/888), see reg 4.

[392]   Disclosure of Adoption Information (Post-Commencement Adoptions) Regulations 2005, regs 5 and 6.

[393]   Adoption agencies are permitted to disclose other information: ACA 2002, s 58.

[394]   ACA 2002, s 59, and Disclosure of Adoption Information (Post-Commencement Adoptions) Regulations 2005, reg 21.

[395]   ACA 2002, s 60.      [396]   [1991] 1 FLR 255, CA.      [397]   ACA 2002, s 60.

disclosure of protected information and none of the information is about a person who is a child at the time of the application, then the agency is not required to proceed with the application unless it considers it appropriate to do so. If it does proceed, it must take all reasonable steps to obtain the views of any person the information is about as to the disclosure of the information about him. The agency may then disclose the information if it considers it appropriate to do so. In deciding those matters the agency must consider the welfare of the adopted person, any views obtained, and all the circumstances of the case. Where any of the information sought is about a person who is a child at the time of the application, then section 62 applies. The same approach as described for section 61 is taken, except that the agency must take all reasonable steps to obtain the views of any parent or guardian of the child, and the views of the child, if the agency considers it appropriate to do so having regard to his age and understanding and to all the other circumstances of the case. If the information relates to an adopted child, the child's welfare must be the paramount consideration, or in the case of any other child, the agency must have particular regard to the child's welfare.

An adoption agency must provide written information about the availability of counselling to any person who is seeking information under section 60, 61, or 62 of the Act,[398] and there is a duty to secure counselling for those who wish it.

In *Re X (Adopted Child: Access to Court File)*[399] a daughter sought[400] access to the court file relating to her father's adoption 84 years earlier, in order to gain information about her paternal grandmother. Granting the application, Munby P said that the court had discretion, to be exercised justly in the circumstances, albeit with an eye on maintaining confidence in the confidentiality of adoption files.

### 7.8.2 Post-adoption contact

The most extensive aspect of openness is, of course, post-adoption direct contact with the child's natural family.[401] The value of such contact is a matter which has been hotly debated amongst commentators, as have the inferences which can validly be drawn from research evidence.[402] Several arguments can be put in favour of open adoption.[403] Ryburn[404] has suggested that while each case must be looked at individually, the starting point should be recognition that post-adoption contact may have benefits for all concerned. Ryburn argues that contact may help birth parents to resolve the grief of their loss of the child; it can serve the information needs of the child and in some cases this may mean that facts can helpfully replace the child's possibly negative speculation or fantasy about the birth parent(s) (eg about the nature of a parent's mental illness). Contact may also provide adopters with a source of up-to-date information with which to deal with the child's questions, together with a sense of security and permanence in the parenting role. Smith and Logan,[405] in a review of research, have observed that there is certainly evidence from several studies that 'children, adoptive

---

[398] Ibid, s 63 and Disclosure of Adoption Information (Post-Commencement Adoptions) Regulations 2005, reg 16.

[399] [2014] EWFC 33, Sir James Munby P.　　[400] Under ACA 2002, s 79(4).

[401] See J. Masson, 'Thinking about Contact—A Social or a Legal Problem?' [2000] Child and Family Law Quarterly 15. Masson argues that it is preferable to think of contact in terms of social rather than legal problems, noting that even though the courts have been wary of post-adoption contact in the face of adopters' opposition, a social work practice surrounding openness and adoption has emerged.

[402] See the debate surrounding the evidence in the following: D. Quinton, A. Rushton, C. Dance, and D. Mayes, 'Contact Between Children Placed Away from Home and Their Birth Parents: Research Issues and Evidence' (1997) 2(3) Clinical Child Psychology and Psychiatry 393; M. Ryburn, 'In Whose Best Interests?—Post-Adoption Contact with the Birth Family' [1998] Child and Family Law Quarterly 53; D. Quinton, J. Selwyn, A. Rushton, and C. Dance, 'Contact with Birth Parents in Adoption—A Response to Ryburn' [1998] Child and Family Law Quarterly 349.

[403] For arguments on the benefits of openness, see eg A. Mullender (ed), *Open Adoption: The Philosophy and Practice* (London: BAAF, 1991); M. Adcock, J. Kaniuk, and R. White (eds), *Exploring Openness in Adoption* (Significant Publications, 1993); J. Fratter, *Adoption with Contact* (London: BAAF, 1996), Ch 1; J. Triseliotis, J. Shireman, and M. Hundleby, *Adoption; Theory, Policy and Practice* (London: Cassell, 1997), Ch 4.

[404] M. Ryburn, 'In Whose Best Interests?—Post-Adoption Contact with the Birth Family' [1998] Child and Family Law Quarterly 53.

[405] C. Smith and J. Logan, 'Adoptive Parenthood as a "Legal Fiction"—Its Consequences for Direct Post-Adoption Contact' [2002] Child and Family Law Quarterly 281.

parents and birth family members value contact and can *experience* it as beneficial',[406] and conclude from their survey:

> First, there appears to be increasing professional support for post-adoption contact and many adoptive parents are willing to facilitate this. Secondly, it is possible to maintain helpful contact with birth parents, notwithstanding their opposition to adoption. Thirdly, many adopters experience contact as beneficial for their children and for themselves and express satisfaction with contact arrangements. Fourthly, adopted children may value contact and want it to continue. Fifthly, contact does not seem to interfere with adoptive parents' sense of security or their perceived status as parents.[407]

Smith and Logan's own research, interviewing adoptive parents in 61 families, also shows, however, that for some adoptive parents the practical and emotional burdens of contact are not insignificant (eg having to take days off work to facilitate it and having to encounter parents with very different social backgrounds and parenting expectations to their own).[408]

While there is some evidence about how contact is *experienced*, there is little evidence of the impact (if any) that post-adoption contact has on long-term *outcomes* for children. Grotevant and Roy studied 171 children[409] aged between four and twelve who were adopted as babies and compared child outcomes according to the openness of the placement (including completely closed adoption, those with indirect contact, and those with fully open face-to-face contact with birth parents[410]). The research found no significant differences 'for self-esteem, curiosity, satisfaction and socio-emotional adjustment by openness level'.[411] The authors commented that these results 'are not compatible with assertions raised by critics of openness stating that such arrangements will damage children's self-esteem and cause confusion. But neither do these findings support the hypothesis that more openness enhances these outcomes.'[412] This research is useful. However, one should be cautious about generalising its findings in relation to 'baby adoptions' to other adoptions, such as the many adoptions which now take place through the system of state care when children are older. As Quinton and Selwyn observe:

> We know little about the consequences of contact for adult adjustment, especially for children with the experiences and profiles of those currently being placed. Moreover, the extent of difficulties many of the children face may militate against finding substantial differences in outcome related to contact, since many improvements in emotional and behavioural adjustment may be hard won, whatever the circumstances.[413]

---

[406] Citing H. D. Grotevant and R. G. McRoy, *Openness in Adoption: Exploring Family Connections* (Thousand Oaks, CA: Sage, 1998) (adoptive parents less fearful); J. Logan and C. Smith, 'Adoption and Direct Post-Adoption Contact' (1999) 23(4) Adoption and Fostering 58 (adoptive parents in 61 families interviewed; advantages identified for 92 per cent of the children concerned); R. P. Barth and M. Berry, *Adoption and Disruption: Rates, Risks and Responses* (New York: Aldine DeGruyter, 1988), p 120 (79 per cent contact, 31 per cent found helpful); M. Ryburn, 'A Study of Post-Adoption Contact in Compulsory Adoptions' (1996) 26(5) British Journal of Social Work 627 (adopters indicated advantages); J. Fratter, *Adoption with Contact: Implications for Policy and Practice* (London: BAAF, 1996) (perceived as contributing to child's welfare).

[407] 'Adoptive Parenthood as a "Legal Fiction"—Its Consequences for Direct Post-Adoption Contact' [2002] Child and Family Law Quarterly 281 at 285.

[408] J. Logan and C. Smith, 'Adoption and Direct Post-Adoption Contact' (1999) 23(4) Adoption and Fostering 58.

[409] Sourced from 190 adoptive families from 35 agencies across the USA.

[410] Note that a study by Neil compared letterbox contact with direct contact but did not find any significant differences in terms of child outcome: see E. Neil, 'Post-Adoption Contact and Openness in Adoptive Parents' Minds: Consequences for Children's Development' (2009) 39 British Journal of Social Work 303.

[411] H. D. Grotevant and R. G. McRoy, *Openness in Adoption: Exploring Family Connections* (Thousand Oaks, CA: Sage, 1998), p 103.

[412] Ibid.

[413] D. Quinton and J. Selwyn, 'Adoption: Research, Policy and Practice' [2006] Child and Family Law Quarterly 459.

The debates surrounding post-adoption contact have not gone unnoticed by the judiciary. Lord Carswell commented in *Down Lisburn Health and Social Services Trust v H*:[414]

> There have been some differences of opinion in the published literature about the desirability of contact, which is propounded by some as universally beneficial, while others are more cautious and urge a degree of flexibility of approach and avoidance of doctrinaire policies. They point out that in the wrong case contact can lead to disturbance of the children and impose a significant burden on the adopting parents. There is, however, general agreement that in appropriate cases contact can contribute to reassurance and security and a feeling of identity for adopted children and help to dispel feelings of rejection . . .[415]

His Lordship therefore went on to caution that when 'considering post-adoption contact courts must exercise care in assessing the effect which contact is likely to have on the particular child in the particular circumstances of the case, bearing in mind the paramountcy of the welfare of the child'.[416] As a matter of the courts' general approach, however, post-adoption contact between children and their birth parents has historically been perceived as highly exceptional, and the effect the 2002 Act has had on this approach is rather unclear. In the pre-Children Act 1989 case, *Re C (A Minor) (Adoption Order: Conditions)*,[417] Lord Ackner commented that:

> [t]he cases rightly stress that in normal circumstances it is desirable that there should be a complete break, but that each case has to be considered on its own particular facts. No doubt the court will not, except in the most exceptional case, impose terms or conditions as to access to members of the child's natural family to which the adopting parents do not agree. To do so would be to create a potentially frictional situation which would be hardly likely to safeguard or promote the welfare of the child. Where no agreement is forthcoming the court will, with very rare exceptions, have to choose between making an adoption order without terms or conditions as to access, or to refuse to make such an order and seek to safeguard access through some other machinery, such as wardship. To do otherwise would be merely inviting future and almost immediate litigation.[418]

Indeed, in early case law the Court of Appeal went so far as to suggest that on-going contact between a child and his or her birth parent(s) was repugnant to the purpose of adoption to effect a transplant of legal parenthood and parental responsibility; in other words, if contact were appropriate, it could be doubted whether the severance of the legal ties which adoption effects is the necessary intervention.[419] After implementation of the Children Act 1989, even against a background of post-adoption contact becoming more common in practice, and of increasing judicial recognition of the value of post-adoption contact,[420] court-imposed post-adoption contact was still perceived to be highly unusual.[421] As the Court of Appeal put it in *Re R (A Child) (Adoption: Contact)*,[422] 'the imposition on prospective adopters of orders for contact with which they are not in agreement is extremely, and remains extremely unusual'.

However, section 46(6) of the 2002 Act now provides that before making an adoption order, 'the court must consider whether there should be arrangements for allowing any person contact with

---

[414] [2006] UKHL 36, [2007] 1 FLR 121, [2007] 1 FLR 121, a case on appeal from Northern Ireland.

[415] Ibid, [44]. See Department of Health, *Adoption Now: Messages from Research* (Chichester: Wiley, 1999) for an overview of research findings in this context.

[416] [2006] UKHL 36, [2007] 1 FLR 121, [2007] 1 FLR 121 at [44].     [417] [1989] 1 AC 1.

[418] [1989] 1 AC 1 at 18.

[419] See *per* Oliver LJ in *Re V (A Minor) (Adoption: Dispensing with Agreement)* [1987] 2 FLR 89 at 98.

[420] *Re G (Children: Contact)* [2002] EWCA Civ 761, [2002] 3 FCR 377 and in the dissenting speech of Baroness Hale of Richmond in the Northern Ireland case of *Down Lisburn Health and Social Services Trust v H* [2006] UKHL 36, [2007] 1 FLR 121.

[421] See eg *Re T (A Minor) (Contact after Adoption)* [1995] 2 FCR 537.

[422] [2005] EWCA Civ 1128, [2007] 1 FCR 149 at [49].

the child; and for that purpose the court must consider any existing or proposed arrangements and obtain any views of the parties to the proceedings'. Furthermore, section 51A, inserted by section 9 of the Children and Families Act 2014, allows a court to make an order for contact between the child and a named person, or prohibit the same. An application can be made by the person who applied for the adoption order, the child, or any person who has obtained the court's leave. In *Re P (Placement Orders: Parental Consent)*,[423] the Court of Appeal indicated in relation to the predecessor of section 51A, section 26(5), which is now repealed, that the 2002 Act thus 'envisages the court exercising its powers to make contact orders post adoption, where such orders are in the interests of the child concerned'.[424] In *Re P* there was universal recognition that the relationship between siblings needed to be preserved and in such circumstances it was the court's responsibility to make orders for contact.[425] Indeed, the court went as far as to say that it was highly likely that a plan to place the children with adopters who were unwilling to facilitate sibling contact would provide a basis for granting leave to apply to revoke the placement order concerned.[426] The court was unclear, however, whether its 'views on contact on the facts of this particular case presage a more general sea change in post adoption contact overall'.

In *Oxfordshire County Council v X, Y and J*[427] the Court of Appeal did not see the discussion of the implications of sections 26, 27, and 46(6) of the 2002 Act in *Re P* as affecting the approach to contact where an adoption order has already been made. The court held that in such a case the judge must apply the checklist in section 1(3) of the Children Act 1989, together with the approach set out in *Re R* (ie, that contact against the wishes of the child's adoptive parent(s) would be extremely unusual). In that case, the child's natural parents sought an order that the adoptive parents provide to them an annual photograph of the child. The adoptive parents did not object to the parents viewing a photograph annually, but objected to the parents retaining the photograph, fearing that the parents might use it to trace the child, perhaps by placing a copy on the internet. The judge at first instance, assessing the risk of disruption to the placement as very small, granted the application, but the Court of Appeal overturned it. The judge had failed to apply the correct approach as set out in *Re R*. The 'essential question was whether the adoptive parents' fear of such a risk was unreasonable in the sense that it had no reasonable basis'[428] since the court's focus had to be on the child's welfare and in the court's view there was a clear link between the fears of the adoptive parents, and their sense of security, and the welfare of their daughter. The court commented:

> It is beyond argument that the welfare of so young a child in the early stages of her adoption depended upon the stability and security of her new parents, the adoptive parents. To undermine that stability by fuelling or failing to heed their fears that their daughter's natural parents might seek to trace her is to damage her welfare.[429]

The court observed that given the effect of an adoption order 'it is very far from obvious, to say the least, that the natural parents can thereafter have any Art 8 rights at all vis-à-vis a child who is no longer their child'.[430] Since, however, the point had not been fully argued before the court, the court said no more about it, except to make clear that even if the natural parents had Article 8 rights capable of being engaged in the application (and the court did not assume, let alone decide, that they did), those rights would not have sufficed to tip the balance in their favour.[431] Kirsty Hughes and Brian Sloan are critical of this aspect of the decision, arguing that there was scope

---

[423] [2008] EWCA Civ 535, [2008] 2 FLR 625.    [424] Ibid, [154].    [425] Ibid, [151].    [426] Ibid, [150].
[427] [2010] EWCA Civ 581, [2011] 1 FLR 272. For comment, see K. Hughes and B. Sloan, 'Post-Adoption Photographs: Welfare, Rights and Judicial Reasoning' [2011] Child and Family Law Quarterly 393.
[428] [2010] EWCA Civ 581, [2011] 1 FLR 272, [28].    [429] Ibid, [29].
[430] Ibid, [43]. The position in the Strasbourg jurisprudence is rather unclear; see for discussion K. Hughes and B. Sloan, 'Post-Adoption Photographs: Welfare, Rights and Judicial Reasoning' [2011] Child and Family Law Quarterly 393.
[431] [2010] EWCA Civ 581 at [43].

for the court to have required full argument on this important issue, and also to engage more fully with all the Article 8 interests that were involved, for example the child's right to respect for private life, in the sense of the child's interest in her image and its retention by others.[432] In a more recent decision, *Re C (Indirect Contact)*,[433] the Court of Appeal, in a short judgment which does not make clear the full circumstances of the case, held that the judge had been wrong to order indirect contact to the child's natural father by way of an annual small photograph. The court found that, given the background to the case, the judge's order paid 'scant regard to the interests and rights of the child', although the court did not engage in any detail with the nature of those rights and interests.

## 8 Special guardianship

The ACA 2002 introduced another option for permanency planning for children who are unable to live with their birth parents, namely a special guardianship order (SGO).[434] Section 115 of the 2002 Act inserted sections 14A–14F of the Children Act 1989, making provision for such orders.[435] Their purpose was to provide an option for meeting the needs of some children for a permanent family placement without the complete transplant of legal parenthood involved in adoption.[436] The aim was to meet the needs of children 'where adoption is not appropriate, and to modernise the law so as to reflect the religious and cultural diversity of our country today'.[437] As the White Paper that preceded the 2002 Act commented:

> Adoption is not always appropriate for children who cannot return to their birth parents. Some older children do not wish to be legally separated from their birth families. Adoption may not be best for some children being cared for on a permanent basis by members of their wider birth family. Some minority ethnic communities have religious and cultural difficulties with adoption as it is set out in law. Unaccompanied asylum-seeking children may also need secure, permanent homes, but have strong attachments to their families abroad. All these children deserve the same chance as any other to enjoy the benefits of a legally secure, stable permanent placement that promotes a supportive, lifelong relationship with their carers, where the court decides that is in their best interests.[438]

Section 14A of the Children Act provides that a 'special guardianship order' is an order appointing one or more individuals to be a child's 'special guardian' (or special guardians).[439] A special guardian must be aged 18 or over and must not be a parent of the child.[440]

---

[432] K. Hughes and B. Sloan, 'Post-Adoption Photographs: Welfare, Rights and Judicial Reasoning' [2011] Child and Family Law Quarterly 393.

[433] [2012] EWCA Civ 128, [2013] 2 FLR 272.

[434] A similar concept, custodianship, had been introduced by the Children Act 1975, following a recommendation of the Houghton Committee's Report (Cmnd 5107, 1972), aimed at providing long-term security for care of a child without the need for adoption. For the history, see S. Cretney, *Family Law in the Twentieth Century—A History* (Oxford: Oxford University Press, 2003), Chs 17 and 20. The provisions were elaborate and little used and were not implemented until 1988, by which time the adoption provisions of the 1975 Act had been consolidated in the Adoption Act 1976: see *Re S (Adoption Order or Special Guardianship Order)* [2007] EWCA Civ 54, [2007] 1 FLR 819 at [5]–[9].

[435] Implemented on 30 December 2005. The provisions are supplemented by the Special Guardianship Regulations 2005 (SI 2005/1109), and with guidance: see Department for Children, Schools and Families, *The Children Act 1989 Guidance and Regulations Volume 1: Court Orders* (London: TSO, 2008), paras 2.59–2.66.

[436] See generally, L. Jordan and B. Lindley (eds), *Special Guardianship: What Does it Offer Children Who Cannot Live with Their Parents?* (London: Family Rights Group, 2006).

[437] White Paper, *Adoption: A New Approach* (Cm 5017, 2000), para 5.9.     [438] Ibid, para 5.8.

[439] Children Act 1989, s 14A(1).     [440] Ibid, s 14A(2).

> ### Key legislation
>
> Those who are entitled to apply for a SGO are:
>
> (a) any guardian of the child;
> (b) any individual who is named in a child arrangements order as a person with whom the child is to live;
> (c) any individual listed in subsection (5)(b) or (c) of section 10 (as read with subsection (10) of that section);
> (d) a local authority foster parent with whom the child has lived for a period of at least one year immediately preceding the application;
> (e) a relative with whom the child has lived for a period of at least one year immediately preceding the application.[441]

The order can also be made in family proceedings, either on application or of the court's own motion.[442] Three months' notice of the application must be given to the relevant local authority (either the local authority for the area in which the potential applicant lives or a local authority which is looking after the child concerned).[443] The local authority then has to investigate and prepare a report. Section 14A(11) makes clear that the 'court may not make a special guardianship order unless it has received such a report'. A court cannot therefore make an order of its own motion unless a report has already been prepared, although it will suffice merely to provide any information which may be missing from existing reports before the court, rather than producing an entirely new report.[444]

> ### Key legislation
>
> The effect of a SGO is that while the order remains in force:[445]
>
> (a) a special guardian appointed by the order has parental responsibility for the child in respect of whom it is made; and
> (b) subject to any other order in force with respect to the child under this Act, a special guardian is entitled to exercise parental responsibility to the exclusion of any other person with parental responsibility for the child (apart from another special guardian).[446]

However, this does not affect the operation of any enactment or rule of law which requires the consent of more than one person with parental responsibility in a matter affecting the child; or any rights which a parent of the child has in relation to the child's adoption or placement for adoption.[447]

While a SGO is in force with respect to a child, no person may cause the child to be known by a new surname or remove him from the UK, without either the written consent of every person who

---

[441] Ibid, s 14A(5). Section 9(3) applies in relation to an application for leave to apply for a SGO as it applies in relation to an application for leave to apply for a section 8 order (see s 14A(4)).

[442] Ibid, s 14A(6).

[443] Ibid, s 14A(7). On provisions relating to notice and leave within s 14A, see *Birmingham City Council v R* [2006] EWCA Civ 1748, [2007] 1 FLR 563 (and see tables on who can apply as of right and who needs leave).

[444] *Re S (Adoption Order or Special Guardianship Order) (No 2)* [2007] EWCA Civ 90, [2007] 1 FLR 855 at [14] and [15].

[445] Unless discharged earlier, the order comes to an end upon the child's reaching age 18: Children Act 1989, s 91(13).

[446] Children Act 1989, s 14C(1).    [447] Section 14C(2).

has parental responsibility for the child or the leave of the court.[448] However, on making a SGO the court may give leave for these purposes.[449]

An application can be made to discharge a SGO,[450] including an application by the child concerned, although in such a case the court may only grant leave if it is satisfied that he has sufficient understanding to make the proposed application.[451] A step-parent who has parental responsibility, or any person who immediately before the making of the SGO had parental responsibility, also requires the leave of the court to apply to discharge the order. The court may not grant leave to such persons unless it is satisfied that there has been a significant change in circumstances since the making of the SGO.[452] In *Re G (Special Guardianship Order)*[453] it was held that there was no relevant difference between the 'significant change in circumstances' test in section 14D(5) and the 'change in circumstances' test in section 24(3) of the ACA 2002. Therefore the same approach as adopted in relation to section 24(3) should be taken, as set out in *M v Warwickshire County Council*.[454] So the welfare of the child and the prospects of success of the application must be weighed.

A SGO discharges a care order and an order under section 34 of the Children Act 1989.[455] A SGO also discharges a child arrangements order with respect to the child's living arrangements.[456]

In *Re S (Adoption Order or Special Guardianship Order)*[457] the Court of Appeal provided some general guidance on the nature and use of SGOs,[458] and particularly on how the court should approach a choice between adoption and special guardianship. The court emphasised the importance of the issues raised by special guardianship, explaining that:

> special guardianship is an issue of very great importance to everyone concerned with it, not least, of course, the child who is its subject. It is plainly not something to be embarked upon lightly or capriciously, not least because the status it gives the special guardian effectively prevents the exercise of parental responsibility on the part of the child's natural parents, and terminates the parental authority given to a local authority under a care order (whether interim or final).[459]

The court explained that the examples given in the White Paper 'are only illustrations' and that there can be 'no routine solutions'[460] and that:

> [t]here is nothing in the statutory provisions themselves which limits the making of a special guardianship order or an adoption order to any given set of circumstances. The statute itself is silent on the circumstances in which a special guardianship order is likely to be appropriate, and there is no presumption contained within the statute that a special guardianship order is preferable to an adoption order in any particular category of case. Each case must be decided on its particular facts; and each case will involve the careful application of a judicial discretion to those facts.[461]

---

[448] Section 14C(3). This does not prevent the removal of a child, for a period of less than three months, by a special guardian of his (s 14C(4)).

[449] Section 14B(2). See for a case in which grandparents' application for change of surname was rejected, *Re L (Special Guardianship: Surname)* [2007] EWCA Civ 196, [2007] 2 FLR 50.

[450] Section 14D. The persons who can apply are listed in subs (1).     [451] Section 14D(4).

[452] Section 14D(5).     [453] [2010] EWCA Civ 300, [2010] 2 FLR 696.

[454] [2007] EWCA Civ 1084, [2008] 1 FLR 1093.     [455] See Children Act 1989, s 91(5A).

[456] *Re S (Adoption Order or Special Guardianship Order)* [2007] EWCA Civ 54, [2007] 1 FLR 819 at [30].

[457] [2007] EWCA Civ 54, [2007] 1 FLR 819.

[458] The guidance was endorsed by the then President of the Family Division, Potter P, and also incorporated in, and endorsed by the judges in, two other cases: *Re M-J (Adoption Order or Special Guardianship Order)* [2007] EWCA Civ 56, [2007] 1 FLR 691 and *Re AJ (Adoption Order or Special Guardianship Order)* [2007] EWCA Civ 55, [2007] 1 FLR 507. For discussion of the case law, see A. Hall, 'Special Guardianship—Themes Emerging from Case-Law' [2008] Family Law 244.

[459] Repeating what the court had said at [78] in *Birmingham City Council v R* [2006] EWCA Civ 1748, [2007] 1 FLR 563.

[460] *Re S (Adoption Order or Special Guardianship Order)* [2007] EWCA Civ 54, [2007] 1 FLR 819 at [43].

[461] Ibid, [47]. See, however, the findings in A. Hall, 'Special Guardianship and Permanency Planning: Unforeseen Consequences and Missed Opportunities' [2008] Child and Family Law Quarterly 359 and 'Special Guardianship: A

The court drew attention to the distinctions between the status of children who are adopted and those who are subject to a SGO,[462] and also to the equally fundamental differences between the status and powers of adopters and special guardians.[463] The court recognised that 'it is a material feature of the special guardianship regime that it is "less intrusive" than adoption'.[464] It also observed that when a child is adopted by a member of his own family 'the "skewing" or "distorting" effect of adoption' is 'a factor which the court must take into account'. However, the court noted that, as the cases illustrate, different weight will be placed on that factor in different circumstances.[465] The court observed that where a SGO is made a parent still has a right to apply for any section 8 order other than a residence arrangements order, and therefore 'it must be accepted that special guardianship does not always provide the same permanency of protection as adoption'.[466] This 'is a factor, which, in a finely balanced case, could well tip the scales in favour of adoption'.[467] Finally, the court indicated that it has jurisdiction to impose a SGO on an unwilling party,[468] but whether or not it should do so will depend on the facts, the nature of the refuser's case, and the welfare of the child. The court was clear, however, that if the court concludes that a SGO would best serve the child's welfare then the court should make it.[469]

In *Re S (Adoption Order or Special Guardianship Order)*[470] the Court of Appeal upheld a judge's decision to make a SGO in favour of the child's foster mother rather than an adoption order because of the close relationship between the six-year-old child and the natural mother.[471] Applying its assessment set out early, that is, that each case must be assessed on its own facts, the court rejected the foster mother's argument that SGOs were intended to be used only in cases where family members would otherwise adopt, and not to replace adoption applications by non-family members. By contrast, in *Re M-J (Adoption Order or Special Guardianship Order)*[472] and *Re AJ (Adoption Order or Special Guardianship Order)*[473] the Court of Appeal upheld the judges' decisions to make adoption orders rather than SGOs in favour of relatives where the children had not been looked after by their respective parents since the age of six months, and where the adoption met the children's long-term needs for security and stability. Similarly, in *N v B and Others (Adoption by Grandmother)*,[474] the court made an adoption order in favour of the maternal grandmother of two children aged nine and three, whose father, who had murdered the mother, would serve a minimum of 14 years' imprisonment. The court recognised that an important factor in such a case is the skewing effect which an adoption order has on the family relationships,[475] but the children would still be aware of the realities of their family relationships, and the children's permanence and long-term safeguarding required adoption rather than special guardianship.[476]

Missed Opportunity—Findings from Research' [2008] Family Law 148 that aspirations for reducing the number of looked after children may not have been met.

[462] *Re S (Adoption Order or Special Guardianship Order)* [2007] EWCA Civ 54, [2007] 1 FLR 819 at [44].

[463] Ibid, [46]. For a full account of the differences, see the table set out in *Re AJ (Adoption Order or Special Guardianship Order)* [2007] EWCA Civ 55, [2007] 1 FLR 507 at 524–525.

[464] *Re S (Adoption Order or Special Guardianship Order)* [2007] EWCA Civ 54, [2007] 1 FLR 819 at [49].

[465] Ibid, [51].

[466] Note, however, that a restriction under Children Act 1989, s 91(14) could be imposed: see eg *Re K (Special Guardianship Order)* [2011] EWCA Civ 635.

[467] Ibid, [68].     [468] Ibid, [74].     [469] Ibid, [77].     [470] [2007] EWCA Civ 54, [2007] 1 FLR 819.

[471] See also *Re I (Adoption: Appeal: Special Guardianship)* [2012] EWCA Civ 1217 (application for permission to appeal), in which McFarlane LJ said that where it is common ground that the natural family will play a meaningful part in the child's life, the possibility of special guardianship, and the distinction between it and adoption, should be uppermost in the court's consideration.

[472] [2007] EWCA Civ 56, [2007] 1 FLR 691.     [473] [2007] EWCA Civ 55, [2007] 1 FLR 507.

[474] [2013] EWHC 820 (Fam) (Theis J).

[475] The children's parents were cousins and the children lived with maternal aunts and uncles who, if the children were adopted, would become half-siblings, and the father would become the children's cousin.

[476] Ibid, [24] and [31].

# Discussion Questions

1. When, if at all, should the law permit a child's adoption without a parent's knowledge? Is the courts' approach to this issue satisfactory?

2. Does English law adequately protect the interests of the birth parent in the adoption process? Should the law treat a child's welfare as paramount when considering whether to dispense with parental consent to adoption? Is the courts' approach to post-adoption contact satisfactory?

3. When, if at all, should it be possible to revoke an adoption order? Are policy considerations more important than justice in this context?

4. What are the differences between adoption and special guardianship? How do the courts choose between these orders?

# Further Reading

BRIDGE, C., 'Adoption and Contact: The Value of Openness' [1994] Journal of Child Law 147

BRIDGE, C., 'Adoption Law: A Balance of Interests' in J. Herring (ed), *Family law: Issues, Debates, Policy* (Cullompton: Willan, 2001)

BRIDGE, C. and SWINDELLS, H., *Adoption: The Modern Law* (Bristol: Family Law, 2003)

CASEY, D. and GIBBERD, A., 'Adoption and Contact' [2000] Family Law 39

CURRY-SUMNER, I., '*EB v France*: A Missed Opportunity?' [2009] Child and Family Law Quarterly 356

DEY, I., 'Adapting Adoption: A Case of Closet Politics?' (2005) 19(3) International Journal of Law, Policy and the Family 289

DOUGHTY, J., 'Myths and Misunderstanding in Adoption Law and Policy' [2015] CFLQ 331.

EEKELAAR, J., 'Contact and the Adoption Reform' in A. Bainham, B. Lindley, M. Richards, and L. Trinder (eds), *Children and Their Families: Contact, Rights and Welfare* (Oxford: Hart, 2003), pp 253–74

HALL, A., 'Special Guardianship and Permanency Planning: Unforeseen Consequences and Missed Opportunities' [2008] Child and Family Law Quarterly 359

HALL, A., 'Special Guardianship—Themes Emerging from Case-Law' [2008] Family Law 244

HARRIS-SHORT, S., 'Holding onto the Past? Adoption, Birth Parents and the Law in the Twenty-First Century' in R. Probert and C. Barton (eds) *Fifty Years in Family Law: Essays for Stephen Cretney* (Cambridge: Intersentia, 2012), p 147.

HITCHINGS, E. and SAGAR, T., 'The Adoption and Children Act 2002: A Level Playing Field for Same-Sex Adopters?' [2002] Child and Family Law Quarterly 60

HUGHES, K. and SLOAN, B., 'Post-Adoption Photographs: Welfare, Rights and Judicial Reasoning' [2011] Child and Family Law Quarterly 393

JORDAN, L. and LINDLEY, B. (eds), *Special Guardianship: What Does it Offer Children Who Cannot Live with Their Parents?* (London: Family Rights Group, 2006)

LEWIS, J., 'Adoption: The Nature of Policy Shifts in England and Wales, 1972–2002' (2004) 18(2) International Journal of Law, Policy and the Family 235

LOWE, N. V., 'English Adoption Law: Past, Present and Future' in S. Katz, J. Eekelaar, and M. Maclean (eds), *Cross-Currents: Family Law and Policy in the US and England* (Oxford: Oxford University Press, 2000), pp 307–40

SLOAN, B., '*Re C (A Child) (Adoption: Duty of Local Authority)*—Welfare and the Rights of the Birth Family in "Fast Track" Adoption Cases' [2009] Child and Family Law Quarterly 87

SLOAN, B. 'Adoption Decisions in England: *Re B (A Child) (Care Proceedings: Appeal)* and Beyond' (2015) 37(4) *Journal of Social Welfare and Family Law* 437–57.

SLOAN, B., 'Post-Adoption Contact Reform: Compounding the State-Ordered Termination of Parenthood? (2014) 73(2) Cambridge Law Journal 378–404

SMITH, C. and LOGAN, J., 'Adoptive Parenthood as a "Legal Fiction"—Its Consequences for Direct Post-Adoption Contact' [2002] Child and Family Law Quarterly 281

Visit the Online Resource Centre at **www.oxfordtextbooks.co.uk/orc/gilmore_glennon5e/** for a range of further features including a detailed bibliography and self-test questions.

**online
resource
centre**

# Index

abandoned children 675–6
abduction 25, 537, 540, 572, 574–6,
    578, 580–8; *see also* international
    child abduction
abortion 352–3, 437, 443, 445, 452,
    589, 700
    advice 437–8
abroad, taking children 510,
    544, 547–61
absent parents 188, 409, 512–13,
    518–19, 521, 536–7, 657
abuse *see also* children needing
    services, care, and protection;
    domestic violence
    access to children 595–6
    allegations 401, 526, 541, 624,
        634, 657–66, 676–82
    care, in 608–9
    children's guardian, role of 651
    Cleveland Child Abuse
        Inquiry 596, 650
    domestic 97–101, 106, 110–12,
        154–5, 157, 578, 585
    emotional 98–100, 115, 618, 628,
        634, 643, 724
    non-physical 100, 115, 121
    parental responsibility 415
    sexual abuse 520–1, 531–2, 658,
        660–2, 664–6, 682, 684
    significant harm
        threshold 658–61, 666
    Waterhouse Inquiry 702
    welfare checklist 682
accommodated children 481, 487,
    490, 601, 608, 611–12, 614
accommodation, *see* homelessness;
    local authority accommodation
    for children
acquired gender 17, 21, 30–1,
    33, 374
actual intentions 263,
    268–70, 302–3
adopters 701–2, 708, 713–14,
    725–6, 731–2, 735–6, 739–41
    potential 705, 707, 713, 723
    same-sex 708
adoption 56, 383–5, 413–14, 470–1,
    482–6, 655, 678, 700–43
    access to information 739
    address, adopters living at
        same 726–7
    adoption orders 484, 686, 700,
        712, 733–8
    Adoption Service 703–4

age
    children 712–13, 731
    parents 726–7
agencies 703, 703–8, 712–13,
    715, 720–2, 731–3, 739–40
    assessing suitable adoptions,
        role in 705–8
    counselling 740
    decision-making 704, 707
    information 739
    panels 707–8
    placements 712–25
    regulation 704
    reviews 704
appeals 724, 733–7
applications 704, 718, 726, 731,
    733–5, 743, 747
assessments 705–8, 720
authorisation to place, effect
    of 721–2
babies 700–1, 741
background of child 737
best interests test 718, 730, 738
birth certificates, access to 739
birth parents
    adoption, by 726, 729–30
    on-going contact 738–43
    parental responsibility,
        extinguishment of 700
British citizenship 736
British Nationals (Overseas) 736
care orders 686, 724, 733
case files 707
change of
    circumstances 723–5, 733
child arrangements orders with
    respect to residence 720, 722
child assessment orders 720
civil partners 41, 726
cohabitants 55
conditions 703, 716, 731, 733
confidentiality 709
consent 712–13, 732
    age 712–13
    dispensing with
        consent 704, 716–18
    fathers 709, 712, 737–8
    rules 712
    withdrawal 714
consequences of placement
    orders 720–1
contact
    advantages and
        disadvantages 740–2

letterbox 739, 743
on-going 738–43
post-adoption contact 740–3
register 738
siblings 742
counselling 740
couples 703, 707–8, 726–7
criminal offences 722
decision-making 704, 707
deductive reasoning 719
delay 703–4, 711
discretion 725, 734–5
discrimination 708
dispensing with
    consent 704, 716–18
disruption of placement 701
divorce 700
domestic violence 710
domicile 726
duration of orders 722
early permanence
    placements 714
effect of adoption orders 735
effect of placement or
    authorisation to place 721–2
eligibility 703, 707–8, 726–30
enhanced welfare test 716
fathers
    adoption by fathers 726, 730
    consent 709, 712, 737–8
    identity 708
    parental
        responsibility 389, 709
    private and family life, right to
        respect for 711–12
    withholding
        information 708–12
habitual residence 726
home environment, sufficient
    opportunities to, *see*
    children in 732
Human Rights Act 1998 723–4
information 707–12
    access 739
    criminal offences 739
    exceptional circumstances,
        withholding
        information in 710
    protected information,
        definition of 739
    withholding information
        from fathers and other
        relatives 708–12
inherent jurisdiction 709

**adoption** (*Cont.*)
injunctions 724
  judicial review 724
  leave to make applications where
    conditions not fulfilled 732
  leave to oppose
    adoption 733, 735
  letterbox contact 739, 743
  live with adopters, children
    must 730-1
  local authorities 700-5
  looked after children 700
  maintenance,
    termination of 736
  married couples 51
  medical examinations and
    reports 707
  mothers, adoption by 726, 730
  natural justice 736
  notice of intention to adopt and
    report 732
  on-going contact 743
  openness in adoption 743
  opposition 720, 722, 735
  orders 412-13, 704, 712-14, 720,
    722-3, 726-38, 742-7
  panels 707-8
  paramountcy or welfare
    principle 704, 711, 716, 725,
    730, 740, 742
  parental responsibility 389, 413,
    700, 709, 712, 735-6, 742
  permanence reports 707
  photographs 739, 743
  placement 712-25
    authorisation to place,
      effect of 721
    conditions for orders 715-16
    consequences of orders 720-1
    definition 713
    duration 722-3
    effect of placement 721-2
    orders 703, 714-22
    plans 708
    removal 722
    reports 708
    return of children, revocation
      of orders without 725
    revocation 723-5, 737
  placement orders 703, 705, 712-
    13, 715-26, 733, 735, 743
  police checks 707
  policy 700, 703, 711, 737
  post-adoption contact 484,
    704, 739-43
  potential adopters 723
  preliminaries 731
  preparation 708
  private and family life, right to
    respect for 711-12, 730, 743
  procedural irregularity 737
  procedure 715

process 703-5, 708, 712, 714,
  723, 726, 733
prohibited degrees of
  relationship 736
prohibited steps orders 720
proportionality 730
prospective adopters 712, 723
protected information,
  definition of 739
reasons for decisions 708
registered adoption
  societies 704-5
relatives, withholding
  information from 708-12
religion 704, 707, 737-8
removal from placement 722
reports 708, 732
return of children 722
reviews 704
revocation of orders 723-5, 737
same-sex couples 703,
  707-8, 726
section 8 orders 484
section 20 agreements 610-12
separated couples 727
setting aside orders 736-8
sexual offences 736
siblings, contact with 742
single people 703, 727-30
social workers 707, 720, 727
special guardianship orders 747
specific issue orders 720
status conferred by
  adoption 736
suitable adoptions, assessment
  of 705-8, 732
supervision orders 720
time limits and target
  figures 702
unmarried couples 703, 708
welfare checklist 705, 716
who may adopt 703,
  707-8, 726-30
who may be adopted 731
withholding information
  from fathers and other
  relatives 708-12
**adoptive parents** lxxii, 385-6,
  484-5, 700-2, 736-8, 740-1, 743
sole 730, 736
**adult children** 219, 330, 335-6,
  338-9, 418, 516
**adultery** 46-7, 65-7, 70-4, 89, 91,
  348, 350
**advancement, presumption of** 257
**age**
  accommodation for
    children 613
  adoption 712-13, 727, 731
  child arrangements
    orders with respect to
    residence 493-5, 569

child support 331, 333
children, rights of 427
  of consent 9, 12, 35, 38
  contact orders 569
  of discretion 433-4
  looked after children 605
  money and property
    distribution on marriage
    breakdown 191
  section 8 orders 569-70
**alcohol** 103, 121-2, 395, 407, 615,
  639, 666
**allocation of parental
  responsibility** 388-413
**ancillary relief,** *see* money
  distribution on marriage
  breakdown and property
**annulment** 16, 19, 21-2, 25-6,
  40-1, 46, 95
**ante-nuptial agreements** lxvii,
  211, 229-35
  disclosure 230
  enforceable 234-5
  Europe 234
  forum shopping 234
  guidance 230
  improper pressure 223
  post-nuptial agreements 231
**antisocial/narcissistic personality
  and domestic violence** 104
**anxiety** 104, 108, 483-4, 486,
  529-30, 619, 626
**appeals and rehearings**
  adoption 723-4, 733-7
  divorce 72-3
  lump sums 239-41
  matrimonial home 238, 240
  money and property
    distribution on marriage
    breakdown 237-49
  periodical payments 239-41
  separation agreements 239
**armed forces, overseas
  marriages of** 29
**arranged marriages** 19, 25-6, 30
**arrest**
  emergency protection
    orders 634
  exclusion requirement 650
  harassment 154
  non-molestation orders 114,
    117, 123
  occupation orders 113-14, 151
  powers of 28, 118, 122-4, 147-8,
    150, 152, 635
  warrants 123, 155
**assessments**
  adoption 705-8, 720, 732
  child assessment
    orders 625-6, 720
  Cleveland Inquiry 649
  competency 650

directions 644–50
  inherent jurisdiction 650
  interim care and supervision
    orders 650
  looked after children 605, 607
  medical or psychiatric
    assessments 645–50
  psychotherapy 647–8
  refuse, child's right
    to 645, 649–50
  residential
    assessments 641, 645–9
  significant harm 628
  treatment, distinguished
    from 647–8
assets 183–5, 197–202, 204–10,
  219–20, 231–3, 238–40, 245–8
  capital 171, 177, 196, 202, 205,
    208, 240
  limited company 184
  matrimonial 69, 183, 196,
    208, 313
  pool of 192, 204, 207
**assisted fertilisation**
  agreed fatherhood
    conditions 370
  autonomy 365
  biological connection 361,
    363, 371
  civil partnerships 371, 374
  consent 364–5, 374
  counselling 364
  death, use of sperm after 373–4
  egg donations 361, 363
  embryos, father's consent to
    destruction of 365
  embryos after mother's partner's
    death, use of 374
  fathers and
    fatherhood 363, 365–74
  Human Fertilisation and
    Embryology Act 1990 364–9
  Human Fertilisation
    and Embryology Act
    2008 364, 369–71
  Human Fertilisation and
    Embryology Authority 364–5
  legal but not biological
    fathers 369
  lesbian couples 371
  licence conditions 364
  licensed treatment 365, 370
  life, right to 365
  margin of appreciation 365
  motherhood 361, 363
  mothers, husbands of 367
  parenthood 371
  private and family life, right to
    respect for 365
  same-sex couples 41, 43,
    337, 371
  sperm donors 369, 371–4

  surrogacy 367
  unmarried couples 367
  woman and man together,
    services provided for 367–9
**associated persons** lxvi, 61, 110,
  114–20, 129, 157, 640
  definition lxvii, 119
**attachment (between children and
  parents)** 394–5, 407, 410, 484–5,
  550, 557, 711
**Australia** 245–6, 320, 459, 506–7,
  509, 558, 560
**authorised persons** 11, 14, 598,
  625, 630
**autonomy**
  assisted fertilisation 365
  children, rights of 422, 425,
    427–38, 450, 453
  cohabitants 52, 57–8
  medical treatment of children,
    consent to 431–8
  parental responsibility 421
  religion 686

**babies** 135, 493–5, 615–16, 666–7,
  672–4, 700–2, 709–10
  adoption 700–1, 741
**balance of harm test** 133–5,
  138, 141–4
**balance of probabilities** 154–5,
  358–9, 542–3, 660, 664–5,
  671, 673
**bankruptcy** 298, 337
**Barder principles** 238–42
**behaviour fact for
  divorce** 74–6, 89, 91
**best interests test** 357–8, 420–1,
  433, 435–8, 442–5, 449–51,
  468–74; *see also* paramountcy or
  welfare principle
  accommodation for
    children 614
  adoption 718, 730, 738
  children, rights of 433, 438
  contact 535, 537, 695
  medical treatment of children,
    consent to 442–3, 445, 450–1
  parentage 348–50, 357–8
  residence orders/child
    arrangements orders with
    respect to residence 494–5,
    504, 507
  shared residence orders 504, 507
  supervision orders 689
**big money cases** 69–70, 81, 197,
  201, 204, 209, 211
**bigamy** 6, 16, 94, 181, 388
**biological parents**, *see*
  natural family
**birth certificates** 32–3, 358, 360,
  369, 374–5, 390–1, 561
  adoption 739

  fathers 390–1, 411
  name, change of 561
  parental responsibility 391, 411
  transsexuals 21, 32–3, 375
**birth family**, *see* natural family
**birth parents**, *see* natural family
**birth rate, decrease in** lxvii
**bitterness** 74, 79, 84–5, 89, 96,
  221, 455
**blood tests** 331, 348–51, 354–7,
  359–60, 394, 399, 452
**blood transfusions** 447–51, 497,
  547, 571–2, 736
**Booth Committee** 67, 74, 84
**Border Agency** 573, 597
**breakdown of relationships**, *see*
  money and property distribution
  on marriage breakdown;
  property disputes of cohabitants
  on relationship breakdown
**Brussels II Revised** 68, 70, 81, 574,
  582, 585, 587
**burden of proof** 293, 370, 518, 659,
  662, 664–6, 672
**businesses, contributions
  to** 281–3

**Cafcass (Children and Family
  Court Advisory and Support
  Service)** lxxvi, 384, 524–5, 535,
  651, 665, 684–5
**Cafcass officers** 515, 521, 525, 535,
  543, 559, 568
**capacity**
  children, rights of 425–6
  consummation 17–18
  forced marriages 6
  learning disabilities, persons
    with 668
  marriage 5–6, 18, 20–2, 29, 42
  mental disabilities/illness,
    people with 6, 20, 22, 35,
    122, 191
  overseas marriages,
    recognition of 29
  parental responsibility of
    fathers 391
**capital** 171–2, 177, 183, 195–6,
  204–6, 240, 244–5
**capital sharing, presumptions
  of** 192, 204
**care orders** 510–11, 570–2,
  639–42, 644–6, 651–9,
  674–87, 689–94; *see also* care
  proceedings; interim care and
  supervision orders
  adoption 686, 724
  care plans 684
  child arrangements orders with
    respect to residence 511
  contact with children in
    care 480–1, 491–2, 693–8

**care orders** (*Cont.*)
discharge of orders 510, 692, 746
discretion 692
emergency protection
orders 690
grounds 595
issue estoppel 692
legal effect 685–7
looked after children 686
monitoring 690
paramountcy or welfare
principle 595, 686–7, 692
parental
responsibility 684–7, 692
religion 686
significant harm threshold 640,
646, 653–64, 687
special guardianship orders 746
supervision orders 691
welfare checklist 682–3, 692
**care plans** 676, 679, 683, 683–5,
687, 691, 693–5
**care proceedings** 457–8, 595, 619,
639–44, 648, 651–84, 737–8
allegations 682
balance of probabilities 664–5
burden of proof 664–6
final hearings 653–83
interim care and supervision
orders 639–52
parental control, where child is
beyond 677
proof 657–66
reasonable parental
care 666–77
significant harm 653–77
standard of proof 664–6
threshold test of significant
harm 653–77
welfare checklist 683
**carers** 599, 613, 615, 654, 657–8,
670, 723
as home-sharers 62
primary 177, 300, 341, 343,
548–50, 552–3, 670
sole 581, 694
substitute 413, 480, 595
**Carlile, Kimberley, inquiry into
death of** 596
**ceremonies**
civil lxx, 4, 10–14, 18, 45
non-religious belief 12
religious lxx, 4, 10–13, 18, 40,
45, 80–1
**certainty** 234–7, 356–7, 360, 362,
368, 384–5, 410
**change of circumstances** 244, 493,
641, 680, 723–5, 734, 746
**checklists** 133–6, 138, 141–2,
145, 492–3, 516, 681–2; *see also*
welfare checklist

**child abuse** 164, 520–1, 594, 596,
609, 623–6, 682–3
**child arrangements**
**orders** 412–14, 474–6,
479–81, 490–1, 510–12, 533–5,
542–5; *see also* contact orders;
residence orders; specific
issue orders
best interests test 535, 537
capacity 491
child of the family 479
concerning contact 512–31
consent 479–80
consents 479–80
definition 475, 492
distress caused to residential
parents 520, 523, 528–30
enforcement 535–44
facilitation 533–5
parental responsibility
conferred by 412
with respect to
residence 492–8, 511
adoption 720, 722
background of child 498
best interests test 494–5
care orders, discharging 510
change of circumstances 493
consent 479–80
cultural heritage 498
discharge 746
discrimination 494–7
fathers, against 494–5
religion 496–7
sexual orientation 496
foster parents 480
gender, relevance of 493–5
guardian, appointment of 511
Jehovah's Witnesses 496, 498
legal consequences 510–11
lesbian couples 467,
469, 493–6
local authority care 479–80,
490–1, 511
mothers, best interests of
babies to be with 493–5
paramountcy or welfare
principle 497–8
parental
responsibility 412–14, 419,
480, 499, 501, 510–11
relatives 480
religious practices and
beliefs 496–8
removal from UK 544
responsibilities and rights,
conferring 510
sexual orientation of
parents 496
siblings to be kept
together 495

status quo, bias towards
the 493–5
who can apply 480
wishes and feelings of
child 493
**child assessment orders** 624–7,
630, 634, 720
**child labour** 428
**child liberationist ideology** 427
**child protection,** *see* children
needing services, care, and
protection
**child support** lxxv, lxxvii, 319–24,
326–7, 333–4, 343, 408
adoption, termination on 735–6
adult children,
applications by 336
against whom orders can be
made 337
age 333
another child, where
non-resident partner is
maintaining 325
applications 324, 335–6
apportionment 325
available orders 332, 336
capital provision 330
capital transfers 327
care, orders against a person
with 330
child, definition of 323
Child Maintenance and
Enforcement Commission
(C-MEC) 321, 324
Child Maintenance and Other
Payments Act 2008 321
child of the family, concept
of 330–1, 337
Child Support Act 1991 319–28
Child Support Agency 320–2
Children Act 1989 335–43
civil partners 330
clean break 320
collection, applications for 323
county court, powers of 330
court's powers 330–43
court's residual role with respect
to maintenance 330
criticism, response to 321
departure directions 321, 327
dependants, children as 333–5
discretion 332, 343
duration of orders 333, 337, 340
during marriage 250
educational expenses 329
enforcement 324, 327
expenses 327–9
fair hearing, right to a 327
flexibility 320–1
gross income scheme 322
habitual residence 323

Henshaw Report 321–2
High Court, powers of 330, 337
legal parenthood 320
liability orders, applications
    for 327
lifestyle choices 327, 343
loss of confidence 321–2
lump sums 330, 335, 337
magistrates' courts 327, 336
maintenance agreements 321,
    324–5, 343
maintenance
    calculation 320, 324–7
    applications 323
    apportionment 326
    basic rate 323, 325
    flat rate 325
    nil rate 325
    reduced rate 325
maintenance orders 323, 325
marital status 330
Matrimonial Causes Act
    1973 330–6, 339
nil rate 325
non-parents, maintenance
    by 332–3
paramountcy or welfare
    principle 338–9
parent, definition of 323
parental responsibility 320, 337,
    403, 417
paternity, lack of
    knowledge of 331
periodical payments 250, 330,
    332–3, 336, 340, 342–3
problems 320–1
property adjustment
    orders 336–7, 339
property transfers 327, 331, 337
qualifying child, duty to
    maintain a 323–4
reduced rate 325
review of system 321–2
same-sex parents 337
Secretary of State 321
secured periodical
    payments 332–3
social parenthood 320, 337
special expenses 327
sperm donation 337
standard of living 332, 338–43
topping up orders 328
unborn children 331
unmarried parents 335–43
    against whom orders can be
        made 337
    applications on behalf of the
        child 335–6
    available orders 336–7
    Children Act 1989 335–43
    discretion 343

duration of orders 337
who can apply 335–6
variations 321, 328, 342
welfare benefits 319–20, 322
who can apply 335
to whom Act applies 323
**children** *see also* adoption; child
    support; Children Act 1989;
    children needing services,
    care and protection; consent to
    medical treatment of children;
    local authority accommodation
    for children; paramountcy or
    welfare principle
abduction 547
advancement,
    presumption of 257
attachment between children
    and parents 394–5, 407, 410,
    484–5, 550, 557, 711
babies 135, 493–5, 615–16,
    666–7, 672–4, 700–2, 709–10
bankruptcy 298
behaviour allegations in
    divorce 74
in care 458, 480, 482, 589, 595,
    651, 693–5
child assessment
    orders 625–6, 720
civil partners 41, 330
clean break 177
cohabitants 52–4, 57–8, 299
    Child Maintenance
        and Enforcement
        Commission 54
    definition of cohabitation 60
    maintenance 54
    rights and responsibilities 56
    section 8 orders 55
    vulnerability 53, 58
competency 357, 429–53,
    565, 650
definition 414, 418
delinquent 595, 614
disabilities, with 191, 329,
    599, 601
divorce 72, 74, 81, 86
domestic violence 102,
    108, 163–4
family, child of the 181–2,
    330–3, 337, 480
higher education or
    training, in 72
marriage 50
matrimonial home 182
money and property distribution
    on marriage breakdown 181,
    188, 202
name, change of 31–5, 162–3,
    238, 268, 560–8, 723–5, 733–4
in need 546, 598–600, 602–3

non-molestation
    orders 115–17, 120
occupation orders 120, 132–49
orphans 676
parental responsibility, *see*
    parental responsibility
property disputes of
    cohabitants 56, 256,
    300–1, 310–11
rights of 424, 438, 717
    adulthood, boundary
        with 427–8
    age 427
    autonomy 425, 452–3
    basic interests 429
    best interests test 433, 438
    capacity 425
    categorisation 429–30
    child labour 428
    child liberationist
        ideology 427
    childhoods 427–9
    Children Act 1989 430,
        437, 453
    competency 429, 431–8, 452–3
    conceptions of a right 424–5
    consent to medical
        treatment 431–8
    contraceptives 430–7
    corporal punishment 453
    criminal law 430
    cultural pluralism 428
    developmental
        interests 429–30, 435
    different childhoods 429
    discretion, age of 433, 436
    discrimination 427
    dual parenting 410
    European Convention on
        Human Rights 451–2
    fair hearing, right to a 452
    freedom of expression 452
    fundamental debates 429
    future-orientated consent 430
    Gillick competency 357,
        431–53, 565
    Human Rights Act
        1998 437–8, 450–2
    inhuman or degrading
        treatment 451
    interest theory 424–5
    interests children can
        plausibly claim 429–30
    legal protection of
        interests 438
    liberal paternalism 430
    life, right to 450
    medical
        treatment 431–50, 453
    paramountcy principle 452–3
    paternalism 425, 427, 430

**children** (*Cont.*)

private and family life, right to
respect for 438, 452
Rawls's theory of justice 430
self-determination 429
should children have
rights 425
social construction of
childhood 427
society's perceptions of
children 429
thought, conscience and
religion, freedom of 452
treaties and conventions 428
voting 427–8
welfarism 429
will theory 424–5
sale of matrimonial home 297–8
same-sex marriages 43
self-esteem 393
separation, dangers to children
after 163–4
Statement of Arrangements for
the Children 72
tenancies, transfers of 298
UN Convention on the Rights of
the Child lxxiii, 253, 353–5
welfare 455–60, 462–7, 469–70,
472–4, 566–72, 597–9, 716–18
welfare reports 72
**Children Act 1989** *see also* section
8 orders
accommodation for
children 601–4, 607–9
child protection 594
child support 335–43
children, rights of 40, 430, 437
Climbié Report 596
complaints and
representations 607–9
decision-making
principles 455–62
family assistance orders 476–7
fathers, parental
responsibility 346,
388–90, 407
Human Rights Act 1998,
compatibility with 471–2
local authorities, duties of 597
paramountcy or welfare
principle 455, 471–2, 474
parental responsibility 346, 407,
411, 421
police protection 639
property disputes of
cohabitants 300–1
significant harm
threshold 26, 617–18
special guardianship orders 744
surrogacy 382, 385
unmarried parents 335–43

**Children Act 2004** 380–1, 390,
412–13, 596–7, 651–2, 701, 707–8
**Children and Families Act
2014** lxii, lxv, 393, 475, 681,
685, 705–6
**Children and Family Court
Advisory and Support Service
(Cafcass)**, *see* Cafcass
**children cases, private law
disputes in** 455; *see also* section
8 orders
**children needing services, care,
and protection** 593–4, 596, 598,
621, 624, 671, 674; *see also* care
orders; supervision orders
access to children in abuse
cases 596
accommodation 601–4, 607–17
background 597
breach of statutory duty 599
Cafcass lxxvi, 597
care plans 683–4, 687
care proceedings, final
hearings in 683
Carlile, Kimberley, inquiry into
death of 596
child assessment orders 626
Children Act 1989 594, 637, 639
Children Act 2004 596–7
children's guardian, role
of 650–2
Children's Trust 597
Cleveland Child Abuse
Inquiry 596
Climbié Report 596
complaints and
representations 607–9
compulsory intervention 595–6,
601, 615, 617–22, 669
contact with children in care 698
cooperation between
authorities 596–7
direct payments 599
disabilities, children
with 599, 601
disciplines, interaction with
other lxxvi
diversity and individuality 593
emergency
intervention 595–6, 628–39
experts lxxvi
forced marriages 250
homelessness 598, 600
inadequacies of previous law 596
inherent jurisdiction to take
child into care 595
International Covenant on Civil
and Political Rights 593
investigations 623–8, 652
keeping families together 601
liberal standard 594

Local Safeguarding Children
Board 597
need, children in 546, 599–601
ongoing practice concerns 596
paramountcy or welfare
principle 595–9
parental responsibility 593, 599
police protection 637–9
provision of services 601
representations and
complaints 607–9
respite care 601
Review of Child Care Law 596
review panels 608
section 37 investigations, court's
power to order 626–7
significant harm
threshold 617–25, 628
social workers lxxvi, 596, 615,
625, 628, 633, 637–9
UK Border Agency 573, 597
UN Convention on the Rights of
the Child 593
wardship 596
wishes and feelings of
child 599, 652
**children's guardian** 610–11, 617,
650–2, 661–2, 672, 675, 736–8
appointment 414
Cafcass officers 651
care plans 683
child arrangements orders with
respect to residence 510
Colwell, Maria, death of 651
duties 650–2
investigations 652
orphans 675
parental responsibility 413
Practice Direction 651–2
records 652
solicitor, appointment of 652
welfare checklist 652, 683
Welsh family proceedings
officers 651
wishes of the child 652
**Children's Trusts** 597
**civil ceremonies** lxx, 4,
10–14, 18, 45
**civil partnerships** 3, 33–55, 94–6,
128–31, 167–8, 311–14, 727–8
adoption 41, 727, 736
agreements 40
assisted fertilisation 371
behaviour, dissolution due to 95
child support 330
children 41, 330
Civil Partnership Act
2004 lxviii–lxix, 36–42,
94–5, 116, 250, 308–9, 330
death, presumption of 95
definition 40

desertion 95
dissolution lxxvi, 40, 65, 68, 95, 237, 313–14
distinguished from marriage 38, 40, 42
domestic violence 38, 40–1
financial provision 40, 95
formalities 40
heterosexual couples 62
home rights 41
irretrievable breakdown, dissolution due to 95
legal consequences 40–1
legal formation 40
legal recognition of families lxviii
lesbian couples 371
marriage 44
nullity 40
occupation orders 128–31, 140–2, 144–5
overseas dissolution 95
overseas partnerships, recognition of 40, 95
parental responsibility agreements 41
property disputes of cohabitants 309
property orders 40, 95
registration 40
residence orders 41
separation 40, 95
statistics 40, 95
surviving spouses 40–1
termination 40
**clean break** 168, 170, 175–81, 184, 191, 217–18, 244–5
children 177, 320–1
contributions 177
deferred clean breaks 170, 180, 191
duration of marriage 177
employment 176
hardship 176–7
just and reasonable test 175
Law Commission 168
lump sum 172
matrimonial home 218–19
orders 175–6, 179–80, 191, 241
past contributions 177
periodical payments 175–80
physical and mental disabilities, persons with 191
policy 175
property adjustment orders 173
public interest 241–2
section 28(1A) directions 180
variation 244, 248
**Cleveland Child Abuse Inquiry** 596, 650
**Climbié Report** 596

**co-ownership** 219–22, 264
**coercive behaviour** vii, 98, 111–12
**cohabitants** 51–61, 95–6, 116–19, 128, 139–42, 253–5, 297–314; *see also* property disputes of cohabitants on relationship breakdown
adoption 55
autonomy 57–8
children 55, 57, 299
    Child Maintenance and Enforcement Commission 54
    definition of cohabitation 60
    maintenance 54–5
    rights and responsibilities 56
    section 8 orders 55
    vulnerability 53, 58
Cohabitation Bills 51, 53, 56–8, 60–2, 312–13
commitment, level of 305–6
common law marriage 53
death 55–6
definition 52, 60, 116
domestic violence 53, 55, 95
financial provision 53
home rights 54, 95
home-sharers 61–2
ideological superiority of marriage, maintaining 311, 314
ideologues, romantics, pragmatists, and uneven couples 53
increase lxvii, 51–2
Inheritance (Provision for Family and Dependants) Act 1975 53, 55
intention of parties with regard to ownership of property 53, 95
intestacy 54–5, 95
Law Commission 51, 54
legal recognition of families lxviii
length of relationships 53
Living Together campaign 53
maintenance 53–5
marriage
    commitment, level of 305–6
    comparison with cohabitation 60, 299, 304–6, 309–14
    ideological superiority, maintaining 311, 314
    policy 314
    reputation of marriage, with 16
    undermining 306
new partners, cohabitation after marriage breakdown with 172, 185–7, 240–2, 249

non-molestation orders 56, 96, 115–17, 119
occupation orders 54–5, 95, 131, 140–5
parental responsibility 56
policy 53, 57, 314
property disputes, *see* property disputes of cohabitants on relationship breakdown
property rights 53–4, 95
reform 56
relationship breakdown 54–6, 60, 96
reputation of marriage, having 16
rights and obligations 3, 53–6, 60, 312
    need for reform 313
section 8 orders 55
social attitudes 51–2, 56
statistics lxvii, 52
tenancies, succession to 55
undermining marriage 306
vulnerability 55, 58, 95–6
wills 55
**Cohabitation Bills** 51, 53, 56–8, 60–2, 312–13
**Colwell, Maria, death** 651
**commitment**
marriage, level of commitment in 60, 306
parental responsibility of fathers 394, 403, 407, 409
property disputes of cohabitants 305–6
unmarried fathers 390
**committal** 124, 149, 512, 514, 538–44, 695
**common intention** 257–8, 260–1, 263–4, 266–8, 272–87, 301–4, 309
inferred 273, 276
**common law marriage myth** 54, 61, 305, 408
**compensation** 25, 112–13, 178, 200–4, 216, 247–9, 543; *see also* damages
**compensation principle** 203–4
**competency**
assessments 650
children, rights of 429, 431–8, 452–3
Gillick competency 357, 431–52, 565
medical treatment of children, consent to 430–50, 452–3
name, change of 565
parentage 357
**competent children** 357, 435, 438–9, 443, 445–6, 596, 603

**complaints and**
**representations** 607–9
**confidentiality** 422, 433, 437,
709, 740
**consent** 17–21, 23–7, 365–7, 370–1,
431–4, 438–49, 712–16; *see also*
consent to marriage; consent to
medical treatment of children
adoption 703, 712–13, 716–20,
732, 737–8
assisted fertilisation 364–5, 374
child arrangements
orders 479–80
divorce 78–9, 90–1
embryos, father's consent to
destruction of 365
family assistance orders 476
fathers
adoption 709, 712, 737–8
embryos, consent to
destruction of 365
financial orders, variation
of 243–4
mothers 352, 382, 609, 714
non-molestation orders 152
occupation orders 152
orders 174, 214, 223–9,
238–44, 249
setting aside in cases of
fraud 226–8
parentage 357–8
parental responsibility 419
section 8 orders 480, 490
separation
agreements 223–4, 229
**consent to marriage** 5
conditional consent 23
duress 19
forced marriages 20, 24, 35
identity, mistake as to 19–20
marriage 18–23
mental disabilities, persons
with 20
mistake 19–20
nullity 19–20
overseas marriages,
recognition of 29
pregnancy by another man 23
**consent to medical treatment of**
**children** 438–50
authorisation of court,
seeking 444
autonomy 431–8, 447, 450
best interests test 443, 445, 450
blood transfusions by
Jehovah's Witnesses, refusal
of 447–51, 572
children, rights of 431–8, 453
competency 430–50, 452–3
consent and refusal, distinction
between 445–6

Gillick
competency 431–50, 452–3
Human Rights Act 1998 450
life-saving treatment 451, 571
paramountcy or welfare
principle 450–1
parental
responsibility 417, 438–9
refusal of treatment 438–50
section 8 orders 571
use of reasonable force 444–5
wardship 441
**constructive trusts** 256–8,
272–4, 276–7, 279–86, 288–90,
294, 303–4
**consummation of marriage** 17–18,
22, 46–7
forced marriage 17–18
incapacity 17–18
religious marriage 17–18
transsexuals 17
voidable marriage 17–18
wilful refusal 17–18
**contact** *see also* child arrangements
orders; contact orders; contact
with child in care
activity directions and
conditions 534–7
adoption 738–43
alienation of parent 527
assumption in favour 518, 520
behaviour of parent during 526
care, children in 480–1,
491–2, 693–8
centres 401, 514, 521
child's interest, contact almost
always in 517
conditions 513–14, 534–7, 540
contempt of court 538–40
court's general
approach 516–20
criminal convictions 530
destabilising present family unit,
risk of 530–1
direct 512–15, 517–18, 520,
525–6, 530–1, 537, 557–8
domestic violence 163–4,
529–30, 537
duration of orders 569
emergency protection
orders 630
enforcement 493, 533, 536, 538
committal 538–9
facilitation of 533
genuine fear 529–30
guidelines 522–6
harm
committal 538
definition of 522
risk 528
section 37 directions 541

hostility of parent,
implacable 528–30, 537, 541
indirect 512–20, 526, 530, 537,
570, 741, 744
intractable disputes 515, 520,
527, 532, 539, 541
local authority care 480,
491, 695–8
monitoring contact and shared
residence arrangements 535
nature of proposed
applications 484
opposition
implacable hostility of
parent 517, 527–32, 536–7,
541, 544
step-parents 531
paramountcy or welfare
principle 517, 520, 527,
534, 537–8
parentage 355–61
parental alienation 527
parental responsibility 480,
491–2, 512
post-adoption 484, 704, 739–43
presumption against 522
private and family life, right to
respect for 514, 535
prohibited steps
orders 475, 544–5
reasonable 510, 612, 629,
688, 694–6
religion 535
section 37 directions 541
specific issue orders 475
step-parents 516, 531
supervised 401, 514, 521, 525,
529, 531, 697
suspended residence orders 540
transsexuals 526
UN Convention on the Rights of
the Child lxxiii
use of residence arrangements
to enforce contact
provision 540–1
warning notices 535
welfare checklist 516
when orders can be made 568–9
**contact orders** 475–6, 512, 529–30,
532–3, 535, 542–5, 693–5; *see also*
child arrangements orders
18, reaching age 569
abuse 520–1, 544
civil partners 41
definition 512
enforcement 517, 532, 539
**contact with child in care**
agreements 694
best interests test 695
committal proceedings 695
consent 479, 481

deny contact, courts authorising local authorities to 695–8
  discretion 694–5
  enforcement 695
  expert evidence 697
  leave to apply 695
  parental responsibility 491–2
  reasonable contact 694–5
  section 8 orders 695
  variation 698
  wishes and feelings of child 695
**contempt of court** 121–5, 147–9, 155, 187, 538–40
**contraceptives** 17, 420, 430–7, 700
**contributions to family home**
  businesses, contributions to 281–3
  clean break 177
  common intention 257, 260–89, 303–4
  constructive trusts 257, 272, 275, 278–85, 288, 303–4
  detrimental reliance 275, 277, 285–7
  domestic contributions 277–80, 284, 287–8, 303–4, 308
  economic disadvantage 310
  financial contributions 256–89, 303–4
  improvements 276–7, 285
  indirect contributions 257, 266, 274–84, 288
  indirect financial contributions 266, 278–84, 288
  joint names cases 255–6, 258, 277, 280, 284, 287, 303–4
  money and property distribution on marriage breakdown 210
  past contributions 177
  proprietary estoppel 289–95
  purchase price 257–8, 276, 280, 285–7, 313
  qualifying contributions 310
  reform 308, 310
  resulting trusts 256–64, 271, 285, 288–9
  sole name cases 258, 272–89
  special contribution argument 208–10
**control, children beyond parental** 677–8
**controlling behaviour** vii, 98, 102, 111–12
**convenience, marriages of** 24
**corporal punishment** 421, 453
**costs** lxiii, 71, 171, 187, 197, 218, 222
**counselling** 86–8, 91, 364–5, 371–2, 534, 600–1, 740

**criminal offences** 28–9, 111–12, 114, 123–6, 147–50, 152, 154–5; *see also* arrest
  accommodation for children 617
  adoption 722, 739
  bigamy 16, 388
  children, rights of 430, 432
  contact 530
  criminal injuries compensation 112
  divorce 75
  domestic violence 106
  fathers, parental responsibility of 396, 404, 415, 422
  forced marriages 25–6
  fraud 225
  harassment 153–6
  marital rape 106
  money and property distribution on marriage breakdown 195
  non-molestation orders, breach of 114, 117, 126, 149
  parental responsibility 415–16
  removal of children 510, 545, 547
  sexual offences 106, 397, 401–2, 736
**culture**
  children, rights of 428
  name, change of 562, 566
  parentage 361
  pluralism 428
  relocation of children 558
  scientific testing 361
  significant harm threshold 621
**custody rights** vii, 574–5, 577–8, 580–8

**damages** 25, 154–6, 183, 202, 376; *see also* compensation
**de facto relationships** lxviii–lxix, 37, 60, 408, 485, 711–12
**de jure relationships** lxviii, lxxi
**death**
  assisted fertilisation 374
  cohabitants 54–6
  domestic violence, statistics on deaths from 100, 164
  home-sharers 61
  presumption of death, decree of 16, 40–1, 93–4
  property rights 51
  separation agreements 239
  sperm after death, use of 374
**decree absolute** 7, 21, 71–2, 78, 80–1, 243, 478
**decree nisi** 7, 67, 72–3, 78, 80, 92
**decree of nullity** 6–7, 13, 15–16, 18–20, 22–3, 25–7, 298–9

**definition of family**
  law lxvi–lxvii
**delay**
  adoption 703, 705, 725
  children's guardian, role of 652
  contact with child in care 696
  divorce 71, 79, 87, 90
  occupation orders 151
  paramountcy or welfare principle 458, 696, 704, 725
  parental responsibility 419
  residence orders 485
**democratic society** lxxi, lxxiii, 353, 515, 526, 593, 717
**desertion** 65, 76–7, 94–5
**detrimental reliance** 274, 277, 285–7, 290–5, 303–4
**developmental interests** 429–30, 435
**direct contact** 512–15, 517–18, 520, 525–6, 530–1, 568–70, 739–41
**disabilities, persons with**
  child support 329
  children 329, 340, 394, 599, 601, 663, 668
  expenses 329
  mental disabilities 6, 20, 22, 122, 191, 332, 338
  need, children in 599, 601
  parents 619, 668
  respite care 601
  significant harm threshold 619
  wishes and feelings of child 599
**discipline of children** 421, 452
**disciplines, interaction with other** lxxvi, 26
**disclosure** 185, 225, 228, 230, 234, 236, 739–40
  frank 187–8, 225, 632
**discretion**
  adoption 725, 734–5
  care orders 692
  child support 332, 343
  children, rights of 433, 436
  contact 568, 694–5
  financial orders, variation of 244–5
  judges lxxv–lxxvi, 121–2, 142, 146–7, 181, 189–90, 504
  non-molestation orders 120
  occupation orders 131, 133–4, 136–7, 143–6
  parentage 356
  parental responsibility 393, 421
  pensions 217
  property disputes of cohabitants 311
  residence orders/child arrangements orders with respect to residence 493, 568
  rules lxxv–lxxvi

discretion (*Cont.*)
    sale of property 297
    section 8 orders 482, 568–9
discrimination lxxiv–lxxv,
    34–5, 42–3, 161–3, 197–9,
    406, 408–9
    adoption 708
    child arrangements orders with
        respect to residence 494–7
    children, rights of 427
    Convention on the
        Elimination of All Forms
        of Discrimination against
        Women 161–2
    domestic violence 161–2
    European Convention on
        Human Rights 8–9, 31,
        38–43, 62, 405–6
    fathers, against 389–90,
        405–11, 494–5
    home-sharers 62
    marriage 5, 31, 406–8
    marry, right to 5
    money and property
        distribution on marriage
        breakdown 187, 201–2
    parental care, lack of
        reasonable 668
    parental responsibility of
        fathers 389–90, 405–11
    prohibited degrees of
        relationship 8–9
    religion 496–7
    same-sex couples lxix,
        42–3, 496
    transsexuals and marriage 31
    unmarried
        fathers 389–90, 405–11
disease, venereal 17, 20–2, 38
dissolution of adult
    relationships 65–95; *see also*
    divorce
    civil partnerships 40
    cohabitation 96
    judicial separation 91
distress 84, 88–9, 96, 102, 121,
    444, 448–9
    causing
        contact orders 520,
            523, 527–30
        parental responsibility of
            fathers 397, 399–400, 404
        relocation of children 548,
            550, 553, 557, 559
divorce 22–4, 65–96, 167–72,
    188–92, 204–8, 214–23, 232–7;
    *see also* money and property
    distribution on marriage
    breakdown
    1 year bar 71
    2 years desertion for 76–7

2 years separation with
    consent 78, 91
5 years separation 78–9
Acts of Parliament, through 65
adultery
    collusion 65, 72
    definition 73
    intolerability 73
    proof 73
    reconciliation, periods of 74
    waiting period 91
appeals 71
attendance at court 73
behaviour 74–6, 89, 91
big money cases 70, 81
Booth Committee 67, 74, 84
Brussels II Revised 68, 70
children
    16, under 72
    before divorce, making
        arrangements 86
    behaviour allegations 74
    Children Act 1989 72
    higher education or
        training, in 72
    legal effects of divorce 81
    parental responsibility,
        continuation of 81
    policy 72
    Statement of Arrangements
        for the Children 72
    welfare reports 72
collusion 65, 72
condonation 65–6
consent 78, 91
constructive desertion 77
criminal offences,
    conviction of 75
criticism 83–6
decrees absolute 7, 21, 71–2, 78,
    80–1, 243, 478
decrees nisi 7, 67, 71–3,
    78, 80, 92
defended divorces 73
delay 71, 79, 87, 90–1
desertion for 2 years 76–7
developments in procedure 67
domestic violence 81
domicile 68, 82
EU law 81
Family Law Act 1996 86–9
fault 85, 91
five facts 70–80
forum shopping 69
future of divorce law 90
habitual residence 69
hardship 78–80, 87
Hemain injunctions 80
higher education or training,
    children in 72
history 65–7

illness, behaviour arising
    through 76
information meetings,
    attendance at 86, 88, 91
Inheritance (Provision for
    Family and Dependants) Act
    1975 81
intolerability 73
irretrievable breakdown 70–1,
    74, 84–7, 89
jurisdiction to hear a
    divorce 70, 81
Law Commission 23, 66, 79, 84–9
legal effects 80
living together
    behaviour, after 76
    desertion for 2 years 76–7
    living apart 77–8
    same household, in the 78
Matrimonial Causes Act
    1973 70–81
mediation and
    counselling 86, 91
mixed system of fault and
    no-fault divorce, proposal
    for 84, 89
Morton Commission 66
no-fault 66, 79, 89, 167, 192
nullity, distinguished from 7, 23
obtaining a divorce 89
occupation orders 139
offences 65–6
oral evidence 67, 73
orders 87
overseas divorce, recognition
    of 81–3
parental responsibility,
    continuation of 81
petitions 7, 70–2, 90, 94, 171
policy 73–4, 90
preventing divorce, orders 87
procedure 71–2
promotion of institution of
    marriage 90
Putting Asunder report 66
Queen's Proctor,
    intervention by 72
reconciliation
    adultery 74
    certificates 71
    condonation 65–6
    encouraging 71, 73, 76, 79, 84
reflection and consideration,
    period for 87–8, 90
reform 66–7, 84, 88–90, 167, 319
    proposals 91–3
Scotland 91
separation
    2 years with consent,
        for 78, 91
    5 years separation 77–9

special preparation 78–80
special procedure 67
state, interests of the 89
Statement of Arrangements for
the Children 72
statements of marital
breakdown 86–7
stay of proceedings in England
and Wales 70
stigma 22–3
talaq (Islamic divorce) 82–3
timetable 72–3, 87, 90
unilateral demand 90
waiting period 90
**DNA testing** lxxiii, 348, 352–3,
356, 358, 361, 406
**domestic abuse** 97–101, 106,
110–12, 154–5, 157, 578, 585;
*see also* domestic violence
coercive behaviour vii,
98, 111–12
controlling behaviour vii, 98,
102, 111–12
police response to victims
of vii, 110
**domestic contributions** 277–80,
284, 287–8, 303–4, 308
**domestic violence** lxi–lxii, 25, 53,
87–8, 96–167, 521–5, 642–3; *see
also* non-molestation orders;
occupation orders
adoption 710
aggravating factors 106
alcohol 121
and alcohol 121
antisocial/narcissistic
personality 104
asymmetry 101
attrition, high levels of 108–9
children
contact 163–4
effects on
children 101, 163–4
separation, dangers of contact
after 163–4
civil law remedies 109, 113–27,
150, 156
civil partners 40–1
cohabitants 53–5, 95
contact 529–30, 537
Convention on the
Elimination of All Forms
of Discrimination against
Women 161–2
criminal injuries
compensation 112–13
and criminal law 106–10
deaths, statistics on 100, 164
definition 97, 99–100, 157–8
dependency, relationships of 104
divorce 81

Domestic Violence
Disclosure Scheme
(DVDS) 110
and drug abuse 103, 121
emotional and psychological
abuse 98–102, 114–15
explanations 105
failure to report abuse 100, 107
fair hearing, right to a 160
family violence, use of term 98
feminist explanations 105
forced marriages 25, 27
gender-based violence 99–101,
104–5, 162
guidelines 522
harassment 153–6
harm, definition of 522
HMIC Report 110–11
home-sharers 61
homelessness 157–60
human rights 160–3
inhuman or degrading
treatment 161
injunctions 154–6
interim care and supervision
orders 643
international human rights
law 161–2
Law Commission 152–3
leave relationships, reasons for
not 102, 104
life, right to 160
local authority housing 160
men, against 100–1, 109
multifaceted phenomenon 105
parental responsibility of
fathers 403
patriarchal social order 105
persons not protected 153
police, attitudes 106
positive obligations 161
prevalence 100–3
private and family life, right to
respect for 160
protection notices 109
protection orders 109–10
psychological explanations 104
Sentencing Guidelines
Council 106
separation, violence
after 103, 163–4
significant harm threshold 618
social structural
explanations 105
Specialist Domestic Violence
Courts 107
statistics 100, 108, 164
structural inequality 105
terrorism 99
threatening or intimidating
behaviour 98–9

treaties and conventions on
human rights 161–3
UN Declaration on Elimination
of Violence against
Women 99–100
under-reporting 107
United Nations 98, 100, 160, 162
vulnerability 158–9
women's refuges 105
**domicile** 29, 68–9, 380, 411, 726
**donor sperm** 352, 367–9, 371,
373, 576
**driving licences** 327, 544
**drug abuse** 103, 121, 146, 614,
666, 679
**duress** 9, 17–20, 23–6, 223, 230,
233, 610
forced marriages 18, 20, 24, 26
marriage 18–19, 23–4, 35
overborne will 19
**Duxbury formula** 172, 197, 245
**DVDS (Domestic Violence
Disclosure Scheme)** 110

**early permanence placements** 714
**earmarking orders** 216–18
**earning capacity** 170–1, 178–9,
182, 184, 205–6, 247–8, 337–8
**economic disadvantage** 56, 201,
248, 304, 308, 310–12
**education** lxiv–lxv, 72, 398–9, 459,
463–4, 497–8, 606
full-time 159, 219, 323, 330, 334,
339, 418
**egg donations** 345, 363
**embryos, use of** 365, 374
**emergencies** 150, 629, 632–4,
675, 688; *see also* emergency
protection orders (EPOs
child protection 596, 639
police protection under Children
Act 1989 637–9
significant harm
threshold 629–30
**emergency protection orders
(EPOs)** 413–14, 571–2, 596,
615–17, 619, 623–5, 627–39
arrest 634
best interests test 630
care orders 690
causative link requirement 631
challenging EPOs 636
contact, directions with
regard to 630
discharge, applications for 635
enforcement 634
enquiries 630
exclusion requirement 634–5
extension 629
frustrated access grounds 630
grounds 634

**emergency protection orders (EPOs)** (*Cont.*)
  inherent jurisdiction of High Court 636
  interim care and supervision orders 641
  medical examinations or assessments 629, 633, 635
  obstruction 628
  parental responsibility 628–9
  police 637–8
  proportionality 632, 638
  removal for protection 629
  significant harm 629–30, 634–5
  social workers 633, 635
  undertakings 634
  without notice 630, 635
**emotional abuse** 98–100, 115, 618, 628, 634, 643, 724
**emotional and psychological abuse** 98–102, 114–15
**employment**
  child labour 428
  clean break 176
**enforcement orders** 535, 542–3
**engagement** 13, 20, 40, 116, 225, 240
**EPO**, *see* emergency protection order
**EPOs**, *see* emergency protection orders (EPOs)s
**equal sharing principle** 204–5, 207, 211, 232
**equality** 197–200, 205–6, 209, 219–20, 464–5, 498–9, 506–7
  yardstick 69, 197, 205
**estates** 5, 51, 53–5, 57, 96, 129–30, 145–6
**estoppel**, *see* proprietary estoppel
**European Convention on Human Rights** *see also* fair hearing, right to a; life, right to; private and family life, right to respect for
  child protection 593
  children, rights of 438, 451–2
  discrimination 8–9, 31, 38–43, 62, 405–6
  inhuman or degrading treatment 161, 628
  liberty and security, right to 151
  life, right to 161, 450
  living instrument doctrine 42
  margin of appreciation 31, 365, 375
  marry, right to 5, 24, 31–3, 42
  same-sex marriages 38, 42
  thought, conscience, and religion, freedom of 452, 686
**exceptional circumstances** 143, 146–8, 243–4, 298, 503, 518, 522
**exclusion orders** 297, 634

**exclusion requirements** 132, 142, 297, 571, 634–5, 640, 650–1
**executed mutual wills** 266
**experts** 562, 646, 661–3, 678, 681, 694, 697
  child protection lxxvi
  contact with children in care 697
  disagreement amongst experts 662–4
  section 37 directions 541
  significant harm threshold 664

**face-to-face contact**, *see* direct contact
**fact-finding hearings** lxiii, 524–5, 532, 662, 667, 672
**fair balance** lxxiii, 31, 353, 515, 582
**fair hearing, right to a**
  child support 327
  children, rights of 452
  committal 539
  domestic violence 160
  interim care and supervision orders 641
  occupation orders 151, 161
  section 8 orders 566
**fairness** 69, 197–8, 200–1, 218–19, 246, 263–4, 300
**false imprisonment** 25–6, 422
**family**
  child of the 181, 330–3, 337, 479
  natural lxxii–lxxiii, 355, 464–71, 700–1, 709–11, 730, 736–44
**family assistance orders** 476–7, 533, 683
**family home**, *see* matrimonial home; property disputes of cohabitants on relationship breakdown
**family life** lxi, lxx–lxxii, 161, 356, 519–20, 593–5, 711–12
  right to respect for, *see* private and family life, right to respect for
**family proceedings, definition** 477–8
**family stability** 49, 59
**family units** lxviii–lxix, 36, 66, 76, 531, 671, 673–5
**fathers and fatherhood** *see also* parental responsibility of fathers; parents
  adoption
    consent 709, 712, 737–8
    by fathers 727, 729–30
    identity 708–9
    parental responsibility 709
    private and family life, right to respect for 711–12
    withholding information 712

  agreed fatherhood conditions 370
  assisted reproduction 363, 374
  biological connection 372
  child support and lack of knowledge of paternity 331
  consent
    adoption 709, 712, 737–8
    embryos, destruction of 365
  death, use of sperm after 373–4
  discrimination 389–90, 405–11, 494–5
  embryos, father's consent to destruction of 365
  genetic connection 363
  Human Fertilisation and Embryology Act 1990 363–4
  Human Fertilisation and Embryology Act 2008 363–4
  identity 708–9
  information on fathers 391, 410–11, 708–12
  knowledge of paternity, lack of 331
  legal parenthood 362–4, 387
  legitimacy, presumption of 347–50, 359, 366
  lesbian couples 364, 373, 387, 399, 401, 496–7
  paternity, child support and lack of knowledge of 331
  private and family life, right to respect for 711–12
  sperm donors 352, 355–6, 369, 372, 374, 387
  transsexuals and marriage 375
  withholding information 712
**fault** 84–5, 89–90, 194–5, 247, 538, 668, 677
**features of family law** lxxv–lxxvi
**feelings of child**, *see* wishes and feelings of child
**female genital mutilation**, *see* FGM
**feminist writers**
  definition of family law lxvi
  domestic violence 105
**fertility treatment**, *see* assisted fertilisation
**FGM (female genital mutilation)** viii, 98, 622–3
**finality** 180, 191, 226, 228, 238, 241–2, 736
**financial contributions** 178, 209, 256–90, 303–4
**financial needs** 136, 170–1, 197–8, 201–2, 211–12, 246, 311–12
**financial obligations** 50, 54, 168, 170, 187–8, 334, 341

**financial orders** 168–9, 181–4, 204–5, 210–11, 228–9, 236–7, 251
**financial provision**, *see* money and property distribution on marriage breakdown; property disputes of cohabitants on relationship breakdown
**financial settlement orders** 61, 312–13
**financial support** 319–20, 322, 324, 326, 328, 330, 332
**forced marriages** 4, 6–7, 9, 18–20, 24–9, 56, 576
  arranged marriages distinguished 24
  arrest, protection orders with 28
  capacity 6
  Children Act 1989, significant harm under 26
  civil remedies 26
  consent 18, 20, 24, 26–7
  consummation 17–18
  criminal offences 25–6
  damages 26
  definition 24, 27
  domestic violence 25, 27
  duress 18, 20, 24, 26
  false imprisonment 26
  family law remedies 26
  forced marriage protection orders 26, 28
  Forced Marriage Unit 24–5
  harassment 26
  inherent jurisdiction of the High Court 26
  injunctions 25
  multi-agency approach 26
  nullity 24, 26–7
  oral evidence 26
  overseas, entered into 26
  time limits 27
  trespass to the person 26
  undertakings 28
  void marriages 24
  voidable marriages 24
  wardship and inherent jurisdiction of High Court, protection under 25–6
**formalities** 3, 6, 9–16, 24, 29, 31, 39
**formation of adult relationships** 3–62
  civil partnerships 42
  cohabitation 51
  home-sharers 61–2
  marriage 3–51
  non-formal relationships 51–62
**former relevant child** 605–7
**former spouses** 8–9, 116, 137–8, 142, 145, 211–14, 245–6
  non-entitled 137–9, 141
**forum shopping** 69, 234

**foster parents** 480, 489–92
**France** 232, 348, 352–3, 557, 586, 708
**frank disclosure** vii, 187–8, 225–8, 632
**fraud** 82, 222, 230, 236, 238, 255, 259
  and consent orders 226–8
**fraudulent non-disclosure** vii, 225–8
**freedom of expression** 452
**full-time education** 159, 219, 323, 330, 334, 339, 418

**gender** *see also* fathers and fatherhood; mothers and motherhood
  acquired 17, 21, 30–1, 33, 374
  child arrangements orders with respect to residence 493–5
  Convention of the Elimination of All Forms of Discrimination against Women 161–2
  domestic violence 98–101, 105, 162–3
  dysphoria 30, 33, 374–5
  human rights 162
  marriage 29–35
  patriarchal social order 105
  stereotyping 386
  UN Declaration on Elimination of Violence against Women 99–100
**gender reassignment**, *see* transsexuals and marriage
**gender recognition certificates** 21, 33–4, 374–5
**genetic connection** 345–6, 362, 372, 385–6
**genetic relationships**, *see* biological relationship
**genuine fear** 405, 529–30
**gifts** 116, 254–5, 257, 265, 273, 287–8, 293–4
**Gillick competency** 320, 357–8, 420, 431, 431–53, 565
**good faith** 237, 383
**grandparents** 388, 480–3, 492, 496–7, 540–1, 581, 711
**gross weekly income** 329
**guardians**, *see* children's guardian, role of; special guardianship orders

**habitual residence** vii, 69, 82, 574–82, 584–5, 587, 726
  country of 581, 584–6
  and international child abduction 575–9

**harassment** 101, 106, 109, 111–12, 114, 118, 153–6
  arrest 154
  civil remedies 153–4
  contempt of court 155
  course of conduct 154–5
  criminal offences 156
  damages 154–6
  definition 154
  domestic violence 153–6
  forced marriages 26
  injunctions 154, 156
  non-molestation orders 114–15, 119, 125, 154, 156
  occupation orders 149
  private nuisance 153
  Protection from Harassment Act 1997 118, 149, 153–6
  restraining orders 155–6
  sentencing 125
  stalking 153
  standard of proof 154
  telephone calls 153
  tort, creation of a 118, 153–4
**hardship**
  clean break 176–7
  divorce 78–80, 87
  financial orders, variation of 244
  judicial separation 91
  property disputes of cohabitants 298–9, 307, 309, 314
  significant lxii, 179, 188
  tenancies, transfers of 299
  undue 170, 176–7, 179, 181, 244
**harm** *see also* significant harm threshold
  balance of 133–5, 138, 141–4, 297
  committal 538
  contact 521, 528, 535, 538
  definition 522
  disruption causing harm 485–6
  domestic violence 98, 113–14
  emotional and psychological harm 98–102, 114–15, 528–30, 541, 583–5, 633, 643
  irreparable 428, 430, 436, 439
  section 8 orders 485–6
  section 37 directions 541
  significant 133–5, 143–7, 617–31, 637–41, 656–61, 673–7, 682–4
**health** 120–2, 135–6, 144, 597–9, 619, 625–6, 702–3
  mental 10, 20, 120, 433, 437, 597, 599
**Hemain injunctions** 69–70, 83
**Henshaw Report** 321–2
**High Court**, *see* inherent jurisdiction of the High Court
**HMIC Report** 110–11

**holiday, taking children on** 510, 547
**home rights** 41, 55, 128–31, 133, 137–8, 140, 253
  cohabitants 54, 95
  divorce 80
  marriage 50, 129
  non-molestation orders 114
  occupation orders 128, 130–3
  property disputes of cohabitants 253
**home-sharers** 3, 51, 56, 61–2, 308–9
**homelessness**
  children 159, 598, 600, 606–7
  Code of Guidance 160
  definition of homelessness 157
  domestic violence 157–60
    Code of Guidance 160
  intentional homelessness 160, 598, 600
  looked after children 606–7
  priority need 159, 606
  vulnerable persons 159
**homosexual couples**, *see* civil partnerships; same-sex couples; same-sex marriage
**hostility** 36, 74, 79, 84–5, 89, 398, 529
  implacable 517, 527–32, 536–7, 541, 544
**housing** 135–6, 138–9, 159, 188–9, 299, 598, 607; *see also* homelessness; local authority accommodation for children; matrimonial home
  domestic violence 156–60
  occupation orders 136
**housing fund** 233, 342–3
**Human Fertilisation and Embryology Authority (HFEA)** 364
**human rights** 5, 42, 351–2, 405–6, 409, 437, 587; *see also* European Convention on Human Rights; Human Rights Act 1998
  domestic violence 160–3
  gender-based violence 162
  International Covenant on Civil and Political Rights 593
  treaties and conventions 161–3
**Human Rights Act 1998** lxix–lxx, 32, 160–1, 451–2, 469–72, 474, 685
  adoption 724
  care plans 685, 687
  child arrangements orders with respect to residence 496
  children, rights of 437–8, 451–2
  Children Act 1989, compatibility of 471–2

discrimination lxix, 496
domestic violence 161–2
list of Convention rights lxx
medical treatment of children, consent to 450
paramountcy or welfare principle 471–2
positive obligations 161
relocation of children 547–8
same-sex couples lxix
transsexuals and marriage 32–3
**identity rights** 351–60
**ill-treatment** 134, 164, 486, 601, 617–18, 622, 631
**illegitimacy**, *see* legitimacy/ illegitimacy
**immigration rules** 5, 9, 24, 72
**improvements to properties** 276–8, 285, 294
**in-law marriages** 8
**inchoate rights** vii, 581
**indirect contact** 512–17, 525–6, 530, 537, 570, 741, 744
**infants** 350, 448, 463, 465, 506, 545, 737
**inferred common intention** 273, 276
**information**
  adoption 707–12, 739
  confidentiality 422, 709
  divorce 86, 88, 91
  exceptional circumstances, withholding information in 710
  fathers, on 391, 410–11, 708–12
  meetings, attendance at 86, 88, 91
  mothers, anonymity of 352
  protected information, definition of 739
  relatives, withholding information from 708–12
  separation agreements 225, 229
  withholding information 708–12
**inherent jurisdiction of the High Court** 6, 26–7, 571–2, 576–8, 588–90, 613–14, 650
  accommodation for children 613
  adoption 709
  assessments 650
  blood transfusions and Jehovah's Witnesses 572
  child protection 595
  emergency protection orders 636
  forced marriages 26
  interim care and supervision orders 650

local authorities 590
parental responsibility 589–90
section 8 orders 566–7, 572–90
wardship 26, 588–90, 595
**inheritance**, *see* succession
**Inheritance (Provision for Family and Dependants) Act 1975** 51, 53, 55, 81
**inheritance tax** lxxiv, 38, 51, 62
**inhuman or degrading treatment** 161, 451, 628
**injunctions** 120–1, 123, 131, 148, 153–6, 160, 724
  adoption 724
  divorce 80
  domestic violence 154–6
  forced marriages 25
  harassment 154–6
  Hemain 69–70, 83
**intent-based parenthood** 385–6
**intentions**
  changes of 270–1
  imputing of 263, 276, 281
  shared 261–3, 266, 280–1, 283, 288–9, 301–3
**interim care and supervision orders** 539, 541–2, 571–2, 615–16, 632, 640–6, 648–51
  assessments 650
  care plans 684
  change of circumstances 641
  child arrangements orders with respect to residence 640
  children's guardian, role of 650–2
  Cleveland Inquiry 649
  decisions on whether to grant order 641
  directions 650
  domestic violence 643
  duration of orders 641
  emergency protection orders 641
  exclusion from home 650
  fair hearing, right to a 641
  guidance 642
  inherent jurisdiction 650
  medical or psychiatric assessments 645–50
  paramountcy or welfare principle 643
  parental responsibility 639–40, 644, 649
  parents, assessment of 644–9
  private and family life, right to respect for 640
  proportionality 642
  psychotherapy 647–8
  reasonable grounds for belief 640

refuse assessments, child's right
to 649–50
residential
assessments 645, 648–9
significant harm 640, 645
threshold 640–1
time limits 640
**interim gender recognition
certificates** 17, 21, 33
**internal relocation** 508
**international child
abduction** lxxv, 552, 572–89
and child's wishes 585–7
and consent/acquiescence 584
criminal offence 573
and grave risk of harm/
intolerable situation 584–5
and habitual residence 575–9
Hague Convention on the civil
aspects 574–87
non-Convention countries 587
prevention 573
recovery of abducted
children 573
rules of return 583–7
and violation of human rights/
fundamental freedoms 587
wrongful removal or
retention 574, 580–2
**International Covenant on Civil
and Political Rights** 593
**intersexuals** 18, 30, 35
**intestacy** 51, 54–5, 58, 94, 96, 738
**intolerability, and divorce** 73
**investigations**
child protection 625–8, 652
children's guardian, role of 652
section 37 investigations, court's
power to order 626–7
significant harm 623–5
**irretrievable breakdown**
civil partners 95
divorce 70–1, 74, 84–7, 89
judicial separation 93
**Islamic State** 618

**Jehovah's Witnesses**
blood transfusions, consent
to 447–51, 572
child arrangements orders with
respect to residence 497
discrimination 496–7
**joint beneficial ownership,
presumption of** 260–2, 264–5,
267–9, 271, 302
**joint names, property in** 254–5,
258–73, 279–81, 287, 287–91,
301, 301–5
**joint residence orders** 60, 502
**joint tenants** 143, 259–60, 262,
270, 272, 297, 299

**judicial review** 607, 609, 611, 616,
623–4, 636, 687
**judicial separation** 6, 22, 65, 68,
93–4, 167, 171
decree of 22, 40, 65, 93–4, 298

**Law Commission**
clean break 168
cohabitants 51, 54
divorce 23, 66, 89
domestic violence 152–3
fathers, parental
responsibility of 411
marriage formalities 22–4
money and property
distribution on marriage
breakdown 193
non-molestation orders 114–15,
119–20, 152
occupation orders 127, 136–7,
140, 145, 150, 152
paramountcy or welfare
principle 461, 467
parental responsibility 411
property disputes of
cohabitants 253, 278–9, 301,
303, 307–11
shared residence orders 499
*Law Commission Report on
Matrimonial Property, Needs
and Agreements* 237
**learning disabilities/
difficulties** lxiii, 586, 600, 610,
619–20, 656, 668–9
**legal advice, lack of** 223
**legal aid** lxii–lxiv, 86, 103, 126,
214, 218, 546
**legal costs**, *see* costs
**legal parenthood** 345–7,
362–84, 387–9, 391, 410–11,
413, 742
assisted fertilisation 369, 371
biology 387
child support 320
consent to 372
criticism of the law 387
definition 346
fatherhood 346–7, 363–4, 387
gender stereotyping 386
Human Fertilisation
and Embryology Act
1990 364–9, 385
Human Fertilisation
and Embryology Act
2008 369–70, 385, 387
intent-based parenthood 385–6
lesbian couples 371, 387
motherhood 361, 363, 411
paramountcy or welfare
principle 386
parentage 347

parental responsibility 346, 387
persons not regarded as
parents 373–4
rationales for attributing
parenthood 387
responsibility/causation 386
social parents 387
sperm donors 373, 387
surrogacy and parental
orders 376, 382–3, 385–6
transsexuals 375
**legitimacy/illegitimacy** 347–8,
350–2, 354, 359, 366–7, 389, 562
Law Commission 389
name, change of 562–3
parentage 347–50, 359
parental responsibility of
fathers 389
presumption of
legitimacy 347–52, 354,
359, 366–7
**lesbian couples** 36, 41, 337, 371,
373, 399, 402
assisted fertilisation 41, 43,
337, 371
child arrangements orders with
respect to residence 467,
469, 493–6
civil partnerships 371
fathers and fatherhood 364, 373,
387, 399, 401, 496–7
legal parenthood 371, 387
mothers 41, 337, 387, 389, 399,
401, 467–8
parental responsibility 41, 43,
337, 389, 399
**life, right to** 160, 365
**life-saving treatment of children,
refusal of** 451, 571
**lifelong welfare** 379–80, 383
**lifestyle choices** 188, 245–7, 335,
343, 550, 639, 667
**limited company assets** 184
**living together after
divorce** 77–8
**local authorities** *see also* care
orders; children needing
services, care and protection;
local authority accommodation
for children; looked after
children; supervision orders
adoption 700–5
Children Act 1989 597
domestic violence and
housing 157–60
family assistance orders 476
functions 679–80
housing 157–60, 598, 606, 624
inherent jurisdiction 590
medical treatment,
consent to 571

local authorities (*Cont.*)
  parental responsibility 417,
    490–2, 571, 590, 604,
    683–7, 692
  prohibited steps orders 491, 571
  resources 476
  section 8 orders 486–91, 571
  specific issues orders 491,
    546, 571
  wishes and feelings of child 487
**local authority accommodation**
  **for children** 601–4
  16, where child is 613
  abuse in care 608
  agreements 614
  best interests test 614
  birth plans 616–17
  care and protection, in need
    of 614, 616
  Children Act 1989 604, 607
  coercion 614, 616
  complaints and
    representations 607–9
  compulsory intervention 616
  cooperation 612
  criminal assaults 617
  homelessness 159, 598,
    600, 606–7
  inherent jurisdiction of High
    Court 613
  looked after children 604–6
  paramountcy or welfare
    principle 613, 617
  parental responsibility 609,
    611, 613–17
  planning 614
  priority need 606
  private and family life, right to
    respect for 612–13, 616
  qualifications to voluntary
    nature 613–16
  residence orders/child
    arrangements orders with
    respect to residence 479, 481,
    490–2, 511, 613
  risk assessment 614, 616
  significant harm threshold 612
  unmarried fathers
    without parental
    responsibility 611, 613
  voluntary nature 617
  wishes and feelings of child 613
**Local Safeguarding Children**
  **Board (LSCB)** 27, 597
**lone parents**, *see* single parents
**long-term supervised**
  **contact** viii, 521
**looked after children**
  accommodation 604–6
  adoption 701
  age 605

assessments 605, 607
background of children,
  consideration of 605
care orders 686
Children Act 1989 607
educational achievement, duty to
  promote 604
eligible child, definition
  of 604–5, 607
former relevant child 605–7
homelessness 606–7
local authorities 604–7
parental responsibility 604
pathway plans 605
personal advisers 605
relevant child
  definition 605
  former relevant child 605–7
safeguard and promote
  welfare, duty of local
  authorities to 604
status 607
wishes and feelings of child,
  parents and persons with
  parental responsibility 604
**lump sums** 172–5, 190–3, 216–19,
  222–4, 240–5, 249–50, 334–6
  appeals 239–41
  child support 330, 332, 335, 337
  clean break 172
  during marriage 250
  Duxbury formula 172
  instalments 172, 242, 244–5
  Matrimonial Causes Act
    1973 168
  matrimonial home 218
  property disputes of
    cohabitants 308, 311
  remarriage 172
  variation 243–5

**maintenance** 171–2, 179–80,
  241–2, 248–50, 319–30, 338–40,
  395; *see also* child support;
  money and property distribution
  on marriage breakdown
  agreements 322–5, 329, 343
  calculation 322, 324, 327–9
  children 50, 70–2, 320–5, 328,
    332–3, 338–9, 457
  cohabitants 53–4, 56, 60
  costs 171
  definition of maintenance 171
  orders 324–5, 328–30, 340
  periodical payments orders 171
  remarriage 242
  suit, pending 171, 242
  variation 242
**margin of appreciation** 31, 62,
  352–3, 365, 375
**marital rape** 106

**marriage** 50; *see also* consent
  to marriage; forced marriage;
  money and property distribution
  on marriage breakdown; nullity
  of marriage
  adoption 50, 736
  age 4, 9
  already married, where
    party is 16
  approved premises, definition
    of 10–11
  armed forces, overseas
    marriages of 29
  arranged marriages 19, 24–6, 30
  banns 10
  bars to relief 21
  bigamy, criminal offence
    of 16, 388
  capacity to marry 5–6, 18,
    20–2, 29, 35
  ceremonies 4, 10, 13–14, 16,
    19–20, 29–30, 375
  civil 4, 10–13, 18
  certificates 10
  children 38, 330
  Christian concept 3, 10, 22–4
  civil ceremonies 4, 10–13, 18
  civil partners
    distinguished 38, 40, 42
  cohabitants
    commitment, level of 305–6
    comparison with
      marriage 299–300, 306,
      309, 314
    ideological superiority,
      maintaining 311, 314
    policy 314
    reputation of marriage,
      with 16
    undermining 306
  commitment, level of 60, 306
  consummation 18, 22
  convenience, marriages of 24
  cousins 8
  death, presumption of 94
  decline in marriage 305
  definition 3
  discrimination 5, 31, 406–8
  duress 18–19, 23–4, 35
  fathers, parental responsibility
    of 388, 405–7
  forced, *see* forced marriages
  formalities
    ceremonies 10–11
    failure to comply 9–16
    overseas marriages,
      recognition of 29
    preliminary formalities 10
    presumptions of marriage 16
  home rights 50
  identity, mistakes as to 19–20

ideological superiority,
maintaining 311, 314
in-laws 9
inheritance tax 38
intersexuals 35
Law Commission 22–4
legal consequences 51
male and female parties 7, 29,
32, 35, 366, 375
mental disabilities, persons
with 6, 20, 22, 35
mistake 19–20
name, change of 565
non-marriages 6, 12–13
by non-religious belief
organisations 11–12
notice 10
overseas marriages, recognition
of 27, 29, 44
parental responsibility of
fathers 388, 405–7
parents
consent of 9
parental responsibility 38
pensions 38
policy 313
polygamous marriages 4, 7
pregnancy by another man 17,
20–1, 23
presumptions of marriage 15–16
prohibited degrees of
relationship 8–9, 736
rape within marriage 106
religion 1, 3, 10–18, 22–4, 29, 44
right to marry 3, 5, 24, 30–3, 43
same-sex marriages 29–44
sham 12, 24, 196
sham marriages 24
state's interest in marriage 5
statistics 304
step-families 8
tax 38
transsexuals 17–18, 21–2, 32, 35
validity 5–44
venereal disease, persons
with 20–2, 35
void marriages 6–35, 94, 323,
366, 375, 388
voidable marriages 6, 16–24
voluntary union, as 3–5
vulnerable adults,
protection of 6
**marry, right to**
discrimination 5
European Convention on
Human Rights 5, 24, 31–3, 42
living instrument doctrine 42–3
same-sex marriages 42–3
sham marriages 24
transsexuals 31–3
**Martin orders** 220–1

**maternity**, *see* mothers and
motherhood
**matrimonial assets** 69, 183, 196,
208, 313
**matrimonial home** 129–31,
143–7, 173–4, 215–21, 253–8,
275–9, 297–8
adulthood, postponement of
realisation of share until
children reach 221
age of parties 189
appeals 238, 240
big money cases 219
charges 221
children 218–20
clean breaks 218–19
co-ownership 219–22
contributions to welfare of
family 192–210
costs 218
court, powers of 218–22
legal aid 218, 221
lump sums 218
mortgages 221
orders for sale 170, 174,
218, 311–12
paramountcy or welfare
principle 182
pensions 216
periodical payments orders 218
postponement of realisation of
one party's share 221
postponement of sale until
specified event 219–21
proceeds of sale 218, 247
property adjustment orders, *see*
property adjustment orders
remarriage or cohabitation with
new partner 240
sale of property 174, 218, 243
sole names, property transferred
in 218–19
statutory charge 218, 221
tenancies, transfer of 221
**maturity** 358, 439, 448–50, 452,
578–9, 583, 585–7
**mediation** lxiv, 84–8, 91–3,
222, 534
**medical evidence** 30, 396, 611, 622,
634, 656, 662
**medical examinations or
assessments** 629, 633, 635,
645–50, 688–9
**medical treatment**, *see* consent to
medical treatment of children
**mental disabilities/illness, people
with** 6, 20–2, 121–2, 191, 332,
338, 444–5; *see also* capacity
**mental health/illness** lxiii, 20, 22,
120–2, 597, 599, 639
**Mesher orders** 177, 219–20

**misrepresentation** 222–3, 227,
230, 238, 402, 438, 616
**mistake, marriage and** 19–20
**molestation** 110, 113–15, 118–19,
121–2, 127, 153–4, 158
**money and property distribution
on marriage breakdown** 167;
*see also* child support;
clean break; lump sums;
matrimonial home; periodical
payments orders; property
adjustment orders
age of parties 189–91
all the circumstances, having
regard to 181, 189
ante-nuptial agreements 229–37
appeals and rehearings 237–49
background to current law 167
Barder test 242
before divorce, making
arrangements 86
big money cases 69–70, 81, 191,
197, 201, 206, 209
capital 185
children 181, 188–9, 249–50
civil partners 40, 95
classification of
property 187, 206
conduct 195, 209
consent orders 244
costs penalties 188, 195
county court,
applications to 249
courts' powers 171–4
criminal offences 195
damages 183
decrees nisi and decrees absolute,
time between 72
deferred orders 169
dependants 188–9
disclosure 188
discretion 181
discrimination 201, 206
divorce 67, 69, 72, 80–1, 86
Domestic Proceedings and
Magistrates' Courts Act
1978 249
duration of marriage 189
during marriage,
orders 249–50
earning capacity 185, 249
equality, yardstick of 69, 206
expectations of inheritance 183
fault 195
finality principle 237–42
financial and property
agreements 221–37
financial needs, obligations and
responsibilities 189
financial provision
orders 169, 249–50

**money and property distribution on marriage breakdown** (*Cont.*)

financial resources of each spouse 183–8

full and frank disclosure 188

general directions 181

hardship 244

High Court, applications to 249

income 185

inequitable to disregard, type of conduct which it is 193–5

inheritance 188, 206

judicial separation 94

Law Commission 169, 193, 210

legal effects of divorce 80–1

legislative framework 169–74

lifestyle choices 245–6

magistrates' courts, applications to 249–50

maintenance pending suit 171–2, 242

Matrimonial Causes Act 1973 169–71

matrimonial/non-matrimonial property, classification of 187, 206

mental disabilities 191

minimal loss principle 169

new partners 186–206, 240, 242, 249

nominal orders 245, 247, 249–50

nullity of marriage 6–7, 35, 44

overseas divorces, recognition of 81–2

paramountcy or welfare principle 181, 244

pensions 169, 181–218, 244–5

physical disabilities 191

policy 181

power of sale 169, 173–4

pre-marital cohabitation 189–91

public interest 237–42

remarriage 186, 216, 218, 221, 240, 242

resources provided by new spouse or partner 185–6

secured periodical payments orders 169, 172, 243–5, 249–50

separation agreements 222–4, 229, 242

settlement orders 173, 312, 335

special contribution argument 208–10

special protection in separation divorces 80

standard of living before marriage breakdown 189

time limit for application for financial provision 212–14

undertakings 174

variation of financial provision orders 242–9

**mortgages** 132, 264–5, 267–8, 270–2, 274–9, 282, 287–90

**Morton Commission** 66

**mothers and motherhood** 337–43, 358–63, 384–92, 395–401, 492–8, 535–41, 557–66; *see also* parents

alcohol and drugs, abuse of 407

anonymity 352

assisted fertilisation 367

best interests of babies 493–5

egg donations 362

fathers, unmarried mothers as less worthy than unmarried 407

genetic connection 362

Human Fertilisation and Embryology Act 1990 363

legal parenthood 362, 411

lesbian couples 41, 337, 371, 387, 389, 399, 401

parental responsibility 388–9, 407, 411

residence orders/ child arrangements orders with respect to residence 467–8, 493

surrogate mothers vii, 366–8, 376–9, 381–5, 387

**name, change of child's**

birth certificates, names on 561

culture 561, 563, 565–6

Gillick competency 565

illegitimacy 562–3

marital status of parents 565

paramountcy or welfare principle 561

parental responsibility 563

religion 566

residence orders 563

specific issues orders 546, 561–6

wishes and feelings of child 564

**natural family** lxxii–lxxiii, 355, 464–71, 700–1, 709–11, 730, 736–44

**need**

children in 546, 598–600, 602–3

principle of 203

**neglect** 593, 595, 597, 601, 628, 631, 682

**new partners, remarriage or cohabitation with** 172, 185–7, 240–2, 249

**no-fault divorce** 66, 79, 89, 93, 167, 192

**nominal orders** 176, 245, 247, 249–50

**non-accidental injuries** 611, 631, 646, 663, 666, 670

**non-consummation** 17, 22, 26, 38, 40, 46

**non-disclosure** 187, 223, 225, 234, 238; *see also* disclosure

fraudulent vii, 225–8

**non-formal adult relationships** 51–62

**non-marriage** 6, 11–15

**non-matrimonial property** 200, 206–8, 210–12, 231, 236, 251

**non-molestation orders** vii, 96–7, 99, 114–29, 147–52, 155–6, 158

alcohol 121

applications 115–20

arrest, powers of 114, 117, 123

associated persons 114–15, 117–20

breach

arrest, powers of 114, 117, 123

criminal offence, as 114, 117, 122–6, 149

sentencing 123–5

children

applicants, as 120

relevant child 115–17, 120

civil partners 41

cohabitants 56, 96, 115–17, 119

consent 152

contempt of court 122–5

criminal offence, breach as a 114, 117, 122–6, 149

criteria 120

definition 114–15

discretion 120, 122

drug abuse 121

emotional abuse 114–15

enforcement 118, 122–6

harassment 114–15, 119, 125, 154, 156

home rights 114

Law Commission 114–15, 119, 152

legal aid 120, 126

mental illness 121–2

occupation orders 120

police, applications by the 152

relevant child 115, 117, 120

research 125–6

same-sex couples 117, 119

sentencing 123–5

standard of proof 120

third parties, applications by 152

threats 114

undertakings 149

unintentional conduct 120–2

victims' right to enforce order in civil courts 124

who can apply 115–20, 152

**non-religious belief organisations** 11–12

**non-resident parents** 218, 323–8, 505, 510–12, 532–3, 537–8, 590
**nuisance** 148, 153–4
**nullity of marriage** 6–7, 13, 19–24, 26–7, 35, 167, 170–1
  civil partners 40
  consent 19–20
  decrees absolute 6–7
  decrees nisi 6–7
  divorce, distinguished from 7, 23
  financial and property consequences 6–7, 44
  forced marriages 7, 20, 24, 26–7
  gender recognition 21
  intersexuals 35
  Law Commission 24
  mental disabilities, persons with 19–20
  mistake 19–20
  non-marriages 11
  pregnancy by another man 17, 20–3
  religion 22–4
  time limits 21, 26
  transsexuals 21, 375
  voidable marriages 21–2, 35
**nuptial agreements** 212, 229–31, 236, 251
  qualifying 236

**occupation, right of**, *see* home rights
**occupation orders** 96–7, 126–37, 139, 141–52, 160–1, 165, 297
  applications 128
  arrest, powers of 113–14, 151
  associated persons 113–14, 128, 130
  balance of harm test 132, 135, 141, 151
  breach 113–14, 149
  causation 134–5
  checklist 133, 135–7, 141–2
  children
    balance of harm test 145
    criteria 132–3
    health, safety, and well-being 136–7
    non-molestation orders 120
    paramountcy principle 134, 136
  civil partners 41, 128–31, 137–9
  cohabitants 54–5, 95, 131, 137–42
  conduct 134–7
  consent 152
  contempt of court 149
  courts, approach of 130–2, 137, 143–7
  criteria 132–3

declaratory occupation orders 128, 130, 133
delay 150–1
discretion 130, 132–4, 136–7, 141–5
divorce 137
duration of orders 137, 141–2
enforcement 132, 147–9, 151
entitled applicants 128–30, 137
ex parte orders 150–1, 161
exclusionary orders 131
existing right to occupy, cohabitants or former cohabitants with no 137, 139
fair hearing, right to a 151, 161
fault 132
financial needs and resources 136
former spouses, civil partners, or cohabitants 137–9
granting occupation rights 139
harassment 148–9
health, safety, and well-being of parties or children 136–7
home rights 128, 130–3
housing needs 136
interim orders 137
Law Commission 134, 136–7, 145, 150, 152
liberty and security, right to 151
living areas, dividing up 130–1
neither party is entitled to occupy, where 142
non-entitled occupants 128–9, 137–42
non-molestation orders 120
orders that can be made 130–2
ouster orders 132
police, applications by the 152
private and family life, right to respect for 151
prohibited steps orders 543–4
regulatory occupation orders 128, 133, 139, 141, 144–5
relationship breakdown 137
rent and mortgage payments, responsibility for 132
repair and maintenance, responsibility for 132
sentencing 148–9
spouses 128–31, 137–9
undertakings 150
who can apply 128–30, 152
**orders for sale** 218, 310, 312
**ordinary trust principles** 254, 258–9, 296
**orphans** 675–7
**ouster orders** 131–2
**overseas dissolutions, recognition of** 40, 95

**overseas divorce, recognition** 81–3
  big money cases 81
  domicile 81–2
  EU law 81
  financial orders 81–2
  habitual residence 82
  Hemain injunctions 83
  refusal of recognition 82
  talaq (Islamic divorce) 82–3
  unconscientiously, oppressively, or vexatiously, acting 83
**overseas marriages** 29, 40, 42, 95
  forced marriages 26–7
  recognition 27, 29, 40, 44, 95
  same-sex marriages 42, 44

**paramountcy or welfare principle** 455–74; *see also* best interests test; welfare checklist
  accommodation for children 613, 617
  adoption 704, 711, 716, 725, 730, 740, 742
  background 455–62
  care orders 595, 643–4, 686–7, 692
  child protection 595–9
  child support 338–9
  children, rights of 452–3
  Children Act 1989 455, 471–2, 474
  contact 517, 520, 527, 534, 537–8, 695–7
  criticism 472–4
  decision-making principles 455–62, 472–4
  definitions 463–71
  delay 458, 696, 704
  directly in issue, welfare must be 457
  fathers, parental responsibility of 394, 396–7
  financial orders, variation of 244
  Human Rights Act 1998 471–2
  impliedly or expressly excluded by other provisions, must not be 457
  interim care and supervision orders 643–4
  Law Commission 461, 467
  legal parenthood 386
  looked after children 604
  medical treatment of children, consent to 450–1
  money and property distribution on marriage breakdown 181, 202
  more than one child 458
  name, change of 561
  occupation orders 134, 136

**paramountcy or welfare principle** (*Cont.*)
no order principle 460–2
paramountcy principle 455, 458, 472, 474
parentage 350
parental responsibility 394, 396–7, 421, 465
police protection 638
private and family life, right to respect for 470–2
private law disputes 455
religion 497–8
relocation of children 548–9, 551, 553–5, 558–60
residence orders/child arrangements orders with respect to residence 497–8, 504, 507–9
section 8 orders 482, 487–90, 568–9
shared residence orders 504, 507–9
significant harm threshold 657, 678
sterilisation 466
supervision orders 643–4, 690
surrogacy 377, 383
transparency 473–4
upbringing or administration of child's property 457
when principle applies 455–8
**parentage** 345–7, 349, 351, 353–5, 359–61, 368–9, 391
anonymity of mothers 352
best interests of the child 347–51, 357–8
consent 357–8
contact 355–61
cultural factors 361
declarations of 323, 347, 349, 372, 403
definition 346
disclosure to children 361
discretion 356
DNA testing 349, 353, 357, 361
evidence 351, 355, 361
failure to comply with directions 359–60
fair hearing, right to a 351
genetic origins, recognition of interests in knowing 350–60
Gillick competency 357
identity rights 351–61
inferences to be drawn from failure to comply directions 361
legitimacy, presumption of 347–50, 359
paramountcy principle 350
parental responsibility 346, 354–8

parenthood 346–7
private and family life, right to respect for 351–3, 357
proof of paternity 349
scientific testing, directions for 348–50, 354–61, 391
sperm donation 351–2, 355, 357
UN Convention on the Rights of the Child 353–5
**parental alienation syndrome** 527–8, 541
**parental control** 433, 457, 653, 669, 677–8, 686, 688
**parental involvement** 409, 416, 459, 483, 515–16, 518, 570
presumption of 416, 459
**parental orders**, *see* surrogacy and parental orders
**parental responsibility** 386–422, 435–8, 499–503, 510–12, 544–7, 609–15, 685–8; *see also* parental responsibility of fathers
abuse, removal of responsibility due to 416
accommodation for children 609, 611, 613–17
adoption 413, 686
agreements 41, 56, 390, 392, 411, 414–15, 730
alcohol and drug abuse 407
allocation 388–413
alone, each holder may act 419
autonomy of child 421
birth certificates 411, 414
care orders 511, 684–7, 692
care plans 683–4
child protection 593, 599
child support 320, 417, 450
Children Act 1989 411–21
civil partners 41
cohabitants 56
complexity of responsibilities 418
confidentiality 422
consent, issues requiring 419
consulted on various issues, right to be 419
contact 480, 491–2, 512
content and scope 419–22
criminal offences 416
definition 396, 418
delay 410, 419
discipline 421
discretion 421
divorce 81
duration 414–15
emergency protection orders 628–9
exercise of 396–9, 401–2, 419, 421–2, 424, 571–2, 745–6
female parents 411

guardians, appointment of 413–14
guidance 418–19
inherent jurisdiction 589–90
interim care and supervision orders 639–40, 644, 649
jurisdiction 653
Law Commission 414
lesbian couples 41, 43, 337, 389, 399, 402
local authorities 412, 415, 417, 490–1, 571, 683–7, 692
looked after children 604
marriage 38
medical treatment, consent to 416–17, 438–9
more than two people with parental responsibility 387
mothers 388–9, 407, 411
name, change of 565–6
nature and scope 417–22
non-resident parents, diminishing responsibility of 510–11
paramountcy or welfare principle 421, 465
parentage 354–8
parental responsibility agreements 411, 414–15
parental responsibility orders 358, 411, 415
position of persons without parental responsibility 416–17
prohibited steps orders 544–5
reasonableness 421–2
religion 421
relocation of children 547
removal 415–17
residence orders/child arrangements orders with respect to residence 412–14, 419, 480, 499, 501, 510–11
restrictions 421–2
section 8 orders 56, 480, 482, 490–1, 571
shared residence orders 499, 501
shared responsibility 418
significant harm threshold 657
special guardianship orders 413, 745
specific issues orders 545–6
step-parents 411–12, 745
supervision orders 690
surrender 419
transfer 419
unmarried fathers 611, 613
wishes and feelings 604
**parental responsibility of fathers** 388–422
acquisition by unmarried fathers 404

adoption 389, 709
age 388
allocation 388–422
attachment 394
bigamy 388
birth certificate, registration
    on 390–1, 411
capacity 391, 396
certainty 396
Children Act 1989 346,
    388–404, 407
commitment, level of 390, 394,
    397, 403, 407
conditional orders 397, 399
criminal convictions 396–7,
    402–4, 406, 415–16, 422
denial, reasons for 404
disclosure of information on
    father 391, 410–11
discretion 393
discrimination and equal
    treatment 389–90, 396–7,
    399, 404–11
domestic violence 403
dual parenting, child's
    right to 410
foreign element 389
how responsibility
    might be exercised,
    focus on 396–7
illegitimacy 389
inappropriate use cases 400–3
interference from fathers 396,
    401, 406
irresponsibility,
    encouraging 409
Law Commission 406, 410–11
lesbian partners 389
local authorities 392
maintenance 394, 396, 408
marriage
    adoption 389
    discrimination 405–7
    reasonable belief in
        validity 388
    void marriages 388
mothers
    married couples 388–9
    no power to override
        decisions 396, 401
non-legal parents 346
paramountcy or welfare
    principle 394, 396–7
parentage 346
parental responsibility
    agreements 390–2
parental responsibility
    orders 368, 392–404, 406,
    410, 415–16, 420, 422
    applications 392–404
    conditional orders 397, 399
    hedging the order 397, 399

reasons for
    applying 396, 400–2
parenthood 346
policy 410
previous behaviour 403–4
private and family life, right to
    respect for 404–6
reasons for applying 396, 400–2
same-sex partners 389
scientific testing 391
self-esteem of child 394
sexual offences 396–7, 401–2
social change and attitudes,
    changes in 408, 410
status, as designed to confer
    a 396, 404, 406
time of birth, unmarried
    at 388–9
unmarried fathers 368, 388–404
    acquisition, by 390–404
    commitment, degree of 390
    discrimination 389–90,
        404–11
    mothers, as less worthy
        than 407
    parental responsibility
        orders 392–404
    time of birth, unmarried
        at 388–9
    unmeritorious
        fathers 389–90, 406–9
unmeritorious fathers 406–9
void marriages 388
**parenthood** 345–7, 363–5, 370–2,
    374–5, 385–7, 422, 468–70
    attribution rationales 385–6
    intent-based 385–6
    legal, see legal parenthood
    and transsexuals 374–5
**parenting** 41, 164, 304, 346, 386,
    409, 618–21
**parents** 323, 334–7, 345–422,
    481–2, 487, 709–10, 714; see
    also fathers and fatherhood;
    legal parenthood; mothers and
    motherhood; parentage; parental
    responsibility
    absent 188, 409, 512–13, 518–19,
        521, 536–7, 657
    adoptive lxxii, 385–6, 484–5,
        700–2, 736–8, 740–1, 743
    assessments 646
    child support 323
    control, where child is
        beyond 677–8
    definition 323
    different senses of parent 345–6
    disabilities, with 619, 668
    interim care and supervision
        orders, see interim care and
        supervision orders
    learning disabilities, with 668

marriage, consent to 38
natural, see natural family
non-resident 218, 323–8, 505,
    510–12, 514, 537–8, 590
parental alienation
    syndrome 527
residential 55, 177, 218, 510–11,
    514, 523, 568
single lxvii, 376, 549,
    703, 727–30
social 320, 337, 345, 354,
    362, 386–7
substitute 456, 470–1
terminology 346–7
unmarried 51, 59, 338–43, 388,
    390, 392, 396
violent 164, 457, 523
wishes and feelings of
    parents 487, 605
**paternalism** 425, 427, 430
**paternity**, see fathers and
    fatherhood
**pathway plans** 605–6, 616
**patriarchal social order** 104–5
**Payne discipline** vii, lxxvi, 471–2,
    508, 548–58, 566
**pensions**
    discretion 217
    duty to consider parties'
        entitlements 215
    earmarking orders 216–18
    loss of entitlements 215
    marriage 38
    matrimonial home, transfer of
        interest in 216
    money and property distribution
        on marriage breakdown 218
    pension-sharing orders 243–5,
        310, 312
    pension splitting 216, 218
    periodical payments 216
    property disputes of
        cohabitants 311
    splitting 216–17
    variation 244–5
**periodical payments orders** 171,
    176–81, 186–7, 201, 204,
    217, 242–50
    appeals 240–1
    capitalisation 240–1, 244–8
    child support 250, 330, 332–3,
        336, 340, 342–3
    clean break 175–80
    consent orders 248
    during marriage 249–50
    extension 244–7
    maintenance 171
    matrimonial home 218
    money and property distribution
        on marriage breakdown 169
    new partners 185–7, 241, 248
    pensions 216

**periodical payments
orders** (*Cont.*)
price fluctuations 239
property disputes of
cohabitants 311–14
remarriage or cohabitation with
new partner 185–7, 241
secured periodical payments
orders 169, 249–50, 332–3
variation 242, 244–9
**personal advisers** 605
**personal identity** lxxi, 31, 351–2,
373, 696
**physical separation** 77–9
**physical violence** 98, 100–2, 115,
137, 145–7, 151, 158
**place of safety orders** 595, 654
**plans**
accommodation for
children 614
adoption 708
birth plans 615–16
care plans 683–5, 687
looked after children 604–5
pathway plans 605
significant harm threshold 627
**police**
adoption and police checks 707
emergency protection orders,
execution of 635
non-molestation orders,
applications for 152
police protection under Children
Act 1989 417, 615, 623–4, 630,
637, 637–9, 642
**polygamous marriages** 4, 7
**possible perpetrators of harm to
children** 670–2, 674, 682
**post-adoption contact** 484,
704, 739–43
**post-nuptial agreements** 224, 230,
230–1, 234, 236
**poverty** 57, 59, 61, 104, 167,
212, 620
**pre-nuptial agreements,** *see*
ante-nuptial agreements
**predictability** lxix, 210, 237, 403
**pregnancy by another man, and
marriage** 17, 20–3
**presumptions**
of capital sharing 192, 204
of death, decree of 16,
40–1, 93–4
of joint beneficial
ownership 260–2, 264–5,
267–9, 271, 302
of legitimacy 347–8, 350–2, 354,
359, 366–7
of marriage 15–16
of parental involvement 416, 459

**primary carers** 177, 341, 548–50,
552–3, 556–7, 580, 670
**private and family life, right to
respect for**
accommodation for
children 612–13, 616
adoption 712, 717, 730
care plans 687
child arrangements orders with
respect to residence 496–8
children, rights of 438, 452
contact 514, 516, 536
domestic violence 160
embryos, father's consent to
destruction of 365
fathers
adoption 712
embryos, consent to
destruction of 365
Gillick competency 438
identity rights 351–3
interim care and supervision
orders 640
occupation orders 151
paramountcy or welfare
principle 470–2
parentage 351–3, 357
parental care, lack of
reasonable 667–8
parental responsibility of
fathers 404–6
positive obligations 352
religion 686
relocation of children 553, 557
sale of property 298
same-sex couples 496
transsexuals and marriage 31,
33, 375
**private law disputes in children
cases** 455–590; *see also* section
8 orders
**private life** 31, 42, 99, 351, 353,
356, 398
**private nuisance** 153
**prohibited degrees of relationship**
adoption 736
affinity 8
biological, moral, and social
reasons 8
consanguinity 8–9
cousins, genetic consequences
for children of marriage
between 8
discrimination 8–9
in-law marriages 8–9
step-parents and step-children 8
**prohibited steps orders** 475, 487,
491, 509–10, 544, 544–5, 571
adoption 720
contact 475, 544

definition 475
local authorities 491, 571
occupation orders 543–4
parental responsibility 544–5
relocation within UK 545
removal, preventing 545
section 8 orders 543–5
**proof** *see also* standard of proof
burden of proof 293, 370, 518,
659, 662, 664–6, 672
care proceedings, final hearings
in 657–66
paternity 347, 349
significant harm threshold 664
**property,** *see* money and property
distribution on marriage
breakdown
**property adjustment orders**
child support 336–7, 339
civil partners 40, 95
clean break 173
duration of marriage 191
during marriage 249–50
fairness and equality 69
history 67
judicial separation 94
legal effects of divorce 80–1
Matrimonial Causes Act
1973 170
periodical payments orders 172
property disputes of
cohabitants 253, 300,
308, 311
property transfer orders 172–3
settlement orders 173
variation 172, 243–5
**property disputes of cohabitants
on relationship breakdown** 52,
253, 314
advancement,
presumption of 256
bankruptcy 298
beneficial ownership
establishing 255–6, 273–87
joint names cases 255, 258–73
quantification 258, 261–72,
280–3, 287–90, 301–2
sole name cases 258, 273–87
trusts of land 295–8
businesses, contributions
to 281–3
children
advancement,
presumption of 256
Children Act 1989 300–1
discretion 311
financial settlement orders,
proposal for 312
reform 56, 310–12
tenancies, transfers of 299

trusts of land 298
choosing to avoid relationship
regulation 52, 304, 311
civil partnerships 309
Cohabitation Bills 51–3, 56–7,
60, 62, 312–13
commitment, level of 60, 306
common intention
ascertainment 263
constructive trusts 257, 273,
301, 304
contributions 257,
260–89, 303–4
detrimental reliance 285–7
evidence 285, 302–3
express common
intention 274–6
household finances,
organisation of 278, 302–3
inferred common
intention 276–8
joint names cases 262, 273,
289, 301, 304
purchase price
contributions 276,
280, 285–7
reform 301–3, 309
resulting trusts 260–4
sole name cases 273–8
constructive trusts 257, 273, 275,
278–85, 288–9, 304
contributions
businesses, contributions
to 281–3
common intention 257,
260–89, 303–4
constructive trusts 257, 272,
275, 278–85, 288–9, 303–4
detrimental reliance 275,
277, 285–7
domestic
contributions 277–80, 284,
287–8, 303–4, 308
economic disadvantage 310
financial
contributions 256–89,
303–4
improvements 276–7,
285, 293–4
indirect contributions 257,
274–84, 288–9
indirect financial
contributions 266,
278–84, 288–9
joint names cases 255–6,
258–72, 287–9, 303–4
purchase price 257–8, 276,
280, 285–7, 313
purchase price resulting
trusts 257–8

qualifying contributions 310
reform 308, 310
resulting trusts 256–64, 271,
285, 288–9
sole name cases 258, 272–89
criteria for determining
applications 297–8
declarations of trust 255,
258–60, 267, 269
deeds 253
detrimental reliance 275, 278,
285–7, 289–95
discretion 298, 311
domestic contributions 277–80,
284, 287–8, 303–4, 308
duration of relationship 52, 60,
265, 308, 310, 312
economic disadvantage 310–11
equity, satisfying 294–5
evidence 285, 302–3
exclusion orders 298
express trusts 255, 259–60
financial
contributions 256–89, 303–4
Fowler v Barron 264–7
hardship 298–9, 307, 309, 313
home rights 253, 298
household finances, organisation
of 278, 302–3
ideologues, romantics,
pragmatists, and uneven
couples 52, 306
implied trusts 255–7, 314
improvements 276–8, 285, 293–4
increase in
cohabitation lxvii, 1, 304
indirect contributions 257,
274–84, 288–9
indirect financial
contributions 278–84, 288–9
inducement 293
joint names cases 255, 258–73,
287–9, 301–4
Jones v Kernott 267
Law Commission 253, 278–9,
301, 303, 307–12
Law Society 308
legal ownership,
establishing 253, 255
lump sum orders 308, 311–12
marriage
commitment, level
of 60, 305–6
comparison with 60, 95–6,
299–300, 304–6, 309–14
decline in marriage 304
ideological superiority,
maintaining 311, 313–14
policy 313–14
undermining 60, 306

non-couple situations 273,
308, 310
opt-in/opt-out schemes 308, 312
orders for sale 311–12
pension-sharing orders 310, 312
periodical payments
orders 311–13
policy 52, 313–14
private and family life, right to
respect for 298
property adjustment orders 253,
300, 308, 311–12
property law principles 253–9
proprietary estoppel 281, 289–95
public opinion 52, 304
purchase price 257, 277, 280,
285–7, 313
quantification of beneficial
interest 258, 261–72, 280–3,
287–90, 301–2
reasonable needs principle 312
reform 56, 301–14
resulting trusts 256–64, 271,
285, 288–9
sale
disputes 298
orders for sale 311–12
trusts of land 298
Scotland 312
separation agreements 311–12
settlement orders, proposal
for 312
sole name cases 258, 273–89
Stack v Dowden 259–73, 279–89
statistics 52, 304–5
tenancies, transfers of 298–300
trusts of land 255–60, 295–8,
301, 309–10
Trusts of Land and Appointment
of Trustees Act 1996 295–8
unconscionability 290
unequal shares, establishing that
property is held in 260
unfair outcomes, property law
principles producing 303–4
vulnerable parties, protection
of 53–6, 306, 308, 310
writing 255
**property ownership** 50, 95, 173,
255, 258–9, 265, 274
**proportionality** 295, 556, 632,
638–9, 642, 678–80, 729–30
**proprietary estoppel** 55, 129, 223,
255, 281, 290–5, 692
assurances or representation
by owners, whether there
were 291
beneficial interests 290
conduct found
insufficient 293–4

**proprietary estoppel** *(Cont.)*
constructive trusts 290
contributions 292–4
definition 290
detrimental reliance 290–5
equity, satisfying the 294–5
improvements 294
inducement 293
property disputes of
cohabitants 281, 290–5
remedies 294–5
**psychiatric examinations** 534,
629, 645, 645–50, 688–9
**psychological factors** *see also*
distress, causing
antisocial/narcissistic
personality and domestic
violence 104
domestic violence 103–4
relocation of children 548–9,
553, 560
shared residence
orders 499, 501–2
**psychotherapy** 647–8, 679
**public interest** 31, 92, 222, 226,
238, 241, 365
**purchase price**
contributions 256–8, 264–8,
270–1, 276, 279–80, 284–7, 313

**Queen's Proctor,**
**intervention by** 72

**rape** 17, 102, 106, 131, 194, 407, 710
**Rawls's theory of justice** 430
**reasonable contact** 510, 612, 629,
688, 694–6
**reasonable force** 444–5
**reasonable parental care, lack**
**of** 421, 595, 653, 659, 666–77
abandoned children 677
causal connection 667
discrimination 668
learning disabilities, parents
with 668
objectively acceptable level, care
must fall below an 667–76
orphans 675–6
private and family life, right to
respect for 667–8
third parties 667
unknown perpetrator cases 672
**reasonableness**
contact with children in
care 694–5
interim care and supervision
orders 641
parental care, lack of
reasonable 666–76
parental responsibility 422

property disputes of
cohabitants 312
relocation of children 550
**reconciliation**
adultery 73
certificates 71
condonation 65–6
divorce 65–6, 71–3, 76, 79,
84, 87–9
encouraging reconciliation 71,
73, 76, 79, 84
reflection and consideration,
period for 87–9
**reform** *see also* Law Commission
cohabitants 56
divorce 66–7, 83–4, 88–90,
167, 319
property disputes of
cohabitants 301
**relationship breakdown,** *see*
money and property distribution
on marriage breakdown;
property disputes of cohabitants
on relationship breakdown
**relatives**
adoption 709–12
child arrangements orders with
respect to residence 480
grandparents 388, 483, 492, 541
siblings 743
significant harm
threshold 653–64
**relevant child** 114–16, 120–2, 133–
5, 138–41, 150–2, 299, 605–7
definition 605
former 605–7
former relevant child 605–7
**religion**
adoption 706–7, 737–8
autonomy 686
blood transfusions and Jehovah's
Witnesses 447–51, 572
care orders 686
child arrangements orders with
respect to residence 496–8
civil partners 38
consummation 18, 36
contact 535
corporal punishment 453
discrimination 496–7
divorce 80, 82
marriage 3–4, 10–16, 18,
22–5, 38, 44
paramountcy or welfare
principle 497–8
parental responsibility 421
private and family life, right to
respect for 686
relocation of children 558
talaq (Islamic divorce) 82–3

thought, conscience, and
religion, freedom of 452, 686
**religious ceremonies** lxx, 4, 10–13,
18, 40, 45, 80–1
**religious upbringing** 421, 463–4,
497–8, 686
**religious worship** 4, 11–12
**relocation of children** *see also*
international child abduction
attachments, importance
of 550, 557
authorisation of the court 548
child arrangements orders with
respect to residence 544
consent 547
criminal offences 510, 545, 547
culture 558
debate and research 559–60
detriment to non-relocating
parent 549, 553, 557, 560
evidence 557–8
genuine and realistic, whether
proposals are 551, 557
holidays 547
Human Rights Act 1998 547–8
internal vii, 508–9, 545
international vii, 547, 551–2,
554–7, 559
lifestyle choices 550
paramountcy or welfare
principle 548–9, 551,
553–5, 558–60
parental responsibility 547
Payne discipline vii, lxxvi,
471–2, 508, 547–58, 566
private and family life, right to
respect for 548, 553, 557
prohibited steps orders 544–5
psychological and emotional
stability of relocating
parent 548–9, 553, 560
reasonable decisions,
interference with 550
relevant factors 550
religion 558
removal from the
jurisdiction 510, 545, 547–61
return to previous home
country 551–7
shared residence 507–9, 550–7
specific issues orders 547, 561
step-parents 550
United Kingdom, within,
*see* relocation of children,
internal
**remarriage or cohabitation with**
**new partners** 171–2, 174, 185–7,
216, 218–21, 240–3, 249
**rent** 132, 220–1, 292,
299–300, 342

**representations**, *see* complaints and representations

**reproduction**, *see* assisted fertilisation

**residence**
age, relevance of 493–5, 569
change of 493, 539
checklist 491, 493
connection with the child 485
continuity 493–4
discretion 493, 568
Human Rights Act 1998 496
interim orders 489, 493–4, 640
prohibited steps orders 475
shared residence, *see* shared residence orders

**residence arrangements orders** 572, 613–14, 682–3, 685, 747

**residence orders** 474–5, 480–3, 485–511, 540–1, 548–51, 566–70, 654–8; *see also* child arrangements orders, with respect to residence
accommodation for children 613
conditions 683
criminal offence of taking or sending child abroad 510
delay 485
duration of orders 569
interim 494, 649
joint 60, 502
name, change of 563
special guardianship orders 746
welfare checklist 682
when orders can be made 567, 569

**residential assessments** 641, 646–9

**residential parents** 55, 177, 218, 510–11, 514, 523, 568

**respite care** 601

**restraining orders** 155–6

**resulting trusts** 184, 256–64, 271, 273, 285, 288–9

**return orders** 574, 586–7

**reversion** 173, 334–6, 338, 341

**right to a fair hearing**, *see* fair hearing, right to a

**right to life** 161, 365, 450

**right to respect for private and family life**, *see* private and family life, right to respect for

**sale of property**
bankruptcy 298
children 298
discretion 297
exceptional circumstances 298

orders for sale 169, 173–4, 218, 310, 312
postponement 296–7
private and family life, right to respect for 298
proceeds of sale 218
property disputes of cohabitants 311
trusts of land 298

**same-sex couples** lxix, 4, 36–9, 41–9, 308–9, 385, 703; *see also* civil partnerships; lesbian couples
adoption 703, 708, 727
child arrangements orders with respect to residence 496
child support 337
discrimination lxix, 42–3, 496
Human Rights Act 1998 496
legal recognition of families lxviii
marriage, *see* same-sex marriage 44
non-molestation orders 117, 119
private and family life, right to respect for 496
tenancies, transfer of lxviii–lxix, 41, 221

**same-sex marriage** lxix–lxx, 3, 30, 36, 41–9, 62; *see also* civil partnerships
children 42
civil partnerships 44
discrimination 42–3
European Convention on Human Rights 38, 42
legalisation lxx, 34, 36, 44–5
marry, right to 42
private and family life, right to respect for 42

**scientific testing** 348–50, 352, 354–61, 391, 457

**Scientology** 4, 11

**Scotland** 91, 311, 405, 420, 494, 535–6, 579

**section 8 orders**
18, reaching age 569–70
adoption orders 484
not the child concerned, where child is 489
children over 16 492
cohabitants 55
conditions 475–6, 567
connection with the child 485
consent 479–80, 490
court's powers 477–8
criteria 487
directions 476
discretion 482, 568–9
duration of orders 567, 569
fair hearing, right to a 566

family assistance orders 476–7
family proceedings, definition of 477–8
foster parents 480, 489–91
free-standing applications 478, 481
harm 485–6, 570–1
inherent jurisdiction of the High Court 566–7, 572–90
interim orders 489
leave to apply 480–91
child concerned 487–9
not the child concerned, where child is 489
restrictions 492, 566, 571
without notice applications for leave 487–91
local authorities
foster parents, restrictions on leave applications by 489–92
medical treatment, consent to 571
parental responsibility 490–1, 571
plans for the child 487
restrictions 491–2
significant harm, risk of 571
wishes and feelings of parents 486–7
medical treatment, consent to 571
nature of proposed applications 484
notice 567
paramountcy or welfare principle 482, 487–90, 568–9
parental responsibility 56, 480, 482, 490–1, 571
parents, wishes and feelings of 487
prohibited steps orders 475, 491, 543–5, 571, 720
no reasonable prospects of success criterion 484
restrictions 489–92, 566–71
specific issue orders 484, 491, 545–66, 571, 720
unmarried parents 479
when orders can be made 567–9
who may apply 480
wishes and feelings of parents 487

**section 20 agreements** 610–12

**secured periodical payments orders** 169–73, 177, 180, 250, 332–3, 336
child support 332
during marriage 249–50
enforcement 172

**secured periodical payments orders** (*Cont.*)
matrimonial home 172
money and property distribution on marriage breakdown 169, 172
variation 242
**self-determination** 429
**self-esteem** 393–4, 409, 620, 741
**self-incrimination, privilege against** 540
**separation** 40, 78–81, 95, 145, 247, 310–12, 506–7; *see also* divorce; separation agreements
children, dangers to 163–4
civil partners 39–40, 94
domestic violence after separation 103, 163–4
judicial 6, 22, 65, 68, 93–4, 167, 171
orders 40, 94, 221, 253, 299
physical 77–9
**separation agreements** 222–3, 230; *see also* ante-nuptial agreements
appeals 239
consent orders 223–4
costs 222
death 239
enforcement 222, 225
full and frank disclosure 229
money and property distribution on marriage breakdown 221
ousting jurisdiction of the court 222
periodical payments orders, extension of 229
private agreements 221–2
property disputes of cohabitants 311
**Serious Crime Act 2015** vii, 111
**settlement orders** 173, 312–13, 335, 338
**sexual abuse** 520–1, 531–2, 658, 660–2, 664–6, 682, 684
**sexual offences**
abuse 659–60, 666, 682
adoption 736
marital rape 106
parental responsibility of fathers 396–7, 401–2
**sexual orientation**, *see* civil partnerships; lesbian couples; same-sex couples; same-sex marriage
**SGOs**, *see* special guardianship orders
**sham marriages** 12, 24, 196
**shared intentions** 261–3, 266, 280–1, 283, 288–9, 301–3

**shared residence orders** 337, 403, 467, 491–2, 496, 498–506, 509–10
50/50 care 499
bases 498–502
best interests test 504, 507
conditions 508–9
criteria 502–3
equality of positions and responsibilities 499, 501–2
exceptional circumstances 503, 505, 507
good existing arrangements, assumption of orders reflecting 504
harmony, where parents are not capable of working in 504
Law Commission 499
paramountcy or welfare principle 504, 507–9
parental responsibility where not otherwise possible, conferring 499–500
presumption, whether there should be a 505–7
psychological benefit 499, 501–2
reality of how children live their lives, reflecting the 498–9, 501, 504, 507
relocation 507–9
wishes and feelings of child 503
**sharing principle** 204–7, 211, 232–3, 248
**siblings**
adoption and contact with siblings 743
child arrangements orders with respect to residence 495
**significant harm threshold** 133–5, 143–7, 150–2, 617–31, 637–41, 653–77, 682–4
accommodation for children 612
actual significant harm 653–64
allegations 658
assessments 627–8
burden of proof 664–6
care orders 640, 646, 653–64, 687
care proceedings, final hearings in 653–76
child protection 617–25, 628
Children Act 1989 617–18
culture 621
definition of harm 618
disabilities, parents with 619
domestic violence 618
emergency action 627, 629–30, 634–5
evidence 653, 656–64
experts, disagreement amongst 662

forced marriages 26
guidance 627
health or development compared with similar child 619–21
inhuman or degrading treatment 628
interim care and supervision orders 640, 646
investigations 623–5
keeping families together 620
paramountcy or welfare principle 678
parental control, where child is beyond 676, 678
parental responsibility, exercise of 657
plans 627
police protection 638
private and family life, right to respect for 662
reasonable parental care, lack of 666–76
relative poverty 620
relatives 653–64
section 8 orders 571
sexual abuse 658–61, 666
social workers 627–8
standard of care 620
standard of proof 617–18, 658–61, 664–6
supervision orders 653–64
uninjured children, protection of 663–4
**single parents**
adoption 703, 727–30
statistics lxvii
**social changes** 3, 51–2, 168, 306–7, 345, 408, 411
**social construction of childhood** 427
**social parenthood** 320, 337, 345, 354–5, 362, 386–7
**social security** 31, 50, 81, 319, 322, 392, 420
**social workers**
adoption 707, 720, 727
child protection 596, 615, 625, 628, 633, 635, 637–9
emergency protection orders 633, 635
interaction with other disciplines lxxvi, 26
police protection 637–9
significant harm threshold 627–8
time limits and targets 702
**sole names** 208, 218, 255, 258–9, 270, 272–89, 299–300
**solicitors, appointment of** 652

**special guardianship orders** 335,
413–14, 714, 720, 722, 735, 744–7
adoption 720, 722, 744, 746–7
care orders, discharge of 746
change of circumstances 746
Children Act 1989 744
notice 745
parental responsibility 745
residence orders,
discharge of 746
step-parents 745
**specific issue orders** 545–66
adoption 720
definition 546
local authorities 491, 546, 571
names, disputes as to
children's 547, 560
nature of proposed
applications 484
need, children in 546
parental responsibility 545–6
relocation 547–61
sterilisation 545
**sperm donors**
anonymity 373
child support 337
death, use of sperm after 373–4
fathers and fatherhood 352,
355–6, 372, 374, 387
identity rights 351–2
intent-based parenthood 385–6
legal parenthood 369,
373, 386–7
parentage 351–2, 355, 357
**stability** 37, 49, 177, 462, 466,
743, 747
**standard of living** 332, 338–43
**standard of proof** 134, 658, 660,
662–6, 670–1, 682, 684
balance of probabilities, *see*
balance of probabilities
harassment 154
non-molestation orders 120
significant harm threshold 617–
18, 658–61, 664–6
**statistics**
civil partners 39
cohabitants lxvii, 52
domestic violence 100, 108, 164
marriage 304
property disputes of
cohabitants 52, 305
single parents lxvii
**step-parents** 331, 333, 336–7,
411–12, 531, 549–50, 666
contact 516, 531
marriage with step-children 8
parental responsibility 411–12,
701, 745
relocation of children 550
special guardianship orders 746

**sterilisation** 463, 466–7, 545–6,
589, 638
**stress** 31, 75, 104, 118, 401, 648, 656
**striking out** 213–14
**substitute carers** 413, 480, 595
**succession** lxvi, 41, 43, 50–1, 53–5,
183, 217–19
expectations of inheritance 183
Inheritance (Provision for
Family and Dependants) Act
1975 51, 53, 55, 81
inheritance tax 38, 62
intestacy 54–5, 96
money and property
distribution on marriage
breakdown 183, 188
surviving spouses 40–1, 51, 55
wills 55, 57, 265–6
**supervised contact** 401, 514, 521,
525, 529, 531, 697
long-term viii, 521
**supervision orders** 627,
639–41, 643–5, 657–8, 673–4,
680–4, 687–92; *see also* care
proceedings; interim care and
supervision orders
additional powers 688
adoption 720
best interests test 689
care orders 691
directions 688
discharge 688
duration 687–8
enforcement 688
interim 640–1, 645, 649
medical or psychiatric
examination and
treatment 688
monitoring 689
parental responsibility 690
reasonable contact of
supervisor 688
responsible person 688–9
significant harm
threshold 653–64
specified activities 688
variation 688–9
welfare checklist 682–3
wishes and feelings of child 688
**surname, change of**, *see* name,
change of child's
**surrogacy and parental
orders** vii, 323, 364, 368,
376–87, 411, 414
Children Act proceedings 384
child's home 379–80
commercial basis, on
a 376, 383–4
conditions 381, 383
deception 385
domicile of applicants 380–1

enforcement 376
expenses 382
genetic relationship, requirement
for 376
Human Fertilisation and
Embryology Act 1990 377
Human Fertilisation and
Embryology Act 2008 377
husbands of mothers 366–7
illegality 376
intent-based parenthood 386
legal parenthood 376,
382–3, 385–6
paramountcy principle 377, 383
parental orders 385–6
policy 382
sums paid to surrogate
mothers 382–5
time limit for application 377–9
who may apply 376
**surrogate mothers** 366, 368, 376,
378, 381–5, 387

**talaq (Islamic divorce)** 82–3
**tax** 29, 38, 41, 51, 59, 61–2, 308
**telephone calls,
harassment by** 153
**tenancies**
children 299
cohabitants 55, 299–300
compensation for transfer 299
hardship 299
matrimonial home 221
occupation orders 131
property disputes of
cohabitants 298–300
relevant tenancy, definition
of 221, 299–300
rent, responsibility for 132
same-sex couples lxviii–lxix,
41, 221
succession lxvii–lxix, 55
transfer 218, 221, 298,
298–300, 308
**tension between utility and
rights** lxxvi
**term orders** 179–80
**terminology**
civil partnership
dissolution 95
divorce law 67, 86
family law lxvi
financial orders 168
parents 346, 389
**terrorism** 99
**thought, conscience, and religion,
freedom of** 452, 686
**threats of violence** 27–8, 110,
114, 146–8, 150, 152–3, 157–60
**transsexuals and marriage**
birth certificates 21, 32–3, 375

**transsexuals and marriage** (*Cont.*)
chromosomal factors, gonadal
factors, genital factors, and
psychological factors 30–2, 35
consummation 17
contact 526
discrimination 31
fatherhood 375
Gender Recognition Act
2004 21, 33, 375
gender recognition
certificates 17, 21, 33, 374–5
Human Rights Act 1998 32–3
legal parenthood 374–5
margin of appreciation 31, 375
marriage
consummation 17
marry, right to 31–3
nullity 375
nullity 375
parental responsibility of
fathers 407
private and family life, right to
respect for 31, 33, 375
retrospectivity 374–5
right to marry 31–3
voidable marriages 21–2
**transsexuals and
parenthood** 374–5
**treaties and conventions** 161–3,
428; *see also* particular treaties
and conventions
**trespass to the person** 25, 441
**trusts of land**
bankruptcy 298
beneficial interests 295–8
constructive trusts 257, 272, 274,
279–85, 288–90, 303–4
criteria for determining
applications 296–7
exclusion orders 297
express trusts 255, 259–60
implied trusts 255, 255–7, 314
property disputes of
cohabitants 301, 309–10
resulting trusts 256–64, 271,
285, 288–9
sale of property
disagreements over 298
postponement of 296–7
trusts for sale 297
Trusts of Land and Appointment
of Trustees Act 1996 295–8
writing, declarations in 255
**twins** lxxii, 357, 367, 371–3, 379,
381–2, 501

**unborn children, child support
for** 331
**unconscionability** 230, 235,
256, 290–2

**undertakings** 28, 80, 149–51, 174,
399, 635, 724
**unfairness** 57, 233, 236, 295, 304,
311, 314
**United Nations (UN)**
Convention on the
Elimination of All Forms
of Discrimination against
Women 161–2
Convention on the Rights of the
Child lxxiii, lxxv, 351, 353–5,
514, 587, 593
Declaration on Elimination
of Violence against
Women 99–100
domestic violence 100, 160, 162
**unmarried cohabitants**, *see*
cohabitants; property disputes
of cohabitants on relationship
breakdown
**unmarried couples** *see also*
cohabitants; unmarried fathers
accommodation for
children 612–13
adoption 703, 708
assisted fertilisation 367
child support 343
parental responsibility 388–404,
611, 613
section 8 orders 479
time of birth, unmarried
at 388–9
**unmarried fathers**
commitment, degree of 390
discrimination 389–90, 405–11
mothers, unmarried fathers
as less worthy than
unmarried 407
parental responsibility 368, 411
time of birth, unmarried
at 388–9
unmeritorious fathers 389, 409
**unmarried parents** 51, 59, 338–43,
388, 390, 392, 396
**unreasonable behaviour** vii, 67,
71–6, 78–9, 89, 91–3, 95
**utility and rights, tension
between** lxxvi

**variation of financial provision
orders** 242–8
capitalisation of periodical
payments orders 244–8
child support 321, 326–8, 342
clean break 244, 248
cohabitation with new
partners 249
consent orders 243–4
deferred orders 243
discretion 244–5
earning capacity 247–8

factors to be considered 244–8
hardship 244
lifestyle choices 245–7
lump sums by
instalments 242, 244–5
maintenance pending suit 242
matrimonial home 243, 247
paramountcy or welfare
principle 244
pension sharing orders 242–3
periodical payments
orders 242, 244–9
property adjustment
orders 243–5
sale of property orders 243
secured periodical payments
orders 242
timing of applications 243
**venereal disease** 17, 20–2, 38, 40
**views of child**, *see* wishes and
feelings of child
**violence**
domestic, *see* domestic
violence
gender-based 99, 162–3
physical 98, 100–2, 115, 137,
145–7, 151, 158
**violent extremism** 618
**void marriages** 6–35, 94, 323, 366,
375, 388
**voidable marriages** 6, 16–24
**voting** 427–8
**vulnerability**
children 53, 58
cohabitants 53–5, 58, 95
home-sharers 61
homelessness 158–9
marriage 6
property disputes of
cohabitants 307–8, 310

**wardship**
child protection 596
forced marriages 26–7
inherent jurisdiction 25, 27,
590, 595
local authorities 589
medical treatment of children,
consent to 441
surrogacy 589
**Waterhouse Inquiry** 702
**welfare benefits** 29, 175,
319–20, 322
**welfare checklist**
adoption 705
allegations 682
care orders 682–3, 692
care proceedings 692
Children Act 1989 460
children's guardians 652, 683
prohibited steps orders 683

range of orders 682–3
sexual abuse, unproven
    allegations of 682
supervision orders 682–3
unknown perpetrators at
    disposal stage 681–2
**welfare principle**, *see* paramountcy
    or welfare principle
**welfarism** 429
**well-being** 135–6, 138, 140–1, 463,
    506, 519–20, 597
    emotional 135, 541, 572

**Welsh family proceedings
    officers** 476, 535, 543, 651
**will theory** 424–5
**wills** 55, 58, 265–7
**wishes and feelings of child**
    accommodation for
        children 613
    child protection 599, 652
    children's guardian, role of 652
    contact 528, 537
    disabled children 599
    looked after children 605

name, change of 564
parental alienation
    syndrome 527
residence 493
section 8 orders 487
shared residence orders 503
supervision orders 688
**women's refuges** 105–6, 525
**wrongful removal or
    retention** 574, 580–2

**yardstick of equality** 69, 197, 205